The
Mississippi Gulf Coast Community College
FOUNDATION

is proud to sponsor this first edition of

Mississippi Gulf Coast Community College: A History

Written and Illustrated by Charles L. Sullivan

The publication of this book is made possible, in part, by a grant from the MGCCC Foundation and the generous contributions of alumni and friends of the college.

In 2002, Mississippi Gulf Coast Community College celebrates 90 years as an educational institution. The MGCCC Foundation gratefully acknowledges the individuals and communities that have sustained the traditions, ideals and mission of the college, and Charles Sullivan, who has captured in great detail the memorable moments of Mississippi Gulf Coast Community College.

PREFACE

By George R. Boggs, President and CEO of the American Association of Community Colleges.

George R. Boggs

America's unique contribution to the educational thought and practice of the Western World is the junior/community college. *Mississippi Gulf Coast Community College: A History* is the most comprehensive treatment of the evolution of one such institution. In this work, the history of one All-American junior/community college, one can discern, in broad strokes at least, the story of all American junior/community colleges.

MGCCC, as many of her sister institutions throughout the nation, began in the first quarter of the 20th century as an agricultural high school that grew into a junior college which branched into multiple campuses and centers. Beginning with one building on a hilltop in the piney woods in 1912 serving 63 students in one county, MGCCC on the eve of the new millennium counted one hundred structures organized into four campuses and three centers serving 28,000 students in four counties.

While junior/community colleges differ from state to state and section to section, they share common characteristics, and they have responded to national stimuli in similar fashion. For example--the Second World War sparked the rise of vocational-technical education at Perkinston. At war's end veterans attending on the G. I. Bill swelled the institution's enrollment as never before. Precisely the same thing happened to every junior college in the nation.

In addition to a comprehensive treatment of the chronological development of MGCCC, the author included remarkably detailed sections on sports, culture and the arts, and student life. In short, this work is a 608-page lavishly illustrated microcosm of the American junior/community college experience. It is my honor to write this preface to this important work.

"It is, sir, as I have said, a small college, and yet there are those who love it."

Daniel Webster 1782-1852
DARTMOUTH COLLEGE CASE [1818]

To Chuck Bond
a True Son of Mississippi
Charles L. Sullivan
June 3, 2013
at Dedication of Jefferson Davis Presidential Library

Mississippi Gulf Coast Community College: A History

written and illustrated by

Charles L. Sullivan

FIRST EDITION
published by
Mississippi Gulf Coast Community College Press

Printed by
McNaughton & Gunn, Inc.
Saline, Michigan

ISBN: 0-9721992-0-9
Library of Congress control number: 2002108276

DEDICATION

The author dedicates this work to the three Presidents under whom he served, (from left), Barry Mellinger, J.J. Hayden, and Willis Lott, and to the memory of Winfred Moncrief (below), Publicity Director of the college from 1972-1992. Moncrief engineered the founding of the Mississippi Gulf Coast Community College Archives and conceived the idea for this book.

December 30, 1923 - July 28, 2000

TABLE OF CONTENTS

Book II -- Sports, 1912 - 2000

Book III--Performing Arts, Clubs, and Student Life

Appendices

MAPS, LISTS, AND CHARTS

Maps

Lists

Charts

ACKNOWLEDGEMENTS AND NOTES ON SOURCES

At the close of an effort that consumed most of a decade during which I made hundreds of inquiries by letter, phone, fax, and e-mail, I find it impossible to remember all those who aided in this endeavor. Because I know that many of the names of those who helped are lost among scores of thousands of documents in the MGCCC Archives Collection, I was tempted to forego a list of acknowledgements in favor of a general "thank you." I felt I could not do that because those who aid an author in his work judge that work to a large degree on the basis of whether or not their contributions were acknowledged. So, knowing that many names would be missed, I decided to list those names I could remember.

Those who donated photographs were acknowledged in the photograph caption if I knew the name of the donor. Alas, I received a large number of photographs from the Alumni Association, which had been donated over the course of many years (some quite recently), but no donor's name came with them. I know, however, that many of the earliest photographs were the gifts of Hammond "Tom" Davis and his wife Lydean (David) Davis. I just do not know which ones they were.

Alumni Association secretaries who followed Davis collected more early photographs, and these were eventually published in a booklet titled *Pictures of Our Past*. Those involved in that long-running effort known to me were Wyvona Scarborough, Ruth Ford, Louise Brown, and April Grace. In addition to the photographs, the Alumni Association secretaries collected documents, letters, and other primary sources that were available to me when I began my work. Equally important were the primary sources in the form of catalogs, Board of Trustees minutes, and yearbooks collected, saved, and protected by presidential secretaries Ethel Bond and Gloria Breland. To put it in a nutshell, all the finest primary sources related to the institution came from the Alumni Association secretaries and presidents' secretaries. Their diligent efforts over the course of the last several decades made this history book possible.

The other great primary source that made the production of this work possible was newspaper articles--tens of thousands of them. Honors students and regular students in my history classes at Perk did much of that work. Most of the articles were copied (or as we termed it, "shot") from the *Daily Herald* and the *Stone County Enterprise,* with 85 percent of them coming from the former. Students were assigned two rolls to read (or "run" as we termed it) for the purpose of picking out all articles mentioning the institution or the hamlet of Perkinston. The citations were written on special sheets, and then the articles were shot on a microfilm printer on the campus bought for that purpose. Each article was then cut out and pasted on a sheet of paper with the name of the newspaper and date written above each one. In that manner some 15,000 articles covering the period 1888 to 1961 were obtained. These were then placed in line with the thousands of articles remaining from the period 1962 to 2000 cut out by Magnolia Clipping Service and sent to the college.

I must thank the administrators of Jefferson Davis Campus for the single greatest and most valuable gift to the MGCCC Archives. For months student workers George and Diane Haydel and I commuted to JD to run microfilm. That ended when the decision was made by JD Vice President Donnie Taylor, JD Head Librarian Charlie Clark, and JD Media Director Foster Flint to send the *Daily Herald* microfilm 1888-1939 to Perk for use here. The post-1939 microfilm was available via courier anytime we needed it.

Approximately 150 students ran more than 300 newspaper microfilm rolls in four years from 1994 to 1998. But most of those articles were shot, cut, pasted, and their citations written on them by George and Diane Haydel. Moreover, these two also ran articles for a whole summer for seven hours per day as student workers. The contribution of George and Diane Haydel to this effort was vital. The Haydels have more "sweat equity" in this book than anyone other than my wife and I. They worked for three years (year round) as students, student workers, and government workers. They kept working on this book even after leaving Perk for William Carey College.

Two other student workers who stand out in my mind are Vivian Anderson and Bourbon Hughes. Their work was of the same high quality as that of the Haydels'. Their time was shorter and in Hughes's case more specialized. Hughes's special assignment was the Second World War aspect of this work and of another book that he and I wrote jointly titled *Valor Remembered.*

George and Diane Haydel, Vivian Anderson, and Bourbon Hughes were all honors students, and each of them acted in the office of a squad leader, directing other honors (and regular) students who reported to them. I thank them and all the history students who worked so long and diligently to find the articles that fleshed the bare bones of the Board of Trustees minutes, catalogs, and yearbooks and which also provided the information to caption the photographs.

In summer 1998 student worker and computer whiz Rebecca Bull made alphabetical lists of all the known students of the institution from 1912-1944. These lists, which also contained the students' hometowns and years of attendance, were in constant use thereafter. She saved me months of research by making those lists.

My long-suffering wife Jane typed the entire manuscript twice (aggregating in excess of 1,200 single-spaced sheets). She also typed all the photo captions. At least half of this she typed on nights, weekends, holidays, and in the summers on her own time with no remuneration whatsoever. In addition, she typed corrections for five years, year-round. On top of that she typed the 250-page manuscript of *Valor Remembered.* She also did research. In an amazingly determined bit of sleuthing, lasting more than a year and covering half the United States on the internet, she located a relative of Superintendent Thomas Ira Cook, the only chief executive officer of the institution about whom I knew nothing. Ironically, Frank Cook, the relative, turned out to live in Hattiesburg one block from where Jane had lived in 1987 at the time we were married.

The gathering of photographs and documents began in 1992 with retired MGCCC Publicity Director Winfred Moncrief aiding me. In time he switched over to saving archival video, and archives secretary Linda Goble worked on photos and documents for more than a year. In summer 1997 Joyce Rogers began a two and one-half year stint as assistant archivist. She filed, interviewed, captioned photos, inventoried the holdings of the archives, and even roughed out drafts of certain sections. Winfred Moncrief, Linda Goble, and Joyce Rogers created archival order out of documentary chaos. These three were indispensable. Perk Campus librarian Glenda Redmond, in partial fulfillment of her master's degree in library science at the University of Southern Mississippi, cataloged thousands of MGCCC archival negatives. She did a masterful job which enabled me to find many illustrations which otherwise would have been impossible to locate.

The years of shooting and pasting microfilm articles together with the making of multiple copies of many articles finally resulted in 46 tightly packed file cabinet drawers, (40 file cabinet drawers full of documents, and six file cabinet drawers full of photos). Each document file drawer held about 2,000 individual sheets giving a total of approximately 80,000 sheets. The photo drawers held about 200 photos each or 1,200 total. In addition, 146 acid free boxes and 41 regular boxes contained approximately 14,600 more documents and 4,100 more photos. That was the main collection. That is a total of 94,600 documents and 5,600 photos. Boxes containing thousands more documents and photos existed. I raided those for what I needed at the moment. I have no idea of how many documents those boxes contained, but the total was no less than 25,000.

Of the hundreds of persons who aided in this endeavor, most were called on to give specific information about a certain topic, but some were "on call" for all topics in a particular era of time. These people received a phone call from me every time I passed through their era on a different tack. For the history of Perkinston in general, my main source was Randle Dedeaux. For the 1920s and 1930s my main sources were Lydean (David) Davis of Wiggins, Marguerite (Callahan) Boswell of Louisville, and Merrill "Red" True of Picayune. For the 1940s and 1950s, my main sources were Ed and Myra Evans of Wiggins and Bill and Dolores Mauldin of McHenry. For the mid 1950s through the 1980s, my main sources were former MGCJC President J. J. Hayden and Lillian Hayden, former Perkinston Campus Vice President Clyde Strickland and Doris Strickland, Jefferson Davis Campus Vice President Donnie Taylor and Carol Taylor, former Perkinston Campus Business Manager L. D. "Buster" Stringfellow and Virginia Stringfellow, and former Jackson County Vice President Curtis Davis.

Another couple on constant call were Bobby and Tommie Weathers. The first chapter written was the one titled "The Weathers Clan." I did that because Bob's office was down the hall from mine. Because he was first, Bob had to teach me about junior college sports. Since I did not know much about the subject, he had to teach me a great deal about all sports--not just about basketball. He was on call for seven years. His wife Tommie was also on call for seven years because she was the campus records clerk. She finally dubbed me an honorary records clerk and taught me how to access pre-1940s records myself. As this book neared completion in winter 2001, Bob Weathers was on the brink of besting Curtis Davis's forty-one years and seven months record for employment by the institution. Jeanette (Bounds) Thomas, another stalwart, who received many calls from me, was only one year behind Bob. Thomas, who began teaching at Perk in fall 1961, transferred to Jackson County Campus in 1967. [As this book was being prepared to go to press in May 2002, both Thomas and Weathers announced their retirement effective June 30, 2002. Weathers, therefore, logged forty-one years, eleven months, and ten days to set a new record for service to the institution.]

Others who were on call a great deal were former coaches Barbara Ann "Sue" Ross, Doris Smith, Curly Farris, Harold Wesson, Charles Cooper, Clem Dellenger, and George Sekul. Then current athletic director Chris Calcote and then current coaches Cooper Farris, Steve Wright, Mike Gavin, Greg Holmes, Carolyn Patterson, Salomon Kidane, Wendell Weathers, Tommy Snell, and Kelvin Lyon aided me as well.

In the realm of private photographic collections outside the college, two people supplied the archivist with original early photographs. These persons were Sherry Dillard of Dixie Press of Gulfport and Elizabeth Brash of Gulfport Printing Company.

In the realm of interview collections outside the college, the archivist acknowledges his debt to Dr. Charles Bolton of the University of Southern Mississippi Oral History Department for the use of three lengthy copyright-free interviews held in the USM Oral History Collection. Those were the interviews with Cooper J. Darby, J. J. Hayden, and Russell Quave.

I also wish to thank three archivists who contributed photographs from their collections to this work. These persons are Bobs Tusa (Director of the William D. McCain Archives on the campus of the University of Southern Mississippi), Dr. Phillip Thomas Tucker (Keesler Air Force Base Chief Historian), and Jennifer Ford of the John Davis Williams Library on the campus of the University of Mississippi.

In securing copies of Jackson County and George County documents related to the school, I contacted Betty Rodgers of the Jackson County Archives. For Stone County I had Chancery Clerk Gerald W. Bond. For Harrison County my supplier was Tim Barnard of the Harrison County Chancery Clerk's office. All three of those rendered invaluable aid for years.

Another person at the top of my "thank you list" is Perkinston Campus Head Librarian Liz Mixon. Aside from letting me check out books in "virtual perpetuity," she let me wreck her library for four summers in a row--1998, 1999, 2000, and 2001. From May through August, I had between 15 and 30 tables and carrels covered with documents, photographs, and artifacts. Chairs, couches, the tops of bookcases, and the floors on two levels were also pressed into service. At the end of each summer the library looked like a reenactment of Hurricane Camille. When the copy machine used by instructors broke at the beginning of summer 2001, she gave me carte blanche to use a superannuated (but working) copier in the library.

Yet another top of the "thank you" list person is Central Office Director of Printing Mike Anderson. He made an office available to Melissa Ladner and me so that we could compose the book by weaving together the text and photographs. Without exception his staff (composed of Terry Shavers, Larry Falcon, Aldridge Free, and Dianna Beall) aided us in every possible way, particularly in running endless correction copies of book sections. Many times one or another of them would stay after work to run those sections created in our daily "final burst." And when the scanner or the computer went on the blink, either Central Office Coordinator of Information Services Raymond Hatten or Computer Technician Danny Lawson (or both) would come work their wizardry, and we would burst forth again.

In relation to the technical production of the book, four persons performed outstanding service. Mike Sewell spent summer 2000 scanning photographs and matching them with text. Melissa Ladner succeeded him in that position from September 2000 to July 2002. Lori Bultman began the copy work for historical photographs and the making of new photos in summer 1999. Rich Kopp succeeded her in 1999 and continued until the photographic work was completed in December 2001.

As always and in my every historical endeavor for the past 20 years, I acknowledge my perpetual debt to Murella Hebert Powell of the Biloxi Public Library. In 1981 she and I began collaboration in writing *The Mississippi Gulf Coast: Portrait of a People*, and I have relied on her aid ever since.

As always and in my every historical endeavor for the past 20 years, I acknowledge my perpetual debt to Kat Bergeron of the *Sun Herald* newspaper. That newspaper has carried a number of names since its founding in 1884, but the word *Herald* has been a part of its name from the beginning. Some of the earlier names were *Biloxi Herald, Gulfport Herald*, and *Daily Herald*, but by whatever name, the *Herald* has been and is the foremost repository of the local history of the Mississippi Gulf Coast. The *Herald* has not only preserved history, but the newspaper has also made history. In 1916, by its editorial stance, the *Daily Herald*, more than any other agency, saved the institution at Perkinston from annihilation. I estimate that no less than sixty per cent of this present work came from the pages of the *Herald.* A number of illustrations in this work also came from the *Herald.* Each one of those is credited in captions, and I thank *Sun Herald* publisher Roland Weeks for permission to use those.

Not only did the *Sun Herald* provide me with a treasure house of local history, but the paper also stepped in to help me in locating new information on the toughest research nut I had to crack--the Perkinston institution's dead of World War II. By early 2001, I had been collecting information on Perkinston's class of the dead (one teacher and 31 students) for over a decade. With time running out and spurred by the in-progress renovation of the Gregory War Memorial Chapel to be rededicated in honor of the dead on homecoming day, October 27, 2001, I called Senator Trent Lott's office, and I called Kat Bergeron. Myrtis Franke of Senator Lott's office began searching, and Kat Bergeron wrote an article for the *Sun Herald. Sun Herald* Executive Editor Stan Tiner approved the Memorial Day, May 28, 2001, article which covered parts of four pages (including page one) and which included photographs of all 32 dead. A few days later the *Pensacola News Journal* ran a short article specifically seeking information on the two Florida natives on the death list. In the historical firestorm set off by all that, I received much information that I could never have gotten any other way. I entered the new information in the book and wrote *fini* to the war dead section on September 1, 2001, though many questions still remained unanswered.

I have to back up a year to continue the saga of the search for the Perkinston war dead. Some time in early 2000 Mitchell Cirlot of Ocean Springs called me to ask for a copy of *Valor Remembered.* Since he is a military researcher, I sent him one of the few remaining copies. By way of thanks he asked if he could do anything for me. I said, "Yes, you can tell me what happened to Marjorie Stallings, Perk's only woman to die in the Second World War." A few days later he called and said, "She is buried in Evergreen Cemetery in Gulfport. You can get the death date off the stone and get an obituary." So I did. I will not go into why I had not thought of something as obvious as that, but I had not. After all, I knew she was from Gulfport. Determined not to make that mistake again, I called Susan Galbo at Gulfport City Hall, who has access to the Evergreen Cemetery files, and read off the names of all the Perkinston war dead I felt might be there. She told me which ones were buried there and which not. I did not read her the name of Madison Kent "Jack" Moorman because he had been killed in action aboard a Motor Torpedo Boat in the Mediterranean Sea. I assumed the boat had sunk, carrying him to the bottom of the sea. (Never assume anything). I did read her the name William Martin Anderson. He was not at Evergreen.

I then called Sharon Hinkle of Riemann Funeral Home in Gulfport and read her the same list I had read to Susan Galbo. She told me which ones Riemann's had records for. I asked her about William Martin Anderson. She had nothing. To digress, I did not ask her about "Dad" Warnell, the Perk Campus engineer of the 1920s through 1940s for whose grave I had been in search of for years. I knew that Dad Warnell was buried in the unmarked grave next to that of his son, Newman, in the Perk Cemetery. I assumed that there was no way Riemann's could have been involved in Warnell's burial. I called Mike Lott at

Moore Funeral Home in Wiggins. When he found he had no record on Warnell, he called Sharon Hinkle at Riemann's. She sent him the records, and he sent them to me. It turned out that after Warnell retired, he lived closer to Gulfport than Wiggins, so Riemann's brought him home. Oh, well--never assume anything. And remember--no one can help you if you do not ask.

As stated earlier, on September 1, 2001, I put the Perkinston World War II dead to rest. On September 4, Mitchell Cirlot called. He had heard that I had been asking recently for more information about Perk's war dead. He said, "Why didn't you ask me about the others a year ago?" I replied, "I didn't think about it." So while I was writing these acknowledgements Cirlot was calling me daily, answering question after question for which I had previously had no answers. He was also answering questions I did not know I had, and he was proving wrong some of the information I had already put in the book. It turned out that Cirlot's father was in the same Motor Torpedo Boat Squadron as that of Madison Kent "Jack" Moorman at the time the Germans killed Moorman off the coast of Corsica and had served in the honor guard at Moorman's original burial. As I said previously, I had "assumed" that since Moorman was on a boat that it had sunk to the bottom of the Mediterranean with him on board. Well, it did not sink, and Moorman, after being buried twice in Europe, was returned for final burial in Evergreen Cemetery in Gulfport. Cirlot called and told me Moorman was in Evergreen. I probably walked beside his grave the day Jane and I went to visit Marjorie Stallings's grave.

There was one KIA I did consistently ask everyone about (except Cirlot), and that was William Martin Anderson. And I checked every record in every cemetery in South Mississippi, including Biloxi National Cemetery, for him. To the bitter end, I had never uncovered one single fact about him. Myrtis Franke found out for me that Anderson, a lieutenant in the Army Air Corps, had been Killed in Action in Europe on January 3, 1943. I had wanted more specifics than that, but I was happy to get that much.

Three days after I finally asked Cirlot about Anderson, he called to say that Anderson's B-17, called *Panhandle Dogie*, had been hit by German flak over St. Nazaire, France. Dare I think he was bombing the U-Boat pens there? (I am afraid to assume anything anymore.) Cirlot knew the burial places of all the crewmen known to have been killed in the crash of the *Panhandle Dogie*. Anderson was not among them. Two days after that Cirlot called and said he knew where Anderson was buried but that I had to guess. I named all the U. S. cemeteries in Europe one after another. Then Cirlot laid it on me: "He is buried in the Vicksburg National Military Park." If I lived to be 100, the Vicksburg National Cemetery would have been very likely the very last one I would have checked for Anderson. I asked Cirlot, "Why did you check Vicksburg?" He replied, "Why not?"

So I held the Perkinston dead of World War II section open while the book was being indexed. In every case where Cirlot found anything new, the information was placed at the bottom of each profile and noted as being from Cirlot. I surely am glad people do not read acknowledgements. I would hate to think that everybody (including my major professors at the University of Southern Mississippi and at Ole Miss) would know that Cirlot located more in six months on the Perkinston dead than I did in a decade. On the other hand, I finally had sense enough to ask him. That ought to count for something.

Last, but as they say--certainly not least--I wish to thank my editor-reader Perkinston English instructor Duke Sutherland for reading and correcting draft after draft of this work. He even took drafts on vacation with him. As Jane and I slaved day and night in the summers, it was particularly gratifying to read little notes on the corrected pages such as, "Wish you were here. The sun has just dropped behind Jamaica tinging the azure waters of the Caribbean with gold." On the other hand as Jane typed his corrections, she often enunciated her fervent desire to strangle him. Even so, he did a terrific job, and he told me what "worked" and what did not. I nearly always took his advice. But if the reader should chance upon a misspelled word or a dangling participle or whatever, Duke would be glad to take the reader's calls at his office in Denson Hall.

In addition to those named in the foregoing, the author wishes to thank the persons named in the following list for their aid in gathering the resources used in writing this book:

Charles Acres, Johnny Adams, Lisa Alexander, Mary Ellen (Watrous) Alexander, Nettie Alexander, Pat Alford, Todd Anderson, Walter Atchison, Lucille Bailey, Jeff Balfour, Cassie (Breland) Batson, Marjorie Baxter, Steve Bessette, Lucy (Huff) Bishop, Bettye Jo Blakeney, Edna Bond, Willie A. Bond, William Charles Boone, Randall Bradberry, Paul Brauchle, Kathy Braun, Will Bramlett, Carolyn Breland, Hanson Breland, Wanda Brignac, Elaine Brockmeyer, Gertie Brown, James Obie Brown, Norvell Louise (McDonald) Brown, Rusty Brown, Tom Brown, Wilton "Red" Brown, Jerry Bryan, Trudy Bryan, Melvin Carpenter, Brian Carriere, Paul Cartwright, Nica Cason, Wayne Catlett, Don Christensen, Grace Clayton, Marsha Cluff, Corece Colvin, Lorette (Rouse) Compton, Frank Cook, Charles Cooper, Mr. & Mrs. Robert Cossey, Reba (Moffett) Counselman, Jane (Denson) Covington, Walter Cowan, Greg Crochet, Denise Daniel, Curtis Davis, Sylvia Davis, William E. Davis, Sal D'Aquilla, Johnnette Dees, Clem Dellenger, Donald DeMetz, Brenda Donahoe, Jeff Donahoe, Betty Drake, L. A. Drago, Laurie (McBryde) Draper, Estella (Johnson) Drevar, David Dueitt, Marla Eason, Tom Eason, James Estes, Janie (Morris) Estrada, Sistie Farris, Dr. Travis Ferguson, David Fitch, Joan Fitch, Rebecca Ford, Stacy Fore, Terry (Price) Fountain, William Frantzen, Harry Carson Frye, Virgel Fulcher, Jimmy Gammage, Ed Gardner, Jerry Gardner, Gerald Gartman, Dr. Bobby Garvin, Mike Gavin, Daunton Gibbs, G. C. Golden, April Grace, Dr. Mary Graham, Ina Sue Gregory, Dr. Frank Gruich, Sybil (Lasseure) Hagen, Alice Hague, Mary Ida (Ferry) Harris, Colleen Hartfield, Clyde Hatten, Dee Dee Hatten,

Roxie Hatten, Russell Hatten, Barbara Haygood, Warren Heath, Martha Heffner, Dr. Marie Heim, Misty Heywood, Gary Higginbotham, Jay Higginbotham, Carol Holley, Patti Holloway, Bobby Holmes, Rhonda Fisher Hood, Clare (Sekul) Hornsby, Zenobia Ruth (Denson) Houston, Grady Howell, Kenneth Hughes, Abe Hutto, Charles Iversen, Angela James, Mary Ann (Reddell) James, Ralph Jenkins, Glendon Johnson, Sanja Johnson, Virginia Johnston, Kim Jones, Kristy Jones, Joel "Cotton" Jordan, Mercedes Jordan, Anna Fay Kelley, Sam Kirsch, Dr. David Knowles, Myrtis Krohn, Andrea Ladner. Herman Ladner, June (Jefferson) Ladner, Pam Ladner, Danny Lawson, Amber Leatherwood, Jon Lewis, Kathryn Lewis, Dr. Bill Lipscomb, Marilyn Lott, Michael J. Lott, Dr. Nelda Lott, Dr. Willis H. Lott, Dr. Woodley Lott, Dr. Royce Luke, John Lynn, Betty Malone, Noel Mann, Doug Mansfield, Richard Marlowe, William Martin, Eleanor Mashburn, Don Massengale, Debra Matthews, Lena Melton, Dr. Barry L. Mellinger, Davis Melton, Claude McBryde, Jean McCool, Glynn Alton McDaniel, Hersel McDaniel, Albert Earl McDonald, Carol McReedy, C. L. Miles, Ronnie Mizelle, Jaclyn Moffett, Marlene Moore, Dr. Houshang Moradmand, Rebecca Moreton, Mike Murphy, Hilton Murray, Nell Murray, Hazel (Bridge) Necaise, Mary Nelson, Charlie Neumann, Leada (Farragut) Niolet, Dorothy Nunnery, Deanne Nuwer, C. G. Odom, Patt Odom, Maurice O'Keefe, Arl O'Neal, Dowey D. O'Neal, John Russell O'Neal, Betty Oswald, Lyle Page, James Palencia, Carole Pearce, Virginia Perkins, Kathleen Pickett, Howard Pollock, Charlie Probst, James O. Rabby, Helen (Taquino) Raborn, Emogene Rainey, Randy Randazzo, Flo Reese, Margo Reeves, Martha Richardson, Morris Richardson, Brenda Roberts, E. J. Roberts, Margie (Rabby) Roberts, Becky Rogers, Robert Rominger, Sue Ross, Eloise Rouse, James Rutledge, Jim Salley, Suzette Salley, Elise (Bayless) Sanders, David Sansing, Margaret (Niolet) Scurfield, Diane Sekul, Michelle Sekul, Charles Serpente, Janice (Felsher) Seymour, George P. Scherer, Dean Shaw, Tommye (Switzer) Skinner, Joel Simpson, Laura Simpson, Kay Sims, Ronald Sims, Leonard Slade, Hilliard Slater, Claude Smith, James Pat Smith, James Ray Smith, Janet Smith, Robert Smith, Charles Spence, Bill Spicer, Sherri Stanford, Creg Stevenson, Arris Stribling, Carson Stribling, Harold Stribling, Webb Stribling, Janice Strohm, Larry Strohm, Ruby Lee (Johnson) Probst Strong, Sarah Stopson, Delores (Parker) Sumrall, Linda Switzer, Lance Taylor, Jeanette Thomas, Bary Thrash, Walter Tienken, Johnny Tynes, Bobby Underwood, Wilma (Profitt) Valentine, Bennie Van Court, Marilyn (Skellie) VanCourt, Jennifer Vickers, Wallene Vogle, Daisha Walker, Roney Walker, Bob Watts, Tammie Weathers, Lanie Wesson, George Westerfield, Ouida White, Jean Williams, Ona Mae Willingham, Debra Willis, Ed Wilson, Sue Wing, William Wilson, Terrell Wise, Darlene (Kapp) Wixon, Tommy Wixon,

PROLOGUE

The prologue of a book is the section accorded an author where he may share the triumphs and the tragedies and the agony and ecstasy of word smithing in perfect equanimity and with the absolute knowledge that the product of his freewheeling internal reverie will remain secret. Nobody reads prologues.

While I do not wish to write a book about writing this book, I feel I should record the salient events that led to my spending nearly one-sixth of my life (to 2001) working on this book. Let what I have to say here serve (1) as a history of the Mississippi Gulf Coast Community College Archives, and (2) as a history of the *Mississippi Gulf Coast Community College: A History* and (3) as a warning to anyone else who might be thinking of blundering into the quicksand of an institutional history.

A History of the Mississippi Gulf Coast Community College Archives

I was an innocent bystander in the establishment of the Mississippi Gulf Coast Community College Archives. MGCCC Publicity Director Winfred Moncrief founded the MGCCC Archives, and he did it as he did everything else to me in the last two decades of the second millennium. As publicity director of the college he dealt with everyone in every level of the institution. He was an able, intelligent hard worker, and a great idea man. Not only were his ideas worthwhile, but he possessed that rare ability to pull people wholeheartedly into a project and make them think the idea was theirs. In my case he set up a triangle leading from him to me and from him to the president of the college and from the president back to me. *The Magnolia Series* of video documentaries which absorbed my energies (and his and Doug Mansfield's at Jackson County Campus) from 1987 to 1992 was a perfect example of how he operated. Moncrief told me that President Barry Mellinger wanted the *Magnolia Series* done. He told Mellinger I wanted to do it. Once he got that far, Doug Mansfield, the television technician, did not have any choice but to "volunteer" for the effort. So seven years passed and four video documentaries hit the table.

As Moncrief approached retirement in 1992, he triangulated Mellinger and me on the idea of a college archives. He told me it was Mellinger's idea. Maybe it was. I was not privy to their discussions. All I know is that it was not my idea. So Mellinger named me college archivist in June 1992 and put Moncrief with me as a consultant to the archives after Moncrief's retirement in July. So Moncrief and I began sifting through thousands of unidentified photos and slides, thousands of negatives, hundreds of videotapes, and tens of thousands of newspaper articles.

The History of Mississippi Gulf Coast Community College: A History

One day in 1994, while Moncrief and I were identifying photographs, he said, "You know, I think Dr. Mellinger's right about there being no point in doing this unless a history of the college is written." Years later I asked Mellinger if he said that. He replied, "I don't remember saying that."

I find a document (dated June 1994) among my souvenirs, informing Mellinger that I would write the book if he would give me five years (five summers) to do it. I figured he would counter offer four years. He agreed to three. It took seven years to do the job. That is as long as Michelangelo "agonized and extasyed" as he painted the ceiling of the Sistine Chapel. That is longer than the United States fought in World War I, World War II, and in Korea. In the final four and one-half years I worked seven days and nights per week all year round, with the exception of exactly 20 days off which included four Christmas Days. In that period my wife, Jane, built a new house that I seldom saw in daylight. She mowed the acre and a half-sized lawn four summers, including one in which the Big Wheel Johnson mower's pulling mechanism would not work because the tires were nearly flat. She did not know what was wrong, and I would not take time to look.

A Warning To Anyone Who Might Be Thinking Of Blundering Into The Quicksand Of An Institutional History.

Having spent three hard years writing *Mississippi Gulf Coast: Portrait of a People* completed in 1985 and one hard year writing *Hurricanes of the Mississippi Gulf Coast* in 1986, I felt I could knock down a junior college in three years--surely! I was in error for several reasons. In the first place, the documents I used to write the first book had been collected for me by Coast historian M. James Stevens in 40 years of digging, and the *Sun Herald* staff collected most of the documents for the hurricane book. Having seen the "forest" of documents on MGCCC, I had not yet discovered that few of the "trees" from 1888-1961 were in that great mass of material. So I had to first pull an "M. James Stevens" before I could even begin to write. Using honors student labor, in three years 15,000 newspaper articles from the *Daily Herald* had to be copied from microfilm before I could even begin to write. In the second place, except for some good work done by past alumni secretaries, I had to amass and caption the pictures for this work. In the case of both my other books, someone else had done that work.

In dealing with the thousands of mostly undated and generally uncaptioned photographs, I at first rejoiced on those rare occasions when a photograph was found to have names and dates on back. Soon, though, I learned to ignore the names and the dates on pictures because so many were in error that it took less time to start from scratch than first to prove the errors and start over. Many of the 1,230 photographs in this book required a whole day each to caption. Some required several days.

Then came another revelation. After I wrote the book and selected and captioned the pictures, I then had to seat each photograph in place because the job was too complicated for anyone else to do it. I could not work the computer, so Melissa Ladner was hired to do the technical work. For 800 hours I pointed to what I wanted where, and she put it there. That little layout and design tidbit was not in my original agreement for sure, because I had no idea that it would have to be done at Perk and much less that I could or would be doing it.

In composing this work, I was dealing with great masses of material much of which was in error. So much was erroneous that in some causes I had to print the most plausible error. In many cases, names, dates, and photographs pertaining to the same event did not jive. The dates on student records did not agree with the dates on newspaper articles which did not agree with the dates in the yearbook which did not agree with the dates written on pictures which did not agree with the dates on trophies. The names on the student records did not agree with the names in the newspapers which did not agree with the names in the yearbooks which did not agree with the names written on pictures which did not agree with what participants remembered. Did I say, "remembered"? Three years into this I stopped asking people to tell me what they "remembered." The results of memory were so awful and cost me so much time that if I could not find a contemporary written account, I just sidestepped the issue if I could. I had whole scrapbooks full of newspaper clippings without a date anywhere on a single article much less a notation to what newspaper published them. I had scores of theatre posters for plays that would be performed "next Thursday" or on "October 20th"--in perpetuity.

All the sports teams were difficult to deal with, but the spring sports were a very special horror. I never could figure out if I was reading in the 1962 yearbook about the 1962 baseball or tennis teams or the 1961 baseball or tennis teams because the yearbooks often went to press before the "present" season ended--but not always.

It was not that I had not had to deal with such things when I wrote the *Mississippi Gulf Coast: Portrait of a People* and *Hurricanes of the Mississippi Gulf Coast*, it was just that I did not deal with them very much. I did not do it because I did not have to do it. Why? Because both of those works were general histories. If I could not find the end of an historical path through the "documentary forest," I simply took another path.

I can now say without fear of contradiction that writing a general history in no way prepares an author to write the history of an institution such as a college. Why? Because the historian absolutely can not deviate from a set path. When I was writing about the Hurricane of 1901, if I could not find out what happened in Bay St. Louis, I told what happened in Pass Christian and let it go. When I started trying to find out who really won the 1927 Mississippi junior college state football championship, there was no way to change the subject or to ignore the missing information.

MY VIETNAM--THE STRUGGLE TO FIND OUT WHO WON THE 1927 MISSISSIPPI STATE JUNIOR COLLEGE FOOTBALL CHAMPIONSHIP--An Example of Why One Should Avoid Writing an Institution History

Any state championship, in my book, (no pun intended) is important. The 1927 football championship was more important than any other because it was the first state championship claimed by this college. At first glance there was no problem. I had the *1927-1928 Catalogue* with the photograph of the football team on page 37 clearly marked "State Champions." I had the photographs of the 1927 team members who returned to Perk in 1977 to celebrate the golden anniversary of their great victory. I had personally known two of these men for many years and saw them from time to time until both died.

The problem began when I obtained a copy of *The Wildcat's Roar*, Pearl River Community College's counterpart to MGCCC's *Athletic Review*, and found that PRC claimed the 1927 football championship as well.

I called Gary Higginbotham (MGCJC class of 1965), whose hobby is collecting Perk's football scores, and asked him about PRC's claim. He said he knew about that and did not know which team won it. Higginbotham has collected what is believed to be the score in nearly every football game Perk played from 1914-2000. From 1926, when the junior college team was first fielded at Perk, he has what is believed to be every single score except that of one game--the November 19, 1927, game against Hinds Junior College played at Perk. Not a bad record--he lacked one game out of more than 700. I set out to find an account of that game. Over a period of five years I estimate that I spun the microfilm of no less than 10 newspapers, no less than 50 hours and made a trip to Hinds to check their archival holdings. I still do not have an account of that game. I had the score of the game from the hands of a member of the 1927 team, but I wanted to verify it. Unable to find an account of that game, I ran microfilm for 15 more hours to get accounts of all of PRC's games for 1927.

PRC's 1927 football season:

Date	PRC score	Opponent	Opponent score
October 1	6	Hammond Junior College	0
October 8	0	Clarke Junior College	0
October 15	0	LSU Freshmen	13
October 28	0	Loyola Freshmen	24
November 5	13	Perkinston	0
November 11	0	State Teacher's College	15
November 19	6	Spring Hill	13
November 24	25	Hinds Junior College	0
Total Points	50		65

PRC's 1927 record: 3 wins, 4 losses, 1 tie

Perkinston's 1927 football season: (scanned from A. I. Rexinger's letter of April 23, 1977:

Record

Perkinston	0-	Miss. State Teachers	0
"	31-	Goodman Jr. College	0
"	31-	Miss. College Fresh.	7
"	13-	St. Stanislaus	6
"	0 -	Poplarville Jr. College	13
"	6 -	Clark College	6
"	25-	Raymond Jr. College	0
Total	106		32

Perk's 1927 record: 4 wins, 1 loss, 2 ties

When I first found Rexinger's scores in his letter of April 25, 1977, I immediately doubted them because the Higginbotham Report carried a game that Rexinger did not include. That game, played against Gulf Coast Military Academy on October 26, 1927, had resulted in a 6 - 6 tie. The October 24, 1927, *Daily Herald* carried an account of that game in which the reporter said the GCMA Cadets tied the "Perkinston Bulldogs" (actually the Cadets tied the Perkinston "Bull Pups" or AHS team--not the college Bulldog team.) The October 29, 1927, *Times Picayune* stated that "Perkinston . . . Junior College did not play last weekend." Thus I learned that Rexinger had not included the GCMA game because it was not a college match.

And there was another problem. The Higginbotham Report said the 1926 Bulldogs beat St. Stanislaus 16-6 while Rexinger said the score was 13-6. The October 31, 1927, *Daily Herald* headline clearly stated that the score was 16-6, but in reading the play by play scoring in the article, the score was actually 13-6 just as Rexinger said it was.

Rexinger's record of 1927 scores claims that Perk beat Hinds (Raymond Jr. College as he put it) 25-0. The next weekend Pearl River beat Hinds 25-0. There is no reason why both Pearl River and Perk could not have beaten Hinds by the same score. My problem was that I could find verification of the PRC-Hinds score and could not find verification of the Perk-Hinds score.

What I finally came to was this. Every time I thought Rexinger was wrong, he proved to be correct, so I am going to believe him.

As to the thought that the 1927 Perk-Hinds game might have been cancelled, then consider these facts. The *Jackson Daily News*, Tuesday, November 15, 1927, stated, "The [Raymond] Aggies will play the Perkinston Junior College at Perkinston Saturday." This is just five days before the game. A year later the *Clarion Ledger*, November 24, 1928, carried the following notation regarding the Hinds-Perk game of that date, "They [the Perk Bulldogs] will come with the reputation of having never been beaten by Hinds Junior College in the history of the two schools." So, whatever the score was in 1927, the 1928 *Clarion Ledger* agrees that it was a Perk victory. After all, in 1928 the Bulldogs and the Eagles had only played twice in "the history of the two schools."

With the Hinds-Perk game of November 19, 1927, thus laid to rest, my problems were over, right? Wrong. The MGCCC Archives Collection contained a silver regulation-sized football trophy reading "Mississippi Junior College Champions, 1928." That date is certainly wrong because in 1928 Perk lost every game it played except for a 6-0 victory over Carthage Junior College and a 13-13 tie with the Millsaps College Freshmen. In the 1928 season, Perk scored 27 points and gave up an incredible 203 points, including a 97-0 loss to Marion Institute of Selma, Alabama.

The erroneous date on the trophy explains why W. C. "Bill" Denson, the coach of the 1927 team, replied as he did in his thank-you letter for his "distinguished coach's plaque" awarded at homecoming 1975. In the letter dated November 28, 1975, he wrote, "There is one little error in the plaque. The first state championship won by Perkinston was 1927. Since no one here [Houston, Texas] will know the difference, I will just proudly display it as is." The "one little error on the plaque" was caused by the "one little error on the trophy." The trophy says 1928 when it should say 1927.

Next I called Pearl River and asked the athletic director if PRC had a silver football reading "1927." He could not locate one so inscribed, but he had one reading "1928" just as I did. I was unable to find out when this misdated trophy was awarded to Perk or who awarded it. It is here, and it should say "1927" instead of "1928."

As to PRC's claim to the 1927 state football championship, I submit the following from the *Hattiesburg American* of November 25, 1927--"The Wildcats of Pearl River Junior College defeated the team from Hinds Junior College for the championship of the state for colleges of this rank on the local field Thursday afternoon. Pearl River won the state championship by tying Clarke 0-0, winning from Perkinston 13-0 and smashing Hinds 25-0." This report was sent to the *Hattiesburg American* from Poplarville and not written by a disinterested party.

PRC claimed the 1927 State Football Championship on the basis of two conference wins (over Perk and Hinds) and one conference tie with Clarke. Perkinston's record was two conference wins (over Goodman and Hinds), one conference tie (Clarke), and one conference loss (to PRC). Perk played four conference games while PRC played only three. In a variation of the PRC dispatch printed in the *Clarion Ledger* of November 25, 1927, PRC claimed the championship "under rules adopted at the first of the season." One wonders what these rules were, but one would assume they required that all teams play the same number of conference games.

In 1935 the Perk Bulldogs played their first undefeated football season (5 wins and 1 tie). Even though that was the best record in the state, Perk was disqualified for the championship title for not playing enough conference games. Perk's 1935 conference record was three wins and one tie with one of the victories being Perk's first defeat of Pearl River. Perk failed to play Holmes in 1935 due to the death of a Perk student the day before the game, and that situation likely cost Perk the state championship for that year. In 1935 Perk was disqualified for the state football championship with a better conference record than PRC had in 1927. In 1927 Perk did play Holmes, but PRC did not play Holmes that year. Yet PRC claimed the 1927 state football championship based on a paltry two win and one tie conference record. Perk claimed the 1927 state football championship on the basis of an overall 4-1-2 record which bested PRC's overall 3-4-1 record.

Perk's claim to the 1927 title was backed by the *Daily Herald* in 1928. On October 29, 1928, the paper noted that the Clarke Panthers "suffered little difficulty in defeating Perkinston, last year's Junior College Champions. . . ." On November 2, the paper stated that "Perkinston won the State Junior College Championship last year." The paper of November 6 referred to the "Mississippi Junior College Championship" which Perk won last year. The November 16 paper put it best of all in avowing that, "The Pearl River squad is making a strong bid for the Mississippi Junior College Championship which Perkinston won last year." The November 23 issue again referred to Perk's 1927 football championship. In my opinion the weight of the evidence points to Perkinston having won the 1927 football state championship.

Apparently Richard "Dick" Lightsey, sports writer for the *Daily Herald* in the 1960s, ran into the same problems over this that I did. On November 21, 1966, he called the 1927 championship a tie between Perk and Pearl River. However, he offered no evidence for his claim.

The 1927 state football championship was by no means the only quagmire I wandered into during the grueling seven-year attempt to write the history of Mississippi Gulf Coast Community College. It was just the longest and most frustrating crawl through the historical swamp.

I might add that the 1928 State Football Championship might be a swamp some other Bulldogs (namely Holmes) might like to sniff into. Apparently most every team in the state except the Bulldogs of Perk and Holmes were "co-champions" that year. Pearl River, Clarke, and Sunflower claimed the only three-way championship tie in the 20th century for that one. I guess all three got a 1928 silver football. However, I accidentally struck a *Clarion Ledger* article of November 28, 1928, which reprinted a dispatch from Goodman in which Holmes claimed "the state championship as they are the only junior college team in the state that has won more than three conference games." So as Bulldog to Bulldog, there it is. Since I do not have a dog in that hunt, I will not be looking further. By way of appreciation I am sure that Holmes will be sending the 1936 State Championship football trophy to Perk since the January 19, 1937, *Daily Herald* noted that two members of the Holmes team had been disqualified thereby turning Perk's only defeat of 1936 into a victory and thus making the Perk Bulldogs instead of the Holmes Bulldogs the 1936 champs. If Holmes does not have this trophy, the state junior college commissioner owes Perk a new trophy dated "1936."

I must say I have tried to straighten out some of this stuff. The *Wildcat's Roar* was missing six years of football scores and in 1999 was claiming 42 victories over Perk against 26 losses. I phoned the PRC athletic director and demanded that he change those lying numbers. He did not act very pleased until I told him that the real figures were 48 wins against 26 defeats. Then my athletic director was not very pleased.

In closing, I would advise anyone desiring to write an institutional history to consider the time involved. From June 1994 to June 1997 I worked more or less regular hours, collecting documentation for the book. On June 6, 1997, I began the blitzkrieg in earnest--seven days a week--estimating it would take two years to finish at that rate. I wrote and researched straight through until November 11, 2001. That is four years, five months, and five days or 1,618 total days. During that time I took off 20 days, so I wrote and researched for 1,598 days. On Mondays, Wednesdays, and Fridays during school sessions, I wrote for approximately five to six hours per day. On holidays, Saturdays, and Sundays I worked 10 to 13 hours per day. So using five hours as the usual on class days and 10 hours as the usual on the other days, then I worked approximately 14,000 hours on this book or on the archives just in the blitzkrieg period. The time devoted to the project in the three years before June 6, 1997, and the months after November 11, 2001 would easily push the figure to 20,000 hours.

Each night when I went home between 8 p.m. and 10 p.m. Jane was required to ask, "Would you have done this if you had known how hard it was going to be?" Each night I answered, "No." I meant it, too. If I could have foreseen the cost I would have quailed in the face of it. But once I said I would do it the only thing I could do was do it. Like somebody said, "The only thing on this planet besides God that approaches omnipotence is determination." I believe that because it is true.

Am I proud of this book? You bet I am! Even with all its faults and mistakes, it is, I believe, the most comprehensive junior/community college history in history. And I am proud of the junior/community college as an institution. The junior/community college is the only educational institution founded in the United States. All other educational systems from kindergarten through university are European in origin. As the higher educational expression of grassroots democracy, the junior/community college celebrates American "know how" and "can do" spirit as no other educational entity. It is my hope that this effort in detailing the evolution of one such institution might be of value in understanding the growth of the one thousand others spread about this land.

fini January 31, 2002

Author's Notes

1. In formal historical writing a person is fully identified once and thereafter addressed by his or her last name. In the case of baseball coaches Curly and Cooper Farris, I obviously could not do that and therefore addressed them by their first names. I did likewise in the case of basketball coaches Bob and Wendell Weathers.

2. Throughout this work in nearly every case involving Perkinston Campus, Jefferson Davis Campus, and Jackson County Campus, I addressed them in that order. I did that because I do not think "alphabetically"; I think "geographically." I was writing at Perk, JD was next nearest to me, and JC farthest from me. Ironically, the way I addressed the campuses is reverse alphabetical order. In writing *Mississippi Gulf Coast: Portrait of a People*, I consistently addressed the cities on the Gulf rim from west to east for the same "geographical" reason.

3. In the captions of photographs copied from published sources (yearbooks, catalogs, brochures, *Action* magazine, etc.), I gave the location of the source. In the case of photographs loaned for publication in the work, I recognized the gift with a courtesy line. If the caption carries no source or courtesy line, then the photo may be assumed to be an original held in the MGCCC Archives Collection.

4. This book is a 20th century history and contains historical information up to 11:59 p.m. December 31, 2000. Research and writing continued through the year 2001 and to the early part of 2002, but no rendition of historical events occurring after midnight, January 1, 2001, was included. If I interviewed persons or received information about 20th century events after midnight January 1, 2001, those sources were noted and dated.

5. Out-of-state towns are followed by the appropriate state name. If there is no state name following the town or village, it is understood to be in Mississippi.

6. Melissa Ladner and I thought we had finished on January 31, 2002. When the indexer hired by the college proved unable to do the job (through no fault of his own), Melissa and I had to perform that task as well. On June 18, 2002 the MGCCC Foundation Board authorized the printing of the book. The CD containing the book was mailed to Michigan on June 20, 2002. When that one failed to arrive, another one was sent on July 2, 2002.

Book Statistics: 608 pages containing 1,232 photos, and 320,900 words.

BOOK I

From Agricultural High School to Multi-Campus Community College

HISTORY OF PERKINSTON

John Perkins photo courtesy of his great-grandson Ralph Jenkins.

John Perkins

Only one battered photograph of John Perkins was in the collection of the MGCCC archives in 2000, but a much clearer word picture of him was penned by Bostick Hanson "Crab" Breland in the *Daily Herald* on June 22, 1945:

"Uncle John Perkins

We don't remember having paid our respects to that interesting old character the late John Perkins in honor of whom the town of Perkinston and the Junior College was named. We call him uncle not as a figure of speech, but because his first wife was Mary Breland, our own blood aunt. Uncle John was married four times, but be it said to his credit he never had but one wife at the same time. He was wholly illiterate but endowed with plenty of "hoss sense" and as full of energy as an egg is of meat. He was not too religious, but did more to support the churches, and took care of the poor and needy far better than the average man. He was not a very large man, but had the strength and staying qualities of an ox. He told us that Martin Breland was the only white man that could out wind him. He proved this when they were chasing a bear one hot day in August, when the animal led off down Red Creek, and they undertook to keep up with the bear and dogs. But at the end of six miles, he gave out, and melted down and Mart beat him to the stand, and killed the bear. Uncle John was a great farmer, a great log man and a great hunter."

Samuel and Charity Perkins moved west from Georgia in the early 1820s, settling in Perry County. The place where they settled was called Red Hill, an eminence overlooking Black Creek at the point where Fairley's Ferry was located. John, the first of six children, was born October 20, 1824. At the next farm down the road lived the Brelands who had come overland from South Carolina. At the age of 26 John Perkins married 19-year-old Mary Breland, and they had a child named Sarah. Mary died shortly after the birth of the child, and on April 25, 1855, John married Emily Hester. By the outbreak of the Civil War in 1861, John and Emily, together with Sarah and a newborn daughter named Lucy, lived in a rough hewn cabin in the forks of Red and Ten Mile Creeks at the place that would later be called Perkinston. After the fall of Vicksburg, the draft age was raised to 50, and Perkins, then nearly 40, was conscripted into the Confederate Army. On October 1, 1863, at Enterprise, Perkins signed the muster roll of (New) Company H, 3rd Mississippi Regiment. In February 1864, he was listed as "absent without leave." In the words of his great-granddaughter, Bettye Jo Blakeney, "He deserted and came back and hid out in the swamps between Red and Black Creeks. The family would leave supplies he needed at a location in the swamps." Apparently Perkins eluded the grand sweep of the Confederate Army which netted 1,000 deserters in the piney woods in summer 1864, and the family escaped the depredations of the "jayhawker" bands roving the area. On December 21, 1864, the Perkins had another daughter, Jerusha. The next year as the war ended they buried four-year-old Lucy in the family cemetery one mile north of Red Creek. In 1869 the Perkins had their last child, a son named David V., known as "D.V." Emily died January 13, 1871, and on June 14 John married her older sister, Mariam Hester. In 1879 Perkins received title to 160 acres of land under the terms of the Homestead Act and in subsequent years added to the tract by purchase. In 1880 Perkins reported his agricultural production as 200 bushels of Indian corn, 120 bushels of oats, 300 bushels of sweet potatoes, 100 pounds of tobacco, and 4 bales of cotton. He owned 12 working oxen, 13 milk cows, 20 swine, and 150 sheep.

On October 27, 1886, John's daughter Jerusha married Richard Nixon "Nick" Davis, a widower with five small children. In time they had eight children of their own bringing the total to 13. Mariam died in 1893, and the following year Perkins deeded his land and house to the Davises. Then John and his son, D.V., became partners in a sawmill with Frank Lott at Inda, two miles northeast of Perkinston. On April 24, 1897, John married his fourth and final wife, Sarah Bond. According to his great-granddaughter, Bettye Jo Blakeney, "He walked the railroad trestle to the Inda sawmill and he was nearly deaf. He was struck by a train on the trestle and killed." After his death on November 21, 1901, John Perkins was buried in the family graveyard between Emily and Mariam.

In the 1890s the Perkins-Davis family pose with their oxen, horses, and wagons in front of the original cabin built by John Perkins. Photo courtesy of Ralph Jenkins.

The John Perkins house, located beyond the east end of Perkins Street in Perkinston, as it appeared on December 14, 2000. The original cabin constructed by John Perkins was contained under the highest middle portion of the roof. In December 2000 the ax strokes made by Perkins in squaring the timbers in the Civil War era were clearly visible in the walls of the back right corner room. The carport at right and the rooms at left were added by the mid-20th century.

Photo by Richard Kopp

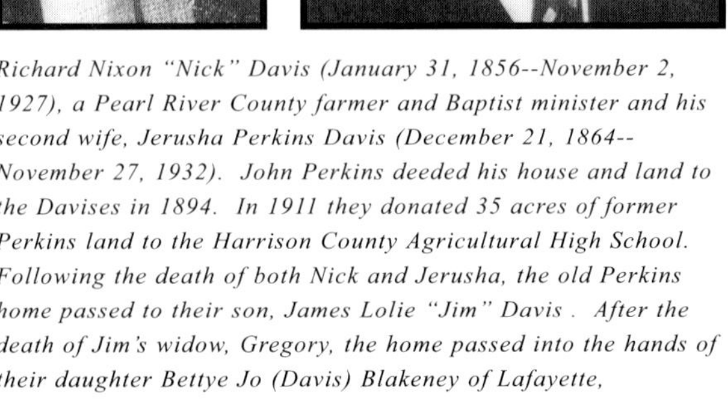

Richard Nixon "Nick" Davis (January 31, 1856--November 2, 1927), a Pearl River County farmer and Baptist minister and his second wife, Jerusha Perkins Davis (December 21, 1864--November 27, 1932). John Perkins deeded his house and land to the Davises in 1894. In 1911 they donated 35 acres of former Perkins land to the Harrison County Agricultural High School. Following the death of both Nick and Jerusha, the old Perkins home passed to their son, James Lolie "Jim" Davis . After the death of Jim's widow, Gregory, the home passed into the hands of their daughter Bettye Jo (Davis) Blakeney of Lafayette, Louisiana.

Bostick Hanson "Crab" Breland

Sketch of Crab Breland by staff artist Robert Christy published November 4, 1984, used by permission of the Sun Herald newspaper.

Most of the early information on Perkinston and the north Harrison County area of the piney woods came from the pen of Bostick Hanson Breland. He was born July 24, 1861, at Red Hill in Perry County. He was the third of 11 children born to Bostick and Elizabeth Breland. Shortly after his father returned home from the Confederate Army at the close of the Civil War, the family moved 15 miles south to an area of north Harrison County (a part of Stone County after 1916) known as Big Level. This 25-square-mile area of gently rolling land, which resembled Kansas more than the pine covered hills surrounding it, was named for its topography. In a one-room school at Big Level, Breland received a formal education aggregating 18 months. His education was augmented by reading enough books in Breland's words, "to load a battleship." As he rode about the piney woods working in various sawmills, he observed the life around him and sent occasional articles to the *Handsboro Democrat*. By 1888 he was writing a weekly column for the *Pascagoula Democrat Star* under the pseudonym "Snap Beans in the Saddle." But when a young lady he was courting told him he was "the sourest old thing she had ever seen," he took the name "Crabapple." Later as he became "less sour" he dropped the "apple" and became just "crab." His desultory columns virtually ceased after his 1889 marriage. For the next 23 years he worked as a country store proprietor, a postmaster, a schoolteacher, a constable, a deputy sheriff, a census taker, and as a game warden, among other jobs. Through it all, he recorded in his mind impressions of piney woods and Coast life. After a two-decade hiatus as a country correspondent, Breland resumed writing for the *Wiggins Enterprise.* Shortly thereafter he acceded to the wishes of Walter Wilkes, editor of the *Daily Herald*, for him to serve a wider audience. On February 13, 1913, the first column of "Crabology: Criticisms and Comments by Crab of Big Level" appeared in the *Daily Herald.* From then until shortly before his death on May 20, 1949, Crab poured forth nearly 1,700 articles. These articles contained "down home philosophy," observations on national and international current events, folklore, historical reminiscences, and eyewitness accounts of doings in the piney woods. Breland so admired Will Rogers, the "cowboy philosopher," that he tried to make himself a carbon copy of him. In doing so he failed to realize that the real value of his writing was not in emulating Rogers, but in preserving the written record of the history and culture of south Mississippi in general and the piney woods in particular.

Bostick "Crab" Breland married Flora Jane Myers in 1889. Photo courtesy of Corece Colvin, granddaughter of Crab and Flora Breland.

Crab (left) began writing for Walter Wilkes, editor of the Daily Herald on Feb. 13, 1913. Photo courtesy of Hanson Breland, grandson of Crab and Flora Breland.

Uriel Wright Plat of Perkinston 1896

Harrison County Civil Engineer Uriel Wright surveyed the plat of Perkinston in1896. Wright filed the plat in the Harrison County Courthouse on February 7, 1898. With the establishment of Stone County in 1916, a copy of the plat was placed in Stone County Record Book 1, page 4. Stone County Chancery Clerk Gerald W. Bond sent a copy of the plat to the MGCCC Archives on May 26, 1998.

Most, if not all, of the area shown on the plat originally belonged to John Perkins. In 1896 Wright named the owners of the area platted as, "R. N. Davis and William Morris." R.N. Davis was John Perkins's son-in-law.

The adaptation of the 1896 Uriel Wright plat of Perkinston used in this work replicates the layout of the lots, avenues, and streets of the original, but section lines and surveyor's notations have been removed. To avoid confusion, block numbers have been rendered into words. For example, Block 7 is styled as Block Seven. On the plat all northwest-southeast tending thoroughfares were styled "streets." The thoroughfares crossing them were styled "avenues." By 2000 all the remaining thoroughfares in Perkinston had been signed "streets." Locations of certain structures were added by the author.

Why 1st Street and 2nd Street were shown by Wright as stopping a block north of the Gulf and Ship Island Railroad tracks was not known to this author. They certainly went to the tracks later. Apparently the blank area north and south of the tracks was intended as a commercial district. The Graves (Swetman) Store was located in this area adjacent to and south of the tracks by 1887. The Dees Store was located in this area adjacent to and north of the tracks by 1911.

All the numbered lots on the plat were 104.5 feet wide. All the lots in the upper tier of blocks (Block Two to Block Sixteen) were 225 feet long. All lots in the tier formed by Blocks One through Fifteen were 230 feet long. All whole lots in Blocks Seven, Twelve, Fourteen, and Six were 200 feet in length. The lots in Block Five varied in length due to the meanders of Ten Mile Creek. Triangular Block Thirteen became the Old Athletic Field of the junior college in 1925.

After the selection of Perkinston as the site of the Harrison County Agricultural High School, the Board of Trustees in September 1911 used most of the $626 donated by the founders to purchase Blocks Seven, Eight, and Nine as the site of the campus. Charlie Swetman, who had donated 40 acres to the school, sold all of Blocks Seven and Eight to the Trustees for $250. Lots 3, 4, and 5 of Block Nine were included in the 35 acres given by R. N. and Jerusha Davis. Uriel Wright sold Lots 1 and 2 of Block Nine to the Trustees for $70. U. B. Parker sold Lot 6 of Block Nine for $125, and Harry H. Lewis sold Lots 7 and 8 of Block Nine for $70. Huff Hall, the original structure of the HCAHS, was built on the Lewis lots.

The school first expanded by building from the top of Perk Hill down to the tracks. In the 1930s the school began expanding to the west, purchasing in time Blocks Ten, Eleven, Twelve, Fifteen, Sixteen, and most of Block Fourteen. In the 1930s the school also began purchasing lots in Block Eight. In 1975, with the purchase of Lots 1 and 2 as the site of Liaison, all of Block Eight became school property. By 2000 the college owned approximately three-quarters of the 1896 Uriel Wright plat.

In the beginning, 4th Street on the plat may have been the original principal northwest-southeast artery for the town. But as 4th Street disappeared into the campus, 3rd Street supplanted it, describing a hairpin turn to the southwest down Cedar Street to connect with an extension of the line of 4th Street to the northwest toward Magnolia and Stillmore. The hairpin curve at the corner of 3rd and Cedar remained until straightened with a new cut road about 1962. The course of Cedar Avenue to the right of 3rd Street is shown on the plat but did not develop into a modern thoroughfare due to a deep ravine. Myrtle Avenue and Perkins Avenue were both cut at 3rd Street by the formation of the campus. In 2000 the former course of Myrtle Avenue (renamed Church Street) connected 3rd Street and 1st Street. That change likely occurred when the Perkinston Baptist Church was moved from its former site in the Perkinston Cemetery to the corner of Myrtle and 1st Street in 1927. That wooden church, though, faced 1st Street. The brick church, which replaced the wooden structure in 1973, faced Church Street. The name "Myrtle" was moved up and placed on the 16-foot-wide alley that split Blocks Two and Three between 1st and 3rd Streets. Perkins Street in 2000 only extended from the Perkins house to 2nd Street.

Uriel Wright Plat of Perkinston 1896

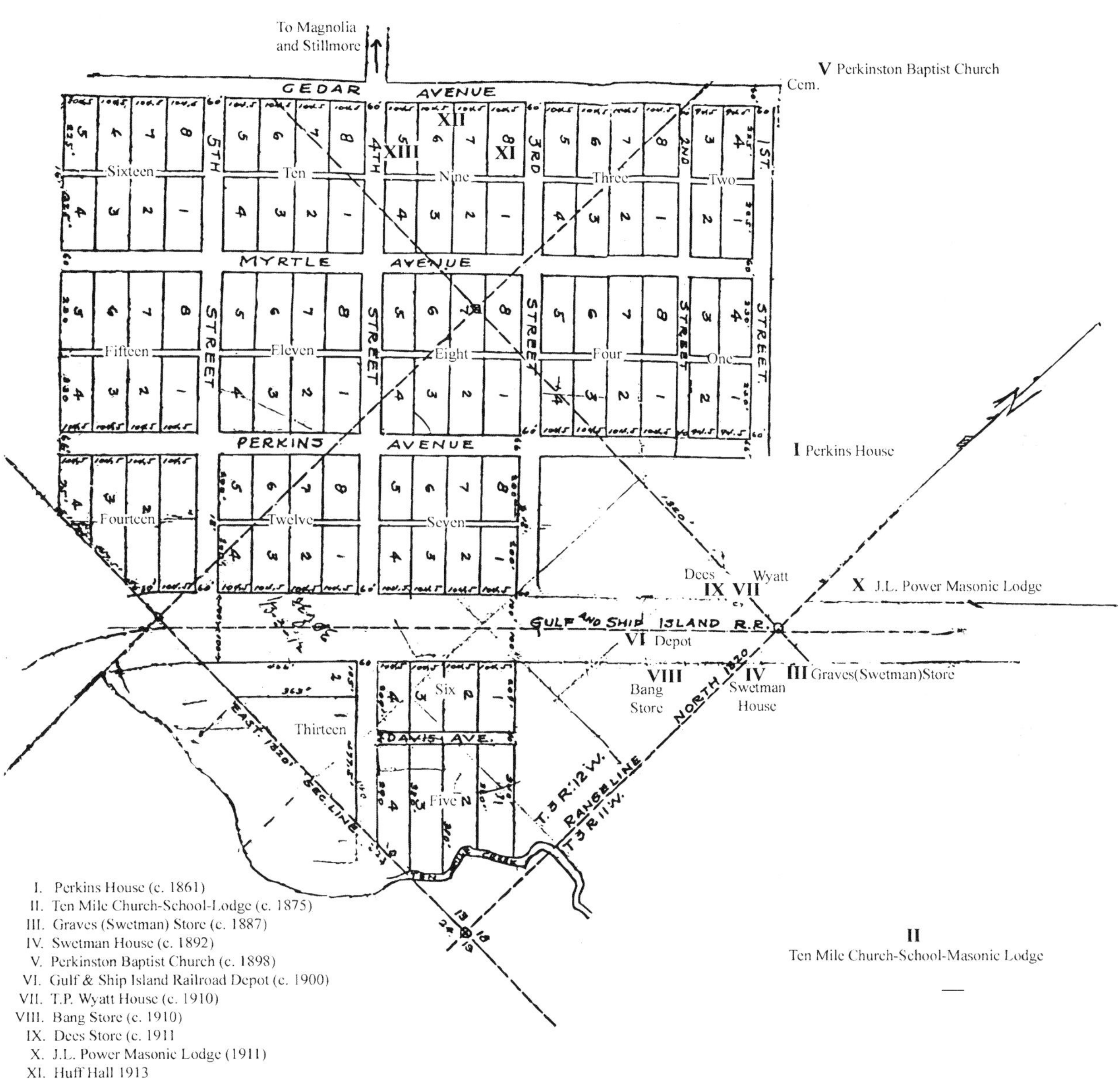

Perkinston and the Gulf & Ship Island Railroad

While building the New Orleans and North Eastern Railroad (NO&NE RR) from New Orleans to Meridian, which he finished in 1883, railroad promoter William Harris Hardy was already planning another line--the Gulf & Ship Island Railroad (G&SI RR). He had selected a point on the NO&NE RR 72 miles due north of the Ship Island anchorage as the junction for the other railway he intended to build from the Coast to Jackson. On that site he erected a depot and platted a town that he christened Hattiesburg in honor of his second wife, Hattie (Lott) Hardy of Mobile.

With settlers buying lands along the proposed route, Hardy secured a bond issue in 1887 and bought land at the southern terminus where he planned another town to be his port on the Gulf--Gulfport. He then leased convicts from the Mississippi State Penitentiary and began grading the roadbed from three points. The crews graded north from Gulfport, south from Hattiesburg, and both ways from the mid-point near the John Perkins house located in the forks of Red and Ten Mile Creeks.

Hardy built a stockade in 1887 on the banks of Ten Mile Creek a quarter mile from the Perkins house and filled it with convicts. Bostick Hanson "Crab" Breland of Big Level, who hired on as a guard, was present when G&SI RR Superintendent of Construction James Hoskins, standing 200 yards from the Perkins house, threw the first shovel full of dirt in the air as the signal

United States of America

No 477 $100

THE COUNTY OF HARRISON,

State of Mississippi.

Twenty Years after date the County of Harrison in the State of Mississippi, undertakes and binds itself to pay to the GULF & SHIP ISLAND RAILROAD COMPANY, or Bearer, One hundred Dollars, with interest thereon at the rate of six per centum per annum, payable annually on the first day of April, of each successive year, at the office of the County Treasurer of said County, upon the surrender and delivery respectively of the Coupons for interest annexed hereto. Provided however that this bond may be called, and re[illegible] at any time upon the payment of the principal thereof and interest accrued at the matu[illegible]

This bond is One of a [illegible] Fifty thousand Dollars [illegible] in [illegible] order of the Board of Supervisors of Harrison [illegible] Mississippi [illegible] of a subscription to the Capital Stock of the [illegible] Ship Island Railroad Company [illegible] to, by the qualified voters of said County [illegible] the [illegible] and laws of said State, on the fourth day of Janua[illegible] of the Legis[illegible] the State of Mississippi, entitled "An act to incorporate the Gulf and Ship Island Railroad Company" Approved February 23rd 1882.

In testimony whereof, the President of the Board of Supervisors of said County hath hereto set his hand, and caused to be affixed the Seal of said County at Mississippi City, the First day of April A.D. 1887.

CANCELED

Countersigned & Registered,

F. S. Hewes Clerk Chancery Court
Ex-officio Clerk of the Board of Supervisors, Harrison County.

Prest. Board Supervisors, Harrison County.

$100

A Gulf and Ship Island Railroad bond issued in 1887 courtesy of Randy Randazzo.

G&SI RR construction train from The Book of Harrison County by Cox and Martin, 1905, p. 33.

to begin work. Near the point where Hoskins broke ground, Henry T. Graves of Hazelhurst, whose wife was the former Susan Swetman of Handsboro, was already constructing a mercantile establishment. The post office in that fledgling "town" was established December 29, 1888, with Dr. Walter T. Bolton as postmaster. Bolton, a physician for the G&SI RR, who had secured quarters in the Perkins home, named the post office "Perkinston" (short for Perkins Town). Bolton soon moved the post office from the Perkins house to the Graves Store.

Perkinston postmaster Arl O'Neal stands on the front porch of the Graves (Swetman) Store in 1960. Photograph courtesy of Arl O'Neal.

By 1892 the railroad bed had been graded from Hattiesburg to Gulfport and the tracks laid 20 miles inland to Bernard Saucier's place. First known as "Bernard Station," the name of the place soon changed to "Saucier." At Saucier, construction halted due to the bankruptcy of Hardy's company.

In spring 1892 H. T. Graves sold his store to his brother-in-law, Charlie Swetman. On April 4, 1892, Swetman succeeded Bolton as postmaster of Perkinston. From then until May 2, 1935 (except for the 14 months between September 9, 1896 and November 6, 1897, when Charles A. Sheeley was postmaster), either Charlie Swetman or his wife Gratia (Myers) Swetman was postmaster of Perkinston.

In 1895 financier Joseph T. Jones of Buffalo, New York, bought the G&SI RR, and construction on the line resumed. The first G&SI RR train to run the line from Gulfport to Hattiesburg passed through Perkinston on October 4, 1896. When the G&SI RR constructed its depot a few years later, the railroad stop was given the same name as the post office—Perkinston.

Though Perkinston was not incorporated as a village, much less a town in the 20th century, the Perkinston post office came to serve an area as large as Belgium. On April 3, 1914, the *Daily Herald* gave notice that the Perkinston post office would begin a Rural Free Delivery (RFD) route on May 1. This route ran from Perkinston across Red Creek Bridge and followed the north side of Red Creek to Cable Bridge near Ramsay Springs. After crossing Cable Bridge back to the south side of the creek, the route followed Old Wire Road back to the point of origin. The name of the carrier was not given, but Thomas P. Wyatt, who lived next door to Dees Store in Perkinston, was the motorcar operator of the route in 1920, which by then had grown to 80 miles in length. The longest in south Mississippi, the route passed through portions of Stone, George, and Jackson counties.

According to retired postmaster, Dolores (McHenry) Mauldin, one of her rural carriers, Flossie Brown, was running a rural route out of Perkinston to the east in 1973 that was 158 miles long. According to Mauldin that route was, at that time, the longest in the United States.

In 2000, the Perkinston rural routes totaled a distance of 599.5 miles. These routes served portions of the counties of Stone, George, Jackson, Pearl River, Harrison, and Hancock. At the close of the 20th century, Perkinston, exclusive of the community college campus, was scarcely larger than it had been in the first decade of the century, but people in all six counties of the Mississippi Panhandle had a Perkinston address.

A circa 1920 Ramsay Springs advertising postcard gives the address of the "One-Galus Resort" as Perkinston post office, 20 miles distant. Courtesy of Willie A. Bond.

On April 25, 1962, Postmaster Arl O'Neal moved his postal machinery from the Graves (Swetman) Store to this post office building on Main Street, Perkinston.

Photo by Richard Kopp

On April 25, 1998, the first envelopes were stamped in the newest Perkinston post office located on the frontage road facing "new" U.S. Highway 49.

Perkinston and U. S. Highway 49

The Mississippi state legislature's 1908 Agricultural High School Law had been born out of the need for agricultural instruction in a state still dependent on horse-drawn vehicles traveling roads that were terrible in any season and impassable in some. Hence, the schools had to be boarding institutions with dormitories.

Photo of an automobile in front of a Wiggins home circa 1912. From the Annual Catalogue of Wiggins High School, Session 1912-1913, p. 41, courtesy of Myrtis Krohn.

Almost simultaneously the advent of the automobile resulted in a cry for good roads. The improvement in roads and transport resulted in school consolidation, which rendered the AHSs unnecessary. The AHSs had been born at the last moment they could have been.

Jasper County established the first AHS in Mississippi at Bay Springs in 1908. Prentiss County established the fifty-first and final one in Booneville in 1919. The importance of the agricultural high school in Mississippi had very little to do with its original purpose. Its great legacy lay in the fact that twelve counties found another use for their AHS campuses. They turned them into junior colleges. Prentiss County founded an AHS solely to make it a junior college. It never served as an AHS. Some AHSs, which later spawned junior colleges, remained in operation for many years in conjunction with them. This happened at Perkinston.

It was no accident that all the main contenders for the site of the Harrison County AHS lay on the G&SI RR. The only viable way for students who lived in the Coast towns and cities to travel to and from the school was via the railroad. The railroad, though, spawned roads.

With the completion of the G&SI RR, a serpentine dirt road grew along the tracks, connecting the turpentine stills and lumber mills located along its length. In the more settled areas the road whiplashed back and forth across the tracks, creating a dangerous situation which resulted in many train-wagon (and later train-automobile) collisions. In certain areas, particularly in the Black Creek swamps near Brooklyn, no track-side road existed.

In June 1908 the residents of Perkinston witnessed the pioneering automobile excursion from the Coast to Hattiesburg. Seafood tycoon W. K. M. Dukate of Biloxi took his family on a jaunt to Hattiesburg in a Thomas Flyer. The trip via Gulfport, then north along the sandy roads connecting the villages flanking the G&SI RR, required a day and a half. The intrepid party spent a good portion of their first day using a mule team to haul the stalled vehicle out of Turkey Creek. The rest of the trip through Nugent, McHenry, Perkinston, and Wiggins was relatively uneventful until Dukate lost his bearings near Maxie. There he hired a pilot to guide him through the Black Creek swamps to Brooklyn where the family spent the night. The party reached the Hub City the next morning and then returned via the route they had come. The return required only one day, since only two hours were lost—one for lunch and the other for a flat tire. In their peregrinations the Dukate party covered 255 miles and burned 66 gallons of gas. The general route they ran from Gulfport to Hattiesburg would, in time, become U. S. Highway 49.

Five years after the Dukate trip, the students and faculty of the first session of the Harrison County AHS witnessed more automotive history. A car passed through Perkinston four times in two trips made by the same two men two months apart for the same reason. Henry Janin, the Ford dealer in Biloxi, had his chauffeur Matteo Bersich drive him from Biloxi through Gulfport and up the road following the G&SI RR to advertise the durability of the Ford cars he had for sale. Helena, (later renamed Carnes) located six miles southwest of Brooklyn, was the destination both times. Janin did not want to go through the Black Creek swamps.

The first trip took place on January 17, 1913. Bersich and Janin left Biloxi at 7 a.m. and made short stops in all the towns including Perkinston. They made it back to Biloxi at midnight. According to Janin, the roads were bad because of the grading being done on them and "had they gone in a large touring car

A child stands on the running board of an automobile in the piney woods circa 1914. Elmira (Williams) Lee in 1982 recalled an automobile trip from her home in Wortham to Poplarville circa 1914. There being no road, she and her husband used a compass as a guide through the forests to their destination. In her words, "There were so many pine trees and so much straw on the ground until everything was clean and pretty. You never saw any brush growing anywhere." Photo courtesy of Myrtis Krohn.

they would have had to abandon the trip early in the journey." The *Daily Herald* considered this an exceptionally quick trip and deemed Janin and Bersich to be "highly elated." They had made 150 miles in 17 hours. Taking two hours out for stops that was an average of ten miles per hour.

Janin and Bersich reprised the trip on March 19, 1913. That time the journey took two days because of recent rains. Janin said the second trip was "more trying on the machine" than the previous one. He said there would be no more trips until the roads were improved. A correspondent from Perkinston quoted in the *Daily Herald* of February 7, 1913, put it plainly, "If Harrison County had no money nor Supervisors or Road Overseers our roads could not possibly be any worse in this neighborhood."

A road crew at work in Stone County in February 1917. Photo courtesy of Myrtis Krohn.

Plans for the Mississippi Centennial provided the impetus for building a real north-south highway between Gulfport and Jackson. Gulfport was to host the exposition which was to open on December 10, 1917. By mid-March a thousand men were at work at various points between Gulfport and Jackson. Three thousand more were to join those within three months. The workers aimed to complete the graveled highway from Jackson to Gulfport by the opening of the exposition thus "making possible an eight-hour trip from the state capital to the sea coast."

On March 15, 1917, a convoy of cars driven by Centennial Highway "Boosters" and led by Mississippi Governor Theodore G. Bilbo approached the Harrison-Stone AHS from the south. The boosters traveled the whole five miles from McHenry to Perkinston in just 30 minutes. The governor and many other dignitaries addressed the student body assembled in the auditorium. After refreshments the convoy proceeded north toward Jackson. At Florence one automobile dropped into a hole in an otherwise smooth road and broke its front axle. Then the rains came, and the eleven miles from Florence to Jackson required 4 hours and 45 minutes to traverse. Still, with unlimited man power and mule power, the highway could be built by December.

American entry into the Great War on April 6, 1917, torpedoed the Mississippi Centennial and the Centennial Highway. Nearly two decades would pass before the momentum in road building lost at this time would be resumed.

The north-south main road through Stone County in 1917 was described as 30 feet wide with no surfacing of any kind other than dirt. A correspondent to the *Daily Herald* on August 8, 1917, said the road was wide enough to permit "three autos to go abreast at good speed." Culverts of heavy timber carried the road across marshes. There were no signs of any kind. This road was still styled the Centennial Highway but was also referred to in various period documents as the Meridian Highway, the Jackson Highway, the Burlington Highway, and the Dixie Highway. The grandiose names did not make it any more passable when it rained.

Roadwork in this period was carried out by supervisors pressing the able-bodied men of their beats into work gangs for a few days each year. Those refusing to work were forced to pay a fine of $5 which was a considerable amount when the minimum wage was about $1 a day. This method of roadwork, dating back to the Middle Ages, was to say the least, very inefficient. An eloquent testimonial of how ineffective road gangs were was printed in the *Daily Herald* of January 7, 1919. The article was entitled "North and South Road in Bad Shape" and subtitled "Waterloo for Autos."

"Henry Walker of Wortham is in the city today. The home of Mr. Walker is near the centennial highway, and a few days ago an army physician came to the field where he was at work and asked for his help in extricating his auto from a mire on the road a short distance away. When he reached the spot where the wheels of the machine were buried in the mud, he saw three others which had suffered a similar fate in trying to pass the one already stuck. As one was pulled to dry land it would be hooked to another in the mud, and the work continued until all were freed. During that day, Mr. Walker claims that he assisted in liberating nine machines stuck at the same point. In fact the work was so continuous that he gave up the job he was doing in a near by field and went to another where he could not be found by stranded automobiles."

By 1925, a rise in automobile ownership had given rise to good roads advocates determined to do whatever was necessary to call attention to the development of the Magnolia Route envisioned to run from Gulfport 1,050 miles north to Chicago. As part of the hype, Magnolia trees had been planted a distance of 600 miles along the route from Gulfport to

The non-stop "Special Six" Studebaker car is pictured in the Daily Herald on Saturday, April 18, 1925, before its history making 1,050 miles, 44 hour and 50 minutes, run to Chicago along the Magnolia Route which began at 10 a.m. on the following Monday. Good highways promoter Colonel W. B. Royster is standing near the front wheel with cap in hand. Lead driver Arthur Lang is leaning against the rear of the car. Relief driver Donald DeMetz of Pass Christian, who later served as a Trustee of Mississippi Gulf Coast Junior College, is standing at the extreme right. Mechanic R. H. Eicholz (pronounced "Iko"), dressed in coveralls, is standing just to the right of Col. Royster. The Non-Stop stunt marked the birth of U. S. Highway 49 and touched off the demand to pave it. Paving began on the Harrison County section the following year, but many years elapsed before the pavement crossed Stone County. In 1925 Sheriff Peter Lott reported 756 license plates sold in Stone County. That same year 176,085 autos were reported in Mississippi, quite a gain from one auto reported in the state in the year 1900. In 1925 the nationwide automobile total reached 20,200,000. The year 1925 marked the coming of the "Automobile Revolution in America." The Mississippi State Department of Education that year reported 1,200 motor buses against 1,400 school wagons carrying children to schools in Mississippi. On the last day of 1925, the trolley cars ran the tracks from Biloxi Bay to the Bay of St. Louis for the final time. The next morning, New Years Day, 1926, motor buses went into service. Photo used by permission of the Sun Herald.

Clarksville, Tennessee. Many main streets of small towns (including Wiggins) along the way had been named Magnolia Street.

On Monday, April 20, 1925, HSAHS Superintendent J. L. Denson dismissed classes. All the students and teachers of the HSAHS gathered along the highway in front of the school to watch history in the making.

Shortly before 10 a.m. in Gulfport on that Monday morning, the lead driver, Arthur Lang, got behind the wheel of a Studebaker "Special Six" in front of the Splendid Café. He was then securely chained and locked to the wheel. Magnolia Route "booster" Colonel W. B. Royster took the "shotgun" position to serve as pilot. Relief driver Donald DeMetz, got in the backseat with "mechanician" R. E. Eicholz. After a complimentary curb service breakfast, the intrepid foursome drove to the Gulfport Post Office at the corner of 13th Street and 25th Avenue.

At precisely 10 a.m. a uniformed Gulfport policeman raised his service revolver, fired, and they were off to run 1,050 miles of unmarked gravel and dirt roads liberally pocked with potholes. They intended to negotiate these roads, dodging wandering farm stock, slow-moving wagons, and other cars and be in Chicago in 48 hours.

Shortly after 10:30 the non-stop car clattered over the planked Ten Mile Bridge and roared into Perkinston to be greeted by the cheers of students and townspeople. Driver Lang swerved to the left and slung gravel as he made the tight curve to the right and disappeared down the main drag of Perkinston in a cloud of dust. HSAHS freshman Frank Eicholtz cheered longer and louder than anyone else did that day at Perkinston because his father was the mechanic sitting in the back seat of that historic car. The non-stop car thundered into Chicago 44 hours and 50 minutes after it left Gulfport. Only 40 hours of that was actual driving time, the balance being pit stops. Royster's "Non-stop Trip" made national headlines, and within seven months the southern extremity of the Magnolia Route received the numerical designation, "U. S. Highway 49," the designation it still bore in 2000.

Roaring 20s boosterism gave the highway a number on the national map, but little was done in the way of improvement of the road surface until the Great Depression. U. S. Highway 49 was constructed as part of a Public Works Administration program authorized by U. S. President Franklin D. Roosevelt.

Right of way clearing for "new" U. S. Highway 49 began in the Perkinston area in November 1933. "Old" Highway 49, with its many railroad crossings and curves, was to be replaced by a new highway following an "airline" or "as-the-crow-flies" route.

The Illinois Central Railroad (IC RR), which had purchased the G&SI RR in 1925, was to have its line crossed by vehicular traffic at only one place between Gulfport and Jackson. That point was Perkinston. The route of new Highway 49 lay east of the IC RR from Gulfport to Perkinston and west of the IC RR from Perkinston to Jackson. Work on the 434-foot long, 24-foot wide viaduct, designed to loft vehicles over the IC RR at Perkinston, began in late April 1936. The bridge was completed in 1937. The paving of new Highway 49 from Gulfport to Jackson was completed in June 1938.

The four laneing of Highway 49 began in the late 1950s and was completed from Gulfport to Jackson in October 1967. As part of the four-lane project, a second Perkinston viaduct had been completed east of and adjacent to the original one in 1965. The 1938 viaduct span was replaced with a new bridge in 1992.

(Above) The original 1937 viaduct, minus its northern span, stands ready for demolition during the 1991-1992 replacement of the bridge. With it went generations of Perkinston students' graffiti.

Photo by Richard Kopp

The 1992 span that replaced the original 1937 bridge is in the foreground. The bridge in the background was built c. 1965. The Perk bridges were the only viaducts between Gulfport and Jackson in 2000, and Perkinston was the only place that U.S. Highway 49 crossed the railroad between Gulfport and Jackson.

(Left and Below) The apron of the circa 1965 viaduct serves as the canvas for Perkinston campus art instructor Charles Acres and his students and graffiti artists.

A Perkinstion Photo Album

A late 1930s view of Perkinston shows (1) the Illinois Central Railroad Depot (originally the Gulf and Ship Island Railroad Depot built about 1900). The building (2) to the right of the depot across old U.S. Highway 49 should be the Bang Store. The Dees General Store (3)is located left of the Depot across Main Street. The large two-story white building (4) north of Dees's Store is the J. L. Power Masonic Lodge. The road crossing the tracks in the foreground is 3rd Street. Straight up the tracks in the far distance (5) the Perkinston viaduct (completed 1937) lofts new U. S. Highway 49 over the tracks.

Photo by Richard Kopp

The Charlie Swetman House (built c. 1892) faces old U.S. Highway 49 in Perkinston in 2000. The Graves (Swetman) Store was located to the left of this structure.

(Left) Circa 1892 Miss Augusta Holden of Union stands with her pupils in front of the combination Ten Mile Church-Ten Mile School-J. L. Power Masonic Lodge. Many rural communities erected two-story rough hewn structures which then did triple duty as a church-school-lodge. Ten Mile Church was organized in 1870, and the congregation built the structure in the photograph sometime after that date. The church and school met downstairs, and the lodge met upstairs. The original members of Perkinston Baptist Church split from the Ten Mile congregation in 1897 and built an 1898 church building in the Perkinston Cemetery. Shortly thereafter the remnants of the Ten Mile congregation removed four miles to the north and established new Ten Mile Church on a site between Inda and Big Level. Ten Mile Church was named for Ten Mile Creek, which flowed near the church. Ten Mile Creek derived its name from the fact that the creek measured ten miles from its source to its confluence with Red Creek. The Daily Herald on May 5, 1912, reported that the first session of the Harrison County AHS would be held in "the old school building in the town." The only "old school building" in Perkinston was the old two-story Ten Mile church-school-lodge building. Photo from M.S.C.W. Alumnae News, (October 1967) p. 15.

(Above) The circa 1910 wooden Perkinston Baptist Church faces 2nd Street. The Doric columns of the circa 1973 brick Perkinston Baptist Church are visible behind the wooden church. The brick church facing Church Street (photo, right) supplanted the old wooden church, but the old wooden church remained standing for some years, serving as the educational department for the new church. The wooden church was moved to the site in the photograph (above, Uriel Plat Block Four, Lot 8) in 1927 from its former location 200 yards to the northwest. The wooden church formerly stood in the north half of the Perkinston Cemetery. There, it had replaced a circa 1898 wooden structure which burned on August 4, 1909, when lightning struck at the beginning of a revival meeting shocking five persons. Throughout the rest of 1909 and into 1910, as the wooden structure in the photograph was being built, the congregation met in the then abandoned former Ten Mile Church building on the north bank of Ten Mile Creek east of the Swetman Store.

Photo by Richard Kopp

(Above) A circa 1960 view of Dees's General Store established circa 1911 at the corner of 2nd Street and Main Street by Calvin Elias Dees of Ocean Springs. In 1925 "Uncle Cal," as he was called, branched out into the funeral business and purchased an automobile hearse. The store annex, at left in above photo, served as Stone County's first mortuary until Uncle Cal's son, John, built Dees Funeral Home in Wiggins.

(Left) Calvin Eugene "Gene" Dees, another of Uncle Cal's sons, stands behind the candy counter in Dees's Store circa 1960. Photograph courtesy of Johnnette Dees.

In 1956, Gene Dees became the recipient of Perkinston Junior College's initial Sam Owen Trophy, awarded for outstanding service to the college. He died on April 26, 1965. In 1968 Dees Hall on the Perkinston Campus was named in his honor. (Below) In 1966 Elwood Taylor purchased the Dees Store, demolished the old mortuary wing, and constructed Taylor's Store which still stood in 2000 on that site. The new store was completed by Thanksgiving 1966, and the stock from the Dees Store next door was immediately transferred to the new building. The circa 1911 Dees store structure was razed by the end of 1966, its former site becoming the parking lot for Taylor's store. The T.P. Wyatt House stands next to the Taylor's Store parking lot.

Photo by Richard Kopp

(Left) The T. P. Wyatt house, built circa 1910, was the home of Thomas P. Wyatt, who was probably the first rural route mail carrier in Perkinston. On July 1, 1999, the T.P. Wyatt house became the Wesley Foundation United Methodist Student Ministry House for the Perkinston Campus.

Photo by Richard Kopp

(Above) The J. L. Power Masonic Lodge. The September 5, 1911, Founders Proposal, which secured the site of the HCAHS for Perkinston, offered free use of "the Perkinston High School Building, which will soon be under construction and will be completed by October 1, 1911, until the agricultural high school is built." Obviously the lodge members wanted the new Harrison County AHS so much that they called their nearly completed lodge hall "the Perkinston High School building" in the document. On December 2, 1911, the lodge members leased the two rooms of the first floor to the trustees of the Perkinston Separate School District. The lease extended for 50 years and the lodge members reserved the right to use the first floor when school was not in session. The lease was terminated in 1922, when the Perkinston Consolidated School was built next door to the lodge. The membership of the lodge razed the grand old historic landmark in 1988 and built a concrete block building across from its site on the south side of the tracks.

Classes at the HCAHS were certainly held in Huff Hall in session 1912-1913, and very likely also in one, two, or three other places—the new J. L. Power Masonic Lodge, the old Ten Mile Church-School-Masonic Lodge, and at the Perkinston Baptist Church in the cemetery.

THE HARRISON COUNTY AGRICULTURAL HIGH SCHOOL AT PERKINSTON: BACKGROUND AND FOUNDING

Professor Benjamin L. C. Wailes of the University of Mississippi drove a carriage through the piney woods of South Mississippi in 1852 and reported seeing a rude cabin an average of every ten miles. The vast coniferous forests had the appearance of a park. The virgin pines shot up ninety feet before blossoming into a needle-leaf crown of twenty feet more. The canopies of the trees touched, shading out most undergrowth except along the occasional stream bank. The trees were so widely spaced that early settlers reported riding at full gallop through the forests. Little had changed even as late as 1888, when a *Biloxi Herald* reporter dubbed the whole area north of the coast "a howling wilderness." The sparse population of subsistence farmers, cattle herders, and woodcutters had remained static since the first decade of the 19th century because the economic strike zone of a caralog extended no more than four miles from a creek.

All that changed when the Gulf and Ship Island Railroad (G&SI RR) snaked its way through this wilderness to connect the hamlet of Hattiesburg with a few shacks on a bed of sand known as Gulfport. The G&SI RR began official commercial operations between Hattiesburg and Gulfport on January 1, 1897. On July 3, 1900, the main trunk line reached Jackson. Dummy line railroads radiating out into the forests from many points along this line exposed the whole primeval forest to the sawyer's blade.

Sawmills and turpentine stills sprouted at average intervals of three miles along the main track. For the first time large numbers of people poured into the piney woods, and towns grew up around the mills and stills. Hattiesburg and Gulfport grew into cities. McHenry and Wiggins grew into fair-sized towns, and these two brash newcomers would engage in dubious battle for economic and political supremacy in north Harrison County, catching the more ancient village of Perkinston in the crossfire. The secessionist tendencies of McHenry and Wiggins threatened Perkinston's chance of becoming the site of a Harrison County agricultural high school. If the seceders succeeded, Perkinston would no longer be in Harrison County, and no new county formed out of old north Harrison would possess the tax base to support an AHS.

In the mid-1880s, in response to advertisements for settlers in south Mississippi, a colony of Michiganders settled on the proposed route of the G&SI RR. The colonists first platted out the proposed town as Niles City, but that name soon gave way to McHenry in honor of their leading citizen Dr. George Austin McHenry. A decade passed before the vicissitudes of the G&SI RR were resolved and the railroad actively began operation.

With the coming of the railroad, a settlement grew up ten miles north of McHenry and it, too, took the name Niles City. The post office at this place, though, became known as Wiggins in honor of Wiggins Hatten, an early settler of the area. Shortly thereafter the name of the post office supplanted the original name of the town.

Soon nearly 7,000 people inhabited north Harrison County. As population grew in the area, many of the citizens began to resent having to travel to the courthouse in Gulfport to conduct their legal affairs.

On July 27, 1905, the people of Wiggins held a mass meeting and voted unanimously to form a new county, and they set up a committee to accomplish this task. The proposed new county would divide Harrison

George Hess Bilbo of Jackson County stands with his ox whip or "cracker" in hand as his oxen await the command to pull the caralog to the nearest creek. Circa 1890 photo courtesy of Bilbo's great-grandson, Clifton D. Taylor, who was Mississippi Gulf Coast Community College Jefferson Davis Campus vice president in 2000.

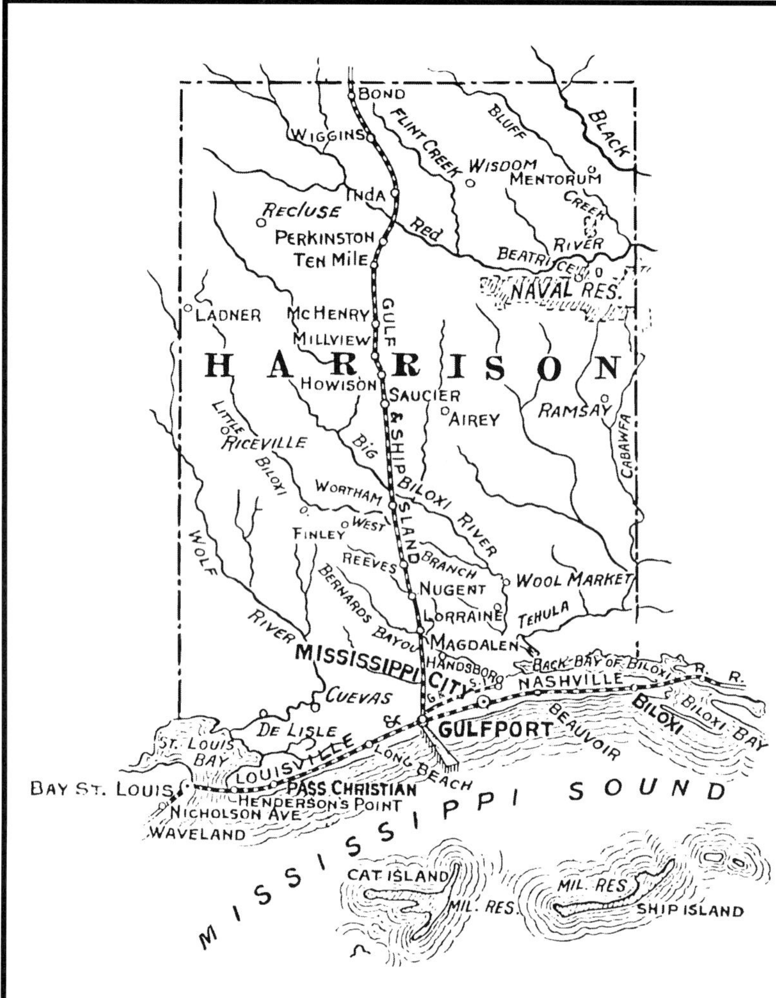

A Map of the Gulf & Ship Island Railroad through Harrison County

The Gulf and Ship Island Railroad, which began commercial operations between Gulfport and Hattiesburg on January 1, 1897, spawned a number of towns, villages, and settlements in Harrison County as shown on this December 1904 map from The Book of Harrison County by Cox and Martin 1905, front.

The 1906 Mississippi legislature set the number of inhabitants for a city at more than 2,000 inhabitants. Towns were classified as having 300 to 2,000 inhabitants, and villages at 100 to 300 inhabitants.

Populations of incorporated areas 1890-1910

	1890	1900	1910
Hattiesburg (City)	1,172	4,175	11,733
Wiggins (Town)			980
McHenry (Town)			627
Saucier (Village)			255
Gulfport (City)		1,060	6,386

The distance from the center of Hattiesburg to the center of Gulfport is 70 miles. Wiggins is approximately equidistant from both cities.

County on an east-west line a mile and a half below McHenry. While the new county would include primarily the northern third of Harrison, it would also claim sections of several neighboring counties as well. Naturally the Wigginites felt that Wiggins should be the seat or capital of the new political entity.

One month later the people of McHenry held a mass meeting and decided to petition the state legislature to divide Harrison County into two judicial districts with McHenry, of course, having the second courthouse. The McHenryites figured to steal the march on the Wigginites because it was easier to form a second judicial district than to form a new county.

The Mississippi state legislature mandated a plebiscite on the subject of a second Harrison County judicial district to be held in the proposed new judicial district area on September 24, 1906. Governor James K. Vardaman appointed three special commissioners to oversee the election. The head commissioner was Dr. G. A. McHenry. After the election, Dr. McHenry reported the McHenry box as registering 297 for the district and 11 against. Perkinston straddled the fence at 43 for and 42 against. Wiggins reported 12 for and 130 against. Dr. McHenry and the other two commissioners, both good friends of his, reported the total vote from all boxes at 386 for and 385 against.

So, by a majority of one vote, the commissioners declared McHenry the seat of the Second Judicial District of Harrison County. But the commissioners never filed the election returns consisting of the tickets, tally sheets, and ballot boxes. The ballot boxes, by the way, were cigar boxes, which was not really a problem, but the cigar boxes had no locks, which was a problem. The election commissioners actually took the ballot boxes to Gulfport the day after the election. However, the commissioners refused to recount the ballots in the McHenry box even in the face of charges by some citizens present that they knew 33 and not 11 votes had been cast in McHenry against the division. The commissioners returned to McHenry with the boxes. The day after that on September 26, 1906, the most violent hurricane in a century swept over Harrison County destroying millions of dollars worth of pine timber. A disputed election in the devastated area suddenly seemed unimportant.

A month later, Native Lumber company, which among other lumber companies owned most of north Harrison County, filed suit to overturn the election on the basis of fraud. The lumber companies did not want the new second judicial district because, as the major tax payers in the district, they would have to foot most of the bill for the new courthouse and appurtenances thereto. The destruction wrought by the 1906 hurricane made them even less willing to do that than before.

Dr. George Austin McHenry stands with family members in front of his home in the town that he founded. Photo courtesy of Dolores (McHenry) Mauldin, Dr. McHenry's granddaughter who resided in the home with her husband, Bill, in 2000.

In 1907 the Harrison County Board of Supervisors ordered the three commissioners to file the election returns in the courthouse in Gulfport. By then Dr. McHenry had taken an extended European vacation, and the two other election commissioners said they did not have the ballot boxes. The board of supervisors fined the other two commissioners $50 each for non-compliance. When Dr. McHenry returned from Europe, he testified that before the journey he had placed the cigar ballot boxes in a steel trunk in a locked room in his law offices in McHenry. When he returned, the door had been broken open and the trunk was gone.

In December 1907, Circuit Judge William Harris Hardy ruled that in absence of the election returns the election was null and void. He assessed the plaintiffs the cost of the suit and dismissed the fraud charges against the commissioners on the basis of lack of evidence. The Harrison County Board of Supervisors even forgave the fifty-dollar fines levied against the two election commissioners.

On January 6, 1908, the Mississippi legislature passed a bill creating Forrest County. That action so inflamed the "secesh" fever in north Harrison County that Wiggins and McHenry united behind a bill authored by Mississippi State Senator Theodore G. Bilbo to form a new county. The bill failed and Harrison County again emerged from the fray intact.

The impetus for the founding of an AHS in Harrison County came from what, at first glance, seemed an unlikely source. The Gulfport Commercial Union, which in time evolved into the Gulfport Chamber of Commerce, was an association of businessmen devoted to fostering the growth of trade and commerce and the general well being of the city.

In seven years since its incorporation on July 28, 1898, the population of Gulfport had soared from a few hundred souls to more than 5,000, and the booming city claimed the title, "Yellow Pine Export Capital of the World." But in 1908 experts predicted that the present rate of the demolition of the forests spelled their doom within fifteen years.

Facing the prospect of a hinterland denuded of forests and heartened by the example of adjacent Long Beach, the Gulfport Commercial Union decided to fill up the interior cutover lands with farmers of all types but particularly "truck farmers." The dwellers of Long Beach, through intensive farming methods, had made big business out of small food crops, especially radishes. Long Beach claimed to be the "Radish Capital of the World."

In their vision the Gulfport Commercial Union saw the ever expanding cutover lands of south Mississippi as a great garden. This garden would pour forth a cornucopia of lettuce, watermelons, cucumbers, okra, peas, and all other manner of "truck" to fill the holds of ships in the port by the time the last great virgin pines fell. Not only truck but also cattle, sheep, and hogs could be exported. Had not the piney woods been the home of the herder since French colonial times? And what of corn, cane, pecans, citrus, and maybe even cotton? The prospects were endless.

The Gulfport Commercial Union quickly enlisted the support of the officials of the G&SI RR and also those of the great lumber companies such as Dantzler, Finkbine, and Native. After all, they were all in this together. The lumber companies needed production from their cutover lands. The G&SI RR needed something to haul. To be a port, the city on the Gulf needed something to export.

But, could it be done? Nobody really knew. Cropping above subsistence level had never been tried on poor piney woods soil. They could not give it the "old college try," because the Gulf Coast had missed becoming the site of the University of Mississippi by one vote in the antebellum era. However, they could give it the "new agricultural high school try," and that they were determined to do. They wanted to bring in farmers from all over the nation, and they wanted an AHS to train these newcomers and their children in the newest and best scientific farming techniques.

The idea of advertising for immigrants to come to the Mississippi Gulf Coast dated back to the French colonial settlement of John Law in the 1720s. Colonists from New England had founded Handsboro in the 1840s. The Michigan settlement at McHenry had come about in the same way in the 1880s.

With the line of march now clearly understood, the Gulfport Commercial Union set up two standing committees in 1908. W. H. Bouslog headed the committee on agriculture and immigration. Professor J. T. Cornell, Superintendent of Gulfport Schools, chaired the agricultural high school committee.

Bouslog, who also happened to be the industrial and immigration agent of the G&SI RR, undertook a national advertising campaign that painted the cutover lands of south Mississippi as the nation's coming Garden of Eden. Bouslog also commissioned a series of rail-borne farmer's institutes conducted by professors of the Mississippi Agricultural and Mechanical College (in 2000 called Mississippi State University). The professors lectured groups of farmers who gathered at various points along the G&SI RR on the subject of piney woods agriculture.

Cucumbers are being unloaded in Wiggins in 1910. Finkbine Lumber Company, seeking a way to use cutover lands for production, established the pickle plant that eventually gave rise to Wiggins's claim as "Pickle Capital of the World." But, poor Stone County soil never produced enough cucumbers to supply the plant. Most of the cucumbers arrived the same way that the pickles departed--via rail.

(Below) Long Beach radishes being packaged for shipment out of Gulfport circa 1909. Postcard courtesy of Jon Richard Lewis.

(Left) This 1952 L. N. Dantzler Lumber Company of Perkinston photograph shows a few of the remaining virgin pines not cut in the early 20th century. These huge trees dwarf the man in the central foreground and the second growth pines around them. The experts who predicted the destruction of the virgin forests in a single generation once the railroads penetrated the piney woods were correct. The great forests of the Mississippi Panhandle were mostly cut over by the mid 1920s. The business leaders in the Gulfport Commercial Union should have pushed for forest management--selective cutting and reforestation. They did not realize that poor piney woods soil grew pine trees and very little else. The intensive labor and fertilizer necessary for the production of large-scale truck crops in such soil was not economically feasible. The word "truck," by the way, has nothing to do with a mode of transport but derives from the French root "to barter." For thousands of years farmers had grown vegetables and other food crops for their own use and then traded or bartered the excess to nearby town dwellers for goods and services. Truck cropping for a living in early 20th century Harrison County was very difficult. The truck croppers of Long Beach who so inspired the Gulfport Commercial Union men lasted one generation. The second generation sought professions less arduous and more lucrative. John H. Lang of Pass Christian in his 1936 History of Harrison County, in considering the Harrison-Stone-Jackson Junior College at Perkinston, wrote, "This college was intended to teach our children agriculture and mechanics but I have yet to find one of our citizens who has been educated there engage in farming. If they have followed agriculture they evidently have gone into other states." Photograph courtesy of Johnnette Dees.

G&SI RR Hattiesburg to Gulfport in Pictures

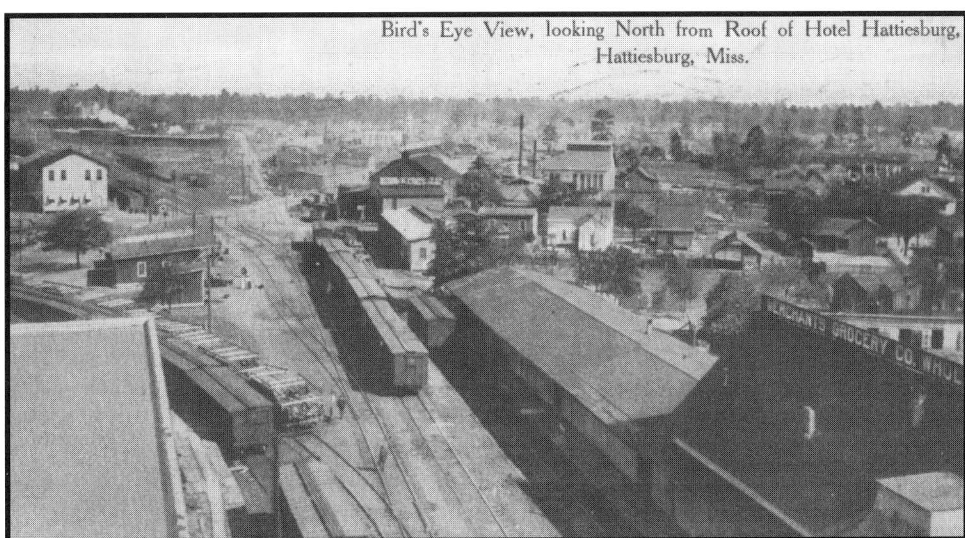

A Gulf & Ship Island Railroad train heads north toward Jackson circa 1908. The G&SI RR tracks had reached Jackson on July 3, 1905.

A circa 1904 view of Wiggins looking south with G&SI RR employees in foreground. The original two-story depot (center) burned along with most of the business district on January 21, 1910. In the wake of the fire, the mayor and board of aldermen permitted only brick buildings downtown. The G&SI RR depot, though, was rebuilt as a single story wooden structure. Photo from The Book of Harrison County by Cox and Martin, 1905, p. 82.

The G&SI RR tracks are at right in this circa 1913 view of Front Street, McHenry, looking south. Postcard courtesy of Jon Richard Lewis.

A train of the G&SI RR steams south toward Gulfport across the Biloxi River trestle circa 1915. Photo courtesy of Randy Randazzo

Burns' Boom: Showing Largest Stock of Timber in One Body in the U. S., Gulfport, Miss.

Lumber schooners await their loads in Gulfport circa 1909. Postcard courtesy of Jon Richard Lewis.

Cornell secured a copy of the lately passed Agricultural High School Bill of 1908 and aimed to secure such an institution for Harrison County. In the new AHS Law, the state legislature promised to appropriate $1,000 annually for the support of a school in any community that would donate at least twenty acres of land and secure a county-wide tax to provide further funding for the institution.

Cornell enlisted the aid of Harrison County Superintendent of Education J. J. Dawsey. Dawsey, armed with a liberal land grant for a school site from the Finkbine Lumber Company of Wiggins, made an impassioned plea for tax support before the Harrison County Board of Supervisors on July 18, 1908. Dawsey pointed out to the members that they ought to pass the levy and get the school, otherwise Harrison County would be paying general fund taxes to other counties that benefited from the law while Harrison County did not.

Dawsey's plea fell on deaf ears. The board, bowing to the opinion of Supervisor Frederick William Elmer Sr. of Biloxi, refused to authorize the levy for an AHS. Elmer opposed the granting of money to a rural high school when, in his opinion, the county rural public schools were in such poor condition.

Repeated efforts failed to move the Harrison County Board of Supervisors to establish an AHS. On August 25, 1908, the editor of the *Gulfport Daily Record Tribune* wrote,

"It is understood that the Harrison County supervisors argue that it is right that they should bring the rural schools already established to the highest point of perfection before they would be justified in authorizing another levy for school purposes. They overlook the fact, however, that the rural schools are already in good condition...therefore...this argument is invalid and it would be unjust to use the rural schools to prevent the establishment of the agricultural high school...which is everywhere admitted would prove a great boon for the country people."

The battle had been joined, and Cornell carried the fight to the Harrison County Teacher's Association at a meeting held at Gulfport Central High School on November 28, 1908. In his speech, titled "Why Should Harrison County have an Agricultural High School?," Cornell stated that the AHS movement sweeping Mississippi was a harbinger of the coming revolution in schoolwork. This revolution would result in the industrialization of the schools and the creation of an aristocracy of labor. The schools would, as in the past, continue to teach students to "be good" but in the future also teach them to "be good for something." The AHS would produce boys who would be master mechanics and master farmers and girls who could actually cook a meal, make garments, and keep house. According to Cornell the purpose of education was preparation for life, and the philosophy of the AHS recognized that supreme fact and actually put it into practice. Moreover, by raising the status of labor, the AHS revolution would do much to establish real democracy in the South.

On June 16, 1909, in an interview printed in the *Daily Herald*, Supervisor F. W. Elmer Sr. stated that nothing had been done by the Harrison County Board of Supervisors regarding the AHS issue because the board wanted to see how such schools were going to work out upstate. If the school worked well in predominantly agricultural counties then the board, according to Elmer, might try it in Harrison, "an essentially non-agricultural county." Then he said,

"There is another problem that enters this matter. That is the question whether or not an education in such a school makes a farmer of a boy. It has been the general observation of a number of men with whom I have talked that there was a tendency among boys so favored to drift into the cities and seek less arduous work than that encountered on the farm."

The Harrison County School Board held the power under the law to select the site of the school and order it built. But, if the Harrison County Board of Supervisors decided not to fund the school, then that left an order to build it dead in the water.

On July 5, 1909, Harrison County Superintendent of Education Dawsey, who was likewise president of the Harrison County School Board, presided at a meeting of that board in Gulfport. The school board ordered the school built and called for bids of land, structures, and money from any interested community in the county. Dawsey advertised the basic requirements as dormitory space for forty boarders, tuition-free classroom space for those and all other Harrison County students who wished to attend on a daily basis, and a curriculum which included practical farming for boys and domestic arts for girls.

Bids poured into Dawsey's office from ten Harrison County communities. Heartened by the response and fed up with the foot-dragging of the board of supervisors, Dawsey redoubled his efforts.

More fuel fed Dawsey's fire when he read of the gala opening of the Pearl River County Agricultural High School at Poplarville on September 8, 1909. Pearl River County, with a far smaller tax base than that of Harrison County and the same soil, had poured more money into its new AHS than any other county in the state. Of twenty-five Mississippi AHSs, Pearl River had the most pretentious. Dawsey had nothing to show for more than fourteen months of effort.

When the Harrison County Board of Supervisors met on September 13, 1909, Dawsey and a number of other AHS advocates were in attendance. He also had a petition "numerously signed" asking that the supervisors declare a countywide vote of the people on the question of establishing the school. The board heard his speakers and decided to postpone action on the matter until Dawsey secured more names on the petition.

Dawsey had no opportunity to get more names. The first storm warning came three days after he appeared before the board. Four days after that a hurricane equal in power to that of the 1906 storm smashed into the Mississippi Gulf Coast. The effort to establish an AHS was gone with the wind for another year.

In summer 1910 the Gulfport Commercial Union once more marshaled its forces and prepared to fight once again for an AHS. At the July 21 meeting of that body, J. L. Taylor accepted the chairmanship of the AHS committee, and he selected 26 of the most prominent men of the region to serve on the committee.

The *Daily Herald,* in article after article over the next month, detailed the deliberations and announcements of the committee. In a broadside delivered on August 27, Chairman Taylor shelled the corn. Armed with a copy of the Agricultural High School Law, as revised in 1910, Taylor informed the Harrison County Board of Supervisors via the press to get ready to make an appropriation. The 1910 law required a board of supervisors to make an appropriation for an AHS upon request of a county school board. Taylor stated that Harrison County Superintendent of Education Dawsey would be along to get the money very soon after September 3, because that was the day the site of the school was going to be chosen. As to the site of

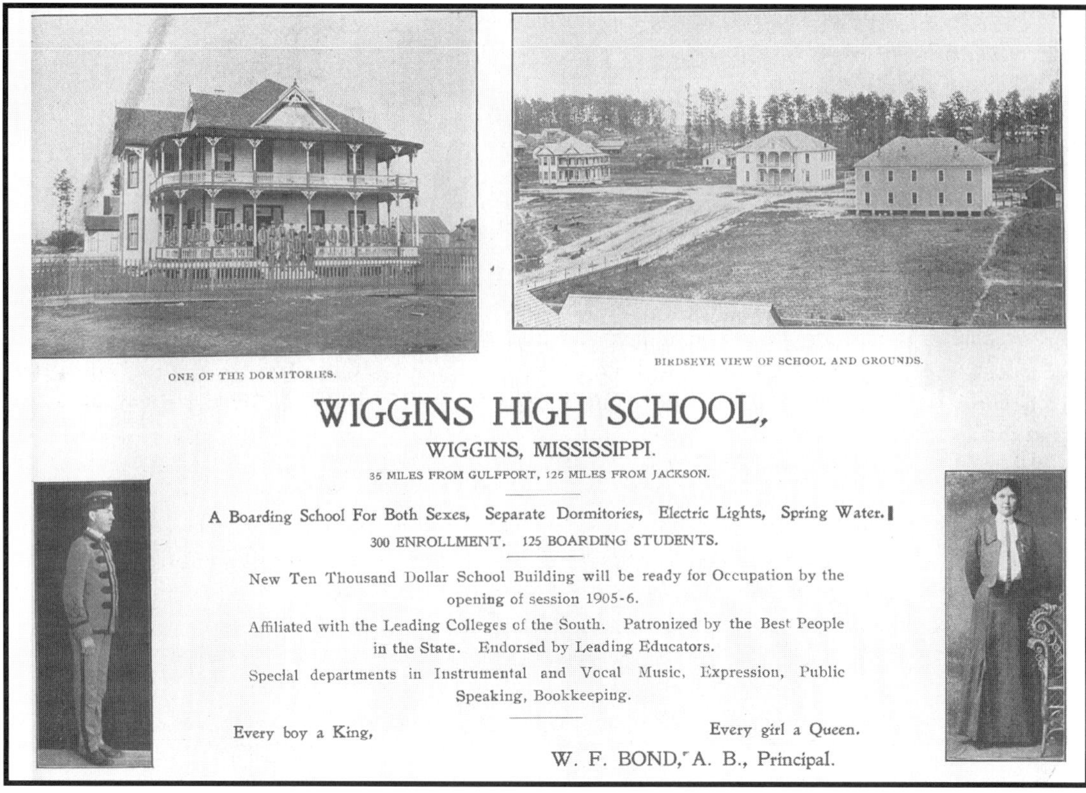

Wiggins offered the facilities of the Wiggins Boarding High School as an inducement to secure the site of the Harrison County Agricultural High School. This circa 1904 advertisement did not include a new structure built in 1905. Perkinston, with no facilities, won the day because the people of Perkinston donated the most land. Advertisement from The Book of Harrison County by Cox and Martin, 1905, p. 83.

the school, continued Taylor, the only thing he could say was that it would not be Gulfport. The site of the school would be located at an easily accessible interior spot of the county where the character of the soil suited instructional purposes. Since northern Harrison County had no good roads, the site would be on the G&SI RR.

On Saturday, September 3, 1910, at 11 a.m. in the courtroom of the Harrison County Courthouse in Gulfport, Dawsey called to order the meeting of the Harrison County School Board. The members of the board were John P. Krohn of Beat 1 (Seymour Post Office north of Biloxi), Icham Reeves of Beat 2 (Lyman), Florian Dedeaux of Beat 3 (Pass Christian), D. W. "Dan" Price of Beat 4 (northwest Harrison County), and Rankin Bond of Beat 5 (Perkinston). Delegations of citizens representing three communities were present. Professor Willard F. Bond of the Wiggins Boarding High School led the delegation from his town. Charles Clay '"Charlie" Swetman represented Perkinston. Professor W. H. Wood of the Saucier Boarding High School represented his village.

Dawsey addressed the assemblage and then recognized J. L. Taylor of the Gulfport Commercial Union, who made his remarks. Board member Rankin Bond of Perkinston then made a motion to establish the Harrison County Agricultural High School. The motion carried unanimously.

Swetman offered $200 worth of lumber and 290 acres of land "free from stumps" in scattered tracts near Perkinston. The land he said was valued at $25 per acre. Wood of Saucier offered a school building worth $4,000, a dormitory with sixteen furnished rooms, and land in scattered lots aggregating 94 acres. W. F. Bond of Wiggins offered the town high school building and dormitory with two years free water and electric lights, 1,500 acres of land, and $10,000 cash to be raised in a town bond issue.

John P. Krohn voted for Wiggins, Icham Reeves and Florian Dedeaux voted for Saucier, and Rankin Bond and Dan Price voted for Perkinston. With the vote deadlocked between Saucier and Perkinston, Dawsey adjourned the meeting until 3 p.m. Apparently the school board members were unable to break the deadlock after they resumed. One thing is certain. The reporter who covered the meeting for the *Daily Herald* missed the deadlock altogether by failing to take into account the two votes for Saucier.

The report published in the *Daily Herald* Monday, September 5, bore the headline, "Perkinston Gets the Big High School." In the accompanying article the reporter asserted that three of the five members of the new HCAHS's Board of Trustees had been named. Dawsey was a Trustee by virtue of his position as Harrison County superintendent of education. The school board, according to the report, had named as Trustees Dr. E. M. Fahnestock of DeLisle and W. E. Batson of Recluse Post Office. The other two Trustees were to be named the following week by the supervisors when they appropriated the money for the HCAHS.

The report closed with the good news that the State of Mississippi had just raised its support for AHSs from $1,000 to $1,500 per annum.

Three days later under the headline, "No High School This Year," the *Daily Herald* admitted its error in not reporting the votes for Saucier by Reeves and Dedeaux. The retraction concluded with the announcement that the Harrison County school board, having used up all its legal meeting time for 1910, could not be reassembled.

On September 5, 1911, one year and two days after the original deadlock, the drama resumed with the same principal characters. The stage changed to Dawsey's office in Gulfport. The contending communities remained the same, but two of them, Perkinston and Wiggins, had changed their offers.

Wiggins offered four separate propositions: (1) 200 acres of land (20 of which was under cultivation and 20 more of which was fenced) valued at $6,000 plus $3,000 in cash. (2) 200 acres of land a half mile north of the depot and $2,500 in cash. (3) A 35-room dormitory, four acres of land near center of town, 68 acres of other land under fence, and $1,500 in cash. (4) $8,000 in cash.

Perkinston offered 566 acres of land, $626 in cash, and use of the "public school building as long as it might be needed." The land consisted of one tract of 320 acres "in or near the town of Perkinston." The remaining 246 acres fell in scattered forty-acre tracts within a mile east and west of the town. The land was said to be high and dry farmland worth $14,150.

Perkinston received three votes, Wiggins received two votes, and the paper did not publish who voted for which. The *Daily Herald* headline on September 6, 1911, read, "Harrison County's Agricultural High School to be at Perkinston."

Appointed to the first Harrison County Agricultural High School Board of Trustees were W. E. Batson of Beat 4 (Recluse Post Office) and J. L. Jones of Beat 3. As before, Dawsey became a Trustee by right of his office. The other two were to be appointed by the Harrison County Board of Supervisors. Those appointed were Rankin Bond of Perkinston and Frederick William Elmer Jr., the 30-year-old son of the Beat 1 Supervisor from Biloxi. The initial meeting of the Board took place on September 18, 1911, at Dawsey's office in Gulfport. The Board members elected F. W. Elmer Jr. as President of the Board and Dawsey as secretary. The Board then officially selected Perkinston as the site of the school and discussed budgets and buildings.

The Uriel Wright Perkinston Plat of 1896 consisted of 16 blocks. The middle tier, composed of blocks seven, eight, and nine, aggregated twelve acres and gradually rose in a straight line from the G&SI RR tracks climbing to an eminence called Perk Hill which was twenty feet higher than the altitude of the railroad. The HCAHS Board decided to buy all three middle tier blocks for the site of the HCAHS campus. The first buildings would crown the ridge in block nine.

As 1912 dawned, the people of Perkinston looked forward to the building of their new Harrison County Agricultural High School. And newly elected 36-year-old Gulf Coast District Senator Andrew Wiggins Bond of Wiggins looked forward to building a new county out of north Harrison and parts of adjacent counties.

At the 1912 legislative session in Jackson, A. W. Bond and his cohorts planned well and sprang the trap without warning. The bill was on the way to passage before Perkinston and other areas opposed to a new county even knew about it. The proposed county line ran across north Harrison County just three miles below Perkinston and, that is to say, two miles above McHenry. Senator Bond thus left Wiggins as the only contender for the position of county seat. This meant he would have to gouge out sections of other counties to meet the legal size requirements for the new county, but that was better than a brawl with McHenry. Bond named his fledgling political entity for former Confederate colonel and popular two-time Mississippi Governor John Marshall Stone.

Citizens of Perkinston gathered in a mass meeting to voice opposition to the bill. They opposed it on the basis of loss of the HCAHS and high taxation. One wag suggested that the new county either be named "Creeks" or "Bridges" since all the county would possess was 18 creeks crossed by 45 bridges and that all the homes in the county would have to be sold to pay the taxes necessary for upkeep of the bridges.

The state legislature passed the Stone County bill and set the date of the plebiscite of the people living within its proposed borders for March 19, 1912. Wiggins went 150 to 3 for the proposition and Perkinston weighed in 53 to 4 against. The election carried all totaled 305 for and 185 against with 8 votes contested.

According to the *Daily Herald* of March 22, "State Senator A. Wiggins Bond of Wiggins, Stone (nee Harrison) County, whose hometown is to be the county seat of the eightieth Mississippi County, reached the capital yesterday." Bond was seeking a proclamation from Governor Earl Brewer naming the provisional county officers. Brewer was not in Jackson.

As Bond awaited the return of the governor, he noticed a few flaws in the bill creating Stone County. He corrected the flaws—ten of them. Secretary of State Joseph Power charged Bond with altering a public record and put him under bond until the June term of court. Because of the legal problem, Governor Brewer refused to issue the proclamation creating Stone County. Eventually the courts exonerated Bond

In 1911 Architect William Drago of New Orleans produced this artist's conception or "strategic plan" of the coming Harrison County Agricultural High School. The circular campus gave way in actual execution to a quadrangle. The two flanking structures, Huff Hall to the right and Stone Hall to the left, did resemble this artist's conception. But Bennett Hall, which was built in the central position, was a Romanesque structure with Corinthian columns. The Dees Building occupied Bennett Hall's former site in 2000. The names, Huff, Bennett, and Stone were not placed on these buildings until decades after they were built. Each of these buildings and others built on the campus later were initially given names in accordance with their functions at any particular time. The functions changed and so did the names. Only one of the three buildings (Huff Hall) had been completed when the first classes began on September 17, 1912. Shortly after Bennett Hall was completed in 1913, J. C. Muerman, a field observer for the Bureau of Education in Washington, D.C., praised the combination of European and Japanese architecture to be found on the HCAHS campus. Stone Hall, the other building suggestive of a Japanese temple, was completed in 1915. Artist's conception from 1912 Announcement, p. 7.

of wrongdoing, but in the interim Stone County sank, well, like a rock.

Having once again been delivered from the clutches of the seceders, the people of Perkinston breathed a sign of relief. The Harrison County AHS Board of Trustees, assured that Perkinston still lay in Harrison County, continued planning for the HCAHS's first session.

At the meeting of May 5, 1912, the HCAHS Board accepted bids on a dormitory of the following specifications,

"This dormitory is to be of brick and will be 110 feet long, 42 feet wide and two stories high with a hall 9 feet wide running the full length of the building. The plan of the building further provides that the first story shall be 11 feet from the floor to the ceiling, and on the second floor the distance from the floor to the ceiling shall be 10 feet, and that each room shall be 12x14 feet in size, and shall be finished in a hard plaster and tinted in different colors. The roof of the building to be slate."

The Gulfport firm of Chevalley and Fursdon, took the contract with a low bid of $13,900. The contractors had finished the concrete foundation for the structure by June 11, and brick laying was about to begin. Work was completed by September 17, 1912, and it was the only building on the campus when the first session of the HCAHS opened. This dormitory bore several designations until September 17, 1952, when it was christened "Huff Hall" in honor of the HCAHS's first principal—James Andrew Huff.

BOYS' DORMITORY

Huff Hall in 1912 was termed the "boys dormitory" even though girls lived in it as well. The girls dormitory, though on the drawing board, was not completed until May 1915. In renovations over the years the balconies have disappeared, and the wooden window frames have been replaced by aluminum ones. Other than that the façade of the building remains much as it was when first constructed. The interior has been changed from a dorm into a Learning Lab. The ground in front is no longer the level of 1912 having been sloped for drainage in the late 1960s. Early Huff Hall photo from Second Annual Catalogue 1913-1914, p. 9. (Below) Huff Hall in 2000.

Photo by Richard Kopp

(Above) Huff Hall and it's Cafeteria Annex from a c. 1970 aerial photograph. (Right) The Huff Hall Cafeteria Annex as it appeared in 2000. The administration, faculty, staff, and students of session 1912-1913 lived in Huff Hall and ate in the Cafeteria Annex. Huff Hall and its annex were the only facilities on Perk Hill in the first session of the school.

Photo by Richard Kopp

Student Roll—Session 1912-1913 *from* *Second Annual Catalogue 1913-1914.*

The student roll of the first session of the Harrison County Agricultural High School contained 63 names (39 boys and 24 girls). The list was alphabetized, but the 1912-1913 spelling was left intact. Many of these family names were on the student rolls of Mississippi Gulf Coast Community College (Perkinston Campus) in 2000, signaling five generations of attendance for some families.

The capacity of Huff Hall that first session was given out as 40 boys and 24 girls which is precisely the number of girls on the list and one more than the number of boys on the list. Perhaps not all of the students on the list lived in Huff Hall. Some may have commuted from Perkinston or Ten Mile.

Alexander, Alvah, Perkinston, Miss.
Alexander, Clark, Perkinston, Miss.
Baker, Orion, Ocean Springs, Miss.
Bang, Estus, Perkinston, Miss.
Baxter, Emery, Perkinston, Miss.
Baxter, Flora, Perkinston, Miss.
Bond, Howard, McHenry, Miss.
Broadus, Buren, Wiggins, Miss.
Caraway, Annie Lou, McHenry, Miss.
Caraway, Pearl, McHenry, Miss.
Caraway, Willie, McHenry, Miss.
Cassibry, Louise, Saucier, Miss.
Clayton, Bessie, Perkinston, Miss.
Clayton, Alma, Perkinston, Miss.
Clayton, Maud, Perkinston, Miss.
Cruthirds, Orvis, Lyman, Miss.
Cuave, Eran, Perkinston, Miss.
Daffin, Ruby, Wiggins, Miss.
Davis, Merritt, Perkinston, Miss.
Davis, Noel, Perkinston, Miss.
Davis, Otis, Perkinston, Miss.
Davis, Searcy, Perkinston, Miss.
Davis, Willie, Wiggins, Miss.
D'Olive, Egnes, Ten Mile, Miss.
Duncan, James, Ten Mile, Miss.
Fillingame, Andrew, Gulfport, Miss.
Fillingame, Print, Gulfport, Miss.
Garner, Elward, Ten Mile, Miss.
Garner, Eoloen, Ten Mile, Miss.
Garner, Ester, Ten Mile, Miss.
Garner, Eulalah, Ten Mile, Miss.
Hatten, Bertha, McHenry, Miss.
Hatten, Floy, McHenry, Miss.
Hickman, Judson, McHenry, Miss.
Hickman, Lowry, McHenry, Miss.
Huff, Charles, Perkinston, Miss.
Lewis, Jessie, Perkinston, Miss.
Lewis, Mary, McHenry, Miss.
McLeod, Hattie, Ten Mile, Miss.
Montgomery, Charlie, Wiggins, Miss.
Moran, Willie, Gulfport, Miss.
NeCaise, Randolph, Kiln, Miss.
Nelson, Cassie, Ten Mile, Miss.
Nelson, Willie, Howison, Miss.
Oneal, Allie, Beatrice, Miss.
Oneal, Dumont, Beatrice, Miss.
Oneal, Wallace, Beatrice, Miss.
Ott, Johnnie, Saucier, Miss.
Pittman, Clara Belle, Perkinston, Miss.
Price, Vera, Ten Mile, Miss.
Rigby, Elmer, Ten Mile, Miss.
Rippy, Willie, Gulfport, Miss.
Ruble, Tom F., McHenry, Miss.
Robinson, Calvin, Blackwell, Miss.
Smith, LeRoy, Perkinston, Miss.
Sugden, Dewey, Long Beach, Miss.
Tisdale, Leo, McHenry, Miss.
Urie, Clinton, Howison, Miss.
Webb, Louie, Mobile, Ala.
Worrell, Elizabeth, Perkinston, Miss.
Worrell, Mary, Perkinston, Miss.
Worrell, William, Perkinston, Miss.
Wyatt, James, Perkinston, Miss.

The Founders' Proposal

Perkinston Miss. 9-4-11

To the Honorable School Board of Harrison County Mississippi

Gentlemen: Noting that your Honorable Body will close bids on September 4th 1911, for the County Agricultural High School, and feeling that Perkinston would be the ideal location, owing to its many natural advantages, we herewith offer your honorable body, as an inducement for the location here of the said school, the following donations:

Any building site in Perkinston, that the Board may select together with the following lands, which are as you know as valuable as any lands in Harrison County:

160 acres donated by the L. N. Dantzler Lumber Co.
80 " " " W. W. Farnsworth
50 " " " Garner Estate
40 " " " C. J. Miller
40 " " " Van O'Neal
40 " " " C. C. Swetman
40 " " " Peter Lott
40 " " " W. C. Welborn
35 " " " R. N. Davis
20 " " " Hamilton Johnson
20 " " " W. M. Davis
1 " " " Hamilton Johnson

Total——566 acres. 300 acres of this is in a solid body, adjoining the town of Perkinston, the balance within one mile of Perkinston.

Figuring our land values at the same as what our neighbors are selling for ($25.00 per acre), would make our offer worth $14,150.00.

Also cash donation of $626.00

We further offer the free use of the Perkinston High School Building, which will soon be under construction, and will be completed by October 1st, 1911, until the Agricultural High School is built.

We most humbly beg a favorable consideration at your hands, of the above offer, which in addition to the natural advantages of the location, such as drainage, different types of soil, as shown by the Government Soil Survey, water, shade trees, healthfulness of the community, etc.

We will have right at the door of this institution, two of the most beautiful running streams in South Mississippi, namely: Ten Mile and Red creeks, which afford at all seasons of the year, an abundant supply of water for all kinds of stock, bathing, etc.

Perkinston being in the centre of the farming and stock raising district of Harrison County, we feel that you would make no mistake by locating the Agricultural School at this place.

Again thanking you for a favorable consideration, we submit the above proposition.

Very truly yours,

W. M. Davis
C. C. Swetman
Jos. A. Gunn
Committee

The text of the document delivered to the Harrison County School Board on September 4, 1911, is given above. Perkinston's offer, being far in excess of the other contenders, won the day.

In regard to the land donors mentioned in the Founder's Proposal, L. N. Dantzler Lumber Company, which owned the big Ten Mile Lumber Mill one mile south of Perkinston gave the most land. W. W. Farnsworth of the Calamity Land Company weighed in second. The estate of Thomas T. Garner came in third. The Garner family had lived in the area even before John Perkins. The Reverend Richard Nixon Davis and his wife, Jerusha, a daughter of John Perkins, lived with their family in the original Perkins home in Perkinston in 1911. Peter Lott was the owner of a large mercantile establishment in Wiggins, and he later became sheriff of Stone County. Charles Clay Swetman and his wife Gratia (Myers) Swetman owned the general store that contained the post office in Perkinston. The new "Perkinston High School Building" referred to in The Founders' Proposal could only have been a reference to the recently completed J. L. Power Masonic Lodge.

J R PRATT GEO R BURTON J R HILL

TEN MILE LUMBER COMPANY

PERKINSTON, MISS.

MANUFACTURERS OF

Long Leaf Yellow Pine Lumber

Special attention given to local orders
You can save money by buying your timber from us
Let us make you prices on anything you want

FLOORING, CEILING AND FINISHING, EXPORT AND BRIDGE TIMBER

Advertisement for the Ten Mile Lumber Company from the Biloxi Daily Herald, November 27, 1900, reprinted courtesy of the Sun Herald. Perkinston is located near the confluence of Ten Mile Creek and Red Creek. The L. N. Dantzler Company set up a mill below Ten Mile Creek about one mile south of Perkinston and named the mill for the creek. The settlement that grew up around the mill took the name of the mill. The settlements of Ten Mile and Perkinston were so closely connected they functioned virtually as one entity. In fact, in the advertisement, the Ten Mile Lumber Company gives its location as Perkinston. The L. N. Dantzler Lumber Company gave 160 of the 566 acres donated to secure the location of the Harrison County AHS for Perkinston.

A Ten Mile Lumber Company locomotive under steam c. 1910. Engineer Albert James McDonald stands at right. The bell on the locomotive is a duplicate of the one given to Harrison-Stone-Jackson Agricultural High School and Junior College by L.N. Dantzler Lumber Company about 1928 for use as a dinner bell. In fact, it may be the same bell. Photo courtesy of Tom Brown, grandson of Albert James McDonald.

L.N. DANTZLER LUMBER COMPANY

(Below) L.N. Dantzler Lumber Company letterhead 1923 from the Crab Breland Collection.

All Contracts are conditional upon strikes, floods, inability to secure cars, and other causes beyond our control. All Orders and contracts are taken subject to the approval of the main office, Moss Point, Miss. All quotations are made for prompt acceptance and subject to previous sale and market change without notice.

ANNUAL CAPACITY 125 MILLION FEET

L.N. Dantzler Lumber Co.

MOSS POINT, MISS.

MILLS: MOSS POINT, HOWISON, TEN MILE, CEDAR LAKE

CABLE ADDRESS "DANTZLER"

CODES: SOUTHARD'S, WATKINS, LIEBER'S, MOTEK AND A. B. C. 5TH ED.

BRANCH OFFICES GULFPORT, MISS. HAVANA, CUBA

SHIPPING POINTS: MOSS POINT, PASCAGOULA, SHIP ISLAND, GULFPORT

HARRISON COUNTY AGRICULTURAL HIGH SCHOOL FIRST *ANNOUNCEMENT* COVER

(Left) Cover of the first Announcement - Harrison County Agricultural High School published in 1912 by Connell Printing Company of Gulfport.

The first Announcement of the Harrison County Agricultural High School acknowledged the debt of the educational system of the Western World to ancient Athens. On the cover two caryatids modeled on those that support the roof of the porch of the Erechtheum on the Athenian Acropolis are depicted reading scrolls of learning. The Announcement declared "a sound mind in a sound body" as the educational ideal of the school. Those words echoed across the hush of 24 centuries from ancient Athens.

(Above) The Logo of the MGCCC Archives was adapted from the cover of the 1912 Announcement.

The mission statement of the institution given in the 1912 Announcement reads in part:

"The purpose of this school is to give as thorough preparation as possible for complete living. . . . This school will endeavor to educate as well as instruct. To form character as well as give information. The morally developed heart, the deft hand, and the trained mind are indicative of a successful life."

Such words deserve to be emblazoned on bronze and set in stone, and they are. These words are on a plaque at the base of the flagpole located in the quadrangle of the Mississippi Gulf Coast Community College, Jefferson Davis Campus. The 1967 Mr. and Miss Jefferson Davis Campus, Danny Williams and Joan Peregoy, stand by the flagpole base emblazoned with the 1912 Announcement mission statement. Photo from 1967 Junior College District Perkolator, p. 12.

HUFF AND THE ESTABLISHMENT OF THE AGRICULTURAL HIGH SCHOOL AT PERKINSTON JUNE 1912 - JULY 1917

Huff and the HCAHS June 1912 to December 1915

James Andrew "Jim" Huff was born in Jasper County on July 22, 1868. He was the son of Philip Huff of Georgia and Frances (Ducksworth) Huff of South Carolina. He was the youngest of a family of nine children which consisted of four boys and five girls. J. A. Huff received his early education at private schools and graduated from Sylvarena Academy, a tuition supported high school established by William Harris Hardy in Smith County before the Civil War. He acquired his college training at the Mississippi Agricultural and Mechanical College and the University of Illinois. On September 16, 1891, Huff married the former Julia May McCurdy of Jasper County. This union produced five children. In order of their birth these were Charles Hatton Huff, Lillian May Huff, Howard Payne Huff, John Charles Huff, and Virginia McCurdy Huff. Huff's first teaching appointment came at Sylvarena Academy. From 1892 until 1896 he served as Smith County superintendent of education at a salary of $18 per month. From 1896 until 1898, he served as principal of the high school at Raleigh, the Smith County seat. In 1898 he became superintendent of schools in Forest, the Scott County seat, and remained in that position until 1912. From 1900 until 1910 he served also as mayor of Forest. In 1912 he left Forest to become the first principal of the Harrison County Agricultural High School at Perkinston. In 1917, Huff left Perkinston to become the superintendent of Pearl River Agricultural High School. He presided over that institution's evolution into a junior college and served as superintendent of the junior college from 1921-1926. His first wife died in June 1927, and in March 1929, he married the former Emma Lucille Paige of Covington, Louisiana. This union produced one daughter, Jimmie Lucille. Huff died June 24, 1931.

On June 4, 1912, the HCAHS Board met and elected Professor James Andrew Huff of Forest, Mississippi, as principal of the Harrison County Agricultural High School. His wife, Julia May (McCurdy) Huff, was to be the matron of the school. The Board set the salary of the Huffs at $1,200 on a twelve-month contract guaranteed for a period of three years.

The first *Announcement* or "bulletin" of the HCAHS was a fifteen-page pamphlet containing all of the necessary information for enrollment. Classes were to begin on Tuesday, September 17, 1912. The only dormitory completed (Huff Hall) would be co-educational. The dormitory was furnished with toilets, baths, steam heat, and electric lights. Every room, in addition to light and heat, contained one dresser, one table, one wash stand, two chairs, two closets, and two bedsteads with mattresses. Each pupil was to supply one pair of sheets, one feather pillow, one pair of pillowcases, one quilt, one white bedspread, one pair of plain white sash curtains, one dresser scarf, one wash stand scarf, one laundry bag, six towels, and all toiletry articles. Laundry expense would be about a dollar a month. Board was $10 per semester in advance. After the first year this price would be changed to actual cost. Tuition was "free to all boys and girls under twenty-one" living in Harrison County. All others were to pay $3 tuition per month in advance. Students could work off part or all of these charges at the rate of 10 cents an hour for "good work."

Under the heading "Discipline" the *Announcement* stated that the school "in a sense will be one large family," and the school would be run in the manner of a family insofar as practicable. On the other hand, "by some manner of means wholesome discipline" would be maintained. The boys and girls would be cared for with the "strictest diligence."

In extolling the virtues of the town of Perkinston, the writer of the *Announcement* stated: "The town is just large enough to supply the school with necessities and conveniences without furnishing any distracting influences to interfere with study and work. In fact, the pupil sees and hears just enough to give him necessary inspiration and relish for his work." In 2000 the "town" furnished fewer "distracting influences" than it did in 1912.

Most of the *Announcement* was devoted to the main purpose of the school--course offerings. A year's worth of remedial 8th grade instruction was offered to those not adequately prepared for the first year of high school if they obtained the consent of the Harrison County School Board. So, in effect, the school was open to those students who had completed the 7th through those who had completed the 11th grade.

The complete four-year offering of the school as published in the *Daily Herald* on July 15, 1912, follows:

"The course for the first year includes: English, grammar, arithmetic, elementary botany, English history, elementary agriculture, knife work and bench work for the boys; sewing and cooking for the girls.

"Second year: Composition and rhetoric, algebra to quadratics, ancient history, elementary physics, agriculture for the boys and bench work; cooking and sewing and general home science and free hand drawing for the girls.

"Third year: English literature, plane geometry, civil government, chemistry, bookkeeping, advanced agriculture for the boys, home care of the sick for the girls.

"Fourth year: Literature and themes, trigonometry and farm surveying, medieval and modern history, American history, agriculture for the boys, garden making for the girls. And in addition, for the boys a year's work in one of the following subjects--horticulture, animal husbandry, dairy husbandry, soils and crops; and for the girls a year's work in one of the following subjects--mechanical drawing and farm mechanics, political economy, pedagogy, and a foreign language.

"Two periods a week of practical work on the farm will be required of all boys in all classes."

On August 30, two weeks before opening, only two faculty members had been hired. James Riggs Vaughn was to teach agriculture and allied sciences. Miss Odessa Banks was to teach domestic science assisted by Julia Huff. J.A. Huff would teach mathematics in addition to his other duties.

On Saturday, September 7, 1912, the people of Perkinston celebrated the early completion of Huff Hall with a gala barbecue and picnic. The town had been cleaned, and the trunks of scores of stately oaks had been whitewashed. According to C. U. Porter of McHenry who was present, the trees "gave the appearance of a miniature painted forest." Seats, tables and a speaker's platform were arranged in a hollow square in the oak grove surrounding the public school (the Masonic Lodge housed the public school).

State Superintendent of Education Joseph N. Powers spoke on consolidation of schools and the efficacy of supporting agricultural schools. Since he was standing next to a public school and there to honor the HCAHS, his speech was right on the subject and well received. Pat Harrison, United States congressman from Mississippi, used his time to praise Woodrow Wilson, whom he predicted would be the next president of the United States.

His prophecy came to pass two months later. At the conclusion of Harrison's speech, master of ceremonies J. F. Wilder of Perkinston bade the assemblage to "eat until they got enough if there was enough but if there wasn't to eat until they ate it all." There was enough and more to spare, and after the meal, Huff delivered an address. The festivities closed with a game of baseball played between the public school teams of Perkinston and Wiggins. Perkinston's victory was the perfect ending for perhaps the most joyous event in the history of the village to that time.

The HCAHS Board of Trustees joined the administration, faculty, and staff at the school on opening day, September 17, 1912. After four years of arduous struggle, all the various agencies and individuals in whom and for whom the institution existed came together to give it life.

Trustee W. E. Batson, a resident of Recluse, ten miles to the west, reported that some of the citizens of Perkinston were so enthusiastic over the future growth of the town that they predicted that Recluse and Perkinston would some day share the same streetcars. Batson, according to the *Daily Herald* of September 20, 1912, "witnessed the turning on of the electric lights at 6:30 o'clock in the High School Building which was the first electric light to flash in Perkinston. The lights still gleamed in Huff Hall in December 2000, but Perkinston never had a streetcar, and by

William Edmund Batson stands in his yard circa 1950. As a Harrison County AHS Trustee, Batson attended the opening day of the institution on September 17, 1912. Photo courtesy of Jim Rabby, grandson of W. E. Batson.

The girls at left toss a basketball in front of Huff Hall in 1912 as the girls at the right look on. The goal is out of camera range to the left. A pile of bricks left over from the construction of the building is visible in the foreground. Huff, the school's first principal, advertised the school as a family and the administration, faculty, and students all lived in the same home--Huff Hall. From September 1912 until the completion of Girls' Dormitory Number 1 (later named Stone Hall) in May 1915, Huff Hall was a "co-educational dorm" with a capacity of 24 girls downstairs and 40 boys upstairs. The dorm accommodated fewer girls than boys because "Daddy" and Mrs. Huff, who served as the school matron or "dorm mother," lived in an apartment on the first floor (entered via the door visible in the photograph at left). The student entrances were at both ends of the structure. Men teachers lived upstairs with the boys and women teachers lived downstairs with the girls. Daddy Huff really was the father of Charles Huff, who attended the HCAHS in its first session. Until the construction of Stone Hall, the cafeteria was located in an annex built behind Huff Hall and connected to it by a 12-foot-long covered walkway. After the cafeteria was moved to Stone Hall, the Huff Cafeteria Annex served as faculty housing, a role it still performed in December 2000.

(Below) Boys and girls learn how to shuck corn "scientifically" by doing it in a classroom without walls in a field of the HCAHS during the first session of 1912-1913. Photo from Second Annual Catalogue 1913-1914, p. 12.

2000 one needed a guide and a machete to find the site of Recluse Post Office.

The next day, Wednesday, September 18, 1912, the Mississippi Normal College opened in Hattiesburg. Thus the Mississippi Gulf Coast Community College is one day more ancient than the University of Southern Mississippi.

The pages of the *Daily Herald* recorded no first person accounts of the doings at the school by anyone there during that first session of 1912-1913. No doubt the beleaguered Huffs and their two teachers were too busy taking care of the 63 boys and girls to write about it. Classes were held in various nooks and crannies of Huff Hall and the Cafeteria Annex. Very likely some classes were held in the Masonic Lodge, the Perkinston Baptist Church located a block away, and the old Ten Mile School building east of Swetman's Store.

Certainly the land about the school served as a classroom without walls because in that first year the school obtained a pair of mules, three jersey milk cows, and some Duroc jersey pigs. With the latest and best cultivators, discs, and spring tooth harrows at his disposal, Huff led his charges in planting twenty acres. The land began to yield crops of corn, cane, potatoes, peanuts, peas, soybeans, velvet beans, watermelons, tomatoes, and more good things to eat.

On February 3, 1913, the G&SI RR Agricultural Special, a farmer's institute on wheels, chugged into Perkinston and stopped at the depot. The *Daily Herald* reporter present on the train recorded a glimpse of the HCAHS students:

> "At Perkinston the Agricultural High School pupils came down from their handsome school buildings on the hill in a body and clustered around the lecturers where many of them took out note books to jot down valuable information. When the clouds insisted on pouring out some of their contents, the people went into the lecture car and heard the agricultural gospel from there."

A Perkinston correspondent to the *Daily Herald* who was present shed more light on the reporter's words. The students were taking notes because they had been assigned to write an essay about what they saw and heard on the train. As to the reporter's reference to "handsome buildings," the correspondent wrote, "Work on the main building for the Agricultural High School is moving along nicely and when completed will be the best of its kind in the State of Mississippi." This "main building" was the new administrative building that was rising at the crest of Perk Hill.

The first *Announcement* of the HCAHS contained no school calendar, but presumably the 1912-1913 session ended about the third week in May. No notice of this event was given in the *Daily Herald,* and no graduation exercises were noted either.

On July 9, 1913, the *Daily Herald* published a detailed description of the new administration building, which had been accepted by the HCAHS Board of Trustees in session in the building on July 5. This building, given the name "Bennett Hall" in April 1960, was a two-story brick structure with a portico flanked by two huge Corinthian columns. New Orleans architect William Drago, who had drawn the original artist's conception of the campus, was at the meeting. For whatever reason, Drago had completely changed the original aspect of the building. Also present were L. L. Chevalley and Thomas Fursdon, the Gulfport contractors who had built it.

The building was described as having two stories, but in actuality the basement served as a third story. The concrete basement was divided into four rooms mainly given over to scientific laboratory work of various kinds. The floor above the basement contained the library and study hall, four classrooms, and the office of the "president." (Three times in this article the reporter termed Huff a "president." Only a few original documents produced by this institution remain, but all of them invariably refer to Huff as a principal.) The top floor contained two classrooms and a well-lit auditorium that soon became the pride of the community.

The 1913-1914 or second session of the HCAHS began with matriculation and registration on Monday, September 8, 1913. James Riggs Vaughn returned to teach agriculture. Odessa Banks gave up her domestic science classes to Miss Mary Etta Eichelberger and switched to history, English, and Latin. W. A. Wellinghoff signed on as the new manual training instructor in blacksmithing, carpentry, mechanical drawing, and tool and bench work. Miss Grace Ruble of McHenry added a dash of culture to the curriculum with her classes in instrumental music, voice, and expression. J. A. Huff continued his duties in the teaching of mathematics, and Julia Huff continued, of course, as matron.

According to the *Second Annual Catalogue* the price of boarding in the dormitory declined to $7.50 per month. Laundry "not including collars" would be about thirty cents a week, which was a bit of a rise from the previous year. But students wishing to engage in honest work, as in the first session, could exchange this labor to pay off these charges at the going rate of ten cents an hour. In the words of the *Second Annual Catalogue,* "Preference in the work is given to those who try to earn what we pay them, and those who fail to try to give value received for the money are soon dropped from the payroll. Last year a few of our pupils paid all their expenses from their labor."

The calendar of the session listed no holidays save Thanksgiving and Christmas. The Thanksgiving holiday lasted one day--Thursday, November 27. The Christmas holidays began on Friday, December 19 and ended Monday, December 29. The session ended May 21, 1914.

(Left) The first administration and faculty consisted of J. A. "Daddy" Huff, principal and teacher of mathematics; Mrs. J. A. Huff, matron; John Riggs Vaughn, teacher of agriculture and allied sciences; and Miss Odessa Banks (not pictured), domestic science. The faculty doubled at the beginning of the second year of operations. W. A. Wellinghoff signed on to teach manual training. Grace Ruble opted for music and expression. Odessa Banks (not pictured) changed to teacher of history and Latin, giving her domestic science classes to Mary Etta Eichelberger. Photo from Second Annual Catalogue 1913-1914, p. 6

(Below) Bennett Hall as it appeared in a circa 1920 photograph. The walks and round concrete fountain at the hub of the walks were probably completed in spring 1917. Photo from HSAHS Catalog of Session 1920-1921, p. 11.

School Wagons

We build the strongest and most comfortable, and can do the work on short notice. Consolidated School Trustees are invited to take the matter up with us. We build auto truck bodies in any style.

J. S. Randolph & Son
GULFPORT

(Right) This school wagon is believed to be in South Mississippi circa 1912, but the exact location is unknown. The photo is published courtesy of Myrtis Krohn of Wiggins. The Mississippi State Legislature in 1910 authorized the use of school wagons to transport children to consolidated schools. According to State Superintendent of Education Willard Faroe Bond, Harrison County was the first to use the wagons, and Woolmarket formed the first official consolidated school under the new law. Mississippi State Department of Education Bulletin No. 8 issued in 1913, recommended that any school with an enrollment of less than twenty be combined with a similar or larger school because transporting the children was cheaper than building a school for one teacher. "Transportation" averred the Bulletin "is accomplished by conveying the children in safe and comfortable vehicles, holding from fifteen to twenty-five children and driven by men under contract and bonds to perform their duties in a satisfactory way." On August 8, 1916, the Daily Herald announced that Harrison County "school authorities are now planning to use motor trucks to convey children to various houses this winter." School Wagon ad from Daily Herald July 13, 1917, courtesy of the Sun Herald.

In addition to the training offered to the students, the HCAHS in the *Second Annual Catalogue* promised to offer teacher training courses or "normals" for public school teachers. In this way the work of the HCAHS could reach all the children of Harrison County.

The HCAHS advertised its role in community service to teachers, children, farmers, and anyone else who wished to come on Friday, October 17, 1913. On that day the HCAHS held a combination Farmer's Union Fair, Institute for the Harrison County Teachers' Improvement Association, and a field day for area schools. An estimated 1,000 people showed up for it.

The theme for the day was the future of agriculture in Harrison County. Huff brought in successful dairymen, stock raisers, home demonstration agents, and C. A. Cobb of the Mississippi Agricultural and Mechanical College at Starkville. Farm exhibits filled Bennett Hall and spilled onto the grounds to merge with the livestock displays. The Girls Canning Club prepared to demonstrate the skills necessary for the finest preservation of fruits and vegetables.

The students at Magnolia High School started the fifteen-mile journey to Perkinston before dawn. As the sun rose on their quarter mile-long procession of flower bedecked horse-drawn school wagons, the children began to sing songs of their own composition. The wagons reached the northeast corner of the HCAHS at about 10:30 and, to the amazement and delight of the throng, did not stop but proceeded down the hill by the school into the town itself. The procession crossed the G&SI RR tracks, turned left, and went up to Charlie Swetman's Store, where the wagons rumbled across the tracks again by the Masonic Lodge Public School and kept going until once again the HCAHS was reached. The pupils alighted to applause and marched to the front of Bennett Hall singing "Magnolia--the Best School in Dixie." At the conclusion of the song, the Magnolians went into Bennett Hall and set up a mouthwatering display of pears, pomegranates, quinces, scuppernongs, cane, jellies, peaches, and figs.

It was a day of speeches and seminars, music and singing, exhibits and demonstrations capped by a "monster picnic." A nearly perfect day it was, except that some "fruit mouthed thief" slipped in and absconded with the whole delicious Magnolia Exhibit. The theft of the Magnolia Exhibit was doubtless an early foraging expedition carried out by denizens of Huff Hall.

Harrison County Canning Club Girls labeling the cans of tomatoes they have canned circa 1913. Photo courtesy of Mary Ellen (Watrous) Alexander.

Likewise, during the spring holidays of 1971, the duck in the duck pond at the entrance to the campus disappeared. Feathers were found behind Huff Hall near a greasy grill belonging to a certain history teacher who then lived in the old Huff Hall Cafeteria Annex. Years later one of the malefactors confessed that he and his roommate who was, in 2000, a Lieutenant Colonel in the United States Army, did capture, kill, pluck, cook, and eat said duck. They did it, he said, because (the cafeteria being closed) they were forced to forage for food. Furthermore, according to the confessor, the history teacher had sealed the duck's fate. Having been required to read *All Quiet on the Western Front* and being moved by the portion of the book in which Kat and Paul stole and cooked a goose, the hungry Huffers re-enacted that moment with the nearest thing to a goose that they could find.

In the combination fair, field day, and institute, the HCAHS demonstrated what it was and what it meant to the community. The connection established that day had lasted for more than eight decades in 2000.

Apparently the first two clubs organized at the HCAHS were the Girls' Literary Society and the Boys' Literary Society. Each society sponsored a public debate on Wednesday night, December 17, 1913. With Christmas holidays two days off, the girls debated the question, "Should a child be deceived of Santa Claus?" Following a spirited debate, the judges came down on the side of the negative. The boys debated the subject "Should Stone County be Created?" The judges decided in favor of the affirmative.

The Boys' Literary Society obviously chose its topic because the creation of Stone County had recently, once again, entered the realm of "current events." On December 3, a thousand people had attended a picnic and barbecue in Wiggins for the purpose of stirring up enthusiasm for a Stone County bill to be placed before the 1914 Legislature in January. Andrew Wiggins Bond, of course, had led the voices shouting "Yea." The speakers from Perkinston and vicinity had led the opposition.

The introduction of another Stone County bill in the 1914 Legislative session once again put the HCAHS on the rack. In particular, the push for a new girls' dormitory went aglimmering. A number of organizations and many individuals had gone on record in opposition to Huff Hall being a co-ed dorm even though the boys and girls were on separate floors. Added to that, according to the February 17, 1914, *Daily Herald*, the school had turned away "nearly a hundred students" for lack of living space. But the Harrison County Board of Supervisors and the south Harrison County members of the HCAHS Board of Trustees refused to act until they knew that the school was going to remain in Harrison County.

A way out of the AHS imbroglio existed if anyone cared to take it. The Mississippi Agricultural High School Law, as amended in 1910, stated that two counties could unite to form a bi-county school. This solution would actually garner more funding from the state because the legislative appropriations authorized by the act remained the same for both counties, thus doubling state support for a single school. However, F. W. Elmer Sr. and W. F. Gorenflo, the heads of the two boards (Harrison County supervisors and HCAHS Trustees respectively) who could make the bi-county support a reality, publicly opposed the idea.

In an effort to torpedo the Stone County bill, Huff, Charlie Swetman, W. E. Batson, and others of the Perkinston area traveled to Jackson to lobby the legislators. A. W. Bond struck back. Since Bond chaired the legislative committee that authorized the pay for Huff and his teachers, pay stopped in early March. Other state support for the HCAHS ceased as well.

On March 9, 1914, the Stone County bill passed the Mississippi State House of Representatives with only one dissenting vote. Unlike the complex bill of 1912, which had involved parts of several counties, the 1914 version was simple and direct. Stone County would decapitate the northern two-fifths of Harrison County. The price of avoiding problems with adjacent counties, though, meant another scrap with McHenry because reaching the statutory size mandated for a county required the line be drawn south of that town.

Three days after the House passed the bill, W. F. Gorenflo announced his impending resignation from the HCAHS Board of Trustees. In Gorenflo's opinion Harrison County bore no further responsibility for "a Stone County AHS." In an obvious attempt at reconciliation, Senator A. W. Bond sent Gorenflo a letter on March 20, informing him that the funds for the HCAHS were once again available.

The Stone County bill sailed through the Mississippi State Senate without a single dissenting vote. On March 24, 1914, Mississippi Governor Earl Brewer, citing the bill as unconstitutional, vetoed it. According to Section 230 of the Mississippi State Constitution, a vote on a county could not be held more often than once in four years. Since one had been held in 1912 another could not be held until 1916. So Senator Bond and his cohorts would have to plan for the next legislative session to launch yet another of their by then perennial biennial secession movements.

Gorenflo, now mollified by the demise of the Stone County threat, withdrew his resignation from the HCAHS Board of Trustees and remained as president.

On April 13, 1914, Huff announced in the *Daily Herald* that the HCAHS had 125 students on the rolls, sixty of whom lived in the one dormitory. Where the other 65 students were staying was not stated. Many students had been turned away at the beginning of the

1913-1914 session, and he had 75 applications on file for the 1914-1915 session already. In addition, the faculty now numbered six. Then, as Huff had done many times before, he appealed for a new dormitory.

Turning to other matters, Huff reported that fifty acres had been cleared of stumps and planted for a fall harvest. This land had been enclosed in a fence composed of wire affixed to concrete posts costing 21 cents each. The new barn, built by the students, had been inspected on March 6, 1914, for the Board by Trustee Rankin Bond and now housed the livestock of the school. The farm had become such a demanding and going concern that some of the boys were going to remain through the summer to tend it.

The 1914 student-built barn (above) burned on June 14, 1925, when a lightning strike destroyed it by fire. In the 1924 photograph, agriculture teacher E. B. Colmer (third from right) stands together with school personnel and students preparing to go to the fields with their tractors and mule team. From Announcements Brochure, 1924-1925.

In a dispatch to the *Daily Herald* from Perkinston dated June 28, 1914, Huff was reported as the owner of a fine new automobile. On the same day a quarter of the world away a Serbian high school student assassinated Austrian Archduke Franz Ferdinand and his wife, Sophie, in their fine automobile in Sarajevo, Bosnia. At the time nobody thought that event would affect Perkinston, but it did. The assassination touched off the Great War. A month later the great powers of Europe slithered over the brink and into the boiling cauldron of war. In less than three years the United States would enter the fray as well.

On Saturday, July 11, 1914, Huff attended the board of supervisor's meeting in Gulfport and asked that body to appropriate $10,000 for a new dormitory. He also asked for a dipping vat and five more cows. The dipping vat would be available to all cattle owners of the area who wished to use it to rid their cows of ticks. The supervisors told Huff to meet with the HCAHS Board of Trustees and submit a proposal for the needs of the school at their next meeting.

Huff submitted a detailed proposal at the August meeting of the supervisors. Much to his surprise and delight, the supervisors decided to issue bonds in the amount of $17,000 to give him all he had asked for plus more agricultural equipment.

The summer of 1914 also marked the first offering of summer school by the institution. The summer school, which ran from July 20 to August 15, was held in conjunction with the Sixth Gulf Coast Normal. Scores of teachers and nearly 100 students, ranging from primary grades up, attended from Harrison, Hancock, Jackson, George, and Pearl River Counties. When the accommodations at the campus proved inadequate, many teachers and students boarded in private homes in Perkinston. The faculty, assembled for this unprecedented learning experience, taught both students and teachers. On the last two days of the normal, the faculty administered examinations for state teacher's licenses.

Four days before the combination summer school/normal closed, Harrison County Superintendent of Education J. J. Dawsey met with the trustees of the various Harrison County consolidated schools in his office in Gulfport. Trustees of the newly created Perkinston Consolidated School, which had supplanted the Perkinston Separate Rural District three months earlier, were in attendance. The *Daily Herald* of August 15, described the resolution made by the assemblage:

"The resolution provides for the adoption in the ninth and tenth grades of all consolidated schools of the county the same course of study pursued in the same grades in the agricultural high schools of the state. This means that when a student has finished the consolidated school he may enter the agricultural high school and complete its courses in two additional years."

This resolution portended the death of the agricultural high school movement in Mississippi. School boards in county after county all over the state adopted similar resolutions. Later, as the consolidated schools added the 11th and 12th grades, they incorporated the whole curriculum of the agricultural high schools.

The biggest story of the third session of the HCAHS was the building of a new dormitory. The Bank of Biloxi issued the bonds for it on November 2, 1914. The HCAHS Board of Trustees advertised for bids on November 21. Burkes Brothers Construction Company of Hattiesburg took the contract for it with a low bid of $12,600 on December 19, promising completion in 120 working days.

In the circa 1920 photograph of Stone Hall Dining Room, the man at the left is standing in the door which led, via a short screened walkway, to the kitchen annex that was enlarged seven years later. The woman with her back to the column at left may be Jane "Ma Fanny" Fahnestock, the school dietician. The eight-seat tables are the ones described by William Albert "Ship Island" Frantzen. The wall at the far end of the room separated the superintendent's quarters from the Dining Room. Contractors replaced the wooden columns in the room with steel columns during the renovation of 1995-1996. In trenching under the floor the plumbing contractor encountered a three-foot thick pine stump blocking the way of a new pipe. This stump had to be grubbed out by hand in the old way once done by students of the institution. Photo from the Bulletin Session 1920-1921, p. 5.

Stone Hall, built in 1915, appears in a 1927 photograph showing the east side of the building. The Dining Room occupied two-thirds of the ground floor to the left in the photo. One third of the ground floor to the right, according to Ruby Lee Johnson Probst Strong, was the apartment of the superintendent of the school. Girls occupied the upper floors. The building has undergone several renovations since 1915. The balcony and the chimney have disappeared and the arrangement of the windows in the central section of the façade have been altered, but the general aspect of the building is recognizable by a student of any era of the institution. The interior was completely gutted and converted into offices in the latest renovation completed in 1996. Photo courtesy of Dixie Press of Gulfport.

A view of the campus as it appeared in 1922. Huff Hall is at right. Bennett Hall is at the crest of Perk Hill, and Stone Hall is at left. The fence in the foreground kept the cows out and the students in. From Announcements for Session Beginning September 11, 1922, p. 10.

The new girl's dormitory, christened Stone Hall at Homecoming on October 13, 1956, opened for occupancy on April 1, 1915. The building was steam heated, contained four bathrooms, and had a dining hall on the ground floor that seated 150 persons.

The fourth session of the HCAHS opened on September 6, 1915, with 140 pupils, an increase of 60 percent over the previous year. Ninety of the students boarded at the school. Fifteen, according to the *Daily Herald* of September 20, "are riding from three to six miles." What they were riding was not given, but an unofficial automobile census of Wiggins found 18 of the machines permanently in town with more in the countryside. What the other 35 students were doing for accommodations was not given either. Presumably they either lived in Perkinston or within less than three miles. Ninety percent of the students of the previous year were back, and seventy-five percent of all the students were boys.

The school farm was estimated to yield for the year about 400 bushels of corn, 500 bushels of potatoes, 600 gallons of molasses, and hay and oats in sufficient quantity to feed all livestock. The school dairy had begun operation, furnishing all needed fresh milk and butter. The hog pens were to yield three to four thousand pounds of pork.

The roster for the 1915-1916 session contained a number of new names and subjects. W. M. Sellers would teach agriculture. George N. McIlhenney took over manual training. Miss Lois Rankin offered business methods and stenography. Miss Fannie Noblin would instruct in piano, voice, and expression. Miss Mary Eichelberger retained her post in home science. Very likely the Mrs. Edith Sloan in English and history

Students at Perkinston in 1963 "grub" a stump in time-honored fashion--by hand. Photo from 1964 Perkolator, p. 17. According to Jesse Buras, a student interviewed December 31, 1915, all male students had to grub stumps in the early days of the institution, but later this backbreaking task became a punishment levied to work off demerits. The malefactor had to dig a wide deep pit around the stump in a radius far enough out to expose all roots. Then mule teams, and later tractors, pulled the stump out by means of chains. Many of these stumps were three feet or more in diameter.

was the former Miss Edith Banks. Huff continued to teach mathematics, and his wife continued as matron.

Huff stated that the medical bill for the entire student body had been less than $35, and the healthfulness of the school was matched in the moral tone of the town. Huff declared that there were no "blind tigers" in Perkinston. A "blind tiger" was, in the slang of the time, a place for the dispensing of alcoholic beverages.

The Christmas Holidays of 1915 began on Christmas Eve and extended to January 3, 1916. Either some of the students remained on campus through the holidays or returned early because a *Daily Herald* reporter interviewed Jesse Buras at the school on December 31. Buras told the reporter that male students spent several hours each afternoon grubbing stumps. Only rain interrupted this difficult chore. Once the stumps were removed, the ground thus cleared came under the plow and the harrow. In this manner the farmland was extended year by year. Young Buras allowed that discipline was rigid but that the students were fond of every member of the faculty.

The HCAHS and the Final Battle to Divide Harrison County, January to September 1916

The new year of 1916 brought a new legislature and Andrew Wiggins Bond a new opportunity to realize his dream. On January 6, Governor Brewer signed the bill calling for a plebiscite on the question of the creation of Stone County with Wiggins as its new county seat. This time there would be no battle with McHenry over the site of the capital of the county because the bill named Wiggins as the capital. The new county would consist of most of Harrison County Supervisor Beats 4 and 5, an area which made up about two-fifths of the old county. The vote would be held on May 8.

Partisans on both sides of the issue flocked to Gulfport to register for the vote. A citizen from McHenry told a *Daily Herald* reporter on January 14, "There is no enthusiasm at McHenry for the new county. In fact there is no enthusiasm anywhere for Stone County outside of Wiggins, and it looks now like it will be a fight between Wiggins and the rest of the territory to be embraced within the new county." Huff and others in Perkinston would lead the fight against Stone County.

In case they lost, the people of Perkinston would need friends in Harrison County. One of the most important AHS advocates, J. J. Dawsey, would no longer be in a position to help. Dawsey had decided not to run again for the position of Harrison County superintendent of education in the election of 1915. Instead he had taken the position of principal of the Lamar County Agricultural High School in Purvis.

W. H. Wood of Biloxi had defeated C. H. Bass of McHenry in August 1915, to become Harrison County superintendent of education. The Perkinston precinct had cast 38 votes for Bass and five for Wood. Politicians tend to remember things like that at tense moments. Also, W. H. Wood's brother, W. N. Wood, lived in Saucier. The Woods had put forth Saucier's offer to be the site of the HCAHS in 1911 and had lost to Perkinston. People tend to remember things like that at tense moments.

As the time for the vote on Stone County neared, interest in the election intensified. On April 25, 1916, Huff hosted an Anti-Stone County rally at the HCAHS. No one from Wiggins attended. The rally produced a committee pledged to wage a strong campaign to defeat the new county.

On May 6, two days before the election, this committee bought a full-page ad in the *Daily Herald* entitled, "Is Stone County Good for us?" Then in about 2,000 words in small type, the ad answered the question in a great many negatives. The document carried the names of the committee. Among the names were J. A. Huff, C. C. Swetman, Rev. R. N. Davis, W. H. Davis, Rankin Bond, C. E. Dees, and Dr. G. A. McHenry. The 33 names on the document read like a Who's Who of the Perkinston-McHenry area. Many were closely connected to the HCAHS, and all of them supported it.

In the Stone County plebiscite held on May 8, 1916, Wiggins, not surprisingly, voted 247 for and 1 against. Perkinston went 53 against and 6 for.

Official Ballot
STONE COUNTY
SPECIAL ELECTION, JUNE 26, 1916
LITTLE CREEK PRECINCT

SPECIAL ELECTION

Stone County, Mississippi

June 26, 1916

For Sheriff and Tax Collector
Vote For One

Jno. B. Brown ......
J. C. Locke ......
D. B. Scarborough ......

For Treasurer

J. R. Davis ......

For Representative
Vote For One

A. Batson ......
S. C. Culpepper ......

For Chancery Clerk
Vote For One

R. L. Brown ......
W. A. Davis ......
D. C. Smith ......

For Circuit Clerk
Vote For One

B. H. Breland ......
Geo. W. Breland ......
W. L. Currie ......
S. B. Davis ......

Supt. of Education
Vote For One

C. H. Bass ......
Robert Hester ......

For Assessor
Vote For One

O. E. Batson ......
J. A. McMurphy ......
W. A. Smith ......

For County Attorner
Vote For One

W. C. Batson ......
E. R. Davis ......

For Surveyor

F. L. Quarles ......

For Coroner

C. A. Herrington ......

FOR BOARD OF SUPERVISOR

District One
Vote For One

A. W. Bond ......
O. E. Hairston ......

District Two

D. J. Brown ......

District Three
Vote For One

J. C. Fore ......
R. A. Switzer ......

District 4
Vote For One

Rankin Bond ......
S. M. Oneal ......

District Five
Vote For One

A. J. Bond ......
E. R. Smith ......

JUSTICE OF PEACE

District One
Vote For Two

Jno. N. Dale ......
E. E. Burns ......

District Two

Shaw Enochs ......

District Three

J. F. McCarty ......

District Five

R. W. Hatten ......

FOR CONSTABLE

District One
Vote For One

F. D. Lovitt ......
D. M. Miles ......

District Two

W. T. Linhart

District Five

B. A. White

(Above) Andrew Wiggins Bond, the "Father of Stone County," was born September 29, 1876, in north Harrison County in the area of the coming town of Wiggins. He was the son of Elisha Warren Bond and Almedia (Hatten) Bond. Educated in a log cabin school, Bond worked in sawmills and read law at night. Admitted to the bar on December 18, 1909, he began the practice of law in Wiggins and served the town as alderman and town clerk from 1909 to 1911. He married the former Leona Sisson of Hickory. Elected to the State Senate on November 7, 1912, he became the chairman of the local and private legislation committee, a position that he used to create Stone County. Bond suffered setbacks in his county building efforts in 1912 and 1914 but succeeded in 1916, becoming the first president of the board of supervisors of Stone County. He was the publisher of the Wiggins Enterprise, which became the Stone County Enterprise. Photo from 1912 Mississippi Official and Statistical Register p. 369.

FIRST BALLOT OF STONE COUNTY

Front and back views of a ballot from Stone County's first election, June 26, 1916. From the Crab Breland collection.

After the May 8, 1916, plebiscite, Mississippi Governor Theodore G. Bilbo, formerly a teacher at Wiggins High School, issued the proclamation forming Stone County. Photo from 1917 Mississippi Official and Statistical Register, p. 495.

McHenry tallied 92 against and 18 for. The total vote came in at 428 for the county and 329 against. By the people's will the former beats 4 and 5 of old Harrison County became Stone--Mississippi's 81st county. State Senator Bond at last had his victory. Governor Theodore G. Bilbo, who had taken the reins of power from Brewer in January, issued the proclamation forming the new county and appointed a provisional government until elections for office could be held.

Gloom settled over the HCAHS. The *Daily Herald* on May 13 noted the plight of the school:

"The law fixes 35 boarding pupils as the minimum for the operation of an agricultural high school, and this number has never been reached by that portion of the county, which now constitutes Stone County. It is understood that there are now present fifteen boarding pupils from Stone County and fifty-five from Harrison County. As the school is apparently beyond the means of Stone County to support it and as its location is suited to answer the needs of both Harrison and Stone Counties, it may not be impracticable for the two counties to get together and operate the school jointly."

On Thursday, May 18, the HCAHS graduated the Class of 1916. Everyone present at the exercises was aware that the birth of Stone County portended the doom of the HCAHS.

On May 20, the *Daily Herald* carried notice of the resignation of Huff as principal of the "Harrison-Stone Agricultural High School." For those who collect "firsts" this is the first time the name "Harrison-Stone Agricultural High School" appeared in print. The name is wrong because that is not what the school was yet and might never have become. Two days later the *Daily Herald* stated that Huff "has arranged to go to Vicksburg to engage in the automobile business." He did not, in fact, resign at that time, and he never went to Vicksburg to engage in the automobile business.

The official birth of Stone County was fixed at

Second District Circuit Judge J. H. Neville swore in Bilbo's provisional county officers on June 5, 1916. Photo from 1917 Mississippi Official and Statistical Register, p. 553.

9:30 a.m., Monday, June 5, 1916. At that moment Judge J. H. Neville administered the oath of office to the newly appointed county officers. These would serve until an election could be held. One appointment was of particular interest--Provisional President of the Stone County Board of Supervisors Andrew Wiggins Bond.

On June 16, P. L. Hatten and Rev. R. N. Davis of Perkinston filed suit in the Harrison County Chancery Clerk's office to annul the election that created Stone County. The suit specifically named A. W. Bond and the other four interim Stone County supervisors as defendants. This came at the moment these men were trying to get the funds from Harrison owed to Stone. Harrison County refused to release any funds until the suit was settled. Likewise no lending institution would deal with the challenged county.

The new imbroglio prompted a *Daily Herald* editorial to the effect, "They are still fighting in Europe, they are still fighting in Mexico, and they are still fighting in Stone County. It looks now like Europe and Mexico will whip themselves fighting and it also looks like a few anti-Stone County men are determined to do the same thing."

The people of Stone County ignored the litigation and held their first election on June 26. When the names of the candidates were released, the *Daily Herald* made another editorial sortie:

"In a community or county like this where large families are the rule, it is to be expected that many of those seeking political favor would bear the same name and this certainly is the case in this campaign. The Smiths, Browns, O'Neals, and Brelands are mixed up in the fray considerably but the Batsons and Davises have capped it all off by switching in a combination named in the person of Batson Davis."

The newly elected Stone County Board of Supervisors were Andrew Wiggins Bond, Beat 1; D. J. Brown, Beat 2; R. A. Switzer, Beat 3; S. M. O'Neal, Beat 4; and E. R. Smith, Beat 5. C. H. Bass became the new Stone County superintendent of education.

As the new county got down to business, 40 damsels belonging to the Canning Club Girls and the Poultry Club Girls of Harrison County arrived at the

(Above) Automobiles line First Street, Wiggins c. 1916 at the time the town became the seat of Stone County. Photo courtesy of William Wilson.

(Left) The Stone County Courthouse, built in 1917, crowns a hill in Wiggins. This c. 1929 view shows the Stone County Jail at right and the Grover Bond Filling Station at the base of the hill. Construction on the filling station began November 3, 1927. Postcard courtesy of Jon Richard Lewis.

HCAHS for a week-long Demonstration School beginning June 19. After the girls departed, the HCAHS hosted Mississippi's first Demonstration School for Corn and Pig Club Boys. The 50 boys had such a fine time they voted to make the demonstration school an annual event.

The last boys departed on July 1, and in retrospect, Huff must have been glad of that. The July Storm struck four days later. The New Orleans weather service apparently had closed for the Fourth of July leaving no one at the helm because the hurricane struck the Gulf Coast without warning at dawn on July 5. The eye passed west of Pascagoula, so northeast winds struck Stone County with nearly the same velocity as the 1906 hurricane. In 16 battering hours the July Storm destroyed the crops of the new county of Stone, both in the fields and the harvest in the barns that collapsed. At least 200 sheep drowned in the ten-inch cloudburst spawned by the storm. Thousands of pines snapped off or uprooted. Fledgling citrus orchards and vineyards ceased to exist. The damage to the towns and villages was blessedly slight except at McHenry where the winds toppled the steeple of the Baptist Church and unroofed several stores.

Two days after the storm, though, the *Daily Herald* noted that Stone County Superintendent of Education Bass would soon appoint two members of the HCAHS

Board of Trustees. Bass expected the Stone County Board of Supervisors to appoint their two as well. He, by virtue of his office, was the fifth trustee. Under the AHS Law of 1910, Harrison County could join with Stone, selecting five trustees in the same manner. These ten would then elect an eleventh to prevent tie votes.

On July 15, 1916, the Stone County School Board served notice through the *Daily Herald* that it wished to enter a bi-county plan with Harrison to support the HCAHS. Bass said he would accept any feasible and practical plan on the part of Harrison to accomplish this union. This included letting Harrison have six trustees to Stone's five thus placing the balance of power in the older county's hands. Harrison County Superintendent of Education Wood remained silent. Huff opened up the month-long Gulf Coast Normal at the HCAHS on July 24. While the teachers learned, the clock ticked. Would there be a 1916-1917 session of the HCAHS?

On Friday, July 28, the Harrison County School Board met and decided not to join Stone County in supporting the HCAHS. Wood refused to release a copy of the board resolution to the press and refused to make a statement. The next day Wood claimed to be confined at home with an "indisposition" and still refused to comment.

Dr. E. M. Fahnestock, a member of the Harrison County School Board known to favor the HCAHS, complained that he had received notice of the school board meeting too late to be present. Then he continued, "I want to say, that had I been present I would have registered my protest against closing the [HCAHS]. . . . It was built by Harrison County for Harrison County's boys and girls. . . . This aspect of the case has not been changed by an imaginary line which has recently been drawn between the north and south end of the old county."

Stone County Superintendent of Education Bass echoed Fahnestock's sentiments. He then reiterated Stone County's willingness to let Harrison control the governing body of the school by six Trustees to Stone's five. By all reckoning, he added, Harrison would educate three boarding students to every one sent by Stone. Also, under the county division agreement, Harrison actually owned 12/15 of the school's physical plant. Surely Harrison County would not want to abandon that, Bass reasoned.

On Monday, July 31, Wood, still at home and still reported "ill," refused to comment and refused to release the resolution of the previous Friday's meeting. J. C. Clower, a member of the Harrison County School Board who had been present at the meeting, said he would be willing to reconsider his vote if a permanent, legal bi-county agreement could be hammered out.

On Wednesday, August 2, Superintendent Wood dropped a bomb in the form of a front-page statement in the *Daily Herald*. Wood stated that, "The people of Harrison County have too much pride to undertake to maintain a school in Stone County. The proposition is a parallel to a farmer building his barn several miles away in his neighbor's barnyard. I can see that we are under no obligation to Stone County to maintain an agricultural school for them. They divorced themselves from us, and should be satisfied with what they acquired."

Wood then stated that Harrison County hoped to spend $60,000 in the 1916-1917 session outfitting the new consolidated high schools to do everything the HCAHS was doing even to the point of using the same books and curriculum. Therefore, he saw no reason for Harrison to support a school in another county just so its students could leave home to gain the same knowledge. He opposed further taxation of Harrison County citizens recently devastated by the July Storm. While on that same subject, he said he had it on good authority that the HCAHS had suffered over $2,000 in damage to its buildings, necessitating even higher taxes to put them in order.

On yet another front, Wood brought up the pending lawsuit to annul Stone County. He pointed out that the success of the suit would nullify any support by Stone County to the school. In essence, Wood said Harrison County would later build its own AHS if it wanted one, and if not, not. Wood then stated, "In conclusion, I wish to say that I have talked to a great many people in Harrison County, and I have found that about ninety percent of those to whom I have talked are opposed to a bi-county school with Stone County."

Apparently at the same time Wood was preparing his statement, the five Harrison County consolidated school principals under his command had met and prepared their own broadside. The two documents in many places are so similar, one wonders if perhaps Wood and the principals collaborated in producing both simultaneously. With that suspicion in mind, the principals' broadside will be treated here in conjunction with Wood's statement and emphasis placed on certain differences.

The principals were so anxious to get their broadside on the front page that they sent the document along with a cover letter offering to pay advertising rates to achieve that end. The *Daily Herald* had since its inception exercised its editorial rights, but the paper usually placed an editorial on a special page a day or two after it printed a statement or covered a story. In this case, the paper slaughtered a statement as it printed it.

The *Daily Herald* editor printed his editorial together with the consolidated high school principals' cover letter and their broadside and Wood's statement and put the whole shebang on the front page. In answering the offer by the principals to pay advertising rates in order to get a front-page slot, the editor informed them, "In line with its well-known policy to print all the news, the *Herald* gladly gives space . . . without charge. The *Herald* is not a one man . . . one town . . . or one county paper. . . . Its aim is to serve the whole public . . . with impartial exactitude."

The principals dedicated their broadside, to which each affixed his signature, to the "Honorable School Board of Harrison County," of which, of course, Wood was the president. The broadside contained ten numbered reasons why Harrison County should not support the AHS at Perkinston and ended with these words, "Yours for Harrison County schools for Harrison County boys and girls. This letter is given to the public without the knowledge or consent of Supt. W. H. Wood and the Harrison County School Board." Whew.

As to the body of the broadside itself, the contention that the consolidated high schools were offering the same agriculture curriculum as the HCAHS had at least a modicum of validity, so the *Daily Herald* editor did not touch on that. As to the desire of the principals to have the money accrue to them that would have been given to the HCAHS, the *Daily Herald* editor let that one go, too. After all, these men were only looking out after their own interests. The contention that food would have to be purchased for the HCAHS cows due to crops lost to the July Storm was let go for the moment.

The *Daily Herald* editor, though, went after Points 7 and 9 with a meat cleaver. These two points are reprinted verbatim below:

"7th The agricultural and the horticultural possibilities of Harrison County are quite different from those of Stone County, therefore, the instruction given there in these lines must be different to that given to Stone County students. Local conditions prohibit the same school serving both sections to the greatest advantage.

"9th Owing to the chaotic condition of Stone County affairs, no one could unite with her in this school with any degree of safety."

The *Daily Herald* editor went after Points 7 and 9 together:

"It is ridiculous to say that an imaginary line drawn across Harrison which has been given the name of Stone could make any difference in soil possibilities; and it would seem still more ridiculous to make such a contention in the face of the fact that if the courts were to annul Stone County, Harrison would have again to take charge of the school and operate it as formerly. . . .

"This reason does not do justice to the intelligence of the men who are at the head . . . of the school system of [Harrison] county . . . and sets the stamp of imbecility on the people of the lower end of Harrison, for it was they who worked hardest for the school and finally selected Perkinston as the best point of location.

"Stone County is either Stone County or it is Harrison County. If it remains as Stone County no entanglement can arise by joining it in the operation of the school. If it ceases to remain Stone County, it automatically becomes Harrison and will pay its taxes in the Harrison County treasury as it has always done, causing not the slightest ripple of confusion.

"But will the principals contend that if Stone County were annulled by the suit that has been filed for that purpose, that the school could no longer be serviceable because the "agricultural and the horticultural possibilities" of north and south Harrison are quite different? And if they are different when have they become so? If they are different today were they not different when the school was located at Perkinston four years ago? If . . . so . . . why was the school located at Perkinston at all, and why has the school gone on for four years without this issue having been raised before?

"The whole fact of the matter is this: If the agricultural high school was worth operating last year, it is worth operating this, notwithstanding the principals of the consolidated high schools, to the contrary."

In view of the past and the future of the institution at Perkinston, the demise of which institution the five principals so fervently desired, the names of two of the signatories of the broadside invite comment. One of those names is that of W. A. Wellinghoff, principal of the Harrison and Jackson Line Consolidated School. He had served as the manual training teacher of the HCAHS in its second session. He had departed the HCAHS after that session and now emerged to stab the HCAHS in the back. The other name is that of A. L. May, principal of the Pineville Consolidated School. One can only hope May was dozing at the meeting where this travesty of a broadside was written. Perhaps he was coerced. If not, then one can not help but wonder if he ever thought back to that meeting during the years 1941-1953 when he served as president of the Perkinston Agricultural High School and Junior College.

A. L. May
Photo from Mississippi Today (1928), p. 120.

On August 3, 1916, the *Daily Herald* published notice for the public of Stone and Harrison Counties to meet in the rooms of the Service Club in Gulfport for discussion of the fate of the HCAHS. Champions of the school, including Charlie Swetman, Dr. E. M. Fahnestock, and a number of the high powered members of the Gulfport Commercial Union, made impassioned pleas for the two counties to unite and save the school.

No one spoke against the school, but some of the supporters of the superintendent were there seeking answers to questions raised by Wood and his five principals. Chief among these was W. N. Wood of Saucier, the brother of the superintendent.

The showstopper, though, was the address given by Huff. He said he had two years to go on a three-year contract but that he intended to resign as soon as the two counties could be brought together to save the school. He said he had seen the school grow from one building to three and become, in the words of many prominent educators, one of the best in the state. Last year, he continued, the attendance at the school was 160 with 105 boarders, and the numbers were ever growing with 100 expected from Harrison County alone in the coming session. He told the assemblage that the size of the farm had gone from nothing to 60 stump-free acres in four years. All the labor had been performed by the students and that the average gain in weight by the pupils was 9 7/8 pounds. He pointed out that the real difference between the HCAHS agricultural program and the consolidated school classes came in the actual learning-by-doing for four years as opposed to the study of theory for two.

The damage done by the July Storm Huff placed at $1,000 with most of that laid to crop loss. One building only had suffered any damage. A carpenter with $150 and plaster could fix it, and that could wait if need be.

He reminded those present that the law provided for bi-county operation and that each county got the same amount of funding thus doubling state support. Only one such school (Copiah-Lincoln AHS) existed, but the reports on it were good.

Webb Patton, a student at the HCAHS who wished to return, stood at the meeting and said, "If you give us the school, give us Prof. Huff, too." Stone County Superintendent of Education Bass echoed that sentiment saying Huff had seen the school through its inception, and he should be allowed to stay with it in view of his excellent work.

At this meeting, W. C. Batson of Stone County articulated possibly for the first time something with which few in 2000 would disagree. In effect he said the school had to be saved because the men and women it produced would be the leaders of the area it served from generation unto generation for as long as it existed.

Wyatt Claude Batson, Wiggins lawyer and Stone County legislator. Photo courtesy of Dixie Press, Gulfport.

George P. Hewes, of the Gulfport Commercial Union, reiterated that association's unswerving allegiance to the school because Gulfport's future depended on the development of its hinterland. Then he added that Superintendent Wood, "has made a grave mistake. So far as I am concerned I want to say that nearly all whom I have come in contact with have expressed themselves in favor of the school." The Service Club meeting closed with the adoption of a resolution calling for a joint meeting of the Harrison County School Board and the Stone County School Board.

The next day a committee of five appointed by those present at the Service Club called on Superintendent Wood and presented him with the resolution to call a bi-county school board meeting. Wood refused. He said he did not like what had been said about him at the meeting, and he particularly resented the remarks made by Bass. He stated further that there would be no bi-county School Board meeting until if and when the Harrison County School Board should decide it wanted a bi-county AHS. He said he was going to call a meeting of the Harrison County School Board in about two weeks time and then he said, "I should be very glad to have every citizen of Harrison County who is interested either for or against the proposition of a bi-county school, appear before the board."

On August 16, Wood postponed the school board meeting due to the illness of two of the members, J. C. Clower and A. W. Ladnier. Wood said he wanted a full board present this time since only three had been present at the meeting which resulted in the controversy.

Meanwhile, the Gulf Coast Normal ended at the HCAHS on August 22. The teachers took their teacher's license examinations and departed. At the then deserted campus, Huff could only wait in limbo. With only a couple of weeks to go to the proposed opening date of the school, he had no authorization to hire faculty, and the students were beginning to make other plans for their education.

The editorials in the *Daily Herald* became more strident. On August 26, the editor put it this way, "To put off the meeting of the school board any longer is equal to saying that no session of the Agricultural School will be held . . . for 1916-1917. This will be a hard blow to the children of this county who have been attending the school and who have the right to expect to continue their attendance, but there will be no help for it." Then the editor took another shot at the five consolidated high school principals, "The idea of the five heads of the consolidated schools of Harrison County urging the cost of feeding a few cows as a reason why the foremost school in this locality should not be operated is almost too preposterous for belief. . . . The cattle . . . will have to be fed whether the school runs or remains closed." And once again the editor blasted Wood,

"Superintendent Wood has based his opposition to the school mostly because of the 'cost.' . . . The 'cost.' . . . as figured out by a Stone County man [is] an average of twenty-five or thirty cents a tax payer--or about the cost of a soda water treat. If the school at Perkinston must stay closed, let some other reason than one of cost be given. . . . The fact is, there is not a valid reason that has been advanced or that can be advanced against running the agricultural school at Perkinston.

In justice to Mr. Wood, it might be stated here that no meeting of the school board has been called because of the illness of two members. . . . In this connection it may be stated that only three members of the board were present at the last meeting at which action unfavorable to the school was taken, and therefore, it is believed that no snap shot will be taken if another meeting is held with only three present. . . . To let the school at Perkinston stay closed will not only kill that institution but it will kill the spirit that made it possible."

Then at the close of the tirade came this,

"NOTE: Since the above was put into type, Superintendent W. H. Wood has announced that a meeting of the school board has been called for Wednesday, August 30, at 9 o'clock."

Elsewhere in the same issue of the paper, a *Daily Herald* reporter stated that J. C. Clower and A. W. Ladnier would not be present at the Harrison County School Board meeting due to illness. Superintendent Wood, Dr. E. M. Fahnestock, Dr. Winfield Cox, and P. N. Scarborough would consider the question of the AHS. The editor then called for all interested in saving the school to "let the board hear from them on Wednesday morning."

On August 29, Chancellor Denny, who had already dismissed the bill of complaint filed against Stone County by P. L. Hatten and R. N. Davis, dismissed likewise an amended version of it. The complainants then had only one recourse left--an appeal to the Mississippi State Supreme Court.

On Wednesday, August 30, 1916, the Harrison County School Board went into session at 9:30 a.m. Wood, Fahnestock, Cox, and Scarborough were there as expected, but so was E. Patton, who was not expected. Patton had been appointed to fill the place of Ladnier, who was very ill with malaria and appendicitis. Once more a stellar cast including George Hewes and William F. Gorenflo took the stage to make appeals to save the HCAHS.

Then came the vote. Patton voted "nay". Scarborough voted "nay." Fahnestock voted "aye." Cox voted "aye." All eyes now turned to Wood, and in the words of the *Daily Herald* reporter present at the meeting, "the advocates of the bi-county idea felt the ground slip from under their feet." And Wood voted "aye."

Harrison County Superintendent of Education W. H. Wood as pictured in the Daily Herald August 2, 1915. Photo courtesy of Sun Herald.

As a clap of thunder follows a lightning bolt, the room exploded. The *Daily Herald* reporter said, "His vote was hailed with joy by the friends of the school who almost shook his hand off . . . and then what followed was designated a 'love feast.' Superintendent Wood won the admiration of the county this morning by voting as he did."

In the aftermath Wood said he still did not favor the bi-county idea, but he had come to realize that the people of Harrison County did. Therefore, he would not stand in their way. Wood then called a joint Harrison-Stone School Board meeting for the next day.

The next day the Stone County School Board led by Bass began the journey to Superintendent Wood's office. While the men were enroute to Gulfport, the treasurer of Stone County brought suit against Harrison County for the funds that had been tied up because of the Hatten-Davis suit against Stone County. Fortunately this tidbit of news did not come up at the meeting.

Before he called the meeting of the joint school boards to order, Wood held a conference in which he presented two propositions to the Stone County

School Board members. One of these, he said, must be accepted before the joint meeting or there would be no meeting. Under the first proposition Harrison County would operate the school paying 60 percent for its support if Stone County would delegate to Harrison sole selection of the eleventh trustee. Stone refused. The second proposition called for a fifty-fifty support basis with Stone being allowed to participate in the election of the eleventh trustee but that the trustee must be a resident of Harrison County. Stone agreed.

The meeting then being called to order, Perkinston was selected as the place for holding the agricultural high school. This was a most fortuitous choice since that was where the HCAHS was.

The Harrison County members of the new Bi-County Harrison-Stone Agricultural High School (HSAHS) Board of Trustees were W. H. Hunt of Beat 1, F. L. Patenotte of Beat 2, W. N. Wood of Beat 4, R. S. Williams of Beat 5, and from Beat 3 Superintendent Wood, a member by virtue of his office. W. F. Gorenflo, the former president of the old board, was chosen as the eleventh trustee. The Stone County members were not published, but Superintendent of Education Bass by virtue of his office was one of them.

On September 8, the lawyers for Davis and Hatten appealed to the Mississippi State Supreme Court to nullify Stone County. This was the last ditch effort. So certain was the defeat that Harrison County paid Stone County the $38,000 it owed even before the case made the docket in Jackson. A. W. Bond pledged the Stone County Board of Supervisors to use $33,000 of that money to start on the north-south section of the Centennial Highway which would follow the Gulf and Ship Island Railroad from Gulfport to Jackson. This highway named for the impending centennial of the State of Mississippi in 1917, presaged U. S. Highway 49, which would pass through Perkinston.

Huff's Final Session at the HCAHS, September 1916 to August 1917

The HSAHS Board of Trustees met in Gulfport on September 9 and set September 18 as opening day for the 1916-1917 session of the school. The board elected Huff as principal and elected the following as faculty: J. S. McKewen, agriculture; George N. McIlhenney, manual training; Miss Pauline Triplett of Carthage, music; Miss Hazel Adams of Pass Christian, commercial department; Miss Aida Clower of Biloxi, history and English; Mrs. J. A. Huff, matron. Lillian Huff, fresh from the Mississippi Industrial Institute and College (in 2000 called Mississippi University for Women) at Columbus, joined her parents as a faculty member at the HSAHS teaching home science.

Dr. E. M. Fahnestock, who had done so much to save the school from destruction, attended opening day to enroll his son, Harris. He stated that 80 boarders were on hand the first day and 30 more were expected in the next two weeks. About 25 students from the previous year had gone elsewhere due to the uncertainty of the school's survival, but, said the good doctor, their places were expected to be filled.

Huff called the students and faculty to order in Bennett Hall Auditorium at 2 p.m., and all joined in singing the patriotic song "America." Rev. R. N. Davis then led the assemblage in prayer, and the new session began.

Huff, having deflected the "slings and arrows of outrageous fortune" to save the AHS, then lost a quarter of his combined faculty and administration to Cupid's arrows. J. C. McKewen wed the former Lillian Huff on December 22 and swept her away to Winona, where he took the position of farm demonstration agent of Montgomery County. Huff had to spend Christmas holidays hunting two teachers.

On December 29, Miss Grace Pope resigned her position at Lyman to take the new Mrs. McKewen's place at the HSAHS. A few days later Huff signed on F. A. Rew as the new agriculture teacher.

In February 1917, the *Daily Herald* and the *Stone County Enterprise* both acceded to petitions by the students of the HSAHS for space in which student reporters might publish occasional columns detailing the doings at the school. Both papers granted permission, and the submissions from the school were printed in both papers under the same heading, "Harrison-Stone Bi-County Agricultural High School." In effect the *Daily Herald* and the *Stone County Enterprise* published the HSAHS student newspaper. This publication will be cited herein as the *HSAHS News*.

The February 9, 1917, *HSAHS News* reported that the senior class had met to choose class rings, which was the first mention of such in the history of the school. Another item printed that day noted that, "The Juniors and Seniors passed a resolution to co-operate with the faculty in maintaining discipline and to give first aid in the student government." One might wonder why first aid was necessary in the conduct of the government.

Yet another announcement declared that the senior engineering class had drawn plans for a poultry house for the school, and the contract had been let to a member of the junior class. This "contractor" was to use the other members of his class as a work crew. The questions was, "Is a lock to be installed; less the fellows, who have a desire to live high; must step into the pitfalls of temptation; and lest industrious hens might be disturbed in their occupation." (Translation --How do we save our chickens from the boys who would steal them and cook them on a sandbar barbecue on Red or Ten-Mile Creek? From the time the AHS was built no fowl within two miles was safe. As has already been stated, ducks were disappearing as late as the 1970s.)

Ogden Lott, a former student reminiscing in the *Bulldog Barks* on November 9, 1974, stated, "The boys liked to have chicken fries. And they would steal them from neighborhood chicken houses. One time about 25 boys were having a cookout and they got caught. The residents in town were notified and were told to report how many chickens they had lost, so the boys could pay for them. There were 120 missing." Then he chuckled and continued, "Of course, the residents must have turned in all the chickens they had lost in years, but they sure had fun kidding those boys about eating 120 chickens."

The *HSAHS News* of February 16, 1917, carried notice that the model poultry house was nearing completion. "Contractor Necaise will turn the building over to Architect Swetman in a few days."

Glen Swetman, son of the president of People's Bank of Biloxi and a nephew of Charlie Swetman of Perkinston, attended the AHS from 1915 to 1917. In a 1992 interview at People's Bank he remembered those long ago days. He said when he was of age, his mother, "told me she was sending me to Perkinston because I was more than she could handle at home," and "it cost less to attend . . . than it did to live at home."

Glen L. Swetman (July 4, 1901-April 30, 1994) HSAHS Class of 1917. He later attended Soule Business College in New Orleans, Ole Miss, and the U. S. Naval Academy. In his position as President of the People's Bank of Biloxi, Swetman was credited with saving the Gulf Coast seafood industry with wise lending practices during the Great Depression. In 1989 the Biloxi schooner, Glen L. Swetman slid down the ways as a reminder of legions of the white-winged queens that once crowded the Gulf waters. Swetman also made vital contributions to Beauvoir and other historic sites of the Gulf Coast.

Swetman said the 80 or so students stood in awe of "Daddy Huff," a no-nonsense administrator. In Swetman's words, "Daddy Huff did not allow anything that resembled heavy courting. Dating was allowed only after classes had been dismissed for the day. Boys and girls could sit together around campus or walk to town for a snack or a soda."

Chickens were at risk but watermelons did not have a chance. Huff frowned on all this illicit augmentation of the very generous and delicious school diet, but he could not stop it. Swetman remembered, "Raiding the watermelon patch was great fun. We'd steal the watermelons and bring them back to the campus to eat them. The rinds were evidence we had been up to no good."

Swetman received his first on-the-job business training at his Uncle Charlie's general store and post office in Perkinston. Sometimes Charlie let him manage the store alone.

Some of Swetman's other memories shed light on the lives of the students in general, "Dances were held on a regular basis but they were closely supervised by Daddy Huff and other school officials. Students lived on campus and seldom went home on weekends. Parents would visit, usually on Sunday. Football and baseball were popular sports at the school. We played scrub teams from Gulfport and Wiggins."

The *HSAHS News* of February 16, also contained a futuristic dream sequence called "Just a Dream" by Miss Anna Patten, member of the junior class. In this essay she had Randolph Necaise fall asleep in the "little power house" on the campus and dream the future of the Junior Class of 1917. At one point the "scene shifted to a magnificent bank and who sat at the cashier's desk but Glen Swetman." Well, that did, of course, come to pass, but then she knew that might happen and it did. The point is, though, all the students except one became bankers, lawyers, generals, theater owners, teachers, or factory owners. Jack Lamey became the only farmer. Her dream was F. W. Elmer Sr.'s nightmare--an agricultural high school that produced everything but farmers.

Bostick "Crab" Breland in his "Crabology" of February 23, 1917, called attention to this inattention to farming, "It was ever thus. The path of the agricultural student has always led away from the farm. . . . A nameless longing fills his breast and he gazes to the far off town. If he farms at all, it is by proxy, or else, he 'farms' the other fellow."

Five weeks later the *HSAHS News* gave facts and figures designed to refute the criticism of the "highland crab shuffling up to disturb our dreams." Of fifty young men of the AHS reporting from the year 1913-1914, contended the *HSAHS News*, twenty-four said they were going to be farmers and thirty of forty-four students from 1914-1915 said the same.

The February 23, 1917, *HSAHS News* carried an account of a Mardi Gras holiday for the school. A half-holiday was given by Huff on Tuesday afternoon, February 20. All students were allowed either to go to the coast towns or take a hayride up to Wiggins. On Ash Wednesday, "L. R. Bowen reports a splendid time at Mardi Gras. However, due to the lack of sleep, he was unable to give an account of himself, in chapel when called upon."

Many solutions to the Mardi Gras Holiday problem

had been tried over the years. Finally in early February 1979, the administration took the unprecedented step of allowing the students of the then tri-campus junior college to vote on the issue. A "yes" vote meant that two days would be added to the second semester closing date in order to allow for the holiday. The students overwhelmingly voted for the proposition. This was the best solution because the students took the two days off anyway.

If Crab was worried about the HSAHS not turning out farmers, Dr. B. C. Lowrey, field secretary of Mississippi College, voiced his fears about it not turning out home economists. The March 9 *HSAHS News* quoted a line from his address to the student body in Bennett auditorium, "Keep a watch out for the girl who can play a piano, but can't cook pies and the girl whose bread will kill your birddog."

All through March the *HSAHS News* was full of plans for the school's exhibits at the Mississippi Centennial Exposition to open at Gulfport on December 10, 1917, and to run until June 10, 1918. The boys had built, among other things, a model of the proposed Gulfport to Jackson Centennial Highway.

But the newspapers carried ominous news together with notices of the centennial celebration. As the month of March slipped away, the headlines told of the resumption of German unrestricted submarine warfare, suspected German sabotage, and possible German involvement of Mexico in a war against the United States.

The March 28, 1917, *HSAHS News* took notice of the international scene, "All the fellows are ready to make a stand if the Germans and [Mexicans] invade Harrison and Stone County."

The April 5 *HSAHS News* spoke of the hoisting of the "Skull and Crossbones" on the flag pole four days prior and the subsequent pranks of the "Fools of April." It was a day of short sheeting and sand in the beds. The "artistic class rings" had been received by the seniors. Spring football practice had begun. Prof. and Mrs. Huff and their little daughter, Virginia, had returned from a trip to their old home at Forest.

The next day, April 6, 1917, the United States Congress, at the behest of President Woodrow Wilson, declared war on the German Empire and by extension Austria-Hungary, Bulgaria, and Turkey. Along with the headlines proclaiming America's entry into the Great War came this notation, "Submarines Reported in the Gulf."

The declaration of war spelled the doom of the Centennial Highway as the workmen flocked to the colors. It spelled the doom of the centennial, too, as Gulfport converted the buildings and exposition grounds into a naval training station.

On April 11, William Guild, manager of the Finkbine Lumber Company of Wiggins and D'Lo, told

"Miss Issippi"--symbol of a centennial celebration that never happened. Illustration from the Daily Herald, February 10, 1917,courtesy of the Sun Herald.

the *Daily Herald* editor that so many men had left his mills for the service that he might have to close the plants. That same day the *HSAHS News* proclaimed, "The AHS . . . has been practicing militarism throughout this session. Strenuous drilling and military exercises are given every morning after arising. The dormitories are controlled entirely by military government. This training is not only of great value should the youth be pressed into service, but affords the greatest healthful exercise."

Citing the fact that April 11 was being observed in Mississippi as Food Supply Day, the *HSAHS News* continued, "Harrison and Stone Counties can do their part by growing crops, cattle and hogs. Every available plot should be planted to corn, peas, beans or something of equal value. . . . This will call for more work and more intensive methods of farming. The young man who enlists is patriotic, for he has the respect of his nation. . . . The man who is not able to enlist can be just as patriotic by raising the foodstuff for his brother at the front."

On April 25 the *HSAHS News* noted stepped-up mobilization procedures at the campus:

"The period of Military Drill has been lengthened from fifteen minutes to half an hour each morning. Immediately after a student enlists with the A.H.S. corps, he is supplied with a dummy gun which is made by the Manual Training Department. Military training is compulsory for the dormitory boys. The officers in charge have planned a series of hikes to be made by the Company. The first one will be Friday, when the 'dusties' will make a short hike of five or six miles. All we need now is a military band. The signal corps have been practicing recently and have met with success in using flags."

Harry McNeil, a young HSAHS warrior overcome by the martial spirit, went off to join the real army. He flunked the physical on account of a "slight defect in one of his ankles" and returned to the accolades of his classmates who admired this patriotic gesture.

The *HSAHS News* of May 2 carried a piece by agricultural teacher F. A. Rew praising the young ladies of the school for volunteering to work in the fields of the school. "Perhaps our young men . . . may have to present their being as food for the war dog, in order to preserve American liberty." But then he added, "Surely young men will be honored in dying for such patriotic heroines."

The next week the *HSAHS News* reported that those "patriotic heroines" were hard workers. "Gee, but our girls up here can out work a Turk, and out boss the Kaiser." The "Aggies" of both sexes were determined to give Uncle Sam what he wanted--foodstuffs. Young professor George McIlhenney, or "Mr. Mack," as they called him, had departed the school to spend a few days at his hometown of Forest. From there he would leave for "the officers training camp in Arkansas."

On May 15, Huff informed the *Daily Herald* that the HSAHS Board of Trustees in session on May 9 had voted to close the school two weeks early to allow the young men the opportunity to return to their homes to aid in planting crops for the war effort. He said nearly all the rest of the boys who did not live on farms would be glad to volunteer to do farm work for anyone who wanted their services. Huff was careful to note that, "This action was taken before any mention was made of exempting farmers from military service." Farmers who needed help could communicate with the school.

Huff said the young ladies had been urged to return to their homes and go to work canning fruits and vegetables and raising poultry. The HSAHS had agreed to take their products at market prices against their board for next session. He ended, "This has been one of the most pleasant and prosperous sessions in the history of the school. Notwithstanding our late opening we have enrolled about 90 boarding pupils, and are closing with 65 boarders in regular attendance." As the Class of 1917 said farewell and began new lives so did Huff. The *Daily Herald* of June 16 carried notice of his resignation effective August 15. Professor J. A. Huff left the Harrison-Stone AHS to take the head position of the Pearl River AHS at Poplarville. In time he would lead that school in its evolution from agricultural high school to junior college, the first in Mississippi to make that transition.

In the long hot summer of 1917, as the nation prepared for "wheatless" Mondays and "meatless" Tuesdays, the home demonstration agents of Stone and Harrison Counties led 67 stalwarts of the Girls Canning Club "over the top" at the HSAHS to see to it that America would not lack for preserves or pickle relish on any day of the week. At the conclusion of this grand offensive, agents Pauline Quarles of Stone and May Quarles of Harrison led their charges in a great victory celebration:

"The girls voted sending a telegram to President Wilson assuring him that they would do their part in the conservation of foods and that each would put in a "War Garden." This action was followed by several rousing yells for the Chief Executive, and America, and the singing of the patriotic songs by every one present."

As the girls left the front for well-earned rest and recuperation, 46 replacements of the Corn and Pig Club Boys poured in to hold the line.

As the nation hunted spies and hounded slackers, 122 Stone County draftees received notice that they would soon follow their 80 brothers who had already volunteered. On July 12, U. S. Secretary of War Newton D. Baker announced Hattiesburg as the site of a new national military training site. Thirteen days later the G&SI RR served notice that it would build a spur line into this military installation which, by then, had a name--Camp Shelby.

The huge lumber mills of south Mississippi added extra shifts as U. S. Government orders for materials for Camp Shelby and Allied Powers orders for timber to shore up the crumbling bunkers and trenches of the Western Front poured in. Orders for ships' timbers and naval stores came from the shipyards of Pascagoula. The guns of the Great War sounded the death knell of the virgin pine forests of the Mississippi Panhandle.

The aftermath of a much smaller, though no less partisan conflict, also played itself out in the summer of 1917. On June 20 the Stone County board of supervisors let the contract to the Standard Construction Company of Meridian to build a $25,147 courthouse in Wiggins. A few days later McHenry, the loser in the Stone County "war," surrendered its town charter and slipped into unincorporated oblivion.

The Canning Club Girls and the Poultry Club Girls, together with representatives of various area Mothers' Clubs, pose on the steps of Bennett Hall in June, 1917. May Quarles [later Watrous], director of the Harrison County Canning Club Girls, is third from right in the first row standing. Photo courtesy of Mary Ellen (Watrous) Alexander, daughter of May Watrous.

May Quarles [later Watrous] (back to camera) leads her militarized Canning Club Girls in exercises on the lawn in front of Bennett Hall at the HSAHS in June 1917. Not a single German, Austro-Hungarian, Bulgarian, or Turkish soldier penetrated the perimeter of the campus on the Canning Club Girls watch. Their unrelenting barrage of Banner Spain chutney pickles, tomatoes, and other foodstuffs emanating from their war gardens helped defeat the Central Powers a mere 17 months later. Photo courtesy Mary Ellen (Watrous) Alexander.

BENNETT AND THE GREAT WAR ERA AUG. 1917 - MAY 1920

On Wednesday, July 6, 1917, the Harrison-Stone Agricultural High School Board of Trustees unanimously selected 38-year-old Professor Claude J. Bennett out of a field of fourteen applicants to replace Huff in August as principal of the HSAHS. Claude and Grace (McVey) Bennett arrived at Perkinston around August 1. Two weeks later the *Daily Herald* carried an account of the welcome given to the Bennetts. They were welcomed in the auditorium of the building that forty-three years later would be named Bennett Hall:

"A reception was given in the auditorium of the A.H.S. Tuesday evening at 8 o'clock in honor of Prof. and Mrs. Bennett. Miss Ruble and Miss Howard furnished delightful music, Miss Vivian Davis gave a reading, after which dainty refreshments were served by Misses Viola Deiter, Annie M. Alexander, Vivian Davis, Mayme Jordan and Eunice DuBose."

At the August meeting of the Board of Trustees held in Gulfport, the AHS Trustees elected Grace Bennett as domestic science teacher and named Robert H. Harmon of Gulfport teacher of math and science. The board set the opening day of the 1917-1918 session for September 10.

As the session drew nigh, the last of the faculty came on board. Sarden F. O'Neal (agriculture), R. M. Coman (farm mechanics), Mrs. R. M. Coman (librarian), Miss Aida Clower (history and English), and Miss Grace Ruble (music and expression), who soon became Mrs. Robert Harmon.

The HSAHS opening on September 10 was touted as a record-setting enrollment. Besides a dozen day students, 86 boarders filled the dorms with more expected to come. Harrison County Superintendent of Education W. H. Wood and Stone County Superintendent of Education C. H. Bass welcomed the students.

Ormond Hughes of Gulfport, one of the HSAHS students who moved into Huff Hall that opening day, had been turned down as a volunteer by Uncle Sam. The army had refused him because he was only 14 years old. Two enrollees from Julia, Louisiana, were worthy of note. Their "old home place" lay only three blocks from the campus. They were grandchildren of John Perkins, for whom the town was named. Their father, John's son D. V., had brought young John and his sister Stella home to go to school.

Claude Bennett was born February 14, 1879, at Silver Creek, Lawrence County, one of five children of Drury Burton Bennett and Elizabeth (Burkett) Bennett. He attended Mississippi College for three years. He received his bachelor of arts degree in 1908 at Trinity College (later Duke University). In 1926 he received his masters of arts degree from George Peabody College (later Vanderbilt University).

Bennett served as principal of various Lincoln County schools and then became Lincoln County superintendent of education from 1908 to 1912. He served as principal of Hattiesburg High School in the 1912-1913 session and held the principalship of Moss Point High for the next two years. On September 3, 1914, he married the former Grace McVey of Highland, Ohio, and eventually they became the parents of three daughters--Margaret Nan Bennett, Grace McVey Bennett, and Mary Ellen Bennett.

In 1915 he returned to Hattiesburg to serve as vice-president of Mississippi Woman's College (later William Carey College). Bennett left Mississippi Woman's College in July 1917, to serve three years as the superintendent of Harrison-Stone Agricultural High School at Perkinston.

Bennett left Perkinston in 1920 to become superintendent of Biloxi Schools for three years. In 1923 he became the first supervisor of agricultural high schools and junior colleges in the Mississippi State Department of Education. He served in that capacity until 1928, when he accepted the presidency of Mississippi State Teachers College (later the University of Southern Mississippi).

In 1933 Bennett, a New Deal Democrat, accepted a position with the United States Treasury Department. He served in the Laurel office as chief of field division, United States Bureau of Internal Revenue, throughout the presidency of Franklin Delano Roosevelt (1933-1945).

Grace Bennett died on August 30, 1940. On May 1, 1943, Claude Bennett married the former Mary (Bentley) Gavin of Stafford Springs, Jasper County.

Bennett maintained his connection with the Perkinston institution throughout his life both officially and privately. He delivered the October 18, 1952, Homecoming Day keynote address commemorating the 40th anniversary of the institution. In his speech Bennett praised his predecessor, J. A. Huff, and announced the naming of the institution's initial structure in that first principal's honor--Huff Hall. Eight years later the Board of Trustees honored Bennett in a similar fashion by naming the institution's second building Bennett Hall.

Crab Breland decided to pay the HSAHS a visit on Saturday, September 22. As he waited for the train in Wiggins, Bennett happened to drive by and offer him a ride. Crab said Bennett "automobiled" him down the "Dixie Highway" and took him to dinner in the "spacious dining hall" and "wined and dined [him] with only the wine left out." At the behest of Bennett, Crab gave an impromptu after-dinner talk to the students after which the Bennetts whisked him away by auto to Howison. Crab said that sometimes the car bucked like a mustang because there were places near Howison where the mode of travel should have been a mustang. On the flying trip back they dropped in on Dr. G. A. McHenry where they settled a few questions of the day--the war in Europe, for example. Returning to Perkinston they "run in" on both Charlie Swetman and C. E. Dees at their respective general stores. Bennett then took Crab back to Wiggins, where he caught another ride to his home at Big Level.

The last extant issue of the *HSAHS News* appeared in the *Stone County Enterprise* on October 13, 1917:

"It may be of interest to some of the friends of the school to know that we have a pretty fair crop on the farm, we estimate that we will make 450 bushels of corn, 4 or 5 hundred gallons of syrup, several hundred bushels of potatoes, besides peas, hay, peanuts, etc.

The first month of the Agricultural High School has just closed and in spite of the troubles with the light and water plant it has been a most satisfactory one."

A single-cylinder engine in a shed supplied the power for the campus. Apparently it was malfunctioning and the war made replacing it difficult.

As the three million-strong American Expeditionary Force poured into France, the news from "over there" dominated the *Daily Herald* and casualty lists replaced the *HSAHS News* as 116,000 young Americans died.

As to the service of Harrison-Stone AHS students in the Great War, only one statement touching on this had surfaced by 2000. The statement appeared three months after the Armistice and it read: "More than fifty [Harrison-Stone] agricultural high school boys have been or are now in the United States Army or Navy." Because of the lack of student rosters in this period, their names will probably never be known.

Once again the session ended two weeks early because of the war. The school held graduation exercises on May 14, 1918.

Once again that summer, the school hosted the Canning Club Girls and the Pig Club Boys. The only thing unusual was that the girls were shown a picture show. Wiggins had movie theaters, but this was the first mention of movies being shown at the HSAHS.

The 1918-1919 session of the school opened with its largest enrollment in history on Monday, September 9. The final count of boarding students stood at 110. This figure included 64 from Harrison and 34 from Stone. The balance came from seven other counties and three other states. In addition to the boarders, about 15 day students attended from the Perkinston area. Boys filled Huff Hall, but so many girls poured into Stone Hall that the parlors had to be converted into sleeping rooms.

The registrants of 1918 faced a unique change in dress. According to the *Daily Herald* of September 13, 1918, "Uniforms will be worn by all students this session. The boys will wear the khaki uniform and the girls blue serge." The boys' uniforms came through membership in the para-military Boys Working Reserve and consisted of coat, trousers, shirt, hat, and leggings, all for $11.00. Notice came simultaneously of a unique honor--graduates would no longer have to take an examination in order to teach in Mississippi public schools. By a 1918 legislative enactment a teacher's certificate would be granted to any AHS graduate in the state who took two Carnegie units of education in the 15 required for graduation, and who also attended a summer normal of not less than 25 days duration.

Movies had come to stay and were shown occasionally in the Bennett Hall Auditorium. According to one of the students remembering those days in 1995, these picture shows left a lot to be desired. A student worker hand-cranked the movie reel, and the images on screen speeded up or slowed down depending on the elan or the fatigue of the cranker.

Every morning at 8:00 the student body assembled in the auditorium for "chapel." Bible verses were read, hymns sung, announcements were made, and the students filed out to their various classes. Sometimes speakers addressed the students in chapel. As the American Army attacked the Germans in late 1918, the speakers tended to be connected with the war effort. Prof. Robert H. Harmon's brother, Rev. Nolan Harmon, addressed the HSAHS student body in late September regarding the Young Men's Christian Association service in France. In early October Sergeant Tom Cunningham of Perkinston, home on furlough after ten months in the hospital, shared with the students what happened in a gas attack. His brother, William, was engaged in battle on the Western Front as he spoke.

At the eleventh hour of the eleventh day of the eleventh month 1918, (Paris time) the Germans signed the Armistice in a railway car in the forest near Compeigne on the Western Front. But the time of day on the Mississippi Gulf Coast was 1 a.m. The bells in the churches in Biloxi and the other coast cities began ringing by 1:45. Shortly thereafter the people of Wiggins began to celebrate with bells, whistles, and gunfire. By 8 a.m. people from the surrounding countryside, including the students of the HSAHS who had trooped up, were marching through the streets of Wiggins. Bennett, among other dignitaries, addressed the joyous crowd at the Stone County Courthouse. The Great War was won.

Ten days later the Great Spanish Influenza Epidemic reached Stone County. Two hundred people came down with the dread disease. Before the end of the year millions had died worldwide, and nearly 100,000 had succumbed in the United States and Canada. Much sickness but no deaths were reported in Stone County.

The students at the HSAHS got a long Christmas vacation that session. Because of the flu epidemic the school did not reopen until January 27, 1919. Even then all wishing to re-enter had to bring a doctor's certificate stating that there was no flu at their homes and stating further that they had not been exposed.

At Christmas time the *Daily Herald* published a notice that Bennett would be leaving for a job in Poplarville in January. J. J. Dawsey, who had long championed the school, applied for the position of principal. Surprisingly Harrison County Superintendent of Education W. H. Wood, who had nearly killed the school, signified his willingness to accept the position if offered. But Bennett decided to stay and was back at his post when the HSAHS opened in late January.

The *Daily Herald* noted another first in the life of the AHS on the day it reopened:

"The Harrison-Stone Bi-County Agricultural High School has received a warrant for $625 from the federal government in consideration of the fact that the school is now operated under the Smith-Hughes law. This amount will be paid twice a year into the treasury of the county for the benefit of the school as long as the board of trustees of the school run the school under the provisions laid down by the federal government."

The Smith-Hughes Act, approved by Congress on February 23, 1917, was the foundation of American vocational education. Under the provisions of this act, appropriations were provided for the promotion of vocational education in agriculture, home economics, trades, and industry, and for the training of teachers in those fields. The funds given to the HSAHS in January 1919 marked the institution's first foray into the realm of federal funding. Only 20 other schools in Mississippi qualified for Smith-Hughes money that year. The federal government was giving money to the schools but none to the military.

Now that "The War to End War" was over, Camp Shelby was demobilized and abandoned. The ships under construction at Pascagoula were left unfinished on the ways as the workers departed. The much-vaunted armistice really was exactly that--a cease-fire. The United States would have to build an army from scratch again in only 20 years.

The HSAHS demobilized, too. No more was said of marching and drilling. The Friday night movies in the auditorium featured America's Sweetheart, Mary Pickford and "six gun totin'" William S. Hart.

The greatest excitement the second half of that session occurred on March 1, 1919. An "aeroplane" flew right over the campus.

On May 10, 1919, the *Stone County Enterprise* reported that "Superintendent Claude Bennett" had been in Wiggins discussing the AHS with a "number of citizens." Due to the dearth of official documents from the school in this period, it is not possible to state with any accuracy precisely when the official title of the head of the HSAHS became "superintendent" instead of "principal," but it had happened by this time.

The subject under discussion in Wiggins had been the proposition of putting the HSAHS on a paying basis. In Bennett's words, "If I stay at Perkinston, I want to place the farm department on a business basis and show the boys that money can be made by farmers in South Mississippi. Like it has been in the past, the products of the farm, and dairy as well, has been used in the boarding department in order to reduce the cost of board to students and in so doing the farm has never received due credit for its products." Bennett pointed out that Douglas L. Ott of Hovey, soon to be a graduate of the school, had cleared $206 on a cabbage patch measuring 75 by 120 feet. The young man's work, in Bennett's opinion, proved his point and served as an inspiration to all other Mississippi agricultural high school students.

In advertising the 1919-1920 session of the HSAHS slated to open on Monday, September 8, 1919, the school pointed with pride to its low boarding rate of $12 per month. This was far lower than the $20 charged by the Mississippi Agricultural and Mechanical College in Starkville or the $19.50 demanded by the State Normal College in Hattiesburg.

A two-page *Bulletin* issued at registration time informed the public that all dormitory spaces had been filled and that the HSAHS was the best of 50 such schools in the state. In the realm of community service, the *Bulletin* announced that, "The forces of the Agricultural High School will be only too glad to do Extension work in the way of vaccinating hogs, terracing land, making farm surveys, helping in the construction of hog houses, brooders, etc. The only cost to the farmer will be the material used in vaccinating and building. Any school thinking of putting on Community Fairs or teaching Community Games can get help by applying to the school."

All the teachers at the school, continued the

Bulletin, were college graduates and all of them were going to live on the campus for the coming session. Instruction in typewriting and shorthand were going to be offered at one-third the rate of a regular business college. The new faculty for the 1919 year included Miss Beulah Delano (home science), W. J. Edens (assistant agriculturist), Miss Kate Atkinson (English), and Miss Mary Clark (matron).

(Left) Ruby Lee Johnson and a friend at Perkinston in 1922. Photo courtesy of Charlie Probst.

The students had much more in the way of entertainment to look forward to in the coming session. A new "stereopticon outfit" had been added to the audio-visual holding of the school. The students were playing volleyball and other games each afternoon.

The *Stone County Enterprise* of September 13, 1919, carried this notation concerning the opening of the 1919-1920 session, "Mr. and Mrs. H. Johnson of D'Lo, were in town Monday to place their daughter, Miss Ruby in the A.H.S."

Ruby Lee Johnson was aged 16 at that time. On Homecoming Day October 19, 1996, Ruby Lee (Johnson) Probst Strong returned to the campus. In an interview conducted that day, she shared with the archivist her recollections of 80 years prior.

"Ship Island" Frantzen in 1923 as center on the HSAHS football team.

The same day Ruby Lee Johnson came to the HSAHS with her parents, the school's first foreign-born student arrived by train from the coast--fifteen-year-old Norwegian-born William Albert Frantzen. The day he arrived at the G&SI RR Depot at Perkinston, Frantzen received a nickname that stayed with him for life. According to Frantzen, "One of the things that we had was bedding and clothing in a trunk . . . everybody was down there . . . to see if their trunk had come in. Some knowing first one and then another . . . would say, 'There's Biloxi' or 'There's Pass Christian.' Most of them knew where I had come from and had seen me out there [but] many didn't know my name. [Then someone said] 'There comes Ship Island.' It stuck from that time." "Ship Island," "Ship" Frantzen, had found a new home.

Stone Hall girls pose in one of Perk's mule drawn wagons circa 1919. "AHS" is written in black paint on the side of the wagon. This and similar conveyances were used to transport students and baggage from the G&SI RR Depot in Perkinston up to the residence halls at the top of Perk Hill. Photo courtesy of John Russell O'Neal.

At the depot the boys piled their trunks on a mule drawn wagon and followed it up the hill to Huff Hall. The girls' trunks were placed on another similar conveyance bound for Stone Hall.

Ruby Lee Johnson had a room on the top floor of Stone Hall directly above the matron's quarters, "so she knew everything I did." In describing the bathroom she said, "you went down the hall and there was a bathroom. We had, I think two stalls...or three...and they had tubs back then."

The dining room and kitchen were on the ground floor of Stone Hall. According to Ruby Lee Johnson, the superintendent's apartment occupied the northern half of the basement with the dining room being in the other portion.

Ship Frantzen recalled how the food was served:

"It was put on the table family style and there were six or eight people [per table]. The girls that served the table for part of their board...put the food on the table from the kitchen. When the meal was over they would...bring two dishpans out. One was their wash and the other they rinsed in...and then they dried [the plates] with a towel and put it back in place upside down so it would be protected. That's how the dishes were washed. Of course, the Board of Health would turn handsprings now."

Frantzen said whatever chair you sat in the first day was yours from then on. The same situation applied to dormitory rooms, "Dormitory rooms...were not

HSAHS girls pose circa 1919 with a horse and buggy in front of Stone Hall, the only girl's dormitory on the campus at that time. Photo courtesy John Russell O'Neal.

assigned. You find one, you moved into it. My first time you can bet I had a lousy room because I didn't know you were supposed to grab that way but the second time I did it that way. I had a good room 'cause I got there early and took one."

The school buildings were electrified, but the power came from "a single cylinder horizontal" engine down by the railroad. Every night at about 9 p.m., Lyman Bradford, the student who ran it, shut it down. According to Frantzen, "When they turned the lights off if you wanted more light you had a kerosene lamp. You could stay up all night if you were foolish."

Bennett's desire to put the school on a paying basis resulted in innovative class scheduling. In Frantzen's words,

"My first year when Bennett was principal the school was run strange in that by 12 noon all classes were over. We could get out and work for 10 cents an hour if you had a job. That first job that I got, I think it was for Mr. [Charlie] Swetman . . . bailing hay. I had never seen a hay bailer before, but I enjoyed meeting a lot of fellows then. It was all strange to me and so new to me--living on a farm. It was very fortunate that it was a vocational farm school-high school at that time because I learned, among other things, that I would never make a farmer. That didn't mean that I didn't enjoy it."

As to the relationship between the sexes, Frantzen remembered, "We would talk to a girl once in a while on campus if they didn't catch you, but that old administration building was wonderful. [It] had more hidden corners."

Ruby Lee Johnson, when asked about holding hands with boys, said, "We didn't do too much of that. I think the girls and boys back then were more refined than they are now."

When asked if she courted the boys, she replied, "Yes. That was the main thing. That is the reason I didn't make better grades. We would walk. The teachers would go with us . . . down to the spring [an artesian well flowed by the railroad for many years]. The boys would climb a tree and get us magnolias. We would pick other kinds of flowers and just walk."

Sometimes, she said, the girls received permission to go to the stores in town to get gum and candy. Once in a great while the teachers would take the girls to Red or Ten Mile Creek so they could wade. They did not swim.

Perhaps the boys were not as refined as Ruby Lee Johnson remembered. Ship Frantzen recalls the night that one of the denizens of the second floor of Huff Hall dressed up like a girl, wig and all, and walked between the kerosene lamps and the shades. This singular development set off a "riot" among various and sundry officials and faculty of the school who searched Huff Hall "until daylight" to try to find who was up there. They found nothing. The culprit, having achieved his aim of sewing great consternation, had thrown the dress and wig up into the attic by way of a trap door. He was in bed and pretending sleep by the time the authorities arrived on the scene.

So far as Frantzen remembered none of the Huffers summoned up the nerve to reprise the "shadow on the shade" incident, but "slat popping" went on constantly. The boys slept in single beds with pliable slats to hold the mattresses in place. In Frantzen's words,

"Late at night when things were finally quiet, sneakers would sneak inside a room . . . and just lay a slat on the floor . . . and if you can hold back on the slat with your foot so you could get a good steam on it, when you turned it loose and hit the floor it went off like a gunshot. As soon as you popped that thing you scooted to your room. There was more than one board laying [around] you couldn't tell which room it came from. . . . It was better than going to the movies."

Smoking was against the rules but, according to Frantzen, those with a letter from home could indulge. Still the school officials, he said, "looked down on everything except a pipe. There were restrictions on smoking but there was quite a bit of it going on. The cheapest was Bull Durham. Most of the fellows who smoked would use a pipe so there wouldn't be any argument about it."

In the 1919 era there was no grill or snack bar or bookstore on the campus. Frantzen remembered, "Any book we bought, we bought at Charlie Swetman's store. And I found, among other things, that if you were going there at the time he wasn't busy and bargain with him you would get a whole lot better deal because he enjoyed it and I know he softened up just for the pleasure of it. If you couldn't afford new books . . . you bought an old one. You bought every book that you had."

Dees General Store was the largest in town, but the students went to Swetman's more because it contained the town post office in one corner and because it served as the bookstore for the AHS. Another smaller store near the G&SI RR depot run by a Mrs. Bang sold gum, candy, soda pop, and sandwich fixings. Bang's Store served in the office of student grill.

The school had no laundry at this time either. Neighborhood washerwomen came to the dorms to pick up the clothes. Frantzen always gave his laundry to a black woman named Beulah White, whose husband was named Jack. Frantzen visited them every time he returned until their deaths years later.

As for automobiles in 1919, Frantzen recalled that C. E. Dees and Charlie Swetman had them in town. At the HSAHS the principal and at least one teacher had cars. The numbers grew over the years. Sometimes the ball teams used these cars to go to games, but if the roads were wet, they spent as much time pushing them as they did riding in them.

At a meeting of the HSAHS Board of Trustees on Monday, April 13, 1920, the trustees elected J. J. Dawsey at a salary of $3,000 to succeed Claude Bennett as superintendent of the Harrison-Stone Agricultural High School for the 1920-1921 session. Dawsey had recently resigned as superintendent of Gulfport public schools. Bennett had recently accepted an offer to become superintendent of the Biloxi public schools.

William and Etta Frantzen, Mississippi Gulf Coast Community College's Greatest Benefactors of the 20th Century.

William Albert "Ship Island" Frantzen was born Wilhelm Albert Chnur in Frederickstad, Norway, on February 2, 1904. After the death of his father, his mother, Anna, married Oscar Frantzen, a Norwegian-born naturalized American citizen who worked as a ship's pilot at the United States Public Health Quarantine Station at Ship Island. In 1916 young William, his sister, and mother sailed from Norway with Oscar Frantzen bound for Ship Island. In the crossing the ship sailed into a North Atlantic gale which ripped the lifeboats from their davits. After the harrowing voyage, the ship docked in Newport News, Virginia, and the family traveled by train to Biloxi. Twelve-year-old William could speak no English, so the Frantzens, though they lived on Ship Island, maintained a second seasonal residence in Biloxi so that he could attend school and receive special tutoring from the local Lutheran minister. When William reached high school age, his parents sent him to the HSAHS at Perkinston because it was the nearest place he could board so economically. On his arrival at Perkinston, he was dubbed "Ship Island" or "Ship."

In Frantzen's words, "I reached Perkinston, Mississippi, in September 1919, as the first foreign student there. I started adding to my vocabulary and learning American customs. The instructors were my friends and things were wonderful. I played center on the football team, taught Sunday School, was involved in church activities, worked on the school farm, swept floors, milked cows, worked in the power plant, became acquainted with people throughout the county, and in general stayed busy."

He graduated from the HSAHS on May 24, 1924, and worked at a number of jobs before returning to Perkinston in 1927 to enter the junior college, which had been founded the year after his graduation from high school. One of his freshman junior college classmates was Etta V. Clayton.

Frantzen had first met Clayton at a field day in 1923, when he was a senior in high school, and she was a junior high student whose family had recently moved to Perkinston from Lufkin, Texas. He had never forgotten her, and when she invited him to her home for Christmas dinner in 1927, he accepted.

Frantzen left Harrison-Stone-Jackson Junior College to begin a 47-year career as a quarantine inspector for the United States Health Service. Clayton stayed on at Perk, graduating as valedictorian of her class on May 31, 1929. She then earned a chemistry and teaching degree from the University of Mississippi and began a lifetime career as a high school chemistry teacher.

Ship and Etta married in 1932. Etta taught at Biloxi High School while Ship served in the Coast Guard during World War II. Following the war the couple moved to Mobile. The Frantzens never had children, and after Etta's death on June 29, 1995, Ship re-established his connection with the place that had given him his start and where they had met--Perkinston. Ship established the Etta V. Clayton Scholarship Fund and the Etta V. and William A. Frantzen Fund. The endowment for the two funds totaled $1,050,000--by far the largest gift to the institution in the 20th century.

In a letter sent to Perkinston, Frantzen closed with these words, "Thank you Perkinston, for giving me a good start, and thank you America, for letting me become part of you." Frantzen, as the adopted son of a naturalized American citizen, was not required to go through the naturalization process himself. But he did it anyway. After receiving his naturalization papers he considered himself more American than those who were native born because as he put it, "I earned the title."

In addition to the monetary gift to the school, Frantzen also made a substantial contribution to the history of the institution. His memories, quoted at length in this work, were vital in reconstructing the way of life at Perk in a time when very little in the way of documentation survived.

Ship Island Frantzen died on September 11, 1998. He was buried beside Etta in Southern Memorial Park near the beach in Biloxi.

THE DAWSEY - COOK INTERREGNUM SEPT. 1920 - MAY 1922

On August 18, 1920, the 19th Amendment to the United States Constitution passed, giving women the right to vote. On September 8, 1920, Crab Breland visited the AHS on opening day to see a lot of old male politicians from Harrison and Stone Counties and "the young women destined to replace them." Crab said, "Prof. Claude Bennett, the old superintendent whom everybody loves was there and Prof. Dawsey, the new superintendent and his faculty were there." After a big dinner Crab predicted a successful session and departed.

J. J. Dawsey made a number of changes in Bennett's regime. School ran all day from 8 a.m. to 3:30 p.m., and the "rising bell" rang at 6 a.m. at which time all students would sweep their rooms out and make their beds. From 6:25 to 6:55 all students were to take "setting up exercises" in response to the Physical Education Law passed at the previous session of the state legislature. Breakfast followed at 7 a.m. to 7:45. After classes the students could choose athletics or work from 3:30 to 5:30. Supper was served 6:00 to 6:45. Study hours were set at 7 p.m. to 9 p.m. "Lights out" at 9:30 meant exactly that because that was when Lyman Bradford pulled the plug. On the subject of lights, Dawsey decreed, "Special attention is called to the fact that students are expected to furnish light bulbs. . . . These can be bought jointly by roommates and expense will be very light."

Interestingly, the "lights out" days were revisited in the late 1960s and early 1970s when "latter day Lyman Bradfords" plagued Perkinston. The power company replaced a light pole undercut and washed away by Red Creek with a new pole on which, some observant students noticed, was a brand new switch box. For years after, particularly during exams, the campus as well as the town would suddenly be thrown into the dark. The switch box was locked, but bolt cutters defeated the locks. That "lights out era" ended only after the switch box was removed.

Dawsey made some other changes in 1920, too. He wrote, "We have no preparatory department. Only students who completed the eighth grade in our public schools will be admitted. Any student failing to make as much as 75 percent in three subjects . . . will be required to take up work at a lower grade. Under the law we have no right to refuse admittance to any worthy students, but, we are frank to say, we are not running a reform school, and students who can not attend school at home because of their conduct are classed

John Jefferson Dawsey, a son of Thomas and Mary Dawsey, was born in Dothan, Alabama in 1870. Dawsey's penchant for agricultural high schools started early. He graduated from South East Alabama Agricultural High School. After that he attended Howard College, where he earned his bachelor of arts degree, and he engaged in further study at Peabody College in Nashville, Tennessee. He married the former Virginia Armstrong and began teaching in Brandon about 1895. Removing to the Coast, Dawsey taught at McHenry before serving eight years as Harrison County superintendent of education (1907-1915).

During his years as superintendent, Dawsey inaugurated a series of athletic and literary competitions among Harrison County schools known as Field Day. Simultaneously, he became a champion of the consolidation of rural schools and helped establish Woolmarket as the first consolidated school in Mississippi in 1910. In light of this present study, he played a vital role in the establishment of the Harrison County Agricultural High School at Perkinston. From 1915 to 1918 Dawsey served as principal of the Lamar County Agricultural High School at Purvis.

Resigning from that post to make an unsuccessful bid for a U. S. Congressional seat, Dawsey returned to the Coast. He served one year as principal of the Orange Grove Consolidated School before becoming superintendent of Gulfport schools. In session 1920-1921 Dawsey became superintendent of the Harrison-Stone Agricultural High School. From Perkinston he removed to Wayne County where he continued his career in education by serving as superintendent of the Wayne County AHS and as principal and teacher at various consolidated schools. He died at his farm near Waynesboro on November 15, 1946, and was interred at Smyrna Cemetery in Dothan, Alabama. He was survived by his wife and their three children, Wilfred L. Dawsey of Philadelphia, Pennsylvania, Dr. Lynn H. Dawsey of Buffalo, New York, and Virginia (Dawsey) Renfroe of Frankfurt, Germany. Lucille Bailey of Waynesboro, remembering J. J. Dawsey 54 years after his death, termed him "one of the finest Christian men" she had ever known and noted that the addition to the Waynesboro First Baptist Church had been named "Dawsey Hall" in his honor. Photo courtesy of Leonard Slade.

everywhere as undesirables. Firearms must be turned over to the principal for safekeeping. Each student shall sign the following pledge: 'I pledge my word of honor to obey the rules and regulations of the Harrison-Stone Agricultural High School so long as I may be a student of same.'"

Boys were to wear Federal Working Reserve uniforms purchased at the school. The girls were to wear caps and gowns, purchased at the school, for all public occasions. White shirtwaists and blue serge dresses or skirts were to be worn with the caps and gowns. A simple muslin dress was to be worn to school entertainments, and middy blouses and skirts and gingham dresses were worn to class.

Dawsey informed the poorest students that they could work their way through school, and he stated flatly, "In this way the dignity of labor is taught. . . . Thus poverty is often a blessing." The school was then paying 15 cents an hour for work. On the other hand, board was up to $14 a month.

Dawsey continually exhorted the students with "The Country Boy's Creed." In part this creed read, "I believe that the Country, which God made, is more beautiful than the city which man made . . . and . . . that success depends . . . not upon luck, but upon pluck."

The faculty for the 1920-1921 session consisted of R. M. Coman (agriculturist), J. T. Brent (assistant agriculturist), R. J. Koonce (math and science), Miss Beulah Delano (home science) and Miss Ethel Ziert (music and expression). Mrs. E. M. Fahnestock served as matron. Her first name was Jane, but she became known as "Ma Fanny" to the students.

The Christmas holidays in the Dawsey session ran from December 23-29, 1920. "Mid-term" examinations were to follow on January 10-15, 1921. The school year was divided into six "terms." The third term ended in January; hence "midterm," or what really ought to have been termed "mid-session" exams occurred then.

In mid-March 1921 the "student body of the Harrison-Stone AHS" published Volume One, Number One of the *Perkinston Aggie*. This is the first known campus newspaper published for distribution by the students. The *HSAHS News* of the World War I era may never have existed in any other form than publication inside the *Daily Herald* and the *Stone County Enterprise*. The *Perkinston Aggie* bore no date, but by internal evidence it appeared between March 11 and April 1, 1921. The paper is composed of four numbered pages consisting of a single sheet 8 1/2 x 11 folded. No later issues had surfaced by 2000.

The most interesting piece of information contained in the *Perkinston Aggie* in light of the future follows,

"The Harrison-Stone A.H.S. has been making progress all along the line for the ten years it has been running. Besides the many material improvements the Southern Association of Colleges has placed us on the Accredited List of High Schools this year. This is the most distinctive honor ever bestowed on the school. Our graduates now can enter any standard college in the South without an examination. If we had space to print all the rules required by the colleges before this school could get on this list the reader would appreciate what honor this standing of the school carries with it. A great many of the High Schools cannot get on the Affiliated List in Mississippi, much less the Accredited List of the South."

In the realm of improvements, according to the *Perkinston Aggie*, 24 pear trees had been planted, and many pecan trees had been added to the eight acres already bearing. A small equipment room had been added to the kitchen behind Stone Hall, and also a laundry room had been attached to that dorm for the convenience of the girls.

The students listed many reasons why prospective students obtaining a copy of this paper should come and join them. "Our boys and girls are the happiest and healthiest in the state," proclaimed the *Perkinston Aggie*, and this was due to hard work, hard play, plain food, and eight hours sleep every night. But then came the admonition:

"Frankly, if you have played out in your home school, or if your parents are sending you to us to get rid of you, we prefer that you go elsewhere. If you are not willing to work--do all kinds of work, this is not the place for you.

"The Senior class this year is composed of ten boys and nine girls, who have come from two states and assembled here to put the last touch to their High School course. There are very few in the class that started here as freshmen.

"The Senior class has braved the storm of Agriculture and Home Science. They have been bathed in an atmosphere of History and Literature. They have been tried as if by fire in Geometry and deluged in a flood of Chemistry, and have come out scarred and battle-torn in some cases, but with a smile on their face. They are struggling now with the fond hope of getting the last quarter behind them and then enter that peaceful land where schoolteachers cease to bother and the flower of life is in perpetual bloom."

On July 20, 1921, the following items appeared in the *Daily Herald* under the heading "Stone County News:"

"Mrs. J. J. Dawsey of Perkinston has her sister, Mrs. C. C. Chastain of New Orleans with her for a visit.

"Mrs. Pearl Vick and daughter Miss Phyllis Muriel of Hattiesburg are visiting Mrs. Thomas I. Cook at Perkinston.

"Prof. Thomas I. Cook and family of Hattiesburg are now occupying the dormitory at the Agricultural High School. Prof. Cook is the new Superintendent of the school."

Dawsey left Perkinston to take over as superintendent of the Wayne County Agricultural High School in Clara. He spent the rest of his life as a school administrator and teacher in Wayne County.

The *Daily Herald* noted the opening of every school in Harrison and Stone County in the fall of 1921 except the HSAHS. The only thing noted for months was the numerous speeches made by Cook at schools throughout Stone and Harrison Counties. His topic was always "better schools." This lends credence to Ship Frantzen's memory of the man, "Thomas Ira Cook--He was a tall, skinny man and every time I saw him he had a briefcase. He was always either going somewhere or just coming back." Ruby Lee Johnson provided one other glimpse of him, "Mr. Cook was the principal in my senior year and he loved to walk and loved for us [students] to sing while we walked. One [song] he liked was 'My Little Margie.'"

On January 31, the *Daily Herald* told of the building of a blacksmith's shop at the HSAHS. Agriculture instructor R. M. Coman was directing his students in building the shop that was to be fully outfitted with a forge, anvil, and smithing tools.

On February 11,1922, the *Daily Herald* carried another bit of news about the AHS:

"Prof. T. I. Cook, Supt. Of the Agricultural College, stated Saturday that it was quite lonely about the campus of the college, as almost the entire student body were spending the weekend at their homes. The students are allowed to leave the [school] only once every six weeks without special permit, according to the rules."

The HSAHS Board of Trustees met at Perkinston on Wednesday, May 3, 1922. The most interesting statement about the meeting in the *Daily Herald* was this: "The election of a principal was deferred until the next regular meeting in June."

The *Stone County Enterprise* of May 16, 1922, quoted Cook in regard to the upcoming commencement exercises for the HSAHS. He said he was going to give the diplomas. He did sign them. Well, he signed Ruby Lee Johnson's, but on graduation night, Monday, May 22, President of the Board of Trustees W. F. Gorenflo gave out the diplomas. Cook was not mentioned as being present.

The coverage of events at the HSAHS by the *Daily Herald* during the successive year-long tenures of J. J. Dawsey and T. I. Cook was slight when compared to the coverage accorded the school both before and after their tenures. The lack of news coverage coupled with the disappearance of Perkinston Minute Book 1 rendered impossible anything approaching a comprehensive reconstruction of events at the HSAHS during the Dawsey-Cook era. However, the remarks of the new superintendent, who took the helm of the HSAHS in summer 1922, offered a backward glance at the school's situation before he arrived.

Thomas Ira Cook was born December 5, 1889, in Scanlon, Newton County, the second of seven children born to James Henry Cook and the former Alice Amanda Gardner. He was a graduate of Mississippi Agricultural and Mechanical College in Starkville. By January 7, 1920, Cook was a farm demonstration agent living in Prentiss, Jefferson Davis County, with his 23 year-old wife, Eva Elma Hathorn, a native of that place. The couple had a six-month-old daughter, Mary Ruth, at that time. In 1921, the year the Cooks moved to Perkinston, a son, Charles, was born to them. After departing Perkinston the Cooks had a third and final child, Lillian Alice. Following his year-long stint as superintendent of the Harrison-Stone AHS, Cook followed a career with the General Land Bank as a field representative and with the Mississippi State Highway Department. He died March 17, 1937, near Stratton, Newton County, and was buried at New Hope Cemetery. Photo courtesy of Frank Cook, nephew of T.I. Cook.

The 1922 Harrison-Stone AHS senior class boys are posed at A. N. Johnson's Grand View Satsuma Farm two miles southeast of Wiggins. The 900-tree orchard flourished for a time, but the freeze of 1924 ended dreams of Stone County becoming a rival to Florida. Casa Winfield Hatten is standing fifth from the left on the back row. The military-type uniform he is wearing is that of the Federal Working Reserve, which, according to the Harrison-Stone AHS Catalog of Session 1920-21, was required attire for all male students at the school. All boys were required to take four years of agriculture, and the occasion is almost certainly a field trip in connection with an agriculture class. Photo courtesy of Clyde Hatten, son of Casa Hatten.

FORBIS TAKES COMMAND JUNE 1922 - JUNE 1924

J. H. Forbis held positions in Georgia and Tennessee before coming to Perkinston. In two years as superintendent, he put the school back on the beam and then departed. Photo from Announcements for Session Beginning September 11, 1922, p. 2.

Apparently the Harrison-Stone AHS Board of Trustees conducted a regional search for a replacement for Superintendent T. I. Cook for several weeks. At the June 1922 Board meeting at Perkinston, Cook's successor J. H. Forbis was introduced. The *Daily Herald* reporter covering the meeting stated,

"The new principal is a middle-aged man and has had long experience in school work, having taught in a number of schools in Tennessee and Georgia. His last school was at Grand Junction, Tenn., from which point he will come to Perkinston. He finished at Davidson College, N.C., and did special work at the University of Georgia. He has also been a regular attendant at summer schools to further perfect himself in his profession.

"Mrs. Forbis was made matron of the school, Mrs. E. M. Fahnestock, who has held the position for the past two years, informing the board that she no longer wished to fill the position.

"The new principal was requested to prepare a list with at least three teachers for each position in the school from which to choose a new faculty, as it [is] the purpose of the trustees to provide as good a faculty as can be secured for the session of 1922-23."

The Trustees wanted a new beginning, and they got it. Along with the new superintendent came a new faculty. At least one of them, like Forbis, was a Georgian. Miss Louise Webb of Americus, Georgia, signed on to teach English and education. Ernest Bert Colmer, lately the agriculturist of the Forrest County AHS at Brooklyn, took over the agriculturist's position at Perkinston. His greatest recommendation was the fact that he had put the Forrest County school on a "paying basis." W. R. Cain of Little Springs, Franklin County, became his assistant. Miss Kathryn Swetman took charge of the home science offerings. Mercer G. Evans of Gulfport took over the classes in math and science and also served as athletic coach. The positions for history and music had not been filled when the *1922-23 Catalogue* went to press in early August.

In this *1922-23 Catalogue*, Forbis in writing of his new faculty said,

"We have worked energetically to select a corps of real teachers and we are proud to say that our faculty is composed of college graduates everyone. . . . We are glad to . . . say further that this is a body of high-toned Christian men and women, who are anxious to make this the very best year in the history of this school. . . . Each teacher [will] devote full time to schoolwork."

In a letter to the *Daily Herald* published on August 7, Forbis told the people of Harrison and Stone counties,

"I am aware that large sums of money have been spent by the tax-payers on this school and . . . some of it has been wasted. But . . . we should profit by the mistakes of the past . . . as the present administration had nothing to do with . . . the sorry work of the past."

In the *1922-23 Catalogue*, Forbis expounded upon the subject of education and students:

"Educating as we understand it, is a drawing-out process and not a cramming-in process . . . but . . . you can not draw water from a dry well.

Ernest Bert Colmer, a World War I veteran with a bachelor's degree from Mississippi Agricultural and Mechanical College in Starkville, joined the faculty of the HSAHS on July 1, 1922. While at Perkinston, he attended Colorado Agricultural College for several summers earning his master's degree in 1928. He remained at Perkinston until September 20, 1935, when he accepted a position as instructor of agriculture at Mississippi State College. Colmer was the first teacher to "put down roots" at Perkinston. His tenure spanned 13 years of service under three successive superintendents.

Miss Zola Emerson, a colleague of Colmer's at Perkinston for seven years, described him in 1973 as the faculty's "most outstanding" member and a "fine man in all respects." Emerson said he made the school farm pay through his "hired hands" who were students. According to Emerson, "He was an example of high manhood to his boys. They admired, loved, and respected him, and marveled that he could cuss for 30 minutes without repeating himself. I was fortunate to be associated with him and his beautiful and charming wife, Bess, during my years at Perk."

On April 20, 1960, three months before he retired as dean of the school of agriculture at Mississippi State, the Trustees of Perkinston Junior college named the institution's first vocational-technical building (completed in 1951) in Colmer's honor. Dean Colmer died at his home in Starkville on July 9, 1972, and was buried in Hattiesburg. Photo from Announcements for Session Beginning September 11, 1922, p. 6. Photographs at right from Announcements Brochure, 1924-25 and from the HSAHS & JC Catalogue, 1924-25 between pages 36 and 37.

(Above) Colmer, standing at far left, lectures to his agriculture class in the HSAHS corn field c. 1924.

(Left) Colmer, standing at far left, shows off his mule and tractor power c. 1924. The rear of Bennett Hall and the north end of Stone Hall are visible in the background.

(Above) Colmer, at center, and his "hired hands" show off part of the HSAHS dairy herd which became one of the finest herds in Mississippi.

"It is the prevailing idea that the purpose of an Agricultural High School is to take up the low-down cut-throats and gamblers whose forefathers as far back as they can be traced were of the same type, and make of them (in one year) a highly educated, cultured gentleman. We can't! Someone has said: It takes a hundred years to make a man. We believe in blood; if we didn't we should not be so careful in breeding better cattle, hogs, horses, chickens, etc.

"We are not running a reformatory primarily for incorrigibles. . . . We have no place for the idle, rough and rowdy type, the profane, the gambler or the cigarette smoker. The strongest measures of punishment will be meted out upon first offense to any student caught gambling in any form, drinking or having strong drinks in his possession in the dormitories or at any time or place while under the discipline of this school. . . . Students caught stealing . . . in any degree, shape or form, shall be dealt with in the most severe terms. If you think you are too big to live under the regulations of our school, we think you are 'too little' to be an inmate of our school. . . . Students expelled from other schools are not solicited.

"Discipline will be kind yet firm, strict and impartial. . . . No student who persists in disobedience or who is exercising a bad influence will be permitted to stay here.

"We have Sunday school and church services every Sunday and the students are expected to take advantage of these. . . . Boys and girls, bring your Bibles."

No student would be allowed to leave the campus without a permit at any time other than the weekends following the close of each six-week term. At any other time a "Home Permit" would be granted upon receipt of a written request from a parent or guardian. Such requests were not to be "too general" and had to be mailed directly to the principal. "Local permits," for example, to go to a store in town, could be signed by any faculty member, but no student could leave the campus without such a written document.

Board was back down to $12.50 per month, but wages were back down to 10 cents an hour. Poor boys and girls of good character were welcomed, and Forbis promised he would help those who helped themselves.

All boys would be given "the benefit of all the work on the farm, plowing, hoeing, driving teams, care of livestock, clearing land, and cutting wood."

The 36-week academic year was divided into six terms of six weeks each. Recitation periods, or class periods, were normally 45 minutes in length except for 90-minute periods in agriculture, home science, and all laboratory courses. Each student was required to take 20 hours of work per week and by special permission could take 25 hours. The regular high school course ran 9th through 12th grade.

Five "housekeeping girls" stand beside Bennett Hall in 1923 with the home economics teacher. According to Marguerite (Callahan) Boswell, a student of the time, "Every six weeks five girls stayed in the Home Ec. Department and kept house. The Home Ec. Teacher had charge of them. They were graded on this." Photo courtesy of John Russell O'Neal.

Proof of completion of the 8th grade was demanded for admission. Those without the necessary proof had to take entrance examinations. But the school did offer a remedial "sub-Freshman Year (eighth grade)."

In regard to the three-year successive offerings of ancient, modern, and American history, Forbis avowed that this course would be so taught that it would, "do away with the idea that history is a dull, dry combination of names and dates, and make it a real live, living subject." Miss Mary Hinton of Mize was hired to teach history as the session began.

Under the terms of the Smith-Hughes Law, all boys had to complete a "home project" and keep accurate records on the same. An additional half credit was awarded upon satisfactory completion. An example of such a project was Douglas L. Ott's inspirational 75 by 125-foot cabbage patch of 1919, but the project could also involve livestock or any other agriculture related subject.

Forbis required every student to be a member of "one of the literary societies" and help in the making and rendering of programs every week. He waxed lyrical about this in a really superb piece of double-

Circa fall 1922 members of "the Barrister's Club Harrison-Stone AHS" stand at the door of Huff Hall. From left the fledgling lawyers are Pierre Bond, Noland Terry of Long Beach, Louis M. Hudson of Gulfport, Jessie Cook of Wiggins, and Leo Scanlon of Gulfport.

This photograph of the Perkinston Consolidated School appeared in the Stone County Enterprise of September 7, 1922. The accompanying article stated that the school was recently completed at a cost of $4,500 and would open Monday, September 11. Randle Dedeaux of Perkinston, who attended the school, stated in an interview conducted on June 11, 1998, that the front door opened into a large auditorium running the length of the building to the point where the hipped roof is visible at the rear of the photo. The stage was located under that section of the roof. Two classrooms flanked the auditorium on the left side and on the right side. The 7th and 8th grade met in the first room to the right. The 1st and 2nd grade met in the next room to the right. 5th and 6th grades met in the first room to the left of the door, and the 3rd and 4th grades met in the next room to the left. Dedeaux recalled that large wood heaters stood in the common corner of each two-room set next to the auditorium. One of the chimneys serving these heaters is visible in the photo. The building was constructed of heart pine. This school had a symbiotic relationship with the Perkinston Campus, adding grades as the AHS dropped them off. Most of the students at this school, including Dedeaux, went from it directly to the AHS and on through junior college. The building was razed after 1941, when a new "Little Perk" was built a block east of Jackson Hall facing 2nd Street. The Perkinston Elementary School of 2000 occupied the site of the circa 1941 structure.

think, "There is power in expression, there is power unseen in oratory. There is a beauty indescribable in silent oratory if we know how and when to see it."

School opened on Monday, September 11, 1922. Forbis laid down the law to the students assembled in the auditorium, one of whom was his daughter, Mary. Crab Breland and a number of parents were there and liked what they heard. Crab said, "His words had the true ring, and sounded the most refreshing to us in any speech we have heard lately."

All through September and into October both the pages of the *Daily Herald* and the *Stone County Enterprise* touted the coming of a new invention destined to have a revolutionary impact on the lives of all Americans. At last on the night of October 24 a crowd gathered on the steps of the Stone County Courthouse in Wiggins and watched as "Mr. Bartlett of the Western Electric Company" turned on the contraption giving Stone County its first radio concert. Among the musical numbers heard by the crowd was a violin solo, "Hot Lips" out of Fort Worth, and "When you and I were young, Maggie" from Atlanta.

The same week as the radio concert, news from the HSAHS told of the enrollment of four new students. This was six weeks after school started. Two weeks after that the *Daily Herald* of November 7 reported: "New students are coming in each week; the enrollment is growing steadily." Apparently this was "open-entry, open-exit" 1922-style.

The November 7 *Daily Herald* also reported on one of Forbis's "Literary Society" doings:

"In the way of declamations . . . the principal event of the evening was the debate on the subject, 'Resolved that if a Ship Sinks in Mid-Ocean it Will Not go to the Bottom.' The principal speaker for the affirmative was Nolan Brewer and William Frantzen for the negative. After a good argument and the bringing out of fine points on each side the negative side was declared the winner."

The same paper carried an account of a Halloween celebration at the HSAHS. On October 31, the dining hall had been decorated for the occasion, and entertainment consisted of games of "Spookdom and the Witch World." The article continued, "On the following morning all gates on the campus were intact owing to Prof. Forbis having the forethought to lock them."

On Friday, November 23, 1922, the *Stone County Enterprise* carried an account of a combined Wiggins-Inda-HSAHS glee club production in the auditorium. This is an early mention of an organized glee club being a part of the school life. Following the performance the performers and friends were treated to a three-course banquet in the dining room. The tables were adorned with flowers in cut glass vases and "electrically lighted Kewpie-dolls, which cast soft shadows on the snow-white linen and the sparkling silver."

On April 20, 1923, in the *Daily Herald,* Crab Breland reported in his "Crabology" column that the HSAHS Board of Trustees in its session that month had retained Forbis for another year "at quite an advance of salary." On May 24, Crab published the agenda for commencement weeks at the AHS and stated frankly,

"We feel that the present session of this school has functioned as never before. . . . We know that in past years the school has not given as much satisfaction or as much good results . . . and . . . has been kicked around by its patrons. . . . So we cheerfully join others in expressing our confidence, and exclaiming 'All praise to Forbis and his splendid force of co-workers.' And . . . we compliment Professor Forbis for his firm and unbending position in the matter of discipline. Orders are orders at the Agricultural School this year, and the boy or girl either, who thinks they can 'run the blockade' while Forbis is at the fleet have another guess coming. . . . We feel safe in saying [the AHS] will become one of the most highly prized treasures of the two counties."

On September 1, 1923, the *Daily Herald* carried a statement by Forbis ten days before the opening of the 1923-1924 session of the AHS. Forbis announced to the people of the two counties that after all debts had been paid from the last session the school still had $6,000 on hand. Then he continued,

"During the last term we placed the farm on a self-supporting basis and repaired the dormitories and administration building. . . . We also installed a new light plant and motor to run the pump, built a new tool shed, remodeled the work shop, screened the boy's dormitory . . . and placed in our library and laboratory books and equipment to more than $1,000.00. . . .

"We have just finished a new cement walk from the fountain to the front gate of the campus, and are now finishing repainting our water tank. . . . We are also installing a new motion picture and stereopticon machine and expect as soon as school opens to organize a Brass Band."

Forbis then announced the faculty for the year. A number of teachers from the year before were retained. The new ones were G. P. Poulk (English and science), Miss Lois Caraway (home science and biology), Mrs. John C. Prince (music and expression), Miss Myrtle Smith (commercial, Latin, and girl's athletic coach), Bennie P. Webb (math and boys' athletic coach).

The *Daily Herald* covered the opening of the HSAHS on Tuesday, September 11. One hundred and forty students enrolled. This figure was one third more than the previous year and the largest in the history of the school. Among the speakers at the event was Harrison County Superintendent of Education-elect Cooper J. Darby. He assured his co-operation with the welfare of the school. Darby would later shepherd the school through the twelve years of the Great Depression.

The *Daily Herald* reporter covering the opening ceremonies closed with these words,

"The Harrison-Stone Agricultural High School has not been just what it should have been in the past few years. It is said that the truth is honorable, and it is true that this institution has been almost a total failure, for the purpose of its origin. In fact, it came very near dying complete. Its fruits were unsatisfactory upon the market of public opinion, and many of those interested gradually lost faith in this institution. . . . But the school is now in a healthy and thriving condition. Last year, under the management of Prof. J. H. Forbis, its course was turned from the channels of debt . . . and is now out of debt and running on a paying basis. This school has a future before it, and with a continuance of the present management, will, in a few years be . . . the school of the South."

Chester H. Rose of the *Daily Herald* went to the HSAHS during the last week of October 1923, and reported on what he found:

"The first place looked into was the workshop. The building is a large, roomy structure with glass windows which afford plenty of light for the young workmen. The building was erected by students of the school and is a very creditable work in carpentry. It is equipped with tools, work benches, and everything needed in a class for manual training.

"The power plant was given the 'once over' then. This plant is a modern one and not only furnishes sufficient electricity for the needs of the school at nominal cost, but the principal part of the homes and business places of the town are lighted by it.

"A commercial course class with a membership of forty-five is now a regular class in training. Seven new typewriters have been installed for the school, besides several students who have bought machines for their own and individual use. This class is steadily growing, with some coming in from the outside."

Crab Breland in his "Crabology" of November 9, expanded on the commuter phenomenon remarked on by Rose. He said students from both Bond and Wiggins were driving cars on the newly graveled Dixie Highway to and from the HSAHS at Perkinston on a daily basis. He reminded his readers that he had predicted the schools of the county would someday be "run on wheels."

On November 16, 1923, the HSAHS staged a cake sale to raise money for the athletic fund. The cake for the most beautiful girl was won by Miss Ruby Mae Terry. Someone, obviously a great admirer of the young lady, paid the astonishing sum of $56.00 for the cake. Sylvester Dedeaux won the most popular boy cake. Tom Dantzler won the cake of soap for laziest boy, and Forbis took the cake of soap for the ugliest. The total raised was $70.75.

By February 1924, the literary societies at the HSAHS had names. One bore the name, Utopian Society, and the other was called the Wilsonian Society in honor of former President Woodrow Wilson. Each society challenged the other to debates concerning topics of national interest.

As spring came around with its rustling shade and apple blossoms filled the air, the HSAHS literary clubs debated the Bonus Bill, and the baseball team lost nearly every game. Crab Breland decried bobbed-haired flappers in men's attire, and an aerial photographer flew near the campus twice. The senior class put on the "Merchant of Venice" and the campus hosted Stone County Field Day, taking many prizes. On Friday, May 23, 1924, Prof. J. H. Forbis handed diplomas to the 26 members of the largest graduating class in HSAHS history.

On Monday, May 26, the HSAHS Board of Trustees appointed Professor Jefferson Lee Denson of George County to succeed Forbis as superintendent of the HSAHS for the coming year. So why after all the praises and raises did this happen?

In further coverage of the Board meeting, the *Daily Herald* reported, "The board discussed the question of inducing some of the neighboring counties to join with Harrison and Stone Counties in the maintenance of the agricultural school. . . . It is hoped to obtain the co-operation of George along with Jackson County, and if this is done, it is said that the Perkinston school will be made the best of its kind in the state." The meeting ended with the Board once again praising Forbis for a "successful year" that ended with a surplus of funds.

The changing of the guard, so to speak, did not seem to faze Forbis. He remained at Perkinston that summer, and Denson spent several days at Perkinston while he was there.

On June 20, the *Daily Herald* commented further on the proposed expansion of the AHS service area including Hancock, along with Jackson and George, as possible supporting counties. The article also tried to correct a slip made earlier, "The report sent out recently that the plan is to make the school a junior. . . college was an error. The school will be maintained as an agricultural school, at least for the present."

It would be maintained as an AHS for precisely one year until the machinery could be put in place to make it a junior college. Simultaneously the plan to bring in more counties for its support would also go forward.

On June 27, 1924, the last item in the *Daily Herald* mentioning Forbis appeared, " Prof. and Mrs. J. H. Forbis, Mary Forbis, C. C. Swetman, and Prof. J. L. Denson were visitors to Gulfport Saturday." After that J. H. Forbis vanished from the annals of this institution. But he made a vital contribution. He came in like an educational six-gun-for-hire, put the place back on the straight and narrow and then rode off into the sunset. In his wake he left his successor, J. L. Denson, to fulfill the school's destiny in becoming a junior college.

The gate to the HSAHS campus circa 1923. The Bennett Building is in the background. Photo courtesy of John Russell O'Neal.

Panorama of the Class of 1924. *Stone Hall is at the left, Bennett Hall is in the middle, and Huff Hall is at the right. The girls' basketball court is visible between Stone and Bennett. An automobile, (see detail below) certainly one of the few on campus, is visible near the base of the western goal. One goal of the boy's basketball court is visible between Bennett and Huff. The other goal is near the water tank, the view of which is blocked by Huff. The first barn,(see* detail below) *destroyed by lightning on June 14, 1925, is visible between Bennett and Huff. The exact date of the picture is unknown, but it was taken after September 1, 1923, because on that date the Daily Herald quoted HSAHS Superintendent J. H. Forbis as saying, "We have just finished a new cement walk from the fountain to the front gate of the campus." Forbis (see detail below) is seated on the left side of the "fountain" facing the camera. The next two men to his left have their feet in the "fountain." No student of the past remembers this cylindrical structure ever having served as a fountain. It never had water or fish in it, but it was called "The Fountain." It finally wound up full of dirt with a flag pole stuck in its middle. Judging from the foliage on the deciduous tree to the left in front of Bennett, the panorama was made before the leaves fell in 1923 or in the green-up of spring in 1924. Mrs. Oren H. Longcoy of Biloxi gave this panorama to the MGCCC Archives in memory of her husband and in memory of her son, James H. Longcoy, both of whom were Perkinston graduates.*

__1925 Panorama.__ This picture was most likely made in early spring 1925. The foliage of the deciduous tree blocking the left side of Bennett's façade indicates that. According to Margurite (Callahan) Boswell of Louisville, Winston County, who is one of the students in this picture, the little girl in the car and the little boy on the tricycle by the fountain in front of Bennett Hall are the children of Superintendent and Mrs. J. L. Denson. The bulldog beside the toy car is "Old Bob," (see detail below) the AHS's first known mascot. The power plant to the right of Bennett Hall was built late in session 1924-1925. When Hersel McDaniel arrived at Perkinston in September 1924, the power plant was a "Fordson tractor" which remained stationary "just north of the boy's dormitory [Huff Hall] and was run by a boy who was working to pay part of his room and board. This tractor was run from dark until about 10 p.m. when 'lights out was the order of the day.'" He also remembered that the belt would fly off and the lights would be off until the belt could be put back on track. McDaniel said this power plant received more "cussing" and "more praise" than any other piece of equipment on the campus. The "cussing" came when it interrupted the movies or a meal. The "praise" came when "we were dating." But, he said, social hour was terminated very quickly in such a case. Later in the session according to McDaniel, "A new boiler for hot water and heat and a small dynamo for lights was to be erected on the spot of our old basketball court just east of the administration building [Bennett Hall]. The firebox of this monster could devour more wood than anything I ever saw." The tin building with the two stacks in the photograph (see detail below) housed the new power plant. McDaniel said the students kept the plant going by innumerable trips to the Ten Mile Sawmill in the old Ford truck. Soon, though, the school switched from wood to coal. The Illinois Central Railroad would sidetrack a coal car at the bottom of the hill and the boys would truck it up to the plant. According to McDaniel, "Dirty was no name for the condition we found ourselves in . . . we got wet with sweat and the coal dust collected on us by the ton it seemed. The only thing white that was visible was our eyes, and they shone like stars. All this for the huge sum of ten cents an hour."

1926 Panorama. *Judging from the dress of the people and the absence of foliage in the deciduous trees this panorama was made in early 1926. Amazingly the small deciduous tree on the left face of Bennett has been joined by a very large tree in front of the left Corinthian column. That tree does not appear in the two previous year's panoramas, so it must have been planted full size. Four magnificent oaks are located in 2000 in front of the Dees Building in the "Garden of the Oaks," but the tree in this photograph is not one of them. The four oaks in front of Dees Hall in 2000 are much younger than formerly supposed by many people on the Perkinston Campus. The man first in line on the far left in the picture is Superintendent J. L. Denson. Fred O. Parsons is next to him. The fifteenth person from the left is Clarence O. Hinton and next to him is W. G. Gregory with one leg and a crutch. According to Jimmy Gammage, who grew up at Perk during the 1950s, Gregory scratched his leg in a boyhood accident. In that pre-penicillin age, the leg festered and had to be amputated.*

The first known appearance of the P Club athletic lettermen can be seen in a line that crosses the sidewalk. At the far right the "new boy's dormitory" (christened Jackson Hall on August 22, 1956) appears completed. The Daily Herald of February 18, 1926, announced that this dormitory which would accommodate 75 boys had been "moved into." The completion of Jackson Hall may have been the reason for the panorama having been made. The Annex behind Bennett was completed at the same time, but it, of course, is not visible. At the far right of the photo stands the AHS Yellow Jackets. Some of them are in their bloomer basketball uniforms, and all of them have on their jerseys. The emblem on the front of each jersey is composed of the stylized initials AHS with a circle around the letters. The fifth yellow jacket from the right is Irene Flurry; the eleventh is Estelle "Bill" David.

Panoramas as a photographic art form began about the turn of the 20th century, reaching their peak of popularity during World War I when practically every military unit in the Great War had one made. Panoramas enjoyed a resurgence during World War II, again for military unit keepsakes, and then became a thing of the past. The panorama photographer arranges his subjects in a semicircle and places the camera near the middle of the arc to be traveled by the lens. The camera is mounted on a tripod with the lens pointing to the cameraman's left. Everyone to be photographed is ordered to be very still because movement smears the negative. The camera is then set in motion, and it slowly turns 180 degrees on the tripod, capturing one long negative. J. L. Denson at the far left was the first person photographed. He and those near him could have crossed the Quadrangle behind the cameraman and wound up photographed again on the far right with the Yellow Jackets. That did not happen here, but it most assuredly has happened in other cases.

(Left) A Fordson tractor runs the belts in the Greene County AHS power house in 1924. The 1924 power source at Perkinston was similar if not the same. Photo from The Antenna, the yearbook of the Greene County AHS, 1924.

(Right) Students began shoveling coal for the school's power from a rail car on the siding at Perk in 1924. This crew carries on the dirty tradition 13 years later. Photo from 1938 Perkolator, p. 44.

DENSON AND THE JUNIOR COLLEGE JUNE 1924 - SEPT. 1929

Newly appointed HSAHS Superintendent Jefferson Lee Denson and his wife visited Perkinston from time to time during summer 1924. On July 24, the family occupied their quarters on the basement floor of Stone Hall, which also contained the school dining room and kitchen.

Denson announced his faculty for the coming year in mid-August. E. B. Colmer, the only holdover from the Forbis administration, remained as agriculturist. Fred O. Parsons signed on as Colmer's assistant. Clarence O. Hinton became the new science and education teacher. Prior to Colmer, Parsons, and Hinton, the roster of teachers changed almost yearly, and few in the past had crossed from one administration to another. Colmer served on into the next administration after Denson. Parsons and Hinton stayed at Perkinston for the balance of their teaching careers. They were the first of many to do so.

Other teachers who hired on that year were W. H. "Billy" Wood (history and boys' athletics), Miss Cliffie Pickering (English), Miss Mary Lillian Peters (music), Miss Julia O. Sigrest (commercial subjects and girls

Jefferson Lee Denson was born March 25, 1889, at Lake Como, Jasper County. The son of Ernest Absalom Denson and Janie (Thigpen) Denson, young "Lee," as he was called, spent most of his youth as the son of a country doctor in the small Jones County communities of Gitano and Soso. On May 30, 1912, Denson graduated from Clarke Memorial College, a Baptist junior college in Newton. Later he received his bachelor of science degree from Mississippi Normal College in Hattiesburg, and he attended the University of Colorado for graduate work.

Denson began his teaching career in the rural communities of Agricola and Rocky Springs in George County. While teaching at Agricola he met and married Mamie Ward, who would in time bear him five children--Curtis Lee, Charles, Laverne (who later took the named "Jane"), Corrine, and Rose Nell. During the school session 1915-1916, he taught and coached at Lafayette County Agricultural High School.

Returning from north Mississippi to George County in fall 1916, Denson became first a teacher and then principal at Lucedale High School from 1916 until 1922. In fall 1922 he went to southwest Mississippi to take the position of principal at Wilkerson County Agricultural High School at Woodville.

Due to his contacts in south Mississippi and his friendship with Governor Theodore G. Bilbo, Denson was chosen to head the Harrison-Stone Agricultural High School at Perkinston beginning in fall 1924. Over the next five years he guided the Perkinston institution in the establishment of its junior college department and more than tripled the number of buildings on the campus. He resigned as superintendent effective September 23, 1929, and embarked upon a new career in the life insurance business. By the time of his death, Denson had risen to the position of district manager of the National Old Line Insurance Company in Jackson. He died of a heart attack on October 29, 1953, at Cumbest Bluff on the Pascagoula River while on a fishing trip. He was buried in Bay Springs. His wife, Mamie (Ward) Denson, followed him in death on January 25, 1990.

The Denson children in front of Bennett Hall circa 1925. From left (standing) Laverne "Jane" Denson, (on tricycle) Curtis Lee Denson, (in car) Rose Nell Denson, and Corrine Denson. Photo courtesy of John Russell O'Neal.

athletics), Mrs. Julia Skinner (home science), and Mrs. E. M. Fahnestock returned as matron. Jane Fahnestock, or "Ma Fanny" as she was called, also had charge of the dining room.

The session opened on Monday, September 8, 1924. Early that morning 150 students showed up, making this enrollment the largest in the history of the school. Most of these poured into and overflowed the dormitories, staking their claims on rooms. At 10 a.m. all attended the required assembly in Bennett Auditorium. Miss Peters directed the assemblage in singing "America." Rev. R. N. Davis read from the Bible. Following the invocation, Stone County Superintendent of Education Buren Broadus and Charlie Swetman, among others, made short talks. Denson introduced the faculty. He then told the students to "be good" and there would be no trouble. He further stated that he and every teacher "would be glad to be a 'big bud' and a 'big sister' to every boy and girl." The Denson years had begun.

When Hersel McDaniel entered the HSAHS as a senior a month after school started, he joined Ferris Batson and Vernon Brown in a room in Huff Hall. As the only boys' dormitory some of the rooms had four occupants. Said McDaniel, "This was to be a new experience for me--I had never stayed away from home a night in my life, also most all the students were strangers."

Having completed twelve and one half units at Magnolia Consolidated High School at Stillmore, McDaniel needed only three and one half units to graduate from the HSAHS. He took four classes. His largest class was the English class taught by Miss Cliffie Pickering, whom he described as, "one of those 'Old Maid' teachers who gave their all through the years for the sheer joy of teaching." He took chemistry under Clarence O. Hinton, whom he described as excellent and credited with instilling in him the love of that subject. As to E. B. Colmer, McDaniel pronounced him "about the best agriculturist--in both knowledge and teaching in the state."

As to the required course in agriculture, McDaniel, being a sawmill town boy, had to learn everything literally from the ground up. What he liked best was molasses making in the sugar cane cutting season. This was a common event to the farm boys but not to McDaniel. As he remembered it:

"Boy, O boy, I can still taste that wonderful juice on those cold mornings. . . . At four in the morning with no heat and no lights, 'cept a candle or a kerosene lamp, the prospect of getting the mule to going around and around turning the mill--the big rollers that squeezed the juice out of the stalks of cane. . . . I can just see the flow of cold juice, and hear the snapping of the stalks of cane as they went through the big rollers. . . . We couldn't work on it very much at a time unless it was on Saturday--then we could be at the job all day . . . stoking the fire [underneath the] cooker . . . and skimming the juice."

Colmer, unable to get money to build a new barn, hit upon the idea of painting the leaky tin roof with thick red paint that was supposed to stop leaks. All he had to do then was to find two students crazy enough to go up on that steep, high, and slick roof for ten cents an hour to apply the paint. He cajoled Hersel McDaniel and Vernon Brown into doing it. These two roped two ladders together, and placed them astraddle the apex of the roof. McDaniel said this "Rube Goldberg" contraption worked until Brown dropped his paint brush and in the lunge for it, knocked over both cans of paint, which then covered both of them in "red paste." McDaniel said, in effect, that he and Brown became human paint rollers. Well, they got it done after a number of death defying acrobatic stunts, and it was all for naught. A few months later lightning struck the barn, burned it down, and the school had to build Colmer a new barn.

Colmer, Parsons, and Denson were in charge of corporal punishment. McDaniel remembered:

"Our 'Shellalah' was a wooden paddle about six inches wide and three feet long with holes bored in it an inch or so apart and it was used quite often that first year . . . [but] the fear of the burning sensation in the area of the seat of the pants kept quite a few of us on the straight and narrow. . . . I am not able to recall a single case of 'Juvenile Delinquent' of that era."

The girls, according to McDaniel, "never got into anything that required such a drastic correction" but the boys did. A group of boys riding in from the fields to the dorm passed a local farmer's watermelon patch, and, in McDaniel's words, "a mighty urge came over the boys--an urge that tasted just like watermelon." The farmer reported the culprits to Colmer. One of these, Henry L. Snead III by name, upon receipt of the summons to Colmer's office deduced the reason and fortified the seat of his pants with two books. In McDaniel's words:

"'Snead' [said Colmer] . . . in his dry humor and speaking through his teeth--it seemed he talked that way most of the time, 'It looks like you are rather overweight in the rear. Could it be that you have reinforced your already thick pants?' Snead . . . had to disarm himself and suffer the consequences.

The way of the transgressor is hard."

The students were under constant scrutiny. A teacher had charge of each floor in both dorms.

Robert Hersel McDaniel in May 1927, at the time he became the first (and that session's only) college graduate of the Harrison-Stone-Jackson Agricultural High School and Junior College.

McDaniel was born near Sandersville, Jones County, on August 27, 1904. When he was a youngster, his family moved to Stillmore, a mill town ten miles west of Perkinston, where his father was a log checker. McDaniel attended Magnolia Consolidated High School near Stillmore until the beginning of his senior year. In September 1924, Julia Lewis, his girlfriend, went to the Harrison-Stone County Agricultural High School at Perkinston, and he went after her. In McDaniel's words, "Julia . . . whom I later married . . . was the main attraction that brought me to Perk in the first place."

After junior college McDaniel attended Mississippi Agricultural and Mechanical College at Starkville on a loan secured for him by Superintendent Lee Denson and chemistry professor C. O. Hinton. In 1929 he married Julia and went to Chicago, where he worked 35 years for the Edison Electric Company. Following his retirement he moved back to Jones County and lived in Estabutchie until his death on November 27, 1980. He was buried beside Julia in the Davis Cemetery near Stillmore. His second wife, Sally, who had accompanied him on many of his jaunts in later years to Perkinston, died November 16, 1993, leaving her body to science. McDaniel maintained his connection with Perkinston, and he bequeathed the institution a historical treasure of real significance. From March 16, 1961, to October 4, 1962, McDaniel sent a series of 35 articles entitled, "As I Remember Perk" for publication in the Stone County Enterprise. These articles, covering the period 1924-1927, are the memoirs of a student who was present on campus in that critical era of transition when the junior college came into coexistence with the AHS. As the Perkinston institution's first junior college graduate, he was the flag bearer in a revolutionary movement, so his eyewitness account is vital. Without his words, the few documents remaining from that time would have yielded very little in the way of a narrative. Hereinafter, all information attributed to Hersel McDaniel was derived from "As I Remember Perk" unless otherwise noted. McDaniel, by the way, followed his words with deeds. Through his fund-raising efforts, the Mississippi Gulf Coast Community College Alumni Association received thousands of scholarship dollars over the years. On Homecoming Day, 1973, MGCJC honored McDaniel with the Sam Owen Distinguished Service Trophy. Photo courtesy of Hersel McDaniel.

On Homecoming Day, 1976 (right), which commemorated the 50th anniversary of the college class of 1927, McDaniel set another record. The entire class showed up for the reunion--him.

From the time McDaniel left Perkinston in May 1927, until the first time he came back in October 1961, much had changed. But enough remained to make the day a nostalgic trip. President J. J. Hayden took the afternoon off to walk the campus with him, a gesture much appreciated by McDaniel.

Bennett Hall still stood on top of the hill then, and Hayden took him to it. As they walked, McDaniel reminisced, "I recall . . . our chemistry lab room which was Prof. Hinton's pride and joy . . . the small home economics room when the girls let us sample their handiwork. As I walked through these places . . . my mind kept wandering back to bygone days. Back over the walks of yesteryear--the old fountain which was the gathering place for couples in love--has been replaced by seats in somewhat of a circle. At this spot which was the center of our campus, many romances blossomed and died--many tears shed and many hearts broken and mended. Looking back in retrospect I can see some of those couples--'Rooney and Helen,' 'Jess and Dot,' 'Hersel and Julia,' 'George and Marguerette.' I wonder how many of these couples married each other and are they still together."

As the walk continued, McDaniel, observing the co-eds of 1961, spoke to Hayden of the strict discipline under Denson. Then McDaniel commented on the modern "co-ed apparel," or rather lack of it, and asked Hayden what his code was. Hayden said he let the girls wear about what they did at home. McDaniel replied, "If anyone had appeared on the campus [in Denson's time] in a pair of shorts--boy or girl--I am sure a trip to the office would have been a must. . . . A girl . . . would have been practically ostracized--that would have been the shock of the century--even the basketball uniforms were the bloomer type. . . . Denson would turn over in his grave if he could see this. Oh, well, how times have changed--sometimes I think for the better and then 'I dunno,' the world is really spinning too fast for us."

The school session of nine months was divided into two terms further subdivided into three six-week sections. Those who made at least a grade of 90 on all three six-week tests in a particular class were exempted from the term examination in that class. This grade of 90 was not an average. The grade had to be attained each time. McDaniel and his roommate, Ferris Batson, figured it was easier to make 90 per test than to study for the term tests, so they were the only boys exempted. McDaniel said some of the other boys, "who were very much in love," asked him, "how anyone could be in love--as I was--and make 90 on any subject, much less all of them?" McDaniel said he was no smarter than they were; he just used his time more wisely.

The HSAHS class periods were 45 minutes in length. These periods were marked by the clanging of the "study bell" which was described by McDaniel as "a huge cast iron bell mounted on a platform outside the administration [Bennett] building." One of the boys had the job of ringing this bell as part payment for his room and board. The bell tolled every activity from rising in the morning to the evening social.

McDaniel's steady job in the 1924-1925 session was sweeping the auditorium in which three chapel services were held each day. The main service was at 11:30 a.m., and singing was a regular feature of this gathering. Miss Mary Lillian Peters, the music teacher, would lead the singing. McDaniel remembered:

"There are two songs that we sang at these chapel exercises that still linger in the back of my mind--one was 'The Marseilles,' the French National Anthem. . . . The First World War had not been over very long and we were still very fond of the French People and their songs--the other . . . the title escapes me unless these lines contain it--'T'was on the eve of bright December and all the world with frost was fair . . . I knelt beside the glowing embers and built castles in the air.'--fond memories of a bygone day and a long time ago."

Meal times were a highlight of the day to the ever-hungry students. Ma Fanny, whom McDaniel supposed would be called a "dietician" in a later time, "was a very noble lady." She was forever "flitting here and there, ever watchful over her charges, the girls who waited on the tables."

During meals, McDaniel remembered Denson "eyeing the ever present young lovers lest they get too close to one another." The mail was brought up from the post office in Charlie Swetman's store by campus mail carrier, Arthur Gullette, and placed on Denson's table. After meals he would make a few remarks and next call out the names of those receiving letters. He particularly delighted in these two names; "Leo Johnson J. Pat Scanlon and Henry L. Snead the Third." Then Denson would nod to Ma Fanny, who would ring a tiny bell at her table, and the students were dismissed.

An evening social of 30 to 35 minutes followed supper in which the boys and girls could mingle outside the dining room on the campus. But the social did not last so long for boys who had girlfriends who were waitresses said McDaniel. Those girls had to spend 20 to 25 minutes washing dishes and resetting the tables, and this was the only time of day that a boy and girl could talk in private. "Study bell" rang at 7 p.m. to begin the mandatory two-hour study period before bed.

Most Fridays or Saturdays a movie, to which a boy could take his girl, was shown in Bennett Auditorium. These movies were still silent, of course, but run by electricity instead of faltering student muscle power. The arms of the auditorium seats had folding desk tops, and these had to be stood up on the edge so that each boy was isolated from his girl. Teachers roamed the aisles with flashlights checking to see that, in McDaniel's words, "everybody was perfectly calm." Then on Sunday afternoon, weather permitting, the social lasted a whole hour during which the young lovers could stroll about the campus or sit on the grass under the ever-watchful eyes of Denson and the teachers. No touching of any kind was allowed. Speaking to a girl at any time other than at the evening social or Sunday social was termed "stealing social."

Across the decades, McDaniel, as did all the students of that era, remembered Bang's Store, Dees's Store, and Swetman's Store. He said that Perkinston, being such a small place, had "the oneness of a big family." He cited three men in the town for their kindness to the students. Those were C. E. Dees, Charlie Swetman, and T. P. Wyatt. He said these three often loaned money to students, and he wondered if they were ever repaid.

He particularly remembered C. E. Dees's four sons. Two of these, Houston and Eugene, were McDaniel's classmates, but he also knew John and Billy Jack.

McDaniel remembered Swetman for many reasons but, like all the other students of the time, particularly in terms of books. Swetman had the books for the county schools, and the students traded in their old books for new ones each year. In McDaniel's words, "The trade in price was always so very low that many times he would allow us much more than was called for." Gratia Leger, Charlie's grandniece and namesake of his wife, in a phone conversation on June 16, 1998, gave the outcome of this generosity, "His love for those kids caused him to die nearly penniless and my Aunt Gratia outlived him by several decades."

Thomas P. Wyatt lived next door east of the Dees Store, and the house still stood east of Taylor's Store in 2000. Wyatt was the rural mail carrier for Route A, Perkinston, and he had a lovely daughter named

Photo by Richard Kopp.

The first known photographs of the Densonian (top left) and Wilsonian Societies (bottom left) are contained on pages 22 and 50 respectively of the Harrison-Stone-Jackson AHS and JC Catalogue of 1927-1928. Both photos were probably made in late October 1927. The literary societies during the administration of Superintendent J. H. Forbis were called the Wilsonian Society, named for U. S. President Woodrow Wilson, and the Utopian Society. When J. L. Denson became superintendent, the Densonian Society, named for him, replaced the Utopian society at the beginning of the 1924-1925 year. Hersel McDaniel served as president of the Wilsonian Society in 1925, and his girlfriend, Julia Lewis, was secretary-treasurer. The Daily Herald of October 11, 1926, stated that these societies met each week to engage in debates and give public programs. The two societies also gave parties for their members on such holidays as Valentine's Day and Halloween. In early 1926 Denson announced that a silver loving cup would be presented to the society winning the school's championship debate contest. The cup was to be kept in the school and retained from year to year by the victorious society. The 16-inch tall cup remained in the collection of the MGCCC Archives in 2000. The inscription reads "Championship Debate, 1928, Densonian." Likely this is the only time the trophy was awarded, and according to McDaniel, these societies met far less than "every week." McDaniel said that country schools had literary meetings every Friday afternoon, and parents would attend these doings to watch their children perform. The societies at Perkinston were patterned on the country school societies, but the realities of campus life precluded Friday afternoon meetings due to work, athletics, and other interests. In McDaniel's words, "We tried debates, charades, imitation, farces, comedy, and all fell down for one reason or another. We did keep the program going but it was quite a struggle and not a very successful one at that."

Velma. She gave parties, which her father and mother co-hosted, for the Perkinston students. Julia Lewis, McDaniel's girl friend, was a friend of Velma's. These elements later coalesced one night into a tangled web that resulted in a meeting between McDaniel and Denson with the old "Shellalah" in the offing.

As the 1924-1925 session drew to a close, the *Daily Herald* carried a number of pronouncements by Denson on a new summer school program to be launched by the HSAHS, but not a word was printed about the coming junior college. Denson did, however, tell the students about it. McDaniel remembered: "As we finished our high school year, Mr. Denson was very much interested in a junior college. . . . Most of us promised Mr. Denson that we would be back if the college was established--most of us really had no choice, 'cause we had no money to go on to a four year school."

On Saturday, May 23, 1925, Superintendent J. L. Denson presented high school diplomas to eleven boys and thirteen girls. Nine of those 24 HSAHS graduates would become freshmen in the institution's first junior college class the next fall.

Because of the loss of *Perkinston Board Minute Book 1,* the precise date that the Board approved the addition of junior college courses may never be known. Therefore, in view of the fact that Denson told the graduates on May 23, 1925, that the junior college had been approved, the date of this graduation was considered an accurate date by the author for the institution's change of name to Harrison-Stone Agricultural High School and Junior College (HSAHS & JC).

Two days after graduation on Monday, May 25, the HSAHS launched its much advertised summer school program. For years the HSAHS had offered periodic summer institutes and hosted summer gatherings for special interest groups, but this was something new. For the first time the school launched a fully accredited summer course of study open to any eligible student desiring to secure units toward a high school diploma. Not only was this a first for the school, it was a first for the state of Mississippi. Denson had secured approval for this unique offering from the State Department of Education. That body had agreed to allow an eligible student to take two classes meeting two hours per day, six days per week for twelve weeks, thereby amassing the required number of hours for two Carnegie units. Naturally, only a few courses could be offered in such a hurry-up session. Those courses cho-

Twenty-eight members of the 1924-1925 Harrison-Stone Agricultural High School senior class pose with Superintendent Denson. This was the last class before the junior college was added and the last before Jackson County added its support to the institution. Most of the students pictured were among the 24 who graduated on May 23, 1925. Eight of those in the photo became junior college freshmen the next fall. The hometowns of those eight were added in the caption. In addition, Evelyn Howell of Perkinston, who is not in the photograph, graduated in May 1925 and became a college freshman in the fall. The students of this class who graduated on May 23, 1925, were told by Denson that the junior college department would be formed in fall 1925. Apparently they were the first members of the general public to be so informed by him.

(From left), first row: Superintendent Lee Denson, Julia Lewis of Stillmore, Estelle "Bill" David of Perkinston, Ola O'Neal, Leola O'Neal, Ina Breland, Alta Linsey. Second row: Una Bond, Irene Flurry of Perkinston, Minnie Lee O'Neal, Ione Hunter of Perkinston, Emma Clara Dean, Lula B. Carmichael. Third row: Mabin Ladner, Louis Hudson, Sylvester Dedeaux of Perkinston, Hersel McDaniel of Stillmore, Millard Hatten of Wiggins, Elmer Avera, Unknown, Aubrey McIntosh. Fourth and fifth rows: Mesker Bond, Nolan Terry, Leo Scanlon, Ferris Batson, Arthur Gullette, Ogden Lott of McHenry, Mal Ward, Aubrey Randolph. Not pictured: Evelyn Howell of Perkinston. Photo courtesy of Martha Heffner.

sen for the first offerings were agriculture, science, history, and English. On March 17, Denson had told a *Daily Herald* reporter why the school had launched its unique summer program:

"The purpose of this summer session is threefold. First, it will shorten a pupil's high school life one year. That is, if a student who is a freshman this year takes work for two units this summer, four the next winter, two next summer, he can graduate the following regular session of 1926-1927; whereas he would graduate in 1927-28 if he did not take advantage of the summer school opportunity.

"Secondly, this summer session is for those pupils who for any reason, might have failed to make a unit in his back work. This will be an excellent opportunity to get that work on which he is behind in.

"Thirdly, there are thousands of teachers in the rural schools of Mississippi who are teaching without a high school diploma. Those teachers can continue to teach in the winter, then come here and work toward a high school diploma.

"Only high school work will be done."

While he had been in Jackson getting approval for this new summer program, Denson was also securing permission to add the first year of junior college in the fall. He, for some reason, kept that a secret.

May slipped away without any publicity about a junior college. Yet the printers at the Dixie Press in Gulfport knew about it because in May 1925, they printed "Volume 1, Number 1" of the *Harrison-Stone*

Agricultural High School and Junior College Bulletin" containing the "*Catalogue 1924-25*" and the "*Announcements 1925-26*." This *Bulletin* detailed everything a student needed to know to enter the junior college at Perkinston down to the minute the doors would open at Perkinston at 11 a.m. on September 14, 1925.

Denson had attended the April meeting of the Stone County Board of Supervisors and had told the supervisors present that the school had outgrown the capacity of its buildings. He told them more specifically that it had come down to building additional structures or stopping "the growth and usefulness of the school." He did not tell them the school was going to "grow" into a junior college or that the new buildings were going to be "used" for that purpose.

The first week in June passed and still not a word about a junior college. That all changed on Wednesday, June 10, 1925, when Denson and several members of the HSAHS & JC Board of Trustees, together with the school agriculturist, E. B. Colmer, went to the office of Harrison County School Superintendent C. J. Darby in Gulfport. The Stone County Trustees present at this historic meeting were President of the Board A. J. Bond of Perkinston, Stone County Superintendent of Education Buren Broadus of Wiggins, and Secretary of the Board Charlie Swetman of Perkinston. The Harrison County members present were Lloyd Blackledge of Saucier, Posey N. Howell of Howison, and of course, C. J. Darby, Gulfport, a member of the Board by virtue of his office.

On Friday, June 12, the *Daily Herald* published an account of the meeting:

"The principal business transacted was the letting of a contract to Harkness & Lockyer, architects, to make plans and specifications for an addition to the administration building of the institution and also for a new boys' dormitory to house about 80 additional students.

"These additions to the plant are made necessary by increased attendance, the school at present being unable to care for those who wish to attend. These additions are to cost about $40,000 and will probably be ready for occupancy about Sept. 15."

The "addition" to be added to the administration (Bennett) building was to be no small structure. Bennett Annex was to be nearly as large as its "parent building" and would be connected to it only by a closed-in, elevated walkway. The annex actually amounted to a building in its own right. Bennett Annex together with the "new boys' dormitory" (which would be christened Jackson Hall on October 13, 1956) in effect, would increase the size of the campus by two-fifths. And all this was to be completed in barely two months in time for the opening of school. The article finished with what amounted to a verbal lightning bolt, "Junior College work will be added to the institution during the coming school year, giving one year in college work. Next year another year in college will be added. There will be thirteen teachers employed at the next session of the school. J. L. Denson will be superintendent and E. B. Colmer will have charge of the agricultural work."

Two days later on Sunday night, June 14, 1925, at 8 p.m., a real lightning bolt struck the school's barn and burned it down in 30 flaming minutes. Two cows and a dog died in the blaze, and all the feed and fertilizer stored in the barn went up in smoke. The mules and other livestock were saved. The loss was estimated at between $6,000 and $7,000 with that figure to go higher unless a storage area could be found for the hay and

The new HSAHS barn built following the June 14, 1925, destruction by fire of the 1914 barn stands at left. In the photograph made in October 1927, two student workers are loading hay at ten cents per hour. Note the cypress water tower located behind Huff Hall visible at the right of the barn. The barn in this photograph, too, succumbed to fire on Thursday, February 13, 1936, at 4:30 a.m. Spontaneous combustion was believed to be the culprit in that case. A third barn, virtually a replica of the one in the photograph, was completed on the same site in fall 1936. That structure still stood in December 2000. Photo courtesy of Dixie Press of Gulfport.

other crops ready for harvest. A new storage area was found until a new barn was completed in mid-August, 1925.

On June 18, the *Stone County Enterprise* noted that work would soon begin "on adequate buildings at the AHS to accommodate the beginning of the junior college work there next session." The article further stated that the Harrison County Board of Supervisors had joined the Stone County Board of Supervisors in passing the respective quotas to provide the funding for the new construction.

Early in July 1925, Superintendent of Education C. J. Darby received a letter from State High School Inspector and Chairman of the State Accrediting Commission (and former Superintendent of the HSAHS) Claude Bennett. In the letter, Bennett told Darby that the State Accrediting Commission had devised a special examination for students who desired to enter the junior college without the required 15 units of high school work. The examination was to be restricted to "students who have an equivalent of a high school education obtained in some manner other than an affiliated high school." The test would be given in Darby's office on July 18.

On July 17, the HSAHS & JC Board of Trustees let the contracts for Bennett Annex and Jackson Hall. The contractors began moving building materials onto the campus on August 11, and the new date for completion of the two structures was set at February 1, 1926.

The opening exercises of the 1925-1926 session, the school's first time to offer one year of junior college credit, began at 11 a.m., Monday, September 14, 1925, in Bennett Auditorium. After a program, which included a violin solo, a duet, and a welcome by Denson, registration began.

According to figures released to the *Daily Herald* by Denson near the end of the session on the following April 9, the enrollment of the 1925-1926 session totaled 212. Of this number, 55 percent were boys and 45 percent were girls. He said 20 students took college work during the session. Interestingly enough 20 students was the exact minimum number of junior college freshmen enrollees required under the terms of the 1924 State of Mississippi Junior College Law "if the said institution offers freshmen work only." The requirement for both years of junior college work was a total of 35 freshmen and sophomores.

Hersel McDaniel, looking back across 35 years, named thirteen of those first year college students and added "there might have been one or two more but I don't recall them." Eight of those he remembered had graduated from the HSAHS with him the past May. These were Julia Lewis of Stillmore, Ogden Lott of McHenry, Millard Hatten of Wiggins, and Irene Flurry, Ione Hunter, Evelyn Howell, Sylvester Dedeaux, and Estelle "Bill" David all of Perkinston. Three more, McDaniel said, had transferred in from other schools. Those were George Rolfe, Velma Hill, and Harold Hammett. Hammett had transferred in from another school, but he was a high school student and not a junior college student. The thirteenth one he remembered was Vernon Brown. According to the school records, Brown graduated from the high school department of the institution in 1926, but did not enter the junior college department until the 1926-1927 session. In McDaniel's words, "Vernon was always there at the start." That was true. Brown left and returned for so many years that very likely McDaniel forgot that Brown was not a college student in 1925-1926 year. So Hammett and Brown must be purged from McDaniel's list leaving eleven entering junior college freshmen and perhaps "one or two more" that McDaniel did not recall. Velma Hill, for whatever reason, would not complete the year and neither would Bill David. In any case, only nine college freshmen would finish the year.

The junior college teachers were E. B. Colmer (agriculture), W. H. "Billy" Wood (history), Miss Frances Bailey (math), C. O. Hinton (science), and Miss Bernice McMullan (English). All of these had a four-year college degree or better because the 1924 Junior College Law mandated that as a minimum for teachers who taught junior college freshmen. That law also mandated at least a year of postgraduate work for those teaching junior college sophomores. According to the session *1925-1926 Announcements,* only Hinton had attained that level of education. Bailey had three summers beyond the bachelor's, Wood had one summer, and McMullan had one summer. That was it.

The junior college faculty, of course, taught high school subjects as well. Those faculty members who taught high school courses only were Miss Dorothy Daughdrill (violin, voice, and orchestra), Miss Mary Lillian Peters (director of music and piano), Miss Julia Skinner (domestic science), Miss Julia O. Sigrest (commercial subjects and girls' athletics), F. O. Parsons (assistant in agriculture and math), Miss Thelma Stevens (English, education, and history), and W. C. Denson, the superintendent's brother, taught science and had charge of boy's athletics. The educational attainments of the high school faculty were not published.

The official name of the institution only recently rendered as Harrison-Stone Agricultural High School and Junior College changed again on September 9, 1925, to Harrison-Stone-Jackson Agricultural High School and Junior College (HSJAHS & JC). The Jackson County Board of Supervisors had placed a special levy of three-tenths of one mill on all assessed property in the county and joined with her two sister counties to form Mississippi's first tri-county AHS and junior college. In the words of a *Daily Herald* reporter

Photo by Richard Kopp.

(Top left) The "New Boys' Dormitory," a two story 75 x 108 edifice, completed and occupied in February 1926, appears in this photograph of the structure contained in the photographic section at the rear of the Session 1925-1926 Catalogue. The building suffered heavy fire damage early on the morning of February 21, 1927, but quick response by students and faculty saved it. By the early 1950s the structure was being referred to as "Varsity Hall." The building was renovated in 1956, and on August 22 of that year, the Board of Trustees renamed it "Jackson Hall." (Bottom left) In the 1956 renovation the balconies were removed and the aspect of the façade changed by sealing the front entrance and respacing the windows in the mid-section. At that time the southern door became the main entrance. (Top right) In 1988, the year after the opening of Hayden Hall, Jackson Hall, no longer being needed as a men's dorm, was transformed into offices for personnel of the MGCCC Central Office. At that time the old front entrance facing the Quadrangle was reopened. In summer 2000 Central Office personnel occupying the building were removed to temporary quarters and massive renovations undertaken. In December 2000, (bottom right) the renovation included the addition of covered porticos on all three entrances.

published September 16, "Jackson County boys and girls will receive the full rights and benefits of the school plant, but Jackson County will not be called upon to assume or pay any part of the bonded indebtedness incurred by Harrison and Stone Counties to build the school."

Many of the early "catalogs" or "bulletins" or "announcements" of the institution, were not held in the collection of the MGCCC Archives in 2000, so it can not be said with certainty that the session *1925-1926 Announcements* carried the first list of "officers" of the institution, but it carries the first known list. J. L. Denson, of course, led the list as superintendent. The rest of these "officers" were C. O. Hinton (assistant superintendent), Miss Julia O. Sigrest (secretary to the faculty), Miss Irene Flurry (secretary to the superintendent), Miss Estelle David (secretary to the superintendent), Mrs. F. O. Parsons (librarian), Vernon Brown (assistant librarian), Mrs. Jane Fahnestock (matron), and N. A. Warnell (engineer).

This list is the first known indication of the birth of an administrative hierarchy in the form of an "assistant superintendent." Obviously, C. O. Hinton was only a part-time "assistant superintendent" because he was first and foremost a teacher, but this was how the hierarchy began. Just as obviously, the two secretaries to the superintendent were not full-time because both Irene Flurry and Estelle "Bill" David were freshmen college students. Bill David at some point in that year may have become a full-time temporary student secretary to Superintendent Denson. In any case she did not finish the year as a junior college freshman. Later and for many years, Bill David served as full-time secretary to the superintendent.

This list likewise indicates the origin of support services for the faculty in the form of a "secretary to faculty" and a "librarian." The duties of the "secretary to faculty" were not described, but Miss Julia O. Sigrest was a full-time faculty member teaching shorthand, typewriting, bookkeeping, and also the coach of girls' athletics. So, she did not have much time to do much else.

Ethel [Mrs. F.O.] Parsons, the junior college's first librarian.

Mrs. F. O. Parsons's post as librarian was likely her only job. Whether the job was "full-time" is not known, but it likely was because Vernon Brown was her assistant. Mrs. Parsons, in any case, is the first known person associated with this institution to bear the title "librarian." Before 1925 nothing at the institution deserved the name "library." The AHS Laws of 1908 and 1910 did not address the subject of libraries, but the 1924 Junior College Law did. The 1924 Junior College Law mandated a library of at least "one thousand well selected volumes, not including pamphlets or government publications," for freshman work and at least 1,500 such volumes for institutions offering both freshman and sophomore work. Mrs. Parsons, by the way, was not the first faculty wife to work for the institution, for that had happened on a few occasions during the AHS years, but she was the first in the junior college era. Her husband, Fred, did not teach junior college subjects that first year, but he did later. Perkinston, with few exceptions, in 2000 had been a one-industry town since 1912, and before the mid-20th century transportation revolution, spouses worked at the campus if they worked at all.

In Hersel McDaniel's words, "My first year of college at Perk was spent in the same room in the old dormitory [Huff]--Vernon [Brown] of course was my roommate--it seems Vernon was there every year for . . . for a long, long time." Their former roommate, Ferris Batson, had gone on to the Agricultural & Mechanical College in Starkville, so their new third man was Sam "Sambo" Lott, and for a while Hiland Davis made a fourth.

Both dorms were bursting at the seams. All the rooms had three occupants and many had four. Jackson Hall, then under construction, would alleviate the overcrowding for the boys but not the girls.

Crab Breland paid a visit to the campus in early October 1925 and inspected the works in progress. The Athletic Field across the railroad from the campus next to the highway was nearly completed. Crab said Jackson Hall and Bennett Annex were both about 70 percent complete. E. B. Colmer took Crab on a tour of the new barn, the "hoggery," and the dairy facilities. Colmer was about to send the boys out to harvest four acres of sugar cane and had ordered 1,000 gallon cans to fill with syrup. Colmer was also preparing the school's agriculture exhibit to be set up at the Harrison County Fair early the next month.

McDaniel, barred from athletics that year because there was no college team yet, was crushing cane on the side for Colmer at 10 cents an hour and working three school jobs. He swept out the auditorium for one job, put out and picked up the song books for chapel in another, and in addition to those, landed the cream puff job of the campus--taking care of the gasoline pump recently installed by Denson. The first two jobs paid $6.00 each per month. Pumping gas paid in addition a colossal $15.00 per month. McDaniel not only paid his current room and board, but he paid off what he still owed for previous years and had money in his pocket. He did all that in addition to making an "A" in Hinton's chemistry class, a "B" in Miss McMullen's English class, an "A" in Coach Billy Wood's history class, and a "B" in Miss Bailey's algebra class. So what if he slipped and made a "C" in Miss Bailey's trigonometry class? "I found that college work required a lot more studying," he said, and "Our class time was increased to one hour so as to be in line with the four year colleges." But McDaniel thrived on both the work and the studying. In his words:

This first side view of the Bennett Administration Building (right) and the Bennett Annex (left) is contained in the photo section at the rear of the Session 1925-1926 Catalogue. The photo taken from the west shows the two-story Bennett Annex about the time it was completed in February 1926, as an addition to the three-story original 1913 structure. Bennett Annex was, in fact, a separate edifice connected only by a closed-in elevated hallway to the "parent" building. The third floor of the Bennett Building was an auditorium, which was converted into the school library when the larger (50 x 70) auditorium on the second floor of the Bennett Annex came available. Simultaneously the chemistry lab was moved from the basement of Bennett to the basement of the Bennett Annex, and the home economics classes then occupied the vacated basement of Bennett. The commercial classes simultaneously occupied the second floor of Bennett abandoned by the home economics department. A chain reaction movement of this type, and there have been many at Perkinston, is termed "fruit-basket turnover." The 1947 hurricane so damaged the second floor auditorium of the Bennett Annex that it was removed circa 1959. The Bennett Annex finished its life as a squat one-story affair. The whole complex fell to the wrecking ball in 1967 to make way for the Dees Building.

"most of . . . those days were extremely happy ones--and why not--I was in love, my girl was in school with me, I had a third job, my finances were shaping up real good, I was doing good in my studies, I had no worries at all, the teachers and my roommates were most congenial so--'Life was just a big bowl of cherries.'"

In mid-February 1926, Crab Breland made another trip over to the campus and found that the Athletic Field had not only been finished but also fenced. The new boys' dormitory (Jackson Hall) had been finished and occupied and so had Bennett Annex. Denson told Crab that next he was going to have to have a new girls' dormitory.

The Bennett complex was quickly put to use complying with the requirements of the 1924 Junior College Law. The new, larger auditorium on the second floor of the annex enabled Denson to convert the older, smaller auditorium into the first real library in the history of the school. The stage was left in place for play rehearsals and speech training in conjunction with the English classes that occupied the classrooms adjacent to the old auditorium. The seats of the auditorium were cleared out, bookcases were set up to contain the 1,000 volumes then held by the school, and reading tables were placed about the room. McDaniel commenting on the new facility said, "Our reference books increased tremendously and it was really a treat to visit the library now."

With the library on the road to compliance, Denson reorganized the rest of the space in the Bennett complex to fulfill the laboratory requirements mandated by the 1924 Junior College Law. The law stated that, "The laboratory equipment shall have an aggregate value of not less than $2,000." So, according to McDaniel,

"Our chemistry lab was moved to the basement [of Bennett Annex]. . . . Our old lab [in the basement of the original Bennett Building] was taken over by the Home Ec. Girls and their room [second floor of Bennett] was taken over for the commercial work."

At dawn on April Fool's Day, 1926, 50 boys and girls slipped away from the campus before the rising bell. When Denson went to breakfast that morning, every table in the dining room had at least one empty seat and some had four or five. Denson was not amused. That evening as the truants straggled back from their hooky holiday, Denson checked off their names as they entered the dorms. McDaniel said none of them got a whipping, but "all of them were campused for a long, long time." Ironically this rebellion in the ranks redounded to the benefit of McDaniel and his fellow collegians:

AHS girls at work in the home economics laboratory in Bennett Hall in October 1927. The December 1928, issue of the Perkolator, the campus student newspaper, carried notice that, "A Home Economics Club has been organized for the first time at Perkinston." The club, sponsored by Miss Winnie J. Hood, the home economics instructor, had Christmas fruitcakes for sale as their first fundraiser. This club continued until the home economics program was discontinued in 1986. Elaine Ogden was the last home economics instructor. Photo courtesy of Dixie Press of Gulfport.

"It made Mr. Denson beam with pride when he read off the names of those taking the day off--when not one college student was on the list. Maybe that is why the punishment was so mild--'cause Mr. Denson was so happy about the college students. Mr. Denson thought he had done a wonderful thing in getting the college in the first place, and he had. No other school had one and that in itself was a thing to be proud of, and Mr. Denson surely was."

Maybe McDaniel did not know it, but Pearl River County AHS had added freshman college work in 1921, and Hinds County AHS had done so in 1922; but in fact, neither had finished the process of evolving into a full-fledged two-year junior college by the 1925-1926 session.

Because Denson was so proud of the junior college students, they had special status. As McDaniel put it, "We were to be shining examples for the AHS group both in deportment and school work." By not joining in the April Fool shenanigans, the college students had justified Denson's faith in them, so he rewarded them with the unheard of privilege of going to downtown Perkinston any time at their discretion without written permission. As McDaniel put it, "boy that was really sompin'--and did we enjoy it very much and were really grateful."

On Tuesday, April 6, 1926, the addition of the second year of junior college work at Perkinston became an assured fact. The HSJAHS and JC Board of Trustees met in Gulfport and appointed the necessary funds to bring the school's library holdings up to 1,500 volumes and to purchase all laboratory equipment necessary to satisfy the requirements of the 1924 State Junior College Law. Going further, a department of modern languages would be added to the offerings of the school, and three new teachers would be hired for that and other requirements of the college department.

After the April 6 meeting, Denson also announced that, as before, a high school summer school would be offered. Twenty courses would be offered this time, but these would be taught by two of his faculty plus adjunct teachers from other institutions. He, and nearly all the present faculty members at Perkinston who were to remain through the coming session of 1926-1927, would be away taking post graduate college classes to meet state requirements for college teachers. He, Hinton, and Colmer would be going to Colorado Agricultural College. Other members of the faculty would be going to Tulane in New Orleans and Peabody in Nashville.

So why were the Perkinston teachers going so far away when the Mississippi State Teacher's College was only 35 miles away in Hattiesburg, and Delta State Teacher's College was then at Cleveland in Bolivar County? They could not go to those colleges because those institutions did not possess the resources for accreditation by the Southern Association of Colleges and Schools. The Mississippi State Legislature had founded them but failed to appropriate the funds to bring their libraries and laboratories up to standard.

Denson had much to be proud of. His dream of a junior college was becoming a reality, and simultaneously, he received a letter published in the *Daily Herald* of April 7, 1926, from the board of examiners that had given the tests for teachers licenses to six of his girls recently at Wiggins. All six had passed with flying colors, demonstrating a "thorough knowledge of the facts covered" and also "a general literary excellence superior to that shown by any applicants" that the board had ever examined.

On April 18, the *Daily Herald* carried word that HSJAHS senior Gordon Vancleave had been announced the winner of the Mississippi state prize given by the American Chemical Society of New York for his essay entitled, "Chemistry and Its Relation to Agriculture." Vancleave received for his 2,500-word effort not only a first prize certificate but also $20 in gold.

But what goes up must come down. On April 20, a play called "The Wren" was staged in the Bennett Annex Auditorium. Many students and teachers performed, but the star was one of Colmer's prize registered pigs. The pig, beautifully groomed, was brought in a sack onto the dogwood and wild azalea embellished stage. After a crowd-pleasing romp, the scene stealing porcine thespian was returned to the sack. Improper securing of the sack resulted in the pig escaping from both sack and the confines of the building. Following an all-night search involving the inhabitants of the countryside, the no longer immaculate "pork player" was recaptured and repenned.

Then Hersel McDaniel, like the pig, broke out. Velma Wyatt, pretty young daughter of the T. P. Wyatts, who lived east of Dees's Store, gave a party, and Denson would allow only girls to attend. McDaniel's girlfriend Julia went, so McDaniel wanted to go, too. Many of the boys wanted to go.

Hinton was the teacher selected to escort the girls to the Wyatts' and to retrieve them at midnight. McDaniel made common cause with Bill Shattles, who was by then rooming with him and Vernon Brown, to dare all and go. So they went. They had a fine time until Hinton showed up early at the Wyatts', so they had to make a run for it. McDaniel and Shattles made it back to Huff Hall, undressed and got in bed as fast as they could. Hinton though, who had already smelled a rat because the two had not been in their rooms when he had made an earlier inspection, put the girls in their dorm quickly and then double-timed it to Huff Hall. Hinton woke up Vernon, who really was asleep and innocent. McDaniel and Shattles, feigning sleep, heard Hinton walk across their room. He picked up their clothes and muttered, "Still warm." Then he left.

McDaniel and Shattles remained in fear for a week, waiting for the bomb to fall. Then came a summons to McDaniel to go to Denson's office. He knew the jig was up and the "Old Shellalah" was coming down. Denson had just hung up the phone when McDaniel went in. Denson said, "Well, Hersel, you not only got yourself into trouble, but you also got your girl into it, too." McDaniel knew he was in for it then, but he noticed that for some strange reason Denson could not stop smiling. McDaniel attempted a feeble excuse on the lines that college students could go to town at their discretion at any time. Denson said it did not apply in this case, but he said he would forget about this escapade if it did not happen again. McDaniel found out later that the reason Denson was so happy was that the phone call had been from Mississippi Governor Theodore G. Bilbo telling him that a new girls' dormitory was a sure thing. That dorm was not built for more than a year, but it saved McDaniel.

In recalling this escapade, McDaniel said, "the old proverb that says, 'The Lord takes care of fools and drunks,' must have applied to Bill and me. We weren't drunk, so we must have come under the other classification." Very likely Denson was the power watching over Hersel McDaniel. The classification McDaniel came under was "Harrison-Stone-Jackson Junior College Freshman"--something Denson desperately needed more of and certainly could not afford to lose any of. Not only was McDaniel a college freshman, he was president of the college class of nine students that Denson thought was 20.

On May 13, 1926, Denson went to the Great Southern Hotel in Gulfport to speak to the Rotary Club on the subject of the Mississippi AHS movement in general and the Perkinston school in particular. Of the AHSs established since the beginning with the AHS Law of 1908, forty-nine (48 white and one black) still remained in operation. Some of these were becoming junior colleges, and he assured his audience that the Perkinston institution would not only achieve full junior college status in the coming session but also come up to the standard set by the Southern Association of Colleges and Schools. He invited the Rotary Club members to come up and visit their college at any time, and he closed with some statistics related to the AHS movement in the state:

"Since the establishment of the AHS in Mississippi; 11,000 students have graduated from these institutions, fifty-two percent of this number are now engaged in some class of agricultural pursuits and two thousand are now teaching in the schools of the state . . . not one has gone to the penitentiary or the poorhouse and none have been buried in potter's field."

The 1926 graduation was both unique and mysterious. And, for the first time, detailed descriptions of the commencement week ceremonies survived.

The festivities began on Friday, May 21, with a senior class banquet at the Masonic Lodge in Wiggins catered by Duggan's Restaurant with Denson as toastmaster. The school glee club entertained at the banquet. At the baccalaureate sermon in Bennett Annex Auditorium on Sunday, both the glee club and the school orchestra performed. The orchestra played the processional and the recessional, which indicated that the graduates marched in before Baptist minister J. N. Miller's sermon and marched out after it.

Earlier in the year Denson had announced that trophies and gold medals would be awarded at the 1926 graduation. There were two trophies. A silver loving cup was to be presented to the class having the best average of scholarship and deportment at the end of the session. This cup was to be inscribed annually with the name of the winning class. A second silver loving cup was to be awarded to the society winning the school's championship debate contest. The competing societies were the Wilsonian Society, named for former President Woodrow Wilson, and the Densonian Society, named for Denson. These loving cups were to remain in the possession of the school, and in 2000 they were part of the permanent collection of the MGCCC Archives.

Five gold medals were to be presented. Two of these--"boy student giving the best declamation" and "girl student giving the best reading" were restricted to HSJAHS students. Two others were specifically for best oration by a college man and best oration by a college woman. The fifth gold medal, given for best all-around student, bore no restrictions based on class or gender.

The contests for the four gold medals for speaking took place in Bennett Annex Auditorium on Tuesday, May 25. All nine college freshmen, five men and four women, vied for the two oration medals. Hersel McDaniel gave his rendition of "The Crucible of Democracy," and Irene Flurry held forth on "The Value of Good Literature." Various HSJAHS boys and girls competed for the other two gold medals.

On graduation night, May 28, 1926, Denson and Rev. R. N. Davis of Perkinston led the graduates to their places on the stage of Bennett Annex Auditorium to the strains of the Grand March from "Aida" played by the school orchestra. The stage was described as "beautifully decorated with a color motif of orchid and pink--the class colors. Tall baskets of Easter lilies and sweet peas, gladioli and ferns banked the stage."

Rev. Davis gave the invocation after which salutatorian Arvid Lindsey of Perkinston and valedictorian Gordon Vancleave of Ocean Springs made their presentations. The orchestra then played "The Mill Wheel" and "Come Where the Lilies Bloom."

Next came the commencement speaker in the person of George D. Riley, State auditor and gubernatorial candidate, who spoke on "Character Building." As Riley finished, the orchestra struck up "Massa's in de Cold Cold Ground" and then revved things up with "Boosting the Old High School" as Denson came forward to award the gold medals and trophies.

Lorraine Casey of Gulfport took the high school girl's best reading medal. Houston Ramsay of Gulfport won the gold for the high school boy's best declamation. Irene Flurry of Perkinston took the prize for oration by a college woman, and Hersel McDaniel won the medal for oration by a college man. Denson also presented to McDaniel, in his capacity as president of the college freshman class, the silver loving cup for class scholarship. The best all-around student gold medal was not mentioned, and neither was the debating society silver loving cup.

Following the presentation of the cup and the medals, Denson presented diplomas only to those AHS seniors present who had completed requirements for graduation. The other seniors seated with the graduates would receive their diplomas, presumably after summer school, and without further ceremony. The diplomas delivered that night bore the new appellation--Harrison-Stone-Jackson Agricultural High

The picture below contains the nine students who finished the first year junior college course at the Harrison-Stone-Jackson AHS and Junior College at Perkinston on May 28, 1926, together with the junior college class sponsor, Miss Frances Bailey, and Harold Hammett, an AHS student who graduated that night. Of the nine freshman junior college students in this photograph only one, Hersel McDaniel, would complete the second year course of study the following year, and he alone would graduate at the close of the next session, 1926-1927. None of the other freshmen of 1925-1926 ran the gauntlet with him to that first junior college graduation. Julia Lewis, his girlfriend and future wife, stopped out the next year and returned the year after. Irene Flurry could not carry a full load because of her secretary-to-the-superintendent job. Evelyn Howell stopped out until 1930 and then returned again, believe it or not, in 1980. The others, in McDaniel's words, "dropped out or fell by the wayside."

Bottom row (from left) Julia Lewis of Stillmore, Irene Flurry of Perkinston, Ione Hunter of Perkinston, and Evelyn Howell of Perkinston. Middle row (from left) Harold Hammett of Gulfport, Ogden Lott of McHenry, Hersel McDaniel of Stillmore, Sylvester Dedeaux of Perkinston, and Millard Hatten of Wiggins. Top row (from left) George Rolf and Miss Frances Bailey (sponsor).

According to Hersel McDaniel this picture "is of our graduation class for the first year of college." Why there should have been a graduation exercise complete with a diploma for the first year of college is not known to this author, but apparently this was the case. In McDaniel's words, "Dad Warnell," the campus engineer in charge of the Power Plant, "had a wonderful flair with the pen--he really could write a beautiful hand--in fact he wrote the names on our diplomas when we finished the first year of college." McDaniel furthermore stated in regard to the picture, "These ten students formed the whole class--this picture is one of the class near the end of the school term. There were two or three more at the beginning of the year--Vernon Brown for one." McDaniel was wrong about Vernon Brown, who is not in the picture, and he was wrong about Harold Hammett. Neither Brown nor Hammett were college freshmen that year. In fact, both are on the proposed list of high school graduates for that year. Vernon Brown became a junior college freshman the following year. There is no record that Harold Hammett ever enrolled in the junior college at Perkinston, but he certainly was not a college student at this time. His presence in the photo is a mystery.

This picture, taken at the base of the Corinthian columns that flanked the front door of the Bennett Building, was almost certainly made on one of two occasions. It could have been snapped on Tuesday, May 25, when each junior college student of the school--which is every student in the picture except Hammett--made a speech in Bennett Annex Auditorium. On the other hand, the picture may have been made at graduation on Friday, May 28. The Daily Herald article of May 20 which described what was going to happen on graduation night and the Daily Herald article of June 5 that described what did happen had something in common. Neither article said anything about anyone other than high school students graduating. Some of the junior college students received medals and the freshman junior college class as a whole received the campus Class Scholarship Loving Cup that remained at the school to be inscribed annually. The freshman junior college "graduation" of 1926 remains a mystery.

Photo by Richard Kopp.

The 16-inch tall Class Scholarship trophy was first awarded to the College Freshman class of 1925-1926. This cup would continue to be presented through the year 1936 when the engravers ran out of space to engrave another class name.

School. With the benediction the ceremonies ended.

At the opening of the school in September 1926, 243 students, the largest enrollment in the history of the institution, crowded the Perkinston campus and more were expected. Every room in Stone Hall held four girls and some had five. Trunks and other personal possessions lined the halls to the point that they made passage difficult. A few of the girls were living on a rotating basis (of one month each group) in the suite of home demonstration rooms recently fashioned in the home economics section of Bennett Hall, but only a new girls' dormitory could alleviate such congestion. The dining room in the basement of Stone Hall was so packed that only with the greatest difficulty could Ma Fanny and her girls cope.

Parents and students at Powers Community, east of Big Level, petitioned Stone County Superintendent of Education Buren Broadus for a novel solution regarding the crowded dormitory conditions at the HSJAHS & JC. They wanted daily transportation to and from the school. They got it, too. Crab Breland, who caught a ride to Wiggins on the school truck in late September, said "The Powers to Perkinston school

On August 12, 1924, the Daily Herald published newly elected Superintendent Lee Denson's announcements for the coming 1924-1925 session of the Harrison-Stone Agricultural High School. Among these was this: "Girl Reserve and Boys Hi-Y . . . will be organized and encouraged." These organizations would be officered by students and directed by faculty members. The Girl Reserve was the high school wing of the Young Women's Christian Association (YWCA) and Boy's Hi-Y was the high school wing of the Young Men's Christian Association (YMCA). Their purpose was the same. Both organizations held religious services and fostered Christian ideals even to the point of leading anti-cheating movements on campus. They also staged plays and "womanless weddings" and sponsored poetry readings, musical programs, and banquets. In time, as the junior college program grew larger than that of the high school, the organizations dropped their high school names and became instead the YWCA and YMCA. The hut or cabin shown in the photo of the Girl Reserve was constructed of poles or logs taken from the abandoned Ten Mile Sawmill. The boys hauled the logs to the site of the cabin located just north of Stone Hall and west of Bennett in a half-ton Ford truck. In Hersel McDaniels' words, "If any truck . . . ever underwent such rough treatment as this truck did--well it would be a record. . . . We would drive right out through the woods over logs or anything that was in the way." On Saturday, February 26, 1927, while hauling poles for the hut, the boys got too rough. They had a trailer hooked to the truck, and eighteen-year-old Otis Barron fell and the back wheels of the truck and those of the trailer crushed him. Barron died an hour and a half later. School officials carried the body to Braxton for burial. This was the first serious accident in the history of the school. The boys finished the hut in April, and it was named the Dorothy Hinton Hut in tribute to Prof. and Mrs. C. O. Hinton's small daughter, who had died two years prior. This was done because of Hinton's service to the YWCA, but the structure was usually referred to as the Y-hut. A fireplace was added to the hut in January 1928, and it became a favorite meeting place for student organizations of all types. Eventually the Y-Hut was planked, and it remained on its original site until construction of Dees Hall began in 1967. At that time the Y-Hut was removed to the site where Weeks Hall was to be built in 1973. At that time the Y-Hut was removed yet again to the site it occupied in 2000 which was behind Hayden Hall. The above photos of the 1927 Girl Reserve and Boys Hi-Y courtesy of Dixie Press of Gulfport.

truck . . . runs from Powers to the Agricultural High School and Junior College daily for a dozen students." The route ran west to Wiggins and then south to Perkinston making a 50-mile per day round trip. This is an early example of bussing or rather "trucking" students to and from the campus. It was an idea whose time would come, but at the time, it was merely a novelty and not a solution.

Denson invited the Harrison County Board of Supervisors up for the day that September and showed them the problems and told them he expected enrollment to double in two years. Therefore, he wanted a $135,000 tri-county bond issue to bankroll not only the desperately needed new girls' dormitory but also a number of other facilities. He wanted all the partitions knocked out of the basement of Stone Hall to double the size of the dining room. He wanted an annex built behind or west of Stone Hall to house the kitchen, the storerooms, the pantry and a refrigeration unit. He wanted a superintendent's house, so he could move his family out of Stone Hall. He wanted a new power plant, a gymnasium, and a laundry. Denson then began promoting this audacious building plan to the supervisors of Stone and Jackson Counties and to his own Board of Trustees.

The school added the second year of college at the

(Above) Claude Smith (AHS Class of 1928) of Lucien, Franklin County, herds cows at Perkinston circa 1927. Bennett Hall and Annex is at right, the northern end of Huff Hall is behind Smith, and the cypress water tower is at left. On the back of the photograph, Smith wrote, "I milked these cows and worked my way through school."

Hersel McDaniel said of the milking that, " Sterilized bottles and milk cartons belonged to the future. Two of the boys had the job of milking the cows night and morning, rain or shine, seven days a week--so I would say they had it pretty tough. . . . The boys would have to get up at four and four-thirty--it took a couple of hours to get the job done--then be ready for meals and classes . . . but the boys never failed. . . . Then too this job paid the very liberal sum of . . . six dollars a month. . . . This milking, of course, was done by hand in big open pails. . . . The milk was brought to the kitchen in big five gallon cans, strained, [and] put in the ice box. . . ." McDaniel said the ice was delivered each day from the ice plant in Wiggins. He said the milk, though, never got very cool because "we really put it away." Photo courtesy of Claude Smith.

(Above) Claude Smith feeds the pigs at Perkinston circa 1927. The 1925 barn is at left. The bull barn is in front and east of it. The poultry house is at the far right. In writing of swine feeding, Hersel McDaniel, a classmate of Smith's, remembered that the skimmings from the sugar cane juice being boiled into molasses had to be fed in small quantities to the pigs because the skimmings contained quite a bit of alcohol. Said McDaniel, "I remember my surprise when I saw my first pig that had imbibed too freely--it was really a funny sight." Photo courtesy of Claude Smith.

beginning of the 1926-1927 session, and William G. Gregory came from Kentucky and remained for decades as a math teacher. Denson said later that the college department rose from 18 to 86 in one year. According to the known facts, he was once again "seeing double" when he looked at college students. The *Perkolator*, the campus student newspaper founded in the fall of 1926 by English teacher Miss Minnie Kay Pearson, printed a list of the 25 students in the freshman junior college class on December 13. Of the original nine junior college enrollees of the previous year, only Hersel McDaniel, Irene Flurry, and Ogden Lott are known to have returned as sophomores, but the records are incomplete. Students were still enrolling in December, and their classification is unknown. Apparently Denson had the statutory 35 college students when the state inspectors came, or he was so close they let it go.

The school joined the recently organized Mississippi Association of Junior Colleges (MAJC) at the beginning of the 1926-1927 session, and for the first time fielded junior college teams in athletics and debate. The debate team lost to Pearl River Junior College in the state junior college championship held at Poplarville on March 11, 1927, but the team members vowed to bring home the trophy next time.

As a new junior college, Perkinston was eligible to compete for the first time in the 1927 MAJC Field Meet. This huge one-day affair was staged that year on April 15 at Raymond. Students of all the state junior colleges took part in a wide variety of competitions including athletics, fine arts, home economics, agriculture, history, English, chemistry, mathematics, and virtually anything else offered in the junior college curriculum. Trophies and medals were awarded to first place individuals and teams engaged in various competitions. Each time individuals or teams placed in a category, points were awarded to their respective junior colleges. At the end of the Field Meet the institution with the most points was awarded the State Cup or "Big Loving Cup." That lucky institution displayed the prize for one year. At the time of the next State Field Meet, the superintendent of the defending junior college returned with his students and the State Cup and retained or lost it for another year.

Perkinston placed second overall behind Hinds Junior College in the 1927 MAJC Field Meet but took first place in sixteen competitions and numerous second place slots. At the close of this field meet, Denson pronounced that Perkinston would enter in every course in the meet and take the State Cup in 1928 "even if he had to climb a greased pole." Greased pole climbing actually was one of the competitions.

Two weeks after the State Field Meet, Denson received a letter informing him that his institution was exactly what its name avowed--a fully recognized "accredited junior college in Mississippi." This letter dated April 30, 1927, and signed by M. Latimer, Chairman of the Junior College Commission, praised Denson for his dedication and vision and extended congratulations for a job well done. Next Denson wanted membership in the Southern Association of Colleges and Schools, and he intended to get it.

On May 20, 1927, Hersel McDaniel became the first college graduate of the HSJJC. On graduation night he had to march with the high school graduates, and he resented it because he was a college sophomore. "But," as McDaniel put it, "I was the only one and they wouldn't give me an exercise by myself." The speaker that night was Gov. Bilbo, and McDaniel remembered, "He made a great speech. One of the best I have ever heard."

Denson's ardent support for the "Stormy Petrel of Mississippi Politics--the man Bilbo" did not get him any state money for Perkinston because state support was illegal under the provisions of the 1924 State Junior College Law. But Denson's politics did assure that Bilbo would use his influence on behalf of the school.

When the 1927-1928 session opened on Monday, September 5, 1927, the girls had a new dormitory, later christened Fahnestock Hall in honor of Ma Fanny. The dining room had doubled in size, occupying the whole of the basement floor of Stone Hall, and a new kitchen annex stood behind Stone. A new gymnasium stood at the base of the hill. Across the

The "New Girls Dormitory" of 1927 was renamed Fahnestock Hall on May 14, 1960, in honor of Sarah Jane "Ma Fanny" Fahnestock, matron and dietician of the school 1920-1922 and 1924-1934. She was the wife of Dr. E. M. Fahnestock, who helped to save the school in the flap over the formation of Stone County in 1916. She was born in 1876, died in 1962, and was buried in Evergreen Cemetery in Gulfport. Denson got every structure in 1927 he had asked the Trustees for except the laundry. He got that in 1928. Photo courtesy of Tom Brown.

The remodeled and extended Stone Hall Dining Room as it appeared in October 1927. The south door or student entrance is visible in the distance. The doors to the right lead to the newly constructed Stone Hall Kitchen Annex. Dishes are stacked upside down on shelves beyond those doors in the foyer of the kitchen. Photo courtesy of Dixie Press of Gulfport.

The "Old Gym" opened for use on September 5, 1927. This brick-veneered structure, which remained standing on the Perkinston Campus in 2000, was the first of its kind in the region. It functioned for years as a miniature "Piney Woods Coliseum" and was the site of many basketball tournaments for the area and even Coast leagues serving elementary through college teams. Photo courtesy of Dixie Press of Gulfport.

Occupied by the Densons in fall 1927, the Superintendent's Home served as the residence of the junior college's chief executive officer until President and Mrs. J.J. Hayden moved into Liaison in March 1976. The old Superintendent's Home served as administrators' housing until it was closed for remodeling in 1987 and reopened as the Alumni House in April 1989. Photo courtesy of Dixie Press of Gulfport.

Quadrangle from the new gym was a new brick power plant next to a large pond.

Directly across from the new power plant just south of the gymnasium, a new Superintendent's Home was nearing completion. This structure had its genesis in the Board Meeting of July 5, 1927, in Gulfport:

"Ordered that Supt. J. L. Denson be allowed to build a superintendent's home on the property of the school at his own expense and the Board of Trustees agrees to refund to J. L. Denson . . . the cost of the home out of the school funds when available after the other obligations are paid now made by the present building program. The building of the home not to exceed $10,000 as provided in the budget."

Denson already had one son and three daughters and another child on the way. The renovations of Stone Hall had driven him from his living quarters on the basement floor up to the floor above. He wanted out of that dorm not only to house his still growing family but also to make his apartment in Stone Hall available to students or teachers. He wanted the new home so much that he was willing to front the money himself. If he did, indeed, pay for this house, there is no subsequent record that he was repaid for the construction costs. Denson and his family moved into the new Superintendent's Home by the middle of the fall semester, and the child, a son, the Densons' last, was born December 8, 1927.

The 1927-1928 session recorded the largest enrollment in the school's history. In the *Stone County Enterprise* of September 22, 1927, Denson pegged the total number registered at 262, of which 85 were college students. All classes were full and many classes were being divided and "still large." The *Daily Herald* of October 5, using figures supplied by the Board of Trustees, reported all four dormitories full with 182 boarding students. In addition, and for the first contemporary use of the term, the paper reported 20 "day students." Denson reported 60 more students than the Board did, but that was not unusual.

Several new faculty members joined the ranks of the college in 1927. Miss Noby Ruth Denson, a cousin of superintendent Denson came from Bay Springs to begin a power-packed five-year tenure during which she made astonishing contributions in music, girls athletics, and the arts. Best of all, she created and kept a photographic record of those five

The College Club, pictured in October 1927, existed primarily to promote social events. The 70 students in the picture should all be freshmen or sophomore junior college students. Photo courtesy of Dixie Press of Gulfport.

years. Miss Zola Emerson arrived from Selma, Alabama, to teach history, remained for seven years, and decades later composed excellent and incisive pen sketches of the place and the people of her time. Miss Lillian Weinstein hired on to teach Latin, and for the first time in the history of the institution, Spanish. Miss Weinstein was also memorable because of her participation in the following incident described by Miss Zola Emerson 46 years later.

The faculty was well aware of Denson's overwhelming desire for recognition of his programs by the Southern Association of Colleges and Schools (SACS). Miss Emerson remembered, "I recall, an inspector for the Association came and was introduced to us at a faculty meeting shortly before lunch. He impressed me as being a pompous ass, but I noticed the Phi Beta Kappa key on the watch chain across his prominent bay window." Miss Minnie Pearson, who was beginning her second year as an English teacher at Perk, together with Miss Weinstein unbeknownst to Miss Emerson, shared both her assessment and her observation. At the afternoon meeting, Pearson, Weinstein, and Emerson returned with their Phi Beta Kappa keys "prominently displayed." Said Miss Emerson, "We were all in our early twenties, so we had a hard time suppressing our giggles at our unaccustomed display. Maybe we impressed the inspector. . . . Anyway, Perk became a member of the Association in short order."

In the *Daily Herald* of December 13, 1927, Denson announced that SACS had accepted the High School Department of the Perkinston institution as a member. He was proud of that, but he still had to win acceptance for the junior college department.

During the 1927 Christmas holidays Huff Hall was made available for boys who for one reason or another remained on campus. In 1927, Warren Heath and Ship Frantzen stayed in Huff for the holidays.

Ship Frantzen had returned for the session 1927-1928. After his graduation from the HSAHS four years prior, he had gone to Birmingham, Alabama, to work for his sister and brother-in-law in their dairy products store. When they sold the store, he had returned to the Coast to look after his mother and stepfather, and he entered the junior college. In Frantzen's words:

"Things were sort of tight and the depression was starting to come on. I had to find a place where I could live and eat, so believe it or not, the cheapest place that I could live was at Perk, so I went to school there because I could afford to pay my room and board there, and I had a job nobody wanted."

The Depression did start in the South before it started in the North. The job he had that nobody else

Fred Warren Heath (AHS Class of 1929) on the golf course in April 1999. Heath was then a resident of Baton Rouge, Louisiana.

Perk Students stand in front of Mack's Corner directly across the tracks from the college circa 1935. Mack McDonald owned the establishment. Photo from 1936 Perkolator p.52.

wanted was shoveling coal for Dad Warnell at the new campus Power House from 8 p.m. until midnight. At Christmas, Frantzen could get in a lot of extra hours because fewer students were there to work, and Dad Warnell always celebrated a lot at that time of year. The food was good, too. There was an oven fashioned of spare firebricks in one corner of the Power House. All one needed then was a pan, some lard, the blowtorch, and a neighborhood chicken or a fish from the pond located by the Power House.

The pond, which used to be far larger than it was in 2000, apparently came into being with the Power House as overflow from the well, the waters of which were pumped up the hill to the school water tower. E. B. Colmer had pressed this pond into service to raise fish as part of his agricultural program.

That Christmas, Ship received an invitation to the most memorable meal of his life. Years before when he had been a senior in the HSAHS, he had attended a field day and had seen there a young lady he had never forgotten. When he returned as a freshman in college in 1927, she had graduated from the HSJAHS in August and had entered as a freshman in the junior college, too. Her name was Etta V. Clayton. She invited Ship home for Christmas dinner. This was the beginning of a lifetime together.

Warren Heath went to another "dinner" that Christmas season that he clearly remembered in a 1997 interview. It all started at Mack's, "the home of the world's most delicious hamburger," according to many in 2000 who still remembered the little establishment that once stood in the curve of Old Highway 49 next to the Athletic Field. There Heath encountered a Perkinston student who invited him to a "chicken fry" to be held on a sand bar of Ten Mile Creek behind the Athletic Field that night. Another Perkinston student, who lived in the town, hearing the tail end of the conversation, asked if he could attend as well. The invitation was extended to this student, too, who shall be called "Bernard." Heath knew the basic scenario of the coming drama but he did not know who the actors would be. Bernard knew nothing.

The students gathered on that cold, clear, star-lit night by a blazing fire on the sand beside the swift icy waters of Ten Mile Creek. As those who had gone before them back to 1912, the boys waited until the cauldron boiled and bubbled and then dropped in those succulent chicken breasts, thighs, wings, and legs and settled back in anticipation of the feast.

Then came a voice saying, "I done told you boys about stealing my chickens!" The boom! boom! of a double-barreled shotgun followed this hearty remonstration. Bernard, without hesitation, leapt head long into the freezing creek, swam across, and clung to the cypress knees in the swamp on the other side. Much laughter on the part of the others present and cries that it was a joke failed to entice Bernard back to the sandbar. Heath, feeling the weight of responsibility wrought by guilt, had to go pull him back across the creek. As the two swimmers emerged, dripping wet, the disembodied voice once again swore vengeance on all chicken thieves. This was followed once again by twin gun flashes and loud booms. Bernard went back in the creek, but this time he went down it. Heath went after him and dragged him out a quarter mile down stream behind Charlie Swetman's house. Slipping through yards and crossing the railroad tracks, Heath escorted the shivering, terrified Bernard to Bernard's parent's house, and then Heath headed back to Huff Hall. As Heath stumbled into the room, bruised, hungry, and half-frozen, he found his roommate, Ship Frantzen, sitting in a chair. Heath opened the closet to get some dry clothes and saw a shot gun propped against the wall in the corner of the closet. He could smell burnt powder. He looked at Frantzen, who smiled back at him. Then Heath knew who the shooter had been.

Many "Bernards" in most colleges have fallen victim to variations of the Great Perkinston Chicken-Fry Shoot-Out of 1927. In more modern times, though, the theme of the tableau concerned "chicks" rather than chickens.

On Wednesday, May 23, 1928, the AHS graduated 53, and the junior college graduated ten. The junior college graduates were Julia Lewis of Stillmore, Ogden Lott of McHenry, Elizabeth Curriden of Ocean Springs, Virginia Switzer of McHenry, Eddie Dedeaux of Sellers, and Irene Flurry, Estelle "Bill" David, Laverna Ladner, Ruby Breeland, and Clyde Batson of Perkinston. The first four students on this list were members of the first freshman college class and were, for one reason or another, graduating a year later. Of the other six graduates, Miss Clyde Batson is notable because she was the first student to receive a diploma in piano from the junior college.

Under the terms of the 1928 Junior College Law, the Mississippi Legislature had removed the prohibition against state aid to junior colleges contained in the 1924 Junior College Law. On July 1, 1928, state authorities announced that $42,000 would be divided among ten junior colleges. Four of these, Raymond, Moorhead, Poplarville, and Perkinston were already offering two years of junior college work. The other six were offering one year with the second year to be added within two years. These were Goodman, Ellisville, Scooba, Senatobia, Carthage, and Mendenhall. Of these, Carthage (Leake County) operated until it later merged with East Central at Decatur, and Mendenhall (Simpson County) ceased operation after one year. Simpson County joined with Co-Lin in 1934.

The good news about state money set off another ambitious expansion program at Perkinston. The Board of Trustees met in Gulfport on July 3. The only item Denson had asked for in 1926 and not gotten in 1927 was a laundry. The laundry machinery appeared on the bid list for this meeting along with the call for bids of materials to repair Huff Hall, landscape and fence the campus, and construct a 1,400 foot long concrete tunnel for steam and hot water lines. A building committee of three, composed of C. J. Darby, C. C. Swetman, and C. O. Batson, set to work to draw up plans for a new administration building, a men's dormitory, a women's dormitory, a hospital, and several instructors' homes "in the near future." The reason cited for this new building program was heavy enrollment.

The enrollment figures for the school in the Denson era were often unintelligible. At the beginning of the previous session Denson had said he had a total of 262. The Board of Trustees had given out a figure of 202. Then at the beginning of the 1928-1929 session, the figure given for the past session was 316. The list of names printed in the official roster of enrollment for that year totaled exactly 300 regular students and seven special students.

The school calendar for the coming 1928-1929 session contained for the first known time the official use of the word "semester." This word may have been used a year or even two years earlier, but those calendars were not in the MGCCC Archives Collection in 2000. Each semester contained three six-week terms. The third term test was to be given Friday, January 11, 1929. This was to be followed by first semester examinations on Thursday, January 25 and Friday, January 26. On Friday, May 24 the sixth term test would be given and then followed on Thursday, May 30, and Friday, May 31, with "second semester examinations." Since "Graduation Exercises" were slotted for 8 p.m. on May 31, the last day of "Second Semester Examinations" must have been a thrilling cliff hanger of an experience for teachers, records clerks, possible graduates, and their families.

The August 23, 1928, *Daily Herald* in announcing the opening of the 1928-1929 session described certain members of the faculty as "department heads." This was not the first time the term "department head" had been used in the paper, but it was the first time it was used a lot. Miss Zola Emerson was described as "head of the department of history at Perkinston." W. G. Gregory was described as "head of the department of mathematics at Perkinston Junior College." Several others in various disciplines were also described as "department heads." These teachers were not described as such in the official *Announcements* for this year, so it is not clear whether or not these were official titles, but it certainly indicated the currency of the term in popular usage. For the first known time in the *Announcements* though, Jane Fahnestock was listed under "Officers of Administration" as a dietician instead of a matron.

When the session 1928-1929 opened on September 10, 1928, the 9th grade had been dropped from the HSJAHS's offerings by order of the Board of Trustees for the purpose of easing congestion in the dormitories. This decision, having been advertised for nine months, enabled the Perkinston Consolidated School in the town to add the 9th grade so that local students would not suffer.

In September 1928, the Board was considering dropping the 10th grade to further reduce the strain on the facilities. In addition, Board members began meeting with the supervisors of the three counties to secure funds for the new building program.

At the meeting of the Board of Trustees held in Gulfport on November 13, 1928, the push for a new administration building began in earnest. To quote the minutes, "Collins and Norwood were employed as architects, Vincent Smith as consulting architect, and W. F. Harkness as supervising architect." The *Daily Herald* issued a report on that meeting on the date it was held stating that "An average of 250 students are in attendance at the institution at the present time and many more could be secured if there were room to

The new administration building was showcased on Perkinston's first homecoming day, November 23, 1929. On May 14, 1960, the structure was named Denson Hall in honor of Superintendent Jefferson Lee Denson. At the close of the 20th century, Denson was the only person for whom two buildings on the Perkinston Campus had been named. "Old" Denson Administration Building was condemned in 1971. "New" Denson classroom building across the Quadrangle was dedicated on April 29, 1972. Photo courtesy of Elizabeth Brash of Gulfport Printing Company.

care for them at the school."

Sketches of the new administration building were received and accepted at the January 8, 1929, meeting of the Board. Also at this meeting, bids were ordered to be let and accepted up to 10:00 a.m. on February 5, the next regular Board meeting. On February 5 the low bid for the general contract work went to John McDonald and Sons. Construction began within a month. The source of the bricks for the building was never specifically stated, but likely the bricks came from the six-month old Perkinston Brick Works founded by the Dedeaux family and others south of the Ten Mile Creek Bridge just below the town of Perkinston.

The ready availability of bricks from a yard less than a mile away resulted in other brick structures on the campus. The March 7 Board minutes contained an order “that the Hi-Y Boys be allowed to build a brick building for a Hi-Y."

In a speech to the Gulfport Kiwanians on Wednesday, March 22, 1929, Denson stated some facts and figures summing up the Tri-County School's rapid growth during his tenure. He said that upon completion of the new administration building the worth of the school plant would aggregate half a million dollars. Harrison County owned 83 percent of the plant, Stone County owned 17 percent, and Jackson County owned nothing. "But," continued Denson, "the 1928 Junior College Law would enable Jackson County to contribute to the building fund and receive pro rata ownership in the physical plant." In the 1928-1929 session, according to Denson, the school had served 252 students (yet a different figure from any others given). Those from Harrison had totaled 116 (32 college and 84 AHS); the students from Stone had totaled 95 (41 college and 54 AHS), and the students from Jackson County had totaled 41 (13 college and 29 AHS). The cost per student per year at the institution came to $131. Because of the pro rata ownership of the school plant, Harrison paid $57 out of county funds for each of its students while Stone paid $76 and Jackson $88. The balance came from the state and the student.

The next day Denson hit the Gulfport Rotarians on another front. The school's new emphasis on dairy farming in southern Mississippi had resulted in his declaration of war on ticks. In his words, "tick eradication is essential to dairying and dairying is essential to the agricultural development of South Mississippi." "Therefore," continued Denson with typical flamboyancy, "we expect to have every tick dead by January 1, 1930."

Denson's team did not take the "Big Loving Cup" in the MAJC State Junior College Field Meet held in Moorhead on May 10, 1929, but the Perkinston students did take eight first place trophies: Etta V. Clayton in organic chemistry, Vernon Robertson in English grammar, Mrs. Ethel Parsons in composition, Lamont Smith in trigonometry, Velma Hill in expression, Laverne "Jane" Denson (the superintendent's daughter) and Margurite Holleman in piano ensemble, and the Perkinston Little Theater group in theater. Zola Emerson and Minnie Kay Pearson directed the theatrical victory.

On May 31, 1929, the school graduated its largest class in history. The HSJAHS awarded 48 diplomas, and the HSJJC awarded 28 certificates.

On July 23, 1929, the *Daily Herald* reported that in the absence of Denson, E. B. Colmer was in charge of the 75 students in the summer school at Perkinston. Colmer said he expected Denson to return in a week or ten days.

On August 8, Denson attended the Board of Trustees meeting in Gulfport and submitted a "Report . . . on his work and trip for the past summer." He also submitted his list of teachers and their salaries for the coming year. He then read to the Board a number of bills he had prepared for Governor Bilbo to have introduced into the legislature. The Board instructed him to travel to Jackson and "undertake to secure the passage of the . . . legislation." The Board next authorized the building committee to inspect the new administration building then in the process of construction for the purpose of suggesting to the contractor any alternation or additions. Then the board adjourned.

Twelve days later on Tuesday, August 20, 1929, the following item appeared in the *Daily Herald*:

"J. L. Denson, superintendent for five years of the Harrison-Stone-Jackson Counties Agricultural High School and Junior College at Perkinston tendered his resignation to the board of trustees last night, effective at the terms of the contract held by Denson or at the discretion of the board.

"During the five years and two months in which Prof. Denson has headed this school it has grown from a high school whose credits were accepted with reservations even by the state of Mississippi to a fully accredited high school accepted by the All Southern Association of Secondary Schools; has added two years of standard college work for which application has been made for recognition by the association; has increased its enrollment from 110 to 387 last year, and has expanded a plant worth approximately $200,000 to one which will be valued at about $600,000 when new construction is completed.

"This morning Prof. Denson said he had no statement to make regarding his action in resigning nor his future connections."

On Monday night, September 2, while enroute from Lucedale back to Perkinston with his wife, Denson drove his Dodge Sedan down to the ferry landing on the Pascagoula River. Not noticing that the ferry flat was on the other bank, he drove the car off into the river and sank in 15 feet of water. Both he and Mrs. Denson managed to get out of the car and make their way to the bank. At least two other cars in earlier years had driven into the river at the same place.

Despite his frightening experience, Denson made it to Gulfport on Thursday, September 5, 1929, for his last Board Meeting as superintendent. The minutes of the meeting put it succinctly, "Prof. Denson's resignation was received and accepted. Ordered that a committee be appointed to draft Resolutions of Appreciation of his interest and work in the school during his supervision of the school." Superintendent Denson's brother, Coach W. C. "Bill" Denson, obviously had already resigned because at this meeting the board elected Lee Roy Weeks as instructor of athletics and physics to replace him.

Before the meeting adjourned, the Board members appointed Cooper J. Darby to succeed Denson. The Board offered Darby a salary of $4,800 (a sum $1,200 more than Denson had earned.) Darby asked for time to think. Denson agreed to stay in office until September 23. Then Denson turned over his books along with the letter from auditor James O. Jones stating that the books were all in order from 1924-1929.

On Saturday, September 7, Darby agreed to accept the position as superintendent of the HSJAHS & JC. He said, though, he would have to remain Harrison County superintendent of education until September 23 to give the county time to find a replacement.

Both Denson and Darby attended the opening day at Perkinston on September 9. Classes began on September 10 with approximately 157 students. The new administration building, the last structure of the Denson era, was completed by that time.

When Denson first came to the campus only three major buildings stood on the crown of Perk Hill. In five short years, Denson renovated all those, adding annexes to two of them, then marched down the hill to the railroad with six new major brick structures, which tripled the size of the campus and created the Quadrangle that still existed in 2000.

Denson was the first chief executive of the Perkinston institution who had the right to bear the name "president," but he never did. Not once did any contemporary newspaper article refer to him other than as "superintendent" or "Mr." and most often as "Prof." As Ship Frantzen put it, "All the men at the school had the same first name--'Prof'."

According to *The Mississippi Junior College Story: 1922-1972* by James B. Young and James M. Ewing, the term "president" did not come into vogue until after the 1928 Junior College Law was passed. Apparently the appellation did not come into vogue at Perkinston for a dozen years after 1928.

Denson, in addition to being the prime mover and builder of the Harrison-Stone-Jackson Junior College, had an impact on junior colleges in the state as a whole and in the nation at large. At the fourth meeting of the Mississippi Junior College Commission held on February 7, 1929, Denson articulated the motion to accept the "zones" (later called districts) and the standards for those zones proposed by State Junior College Commissioner Knox M. Broom. The state of Mississippi was therefore divided into 14 zones wherein only one institution, usually an AHS, meeting very high standards could form into a junior college. Because of such planning only the very best and strongest institutions survived to evolve into the first state system of junior colleges in the nation. Other states such as Illinois had older junior colleges and California had more, but these and other states had collections of junior colleges. Only Mississippi, by zoning such institutions, insured a "systematic" geographical distribution that made educational opportunities accessible to practically every student in the state.

Denson was one of those pioneer junior college men who developed county agricultural high schools into junior colleges in eleven zones by 1929. These were in order of establishment by year in the fall of which they offered the first year of junior college work,

1921 Pearl River at Poplarville
1922 Hinds at Raymond
1925 Harrison-Stone-Jackson at Perkinston
1925 Holmes at Goodman
1926 Sunflower at Moorhead
1927 Kemper at Scooba
1927 Jones at Ellisville
1927 Tate at Senatobia
1928 Copiah-Lincoln at Wesson
1928 Newton at Decatur
1929 Pike at Summit

All eleven of these county agricultural high schools had begun their offering of the first year of college work by September 23, 1929, when Denson left the profession. No more county AHSs would develop into junior colleges for eighteen years after 1929. Meridian did, however, develop a unique municipal junior college in 1937.

Denson's dream of achieving Southern Association of Colleges and Schools accreditation for his junior college was realized two months after he resigned. Only two others of the original eleven had achieved that benchmark by 1929. Pearl River achieved it in 1929, and Hinds had achieved it in 1928.

Denson had taken charge of the three-building campus of the Harrison-Stone Agricultural High School in 1924, but he departed from the ten-building campus of the Harrison-Stone-Jackson AHS and Junior College in 1929. True, he did most of it on borrowed money and his successor, Cooper J. Darby, had to pay off the then staggering debt of $98,000 that Denson left in his wake. But Perkinston benefited both from Denson's profligacy and Darby's parsimony. Fiscally speaking, Denson was a flamboyant Roaring 20s promoter and Darby was a no-nonsense Great Depression accountant. "But," as Mississippi Gulf Coast Junior College President J. J. Hayden rhetorically asked in an interview 40 years later, "If Denson had not built in the 20s how would Darby have handled the high enrollment of the 30s?"

Darby did not agree with Denson's methods or his results, but in a letter written on February 23, 1973, Darby paid Denson a number of compliments, backhanded though some of them were. Darby summed up Denson thusly,

"Denson was the arch politician of the junior college men and cared very little about hard facts and logic, but devoted his tireless energies in trying to develop an impressive image and promoting the men or the cause which he happened to espouse for the sake of expediency. . . . He never allowed his lack of logic to disturb his composure. Even so, Denson had valuable qualities worth noting. He had abundant energy and copious buoyant enthusiasm. He was an incurable promoter who never knew when he was whipped.

"Denson left Perkinston . . . but he borrowed money, went to the University of Colorado, and took courses in agricultural extension work. Governor Bilbo tried to make him Director of Extension in Mississippi but the effort was blocked by some means through the Federal Government which participated in the cost of such work. Denson then . . . started selling life insurance without money to buy a solid meal. He struggled to the top . . . of his company. [He] died of a heart attack on the banks of the Pascagoula River while on a fishing trip. I venture the guess that he had just finished a hearty laugh at some joke."

Miss Zola Emerson, who taught history during the last years of Denson and the first years of Darby, paid both men the highest compliment possible from a teacher's point of view in a letter dated June 18, 1973.

"J. L. Denson and Cooper J. Darby were superintendents during my 1927-1935 career at Perkinston. Both strong and capable administrators--but very different in personality--who attended to administering, selected good faculty, and left teaching up to faculty. No lesson plans, no interference with one's way of teaching or with teacher-pupil relationships. (Otherwise I would have looked elsewhere for a teaching job, thoroughly enjoyed 8 years there; left only because salaries going down--from $150 a month to $135 when I left for a job in Washington.)"

Emerson never forgot Denson or Darby or Perk. Forty years after she departed, she established, in memory of her mother, the Sarah Bailey Emerson Scholarship-Loan Fund for graduates of Gulf Coast wishing to attend senior college. Prior to her death in Alexandria, Virginia, on July 3, 1989, at the age of 84, she contributed thousands of dollars to this fund.

Students sit on the bridge over Perk Pond circa 1938. The artesian well pump house is at center on the peninsula in front of the brick Power House, which began operation in September 1927. Harrison Hall is at right up the hill. Student ten-cent-per-hour labor gangs dug the pond, built the bridge, and hand-carried the bricks to the masons who built the Power House. The Power House supplied electricity via electric lines to the campus and the community and pumped cold water via an underground aqueduct to the water tank on top of Perk Hill. Hot water and steam heat was supplied to campus structures via pipes laid in tunnels leading from the Power House to each building. Rural Electrification Administration (REA) power lines reached the school in late 1941, but the Power House continued to supply heat and water to the campus until June 1957, when the Board of Trustees mandated a policy of individual heating for campus buildings. The Power House was destroyed and most of Perk Pond filled in 1959 to provide a site for Hinton Hall. A new road was built on the east side of the pond at the same time to provide a new main entrance to the campus and which remained the main entrance in 2000.

"Dad," "Runt," the Power House, and the Warnell Medal

Newman Asa Warnell, born in Savannah, Georgia, in July 1870, was the engineer of the school and had charge of the Power House. He was one of those rare people described as a "real character" by everyone who knew him, and for at least eighteen years beginning in 1924 every boy who worked his way through school did know him. Although his given name was Newman, his peers called him "Warnell," and the boys who worked for him called him "Dad" or "Dad Warnell." He was a rough-edged, thick-set, bull-necked man, and according to Warren Heath, one of his student workers in the late 1920s, he had a "mustache, no teeth, chewed tobacco, and was very intelligent." Ship Frantzen, another of his charges and a contemporary of Heath's, recalled "Dad's fondness for white lightning most any time but particularly on the Fourth of July and at Christmas." All who knew him agreed that he wrote the most beautiful hand in the region. He inscribed nearly all the AHS and junior college diplomas of his time.

Dad's wife had died and he had sole charge of his son, Newman, who was known to all as "Runt." Runt entered the 9th grade at the AHS in September 1924, which is almost certainly when Dad and Runt came to Perkinston. Runt gave his hometown as Barth, which was a "boom and bust" sawmill town in east Pearl River County. Dad had dealt with steam engines, mainly in relation to railroads, all his working life, and his arrival at Perkinston neatly coincided with the purchase of a 60-horse-power 13,000-pound boiler installed for the purpose of steam heating the buildings of the AHS.

To Merrill "Red" True, a high school freshman in 1930, 20-year-old Runt Warnell, a junior college football star, was his idol. In describing Runt, True compared him to "Hulk Hogan the wrestler." He said Runt was a body builder with a thick neck and huge chest and legs with such over-developed calves that when he ran, his legs did not bend and the soles of his feet struck flat on the ground.

After he graduated in 1932, Runt joined the Marine Corps. According to the *Stone County Enterprise* of November 29, 1934, Runt's badly bruised body had been found beside the highway near Quantico, Virginia. Runt had been enroute to the U. S. Marine base there when he died. Foul play was suspected and a suspect arrested. Runt was buried in the Perkinston Cemetery under a government marker that reads:

Newman
Bradley
Warnell
Pvt.
U. S. Marine Corps.
July 17, 1910
Nov. 18, 1934

At graduation in May 1935, Dad Warnell presented the first Newman Bradley Warnell Memorial Award or "Warnell Medal" in honor of his son. In broad strokes at least, the Newman Warnell Memorial Award presaged the Sam Owen Award which began in 1956 and continued in 2000. Both Dad Warnell and Sam Owen wished to recognize outstanding service to the college, but the Sam Owen Award was open to anyone with any connection to the college and not restricted to students and former students as was the Warnell Medal. The last Warnell Medal was given at graduation in May 1941. Dad Warnell died August 4, 1944, and was buried in an unmarked grave next to Runt.

(Above) Students unloading coal for the Power Plant. 1938 Perkolator p. 46.

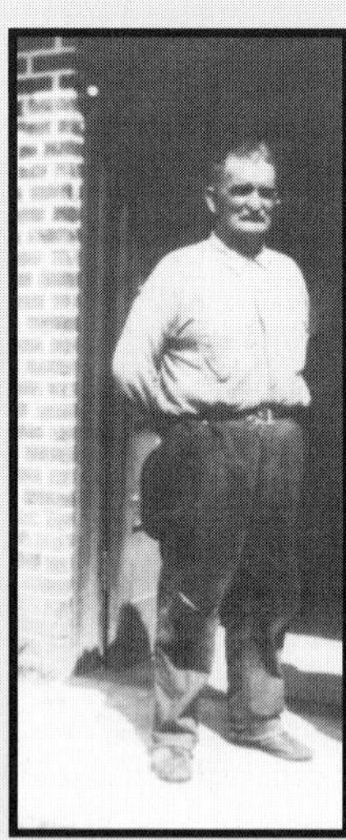

(Left) N. A. "Dad" Warnell, campus engineer 1924 to about 1942 stands in the Power House doorway. Photo courtesy of Lydean (David) Davis.

The Warnell Medal is 7/8 inch in diameter and reads: "Warnell Memorial Award for Outstanding Service, 1940." This particular medal was awarded to Hammond "Tom" Davis, husband of Lydean (David) Davis.

Newman Bradley "Runt" Warnell

The Power House boilers. The plates on each boiler read, "The Casey-Hedges Co., Chattanooga, Tenn. Harrison-Stone-Jackson Agricultural High School and Junior College, 1927." Merrill "Red" True, (above in baseball uniform) an AHS and JC student from 1930 to 1937, came to know these boilers very well. Coal from rail cars (above right) on the sidetrack of the Illinois Central Railroad in front of the Power House was transported by truck to the coal hoppers in the Power House. The boiler on the right was a "self feeder," but the left one was supplied with coal by a student with a shovel. Each boiler contained 70 horizontal tubes each 18 feet long and four inches in diameter. These had to be cleaned by a student standing on a saw horse scaffold. The student pushed a 19-foot-long wire brush through each tube and stood enveloped in a cloud of black coal dust the whole time. True worked his way through both high school and junior college at the Power House on the 2 a.m. to 6 a.m. shift.

DARBY AND THE DEPRESSION SEPT. 1929 - AUG. 1941

The Harrison-Stone-Jackson Agricultural High School and Junior College Board of Trustees by unanimous vote appointed Cooper J. Darby as superintendent of the school on September 5, 1929, and fixed his salary at $4,800 per year. Darby, then in his second term as Harrison County superintendent of education, notified the Harrison County Board of Supervisors that he would continue to serve in his current position until September 23, by which time a replacement had to be found. Darby and Denson shared joint control of the school until September 23, when Darby officially assumed his duties at Perkinston.

The culmination of Denson's superintendency came just over ten weeks after his departure. Though Darby held the reins of power when it happened, Denson deserved the credit. On December 11, 1929, the Southern Association of Colleges and Schools (SACS) welcomed the junior college at Perkinston into its ranks as a fully accredited institution. On the same day SACS also extended full accreditation to Pearl River County Junior College at Poplarville and the Mississippi State Teachers College at Hattiesburg.

Although they were both products of rural Mississippi, Denson and Darby developed very differently. Whereas Denson had been a flamboyant promoter and builder, Darby was far more conservative. Oddly enough, Perkinston needed each of them at the precise time it got them. Denson built the college in the Roaring 20s. Darby saved the school in the Great Depression.

In the closing years of the 19th century, Darby's parents, Henry Clark Darby and Martha Ann (Johnston), Darby lived on a homestead near Perryville about four miles south of Perkinston. Cooper was born January 26, 1896, at Purvis, the home of his maternal grandparents, because his mother had gone to her parents in order to be near a hospital. As soon as she was able to travel, Mrs. Darby took the new baby, her fifth and last child, back to Perryville.

Henry Clark Darby died when his youngest son was aged 12, leaving little behind to sustain his family after a life in rural school teaching and logging. Young Cooper had to work to support the family, but his mother never let him give up on his schooling because she saw it as his only way out of poverty. The early burden of responsibility, coupled with a strict Baptist upbringing, produced a man both straight-laced and resolute but not entirely humorless in his view of life.

He managed to finish in the local three-teacher school that went to the 10th grade. In 1914 he enrolled in the Mississippi Normal College at Hattiesburg in a summer institute and obtained a teacher's license. He then began a life of teaching in rural schools in the piney woods while attending the Mississippi Normal College in the summers.

Cooper J. Darby as he appeared in the 1939 Perkolator. The caption under the photograph referred to him as "President," a title used intermittently only in his last two years at Perk. The writer of the 1939 caption, in recalling Darby's initial session (1929-1930) as head of the school, stated, "In the spring of 1930 several important experiences came in rapid succession. Within the space of a little less than thirty days he experienced a bank failure where the school had its funds, conducted his first graduating exercises at the junior college, had an operation for appendicitis, and was married to Miss Grace Quarles of Long Beach, Mississippi." Photo from 1939 Perkolator, p. 15.

In 1918 he enlisted in the United States Army and traveled with ten other young men from Harrison County to Camp Mabry, Texas. In summing up his brief military career, he later recalled, "I kept every German out of Camp Mabry for thirty-one days. [Then] the old Kaiser heard I was coming and surrendered."

A civilian once again, Darby continued as before to alternate teaching and study. In 1923 he ran for the position of superintendent of Harrison County schools and won. Taking office in January 1924, he became a member of the Board of Trustees of the Harrison-Stone Agricultural High School by virtue of his office. He remained in this position throughout the balance of the 1920s, helping to guide the Perkinston institution in its evolution into a junior college.

Meanwhile, Mississippi Normal College had evolved into State Teacher's College, and by transferring his summer credits from Peabody and Tulane to the Hattiesburg institution, Darby secured his B.S. degree in 1928. Recalling that achievement from the perspective of half a century, Darby quipped, "I frequently remark on how brilliant I was. It didn't take me but fourteen years to get a B.S. degree."

Armed with this new degree, Darby was in the position to accept the appointment as superintendent at Perkinston when

Denson resigned. Even though he had served on the college Board of Trustees throughout the Denson era, Darby did not know the financial condition of the school. He recalled, "I got up there and found the school was about ninety-eight thousand in debt. That was a whale of a debt in those days."

As far as Darby could ascertain, wealthy lumbermen at the behest of Governor Bilbo had loaned the money to Denson and the Board because Denson was a Bilbo supporter. Darby was not a Bilbo man. In Darby's words, the lenders "were very much concerned about that debt." There being no legal authority to make such loans, Darby observed, "I think . . . the debt could have been repudiated but it was an honest, actually a moral debt . . . and it expanded the facilities of the institution."

While he considered Denson to be, in his words, "kind of a heedless spendthrift," Darby agreed with the Trustees that an honest debt should be paid. Therefore, Darby and the Trustees petitioned the state legislature to validate the debt, which it did. So, at the onset of the Great Depression, Darby set forth to pay off Denson's building program. He continued to do so in the face of tremendous cuts in state and county appropriations, which ironically coincided with rising enrollments.

Darby assumed the office of superintendent at Perkinston five weeks before the stock market crash of October 1929 detonated the Great Depression, and he resigned three and one half months before the Japanese attack on Pearl Harbor primed the war-fueled economic pump which ended it. By the time he departed, the college debt stood at only $10,000.

Zola Emerson, who taught history for Darby during the Depression, remembered him fondly forty years later:

> "Cooper J. Darby managed finances so successfully that he should have become a Wall Street financier. Perk was one of the few places in Mississippi or Alabama where teachers were paid regularly by checks convertible into money and not in script during the depression years."

She recalled also that only in 1933, when all banks were closed, did the checks stop coming. When the banks reopened, the checks resumed.

In February 1931, the faculty volunteered to take salary cuts of ten per cent. In April 1932, Darby and the Board cut teacher contracts from twelve to nine months and then reduced the nine month salaries ten per cent. When yet another ten percent salary cut, proposed in May 1934, threatened Emerson's $135 per month salary, she sought better paid work in Washington, D.C. She left with regret and

Front view of the Darby-era campus in December 1937. The south end of Harrison Hall, completed in November, is located uphill from the Power House. Bennett Hall crowns Perk Hill, and the original cypress water tank stands on a tower to the right of Bennett behind Huff Hall. Photo courtesy of Elizabeth Brash of Gulfport Printing Company.

The façade of Harrison Hall shortly after the structure was completed in November 1937. Harrison Hall remained the premiere women's dormitory at Perk until the completion of Andrews Hall in August 1979. In 1982 Harrison was converted to a men's dorm. Photo from 1938 Perkolator, p. 9.

without rancor. She and all the other faculty members knew that Darby had taken substantial cuts in his pay. He had not asked of them anything he was not himself willing to do.

Oddly enough, Darby left Perkinston for the same reason Emerson did--low pay. He had married Grace Quarles of Long Beach in June 1930, at the close of his first year as superintendent. In time they had one child, Joyce. Darby had never forgotten the struggle facing his family at the death of his father, and he had no intention of leaving his wife and daughter destitute. There being no Mississippi teacher's retirement program at the time and unable to save money from his salary, Darby felt he could not afford to remain. In his words, "I left Perkinston . . . not because I didn't like it, I loved it. . . . I left largely in order to make a little more money . . . and I did make much better." He took leave to make the race for the position of Chancery Clerk of Harrison County in the summer of 1941. He won the race and held that office until his retirement in January 1972. Darby died February 8, 1983.

Darby's Building Program

During his twelve-year tenure at Perkinston, Darby initiated the construction of only one major building, but it was the largest structure yet built on the campus. Rising enrollments in the mid-1930s caused Darby and the Board of Trustees to consider building a new woman's dormitory. With funding and labor made available through the Works Progress Administration (WPA) and the Public Works Administration (PWA) together with a bond issue in Harrison and Stone Counties, the new women's dormitory rose on the Quadrangle opposite Denson Hall.

Darby wanted to name the edifice "Pat Harrison Hall" because that congressman had done so much to secure the WPA and PWA funding for it. But, remembered Darby, "We had some trustees that weren't too favorable to Pat Harrison . . . . So, we had to call it Harrison Hall, [not saying] whether it meant Harrison County or Pat Harrison." The dedication of 62-room Harrison Hall was held in conjunction with homecoming on October 30, 1937, but actual occupancy was not approved until November 20.

Two women study in a typical room in Harrison Hall shortly after the dormitory began service. Photo from 1938 Perkolator p. 9.

One month before Harrison Hall opened, Darby and the board accepted bids on a new 25,000-gallon steel water tank and tower to replace the original cypress tank and steel tower. The new tower, constructed by R. D. Cole Manufacturing company of Newman, Georgia, was completed in March 1938. The board ordered the destruction of the old cypress tank as a "menace" to the campus in December of that year.

Aside from Harrison Hall and the water tower, new structures in the Darby era were limited to a few faculty houses. On the other hand several buildings of the Denson era were renovated and improved or even added to. One of Darby's

Front view of the Darby-era campus in March 1938 showing the newly completed steel water tower located between Bennett Hall and Huff Hall. The school's original cypress water tank and tower, which remained standing until removed in December 1938, is visible behind Huff Hall. The steel water tower in this photograph, which was completed in March 1938, dominated the skyline of the campus first beside Bennett Hall and later behind Dees Hall for 60 years. Workers began dismantling the 1938 tank and tower on August 28, 1998, and completed the job four days later. A new "golf ball and tee" style tower located in the field behind Dees Hall began service a couple of months earlier.

last acts was to build an addition to the Old Gym "of sheet metal in imitation of brick." This storeroom, which still existed in 2000, provided a place for athletic equipment, which freed space in the Denson Administration Building to expand the bookstore.

If Darby built few structures, he certainly improved the infrastructure of the campus. All the campus buildings were connected to a centralized steam heating plant, the campus was beautified, an "artistic sign" placed at its entrance, and the streets about the Quadrangle were paved. Darby also added concrete tennis courts on the Quadrangle across from the Old Gym and a nine-hole golf course northwest of the barn.

Darby also replicated a Denson-era building. The large barn built in 1925 (to replace the 1914-era barn destroyed by lightning) fell victim to spontaneous combustion on the morning of February 13, 1936. By mid-August, Darby had replaced it with a near perfect copy for less than $100 over the insurance collected. Furthermore, in 1941, he built a small concrete block dairy barn next to the large barn in order to sell surplus milk to "concerns supplying the soldiers at Camp Shelby." Darby's successor later built additions to both ends of the dairy barn to create the Dairy and Pasteurizing Plant Building in January 1953.

Looking back over his tenure, Darby estimated that he spent about $150,000 in buildings and revamping the campus. Then he added, "that was a whole lot of money in the depression days."

If Darby had remained at Perkinston he would have built more new structures. In June 1940, he and the board announced their intentions to seek a bond issue to build a new two-story apartment building and a new two-story combination dining hall and science hall. No action was taken on the project. These two new proposed structures would remain on hold until after the Second World War.

George County Joins the District:

A change in titles (superintendent to president) and a change in names (Harrison-Stone-Jackson Junior College to Perkinston Junior College)

Perkinston Minute Book 3, p. 12, October 3, 1934.

"Supt. Darby reported to the Board that he had just visited the Board of Supervisors and County Superintendent of Education of George County and that the Board of Supervisors and Superintendent were interested in the proposition of joining in the operation of the college but that no definite action had been taken. After considerable discussion pro and con, it was ordered that the Board of Trustees go on record as favoring George County's joining in the operation of the college as provided by law."

Perkinston Minute Book 3, p. 48, September 4, 1935.

"Supt. Darby reported that George County Board of Supervisors had indicated a desire to join in the operation of the college by appropriating one mill for the maintenance and operation of the school with the understanding that they would be represented on this Board of Trustees by one member, the County Superintendent of Education. . . . "

The Perkinston Board then passed a lengthy official resolution inviting George County to join with Harrison, Stone, and Jackson Counties in support of the school, but George County officials, for whatever reason, took no action.

Perkinston Minute Book 4, p. 175; October 15, 1941.

"The Superintendent [A. L. May] reported that the County School Board and Board of Supervisors of George County, by unanimous vote of both bodies, had expressed a desire to join the Harrison-Stone-Jackson Agricultural High School-Junior College and cooperate in the maintenance of it, and that one-half mill had been levied on all the property of George County by the Board of Supervisors for the support of the school for 1941, and that it was the intention of the Board of Supervisors of George County to levy one mill for 1942 and hereafter.
Motion was made by Mr. T. W. Lott and seconded by Mr. D. D. O'Neal. . . .
Motion was carried.
It is hereby understood by the Board of Trustees that George County is to have representation on this Board by the County Superintendent of Education and one other member, elected by the Board of Supervisors (Section 6678, Chapter 163, Mississippi Code of 1930)."

Perkinston Minute Book 4, p. 177; November 7, 1941.

"President Vinson Smith extended welcome to the George County Trustees, Mr. M. A. Eubanks and Mr. M. L. Malone." Maurice L. Malone was then Chancery Clerk of George County. Malone had been elected to his Trustee post by the George County Board of Supervisors. M. A. Eubanks, then current George County Superintendent of Education, was an ex-officio Trustee by virtue of his office. His first act at his initial Trustee's meeting was to second the motion changing A. L. May's official title from that of "Superintendent of Harrison-Stone-Jackson Agricultural High School and Junior College" to that of President of the Harrison-Stone-Jackson Agricultural High School and Junior College.

"Motion was made by Mr. H. P. Heidelberg and seconded by Mr. M. A. Eubanks that the head of the junior college be designated as President.
Motion carried."

Perkinston Minute Book 4, p. 195; April 15, 1942.

"The following resolution was unanimously passed by the Board:
WHEREAS, the name of the school has heretofore been known as Harrison-Stone-Jackson Agricultural High School and Junior College, and
WHEREAS, George County has levied a tax for the support of the institution and has joined in with the other three counties in completing the region as zoned by the State Department of Education for junior colleges of the State, and
WHEREAS, adding another county to the name would prove to be too long, and
WHEREAS, the school is generally known by students, alumni, and the general public as Perkinston Junior College;
NOW, THEREFORE, BE IT RESOLVED that the name of the institution be changed from Harrison-Stone-Jackson Agricultural High School and Junior College to Perkinston Agricultural High School and Junior College, and that this action will become effective after the Boards of Supervisors of the four counties approve the action of the Board of Trustees by resolutions of their action which will be spread on the minutes of the Board of Trustees."

Author's Note: This resolution will hereinafter be styled "The Perkinston Agricultural High School & Junior College Resolution of April 15, 1942."

Jackson County Board of Supervisors, Minute Book 19; p. 206.

"The Perkinston AHS and JC resolution of April 15, 1942, was spread upon the minutes of the Jackson County Board of Supervisors on May 4, 1942 along with the order to change the name of the school."

Clarion Ledger (Jackson) newspaper, May 12, 1942.

"Supervisors Authorize Name Change at Perk. The board of supervisors of Jackson County adopted a resolution authorizing the changing of the name of the Harrison-Stone-Jackson Agricultural High School and Junior College to Perkinston Agricultural High School and Junior College at their regular monthly meeting on May 4."

With this information reaching newspapers as far distant as Jackson, what prevented the Perkinston board from knowing that the Jackson County Board of Supervisors had authorized the name change?

Perkinston Minute Book 4, p. 199; May 13, 1942.

"A report was made on the change of the name of the school. All Boards of Supervisors had responded except Jackson County. On the suggestion of the Board of Supervisors of Harrison County, motion was made by Mr. D. E. Smith and seconded by Mr. J. H. Breland to suggest to the Boards of Supervisors of the four counties that the name of the school be changed to Perkinston Junior College. Motion carried."

Once again the Trustees promulgated the Perkinston Agricultural High School and Junior College Resolution of April 15, 1942, and once again ordered it "forwarded to the four Boards of Supervisors."

In this same May 13, 1942, meeting, the Trustees let the bid for publishing the bulletin for the coming session to begin September 7, 1942. The advertisement of the bid passed in the April meeting had specified that the cover of the bulletin carry the name "Harrison-Stone-Jackson Junior College." The bid was let to the Advertiser Publishing Company to print 1,500 copies of said bulletin.

Jackson County Board of Supervisors Minute Book 4, pp. 222-223; June 1, 1942.

The Jackson County Board of Supervisors spread the Perkinston AHS and JC Resolution on its minutes again and again approved it and again ordered the Perkinston Trustees to change the name of the school.

Perkinston Minute Book 4, p. 206; June 10, 1942.

"The President reported that all of the counties except Jackson County had reported favorably on the resolution, changing the name of the school from Harrison-Stone-Jackson Agricultural High School and Junior College to Perkinston Junior College."

Perkinston Minute book 4, p. 214; July 15, 1942.

"WHEREAS, the Board of Supervisors of Harrison, Stone, Jackson, and George Counties have passed resolution approving the proposal of the Board of Trustees to change the name of the school from Harrison-Stone-Jackson Agricultural High School and Junior College to Perkinston Junior College and have been certified to by chancery clerks of the Boards of Supervisors,
NOW, THEREFORE BE IT RESOLVED that the name of the institution be changed from Harrison-Stone-Jackson Agricultural High School and Junior College to Perkinston Junior College and that this action will take effect and be in force from and after its passage, July 15, 1942."

Perhaps the key to the riddle of the three-month long hassle to effect the name change lies in the statement above, to wit, "and have been certified to by the chancery clerks of the Boards of Supervisors." Perhaps the Jackson County chancery clerk failed to send a certified copy of the Jackson County Board of Supervisors' name change order until July. Be that as it may, Harrison-Stone-Jackson Agricultural High School and Junior College officially became Perkinston Agricultural High School and Junior College on July 15, 1942. On that day for the first time, the Board secretary recorded the minutes as those of "a meeting of the Board of Trustees of Perkinston Junior College."

Fortunately somebody notified the Advertiser Publishing Company in time to change the name of the school on the bulletin because the session *1942-1943 Bulletin* title page gives the name of the institution as Perkinston Junior College.

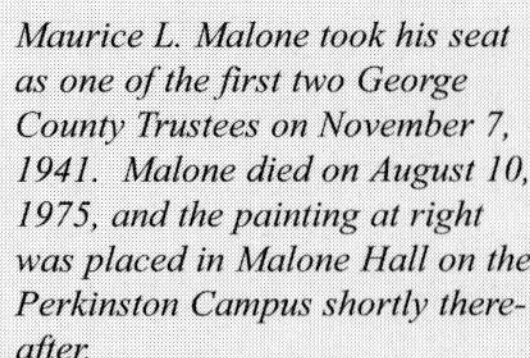

Maurice L. Malone took his seat as one of the first two George County Trustees on November 7, 1941. Malone died on August 10, 1975, and the painting at right was placed in Malone Hall on the Perkinston Campus shortly thereafter.

Albert Louis May Sr.

A. L. May was born August 22, 1892, one of the eight children (three sons and five daughters) of Mr. and Mrs. W. N. May of Brookhaven. Following graduation from high school, he spent two years at George Peabody College in Nashville, Tennessee, taking his bachelor's degree in 1923. He earned his master's degree at Peabody in 1933 and was awarded a specialist's diploma in school administration from Columbia University, New York City, in 1938 after a year's training at that institution.

President and Mrs. Albert Louis May Sr. Photos from 1950 Perkolator p. 3.

May began his teaching and educational career in the rural schools of southwest Mississippi. He served as principal of the Sontag School in Lawrence County from 1914 to 1916. He moved to the Mississippi Gulf Coast in 1916 serving first as principal of Pineville School until 1918 and then as principal at Wood High School in Lyman from 1918 to 1923. In 1923 May was elected superintendent of Biloxi City Schools, a position he held for eleven years. In 1934 he moved to Jackson to become state superintendent of adult education in the State Department of Education. May gave up that position to become superintendent of Harrison-Stone-Jackson Agricultural High School and Junior College on August 20, 1941. On November 7, 1941, the Board of Trustees changed May's title from "superintendent" to "president," and the school officially changed its name to Perkinston Agricultural High School and Junior College on July 15, 1942.

May's term as the chief executive officer of the Perkinston institution coincided with America's involvement in World War II and the Korean War. He took office three months and 17 days before the United States entered the Second World War on December 7, 1941, and died in office 19 days before the signing of the July 27, 1953, armistice that ended the Korean War.

The May era was one of great change. The school suffered dwindling enrollments as the students marched off to war. Simultaneously, though, as part of the national defense program, the school added vocational-technical programs to a curriculum formerly dominated by liberal arts and agriculture.

As the Second World War came to a close, enrollment climbed as veterans poured in to take advantage of the educational provisions of the G. I. Bill, particularly in the realm of vo-tech education. With his experience in adult education, May was remarkably suited to handle the challenges facing the institution as its clientele changed from youths desiring liberal arts education to that of battle-tested veterans seeking vo-tech training. Two of the major May-era structures, the Colmer Building and the Pasteurization Plant, were vocational-technical in nature.

Along with the veterans came military surplus buildings. Of the seven major May-era structures four were of military origin and were erected in a "Military Perk" compound on the west side of the campus. These were (using the names they later bore) Apartment Dormitory, George Hall, Smith Hall, the Cafeteria and Classroom Building, and War Memorial Chapel. On July 9, 1953, the day after his death in the Stone County Hospital after a five month bout with lupus, he lay in state in the War Memorial Chapel from 10 a.m. until his funeral in the chapel at 2 p.m. He was interred at Southern Memorial Park on the beach in Biloxi.

On July 22, 1953, the Board authorized the naming of the largest installation built during the May era in his honor. Thus on homecoming day, October 10, 1953, Perkinston Football Stadium was officially rededicated as A. L. May Memorial Stadium, and the track and football field was named "May Field."

May was survived by his widow, the former Velma Wood, and their son, Lieutenant Commander Albert Louis May Jr., who was then assistant chief of surgery at the U. S. Naval Hospital, Jacksonville, Florida. Dr. May's two sons were Albert Louis May III and Timothy Dayton May.

So ended the career and life of President Albert Louis "Mighty Fine" May. That sobriquet came about because of his penchant for describing groups, individuals, events, the weather, and everything in general as "mighty fine." In addition to his many "mighty fine" accomplishments, he served as president of the Mississippi Junior College Association in 1946-1947 and as president of the Mississippi Association of Colleges in 1950-1951.

MAY ERA
AGRICULTURAL HIGH SCHOOL AND JUNIOR COLLEGE ENROLLMENT AND GRADUATION STATISTICS
Session 1941-1942 through Session 1952-1953

	Regular Session Enrollment						Graduates		Summer Enrollment					Graduates	
Session	AHS	Junior College Regular	Junior College Night	Farm Trainees	Vo-Tech	Total	AHS	JC	AHS	Junior College Regular	Junior College Night	Vo-Tech	Total	AHS	JC
1941-1942	82	194				276	23	42	28*	25			53		
1942-1943	100	199				299	38	43	98	29			127	24	3
1943-1944	85	118				203	27	16	154	35			189	40	3
1944-1945	117**	105				222	47	22	135	46			181	23	5
1945-1946	174***	201				375	48	19	103	112			215	43	3
1946-1947****	102	415				517	36	53	44	73		12	129	4	6
1947-1948	79	332			47	458	38	84	33	55		67	155	5	14
1948-1949	82	289			242	613	26	65	23	78		192	293	1	13
1949-1950	55	306	9	28	235	633	27	73	14	64	8	164	250	1	9
1950-1951*****	95	296	12	25	139	567	20	61	20	47	19	102	188	1	4
1951-1952	109	222	41	19	72	463	25	51	23	24	16	23	86	3	5
1952-1953	174	272	46	6	21	519	38	58	38	39	22	19	118	2	7

*This figure included five "special" students defined as students over 21 who did not possess documentation of 15 units of high school work but who desired special training in certain courses. All five of these students were Central Americans.

**This figure included 26 "special" students, only 11 of which were listed with Central American addresses. Most of the other 15 were a new kind of special student--Vocational-Technical students. One of these was Ed Evans, who in a personal interview, confirmed that he was not then over 21 years of age, and he was taking one vocational course in order to play football. Apparently the school was adapting a pre-existing term to describe a new kind of student

***Eighty students in this total of 174 were designated "special." The explanation given on page 88 of the *1945-1946 Catalog* stated that these 80 students included "full-time Vocational and full-time Technical students and 14 Veterans who graduated as a result of the General Educational Development Test." This was the first time in the official documents of this institution that this new type of "special" student was designated as a vo-tech student. In summer 1946, the college listed 23 "specials" and the AHS seven with no reference as to whether they were vo-tech or not.

****In the regular session 1946-1947, the college listed 16 "specials" and the AHS seven with no reference to vo-tech. Beginning in the summer of 1947 the college created a new reporting category called "Vocational and Technical Special" and listed 12 students. Once the new category was established the term "special student" reverted back to its original meaning and was included in the respective totals of the college and AHS in this chart.

*****In September 1950, the AHS 9th and 10th grades, eliminated in September 1941, were reinstituted.

Junior college night classes, inaugurated during regular session 1949-1950, began with nine students. Enrollment rose to 41 in session 1951-1952 with the matriculation of 20 airmen from Keesler Air Force Base. Nine airmen enrolled for night classes the following year after which attendance by airmen became sporadic and individual. This was, though, the beginning of this institution's educational alliance with Keesler.

THE MAY ERA: THE SECOND WORLD WAR AND THE RISE OF VOCATIONAL-TECHNICAL EDUCATION AT PERKINSTON AUG. 1941 - JULY 1953

Albert Louis May Sr. in 1941, at the time he was named president of the Harrison-Stone-Jackson Agricultural High School and Junior College. Photo from 1942 Perkolator, p. 11.

When Albert Louis May assumed office as chief executive officer of the Perkinston institution on August 20, 1941, America's first peacetime draft, inaugurated the previous September 16, had already impacted enrollment at the school. More than 900,000 men nationwide had been drafted in the original group of 21 to 36-year-olds, and thousands more in the 18 to 20 year old age group had volunteered. Enrollment, which had totaled 393 in Darby's last year, dropped to 276 in May's first September. Not only were potential students flocking to the colors, but younger faculty members as well. On the eve of classes, May had to replace accounting instructor Julius Felicione, who was "granted leave of absence without pay while he was in the United States Army."

That fall, as the war clouds gathered, Civil Defense organizations were formed in the Coast towns and in the piney woods. The Stone County Civil Defense set up four enemy aircraft observer units. One of those served at Perkinston.

While observers scanned the skies over Perk on December 7, 1941, Japanese aircraft slipped unnoticed through the defenses at Pearl Harbor in the Hawaiian Islands and destroyed half of the American Pacific fleet. Following that attack, U. S. President Franklin Delano Roosevelt delivered his "Day of Infamy" speech mobilizing the nation for total war. At Perkinston, May, officially accorded the title of "president" less than a month earlier, delivered an address mobilizing Perk for the war effort:

"The thought I would emphasize is that we shall always need men and women with college training. Government and industry today need more than ever before trained and skilled technicians. We not only need men and women with broad understanding and special aptitudes to serve as leaders in the national crisis, but more efficient leadership will be demanded to manage the post-war world. We all should redouble our efforts to make the Perkinston Junior College render more efficient service in support of our democratic way of life.

"The Junior College is unique in three respects. Preparation is given young men and young women for advanced work at the senior college, university, or professional school. An effort is made to round out and complete the period of general education for some students who cannot undertake senior college work. Training of a vocational nature is provided to students, which training is designed to equip them for immediate entrance into an adulthood that is necessarily earlier than that of the college preparatory group.

"For immediate purposes the Junior College must prepare its students for the different war services, for the production industries, for the production and conservation of foods, and for the civilian defense responsibilities. The fundamentals of mathematics, chemistry, physics, agriculture, home economics, and social science must be emphasized more than ever before. Health and physical education, including first aid, must be greatly intensified. A shop program, including the different trades, must be expanded.

"With the splendid type of student body this school has, with its excellent faculty and adequate buildings and equipment, this college is destined to maintain a leading role among the Junior Colleges and render worthwhile and efficient service to the counties supporting it."

Many of the points May articulated had been hallmarks of the institution since September 17, 1912. Other of May's goals required only a shift in emphasis to accomplish, but his call for the training of "skilled technicians" through a "shop program" to teach "different trades" presaged a new educa-

The Girl's Home Guard stands at attention in the Perkinston Quadrangle in 1942. From left Platoon One Second Lieutenant Helen Cain of Mississippi City, Platoon Two Second Lieutenant Maryanne Passmore of Dallas, Texas, Platoon Three Second Lieutenant Elizabeth Elston of Gulfport, Platoon Three Second Lieutenant Wilma Proffitt of Lexington, Kentucky, Home Guard Captain Gloria Keller of Biloxi, Platoon Three First Lieutenant Marie Giannetto of Gulfport, Platoon Four Second Lieutenant Freda Long of Biloxi, Platoon Five Second Lieutenant Dorothy Bleuer of Biloxi. Photo from 1942 Perkolator, p. 76.

tional role for the institution. The only "shop program" previously sanctioned by the college had been of the "learning by doing" type imparted to the 10-cent-per-hour labor gangs by agricultural teachers. As May began casting about for ways to implement this "new vocational-technical program," the school prepared to do its bit for the defense program.

All teachers and students signed up for an American Red Cross first aid course. The 36-bed infirmary established back in October on the top floor of Fahnestock Hall was put in combat readiness by school nurse Amelia Evans. Nearly every AHS boy and college man joined one of the four "Home Guard" platoons devoted to fire fighting, calisthenics, marching, and drilling. The members of these platoons began converting the physical education and intramural field behind Stone Hall into a military-type obstacle course. Not to be outdone, the AHS girls and the college women organized five uniformed Home Guard platoons complete with cadence-calling officers. Most of the students of the fairer sex also joined sewing and knitting groups to produce clothing for the war effort.

The college sponsored the sale of defense stamps and bonds and started a scrap metal drive. Programs in patriotic music and special short courses in ambulance work, navigation, military Spanish, and growing a Victory Garden were scheduled for second semester.

Some of the more devoted girl and women students and faculty wives joined the Women's Division of the Civil Defense of Stone County. The Perkinston members were responsible for carrying out the dictates of the various committees of that stalwart organization at Perk. The "Committee on Gas Defense," charged "to read and absorb everything on gas" was represented at Perk, not surprisingly, by the wife of chemistry teacher C. O. Hinton. The "Intelligent Committee" was "to investigate and report to the Sheriff any suspicious characters; activities; conversations or anything that would seem to give aid and comfort to the enemy." The names of all the county members of that committee were published in the *Stone County Enterprise* of January 18, 1942, except the one for Perkinston. Her name was blanked out. Perhaps she preferred to remain undercover or incognito or whatever. The Air Raid Observation Committee was "to watch for and report . . . any suspicious planes and parachutists; to seek out and locate any natural landing fields and hiding places where the enemy might hide or land . . . to watch for parachutists . . . [and] . . . call the SHERIFF." The members of the Committee on Blackouts were to see that all lights were extinguished on signal "for protection of civilians, to throw the enemy off the track; to assist our armies to travel in secrecy." Mrs. A. L. May was Perk's member for both Air Raids and Blackouts.

In addition to the various committees, the women organized a "Rifle Squad," a "Bombing Squad," and a "Camuflage (sic) Squad." The "Rifle Squad" women," said the *Stone County Enterprise*," may be trained in the use of light fire arms--for their own protection." Two notable members of this "Rifle Squad" were Second Lieutenant Margaret Rose Eubanks (later Mrs. John C. Dees) and Corporal Word Guild (later Mrs. George Guild) later a globe-trotting foreign languages instructor at the college.

The "Bombing Squad" was "to make a study of the different kinds of bombs; how to distinguish between them; what to do when one falls near; how to extinguish them. Study first aid for bombing victims." The "Camuflage (sic) Squad" was to camouflage roads, trucks, guns, schools, homes, "and our moving armies." The efforts of the Women's Division of the Civil Defense of Stone County were spectacularly successful in that not a single armed German, Italian, or Japanese soldier penetrated the borders of Stone County during World War II. On the other hand, hundreds of German prisoners of war, formerly soldiers in Field Marshal Erwin Rommel's Afrika Korps, were set to work planting pine trees in Stone County, which had the salutary effect of helping to camouflage the land much to the chagrin of their comrades in the Luftwaffe.

The war cost the school women as well as men. In January 1942, May lost Spanish teacher Marion Steele, who resigned to take a Civil Service position as a Spanish translator for the U. S. Army in Miami, Florida. Fortunately, he

The Brick Steam Laundry Building, constructed in 1928, appears in the foreground of this photo taken circa 1939. Perk's initial vocational-technical course, a class in welding, began in a portion of the Brick Laundry in January 1942. After that, May-era vo-tech courses, primarily radio mechanics, were taught in the building as well. The laundry, though, continued to function as a cleaning establishment until 1946. The Brick Laundry was razed along with Bennett Hall and Bennett Annex in 1966 to clear the site for Dees Hall. The 1936 (or third barn) is visible in the central background. The barn still stood in 2000. At right in the photo is the concrete block Darby-era Dairy Barn.

was able to secure the services of Miss Terry Collette of Rolling Fork to replace Steele.

On January 22, four days before second semester classes began, the *Stone County Enterprise* announced that Perk would offer a welding course "intended to appeal to out-of-school youths and . . . fill a real need in the defense program." Facilities for the training of 15 students in the ten-week course had been set up in a portion of the brick laundry building located on the northeast side of Bennett Annex. The name of the instructor was not given.

The Board retroactively blessed the new offering on February 11, 1942, with a "Resolution Approving Application of Harrison-Stone-Jackson Junior College to Carry on Vocational Training Courses in Cooperation with the Mississippi Vocational Board." Citing the need for "trade and industrial training" never before offered by the college, the resolution stated that,

"WHEREAS, the funds are available through the National Defense program of the Mississippi State Board of Vocational Education to furnish equipment and pay for instructional services, supplies for repair and maintenance of equipment, operation, clerical work in connection with the program, and travel and communication in connection with the program, for carrying on courses in welding, electrical work and certain other courses;

"NOW, THEREFORE, BE IT RESOLVED by the Board of Trustees of the Harrison-Stone-Jackson Agricultural High School-Junior College that this Board hereby approve application being made for carrying on vocational training courses in cooperation with the Mississippi State Vocational Board with the understanding that the full expense for carrying on such programs shall be paid by the State Vocational Board. It is understood that space for the shop and supervision of the courses shall be provided by the junior college. It is further understood that separate accounting for such program shall be made."

One month later, the Board, meeting in Gulfport, enshrined its commitment to the new order clearly and concisely. The minutes read, "Motion was made by H. P. Heidelberg and seconded by E. E. Flurry that President May be authorized to proceed with the organization of industrial education as a part of the institution. Unanimously carried."

The *Daily Herald* report covering that historic March 11, 1942, Board meeting noted that the Board had re-instituted the summer session at Perkinston last offered in 1937. The summer session was to run for 12 six-day classroom weeks with both high school and college work being offered. A high school student could earn one and one-half units while a college student could earn 12 semester hours.

College freshmen, by attending the 12-week 1942 summer session, the regular session of 1942-1943, and 1943 summer session, could complete junior college graduation requirements a year early. The value of such acceleration to the student lay in achieving graduation before the then current military induction age of 20. Such graduates stood a greater chance of obtaining officer status in the military or failing that, at least advanced enlisted rank. In addition to the usual university parallel curriculum, though, expanded trade and industry courses would be offered to prepare students for various war services and production industries. Principal trades courses to be offered were metal work, automotive and diesel mechanics, and woodworking.

By late March 1942, government war measures were affecting everyone. With the recent issuance of *Ration Book Number One* limiting sugar purchases, daily shopping had become an exercise in arithmetic.

On Thursday, March 26, the government involved itself in the nightlife of the citizens when Coast Civil Defense directors staged blackout number one. At 9:14 p.m. sirens, church bells, and factory whistles gave the signal to extinguish all lights, including those of automobiles and buses engaged in interstate commerce on U. S. Highways 90 and 49. As the Coast went black, an awed auxiliary policeman asked Gulfport Police Chief John Payne if there would be additional warnings in the event an enemy plane actually flew over the Coast during the test. "Yes," said Payne, "bombs." The test lasted 30 minutes. While no reports of deaths, injuries, or violence marred the test, two recalcitrants, who absolutely refused to co-operate, were arrested. This test, though, had been planned and the public forewarned.

On April 15, 1942, science instructor Linwood P. Ingram notified the Board that he would be entering the United States Army Air Corps at the close of the present session. Ingram, destined to be the sole former faculty member to die in the war, was killed in action when the Japanese shot down his B-25 Bomber over Biak Island on May 28, 1944.

Horace M. Ivy, Perkinston Junior College's first full-time vo-tech instructor taught from May 1, 1942 until January 13, 1943. Photo from 1943 Perkolator, p 17.

Also at the meeting of April 15, 1942, the board hired Horace M. Ivy, holder of a bachelor's degree from Mississippi State College, to teach trades and science. Ivy, who had six years as a "practicing Agricultural Engineer and one and one-half years with the State Vocational Board," was the institution's first full-time instructor to teach vocational-technical subjects. The Board elected Ivy at a salary of $2,000 per year and living quarters "with the expectation that the school would receive from $900 to $1,200 from the United States government to reimburse the salary." In addition, the Board applied to the state vocational board for funds for the purpose of outfitting the shop with internal combustion engines and the necessary experience for instruction in woodworking and mechanical drawing. Ivy's contract began May 1 and summer school was set to start on June 10.

In May 1942, college registrar B. P. Russum received word from the U. S. Navy that Perk had been approved for that service's V-1 Program. Such approval meant that students who met U. S. Naval requirements and who enrolled in prescribed courses would receive a draft deferment until they had graduated from the junior college. Students showing the greatest potential could also receive a deferment until they had completed senior college. In short order, the U. S. Army and the U. S. Marine Corps joined with the Navy in making similar pre-induction agreements with Perkinston students desiring to enlist in the various service programs leading to reserve commissioned officer status.

Perk's martial spirit reached a crescendo on May 14, 1942. On that "Home Guard Mobilization Day," the institution's five platoons of women and four platoons of men staged a grand "regimental review." A large crowd watched as the platoons paraded, and Stone County Civil Defense representatives judged the maneuvers. Platoon Three, commanded by Captain Marie Giannetto of Gulfport, took women's honors. Platoon One, commanded by Lou Campbell of Columbus, and Platoon Two, commanded by John Jackson of New Orleans, Louisiana, tied for first place in the men's category. All first place platoon members received intramural drill squad emblems.

Simultaneously, the school announced the completion of the "barricade course" on the physical education field behind Stone Hall. Modeled on a U. S. Army basic training obstacle course, the half-mile-long run contained at intervals hurdles, ladders, barricades, and vaults designed to involve the use of all muscles in pulling, lifting, balancing, and adjusting.

Close on the heels of the militarization of Perk came the industrialization of the school. On May 25, 1942, the state legislature passed House Bill 622, which made funds available to the junior colleges to purchase shop equipment. Accordingly, the State Board of Education in tandem with the State Board for Vocational Education allotted Perk $4,615.38. President May and the Board of Trustees began deliberations on how best to spend that allotment on June 10, the day Perk's first summer school in five years opened.

Fifty-three students (28 high school and 25 college) started classes on June 10. Some of them reported to Horace Ivy's "shop" located in a portion of the brick laundry beside Bennett Annex. He did not have the whole building. Clothes were being cleaned in part of it. Ivy opened up with whatever equipment he had managed to beg, borrow, or appropriate during the past six weeks, and vocational-technical education at Perkinston began.

Beginning in summer 1942, a summer school program became a regular feature of the Perkinston institution. So strong became the summer program that Perkinston could be described as a year-round teaching institution through summer 1964. The division of the institution into three campuses in 1965 eventually dealt the summer school program at Perkinston a mortal blow. While no summer school graduation ceremony marked the close of the 1942 summer session, such exercises did begin in 1943 and continued in an unbroken line through summer 1969.

Summer 1942 marked a new phase in the development of the institution, and the institution coincidentally received a new name. On July 15 the designation "Perkinston Agricultural High School and Junior College" replaced the designation "Harrison-Stone-Jackson Agricultural High School and Junior College."

In early 1943 Perkinston Junior College men test their agility and stamina in surmounting one of the barricades located on the half-mile-long military type obstacle course built behind Stone Hall. Photo from 1943 Perkolator, p. 48.

Summer 1942 also marked a new phase in German U-Boat activity in the Gulf of Mexico. In July, with American merchant ships being torpedoed within 90 miles of the Mississippi Gulf Coast, military authorities of the Fourth U. S. Army Corps Area instituted draconian dim-out regulations for the duration of the war in Coast cities and towns. The Biloxi Lighthouse, for the first time since the Civil War, ceased to cast its beam into the Gulf. Mississippi Power Company officials extinguished all streetlights within five hundred yards of the shoreline. Southbound motorists were ordered to slow to 15 miles per hour and dim their automobile lights upon reaching the line of the Louisville and Nashville Railroad, which paralleled the Gulf shore from the Louisiana to the Alabama state line. On July 28 the *Daily Herald* reported that 50 to 100 Coast citizens per night were being arrested and fined for dim-out regulation violations and warned that military authorities were threatening to permanently close U. S. Highway 90 from 7 p.m. to 7 a.m.

On August 6, 1942, in the piney woods far above the dim-out zone, Perkinston Junior College President A. L. May, who was by then the Civil Defense director of Stone County, presided at a "lighting-up" ceremony. The patriotic program scheduled that morning was a public gathering at the picnic grounds located three miles west of Wiggins on state Highway 26. The gala barbecue, hosted by state and local officials, celebrated the inauguration of Rural Electrification Association (REA) service for Stone County. A switch thrown at Maxie at 9 a.m. turned on the current, lighting up hundreds of homes in rural Stone County, and relegated the coal oil lamp to the status of a curiosity.

On the night of August 27, in the first test blackout since the original one in March, all the lights in the Mississippi Panhandle from Hattiesburg south to the Coast were ordered shut off. One may suppose that Mrs. A. L. May, in her role as the Perkinston representative on both the Committee for Air Raids and the Committee for Blackouts of the Women's Division of the Civil Defense of Stone County, did her duty. The duty was likely not difficult as summer school had closed five days earlier. At any rate the names of no Perkinston inhabitants were included in the long lists of fined malefactors published in the post-blackout-test *Daily Herald.*

After registration for the 1942-1943 session in September, May reported a gain of about 25 students over the previous session. Total enrollment stood at 299 with 100 of those being high school students. Of the total enrollment, two-thirds were men, and recruiters from all services were at Perkinston in force.

On October 2, 1942, the *Daily Herald* reported football games at Gulfport High, Biloxi High, Pascagoula High, and at Perkinston Junior College. All three Coast high school games had to end at twilight, so the fans could get home by dark. The Perk Bulldogs did not even begin pounding the Holmes County Bulldogs 12-6 until 8 p.m. under the arcs on the Old Athletic Field.

U-boat commanders could not see the lights of Perkinston, but they were sinking the ships bringing rubber and coffee from Brazil to American docks. The Japanese had a strangle hold on the rubber producing region of Southeast Asia. The United States began running out of tires. The *Daily Herald*, October 13, 1942, carried the announcement that the speed limit would be dropped to 35 miles per hour and that gasoline rationing for the purpose of saving tires would begin on November 22. On October 26, the *Daily Herald* announced that coffee rationing would begin on November 28.

On October 27 the *Daily Herald* carried the news that both Pearl River Junior College and Sunflower (Moorhead) Junior College had discontinued football in order to save tires. Perk played the teams still competing, and with a season record of six wins, no losses, and one tie, took the 1942 state championship title. With the advent of gasoline rationing in November, all Mississippi junior colleges suspended all intercollegiate sports competition and beefed up their intramural sports programs.

Prohibitions against outside Christmas lighting along the Coast and appeals to patriotism to eschew such decoration elsewhere, rendered December 1942 even darker than usual. Adding to the general depression in spirit were notices of impending rationing of fat and oil, paper, and canned goods. On the other hand, scrap metal collections rose after New Years Day as Biloxi policemen hurled the battered remains of 35 recently seized slot machines into the collection trucks.

On January 13, 1943, after barely seven months on the job, Horace M. Ivy resigned. Into his position stepped W. D. Smith as Perk's new instructor of trades and science. Smith, like Ivy, had graduated from Mississippi State College. Smith, though, boasted several years of graduate study collectively at Corinth Business School, the University of North Carolina, and Vanderbilt University. His experience included "several years" in public and high schools in Mississippi, six years as supervisor of vocational education in Waynesville, North Carolina, four years as a County Farm Agent, and three years at "Pearl River College."

Vo-tech instructor W. D. Smith (center in hat) instructs a class in woodworking. The woman student at left was a "Rosie the Riveter" type. Smith began his vocational-technical teaching career at PJC in January 1943. He retired in December 1951 and returned to his home in Waynesville, North Carolina. Photo from 1944 Perkolator, p. 42.

A series of photographs from the 1944 Perkolator depicts the unprecedented industrial training carried out on surplus NYA machinery in surplus CCC Camp buildings.

PJC student sheet metal workers.

PJC students welding.

A PJC woman "tool checker."

Smith was the real founder of the vocational-technical education department at Perkinston. In fact, for three and one-half years, he alone was the vocational-technical department at Perk, and during his first semester he taught science also. His classes would run six days per week, year round.

Smith had to conduct his shop classes in the cramped quarters in the brick laundry until mid-April when he moved into far more spacious, well-equipped quarters. A new vo-tech center, secured through the auspices of State Junior College Supervisor Knox M. Broom, was located in the field behind Bennett Hall Annex. The center was composed of six portable units transported to the campus from Civilian Conservation Corps Camp P-81 of Bay Springs. The structures consisted of a 20' x 40' officers quarters, a 20' x 30' dispensary, a 10' x 25' oil house, a 30' x 30' maintenance shop, a 24' x 60' garage, and a 20' x 20' blacksmith shop. In addition, the school had also received as surplus property the machines, tools, and other operational necessities, including wiring, from a National Youth Administration (NYA) cabinet and woodworking shop in Kosciusko. All these structures and resources together with the new machinery and tools purchased with the $4,615.38 appropriated by the state the year before added up to a respectable effort at establishing a viable vo-tech center.

That summer, the session was lengthened to 13 weeks with high school students being allowed to earn three credits and college students 15 semester hours. The school's summer enrollment more than doubled over the previous summer session to 127 (98 AHS and 29 JC). The accelerated program, begun the previous summer, doubtless contributed to the ranks of the 27 (24 AHS and 3 JC) graduates honored in the school's first summer exercises since the only other such ceremony in 1925. These 27 graduates amounted to a total equal to one-third the number of regular May 1943 graduates.

The summer enrollment of 127 had contained only ten more women than men with there being one more man than the number of women among the 29 college students. But on September 6, one week after summer school graduation, the new session opened, and the enrollment figures were nothing less than catastrophic. At 203 the figure was two less than the total enrolled in 1925, the year the institution first offered college courses, and nearly 100 students below the previous September.

The 1943 enrollment contained only 118 college students with women outnumbering the men more than two to one. Only 30 men enrolled as college freshmen. The sophomore class counted 21 women and six men. The lowering of the induction age to 18 in 1943 had devastated the Perkinston junior class of that session. Falling enrollment and rising prices resulted in President May at the December Board meeting requesting and receiving an unprecedented mid-session increase in charges to students for room and board from $18 to $20 per month.

The dawning of the new year, though, brought news that the worst had passed. With the Axis armies in retreat in Europe and Asia, the *Daily Herald*, on January 13, 1944, declared that the war was no longer expected to strike the continental United States. Civil Defense airplane spotters were relieved of their duties. Dim-outs were eliminated nationwide, and practice blackouts were eliminated in all but coastal areas.

On January 15, J. R. Robinson, secretary of the Southern Association of Colleges and Schools (SACS), announced the formation of a Mississippi state post-war educational committee for the purpose of providing educational opportunities for veterans. The committee wished particularly to provide vocational-technical education. Dr. J. M. Ivy of Meridian represented junior colleges on the committee.

Through Ivy's efforts Perk received from Greenwood the contents of a complete NYA sheet metal shop. On March 22, 1944, May reported to the Board that the new shop had arrived and was operational.

On April 10, 1944, U. S. Bureau of Census statistics released in the *Daily Herald* indicated the extent to which the counties served by Perk had been affected by the war. Between April 1, 1940, and November 1, 1943, Harrison County's civilian population had risen 29.3 percent from

40,651 to 65,505. Jackson County's population had risen an incredible 85.1 percent from 20,462 to 37,872 primarily due to the tremendous growth of Ingalls Shipbuilding and related industries. The Harrison County figures did not include the personnel of the Naval (Seabee) Base, Gulfport Field, or Keesler Field. On the other hand the piney woods counties had lost population. Stone County's population had decreased 12.9 percent from 6,155 to 5,362. The figures for George County were not included.

If the population figures skewered by the war seemed strange, so did Perk's graduation figures. On May 24,1944, the institution awarded 16 college diplomas and 27 AHS diplomas for a total of 43. (The last year the school had graduated fewer than that had been in 1927). On August 24, the school awarded three college diplomas and 40 AHS diplomas for a total of 43. The enrollment in the 1944 summer session had reached 189, only 14 students less than in the regular 1943-1944 session. Falling regular session enrollments coupled with rising summer enrollments, had created a situation in which both the regular session and the summer session had produced the same number of total graduates.

The summer enrollment had been driven up by high school boys seeking to achieve as much education as possible before they were drafted into military service. Among the enrollees, though, were a few veterans seeking educational benefits under the G.I. Bill of Rights. On August 3, 1944, according to the *Stone County Enterprise*, Bob Rivers, social studies instructor at Perk, spoke at a special assembly "on the G. I. Bill recently passed by Congress. He interpreted the bill and explained the many provisions."

The "G.I. Bill of Rights" was the collective term for a body of federal legislation passed by Congress to provide education and other benefits to veterans of the Second World War. The original text of the G. I. Bill was embodied in the Serviceman's Readjustment Act of 1944. Signed into law by President Franklin D. Roosevelt on June 22, 1944, the educational benefits were available to any veteran who had served honorably for 90 days or more after September 16, 1940. Under the bill's provisions, a veteran was entitled to one year of full-time training plus a period equal to his or her service. Maximum entitlement for school costs was $500 per year for four years plus $50 per month living allowance for singles and $75 per month for those with dependents. When the G.I. Bill went into effect, more than a million veterans had already been discharged. In time 7.8 million veterans would take advantage of their benefits. The top five occupational fields chosen by them were (in descending order) mechanics, business, construction work, engineering, and metal working. These choices had staggering implications for vocational-technical education.

Regular session 1944-1945 and the summer session which followed proved to be the calm before the veterans' storm. Regular session and summer session enrollment figures

(Above) In 1945, Keesler Field mechanics inspect a B-24 Liberator bomber like the one that crashed at Perkinston. Photo courtesy of Dr. Phillip Thomas Tucker, Chief Historian, Keesler Air Force Base.

On Saturday, March 31, 1945, a B-24 Liberator bomber on a routine training mission out of Keesler Army Air Field caught fire at 4:15 p.m. As the plane went into a dive, two of the eight airmen aboard parachuted to safety. The plane crashed on Perkinston Junior College property north of the campus, killing four of the airmen outright and critically injuring a fifth who died five days later.

Killed in the crash were Second Lieutenant Arnold J. Grein, aged 26, of Lakefield, Minnesota, Second Lieutenant Joseph E. Carr, aged 24, of New Carlisle, Indiana, Sergeant Harold W. Baur, aged 27, of Kingston, Pennsylvania, and Private Neil V. Harrington, aged 21, of Courdersport, Pennsylvania. Private Thomas L. Schweitzer, aged 19, of Crawfordsville, Indiana, who suffered multiple fractures, was removed to the Gulfport Army Air Field hospital where he died on April 4. Private Earl H. Kellam, aged 19, of Calvert, Alabama, survived the crash with only a slight foot injury.

Emma Jean (Byrd) Bookout (PAHS Class of 1949) of Saucier, in a telephone conversation in July 2000, informed the MGCCC archivist that she heard the crash from her home (the Martin house next to the Perkins house) in Perkinston. Then aged 12 she remembered walking with her father to the crash site. She could see the dead pilot (Grein) and co-pilot (Carr) through the windshield of the burning plane. She also remembered a parachute hanging in a tree.

By e-mail of August 5, 2000, Evelyn Carol (Engbarth) Barrett (PJC 1945 summer graduate) of Merimack, New Hampshire, informed the MGCCC Archivist that she had been at her home in Ocean Springs when the plane crashed. When she returned to the campus on Sunday, she learned of the disaster, and she and two other women students walked to the crash site two days later. In her words, "I think we walked less than five minutes to find it. We had no trouble locating it." Barrett remembered that the plane was "silver colored" and lay in the woods with broken pine trees scattered about.

Perkinston Minute Book 4, April 18, 1945, contained the following regarding the incident: "President A. L. May made the report of the plane crash in the field of the Junior College and it was a consensus of the Board that no claims for damages should be made."

Col. Robert F. "Bob" Rivers, a World War I veteran, prided himself on the fact that Superintendent Cooper Darby's last official act was to draw up the contract to hire him as a social studies instructor, and the first official act performed by Superintendent May, when he succeeded Darby in September 1941, was to sign the contract which Darby had inadvertently left unsigned on the superintendent's desk. Rivers held a bachelor's degree from Mississippi Southern and a master's degree from the University of Mississippi. In addition he had attended Louisiana State University for a year of post-graduate work. On October 25, 1944, Rivers became registrar of the institution and served in that capacity until his retirement on March 13, 1963. Rivers died at age 83 in early 1978 in Hattiesburg. Photo 1946 Perkolator, p. 8.

remained very close to that of the previous year, and for the last time, AHS students outnumbered junior college students. The 1944-1945 session, if not markedly different from the previous session, did witness one major indication of a return to normalcy. The state junior colleges resumed intercollegiate competition in some sports.

The 1944-1945 session also contained harbingers of things to come. In November, May requested and received permission from the Board of Trustees to extend Thanksgiving holidays by two days for the faculty of the school to attend a statewide junior college conference in Jackson on the subject of "terminal education." That same month May reported to the Board that printed materials detailing the institution's offerings had been delivered to the counselors at the Separation Center at Camp Shelby. By May 1945, the institution's advertisements in area newspapers emphasized that its course work was "offered to veterans under G. I. Bill."

On May 8, 1945, the faculty and student body gathered in the school auditorium for a special Victory in Europe Day program. According to the *Daily Herald* of May 9, 1945, "The group assembled and heard the victory proclamation by President Truman and Prime Minister Churchill." After a scripture reading by Joe Gillis of Biloxi, Dorven Craft of Lucedale led a prayer. The Perkinston Junior College Junior State Guard presented the colors as the assemblage recited the pledge of allegiance. History instructor Bob Rivers reviewed the European War and told of the fighting ahead in the Pacific. Then Lewis Bangham of Elgin Field, Florida, sounded "Taps" and classes were resumed.

The Japanese surrendered on September 2, 1945, while Perk was in recess between the summer session and the new regular session slated to begin on September 8. All the courses offered by the institution's AHS division and junior college division were, of course, available to veterans, but an unprecedented notice in the institution's *1945-1946 Bulletin* was titled "Additional Offerings to Veterans and Others." This notice read,

"Fees and tuitional charges will be made on the courses listed below based upon the costs for instructional services and for materials and supplies.

"A schedule will be arranged so that veterans may enroll at any time throughout the twelve-month school year. Any veteran of junior college age may be accepted for enrollment irrespective of previous training. Such students will be classified as 'special,' and will not be eligible for graduation until the entrance requirements are met. However, certificates of proficiency will be awarded on the completion of certain courses. Courses will run from short to semester courses.

1. Truck and tractor mechanics
2. Woodworking (included in bulletin)
3. Drafting
4. Painting
5. Spray painting
6. Building trades
7. Blue-print reading
8. Concrete form building and finishing
9. Sheet metal

(Right) The Mississippi Junior State Guard stands at attention on the campus of Perkinston Junior College in March 1945. This unit of the state militia was authorized on September 20, 1944, by the Board of Trustees by contract with the Adjutant General, Military Department of the State of Mississippi. Joe N. Dedeaux, a Perkinston resident and a U. S. Marine Corps veteran of World Wars I and II, was appointed commandant of the unit. Photo from 1945 Perkolator, p. 91.

(Top Right) (From left) In 1946 Commandant Dedeaux stands on the parade field with Student Captain Osborne Thomasson of Weewahitchka, Florida, and Student Second Lieutenant Wallace Bahr of La Lima, Honduras. Photo from 1946 Perkolator, p. 84. The Mississippi Junior State Guard unit at Perkinston had 35 members in 1945 and 45 members in 1946. In October 1947, the unit ceased to exist as its members joined the Wiggins National Guard Unit.

10. Sheet metal lay-out work
11. Electrical
12. Electric welding
13. Acetylene welding
14. Laboratory Technician
15. Photography
16. Pre-Nursing
17. Cooking
18. Business and commerce, including retail, wholesale, selling, transportation, commercial and marketing, doctor and dental assistance
19. Agriculture"

According to this amazing document, any veteran could show up at the school at "any time" and enter any one or more of 19 different courses. W. D. Smith, who was at the time still the school's only vocational-technical teacher was responsible for teaching the first 13 subjects on the list. And these special courses were being offered in addition to his regular courses which consisted of two mechanical drawing classes, automotive and diesel mechanics, woodworking, and a new general shop course that included electric and acetylene welding.

On November 21, 1945, the Board of Trustees hired a new trades instructor, but that did not help Smith. The new instructor, John M. Wallace of Biloxi, was to teach a new course in small business training for vets. Wallace, a graduate of Oklahoma Agricultural and Mechanical College and a World War II veteran himself, had additional duties. He was to serve as veterans' counselor and as a recruiter for the vocational-technical program.

During fall semester 1945, notice of an impending program in radio mechanics, slated to begin in January, began appearing in Perk course advertisements. D. Wiley Murray, a radio repairman with 20 years experience and a U. S. Army Signal Corps veteran of World War II, was secured as instructor. Once again the brick laundry building was pressed into service for a vo-tech program.

On November 30, 1945, eleven veterans already enrolled at Perk met to form the Veterans Club. Wallace predicted a great many more veterans would enroll in January. To ensure that end, advertisements in area newspapers in December extolled Perk's "7 Point Advantage to Vets":

"1. Centrally located, close to Gulf Coast.
"2. A Sound curriculum--Practically any course of High School and College level desired.
"3. Special Vocational and Technical courses with training in related subjects for Veterans who do not meet the high school entrance requirements.
"4. An Intensified Program in Athletics and Physical Education.
"5. An Accelerated program of instruction, by operating 12 months in a year thus enabling Veterans and Others to complete Schooling quickly.
"6. Attractive Campus, Friendly Student Body and Faculty and many school activities.
"7. Plans are being formulated to expand the facilities of the college to better take care of all future requirements of the students."

Then at the bottom of the ad came another, and likely the most effective, enticement--the cost. The ad asserted that attendance at a senior college in Mississippi averaged $500 per year for room, board, and laundry with incidental costs of $50 to $100 more. At Perk, claimed the ad, all expenses

(Above) Early in second semester 1946 D. W. Murray, instructor in radio mechanics, stands in the newly equipped radio shop located in the Brick Laundry Building.

(Top Right) The facade of the Brick Laundry Building built in 1928.

(Right) Early in second semester 1946, two women laundry workers fold and sort clothes in the Brick Laundry building. Apparently the laundry ceased operations shortly thereafter as the Board on May 20, 1946, authorized President May to sell the laundry equipment.

On November 21, 1945, John Wallace signed on to serve as veterans' counselor and instructor in small business training for vets. He organized the Veterans' Club and served as its faculty sponsor until he left in mid-1946 to take a position with the Mississippi Employment Securities Commission.

Session 1945-46 PJC Veterans' Club, first row *(from left) John M. Wallace (Faculty Advisor), Fred W. Strong (Col. Fr.) of Birmingham, Alabama, Phillip Collins Broadus (H. S. Sr.) of Saucier, Charles Douglas Neville (H. S. Jr.) of Hattiesburg, Oscar R. Bragg (Col. Fr.) of Bay St. Louis, Clinton E. Dyess (Col. Fr.) of Robertsdale, Alabama, Ora Clyde Collins (H. S. Sr.) of Gulfport, Robert Hendrix (Col. Fr.) of Gulfport, Drew Hasty Jr. (Col. Fr.) of Perkinston, William P. Stinson (Col. Soph.) of Lucedale, and Barnett Gilmer (Special) of Pascagoula.* ***Second row*** *(from left) Vincent Moran (Col. Fr.) of Pass Christian, Dantzler Joseph Moran (H.S. Jr.) of Pass Christian, Edwin Joseph Neville (Col. Fr.) of Hattiesburg, Edison Dale (Col. Fr.) of Wiggins, Durwood Langley (Col. Fr.) of Biloxi, Isaac Hilton Bourne (Col. Fr.) of Gulfport, Charles W. Maxey (Col. Soph.) of Gulfport, Bernard E. Dessommes (Col. Fr.) of Ocean Springs, and Hervey Winston McLeod (Col. Fr.) of Pascagoula.* ***Third row*** *(from left) John Nick Pitalo (Col. Fr.) of Biloxi, George Finka (Col. Fr.) of Biloxi, Mitchell M. Crawford (H. S. Jr.) of Perkinston, Lester Pepper (H. S. Jr.) of Perkinston, Louis James Baker (Special) of Pascagoula, Albaugh Lee Lewis (Col. Fr.) of Robertsdale, Alabama, Fred L. Jackson (H. S. Sr.) of Gulfport, James D. Cronia (H. S. Jr.) of Hattiesburg, George Cruthird (H. S. Jr.) of McHenry, Willard R. Deforrest (Col. Fr.) of Pascagoula, Elom Thomas Shattles (Col. Fr.) of Brooklyn, and Earl Brewer Johnson (Col. Fr.) of Saucier. Photograph from 1946 Perkolator, p. 85.*

totaled a mere $212.50.

Apparently the ad had the desired effect. Enrollment shot up from September's 225, two-thirds of which were women, to 375 in January 1947, with most of the 150 newcomers being veterans. For the first time since the war began, men outnumbered women at the school. A reporter for the *Bulldog Barks,* February 26, 1946, wrote, "Personally, we are glad to see Perk again become a 'Boy's School.'" One of the "boys" enrolling in radio mechanics that session was Drew Hasty Sr. of Perkinston. He was a veteran not only of World War II but also a veteran of World War I and the Philippine Insurrection of 1901. He was 69 years old.

The 80 "special" students of the 1946-1947 session were described in the session *Catalog* as including a new kind of "special" student enrolled in "full-time Vocational and full-time Technical" courses. Nearly all of these were veterans who did not yet have a high school diploma. Some had not even begun high school. Several of them enrolled in junior high courses at Perkinston Consolidated School located one block northeast of the Perk campus. Fifteen of these veterans passed the General Educational Development (GED) Test and graduated in uniform with the regular Perkinston AHS class of 1946.

As the summer session began, the school, as opposed to offering a wide range of short courses, announced full-time vocational-technical programs for the first time. Four programs were offered, each to run 25 hours per week--wood manufacturing, radio mechanics, auto mechanics, and sheet metal work. The programs begun that summer were announced to be continuous throughout the coming years. A veteran could enter at any time. He could work toward graduation or, if he so desired (as had been established the previous year), he could attend on "special" status, working toward a certificate of proficiency in his chosen craft. The teachers in the new full-time vo-tech programs were W. D. Smith in wood manufacturing, D. W. Murray in radio mechanics, and Allen R. Nye in auto mechanics and sheet metal work. Nye, a recently discharged U. S. Army captain, held a bachelor's degree from Texas Agricultural and Mechanical College.

Also in June 1946, the school hired two vocational agricultural teachers. One of these was Milton D. Blakeney, a veteran of 31 months in the European theatre of war and holder of a bachelor's degree from Mississippi State College. The other was James V. Gammage, holder of a bachelor's degree from Mississippi State and a master's degree from Louisiana State University. Gammage had taught four years at Wilkinson County Agricultural High School and 14 years at Taylorsville.

In the ten days between the end of the 1946 summer school session and the opening of the regular school session set for September 9, workmen rushed to provide extra housing for the expected influx of veterans--especially those with wives and dependents. For the first time, married students would be living on campus.

President May and the Board had begun planning for additions to the post-war campus as early as August 1944. Planning had begun at that time because of provision of the G. I. Bill, which had pledged the U. S. government to supply facilities to schools intending to provide instruction to veterans. Facilities planning begun by May and the Board evolved as U. S. Government surplus structures and equipment became available.

By early 1946, May and the Board had received a solid

The 1946 Perkinston Agricultural High School graduates pose on the steps of Denson Hall on May 29, 1946. ***First row*** *(from left) Ester Banegas of La Lima, Honduras, Iris Rose Shifalo of Pascagoula, Dorothy Lee Broadus of Saucier, Delores Lott of Gulfport, Devida Dorice Mixon of Mobile, Alabama, Jeanne Kelley of Ozark, Alabama, and Helen Hickman of McHenry.* ***Second Row*** *(from left) Philip Collins Broadus of Saucier, Nevelle McKeehan of Mobile, Alabama, Ora Clyde Collins of Gulfport, Dorothy Ann Baughan of Elgin Field, Florida, Paul Baria of Hattiesburg, Ben Briggs of Pascagoula, Clark Henry Alexander of Gulfport, David Still of Sardis, Helen Marie Cobb of Wiggins, Ruby Doris Bond of Bond, Drew Hasty Jr. of Perkinston, Mitchell Crawford of Perkinston.* ***Third row*** *(from left) Willie E. Broadus of Wiggins, Bob Hendrix of Gulfport, Robert Scruggs of New Orleans, Louisiana, Nolan O'Neal of Perkinston, Opal Ivey of Mobile, Alabama, Pio Porta of Port Barrios, Guatemala, Frank Edwards of Saucier, Nora Willis of McHenry, Oscar E. Stevenson of Moss Point, and Robert Ehlers of Moss Point.* ***Fourth row*** *(from left) Clarence Vaughn, Lewis James Baker of Pascagoula, Lester Pepper of Perkinston, Jesse Crawford of Perkinston, Mario Penadas of Guatemala City, Guatemala, John Stewart of Gulfport, Billye Laney Bellande of Birmingham, Alabama, Morgan Thistle of Long Beach, Jerry Collins of Biloxi, Willene Robertson of Perkinston, Doris Louise Bond of Perkinston, Malcolm McAlpin of Gulfport , Ella Ruth Nash of Bond, Rodney Tillotson of Pascagoula, George Willis Cruthird of McHenry, Dantzler Joseph Moran of Pass Christian. Photo courtesy of Wilton "Red" Brown.*

The 1945-1946 Catalog, p. 88, noted that "14 veterans . . . graduated as a result of the General Education Development (GED) test." Fourteen of the 15 uniformed men in the photo are those veterans. Clarence Vaughn, the 15th uniformed man in the photo, was the only one not included in the roster of students for the 1945-1946 session. His name appeared nowhere in the records of the institution. Possibly he alone of the 15 men in the photo opted to take the GED without enrolling in any other courses. All of the others did take other courses, and each of their records noted each of them as having graduated May 29, 1946. None of the records contain any notation regarding the GED, but an assessment of the records indicated that they did not graduate by taking a regular high school course of study. Also, Clarence Vaughn's name, in the official list of graduates published in Perkinston Minute Book 4, August 21, 1946, was added last and out of order.

The 1946 Perkinston Junior College graduates pose on the steps of Denson Hall on May 29, 1946. ***First row*** *(from left) Nancy Lee Horton of New Orleans, Louisiana, Mary Rose Cain of Perkinston, Helen Elizabeth Martin of Wiggins, Kathryn Shanteau of Ocean Springs, Jean Ellen Moore of Wiggins, and Wallace Bahr of San Pedro Sula, Honduras.* ***Second row*** *(from left) Vivian Katherine Kirk of Gulfport, Iza Ruth Geiger of Lucedale, Walean Rustin of Wiggins, Dorothy Bond of Wiggins, Muriel Arcola Miller of Lucedale, and Patricia Louise Collins of Biloxi.* ***Third row*** *(from left) Clarence Hutchins of Gulfport, Joy Vincent of Agricola, Dorven Craft of Lucedale, Alan Moreno of Biloxi, Russell Quave of Biloxi, and Glenn Denson of Wiggins. Photo courtesy of Walean Rustin. The photograph, depicting as it does 12 women and only six men, is indicative of the two-to-one women over men college enrollment during the Second World War.*

government commitment of four two-storied prefabricated barracks measuring 36 feet by 168 feet to be removed from the U. S. Naval (Seabee) Base in Gulfport. These structures were to be dismantled, transported, and reassembled on the campus at no cost to the school except for brick veneer. In addition, the government agreed to supply Perk with 24 surplus "dwelling units" (house trailers) together with a laundry trailer for the purpose of establishing a trailer park for veterans with wives and children. On February 26 the Board authorized the construction of a bathhouse on the site.

When the 1946-1947 session opened on September 19, 1946, "Trailer City" located in a stand of pines adjacent to the campus on the northwest side, was ready for occupancy, and 24 families moved in. By that time, too, the site for the four barracks dubbed, "Military Perk," had been selected on the south west flank of the campus in the area behind Harrison and Fahnestock Halls. Two of the barracks were on site. One of these, the Apartment Dormitory, though not yet brick veneered, was ready for occupancy. Designed to provide quarters for 24 married veterans, the Apartment Dorm was, on the eve of registration, relegated to the housing of six single men per apartment. That action was taken because the other barracks on site (later named George Hall), that was to be a men's dorm, was not ready.

Though no route for it was published, the school's newly purchased bus was placed on line to transport day students. According to the *Stone County Enterprise*, September 5, 1946, the school expected 75 to 100 students to use the bus or private automobile to commute that session.

The record-setting enrollment of 517 in September 1946, included 450 boarders. Two hundred veterans were included among the 350 men. More than half of the 102 high school enrollees were veterans.

For the first time, the Stone Hall dining room was converted to cafeteria style serving. Three shifts were required at each meal in order that all those dining could be seated in rotation.

Throughout session 1946-1947, work continued on Military Perk with the other two barracks being moved on site. Half of one of the barracks was placed in general line with and east of George hall and designated as the "hospital" or "infirmary" (later to be named Smith Hall). The remaining barracks-and-a-half was set up in the form of a "T" across from the infirmary at the east end of the Apartment Dormitory. This structure was named the "Cafeteria and Classroom Building."

In spring 1947, President May and four other members of the War Memorial Chapel committee traveled to Gulfport Field and chose the war surplus chapel destined to become the centerpiece of Military Perk. On May 21, 1947, the Board unanimously authorized the purchase of Chapel building T-3101 as the institution's memorial to its dead in the Second World War.

Five weeks later, May presided over a meeting of the Mississippi Junior College Association at Perkinston, which signaled the end of the restrictions placed on the junior college program during World War II. That early July convocation of Mississippi junior college presidents agreed to restore all pre-war activity programs in music, oratory, little theatre, and to restore the full range of intercollegiate athletics. As they returned to the familiar pattern of junior college life, the presidents assembled gave greater impetus to war-wrought change. They set up planning committees to formulate a "more far reaching program of vocational and technical courses in order to serve the entire state." The presidents agreed that a new purpose of their particular type of institution was to provide college level, full-time instruction to veterans and other adults desiring such training, but who could not meet the entrance requirements of such institutions. The meeting closed with a call for the Veterans Administration to arrange for veterans to take the full-time training.

As May presided over the meeting, a new veterans farming training program was just beginning at Perk under instructor Monroe O. Webb. Beginning that summer, also, Perk created a new category of student termed a "Vocational and Technical Special" and reported 12 of them on hand. After that the term "special" student returned to its pre-war meaning of students over age 21 not possessing documentation of 15 units of high school work but desiring special training in certain courses.

The new *Catalog*, published in summer 1947 for the coming 1947-1948 regular session, contained new information in its "Trades and Industry" section regarding "extensive refresher courses" designed to prepare vo-tech specials for college entrance. The four full-time vo-tech programs established the year before in auto mechanics, radio mechanics, sheet metal, and wood manufacturing still, as before, could be entered at any time and ran for 25 hours per week but carried the extra requirement that the student remain for a "maximum of nine to twelve months." And one program, wood manufacturing, had been so augmented by additional courses in wiring, plumbing, and concrete construction that it might have been more accurately termed "building trades."

As the regular 1947-1948 session opened on September 8, 1947, newly brick-veneered George Hall, containing 37 rooms for men and two faculty apartments, was occupied for the first time. Thus, the Apartment Dormitory, its brick veneer completed as well, became what it originally had been intended to be--a married students' dorm.

Eleven days after the session started, the first hurricane in 31 years struck the Mississippi Gulf Coast. The devastation wrought on the Coast probably accounted for much of the ten percent drop in enrollment for the session. While little outward devastation was evident at Perk, the winds caused hidden structural damage to the older buildings on the campus with Bennett Annex sustaining the most. Years later when the second story of Bennett Annex had to be removed, the architects attributed the cause to the 1947 Hurricane.

The 18,000 square foot brick veneered Cafeteria and Classroom Building containing a band hall, the science department, a kitchen, and a dining hall was completed shortly after the session began. The various sections of the struc-

The four barracks moved from the Gulfport Naval (Seabee) Base appear as they did when photographed for the 1948 Perkolator. (Below right) The Apartment Dormitory began service in September 1946, with six single men assigned to each of its 24 apartments. Brick veneered by September 1947, it was then assigned to married veterans. The structure was demolished in summer 1984. (Below left) "New Boy's Dormitory" (named George Hall on August 22, 1946) was already brick veneered at the time it began service in September 1947. George Hall still stood in 2000, but after the opening of Hayden Hall in August 1987, it became primarily a storage building. (Above right) The Cafeteria and Classroom Building, composed of a brick veneered barracks-and-a-half set up in a "T" formation, was occupied in sections in fall 1947. The cafeteria in the structure opened for service on Halloween, 1947. Fire destroyed the Cafeteria and Classroom Building on January 25, 1958. (Above left) First called the "hospital" or "infirmary" this half-a-barracks structure of wood began service in November 1947, but was not brick veneered until September 1950. On April 20, 1960 the structure was named Smith Hall in memory of former Board of Trustees President Vinson B. Smith Sr., of Pass Christian, who had died December 20, 1943. By 2000, Smith Hall had achieved the distinction of serving in more capacities than any other MGCCC structure. A partial list of Smith Hall's 1947-2000 incarnations more or less in succession (with upstairs and downstairs often serving different roles simultaneously) included services as a hospital, a little theatre, a classroom building, a periodicals library, a store room, a student center ("The Attic"), a print shop, a computer repair center, and an art studio. Smith Hall basically served as a launch pad for new programs and as temporary quarters for refugee instructors from condemned structures awaiting the completion of new buildings.

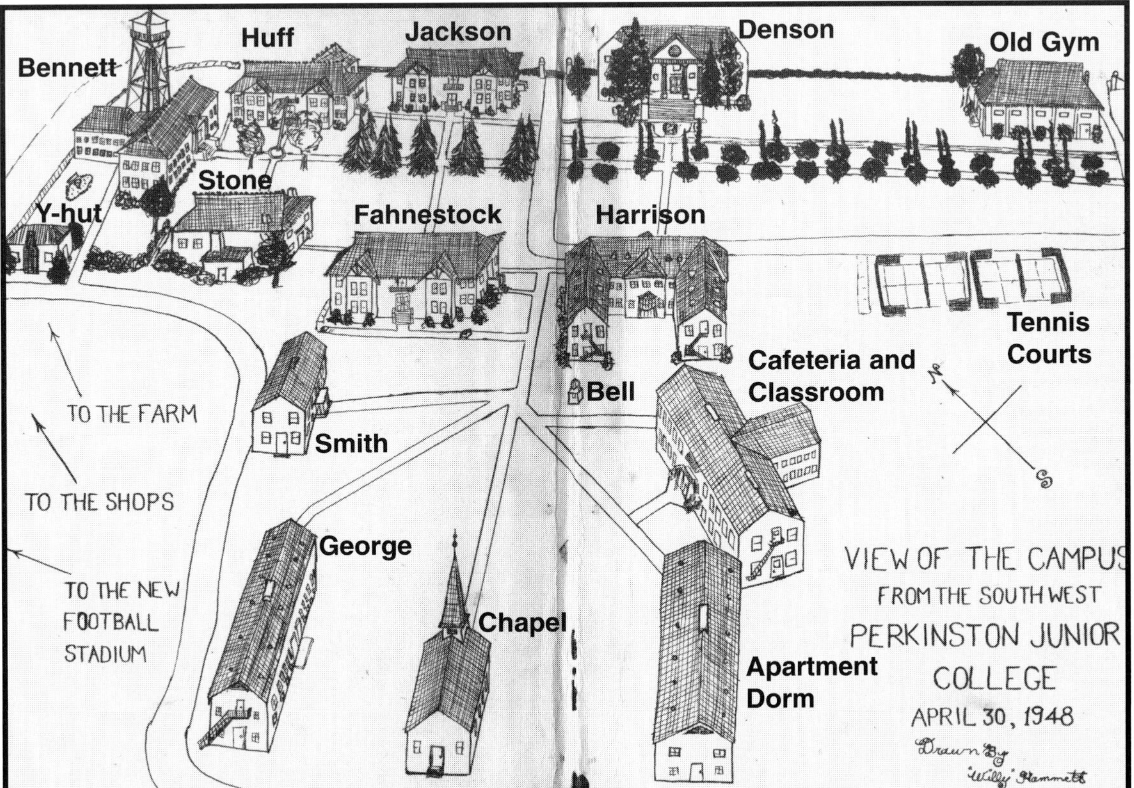

Bobby "Willy" Hammett of Biloxi, a college freshman in session 1947-1948, made this April 30, 1948 drawing, showing the major portion of the campus for the flyleaf of the 1948 Perkolator. The drawing does not include the football stadium, shops, and farm buildings to the left, nor does it include the superintendent's home or the Power House and pond. The drawing is fanciful in depicting building detail but the relationship of the structures to one another is well done. The five structures of Military Perk, including the War Memorial Chapel, which was on-site though incomplete, appear at bottom. The Posey Howell Dinner Bell is depicted behind Harrison Hall at its final point of service in that role. Hammett placed no names of buildings on his drawing but their names of 2000 (or names prior to destruction) were added.

ture were occupied piecemeal as necessary equipment was installed. The first meal was served in the new cafeteria on October 31, 1947. At that point renovation of the old Stone Hall dining room into a new college grill began.

The 20-bed wooden infirmary (Smith Hall) opened in early November with Mrs. George Westerfield, the college nurse, in charge. Apparently the top floor was the infirmary with the bottom floor being converted into a "little theatre" and audio-visual area.

With the addition of the four new buildings of Military Perk, the institution reached an evaluation in material, equipment, and facilities in excess of $1 million for the first time. In a college press release to the *Stone County Enterprise*, February 29, 1948, the writer pointed out that the institution had achieved "million dollar" status at very little cost to its four supporting counties since the state and federal government had funded the post-war expansion.

With the new facilities in place, the stage was set for the largest enrollment in the history of the institution. In the regular session 1948-1949 enrollment broke the 600 mark for the first time, and in the 1949 summer session, enrollment broke the 200 mark for the first time. The 613 regular session students together with the 293 summer school students resulted in the institution exceeding a yearly enrollment of 900 for the first time. Vocational-technical enrollment accounted for most of the gain, and the great majority of vo-tech students were veterans. Regular session vo-tech students quintupled from 47 in September 1947 to 242 in September 1948. Summer session vo-tech students nearly tripled from 67 in June 1948 to 192 in June 1949.

During the 1948-1949 session, five new instructors were hired for the automotive mechanics program alone. Two new instructors were hired in agriculture, and a new program was initiated in vocational agriculture for veterans.

By summer 1949, the Perk vo-tech program had expanded to the point that the Board of Trustees hired the institution's first vocational-technical administrator. On June 20, Reginald Cook, in addition to teaching duties, was hired as "coordinator for vocational-technical programs" at a salary of $300 per month for 12 months. Cook, a native of Meridian, had received his bachelor's degree in vocational education from Mississippi State College. He came to Perk from Raymond where he had served Hinds Junior College in a similar position.

In fall 1949, President May prepared for the dedication of a new facility toward which he had worked for five years--the Perkinston football stadium. The Bulldogs hosted their first game on September 17, 1949, in the stadium later to be dedicated to the president who had it built.

The enrollment of regular session 1949-1950 once again set a record--the apex reached in the May era--633 students. The numbers would have been even higher except that Perkinston Agricultural High School enrollment fell to 55, a figure eight less than the year the school opened in 1912. The reason for the drop lay in the fact that Perkinston Consolidated School, located one block off campus, had in fall 1949 become Perkinston Consolidated High School by adding 11th and 12th grade work. Not only that, but in November the new high school began advertising a high school night class program for veterans to last five hours per night per week.

At the December 14, 1949, Board meeting, May asked for

Reginald E. Cook became the institution's first coordinator of vocational and technical training on June 20, 1949. He held that position until May 1951, when Curtis Davis succeeded him. Photo from 1951 Perkolator, p. 75.

(Right) The interior of the automobile mechanics shop at Perk in 1949. Photo from 1949 Perkolator, p. 21.

Session 1951-1952 Saucier area students pose by their Harrison County school bus, which is parked by Bennett Annex on the PJC campus. Photo from 1952 Perkolator, p. 50.

Beginning in 1912 the Perkinston Consolidated School (PCS) established a symbiotic relationship with the Agricultural High School at Perkinston. When the AHS dropped the 9th grade in May 1928, PCS picked it up. When the AHS reinstated the 9th grade in September 1931, PCS dropped it. When the AHS dropped both the 9th and 10th grades in September 1941, PCS added them. Then in September 1948, for whatever reason, the PCS, styling itself Perkinston Consolidated High School (PCHS), added the 11th and 12th grades and went into competition with the AHS. The AHS enrollment for 1949-1950 plummeted to 55, the lowest in its history.

In September 1950, two years after PCHS was established, Saucier High School in north Harrison County closed, and all four high school grades were bussed to the AHS. Thus the AHS at Perk re-established the full four-year high school offering eliminated by the dropping of the 9th and 10th grades in September 1941. In April 1951, the Perkinston AHS and JC Board voted to accept the high school students from Magnolia Community in western Stone County beginning in September 1951.

On January 23, 1952, the PAHS and JC Board granted the petition of the trustees of the Perkinston Consolidated High School Board to send its high school students to Perkinston Agricultural High School beginning in September 1952. Thus, as May's last session began in September 1952, the AHS enrollment reached 174, a figure equal to the other highest year of AHS enrollment in the May era. Not only did the students of the PCHS come, but some of their teachers and coaches accompanied them, accepting employment at the AHS. Thus ended a strange educational interlude, and Perkinston Consolidated School reverted to grades one through eighth.

and received permission to offer night classes in both the high school and college divisions in cooperation with the veterans Administration. Though no mention was made of PCHS in the Board minutes, it would seem that Perkinston Junior College began its evening class offerings in response to such offerings by PCHS.

The nature of the political aberration that pumped Perkinston Consolidated School up to the exalted status of a second high school in a hamlet was not known to this author in 2000. The situation was never addressed in the Perkinston Junior College board minutes. Suffice it to say the situation did not last long.

The big story in the May era continued to be vo-tech education, and session 1950-1951 proved to be the biggest of all in terms of money spent on the program. The institution's budget for that session allocated $60,935 for the salaries of 24 "regular" (academic) instructors and $31,905 for 12 vocational-technical instructors. Between September 1941, when May assumed office, and September 1950, the portion of the instructional budget allocated to vocational-technical education rose from zero to one-third of the total. The ratio was actually higher still due to a $4,800 vo-tech operational fund, which paid the salaries of a secretary and two "tool checkers." Shortly after the 1950-1951 budget was announced, May and the board awarded the contract for a new vocational-technical building which was to be built across the road in front of the Perkinston Football Stadium.

If the 1950-1951 budget revealed the impact of vo-tech education on the school, it likewise pointed out how little other aspects of the institution had changed. As in 1941, there were still only two full-time administrators--President A. L. May and business manager T. J. Gipson. Each of them had one secretary. Except for this four-person administration, three maintenance men, a dietician, a Harrison Hall housemother, and a school nurse, everyone else whose name was listed on the budget was a teacher. Col. Bob Rivers was a social studies teacher and registrar. L. A. Blackwell was a social studies teacher and dean of men. Reginald Cook was coordinator of the vo-tech program, but he taught as well.

Perkinston Junior College would shortly begin its transformation into a complex institution that would in retrospect view the Perk of 1950 as quaint. The name of the man who would preside over this remarkable change appeared on the faculty list in July 1950. The new social studies instructor was Julius John Hayden Jr. One month earlier a new vo-tech instructor, Curtis Lee Davis of Vancleave, had hired on to teach woodworking. Davis would be Hayden's right hand man in the coming transformation. The changes that set Hayden and Davis in their course began the year both began teaching at Perk.

As the 1950-1951 session began, it became apparent that the G. I. Bill veterans boom had reached its peak the year before. Regular enrollment fell from its previous year's height of 633 down to 567. Vo-tech enrollment plummeted nearly 100 to 139 down from 235 the year before.

As vo-tech enrollment fell, oddly enough, the actual program became stronger and better. The chaos engendered by enrolling veterans "at any time" had been replaced by the invitation for veterans to "enroll at the beginning of each school month." The original four full-time courses in auto mechanics, radio mechanics, sheet metal, and wood manufacturing (building trades) were still being offered, but all four had been raised to 18 months duration. In addition new programs had been added in advanced radio mechanics (9

(Right) The Vocational-Technical Building appears shortly after its completion in late March 1951. On April 20, 1960, the building was named in honor of Ernest Bert Colmer, former head of the institution's agriculture department from July 1, 1922, until September 20, 1935. Photo from the flyleaf of the 1950-1951 Catalogue. As the Colmer Building began service, the vocational-technical department of the institution counted three instructors who would serve the institution throughout their careers. These were, in order of their coming, Willie B. "Willie Boy" Rogers of Perkinston, Curtis Davis of Vancleave, and Winfred L. Moffett of Shipman.

Willie Boy Rogers (standing left) oversees the work of student welders in the Colmer Building in 1952. Rogers first hired on as an assistant auto mechanic instructor on October 20, 1948. While he taught, he attended PJC, receiving his college diploma on May 21, 1952. Rogers's career with the institution spanned 28 years. Photo from 1953 Perkolator, p. 117.

Curtis Davis works at the table saw in the Colmer Building wood manufacturing shop in 1952. Photo from 1952 Perkolator, p.125. Davis began his 20th century record-setting 41and three-quarter-year career with the institution on June 1, 1950, as a wood manufacturing and mechanical drawing instructor. On May 16, 1951, when R. E. Cook resigned, the Board of Trustees named Davis as the vocational-technical coordinator of the institution in addition to his teaching duties.

Winfred Moffett (kneeling right) inspects furniture fashioned by wood manufacturing students in the Colmer Building in 1952. Photo from 1952 Perkolator, p.125. Moffet was hired on September 1, 1951, as an industrial arts instructor and served the institution for 25 years, retiring in October 1976 at the same time Willie Boy Rogers did.

months), display merchandising (18 months), advanced wood manufacturing (9 months), and auto body-fenders repair and painting (9 months).

In addition to offering new courses, the department had taken a new name--"Vocational Trades and Industrial Education." This department taught courses in three groups for three different purposes:

"(1) courses . . . designed to give two years of college training to industrial arts and vocational teachers for employment in the elementary and secondary schools, (2) courses . . . designed to prepare for entrance into industry as advanced learners or junior tradesmen or to upgrade employees that are presently employed in industry, (3) courses designed to give high school youth a general overview of the field of industrial employment and assist them in selecting the type work that is best suited to their needs."

As Perk's vo-tech department stabilized in the wake of the onslaught of World War II veterans, the institution began to prepare for the effects of another war. The *Daily Herald*, December 19, 1950, carried May's thoughts on the Korean War, which had begun the past June 25 with the invasion of South Korea by North Korean forces. In the article, May endorsed the war plan adopted by the American Association of Junior Colleges, which called for "education and military training to go hand in hand." To that end May called for the establishment of a Reserve Officers Training Corps (ROTC) unit at Perk. "Only through getting an educated military force can we gain final victory," declared May.

In his role as president of the Mississippi Association of Colleges for 1950-1951, May saw to it that the March 8, 1951, meeting in Jackson was devoted to the war situation. Despite May's best efforts, ROTC units were not established on the campuses of Mississippi junior colleges during the Korean War.

The Korean War had little discernable effect on Perkinston Junior College except in one area. When Dean of Students B. T. Nash was called to active service, J. J. Hayden assumed his duties and thus attained the position that enabled him to later succeed May as president of the institution.

In late March, 1951, May announced the completion of the college's new vocational-technical building, which was later named in honor of E. B. Colmer, a former Perk agriculture department head. The Colmer Building, built and equipped at a cost of $50,000 of mostly state money, was a one-story 12,000 square foot structure consisting of 12 major rooms. Constructed of Malvern tile brick brought in from Malvern, Arkansas, the new facility contained the school shops and was supposed to contain a pasteurizing plant. Instead, for whatever reason, the Board decided to construct an annex to the pre-existing concrete block dairy barn for that purpose. On July 23, 1952, the Board let the contract for the new addition, which, like the Colmer Building was built of Malvern tile brick.

A reporter for the *Bulldog Barks* on January 14, 1953, noted that the pasteurizing unit was being installed in the completed Dairy and Pasteurizing Plant Building. The milk from the college's herd of 30 milk cows, formerly sold to the Borden Company, was to be sent to the cafeteria in bottles from the Perkinston Junior College Dairy as soon as the plant began operation.

Also in January, the Board let the bids on what was to be the final facility of the May era. The $30,000 35' x 75' swimming pool complete with dressing rooms was projected to be finished by late summer.

By March, President May had entered the Stone County Hospital. In April, Dean of Students Hayden began reporting to the Board on May's behalf. May resigned effective July 3, 1953, and died July 8.

On July 22, 1953, newly-elected President Hayden and the Board memorialized May by naming the football stadium in his honor. Six weeks after May's death, the pool was finished, and simultaneously the first milk bottles labeled "Perkinston Junior College Dairy" came off the line. Had he been alive to witness these occurrences, no doubt May would have pronounced them "mighty fine."

(Right) Dairy cattle mill about the Darby-era concrete block Dairy Barn in 1949. Photo from 1949 Perkolator, p. 21.
(Left) The Dairy and Pasteurizing Plant Building as it appeared shortly after the completion of the structure in January 1953. This building was constructed by adding a short Malvern tile storeroom to the rear of the Dairy Barn and a long Malvern tile pasteurizing plant area to the front of the Dairy Barn. The Dairy and Pasteurizing Plant Building produced its first bottled milk in August 1953 and ceased operation by Board order on March 25, 1959. According to agriculture instructor J. V. Gammage, who was interviewed in the Bulldog Barks, May 25, 1953, the new plant would supply milk to the school at a greatly reduced price and help students majoring in dairying to better understand the process. According to Gammage, the last stop on the conveyor belt in the plant was the automatic bottle capper that sealed the bottles. (Top right) In June 1995, Nettie Alexander, who was at that time courier for the college, found in the barn and gave to the archivist the only piece of ephemera related to the dairy contained in the MGCCC Archives in 2000. The bulldog logo milk bottle cap reads, "PERKINSTON JUNIOR COLLEGE, GRADE A, MIN. B.F. 3.8% PASTEURIZED MILK, PERKINSTON, MISSISSIPPI." Photo of Dairy and Pasteurizing Plant Building from Catalogue, 1952-1953, flyleaf. The Dairy and Pasteurizing Building still stood in 2000 and contained the office of the college engineer and the Central Office computer and office machine repair shop.

This aerial photograph from the 1954 Perkolator taken within a few months of President May's death on July 8, 1953, shows the campus as May left it. The swimming pool, the last facility built in the May era, appears in the Quadrangle between the tennis courts and the Old Gym. The pool, completed in August 1953, is filled but not fenced and the scars of construction still surround it. Most of the other May-era structures are visible as well. The five buildings of Military Perk are visible at left. A. L. May Memorial Stadium is at the top of the photo with the Colmer Building standing complete across the street. Due to the trees, only a portion of the World War II-era vo-tech complex of shops and garages is visible between the Colmer Building and Bennett Hall.

(Following page) The first schematic diagram or map of the institution appeared in An Evaluation of Perkinston Junior College and Agricultural High School April 21-24, 1952. This internal self study, ordered by President A. L. May, was the first evaluation of the school. The study lasted for three school sessions. The original names stated on the 1951 map were reprinted here. The shop (No. 9) and the garages (No. 33) together constituted the first vocational-technical center of the institution. The shop and garage structures consisted of portable buildings transported to the campus from Civilian Conservation Corps Camp P-814, Bay Springs. The five buildings of "Military Perk" appear at left on the map. The only two May-era facilities not yet built when the map was drawn were the swimming pool, located in the Quadrangle between the tennis courts (No. 32) and Old Gym (No. 2), and the enlarged Dairy and Pasteurizing Building.

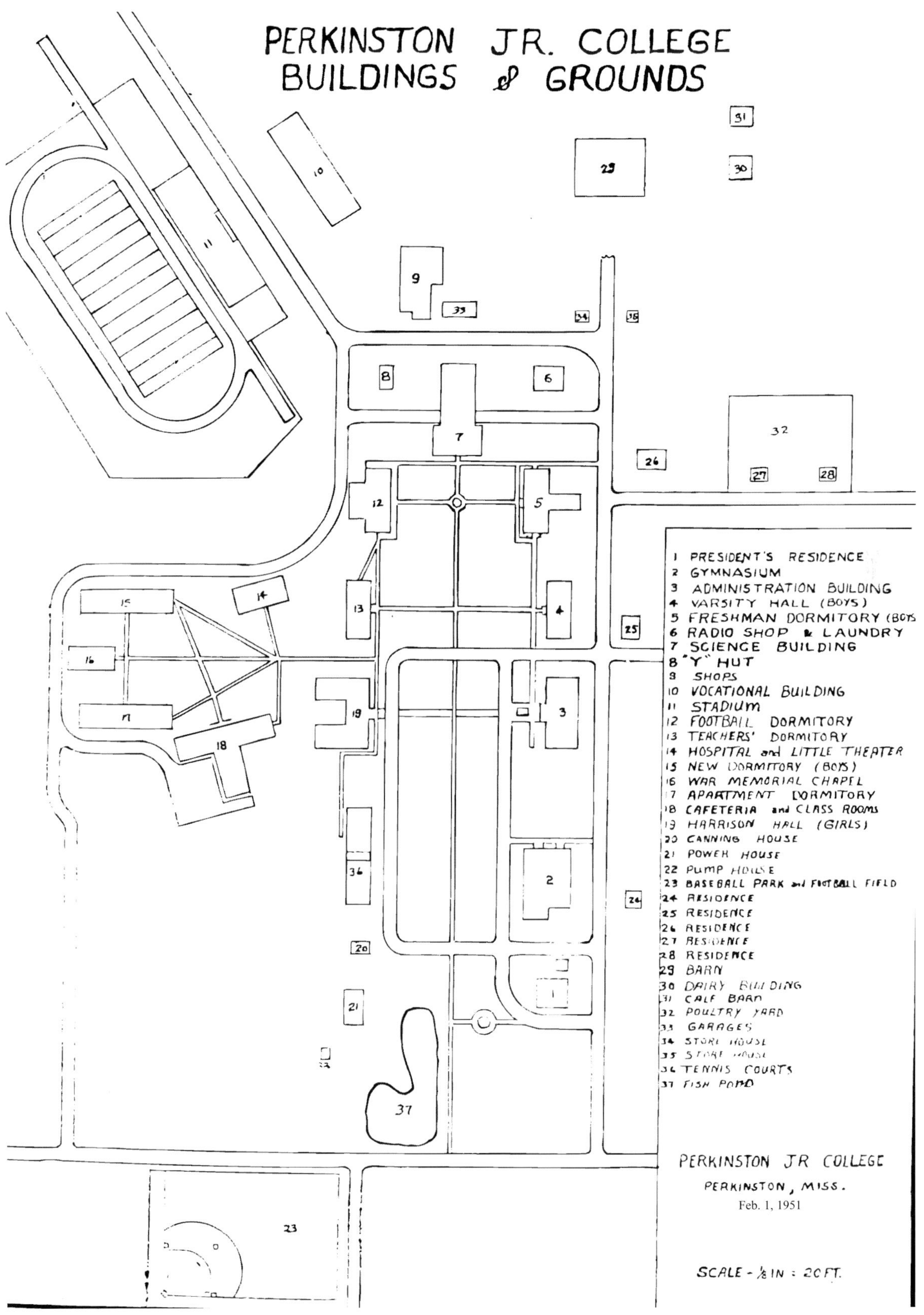
PERKINSTON JR. COLLEGE
BUILDINGS & GROUNDS
1 PRESIDENT'S RESIDENCE
2 GYMNASIUM
3 ADMINISTRATION BUILDING
4 VARSITY HALL (BOYS)
5 FRESHMAN DORMITORY (BOYS
6 RADIO SHOP & LAUNDRY
7 SCIENCE BUILDING
8 "Y" HUT
9 SHOPS
10 VOCATIONAL BUILDING
11 STADIUM
12 FOOTBALL DORMITORY
13 TEACHERS' DORMITORY
14 HOSPITAL and LITTLE THEATER
15 NEW DORMITORY (BOYS)
16 WAR MEMORIAL CHAPEL
17 APARTMENT DORMITORY
18 CAFETERIA and CLASS ROOMS
19 HARRISON HALL (GIRLS)
20 CANNING HOUSE
21 POWER HOUSE
22 PUMP HOUSE
23 BASEBALL PARK and FOOTBALL FIELD
24 RESIDENCE
25 RESIDENCE
26 RESIDENCE
27 RESIDENCE
28 RESIDENCE
29 BARN
30 DAIRY BUILDING
31 CALF BARN
32 POULTRY YARD
33 GARAGES
34 STORE HOUSE
36 TENNIS COURTS
37 FISH POND
PERKINSTON JR COLLEGE
PERKINSTON, MISS.
Feb. 1, 1951
SCALE - 1/8 IN = 20 FT.

HAYDEN AND THE ESTABLISHMENT OF MISSISSIPPI'S FIRST MULTI-CAMPUS JUNIOR COLLEGE JULY 1953 - SEPT. 1965

In his office in Jackson on Thursday, May 10, 1962, Mississippi Governor Ross Barnett signs the legislation creating the Mississippi Gulf Coast Junior College District, the state's first multi-campus junior college. Seated to the governor's right is J. J. Hayden, whose title by stroke of the governor's pen, has changed from that of president of Perkinston Junior College to that of president of Mississippi Gulf Coast Junior College. Standing from left: Representative Karl Wiesenburg (Jackson County), Senator Hudie Pitts (George County), Representative Jerry O'Keefe (Harrison County), Representative Roy Strickland (Stone County), Representative and MGCJC Board of Trustees Chairman M. L. Malone (George County), and Senator Stanford Morse (Harrison County).

Julius John Hayden Jr. was born May 19, 1920, in Pass Christian. He graduated from Pass Christian High School in 1938 and went to Perkinston Junior College to play football at the behest of Coach A. I. Rexinger. At 6' 2" and 135 pounds, he was not built to be a football player. But on May 4, 1940, in the state track meet at Hinds, Hayden, with a time of 4:42, won the state medal for running the mile.

Hayden joined the Army Air Corps in fall 1940. When a bout with the flu knocked him out of cycle in flight training, he took a separation from that service and joined the United States Coast Guard Reserves with the rating of Coxswain, just before the bombing of Pearl Harbor. Placed in charge of a 72-foot cutter, he patrolled for submarines out of Eastport, Maine, and other East Coast ports. On April 23, 1943, he married his high school sweetheart, Lillian Ruth Aschbacher, also of Pass Christian.

Discharged from the service at war's end, Hayden entered the freight boat business in Lubec, Maine, with the family of a Coast Guard friend. In Hayden's words the money was "fabulous . . . being a poor Mississippi boy," but it was seasonal, and "I guarantee you that both the smoked fish and the pickled fish [we hauled] were fragrant." The fish were so fragrant that his wife insisted he leave his work clothes in the yard before entering the house.

For years Hayden had thought about being a history teacher and coach, so he returned home and entered Mississippi State in January 1947 under the G.I. Bill. Two years later he finished his bachelor's degree in secondary education with a major in social studies and went directly into the master's program in history.

In fall 1949, Hayden took a job as coach and history teacher at Lee Road Elementary-Junior High School fifteen miles north of Covington in St. Tammany Parish, Louisiana. He taught three different history courses, coached both girls' and boys' basketball, and taught all the recreation classes.

Somehow he found time to continue work on his master's thesis, *The History of Pass Christian 1699-1900*. He completed the thesis and received his master's degree in history in summer 1950. Soon thereafter he heard of a temporary vacancy for a history teacher at Perkinston. Nollie Wade Hickman was taking a leave of absence to return to the University of Texas to work on his monumental dissertation entitled, *History of Forest Industries in the Longleaf Pine Belt, East Louisiana and Mississippi, 1840-1915*. Hayden applied for the job and got it.

In session 1950-1951 Hayden taught five classes with four different preparations--world history, economics, sociology, and government. His favorite was the government class that was a vocational-technical related course for veterans attending on the G.I. Bill. The students knew that Hayden's father was the supervisor of Beat 3, Harrison County, so the class came to focus primarily on local government. The principles of this class were soon to become very important to Hayden in his impending rise to power, which was destined to be nothing less than meteoric.

In his second year, session 1951-1952, Hayden chaired two committees on the self-study of the school--pupil population and the college community and social studies. In addition, he served on several other committees--philosophy and educational needs of students, core programs, library services, and guidance. President A. L. May was impressed with his performance in these areas. Consequently, when the United States Naval Reserve called up Dean of Students Truett Nash for service in Korea that session, May asked Hayden to assume Nash's duties until his return. Hayden accepted and was still filling in for Nash when May became ill with a rare form of leukemia in January 1953.

At the time there were really only three officers of the college--Dean of Students Hayden, Business Manager L. A. Krohn, and Dean of Instruction/Registrar Col. Bob Rivers. Krohn was even newer than Hayden, having recently come on board to replace Thomas Gipson who had died in an automobile accident. "Col. Bob" as he was affectionately known, was near retirement.

(Left), Nineteen-year-old J. J. Hayden (right) stands next to track coach J. O. Brown during practice at Perk in 1940. Hayden was state junior college medallist in the mile run that season. Sitting from left are Alvaro Facio and Charles Wilson. Photo from 1940 Perkolator, p. 98.

Hayden's childhood sweetheart, Lillian Ruth Aschbacher, Perk cheerleader (third from left) attended Perk in Session 1939-1940 because, in her words, "J. J. was there." Photo from 1940 Perkolator, p. 88.

(Left), Chief Boatswains Mate, J. J. Hayden married Lillian Ruth Aschbacher on April 23, 1943. Photo from 1975 Perkolator, p. 95.

HAYDEN PHOTO ALBUM

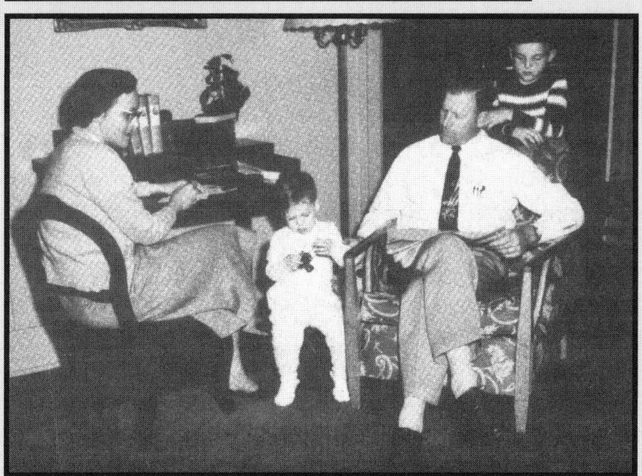

The Haydens in the 1927-era President's Home in late 1954. (from left) Lillian, Glover Richard, J. J. Jr., and Julius John III known as "Jay." A daughter, Susie Stafford, was born later. All three Hayden children graduated from Perk. Photo from 1955 Perkolator, p. 134.

Hayden sits in his office in the Old Denson Building shortly after becoming president.

According to Hayden, "the three of us formed a little committee to operate the college--no official action, nobody told us to or not to." Col. Bob and Krohn asked him to lead their group, so in Hayden's words, "I started going to the board meetings," and "I would confer with Mr. May." Hayden continued as acting-president for several months. As his illness worsened, May sent a letter of resignation to the Board dated July 3, 1953. He died five days later.

In a special board meeting on July 15, six names were placed in nomination for the position of President of Perkinston Junior College. Two of the nominees, one of whom was Hayden, were present. The board granted each man ten minutes to speak. The other contender spoke of his qualifications for six minutes. Hayden spoke for five and got the job. At the age of 33 Hayden became the youngest chief executive officer in the history of the institution. His term of two years at $6,000 per annum began immediately.

In Hayden's first regularly scheduled board meeting on July 22, 1953, the football stadium was given the name "A. L. May Memorial Stadium," and the track and football field became "May Field."

Soon after assuming office, Hayden said, "We intend to continue the junior college philosophy of offering every student who desires two years of college education a chance to attain that goal." His major problem in the realization of this philosophical goal was the isolation of the college. The institution had been founded as an agricultural high school in a rural area. Even so, it had evolved into a junior college and had served its region well as long as the coastal towns had remained relatively small. But the Mississippi Gulf Coast,

The Perkinston Junior College Board of Trustees, composed of 24 total members (six for each District county), poses for the camera during a meeting in the conference room in the Denson Building at Perkinston in 1954, the year after Hayden became president.
(From left standing) *Mrs. Charles M. (Ruth) Carr of Ocean Springs; (to Carr's front) Bruner A. Lott of Wiggins; (right of Carr) Leonard Blackwell of Wiggins; (right of B. A. Lott) Lester Mack of Escatawpa; (right of Len Blackwell) J. J. Hayden; Charles S. "Vester" Wentzell, President of the Board; C. E. "Gene" Dees of Perkinston; Mack M. Morgan of Pascagoula; (partially hidden behind M. M. Morgan) W. W. Taylor of Wiggins; K. G. Brown of Lucedale; M. L. Malone of Lucedale; A. M. Dantzler of Pass Christian; J. L. Cochran of Lucedale; Duncan E. "Dunk" Smith of Perkinston; L. A. Krohn (business manager).*
(Seated from left) *B. A. Evans of Perkinston; Robert G. Carson of Biloxi; Gavin M. Hamilton of Moss Point.*
Not pictured: *R. L. Ladner of Gulfport; W. H. Caraway of Gulfport; R. J. Moran of Lyman; Carl Megehee of Pascagoula; Norman Flurry of Perkinston; Leo Rouse of Lucedale; M. L. Pope of Lucedale; W. T. Moore of Perkinston.*

which had entered the Second World War as a peripheral province, had, in a few short years, joined America's military-industrial complex. The erstwhile quiet towns which had dotted the littoral in the pre-war era were now becoming wide-awake cities growing rapidly toward one another and rimming the coast.

Many of the coast's war-born installations and industries remained intact even after the guns cooled as the United States for the first time embraced the concept of "Cold War" and consequently, military preparedness. Keesler Field, even after demobilization, remained a city within a city with a population of 20,000. Ingalls Shipbuilding retooled for civilian production but retained its favored status as a ship fabricator for the peacetime navy. Tourism, always important, became big business in 1951, when the U. S. Corps of Engineers pumped in a sand beach to protect the seawall, which was protecting U. S. Highway 90--the nation's first transcontinental four-lane coast-to-coast military superhighway.

The new coast industries and businesses needed skilled technicians and educated workers, and the only mature, established educational institution in the area was Perkinston Junior College. But could a small isolated junior college supply the demand?

In Hayden's first year as president the total enrollment for

Radio-television repair students "learn by doing" in the Colmer Building at Perk in 1954. This two-year terminal program initiated the year before was the first of its kind in Mississippi. Photo from 1955 Perkolator, p. 97.

the regular session reached 583, a gain of 63 students over the previous year. Of these, 188 were AHS students, 316 were junior college academics, 44 were junior college night students, 30 were vocational-technical majors, and five were farm trainees. The boarding capacity of the school stood at 340. Two bus routes--one originating in Lucedale and the other in Biloxi--continued to transport day students as they had since their establishment in the last year of the May Era.

Under the direction of Vocational-Technical Director Curtis Davis, the vo-tech offerings of the college grew. In 1953 the college announced Mississippi's first two-year terminal radio-television program. 1956 saw the addition of electronic technology and drafting technology. The school added another bus route that year, and total enrollment grew to 727.

Regular session enrollment showed steady growth while summer school attendance averaged about 100 in the early Hayden years. But Hayden knew that the enrollment would skyrocket if he could find a way to make the college offerings more available--especially to working people.

In January 1957, Hayden announced the establishment of a new Evening College at Perkinston. This Evening College was envisioned to be a great improvement over the hit-or-miss night class offerings of the past. Specifically aimed at the working population of the region, the Evening College had its own director, Charles Clark, and offered, at first anyway, nearly all the day classes of the institution so that an enrollee could actually get a junior college degree (academic or vocational-technical) at night. All any coastal town dweller had to do was work all day and then drive 40 to 65 miles up a two-lane highway, sit in class from 6:30-9:30 and then drive 40 to 65 miles home and study. It was strictly up to the student to choose to do this one to four nights a week. Depending on his choices, the student would have to attend in this manner between two and one-half and ten and one-half years in order to graduate. The Evening College at Perkinston served the people of McHenry and Wiggins, and not many of them, because the offerings fell precipitously in a short time.

To paraphrase the founder of Islam--If the mountain would

not come to Perkinston, Perkinston would go to the mountain. In May 1957, Hayden announced a study for the purpose of establishing a Perkinston Junior College Coast Center. Simultaneously he announced the beginning of a practical nursing program to be taught in alliance with the hospitals in the four county areas served by the school. Groups of 20 practical nursing students would take three months of pre-clinical classroom study at the campus followed by nine months of clinical training at participating hospitals. Practical nursing students had to be over 18 with a 10th grade education and could ride the free Perk buses for the pre-clinical phase, but they had to buy two uniforms, one pair of shoes, and a watch. Lunch was not included. Completion of the program earned the student a certificate, but only the passing of a state-administered examination conferred the coveted title of Licensed Practical Nurse (LPN).

In session 1957-58, Patricia Martin (front row right in the white uniform of a registered nurse), who began teaching at Perk in June 1957, stands on the front steps of the Infirmary (renamed the Smith Building in 1960) with a group of enrollees in the licensed practical nursing (LPN) program. ***First row*** *(from left), Zadie Sbardella of Biloxi, Ruth Oakes of Pass Christian, Constance Spooner of Gulfport, Darline Miller of Wiggins, Annie Thomas of Gulfport, Patricia Martin, R.N. (instructor)* ***Second row*** *(from left), Olivia Jones of Gulfport, Joyce O'Dell of Biloxi, Alice Williams of Mississippi City, Amanda Pabon of Ocean Springs, Virgie McLeod of Perkinston, Johnnie Starcher of Gulfport, Fleta Carrington of Biloxi.* ***Third row*** *(from left), Gertrude Scruggs of Biloxi, Floy Bond of Lumberton, Irene Shifalo of Gulfport, Reba Malley of Saucier, Betty MacFarland of Biloxi, Eileen Porter of Biloxi, Fannie Drury of McHenry, and Mary Sammon of Biloxi. Photo from 1958 Perkolator, p. 68.*

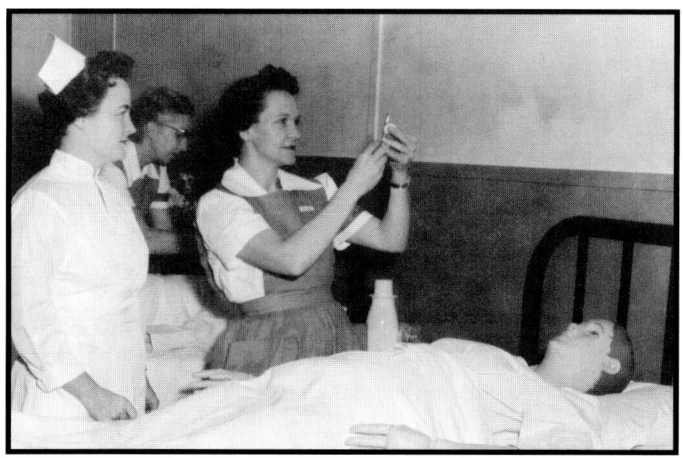

Patricia Martin (left) instructs an LPN student in the Infirmary at Perk in session 1957-1958. By 1959, LPN classes were being taught also in the Evening College at the O'Keefe home in Ocean Springs. When the home caught fire, Curtis Davis had to restrain firemen from risking their lives to save the "man in the bed" which was actually an anatomical dummy like the one in the photo. Photo from 1957-1958 Catalog, p. 85.

The new Coast Center was to offer eleven major fields divided into 43 pre-professional programs and nine terminal programs. In August, Hayden told the Biloxi Chamber of Commerce that the Coast Center should be in the vicinity of their city because it was near the geographical center of Perkinston's four-county area.

On August 29, 1957, Hayden hosted the organizational meeting of the Technical Advisory Committee for the college's new Technological Education Division headed by Curtis Davis. The members of the committee meeting that night in the Cafeteria and Classroom Building at Perkinston represented twenty of the most important firms of the New Orleans to Mobile region. Among the firms represented were Ingalls Shipbuilding Company of Pascagoula, Irby Brothers Machine and Iron Works of Gulfport, International Business Machines (IBM) of New Orleans, Texaco of New Orleans, Mississippi Aluminum Corporation of Gulfport, the *Daily Herald* Newspaper of Biloxi, Frank P. Corso, Inc. of Biloxi, and the A. M. Dantzler Lumber Company of Perkinston. In addition, representatives of government agencies such as Keesler Air Force Base of Biloxi, the Naval Construction Battalion of Gulfport, and the Biloxi Veteran's Administration Hospital were present.

Hayden and the college administration and teachers present explained the unique position occupied by the junior college in American education. Curtis Davis told the assemblage that the purpose of the junior college in the vocational-technical area at least was to teach exactly what the business and industrial leaders of the area wanted taught. The purpose was to prepare a student to go immediately into the workplace with the precise skills necessary to do a job that already existed. The only way to do this was close cooperation between the junior college and the employer.

George W. Ingles of Ingalls said his company wanted a strong technical program at Perkinston and offered to help plan the courses. Major E. A. Hiller said the Biloxi Veterans Administration Hospital wanted trained nurses, x-ray technicians, dental technicians, and other medical personnel. T. W. Crump of IBM said he wanted two-year training for new employees (five months later Crump gave the college it's first "computer trainer kit"). At this meeting the college forged its continuing alliance with the businesses and industries of its service region.

The next month at fall registration, temporary housing was set up in the Old Gym for some men. After that, students were turned away and encouraged to use the bus routes. Perkinston's facilities were not adequate for the demand. Hayden redoubled his efforts for a Coast Center.

On December 27, 1957, Mississippi Junior College Commissioner B. L. Hill approved Hayden's request for a survey team to determine the need for establishing a Coast Center. The five-man team, including Hill and junior college experts from Florida and Texas, met at Perkinston on January 14, 1958, and began to gather data.

On January 25 at 4:30 a.m., Stone County Deputy Sheriff

Ford O'Neal, patrolling the western part of the county several miles from Perkinston, saw the glow of flames. When he arrived at the campus, he found the Cafeteria and Classroom Building burning and no one aware. He awakened Hayden, who sounded the college fire alarm. The fire departments of Wiggins, Gulfport, and Hattiesburg arrived on the scene and their action saved nearby buildings which included the new $216,000 Wentzell Center Gymnasium, Harrison Hall, and the Apartment Dormitory.

Perk students hose the smoldering Cafeteria and Classroom Building on January 25, 1958. Photo from 1958 Perkolator, p. 45.

Jerry Bennett (PJC Class of 1959) stands in the rubble of the gutted Cafeteria and Classroom building in a snapshot taken by George Scherer (PJC Class of 1958).

The Cafeteria and Classroom Building was a total loss. The biology department and its laboratories no longer existed. The music department no longer existed. The band instruments, the pianos, and all the other accoutrements of the choir and band were lost. The campus no longer had a publicity office, a photo lab, a kitchen, or a cafeteria. No one was certain of the contents of all the destroyed storerooms, but choir director Eugene Clement estimated the loss at $250,000.

The destruction of the Cafeteria and Classroom Building occasioned what is termed a "fruit-basket turnover" as the already overcrowded facilities were forced to do extra duty. Fortunately, the recently completed Wentzell Center contained a new student grill, so the cafeteria could be returned to the quarters it had occupied from 1915-1948 under Stone Hall. The recently completed library building, soon to be christened Darby Hall, made the old library space in Bennett Hall available. Bennett Hall and Annex, which had become the AHS classroom building, now served college students once again, particularly in the realm of science instruction. Unfortunately the top floor of Bennett Annex, which had sustained structural damage a decade earlier in the 1947 Hurricane, was becoming more and more unstable.

As Hayden and the Perkinston Board began long range planning to build facilities to replace those destroyed by fire, a threat arose to the future of the college far greater than the loss of a building. Ironically, this threat came from Hayden's hometown. Mayor Francis Hursey of Pass Christian knew of the Perkinston survey to establish a Coast Center since it had been in the newspaper. He advanced an opposing plan to establish a Harrison County junior college on the site of the defunct World War II-era Merchant Marine Academy at Henderson Point at Pass Christian. Hursey envisioned this new junior college as the first step in the growth of a major four-year college or university for the coast. The 25-acre site contained a number of large stucco and tile buildings, tennis courts, an athletic field, paved drives, and a pier. Keble

Darby Hall (library/administration building) -- Because of limited funding from the state, the Board elected to build a structure on steel beam stilts with an eye to enclosing the understory at a later date. Work on the $73,000 library began in spring 1957. In July the Board borrowed $10,000 to add air-conditioning--a first for Perk. The library opened in fall 1957, and in February 1958, the Board began planning to enclose the lower floor for use as administrative offices. On August 20, 1958, the Board of Trustees abandoned the sweltering conference room in Old Denson and held a meeting in the air-conditioned library. The Board never returned to Old Denson. Apparently the enclosing of the administrative lower floor was completed in fall 1959. On May 14, 1960, the library/administration building was dedicated and named Darby Hall in honor of former Perk Superintendent Cooper J. Darby, who was present at the ceremony.

Wentzell Center ("New" Gym)--The Board of Trustees accepted the $196,000 structure which contained a gymnasium seating 800 and a student grill on April 17, 1957. Mississippi Lieutenant Governor Carroll Gartin spoke at its dedication at 3:00 p.m., homecoming day, October 5, 1957. In ceremonies held May 14, 1960, the day before graduation, the structure was named and dedicated to the memory of Charles S. "Vester" Wentzell. Wentzell, who had died December 28, 1957, had been President of the Board of Trustees at the time of the construction of the edifice.

College, a private four-year institution, had actually begun operation on the site in 1951 but had failed after a year due to lack of financing. Hursey believed that a public college on the site would flourish, and he secured the endorsement of the mayors of Long Beach, Gulfport, and Biloxi for the project.

The Coast had desired a university since the antebellum era. In 1841, Harrison County was born with its seat at Mississippi City. In that same year State Senator John J. McCaughan entered Mississippi City in the race as the site of the University of Mississippi. When he lost Ole Miss to Oxford by one vote, the 280-pound, fiery Scot-Irishman wielded his gold-headed cane against the skull of an opposing senator.

Many senior colleges and universities had opened extension centers on the Coast at Keesler Air Force Base, at high schools, and in any facilities they could obtain after World War II to serve the needs of veterans desiring educational opportunities under the GI Bill. Among these were Louisiana State University, Tulane University, Mississippi Southern College, and the University of Mississippi. The four-year institutions offered only junior level courses because all of them required seniors to attend class on campus. By 1951, though, Ole Miss was offering freshman and sophomore classes on the coast. When President May and the Perkinston Board heard about that, they delivered a two-page broadside dated June 20, 1951, which contained 14 whereases capped with a resolution deploring this educational imperialism in very clear and unmistakable terms. Copies were sent to the presidents of every Mississippi junior college, to the Board of Trustees of Higher Learning, to the Mississippi Junior College Association, the Mississippi Junior College Accrediting Commission, and to the Chancellor of the University of Mississippi.

Ole Miss stopped offering the freshman and sophomore courses but then proposed an alliance with the private women's junior college at Gulf Park to set up a permanent Ole Miss Center. Ironically Gulf Park College at Long Beach occupied the former site of Rosalie, the home of John J. McCaughan. Perkinston managed to postpone that movement until it evaporated.

Perkinston did not oppose four-year colleges offering upper division courses on the Coast. In fact, all the announcements that related to the survey being conducted for a Perkinston Coast Center touted the coming branch as a place where Coast citizens could obtain three years of college work. Perkinston would have been glad for the four-year colleges to offer both junior and senior courses. The four-year colleges themselves refused to do so because of their own residency requirements. Perkinston objected to four-year colleges offering lower division courses because it was a duplication of effort and would kill the junior college. In Hayden's words, "I could see Harrison County flying away out of our fold . . . . I knew that Perkinston . . . could not support [itself alone] because most of our finances as well as everything else came from Harrison County at that time."

Once again, as in 1916, imaginary lines on a map threatened the institution's existence. Some in Harrison County still did not like supporting a junior college in Stone County. Probably these persons did not know, and if they did, did not care that the Harrison County Agricultural High School and the Perkinston community had fought the formation of Stone County to the last ditch for four years. Some Perkinston inhabitants had carried the fight on even after defeat by trying to get the new county annulled. So, having once fought to stay in Harrison County and lost, the institution would now have to engage in dubious battle to keep the support of her parent county. The Harrison County mayors were a problem, but the battle would be won or lost in the meeting room of the Harrison County Board of Supervisors, and Hayden's father was no longer a member of that board.

On February 11, 1958, six days after Hursey's proposal for a new junior college at Henderson Point appeared in print, Hayden went before the Harrison County Board of Supervisors and outlined a four-point plan. (1) He needed funds to replace the burned Cafeteria and Classroom Building; (2) he needed general improvement funds for college and AHS building renovations and equipment; (3) he desired the establishment of a Perkinston Coast Center; (4) he desired the establishment of a Negro junior college to meet the demand "that must be faced sooner or later." This last referred to the separate but equal doctrine embraced by the state of Mississippi in educational matters.

In further reference to the AHS, Hayden told the supervisors that the funds then available for the AHS were insufficient, and money earmarked for the college was being used to support the AHS. This could not continue. He said the AHS currently served 104 day students from Stone County and 99 from Harrison. The AHS boarding students numbered 30, and 25 of those were from Harrison County.

When Beat Two Supervisor Roy Dedeaux reminded Hayden of the four mayors' plan for a new junior college at Henderson Point, Hayden labeled that proposal "impractical." He further stated that he doubted that the State Junior College Commission would approve a site in such close proximity to both Pearl River Junior College, which served Hancock County just across the Bay of St. Louis, and Perkinston, which served Harrison County. Besides, Hayden continued, "It would cost less in the long run to build the proposed new Perkinston Center which should logically be established near the population center of Biloxi-Gulfport." Hayden later said he wished he had waited for the findings of the Survey Team before saying anything about a site.

On August 20, the Survey Team reported to the Perkinston Board that the site for the new Coast Center should be at the geographical center of the coastline extending from Pass Christian to Pascagoula. Thus, the committee recommended a site on the line between Biloxi and Ocean Springs. The Board approved the report and sent it to the Mississippi Junior College Commission for approval.

The four counties approved a bond issue to replace the facilities lost by fire at Perkinston. On February 18, 1959, the Perkinston Board approved bids for the construction of a cafeteria/music building (later to be called Heidelberg Hall) and an addition to Darby Hall. The addition really entailed the enclosure of the patio of the library. Darby Hall had been built on stilts of steel beams with the idea of later enclosing the area underneath as a first floor. Simultaneously the Board approved advertising for bids for a new science building (later to be named Hinton Hall).

By mid-April the campus at Perkinston was in the midst of the greatest building and renovation boom in its history. Sites for Heidelberg and Hinton were being bulldozed, and the bottom floor of Darby was being prepared for enclosure to serve as the office of the Perkinston Campus academic dean. Renovation had already begun in George, Stone, and Jackson dormitories. The number of boarding college students in those three halls together with the 128 students in Harrison Hall for women had already reached 400 and would go higher.

Tennis courts to replace the old ones destroyed for the site of Wentzell Center were being constructed. The Hurricane-damaged second floor of Bennett Annex was being removed and the roof lowered to the first floor. The inadequate water system and mains were being reworked. A row of new faculty duplexes was being built and old faculty houses repaired.

Heidelberg Hall (cafeteria/band and music building), Perk's only round building, was constructed to replace the Cafeteria-Classroom Building which had burned January 25, 1958. The Board of Trustees accepted the $210,000 tri-level structure on February 24, 1960, and dedicated it and named it for former President of the Board of Trustees Hinkle P. Heidelberg on May 14, 1960. The new cafeteria began service at some point between late February and early May as the dedication banquet was held in it. So at some point in spring 1960 the 1915-era Stone Hall dining room, pressed into service after the Cafeteria-Classroom Building fire, ceased operation for the last time. Photos from 1960 Perkolator, p. 112.

Megehee Building (home economics building)--Constructed as a laboratory and practice house for the homemaking program, the $45,000 steel, concrete, and brick structure was accepted by the Board on January 17, 1962. Home economics teacher Juanita McInnis opened her second semester classes in the facilities a few days later. In ceremonies held May 22, 1963, the building was dedicated to the memory of A. Forrest Megehee, former member of the Board and former Jackson County superintendent of education who died October 18, 1951.

FINAL STRUCTURES AT PERKINSTON BEFORE THE TRI-CAMPUS ERA

Hinton Hall (science)--The square concrete brick and steel structure with an open central patio was built on the site of the 1927 power plant and on a filled in portion of the power house pond. Simultaneously, a new road was cut from the lower end of the Quadrangle to the Perkinston-Silver Run Road in order to provide a new main entrance to the college. That action resulted in filling even more of the pond. The board accepted the $118,500 structure on February 24, 1960, predicting occupancy within 30 days. On March 14, 1960 the new science hall was dedicated and named for Clarence O. Hinton, former science department chairman and administrator at Perk, then a druggist in Wiggins. Hinton died September 24, 1967.

The enclosure of the lower floor of Darby Hall was completed circa Fall 1959.

On April 18, 1959, the Mississippi Junior College Commission announced that Perkinston Junior College had been granted authorization to establish a Coast Center at a yet undetermined location. While other junior colleges in other states had similar centers, this was a first for one of the 15 junior colleges in Mississippi.

At the Perkinston Board meeting on April 22, Commissioner Hill visited to tender his congratulations. Hayden and the Board invited Hill and the other members of the Survey Team of the previous year to select the site and to recommend curriculum and facilities.

In early July, as the Survey Team searched for a site for the Coast Center, Charles Clark, director of Perkinston's Evening College, announced that facilities for holding night classes for the coming fall had been rented by the college in Ocean Springs. Some academic courses and practical nursing classes and other vocational courses would be held in the old Trilby's Restaurant building also known as the old O'Keefe Home.

The rental of night class facilities in Ocean Springs fueled speculation in Harrison County that the site of the Coast Center might be in Jackson County as well. Speculation about the Coast Center inevitably led to speculation that the Coast Center would inevitably become the genesis of Mississippi's greatest university, and the fuse on the political powder keg began to burn.

In a letter to the editor of the *Daily Herald* on July 8, Earl Noland of Saucier wrote,

"About one-hundred-fifty years ago Harrison County by one vote in the State Legislature lost the privilege of having the University of Mississippi located within its boundaries.

About fifty years ago . . . the county lost what became a junior college when Stone County was formed although Harrison was the principal supporter.

Now Harrison County is doing nothing to secure the location in the county of the Coast Center for Perkinston Junior College although this center may--according to an article in today's Herald become a four-year college. This college should be in Harrison County and west of Biloxi."

On July 28, Ed Larson of Gulfport wrote,

"The people of Harrison County have for years contributed to the support of a Junior College in Stone County. Now we are being conditioned and readied to support one in Jackson County. Thus we will be in the position of supporting educational facilities in two counties adjoining our own . . . . Surely Mississippi's second most populated county should have a junior college . . . in its own boundaries.

I sincerely hope that Harrison County civic leaders and politicians will awaken . . . and lead a fight to have the Perk Extension located here or to build a junior college of our own, independent of Perk."

In late August the Gulfport Chamber of Commerce proposed the mothballed Gulfport Navy Base (also known as the Naval Construction Battalion Base or CB--"Seabee"--Base) as the site of the Coast Center. Simultaneously the Harrison County Board of Supervisors informed Hayden that the Coast Center should be sited at the population center of Perkinston's service area in Harrison County and not at the geographical center in Jackson County.

On September 23, 1959, at Perkinston, the Survey Team made its report to Hayden and the Perkinston Board. The Survey Team had considered five sites, all of which were in Jackson County and decided on one in Gulf Hills just north of Ocean Springs. Hayden and the Perkinston Board approved the report and ordered it forwarded to the Junior College Commission for final approval. Each Board member was requested to invite his or her appointing supervisor to a special meeting at Perkinston on October 1. The Harrison County supervisors were to be cultivated with special diligence, as the money for the Coast Center site was needed. The *Daily Herald* printed the account of this Perkinston Board meeting the next day. While there was no great outcry, Harrison County officials went into a posture of passive resistance.

In a speech to the Gulfport Civitan Club on October 9, Hayden noted that the five members of the Survey Team were experts from upstate Mississippi or out-of-staters with no personal stake in the outcome. He also warned that the failure of the coast to show popular support might result in disapproval of the Coast Center on the part of the junior college commissioner. His remarks had no effect.

A month after Hayden and the Board approved the Survey Team's site, the fireworks began. Biloxi Mayor Laz Quave, together with other Biloxi city officials, sent a missive to the Perkinston Board of Trustees. In the letter they stated their position clearly and unequivocally: "We do not want to take anything away from Jackson County, but we feel that it is unfair to the taxpayers of Harrison County to place a school there." The letter furthermore stated that not only was western Jackson County not the population center of Perkinston's service area, it also was not the geographical center either. Quave and his commissioners ended by saying they would like for the Perkinston Board to reconsider and select a site in Harrison County.

In early November the owners of the first choice site in Gulf Hills withdrew their offer due to delay in acceptance. Hayden and the Board requested more time from the junior college commissioner to check on the purchase of the other recommended sites. Failing that, the college wanted a new survey. In December Hayden told the Board of rumors that Harrison County was moving to set up a new junior college. He told the Board, however, "not to be alarmed, yet."

Then came some real fireworks. A blaze gutted the O'Keefe Home in Ocean Springs, where the Evening College classes were being held. Curtis Davis, who oversaw the practical nursing classes as part of his duties as vocational-technical director, received a call from the Ocean Springs Fire Department. He raced from Perkinston to the scene of the

1960 Perkinston Junior College associate degree nursing class in front of Singing River Hospital.
***First row** (from left), Bennie Warnock and June Calfas, Moss Point; Sandra Schatmeyer, Pascagoula; Carrol Townley, Biloxi; Betty Scheffler, Ann Byrd, Gloria Odom, and Jean Coats, Pascagoula; Cora Mae Johnson and Alene Bonner, Laurel.*
***Second row** (from left), Katherine Parent and Joan Cubberson, Biloxi; Jane White, Perkinston; ADN instructor Mrs. Katherine Webb, Pascagoula; PJC Vo-Tech Director Curtis Davis; PJC Director of Nursing Margaret Kingman, Gautier; PJC President J. J. Hayden; instructor Miss Lois Dickson, Moss Point; Mary Williford, Laurel; Elaine Philen, Biloxi; Irene Murphy, Pascagoula.*
***Third row** (from left), Helen White, Hattiesburg; Wallace Parent, Biloxi; Tommy Wood, Laurel; Catherine Jameson, Moss Point; Yvonne Dill, Hattiesburg; Katie Rayburn, Pascagoula; Edna Earl Davis, Moss Point; Joann Dufek, Gautier; Zula Mae Sanders, Moss Point; Anita Blanks, Meridian; Jean Burnham, Perkinston; Edna Touchstone, Wiggins; Dorothy Easterling, Broome; Joyce Cranford and Jeanette Crimm, Pascagoula. Not pictured is Ann Gunter of Kreole. Photo courtesy of Wanda Brignac.*

blaze and, with greatest difficulty, stopped the firemen from risking their lives to save "the man in the bed upstairs." Davis finally got them to understand that the "man" was really the anatomical dummy used in the practical nursing classes.

In the semester following the fire, the 55 students enrolled in academic classes met at the Gulf Coast Research Laboratory in Ocean Springs until quarters could be rented in the Dale Building, and the 12 practical nursing students were transferred to Pascagoula High School.

Hayden and a committee of the Board requested a face-to-face meeting with the Harrison County Board of Supervisors. Beat Two Supervisor Roy Dedeaux ignited the powder keg. He stated that 65 per cent of Perkinston's annual budget came from Harrison County, and in his opinion the "golden goose providing an abundance of golden eggs" ought to be able to decide the site of any Perkinston Coast Center. While he was at it, he blasted the numerical makeup of the 24 member Perkinston Board of Trustees. Each of the counties had six trustees--one appointed by each of the five supervisors in each county plus the superintendent of each county school system as an ex-officio member. Therefore, Harrison County, which supplied two-thirds of the funding, had a one-quarter voice in the running of the school. In his estimation, Dedeaux thought the only viable solution to the problem was for Harrison County to establish its own junior college and eventually advance it to a senior college. Dedeaux then requested that the Harrison County superintendent of education undertake a survey to do just that. This was a most interesting development since Superintendent Esco Smith was in attendance with Hayden as a member of the Perkinston Board. Thus ended Perkinston's first attempt to establish a Coast Center.

In the aftermath of the Coast Center defeat, Hayden told the Perkinston Board, "Let's just stay at Perk and improve Perk." The Board agreed and all off-campus operations except the practical nursing interchange with area hospitals were suspended.

A few days later, on May 12, 1960, Perkinston expanded its commitment in the field of nursing training far beyond the pre-clinical nursing curriculum offered since 1944. Margaret Kingman was named director of nursing for a program aimed at producing registered nurses (RNs).

The new associate degree nursing (ADN) program was the result of an agreement worked out by Vo-Tech Director Davis between the National League of Nurses and the Mississippi State Department of Education. Northeast Mississippi Junior College at Booneville was offering a three-year ADN program. Davis and the National League of Nurses wanted an 18-month program. The state superintendent of education compromised by decreeing that the new program would run two years and two summers. All instruction was to be carried out by Perkinston Junior College instructors both on the campus and in participating hospitals until the second summer when the nursing students were to receive their final training at the State Hospital at Whitfield.

Lester Tuck, chief administrator of the Singing River Hospital in Jackson County, was so impressed by the new ADN program that he had a dormitory built next to the hospital. The students lived in the hospital dormitory and were bused to the campus at Perkinston on certain days of the week for classes. At the end of their training, the students received the associate degree in nursing, but as in the case of LPNs, only the passage of a state examination conferred the title of RN.

On May 25, 1960, in an effort to bring as many students to Perkinston as possible, the college advertised the expansion of its bus routes to five. The new routes served the Coast towns from Pass Christian to Pascagoula. All told, the buses brought in 174 students daily to swell the fall enrollment to 958. The Pascagoula bus, which departed at 6:30 a.m. and ran the longest round trip of 110 miles, was designed to carry 37 but instead carried 50.

In late September, reports reached Perkinston that senior colleges were once again offering freshman and sophomore

Drivers ready the PJC bus fleet for action in front of the Colmer Building in 1956. The college began busing college students to Perkinston on September 1, 1952, with two routes--one originated in Biloxi and the other in Lucedale. By 1962 the routes numbered seven and served practically every main road in the four county district. Bus service ended with the opening of the coast campuses in September 1965, except for the Lucedale route which continued until October 18, 2000. Photo from 1955-1956 Catalog, p. 12.

BUS SCHEDULES
MISSISSIPPI GULF COAST JUNIOR COLLEGE DISTRICT
(PERKINSTON)

ROUTE 1

Leave Hurley Community .... 6:10 a.m.
Leave Wade Community .... 6:25 a.m.
Lampton Road (63) to Highway 26. Highway 26 to Wiggins. Highway 49 to Perkinston.

ROUTE 2

Leave Agricola, High School .... 6:30 a.m.
Old Highway 63 to Lucedale
Leave Lucedale, Courthouse .... 6:45 a.m.
Highway 26 to Wiggins
Leave Wiggins, Bus Station .... 7:40 a.m.
Highway 49 to Perkinston

ROUTE 3

Leave Biloxi, East End of Howard Avenue .... 6:45 a.m.
Howard Avenue to Porter to Highway 90
Highway 90 to Lorraine Road to Handsboro
Leave Handsboro, Corner Pass Road and Lorraine Road .... 7:05 a.m.
Lorraine Road to Dedeaux Road
Dedeaux Road to Highway 49
Leave Orange Grove, Corner Dedeaux Road and Highway 49 .... 7:25 a.m.
Highway 49 to Perkinston

ROUTE 4

Leave Biloxi, West Gate of Keesler Field .... 6:45 a.m.
Pass Road to Gulfport
Leave Gulfport, Corner 25th Avenue and Pass Road .... 7:15 a.m.
Highway 49 to Perkinston

ROUTE 5

Leave Pass Christian, Corner Henderson Avenue and 2nd Street .... 6:45 a.m.
East on 2nd St. to Fleitas Avenue
Fleitas Avenue to Highway 90 to Long Beach
Leave Long Beach, Corner 2nd St. and Jeff Davis .... 7:00 a.m.
Jeff Davis to Railroad Street to Gulfport
Leave Gulfport, Corner 25th Avenue and Pass Road .... 7:15 a.m.
Highway 49 to Perkinston

ROUTE 6

Leave Pascagoula, Corner Market and Highway 90 .... 6:30 a.m.
Along Highway 90 to Ocean Springs
Leave Ocean Springs, Washington Avenue .... 6:50 a.m.
Old Highway 90 to St. Martin
Leave St. Martin, School .... 7:00 a.m.
Highway 67 to Saucier
Leave Saucier .... 7:40 a.m.
Highway 49 to Perkinston

All buses leave Perkinston on return trip at 3:15 p.m.

Buses begin running Tuesday, September 4.

REGISTER NOW!!

courses at facilities along the Coast. For the first time Hayden and the Perkinston Board made no public comment on the issue.

In late October, Hayden attended a college conference in Meridian. There he met Dr. C. C. Colvert, Chairman of the Department of Junior College Education at the University of Texas, who was then engaged in a study of Mississippi junior colleges. This fateful meeting set in motion a chain of events of immense proportions. Colvert knew all about the previous year's failed attempt to establish a Coast Center because one of his colleagues had been a member of the Survey Team.

Hayden reported to the Perkinston Board about Colvert's work. He then reminded the members that the visiting team of the Southern Association of Colleges and Schools (SACS) at the time of the previous year's self-study at Perkinston had suggested the implementation of a long-range plan for the college. Hayden suggested Colvert as the man to develop such a plan.

In mid-February, 1961, Hayden and a few members of the Perkinston Board attended a two-day junior college workshop at the University of Texas. On September 20, the Board hired Colvert as "a consultant for the long range campus planning . . . " including . . . "The coast center problems."

Hayden and the Perkinston Board had proclaimed the session 1961-1962 the "Golden Year," as it marked the 50th anniversary of the founding of the Harrison County Agricultural High School. That September, enrollment rose to 1,091, breaking the thousand mark for the first time in the institution's history. The total would have gone higher, but boarding students had been turned away after the 440-space capacity had been reached.

The record-breaking total of 1,091 included yet another record. AHS students numbered 281, the most ever. So the AHS was to die at the crest of the wave. Shortly after the term began, Hayden and the Perkinston Board informed the school officials of the counties of Harrison and Stone that the Perkinston AHS would be discontinued at the end of the session. According to the official press release given out by the Perkinston Board, this action was made necessary by SACS, which accredited both the AHS and the junior college. SACS declared that the AHS operation was not self-supporting and that junior college funds could no longer be diverted to it. But the final nail in the coffin was the ramshackle condition of Bennett Hall, the AHS classroom building. The college architects deemed it unworthy of renovation. Thus the AHS was to cease operation one summer shy of the 50th anniversary of its opening.

As Perkinston began its Golden Year celebration, Harrison County continued to seek ways to establish a rival junior college. That fall the Biloxi School Board came up with the novel idea of establishing a 13th and 14th grade in the Biloxi school system, but the Biloxi City Council failed to endorse the proposal.

Meanwhile, a potentially far more dangerous movement began in Gulfport. On October 23, 1961, at a meeting of the Gulfport Chamber of Commerce, Supervisor Roy Dedeaux seconded the motion of Jim Reese to investigate the possibility of establishing a junior college. Reese, the manager of

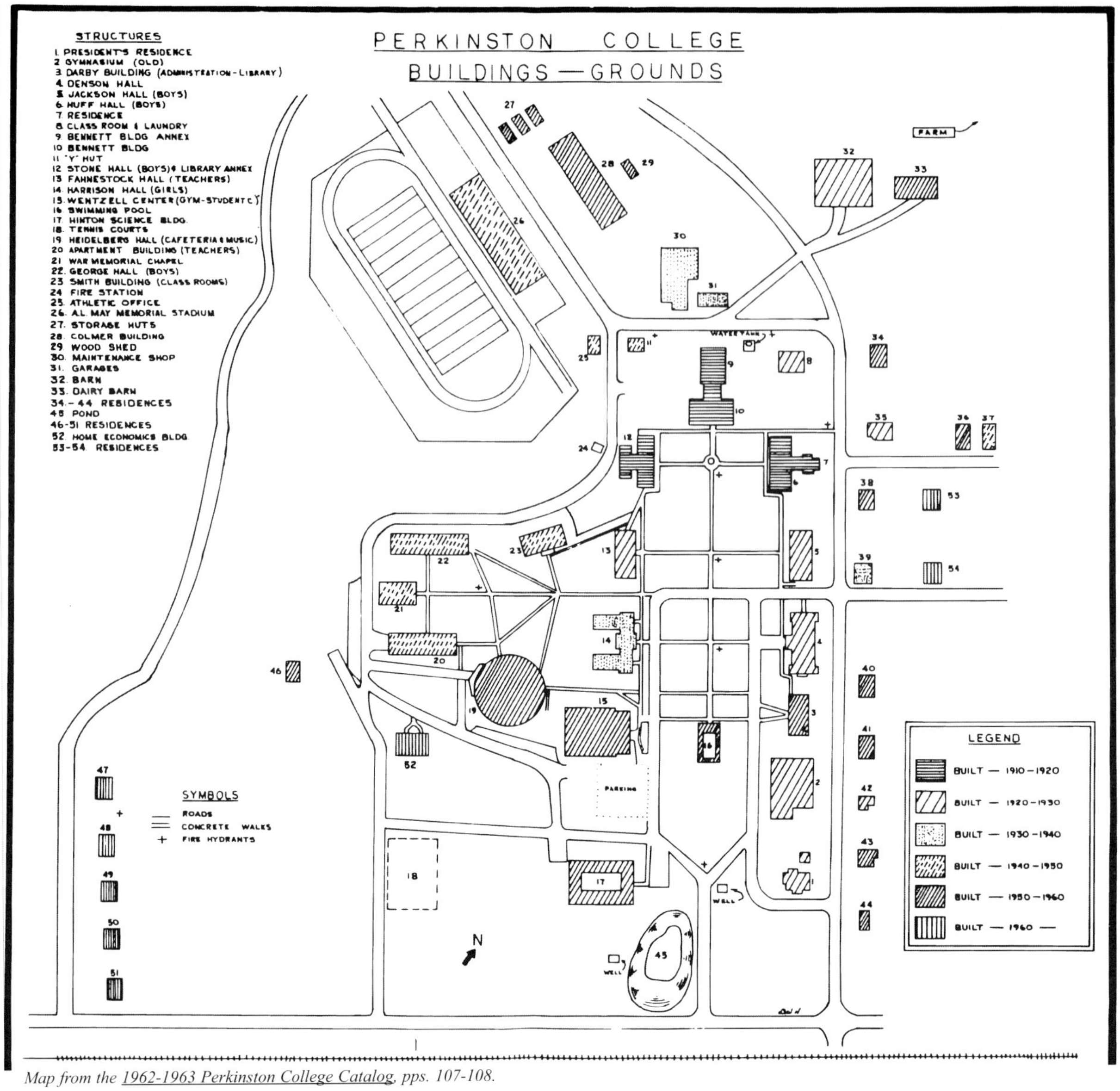

PERKINSTON COLLEGE
BUILDINGS — GROUNDS

STRUCTURES
1. PRESIDENT'S RESIDENCE
2 GYMNASIUM (OLD)
3 DARBY BUILDING (ADMINISTRATION - LIBRARY)
4 DENSON HALL
5 JACKSON HALL (BOYS)
6 HUFF HALL (BOYS)
7 RESIDENCE
8 CLASS ROOM & LAUNDRY
9 BENNETT BLDG ANNEX
10 BENNETT BLDG
11 "Y" HUT
12 STONE HALL (BOYS) & LIBRARY ANNEX
13 FAHNESTOCK HALL (TEACHERS)
14 HARRISON HALL (GIRLS)
15 WENTZELL CENTER (GYM-STUDENT C.)
16 SWIMMING POOL
17 HINTON SCIENCE BLDG.
18. TENNIS COURTS
19 HEIDELBERG HALL (CAFETERIA & MUSIC)
20 APARTMENT BUILDING (TEACHERS)
21 WAR MEMORIAL CHAPEL
22. GEORGE HALL (BOYS)
23 SMITH BUILDING (CLASS ROOMS)
24 FIRE STATION
25. ATHLETIC OFFICE
26. A.L. MAY MEMORIAL STADIUM
27. STORAGE HUTS
28. COLMER BUILDING
29 WOOD SHED
30. MAINTENANCE SHOP
31. GARAGES
32. BARN
33. DAIRY BARN
34.-44 RESIDENCES
45 POND
46-51 RESIDENCES
52 HOME ECONOMICS BLDG
53-54 RESIDENCES

SYMBOLS
ROADS
CONCRETE WALKS
FIRE HYDRANTS

LEGEND
BUILT — 1910-1920
BUILT — 1920-1930
BUILT — 1930-1940
BUILT — 1940-1950
BUILT — 1950-1960
BUILT — 1960 —

Map from the *1962-1963 Perkinston College Catalog, pps. 107-108.*

The new cut road between the barn and the Colmer Building is visible in this detail of a north view aerial made the same day as the aerial on the next page. The Bennett Building Annex second-story was removed in 1957 due to damage suffered in the 1947 Hurricane. The road between Bennett and Bennett Annex is visible. The Y-Hut is the frame structure to the right of Bennett. When Dees Hall was built in 1968, the Y-Hut was removed first to a site behind Gregory War Memorial Chapel and later to its 2000 location, behind Hayden Hall. The Huff Hall Cafeteria Annex (built 1912) can be seen in the photo, and so can the Stone Hall kitchen annex. The Stone Hall annex (built in 1927) was razed ca. 1970. In 1995 another Stone Hall annex was built on the site of the original. The Brick Laundry Building is left of Bennett Annex.

Aerial photograph of Perkinston Campus circa 1965 at the time of the opening of the two coast campuses. The map of the campus(previous page) used as the key to the above aerial photograph, came from the 1962-1963 Catalog. The numbers referred to below are derived from the diagram.

The principal Hayden-era buildings (initiated after July 1953) were:
(Refer to the previous page for locations).

No. 3 Darby Hall
No. 15 Wentzell Center
No. 17 Hinton Hall
No. 19 Heidelberg Hall
Nos. 47-51 are faculty houses finished in summer 1961. Nos. 47 and 51 were single family dwellings while Nos. 48, 49, and 50 were duplexes. In summer 1999 all Faculty Row inhabitants were notified to vacate by summer 2003 as Faculty Row houses had been slated for removal or razing. Nos. 53 and 54 are faculty houses built in 1963.
No. 52 Megehee Building

The main road entering Perkinston from the west in the above photo bore the name 3rd Street on the Uriel Wright Plat of Perkinston 1896. Once the road left Perkinston, it bore no official name until the mid-1990s when a sign went up proclaiming it Wire Road West. Historically this designation is erroneous because Old Wire Road ran from Mobile to New Orleans passing south of Perkinston. The Uriel Wright Plat contained names for all the streets in Perkinston. But no signs were erected until the mid-1990s, and no one in Perkinston knew the names of the streets. The original road going west out of Perk made a 90° turn and passed behind the Bennett building (site of Dees Hall in 2000) then curved again to pass between the sites of A. L. May Memorial Stadium and the Colmer Building. About 1962, a new road was cut through the 90° curve to take the road out of Perk between the barn and the rear of Colmer. In October, 1997, the old road was partially destroyed beyond Ken "Curly" Farris Baseball Field to end its days as a thoroughfare.

James Elbert Reese, a native of Huntsville, Alabama, born September 4, 1921, began his association with the Perkinston-based institution in 1961. As manager of Radio Station WGCM in Gulfport, Reese became the "voice of Perkinston" spreading the vision of the coming tri-campus junior college to thousands of listeners. He served as an MGCJC Trustee from January 1, 1964, until February 1976. In April 1977, Reese became the first MGCJC administrator to hold the title Director of Institutional Relations. He retired from MGCJC in November 1986 and died February 14, 1987 at his home in Brookhaven.

Radio Station WGCM in Gulfport, pitched the proposition to his listening audience. The constant bombardment of his deep bass voice began to bring results. Harrison Countians became keenly interested, particularly as Reese told them such a junior college could easily develop into "the largest university in Mississippi." To back up such assertions he noted the overcrowded condition in state public institutions and particularly at Perkinston, which was being forced to turn students away.

Actually a site for such a junior college already existed--the Seabee Base. The commander of the mothballed base informed Reese that two barracks buildings and a hospital stood ready for conversion to educational use. For the clincher, Reese, formerly of Alabama, had as a friend the president of a junior college in that state. So the Chamber of Commerce invited President David Roland of Walker Junior College in Jasper, Alabama, to come and to share his expertise the first week in November.

Hayden and the Perkinston Board members figured that they had better get their expert and his proposal before the people of Harrison County before Reese's expert arrived. On October 31, Hayden and members of the Perkinston Board staged a well-publicized meeting with Colvert present at the Markham Hotel in Gulfport. In a stellar performance, Colvert announced that he would conduct a survey to determine the possibility of establishing two Coast Centers of Perkinston Junior College. One of these should be in the Biloxi-Gulfport area of Harrison County and the other should be near Pascagoula in Jackson County. With that formula, Colvert really perked things up. Hayden had sold Colvert to the Perkinston Board as a "real diplomat and more . . . a real smooth operator." That he was. Colvert had discerned the political realities. Neither Harrison nor Jackson County would have been satisfied to let the other have the site of a single center. The only solution was to build one in each. The same political situation existed vis-à-vis Gulfport and Biloxi. The only solution was to build the Harrison County Center on neutral ground between them.

President Roland did come and speak, but by then he was not a potentially divisive influence. His remarks, in fact, helped to fuel Colvert's vision.

On November 13, Hayden spoke before the Gulfport Chamber of Commerce, the progenitor of which, it should be remembered, was the Gulfport Commercial Union. And it was the Gulfport Commercial Union, which, more than any other entity, had birthed the Harrison County Agricultural High School, which lead to the development of Perkinston Junior College. One of the Chamber of Commerce members present for Hayden's speech was Harrison County Chancery Clerk Cooper J. Darby, who was always ready to do his part for the school he had led through the Great Depression. Also present was Jim Reese, who was about to become one of the school's greatest supporters.

In his speech that day, Hayden explained the salient reasons why the two new centers should be formed as branches of Perkinston. First, as extensions of a mature, established college, the centers would be accredited by SACS at birth and not have to go through a five-year long initial accreditation process. Second, a four-county alliance to support the centers was already in place. Third, the machinery to administer and conduct classes in the centers already existed. In his view, said Hayden, the centers would in time achieve maturity themselves and form with Perkinston an educational "tripod" serving all the citizens of the four-county area. At the close of Hayden's speech, Reese made a resolution commending Perkinston on its Golden Anniversary and commending Hayden, faculty, and staff for the work accomplished by the college.

One week later Hayden introduced Reese to Colvert, and things really started to move. In Hayden's words Reese "was the catalyst [and] Dr. Colvert was the mediator and the person that worked out the problems." Reese's WGCM became the "voice of Perkinston," while Colvert prepared a report destined to change the course of junior college history in Mississippi.

Once again, in order to establish a presence in the Coast towns, the Perkinston Board, at its December meeting, ordered the Evening College, then under the direction of Charles Probst, to secure facilities for second semester night classes in Gulfport, Biloxi, and Pascagoula. This attempt met with greatest success in Pascagoula, where the Arts Building of the Jackson County Fairgrounds was secured. Seven teachers and administrators served there second semester, teaching 98 students. Mississippi State College offered junior, senior, and graduate courses there in conjunction with Perkinston.

Colvert presented his finalized report to the Perkinston Board in January 1962. Basically the Colvert Report recommended the organization of the four-county support area of the school into the Mississippi Gulf Coast Junior College District (MGCJCD). Composed of three junior colleges each with a dean responsible to President Hayden and the MGCJCD Board of Trustees.

The MGCJCD Board of Trustees was to be composed of no more than 14 members and have the revolutionary power to draw up a budget which the county boards of supervisors were required to fund by a levy of up to six mills. Colvert did not want a unwieldy board of 24 members, and he certainly did not want the president and the Board to have to go hat in hand to four different groups of supervisors to beg for funding each year. Besides, under this plan each citizen in all four counties would pay the same millage to the school.

Under Colvert's plan, George and Stone were to have two Trustees each, Harrison was to have six and Jackson four. The Perkinston Board deadlocked when George and Stone refused to give up any of their six members. The Harrison Trustees, no longer willing to have a one-quarter say in running the school, then bolted and joined the Harrison supervisors who were already chafing under the requirement to give up their taxing powers. Again Harrison County stood on the verge of secession as her officials called for the establishment of an independent Harrison County Junior College.

But this time the officials had no grassroots support. Hayden attributed this turn of events to Reese and his radio station. In Hayden's opinion, no supervisor who stood against the new district would have been re-elected. And there was another force at work. As Harrison County Chancery Clerk, Darby used his immense prestige to influence all the parties engaged in this internecine strife. He told the deadlocked Perkinston Board that they would have to reach a compromise on proportional representation in order to clear the way for the supervisors to surrender taxing power.

On October 24, 1964, President J. J. Hayden stands with Susie, the Hayden's last child and only daughter, as Harrison County Chancery Clerk Cooper J. Darby speaks at a lectern set up on the island in the Perkinston Campus Pond. Darby is eulogizing recently deceased Duncan E. "Uncle Dunk" Smith. As the institution's first Trustee to cross the 30-year service mark, Uncle Dunk set the 20th century record for service by a Stone County Trustee with 31 years, four months. Between Susie Hayden and Darby is a cloth covering a stone marker bearing Smith's name. The spray fountain placed in the pond and dedicated to the memory of Smith this night later disappeared, but the stone marker remained in 2000. Darby, who served as superintendent of the institution 1929-1941 supported Perk throughout his life. In the struggle to establish the tri-campus college, Darby used his political power and prestige to assure Harrison County support for the venture.

The Perkinston Board, after many votes, finally reached a compromise. Five members would be added to make a total of 29 members. George and Stone would retain their six members. Jackson would have seven and Harrison ten. With this "victory" in hand, Darby and his friends moved against the supervisors and in his words, "beat their ears down." On March 5, 1962, the Harrison County Board of Supervisors endorsed the proposed district.

In mid-April, House Bill 597, authored by Perkinston Board attorney Joel Blass for the purpose of establishing the Mississippi Gulf Coast Junior College District, was reported out of committee in the legislature with a unanimous "do pass" vote. On May 9, the Senate registered another unanimous vote on the bill, and Mississippi Governor Ross Barnett signed it into law the following day. This landmark legislation then became the model for the formation of junior college districts throughout the state.

House Bill 597, General Laws of 1962, Regular Session of the Mississippi State Legislature, had birthed a new educational entity called the Mississippi Gulf Coast Junior College District (hereinafter referred to as MGCJCD or as the "District"). This District was placed under the direction of Hayden and a 29-member Board of Trustees, which hereinafter will be referred to as the "Board."

In the first meeting after the formation of the MGCJCD held on May 23, 1962, at Perkinston, the Board appointed three committees to select "sites for the new colleges." These were the Harrison County Site Committee made up of the ten Harrison County trustees, the Jackson County Site committee made up of the seven Jackson County trustees, and the "Negro College Site committee" composed of two trustees from each District county.

This last committee, which soon became known as the "Fourth Site Committee," eventually selected the point where U. S. Highway 49 would cross the future line of Interstate 10. Ironically, from the hindsight of nearly four decades, that location would have been the finest site for a college in South Mississippi. But the passage of the Civil Rights Act of 1964, which tied federal education grants to compliance, resulted in Board acquiescence to that law in early 1965, thus rendering the Fourth Site Committee obsolete.

The only installation of the MGCJCD up and running at the birth of the District had, since 1942, been called Perkinston Junior College. On October 17, the Board gave that installation a new name: Perkinston College (hereinafter referred to as "Perk").

The coming installations to be sited in Harrison County and Jackson County were referred to in Board minutes and the media usually as "centers" or "attendance centers" or "branches." Sometimes, though, they were referred to as "junior colleges" or "colleges." Only rarely were they termed "campuses."

The appellation "Jackson County" always appeared before whatever term denoted the installation to be founded in the District's southeastern-most member county. Apparently someone suggested "Singing River" be used in the title. But in the board meeting of November 18, 1962, it was recorded that the L. L. Stine deed to some of the property eventually purchased for part of the site contained a proviso denying the MGCJCD the use of that name. One month later the Board formerly adopted as the official designation of the center the name: Jackson County Junior College (hereinafter referred to as "JC").

"Harrison County" quite naturally prefaced any designation given to the site in that county. On February 19, 1964, the Board adopted as the official name of that center: Jefferson Davis Junior College (hereinafter rendered "JD"). Inexplicably for months after the Board adopted the official name, JD still continued to be called by the name "Harrison County Junior College" in the official Board meeting minutes. Understandably the media took even longer to make the change.

In early summer 1962, the Board placed advertisements in the newspapers seeking two tracts in the 100-acre range located near the coastline with one in or near the Biloxi-Gulfport area and the other in or near the Pascagoula-Moss Point area.

Meanwhile, Colvert began a new study to determine curriculum, types of classrooms, laboratories, and placement of buildings. The Harrison County site was to be readied for 850 full-time equivalent students and the Jackson County site readied for 450.

Eleven sites were proposed in Jackson County. By July 18, the JC Site Committee had made its choice. JC would be located near the junction of Vancleave Road and U.S. Highway 90 in Gautier. The Committee also advised the acquisition of the Longhorn Saloon facing Highway 90 and surrounded on three sides by college property. That took a bit of dickering, but the negotiations eventually bore fruit.

Meanwhile, the Harrison County Site Committee, besieged with 22 offers on a line from Bay St. Louis to Biloxi Bay, bogged down in the political mire. Once again, Jim Reese formed his own committee and entered the fray, using his considerable influence to guide and protect the Board's site committee.

As the opening of fall classes drew near, Evening College Director Probst advertised numerous offerings at the Arts Building at the Jackson County Fairgrounds in Pascagoula. Nine classes made. Other huge ads listing four classes per night from Monday through Friday nights at the Seabee Base in Gulfport were not so successful. Apparently only one of the 20 classes developed--an English Composition class for Perkinston instructor Woodley Lott.

One Harrison County site lay at the end of Debuys Road, the border between Beat 1 (Biloxi) and Beat 2 (Gulfport). Neither city had reached Debuys Road yet, but they were growing toward it. A journey up Debuys in 1962 brought the traveler to its junction with Pass Road, Harrison County's earliest east-west artery dating back to colonial times. The area where Debuys Road and Pass Road joined was known as Fernwood, and a school by that name lay on the southwest corner of the point where the two roads crossed. One-quarter mile north of the crossing, Debuys ended in a field on the south shore of Bayou Bernard, an extension of Back Bay Biloxi. That field lay in the eastern-most extremity of an antebellum village known as Handsboro.

That field in Handsboro, which lay in the no man's land between Biloxi and Gulfport, was the only politically viable site for JD. The only way to avoid a conflict between Gulfport and Biloxi over JD was to place it between the two rivals and not in either.

Reese recommended the Handsboro site as early as September 19. In October, the Chambers of Commerce in both Biloxi and Gulfport added their endorsements. The Board ordered the purchase of a 124-acre site there in late November. In order to secure the tract, portions of which were owned by five families, the Board had to agree to allow aged Miss Effie Newman, her younger sister, and their parrot to remain at their home on the tract for the rest of their lives.

Assistant Vocational Technical Coordinator Barry L. Mellinger

Also in late November the Board called for a bond election in the amount of $3,200,000 for the construction of JD and JC. The voters of the District approved the bond issue on February 5, 1963. In March, the college architects presented the preliminary schematics of JD and JC to the Board, and the Board formally requested aid from the supervisors of Jackson and Harrison Counties for constructing and paving roads at the two sites.

As the plans for the sites went into motion, a new name appeared in the lists of employees. At the May meeting of the Board, Barry L. Mellinger entered the lists with the title "Assistant Vocational Technical Coordinator." This meant specifically that he was the assistant to his mentor, Curtis Davis. Years before, Mellinger, at that time a journeyman plumber, had gone to Perk on a job. Davis had met him then and had talked him into enrolling at Perk. After Mellinger graduated from Perk in 1960, Davis secured for him a fellowship at Mississippi State University. So Mellinger, armed with a fresh master's degree, began his career at MGCJC. Among his many duties would be oversight of the MGCJC's recent commitment to develop programs under the nation's new Manpower Training Development Act. The MTDA was specifically aimed at providing employment to unemployed persons over age 18 who lacked the necessary skills and education to secure jobs.

One of Mellinger's immediate duties was to help establish classes both vocational and academic on the site of JC in a pre-existing building. MGCJC had bought the Longhorn Saloon and given the purveyors of spirits until July 1, 1963, presumably at high noon, to vacate the premises.

At the January 22, 1964, Board of Trustees meeting, the Board named the academic deans who were to take charge of the three campuses of MGCJC on July 1. (from left) William P. Lipscomb named academic dean of Jefferson Davis Campus, Curtis Davis named academic dean of Jackson County Campus, President J. J. Hayden, and Charles G. Odom named academic dean of Perkinston Campus (replacing Lipscomb).

The commodious four-room structure then replaced the Arts Building of the Jackson County Fairgrounds as MGCJC's beachhead in Jackson County. According to Hayden, "Our students immediately dubbed it Longhorn University."

The Longhorn's lightning-bolt metamorphosis presented patrons from its former incarnation with "Twilight Zone" experiences. Biology teacher Clyde Strickland, who hauled twenty-four microscopes and several jars of formaldehyded frogs down there each week from Perk, recalls that on several occasions passing truckers who came in to drink remained to gape. In another instance, recalled by math instructor Sal D'Aquilla, a fellow who had quite obviously already visited several of his other haunts, burst into his calculus class and said, "Hey, buddy, I want a beer." Sal replied, "Yeah, me too, but I have to finish teaching this class first."

The success of Longhorn University is measured in its count of 16 classes in session 1963-1964. On the other hand, the Evening College experienced total defeat on its western front at the Seabee Base. No classes made there. Nonplussed the redoubtable Woodley Lott carried MGCJC's lamp of learning into previously benighted George County by establishing an English night class in Lucedale.

By November 1963, the architects' plans and models of JD and JC were complete. Grace and Guild, Architects, of Mississippi City, in association with Architect William R. Allen Jr. of Jackson, produced the plans and model of JD. William R. Allen, in association with Grace and Guild, produced the plans and model of JC. JD was to be a one story, flat rectangle of brick composed of 12 buildings separated by open courtyards and connected by colonnades. JC was to be a futuristic structure built of concrete block faced with light aggregate concrete and composed of a rectangular building connected to two flanking circular structures by covered walks.

The impending multiplication of installations in the District resulted in a multiplicity of administrative units. It had already been decided that each campus was to have a dean responsible to the president. The deans of the two new campuses would in turn and of necessity develop hierarchies similar to the one at Perk. But a supra-hierarchy would also have to develop about the person of the president. Hayden had crossed the line from Perkinston Junior College President to MGCJC District President the moment Governor Barnett signed House Bill 597.

Oddly enough one other administrator crossed the line unheralded. Curtis Davis had been vocational-technical director for some time when the District was formed. He had been based at Perk, but his duties covered all four counties, so the Board took no special action to define his job at the District level. Soon, though, Davis was being referred to as vo-tech coordinator rather than director. Shortly after that the word "District" began to appear in front of his title.

The real birth of the District administration came on January 22, 1964. On that day the Board named L. A. Krohn as Administrative Assistant in Charge of Finances and Harold T. White as Director of Student Personnel and Administrative Assistant in Charge of Public Relations.

In that same meeting, the Board named the deans of Perk, JD, and JC for the coming fiscal year which was to begin July 1. William P. Lipscomb, the current academic dean at Perkinston, was to take charge of the JD campus. Charles G. Odom, the current director of admissions and guidance, was to replace Lipscomb at Perk. Curtis Davis, the current District vocational-technical coordinator, was to have charge of JC.

Lipscomb, a native of New Orleans, graduated from Vancleave High School. He entered Perkinston Junior College in 1938, where he lettered two years in baseball and also played on the football and basketball teams. He graduated from Perk in 1940 in the same class as Hayden. He earned his B.S. and M.A. at Mississippi Southern College, while coaching and teaching social studies at various South Mississippi schools. When Hayden became president in

GROUNDBREAKING AT THE COAST CAMPUSES

Standing in front of a bulldozer during the Friday, May 22, 1964, ground breaking ceremony at Jackson County Campus are (from left) architect William R. Allen Jr.; Jackson County Campus Academic Dean-to-be Curtis Davis; Trustee Warner Peterson; Trustee Robert Slaughter; Trustee R. A. Roberts; Board Chairman M. L. Malone; Trustee Newton Perry Gautier; Trustee Gus Puhle; MGCJC President J. J. Hayden and Trustee Gavin M. Hamilton.

At the groundbreaking ceremony at Jackson County Campus MGCJC President J. J. Hayden gets JC off to a roaring start with a bulldozer.

Standing behind MGCJC Board Chairman M. L. Malone as he hefts a shovelful of dirt during the Jefferson Davis Campus ground breaking ceremony on Saturday, June 13, 1964, are (from left) Trustee Arthur Ball; Trustee John Furr; Trustee James E. Reese; Harrison County Supervisor Laz Quave, Trustee Lyle Page; Trustee Esco Smith; Trustee W. H. Starr and Trustee R. J. Moran.

1953, he recruited Lipscomb, who was principal of Purvis High School, to take his place as Perk's dean of students. Lipscomb became Perk's first academic dean upon the creation of that position in 1959.

Lipscomb was the first MGCJC administrator to seek a doctorate under the Board supported SACS mandated leave of absence policy designed to upgrade junior college instructors and administrators. The Board granted him leave in December 1963, and he enrolled for the winter quarter at the University of Southern Mississippi. But in light of his almost simultaneous appointment as academic dean of JD, there was no way that he could physically be away for nine months. In his words what he actually got was, "leave of absence from serving as academic dean [of Perkinston Campus]."

His duties as academic dean at Perk were parceled out among other campus administrators. His classes at USM were then arranged in such a way that he and Curtis Davis could strike a bargain in which each took on certain responsibilities and duties related to the formation of both JD and JC.

Davis remembered their deal thusly: "My assignment was to supervise the construction of [the] Jackson County facility and Jeff Davis facility and Dean Lipscomb's responsibility was to try to get a faculty together for us so we could start in 1965." This succinct statement is not inaccurate, but there was a whole lot more to it than that. This undertaking was to require efforts of epic proportions on the part of both men.

Davis was to supervise the construction of two campuses located 30 miles apart. As the contractual representative of the Board, he would have the responsibility of inspecting all material and labor. In fact, he would order much of the material. On top of all that, he, too, was enrolled in part-time doctoral studies at USM.

Lipscomb, who was enrolled full-time in a doctoral program, had a great deal more to do than merely hire faculty for JD and JC. In addition, he would order every piece of equipment for every classroom and laboratory, receive them, and store all of it in crates and boxes marked JD or JC. The Bennett Building, derelict since the demise of the AHS, performed its final great service to the institution it had served since 1913. It became the supply depot for the new campuses. Its ground floor began to fill with typewriters, microscopes, Bunsen burners, and all the other paraphernalia of pedagogy. Well, all but chalk. Either Lipscomb forgot to order it, or all of it went to JC because, according to Sal D'Aquilla, not one piece of chalk would make it to JD for the first day of classes.

In addition to equipment, Lipscomb would fill Bennett's deserted rooms with books--5,000 of them for each campus. The first person hired for either of the new campuses was JC Campus librarian, Frances Murry. She and Perk librarian James Burford would spend months cataloging books. Lipscomb would not have to hire a librarian for JD; he would take Burford and the books.

On April 22, 1964, the Board accepted the $857,000 bid of Polk Construction Company of Columbia, Mississippi, to construct JC. On May 14, the Board accepted the $1,319,000 bid of McClendon Construction Company of Gulfport to build JD.

On the afternoon of May 22, six of the seven Jackson County Trustees together with Board President M. L. Malone met with Hayden, Davis, and architect William Allen at the JC site. A shovel is the favored tool for a groundbreaking but not in this case. Mounting a bulldozer parked at the site, Hayden got JC off to a roaring start.

On the afternoon of June 13, seven of the ten Harrison County Trustees and two Harrison County supervisors, together with Malone, joined Hayden and Lipscomb at the JD site. Malone inaugurated construction there with the more prosaic but no less official shovel.

With a bulldozer and a shovel in the summer of 1964, Hayden and the Board made the first scratches in the earth to begin the transformation of lines on paper into the reality of buildings. In little more than a year the concept of the Mississippi Gulf Coast Junior College would translate itself into installations of steel and brick and mortar.

On July 1, 1964, Curtis Davis officially became academic dean of JC and undertook supervision of construction in both Gautier and Handsboro. In addition, Davis retained this position as District vocational-technical coordinator, a job he continued to pursue with diligence.

The precise point at which Davis established MGCJC's in-plant program at Ingalls Shipbuilding is not known. The earliest documentary evidence specifically mentioning instruction at Ingalls is to be found in the minutes of the Board relating to the meeting of July 22, 1964. The statement reads, "On motion of Esco Smith, seconded by Luther Blackledge the board approved that classes at Ingalls Shipbuilding Corp. in Pascagoula be continued."

The Board had approved many different kinds of classes in the Pascagoula area for at least two years but always under the title "irregular classes" with no further specifics. In any case, the MGCJC-Ingalls alliance, which still existed in 2000, was forged at least as early as 1964.

On September 23, 1964, Davis reported to the Board that he and Mellinger had chosen the sites for MGCJC's new Manpower Training Development Act (MTDA) programs. The Seabee Base was to be secured as the site for several offerings. Two buildings in Wiggins would serve as the site for an MTDA program in saw filing to be offered in response to a request by the Lumberman's Association.

As the Board moved to secure the benefits of the federal

Inset - Back of Longhorn as seen from the campus site.

The outline of JC is etched in the earth in the summer of 1964. In the upper portion of the photograph between the campus and U.S. Highway 90, the Longhorn Saloon is barely visible in the midst of its shell drive and parking lot. A motel can be seen across Highway 90, west of the Longhorn. In the insert the rear of the Longhorn Saloon is visible from the construction site of Jackson County Campus in mid-1964. The students dubbed this progenitor to the campus "Longhorn University." The four-room structure served as a classroom building from July 1, 1963, until the opening of the campus buildings in September 1965. The Longhorn also served as the place of registration for the first session of the campus, after which it was razed.

Manpower Training Development Act for the people of the District, Mississippi Governor Paul B. Johnson Jr., signed the State Vocational Training Act of 1964. Johnson, an avid supporter of vocational-technical education, had personally championed this new state law which, among other things, provided matching funds for vo-tech buildings. This meant that if the Board could come up with half the money for a vo-tech building on any one of the three campuses, the state would pay the other half. In time this law would be of great benefit to MGCJC.

In October, Perkinston Academic Dean C. G. Odom gave the statistics for the record fall enrollment. The total count for the District stood at 1,474. Of these, 929 were enrolled in full-time academics at the Perkinston Campus. All dormitories were filled beyond capacity with 460 students. The rest were day students supplying their own transportation or riding the record seven buses operated by the college. The Longhorn was serving 59 part-time academics. Full-time vocational enrollment stood at 111 in auto mechanics, shipfitting, practical nursing, and nurses aide training. An additional 345 students were enrolled in part-time vocational courses.

On November 18, the Board approved a supervisor and eight instructors for Manpower courses. All the personnel and courses, with the exception of Leonard Avera's sawfiling course located in Wiggins, were to be at the Seabee Base. Barry Mellinger's father, Paul, was named Manpower supervisor. The courses to be offered were metal trades, automotive mechanics, auto body repair, small gasoline engine repair, drafting, diesel mechanics, welding, lumber grading, and electronics.

In regard to the electronics course, MGCJC entered an agreement with Mississippi State University to administer the course jointly. MSU, which had recently established the Mississippi Technical Institute at the Seabee Base, was offering the last two years leading to a B.S. in engineering.

At the Board meeting of January 20, 1965, Davis relinquished his title as District vocational-technical coordinator to his protégé Barry Mellinger. The new campuses' administrations began to grow at the same meeting. Royce B. Luke became director of student services for JC. Glen Cadle was appointed to that same position for JD. In addition, JD secured the services of William Vierling as director of admissions and guidance.

Lipscomb's efforts to secure faculty for JD and JC became manifest in February with the publication by the Board of the first tri-campus faculty list. Ten names appeared in the lists for JC and 22 for JD. Some of the names on both lists were those of current Perk teachers. Before it ended, Lipscomb would have recruited over 40 per cent of the 56 Perk faculty members for either JD or JC, and three quarters of those would be assigned to JD. Some Perk administrators were not particularly happy about this "brain drain," but the faculty had the right to choose where they would go. It was, after all, the same college. Lipscomb had been the academic dean at Perk for ten years, and those faculty who were particularly loyal to Lipscomb wished to go with him.

Some had no choice. All the nursing instructors appear on the JD list because JD was to have both the Practical Nursing Program and the Associate Degree Nursing Program. This decision came as a bit of a shock to Curtis Davis, who had set up the ADN Program at Perk in concert with Lester Tuck of the Singing River Hospital. Davis remembered, "Of course I wanted the nursing program when the campuses opened, but the Board gave it to JD because there were more hospitals in Harrison County. Mr. Tuck was not happy." After years of 100-mile round trips for classes, the nurses were to bypass JC for 70-mile roundtrips to classes. The District, of course, would continue to furnish the bus.

Many of the vo-tech personnel at Perk elected to accompany their former director to JC, but there was another reason for their exodus as well. Most of the vo-tech programs were to be moved to either JD or JC. JD, because of its geographical location, was to concentrate in business programs and general building trades such as carpentry, brick masonry, and electrical work. JC, with its proximity to Ingalls Shipbuilding, was to concentrate on welding and other vo-tech programs applicable to heavy industry. Both JD and JC were, of course, to offer adult education courses of all types, and both would offer the typical academic transfer curriculum. Ironically it developed in the public mind that JC was to be only a vocational-technical institution. Davis, after emphasizing vo-tech for so long, suddenly found himself having to emphasize academics in the media and in his talks to various groups.

In addition to hiring faculty, Lipscomb also registered and recruited students for both campuses. At least as early as January, the media began informing the public to make application to enter either JD or JC at Perk. There is no way to tell how many of Perk's current freshmen Lipscomb actually recruited to be the first sophomores of the new campuses, but JD would begin with 149 sophomores and JC with 59. Obviously most of those 208 sophomores came from Perk because there was no other area institution to have produced them in any appreciable numbers.

Perkinston Campus English Instructor Woodley Lott was the first MGCJC instructor to teach in all four District counties.

In February 1965, the District enrollment reports revealed 109 students "engaged in trade-extension courses at Ingalls Shipbuilding Corporation." That was the first time figures were revealed related to an Ingalls program. The Manpower Program at the Seabee Base was off to a good start with 279 enrolled. Five classes were underway at the Longhorn, and one of them belonged to that intrepid circuit rider Woodley Lott. At this point, Lott set the record as both the first and the fastest District teacher to hold a class in all four-district counties. Furthermore he and his four colleagues that semester would be the last faculty of Longhorn University.

In March, the newspapers began to be filled with photos of Curtis Davis standing around construction sites talking to people in hard hats. Article followed article about how many buildings had been completed "as far as masonry is concerned."

In late April, contractor appeals for extensions on the May deadline began to appear in the Board minutes. The Board granted extensions until June.

On June 16, Longhorn University morphed into the JC Registration and Student Services Center manned by JC Student Services Director Royce Luke. One week later the name of the building was changed to JC-University of Southern Mississippi Registration and Student Services Center. Royce Luke was promoted to "JC Student Services Director and Coordinator of the Jackson County Extension Center of USM." A student could then enroll for courses from freshman to graduate (but no senior courses because of the USM residency requirement.) The Board offered the use of facilities to both Ole Miss and Mississippi State, but both declined with thanks, citing their Keesler based extensions as sufficient. Luke might have been able to stand the extra work on two more extensions, but his title could not have stood another extension.

On June 23, the general contractors of both JD and JC reported that the same plumbing and heating subcontractor was holding up progress at both sites. The Board granted another month's extension but sent an ultimatum with a seven-day time limit to the plumbing and heating subcontractor. Then the Board, by motion, second, and unanimous vote, informed the general contractors of the bottom line. Alternate facilities would now be sought, and if JD and JC were not finished in one more month, the contractors would pay the rent on those alternate facilities. The report of this meeting in the next day's *Daily Herald* read, "Construction on Jackson County and Jefferson Davis is progressing on schedule and should be completed in the near future."

The same report noted that Board Chairman M. L. Malone had appointed a Board committee to investigate the possibility of improving the roads in the vicinity of JD before its opening. Harry Stamps, a Perk-JD transfer social studies teacher who traveled DeBuys Road at the time, recalled that the inhabitants of the area were then referring to it as "Ho Chi Minh Trail" due to its resemblance to that muddy, bomb-cratered Vietnamese thoroughfare. When the Board committee queried the Harrison County supervisors about fixing the road, they were informed that the county funds for that year had given out soon after the crews had torn up the road. However, the supervisors offered to let MGCJC use county machinery if the Board wished to supply the workers to complete the project. DeBuys Road continued to be called the "Ho Chi Minh Trail" for months.

With the JD campus unfinished and the time for the school's opening drawing nigh, the Board authorized the renting of two rooms in Fernwood School, on the corner of DeBuys and Pass roads a quarter mile south of the unfinished campus. Lipscomb, Glen Cadle, and Bill Vierling, with Katherine Smith serving as secretary, began registration at Fernwood on July 1. When Lipscomb opened the door that morning, the first applicant to enter was black.

The Coast campuses integrated at their inception. In all, JD admitted ten blacks--two men and two women in academics and six other men in vocational. JC opened with one black woman majoring in business. No blacks applied at Perk that year. Integration came to Perk the following year when Eugene Vanderbilt of Wiggins entered to play on Coach Bobby Weathers's basketball team.

According to Vierling, that July and August was a hectic time. In his words, "we were frantically registering people [at Fernwood] and the construction people were frantically working, trying to get the buildings and everything ready." He recalled a bit of animosity on the part of the people at Perk, "because we kind of depleted their sophomore class."

As in the case of JC, the JD registrars also placed students in night classes to be conducted by the University of Southern Mississippi. The JD campus would open with 21 USM classes operating in addition to its own.

At the Board meeting of July 21, the general contractors reported their recalcitrant plumbing and heating sub-contractor still in arrears. Their ultimatum having failed and there being no "other facilities" to rent, the Board's last order (really a plea) was for all contractors to "pursue with diligence the completion of the [campuses]."

With their backs to the wall the contractors came through. Neither campus was completely finished, but enough facilities at each were completed to open classes on September 7. Students poured into the halls of JD and JC 53 years to the month after the first students had begun classes at the Harrison County Agricultural High School and forty years to the month after Hersel McDaniel and a few others had inaugurated Perk's role as a junior college. The past was prologue. The history of Mississippi's first multi-campus junior college had begun.

Two days later Hurricane Betsy brushed the Mississippi coast en route to New Orleans, delaying late registration and class organization at JD and JC, but caused little damage to the new physical plants. When the winds of Betsy had passed and the smoke of registration had cleared, Perk counted 587 full-time academic, 15 full-time vo-tech and no part-time night students. JD counted 514 full-time academics, 45 full-time vo-tech and 110 part-time night students. JC tallied 286 full-time academic, six full-time vo-tech, and 119 part-time night students, and in addition, at least 10 USM classes made.

Perkinston's full-time academic enrollment of 360 freshmen and 227 sophomores represented a drop of nearly thirty-percent compared to the previous year, but most of those had been commuters. When registration closed at Perk in 1965, 100 students were still on the waiting list for dormitory rooms. Of the seven bus lines running in May 1964, only one, the George County bus, remained operative in 1965.

On Friday, October 22, 1965, Governor Paul B. Johnson Jr. spoke at the dedication of JD at 10 a.m. and then spoke at the dedication of JC at 3 p.m. Johnson emphasized the role of the two campuses in bringing vocational-technical education to the people of the District. He stated that as the state's first multi-campus District, MGCJC would be a model for the development of other such districts in Mississippi.

The institution had been founded as an agricultural high school to produce farmers. A half century later the institution had become a pioneer in leading Mississippi's transition from agriculture to industry.

MGCJC Jefferson Davis Campus, located at the corner of Switzer and DeBuys Road in Handsboro, is pictured shortly after completion in September 1965. At this time the college consisted of 12 buildings connected by covered walkways. These buildings contained 35 classrooms and laboratories. The American Association of Administrators in their annual convention of February 12-16, 1966, issued a special award to the campus for Outstanding Architectural Design. The AASA committee chairman's official comments read in part, "Spaces in buildings and between buildings are well handled. Each unit has a distinctive quality, yet all blend together in a stimulating teaching-learning environment." JD Campus subsequently won recognition from three other entities in 1966-the American Institute of Architects, the National School Board Association, and the United States Office of Education Bureau of Higher Education. President of the Board M. L. Malone, acting in place of Hayden, who had a prior commitment, traveled to Washington, D.C. to accept the U.S. Government Award of Merit on October 18, 1966, from the hands of U. S. Commissioner of Education Harold Howe II. Photo from 1966 Perkolator, p. 12.

Mississippi Governor Paul B. Johnson (left) and MGCJC President J. J. Hayden examine the book collection inside the JD Campus library during dedication ceremonies October 22, 1965. To the right of Hayden is Colonel William Byrd, MGCJC publicity director. Photo from 1966 Perkolator, p. 37.

DEDICATION DAY AT JEFFERSON DAVIS CAMPUS

OCTOBER 22, 1965

MGCJC Jackson County Campus located on U. S. Highway 90 in Gautier in 1965. The circular structure to the left is Building A, containing the academic classrooms, administrative offices, library, and television studio. The rectangular structure in the middle is Building B, containing the vocational-technical unit composed of four shops and two classrooms. The smaller two-story circular edifice at right is Building C, containing the student center, a music studio, a choral room, arts room, and physical education dressing room. The area of the college buildings encompassed 66,000 square feet. Photo from 1966 Perkolator, p. 21.

DEDICATION DAY AT JACKSON COUNTY CAMPUS

OCTOBER 22, 1965

Robert Slaughter, left, MGCJC Trustee and associate vice president Ingalls Shipbuilding Nuclear Power Department, shakes hands with Mississippi Governor Paul B. Johnson Jr., during the October 22, 1965, dedication of the new Jackson County's Campus of MGCJC at Gautier. Shown are MGCJC President J. J. Hayden, second from left, and JC Campus Academic Dean Curtis Davis is at right. Gov. Johnson was the principal speaker at the dedication. The men stand at the main entrance to Building A.

Jackson County Campus Academic Dean Curtis Davis, left, and MGCJC President J. J. Hayden look on as Mississippi Governor Paul B. Johnson Jr., sits at the control panel in the JC television studio on October 22, 1965. At that time JC offered the South's only vocational television program designed to train television production engineers. Equipped at a cost of $75,000, the studio also furnished closed-circuit television to all JC campus classrooms enabling instructors to telephone for instructional films. Davis, commenting on the unique program, said, "We have everything in our studio to operate a television station except a transmitting antenna. It is possible that someday that we . . . will be able to offer college courses for credit via television to people of this area."

Mississippi Gulf Coast Junior College District Jefferson Davis Campus First Administration - Session 1965-1966

William P. Lipscomb Jr.
Dean
(Employment began
Perk 1963)

James V. Burford
Librarian

Glen W. Cadle
Student Services
(Employment began
Perk 1961)

William L. Vierling
Guidance Counselor

Mississippi Gulf Coast Junior College District Jefferson Davis Campus First Faculty - Session 1965-1966

Evelyn Alford
Practical Nursing
(Employment began
Perk 1964)

Ruby Winston Beachem
Physical Education

Robert F .Couch
Social Studies
(Employment began
Perk 1959)

Sylvester D'Aquilla Jr.
Mathematics
(Employment began
Perk 1960)

G. L. Douglas
English & Literature

Kenneth Paul Gilliard
Industrial Electricity

Joseph O. Goforth Jr.
Developmental Reading

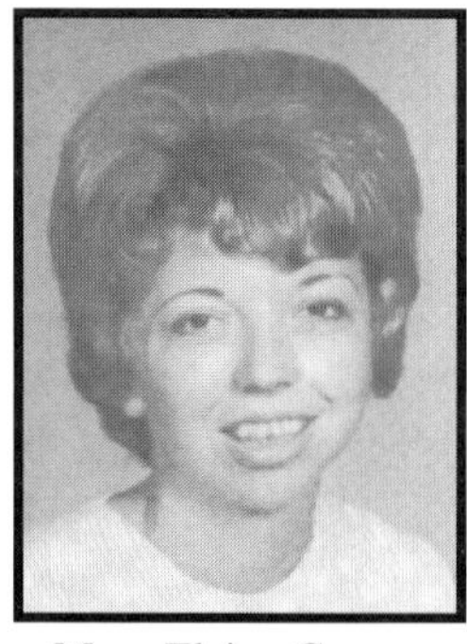

Mary Elaine Graves
Business Education
(Employment began
Perk 1958)

Merrell Hillman Guess
Mechanical Draftsman

Rosemary Henrion
Nursing
(Employment began
Perk 1964)

Louise Jones
Practical Nursing
(Employment began
Perk 1964)

Margaret Kingman
Director of Nursing

Betty June Lee
Business Education

Quincy A. Long
Biology

Betty P. Malone
English

Howard Malone
Accounting
(Employment began
Perk 1963)

Daphne Richardson
Practical Nursing
(Employment began
Perk 1964)

Carlie D. Scofield
Air Conditioning &
Refrigeration

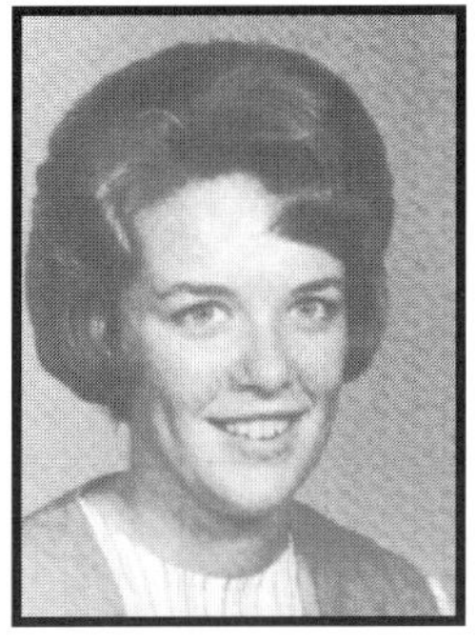
Kathryn Sebastion
Nursing

Charles R. Shows
Social Studies &
Psychology

Robert T. Smith
Business Data
Processing

Harry W. Stamps
Social Studies
(Employment began
Perk 1962)

William S. Thornton
Economics & Business
(Employment began
Perk 1963)

Fred W. Weems
Health & Physical
Education

Mary Wenger
Practical Nursing

Not pictured: Ollie Eason, English; H. Hillman Butler, Math

Because JD was given the nursing program, all nursing instructors were carried on the JD roll in 1965.

Nurses not pictured:

Lois (Dickson) Hicks Crumbaugh (Employment began Perk 1960), Associate Degree Nursing;
Joan Lauraine Livingston (Employment began Perk 1963), Associate Degree Nursing;
Mary Rebecca Craven (Employment began Perk 1964), Practical Nursing;
Mary Easterwood (Employment began Perk 1964), Practical Nursing

Mississippi Gulf Coast Junior College District
Jackson County Campus First Administration - Session 1965-1966

Curtis Lee Davis
Dean
(Employment began
Perk 1950)

Raleigh Travis
Ferguson
Coodinator Supervisor
Ingalls Division

Marshall A. Glazebrook
Vocational Counselor

Royce B. Luke
Student Services

Frances Murry
Librarian

Mississippi Gulf Coast Junior College District Jackson County Campus
First Faculty - Session 1965-1966

Richard J. Beck
Electronics
(Employment began
Perk 1955)

Theo R. Cowsert
Electronics
(Employment began
Perk 1958)

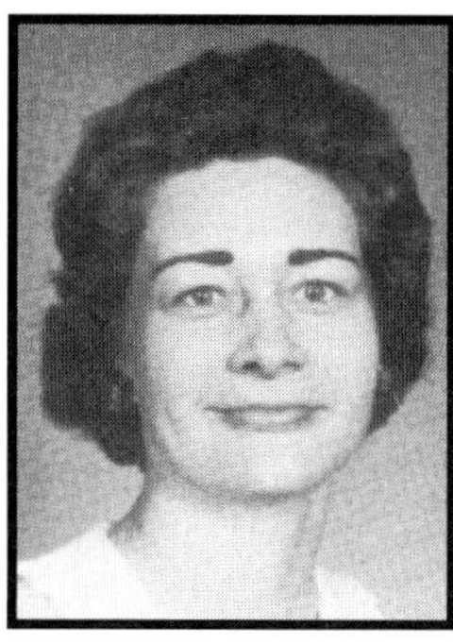
Jane (Dukes) Irwin
Business Education

Gustaf L. Johansson
English
(Employment began
Perk 1962)

Robert L.
Hollingsworth
Biology
[second semester]

Charles A. Keith
Physical Education

Carlana L. Lane
English

Billie Jack Lofton
Mathematics
(Employment began
Perk 1964)

Morris Maniscalco
Biology
[first semester]

Charles L. Munroe
Related Technology
(Employment began
Perk 1959)

Bobbie Pearson
Physical Education

Harold Rouse
Business
Administration

William D. Ruddiman
Social Studies

Harmon Dean Shaw Jr.
Social Studies

Thomas Ralph Smith
Mathematics

Amaryllis J. Stroud
Developmental Reading

Not pictured:

Gilbert Shaw
Electronics

Mississippi Gulf Coast Junior College District Joint First Faculty of Jefferson Davis Campus and Perkinston Campus Session 1965-1966

Robert L. Burnham
English

Mississippi Gulf Coast Junior College District Joint First Faculty of Jefferson Davis Campus and Jackson County Campus - Session 1965-1966

Walter R. Dunn
Physics & Slide Rule

Kathleeen Ellis
Languages

William H. Lane
Chemistry

Lucas Philip Lisotta
Speech & Drama
(Employment began Perk 1962)

Clifton D. Taylor
Music

Not pictured:

James P. Mathis
Art

Jeanette (Bounds) Thomas
(Employment began Perk 1961)

First Faculty Beginning a New Millennium:

Thomas did not transfer to JC in 1965, but she did transfer later. She, together with Charles Keith and Dean Shaw of JC, remained on the faculty roll as the 21st century began.

Clifton "Donnie" Taylor, a joint JC/JD First Faculty member, continued his employment into the 21st century as vice president of the JD campus.

THE BOARD OF THE FIRST SESSION OF THE TRI-CAMPUS COLLEGE -- FALL 1965

The MGCJC Board in the Perkinston Campus library on the second floor of Darby Hall is gathered for the regular meeting of November 17, 1965, two months after the first session of the tri-campus junior college began. Left to right, standing: Arthur Ball, Saucier; W. Luther Blackledge, Saucier; Donald DeMetz, Pass Christian; G. M. Hamilton, Moss Point; M. C. Murrah, Lucedale; W. S. Mauldin Jr., McHenry; W. W. Taylor, Wiggins; Gordon G. Bond, Perkinston; Boyce L. Breland, Wiggins; J. J. Hayden Jr., MGCJCD President, Perkinston; W. T. Moore, Perkinston; L. A. Krohn, MGCJC administrative assistant in charge of business. Seated: Esco Smith, Gulfport; M. H. Mallette, Pascagoula; Leo Rouse, Lucedale; Attis O'Neal, Perkinston; R, H. Slaughter Jr., Pascagoula; Ethel H. Bond, secretary to President Hayden; Warner Peterson, Pascagoula; M. L. Malone, Lucedale; W. H. Starr, Gulfport; M. L. Pope, Lucedale; R. A. Roberts, Moss Point; R. J. Morgan, Gulfport; John Furr Jr., Pass Christian.

On February 21, 1962, on motion by Warner Peterson, seconded by R. J. Moran, the number of Trustees was increased from 24 to 29 with Harrison County having ten, Jackson County having seven, and Stone and George Counties remaining at six each. At the same meeting on motion by Esco Smith, seconded by Donald DeMetz, the Board ordered that the Perkinston Junior College district be renamed the Mississippi Gulf Coast Junior College District (MGCJCD). On May 10, Mississippi Governor Ross Barnett signed House Bill 597, General Laws of the 1962 regular session of the Mississippi legislature, which gave official state sanction to the new entity.

The term of office of all five new board members began June 5, 1962. The new seventh Trustee from Jackson County was R. H. Slaughter. The four new members from Harrison County were John Furr, W. H. Starr, Arthur Ball, and Lyle Page. All except the last were present when the photograph was made. Page attended his final meeting in August 1965 and obviously had not yet been replaced. Others absent when the photograph was made were Ray Elder of Biloxi, James E. Reese of Gulfport, Norman V. Flurry of Jackson County (but who had a Perkinston rural route address), Hiram J. Davis of Perkinston, and Kenneth G. Brown of Agricola. Gus Puhle of Ocean Springs was at the meeting but is not in the photo.

The Board had been meeting in the Perkinston Campus library since August 1958 and continued to do so after the formation of the MGCJCD. Hayden wished to locate the District (or Central) Office at Perkinston permanently. On August 17, 1966, in accepting the first tri-campus building program by a vote of 17-6, the board gave tacit approval to that idea. Sections of Darby Hall became available with the removal of Perkinston Campus personnel to Perkinston Campus buildings. District (Central) Office personnel occupied the vacated sections until Darby Hall became a District (Central) Office structure in March 1971. The conference room in Darby Hall was created by partitioning a section of the former Perkinston Campus library. The Board, over the years, occasionally met at the other campuses and centers, but its primary meeting place in 2000 continued to be Darby Hall.

THE FIRST MGCJCD BROCHURE 1965

The first brochure issued by the Mississippi Gulf Coast Junior College District (MGCJCD) highlights the quandary facing Hayden and the Board over what to call the elements of the trinity (represented on the brochure by a trident)that they had wrought. The original entity is termed "Perkinston College." The two new entities are termed "junior colleges." Inside the brochure a rhetorical question is, "Are Jefferson Davis and Jackson County new colleges?" The answer given is, "No! They are branches of Perkinston College in new buildings located near population centers." Another rhetorical question is, "What about Perk?" The answer given is, "Perkinston College will continue to be a most outstanding Junior College." The Southern Association of Colleges and Schools (SACS) finally solved the nomenclature problem by ordering that the word "District" be eliminated from the name of the college and that the name of the institution be designated as "Mississippi Gulf Coast Junior College with Perkinston Campus, Jefferson Davis Campus, and Jackson County Campus." The Board complied on April 23, 1969, and within a few months, new signs went up proclaiming the three entities as "campuses."

Architect's rendering of Dees Hall, the library-classroom building, constructed on Perkinston Campus on the site of Bennett Hall.

WHAT'S IN A NAME?

Only the buildings at Perkinston Campus are named for people. Those at JD and JC are named for letters of the alphabet. One would suppose that since the buildings at JD and JC are named alphabetically that they would have been lettered in progression through the alphabet as they were constructed. At JD the letters are in progression to a certain extent. The problem at JD is that some newer sections were considered to be annexes to older sections and were given the same letter. At JC the buildings were lettered in progression to a certain time, after which lettering became more whimsical.

At Perkinston Campus the naming of Dees Hall resulted in a change, or really the revocation of the Board policy on naming buildings. Some buildings had been named before the Board adopted its policy on August 22, 1956, but on that date the decision was made to name buildings: "First, for the Counties; Second, for the presidents of the college; Third, for the founders of the college; Fourth, for the president of the Board of Trustees."

In August, 1967, as the site for the new academic building at Perk was being prepared, Hayden recommended to the Board Building Committee that the new building be named immediately so the architects would have plenty of time to prepare the plaque for it. He further recommended that the building be dedicated to the memory of C. E. Dees Jr., and named Dees Hall. According to Perkinston Campus Dean of Business Johnnette Dees, whose office was located in Dees Hall in 2000, C. E. Dees Jr. never existed. Her grandfather was actually named Calvin Eugene Dees and his father was Calvin Elias Dees. The mistake arose because people called her great-grandfather C. E. and his son C. E. Jr., and Calvin Eugene actually signed his name as "C. E. Dees Jr."

Calvin Elias Dees founded Dees General Store in Perkinston circa 1911. He sired four sons, Calvin Eugene, Houston Longino, John Clifton (Johnnette's father), and Billy Jack. The father and the sons were prominent in the history of the area and in the history of the college. The "Garden of the Oaks" located in front of Dees Hall was dedicated to all of them on October 19, 1996.

Calvin Eugene Dees (also known as C. E. Dees Jr.) had served 19 years on the Board but had never been president of the Board. When Hayden recommended naming a new building for him, the Board turned down the request, not because of any objection to Dees receiving the honor but because he did not fit the criteria. At the next meeting, September 20, 1967, the Board's former naming policy was "amended to include officers of the Board of Trustees and such others as the Board may select." The Board then "ordered that the academic building on the Perkinston Campus be named C. E. Dees, Jr., Hall." Fortunately, the architects fabricated the plaque with only the words, "Dees Hall" at the top.

HAYDEN AND THE THREE CAMPUSES SEPT. 1965 - DEC. 1985

Two weeks before JD and JC opened, Hayden sent a letter to Junior College Commissioner B. L. Hill at the State Department of Education in Jackson detailing the immediate building needs of MGCJC. In Hayden's view the most critical needs were larger library facilities, more classrooms, more administrative offices, and more dormitory rooms at Perk. Even with the drop in enrollment at Perk due to the closing of the AHS and the opening of JD and JC, scores of students were being turned away each semester because of the lack of dormitory space.

For years, according to Hayden, the resources of MGCJC had been directed toward building JD and JC while the Perk physical plant, taxed beyond its capacity, had disintegrated. Hayden closed his letter to Hill by informing him that improvements in the realm of library and classrooms had been mandated by the Southern Association of Colleges and Schools (SACS) and would have to be completed by the next self study which was only three years away. SACS accreditation for Perk was now triply important because JD and JC had been established as SACS accredited "branches" of Perk. If that had not been done, both JD and JC would have been required to submit to at least five years of initial scrutiny by SACS before accreditation could have been considered. During the evaluation period no credits earned at JD or JC would have been transferable to senior institutions.

Hayden and the MGCJC Board of Trustees had established Mississippi's first multi-campus junior college. With no precedent to guide them, they were trying to organize the three campuses into something more than a loose confederation but something less than a highly centralized federal union. Yet, for a time at least, Perk had to occupy a preeminent position because SACS accreditation emanated from it. Eschewing the subservience inherent in the term "branch," they had finally elevated Perk to the status of "college" while terming JD and JC "junior colleges." In Hayden's opinion the attempt to confer upon JD and JC a name with higher status unfortunately had resulted in nomenclature which inferred autonomy. The quandary facing Hayden in the matter is evident as he looked back on this foray into "confederated federalism."

"We called them . . . junior colleges . . . rather than branches because we wanted [them] to be degree-granting institutions. We wanted [them] to be independent, except we didn't want them to be separated . . .. [It] was a mistake . . . [to call] . . . them junior colleges. I was sorry after we had done it. Some people still do, [and] it's been hard to wipe out the name, Jefferson Davis Junior College or Jackson County Junior College."

MGCJC President J. J. Hayden (left), receives the 1966 Pacemaker Award on June 30 in Miami Beach from National Education Association (NEA) President Richard D. Batchelder (right). The award, a joint citation issued on an annual basis by the NEA and Parade, a Sunday newspaper magazine with national circulation, recognized the most outstanding school or school system in each state and U. S. territory. MGCJC was selected as Mississippi's "Pacemaker" for making education (particularly vocational-technical education) available to the people of its District through the establishment of two new campuses in heavily populated areas.

So in 1965 Hayden had a crumbling "college" and two rapidly growing "junior colleges" on his hands, and each one considered its needs to be greater than either of the others. Hayden, who had two sons and a daughter, couched his dilemma in terms any father would understand. Dealing with Perk, JD, and JC he remembered, " was like giving your three kids money for the picture show, each one [had] to have an even amount." Then he continued, "Money [was] the main problem. It [had] to be appropriated."

To the extent that he could in the coming 20 years, Hayden did give Perk, JD, and JC equal attention. Five-year plans and ten-year plans tended to overlap and change, but structures tended to go up three at a time in Perkinston, Handsboro, and Gautier. More than once, buildings were dedicated in triplicate--one at each campus.

In 1965, Hayden was also faced with decisions about the location and the nature of another new entity. Dr. C. C. Colvert, whom Hayden considered the chief architect of the tri-campus idea, advised him to locate the District Administrative Office (later termed "Central Office") in some neutral spot on the Coast away from all three campuses. In this case Hayden did not follow Colvert's advice. In the first place, according to Hayden, "The Executive Secretary of the Southern Association of Colleges and Schools stated, 'the President's offices had to be located on the Parent Campus since the accreditation of the two new branches was dependent upon Perkinston College.'" In the second place, the President's home was at Perkinston, and Hayden had no desire to commute daily to an office on the Coast. The Board voted 17 to 6 to locate the District Administrative Office at Perkinston.

The Denson Building, which contained the President's office and a number of classrooms, offered precious little space for the addition of District personnel. Constructed of shoddy materials in 1929, the huge structure had developed a pronounced downhill list that in time grew to be 19 inches off plumb.

Few older buildings in the Perk physical plant were much better. Perk's four men's dormitories, Huff, Stone, Jackson, and George, were each rated only "fair" on the inventory of the time. Designed to hold a combined total of 210 men, they actually held 284.

Harrison Hall, the main women's dormitory, was the only dormitory on the campus with a rating as high as "good." Designed to accommodate 110 women, it held 123. Two other dormitories, each rated "substandard," housed teachers downstairs and women upstairs. Thirty women were crowded into space meant for 24 on the second floor of the Apartment Dorm. Fifty-six women were packed into an area meant for 44 in Fahnestock Hall.

While all the dorms, except Fahnestock, contained fire extinguishers, all of the fire extinguishers were empty. It was not that Dean G. C. Odom did not have these extinguishers inspected and filled, it was just that the students enjoyed spraying the contents about the halls and upon one another. Very likely the absence of the canisters in Fahnestock could be laid at the feet of its denizens as well.

Fahnestock Hall was a textbook case in the area of fire safety, or rather, the lack of it. Access to the second floor was provided by a single set of stairs in the middle of the building. Even though persons unknown, for some mysterious reason, had nailed the upstairs windows shut, there was another way out if fire blocked the stairs. In such a case the women could go to the uphill end of the second floor hallway and open a pair of shutters. Safety lay 15 feet below on a solid slab of cement. There was a fire escape in the form of an iron ladder affixed to the outer wall to the left of this window. But, through some oversight, the left shutter, when opened, covered the top three rungs of the ladder, making it impossible for anyone to mount the ladder.

Odom obviously did not know the exact state of affairs in Fahnestock because he was very fire conscious. He did what he could with what he had--which was not much. At the beginning of each semester he ordered the tires inflated on the museum-quality LaFrance fire truck in the shed by the Colmer Building. The automotive mechanics instructor would come over, crank it, and drive it to the nearest fireplug where the men faculty members were gathered for fire training. Usually in an hour or so, the water not leaking out of cracks in the hose was streaming from the nozzle.

The ramshackled Bennett Building and Annex, having per-

A Corinthian capital lays on the lawn in front of Bennett Hall as workmen on the roof toss debris to the ground. After the razing of 1913-era Bennett Hall and 1925-era Bennett Hall Annex, Dees Hall was constructed on the site. Photo from December 1966 Bulldog Barks.

formed final service as a warehouse for the accoutrements of JD and JC, stood empty and condemned at the crest of Perk Hill. Hayden knew that Perk desperately needed new dormitories, but he also knew that SACS accreditation hinged on a larger library and more classrooms. He wanted to raze Bennett and Annex and build a new multi-purpose classroom/administration building on that site.

Even though he personally felt Perk's needs to be greater at this time, Hayden did not intend to ask the Board to build at Perk without also asking for something for JD and JC. In early March 1966, he and architect Willis T. Guild Jr., toured east coast vo-tech centers to study optimum architectural arrangements of space in a vo-tech structure to insure maximum versatility. Hayden wanted to be certain that the changing demands of industry could be accommodated quickly in a single facility.

At the March 23 Board meeting, Hayden proposed the construction of two new dorms and a multi-purpose building at Perk, together with new vo-tech structures for both JD and JC. For the first time in his career the Board seriously divided over an issue. Some Board members wished to use all available funds for vo-tech structures at JD and JC. Others wanted new dormitories at Perk before the multi-purpose building was built. The impasse was resolved in the August 17, 1966, meeting in which the Board voted to build a $725,000 multi-purpose building at Perk, a $716,000 vo-tech annex at JD, and a $667,000 vo-tech structure at JC. Hayden then contacted Colvert, and the Board soon engaged Colvert's services for a ten-year projection of future building needs for the District.

As the new building program got underway so did the school year 1966-1967. Enrollment figures revealed that Perkinston's full-time academic and technical enrollment had dropped from the previous year's 587 to 554. Special (part-time) student enrollment (which in Perk's case was day students) had risen from one to 13. Vocational enrollment had fallen from five to two. At JD full-time academics and technicals had risen from 514 to 604. Special students (which in the case of the coast campuses were mostly night students) had risen from 110 to 187 and vocational enrollment from 45 to 105. At JC full-time academics and technicals rose from 286 to 461. Specials rose from 119 to 181 and vocationals from six to 15.

MGCJC President J. J. Hayden cuts his birthday cake at a surprise birthday party-picnic held in Magnolia State Park in Jackson County on May 19, 1967. His boat, Conference, was so named that on those occasions when he could get away to fish he could be said to be "in conference." Conference gave way to Conference II which in turn was replaced by Cloud IX.

In the case of District vo-tech offerings apart from those at the three campuses, all but one program was projected to increase. Due to the temporary and short-term nature of some of these programs under the oversight of Barry L. Mellinger, the enrollment in them at any one time was not analogous to the semester-long enrollments at any one of the three campuses. The number of students served in session 1965-1966 was known, but those served in 1966-1967 could not be determined until year's end. In session 1965-1966, 308 apprentices had been enrolled, and 400 were projected in the present session. The Ingalls welding program was expected to grow from 1,944 to 2,000 and the "after hours" program from 1,339 to 2,000. The Manpower Development Training Act (MDTA) program at Ingalls was projected to rise from 201 to 500. MDTA (Gulfport) located at the Seabee Base, which was under the direction of Mellinger's father, Paul, was projected to drop from 311 to 200. Enrollments were falling there because the Navy, which was in the process of reactivating the Seabee Base due to the escalating war in Vietnam, wanted its facilities vacated.

The impending reactivation of the Seabee Base, together with fire damage to the shop building at the Seabee Base Manpower Center in March, 1967, led to the relocation of the center. By January, 1968, the machinery and personnel had been removed to a site provided by the Harrison County Development Commission on the Industrial Seaway near the JD Campus. The relocated center was placed under the administrative control of a supervisor responsible to JD Campus Academic Dean Bill Lipscomb. Thus the new JD Manpower Training Center (later known as the Harrison County Occupational Training Center) became the first satellite of a MGCJC campus. With the precedent set, George County Trustees soon began to

Jackson County Campus Academic Dean Curtis Davis (left) and welding instructor G. A. "Don" Parnell (right) flank the first graduates of JC's vocational welding program on May 26, 1967. The men are standing in what Davis described as "the welding shed behind B Building." The graduates, holding their welding certificates, are (from left) Jimmy Dell McLaurin of Hattiesburg, Jerry Donald Thomas and Jerry Ronald Thomas, both of Gautier, and Ronald Floyd Page of Ocean Springs. A fifth graduate, Exel Dorsey of Pascagoula is not pictured. Photo courtesy of Curtis Davis.

Jackson County Campus Building D appears as a rectangular group of structures located north of original Building B in this early 1968 aerial photograph. Building D was finished in January 1968, an open house was held February 18, 1968, and the official dedication of the facility came on February 9, 1969. The grass airstrip immediately east of the campus is cleared in preparation for offering a vocational-technical program in flying which never got off the ground. To the east of the campus U. S. Highway 90 crosses the Pascagoula River and enters the city of Pascagoula. Ingalls Shipbuilding is located at the far right (or southeast) corner of the photo.

inquire about the establishment of a similar facility in their county, the only MGCJC District county with no installation.

As the JD Manpower Training Center began operations at the Industrial Seaway, the new JC Vocational Technical installation dubbed "Building D" was completed. In mid-February, Academic Dean Curtis Davis had staged an open house to show off the new facility which had added 47,000 square feet to the 65,000 square foot original JC campus composed of Buildings A, B, and C.

JC Building D contained several laboratories, four classrooms, a technical library, an audio-visual room, and administrative and faculty offices. The structure housed the vocational courses in welding, pipe fitting, sheet metal, automotive mechanics, and licensed practical nursing. It also housed the technical courses in electronics, electricity, and the health occupations program which included associate degree nursing, x-ray technology, and medical lab technology.

Though Perk's multi-purpose building (Dees Hall) had not been completed for the opening of classes in fall 1968, the contractor had rushed one classroom to completion. L. D. "Buster" Stringfellow, chairman of the Perkinston math department and coordinator of the new Educational Communications System, recalled that, "Dees was the only building on campus suited for the class. We had to get into it." The course was

Dees Hall appears complete in this circa 1970 aerial photograph of a section of the Perkinston Campus. The kitchen annex of Stone Hall with its attached storeroom, was razed shortly thereafter.

one in engineering dynamics originating at the University of Mississippi to be televised to classrooms in 13 junior colleges throughout the state beginning September 27, 1968.

As Dees Hall neared completion, Dean Odom found himself at the center of the greatest "fruit basket turnover" in Perkinston history. Hayden and the District personnel wanted

Two students take notes as Dean of Men/Mathematics Department Chairman L. D. "Buster" Stringfellow (left) watches industrial arts instructor Winfred Moffett adjust the equipment for the first class in Dees Hall, which began September 27, 1968. This course in engineering dynamics was taught by Dr. George Manifold of the University of Mississippi by means of a television-telephone link between Perk and Ole Miss. The five pre-engineering majors enrolled were James Richardson, David Niolet, David Paul Howell, Perry Stewart, and Don Bradley. As the first such "distance learning" experience in Mississippi junior college history, this course presaged the Community College Network (CCN), which began statewide operation in July 1994. The United States Department of Agriculture funded the CCN as part of a grant to the Mississippi Rural Health Care Corps. The grant funded a site at each of Mississippi's community/junior colleges, but MGCCC funded two additional sites--one for each MGCCC campus. The Perkinston Campus CCN room was placed in the Dees Building near the room used by Stringfellow for his class in 1968.

Odom and the campus administrators to vacate Darby Hall so that it could be renovated and they could get out of the creaking and swaying Denson Building. Social studies and English department instructors, who had taught for years in Smith Hall, freezing in the cold months and sweating in the hot months, wanted out. Not only was Smith Hall not air-conditioned, it did not even have screens on the windows. Some who taught in Smith appointed "special action squads" of students to assassinate the swarms of mosquitoes, wasps, and bees invading the classrooms in the warm seasons.

Odom was in the position of a man being pushed out of his lair by a pride of lions while simultaneously trying to hold back a herd of thirsty steers from a waterhole. To instructors plying their profession in places like Smith Hall and crammed into broom closet offices, the air-conditioned Dees Building with its 12 spacious classrooms (two of which were large teachatoriums), 19 faculty offices, and vast library area seemed a "New Jerusalem."

Odom and the campus administrators began moving into their office area on the first floor even before the Board accepted Dees Hall as completed on October 24, 1968. After acceptance day there was no stopping the instructors moving into Dees, but unassembled steel furniture still lay scattered about the building in crates. No matter. The instructors were glad to assemble the furniture for their offices, and some worked through the Christmas holidays helping to assemble classroom furniture.

Classes had to continue in Smith and other places throughout first semester exams held the second week in January. (From junior college session 1925-1926 until junior college session 1971-1972 the first semester did not end until after Christmas holidays.) When second semester registration began on January 20, 1969, Dees Hall was fully occupied. Classes began on Wednesday, January 22.

The railings for the wheelchair ramp at the north end of Darby Hall are piled on the lawn in winter 1969. By December 1969, the word "district" in relation to the Darby Hall had been changed to "central." Apparently Central Office personnel occupied sections of the building as other parts were renovated. On March 12, 1971, a Bulldog Barks article entitled "MGCJC Centralizes for the First time" noted that "the Darby Building renovation project was inspected and accepted by federal authorities the week of Feb. 15." The article also noted that later that week, "central business office personnel made the trek back downstairs to occupy expanded office space on the first floor." As for the significance of the renovations, the article averred, "For the first time in the history of the college, key central administrative personnel will be located in offices under one roof." Likewise, for the first time, a building (other than the president's residence) located on the Perkinston Campus ceased to be a part of Perkinston Campus. Darby Hall became the initial administrative structure belonging to a new entity called "Central Office." Photo from 1971 Perkolator, p. 43.

In February 1969, the Board approved the renovation and evolution of Darby Hall into the college's District Administration building. The first floor was to contain enlarged business offices and Hayden's office. The second floor, formerly the Perkinston Campus library, was to be rearranged to provide a conference room for the Board, six offices for administrative assistants and a stenographic pool. The renovations

During the 1971-1972 school session in his office in Darby Hall, MGCJC President J. J. Hayden (right) dictates a letter to his secretary, Ethel Bond.

thus described, except for the U.S. Government's requirement for an outside wheelchair ramp, which was added in November 1969, was the way the building remained in 2000.

Dees Hall at Perk and the JD Vocational-Technical Complex (designated Buildings M, N, O, and P on a JD schematic) were accepted as complete by the Board only a week apart. (Dees Hall on October 24, 1968, and the JD Vo-Tech Complex on October 31.) But one class began in Dees Hall in September, and, according to industrial trades instructor Bill Johnson, who was still at his post in the JD Vo-Tech Complex in summer 1999, some instructors were in the JD buildings by the third week in August and some classes began September 14, 1968. In any case the new facilities were in full service when second semester began in January 1969.

The JD Vo-Tech Complex offered technical training in drafting and design, data processing, radio announcing, distribution and marketing, police science, associate degree nursing, and hotel-motel-restaurant management. Vocational training was offered in secretarial science, industrial electricity, electronics, carpentry, trowel trades, metal trades, licensed practical nursing, plumbing and heating, and air-conditioning and refrigeration.

Dees Hall at Perk, the JD Vo-Tech Complex (Buildings M, N, O, and P) and JC Vo-Tech Building D were conceived simultaneously by Hayden and the Board as the first round in giving the "three kids . . . an even amount . . . for the picture show." JC Building D which at first glance was to cost the least, due to cost overruns wound up costing not $667,000 but $728,694 and was up and running nearly a year before the other two. Above and beyond the monies for Building D, Hayden and the Board had decided to spend at least $158,000 more at JC to turn Building C into a cafeteria.

JC Building D was dedicated in ceremonies held on Sunday, February 9, 1969, a full year after it began operation. The JD Vo-Tech Complex (Buildings M, N, O, and P) was dedicated in ceremonies held Sunday, February 23, 1969. Dees Hall was dedicated in ceremonies held Sunday, March 23, 1969.

While Dees Hall, JC Building D, and the JD Vo-Tech Complex were under construction and Darby Hall was being renovated, Hayden and the Board were planning the next round of building. Colvert's new ten-year plan for the growth of the college had been delivered to the Board in late 1967. The plan called for the expenditure of $9.2 million with approximately one-third going to each of the three campuses. Hayden and the Board worked throughout 1968 devising a way to raise the funds using a combination of bond issues, government loans, and increased state and local support.

In July 1968, through the good offices of U. S. Representative Bill Colmer, the college received $735,000 from the Department of Housing and Urban Development earmarked for dormitories at Perk. While this was welcome news, the funds did not permit the construction of a women's dormitory and two men's dorms as originally desired. The

The Jefferson Davis Campus Vo-Tech Complex appears to the immediate northwest of the original buildings in this circa 1968 aerial photograph. Building M is farthest west. Clockwise from Building M in succession is Building N, Building P and Building O. Some classes began in the new complex in September 1968. The Board accepted the complex as complete on October 31, 1968, the complex began full service in January 1969, and dedication ceremonies were held February 23, 1969. Beyond the campus to the north, Bayou Bernard debouches into the western end of Back Bay Biloxi.

decision was made to build twin dorms--one for women and one for men. The long-range plan was to convert both dorms for men's use when a new and larger women's dorm could be built.

Ironically, Hayden knew when the loan for the new dorms was approved that their completion approximately two years away would not add to the capacity to house students at Perk. The two new dorms would merely replace other dorms being condemned as unfit for human habitation.

The 1968-1969 session was the occasion for that once in a decade vivisection called a SACS Self-Study. The visiting committee came down hard on the issue of MGCJC nomenclature. On April 23, 1969, Hayden reported to the Board the recommendations of the committee. By the way, the word "recommendations" in "SACS-ese" means "do it, and do it quickly." Hayden and the Board did it, and they did it immediately:

"On motion by M. H. Mallette, seconded by James E. Reese, the Board of Trustees ordered that "District" be deleted from the name of the college and that the name of the institution would be "Mississippi Gulf Coast Junior College with Perkinston Campus, Jefferson Davis Campus, and Jackson County Campus."

U. S. President Richard Nixon (left) shakes hands with MGCJC President J. J. Hayden while Jefferson Davis Campus Student Council President Ellis Taylor waits his turn. Hayden and Taylor had journeyed to Washington, D.C. for the first Presidents to Presidents Conference sponsored by the National Student Government Association slated for September 19-22, 1969. "To Seek Answers Together" was the theme of the program which featured such topics as student riots, the draft, Reserve Officer Training Corps, and the role of the federal government in higher education in general. In speaking with Taylor, Nixon referred to the devastation wrought by Hurricane Camille scarcely a month earlier saying, "you've had a rough time of it...but...you people have a lot of guts down there, and we wish you the best of luck."

As soon as possible the college letterhead was changed. The logo was changed. The signs at Perk, JD, and JC went down and new ones went up. Mississippi Gulf Coast Junior College was one entity--not three, not four, or any other number.

At this same Board meeting, word came of a federal grant for 40 percent of the $310,000 estimate to build a new business education building at Perk. Once again, as in the case of the coming new dorms, this new structure represented no net gain for Perk. It would merely provide new quarters for the business education instructors, who, like the Central Office personnel, had fled increasingly dangerous Denson Hall for any refuge they could find.

In the following months the Board worked out a plan whereby George County could supply 40 percent and the federal government 60 percent of the funding to construct the long-discussed vocational-technical facility near Lucedale. At the July 23, 1969, Board meeting, Board President M. L. Malone of Lucedale told the Board that the state legislature would have to authorize George County to issue the necessary revenue bonds and also authorize MGCJC to take control of the center once it was completed. Board Attorney Roy Strickland announced that a legislative bill designed to secure such authorization was being prepared for the coming Special Session of the Legislature. Academic Deans Davis, Lipscomb, and Odom departed that July 23 meeting as "executive deans," the new, upgraded title having been conferred that day by the Board.

When newly-promoted Executive Dean Odom went to his home on Silver Run Lake after the Board meeting, he did not know that he would not return from that home for the next Board meeting or that the meeting would be a week later than intended. On August 17, 1969, the most powerful hurricane in American history to strike a heavily populated area made landfall with 230 m.p.h. winds totally destroying Odom's home, 5,661 others, and heavily damaging 13,915 more. The total destruction area in Harrison County alone totaled 68 square miles. Camille injured 8,931 people and killed at least 132, among whom were Sam and Genevieve Owen of Gulfport. Sam Owen was the originator of the trophy for service to the college, which had been awarded since 1956.

Buildings on all three campuses served as refugee centers on that terrible Sunday night and suffered remarkably little physical damage. Ironically, Perk, the campus farthest inland, suffered the most with estimates given at the August 27 Board meeting as $125,000 to $150,000. Hardest hit was Wentzell Center (the "New" Gym). The gym floor had been ruined by rainfall after the wind partially unroofed the structure. Maxine, the large fiberglass bulldog atop Wentzell, suffered injury to her ears and both right legs. At Dees Hall the aluminum frames of the long banks of windows in the third floor façade of the library bent inward under the onslaught of Camille's right front quadrant winds. Rain blew in over and under these window frames, but the metal held and the windows did not break. No books were lost and no refugees were injured in the building.

But Camille was potentially disastrous for the college in

other ways. Lights and power would not be a problem for long at JC, but as one moved west from Gautier, the scaffolding of civilization lessened until it virtually disappeared at Biloxi. From Gulfport to Pass Christian, the area along the beach resembled the bombed-out cities of World War II. By Monday, August 25, Perk and JC had electric power but JD still lay darkened.

For the Board, the immediate problem was fall registration set for September 2 with the dorms at Perk to open on September 1. The long-term problem was the impact of such destruction not only on potential students but also on the tax base of the four county supporting district. The Board postponed registration for one week and began to explore ways to aid students who wished to attend the college. From a variety of private and government sources college authorities acquired funds to aid 74 students at Perk, 88 at JD, and 16 at JC. Not surprisingly, the number of students applying for aid at the various campuses reflected the severity of damage in the service area of each campus.

Enrollment figures released on September 24 revealed that full time enrollment college-wide was down 61 students compared to the previous year. Not good, but by no means disastrous. The dormitories at Perkinston were certainly in much demand. Twenty-four students had showed up with nothing but the clothes they were wearing. The Red Cross had issued the students sheets, toiletries, and extra clothing. Social Studies Department Chairman David Sansing remembered, "Dr. Hayden was afraid we would lose a lot of students. He was wrong. Some of the kids showed up early and were glad to get a Perk dorm room. The dorms were better than what some of them then had at home."

At the October 22 Board meeting, the Board attorney reported that the legislature had passed the "George County Vocational Center" bill and that the governor had signed it. Hayden, though, felt the project should be delayed until the impact of Camille on tax collection could be determined.

The dislocation and building materials shortages caused by Camille had delayed the construction of the two new dorms, but the contractors were hoping to have them ready by the following fall. At the October 22 meeting, the Board named the coming men's dorm "Owen Hall" in honor of Sam Owen. In November the Board named its twin women's dorm, "Moran Hall" in honor of long time Jackson County Supervisor A. P. "Fred" Moran.

The dorms were completed in August 1970, providing excellent quarters for 100 men and 100 women. And they really were twin dorms and they were located facing one another with a “no man’s land” between them. Both were decorated with hollow tile screens, which reached to the second floors. In the words of one perplexed campus security guard frazzled by the constant need to patrol the no man's land between Moran and Owen, "Why did they build a boy's dorm next to a girl's dorm off on the edge of the campus and then run ladders up the fronts from one end to the other?"

Moran Hall is named for A. P. "Fred" Moran (born June 17, 1897--died October 19, 1967), who served a record-setting 35 years as a Jackson County supervisor. Moran, who was president of the Jackson County Board of Supervisors at the time of the establishment of Jackson County Campus, used his good offices to aid that endeavor.

MORAN HALL & OWEN HALL

Owen Hall is named for Sam Owen of Gulfport, who attended Harrison-Stone-Jackson Agricultural High School in Session 1927-1928, and later became one of the school's greatest boosters. Owen and his wife, Genevieve, died on the night of August 17-18, 1969, victims of Hurricane Camille.

Owen Hall (bottom) for men and Moran Hall (top) for women are pictured here as they were in the pamphlet issued for the dedication of the two-story brick and masonry twin structures on April 29, 1972. Occupied since the beginning of fall semester 1970, each contained 21,754 square feet with 50 two-student living units, a two-bedroom dormitory supervisor's apartment and lobby and recreation space. Moran hall was converted to men's use in Fall 1979, when Andrews Hall for women was completed. In fall 1983 Moran Hall once again became a women's dorm when Harrison Hall was converted into a men's dorm.

OLD DENSON AND NEW DENSON

A workman prepares to toss a plank off the top of Fahnestock Hall in summer 1970. By September, the 1927 structure had been demolished. The site was then prepared for the erection of the New Denson Building.

The "new" Denson Building, completed in fall 1971, appears here as it did in the pamphlet issued for the April 29, 1972, dedication of the structure. Then Mississippi Lieutenant Governor William Winter spoke at the combined dedication of Owen, Moran, and "new" Denson Halls. Within a few years the reference to Denson being "new" slipped away as new employees replaced the old ones who had known about "old" Denson.

Central Office Coordinator of Buildings and Grounds Willie Boy Rogers looks on as a Corinthian column is wrenched from its pedestal on the portico of the Old Denson Building in October 1972. By November, nothing remained of the 1929 structure and the site between Jackson Hall and Darby Hall remained undeveloped in 2000.

This aerial of Perkinston Campus in late summer 1972 shows an anomaly which existed only once and for only one year -- the period of the two Denson Buildings. The "new" Denson Building, completed in fall 1971 stands on the site of Fahnestock Hall between Stone Hall and Harrison Hall on the west side of the Quadrangle while "old" Denson, destroyed in fall 1972, stands between Jackson Hall and Darby Hall on the east side of the Quadrangle. The Denson name was transferred to the new structure because the MGCJC Board wished to continue to honor Jefferson Lee Denson, the 1924-1929 superintendent who founded the junior college. From 1972 to 2000 no structure was built on the site of "old" Denson, but should a structure be built there in the future, perhaps it could be dubbed "new" Fahnestock thus completing the transposition of two buildings begun in 1972. At the lower right in the photo, Malone Hall is nearing completion and is likely the reason the photo was made. At lower left the relative position of Owen Hall (rear view) and Moran (front view) is apparent. Stone Hall, between "new" Denson Hall and Dees Hall no longer has its 1927 kitchen annex, that structure having disappeared in the two years prior to this photo.

As Owen and Moran began service, the wrecking ball crashed into Fahnestock Hall to clear the site for the long awaited classroom building designed to replace Denson Hall. Since the new two-story brick and steel structure was also slated to carry on the name "Denson," it will hereinafter be referred to as "New Denson," and the original 1929 structure will be dubbed "Old Denson." New Denson was to be the new home of the business education, language, reading, and journalism departments.

Old Denson, deserted nearly two years before by the Central Office personnel and by the business education instructors, still contained a few foolhardy souls. Among those were the foreign language students under the tutelage of the redoubtable Word Guild and the Perk Players led by the intrepid Kathryn Schledwitz (soon to be Lewis).

During the 1970 Christmas holidays, one part of Old Denson zigged as another part zagged, and the ceiling above the foreign language lab fell, crushing everything in the room. In January 1971 the last die-hard denizens evacuated the building, and it stood derelict and condemned as its namesake rose on the former site of Fahnestock. New Denson, completed in fall 1971, though, was not a full successor because it provided only half of the space and only a portion of the services provided by Old Denson.

With the demise of Old Denson, the campus no longer had an auditorium of any description. The Perk Players staged their next performance in tiny Gregory Chapel. Perk needed a fine arts building.

In February 1971, Hayden and the Board appealed to the Stone County Board of Supervisors to alleviate a problem which had plagued the Perkinston Campus since 1912--loose cows. The small cattle raisers of the piney woods counties had, since colonial times, considered it an inalienable right for their bony, cantankerous cattle to wander freely about the woods grazing on the "open range." These "woods" cows, as they were called, grazed about the Perkinston Campus taking particular delight in consuming the flowers and hedges thereof. This vegetable matter was in the natural course of events deposited about the campus in the form of "landmines" which were particularly effective at night. Also, these cows were a source of great amusement to the student fans of the popular television show called "Rawhide." These "Clint Eastwood" types would stage nighttime roundups and then drive the thundering herds through the campus, shaking the buildings and waking the inhabitants. On at least one occasion these cowboys locked a steer in a room in George Hall on a Friday afternoon wherein it wreaked havoc until the tenants returned the following Sunday night.

One administrator (who shall remain nameless) driven over the edge by the depredations of one particular cow munching his wife's rose garden, fired a shotgun to drive it away. Unfortunately the administrator misjudged the spread of the shot, and one pellet struck the critter in the head. Fortunately the bawling beast had enough momentum to reach the railroad in front of the college where it fell dead right on the tracks. Even more fortuitously a locomotive soon struck the cow and "killed" it again. The owner collected from the railroad.

It was by no means unusual for a cow to be struck by a train or by 18-wheelers or cars on Highway 49 and other roads. The cows liked to lie on warm asphalt, concrete, and on the slag of railroad beds--particularly at night. The Board appeal of February 1971 to the Stone County Board of Supervisors became irrelevant when the passage of a statewide stock law soon thereafter ended the open range.

MGCJC ACTUAL CONSTRUCTION 1963-1973

Estimated Time of Real Occupancy	Construction	Cost
	Perkinston Campus	
1963	Sewage Lagoon & Major Rehabilitation done on several Buildings	75,000
September 1968	Dees Hall--Library/Administration/Classroom Building	899,419
August 1970	Owen Hall--Men's Dormitory	415,209
August 1970	Moran Hall--Women's Dormitory	415,209
Feb. 1969-Feb. 1971	Darby Hall Renovation and evolution into Central Office	75,175
Fall 1971	New Denson-Business Classroom Building	310,000
November 1972	Malone Hall--Fine Arts Building	618,722
	Total	2,808,734
	George County Occupational Training Center	
December 1972	Original Academic/Vocational Buildings A & B	585,582
	Jefferson Davis Campus	
September 1965	Original Campus Constructed--Buildings A,B,C,D,E,F,G,H,I,J,K, and L	2,154,000
September 1968	Vocational Technical Building (Buildings M,N,O, and P)	784,391
Summer 1972	Health & Physical Education Building (Annex to Building L)	935,315
	Total	3,873,706
	Jackson County Campus	
September 1965	Original Campus Constructed (Buildings A, B, and C)	1,337,778
January 1968	Vocational-Technical Building (Building D)	728,694
August 1969	Food Service Facility (Renovation of Building C)	185,279
December 1973	Physical Education & Health Building (Building E)	990,280
	Total	3,242,031

· This chart was adapted from "Alumni Action: Mississippi Gulf Coast Junior College," March 1973, Perkinston, Miss.

· The "estimated time of real occupancy" is the point at which any employee of MGCJC can be ascertained to have established a permanent presence in any part of a structure. This is often the most difficult date to ascertain with accuracy because it almost never appears in official documents. Most official documents favor "acceptance dates," which may occur weeks after real occupancy, and dedication dates, which normally come months after viability has been achieved.

· When the last Perkinston Campus personnel and library books departed Darby Hall at some point in 1969, the structure ceased to be a Perkinston Campus building and became the property of another entity called Central Office. Darby Hall apparently remained occupied at some level until its final evolution was completed. Federal inspectors accepted the renovations as complete in mid-February 1971. At that time Darby Hall became the full functional seat of Central Office.

On March 17, 1971, Hayden and the Board announced a new four-county building program heralded as the capstone of Colvert's Original Ten-Year Plan (1963-1973). Not only would each campus get a new structure but also George County would get its first one. At this meeting it was decided that the "George County Center" to be constructed near Lucedale, would officially become "George County Occupational Training Center (GCOTC)." Perk was to receive a fine arts building, and both JD and JC were to receive health and physical education buildings.

Of the new buildings, the JD Health and Physical Education Building (an annex to original Building L) was finished first, though not in time for graduation which, consequently, had to be held in the JD Student Center on May 14, 1972. The 38,190-square-foot structure, hailed as a "gymnatorium," contained seating for 1,000 persons in addition to classrooms, offices, and conference rooms. An outdoor, heated, regulation size swimming pool complemented the building. This building was to serve as the site of JD's May graduation ceremonies from 1973 until 1998.

The 32,000-square-foot George County Occupational Training Center, which opened in August 1972, was established as a satellite of Perkinston Campus. The Center was composed of two buildings containing four classrooms, administrative offices, a licensed practical nurses suite, and facilities for programs in sheet metal work, welding, pipe fitting, and machine shop.

The Perk fine arts building, dubbed "Malone Hall" in honor of then Board Chairman M. L. Malone of Lucedale, was occupied in November 1972. The 27,000-square-foot brick, concrete and steel structure contained a 467 seat auditorium and facilities for music, drama, and art. The music area held two rehearsal rooms--one for band and one for choral music--ten practice rooms, four offices, and a music library with listening devices. In the realm of art, in addition to faculty offices, Malone Hall contained a ceramics lab, general drawing lab, and the corridors were developed as art exhibition areas. In addition to the stage and lighting facilities, the drama section contained classrooms, a dressing area, and a workroom for building sets.

The Jefferson Davis Campus Health and Physical Education Building was completed in summer 1972. Mississippi State Senator Nap Cassibry (right) receives a barometer from MGCJC President J. J. Hayden as a token of appreciation for making the dedicatory address for the structure on April 15, 1973.

MGCJC Board Chairman M. L. Malone of Lucedale stands in front of the steel skeleton of the building named in his honor on February 23, 1972. Malone served 32 years on the MGCJC Board of Trustees retiring in December 1972. For his last 16 years he served as Board President/Chairman, the title having been changed from the former to the latter on February 18, 1965. Malone was present for the dedication of Malone Hall on April 8, 1973, terming the event, "the greatest honor ever bestowed upon me." He died August 10, 1975.

The Jackson County Campus Physical Education and Health Building (JC Building E) began service in December 1973.

The JC Physical Education and Health Building (JC Building E) was a concrete and steel structure of 35, 477 square feet with an adjacent outdoor, heated, regulation size swimming pool. The building contained, in addition to a gymnasium with a multipurpose stage, six classrooms and six offices. Occupied in December 1973, the facility was dedicated April 7, 1974, with U.S. Representative Trent Lott (R-Miss.) being the principal speaker. Beginning the following month, Building E became the site of JC's May graduation ceremonies until 1998.

As the completion of the structures in the Colvert Original Ten-Year Plan drew nigh, Hayden and the Board announced at the April 1973 meeting that MGCJC was about to embark on a $12 million Second Ten-Year Plan. Accordingly, the Board adopted a resolution calling for the sale of $3.3 million in bonds under the law which had established MGCJC in 1962. This law allowed MGCJC, alone among Mississippi Junior Colleges, to issue bonds without a public referendum.

The following month on May 21, MGCJC added yet another center to its rapidly growing educational network. On that day Keesler Center, conceived as a satellite of the JD campus, began registration for its first course offerings to begin June 4. A full-time staff of four carried out the registration. Sylvester "Sal" D'Aquilla was appointed Keesler Center Director with Elizabeth Locke as his secretary. Gene Rester was named counselor, and Howard Rodgers signed on as social studies instructor.

In the first phase of the Second Ten-Year Plan, Perk received only a token share amounting to about $1 million, much of which was used for renovation and air-conditioning of existing structures. Perk did, however, receive one new facility--a $673,272 vocational-technical complex containing 32,500 square feet--named Weeks Hall in honor of Lee Roy Weeks, a former teacher and coach at Perk from 1929 until his death on May 14, 1942. Weeks Hall, completed in August 1974, contained three classrooms, library space, administrative offices, and housed vocational programs in carpentry, auto mechanics, welding, printing, drafting, and horticulture. The new complex was dedicated February 22, 1975.

Weeks Hall, the Perkinston Campus vocational-technical complex, began service in August 1974.

JD, JC, and Central Office took the lion's share of the first phase funds of the Second Ten-Year Plan. JD and JC together received more than $6 million, and Central Office built a new president's residence named Liaison. On May 24, 1976, Mississippi Governor Cliff Finch, speaking at JC in the morning and JD in the afternoon, dedicated all the new structures at those two campuses. Though Finch did not journey to Perkinston, Liaison was included in the dedication ceremony and was included on the First Phase Second Ten-Year Plan dedication program, an adaptation of which follows:

First Phase Second Ten-Year Plan Dedication Program
May 24, 1976

Building Budget		
Financing:		
Federal Funds (State Dept. Vocational Education)		$326,985
State Funds		2,574,204
Local Funds		3,440,624
Total:		6,341,813
Expenditures:		
JACKSON COUNTY CAMPUS		
Fine Arts Building (Building F)		$1,044,291
Construction Cost	$973,551	
Furniture and Equipment	70,740	
Library-Classroom Building (Building L)		$1,037,182
Construction Cost	$948,587	
Furniture and Equipment	88,595	
Learning Resources Center (Renovation in Building A)		$53,650
Construction Cost	$37,704	
Furniture and Equipment	15,946	
Science & Mechanical Additions (Addition to Buildings A and B)	$516,775	
Construction Cost	$499,985	
Furniture and Equipment	16,790	
Total Jackson County Campus		$2,651,898
JEFFERSON DAVIS CAMPUS		
Fine Arts Building (addition to Building D)		$893,208
Construction Costs	$813,208	
Furniture and Equipment	80,000	
Additions and Alterations		$1,879,524
Learning Resources Center (Addition to Building I)		
Administration Building (Addition to Building J)		
Library Addition (Addition to Building I)		
Student Commons (Additions to Building J)		
Student Center Additions (Additions to Building J)		
Central Utilities Additions (Renovation in Building K)		
Construction Costs	$1,610,851	
Furniture and Equipment	268,673	
Vocational-Technical Complex (Addition to Buildings M, N and O and New Building Q)		$703,948
Construction Costs	$703,948	
Total Jefferson Davis Campus		$3,476,680
CENTRAL OFFICE (on Perkinston Campus)		
President's Residence (Liaison)		$213,235
Construction Costs	$193,235	
Furniture and Equipment	20,000	
Total Central Office		$213,235
Total All Campuses		$6,341,831

FIRST PHASE SECOND TEN-YEAR PLAN DEDICATION DAY MAY 24, 1976

Mississippi Governor Cliff Finch (at lectern) speaks at Jackson County Campus on the morning of May 24, 1976, dedicating two principal new buildings. From left, sitting are Jackson County Supervisor Eddie Khayat and MGCJC President J. J. Hayden. The Library-Classroom Building (JC Building L) (top) appears as it did in the dedication pamphlet. The structure was completed and the books transported to it from Building A in May 1975. Apparently the new library was designated "L" because that is the first letter of the word "library." In any case, the designation of this building ended the practice of labeling buildings chronologically by letters of the alphabet. Building L aggregated 31,150 square feet and, in addition to a 60,000 volume library, contained nine classrooms and eight faculty offices. The Fine Arts building (JC Building F) (second) appears as it did in the dedication pamphlet. Occupied at some point early in second semester 1976, the 19,700-square-foot structure contained a 472-seat auditorium together with fine arts classrooms and space for art exhibits. Building G, a vo-tech addition under construction behind Building C, was not included in the dedication pamphlet because it was not slated for completion before the summer of 1976. The JD Fine Arts Building (third) appears here as it did in the dedication pamphlet. The structure, which began service in March 1975, aggregated 30,145 square feet and contained a 485-seat auditorium, seven classrooms, and eight faculty offices together with painting and ceramics laboratories. Building Q, the hotel-motel-restaurant management building, located adjacent to and east of Building O in the JD Vo-Tech Complex was also dedicated but is not pictured.

Liaison (bottom), completed in March 1976, appears in an early photograph. Trumpeter Al Hirt's home in New Orleans, served as the pattern for Liaison. The dispute over the cost of the house which began with the April 1975 Board meeting, ended the halcyon years of J. J. Hayden's presidency. Photo from 1978 Phases, p. 125.

The circumstances attending the construction of Liaison detonated a dispute between Hayden and a Trustee of the Board, Russell Quave of Biloxi, that in time reverberated throughout the state of Mississippi and beyond.

Russell Quave took his seat on the Board at a Special Meeting held at JC on August 12, 1968. First Vice President W. H. Starr welcomed Quave as a new member and according to the minutes, "Mr. Quave expressed his feeling at being a member of the Board after 22 years absence from Perkinston as a student." Nine days later Quave attended his first regular Board meeting at Perkinston at which time Board Chairman M. L. Malone once again welcomed him as a new member. At the next regular meeting held in September, the question arose of issuing $2,700,000 worth of bonds under the special powers granted MGCJC at its inception in 1962. Ironically, in light of future events, Quave voted for the bond issue.

As Quave later put it,

"I took my place on the board and with the belief that everything was extremely well . . . managed at the college. And I sat on the board for a period of perhaps four years or more and merely became just a fixture. . . . I suppose the spark . . . of the controversy between myself and the college began . . . [with] . . . the effort to build a new president's home. . . . This home was constructed off of the Perkinston Campus."

By way of clarification it should be noted that the house was constructed on land that was off the Perkinston Campus up until the moment the property of Mr. and Mrs. Morris Baker was purchased for the site of the house. The Bakers owned the east half of Block 3 of surveyor Uriel Wright's Plat of Perkinston 1896. The college had owned the western half of Block 3 for many years and had built several college-owned faculty houses there before 1975, all of which still stood in 2000. Once the land for Liaison was purchased, it blended into the territorial integrity of Perkinston Campus. Liaison was not on the Quadrangle like the original 1927 President's home, but the terms "quadrangle" and "campus" were not synonymous. Many structures on the Perkinston Campus were farther from the Quadrangle than was Liaison. However, even though Liaison was built on land on the Perkinston Campus, the house itself, like Darby Hall, was a Central Office structure.

Quave's major objections to Liaison lay in the price tag for the house and also the existence of a cash surplus which enabled Hayden and the Board to fund its construction and other improvements at the college. And Quave worked at a bank. Terming Liaison "a monument to fiscal irresponsibility," he began to scrutinize all the financial dealings of MGCJC with a banker's thoroughness.

In May 1969, the Board had discussed the renovation of the old 1927 president's residence to cost $22,000 to $25,000. Quave was present at this meeting, the consensus of which was to refer the matter to the Board's Building Committee. That body met five weeks later and decided that "because of its age and poor physical condition, it would be better to construct a new residence for the district president as soon as funds [became] available."

The question of whether to renovate or build a new residence continued off and on for years. Then the Bakers, who desired to move to the coast, offered their property and small house to the college for $20,000. In Hayden's words, "We thought that was kind of high for property in Perkinston... [but]...we felt it would be a good addition... since it was close enough to the school to be continuous property. [We] didn't have in mind at the moment to build the president's residence, but that shortly developed."

In April 1975, the Board voted 16-8 to approve the construction on the Baker site the 6,042-square-foot two-story French Colonial-style president's residence at a cost of $184,000. Quave and the others who opposed the house on the basis of high cost pushed for another vote at the May Board meeting and lost that time 17-5. Work on the site was authorized to begin immediately.

Russell A. Quave of Biloxi, a member of the Perkinston Junior College class of 1946, examines a document during an MGCJC Board of Trustees meeting three decades later.

The day following that May Board meeting, Hayden went to his boat and Quave went to the newspapers. Hayden remembered, "I was at a boatyard and [was] called to the telephone by one of the reporters of the *Daily Herald* telling me Mr. Quave had given his release and what was my reply to it?" So it began.

Quave maintained that he would not have opposed a house costing in the $100,000 range. Hayden, speaking of the issue years later said, "the whole project cost right at two hundred and forty thousand dollars. I think it's really something that it didn't cost any more than that. I think we really came out well [and] the general public certainly has its value out of the house." The house was named "Liaison," according to Hayden, because "That is really what it is, a link between the college and its public."

Whatever else Liaison signified, it certainly created a link between Hayden and Quave which lasted the rest of Hayden's tenure. While the house was under construction, Quave publicly began calling for a private audit of the college's finances. Quave's criticism mounted as the Haydens moved into the house in March 1976. By the time the house was dedicated in May, Hayden recalled that Quave was challenging "practically everything the college proposed to do."

At the January 1977 meeting, the Board took up the long deliberated question of approving the construction of a $1.5 million dorm to accommodate 200 women at Perk. According to Executive Dean Odom, the only two dorms for women at Perk--Moran and Harrison--could house only 210 women. The Apartment Dorm, which was substandard by any criteria, was used for those women who would consent to live in it. After that, women were turned away and went to other schools. Men's dorm space was equally limited.

The Apartment Dormitory (above), as seen from the north, was a two-story Second World War-era military barracks which had been moved to the campus from the Gulfport Seabee Base. The structure began service in September 1946, as an apartment house first for single veterans and the following year for married veterans. Brick veneered in 1947, the structure housed nine faculty families and one student couple when it caught fire due to faulty wiring on May 6, 1960. Since only 10 percent of the building suffered damage, the building was repaired. By 1965 the structure held 13 apartments, one of which was assigned to the campus nurse, who oversaw the student clinic located next to her apartment on the first floor south side. Faculty members occupied the other first floor apartments while women students occupied the second floor. By 1979, the brick veneer was breaking loose from the corners of the building and steel flying buttresses were constructed to brace the corners. Slated for demolition by the Board in 1980, so great was the need for housing for married students and for women that the Apartment Dormitory continued to be used. Then, again due to faulty wiring, a fire on the night of February 21, 1984, resulted in damage to 50 percent of the structure. (Right photo) A remnant of the Apartment Dorm stands as demolition proceeds in summer 1984.

But if a new women's dorm could be built to provide 200 spaces, then Moran Hall could be converted to use by men thus providing extra housing for 100 men and 100 women. Quave opposed the new dorm and stated that he had written to the State Building Commission asking that "any application filed by MGCJC be denied." Hayden rejoined that since this dorm was being financed by local funds saved up over a period of years, state permission was not needed. The Board passed the measure to build the new dorm over Quave's objections.

In fall 1977, MGCJC experienced the largest increase in enrollment of any junior college in the state. The figures revealed 3,525 full-time students at the three campuses and GCOTC. Perk's enrollment over the 1976 total rose 52 to reach 694 with an unknown number having been turned away due to lack of dorm space. JD gained 130 to top out at 1,604. JC counted 1,173--an increase of 106. The only decrease came at GCOTC, which dropped 10, winding up with a total of 54. Enrollment in all programs (Manpower, part-time, Keesler, Ingalls, etc.) reached 9,069 up 465 over the same period in 1976.

MGCJC's 1977 enrollment surpassed the figures predicted by Colvert to occur in 1980. A 1978 amendment to the G. I. Bill, which increased educational allowances to veterans, brought more students. Also in mid-1978 MGCJC developed a unique "open entry-open exit" vocational-technical policy which allowed students to enroll the first Monday of any month in vo-tech courses, and enrollment increased again.

Burgeoning enrollments placed great strain on MGCJC facilities but most particularly at JC. There the rapidly growing number of students in health-related courses, coupled with expanding offerings in the health-related field, was creating a problem approaching crisis proportions. Executive Dean Davis wanted a separate vocational-technical structure for JC's human services and health-related programs.

On July 19, 1978, the groundbreaking ceremony at Perk for a new 200-student women's dorm was held. (Andrews Hall, as it was later named, was finished by the time school opened the following fall, and Moran Hall was converted to a men's dorm at that time.)

Full-time enrollment rose 251 college-wide in August 1978, and in September Hayden announced that Colvert's current expansion plan was so conservative that he wished to hire a private consultant to draw up a new plan. He said MGCJC was looking to the legislature for some of the building money but that it was "likely we will have to go to a bond issue" to finance more construction.

Also in September 1978, Quave appealed to the county supervisors in the MGCJC district to reduce capital millage to the college because of the "fat cash surplus" which had enabled the school to pay cash for the new women's dorm in the same way it had paid for Liaison. In Quave's view, MGCJC's major problem was an "abundance of funds."He felt it best for a public institution "to be in a position of always needing funds, rather than having a surplus on hand."

As the Hayden-Quave dispute grew in intensity, so did the media coverage. The media gave particularly extensive coverage to Quave's remarks to local civic clubs. On October 19, 1978, Quave spoke to the Gulfport Rotary Club. The next day the faculty and administration of JC issued a press release detailing their vote of confidence on behalf of Hayden. The press release also deplored the continued adverse publicity and consequent damage to the college and all its employees caused by Quave's "continued insinuations of alleged wrong doings of the President."

Hayden, stung by Quave's remarks before the Gulfport Rotary Club and fed up with his "continued insinuations of alleged wrongdoing" asked Gulfport Rotarians for equal time. In his speech Hayden rebutted all Quave's charges of illegal financial manipulations and ended with the challenge that he "would welcome a grand jury investigation" if that would clear up the matter.

Thelma Andrews stands on a podium erected on the field of A. L. May Memorial Stadium on May 24, 1970 as MGCJC President J. J. Hayden adjusts the cowl of his graduation gown. A few moments later Cooper J. Darby (seated left), the superintendent of the school when Andrews began working there, presented him with an honorary junior college degree.

Andrews, born June 15, 1905, in Perry County, began his employment at the Harrison-Stone-Jackson Agricultural High School and Junior College as a kitchen worker in 1933. He became head cook in 1941 and, except for a two-year stint in the U. S. Army during World War II, remained in that position until his retirement in June 1970. Andrews died March 12, 1979, and shortly thereafter, the MGCJC Board of Trustees voted unanimously to name the women's dorm then under construction "Thelma Andrews Hall" in his honor. Dedication ceremonies attended by Andrews's wife, Bernice, together with several of the Andrews's children, grandchildren, and other relatives, took place on April 18, 1980. A portrait of Andrews in his MGCJC graduation gown was unveiled at the banquet in Heidelberg Hall and later hung in Andrews Hall.

THELMA ANDREWS AND THE BUILDING OF ANDREWS HALL

(Right) Thelma Andrews, wearing his cook's hat, poses on a bench in front of Old Denson Hall shortly before his retirement in May 1970.

(Below, from left) MGCJC President J. J. Hayden looks on as Board member Eula Switzer of Biloxi, Board Chairman William Mauldin of McHenry, and State Senator Nap Cassibry of Gulfport wield shovels in July 19, 1978, groundbreaking ceremonies for the new women's dorm at Perkinston.

(Below) Andrews Hall began service in August 1979. The two-story facility housed 200 women in 19 suites surrounding two courtyards. Each suite had its own living room, work area, and baths. Each floor had its own lobby and recreation area.

A few weeks later Hayden remembered, "I think maybe on a Friday afternoon I got a call from the district attorney's office [asking] me to come before the grand jury the following Monday. The grand jury, Circuit Court of Harrison County, First Judicial District, November Term, 1978 in considering the charges in this case stated, "Based on the evidence presented...in regard to the Mississippi Gulf Coast Junior College, we did not find any violation of the law."

Quave, in recalling the incident stated, "I went to the Grand Jury...but...I came out without an indictment." The grand jury did, however, make recommendations regarding Board minutes, access to records by Board members, and other procedures.

In September 1978, Hayden and the Board had authorized James L. Wattenbarger of Associated Consultants in Education of Tallahassee, Florida, to make a study of the projected needs of MGCJC through 1993. Two other consultants aided in the production of the Wattenbarger Report. One of them was C.C. Colvert, whose five previous reports produced from 1962 to 1976 had guided the development of MGCJC from its inception. The other consultant was Dr. Barry L. Mellinger.

Mellinger, who had resigned his position as MGCJC District director of vocational technical affairs on July 17, 1968, had first gone to Lafayette, Indiana, to further his education. After receiving his doctorate at Purdue University, Mellinger had risen to the position of associate executive secretary of the Southern Association of Colleges and Schools in Atlanta. After nine years at SACS, he had taken a dual position at DeKalb Community College in Clarkston, Georgia, where he was both dean of occupational education and director of the DeKalb Area Technical School. Through it all he had never lost contact with his old friends and mentors--MGCJC President Hayden and JC Executive Dean Davis. When Mellinger re-connected with MGCJC via his work on the Wattenbarger Report, Hayden and Davis advised him to return permanently. On July 18, 1979, eleven years and one day after his departure, the Board approved his re-employment in the Central Office position of executive assistant for instructional affairs.

At that same Board meeting the Wattenbarger Report, which had been presented to the Board two months earlier, began to draw fire from dissident Board members. The Wattenbarger Report called for a building program to be financed by a series of four bond issues totaling $22 million to be issued successively in 1981 ($6 million), 1983 ($3 million), 1989 ($7 million) and 1992 ($6 million). Such bond issues promulgated in 1963, 1968, 1971, and 1973 had financed much of the construction at MGCJC from its birth.

Dr. Barry L. Mellinger appears as he did at the time he resumed his employment in MGCJC's Central Office on July 18, 1979, as executive assistant for instructional affairs.

While a bond issue was nothing unusual for MGCJC, the college's power to issue bonds was unique. Under the terms of the law that had created MGCJC in 1962, its Board alone among Mississippi junior colleges had been given the extraordinary power to issue bonds upon its own authority. Once the Board had passed a resolution to issue bonds, it was required to advertise intent to issue for 30 days. If no protest was filed in that period, the authorities of the four counties were required to raise millage and sell the bonds. If, in that period, interested parties desiring to force a vote on the issue were able to secure the names of 20 percent of the registered voters of the four-county district on a petition for that purpose, an election would be held. Then, for the bond issue to be halted, 50 percent of the registered voters had to vote against the bond issue. In Quave's view this was "not the American way, or the constitutional way, to impose a debt upon any people . . . [because] . . . the [MGCJC bond] law was so written that it would absolutely eliminate any possibility of protest."

Quave was not the only MGCJC trustee with qualms about the college's special bond issuing privilege. At the July 19, 1979, Board meeting, not Quave but Trustee Harold DeMetz, a Gulfport attorney, suggested that the college itself submit so vast a levy ($22 million) to public referendum. In DeMetz's words, "A bond issue of this magnitude cries out for the public to say, 'We agree with you.'" Hayden proposed instead to inform and educate the public regarding the impending issue as had been done in previous cases. The Board voted merely to "seriously consider" use of public referendums in future bond issues.

On January 23, 1980, the Board met to consider the issuance of $6 million in bonds to begin the first phase of the Wattenbarger Expansion Plan. At that time Trustee Alan Santa Cruz of Biloxi joined Quave in opposing the measure. Both men stated that they did not oppose the building plan per se, but they did oppose the method of implementing it. Santa Cruz suggested that the vote be delayed for a month. Quave called for a public referendum. The other Board members ignored both suggestions and voted to issue the bonds.

Quave and Santa Cruz together with seven other citizens of Harrison County, including former Trustee Harold DeMetz, filed a class-action suit petitioning the Harrison County Chancery Court to stop the bond sale and to declare the 1962 MGCJC bond law to be unconstitutional. The sale was stopped, and in May 1980, Chancellor William Stewart heard the case in Gulfport, finding for the complainants. MGCJC appealed the case to the Mississippi State Supreme Court, which, in March 1981, upheld the chancery court decision.

Hayden termed the blockage of the bond issue and the

elimination of MGCJC's special right to make such bond issues to be his "greatest disappointment." Then he added, "The only other thing I regret is that I haven't been able to perform satisfactorily enough to please Mr. Quave."

At the December 1981 Board meeting, Hayden announced that he would retire at the close of his next four-year term. In January 1982, the Board, with two dissenting votes, one of which was Quave's, elected Hayden to a final four-year term to begin July 1. With the limited funds at his disposal Hayden embarked on a last effort to alleviate the most critical needs of each campus.

JC received top priority due to the danger of the health occupations programs being in jeopardy of loss of accreditation. Medical technology was being taught in a non air-conditioned one-room combination classroom-laboratory-office in Building D, which smelled of fumes from the welding operation next door and which leaked when it rained. The licensed practical nursing program, also located in Building D, had accommodations just as inappropriate. Associate degree nursing was being taught in the Library Building L with no medical facilities--not even lavatories. Emergency medical technology was being taught in the noisy student center. The new respiratory therapy program shared those quarters. The x-ray technology program was not even on campus. It was at Singing River Hospital. A $2.4 million Health Occupations Building was authorized by the Board and occupied by the personnel of all JC health programs in January 1983.

The University of Southern Mississippi Jackson County Center appears in this summer 1999 photograph. The Jackson County Board of Supervisors issued $2 million in bonds to construct the facility on the Jackson County Campus. The structure became the property of MGCJC with the right (and intention) that it be subleased to USM. University night classes began in the building circa fall 1982.

The Jackson County Health Occupations Building (JC Building H) began operation in January 1983.

Two years later the enclosure of the open under-story of Building L began with the construction of a new Learning Resources Center.

In Hayden's last term, JD received about $1 million for renovation and minor additions plus a new $2 million satellite called West Harrison County Occupational Training Center (WHCOTC). Conceived as a quadruple effort on the part of MGCJC, Long Beach, Pass Christian and the State of Mississippi, all four entities contributed to the cost of the new installation designed to better serve the western part of the district's most populous county. The groundbreaking for the facility took place on June 6, 1984, and the facility opened in fall 1985, offering both secondary and post secondary vocational courses. High school students from Long Beach and Pass Christian were bused to the center daily for instruction.

In Hayden's last term, Perk received a $190,000 Student Union building which opened in fall 1982. Hinton Hall, Perk's science and math building, was renovated and an annex added at a cost of nearly $1 million. The new facility went into service in fall, 1984. In February 1985 at Hayden's behest, the Board okayed the construction of a $2.5 million men's dormitory (later to be named "Hayden Hall"). At the same time, the Board likewise approved the expenditure of $350,000 to add aluminum bleachers to the west side of A. L. May Memorial Stadium, and on the south side of the stadium a new Field House for the football and baseball teams. GCOTC, Perk's satellite, received in Hayden's last year a new $500,000 structure for the addition of new vocational programs, one of which was cosmetology.

By mid-1984 the Board was considering guidelines and the timetable for selecting Hayden's replacement. By March 1985, the Board's Presidential Search Committee had disseminated word of the impending vacancy throughout the nation. But Hayden made no secret of the fact that he had groomed Dr. Barry L. Mellinger, whom he described as "an outstanding man and educator," to be his successor.

On September 18, 1985, an overwhelming majority of Board members voted to name Mellinger the coming chief executive officer of MGCJC. Hayden, who could have remained at his post until June 30, 1986, had already opted to close out his administration on the last day of 1985. At the stroke of midnight December 31, 1985, the Hayden era ended and the Mellinger era began with the coming of the new year 1986.

Despite the shadow cast by his turbulent last years, Hayden's career as a Mississippi junior college administrator was unprecedented. He took charge of a small rural junior college with facilities valued at just over $1 million and turned it into Mississippi's first multi-campus institution with a net worth of more than $35 million at the time of his departure. In less than a generation the single installation at Perkinston had been joined by six other major facilities serving all four district counties--Jefferson Davis Campus, Jackson County Campus, Harrison County Occupational Training Center, George County Occupational Training Center, Keesler Center, and West Harrison County Occupational Training Center.

In a "fond farewell" published shortly before his retirement Hayden summed up his career thusly:

"When I became president 32 years ago, our 513 students met for lectures in hot, stuffy classrooms. Individualized instruction was unheard of. Today our students enjoy fully air-conditioned facilities and have the benefit of learning labs, developmental studies, microcomputers, high tech machines, and open-entry, open-exit programs. We have been able to realize our potential in providing quality education to our students. The growth in facilities has permitted the college to expand its offerings to include more than 30 university parallel programs, nearly 50 occupational programs, plus adult and continuing education programs. The years for me have been rewarding. My love and support will always be with this great institution."

Quave, who suffered a mild heart attack in February 1986, attended his last Board function in July, less than a month shy of 18 years service. As he bade farewell he said, "I did what I felt was in the best interests of the college.... I feel that Mississippi Gulf Coast Junior College is perhaps the most important institution on the Gulf Coast."

On September 18, 1985, MGCJC President J. J. Hayden (right) applauds the Board's selection of his successor, Dr. Barry L. Mellinger.

AN ERA ENDS, ANOTHER BEGINS

The October 12, 1985, Gulf Coast-Pearl River football game held at 7:30 p.m. Saturday night in Biloxi Municipal Stadium was dedicated to retiring President J. J. Hayden. (above right) U. S. Representative Trent Lott reads a letter at halftime from U. S. President Ronald Reagan commending Hayden on his long and successful career. (Right) With Lillian at his side, J. J. holds up the Reagan letter in a gesture of farewell. Since he had attended Perkinston 47 years earlier on a $6 per month football scholarship, saying farewell on a football field was most appropriate. Coach George Sekul's Bulldogs defeated the Wildcats 10-6 that night which was even more appropriate.

(1986 Perkinston Campus aerial photograph) The major Hayden-era structures completed or initiated on Perkinston Campus prior to his retirement on December 31, 1985, are numbered in order of construction. The date given by each structure is that of the best evidence of real occupancy of the structure (or portion thereof) by MGCJC personnel.

1 *Wentzell Center, spring 1957*
2 *Darby Hall, fall 1957 (Central Office structure)*
3 *Hinton Hall, spring 1960 (Hinton Hall Annex, fall 1984)*
4 *Heidelberg Hall, spring 1960*
5 *Megehee Building, January 1963*
6 *Dees Hall, September 1968*
7 *Owen Hall, fall 1970*
8 *Moran Hall, fall 1970*
9 *"New" Denson Hall, fall 1971*
10 *Malone Hall, November 1972*
11 *Weeks Hall, August 1974*
12 *Liaison (Central Office structure), March 1976*
13 *Andrews Hall, August 1979*
14 *Student Center, fall 1982 (later expanded and named Barry L. Mellinger Student Center)*
15 *Field House, fall 1986 (site not visible due to trees--later renamed S. George Sekul Field House)*
16 *Hayden Hall, fall 1987 (site is cleared)*
17. *Baptist Student Union 1981 (a private religious structure built during the Hayden Era) across the street is a putt-putt golf course built in 1982.*

Visible in the foreground is a line of faculty houses (three duplexes flanked by two single-family dwellings, one of which is visible) finished in 1960. The Perkinston Campus vice president gave the order in summer 1999 to begin vacating the structures so that they could be demolished or removed by 2003.

The area behind or north of the 1936-era barn was developed into the transportation center for the college beginning with the construction of bus sheds in 1970. The 3,000 square-foot metal building directly behind the old barn was erected in 1980 as Central Office transportation office and shop. The bus sheds are to the right of this building.

(1986 Jefferson Davis Campus aerial photograph) All structures are Hayden-era, being either completed or initiated prior to his retirement December 31, 1985. The date given beside each structure is that of the best evidence of real occupancy of the structure (or portion therof) by MGCJC personnel. Except for the Vocational-Technical Complex, JD remained essentially one massive structure under a single roof during the Hayden Era. Expansion was often expressed by covering the open spaces among the original 1965 "buildings." Even large new additions took on the "letter" of the sometimes quite small adjacent original "building." Because of these unique characteristics, an aerial photo of JD does not reveal the quality or the quantity of information made available by aerial photos of Perk and JC.

A-L was the original structure in September 1965. The renovations and additions to the original structure, which resulted in the massive area under one roof in the aerial photograph above, cannot be labeled.

M, N, O, P	*The Vocational-Technical Complex,*	*September 1968*
	Health and Physical Education Building	*Summer 1972*
	Fine Arts Building	*March 1975*
Q	*Hotel-Motel-Restaurant Building*	*1976*
G Annex	*Faculty offices*	*1986 (This last of the Hayden-era structures at JD appears north of the main structure with the black roof.)*

(1986 Jackson County Campus aerial photograph) All structures are Hayden-Era, being completed or initiated before his retirement on December 31, 1985. The date given beside each structure is that of the best evidence of real occupancy of the structure (or portion thereof) by MGCJC personnel. Renovations are not noted. Annexes or expansions on pre-existing structures are not generally noted.

A	*August 1965 - Original Administration and Library Building*
B	*August 1965 - Original Vocational-Technical Building*
C	*August 1965 - Original Student Center Building*
D	*January 1968 - Vocational-Technical Building*
E	*December 1973 - Physical Education and Health Building*
L	*May 1975 - Library Building*
F	*January (?) 1976 - Fine arts Building*
G	*Summer 1976 - Vocational-Technical addition*
S	*Fall 1982 - The University of Southern Mississippi Building*
H	*January 1983 - Health Occupations Building*

THE MELLINGER YEARS JAN. 1986 - AUG. 1998

The financial situation facing the college when Dr. Barry Lee Mellinger took the helm from Dr. J. J. Hayden on January 1, 1986, paralleled that encountered by Cooper J. Darby when he replaced Lee Denson in 1929. Both Denson and Hayden had been expansionists of the "build now, pay later" school of economics. Both Darby and Mellinger subscribed to the "balance the budget, pay-as-you-go plan." Ironically, the college, in the long term benefited from all four of these regimes because the physical plants left behind by the expansionists served during the periods of retrenchment. Unlike Denson though, the bonded indebtedness left by the Hayden regime did not exceed the taxing authority of the Board of Trustees.

The shape of things to come began to appear in the last months of Hayden's term. Hurricane Elena inflicted extensive damage at JC, and on the heels of that disaster, came a \$1.2 million slash in already budgeted state appropriations to MGCJC. The Board mandated the first austerity measures during Hayden's last meeting in December, a hiring freeze and reductions in funds allocated for equipment, supplies, and travel.

By the time Mellinger presided over his first Board meeting in January, 1986, the situation had worsened considerably. Additional legislative budget cuts coupled with an unexpectedly large decrease in second semester enrollment had cost MGCJC a further \$800,000. This meant that the school's \$23 million budget had to be trimmed to \$21 million immediately, and the news from Jackson heralded still more cuts to come. "I would have liked for my coming to have been at a better time," said Mellinger. Then he mused, "We must remain financially responsible."

Mellinger moved swiftly to institute measures to meet the crisis. Scarcely a budget remained untouched. Travel for instructors was virtually eliminated. Equipment purchases became nearly non-existent, and mechanical maintenance contracts for equipment were cancelled. The color pages of the college yearbooks disappeared. Tuition was increased \$50 from \$250 to \$300 per semester. Tenth month contracts given to the faculty in lieu of a raise during the Hayden administration vanished, thus, in effect, cutting salaries. By May the austerity program resulted in the elimination of 48 faculty, staff, and administrative positions, mostly by attrition, but including 22 teaching contracts not renewed.

In a statement to the press regarding the necessity of the state-ordered measures, Mellinger said, "Obviously all these cuts will have an effect on the education process. We tried to make the reductions in areas where we wouldn't undermine and destroy the integrity of our programs. But the overall quality is going to suffer." Trustee Wilbur Ward of Lucedale in reflecting on the action of the legislature, which had

President Barry L. Mellinger makes a point in an early 1986 Board meeting.

caused the situation, prophesied that, "It will take years to recover from the damage being done to education in the state this year." Then he added, "one of the best things we could do for any young person planning to go into the field of education would be to advise him or her to go some place else." Feisty former Perkinston Campus Executive Dean and then Trustee C. G. Odom, in his own inimitable style, remarked, "The Legislature [is] raping education to keep from raising taxes."

In May, 1986, Mellinger's draconian belt-tightening enabled him to present a balanced budget to the Board. Determined, in his words, "never to get caught in that situation again," Mellinger took strategic planning steps which would enable the college to prevent a recreation of that "dark period." This planning paid off in 1990, enabling the college to, in Mellinger's words, "bite the bullet" before a looming five percent legislative budget cut struck. The financial crunch finally ended in 1993 and college employees received a seven per cent raise. By 1995 the college had achieved debt-free status, and all building projects were placed on the "pay-as-you-go plan."

In the blackest part of the "dark period" (1986-1989) the

only construction at MGCJC, other than minor renovation and repairs, was the conclusion of projects launched at the end of the Hayden era. The most noteworthy of these at Perkinston was a 200-bed men's dormitory christened "Hayden Hall" by the Board in May 1986, while it was under construction. The opening of Hayden Hall in fall 1987 signaled the end of the long service as dormitories of Huff Hall, Jackson Hall, and Stone Hall.

Hayden and Mellinger were present at the dedication of Hayden Hall on August 16, 1987. Even as the 47-year old MGCJC President introduced the 67-year old MGCJC President Emeritus to those assembled for the dedication, legislative and Board approval had already been given for a change of name for the institution. Six weeks later on October 1, 1987, MGCJC became Mississippi Gulf Coast Community College (MGCCC). In speaking of the name change, Mellinger said, "The community college offers local programs to meet local educational needs. And we feel we can adapt our educational programs to meet those needs. . . . The 'Community College' is just more descriptive of that."

Mellinger himself was a prime example of just how well the institution he then led could, by any name, meet local needs. Nearly three decades before the dedication of Hayden Hall, Mellinger and Hayden had met for the first time. Then eighteen-year-old Mellinger, a recent graduate of Lyman Consolidated High School, was working as an apprentice plumber in the employ of the Gulfport firm of W. D. Weaver and Sons, Mechanical Contractors.

In 1957 Weaver and Sons had secured the contract to convert the remaining building of the then Perkinston Junior College from central steam heat supplied by the old campus Power House to individual heating systems. According to Hayden, "One Saturday in 1958 I was in the administration (Old Denson) building and I heard a pounding noise in what would become the new boiler room. I went in and saw a pair of legs and feet sticking out from under the tanks and pipes. He [Mellinger] came out and said he had just finished high school and was working to get money to go to college."

Hayden and then Vo-Tech Director Curtis Davis soon became mentors for the young apprentice plumber. Together they convinced him to matriculate at Perk in fall 1958. Mellinger, remembering the day he enrolled at Perk, termed it "one of the highlights of my association with the college." That day was "something I never imagined in my wildest dreams," he continued, and analogous in his mind to the day he was elected president of the institution in 1985. Oddly enough, one of the reasons Mellinger's father, Paul, had removed his family from Colorado Springs, Colorado, to Mississippi in 1950 had been to secure for his children a low cost junior college education.

With his background in mind, Barry Mellinger's description of the role of a junior/community college in American education takes on a deeper meaning:

"A Community College is what I call the people's college. Historically a college education has been reserved for a small, elite group of students. The further back you go, the smaller that group has been. Community College is an open door, open access college that really has no entrance criteria that would exclude any student. We are an open door, people's college."

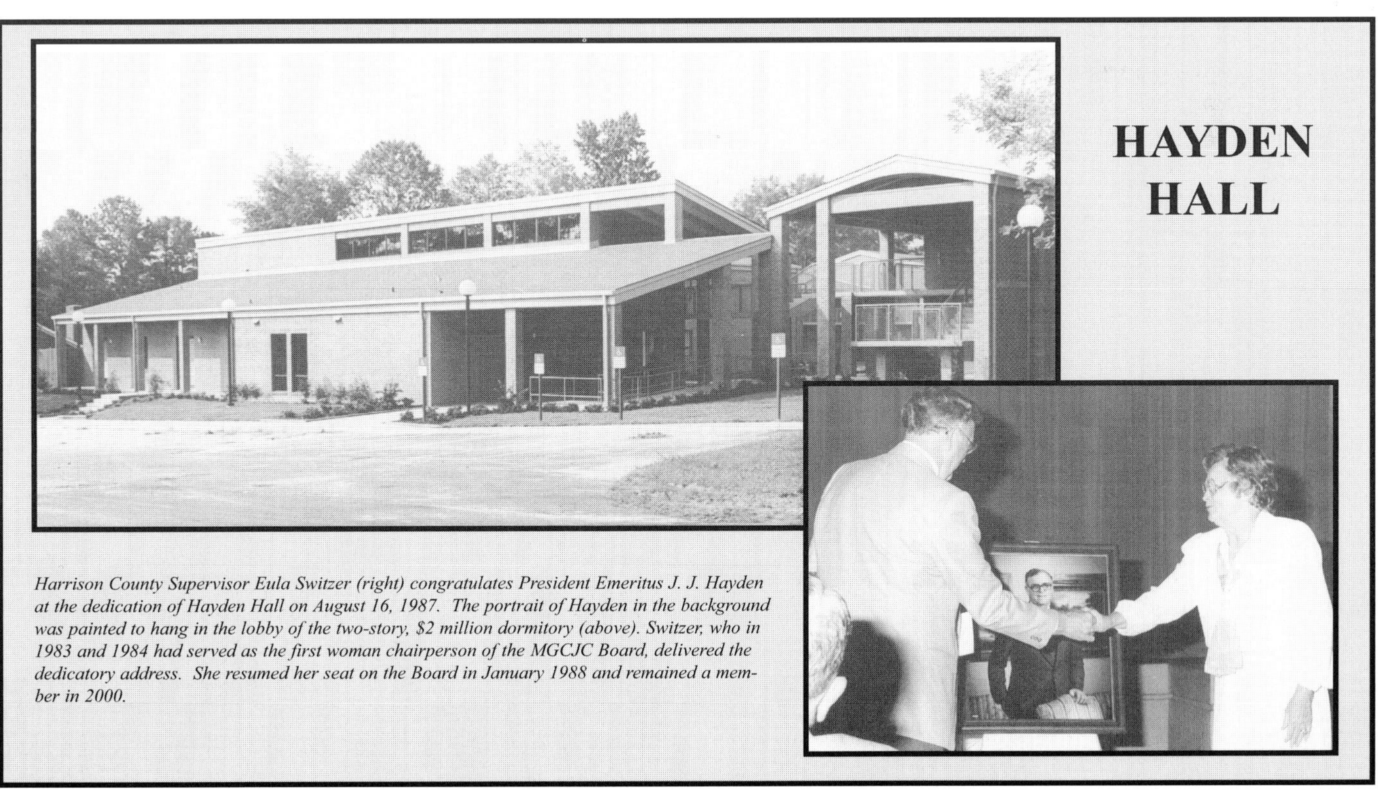

HAYDEN HALL

Harrison County Supervisor Eula Switzer (right) congratulates President Emeritus J. J. Hayden at the dedication of Hayden Hall on August 16, 1987. The portrait of Hayden in the background was painted to hang in the lobby of the two-story, $2 million dormitory (above). Switzer, who in 1983 and 1984 had served as the first woman chairperson of the MGCJC Board, delivered the dedicatory address. She resumed her seat on the Board in January 1988 and remained a member in 2000.

THE MELLINGER FAMILY

Barry L. Mellinger poses with his wife, four daughters and son in Liaison, shortly after he became president. From left, seated are Dr. Mellinger, Dot (the former Dorothy Gwendolyn Bugg of Petal), and Christa Faye. From left, standing are Jared Lee "Jay", Deborah Lynn "Debbie", Miriam April "Mim", and Sharon Rose. All five of the Mellinger's children graduated from MGCCC (Perkinston Campus) while their father was president. Editor's Note: The Mellinger's married on June 20, 1964.

Deborah Lynn "Debbie" Mellinger, died October 4, 1991 of a malignant tumor. A graduate of Stone High School, Debbie was valedictorian of her 1986 graduation class. She was an honor student at Perkinston Campus, where she was named to the Hall of Fame and listed in Who's Who Among American Community Colleges.

Debbie was in her fifth year at Ole Miss where she had the honor of being named the Outstanding Graduate of 1991 in American Pharmacy, the official journal of the American Pharmaceutical Association, and received the Pharmacy School's 1991 Senior Leadership Award.

The Pharmacy Degree that she had nearly completed was awarded to her posthumously by the University of Mississippi.

Dr. and Mrs. Mellinger pose with three-year old granddaughters Courtney Hatten (left) and Tamara Sanders (right) in Mellinger's 1929 Model A Ford Roadster in 1993. Mellinger's hobby was restoring antique cars. In thirty years he restored ten of them.

Mellinger went to unprecedented lengths to provide "open door, open access" that would not "exclude any student." During his term of office, MGCCC literally extended its range of services from the cradle (JC began child care technology in 1987) to the grave (Perk added funeral technology in 1998) and everything in between (the Institute for Learning in Retirement began in 1994). For students needing tutorial aid in specific subjects, he established a Learning Lab at each of the three campuses. That effort which began with a U. S. Government Title III Grant while Mellinger was still vice president for instructional affairs became an integral part of MGCCC's services when he became president. For the academically talented he established full tuition scholarships through the Honors Program in 1987. A prisoner-in-training program for non-violent offenders began the same year. Responding to the Mississippi legislature's appeal to the community college to address Mississippi's 50 percent functional literacy rate, he increased MGCCC's already long commitment to that effort by creating campus literacy managers' positions at all three campuses in 1992. That same year MGCCC joined the U. S. Government Rural Health Corps initiative in training healthcare workers for rural Mississippi. Also in 1992, cognizant of the need to encourage junior high students to plan for college and careers, he took MGCCC into the Alliance for Achievement Program. The next year JC began the Youth Leadership Program for high school seniors designed to get a headstart on developing the next generation of informed and committed local leaders.

In addition to offering something for people of all ages and walks of life, Mellinger specifically targeted vocational-technical education. The Technical Preparation (Tech-Prep) Education Act of 1989, designed to articulate high school and community college technical programs in training qualified technicians, drew his special interest. Testifying before a

U. S. Government Senate sub-committee hearing at JD on April 28, 1989, Mellinger said, "To put the American economy back in the forefront of global competition, our nation must build a world class workforce."

With three campuses, four centers, and on-going training at 20 industrial sites, including the Ingalls Shipbuilding Apprentice program (the second largest such program in America), MGCCC was in a remarkable position to help provide a world class workforce. As Mellinger testified before the Senate subcommittee, events were already in motion to provide a new, "world class" training place.

In June 1988, the Board had approved MGCCC's entry into a dual alliance to build a new technical training center in Jackson County and a second unprecedented quadruple alliance for the same purpose in Harrison County. Each center would be referred to as an applied technology and development center (ATDC).

The Jackson County facility, a joint effort of the State Department of Education ($460,000) and MGCCC ($160,000), was built on the JC Campus in Gautier. Completed in fall 1990, it showcased the latest techniques in automated manufacturing (robots).

The Harrison County installation, eventually named the Mississippi Gulf Coast Applied Technology and Development Center (MGCATDC), was to be located in the Intraplex 10 Light Industry Park just south of Interstate 10 and west of Lorraine Road. The site chosen for the MGCATDC lay about one mile northwest of the Harrison County Occupational Training Center (HCOTC), a long time satellite of JD on the Industrial Seaway. In fact, the MGCATDC was intended as a replacement for the HCOTC but with a greatly expanded role. It was intended not only as a vo-tech training center but also as a regional development center.

Mellinger masterminded the plan that led to the unique funding arrangement involving MGCCC, the State Department of Education, the Harrison County Development Commission, and Mississippi Power Company which produced the MGCATDC. In speaking of this success he said, "This is Mississippi's first real joint partnership between the public and private sector." Within a short time such partnerships became the rule rather than an exception.

MGCCC personnel moved into the MGCATDC in April 1991. At first the MGCATDC, as had its HCOTC predecessor, functioned as a satellite of JD. But on July 1, 1996, the new center, due to the implementation of Mississippi's revolutionary Workforce and Education Act of 1994, became an element of MGCCC's fourth campus--the Community Campus.

Due to the influence of Mellinger and other members of the executive committee of the Mississippi Community College Foundation, the Mississippi Legislature unanimously passed the Workforce and Education Act of 1994. This act, based on studies of foreign and domestic workforce initiatives, proposed to glean the best elements of all such initiatives and forge them into a plan designed to make Mississippi workers internationally competitive.

In recognition of the role of community college leaders in securing the passage of the Workforce Act, the legislature designated the community colleges as the primary deliverers of workforce training. In reading the "intent statement" of the Workforce Act, one is struck by the similarities of its verbiage to that enunciated and published by Mellinger in estab-

THE MGCCC EDUCATIONAL SERVICES CENTERS

Educational Services Centers, designed to bring student-related services and records together under one roof, opened on each MGCCC campus in fall 1996. On the Perkinston Campus, historic 1915-era Stone Hall (below) was renovated and an annex added to the west side of the building. On the Jefferson Davis Campus new Building U (below left) became the Educational Services Center. At Jackson County Campus new Building N (left) became the Education Services Center.

In dealing with Stone Hall the architects, with no knowledge of the earlier aspect of the building, accidentally put the new annex where an old one had stood circa 1927-1970. The roofline of the new Stone Hall Annex was constructed perpendicular to the roofline of Stone Hall while the old annex's roofline ran parallel to it. But for that change, the new annex resembled the old. In preparing the foundation for the new annex the foundation for the old annex was discovered to be solid concrete four feet thick. Workers finally broke the old foundation into boulder sized chunks, each of which amounted to a load for a dump truck.

Photo by Richard Kopp

lishing the MGCATDC years before:

"It is the intent of the Legislature by the passage of this act to provide for the creation and development of a regionally based system in Mississippi for education and training which responds to the needs of Mississippi's work force and employers, is driven by the demands of industry and a competitive economy, makes maximum use of limited resources, and provides for continuing improvement through constant assessment of the results of education and training for individual workers and employers."

In plain words, the Workforce Act aimed to educate uneducated workers, train untrained workers, and efficiently and quickly place them where business and industrial leaders said to place them. The act specified the establishment of "One Stop Career Centers" on each community college campus to provide the services and District Workforce Development Councils (District Councils) to direct the effort.

The act charged the staff of each One-Stop Career Center with over thirty different duties and services in preparing workers to work. The act required that each community college district have an affiliated District Council, the members of which were to be the area's best representatives from the business, professional, industrial, educational, and political milieu. The Act did not specify a membership total, but one member had to be involved in basic literacy training, and eight members were required to be "chief executive officers or plant managers of significant employers of that district." So the District Council provided the direction for preparing a workforce.

Realizing that the One-Stop Career Center was the contact point where worker met job, Mellinger decided to build such facilities on each of the three campuses--not on just one. While he was at it, he decided to expand the scope of the state-mandated services and merge them with regular programs and services already provided to students. This expansion resulted in a new name for the three new facilities constructed by MGCCC--"Educational Services Centers" (ESC). The state One-Stop Career Centers were located inside these facilities. All three ESCs opened in fall 1996.

JD's $1.4 million ESC, Building U, was that campus's first two-story structure. JC's $1.7 million ESC was Building N. Perk's ESC cost less than half the amount of those of either of the other two campuses because only 1,865 square feet of it was new. Rather than destroying historic Stone Hall, Mellinger elected to renovate it and add an annex.

MGCCC Executive Assistant for Development Nell Murray headed the initial effort to put Workforce in place. At first the Workforce director on each campus reported to the vice president of his or her campus and to Murray, who led the effort. In Murray's words, "This lasted about two years, until we realized that the organizational structure caused the effort to break down."

Business and industrial leaders had been promised, according to Murray, "training on the ground, on-site as quickly as possible--24 to 48 hours." Under the original cumbersome set-up, paperwork had to pass from private sector to campus, to Central Office, back to campus, and then back to private sector, slowing response time to two weeks.

MGCCC Executive Assistant for Development Nell Murray served as the first administrator in charge of the Community Campus.

Seeking a way to cut through this bureaucratic Gordian Knot, Murray requested consideration of a solution. According to Mellinger, "When Nell Murray made her request I said, 'DeKalb!'" As Dean of the Occupational Educational Division of DeKalb Community College in Clarkston, Georgia, Mellinger had observed the operation of an organizational structure called a "community campus" designed for the delivery of rapid response to community educational needs. Inspired by that DeKalb model, Mellinger developed the broad parameters of a new "organizational delivery mechanism" designed to streamline the delivery of MGCCC's Workforce training and services to the Coast's business and industrial community.

In June 1996, Mellinger recommended and the Board approved the creation of this new entity to be known as the "Community Campus." The campus began operation on July 1, 1996, with Murray in charge. Murray put off her retirement plans for one year and remained as executive assistant for development in order to set up the machinery of the new "campus." On July 1, 1997, Dr. Mary (Spring) Graham was named vice president of the Community Campus becoming MGCCC's first woman to bear the title vice president.

In the college's first major organizational change since 1962, the Community Campus became a fourth campus equal in stature to Perk, JD, and JC. Unlike those brick and mortar campuses, the Community Campus was, in Murray's words,

Community Campus Vice President Mary (Spring) Graham

"a campus without walls . . . not tied to place . . . but present everywhere."

Actually the Community Campus did gain control of one site--the MGCATDC. Due to the similarity of that center's mission to that of the Community Campus, JD relinquished control of the MGCATDC, and the office of the Community Campus vice president was located there. For the rest, Community Campus personnel were ensconced in all the other campuses and centers of MGCCC and also in industries ranging from Ingalls Shipbuilding and the Chevron Refinery in Pascagoula to the Dupont Plant in DeLisle.

According to Murray, "the structure of the Community Campus was not fixed. . . . We identified our vision, we identified our goals, we identified the mission, and structure more or less evolved." Since the desire to better implement the Workforce and Education Act of 1994 had sparked the idea of the Community Campus, all elements related to the legislation fell under the purview of Community Campus personnel. At its inception, the Community Campus had charge of all non-credit offerings of the college, including Workforce training, adult and continuing education, literacy, small business development, the Institute for Learning in Retirement, and distance learning.

"Distance Learning" was originally an outgrowth of the Community College Network (CCN) established in July 1994 as a project of the Mississippi Rural Health Care Corps for the purpose of training rural health care workers. The CCN connected all of Mississippi's public community colleges in a web consisting of one interactive classroom each, but MGCCC established three such classrooms--one at Perk, JD, and JC. With CCN came access to the Internet and the worldwide web with its endless possibilities for innovation in the realm of the dissemination and gathering of knowledge.

In addition to distance learning accomplished by interfacing instructor and student via the interactive video and computers of the CCN, the Community Campus in August 1996 put its new Mobile Training Unit on the road. The Mobile Training Unit was a 34-foot motor coach fully equipped for instructional purposes. This $120,000 "learning lab on wheels" was loaded with 15 computer stations and a video player and television for instructional purposes. The unit was geared for computer training, basic skills instruction, and occupational assessment and driven to any business and industrial site in the district which applied for its services.

The establishment of the Community Campus was one of many actions designed to keep MGCCC, in Mellinger's words, "at the cutting edge of modern technology" and fulfill the college's "mission [of] aggressive innovation in educational techniques and community service."

Ironically, some of Mellinger's forays into the past wound up being innovations. In 1992 he established the Mississippi Gulf Coast Community College Archives, the avowed purpose of which was to aggressively seek out, discover, and find the remaining documentary and photographic evidence of the institution's role and impact on its district and the state since its inception.

Also, in 1992, again calling on the past as an aid to the present and a boon to the future, Mellinger was instrumental in launching the Building on Our Heritage Campaign. This fundraising effort, unprecedented in the history of the institution, was conceived as a three-year effort on the part of the

The Community Campus Mobile Training Unit.

MGCCC Foundation to raise $1.5 million for college improvements in a variety of areas. The effort yielded in excess of $2 million with the greatest single contribution coming from a former student who had attended in the post-World War I era. William Albert "Ship Island" Frantzen contributed an estimated $1,050,000 in property and money.

Some of the Building on Our Heritage money was spent in remembrance of the more recent past. For one week in April 1997 the Vietnam Moving Wall stood in front of Dees Hall, drawing 8,000 visitors to the Perkinston Campus. For those who remembered Vietnam, it was a catharsis. For the young, with no memory of that war, it was a memorable educational experience.

MGCCC President Barry L. Mellinger (left) stands with William Albert "Ship Island" Frantzen, a member of the Harrison-Stone Agricultural High School class of 1923. Frantzen, a native of Norway and Perk's first foreign-born student, became its greatest benefactor of the 20th century.

A photographer snaps a photo as workers emplace a panel of the Vietnam Veterans Memorial Moving Wall in front of Dees Hall on the Perkinston Campus on April 5, 1996. The one-half scale 250-foot replica of the memorial in Washington D.C. was opened to the public from Saturday, April 6 until Thursday, April 11, 1996.

And what of Mellinger's "brick and mortar" building program? Due to the financial straits in which the state legislature had placed the college at the time he became president, no new structures of consequence were built on any campus before 1990. Structures appeared slowly until 1994, and, with the achievement of debt-free status a year later, they appeared more frequently.

Unlike Hayden, Mellinger did not allot building funds equally among the campuses. Instead, he followed a formula based on student enrollment. Thus in the years 1990 to 1998 (allowing for the final structure being completed in 1999), new construction at JD and its WHCOTC satellite totaled $6,815,101. At JD in succession these buildings were R (Allied Health Building), S (Academic Classroom Building), T (Maintenance and Storage), U (Educational Services Center), V (Vocational Classrooms/Computer Lab), and RA (a second Allied Health Building).

At JC in the same period new construction totaled $7,993,707. In succession, 1990-1998, the new buildings included J(Childcare), T(Applied Technology), L

Jefferson Davis Campus Associate Degree Nursing Department Chairperson Wanda Brignac (left) and Mellinger cut the ribbon at the April 1, 1990 dedication of Building R (Allied Health). Though the structure was not yet completed, it was dedicated early as part of the 25th anniversary celebration of JD campus.

(Library/Classroom Addition), T (Applied Technology Addition), G (Vo-Tech Addition), F (Fine Arts Addition), K (Student Center), M (Classroom/Office Building), H (Health Occupations Addition), N (Educational Services Center).

In the Mellinger Era, Perkinston Campus received only one built-from-scratch free-standing structure--the $900,000 Sam P. Jones Band Hall, which began service on March 24, 1998, at precisely 1:15 p.m. On the other hand, Mellinger spent $3.5 million on renovation and preservation of existing structures. Shortly after he became president he confided, "Not another of the historic buildings of this campus will fall while I am in charge."

The new water tower stands completed in May 1998 with the 1938 water tower behind Dees Hall in the background. The new tower is the third water tower on Perk hill since 1912. All three towers have played and will continue to play an important role apart from their prosaic purpose--the dating of visual images of the campus. The "golf ball" tank was set on the "tee" on the afternoon of March 16, 1998. The tank was then painted and began service that summer. On August 28, 1998, a huge crane lowered the old tank to the ground. The crane then held the tower and lowered it as welders cut the legs off in sections. On September 1, 1998, the tower sections were removed from the campus.

Several of Mellinger's renovation efforts resulted in additional square footage for the Perkinston Campus. In one case the "addition" he built quadrupled the size of the existing structure. The 1982 Student Center was increased from its original size of 3,900 square feet to 16,100 square feet at a cost of $786,326. The $670,559 conversion of Stone Hall into the Perk Educational Services Center in August 1996 resulted in the addition of an annex. The $900,000 renovation of Heidelberg Hall in 1998 included additions for a new kitchen and two new dining areas. A 1998 Weeks Hall addition of 3,896 square feet was made at a cost of $309,198.

Central Office received a 6,000 square foot Central Printing/Central Stores building. This metal structure, occupied on June 6, 1994, cost $308,162. During the Mellinger era two historic structures passed under control of Central Office. Central Office personnel occupied Jackson Hall in summer 1988, and the original 1927 Superintendent's Home became the Alumni House in spring 1989.

Huff Hall, MGCCC's first and most historic building, where classes first began on September 17, 1912, was converted in 1989 into a Learning Lab and offices. Huff's original kitchen annex remained a faculty residence as it had been since 1915.

Nothing was done in the Mellinger era to the MGCCC building possessing the greatest architectural integrity. The Old Gym, remained much as it was when it was built in 1927, the year the college produced its first graduate. But it remained.

In 1997 Mellinger announced a new program of alternative scheduling to meet the needs of those who could not attend classes at "traditional" times. A program of accelerated General Education Core (GECo) courses put a community college degree in reach of adults with full-time jobs. Other classes were offered on weekends and still others scheduled in short term day slots.

By mid-1998, the $8 million effort by Mellinger and the Board, begun two years prior, to place MGCCC in the forefront of the computer revolution was nearing completion. All MGCCC campuses and centers had been wired internally and networked together. Scores of new computers were being placed in offices and classrooms, and the administrators, instructors, and staff members of MGCCC were booting up and going online to the World Wide Web.

Then, at the conclusion of the May 22, 1998, Board Meeting, Mellinger pulled a note from his pocket, unfolded it and read from it: "This college has been my life personally and professionally . . . [but] . . . the presidency is a full-time job, complex and demanding . . . and unanticipated circumstances have changed my plans." He then told the Trustees that he might face medical situations requiring lengthy treatment and closed by announcing his retirement effective August 1, 1998.

Wilbur Ward, a 25-year veteran Board member recalling that moment said, "We were shocked. . . . He talked to no one but his family. We had no idea." The shock waves radiating from the Boardroom passed with lightning speed to the employees of MGCCC.

In the dark days of the beginning of his presidency Mellinger had said, "I would have liked for my coming to have been at a better time." In his final message to the employees of MGCCC, he expressed his gratitude that his departure, at least, came at a better time:

"This college is on the threshold of a very bright future. I am confident that its leadership, the Board of Trustees, and employees at every level will continue the course into the new century. It has been my privilege to serve this institution [with] people who have shared my vision for an institution that has had a life-changing impact on thousands of people."

Dr. Willis Lott succeeded Mellinger as president of MGCCC on August 22, 1998. Mellinger (right) presents Lott with the key to the president's office.

The Perkinston Campus Student Center (above), in ceremonies held April 21, 1999, was officially named the Barry L. Mellinger Student Center.

(Right) Perkinston Campus Vice President Mary (Spring) Graham and MGCCC President Willis Lott flank President Emeritus Mellinger as they stand in front of the new sign which had been affixed to the front wall of the Student Center.

Perkinston Campus aerial photograph taken Wednesday, March 22, 2000 by Will Bramlett Aerial Photography.

The major Barry L. Mellinger-era structures completed or initiated on Perkinston Campus prior to his retirement on August 15, 1998, are numbered on the photo in order of construction. The date assigned to each structure is that of the best evidence of real occupancy or use of a structure (or a portion thereof) by MGCCC personnel.

1. *Central Office Printing (6,000-square-foot metal structure). The move from the Smith Building was completed June 6, 1994. Frank Spring, then MGCCC director of printing, recalled his role in the D-Day landing at Normandy precisely fifty years ago that day.*
2. *Barry L. Mellinger Student Center* — *Quadrupled in size in 1994, the full structure including the 1982 original portion was named for Mellinger on April 21, 1999.*
3. *Stone Hall Annex* — *The two-story, 2,000-square-foot addition together with the rest of the 1915-era structure began service as Perk's Educational Services Center in August 1996.*
4. *Heidelberg Hall Annex, 1998*
5. *Weeks Hall Addition, 1998*
6. *Sam P. Jones Band Hall* — *This 10,340-square-foot brick and masonry structure began service March 24, 1998 at 1:15 p.m.*
7. *Water tower--Erected spring 1998*
8. *Horticulture and golf turf management* — *The first greenhouse was erected in 1982. The facilities were expanded in 1996 and 1997*

Jefferson Davis Campus aerial photograph taken Monday, March 27, 2000 by Will Bramlett Aerial Photography.

The major Barry L. Mellinger-era structure completed or initiated on Jefferson Davis Campus prior to his retirement on August 15, 1998, are numbered on the photo in order of construction with the letter of the building given in parentheses. The date assigned to each structure is that of the best evidence of real occupancy of the structure (or a portion thereof) by MGCCC personnel.

1. R (Allied Health Building)	*The building was dedicated on April 1, 1990, as part of the 25th anniversary celebration for the JD campus though it was not accepted by the Board as complete until June 20, 1990. The masonry structure contained 14,7000 square feet and cost $944,663.*
2. S (Academic Classroom Building)	*Completed in 1994, the structure contained 19,264 square feet and cost $1,024,027. Beginning with S Building, no more flat roofs were built at JD.*
3. T (Maintenance/Storage Building)	*Completed in 1995, the 8,000-square-foot structure cost $487,424*
4. U (Educational Services Center)	*JD's first two-story edifice, the brick and masonry structure contained 21,800 square feet and cost $1,384,292*
5. V (Classroom/Computer Lab Building)	*Completed in 1996, the 11,000-square-foot brick and masonry structure cost $801,089.*
6. RA (Allied Health Classroom Building II)	*Completed in 1999, the 14,700-square-foot masonry structure cost $1,163,219*

Construction of the Arena Theatre, adjacent to and east of the Fine Arts Building, began in spring 1999. The first performance in the $2 million masonry structure took place in September 2000. The Arena Theatre was the initial Willis Lott-era structure completed on any campus.

Jackson County Campus aerial photograph taken Monday, March 27, 2000, by Will Bramlett Aerial Photography.

The major Barry L. Mellinger-era structures completed or initiated on the Jackson County Campus prior to his retirement on August 15, 1998, are numbered on the photo in order of construction with the letter of the building given in parentheses. The date assigned to each structure is that of the best evidence of real occupancy (or a portion thereof) by MGCCC personnel.

1. J (Childcare Building)	*A 2,452-square-foot concrete and brick structure which cost $186,869.*
2. T (Applied Technology Building)	*A 7,575-square-foot brick and concrete structure which cost $297,598.* *Both J Building and T Building were dedicated March 25, 1990, as part of the JC Campus 25th anniversary celebration. Both were accepted by the Board as completed on June 20, 1990, and both began operation in the fall.*
3. L (Library/Classroom Addition)	*Completed in 1991, the 22,890-square-foot brick and masonry addition cost $977,540.*
4. T (Applied Technology Addition)	*Completed in 1992, the 10,300-square-foot brick and masonry addition cost $572,738*
5. G (Vo-Tech Addition)	*Completed in 1992, the 3,887-square-foot addition cost $89,956*
6. F (Fine Arts Addition)	*Completed in 1994, the 16,575-square-foot brick and masonry addition cost $1,116,889*
7. K (Student Center/Cafeteria Building)	*Completed in 1995, the 16,986-square-foot brick and masonry structure cost $1,282,566*
8. M (Classroom/Office Building)	*Completed in 1995, the 19,189-square-foot brick and masonry structure cost $1,113,216*
9. H (Health Occupations Addition)	*Completed in 1996, the 8,528osquare-foot brick and masonry structure cost $600,382*
10. N (Educational Services Center)	*Completed in 1997, the 23,270-square-foot brick and masonry structure cost $1,650,953*

LOTT AND THE EVE OF THE NEW MILLENNIUM AUG. 1998 - DEC. 2000

MGCCC President Willis Hulon Lott Jr. poses for a portrait at Jackson County Campus shortly after taking office.

When MGCCC President Barry L. Mellinger announced his resignation on May 22, 1998, effective August 1, the MGCCC Board of Trustees fortunately had a qualified successor for Mellinger already on contract. Accordingly, the Board named Dr. Willis Lott, then vice president of the Perkinston Campus, as president-elect on July 22, and he took office the day Mellinger departed. Lott, the eleventh chief executive officer of MGCCC and its predecessors back to 1912, was the fourth of those designated "president."

Willis H. Lott Jr., only son and one of two children of Willis Hulon and Marie (Speaks) Lott, was born in Yazoo City on November 6, 1944. His early life was spent in the small Delta town of Louise. When he was aged six, the family moved for a time to Jackson and finally settled in Seminary by the time he was in the eighth grade.

As an avid participant in sports at Seminary High School, Lott set his sights on becoming a high school coach. After earning a bachelor's degree in health and physical education at the University of Southern Mississippi in 1968, Lott began his career in education as a teacher and coach at Bassfield High School. While at Bassfield he married the former Ethel Myers of Collins, a 1966 union which eventually produced two children, Stacey and Shane. Also while at Bassfield he earned his master's degree in counseling and school guidance at USM in 1971.

In March 1975, Lott began his junior college career as a vocational-technical counselor at Pearl River Junior College (PRC). In September of the following year, he became PRC's director of admissions and records, a position he held for nearly a decade. One of his accomplishments of this period was the establishment of a computerized "on-line registration system."

During this period, also, Lott developed the ambition of becoming a junior college president. To lay the groundwork for that goal, he earned a terminal degree in higher education administration at USM in 1979. Elevated to the position of PRC dean of academic affairs in July 1986, he served in that office until December 1991.

In January 1992, at the behest of MGCCC President Barry L. Mellinger, Lott moved to Perkinston to assume his new duties as vice president for instructional affairs. While in that position, Lott guided the development of the $8.6 million technology plan for MGCCC that led to the networking at all MGCCC installations with connection to the Internet. This plan, destined to carry MGCCC into the new millennium, called for the distribution of a personal computer to each faculty member. He also initiated the instructional programs carried over the Community College Network (CCN).

Soon after Perk Campus Vice President Richard Miller suffered a debilitating stroke on September 2, 1994, the MGCCC Board of Trustees assigned Lott the job of Perk Campus interim vice president, in addition to his other duties. In January 1996, the Board approved his lateral transfer to full-time Perk Campus vice president, and he moved from that position to that of president on August 1, 1998.

When Lott presided at his first Fall Faculty Workshop held at the Perkinston Campus later that month, he shared his vision for the college with the massed faculty of MGCCC. For the first time his faculty members experienced the elements of their new leader's style of delivery--the combination of which might be described as "charismatic." The overall effect was that of a "fireside chat" which left each listener with the impression that Lott had spoken to him or her privately. A standing ovation from such an audience on such an occasion is rare, but it happened.

MGCCC President Willis Lott poses with First Lady Ethel Lott in Liaison on homecoming day, October 10, 1998.

Everyone who heard Lott's August 1998 talk with his faculty remembered three words--family, technology, and education. While he had been vice president of the Perkinston Campus, he referred to his charges as the "Perk family." That August he spoke to the "Gulf Coast family," saying "It does not matter what you do for the college. Whatever you do is important to the success of the college. It does not matter what site we work at. We're the same college with the same mission." While the family lived in a four-county district, the education it provided had to be "world class" because, "We have to make sure [our] students can compete in a global market." Finally, the only way the "Gulf Coast family" could ensure a "world class" education for its students was through the medium of technology. He challenged each instructor present to embrace technology and to open all the new doors to teaching and learning offered by technology.

To Lott, modern technology embraced many things, but it always involved computers. While many of the instructors who had been in Lott's audience had already received computers during the Mellinger era, Lott had spearheaded that effort even then. After Lott became president, virtually everybody else in the Gulf Coast family got a computer whether he wanted one or not.

Once the computers were in place, the college instituted a new software program called "Banner," and even the recalcitrants had to follow the flag or face isolation. E-mail became the order of the day as administrative messages formerly distributed via paper vanished from the pigeon holes in the mail rooms. When the final resister, an instructor who had boasted that he was "road-kill on the information highway and proud of it," at last had a secretary check his e-mail, he found more than 800 messages waiting. That same instructor, along with every last-ditch holdout, finally touched a keyboard at mid-term, fall semester 1999. At that point direct input of grades into the computer replaced the time-honored method of penciling the grades on a bubble sheet. Lott had led his educational family members down the information highway and placed them on the Internet. He had accomplished his aim in his typical friendly style without force or rancor simply by shutting off all avenues of escape.

In 1999, realizing that the family needed to get together more than just once a year at the Fall Faculty Workshop, Lott staged the first united MGCCC main graduation since 1969. Since no MGCCC-owned facility offered the space to seat so many graduates, much less the family and friends of the honorees, the Mississippi Coast Coliseum was chosen as the site of the ceremonies held on the night of May 10, 1999. As he prepared to honor a record 933 graduates, Lott reminded the assemblage of the first college graduation of May 20, 1927, when Hersel McDaniel had become the institution's first college graduate and its only class of one.

To Lott all those associated with the institution back to opening day, September 17, 1912, were as much a part of the family as those who came later. While a Hall of Fame for the purpose of honoring former students of significant achievement after leaving the institution had been established in 1971, the college's athletes and coaches had been ignored. So, at the behest of Lott, 15 inductees entered MGCCC's Inaugural Athletic Hall of Fame at a banquet held on the Perk Campus on October 28, 1999. The honorees included coaches and players representing Perkinston Campus, Jefferson Davis Campus, and Jackson County Campus across a span of time stretching from 1931 to 1999.

By 2000, only two years into his presidency, Lott had made clear his intention to forge the college's scattered campuses and centers into a more perfect union. The final computerized networking of all installations, the resurrection of a single graduation ceremony, and the establishment of an Athletic Hall of Fame were three of the more visible manifestations of that intention.

Shortly after assuming the presidency, Lott had begun laying the groundwork for the development of a focused vision of MGCCC's future. Long range planning was nothing new in the history of the institution, but the solicitation of the views of employees, students, alumni, business and industry leaders, and the general public in order to devise the tactics necessary

MGCCC President Willis Lott presents the Strategic Plan 2000 Perkinston Campus Master Plan to the Board of Trustees in the boardroom on February 17, 2000. The CSA Group, Inc., a Mobile, Alabama, based site planning company, completed a comprehensive evaluation of all college-owned facilities and produced a Master Plan schematic for each location in December 1999.

for the development of a grand strategy was new. "Together we are going to make this a better institution" was Lott's motto during 18 months of public meetings and questionnaire mail-outs.

In April 2000, during community college month celebrations, Lott publicly launched "Strategic Plan 2000." Strategic Plan 2000, which was to be the foundation of the college's planning for the opening years of the new millennium contained a "Mission" statement, a "Vision" statement, eight core "Values," and ten "Strategic Initiatives:"

Mission -- We make a positive difference in people's lives every day.
We welcome the responsibility to respond to the educational needs of our community by providing an outstanding learning environment supported by excellent products and services. We achieve this by creating an atmosphere that fosters responsible citizenship and leadership in a dynamic community.

Vision
We envision Mississippi Gulf Coast Community College as a world-class institution. Utilizing appropriate technologies and showcase facilities, we will deliver flexible, responsive programs of the highest quality. Our vision will be realized through outstanding employees who adhere to high standards of excellence while working in partnership with the community.

Values
Core values define the ethics, ideals, and principles that will guide our decision-making, problem-solving, and team-building.

- **Access:** To provide opportunities for participation in quality programs and services.
- **Collaboration:** To unify our efforts to achieve our mission by forging internal and external partnerships and alliances.
- **Excellence:** To set and meet the highest standards.
- **Integrity:** To exemplify honesty, trustworthiness, and good character as we engage in all programs, services, and partnerships.
- **Leadership:** To develop and model leadership skills for our students and our communities.
- **Learning:** To improve the quality of life by providing knowledge and skills.
- **Responsibility:** To ensure stewardship of our resources and accountability to our communities.
- **Unity:** To operate as one college in purpose, plans, priorities, and processes.
- **Vision:** To anticipate, welcome, and embrace future challenges.

Strategic Initiatives

1. **One Unified College**
   As a multi-campus institution, we operate as a single, unified college.
2. **World-Class Instruction**
   Students/graduates will be prepared to compete suc-

(From left) Jackson County Beat 3 Supervisor Tim Broussard, MGCCC President Willis Lott, Jackson County Beat 4 Supervisor Frank Leach, Jackson County Beat 1 Supervisor (and President of the Board of Supervisors) Manly Barton, and Jackson County Campus Vice President Houshang Moradmand participate in groundbreaking ceremonies at the Jackson County Campus on May 25, 2000. The event marked the official beginning of the renovation of and the construction of an addition to Physical Education and Health Building E. The event likewise celebrated the impending construction of a new Administrative Classroom Building. Both projects were conceived and authorized in accordance with the JC Campus Master Plan as set forth in Strategic Plan 2000.

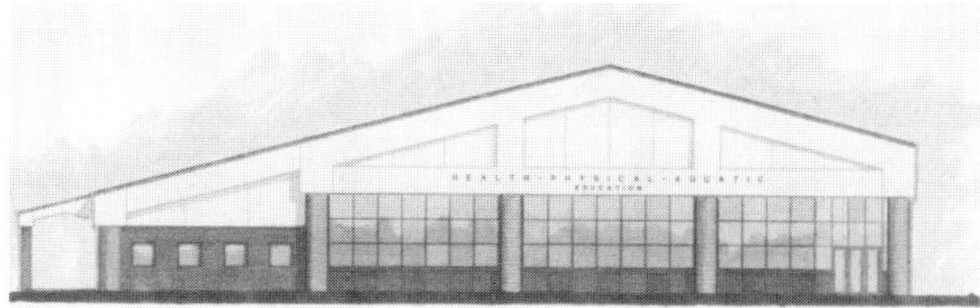

Architect's rendering of the natatorium section of the $1,191,000 renovation/addition to Jackson County Physical Education Building E.

Architects rendering of the façade of the $2,030,000 Jackson County Administrative Classroom Building.

cessfully in the diverse global workplace of the 21st century.

3. **Information Systems Technology**
   MGCCC will provide technology to ensure that our students are successful, that faculty are technologically empowered, that administrative system support is high quality, and to ensure that learning can take place anywhere, anytime.
4. **Human Resources**
   MGCCC will employ qualified, dedicated, and capable personnel.
5. **Student Activities**
   Increase student participation in collegewide activities.
6. **Efficient Processes**
   Customer satisfaction will be consistently rated at the highest level. All who interact with the college will have a high opinion of its effectiveness and efficiency.
7. **Fiscal Resources**
   MGCCC will increase funding sources and will more effectively manage existing resources.
8. **Long-Range Capital Plan**
   The college will be enhanced by a modern learning environment that supports its mission and vision.
9. **Alumni/Foundation**
   Increase support for the college mission by increasing participation (fiscal and otherwise) by individuals and organizations.
10. **Expansion of Higher Education on The Coast**
    To respond to higher education needs by using our assets and opportunities to integrate our programs and services with other higher education institutions. We will create partnerships to expand opportunities for our students without duplicating costly programs, services, and facilities.

Almost at once the bright future envisioned in Strategic Plan 2000 dimmed due to a down-turn in the state's economic growth. In May 2000, for the first time in nearly a decade, the Board of Trustees had to approve a budget cut by state mandate. The $840,000 removed in May was followed by another $1,035,000 cut in October. By the close of the second millennium in December 2000, projected cuts exceeded those experienced in the darkest days of the Mellinger era.

Once again, as in 1986, MGCCC's success in serving the special needs of its unique district had placed the college in the ironic position of suffering proportionally more financial loss than upstate community/junior colleges. While the upstate institutions generally served the so-called "traditional" 18 to 20 year-old full-time student, MGCCC catered to a student population averaging age 27 that required distinctly non-traditional and often part-time service. Unfortunately for MGCCC the archaic state funding formula offered far greater financial support for a full-time traditional student. The long-standing MGCCC dilemma of using funding made available by its static traditional enrollment to finance ever-burgeoning non-traditional services became more difficult as budget cuts deepened.

In 2000, under Lott's guidance, the school continued and even expanded its non-credit and part-time offerings. He did this he said, "because the demand for such services existed in the four-county district."

Weekend classes, short term classes, and distance education received greater impetus under Lott. In January 2000, the college began offering online courses as part of the Mississippi Virtual Community College (MVCC).

Service to the military on the Coast, which had resulted in the establishment of Keesler Center in 1973, was expanded. On August 25, 2000, MGCCC became Mississippi's first Service Members Opportunity College-Navy (SOCNAV) school. Classes began in the fall at the Naval Construction Battalion Center ("Seabee Base") in Gulfport. In November, former JD Campus Dean of Student Services David Drye was authorized to open an office on the base after the Christmas holidays to better serve the 5,000 sailors of the U. S. Navy and U. S. Coast Guard on the base.

On October 4, 2000, the SOCNAV agreement was extended to Naval Station Pascagoula to increase service to the 1,910 sailors quartered on five U. S. Navy vessels and one U. S. Coast Guard cutter stationed at the port. MGCCC had served personnel at Naval Station Pascagoula with special scheduling through Jackson County Campus since 1998, but the SOCNAV agreement, which placed MGCCC in a consortium with 80 other fully accredited colleges and universities, expanded MGCCC's ability to offer weekend, online, and other short-term course options.

As the first multi-campus junior college in Mississippi, MGCCC in 2000 served the most heavily industrialized and fastest-growing area of a state that (with the exception of the Jackson area) remained largely rural. In the 35 years since 1965, the Perkinston institution had grown from a piney woods junior college serving scarcely 1,000 students into a mostly urban entity composed of four campuses and four centers serving nearly 30,000 citizens in credit and non-credit programs. Yet the state, ignoring what the school had become, still financed it on the basis of what it used to be.

On the eve of the new millennium Lott told his "family" that the "coming years look bleak." But then he said, "The people before us faced some hard times. They survived. The institution survived. We will survive these hard times together."

The institution had begun in a single structure on a hilltop in Perkinston on September 17, 1912. At dark on the night of September 17, 1912, Superintendent James A. Huff had ordered the ignition of a farm tractor-dynamo, and Huff Hall had been illuminated by the first electric lights to shine in Perkinston. Huff and his staff of three had then set to work teaching 63 students. In December 2000, the lights still gleamed in Huff Hall, but an electrical grid connecting nearly 100 buildings scattered across four counties then powered them. Likewise, that electrical grid powered the computers which provided instantaneous communication among the personnel located in all those structures and connected them to the world via the Internet. President Willis H. Lott's staff of 781 was then serving 28,371 students. In 88 years of evolutionary growth periodically spurred by revolutionary change, the Harrison County Agricultural High School had become a community college of national renown.

(Above) Completed was the $1,882,835 Arena Theatre, a 14,500 square-foot annex to Jefferson Davis Fine arts Building D. The Arena Theatre was the initial MGCCC structure completed in the Lott era.

On October 4, 2000, a unique "building ceremony" which simultaneously marked the completion of one structure (left) and launched the construction of another, (below) was staged at Jefferson Davis Campus. Both projects were conceived in accordance with the JD Master Plan as set forth in Strategic Plan 2000.

(Above) Architect's rendering of the facade of the proposed 14,600 square-foot, $1,517,000 Math and Computer Science Classroom Building.

THE CENTERS:

MISSISSIPPI GULF COAST APPLIED TECHNOLOGY AND DEVELOPMENT CENTER

GEORGE COUNTY OCCUPATIONAL TRAINING CENTER

KEESLER CENTER

WEST HARRISON COUNTY OCCUPATIONAL TRAINING CENTER

On July 6, 1944 Sergeant Joe Pilior raises Old Glory on a pole in front of the largest Quonset hut at the Gulfport Seabee Base. Twenty years later the Seabee Base, in particular the "Elephant Hut," became the site of MGCJC's first satellite installation. Photo from Bolts & Bullets magazine, July 6, 1944.

Paul Mellinger
MDTA Supervisor
CB (Seabee) Center
1964-1968

MISSISSIPPI GULF COAST APPLIED TECHNOLOGY & DEVELOPMENT CENTER

MGCCC'S OLDEST SATELLITE AND NEWEST INSTALLATION

The title page of MGCCC's 1999-2000 catalog listed the various campuses and installations of the institution. One of these was given as "Applied Technology and Development Center (established 1964--Relocated 1991)." The 1964 establishment date made the Mississippi Gulf Coast Applied Technology and Development Center (MGCATDC) older than any other MGCCC installation except Perkinston Campus. MGCATDC traced its lineage back through several previous incarnations and not one but two relocations.

The federal Manpower Development Training Act (MDTA) of 1962 made funds available to educational institutions for the purpose of training unemployed persons over age 18 in the necessary skills to secure jobs. MDTA funding was administered through the Mississippi State Department of Education, Vocational Division. Specific vocational areas of training were identified and certified by the Mississippi Employment Security Commission. Once the selection of a program had been made, the commission authorized Mississippi Gulf Coast Junior College (MGCJC) to offer the classes, recruit students for those classes, administer the subsistence allowance for the trainees, and place the graduates in jobs. By mid-1964 MGCJC District Vocational-Technical Coordinator Curtis Davis and his assistant, Barry L. Mellinger, were seeking a site in Gulfport for an MDTA training center.

Since MGCJC had been offering intermittent academic night classes at the mothballed, Second World War-era Naval Construction Battalion (CB or "Seabee") Base since 1962, it seemed logical that quarters for a Manpower Center might be found there as well. On September 23, 1964, the two men reported to the MGCJC Board that accommodations at the Seabee Base were in the offing. In October MGCJC acquired a two-story barracks for use as offices and adult education classrooms. The shops were located in a huge Quonset hut--the biggest on the base--which was dubbed the "Elephant Hut."

On November 18, 1964, the Board named Paul D. Mellinger, father of Barry Mellinger, as supervisor of the Seabee Base Manpower Training Center and approved eight instructors. These first instructors and their areas of instruction were Pat Flaherty of Perkinston, small gasoline engine repair; John F. Pachel of Wiggins, metal trades; Robert H. Yoder of Gulfport and Johnny G. Sumner of Biloxi, automotive mechanics; James M. Bankston of Wiggins and G. G. Loftin of Long Beach, automobile body repair; E. G. Laughlin, hardwood grading and literacy training; and Leonard Avera of Jackson, saw filing. This last program was moved to rented quarters in Wiggins near the sawmills.

In February 1965 four instructors were hired to teach electronics. This course was offered jointly by MGCJC and Mississippi State University personnel who were on base at the newly established Mississippi Technical Institute. Also in February, MGCJC hired a drafting instructor, two welding instructors, and two diesel mechanics instructors. One of the latter was Gerald Gartman, who was destined to be involved in and, indeed, preside over most of the quarter century evolution of the Seabee Manpower Training Center into the MGCATDC.

On June 25, 1965, MGCJC officials conducted graduation ceremonies for 251 graduates of the first 11 classes at the Seabee Base Manpower Training Center. Barry Mellinger welcomed the assemblage, Paul Mellinger gave the special awards, and MGCJC President J. J. Hayden presented the certificates.

In 1966 the average enrollment at the base, which had hovered around 300, began to decline as the Navy, due to the escalating war in Vietnam, began to press for the return of its facilities. In addition to that development, a fire in early March 1967 heavily damaged the "Elephant Hut" at the Seabee Base, resulting in all but the welding program being moved to temporary quarters on the

MDTA FIRST FACULTY

John F. Pachel *(pictured right with two automotive mechanic students at Perkinston in 1970)* began teaching metal trades at the Seabee Base in 1964. Leonard E. Avera *(pictured below at Perkinston in 1970)* began teaching MDTA sawfiling in rented facilities in Wiggins in 1964. One of Avera's students *(below right)* prepares to file a saw at Perkinston in 1970 after the program was moved to the campus.

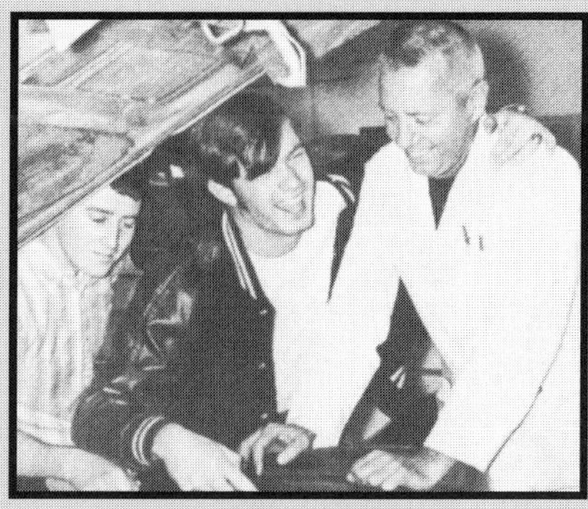

Gerald Gartman, who began his career at MGCJC as a diesel mechanics instructor at the Seabee Base, moved into administration. Gartman *(pictured above in 1971)* directs construction of a new Future Farmers of America camp center in Long Beach, replacing one destroyed by Camille.

base. The welding program was transferred to JC. Clearly, the whole operation needed to be relocated.

In August 1967, the Board accepted the offer of the Harrison County Development Commission for new quarters in two buildings located on five acres of land on the east side of Lorraine Road near the north end of the Wilkes Bridge over the Industrial Seaway. The property was offered for the sum of one dollar until such time as MGCJC no longer needed it for educational purposes. At such time the property would revert to the owner. By mid-January 1968 all equipment had been removed from the Seabee Base to the new installation, and the programs in drafting, diesel mechanics, metal trades, small engine repair, welding, auto mechanics, and auto body repair were ready to begin.

In ceremonies held May 17, 1968, Hayden joined State Senator Tommy Munro, U. S Representative William M. "Bill" Colmer, and *Daily Herald* editor E. P. Wilkes in dedicating the new installation which bore the appellation, "Manpower Training Center, Jefferson Davis Junior College, Mississippi Gulf Coast Junior College District." MGCJC had operated programs administered by the District in temporary off-campus quarters before, but this dedication marked the birth of the college's first satellite. In particular the new Manpower Training Center was a satellite of JD, and Dean Bill Lipscomb attended the dedication ceremony along with the center's new supervisor, Gerald Gartman. Paul Mellinger, who would have been supervisor of the center had he not resigned to become vocational director of the state penitentiary at Parchman, was present as well. The formation of this JD satellite likely had the effect of sparking the movement toward the formation of another. Coincident with the establishment of the JD Manpower Training Center, the George County Trustees began putting forth the proposition that their county should have a center offering MTDA training, vo-tech courses, adult education, and evening classes. George County was, after all, the only one of the four District counties with no permanent installation.

Not only was the JD Manpower Center MGCJC's first satellite, it was also Mississippi's first trade school to be located in the confines of an industrial park. The center performed its mission so well that before the end of its first year of operation it achieved another first for Mississippi. In December 1968 Gartman received word that the United States Department of Health, Education, and Welfare (HEW) had elevated his facility to the status of "Manpower Training Skill Center," one of only 54 in the nation.

To qualify for "Skill Center" status an installation had to be located in a centralized, self-contained facility, operating on a full-time basis, and providing counseling and related services to trainees recruited from a large area. In speaking of the HEW accolade, Gartman said, "Our Manpower program has come a long way since its initiation in 1964 in temporary buildings on the Navy Base in Gulfport. The Skill Center is now operating in permanent buildings . . . in the middle of a growing industrial area." In the four years since the college's MDTA program had begun, Gartman claimed that 75 percent of the program's 934 graduates had achieved immediate employment in related fields at salaries far greater than those they had previously earned.

In 1973 MDTA gave way to another federal program known as the Comprehensive Educational Training Act (CETA). The JD Manpower Skill Center continued to offer training under that program, but on October 1, 1979, the college expand-

EVOLUTION OF THE INDUSTRIAL SEAWAY SATELLITE INSTALLATION

From
Manpower Training Center
to
Manpower Skills Center
to
Harrison County Occupational Training Center

The building on the Industrial Seaway circa 1969.

The HCOTC sign circa 1979.

Gerald Gartman
Supervisor
Manpower Training/Skills Center
1968-1979
Assistant Director/Dean
Harrison County Occupational Training Center
1979-1987

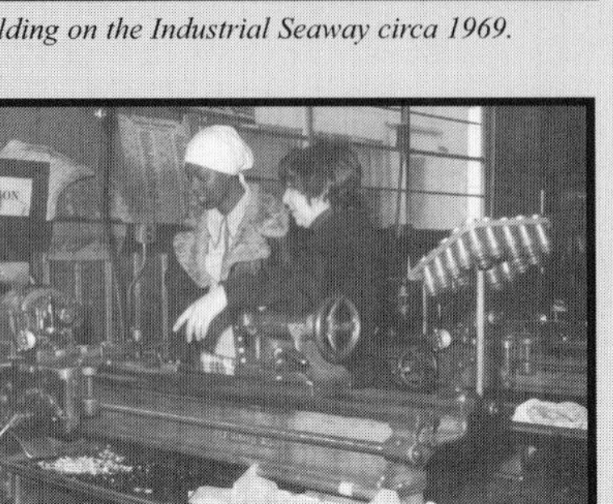

HCOTC women pipefitters circa 1979.

HCOTC automotive mechanics circa 1979.

ed the offerings at the Skills Center to include regular vocational programs and renamed the installation the Harrison County Occupational Training Center (HCOTC). Gartman remained in charge of the new entity with the title of assistant director until June 1983, when, in a college-wide administrative reorganization, his title was changed to assistant dean.

In summer 1985 the HCOTC automotive machinery and programs were moved to West Harrison County Occupational Training Center (WHCOTC). Thereafter, other HCOTC programs were removed to JD Campus or Jackson County Campus until its offerings fell below the minimum number necessary for an assistant dean.

In late 1987, Gartman accepted a lateral transfer to Central Office, taking the position of director of special vocational projects. In January 1988 Johnny Tynes took charge of the HCOTC as part of his recently created position as Central Office industrial training coordinator.

Within a year only Alton McDaniel's welding program still functioned full-time at the HCOTC. But, said Tynes, "We still used HCOTC for short term programs for the Harrison County Sheriff's Department and industrial start up programs for companies such as Mississippi Power Company, Regina Manufacturing, and Avondale Shipyard. We also ran Job Training Partnership Act (JTPA) programs, one of which lasted a year for the purpose of assisting dislocated workers." According to Tynes, JTPA, which had replaced CETA in the early 1980s was nothing more than an extension of the old Manpower Development and Training Act by another name.

Johnny Tynes
Central Office Industrial Training Coordinator/
HCOTC Coordinator
MGCATDC
Administrative Dean
1988-1994

By mid 1988 the ramshackled and virtually deserted HCOTC seemed destined not only to be MGCCC's first satellite but also the first to wither away into oblivion. But on June 22, 1988, the MGCCC Board entered into an agreement with three other entities which reincarnated the HCOTC as the Mississippi Gulf Coast Applied Technology and Development Center (MGCATDC).

The State Department of Education matched MGCCC's $340,000 contribution to the effort while Mississippi Power Company put in a further $1,500,000. The fourth partner in the venture, the Harrison County Development Commission, provided $50,000 but more importantly the site for the new facility.

Under the terms of the 1967 agreement by which the Harrison County Development Commission had leased to MGJC the five-acre site and buildings of what became the HCOTC, the college was to retain control of the land and facilities until no longer needed for educational purposes. Two decades later that time had come, so the commission offered to provide a new five-acre site and reclaim the old when the new facility was completed.

The new site lay one-half mile

northwest of the old HCOTC in the Intraplex 10 Light Industry Park just south of Interstate 10 and west of Lorraine Road. Groundbreaking ceremonies were held November 15, 1989, and the new building was slated for a fall 1990 opening.

That did not happen. Alton McDaniel remembered, "We had to take delivery of furniture and equipment for the new building at the old Harrison County Center because completion of the new building was delayed time after time." On March 19, 1991, the MGCCC Board took the unprecedented step of accepting a portion of a building as substantially complete. The outside sheltered work areas of the new structure were accepted so that heavy instructional machinery could be stored there pending the completion of the interior of the building. HCOTC personnel began moving into the interior of the 40,000 square foot structure on April 15. McDaniel, the last instructor of the final full-time program of the HCOTC, became the first instructor in the initial program of the MGCATDC. According to McDaniel,"Once the welding equipment was in place, the students came for the first time on May 22. We finally got the machines wired and the students started welding on June 13."

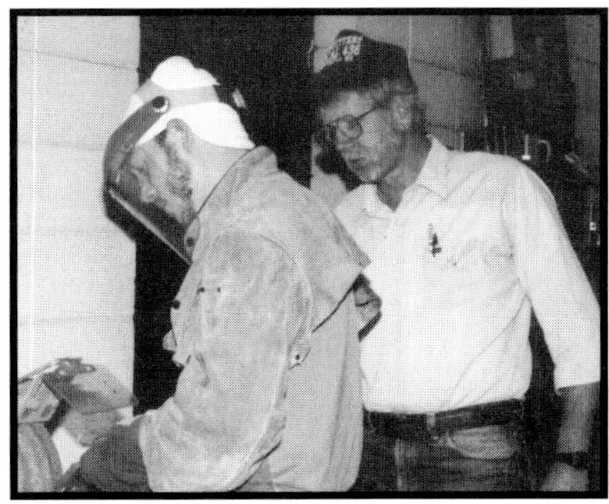

Alton Glynn McDaniel (right) instructs a welding student in the MGCATDC in June 1993.

Johnny Tynes, who had been named administrative dean of the MGCATDC several months before its completion, recalled that the next two programs in the building were especially designed for Mississippi Power Company employees. One program concerned instrumentation control and electricity/electronics. Mechanical maintenance was the other.

On June 26, 1991, former Mississippi Governor William Winter delivered the keynote address at the dedication of the MGCATDC. According to Winter and the other speakers at the dedication, each of the four parties involved in the establishment of the MGCATDC had achieved its specific goal. Mississippi Power Company had its specialized training center. The Harrison County Development Commission had a magnet for prospective industries. The State Department of Education and MGCCC had a new vocational-technical training facility which could serve as a regional development installation. But the sum was greater than its parts. Touted as the product of the first large-scale alliance of business, education, and state and local government entities in

MISSISSIPPI GULF COAST APPLIED TECHNOLOGY & DEVELOPMENT CENTER DEDICATION DAY, JUNE 26, 1991

Former Mississippi State Governor William Winter making the dedicatory address.

Cutting the ribbon at the dedication of the MGCATDC are, from left, Honorable William Winter, former governor; Don Mason, president of the Harrison County Development Commission; David Ratcliffe, president of Mississippi Power Company; Elwyn Wheat, associate state superintendent for vocational, technical, and adult education; and Dr. Barry L. Mellinger, MGCCC president.

The completed MGCATDC.

Mississippi history, the MGCATDC was declared the model for subsequent partnerships statewide.

Tynes remained as administrative dean of the MGCATDC until spring 1994, when he returned to his original post as Central Office industrial training coordinator. Helen Dees, former Central Office assistant director of vocational instruction, then became administrative dean of the MGCATDC.

Helen Dees
MGCATDC Center Director
1996-1997

On July 1, 1996, the MGCATDC, formerly a satellite of the JD Campus, became the administrative center of MGCCC's fourth campus -- the Community Campus.

In the administrative reorganization that followed, Dees's title was changed from administrative dean to that of MGCATDC center director. When Dees retired in 1997, Tynes, who by then was Community Campus industrial services coordinator, served as interim center director until Joe Tillson filled that position. However, Tillson stayed only a year before transferring to the JC campus. Tynes, who was by then Community Campus dean of industrial services, was once again named MGCATDC interim director.

Joe Tillson
MGCATDC Center Director
1997-1998

In April 2000, Tynes, who had an office at the MGCATDC and another office in Stone Hall on the Perkinston Campus, cautioned about too great an identification of the Community Campus with the MGCATDC. In his words:

"Certainly a number of Community Campus administrative offices, including that of Vice President Cliff Quinn, are located in the brick and mortar installation known as the MGCATDC. Certainly the reasons for the founding of the MGCATDC, chief among which were vo-tech training and regional development through industrial, educational, and governmental partnerships, are the heart and soul of the Community Campus. But, because of all that, those of us in the Community Campus must constantly guard against the erroneous perception that the MGCATDC *is* the Community Campus. Sure, all the MGCCC personnel at the MGCATDC work for the Community Campus, but we also have personnel in every other brick and mortar campus and center of MGCCC. In addition, we have personnel at Ingalls, Dupont, and many other industrial sites. We also have a mobile training unit that travels among all these places. The Community Campus is not tied to a 'place.' Its activities not only pervade MGCCC but also the whole southeast Mississippi region."

Johnny Tynes at Ingalls Shipbuilding Corporation. Tynes became MGCATDC director for the third time in 1998 and remained in that position in 2000.

Aerial photograph of the MGCATDC made by Will Bramlett Aerial Photography on March 27, 2000. In this photograph east is at the top.

Mississippi Gulf Coast Junior College (Perkinston Campus)
George County Occupational Training Center
First Administration - Session 1972-1973

Robert Dale Rose
Center Director

Ronnie C. Mizell
Counselor

Mississippi Gulf Coast Junior College (Perkinston Campus)
George County Occupational Training Center
First Faculty - Session 1972-1973

John Ward Cooley
Secondary Building Trades

Freida Mae Davis
Post-Secondary Licensed
Practical Nursing

Johnnette Heidelberg
Post-Secondary
Secretarial Training

Harlis D. Johnson
Secondary Metal Trades

Junius Howard Martin
Post-Secondary
Welding

Georgia Rouse
Secondary Health Occupations

GEORGE COUNTY OCCUPATIONAL TRAINING CENTER

After 1965 George County was the only one of Mississippi Gulf Coast Junior College's four supporting counties with no MGCJC installation. In January 1968, the MGCJC Board began discussing the issue of "establishing a Center in George County in which vocational-technical, MDTA (Manpower Development Training Act), evening extension, and adult education programs could be offered."

Plans for financing the construction of the center were nearly finalized when Hurricane Camille struck on August 17, 1969, causing a delay. A year later, in order to establish a presence in George County, MGCJC officials opened a small MDTA installation in a rented building in Lucedale. In November 1970, the MGCJC Board authorized the purchase of 15 acres of land for $15,000 in south Lucedale at the junction of Highways 63 and 26 as the site of a new vocational-technical center.

In March 1971 the MGCJC Board announced that the new branch of MGCJC's Perkinston Campus would bear the official name, "George County Occupational Training Center (GCOTC)." Five months later the planned $500,000 GCOTC, to be paid for with a combination of federal, state, and local funds, was described as having a total of 32,000 square feet. The center would include four classrooms, administrative offices, a library, a practical nursing suite, and shops for sheet metal work, welding, pipefitting, plumbing, and machine shop trades.

In January 1972, the MGCJC Board of Trustees named 32-year-old Robert Dale Rose as the first director of GCOTC. Rose, a native of Jacksonville, Illinois, had earned both a diploma (1960) and an associate degree in drafting (1966) at Perkinston and had then earned a bachelor's at Mississippi State and a master's at Southern Illinois University. At the time he was chosen as director of GCOTC, he had been a drafting and design instructor at Jefferson Davis Campus for 18 months.

By the end of August 1972, a faculty of five had been assembled: John Ward Cooley of Lucedale, building trades; Harlis D. Johnson of Wade, metal trades; Junius Howard Martin of Pascagoula, welding; Johnnette (Dees) Heidelberg of Pascagoula, secretarial training; and Freida Mae Davis of Lucedale, practical nursing. The last three programs were post-secondary offerings, but the first two were to be offered to George County High School students who were to be bussed to the center five days per week. Ronnie Mizell of Lucedale signed on as counselor.

The MDTA personnel manning the rented facilities in Lucedale relocated to the new center. William D. Taylor taught MDTA welding.

Though the structure was unfinished, in Rose's words, "We began classes in . . . [the] . . . facilities in August to meet the high school schedule." Because the high school program mandated classes in health occupations, Georgia Rouse was hired by November to instruct in Mississippi's only health occupations assistant program. In addition, due to the center's commitment to literacy, a night class in adult basic education was offered that first semester.

The facilities were finally completed in December, and GCOTC began its full range of offerings in January 1973. The center granted its first certificates of completion on March 13, 1973, to six women who had completed the 17-week post-secondary course in vocational secretarial studies.

On March 4, 1973, Mississippi Governor William Waller spoke to approximately 1,000 persons at the dedication of the GCOTC. A week later the editors of the *George County Times* called the dedication a "milestone" and the "fruition of a dream shared for years by many George Countians." The editor then noted that, "The appearance of Governor Bill Waller . . . indicated the importance attached to the opening of the OTC here."

MGCJC President J.J. Hayden (right) presents a barometer to Gov. Bill Waller at the dedication of GCOTC, March 4th, 1973.

In mid-May the announcements for summer school revealed that academic night classes were to be offered for the first time at GCOTC with registration set for May 28. But Rose was not there to register those first academic students at month's end because he resigned to return to Southern Illinois University to work toward his doctorate.

On June 1, 1973, 29-year-old Biloxi native Paul E. Brauchle, an

MGCJC Central Office vocational-technical counselor since joining the college in 1968, replaced Rose. Brauchle, who had earned his bachelor's and master's from the University of Southern Mississippi (USM), had come to Gulf Coast from the Copiah-Lincoln Manpower Center at Monticello.

During his four years as director, Brauchle was credited with the addition of such post-secondary courses as air conditioning/refrigeration and construction maintenance. He also oversaw the establishment of branches of the various clubs pertaining to the particular post-secondary courses of study at GCOTC. In May 1977, Brauchle announced that he was returning to his old position in the Central Office vocational-technical division for a time in preparation for his departure for the University of Missouri to work toward his doctorate.

John Ward Cooley of Lucedale, an instructor at GCOTC since its opening, replaced Brauchle as director on May 18, 1977. Cooley, a 1962 graduate of Perkinston Junior College, had earned his bachelor's and master's at USM and completed additional graduate work at Mississippi State University. For six years prior to his employment at GCOTC he had been a vocational instructor at George County High School.

At the close of his first year as director, Cooley began what was to become a tradition. In May 1978, rather than hold a separate graduation, the GCOTC candidates for graduation traveled to Perkinston to take part in the campus graduation ceremonies.

In December 1978, Cooley inaugurated a novel approach to instructing students involved in building trades. A corporation designated the "Total Occupation Performance Foundation (TOPF)" was organized to solicit donations from various businesses of money and materials with which to build a dwelling complete in all aspects. In this manner, 150 students working under the close supervision of college instructors received "hands-on experience" in building a house, which was then auctioned to the highest bidder. The funds from the sale of the house were used as "seed money" for a second and third house. The demise of the post-secondary building trades program ended the TOPF program in 1984. The profit from the sale of the last house was given to the MGCJC Alumni Foundation to provide scholarships for deserving vocational students.

In June 1983, MGCJC's Board of Trustees changed the title of the administrator in charge of GCOTC. Thus, Cooley, the center's third director, became its first administrative dean.

In 1985 a half-million-dollar addition to the center resulted in new offerings. The program in cosmetology began at that time, and a computer lab was added for the use of high school students.

THE TOTAL OCCUPATION PERFORMANCE FOUNDATION (TOPF)

GCOTC Director Cooley inaugurated the TOPF program in order to give students "hands on experience" in all aspects of building a house.

Left: GCOTC building trades students put the final touches on the roof of the first TOPF house in 1979.

Below: GCOTC building trades students enter a TOPF house nearly ready for auction.

Paul Brauchle
GCOTC Director
1973-1977

John Ward Cooley
GCOTC
Director/Administrative Dean
1977-1992

Cooley retired on June 30, 1992, and Anna Faye Kelley, a native of Lucedale, became the GCOTC's new administrative dean. Kelley, MGCJC (Perkinston Campus) class of 1966, earned her bachelor's and master's at USM. In 1969 she became a business education instructor at Perkinston Campus, a position she occupied for 18 years. In 1987 she moved to Central Office, becoming director of the institutional self-study. The following year, in addition, she became administrative assistant for academic and general instruction and student services. When she began her duties at GCOTC, Kelley became the first woman to assume administrative responsibilities for an MGCCC installation.

Anna Faye Kelley
GCOTC Administrative Dean
1992-2000

Under Kelley's guidance in 2000, GCOTC operated days, nights, and weekends. The secondary programs that year served 228 George County High School students in welding, building trades, institutional food preparation, business computer technology, and allied health occupations. Post-secondary training was offered to 100 students in welding, licensed practical nursing, cosmetology, office systems technology, and surgical technology. In the realm of academics, GCOTC was serving approximately 400 students per semester in evening and weekend classes.

Beginning in August 1999, GCOTC implemented a four-month apprentice electric lineman Workforce training program enrolling 25 students. The lineman program was made possible with shared funding by the State Board for Community and Junior Colleges, rural electric power industries, and a utility contractor.

Heading the list of community services in 2000 was the Adult Basic Education/General Educational Development (ABE/GED) Program, which had been part of GCOTC's mission since its inception. Other community services included on-site access to Mississippi Employment Security Commission job representatives, Small Business Development Center representatives, and other local, state, and federal counseling and aid representatives. The service delivery area in 2000 reached far beyond the borders of George County to include Greene County, eastern Stone County, northern Jackson County and east Mobile, Alabama. Student records covering the 28 years of GCOTC's existence reveal that 1,464 diplomas and certificates had been issued to students completing programs through May 2000. Far more students, though, had entered the workplace as soon as they had obtained a saleable skill.

Apprentice electric lineman Anthony Barfield of Greene County climbs a pole at GCOTC on November 18, 1999. Photo by Richard Kopp.

GCOTC aerial photograph made by Will Bramlett Aerial Photography on April 4, 2000. The apprentice lineman training program's pole field is visible in the upper right hand corner. The two large buildings (center) constitute the original installation completed in 1972. The annex (bottom right) was added in 1985. The small metal building (center right) is a storage building added circa 1979. In this photograph south is at the top.

Dean Belton
GCOTC Administrative Dean
2000-

In July, 2000 Anna Faye Kelley became vice president of the Community Campus. Counselor Ronnie Mizell served as interim director of GCOTC until August 28, when former Central Office Tech-Prep Coordinator Dean Belton assumed the position of administrative dean of GCOTC.

Keesler Air Force Base Boulevard of Flags.

KEESLER CENTER

Perhaps what was the initial offering of Perkinston Junior College at Keesler Air Force Base was recorded in the *Daily Herald* of December 20, 1951, which gave an account of the meeting of the Perkinston Junior College (PJC) Trustees the previous day:

"Walter Pharris, Biloxi, was elected as physics teacher for evening classes at Keesler Field two nights each week. The classes are sponsored by Perkinston."

On January 9, 1952, the PJC student newspaper, *Bulldog Barks*, elaborated on the new offering under the headline, "Twenty-Two KAFB Personnel Attend Perk Night Classes." The article carried notice from PJC President A. L. May to the effect that such classes offered airmen the opportunity to earn four hours of resident credit and that similar classes would be offered on demand.

Throughout the 1950s and early 1960s PJC continued to offer intermittent night classes at Perkinston and at various points along the coast. Apparently, though, no more were offered at Keesler.

At the close of the 1964 summer session, the University of Southern Mississippi (USM), which had been offering upper division classes since 1947 at various sites in Biloxi, moved its center of operations to Keesler Air Force Base. At that point USM apparently began offering freshman through graduate courses at the base. That December the Trustees of the then Mississippi Gulf Coast Junior College (MGCJC), "ordered that the administration explore the possibility of Keesler Field extension courses." Obviously this order was a reaction to USM's offering lower division classes. The Perkinston institution in all its incarnations had steadfastly opposed any public university offering such classes in its four-county district. But MGCJC President J. J. Hayden and the Board did nothing more than "explore the possibility" occupied as they were at that time in the tremendous effort to establish a tri-campus college.

With the opening of the Jefferson Davis Campus (JD) and the Jackson County Campus (JC) in September 1965, MGCJC provided USM with quarters on both campuses in which to offer upper division courses. Hayden requested that USM offer sufficient junior and senior courses to allow Coast citizens to earn a four-year degree. The Hattiesburg institution, as it had always done in all its incarnations and in league with all its sister universities, refused. No Mississippi university would grant an off-campus degree. The senior year had to be taken in residence. The MGCJC Board, fed up with this rule, appointed a committee in November 1965 to press the Board of the Institution of Higher Learning (IHL) into revoking the rule.

In July 1966 while Hayden was locked in dubious battle with the IHL Board over the degree-granting rule, authorities of Keesler Air Force Base proposed to allow civilians to attend classes on the base. Hayden attended a meeting on the issue and voiced his objections because it meant that civilians could take USM freshman and sophomore courses at Keesler. His objections were ignored.

For seven years the classes were offered on a first-come, first-served basis. Then Keesler adopted a preferential admissions policy which required students to sign up for classes in descending order as per the following list: active military, Department of Defense civilians, retired military, reserves, national guard, military dependents, and off-base civilians.

Success, though, eventually came in the battle with the IHL Board in fall 1972. USM-Gulf Park became Mississippi's first university branch empowered to offer upper division courses and grant degrees. That success, strangely enough, led to victory on the other front. So long as the USM-Keesler Center was administered directly from Hattiesburg and so long as USM had no degree-granting branch on the Coast, its location on a United States military reservation rendered it untouchable. But, with the establishment of USM-Gulf Park, USM- Keesler Center became a branch of a branch that could not offer lower division courses due to IHL rules, so neither could the Gulf Park Keesler Center.

Hayden wasted no time. On August 23, 1972, the MGCJC Board approved a plan to be submitted to the Mississippi Junior College Commission, the aim of which was to offer the same courses available to MGCJC students to the personnel at Keesler. The courses were to be administered by the college through the JD Campus.

In January 1973, the American Association of Community and Junior Colleges (AACJC) designated MGCJC as a "Serviceman's Opportunity College (SOC)." The AACJC had created the SOC concept in partnership with the United States Department of Defense while developing a philosophy of education for colleges serving the military. Hayden pledged MGCJC to follow the precepts of that philosophy which included among other things non-traditional class scheduling and permitting servicemen to complete a course by special means when military obligations interrupted their education. With that hurdle cleared, Hayden announced that MGCJC would begin offering classes at Keesler on June 4, 1973.

MGCJC President J.J. Hayden Jr. (center) meets with Keesler Air Force Base Commander Major General Bryan M. Shotts (left) and his aide, Capt. Robert Whelan Jr (right) on May 4th 1973 at Darby Hall on the Perkinston Campus.

On May 4, Keesler Air Force Base commander Major General Bryan M. Shotts and his aide, Captain Robert Whelan Jr., toured MGCJC's three campuses. Beginning at JD that morning, Executive Dean Bill Lipscomb explained how his campus would administer the program. At mid-day the general toured Perkinston Campus where Executive Dean C. G. Odom reviewed the functions of his campus in the matter. Odom then took the general to the Central Office where Hayden and his administrative assistants briefed Shotts on the role of the central administration. Late that afternoon in Gautier, Executive Dean Curtis Davis told the general how JC would support the Keesler effort.

Sylvester J. "Sal" D'Aquilla Jr., then teaching undergraduate courses for USM-Keesler, found himself in an odd position. D'Aquilla, a native of Woodville, had received his bachelor's degree in 1959 and his master's degree in 1960 from the Hattiesburg institution. The year he received his master's, D'Aquilla had signed on at the Perkinston institution as a math teacher. In 1965, with the opening of the JD Campus, he had accompanied Dean Bill Lipscomb to the new campus to serve as chairman of the math department. In May 1967 he had resigned that position to teach at USM in Hattiesburg and to take more graduate courses in mathematics. He taught at the main campus from 1967-1970 at which time he transferred to USM Keesler Center to teach freshmen and sophomore courses.

In D'Aquilla's words from a letter written October 28, 1997:

"In 1973 when USM got degree granting privileges on the coast, the State Board of Higher Education mandated that USM could not teach any of the freshman and sophomore level courses on the coast. This meant that the first two years of college had to be taught by the junior college. When all of this happened I had no courses to teach for USM-Gulf Park, so Dr. Joe Holloway, who was the Dean at Gulf Park, got with Dr. W. P. Lipscomb, Dean of Jefferson Davis Campus, to hire myself and Howard Rogers to work at the Keesler Center for MGCJC. I was the director and Howard Rogers taught history. When we began classes that summer of 1973, our office was housed in an old wooden military building, and we taught 187 students in 17 classes at Allee Hall. All of the classes except the two that I taught and the four that Howard Rogers taught were taught by adjunct instructors or as overloads by instructors from the junior college."

The JD-Keesler Center classes were taught on the quarter system (with credit given in semester hours) consisting of four terms of 11 weeks with a Friday night extra for each class -- fall, winter, spring, and summer. To accommodate the military, this system remained in effect for MGCCC classes in 2000, even though MGCCC had always been on a semester system. The shorter term

Standing in the JD-Keesler Center office circa 1976 (from left) are Elizabeth Locke, secretary to the director; Sal D'Aquilla, JD-Keesler Center director; Hope Johnson, office secretary; and Dr. Clara (Lopez) Campbell, instructor of English and history. Photo courtesy of Sal D'Aquilla.

enabled military personnel to earn more credit hours in a year's time. Oddly enough USM, which had been on a quarter system for decades, changed its classes on the main campus to the semester system in the 1970s, but USM Keesler classes stayed on the quarter system until the early 1990s when those were changed to the semester system as well. According to D'Aquilla this action was taken because the USM professors who taught at Keesler did not want their holidays interrupted.

D'Aquilla remained in charge of the Keesler Center for a quarter century. He held the title "director" until June 1983, when his title became "administrative dean." Throughout that period he taught two math classes per quarter. Howard Rogers remained a full-time instructor, teaching four classes per quarter until his retirement in 1976. Dr. Clara Campbell, who later became Mrs. Sal D'Aquilla, replaced Rogers and taught history and English full-time until her retirement in 1996. When she retired, no full-time instructor replaced her.

In the late 1970s JD-Keesler Center moved into Sablich Hall, Keesler's newly constructed personnel building. After that, according to D'Aquilla, "The Center grew to over 800 students by 1981. Over the years the fall and spring terms had enrollments from 600 to 800 students; winter and summer terms had enrollments from 500 to 700 students."

The original 1973 complement of four full-time persons at JD-Keesler Center remained the norm nearly to the close of the D'Aquilla era--himself, one full-time instructor, a counselor, and a secretary. Gene Rester, the original counselor, remained until 1978, when he returned to JD Campus.

JD-Keesler Center personnel on the eve of Sal D'Aquilla's retirement in 1998 included (from left, standing) Melissa Morgan, secretary to the administrative dean; Tammi D'Antoni, office secretary; Rachel Rushing, office secretary; and Jerry White, counselor. Administrative Dean D'Aquilla is seated. Photo courtesy of Sal D'Aquilla.

Tommy Adkins, who replaced Rester, served JD-Keesler Center for the next 17 years. Two secretaries, Elizabeth Locke and Lori Sutton served in succession for two decades. No extra staff people were added until the early 1990s when JD-Keesler Center, in D'Aquilla's words, "got on line with the computer center."

D'Aquilla closed his October 28, 1997, letter with these words:

"As for myself I am looking forward to joining my wife, Clara, in retirement in June 1998. This will end 25 years at the Keesler Center and a total of 32 with MGCCC and 6 with USM. I am sure that the Keesler Center will continue to serve Keesler AFB . . . as successfully in the future as it has in the past. The Center has always generated enough revenue to support all its activities."

On July 1, 1998, Robert Rominger succeeded D'Aquilla as administrative dean of JD-Keesler Center. A native of Pensacola, Rominger earned his bachelor's degree and master's degree from the University of West Florida. Hired as a social studies instructor at the Perkinston Campus in 1970 he served in that capacity for 18 years. Rominger then moved into administration serving as dean of student services from 1988-1991 and thereafter as dean of academic and general instruction until his appointment as administrative dean of JD-Keesler Center.

Gene Rester
Counselor
JD-Keesler Center
1973-1978

Tommy Adkins
Counselor
JD-Keesler Center
1978-1995

Robert Rominger
Administrative Dean
JD-Keesler Center
1998-

Sablich Personnel Support Center or Sablich Hall is the site of MGCCC's classes at Keesler Air Force Base.

Keesler personnel try their luck in MGCCC computer class in Sablich Hall in 1995.

In Sablich Hall on September 8, 1997, MGCCC President Barry L. Mellinger looks on as Keesler Staff Sergeant Todd Peach cuts a cake celebrating him as the 9,500th enrollee in MGCCC degree/diploma programs that fall. At the time this enrollment was the largest in MGCCC history.

Mississippi Gulf Coast Junior College (Jefferson Davis Campus) West Harrison County Occupational Training Center First Faculty and Administration - Session 1985-1986

Sam Kirsch
Administrative Dean
1984-1990

* Tommye (Switzer) Skinner
Secondary Vocationl Counselor

Russell "Bob" Acuff
Post-Secondary Drafting

* Daniel Eugene "Gene" Anderson
Secondary Auto Body & Frame Repair

David Arkwright
Post-Secondary Auto Body & Frame Repair

Bill Donna
Post-Secondary Automotive Mechanics

* Marla Eason
Secondary Health Occupations

Ernie Giles
Secondary Quantity Food Preparation & Service

Ross Irby
Post-Secondary Metal Trades

J. Hal Kibler
Secondary Metal Trades

Charles "Chuck" Lewis
Secondary Automotive Mechanics

Ray Phillips
Diversified Technology

* Wendell Smith
Post-Secondary Quantity Food Preparation & Service

Jessie Stever
Intensive Business Training

* Sarah (Varnadore) Mulvaney Stopson
Secretary/Post-Secondary Secretarial

* Thomas Stopson
General Electricity/Electronics

Bary Thrash
Secondary Drafting

George Wilson
Post-Secondary General Electricity

Marvin "Bud" Zimmerman
Secondary Auto Body & Frame Repair

Not Pictured:

Linda Arnold
Sales & Marketing/ Diversified Occupations

Steve Leker
Secondary Horticulture

* Still employed at WHCOTC as of Dec. 31, 2000

Digging in at the June 6, 1984 groundbreaking for the WHCOTC are (from left) Jefferson Davis Campus Vice President Glen Cadle, MGCJC President J.J. Hayden Jr., and WHCOTC Administrative Dean Sam Kirsch.

Facade of the administrative/classroom building at the West Harrison County Occupational Training Center located in the Long Beach industrial park at the corner of Espy Avenue and B Street. Photo from 1993 Beauvoir, p. 4.

WEST HARRISON COUNTY OCCUPATIONAL TRAINING CENTER

On March 20, 1983, the MGCJC Board of Trustees entertained a proposal to study the possibility of establishing a vocational-technical facility for high school and college students in the Long Beach Industrial Park. Authorities of the Pass Christian and the Long Beach Municipal Separate School Districts wished to join MGCJC in a tripartite agreement to pay half the cost of the proposed $2 million facility. The vocational department of the State Department of Education was to pay the other half in a matching funds agreement.

Trustee Murrell Hilton of Long Beach urged the MGCJC Board to approve the study. Hilton stated his case thusly: "This is a once in a lifetime opportunity to bring all these parties together in West Harrison County. . . [and] . . . we need technical training to get more adults employed."

MGCJC President J. J. Hayden averred that both Hinds Junior College and Pearl River Junior College had set the precedent for such a facility, but he cautioned, "We can't go into it unless we can show a need." The MGCJC Board agreed to the study.

The study revealed that 45 percent of the high school graduates of the Pass Christian-Long Beach area did not attend college. Therefore, such a facility would be ideal not only for training high school students who would be bussed in daily from 8 a.m. to 3 p.m. but also for training adults in college classes in the evenings.

In December 1983 the MGCJC Board decided to enter the consortium to build the facility on 14 acres at the Long Beach Industrial Park donated by the Harrison County Development Commission. This was done with a stipulation on Hayden's part that the Commission would sell to the consortium an adjacent 10 acres to provide for future expansion. All parties involved agreed to the purchase, and, for a payment of $60,000, the site was expanded to 24 acres.

On February 22, 1984, the MGCJC Board approved the plans of the architectural firm of Grace and Guild of Gulfport for a facility composed of two brick buildings aggregating 40,500 square feet and linked by a covered walkway. One building was to house administrative offices and programs in quantity food preparation and service, industrial electricity/electronics, health occupations, general and industrial drafting, and intensive business training. The other structure was to include shops for automobile body and frame repair, metal trades, and automobile mechanics. All the programs were to be offered first on the secondary (high school) level. In time those programs achieving sufficient adult enrollment would be offered on the post-secondary (college) level. Bids were to be let in April, contracts were to be awarded in May, and the projected completion date was set for July 15, 1985.

In March 1984 Jefferson Davis Campus Vice President Glen Cadle announced that the college, through the JD Campus, would administer the new West Harrison County Occupational Training Center (WHCOTC). On June 6, 1984, Cadle, Hayden, and newly selected WHCOTC Administrative Dean Samuel H. Kirsch participated in groundbreaking ceremonies at the site.

Kirsch, of Pueblo, Colorado, a 26-year veteran of the United States Naval Construction Battalions (Seabees), had begun his service to MGCJC on August 27, 1973, as an air conditioning instructor at the JD Campus. In the ensuing years, he had earned his bachelor's and master's at the University of Southern Mississippi. He was associate dean of the evening college at the time of his elevation to the position of administrative dean of WHCOTC.

In early 1984, Kirsch, together with secretary Sarah Mulvaney and vocational counselor Tommye (Switzer) Skinner, began working in temporary quarters in the licensed practical nurses building (JD Building N) preparing for the opening of the new installation. According to Kirsch, on March 29, 2000, "While I had been chosen to be administrative dean of the West Harrison Center, I still had my job as associate dean of the evening college and additional duties due to the death of G. L. Douglas (JD dean of instruction). So, I was doing two jobs and trying to order equipment and hire faculty for the new center. I wouldn't care to go through that again." Then he finished, "Even though I was at the groundbreaking, neither my job nor my pay as administrative dean of the center began until July 1."

According to Marla Eason, WHCOTC's first health occupation's instructor (who was still at her post in March 2000), "We entered the new buildings in July 1985. We were still moving in furniture and setting up our desks when the first buses arrived from Long Beach and Pass Christian High Schools in late August. It was hectic, thrilling, and a little frightening because most of us had never taught before."

All the secondary courses were up and running by the time the center opened, but the only post-secondary courses were those in automotive mechanics and body work. The automotive machinery for those classes together with instructor Marvin "Bud" Zimmerman had been moved to the WHCOTC from the old Harrison County Occupational Training Center on the Industrial Seaway. "After Christmas," remembered Eason, "we added some other post-secondary classes."

By the time Kirsch retired on July 1, 1990, post-secondary programs included those in auto body and frame repair, automotive mechanics, precision metal work, industrial electricity, drafting, secretarial training, landscape construction and design, and cooking/baking. Also, in the vocational field, a new program in emergency medical technology/paramedics had been added.

Larry Garvin, a former Leland School District superintendent with a bachelor's from Mississippi College and a master's from Delta State

Larry Garvin
WHCOTC Administrative Dean
1990-1992

University, replaced Kirsch. Garvin, however, stayed less than two years, leaving in August 1992.

On October 1, 1992, Donald Christensen, possessor of a bachelor's and master's from Mississippi State University with a specialty in vocational/agricultural administration, replaced Garvin. Christensen used his specialized knowledge of agriculture to interest business, educational, and political leaders in lending their support to an effort to secure a new program at WHOTC.

Coast legislative representative Diane Peranich of DeLisle, Glen Endris of Gulfport, and upstate repre-

Don Christensen
WHCOTC Administrative Dean
1992-

sentative Billy McCoy of Rienzi, a personal friend of Christensen and head of the House Appropriations Committee, spearheaded a $715,000 special state appropriation for the purpose of establishing at WHCOTC both a secondary and post-secondary program in aquaculture -- the technical name for fish farming.

Aquaculture instructor Gregory Crochet, who earned his degree at the University of Southwestern Louisiana, came to WHCOTC in 1994. The following year aquaculture instructor Michael Murphy, who took his degree from Colorado State University, joined Crochet, forming WHCOTC's aquaculture team. Both were present as tour guides on July 28, 1995, at the dedication of the WHCOTC Aquaculture Facility, the first of its kind in Mississippi. The new facility consisted of an instructional building containing two classrooms, two labs, a reference library, a walk-in cooler, and several large fish tanks. On the grounds were three 125 foot x 50 foot culture ponds and a 125 foot x 20 foot wetlands filtration pond.

Speaking at the dedication, Rep. Peranich said she believed that the new facility would ensure future generations of fishermen the opportunity to learn new technologies and skills and remain in the seafood business. Then she added, "We would not have been able to do it . . . without the excellent support of the college and Don Christensen."

Secondary classes in aquaculture had already begun the August before the dedication for 30 high school students from Pass Christian and Long Beach. The two-year college program began the month after the dedication.

In speaking of the aquaculture program on March 29, 2000, Christensen said, "Our high school enrollment in the program is full, and we turn away 60 to 90 high school students per year. The post-secondary is maxed-out at 12 because the training is so intensive and requires so much lab work." When asked about the ponds, he said, "We have 18 now and we are getting ready to add two more for crawfish and one more wetlands pond." When asked about the fish in the ponds he said, "We have shrimp, oysters, and many kinds of fish -- rainbow trout, catfish, even albino catfish. When we get too many fish we release them into streams and rivers and public lakes." Aquaculture instructor Murphy speaking of catfish in particular said, "Catfish is the third largest crop in the state. The only two that are more important to farmers are cotton and chickens."

Aquaculture instructor Crochet, in speaking of the future, said:

"We have gotten a $75,000 fishing bait grant from the Tidelands Fund of the Mississippi Department of Marine Resources. Three of our ponds are being used now for this project to teach students how to grow bait for the bait industry to sell to recreational fishermen. By weight, bait is of greater value than food fish. We are starting a move toward growing more saltwater species such as red fish and red snapper, and we hope to get into restoration programs for aquatic species in fresh and salt water. Mississippi is the largest aquaculture producing state in the nation and aquaculture is the fastest growing segment in the agriculture industry. MGCCC is the only community college in Mississippi with an aquaculture program of this breadth. Mississippi Delta has an aquaculture program but only for catfish."

Asked to sum up his years at WHCOTC, Christensen said:

"When I came here in 1992 we had 150 high school and 87 post-secondary students. Now, through incentive type scheduling and other recruitment techniques, we have a total of 475 high school students arriving for four ninety-minute periods a day. We also have 155 post-secondary students. Some programs are closed in both areas and others are at maximum enrollment."

Then he added, "You might say we are already using everything but the broom closet to teach in now. I can't add anything else without more buildings."

WEST HARRISON COUNTY OCCUPATIONAL TRAINING CENTER
FROM POND TO PLATE: TWO UNIQUE MGCCC PROGRAMS

WHCOTC's unique programs in aquaculture and food production and management technology complement one another. Student fish farmers supply fledgling chefs with items for the menu.

Aquaculture students Elizabeth Arndt (left) of Biloxi and Frank Kubiak (right) of Gulfport check spawning cans for catfish eggs in one of WHCOTC's stock ponds on June 13, 2000. Photo by Richard Kopp.

Student chef Joel Newman shows off a completed meal circa 1997.

Aerial photograph made by Will Bramlett Aerial Photography on March 22, 2000. The two large buildings (top) are the original WHCOTC structures completed in 1985. The larger structure is the administration/classroom building. The other is the classroom/shop building. The rectangular structure left of center is the aquaculture building. The aquaculture ponds are to the north and to the east of this structure. In this photograph west is at the top.

THE TWO-YEAR INSTITUTION AT PERKINSTON AND THE FOUR-YEAR INSTITUTION AT HATTIESBURG AND THEIR 20TH CENTURY EXPANSION ON THE GULF COAST

Author's note

The Harrison County Agricultural High School at Perkinston began operation on September 17, 1912. Mississippi Normal College opened for classes the next day in Hattiesburg. The AHS evolved into a junior college in 1925 and then into the tri-campus Mississippi Gulf Coast Junior College in 1962, which became Mississippi Gulf Coast Community College in 1987. Mississippi Normal College became Mississippi State Teacher's College in 1924, Mississippi Southern College in 1940, and the University of Southern Mississippi in 1962.

The history of Mississippi Southern College on the Coast began in 1947 with three classes taught in Van Hook Hall at the Methodist Seashore Assembly in Biloxi. Mississippi Southern continued to offer classes there for more than a decade. Since none of the classes were at the freshmen or sophomore level, the administration of Perkinston Junior College had no objections and in fact aided the effort by supplying some instructors for the program.

In 1958 Mississippi Southern moved its center of operation from the Methodist Seashore Assembly to the facilities of Mary L. Michael Junior High School in Biloxi. For the first time Southern assigned a permanent instructor-administration to run the center. The other instructors, all part-time, came from Hattiesburg or Perkinston or the local community. At the close of the 1964 Summer Session USM moved its center of operations once again, that time to Keesler Air Force Base.

The next July, with the impending September opening of the new MGCJC campuses at Handsboro and Gautier, MGCJC President J. J. Hayden publicly announced that the facilities of the Jefferson Davis Campus and the Jackson County Campus had been made available to USM. Dr. Paul C. Morgan, dean of the USM Division of Continuing Education, in accepting the offer, stated that junior-year level and graduate level courses would be offered at the two new USM extension centers. According to the rules of the Board of the Mississippi Institutions of Higher Learning (IHL

In May 1922, Mississippi Normal College awarded its first baccalaureate degree to Kathryn B. Swetman of Biloxi, a 1916 graduate of Harrison-Stone Agricultural High School at Perkinston. Swetman was the first of thousands who would repeat her achievement as the Perkinston-based institution became a main feeder to the senior college in Hattiesburg. In September 1922, Swetman returned to Perk to teach, becoming the first of scores of instructors to make the "Perk to Hattiesburg and back to Perk circuit." The connection between the two schools, typified by the case of Kathryn Swetman, deepened in the 1930s as students began to flow both ways between the two institutions. This arrangement was particularly reciprocal in the case of foreign students sent from Hattiesburg to Perk to upgrade their English skills before resuming senior college work. By the 1990s some students, particularly foreign students, were enrolled in both institutions simultaneously. Not only did the institutions share students but teachers as well. Over the years many classes were taught for the four-year school by the faculty from the two-year school. The two schools shared a close relationship for three quarters of a century. Photo courtesy of the McCain Archives (USM).

Board), at least one year of senior college credit had to be earned while in residency on a senior college campus. Hence, USM would offer no senior level courses.

The JD-USM Extension Center opened with ten classes. The JC-USM Extension opened with nearly twice that many. But, according to the rules of the time, no resident of the second most populous region of the state (after Jackson) could earn a senior college degree without living at least 70 miles away or traveling at least 140 miles roundtrip to Hattiesburg per day for a year. Coast residents did not like this. Neither did Hayden and the MGCJC Board, and they moved to do something about it.

On November 17, 1965, the MGCJC Board appointed a committee to negotiate an arrangement with any state senior college that would offer both junior and senior level courses and grant degrees on the Coast. This committee was empowered to offer such a senior institution the use of MGCJC facilities for this purpose or to offer aid in establishing an "adjacent campus."

The MGCJC committee struck the IHL Board's stone wall blocking off-campus degrees and made no progress for a year. Then in mid-October, 1966, the news came that the trustees of the IHL Board had approved a Universities Center for Jackson which would offer graduate level programs administered by a consortium composed of USM, Mississippi State University, and the University of Mississippi. Accordingly, on October 21, the MGCJC Board issued a public statement urging local and state authorities to consider establishing a similar Universities Center on the Coast which could grant both baccalaureate and graduate degrees.

In August 1967, Hayden told the MGCJC Board that Biloxi Mayor Danny Guice was planning a survey of higher educational needs on the Coast. Hayden further stated that Guice's aim was to incorporate the junior college's operation and not to supplant it by founding a new university.

On February 9, 1968, in a meeting held on the JD Campus, Guice released the results of the survey conducted by Dr. S. V. Martorana, Executive Dean, Junior College Division, New York State System of Higher Education. The survey, entitled, "A Plan for a Gulf Coast Universities Center," called for construction of a $1.9 million physical plant. At this meeting it was suggested that the plant be constructed on the JD Campus so that if future expansion of the Universities Center necessitated a move to another site, the junior college could use the facilities for its own expansion. The steering committee named by Guice at this meeting was composed of a dozen of the most influential men of the day. Among them was, not surprisingly, Jim Reese of radio station WGCM who was by then an MGCJC trustee. On February 21, the MGCJC Board formally voted its support for Guice's plans.

In late April 1968, Guice announced that the IHL Board Executive Secretary E. R. Jobe had notified him by letter that the state had approved the plan to establish a Coast Universities Center. Jobe's letter stated that the center could offer junior, senior, and graduate level courses but would not be allowed to grant degrees. Guice, obviously fighting one battle at a time, accepted the offer.

Reese, who had been present in the meeting with the IHL Board as a member of Guice's steering committee, told the MGCJC Board at its April meeting that work on the Universities Center might start as early as the coming fall if the state money was available. Reese also stated that the establishment of the center should finally eliminate the idea that JC and/or JD would become four-year colleges.

Apparently the Southern Association of Colleges and Schools (SACS) did not agree with Reese's assessment. In November, Hayden apprised the MGCJC Board that SACS had criticized the plan to locate the center on the JD Campus because it seemed as if JD was becoming a four-year college. So the MGCJC Board began to support a new plan to purchase the Markham Hotel in downtown Gulfport as the site of the Universities Center.

Proposals and counterproposals for a Universities Center site continued until August 17 of the next year when Hurricane Camille turned coastal residents' attention to mere survival. Ironically though, Camille solved the problem of a site. The impact of the disaster on Gulf Park College, an exclusive women's junior college located in Long Beach since 1919, proved to be too much. The storm was the economic *coup de grace* for the school already suffering from falling enrollments in a time when co-educational institutions had become the norm.

On January 20, 1971, JD Director of Admissions Clifton "Donnie" Taylor in a speech to the Biloxi Rotary Club said he was frequently asked when would JD become a four-year college. He told the members that such a day would never come because the philosophy of a junior college was to remain a broad-spectrum institution and not to become a senior college. He then told the audience that a movement was underway aimed at establishing a branch of USM on the Coast, which would enable a student at JD to then take two more years at the branch and earn a bachelor's degree at home.

The next month USM upgraded its MGCJC Jackson County Campus USM Extension Center to "Resident Center" status, thereby placing it on a equal footing with the USM Resident Centers established earlier at JD and at Keesler. The main difference between an "extension center" and a "resident center" was that courses taken at the latter were considered equal in quality to those offered on the main campus in Hattiesburg.

In April the trustees of Gulf Park College announced that the institution would close its doors after the May, 1971, graduation. Hayden and the MGCJC Board immediately began a feasibility study to consider the incorporation of Gulf Park into MGCJC as a fourth campus but scrubbed that idea when USM expressed its desire to secure the property as a branch campus. In view of this new development, the MGCJC Board authorized Hayden to make the following statement: "We support the idea of having an upper division degree-granting college but we are opposed to adding another institution to handle freshmen and sophomores."

Gulf Park College issued its last diploma to Debra Ann Wright of Mountain Brook, Alabama, on May 30, 1971, and closed its doors. For the next ten months Trustees of the IHL Board tried to decide whether to make Gulf Park a branch of USM or to make it a Universities Center like the one in Jackson.

Throughout it all MGCJC called for an upper division degree-granting university by any name. On February 19, 1972, the IHL Board announced that the facility would be known as the "Harrison County Residence Center of the University of Southern Mississippi." That merely amounted to moving the pre-existing JD Campus USM Resident Center

The women of Gulf Park College are gathered for graduation on May 31, 1927. Gulf Park College became University of Southern Mississippi Gulf Park Campus.

to Gulf Park. Registration for spring quarter was held at JD Campus in late February for classes to begin on March 6 at the new site. Dr. A. C. Johnson was named Director of the Gulf Park Center. He was assigned an administrative assistant, a counselor, and five full-time faculty members who would teach at both Gulf Park and Keesler. USM Keesler, by the way, was considered a satellite of Gulf Park while USM Jackson County Campus remained a separate Residence Center.

In fall 1972 Gulf Park became Mississippi's first university branch empowered to grant degrees. The new institution graduated its first class on May 12, 1973. Nine days later the Mississippi Gulf Coast Junior College Keesler Air Force Base Center opened as a satellite of the JD Campus to provide freshman and sophomores classes in conjunction with USM-Gulf Park upper division offerings at the base.

In August, 1974, a joint MGCJC-USM articulation committee was formed to correlate course offerings so that students could make a smooth transition from MGCJC to USM in general and Gulf Park in particular. It seemed that the higher education problems of the Gulf Coast had at last been solved--but not so.

USM Gulf Park granted certain degrees, but offered only night classes, and a student was restricted to taking only two courses per term. This restriction doubled or even tripled the number of years necessary to earn a degree. Inability to enroll at Gulf Park full-time eliminated student attendance on the GI Bill and disqualified many other students for loans that required full-time status. Of course, that was the aim of the rule. USM and all the other senior colleges wished to limit full-time students to attendance at main university campuses.

The controversy erupted publicly in February, 1976, in the form of two bills in the legislature. One bill called for the formation of the four-year degree-granting University of Long Beach to be formed at Gulf Park. The other bill sought to smash the two-course restriction. Resolutions adopted by various local government and civic groups supporting one bill or another poured into the legislature not only from the Coast but also from Natchez where USM had established a branch similar to the one at Gulf Park.

Hayden and the MGCJC Board stated their total opposition to the creation of the University of Long Beach and their complete support for the elimination of the two-course restriction. The University of Long Beach bill failed, but the legislature increased the number of courses that could be taken by students at an off-campus center to three per quarter.

On May 17, 1976, Mississippi Governor Cliff Finch spoke at the dedication of new buildings at both JC and JD. In his remarks the governor praised the MGCJC leadership and said he believed the junior college would "one day in the foreseeable future be a university" and that he knew of "no one better qualified to run a university than J. J. Hayden Jr." Mercifully Finch ended by noting that he had "no definite plans" to promote this coming institution.

On July 22 at a press conference held at the Ramada Inn in Biloxi, Hayden together with USM President Aubrey K. Lucas and USM Vice President for Administration and Regional Campuses Shelby F. Thames announced the Two Plus Two Program. In this landmark agreement MGCJC and USM combined a number of old and new elements into a formal alliance to provide Coast residents the opportunity to secure a four-year college degree in 17 fields at USM Gulf

(From left) Dr. Shelby F. Thames, USM vice president for administration and regional campuses, Dr. Aubrey K. Lucas, USM president, and Dr. J. J. Hayden, MGCJC president announce the Two Plus Two Program in a press conference at the Biloxi Ramada Inn on July 22, 1976. The Two Plus Two Program advertised to Coast students that 17 four-year degree-granting programs were available to them through attending a campus of MGCJC for two years and USM-Gulf Park for two years more. Photograph from The Scene at Southern, July 31, 1976.

Park Regional Campus.

MGCJC-USM articulation of coursework to provide smooth transition from the junior college to the university with little or no loss of credits had been constantly improved for decades. USM-Gulf Park had been granting degrees since 1973. The new element in the mix that made Two Plus Two viable was the recent three course per quarter allowance. Three courses in a quarter translated into minimum full-time status for a student and thus made available GI Bill benefits and also qualified students for government loans.

More than anything else the Two Plus Two agreement was a media event which educated the public about the opportunities which existed to acquire a four-year degree locally. Of course, the Two Plus Two agreement was as applicable to entry into the 104 degree programs offered on the main USM Campus at Hattiesburg as it was to the 17 offered at USM Gulf Park. But the 17 programs initially offered at USM Gulf Park had been selected with an eye to achieving the greatest possible enrollment on the Coast.

Hayden termed the Two Plus Two announcement a "joyous occasion" and the culmination of years of effort in securing "four years of college work [for] the people of the Coast." Hayden termed Two Plus Two as a major step in USM-Gulf Park becoming a full upper-level university similar to thirty such junior-senior college partnerships known to have developed in the United States. "I won't be satisfied until it happens," he said.

In January, 1977, USM entered into a similar Two Plus Two agreement with Copiah-Lincoln Junior College in relation to the Natchez Regional Campus. On April 5, 1977, USM brought Pearl River Junior College into the Two Plus Two fold as a feeder to both the Hattiesburg Campus and Gulf Park.

In November 1978, USM and Pearl River went into partnership offering combined classes in Bay St. Louis. Eventually this resident center was relocated to the National Space Technological Laboratories (later re-named Stennis Space Center).

So by late 1978, USM had established installations in all three coast counties--Hancock, Harrison, and Jackson. In mid-1979 the Jackson County Board of Supervisors initiated a unique plan to upgrade USM's presence in Gautier.

In June the Jackson County Board of Supervisors adopted a plan to use county money to construct a classroom building on MGCJC's Jackson County Campus for the purpose of having MGCJC lease the structure to USM in order to secure an upper division degree-granting program for their county. Talks with officials of both schools were successful, and on August 8, Hayden and Lucas met with the Jackson County Board of Supervisors to accept its offer.

(From left) Dr. Aubrey K. Lucas, USM president, Edward A. Khayat, president of the Jackson County Board of Supervisors, and Dr. J. J. Hayden, MGCJC president, confer at the August 8, 1979, Jackson County Board of Supervisor's meeting regarding plans for a USM classroom building to be constructed on MGCJC's Jackson County Campus in Gautier.

The USM-Jackson County Resident Center Building constructed in 1982 located on the MGCCC Jackson County Campus. USM-JC was the easternmost installation of an entity that was in 1999 termed "USM Gulf Coast." The other major installations were USM Stennis Space Center, Gulf Park Campus, and its satellite Keesler Air Force Base Center.

In April,1980, Mississippi Governor William Winter signed a bill enabling Jackson County to issue $2 million in bonds to finance the project. On April 14, 1981, officials of both colleges joined the Jackson County supervisors in groundbreaking ceremonies. On November 22, 1982, officers of those three entities joined once again to dedicate the completed structure.

The USM-MGCJC alliance on the Gulf Coast did bring about a situation in which a Coast resident could earn a baccalaureate degree or even a master's degree but not easily and not quickly. The three night-course per term rule, together with intermittent course offerings for even the relatively few programs allotted by USM to Gulf Park, in effect, still necessitated a long commute or even residency in Hattiesburg for many. Thousands of Coast students elected instead to commute to the University of South Alabama in Mobile or to the University of New Orleans or Tulane. Then came the casinos and more industry. Coast population swelled, and the desire for higher education grew while USM-Gulf Park continued to trickle forth an average of 130 graduates per year. After that first on-site graduation in 1973, even candidates for graduation had to journey to Hattiesburg for the baccalaureate ceremony. As year followed year the frustration thus engendered stored up a tremendous potential that only awaited a spark to touch it off.

Hayden retired as president of MGCJC on December 31, 1985, and Dr. Barry L. Mellinger assumed power the following day. On October 1, 1987, the college substituted the word "community" for the word "junior" in its official name becoming Mississippi Gulf Coast Community College (MGCCC).

Mellinger, as had Hayden before him, continued to strengthen the Two Plus Two alliance with Lucas. When the 1989 State Legislature lifted some of the restrictions on day classes at USM-Gulf Park, Mellinger applauded this action, which enabled Coast students to earn USM degrees more quickly. While day classes were a step forward, access to them was hedged about with obstacles, and, in retrospect was too little too late.

Lucas retired as USM's president and was succeeded by Dr. Horace W. Fleming on January 1, 1997. Many Coastians unhappy with the slow growth of USM's presence in the area perceived Fleming as more "Coast friendly" than his predecessor, and they were correct in that assessment. USM's evolutionary growth on the Coast under Lucas gave way to revolutionary changes under Fleming.

Various civic and political groups on the Coast had long supported a greater USM presence. Some, going further, desired the establishment of a new ninth Mississippi university. Perhaps the most vocal and most influential of these groups bore the name "Coast 21" and counted among its ranks a stellar array of professional, business and political leaders.

State Representative Diane Peranich of DeLisle, a Coast 21 advocate, in a speech to the State Legislature in January, 1997, said, "We would like to at long last, realize our dream of a four-year university on the Coast." Forthwith she introduced legislation to that end. Peranich, a long time supporter of the state's community college program in general and MGCCC in particular said also, "We would not do anything to harm our viable junior college system."

Peranich's plan called for admitting 150 freshmen at USM-Gulf Park the first year and then continuing to admit both freshmen and sophomores until a total of 750 had been reached. Capping enrollment at 750, according to Peranich, would protect MGCCC.

Cognizant of the fact that the only viable test of a bombproof shelter was to drop a bomb on it, the MGCCC administration was understandably not so certain of that protection. Mellinger confined his remarks regarding the issue to the following statement: "Additional degree offerings at the upper division levels at USM-Gulf Coast would complement the mission of the Gulf Coast Community College." MGCCC had championed unlimited upper division offerings on the Coast by USM and/or any other senior college or university for decades. Conversely, MGCCC had just as strenuously opposed all attempts by Mississippi public institutions of higher education to offer freshman and sophomore classes anywhere in MGCCC's four-county district.

From the view point of the supporters of Peranich's bill, the 750 lower-division students at USM-Gulf Coast's Gulf Park Campus were needed in order to provide the funds necessary to pay for more upper-division classes. The fairness of such a system of charges might have been debatable, but the fact of its existence was not, and for that reason a student could obtain two years of instruction at a community college for one-third the cost of attending the first two years at a senior college.

And what of the future? By 1997, USM's jungle of former branches and branches of branches and interconnected twigs and vines clambering along a trellis stretching 70 miles from Stennis Space Center in the west to Gautier in the east, had come to be styled "USM Gulf Coast". This new designation having, in effect, unified all the former USM installations into one entity, then what was to confine USM's offerings of freshman and sophomore courses to Gulf Park Campus alone? Why not also offer these courses at Stennis, Keesler, and at the USM Gulf Coast Center on the MGCCC Jackson County Campus?

The legislative battle to make USM Gulf Coast a four-year degree-granting branch of USM proved to be the opening of a Mississippi educational Pandora's Box. Mississippi, the nation's poorest state, already had eight universities it could not afford. Some of those had branches, too. Would those develop also into four-year degree-granting branches once USM Gulf Coast had set the precedent? Would not USM Gulf Coast someday develop into a ninth university? If so, what of the other universities' branches? Why could they not also achieve their manifest destiny? In this milieu, what would be the fate of the state's 15 public community colleges surrounded by university branches?

The 1997 legislative initiative to create a four-year institution at USM Gulf Coast's Gulf Park Campus failed. Peranich, however, did manage to achieve the passage of a bill "to study the need and advisability of offering courses for college credit at the lower undergraduate level at off-campus sites of institutions of higher learning. . . . " This study was to be carried out under the auspices of the IHL Board in cooperation with the State Board for Community and Junior Colleges (SBCJC).

In obedience to a legislative fiat empowered by a $250,000 appropriation, the IHL Board selected the prestigious College Board of New York (CBNY) to carry out the study. Officials of the CBNY, a nationwide association of 2,500 colleges and high schools, were to inventory the current higher education offerings in Mississippi, assess needs, and prepare recommendations for action to the 1998 legislature.

CBNY researchers arrived on the Coast in August, 1997. Over the next two months they met with administrators of every institution of higher education involved in offerings in south Mississippi. These institutions included USM, MGCCC, William Carey College, the University of South Alabama, the University of New Orleans, Mississippi State University, and Pearl River Community College to name the major ones. In addition CBNY researchers held meetings with educational civic and political groups, conducted student surveys, and monitored telephone call-in message lines. In December the CBNY team submitted to the IHL Board its 81-page Policy Report: *The Academic Program Needs Of the Gulf Coast Region.* The Policy Report contained the following general statement: "Mississippians . . . appear to be convinced that eight public universities are too many. We heard that repeatedly. They know that the state has limited resources to support eight institutions. Mississippians are also convinced of three other matters, according to most of those we interviewed: No Mississippi university can be closed; none can be moved; and none can be combined with another."

Former state legislator Ray Vecchio had been one of the most vocal respondents at a CBNY September meeting conducted in Jackson County. At that meeting, Vecchio had intimated that, in his experience, Mississippians tended to spend hundreds of thousands of dollars to bring in outside experts whose advice they then refused to follow. In his remarks he cited the case a few years prior in which experts had conducted a costly study that had recommended the closing and combining of some of the state's eight universities and that the legislature had refused to do it. With that in mind he opposed the formation of a ninth university.

The CBNY report contained a list of ten "alternative arrangements" for the delivery of higher education on the coast originating from its research. The most popular of these were,

(1)GULF COAST UNIVERSITY CENTER in which any of Mississippi's eight public universities could offer complete bachelor's, master's and doctor's degrees. State officials were to decide which university would offer which degrees in order to avoid duplication.

(2)UPPER DIVISION/ GRADUATE USM/ON THE GULF COAST in which all required courses could be offered on the Coast. MGCCC and Pearl River Community College, in their respective districts, were to provide the freshman and sophomore courses.

(3)COMPREHENSIVE USM ON THE GULF COAST would provide all courses beginning with the freshman year.

(4)GULF COAST UNIVERSITY would be a new ninth comprehensive public university.

The recommendations of the CBNY study turned out to be a combination of Alternative Arrangements one and two. USM Gulf Coast should greatly increase its offerings especially in the mornings on the Gulf Park Campus. MGCCC instructors should offer freshman and sophomore courses not only at Perk, JC, and JD but also at Gulf Park. The enhanced linkage between USM Gulf Coast and MGCCC should lead to "seamless transition for students" even to the point of joint enrollment by students in both institutions simultaneously. The partnership between the University of Texas-Brownsville and Texas Southernmost College was cited as the model for integration so close that the two institutions shared administrations and faculty and jointly offered all programs.

The CBNY study further recommended that USM Gulf Coast should contract with other public universities both inside and outside Mississippi to offer courses to students that USM normally did not. With the consequent shift from supply-oriented scheduling formerly dictated from the USM main campus to the student-demand orientation of an expanded and greatly empowered USM Gulf Park, the chief executive officer's title should be elevated from that of associate vice-president to that of a vice-president reporting directly to the USM president.

In January, 1998, the IHL Board submitted the CBNY study together with the recommendations to the legislature. On February 12, Mississippi senators voted 50-2 to make USM Gulf Park Campus a four-year degree-granting branch of USM. The bill authorized the admission of 750 freshmen and sophomores and offered to increase that number contingent on the agreement of the State Board of Community and Junior Colleges (SBCJC). The senate proposal also authorized Gulf Park to have gyms and dormitories but did bar Gulf Park from "fielding its own college sports teams that duplicate those at USM." IHL Board member, Roy Klumb of Gulfport, stunned by this development, said, "The next thing you'll hear is they need autonomy for USM Gulf Park. That's going to start a ninth university."

The 1998 initiative to form a four-year USM Gulf Coast died in committee in the House of Representatives. Representative Norma Bourdeaux of Meridian who headed the effort to kill the bill said of her actions, "If we did this, every other institution with a regional campus will want the same thing."

MGCCC President Willis Lott (left) and USM President Horace Fleming participate in an August 4, 1998, press conference announcing the "seamless single campus degree" in industrial engineering to be offered on the Jackson County Campus.

State board of Community and Junior Colleges Executive Director Olon Ray (left) and Institutions of Higher Learning Board Commissioner Tom Lyzell pause for a moment of reflection during the September 24, 1998, USM Gulf Coast-MGCCC hosted Visions for Leadership lecture series held at USM Gulf Park.

The writer of an editorial in the Jackson *Clarion Ledger* on March 3 stated:

"Mississippi already has eight public universities and 15 two-year colleges. It doesn't need a ninth public university. The issue is proper utilization of the two-year college system. Why should a four-year school (USM) compete with a two-year school, Gulf Coast Community College? Why should taxpayers pay for such competition."

In June, representatives of MGCCC met with officials of USM and the IHL Board and pledged to carry out the CBNY recommendations if such a thing would be allowed. That same month representatives of Mississippi State University, Jackson State University, Alcorn State University, and the University of Mississippi made overtures to USM and the IHL Board to implement CBNY's Universities Center recommendation. But neither IHL Commissioner Tom Lyzell nor USM President Fleming seemed overly concerned with the CBNY recommendations. Lyzell was quoted that month as saying, "Eventually you will see a four-year university on the Coast." Fleming agreed with that assessment opining, "A four-year university (on the Coast) is inevitable."

At this critical juncture MGCCC President Mellinger retired due to reasons of ill health, and Dr. Willis Lott, former Perkinston Campus vice president replaced him on August 1. Three days later Fleming and Lott announced USM-MGCCC's first "seamless, single-campus program." The coming industrial engineering technology degree was to be offered in the fall jointly at MGCCC's Jackson County Campus. This program, according to USM Gulf Coast Vice President James Williams, was the first in a line that would eliminate the Two Plus Two USM degrees that had required shuffling among USM campuses in Hattiesburg, Gautier, and Long Beach.

As USM and MGCCC forged closer ties and the universities upstate continued to press for a Universities Center on the Coast, Attorney Ron Peresich of Biloxi, spokesman for Coast 21, decried these initiatives and launched another offensive for a four-year university. In mid-September he called for an end to MGCCC's veto power through the SBCJC to stop freshmen and sophomore courses from being offered in its district.

In mid-October Fleming unveiled his plan to make USM a "dual university" with a residential campus at Hattiesburg and a co-equal Metropolitan Campus at Long Beach as early as spring 1999. This plan, in effect, conferred four-year status on USM Gulf Coast. He asked the IHL Board to back the plan and began an initiative among legislators to remove the SBCJC's power to veto university expansion.

Coast 21 and other Coast groups embraced Fleming's dual campus idea with alacrity. Peresich requested an opinion from State Attorney General Mike Moore on the question of a dual campus. Moore's opinion delivered November 12th turned out to be a bombshell. Community colleges under the law did have the power to stop university "branch" campuses from offering lower division classes in their districts, but if USM wished to designate the Gulf Park Campus as a "dual" campus, co-equal with the campus in Hattiesburg, then the Gulf Park Campus, no longer being a "branch," no longer came under SBCJC veto. Furthermore, according to Moore, the power to officially designate USM as a dual campus university lay within the purview of the IHL Board and required no action on the part of the legislature. The legislature, of course, retained the power to fund the venture.

On January 21, 1999, the IHL Board by a vote of 7-5 blessed Fleming's dual campus concept thus establishing USM Gulf Coast as a four-year degree-granting college. At the same time, the IHL Board approved the creation of a USM-administered Universities Center wherein Mississippi State, the University of Mississippi, Jackson State, and Alcorn State would offer programs that USM Gulf Coast did not. USM Gulf Coast requested $1.1 million for the enrollment of 150 freshmen in fall 1999, and $900,000 to create the Universities Center. These funds represented a $2 million increase in USM Gulf Coast's annual $8.5 million operational budget.

In commenting on the IHL Board's actions MGCCC President Lott said:

"We are pleased that the university center concept was part of the proposal approved by the IHL Board. However, we are concerned that limited resources and splintered efforts to establish a dual campus as well as a university center will not lead to high quality offerings at the junior and senior levels."

Although advocates for USM Gulf Coast had won the war, they lost that year's budget battle. Representative Ed Blackmon Jr. of Canton said, "No one is being fooled into viewing USM Gulf Coast as a mere expansion of the Hattiesburg campus. It's a university by whatever name you want to call it."

Some lawmakers opposed USM Gulf Coast on the basis that it was a "ninth university." Others, particularly black legislators, were unsure of its impact on the Ayers Case financially and otherwise. This college desegregation case, which had originated in 1975 when the late Jake Ayers of Glen Allen sued the state for long time neglect of historically black universities, came into play when USM Gulf Coast placed unique admission requirements designed to limit enrollment in its proposed initial freshman class at Gulf Park. Applicants were required to write an essay stating why they wished to pursue a degree at USM Gulf Coast, and only applicants living in the "Gulf Coast area" were sought.

United States District Judge Neal B. Biggers Jr.

Alvin Chambliss Jr., who represented the plaintiffs in the Ayers Case, took USM to federal court. Judge Neal Biggers Jr. on March 24, 1999, enjoined USM Gulf Coast from enrolling freshmen and charged USM Gulf Coast to amend its discriminatory application procedure to conform to the norm for colleges in Mississippi.

In the transcript of his Court Order signed March 24, 1999, Biggers addressed a paradox raised by the attempt to make USM Gulf Park a four-year institution. Biggers stated:

"The [IHL] Board came to the court in 1994, arguing that the present number of eight four-year campuses in the state should be reduced to six in the name of educational and financial efficiency and to promote desegregation. Now, paradoxically, the [IHL] Board comes to the court suggesting that it is educationally and financially efficient and sound to have not six, but nine four-year campuses. . . . "

In his court order Biggers quoted the following exchange with USM Gulf Coast Vice President James Williams at the hearing of March 17, 1999, when Williams appeared before him as a witness for the IHL Board:

"THE COURT: Dr. Williams, where did this idea of establishing a four-year program on the Gulf Coast come from, and what rationale supports it? Who started this idea?
THE WITNESS: The idea really comes from the community, and they point out the disparity in the proportion of the adult population who have four-year degrees as they compare it to places like Jackson and Hattiesburg. They also use figures that show at the point of high school graduation --
THE COURT: You say 'the community,' and who is this? A motel owner or Presbyterian preacher or who?
THE WITNESS: People from the business community; people from the professional community; people who head media; mayors; board of alderman members; councilmen; legislators.
THE COURT: Well, are they aware of the program that you've got with the Gulf Coast Community College whereby they can go two years at the Gulf Coast and then go two years to Southern to get a four-year degree if they want to get a degree?
THE WITNESS: Yes, sir, they are aware of that. We have over the years done a substantial -- made a substantial effort in terms of getting that word out that it is available, yes, sir."

On the subject of community college-university cooperations, Biggers offered the following in his court order:

"There exists at this time an excellent community college system on the Gulf Coast, offering freshman and sophomore courses from which graduating students may directly enter the upper level courses at the existing USM campus on the Coast and graduate from USM without ever leaving the Gulf Coast area. This is the same type system that is in existence in other parts of the state. In Tupelo, there is an Itawamba Community College (ICC) and University of Mississippi (UM) joint campus which provides access to the same type of 'place bound' students that USM is proposing will be benefited by its new campus on the Gulf Coast. The students can enter ICC the first two years and then progress to the University of Mississippi program for the last two years, receiving four-year degrees in such programs as business and accounting, all the while remaining in the Tupelo area holding down employment and/or family responsibilities.

"A similar program exists in the Northwest Community College (NWCC) area in DeSoto County in conjunction with the University of Mississippi, whereby a student can obtain a four-year degree in such programs as education, accounting, and business. The DeSoto Center houses both the NWCC and the UM offices and classrooms, with NWCC offering the lower level courses the first two years and UM offering upper level undergraduate courses the last two years. In addition, a similar program is working in Meridian operated through the auspices of Meridian Community College and MSU (Mississippi State University).

"There has been no evidence submitted to the court to explain why the successful programs in Tupelo and DeSoto County effectively operate for place-bound students in North Mississippi, but are inadequate for the USMGC and Gulf Coast Community College joint venture on the Gulf Coast; and there has been no educationally justified rationale offered on which to base the addition of a four-year campus of USM on the Gulf Coast, less than 100 miles from the main campus at Hattiesburg.

"The Board predicates its proposed creation of the four-year campus on the Gulf Coast as one meeting the needs of "place bound" students, who do not wish to experience the usual college experience of campus life and would presumably be students age 21 or older, who are regularly employed, perhaps married, with families. Yet, at the time of the initial March 15 deadline for applications to attend the new proposed campus, over two-thirds of the applicants [The March 18, 1999, *Sun Herald* reported 75 applicants] were the traditional first-time freshmen enrollees, i.e., recent high school graduates, ages 17 to 19, who could choose to attend a state community college on the Coast the first two years, or go 75 miles to the Hattiesburg campus or attend one of the other universities. There were only 16 applicants age 21 or older."

In addressing the legal right of the State Board of Community Colleges to stop the expansion of USM Gulf Coast and the opinion of Mississippi Attorney General Mike Moore on that matter, Biggers wrote:

"Section 37-4-3, Mississippi Code Annotated [hereinafter referred to as "the 1972 Law"] provides as follows: '. . . the State Board for Community and Junior Colleges [must] approve any university branch campus offering lower undergraduate level courses for credit.' The State Board for Community and Junior Colleges withheld its approval for the offering by USM of lower undergraduate courses at a Gulf Coast campus. The [IHL] Board presented to the court a letter from the Mississippi Attorney General to a Gulf Coast legislator which . . . sets forth an advisory opinion that the proposed USMGC four-year campus is not a 'off-campus site' therefore obviating the necessity to receive the approval of the State Board for Community and Junior Colleges for the building of this proposed campus. The [IHL] Board cited this letter in support of its position that the proposed campus is also not a 'branch campus.' This interesting interpretation that the USM campus on the Coast is neither an 'off-campus site' nor a 'branch campus' has not been considered by any state court."

But Biggers said he was not going to get into collateral issues. He enjoined the IHL Board from admitting freshmen to USM Gulf Coast because of unique and discriminatory admission policies not practiced by any other state supported four-year institution. These "discriminatory" practices included having applicants write an essay on the subject of why he or she wished to attend USM Gulf Coast. Also, the admission policies restricted applications to "several counties only" which to Biggers's ears sounded more like a four-year community college than a university. Finally, the admission policies sought to select the applicants on the basis that "would reflect the diversity of the residents of the area." Such nebulous racial, or cultural, or socio-economic criteria were unacceptable.

Five days after Biggers ruled, the legislature decided against the special appropriation for USM Gulf Coast. Law makers, though, tempered that decision with promises to make the appropriations the following year. Some solons even urged USM to go on and spend the money to admit freshmen with the promise that they would reimburse the funds the following year.

The IHL Board moved swiftly to bring USM Gulf Coast's admission policies into line with the state's other four-year institutions. Since that was the only legal objection in Biggers's court order, the IHL Board intended to remove that obstacle in time for fall enrollment in August.

The state's other community/junior college leaders, who had been watching the USM-MGCCC *tete-a-tete* from the sidelines, suddenly realized the implications of the precedent about to be set. If USM Gulf Coast were allowed to call USM Gulf Coast a dual campus and admit freshmen, there was no reason why the University of Mississippi could not do the same in Tupelo. There was no reason why Mississippi State University could not do the same in Meridian. There was no reason why any and every university partnered with any community college in several other places could not do the same either. The 1972 Law passed by the legislature to protect taxpayers against just such an eventuality had been first nullified by the attorney general and then ignored by the legislature as if it did not exist.

The SBCJC met in Jackson on June 3, 1999, and the local struggle between USM and MGCCC suddenly became a state-level issue. The SBCJC voted to request state permission to hire a lawyer. The request, of course, went to the state's chief law officer, Attorney General Mike Moore, who had authorized the decision being challenged.

Moore gave the SBCJC permission to hire a private lawyer to examine legal issues related to the USM Gulf Coast expansion. According to the *Clarion Ledger*, July 1, 1999, Moore tempered his magnanimity with a warning, "I won't give permission for one state agency to file a law suit against another agency."

On November 29, 1999, Biggers approved USM Gulf Coast's amended admission standard thus paving the way for the admission of 150 freshmen to USM Gulf Coast in June, 2000. On December 2, the SBCJC met in Jackson and passed a resolution giving SBCJC Executive Director Olon Ray authority to sue the IHL Board. The administration of all 15 state supported community/junior colleges, together with the

Mississippi Community and Junior College Faculty Association and the Mississippi Community College Inter-Alumni Association, endorsed the SBCJC resolution.

On December 22, 1999, the SBCJC filed suit against the IHL Board in Hinds County Chancery Court to stop USM Gulf Coast from becoming a four-year college. The suit was filed without the permission of State Attorney General Mike Moore. The *Sun Herald*, December 24, 1999, carried the comments of Olon Ray regarding the matter: "We're essentially asking that [IHL] Board to uphold the law. . . . We got to the point where there were no other realistic options."

On March 16, 2000, MGCCC Board of Trustees Chairman Don Massengale sent a "Special to the *Sun Herald* Forum" entitled "USM expansion doesn't meet demand for more degree programs." This special, summing up the official position of MGCCC regarding the dispute, is reprinted in full:

"Debate about a ninth university in Mississippi is stalling any action in bringing more higher education options to the people on the Coast. The media is portraying the issue as a turf battle between the community college and the university. Articles and editorials in the *Sun Herald* present a one-sided view of the issue by promoting the addition of freshmen and sophomore classes at USM Gulf Coast in Long Beach as the only way to expand higher education.

"For the record, the Mississippi Gulf Coast Community College Board of Trustees supports the expansion of higher education on the Coast. It endorses a university-center model that encourages expansion, not duplication, and collaboration, not competition. Our goal is to work with Mississippi universities to bring more bachelor's, master's and doctoral degrees to the people of the Coast.

"The rationale for the board's position is based upon recommendations made by The College Board [CBNY] in its report, *A Study of the Academic Program Needs of the Gulf Coast Region.* Conducted in coordination with the IHL Board, the purpose of the study was to determine if expansion of the University of Southern Mississippi Gulf Coast was warranted. The *Sun Herald* and Coast 21 leaders have chosen to ignore the findings of the $250,000 study which was requested by the Legislature and paid for by the taxpayers.

"The IHL proposal to add freshman and sophomore courses at USM Gulf Coast in Long Beach does not address the core issue and primary higher education demand as documented in the study: more bachelor's and master's degrees offered and scheduled more conveniently for time and place-bound Coast residents.

"The proposal to make USM Gulf Coast a dual campus of the University of Southern Mississippi does not meet the need of MGCCC graduates who want to continue their education on the Coast. The current USM five-year plan does not include any new bachelor's or master's degree programs. A university center with new degree programs delivered by multiple universities is a better solution for expansion.

"However, while the concerns of our board are local, the issue of higher education expansion is very much a state-wide issue. Expanding higher education is not a one-time, one-institution or one-region issue.

"In the study, The College Board [CBNY], a nationally recognized expert in higher education, concluded, 'Creating an entirely new four-year institution in the state of Mississippi does not appear to The College Board to be a realistic financial, political, or necessary action.'

"As an advocate for a multi-institutional partnership, the community college continues to promote collaboration with other colleges and universities to eliminate barriers for students and avoid costly duplication of programs. The MGCCC board has adopted what it considers to be the 'right' position, albeit an unpopular position with some leadership groups on the Coast.

"The community college does not view university expansion as a threat to its enrollment. The market will decide who will thrive and who will flounder. It is a cost issue to determine the most effective use of available funding. It is a cost concern for students and taxpayers.

"Despite the rhetoric, the bottom line is the timing and delivery of courses in a manner that is convenient and available at the right price for time- and place-bound Coast residents.

"The Coast's need for higher education should be addressed in an innovative manner that serves a practical statewide model. Recognizing that collaboration is not easy unless there is something to be gained, the community college carefully researched model higher-education partnerships throughout the nation and found at least five common characteristics at successful university centers.
These centers:

- Increased access to higher education--more degree programs, more places, more often;
- Avoided duplication of programs and services offered by the institutions in the partnership;
- Utilized technology and distance education to increase access;
- Maximized the strengths of each institution to provide high quality, cost-efficient programs for students and tax payers; and
- Presented a plan to expand higher education that was futuristic and entrepreneurial, as well as politically and economically feasible.

"Today's higher-education consumers are driven by a mobile, 24-hour service economy. We must meet the need, but not with the same old educational model. The expansion of higher education is achieved by access to convenient, flexible and quality programs and services.

"Let's move forward. Collaboration and expansion are mutually beneficial for the community colleges and the universities, but especially for the people of the Mississippi Gulf Coast."

On Monday, March 21, 2000, the *Sun Herald* reported that 27 applicants out of a pool of 90 had been accepted as members of the first freshman class of USM Gulf Coast. Vice

President Williams was quoted as saying, "This is a big step for us. . . . We will begin teaching the freshman class this summer to a smaller group of students. Our freshman cohort will actually begin in the fall semester." Williams's plans, though, were contingent on securing state funding by then in jeopardy from impending budget cuts and on the outcome of the SBCJC suit.

On April 25 Hinds County Chancery Judge William Singletary refused to dismiss the SBCJC suit against the IHL Board. Singletary then set October 30 as the trial date.

On April 30 the Mississippi State House of Representatives voted 120-0 and the Mississippi State Senate voted 41-0 to approve a $700,500,000 budget for state universities in fiscal year 2000-2001. The bill included $250,000 to admit freshmen at USM Gulf Coast. On May 10 Judge Singletary barred USM from admitting freshmen or sophomore students until the trial in October, thus, in effect, halting summer or fall classes for such students. The legislature promised to save the money appropriated for that purpose until the trial was over.

On July 20, 2000, the IHL Board approved its 2001-2002 budget of $699,000,000, which included $1,750,000 for USM Gulf Coast with $350,000 earmarked to add freshman and sophomore courses. According to the July 21, 2000, *Sun Herald*, USM President Horace Fleming regarded the IHL Board's budget request as a favorable sign. He also pointed out the 1972 Law as the main obstacle to the offering of lower division classes at USM Gulf Coast, but, he said, "The Legislature could easily solve this by changing the law."

On August 14, 2000, the Mississippi Supreme Court granted to the IHL Board an interlocutory appeal in regard to Singletary's May 10 decision. The appeal process derailed the proposed October 30 trial.

By October the SBCJC and the IHL Board found themselves united in facing another kind of trial--budget cuts. State mandated cuts to state-supported educational institutions caused by a down turn in the Mississippi economic growth rate begun in May had worsened. By year's end the projected cuts had reached crisis proportions. The IHL Board had been told to expect an $89 million cut in its already approved $700 million budget. The community/junior colleges were confronted with a cut proportionally even worse.

In the specific case of USM the budget cuts had resulted in a loss of $2 million in 2000. The university had been informed of an impending cut of $3 million more early in the new year and told of a further cut of $11 million the following year.

As the 20th century ended, the economic pillars of higher education were crumbling in Mississippi, and the IHL Board was considering the declaration of a financial state of emergency. Yet, in the face of all that, personnel at USM's "Dual Campuses" in Hattiesburg and Long Beach were preparing to lobby the legislature during its first session of the new millennium to appropriate the funds to admit underclassmen at USM Gulf Coast. But the case of Olon Ray, et al. versus the Board of Trustees of the State Institutions of Higher Learning, which had barely managed to halt that outcome, was still alive. And some who had condemned that suit as community/junior college "turf protection" were beginning to regard that legal case for what it had long been advertised to be--a last ditch effort to save the State of Mississippi from costly and unnecessary duplication of educational services to its people.

SIGN OF THE TIMES

The period of time covered by this work ended on December 31, 2000. But since the Mississippi State Supreme Court rendered its decision in the suit of the SBCJC against the IHL Board before this book went to press in May 2002, the author decided to include the outcome.

On Thursday, February 28, 2002, the Mississippi State Supreme Court ruled that freshmen could enroll at USM Gulf Coast. By majority of 7-1, the justices cited three basic reasons for their decision: 1. Since Mississippi State Attorney General Mike Moore did not give his consent for the suit, then the SBCJC could not legally sue the IHL Board. 2. Since state law did not designate a specific location for USM, then dual campuses in Hattiesburg and Long Beach were not prohibited. 3. Most importantly the SBCJC, which was created by legislative statute, could not exercise veto power over the IHL Board, which exercised a constitutional mandate.

The Sun Herald, May 16, 2002, stated that three freshmen, one of whom was Angela Brown, were the first to complete registration for classes at the new dual USM Gulf Coast campus. The three had registered on Wednesday, May 15, the day USM Gulf Coast became a four-year university. Summer quarter classes were slated to begin May 27, 2002. All told, 131 freshmen had applied for either summer or fall classes by mid-May.

Gary West, left, and Lynn Davies, physical plant workers at the University of Southern Mississippi Gulf Coast, set up a sign on the Gulf Park Campus in Long Beach announcing the school will start admitting freshmen students for the first time. Photo courtesy of USM News.

The Parable of the Monks and the Friars

by Charles L. Sullivan

And it came to pass in days of old that two monasteries began service one day apart some distance apart. In time the younger of the two monasteries grew large while the older remained small. The larger monastery had many learned monks who were regarded as the saviors and protectors of scriptures handed down from generation unto generation. And the most erudite of these monks thought great thoughts and authored great tomes to the glorification of knowledge, and this was good. As these monks labored in their vast scriptorium, they directed acolytes who aided them in this endeavor.

And this monastery was a boon to the laity residing in the vicinity as the monks imparted knowledge unto them and even boarding those who came from afar seeking wisdom. Alas, the most learned monks, charged as they were with the imperative to produce new parchments, caused novices to be gathered in great multitudes to hear their words or else assigned their teaching chores to their acolytes who were, in some cases, less wise than their masters.

Now, the other smaller monastery developed along different lines. The monks there decided to become friars and to expend their energies in working more closely with the laity. But the large monastery was very important to the little one, and many of the friars spent years journeying to or boarding there in order to absorb some of the wisdom of the monks.

These friars, while perhaps not as wise as the monks, were more wise than the monk's acolytes. And being friars they themselves had no acolytes, so they spent all their energy in teaching the laity rather than in scripting lest they slip in the hierarchy of monkdom. So as year followed year the friars imparted the truths gleaned from their days at the feet of the masters and from reading the writings thereof to the sons and daughters of the laity, and it was good. Soon too, the friars began to teach the lay people how to make a living as well as how to live, and that was good, too.

Conversely, in the fullness of time the friars became of some importance to the monks by sending unto them a steady procession of their best novices. Some of these became acolytes and later friars and in rare occasions even entered the hallowed ranks of the monks. Virtually all these novices became at least lay defenders of the faith.

While the monks remained locked in the towers of their large monastery, the friars established a number of priories about the region the better to serve the people. Always the friars restricted their teaching to the rudiments of culture and living because they did this better than monks and because they saw it as their mission to do the greatest good for the greatest number.

Then, it came to pass that large numbers of laity gathered to live in an area around the friars but far distant from the great monastery. And the people said unto the friars, "You have been taught by the monks and are as such incipient monks so we wish for you to turn your priories into monasteries and be as monks that you might impart unto us monk knowledge." But the friars protested saying, "Nay, we are not junior monks but rather we are full grown friars, and though we can not and will not do what a monk can do, we do things for you they can not and will not do."

But when the laity became more restive in their pursuit of the vast knowledge of the monks, the friars sent an emissary to the great monastery requesting that monks journey to their priories to impart their knowledge to the people of the friars' region. At first the monks were reluctant, but, in time, lured by special quarters secured for them by means of the friars working among the laity, they came. But still this was not enough to satisfy the laity, so the friars offered to go into a partnership with the monks to provide all that the laity desired. Such a fellowship in the estimation of the friars would provide the laity with the best offerings of both the friars and monks. But then the monks decided that they wished to build another great monastery at great cost to the people in the midst of the new concentration of laity. So expensive was the construction of a new great monastery that the monks said unto the friars, "You have done well in preparing your people for us, but now we must teach your novices so that we will gain their fees to support our works." Hurt and confused, the friars proposed that convocation of provincial clergy be called to mediate. This convocation invited disinterested vicars from another land to come to the region to assess the situation and offer solutions, and this was done.

These vicars after much study decided that a partnership of friars and monks would provide the laity with the best efforts of both the friars and the monks. A large majority of the laity agreed with the wisdom of the decision. The friars accepted the recommendation with alacrity and offered many garlands of friendship to the monks and placed lists of concessions of all kinds in the hands of the monks for they wished nothing more that to join them in aiding the laity.

But the monks refused the overtures of the friars saying, "What care we for the flawed advice of distant vicars whose errors are made manifest by their failure to see our vision. That the laity be pauperized to build our mighty edifice is small price indeed and if they grow hungry--let them eat knowledge. As for you friars--ye, too, have fallen in to error as ye dare to defend friar turf. In our magnanimity we leave to you the teaching of mundane matters only. Ye may continue to teach the people to make a living while we and our acolytes will teach them en masse the meaning of life and thus reap the benefits thereof to support a new and great scriptorium." And the friars did gaze in deep amazement as they pondered the burden of a ninth Monastery-Scriptorium upon the bowed backs of a people unable to adequately support the other eight in the province.

And what is the point of the parable? Let the monks consider that after they solve the eternal question of how many angels can dance on a pinhead. In my mind it has no moral, but then what matter that? For I am only a friar.

BOOK II

Sports
1912-2000

AGRICULTURAL HIGH SCHOOL SPORTS GLIMPSES AND HIGHLIGHTS 1912 - 1924

The writer of the Harrison County Agricultural High School's first official *Announcement* published in summer 1912 penned the school's first athletic policy: "All work and no play makes Jack a dull boy. Daily moderate exercise, which always stops short of fatigue, is one of the best laws of health; so in addition to the farm and garden we expect to have tennis, baseball, and basketball grounds so that real work may be tempered with pleasurable games."

If the school built a tennis court, nothing was said of it for the next fifteen years. The school, though, did build "baseball and basketball grounds" in its first session, 1912-1913.

By spring 1913 the Harrison County Agricultural High School (HCAHS) was competing in track and field events. On Saturday, March 29, 1913, J. A. Huff, of the HCAHS, along with the other high school principals of Harrison County, assisted Harrison County School Superintendent of Education J.J. Dawsey in hosting and judging the events of the Annual Harrison County Field Day held that year in Gulfport. Dawsey had initiated Field Day, and the first one had been held April 9, 1909. Field Day contests pitted school against school for prizes in oratory, music, and athletics. This "healthy rivalry," according to Dawsey, not only stimulated interest among teachers and students but also brought "the schools before the people in the endeavor to arouse school interest and enthusiasm."

At Field Day 1913, Andrew Fillingame of Gulfport garnered the HCAHS's first laurel in athletics or anything else for that matter. In the running broad jump for boys over age 14, Fillingame won first place with a leap of 15 feet 9 inches.

The HCAHS baseball team began competition in spring 1913. On Saturday, April 19, 1913, on the diamond at the Gulfport Fair Grounds the "Perkinston Agriculturalists" met the "Soldiers" of Gulf Coast Military Academy. In the game, which ended with a score of 8-1, the Soldiers won their academy's first victory (GCMA opened in 1912, too) and the HCAHS baseballers suffered their second defeat in seven games played.

The following Wednesday the soldiers traveled up the Gulf & Ship Island Railroad (G&SI RR) to play the HCAHS at home. The Perkinston Agriculturalists (that appellation soon gave way to the sportier "Perk Aggies") were only one point behind until the ninth inning. At that point the HCAHS team switched in its lefty to throw the Soldiers a curve, but the Soldiers were used to left-handed pitchers. When the smoke cleared, the score stood at 16-9 the Soldier's way. Two defeats at the hands of the same team in five days left the Agriculturalists a bit huffy, which they expressed with parsimony. This from the *Daily Herald*, April 25, 1913:

The first baseball team of the Harrison County Agricultural High School won 12 of 15 match games in the 1912-13 season. Two of the losses came one week apart to the Gulf Coast Military Academy founded the same session. Photo from Second Catalogue, p. 11.

"The G.C.M.A. feel a little aggrieved at the A. H. S. boys for what they consider shabby treatment. Col. McGehee states that it was understood that the A.H.S. was to pay the railroad fare and all expenses to Perkinston and back for twelve men, but that after the game was over the High Schools boys would pay the railroad fare of eleven men only and that the visitors had to buy their own dinners and suppers."

The day after that the Agriculturalists snapped, "The AHS claims the Championship over any high school team in the county and is ready to defend the championship." Apparently the Aggie team did not lose any more games that year because they finished the season with 15 wins and 3 losses.

The writer of the *Second Annual Catalogue* heralding the HCAHS's second session to begin in September 1913, shared some new and rather pointed admonitions regarding athletics and discipline doubtless gleamed from the fires of experience during the first session. The writer (probably J.A. Huff) stated:

"We have . . . baseball and basketball. No pupil will be allowed to play on our match teams whose class work is not satisfactory. Drinking and cigarette smoking not only bars one from athletics, but from school. We have a few regulations the enforcement of which is necessary for the good of all concerned and if you do not intend to stand to and abide by them, choose some other school."

The HCAHS roundballers were playing match games in early 1914. On Saturday, February 1, the Perkinston Aggies defeated McHenry High School by a score the *Daily Herald* reporter rendered as "too bad to tell." A week later the McHenry High varsity team journeyed to Perkinston for a rematch and lost to the HCAHS Aggies by a score of 11 to 6. On February 27, the HCAHS Aggies went down in defeat in Brooklyn to the boys of the Forrest County Agricultural High School.

Football debuted at the HCAHS in fall 1914. Alvah Alexander, an early HCAHS football player, when interviewed in 1952 recalled, "The team was ill equipped with shoulder pads made from horse's collars. Work shoes with nails driven in them for cleats were used for football shoes. Instead of a dummy, a man was used for blocking practice. Despite these odds a winning team was produced." The surviving records revealed a big win but also some big losses.

On Saturday, October 24, 1914, the HCAHS played its first football game. In the game, played in Gulfport, the Soldiers of the Gulf Coast Military Academy defeated the Aggies 32-0. A *Daily Herald* reporter described the defeat as "ignominious" but softened this verdict by saying, "The Perkinston boys seemed to lack experience, but played a plucky game." Of course they lacked experience--they had never before competed. On Saturday, November 21, 1914, the Gulfport High Eleven traveled to Perkinston in automobiles, and according to the *Daily Herald*, "When they arrived at their destination, the country lads ran out of the way, having never before seen wagons run without horses." This last was obviously in jest, but, be that as it may, the Aggies ran over the visitors inflicting, in the *Daily Herald* reporter's words, "a terribly ignominious defeat of 86-6." Alas, on November 26, the worm turned in this institution's first contest against the school destined to become its bitterest rival. The *Poplarville Free Press* touted the score of 51-0 under the title, "Poplarville Wins Easily." The Perkinston-Pearl River conflict had begun.

On Saturday, February 9, 1915, the HCAHS Aggies took on the Pearl River County Agricultural High School in a series of three basketball games played at Perkinston. The Aggies won the first game 19 - 10 and lost the second 26 - 16. In the third and deciding tilt, the score see-sawed back and forth, and the teams were tied four times before Perkinston finally won 21-19.

On Monday, April 26, 1915, the Aggies met Pearl River on the baseball diamond. This, too, was a three game series, and it turned out much like the basketball games. The Aggies won the first game 5-2, lost the second 1-3, and then won the third and deciding game 11-1.

By 1916 the HCAHS girls were playing competition basketball. On Wednesday, February 8, the HCAHS girls hosted the McHenry High girls' team. The game began on the dirt court at 3:40 in the afternoon with Lois Rankin, the HCAHS business teacher, officiating. At the half the score stood at 7 - 2 McHenry's way. Miss Rankin was so excited that she could not referee the second half, so Professor C. H. Bass of McHenry took over for her.

The 1918 Harrison-Stone Agricultural High School Mississippi State Basketball Championship team. *(From left) Charlie Terry of Long Beach, Gene Barnett of Moss Point, Professor Robert H. Harmon of Perkinston, Noll P. Davis of Perkinston, and Forstall A. Kelly of Biloxi. Apparently Harmon, who taught math and science at the HCAHS, was the team coach and also a player on the team. In the accounts of the time other "profs" from other high schools were listed as players. Harmon is sitting because, according to the Daily Herald of January 29, 1918, "Mr. Harmon recently broke his ankle while playing basketball." A later account of the season lists Joe Kelly as "scrubbing for Harmon." Noll Perkins Davis in the photo was the grandson of John Perkins for whom Perkinston was named.*

McHenry defeated the HCAHS girls 18 - 2.

The Harrison-Stone AHS (HSAHS) football team made history in November 1916, by playing the Wiggins High School team at the first Stone County Fair in Wiggins. Bostick "Crab" Breland of Big Level, who attended the game, summed up the game laconically, "The Wiggins boys were clean outmatched and lost the game by a score of nothing to everything."

On November 27, 1916, the *Daily Herald* published a more detailed account of a HSAHS football game against the Soldiers on the field of the Gulf Coast Military Academy. The Soldiers pulverized the Aggies 26 - 6. The Aggies made their only score four minutes before the end of the game by using "line bucks" and a forward pass thrown "behind the goal."

The February 9, 1917, *HSAHS News* reported that the Aggie basketball team had met defeat in Biloxi at the hands of the Seashore Campground roundballers. This defeat, though, had served only to spur the Aggies on to "greater zeal and determination" for the future. The team was next "preparing for a crash with the Pearl River AHS." The writer probably meant "clash" but "crash" was likely more accurate.

In 1918 the HSAHS roundballers exhibited unprecedented zeal and determination. The team defeated Millsaps College in the state championship match to take Perkinston's first ever state title.

Alas, next season the state championship basketball team began the slide to failure due to Success. Success High School sent it down to defeat on March 5, 1919. Then in another game, star roundballer Noll Davis broke his collarbone and that was that.

In spring 1921 the Aggie baseball team celebrated the completion of a new diamond on the hill behind Bennett Hall. Coach R. J. Koonce issued the team a full uniform and announced his intention to lead them to victory. "Pep" and "BULL-DOGGISHHANGONITIVE-NESS" was their slogan. (This was the first mention of that fierce canine in relation to the school. Four years later the "Aggies" would become "Bulldogs.") In early March, Chandler Bradford and Clifton Bond demonstrated the fierce elan of the baseball team in practice by running together so forcefully on the diamond that each suffered a broken leg.

In baseball action that spring the Aggies beat Wiggins, Bond, Brooklyn, and the team of the Mississippi Industrial Training School of Columbia. On the other hand, the Pearl River AHS beat them 11-5, and the Soldiers of the G.C.M.A. defeated the Aggies 5 - 0 in one game and 18 - 1 in another.

The lack of triumphs and the tragedies of the HSAHS football team dominated the headlines in fall 1921. According to the *Daily Herald*, on Saturday, October 8, the Gulfport High School team went to Wiggins to play the HSAHS, "because the Stone County Fair is going on there and because there is no good field at Perkinston." Gulfport scored in the first four minutes. "After this it was only a question of how big the score would be as the Gulfport boys gained at will." At game's end the score stood 32-0 Gulfport's way. Marion Cox, an HSAHS player from Woolmarket said after the loss, "We had no training hardly and did not stand a chance."

On Saturday, November 19, 1921, four Aggies--Louis and Steven Gorenflo, Nelson Douglas, and Eugene Coman--hired Wiggins taxi driver Guy Forbes to drive them to Pascagoula for a game. There the team did much better, losing by a score of only 3-0. According to the *Daily Herald*, at 6:15 Saturday evening, enroute back to Perkinston, Forbes, "not knowing the roads, and intending to drive to the Ferry, miscalculated." Instead of turning from Delmas Avenue onto the ferry road, he drove to the docks. The five passenger Ford shot off the dock still clocking 25 miles per hour and splashed down in the middle

The 1921 Harrison-Stone AHS "Aggie" football team *poses in front of Huff Hall. (From left) Louis M. Hudson of Gulfport, "Bogie," Lloyd Gates, "Music Teacher," Tom Dantzler of Moss Point, Marion Cox of Woolmarket, and James Bell of Gulfport. The "Music Teacher" of the time was Miss Ethel Ziert.*

of the Pascagoula River and settled to the bottom in 22 feet of very cold water. Two cars following closely on the Ford managed to stop in the nick of time. In the words of a *Daily Herald* reporter, "Not enjoying sitting in a car under water, the boys crawled out as best they could. Louis breaking through the isinglass at the back and Steve coming out from the side." When the boys emerged from the river shivering and wet, H. E. Fredericks of Pascagoula loaned clothes to two of them, and the Pascagoula High principal bought clothes for the other three. The Perkinston coach bought tickets, sending the Gorenflo boys to Biloxi and the other three to Gulfport. Crab Breland in an article entitled, "Fording a River in a Ford," got in his licks on the incident. He quoted Forbes, then high and dry, as responding to his jibes with the reply, "You just can't keep a good man down."

On December 3, the Aggies sallied forth one last time in a post-season game against Biloxi. That time they sank 39-7.

The 1922 HSAHS football team in combat array. First row *(From left) Leo J. Scanlon of Gulfport, Sheely Davis of Wiggins, Ernest Bufkin of Petal, William Albert "Ship Island" Frantzen, Houston Dees of Perkinston, Lawrence "Lefty" Blake of Hattiesburg, and Paul Heard Anger of Algiers, Louisiana.* ***Second row*** *(from left) Forrest Runnels of Hattiesburg, John Perkins of Perkinston, Louis Hudson of Gulfport, and Tom Dantzler of Moss Point.* ***Third row*** *(from left) Professor W. R. Cain (assistant agriculturist), Cooper Rouse of Saucier, Nolan E. Terry of Long Beach, Royal Daniels, James Bell of Gulfport, Welton Shaw of Perkinston, Fred Sargent (Mascot) is on window ledge behind Shaw, Othman Seaman of Moss Point, Superintendent J. H. Forbis, and Coach M. G. Evans. John Perkins was the grandson and namesake of the founder of Perkinston. His wife, Virginia Perkins of Tuscon, Arizona, sent the photo to the MGCCC Archives in 1998 and identified him in this photo.*

The 1922 HSAHS football team. *(Front) Fred Sargent (mascot) of Vicksburg.* ***First row*** *(from left) Leo Scanlon, Sheely Davis, Ernest Bufkin, Paul Heard Anger, William "Ship Island" Frantzen, Houston Dees, and Lawrence "Lefty" Blake.* ***Second row*** *(from left) Nolan Terry, Welton Shaw, Forrest Runnels, John Perkins, Royal Daniels, Louis Hudson, Thomas Dantzler, and Othman Seaman.* ***Third row*** *(from left) Coach M. G. Evans, Professor W. R. Cain, Herb Rogers, Elmer Avera, Cooper Rouse, James Bell, and J. H. Forbis. Photo courtesy of John Russell O'Neal.*

In summer 1922 J. H. Forbis became the new principal of the HSAHS and instituted a sweeping reform program that emphasized athletics. Forbis encouraged all students to participate in athletics because sports diverted the mind "from idle thoughts and acts of mischief and fostered school loyalty." Because not everyone could make the varsity team, "scrub" or second teams would compete with one another and with second teams from other schools.

Coach M. G. Evans took his Aggie varsity footballers to Laurel for their initial outing of the season on Friday, September 30, 1922. Laurel beat them 36-0. One week later Evans invaded Jones County again to take on Ellisville and did much better coming out with a 6-6 tie. Evans said, considering that Ellisville had 275 men to pick from to his 75, he was happy with the outcome. Besides, he said, "Perkinston's team is made up mostly by men who have never seen a football before."

Evans's Aggies did not win many games that year, but they surely did impress a *Daily Herald* reporter who covered their battle with Gulfport High on Saturday, November 4. The reporter described the game as, "The most sensational and most furiously fought gridiron combat ever seen on the Mississippi Coast. The score was 14 to 0. The game was replete with brilliant runs, bucks, forward passes, broken field running, lightning quick formation shifts, and all the efficient plays known to the science of football. The Perkinston team, while being defeated certainly did put up a wonderful game. They never once failed to fight and they have a good, heavy, well-drilled squad."

Later that month the Aggies actually won a game. They beat the Forrest County AHS 20-0 at the Stone County Fair on November 24.

Forbis, true to his word, had organized all teams at the HSAHS into first and second squads. On February 20, 1923, the HSAHS girls "first team" basketeers defeated the McHenry High School "first team."

On May 13, 1923, Forbis convoyed the girls "first and scrub" basketball teams together with most of the HSAHS student body to Wiggins for a tournament. This action not only bespoke Forbis' devotion to athletics but also indicated that the HSAHS marshaled sufficient motorized vehicles to transport nearly 100 persons to a sports event. Stone County Sheriff Peter Lott reported licenses sold for 600 automobiles in the county in 1923.

At the close of the 1922-1923 session, Forbis announced a revolutionary new policy. Until that time men and women who first and foremost had been faculty members had coached. Beginning in September 1923, men and women who were first and foremost coaches would have charge of the HSAHS teams. In Forbis's words, "We are also going to have athletic coaches for both boys and girls, while we don't mean to cast a reflection on those who did this work the past year, yet we must make this phase of the work more effective by giving the coaches time to do this work."

In announcing the faculty for the 1923-1924 session, Forbis published Miss Myrtle Smith as "girl's athletic coach" and teacher of commercial subjects and Latin. Bennie P. Webb was given out as "boy's athletic coach and math instructor." Forbis certainly left no doubt that Bennie Webb was first and foremost a coach. In introducing Webb to the students and faculty, Forbis said,

"We have a man at the head of the athletics who is able to make the strongest team in the state if we will furnish him with material. Mr. Webb [played] four years on the Georgia Tech teams and starred in them all and reached his four letters from that university; he has also coached two years. Now boys we do not mean to place too much stress on athletics, but we do believe it

The 1923-1924 Harrison-Stone AHS girl's basketball team of Coach Myrtle Smith poses behind Bennett Hall. *Photo courtesy Dowey D. O'Neal.*

***The 1923 Harrison-Stone AHS football team** poses between Huff Hall (right) where the boys live and Bennett Hall (administration building). Sitting (from left) Archie Lavasseur of Moss Point, Nolan Terry of Long Beach, Thomas Henry Dantzler of Moss Point, Forrest Charles Runnels of Hattiesburg, and Frank Bettis Atchison of Bond. Kneeling (from left) Houston Longino Dees of Perkinston, Louis Lavasseur of Moss Point, and Earl Paul Long of Leesburg. Back row (from left) Coach Bennie P. Webb, Paul Heard Anger, of Algiers, Louisiana, William Albert "Ship Island" Frantzen, Foster Rouse of Saucier, Vernon Brown of Stillmore, and Larue Breland of Perkinston. According to Ship Frantzen in a 1996 interview, "The rules were nothing to resemble the present play rules except the number of people on the field. For example, a player leaving the field for any reason could not play again in the same quarter. The uniforms that we had were mostly scrap stuff that protected you some." He said the campus field, located then behind the Bennett Building, was more like an uneven gravel pit, so the game required a lot of endurance. The team traveled to Laurel or to the Coast by automobile, but by train to New Orleans. He remembers that the New Orleans field, "was easier to play on and more comfortable. Of course, we were a raggy looking bunch because we were more the poor folks playing." Photo courtesy of Walter Atchison, son of Frank Bettis Atchison.*

has a place in all well regulated schools and we believe you are missing a good chance to learn clean wholesome athletics and at the same time be on the winning team, if you don't take advantage of this opportunity."

Coach Bennie Webb's Aggie footballers won a few and lost a few and refused to play one. The Aggies beat the Forrest County AHS 6-0, lost to the Soldiers of the GCMA, and smashed Gulfport 31-0. The Gulfport "Fighting Tigers" demanded a rematch. The Aggies went down to Gulfport to play the post-season game, but backed out. In the *Daily Herald* of December 8, 1923, the Tigers showed their claws:

"Seeing plainly the woeful handwriting on the wall, the Perkinston foot-ball players refused to battle the fighting tigers after they had journeyed down for that purpose, supposedly. They claim one of our men must be removed out of the line-up else they would quit the field. They were not anxious to play and seemed highly delighted, when we failed to comply with their silly whim. Our tiger's mouths watered to tear them up but our coach chose the moral victory instead. Perk had better look out next year!"

Webb's reply three days later put the impasse in a new light. He said his team had beaten Gulfport 31-0 and did not care to "waste time" whipping them again. In response to repeated entreaties he had, though, gone down to give them a rematch. The trouble arose when the Perkinston boys saw a former student from the AHS who had been expelled standing in the ranks of the Gulfport team. Webb said expelled students from any school could not legally play for any other. Webb said he had already told the superintendent of Gulfport schools and the coach of Gulfport High that his team would not play if that person appeared on the field. They promised Webb the boy would not be there. He was, so the Aggies departed.

Coach Webb's Aggie roundballers hit the court in January 1924. They won eight games in a row, but their forward progress was stopped by Progress. Progress High School of McLain broke their streak with a heartbreaking 14-13 defeat.

Forbis turned over the reins of power to Jefferson Lee Denson in June 1924. Denson aimed to add a junior college curriculum to that of the HSAHS. He also aimed to add a junior college athletic program. Denson's first session, 1924-1925, (the last solely AHS year), saw the beginning of the metamorphosis into a new entity--a combination junior college and agricultural high school.

***1923-1924 HSAHS basketball team** poses by the Perk cypress water tower because that was the location of the court prior to 1925. The goal backboard is visible behind the head of the next to the last player in the photo. Vernon Brown is first in line, Paul Anger is next, other members of the team were Jesse Cook, Forrest Runnels, Tom Dantzler, and Frank Bettis Atchison Photo from 1924-1925 Announcement Brochure.*

SPORTS IN THE DENSON ERA 1924 - 1929

According to Hersel McDaniel, a Denson-era student, the county high schools such as Magnolia, Silver Run, Inda, Deep Creek, and Carnes turned out fine basketball players but not football players. According to McDaniel, any farm boy could nail a barrel hoop to the barn wall; then all he needed was a basketball and he was in business. County schools played basketball year round and very little else. Football required far more expensive equipment and a special field, so only the city schools such as Pass Christian, Gulfport, Biloxi, Ocean Springs, and Pascagoula turned out football players. As football was the major sport at Perkinston, the city boys who went out for the team had the edge on the country boys who knew very little about the sport.

W. H. "Billy" Wood was the combination coach/history teacher when McDaniel entered the Harrison-Stone County Agricultural High School (HSAHS) in September 1924. Coach Wood had wanted all the football players to come to the campus two weeks early for training, but McDaniel and many of the others who lived in the country could not do that. In McDaniel's words, "I had never played football before entering Perkinston--and entered late at that. . . . I thought I would like the game, which I did and do but BROTHER was I in for a surprise, and a very sore surprise at that. . . . I tell you I have never been so beat upon and dragged around and stomped on--and sore. . . . Well, I was learning the hard way and I do mean HARD."

Aside from being untested and untried, many of the boys were small, and they were going up against high schools with much better material and much larger enrollments from which to draw. Despite the formidable odds coach Wood did his best. McDaniel remembered his coach, "He was a star at State Teachers College and while playing had a broken neck and almost died, still he was a good football coach and sometimes mixed it up with us pretty rough. He was one of the finest Christian gentlemen I have ever met."

Coach Wood was delighted that his team rated a special training table in the dining hall. McDaniel said he did not think the food was really any different, though always plentiful and good country fare, but coach Billy "hovered over us as a hen does her chicks."

As to the 1924 football team record, McDaniel summed it up, "We won a few games--in a few we were slaughtered and a few were pretty close."

1924 - 1925 Harrison-Stone Agricultural High School Football Team poses in front of Huff Hall.

First row *(from left) Ferris Batson of Perkinston, unknown, unknown, unknown, J. S. Calhoun of Hattiesburg, unknown, Wendell Callahan of Perkinston, Arthur "Gullet" Gullette of McLaurin, and unknown.* ***Second row*** *(kneeling from left) unknown, unknown, unknown, unknown, Newman "Runt" Warnell of Perkinston, unknown, J. C. "Wagon" Handsborough of McLaurin, unknown, unknown, and Hersel McDaniel of Stillmore.* ***Third row*** *(standing from left) Jessie Cook of Wiggins, unknown, Harold Nelson of Kreole, unknown, unknown, Vernon Brown of Stillmore, James Miller of Piave, unknown, Clyde McDonald of Ten Mile, unknown, and Coach W. H. "Billy" Wood.*

Other members of the team were George Lemon, Mal Ward, Nolan Terry, Breland, and Davis. Photo courtesy of Margurite (Callahan) Boswell, sister of team member Wendell Callahan.

According to the *Daily Herald* on November 22, 1924, coach Wood's boys engaged in at least one slaughter of their own. In that game, played against Brooklyn in Wiggins, the Aggies won 40-0 "before the largest crowd that . . . ever witnessed a game on the Wiggins field." In the game, Arthur "Gullet" Gullette, Captain and halfback of the HSAHS team, made "the most spectacular run ever seen on the Wiggins field." Jesse Cook caught a Brooklyn kick in the second half and handed the ball to Gullette, who made a 95-yard touchdown run.

Because the country schools emphasized basketball, the HSAHS 1924-1925 basketball teams fared well on the court. McDaniel remembered:

The nine members of the 1924-1925 Harrison-Stone Agricultural High School Men's Basketball Team.

First row *(from left) Arthur "Gullett" Gullette of McLaurin, Jessie Cook of Wiggins, Larue "Rooney" Breland of Perkinston, Hersel McDaniel of Stillmore, and Ferris Batson of Perkinston.* ***Second row*** *(from left) Mabry Breland of Wiggins, Walter Allen of Vancleave, Aubrey McIntosh of Wager, Alabama, and Hilton Shirley of Liberty.*

In speaking of this picture, Hersel McDaniel remembered the effect that scarcity of money had on his dress during these hard times. "I have shoes of different kinds, and also there are holes in the toes of each shoe. . . . The suits we wore had been in use several years--faded and not fitting too good." Photo courtesy of Martha Heffner.

"Our basketball court was just an oblong place cleared away and the dirt was packed hard--in fact all the schools in Stone County had dirt courts. Our ball court was just north of the boy's dormitory [Huff Hall]--about fifty feet or so--the spectators were the students--very seldom anyone else--and there was no charge for the game . . . 'cept when we played a city school that had a gym."

McDaniel said basketball was a much rougher game in the 1920s than later, or either the rules were less strict, because almost no one ever fouled out of a game. As he put it, "Those were the days of passing and blocking--days of low scoring games--if a team got as many as 25 or 30 points they were doing good. Very seldom did any player shoot from any further out than the foul line--passing was the creed of the day. A few players developed the shot from the corner crosswise to the hoop or goal as it was called in those days. The overhand shot was also used quite a bit by some of the players."

Coach Wood was in charge of all boys' athletics, and Miss Julia O. "Jo" Sigrest had charge of commercial subjects and girls' athletics. Sometimes Wood and Sigrest sallied forth together with their respective teams for a double-header.

The girl's basketball team by 1924 carried the appellation, "Yellow Jackets." The girls certainly lived up to the tenacious fighting ability of their namesakes. In the game against Ellisville at that town on November 21, 1924, Estelle "Bill" David suffered a broken shoulder and collarbone. In a later brawl with Bay St. Louis, Yellow Jacket Leola O'Neal suffered a badly bruised knee that cost her a week of school.

By February 20, 1925, when the HSAHS teams journeyed to Biloxi by automobile for a double-header against that high school's teams, the Yellow Jackets were undefeated. The Aggies though had won a few and lost a few. Both, however, were victorious in that double-header. The *Daily Herald* coverage of the contest included the statement that the Perkinston teams won "with the aid of their cheer leaders and rooters who accompanied the teams."

On February 25, 1925, the Yellow Jackets lost their first game of the season to Orange Grove. They lost by only two points.

On March 6 and 7, 1925, both the Yellow Jackets and the Aggies returned to Biloxi to compete in the First Annual Tournament of the Mississippi Coast

Photo by Richard Kopp.

Yellow Jackets of 1924-1925

The Harrison-Stone Agricultural High School "Yellow Jackets" with their trophies for the school year 1924-1925. The team won the silver loving cup in the hands of the player at the far right with their victory in the First Annual Tournament of the Mississippi Coast Schoolmasters Club held in Biloxi on March 6-7, 1925. The silver loving cup had vanished, but the silver regulation-size basketball trophy in the hands of the player at the left at the head of the line was in the collection of the MGCCC Archives in 2000. The base is gone and the basketball dented and blackened with age. It reads "Gulf Coast Region Champions, 1924-25, Harrison-Stone Agricultural High School." The account of the March 6-7 tournament stated that the Yellow Jackets would have to play Orange Grove for this trophy "at a date of play to be arranged later." No account of this game had surfaced in 2000, but obviously the Perkinston team won because the trophy is in the picture.

(From left) Beatrice Brown of Barth, Lorraine Casey of Gulfport, Estelle "Bill" David of Perkinston, Emma Clara Deane of McLaurin, Mildred "Dago" Davis of Bond, Irene Flurry of Perkinston, Minnie Lee O'Neal of Wiggins, Lula B. Carmichael of Goss, Leola O'Neal of Saucier, and Coach Julia O. "Jo" Sigrest.
Photograph of the Yellow Jackets from HSAHS and JC Catalogue 1924-1925 folded between pages 16 and 17. Players and coach identified by Margurite (Callahan) Boswell.

Lydean (David) Davis, who later attended Perkinston and played on the basketball team as well, explained in a 1998 interview why a pretty young girl like Estelle was called "Bill." Lydean said it was faddish at the school in the 1920s to call a girl by her father's first name. She did not know if this fad existed nationally or regionally, but it existed locally. Consequently, many girls were addressed by men's names. Sometimes that was all that appeared in print about them and was the only name many of their classmates remembered. In addition, some girls were christened with a name usually given a boy. Conversely, some boys were christened with names usually reserved for girls. Hence, accurate identification of students in photographs of the 1920s era was sometimes difficult or impossible.

Schoolmasters Club (MCSC). The MCSC was an association of superintendents and principals of high schools in the six counties of the Mississippi Panhandle designed to promote athletic, scholastic, and musical competition among the schools. The MCSC tournaments resembled "field day," but the competition was restricted to high school entries. The regional victors could also go up the line to compete for Mississippi state prizes.

The *Daily Herald* report on the tournament recorded a defeat for Wood's Aggies and the following about Sigrest's Yellow Jackets, "The girl cagers representing the Agricultural High School of Perkinston pleased those who witnessed the games as they wore uniforms which gave them the appearances of Scotch lassies, and after defeating Lucedale they battled Pass Christian in the finals by 41-37. This was the hardest fought game of the entire two days play and each side secured the lead during the first and last half." The Yellow Jackets won a silver loving cup for their victory that night. For the Gulf Coast Regional Championship they had to play Orange Grove at a date to be arranged later. The Yellow Jackets won the championship.

Coach Wood's 1924-1925 baseball Aggies started off the season with a victory over Wiggins at Perkinston on April 3, 1925. Then in succession the Aggies defeated Biloxi, Picayune, and Lumberton. On May 18, 1925, the executive committee of the MCSC met in Gulfport and declared the Perkinston Aggies to

Photo by Richard Kopp.

The 1924-1925 Harrison-Stone Agricultural High School "Aggie" Baseball Team *poses on the steps of Huff Hall. On May 18, 1925, the executive committee of the Gulf Coast Schoolmasters' Club named this team, on the basis of its record, as Gulf Coast regional champions. A foot-tall loving cup in the collection of the MGCCC Archives bears this inscription: "Gulf Coast Region Champions, 1925, Harrison-Stone Agricultural High School." No further information is given on the trophy, but by a process of elimination it must be the team's cup. The bulldog in the photograph is "Old Bob" the school's first bulldog mascot.* ***First row*** *(from left) Herbert Easley of Barth, Harold Nelson of Kreole, Morris "Babe" Baker of Ocean Springs, Mal Ward of Lucedale, and Harmon Blaylock of Wiggins.* ***Second row*** *(from left) Manager Kenneth Frater of Gulfport, Sheely Davis of Petal, Hilton Shirley of Liberty, Newman "Runt" Warnell of Perkinston, Jessie Cook of Wiggins, Walter Allen of Vancleave, Arthur "Gullet" Gullette of McLaurin, J. C. "Wagon" Handsborough of McLaurin, Aubrey McIntosh of Wager, Alabama, Larue Breland of Perkinston, and coach W. H. "Billy" Wood.*

be the Gulf Coast Regional Baseball Champions of 1925. The committee members, two of whom were HSAHS Superintendent J. L. Denson and Superintendent of Biloxi City Schools (later president of Perkinston Junior College) A. L. May, gave this award based on the team holding the best record as of May 15. The team thus chosen would represent the region in the state championship meet. McDaniel remembered that state championship game held at Picayune. According to McDaniel, Morris "Babe" Baker was the best pitcher on the Aggie team. Because Baker was the best, he threw until he hurt his arm, and the Aggies lost the game. Baker never pitched again in his school career.

The Picayune coach at the time of that state championship game was William C. "Bill" Denson, brother of J. L. Denson. At the beginning of the next term of the HSAHS, as the junior college was added, J. L. brought W. C. in to replace Coach Wood, relegating Wood to the teaching of history only. McDaniel said that J. L. and coach Wood had been friends for years and that the change was made "without any hard feelings--outwardly anyway." But Coach Wood stayed at Perkinston only one more year.

McDaniel said that the HSAHS played only football, basketball, and baseball in this era. Occasionally a member of one of these teams would participate in track and field events at some field day or other, but track and field was not yet part of the Perkinston athletic program.

McDaniel graduated from the HSAHS in May, 1925. He could not participate in any sports during the 1925-1926 session because there were only ten college students that year, six men and four women. No college team could be made from so small a number, and none of them could play on the HSAHS teams. Other agricultural high schools, like Harrison-Stone, were also adding junior college programs, but there could be no junior college teams until enough junior college students existed to supply the men and women for them. Oddly enough, high school students could play on the junior college teams but not the other way about. Coaches in the position of W. C. Denson had to shepherd their athletic programs through an era of transition to the point they had enough college material to justify the virtual elimination of the AHS teams. In his four-year career at Perkinston, Coach Denson would do just that.

On August 25, 1925, the *Daily Herald* noted that, "A new athletic field consisting of five acres and located on the highway has been purchased by the trustees of the Perkinston Agricultural High School through Superintendent J. L. Denson. Work on putting it in shape for athletic events commenced yesterday morning, the football field being the first matter to receive attention. Fencing material is on the ground and the fence will be put up at once. Football practice will commence on September 7, although the school does not open until September 14."

The problem with terming anything "new" is that at some point it suddenly becomes "old" the moment anything "newer" takes its place. This 1925 athletic field was designated "new" in 1925 to differentiate it from the "old athletic field" located north of Huff Hall. A quarter century later with the construction of A. L. May Memorial Stadium, the "new athletic field" of 1925 suddenly became the "old athletic field," a designation it still bore in 2000. In 2000 it served primarily as a practice field for the Band of Gold. Hereinafter until the building of A. L. May Memorial Stadium, this facility will be termed simply the "Athletic Field" in capital letters since it never bore any other name. The Athletic Field was built where the Magnolia Highway, designated U. S. Highway 49 in fall 1925, curved due south as it exited the west end of Perkinston and crossed Ten Mile Creek. Thus U. S. Highway 49 bordered the Athletic Field on the east, and the railroad bordered it on the north. The southwest boundary of the Athletic Field was Ten Mile Creek. When "new" Highway 49 was completed east of Perkinston in the late 1930s, upkeep on Old Highway 49 at Perkinston virtually ceased. In the 1980s the Old Highway 49 bridge over Ten Mile Creek collapsed. After that the Old Athletic Field became a cul-de-sac.

As the Athletic Field was being built, the AHS lost its first mascot. On Tuesday, September 22, 1925, according to the *Daily Herald*, "Old Bob, the large white bull dog that belonged to the AHS, was killed suddenly Tuesday night by 3 shots which some unknown person fired."

The Aggies played their first game of the 1925-1926 session season on the not yet completed Athletic Field on Friday, September 25, 1925. In that game Varnado (Louisiana) High School beat the Aggies 13-7.

Two weeks later Crab Breland went to Perkinston for a visit and found Superintendent Denson engaged in several projects. One of these projects was "looking after the finishing touches of the new athletic grounds. . . ." In the curve of Highway 49 just opposite the Athletic Field Crab found J. T. Hall in the process of opening a new combination store and "drive-in filling station."

According to McDaniel, a road running just west of Stone Hall went down the hill to join Highway 49 at the bend. The students used this road to get to the Athletic Field. McDaniel was one of a work gang of students who "raided the Ten Mile Mill" for lumber for use at the Athletic Field. The Ten Mile Mill did not operate for several years in this period, and the school used a great deal of wood from the mill. A high board fence was built to block the view from the highway and the railroad so that spectators, for the first time, had to go to a gate and pay admission to the games. McDaniel said the students also secured sufficient lumber to build a "basketball floor" on the athletic field. In his words, "This floor wasn't exactly level and was not covered so when it rained water would stand in spots and the floor would become quite slippery--but it was better than the dirt one we had been using."

Coach Denson fielded two football teams in fall 1925. Both were high school teams, but one was termed "varsity," and the other was the "scrub" or sec-

The 1925-1926 Harrison-Stone-Jackson Agricultural High School "Bulldogs" pose together with the HSJAHS "Bull Pups." The Bulldogs were high school varsity players, and the Bull Pups were the high school second or "scrub" team. The 1925 team was the first to be named for the fierce canine, and the next year the Bulldogs became the Harrison-Stone-Jackson Junior College team.

***First row** (from left) Clyde McDonald of Ten Mile, Sherman Wright of Ocean Springs, Carlton Sparks of McHenry, W. J. Calhoun of Hattiesburg, Newman "Runt" Warnell of Perkinston, and Perry Bond of McHenry. **Second row** (from left) Hilton Shirley of Liberty, William Albert "Bo" Curtis of Hattiesburg, Keith Cox of Howison, J. C. Poole of Gloster, Posey Godard of McHenry, Herbert "Red" Easley of Barth, Lemon Bryant of Collins, Horace Watson of Gautier, and Mabry Breland of Perkinston. **Third row** (from left) Robert "Bob" Carleton of Lucedale, Jessie Cook of Wiggins, Jimmy McManus of Gulfport, Larue Breland of Perkinston, Bill Shattles of Perkinston, coach W. C. "Bill" Denson, Vernon Brown of Stillmore, George Lemon of Ocean Springs, Travis Scoggin of Ellisville, Everett Davis of Escatawpa, and J. C. "Wagon" Hansborough of McLaurin.*

ond-string team. Both the varsity team and second-string team took new names that year. The *Daily Herald* of November 7, 1925, carried an account of play of one of the new teams: "Much credit is due the bull pups of Perkinston because of their victory over the Wiggins eleven. Although the Wiggins team was more successful in line plunges, the Perkinston puppies showed a superiority in their aerial attacks and end runs." The "Bull Pups" won the game 20-0.

The *Hattiesburg American* of November 9, 1925, carried an article describing another game played the same week that the Bull Pups played in Wiggins. In this other game, played on the Athletic Field at Perkinston, "The Perkinston Bull Dogs defeated the Purvis A.H.S. 6 to 0." So both teams played the same week under the new names. The Bulldogs were the varsity players and the following year evolved into the school's first junior college team. Simultaneously the Bull Pups became the high school team.

During the 1925-1926 basketball season the name "Bulldog" achieved currency among *Daily Herald* sports writers who began to use it to describe the Perkinston varsity basketball team. Both the Bulldog roundballers and the Yellow Jackets won the Gulf Coast Championship in 1926.

The 1925-1926 HSJAHS baseball team won five of its first six games but by that time, according to *Daily Herald* article of April 22, 1926, Coach Denson report-

The 1925-1926 Harrison-Stone Agricultural High School Yellow Jackets *won a 10-inch x 8-inch plaque inscribed, "Girl's Basketball, Gulf Coast Champions, 1926."* ***Sitting*** *(from left) Eudora Cox of Gulfport, unknown, Lula B. Carmichael of Goss, and Dorothy Oliver of Moss Point.* ***Kneeling*** *(from left) Neva O'Neal of Perkinston, Lorraine Casey of Gulfport, Ola O'Neal of Perkinston.* ***Standing*** *(from left) Coach Julia O. "Jo" Sigrest, unknown, Minnie Lee O'Neal of Perkinston, Emma Clara Deane of McLaurin, Beatrice "Bee" Brown of Barth, and Mildred "Dago" Davis of Bond. Photo from HSJAHS and JC Catalogue 1925-1926, p. 52.*

The 1925-1926 Harrison Stone Agricultural High School "Aggie" Basketball Team *won a 9-inch tall trophy in the form of a boy holding a basketball. The inscription on the base of the trophy reads "Gulf Coast Champions, 1926."* ***Kneeling*** *(from left) Mal Ward of Lucedale, Hilton Shirley of Liberty, unknown, Everett Davis of Escatawpa, and Carlton Sparks of McHenry.* ***Standing,*** *(from left) Aubrey McIntosh of Wager, Alabama, Jessie Cook of Wiggins, Larue Breland of Perkinston, J. C. Handsborough of McLaurin, Mabry Breland of Wiggins, and Coach W. C. "Bill" Denson.*

ed his team in a badly crippled condition. One had a sprained ankle, one a fractured foot bone, one was in bed with malaria, and Jesse Cook, his best pitcher, was out with a "Cholly hoss."

At the beginning of the 1926-1927 session, the Harrison-Stone-Jackson Agricultural High School and Junior College joined the recently organized Mississippi Association of Junior Colleges (MAJC) and entered upon its career in junior college sports. Throughout the 1926 football season, *Daily Herald* reporters alternated between calling the varsity team "Aggies" and "Bulldogs" but left no doubt as to the standing of the team. On October 27 a reporter stated, "Perkinston played in the high [school] class last year, but is now considered a junior college." On October 29 a reporter noted that, "Perkinston . . . frequently steps out of its class as a junior college and trades wallops with college outfits . . . [such as] . . . Mississippi State Normal." And on November 6 a *Daily Herald* reporter made it crystal clear, "This was Perkinston's first year in the junior college conference having heretofore been rated as a preparatory school."

The 1926 high school football team was styled "Bull Pups," but all but two of ten known Bull Pups showed up also in the Bulldogs' listings. Of these eight crossovers all but one were listed as "substitutes" on the Bulldog roster. Hersel McDaniel appeared as a substitute Bulldog, too, but he did not appear on the Bull Pup list because he was a junior college sophomore that year. Newman Warnell, who was the Bull Pup quarterback, was a Bulldog second stringer. Coach Denson raised Bulldogs from Bull Pups.

On Friday, September 24, 1926, the HSJAHS & JC Bulldogs played the Perkinston institution's first college game. In the game, played on the Athletic Field, the Bulldogs defeated the Mississippi Industrial Institute of Columbia by a score of 32-9.

In the next game of that initial college season, the Bulldogs set a school record for scoring that still stood in 2000 by destroying Chamberlain-Hunt Military Academy of Port Gibson 69-0. Following that victory the Bulldogs posted a win, two losses, and a tie. Then, the Bulldogs went up against the Pearl River Junior College Aggies for the first time in junior college history. In time the Poplarville team would be known as "Wildcats," but in 1926, like many other teams from an agricultural school, it bore the almost generic designation "Aggies."

This first Perkinston-Poplarville college football clash took place on November 5, 1926, at the Gulfport Fairgrounds. A. G. Johnson, Secretary of the Gulfport Fair, prevailed on Superintendent Denson to hold the contest at the fair in order to boost attendance. Johnson laid out a new 100-yard gridiron on the fair field just for the occasion. According to the *Daily Herald* of November 6, "It was a hard fought game that handicapped the players on the new gridiron that was left soft from the plow. And the two junior colleges plowed through the soft ground for the victor of the game that would declare them the champions of the Mississippi Junior colleges." (One wonders how this

The 1926-1927 Yellow Jackets pose beside Bennett Annex. *The women wear jerseys with a stylized AHS in a circle and the basketball carries the legend AHS as well. But Irene Flurry (back row, second from left) was a college student and the team captain that year. Bill David (second row, third from left) was a college student, but Lydean (David) Davis (front row, left) was a high school student. Since high school students could play on college teams but not vice versa, then this team must be the first women's basketball team to compete on the college level. By the next season the women wore jerseys carrying the legend "Perkinston." The woman standing (top row, far right) is Coach Frances Rednick.*

The 1926-1927 Harrison-Stone-Jackson Junior College Men's Basketball Team *lost the Mississippi junior college championship to Pearl River.* ***First row*** *(from left) Carlton Sparks of McHenry, Don Newcomb of Ocean Springs, unknown.* ***Second row*** *(from left) Everett Davis of Escatawpa, Grant Eighmy of Wiggins, Hersel McDaniel of Stillmore, and unknown.* ***Third row*** *(from left) Coach W. C. "Bill" Denson, Mabry Breland of Perkinston, Jimmy McManus of Gulfport, and Vernon Brown of Stillmore.*

could be the junior college championship game when Perkinston still had two conference games on line after it, but maybe the others had lost more than either Perkinston or Poplarville.)

In coverage of the game the *Daily Herald* reporter noted that:

"Squabbles and arguments about penalties that resulted in the referee pulling out his rule book and convincing the Poplarville captain that he was not trying to rob him, made the game tiresome in the last quarter. . . . Poplarville was penalized 15 yards at one time for their coach coming out on the gridiron without permission. Outside of the arguments and the dull moments that it caused the game was hard fought and interesting. Poplarville won the 'titular game' by a score of 6-0."

On November 13, the Bulldogs lost to Clarke Junior College 17-0. The season ended on November 19 with a 6-0 Bulldog win over Hinds County Junior college. Perkinston finished the first junior college football season with four wins, four losses and one tie.

In men's basketball action in the 1926-1927 session, Poplarville defeated Perkinston for the state title. In the state tournament held at the Mississippi College gymnasium in Clinton, the *Stone County Enterprise* of March 3, 1927, reported a 20-18 defeat for the Bulldogs. Poplarville made the winning goal two minutes before the end of the game. Hersel McDaniel played for his alma mater for the last time in this contest.

In the realm of women's basketball, the Yellow Jackets apparently began junior college competition in the 1926-1927 session. Miss Frances Rednick, a commercial subjects teacher from Alice, Texas, had charge of girl's athletics that year. According to the *Stone County Enterprise* of March 17, 1927, Yellow Jacket Captain Irene Flurry spoke at the athletic banquet in the dining hall regarding the team's record, but the paper neglected to publish what she said. But Irene Flurry was a college student, so her presence on the team indicates collegiate participation. The girls' HSJAHS basketball team definitely continued to function for at least another year, so the women's college and the girl's high school teams co-existed, as did two teams in other sports at the school.

On March 21, 1927, the *Stone County Enterprise* reported that Hubert "Red" Easley had been named captain of the 1927 Bulldog baseball squad. The south Mississippi newspapers failed to record the scores of the games of the 1927 baseball team, but the team was slated to play Clarke and Raymond, both junior colleges.

Sufficient evidence exists to state unequivocally that in the session 1926-1927, Coach Denson carried football, men's basketball, and baseball across the line from high school to junior college competition. In addition, he retained the high school football and basketball teams in order to train players for the college teams. His female counterpart, Miss Rednick, apparently carried the women's basketball team to college competition under their former name, "Yellow Jackets." In addition to basketball, baseball, and football, which crossed the line from high school to college competition, new sports debuted in the Denson era. The principal new sports were tennis and track.

Together, Coaches Denson and Rednick inaugurated men's and women's tennis as a competitive sport in spring 1927. At the MAJC State Field Meet at Raymond on April 15, 1927, the Perkinston men's and women's tennis teams took second place. Dan Newcomb and Sherman Wright formed the men's team, and Mildred Davis and Lillian Tucker made up the women's team. Apparently these two doubles teams competed only at the day-long Field Meet. The time of the "tennis season" culminating in a state championship tournament was still in the future.

As in the case of tennis, Perk's junior college track

and field competition began at the 1927 State Field Meet. Both the Perk men and women won or placed at Raymond that day. Also, as in the case with tennis, several years passed before the inauguration of a regular track and field season.

At the beginning of the 1927-1928 session, Coach Denson set in motion the machinery that would, in time, result in a competitive track team for the college. Beginning in fall 1927 the school instituted gym classes for all students for the first time. This can be stated without equivocation because the school did not have a gym before the opening of this session.

The new brick veneered gym, ready for use as the session opened, was the first structure of its kind in the south Mississippi piney woods. Naturally it became known as the "gym" until the construction of a newer gym in 1957. The newer gym was christened Wentzell Center in May 1960, but in 2000 it was most often simply referred to as "the gym" and the 1927 structure as the "Old Gym." Hereinafter the 1927 gym will be referred to as the Old Gym in capital letters.

In regard to the beginning of gym classes in 1927, Coach Denson was reported in the *Daily Herald* of

The Catalogue of 1927-1928, p. 19, described the Old Gym in these words, "This gymnasium has in it a basketball court, dressing room with showers for visiting teams, seating capacity for 800, office and store room." This photograph shows the Harrison-Stone-Jackson Agricultural High School girls on the floor of the Old Gym in October 1927, one month after it began service. The girls are wearing bloomers and jerseys marked with a stylized AHS in a circle. All of them sport the controversial boyish "bobbed" hairstyle of the time. Coach Noby Ruth (Denson) Houston is at the far left. The Old Gym in 2000 still served the campus as a center for myriad activities but especially as a site for intramural sports. Photo courtesy of Dixie Press of Gulfport.

(Left) On March 15-16, 1929, the Old Gym served as the site of the Mississippi State Junior College Basketball Tournament. No other tournament of this magnitude occurred again in the Old Gym. By the time Perkinston was once more accorded the honors of host in 1962, the Wentzell Center had been built. Photo from 1927-1928 Catalog, p. 19.

(Below) ***The 1927-1928 Yellow Jackets Junior College Team*** *stands in front of Huff Hall in October 1927 with their coach (far right) Noby Ruth (Denson) Houston. The coach wears bloomers but the team members wear shorts. Photo courtesy of Dixie Press of Gulfport.*

October 22, 1927, as intending "to pick most of his track men from the gym classes." Thus the Old Gym provided the training facility for Perk's initial track program.

The biggest sports story of fall 1927 was the state championship won by the Bulldog footballers. The season opened on October 1, with a nothing to nothing tie with Mississippi State Teachers College of Hattiesburg. In the second game on October 8, the first conference tilt of the season, the Bulldogs faced the Goodman's Aggies. This game, played in a blinding rainstorm at Perkinston, resulted in a 31-0 victory for the Bulldogs. On October 17 in a non-conference conflict, the Bulldogs beat the Mississippi College Freshmen 31-7. On October 29, non-conference St. Stanislaus of Bay St. Louis, fell 13 to 6.

Then on November 5, 1927, Poplarville came to call in a conference game on the Athletic Field. The game was unusual, regrettably not because Perkinston lost it 13-0, but because the *Daily Herald* report on the game carried an account of bands being present:

"The faculty and students stood on the sidelines as close to the team as they could get, and showed their feelings by the noise they made. Although the band had no place to sit, the members did their best to help win the game. If you are one of those two people who missed the game, just look at the swollen and blistered lips of the band members and you will not doubt their whole-hearted support. The opponents, also, had their entire student body and band."

On November 12, the Bulldogs engaged in a brutal 6-6-conference standoff with Clarke Junior College of Newton. One week later the Bulldogs clinched the 1927 Mississippi State Football Championship in a 25-0 victory over Raymond.

In basketball action in the 1927-1928 year, both the Bulldogs and the Yellow Jackets made it to the state tournament in Clinton. The Clarke Junior College

Photo by Richard Kopp.

The 1927 Harrison-Stone-Jackson Junior College State Championship Football Team.
First row *(from left) Dewitt Byrd of Wiggins, Newman Bradley "Runt" Warnell of Perkinston, Stanford O. "Cotton" Carraway of Gulfport, Dan Newcomb of Biloxi, Albert I. "Rex" Rexinger of Eudora, Arkansas, Everett Davis of Escatawpa, Jewel Holcomb of Nicholson, W. W. Mills of Richton, and George Benton of Ocean Springs.*
Second row *(from left) Kenneth Frater (Manager) of Gulfport, Jimmy McManus of Gulfport, Harold Nelson of Kreole, William "Bill" Parker of Lyman, Sherman Wright of Ocean Springs, Lowell M. "Sam" Lott of Bond, Vernon Brown of Stillmore, William "Bud" Parr of Eudora, Arkansas, James Miller of Piave, Nathan Dunham of Neeley, and coach W. C. "Bill" Denson. The 1927 Bulldog football team won Perkinston's first college state trophy. The team's record was four wins, one loss, and two ties. Unfortunately the football-shaped silver trophy, which is in the collection of the MGCCC Archives, bears the date 1928. This is obviously incorrect since the team record for 1928 stood at one win, seven losses, and one tie. Photo courtesy Albert I. "Rex" Rexinger who got it from Mrs. S. O. "Cotton" Carraway. The original photo was taken in late October 1927 by photographer Pruitt of the Universal Photo Service of Gulfport for inclusion on page 37 of the Catalogue of 1927-1928 published by the Dixie Press in summer 1928.*
(Left) The regulation-size silver-plated football affixed to a 5 1/2 inch diameter Bakelite base reads "Mississippi Junior College Champions, 1928." The date is in error. It should read "1927."

(Left) MGCJC President J. J. Hayden shakes hands with former 1927 state championship football player Albert Isaac Rexinger on homecoming day, November 5, 1977, in Heidelberg Hall on the Perkinston Campus during the golden anniversary celebration of the team's victory. The 1927 championship was the college's first state championship of any kind. Rexinger, who had served as head coach at Perkinston from 1937 to 1942, was then the owner of a sporting goods store in Natchez.

Record

Perkinston	0-	Miss. State Teachers	0
"	31-	Goodman Jr. College	0
"	31-	Miss. College Fresh.	7
"	13-	St. Stanislaus	6
"	0 -	Poplarville Jr. College	13
"	6 -	Clark College	6
"	25-	Raymond Jr. College	0
	106	Total	32

(Above) On April 25, 1977 Rexinger typed the scores of the 1927 team and mailed them in a letter to the college alumni secretary. His record of the score of the November 19, 1927, victory over Hinds Junior College (Raymond) was the only such record known to exist by the college archivist in 2000. In summer 1977, Rexinger became one of the first men to be inducted in the Mississippi Coaches Hall of Fame. He died May 30, 1990.

Panthers knocked the Bulldogs out of the semi-finals competition by a score of 57-39 on March 2, 1928. The Yellow Jackets faced Hinds in the finals for the state championship on March 3 and lost 63-24. Whether or not a trophy was given for the Yellow Jackets' second-place finish was not addressed in accounts of the tournament.

The names of the eight colleges that played in the state basketball championship tournament at Clinton were published by the college name and by town. Prior to this time the newspapers tended to give only the name of the town. The contenders were:

Leake County Junior College of Carthage
Sunflower County Junior College of Moorhead
Pearl River County Junior College of Poplarville
Tate County Junior College of Senatobia
Jones County Junior College of Ellisville
Hinds County Junior College of Raymond
Clarke Junior College of Newton
Harrison-Stone-Jackson Junior College of Perkinston

This last was the only triple-county college at the time, and apparently Copiah-Lincoln Junior college at Wesson, the only double-county junior college of the day, did not have a very good basketball team in 1928 since it is not on the list.

On March 7, 1928, the Harrison-Stone-Jackson AHS and JC hosted a tournament of its own--the Stone County Elementary School Basketball Tournament. It must have been quite a thrill for the youngsters to come and play at the Old Gym. Denson gave a trophy to the victorious school--Magnolia Elementary. In presenting the trophy, he spoke to the children on the origin of sporting contests in the western world. He compared their tiny tournament with the Olympic Games of Ancient Greece, citing Magnolia as the victorious city-state. Then he told the children to take pride in their schools but to remember that they were part of a greater community--the nation. He reminded the children that even though the Greeks lived in their city-states, they also felt allegiance to the concept of Hellas (all Greece), and that spirit resulted in the celebrated and fabulous sacrifice of the 300 Spartans at Thermopylae. According to the account in the *Stone County Enterprise* of March 22, Denson ended his lesson to those assembled with these words:

> "So if the horizon of our girls and boys is to be broadened, if their love is to radiate beyond the boundary of the immediate communities, if their interest is to be nation-wide and world-wide, we must give them training along the lines that will bring about this desired result."

The children may not have remembered Denson's speech, but they never forgot that they went "to the college" to play in a tournament and that he spoke to them. Such activities have been a part of the Perkinston institution from its inception, but the "tiny tournament of 1928" is one of the best-recorded examples of this type of community service.

Again in 1928 south Mississippi newspapers failed to publish a record of the Bulldog baseball season, but the *Stone County Enterprise* recorded an incident that occurred on the outskirts of Laurel in mid-May. Harmon Blaylock of Wiggins was at the wheel of his father's Ford sedan, driving the Bulldog baseball team back to Perkinston after a game, when an elderly lady walked out into the road in front of his car. When the dust settled, the car full of Bulldogs lay in the ditch with "a smashed wheel and a bursted in top." The elderly lady lay in the road. The Jones County sheriff, believing the woman to be dead, arrested Blaylock and all the other Bulldogs. But when medical personnel finally examined the woman, it was found that she had only fainted, her sole injury being a bump on the head from falling in the road. Blaylock's fast reactions, honed on the diamond, had paid off on the straight-a-way, and likely his father did not mind the damage to the car considering the alternative.

The Perkinston football Bulldogs began the 1928 season as the defending state champions. Many of the stars of 1927 such as Lowell M. "Sam" Lott, then team captain, and Albert I. Rexinger, alternate captain, were back. It looked like another halcyon year. It did not turn out that way.

The *Daily Herald* reported that the preparations for the coming grid season had begun on September 26, 1928:

"At a tryout 'pep' meeting in chapel Monday morning three cheer leaders were elected by the student body. Those elected were: Grace Perry of Gulfport, Sally Merle Lincoln of Bogalusa, and Francis "Red" Meeks of Macon. 'Red' was cheer leader last year and with two able co-workers the Bull Dogs and Pups are assured of plenty of support."

So it is certain that Perkinston fielded at least one bona fide cheerleader in the person of "Red" Meeks in 1927. It is also evident that the same cheerleader or cheerleaders rooted for both the high school and the college teams.

In this same article Coach Denson said he had "only a limited amount of high school material" from which to select. This showed in his first outing on Monday, October 1, when the Gulfport High Tigers clawed his Bull Pups 50-0. This proved to be a harbinger of things to come.

The Bulldogs sallied forth in their first game of the season on Friday, October 5, and lost 12-2 to State Teachers College. On October 13, the Copiah-Lincoln Wolves delivered an 18-0 defeat.

One week later the Bulldogs beat Leake County Junior College of Carthage 6-0. Things were looking up.

On October 27, Clarke Junior College jolted the Bulldogs with a 37-0 defeat. A week later the Bulldogs held the Millsaps College Freshmen to a 13-13 tie. Six days later Holmes County Junior college put them in the loser's column again 12-0.

Then on Monday, November 12, 1928, the Bulldogs journeyed to Selma, Alabama, to take on the Cadets of the Marion Institute. In Selma that night the Cadets set a Perk single-game loss record that still stood in 2000. The Cadets shattered the Bulldogs with a defeat that turned into a rout of sublime proportions. At game's end the score stood 97-0. This score included 15 touchdowns and seven extra points.

Four days later Pearl River Junior College, now styling its team as the "Wildcats" came to Perkinston for the annual clash. Two hundred supporters and a 60-piece band accompanied the invaders. The Pearl River coach on the eve of that contest had boasted that no junior college in the history of his institution had defeated his team and that Perkinston in particular had never even crossed the Pearl River goal line. That was true. Perkinston had lost to Pearl River 6-0 in 1926 and 13-0 in 1927.

The *Daily Herald* account of the contest reported the "bleachers" nearly filled. That was the first mention of such niceties at the Athletic Field. So at last the Perkinston Band-Orchestra had a place to sit and so did everyone else. The whole Perkinston student body was reported in attendance. When the smoke cleared on this game, the Pearl River coach could still claim to be undefeated in junior college play, but Perkinston had violated his goal line. The final score stood at 7-6.

A loss to Hinds on November 14 at last brought that disastrous 1928 football season to a close. The overall statistics for the Bulldogs were one win, seven losses, and one tie. The 1928 team had scored a total of 27 points while giving up a colossal 202.

During the 1928-1929 basketball season the school fielded a men's and a women's college team and a boy's high school team. No mention was made in the surviving records of a girl's high school team. The *Daily Herald* that year referred to the women's college team as the "Perkinston girls" and not as the Yellow Jackets, so apparently, that designation had fallen into disuse.

The Perkinston girls and the Bulldog basketeers did very well in the 1928-1929 season--so well that the school was accorded a signal honor. Previously the state junior college tournament had been held in the Mississippi College gymnasium at Clinton. The *Daily Herald* of Thursday, March 14, 1929, stated:

"The stage is all set for the Mississippi Junior College basketball tournament, which will be played on the local floor tomorrow, and Saturday. This will be the first time that the championship play-off has been staged in a junior college gym and the officials of the local institution announced that they are sure that the tournament will go over with a success."

As the teams converged on Perkinston for the 1929 state basketball tournament, heavy spring rains blanketed the Deep South. Matches had to be rescheduled due to teams being delayed by washed out roads. In addition to the state basketball championship, the state volleyball title was also to be decided at Perkinston. Hinds County Junior College defeated all comers, including Perkinston's men's and women's teams, to take both volleyball titles.

On March 16, 1929, in the Old Gym, the Jones Junior College team eliminated the Bulldogs in the first game of the semi-finals with a score of 47-45. Pearl River won the men's state basketball championship. That same day the Copiah-Lincoln women's basketball team took the state basketball championship by defeating the Perkinston women 44-31.

Apparently after 1929 the state tournament traveled on a round-robin basis among the contenders for the state title. In order to be selected as the site of the tournament, a school's team had to be a contender, so Perkinston did not host the state tournament again until 1962, the second season of legendary coach Bob Weathers.

The 1929 Bulldog baseball team lost only three games that season and made it to the state championship finals. In the championship action Moorhead claimed the title.

Both Superintendent J. L. Denson and his brother, coach W. C. "Bill" Denson, resigned in September 1929. Coach Denson then went to Ellisville to become the assistant coach at Jones County Junior College.

Head coach Bill Denson presided over the transition of the institution's sports program from high school to junior college contention. During his four-year tenure, teams of both sexes in both arenas garnered trophies on both levels. On his watch, two important auxiliaries to the school's sport scene were added--namely cheerleaders and the band-orchestra. His contributions and those of the several women coaches who worked with him were vital in the sports history of the Perkinston institution. They sailed uncharted waters and they did it very well. They set the stage for all the coaches who came after them.

***The 1929 Harrison-Stone-Jackson Junior College Women's Second Place State Championship Team** poses with the team coach and referee. From left, Coach Noby Ruth (Denson) Houston, Marie "Jack" Fiveash of Mclaurin, Lydean (David) Davis of Perkinston, Irma Read of Biloxi, Grace Shattles of Perkinston, Delia Kerr of Long Beach, Clesta Newcomb of Ocean Springs, Ted Black, and Albert Isaac "Rex" Rexinger of Eudora, Arkansas. Rexinger, who graduated from the junior college on May 29, 1929, often served as a referee in basketball games, and he may have been serving as a manager or an assistant to Noby Ruth Denson. Photo courtesy of Lydean (David) Davis.*

This 8-inch tall trophy reads "Mississippi Junior College Second Place, 1929." This trophy is the earliest Mississippi Junior College Association women's trophy in the collection of the MGCCC Archives in 2000 and the highest award taken on the court by a Perkinston women's team for 48 years following 1929.

Photo by Richard Kopp.

BASEBALL
1929 - 1962

The college won two state baseball championships in the 1930s. These came in succession in 1931 and 1932 and are credited to Coach Lee Roy Weeks and his assistant coach, G. E. Gully.

The Bulldogs opened the 1931 season on March 21 at Perkinston with a 9-8 victory over the Jones County Aggies. On April 18, with ten straight victories to their credit, the Bulldogs faced Jones once again, this time at Ellisville, and lost 7-6. This loss tied the two schools in the race for the south division title. But a loss by Jones to East Mississippi three days later gave Perkinston the edge in the south and assured the Bulldogs a berth in the state title match.

Perkinston took the field against Northwest, the northern division champions, at Moorhead on Friday, April 24. Joe B. Denson drew first blood in the second inning on a single from Leemon Baird. At game's end Perkinston had sent the Senatobia boys down to a 5-3 defeat.

On May 22 at the annual athletic banquet, Superintendent Cooper J. Darby praised the champions for their 11-1 overall (9-1 conference) season. Each member of the championship team was presented with a small silver baseball as a memento of the grand occasion. Before adjourning, the team elected Leemon Baird as the captain for the coming season.

By mid-April 1932, the Bulldogs had won five conference games and lost one. The loss to Copiah-Lincoln placed them in a situation where only a double victory over undefeated East Central would gain them a slot in the 1932 State championship game.

Originally the two games were to be played on April 13 and 14, but term examinations at both schools forced a rescheduling of the contests. The two teams met in a double-header at 1:30 p.m. on Friday, April 15 at Perkinston.

The Bulldogs won the first game by a score of 5-4. In the second game Decatur had Perkinston down 5-4 in the top of the sixth inning with the Bulldogs at bat as the light faded. At that critical moment Obie Brown slammed a line drive into centerfield that turned into a home run when the Decatur player muffed the catch. Brown made the circuit, bringing home two other Bulldogs who were on base to rack up a 7-5 victory when the officials called the game on account of darkness. Brown's home run garnered the south division title for his alma mater.

It was Bulldog against Bulldog at Ellisville on April 23 as Perkinston took on the Holmes County Bulldogs for the state championship. Pitcher "Smoky Joe" Denson, making his last stand in a five-year athletic career at Perkinston, held the opposing canines scoreless for seven innings. Meanwhile his team racked up the points. At game's end the score stood at 9-1, bringing Perkinston its second successive state championship.

Once again Superintendent Darby doled out tiny silver baseballs to the victorious team members at the athletic banquet held that year on May 13. Merrill "Red" True, a recipient of one of these miniature trophies, remembering that moment in 1998, said, "We were really surprised to get those little silver baseballs because Mr. Darby didn't spend money for anything he didn't have to. That he gave us anything at all showed how proud he was of us."

The 1931 Harrison-Stone-Jackson Junior College Baseball team displays its trophy on the Old Athletic Field. *No baseball trophies of the Darby Era were held in the MGCCC Archives collection in 2000.* ***Front row*** *(from left) Bill Dietrich(?) of Pensacola, Florida, James Obie Brown of Big Level, O. V. Lee of Lyman, Bernard VanCourt of Ocean Springs, Pat Harrison Morris of Sanford, Columbus "Hinky" Hines of Kentucky, and Leemon Baird of Paris, Tennessee.* ***Back row*** *(from left),Coach Lee Roy Weeks, Paul Bonner of Pensacola, Florida,Unknown, Ford Johnson of Moss Point, Hammond "Tom" Davis of Wiggins, Joe B. Denson of Bay Springs, Newman "Runt" Warnell of Perkinston, and Bob "Cooney" Barnes of Hattiesburg.*

The 1932 Harrison-Stone-Jackson Junior College Baseball Championship team wears football jerseys because the school could not afford baseball uniforms. *According to Merrill "Red" True the Old Athletic Field did double duty, too. After football season the "grid iron" was changed into a "diamond" with home plate located at the corner formed by Old Highway 49 and the railroad. Home-run balls occasionally wound up in Ten-Mile Creek which flowed through the woods behind the team.*
Front row *(from left) Townsend "Skipper" Gifford of Tela, Honduras, Walter "Runt" Alexander of Moss Point, Keble Ramsay of Vancleave, Willie Rogers of Perkinston, Albert McDonald of Perkinston (Captain), Pat Harrison Morris of Sanford, Unknown, Merrill "Red" True of Mississippi City, Archie Porter (?) of Wiggins, and Frank Doubleday of Tela, Honduras.* ***Back row*** *(from left) Coach Lee Roy Weeks, Paul Bonner of Pensacola, Florida, Joe B. Denson of Bay Springs, Leemon Baird of Paris, Tennessee, O. V. Lee of Lyman, James Obie Brown of Big Level, Alexander Roy of Handsboro, Ford Johnson of Moss Point, Hammond "Tom" Davis of Wiggins, and manager Cooper Roberts of Moss Point.*

While the Perkinston Bulldogs won no more state championships prior to World War II, they did take the south division crown in 1934, 1936, and 1937. In each of those years Perkinston lost the championship match to Sunflower Junior College.

The Mississippi Junior College Association suspended baseball from spring 1942 through spring 1945 due to the war emergency. The Bulldog baseball team did play in spring 1946 but apparently only against Coast independent teams. In spring 1947 the Mississippi Junior College league resumed full regular play with a north division, a south division, and a championship playoff.

Coach James D. Stonestreet, a three-year veteran of World War II, led his Bulldogs through a string of baseball victories reminiscent of those of Perk teams of the early 1930s. On May 6, 1947, the Bulldogs riding a seven win and one tie streak defeated the Southwest Junior College Pilots 4-2 at Perk to take south division honors.

On May 13 the Northwest Junior College Rangers, champions of the north division, arrived at Perkinston and thrashed the Bulldogs 6 to 1 in the opening battle for the state crown. The next day, Stonestreet, knowing the Bulldogs had to win both games, threw in ace pitcher Bill Davis of Pensacola, Florida. Davis earned that day the sobriquet "iron man" by hurling both games defeating the Rangers 12-1 in the afternoon and 6 to 1 that night. State Junior College commissioner B. L. Hill presented the 1947 state baseball junior college championship trophy (the first awarded in Mississippi since 1941) to Davis at the end of the double header.

Stonestreet left Perk at the end of the season, and Marvin "Red" Campbell took over as baseball mentor. Only three veterans of the 1947 state championship team returned, but one of them was Bill "Sweet William" Davis. On May 1, 1948, when he burned 11 Wesson Wolves to take the south division crown, Davis earned yet another nickname--"Fireball."

On May 13, the bulldogs journeyed to Senatobia to battle, for the second year in a row, the Northwest Rangers for the state championship. The Bulldogs led in the scoring throughout the first game until the Rangers tied the game 2-2 in the ninth inning. According to the *Bulldog Barks*, May 19, 1948, "a free for all started between the two teams in the [ninth] inning after one of the Senatobia players jumped the umpire because he was called out at home. The spectators came onto the diamond to participate."

Northwest scored in the tenth inning to win the first game. The next day, despite Davis being on the mound all nine innings, Senatobia won again 6-2, dashing Perkinston's hopes of back to back state championships.

1946-1947 Mississippi Junior College Baseball Champs.
First row *(from left, sitting) William Saucier of Saucier, Gerald Ball of Saucier, John Pitalo of Biloxi, and Charles G. Cain of Pensacola, Florida.* ***Second row*** *(from left, kneeling) Claude Locklin of Milton, Florida, Jack Williams of Bond, Unknown, Edwin W. Simpson of Pensacola, Florida, William Elvin "Bill" Davis of Pensacola, Florida, and J. C. McGuire of Saucier.* ***Third row*** *(standing, from left) Claude Lester Stauter of Moss Point, Robert Mohler of Ocean Springs, James L. Caldwell of Como, Bobby Goff of McLain, Daniel Frank Maras of Kincaid, Illinois, E. J. Madden of Wiggins, James Atkinson of Memphis, Tennessee, and Coach James D. Stonestreet of Perkinston. Other men on this team were: Marvin Clem of Athens, Alabama and, (?) Ladner. 1947 team members identified by Bill Davis. Photo courtesy of Bill Davis.*

The state championship baseball pitchers of 1947 *(from left) Bobby Goff, Bill Davis, Charles Cain, and John Pitalo. Photo courtesy of Bill Davis.*

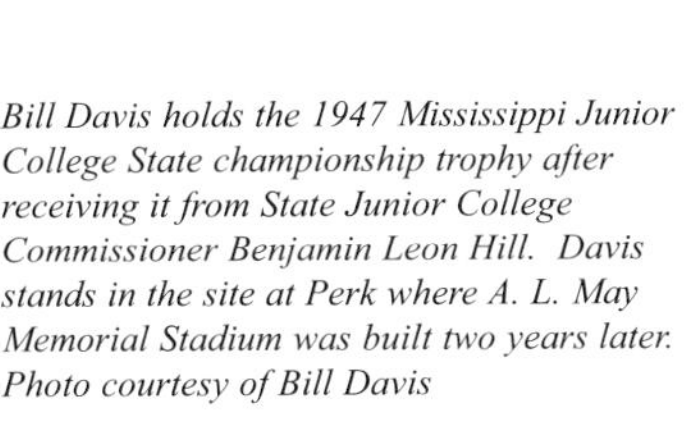

Bill Davis holds the 1947 Mississippi Junior College State championship trophy after receiving it from State Junior College Commissioner Benjamin Leon Hill. Davis stands in the site at Perk where A. L. May Memorial Stadium was built two years later. Photo courtesy of Bill Davis

The 1957 Mississippi junior college state baseball champions sit in A. L. May Memorial Stadium.
***First row** (from left) Mickey Davenport of Pascagoula, Orville Pugh of Milton, Florida, Joe Pinson of Lyman, Rodney Miles of Moss Point, Jay Pinson of Lyman, Larry Brannam of Moss Point, and Ray Moncrief of Pascagoula. **Second row** (from left) Coach Mel Carpenter, Vernon Ehlers of Moss Point, Joe McAnulty of Albermarle, North Carolina, Bill Smith of Mobile, Jerry Sharp of Brooklyn, Joe Gill of Biloxi, Nelson Morgan of Biloxi, and Leroy Wescovich of Pass Christian. Photo courtesy of team Coach Melvin Carpenter.*

Perk's diamond performance in the early 1950s was unexceptional. The only bright spot was Perk's claim to the south division title of 1953 on the basis of an 8-2 record. For some reason no south division or state playoffs were held in 1953 or in 1954. When that situation began or when it ended was not known to this author, but the playoff system was back by 1957.

On April 26, 1957, Coach Melvin Carpenter's Bulldog baseball team faced the Hinds Eagles on the Perkinston diamond for the south division championship. Hinds, which had earlier in the season handed the Bulldogs their only conference defeat, wrested the south division title from the Bulldogs by beating them 3-1. Hinds then prepared to meet north division Itawamba for the state crown.

Then came the stunning announcement that Hinds would not be participating in the state championship playoff. According to the May 8, 1957, Meridian Star, Hinds Junior College President George McLendon said that his school was withdrawing because the Hinds players had "missed too many classes already." McLendon then denied allegations that Hinds had been eliminated from the competition because the team had fielded a professional player. In any case, the Perkinston team, as second in south division, came back alive to defeat the Itawamba Indians and take the 1957 state baseball championship by a score of 9 to 7 at Aberdeen on May 4.

Coach Mel Carpenter contacted at his home in Ocala, Florida, 43 years later said, "We were declared south division champs in 1957 because Hinds was disqualified on the basis of fielding an ineligible player. We took the state title by defeating Itawamba."

The Bulldogs roared out the starting gate in 1958 racking up 14 straight victories, including two victories over Hinds, to take the south division title. When the Bulldogs faced 8-2 East Mississippi at Scooba on May 10, the game seemed a foregone conclusion. But the Lions tallied four runs in the second inning, and Perk made one run in the ninth and lost.

In 1959 the Bulldogs posted a 10-1 record, and for the third year in a row, took the south division title. Once again East Mississippi posted an 8-2 record to take the north division honors, which led to another shootout with Perk for the state crown. In the championship game, played at Perkinston on May 7, 1959, the Lions tallied two runs in the first inning and two in the third, holding the Bulldogs to a lone run in the ninth. As the year before, Scooba defeated Perk 4-1 for the state title.

In 1960 only two south division public junior colleges fielded teams--Perkinston and Southwest. According to Carpenter this situation came about because "the other junior colleges in the south said, 'Perk is going to always beat us so why should we play?' You know just in my time at Perk we sent six or seven players to professional teams."

Perk easily took the south division crown in 1960, and for the third year in a row prepared to fight the Scooba Lions for the state title. But it was not to be. Torrential rains in the Scooba area on the May 4, 1960, game date resulted in cancellation of the contest. In Carpenter's words, "Because we couldn't play the game, the state officials declared Perk and

Scooba co-champions in 1960."

In spring 1961, only Perkinston offered to field a baseball team in the south division. The April 12, 1961, *Bulldog Barks* quoted head Coach Harold White as saying, "We are more than willing to have a team in baseball, but without a schedule it is not practical." No south division junior college fielded a team in spring 1961 or in spring 1962. In spring 1963 Kenneth "Curly" Farris began the resurrection of baseball in the south division.

1959 south division baseball champions pose by the scoreboard on the Old Athletic Field.
First row *(from left) Jack Fleming of Metairie, Louisiana, Lavon Nettles of Gulfport, Vernon Ehlers of Moss Point, George Dewey of Gulfport, John Wells of Lucedale, and Richard Kennedy of New Orleans, Louisiana.* ***Second row*** *(from left) Charles "Poncho" Tillman of Moss Point, Morris Powell of New Orleans, Louisiana, Terry Broadus of Saucier, Gayle Thomas of Moss Point, Bill Koski of Moss Point, Joe Cherry of Ocean Springs, and William James Jussely of Brooklyn. Photo courtesy of Melvin Carpenter.*

1960 State Co-Champions Baseball Team pose on Old Athletic Field.
First row *(from left, kneeling) Charles Purvis of Long Beach, John Wells of Lucedale, Paul Babuchna of Biloxi, Cunningham W. McGrath of Pascagoula, Bert Dale of Wiggins, Roy Baker of Gulfport, and Charles T. Prevost of Moss Point.* ***Second row*** *(from left, standing) James W. Clark of Gulfport, Jimmy Causey of Florida, Alabama, Joe Cherry of Ocean Springs, Morris Powell of New Orleans, Louisiana,Gayle Thomas of Moss Point, and Roger Benton of Dothan, Alabama. Photo courtesy of Melvin Carpenter.*

Baseball 1962 - 2000

THE FARRIS DYNASTY

Kenneth Callie "Curly" Farris was born July 1, 1927, in Michie, Tennessee, the son of Henry Clay and Pettie (Flanigan) Farris. He and his two brothers, Vernon and Bill, lived on a farm with their parents until Curly was age seven, at which time the family moved to Corinth. At Corinth High School he lettered four years in football, baseball, and basketball, but his high school career was interrupted by a stint in the U.S. Navy during World War II. He graduated from high school in 1947 and entered Hinds Junior College at Raymond, where he lettered two years in baseball and football. In 1950 he went to Mississippi Southern College, where he played one year of baseball and made the All Gulf States Conference Football Team. At Southern he met and married Ruth "Sistie" Warrick of Kingsport, Tennessee.

Following graduation from Mississippi Southern in 1952, Curly served as head football and baseball coach at Lumberton for a short time. Then he returned to his hometown of Corinth to become assistant baseball coach and assistant football coach under Harold Wesson. Both Curly and Wesson were Corinth natives and had known one another most of their lives.

The Wesson connection was very important because it eventually led Curly to Perkinston. In coaching together for three years at Corinth, Curly and Wesson developed a close working relationship, but in 1955 Curly took a job as head coach at Tupelo High School. Three years later he moved on to Greenville High School where his team won the "Big 8" football championship in 1958 and the 3A Baseball State Championship in 1961.

In May 1962, when Wesson became the first head football coach of the newly established Mississippi Gulf Coast Junior College (MGCJC) at Perkinston, he offered Curly a job. The salary Wesson could offer was little better than Curly's salary at Greenville High School, but there were some perks. The demise of the Perkinston Agricultural High School in May 1962 had made available the home economics section of Bennett Hall as free living quarters. Free meals for the family in the college cafeteria sweetened the pot, and the offer to move Curly's furniture sealed the deal. There was another reason Curly wished to come to Perk. Hattiesburg was only thirty-five miles away, and he wanted to earn a master's degree at the University of Southern Mississippi. In July 1962 Curly and Sistie moved into Bennett Hall with their two children, nine-year old Cooper and five-year old Peg.

Curly was quick to say, "My greatest love has always been football." One must credit this coming from the man himself, but the degree of his love of baseball must have been infinitesimally less. When Curly arrived at Perkinston, baseball had been dead for two years. In 1960 Coach Mel Carpenter's team had won the south division championship in baseball. That victory was not that great an achievement since there was only one other team (Southwest Junior College) in the south division. Carpenter played only ten games in 1960 but wound up with a state co-championship. When he left at the end of the season to take a job in Florida, baseball ended at Perk, and the "south division" ended as well. Perkinston had fielded championship baseball teams as far back as 1931, and north division baseball remained as strong as ever in 1962 with six teams. With the coming of Curly Farris, the south would rise again. Curly's first year at Perk bore the designation 1962-1963, and he fielded his first team--the 1963 team--that first year.

Curly Farris (right) talks with his friend and colleague, head football coach Harold Wesson, in A. L. May Memorial Stadium in 1963. In 1962 Wesson, a fellow Corinthian, brought Curly to Perkinston to be his line coach in football. Curly resurrected baseball as a sport at MGCJC and served as the head baseball coach for 27 years.

The resurrection of baseball at Perk began with Curly's call for players in the February 27, 1963, *Bulldog Barks,* "We expect practice sessions to begin immediately following completion of football spring training which should be about March 20." Baseball, of necessity, had to wait until after football spring training because the diamond had to be laid out on the football training field across the tracks from the college--the original Old Athletic Field.

Curly knew that Southwest had played in the south division against Mel Carpenter two years prior, so he called Coach Jerry Reid in Summit, and their two teams became the south division of 1963. In their first meeting on the Old

Baseball Makes A Comeback At MGCJC With Ken "Curly" Farris

*No team picture was made in 1963. The returning lettermen of Curly's first team (1963) sit with him in the bleachers of Wentzell Center in 1964. **Front row** (from left) Frank Pates of Biloxi, Jackie Smith of Gulfport, Frank Singletary of Ocean Springs. **Back Row** (from left) Frank Pinnix of Long Beach, coach Curly Farris, Willis Clay "Bubba" Boyd of Pascagoula. Other members of the original 1963 team were Ogwin Clark and Tommy Seaman both of Pascagoula. Photo from 1964 Perkolator, p. 101.*

***The 1965 Bulldogs pose on the Old Athletic Field for the first full team photo of the Curly Farris era.** The team garnered Curly's third consecutive south division title and finished with a 12-3 record. **Front Row** (from left) Bob Goodwin (manager) of Gulfport, David Drye of Gulfport, Walter E. "Junie" Ross of Biloxi, Geoffrey Malpass of Biloxi, Al Turner of Moss Point, Tony Wilberding of Brooklyn, David Norris of Gautier, Jerry Wilson of Lyman, Roy Caldwell of Lucedale, Wesley Leroy Hyatt of Moss Point. **Back Row** (from left) Coach Curly Farris, Bobby Boggs of Gulfport, Irvin Favre of Gulfport, John Richardson of Biloxi, Larry Henry of Pascagoula, Jimmy Shields of Moss Point, John Kitchens of Pascagoula, Richard Dambrino of Biloxi, D. J. Ziegler of Mississippi City, Glenn Johnson of Gulfport, and James Graves of Pascagoula. Photo courtesy of Curly Farris.*

Athletic Field at Perk, Southwest won with a score of 9-3. The two met three more times that season, and Perk triumphed all three times and thus captured the south division crown.

In other play, the 1963 Bulldogs downed Pensacola Junior College twice, Belhaven College twice, Clarke Junior College three times, but lost to Clarke once. The MGCJC team also won one and lost one with East Mississippi and lost one to William Carey College. Curly's team wound up their first season 11-4 overall and 3-1 in south division.

When the Bulldogs met north division champion Mississippi Delta at Moorhead to decide the 1963 State Championship, Delta shut them out 6-0. Some of the players on the victorious Delta team had been members of Curly's Greenville High 3A Championship team the year before.

Curly had reorganized baseball at Perk and in South Mississippi in 1963 on his own hook and without pay. At the conclusion of that successful season, the administration recognized him as head baseball coach and decided to pay him the next year.

***Curly Farris's 1966 team poses at William Carey College in Hattiesburg, the site of his first state championship win. Kneeling** (from left), Ivan Thomas (manager) of Vancleave, Geoffrey Malpass of Biloxi, George Rasco of Pascagoula, Leslie Breazeale of Biloxi, Don Barron of Pascagoula, Jimmy Ethridge of Pascagoula, Bobby Boggs of Gulfport, Gary Dubuisson (manager) of Pass Christian. **Standing** (from left), Coach Curly Farris, Harold Sablich of Biloxi, Roy Caldwell of Lucedale, Steve Goff of Lucedale, Pat Ladner of Pass Christian, Kirby Carlisle of Gulfport, Tommy Boutwell of Gulfport, George McCall of Gulfport, David Drye of Gulfport. Not pictured: Scotty Waldvogel of Brooklyn, Billy Burke of Gulfport, Larry Henry of Pascagoula, and Tommy Taranto of Biloxi. The 1966 state championship was the first of ten consecutive state championships in what was later termed the "Gulf Coast Baseball Decade." The old uniforms embossed with the term "Perk" or "Perkinston" gave way in 1967 to new ones emblazoned with the term "Bulldogs." For three more years the caps carried a "P," which was then replaced by "GC" for "Gulf Coast." Photo from 1967 Perkolator, p. 113.*

Catcher Scotty Waldvogel of Brooklyn and umpire Dan Vernon of Perkinston at the Old Athletic Field at Perk in 1966.

KEN "CURLY" FARRIS' FIRST STATE BASEBALL CHAMPIONSHIP TEAM 1966

Copiah-Lincoln Junior College became the third member of the up and coming south division in the 1964 season. Once again Perk took the south division title and once again lost the state championship, this time 7-5 in ten innings to East Mississippi. The championship game, played on a neutral field at Clarke Junior College in Newton came the day after graduation. The team record stood at 12-4 overall at season's end.

The south division roster grew to four teams in 1966 with the addition of East Central at Decatur. The Bulldogs traveled to Decatur to defeat East Central in Perk's first conference test of the 1966 season.

The two most memorable games of the 1966 season took place in Hattiesburg on the William Carey College Field. In the first game the Bulldogs took on William Carey and set a 20th century MGCJC record. Bobby Boggs, a slender right-hander from Gulfport, pitched the whole 4 1/2 hour, 17-inning game to vanquish William Carey. Jeff Malpass caught for Boggs for the entire seventeen innings. Curly remembered, "I'll bet Bobby didn't weigh 135 pounds soaking wet, but he was a real competitor. When he had that knuckler working he was tough to hit. There never was another 17-inning game in my career." The game stayed deadlocked 4 to 4 until Harold Sablich drove in the winning run in the bottom of the 17th.

In the second game, played on Saturday, May 22, 1966, the south division champion Bulldogs took on the north division champion East Mississippi Lions at the William Carey College Field for the state baseball title. The Bulldogs, remembering their drubbing by East Mississippi for the state crown the year before, were out for blood.

In the bottom of the fifth inning, David Drye, who had worked the East Mississippi pitcher for his only walk of the game, advanced to second base on a sacrifice bunt by Bobby Boggs. Seeing third base uncovered on the play, Drye went on to third. The East Mississippi player who fielded the bunt attempted to throw Drye out at third, but the ball went into the outfield, and Drye came in for the only run of the game which was rained out in the top of the eighth.

At game's end, Boggs, the Bulldog pitcher, in addition to bunting in Drye, had given up only three hits. Boggs took the most valuable player award in the 1-0 shut out that gave Curly his first state baseball championship.

As Curly took his first state crown, Bob Weathers took his second, and the next fall George Sekul became head football

Football line Coach Curly Farris (above left, kneeling and above right, standing) conducts blocking drill in the "chute" on the practice field behind Gregory War Memorial Chapel in 1967. The offensive player launches off the strip of muddy canvas and strikes the defensive player in the mid-section driving him back. If one stood up too high one launched one's head against the 2 x 4 lintels nailed to the posts. Photos from 1968 Perkolator, p. 64.

coach and took his first. So the calendar year 1966 saw Gulf Coast garner three state titles for its first Triple Crown Year. Curly took one of those on his own but deserves partial credit for another because he was line coach in football. In Curly's words:

"People identify me so much with baseball, they forget I was assistant football coach in charge of offensive and defensive line from 1962 to 1975. In that time, we won several state football championships and one national championship, and I was athletic director from 1975 to 1985 when we took more state football championships and another national title was won."

One might be forgiven for not knowing that Curly ever coached football, considering what he did in state baseball in the decade beginning with 1966. He won ten consecutive south division and state championships. In the midst of Curly's chain of victories, one often defeated Mississippi junior college baseball coach observed, "Why not just give Gulf Coast the crown and let everybody else play for second place."

Alvin Husband of Wiggins, a member of the 1968 state championship team, was MGCJC's first black baseball player.

In 1967 Holmes Junior College at Goodman, which is 50 miles above Jackson, joined the south division in order to bring the two divisions to five teams each. Curly's Bulldogs beat Holmes's Bulldogs that year for the south division championship and then defeated Northeast for the state crown.

In 1968, Jones Junior College joined the south division. Then, of the Mississippi public junior colleges, only Hinds, Utica, and Pearl River had no baseball teams. In time all of them did field teams, so Holmes later rejoined the north division. One wonders if this course of events would have occurred if Curly Farris had not been determined to have a baseball team.

After five years playing on the Old Athletic Field, Curly's Bulldogs moved to a new diamond constructed in a large open field behind Gregory War Memorial Chapel. This field never had an official name, so hereinafter it will be called the "Gregory War Memorial Chapel Field."

The inaugural game on the new field opened the 1968 season on March 23 against Kalamazoo College, a four-year college in Michigan. This season saw another first as well. Alvin Husband of Wiggins became the first black to play on a Gulf Coast baseball team.

The Bulldogs, as usual, won the south division championship. In the state championship match, Gulf Coast won (21-1) the first of a best two out of three series against Northwest. Since rain caused the postponement of the other two games beyond graduation, Northwest conceded the championship. Of course, the score of the first game may have influenced that decision. Curly's 1968 team finished 16-3 overall, the best in Region VII of the National Junior College Athletic Association (NJCAA). Describing this team as "the finest in the school's history," Curly decided to enter the NJCAA Eastern District Tournament. The best teams in Region VII and Region X played in this tournament, the winner of which would go to the NJCAA World Series in Grand Junction, Colorado. Curly's paperwork arrived at the NJCAA offices four days beyond the deadline. The NJCAA's requirement that one loss be added to the team's record for each day late disqualified Gulf Coast. These losses were administrative only and were not reflected in Curly's true win-loss record, which for the 1968 year was 16-3.

In 1969 Curly's state champion Bulldogs did go to the NJCAA Eastern District Tournament in Louisburg, North

Tommy Thompson of Biloxi swings the bat in the 1969 State Championship game against Mississippi Delta at Gregory War Memorial Chapel Field at Perkinston. MGCCC won the game 7-2. Some of the players wear 'Perk" shirts while others wear "Bulldog" shirts. All wear "P" caps except for the two with bats who wear helmets. (The "GC" caps made their appearance the next year). Cooper Farris, Curly's son and successor, sits second from the right end on the bench. Tommy Thompson's son, Doug, became a Cooper Farris star baseball player a generation later.

Curly (left), his wife Sistie (center), and daughter Peg, celebrate after the state championship of May 10, 1971 in which MGCJC defeated East Mississippi 3-2. Peg, who became a Bulldog baseball bat girl five years later, is holding the 1971 state championship trophy.

A Farris Family Portfolio

On May 5, 1973, Ray Busby, state junior college commissioner of athletics, presents the 1973 championship trophy to Curly on the field that would later bear his name. MGCJC defeated Northwest 4-2.

***The 1973 championship baseball team** was the first to play on the recently completed baseball field which would 17 years later be named the Ken "Curly" Farris Baseball Field. The player on the right end of row two is Curly's son Cooper. **First row** (from left), Kim Letort of St. Martin, Rodney Fountain of Biloxi, Mike Moran of Biloxi, Vincent Lionel "Pete" Bosarge of Biloxi, Tom Davenport of Pascagoula, Tony Havard of Lucedale, Eddie Hutchinson of Pascagoula, Lucius Kennedy of Gulfport. **Second row** (from left), Lee Trahan of Biloxi, Gary Dronet of Biloxi, Kevin Covacevich of Biloxi, Clay Andrew of Gulfport, Stuart Hodges of Gulfport, Louis Pennell of Moss Point, Steve Odom of Pascagoula, Cooper Farris of Perkinston. **Third row** (from left), Marvin James "Jimmy" Dubuisson of Long Beach, Mitch Hebert of Biloxi, Calvin Rogers of Perkinston, Roger Parker of Pascagoula, Rod Herring of Gulfport, Leroy Trahan of Biloxi, David Pettis of Moss Point, Carl Graham of Gulfport, Percy Fournier of Biloxi, and Danny Baggett of Wiggins. All photos courtesy of Curly Farris.*

Carolina. On May 15, 1969, Gulf Coast lost 2-1 to Garner Webb Junior College of Boils Springs, North Carolina. Even in losing, the Bulldogs established a record, being the first Mississippi junior college baseball team to play in a NJCAA district tournament.

The unbroken line of south division and state championships continued, but Curly's team did not return to the district tournament until 1972. The eighteen-year-old freshman third baseman on this team was Curly's son, Cooper. At the NJCAA Eastern District Tournament held in Columbia, Tennessee, on May 18-20, the Bulldogs won one game and lost two. They did, however, take the NJCAA Eastern District Runner-Up Trophy.

The Bulldogs opened up play in the 1973 season on a new diamond constructed northwest of and adjacent to A. L. May Memorial Stadium, the old diamond having been taken as the site of a new vocational-technical building (Weeks Hall). With the new field came another innovation designed to distract the opposition—bat girls. The bat girls were chosen by Curly primarily for their love of baseball. The bat girls served as combination cheerleaders, nurses, and general all around helpers. They traveled with the team, and, as one of them said, "We support the team, pack the bats, and most importantly, we bring gum to the players."

In 1973, as usual, the Bulldogs won the south division and state championship, and again they went to the NJCAA Eastern District Tournament in Louisburg, North Carolina. They lost. The 1974 season was an instant replay of 1973 except that the Bulldogs went to the NJCAA Eastern District Tournament in Columbia, Tennessee, and lost.

In 1975 the Bulldogs won their 13th consecutive south state championship and their tenth consecutive state championship and went to Louisburg, North Carolina. The Gulf Coast Bulldog Express left Perkinston, bound eastward to Louisburg, on Wednesday morning, May 14, 1975, which was graduation day for all except six baseball players, one baseball manager and two bat girls who were on the bus. Their graduation caps and gowns were in the cargo area of the bus along with one for Curly, another for Perkinston Campus Dean of Men Ed Scarborough, and still another for Perkinston Campus Executive Dean C. G. Odom. The bus contained all the makings for a unique MGCJC commencement exercise.

The bus arrived in Louisburg on Friday, May 16. The baseball team members donned their uniforms, and shortly before the 1 p.m. game time, the nine candidates for graduation exchanged their caps for mortar boards, zippered their gowns over their uniforms and lined up on the third baseline. Then the candidates marched down the baseline to home plate where the trio of Dean Odom, Dean Scarborough, and Curly awarded their diplomas. The Louisburg Junior College choir sang. The new graduates removed their scholarly regalia, and the contest began.

The Region VII teams in the NJCAA Eastern District Tournament were Gulf Coast and Columbia (Tennessee) State Community College. The Region X teams playing in the tournament were Spartanburg (South Carolina) Methodist College, and host Louisburg (North Carolina) College.

Sharon Eubanks of Lucedale, one of MGCJC's first 'bat girls" stands with Curly during the 1973 season. The March 1973 Bulldog Barks mentioned three other bat girls—Darlene Kapp of Long Beach, Karen Farve of Gulfport, and Linda Cachot of Ocean Springs. In time the bat girls evolved into the "Bulldog Babes." Photo courtesy of Curly Farris.

In the game against Louisburg, Gulf Coast pitchers walked 10 batters, a huge number when in the 279 innings of the season just passed they had walked only 69. Many present believed the umpires had walked the batters. The Columbia coach, observing this game from behind home plate, later told Curly that sixty percent of the called balls were, in his opinion, actually strikes. In the bottom of the ninth a Louisburg runner was called safe when nearly everybody in the stands, including the runner's mother, thought he was out. As one unnamed Gulf Coast fan put it after the 5-4 loss, "The NJCAA opened a new deck of umpires for the regional tournament and we got stuck with the two jokers."

According to the *Mississippi Press*, May 18, 1975, Curly summed up his feelings thusly, "I'm so damn sick I can't see straight," and he together with the head coaches of Columbia and Spartanburg, refused to let their teams take the field

Coach Curly Farris dons gown. In the background are Perkinston Dean of Men Ed Scarborough (left) and bat girl Susanne Papania of Gulfport. Photo from 1976 Perkolator, p. 108.

Lined up to receive degrees during commencement exercises on the baseball diamond at Louisburg are (from left) Renee Pucheu of Gulfport, Susanne Papania of Gulfport, John Parker of Pass Christian, Jim Wargo of Gulfport, Kevin Walker of Pensacola, Florida, Mark Taylor of Long Beach, Tommy Robertson of Moss Point, Joe Evans of Gulfport, and Bill Bradley of Gulfport. Photo from Action, August 1975, p. 16.

THE 1975 BASEBALL GRADUATION

again until the umpires were changed. The officials' association replaced the umpires.

A downpour, which began that night, continued all day Saturday, interrupting play. On Sunday, Gulf Coast beat Spartanburg 1-0. On Monday, Gulf Coast beat Columbia 5-1.

With Columbia gone and Spartanburg gone, Curly had eliminated his two allies against the two "joker umpires." They reappeared on the field to call his next game that same afternoon. His opponent, Louisburg, certainly had no objection to those fellows, so the NJCAA officials sent them back in. A cloudburst drenched the field in the fifth inning. Following a short delay, the umpires decided to resume the game over Curly's protest. According to the *South Mississippi Sun* on May 20, "Farris argued with the umpires several times. In the seventh inning a dispute over a foul tip led to the ejection of mild mannered center fielder, Kirk Thompson, and a threat by the umpires to clear the Perk bench."

After nine innings, darkness fell on the unlighted field, leaving the game (tied 4-4) suspended until the next day. On Tuesday at 10 a.m. Louisburg and Gulf Coast resumed the game. Sudden death came to Gulf Coast in the form of a Louisburg run in the bottom of the twelfth inning. Louisburg, triumphant 5-4 again, started packing for the NJCAA World Series. Curly packed up his second NJCAA Eastern District Runner-Up Trophy, gathered up his newly certified scholar-athletes, and said to them, according to the May 21, 1975, *Mississippi Press,* "It's been a long season and we've played a lot of baseball and ya'll battled all the way. I'm proud of ya'." Then the Bulldog Express headed home to Perkinston. That next Saturday Louisburg lost the NJCAA World Series in Grand Junction, Colorado.

And there was more consolation for Curly. In October of that year NJCAA Southeastern Region Director Kermit Smith named him Region VII Coach of the Year. This award was given annually to the coach in the four state (Mississippi, Tennessee, South Carolina, North Carolina) NJCAA Eastern District who had contributed the most to junior college athletics. Gulf Coast counted only one other former recipient—George Sekul for his 1971 National Football Championship. In a letter to Curly concerning the award, Smith stated, "Your dedication to baseball is unsurpassed. And, your continued competitive spirit in Region VII has been evident."

In January 1976, at the behest of the president and the Board of Trustees, Curly became the Athletic Director of the Mississippi Gulf Coast Junior College, a position that had not been filled for twelve years. While he no longer coached football, he remained the baseball coach.

Curly's unbroken run of thirteen south division titles and ten state championship crowns ended in 1976. That year, despite a 31-10 record, the Bulldogs captured no championship for the first time in Curly's career. In 1977 the team went 30-10 and took only the south division championship.

Ray Busby, state junior college commissioner of athletics, holds the 1979 State championship trophy in preparation for presenting it to Curly Farris at Perkinston. MGCJC had just defeated East Mississippi in a double no-hitter 2-0 and 9-0. Following this game, MGCJC took the NJCAA Region VII championship.

On May 5, 1979, at Perkinston, Dale Chatham (left) of Biloxi and Doug Morrison (right) of Ocean Springs pitched the only double no-hitter in a state baseball championship play-off in Mississippi junior college history.

State Baseball Championship 1979

In 1978 the team racked up a smashing 38-7 overall with 11-1 in division play but won no trophy.

In 1979 Curly came back with a record-breaking vengeance. In the best two of three series for south division, the Bulldogs smashed Hinds 4-3 and 4-2. On Saturday, May 5, 1979 at Perkinston, in the state championship battle, the Bulldogs blasted north division champion, East Mississippi, with a double barreled 2-0 and 9-0 doubleheader sweep. Southpaw Dale Chatham of Biloxi pitched the first game, and Doug Morrison of Ocean Springs pitched the second. Said Curly of this moment, "It was the first time there had been a double no-hitter in the state playoffs." This is the only time it happened or would ever happen because a few years later the rules were changed to a double elimination four-team tournament to decide the state championship.

By 1979 the NJCAA had added a best of three series Region VII Championship game to determine Region VII's representative to the Eastern District Baseball Tournament at Louisburg, North Carolina, to begin on May 17. The Bulldogs (season overall 37-6) met Paducah, Kentucky, (season overall 29-8) at Northwest Junior College in Senatobia on Friday, May 12. With a Bulldog double blitz (2-0 and 9-6), MGCJC wrested the NJCAA Region VII title from Paducah. These twin victories set a new Gulf Coast overall season record of 39-6, breaking the old 1978 total of 38-7.

As Region VII victors, the Gulf Coast Bulldogs sallied forth to Louisburg. On Thursday, May 17, Louisburg delivered a 12-5 mortal wound, and Spartanburg finished off the Bulldog team with an 8-3 *coup de grace*. The Bulldogs ended the season 39-8.

In 1980 the Bulldogs won south division and state and lost to Louisburg and Spartanburg in Cleveland, Tennessee, for a change. In 1981 the Bulldogs won south division and state and lost to Louisburg and Spartanburg in Louisburg, but it would be the last time.

Curly suffered from triskadiskaphobia, fear of the number "13." All year he had worried that he would not win the 1981 state championship because it would be his thirteenth. He did win it, but he never won it again. Consequently, he never went to the NJCAA Eastern District Tournament again. He won the south division championship in 1982, 1983, and 1984, bringing his career total of south division championships to twenty.

Ray Busby, state junior college commissioner of athletics, presents to Nick Moore of Moss Point the 13th and final State Championship Trophy won by a Curly Farris team. MGCCC defeated Northwest 12-9 at Perkinston for the title on May 2, 1981. Photo from 1982 Perkolator, p. 149.

State Junior College Commission of Athletics R. L. "Mac" McLellan (left), presents an award of appreciation to Curly Farris for 27 successful years as a junior college coach. The award was presented at the Mississippi Association of Community and Junior Colleges 1989 All-Star Baseball Game.

Curly speaks at the dedication of the Ken "Curly" Farris Baseball field on April 7, 1990.

Curly retired in 1985 but remained on contract for the next four years solely in the capacity of baseball coach. The Bulldogs won many more games, but Curly never won another championship. He went into full retirement on July 1, 1989, his sixty-second birthday.

In twenty-seven years Curly's Bulldogs never experienced a losing season. He had few regrets but among them was his inability to break the jinx of the thirteenth state championship and the fact that he never could win the NJCAA Eastern District Tournament and lead a team to the NJCAA World Series at Grand Junction, Colorado.

The day Curly retired, the Farris baseball dynasty began. At the behest of the MGCCC president and Board of Trustees, Curly's 35-year-old son Cooper took charge of the baseball squad. Like his father before him, Cooper's job description also included football coaching and teaching duties.

As a student at Perkinston Campus, Cooper had played on the 1972 state championship team, which had finished as NJCAA Eastern District Runner-Up that year. He also had played on the 1973 state championship team. In his junior and senior years at Delta State University, he played for the legendary Dave "Boo" Ferriss. Cooper remained at Delta State as a graduate assistant coach under Ferriss, taking his master's degree in physical education in May 1977.

For the next seven years Cooper taught and coached both baseball and football at Stone High School in Wiggins. From 1984 to 1988, he served in that same capacity at Diboll High School in Diboll, Texas. He had just completed his first year at Stroman High School in Victoria, Texas, when his father retired at Perk, and the job he had always wanted came available. His won-loss record and numerous coaching awards placed him first among the five contenders for his father's old job. So Cooper, his wife Beverly, and their two daughters Lindsey and Lauren, moved back home to Mississippi.

In January 1990, an official of the NJCAA notified Curly that he had been chosen for his former profession's highest award. On Friday, May 25, Curly was to be inducted into the NJCAA Hall of Fame in Grand Junction, Colorado, on the eve of the NJCAA World Series. With this news in hand Curly said, "I told Cooper he had to make the World Series and bring the team out there."

Cooper lost the first three games of the 1990 season, but then won 21 out of the next 26. At that point on Saturday, April 7, in official ceremonies, the diamond at Perk was dedicated as the Ken "Curly" Farris Baseball Field. Meridian baptized the field with a doubleheader drubbing of Gulf Coast 16-10 and 14-1.

The Bulldogs continued to bounce from the win to loss column all through that hectic season. Gulf Coast won south division, lost the state championship game, but stayed alive all the way to the NJCAA Eastern District tournament hosted by Mississippi Delta in Moorhead that year.

The resurgent "under Dawgs" battled to victory after astonishing victory at Moorhead until only one opponent stood between them and a World Series berth at Grand Junction. On Sunday, May 20, 1990, Cooper Farris faced his father's nemesis, the Louisburg (North Carolina) Hurricanes and lost 8-4. Cooper finished his first season with a 36-24 overall record.

They did not take any Bulldogs with them, but both Curly and Cooper went to Grand Junction that year. On May 25, officials inducted Curly into the prestigious NJCAA Baseball Hall of Fame. As Cooper viewed the ensuing World Series games, he became imbued with a sense of mission. In his words, "I saw the caliber of ball that was played, and I knew we were at that level. It was just a matter of us working to that end." Cooper mailed Junior College World Series clip-

Cooper Farris

pings to his players with the message, "This is what it is like, and this is where we need to be."

The 1991 Bulldogs, ranked sixteenth in the nation, roared out of the starting gate with six consecutive wins. By the time they won the south division crown with a double-header victory on April 25, the Bulldogs stood 36-6 overall and were ranked third in the nation. Inexplicably, Gulf Coast dropped the state title in a pair of losses, one to Pearl River on May 4, and the other to Mississippi Delta on May 5. With these defeats Gulf Coast fell from the national rankings.

But on May 11, the Bulldogs came back alive by defeating Delgado (New Orleans) Community College to gain a slot in the NJCAA Region XXIII tournament in Meridian. At Meridian, Gulf Coast cleaned the slate and won the Region XXIII Championship. With this win came the Region XXIII Coach of the Year award for Cooper.

Gulf Coast, then 39-9 overall, advanced to the NJCAA Eastern District Tournament in Cleveland, Tennessee. In their first game on Friday, May 18, 1991, the Bulldogs beat fourth-ranked Columbia State 6-2. On Saturday morning Gulf Coast, as so many fateful times in the past, faced the Louisburg Hurricanes, and for the first time defeated them with a score of 7-3. But Louisburg defeated Cleveland, which meant that the Bulldogs and the Hurricanes would face one another in a final meeting on Sunday, which would decide which one would go to the NJCAA World Series.

With their backs to the wall and fired up for vengeance against a team that had cost Curly several titles and Cooper one the year before, the Bulldogs held on like, well, bulldogs. The game went into extra innings. Gulf Coast designated hitter Ronnie Ducksworth, with only one prior home run to his credit in his two-year college career, hit another in the eleventh inning to send the Hurricanes howling to their deaths 5-4. What a score! Curly, who was sitting on the sidelines, remembered those numbers and Louisburg and the year 1975.

For the first time in history, the Bulldogs had won the NJCAA Eastern District crown and were about to go where no Gulf Coast team had gone before—Grand Junction, Colorado. In fact, only one Mississippi team, Hinds in 1989, had previously made that journey.

Gulf Coast (42-9) faced its first opponent, Allegany (Cumberland, Maryland) Community College (40-4), on Sunday, May 26. Gulf Coast lost 6-3.

Wounded but still alive the Bulldogs took on South Suburban (Illinois) Community College (45-23) on May 28. The Bulldogs went ahead 7-2 in the eighth inning with a two-run homer by Robert Dickerson of Gulfport. That made South Suburban Coach Steve Ruzich very unhappy. The score stood at 7-5 in the final inning of play when a South Suburban hitter put a high fly ball that appeared to be a home run over the ten-foot fence. Pascagoula Bulldog Robin Higginbotham, in what was aptly described by an eyewitness as "a major league play", leaped above the fence and caught that ball. This play took the wind out of South Suburban's sails and made Coach Ruzich unhappier still. When the final out came on a foul tip to the Bulldog catcher, Ruzich charged the plate umpire, ran him out of the stadium, and had to be dragged away by tournament officials. The South Suburban players joined the temper tantrum by throwing bats and helmets and dumping trash out of their dugout and chasing the other three umpires out of the stadium.

On Wednesday, May 29, Gulf Coast once again went against Allegany and once again lost. That time the score was 11-6.

The Bulldogs left Grand Junction with a 43-11 season record and a 5th place NJCAA National Baseball Tournament plaque. In this greatest of all MGCCC baseball seasons, the Bulldog team had gone farther and risen higher than any other community/junior college baseball team in

Matt Lawton makes a hit against Jones County Junior College at Ellisville in 1991.

***The 1991 NJCAA World Series 5th place team poses in Sam Suplezio Stadium in Grand Junction, Colorado. First row** (from left) Chris Fairley (No. 2) of Wiggins, Matt Crosby (No. 27) of Long Beach, Sean Sain (No. 3) of Decatur, Illinois, Ray Mabile (No. 1) of Beaux Bridge, Louisiana, Matt Lawton (No. 7) of Saucier, Adrian Carter (No. 16) of Lucedale, Lilo Garza (No. 24) of Victoria, Texas. **Second row** (from left) Rob Holifield (No. 21) of Pascagoula, Todd Dickerson (No. 28) of Lucedale, Brian Summerlin (No. 19) of Pascagoula, student coach Billy Stone, Cooper Farris, head coach, volunteer assistant Mike Odenwald, Jimmy Barta (No. 34) of Gulfport, Brian Howell (No. 13) of Lucedale, Ronnie Ducksworth (No. 12) of Biloxi. **Third row** (from left) Kenny Taylor (No. 15) of Pascagoula, Trace Frazier (No. 5) of Niceville, Florida, Chris O'Brien (No. 10) of Pascagoula, Harold Holton (No. 33) of Gulfport, Geremie Hopkins (No. 35) of Biloxi, Heath Tanner (No. 30) of Lucedale, Jamie Braxton (No. 9) of Gulfport, Teddy Bishop (No. 17) of Pascagoula, Michael Young (No. 8) of Pascagoula. **Fourth Row** (from left) Kenny Lehman (No. 32) of Gulfport, Kraig Hawkins (No. 4) of Lake Charles, Louisiana, Ricky Taylor (No. 31) of Lucedale, Duane Dobson (No. 13) of St. Martin, David Marsland (No. 20) of Biloxi, Robert Dickerson (No. 29) of Gulfport, Alan Roberts (No. 22) of D'Iberville, Jimmy Barta (No. 34) of Gulfport, and Robin Higginbotham (No. 25) of Pascagoula. Photo courtesy of Cooper Farris.*

Mississippi history to that time.

While 1991 remained Cooper's 20th century apex, that season represented no diminution in his drive for victory and excellence. The 1992 Bulldog team won MGCCC's first state championship in baseball since 1981. The 1997 team took the state crown once again. At the close of the 2000 season, Cooper's teams had taken the south division trophy in nine of his eleven seasons, the exceptions being 1993 and 2000.

In 38 seasons (1963-2000) the Farrises together won one 5th place national plaque, one Eastern District championship trophy, two regional titles, 15 state trophies, and 29 south division championships. Those totals included none of the many runner-up trophies, not even regional or district. In comparison the Farrises' predecessors in 37 seasons (1926-1962) had won only four state titles and three south division championships.

On the back of the plaque given to Cooper Farris, at the close of the 1991 NJCAA World Series Tournament in Grand Junction, Colorado, officials wrote "5th place 91 NJCAA." The NJCAA ceased awarding full-fledged 5th place trophies in 1990.

Curly Farris's
Baseball Championships 1963-1989

Year	Record	South Division	State Championship	NJCAA Tournaments
1963	11-4	SD		
1964	12-4	SD		
1965	12-3	SD		
1966	12-4	SD	SC	
1967	9-4	SD	SC	
1968	16-3	SD	SC	
1969	19-3	SD	SC	
1970	20-4	SD	SC	
1971	20-4	SD	SC	
1972	25-10	SD	SC	NJCAA Eastern District Runner-Up
1973	24-6	SD	SC	
1974	16-8	SD	SC	
1975	38-7	SD	SC	NJCAA Eastern District Runner-Up
1976	31-10			
1977	30-10	SD		
1978	38-7			
1979	39-8	SD	SC	NJCAA Region VII Champions
1980	33-12	SD	SC	
1981	47-10	SD	SC	
1982	35-15-2	SD		
1983	39-13	SD		
1984	36-19	SD		
1985	45-11		SC Runner-Up	
1986	50-20			
1987	33-22			
1988	24-20			
1989	29-17			
Total	743-261-2			

The year given for a team is the second or spring semester of a college session.
South division trophies were not awarded during the Curly Farris era.

Cooper Farris's
Baseball Championships 1990 - 2000

Year	Record	South Division	State Championship	NJCAA Tournament
1990	36-24	SD	SC Runner-Up	NJCAA Region XXIII Runner-Up NJCAA Eastern District Runner-Up
1991	43-11	SD		NJCAA Region XXIII Champions NJCAA Eastern District Champions NJCAA World Series 5th Place
1992	33-17	SD	SC	
1993	36-18-1*	SD Runner-Up	SC Runner-Up	NJCAA Region XXIII Runner-Up
1994	33-21	SD	SC Runner-Up	NJCAA Region XXIII Runner-Up
1995	41-16	SD	SC Runner-Up	
1996	39-19	SD		
1997	38-13	SD	SC	
1998	36-19	SD	SC Runner-Up	
1999	38-20	SD	SC Runner-Up	
2000	38-20	SD Runner-Up		NJCAA Region XXIII Runner-Up

*A tie occurred at Goodman because Holmes Community College did not have a lighted field and the officials called off the game at dark.
The year given for a team is the second or spring semester of a college session.
By the time Cooper Farris succeeded Curly Farris, south division trophies were being awarded.

BASKETBALL: JUNIOR COLLEGE AND AGRICULTURAL HIGH SCHOOL 1929 - 1960

In the 31 seasons from 1929 to 1960, the men's junior college basketball team competed in state championship tournaments at least 10 times but failed to win state laurels. In that same period the women's junior college basketball team competed in state championships tournaments at least 12 times with the same result. However, the women did win the 1953 south division championship, thus marking the highest attainment any junior college basketball team fielded by the Perkinston institution during the 1929 to 1960 period.

In the 31-year period the school eliminated men's junior college basketball during the 1942-1943 session and during the 1943-1944 session, but a Perkinston Agricultural High School boys' team did compete in the 1943-1944 season. Full men's intercollegiate play resumed in session 1944-1945 as Allied victory in the Second World War became apparent.

On the other hand, the institution eliminated women's junior college basketball at the end of the 1939-1940 session and did not resume it until the beginning of the 1944-1945 session. Then at the close of the 1954-1955 season, the Mississippi Junior College Association eliminated women's intercollegiate basketball competition and did not reinstate it for 19 years. So, in the period 1929-1960, the men's junior college basketball team competed for 29 seasons. The women's junior college basketball team competed for only 23 seasons.

Throughout the 1930s and 1940s the men's basketball team and the women's basketball team usually traveled together and played a double bill with the women taking to the court first followed by the men. Newspaper reporters used a variety of terms to describe the men's junior college basketball team. Among those were the "Perk quintet" (because five men were on the floor), "Perksters," "Perkmen," "Perkinston cagers," "Perkinston basketeers," and "Bulldogs," but most often "Perk boys." Newspaper reporters called the women's junior college basketball team the "Perk sextet" (because six women were on the floor) but most often they referred to them as the "Perk girls."

On January 12, 1950, for the first time in a document in the possession of the MGCCC Archives in 2000, a *Daily Herald* newspaper reporter referred to the members of the women's junior college basketball team as "Perkettes." Soon the Perkinston Junior College Perkettes were playing the Copiah-Lincoln Junior College "Wolvettes," the Northeast Junior College "Tigerettes," or the Hinds Junior College "Eaglettes." In the early 1950s sports reporters "etted" every women's junior college team that they could.

In Perk's case that proved to be a wise move because at the beginning of the 1950-1951 session, Perkinston put two more basketball teams on the courts. Harrison County school officials discontinued Saucier High School in May 1950. In September 1950, the Saucier students were bussed to Perk. The arrival of the Saucier students resulted in the expansion of the erstwhile 11th and 12th grade Perkinston Agricultural High School back to the full four-year offering abandoned nine years before. The AHS enrollment jumped from 55 to 95, and the students, mainly the ones from Saucier, wanted both a girls' basketball team and a boys' basketball team.

With the formation of these two new teams, the Perkinston institution had four basketball teams--college men, college women, AHS boys, and AHS girls. The dubbing of the college women's team as "Perkettes" the previous year headed off the potential problem of having two "Perk girls' teams." To head off the problem of having two "Perk boys' teams," newspaper reporters began referring to the college men's team as the "Bulldogs." Since that had been the official name of the team for a quarter century, it was about time.

But in the 1950-1951 session, the hamlet of Perkinston was fielding not four but six teams. One block east of the Perkinston AHS and Junior College stood Perkinston Consolidated High School (PCHS), and it had a boys' basketball team and a girls' basketball team. So the "Perk boys" (AHS) and the "Perk girls" (AHS) were adjacent to the "Perk boys" (PCHS) and "Perk girls" (PCHS). Newspaper reporters of the time became confused about which of the two Perkinston high school teams was playing an outside team, but when Perk AHS played PCHS the confusion approached the sublime. In those games, this author failed to figure out who beat whom. Actually the PCHS teams had names ("Eagles" and "Eaglettes"), but the reporters often failed to use them.

In September 1952, Stone County school officials ordered the PCHS to join with Perk AHS, and the Eagles and Eaglettes crossed the road. The combination "Eagles-Perk AHS boys' basketball team" became the "Bullpups." The combined "Eaglette-Perk AHS girls' basketball team" became the "Puppettes."

It all seemed conveniently arranged and permanently settled--Bulldogs and Perkettes, Bullpups and Puppettes--but it was not to be. The new band director, Sam Jones, decided to expropriate the name "Perkettes" for his newly formed college women's combination pep squad and dance team. After that, Perk had Perkettes shooting goals and Perkettes marching and drilling. Some were doing both. Janice Felsher, the first head band-Perkette was also a basketball-Perkette. Margaret Wallsmith was likewise a double Perkette. Geraldine "Jerry" Jordan, a member of the Perkette dance team was also a Puppette. Whew.

On February 11, 1953, Harve Hagerty, editor of the *Bulldog Barks* attacked the "double-ette" problem head on:

"NEW NAME NEEDED . . . .

"It has come to the attention of the staff that there is a conflict in names between the college girls' basketball team and girls' pep squad.

"Up to this year the basketball team had sole rights to the title "Perkettes," but now the name has been taken over by the band majorettes.

"At Holmes Junior College the team is known as the Bulldogettes. Can anyone think of a better name for our basketball girls? - H.H."

Apparently no one thought of a better name because the band-Perkettes remained on the field, and the basketball-Perkettes remained on the court. The Mississippi Junior College Association finally solved the problem by eliminating women's basketball in all Mississippi junior colleges at the close of the 1954-1955 season. After that the basketball Perkettes faded into history to be forgotten by everyone, apparently including the women who had once been basketball-Perkettes.

This author interviewed five women who once were basketball Perkettes, and not one of them remembered being called Perkettes. Yet the MGCCC Archives in 2000 contained photographs from the *Bulldog Barks* which clearly labeled the women's basketball team as Perkettes. Moreover, newspaper reporters (including *Bulldog Barks* reporters) from 1950 to 1955 rarely referred to the school's women's basketball team as anything but Perkettes. On the other hand, the editors of the *Perkolator* yearbook never used the word "Perkette" in reference to women's basketball. The *Perkolator* labeled women's basketball team photos either with the words "Basketball Girls" or even more noncommittally with the words "College Basketball," leaving it to the viewer to discern sex.

The Perkinston Junior College basketball-Perkettes dribbled into oblivion in spring 1955, but the Perkinston Agricultural High School Puppettes played on. The last Puppette team, and the last Bullpup team as well, vanished with the demise of the AHS in spring 1962.

Fall 1960 marked a watershed in the realm of junior college basketball at Perkinston. Coach Robert W. "Bob" Weathers took charge of the Bulldogs, and Barbara Ann "Sue" Ross hired on as a physical education instructor. Weathers was destined to lead the Bulldog basketeers not only to the state glory that had so long eluded them, but to national recognition as well. Ross was destined first to play a vital role in the resurrection of women's intercollegiate basketball in Mississippi and then to lead her Perkinston team to state and national renown.

Basketball 1929-1960 A Photographic Gallery:

The first Bulldog basketball team coached by Lee Roy Weeks poses in front of the Old Gym in session 1929-1930. First row *(from left) Harold McHenry of McHenry, Obry Breland of Wiggins, William B. Nobles of Hattiesburg, Clyde Sylvester of Bay St. Louis, and Maxie Broadus of McHenry.* ***Second row*** *(from left) W. E. Godard of McHenry, Edward Casey (also known as Edward Sherman) of Gulfport, Unknown, Othmar Flurry of Perkinston, Leeman Biard of McHenry, and coach Lee Roy Weeks.*

The person (unknown to this author) who captioned the above photograph many years ago wrote that the little boy holding the ball was named "Doubleday." He is almost certainly Frank Doubleday of Tela, Honduras. According to W. R. "Bill" Woolfolk in a letter published in Action (Winter 1992), "Several of us had come up for high school from Tela, Honduras, in the fall of 1929. The United Fruit Company School there only went through the grammar grades." Once the United Fruit Company established the connection with Perk in the late 1920s, more than 100 Central American students followed. Merrill "Red" True, a student from Mississippi City in the 1930s, informed this author that in a few cases younger brothers of Central American students attended Perkinston Consolidated School while living in the Perk dorms with their older brothers. These youngsters would then enter Perk themselves when they had earned the required credits. If this author interpreted the Perkinston records correctly, Frank Doubleday seems to have attended Perkinston Consolidated School from 1929 or 1930 until 1934. He certainly attended the AHS from 1934 until his high school graduation on June 3, 1938. A check of the Perkinston Campus records revealed that from 1929 through 1944 one hundred and sixteen foreign students attended Perk. One was Norwegian, all the others were Central Americans, the great majority of whom had connections with the United Fruit Company. Not all of the students enrolling from Central America were Hispanic in language and culture. Some were the sons and daughters of British and Anglo-American employees of the United Fruit Company.

1931-1932 Women's Basketball Team.
(From left) Coach Noby Ruth (Denson) Houston, team captain Lydean (David) Davis of Perkinston, Elizabeth Kerr of Long Beach, Mary Alice Ross of Gulfport, Vera O'Neal of Saucier, Elsie Broadus of Perkinston, Zona Bell Turritten of Cuevas, Janelle Heidelberg of Pascagoula, and manager R. L. Roberts of Ocean Springs. The team, the last of Noby Ruth (Denson) Houston's career, made it to the semi-finals in the state tournament held at Goodman in late February 1932. After the tournament, Elizabeth Kerr was named to the All-State team and Zona Bell Turritten was named All-State Honorable Mention.

Members of the 1939-1940 women's basketball team *pose for individual snapshots in front of the Old Gym. This would be the last women's intercollegiate team for four years because the institution eliminated women's intercollegiate sports in favor of physical education on the eve of World War II. Photograph from the 1940 Perkolator, p. 93.*

The women's basketball team gave way to the "Super Duper Blue Devils Tumbling Team," which performed for organizations and schools in south Mississippi during the Second World War. (Above) The Super Duper Blue Devils perform at Perkinston in 1942. The women are dressed in the basketball uniforms of 1940. Women's intercollegiate basketball play resumed in session 1944-1945. Photograph from the 1943 Perkolator, p. 45.

***The 1947-1948 Perkinston Junior College women's basketball team. First row** (from left) Lorette Rouse of Saucier, Helen Davis of Ocean Springs, Bettye Thames of Lyman, Elizabeth Ware of Escatawpa, Louise Penton of Gautier, and Annie Murray of Pascagoula. **Second row** (from left) Flora Shepard of Foxworth, Carmen Tarzetti of DeLisle, Helen Bond of Saucier, Marjorie Hawley of Ocean Springs, and Mildred Daniels of Gulfport. Photograph courtesy of Lorette (Rouse) Compton.*

Lorette Rouse took All-Star honors at the state junior college basketball tournament in 1947 and also was selected All-State. At the 1948 women's state basketball tournament, held in the Old Gym at Perkinston for the first time since 1929, both Rouse and Helen Bond were named tournament All-Stars. In addition, Bond was named All-State in 1948 and again in 1949.

The first "Perkettes"--the 1949-1950 Perkinston Junior College women's basketball team. *On January 12, 1950, a Daily Herald reporter referred to this team for the first time as "Perkettes." The name continued until the elimination of the Perkette team in spring 1955.* ***Kneeling*** *(from left) Betty Jo Davis of Wiggins, Shirley Dean of Logtown, Ruby Helen Simmons of Lucedale, Jenelle King of Biloxi, and Beatrice Ellis of Ocean Springs.* ***Standing*** *(from left) Patti Spruell of Moss Point, Lillian Rouse of Lucedale, Florence Havens of Perkinston, Mary Ellen Brown of Biloxi, Dot Necaise, and Coach Evelyn Prescott. Photograph from 1950 Perkolator, p. 126.*

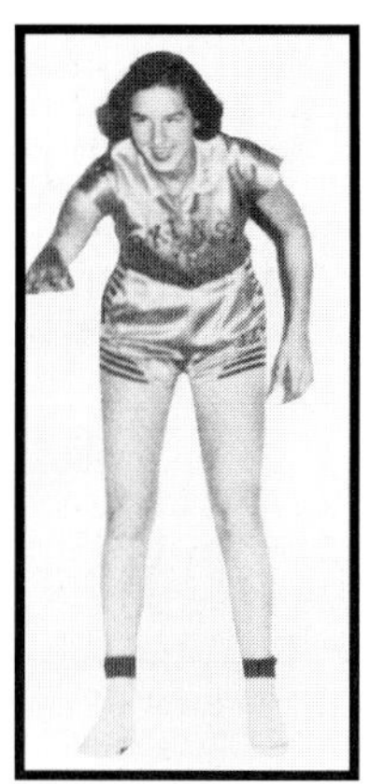

Janice Felsher 1952 basketball-Perkette. Photograph from 1953 Perkolator p. 92.

Janice Felsher 1952 band-Perkette. Photograph from 1953 Perkolator p. 116.

Perkinston, Miss., November 28, 1951 BULLDOG BARKS

PERKETTES . . . .
They are Christine O'Neal, Marietta Morris, De:ores Parker, Mary Ruth Overstreet, Joan Tarzetti, Katherine Gangloff, Lula Mae Guillotte, Ella Wayne Clark, Janice Felshur, Joan Wentzell, Loraine Davis, Elizabeth Laird, Gurdia Kay Broadus; kneeling, Coach Esther Craig and Manager Melba Wall. (Photo by Lautner)

(Above) The 1951-52 basketball-Perkettes team is pictured and named in the November 28, 1951, Bulldog Barks. The next fall, Janice Felsher of Biloxi,(whose name is misspelled as "Felshur" in the Bulldog Barks article) became the first head band-Perkette. Sam Jones, the new band director who replaced J. O. Ware, took the basketball team's name for his newly established women's dance and drill team.

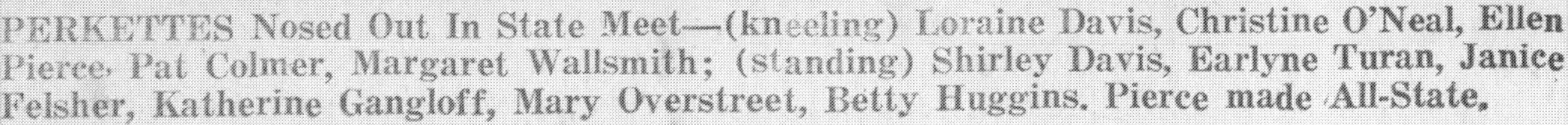

PERKETTES Nosed Out In State Meet—(kneeling) Loraine Davis, Christine O'Neal, Ellen Pierce, Pat Colmer, Margaret Wallsmith; (standing) Shirley Davis, Earlyne Turan, Janice Felsher, Katherine Gangloff, Mary Overstreet, Betty Huggins. Pierce made All-State.

(Above) The 1952-53 basketball-Perkettes team is pictured and named in the March 11, 1953, Bulldog Barks. This Perkette-basketball team won the only Mississippi Junior College Association trophy awarded to any Perkinston junior college team from 1929 to 1960. As the Bulldog Barks caption attests, the team was "nosed out in state meet" for the state championship, but the team did win the south division championship. (Right) The trophy reads "South Mississippi Champs, 52-53."

The Perkinston Agricultural High School Girls' Basketball or "Puppettes." The team poses in the Old Gym in 1952. (From left) Virginia Keesee of Long Beach, June Cox of Perkinston, Geraldine "Jerry" Jordan of Perkinston, Alice Diamond of Howison, Carol Edwards of Saucier, Blondell Broadus of Howison, Carolyn Fay Patton of Saucier, Ann Peterson of Biloxi, Peggy Broadus of Saucier, Betty Jean Rhodes of Saucier, Myrtie Mae Parker of Perkinston, Janet Ellsberry of Perkinston, and Linell Malone of Saucier. Photo from 1953 Perkolator p. 93.

(Right) Perkinston Agricultural High School basketball team "Puppette" Geraldine "Jerry" Jordan prepares to shoot a basketball in the Old Gym in 1953.

(Far Right) Perkinston Agricultural High School and Junior College band-Perkette Geraldine "Jerry" Jordan poses on the portico of Harrison Hall in 1953. Jordan was a member of the original band-Perkette drill team of 1952 and remained a member of the squad until her graduation from the AHS on May 19, 1954. Photographs of Jerry Jordan courtesy of Joel "Cotton" Jordan and his wife Mercedes, who also donated her baton to the MGCCC Archives.

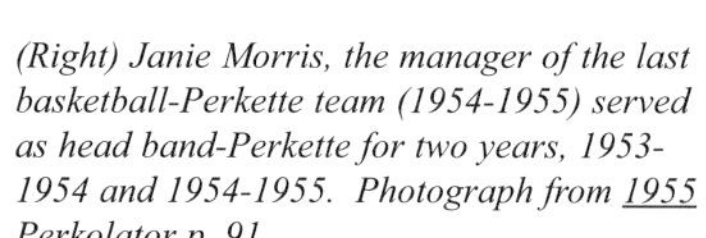

(Right) Janie Morris, the manager of the last basketball-Perkette team (1954-1955) served as head band-Perkette for two years, 1953-1954 and 1954-1955. Photograph from <u>1955 Perkolator</u> p. 91.

(Far Right) Barbara Ann "Sue" Ross, a member of the final basketball-Perkette team of 1954-1955. The team was disbanded after Ross graduated from PJC in May 1955. She returned to Perk to teach physical education, and through her efforts the state of Mississippi re-instituted women's basketball after a 19-year hiatus. Photograph from the <u>1955 Perkolator</u> p. 92.

The Perkinston Agricultural High School Boys' Basketball Team or "Bullpups." *The team poses in the Old Gym in 1952. (From left) Manager Horace Breland of Perkinston, Leroy Coker of Perkinston, James Rouse of Howison, Wesley Scarborough of Saucier, Victor Gipson of Perkinston, Derlyn Bond of Perkinston, Shirley Evans of Perkinston, Edward Ray Coker of Perkinston, Earl Bond of Gautier, Arlan Robinson of Perkinston, Fred Gill of Perkinston, Roddy Daniels of Saucier, Clifford Patton of Saucier, and manager Estus Parker of Perkinston. Photograph from 1953 Perkolator, p. 93.*

The 1956-1957 Bulldog basketball team was the last to play in the Old Gym. *According to Coach Melvin Carpenter, this team scored a total of 2,458 points and ranked second among junior colleges in national scoring. According to the Daily Herald, this team's game against Copiah-Lincoln on January 29, 1957, set a new scoring record in the Mississippi Junior College Conference. Perk lost by a score of 134 to 113. (From left) Raul Rivera of Tiquisate, Guatemala, Joe Pinson of Lyman, William "Hobo" Jones of Marshall, Texas, Jay Pinson of Lyman, Jerry Sharp of Brooklyn, Ernest Schroeder of Pascagoula, Joe McAnulty of Albermarle, North Carolina, Vernon Ehlers of Moss Point, Jerry "Rooster" Rouse of Gulfport, Maxwell Gentry of Gulfport, Leroy Wescovich of Delisle, and Bobby Bradley of McHenry. Not pictured: William "Bill" Smith of Mobile, Alabama. Photograph courtesy of Coach Melvin Carpenter.*

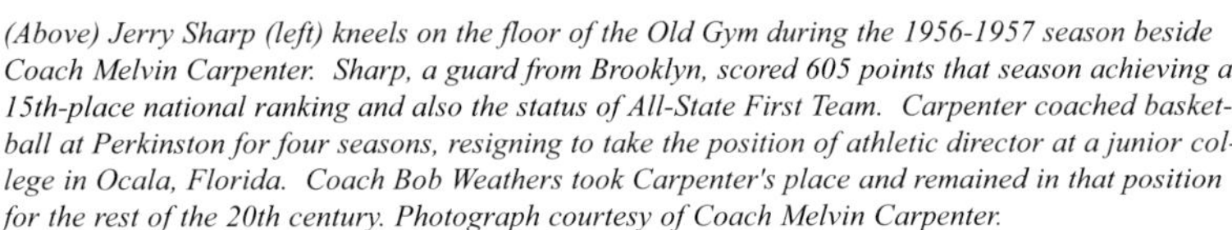

(Above) Jerry Sharp (left) kneels on the floor of the Old Gym during the 1956-1957 season beside Coach Melvin Carpenter. Sharp, a guard from Brooklyn, scored 605 points that season achieving a 15th-place national ranking and also the status of All-State First Team. Carpenter coached basketball at Perkinston for four seasons, resigning to take the position of athletic director at a junior college in Ocala, Florida. Coach Bob Weathers took Carpenter's place and remained in that position for the rest of the 20th century. Photograph courtesy of Coach Melvin Carpenter.

(Above right) In the first game of Coach Melvin Carpenter's Perkinston career, Bulldog center Bill Smith (center of photo) gapes at the airborne action as a Wildcat goes for the goal in the Perkinston-Pearl River game of December 5, 1956. Smith's jersey reads only "Perkinston Junior College" with no accompanying numbers. According to Carpenter in an interview 44 years later, "I knew that those jerseys without numbers on the front were illegal, but it took me a year to get the money to buy new ones." Photograph courtesy of Coach Melvin Carpenter.

(Right) Bulldog guard George Rosetti of Gulfport prepares for a shot in Wentzell Center ("New Gym"). Rosetti's 1957-1958 team was the first to play in Wentzell Center. His jersey carries the number "10" on the front unlike those of the year before, which were numbered only on the back. That season, Rosetti scored 435 points and also earned an All-State First Team ranking. Photograph courtesy of Coach Melvin Carpenter.

Basketball 1960 - 2000

THE WEATHERS CLAN

The Weathers clan poses in the Grand Ballroom of the Hilton Hotel in Jackson on July 16, 1999, the night Bob was named to the Mississippi Association of Coaches Hall of Fame. Front row (from left) Robert Vernon Weathers, Tommie Jean (Dixon) Weathers, Emily Brooke Weathers, Robert Wayne "Bob" Weathers. Back row (from left) Tammie Marie (Callahan) Weathers, Raymond Wendell Weathers, and Ross Anthony Weathers.

Due to the relative isolation of the tiny village of Perkinston, the campus has from its inception been the major local industry. Husband and wife teams have always been a feature of the faculty, staff, and administration. It had not been unusual for second or even third generation members of the same family to serve the college in one capacity or another over a long period, but the Weathers Clan was unique in the realm of so many serving in so many areas simultaneously. Four mailboxes in succession in the campus mail room read: Weathers, Bob; Weathers, Tammie; Weathers, Tommie; Weathers, Wendell.

Robert Wayne "Bob" Weathers, the patriarch of the clan, began his career as head men's basketball coach in 1960. His wife, Tommie, began as campus veterans' affairs officer in August 1973, and in January 1985, became the campus records clerk. Their oldest son, Wendell, joined his father as assistant men's basketball coach and chemistry instructor in 1988. Then aged 31, Wendell came on board with eight years of coaching experience--one year as a graduate assistant at Delta State University in Cleveland, two years at Buras (Louisiana) High School, and five years at Thibodaux (Louisiana) High School. At Thibodaux Wendell amassed an enviable 107-48 game record which earned him the Louisiana District Eight 4-A Coach of the Year award in 1987. Also while at Thibodaux he won the hand of Tammie Callahan. From 1988 to 1999, Wendell and Tammie lived in Andrews Hall where she was resident manager and coordinator of women's activities, cheerleader instructor, and cheerleader summer camp director. In July 1999, Tammie became the Perkinston Campus Bookstore manager and book buyer. In their three children, Ross, Robert, and Emily, lies the promise of the Weathers Clan third generation at MGCCC.

How did it begin? How did it happen? Bob Weathers was born September 16, 1932, in Hattiesburg, Mississippi. Actually he grew up in Oak Grove, a hamlet just west of Hattiesburg. According to Bob:

"I achieved perfection in my very first basketball game and it's been downhill ever since. I was in the fourth grade at Sandy Run Elementary. We played the Oak Grove fourth grade. I made a foul shot in the second quarter, a field goal in the third quarter and another foul shot in the fourth. The final score of that game was 4 to 0. I made all the points in the game. So, I've spent the rest of my life trying to shut out another team but never have been able to do it again."

In any case, Bob's subsequent performances at Oak Grove High netted him the prized title of "Mississippi High School All-State Player" in his senior year of 1950. Then he went "across the road" to Mississippi Southern College (now the University of Southern Mississippi) where he lettered in basketball all four years.

After graduation from college Bob became freshman basketball coach at his alma mater from 1955-1957, racking up a 30-5 record. In the school year 1958-59, he became assistant basketball coach on a graduate fellowship and earned his master's degree in physical education.

In the summers, while coaching at Mississippi Southern, Bob played basketball summer league for the entertainment of guests at resorts in the Catskill Mountains of New York. There he encountered for the first time the idea of summer basketball camps for boys--an idea he would make much of later.

In 1959 Bob hired on as head basketball coach and physical education instructor at Picayune High School in Picayune. His record for the 1959-60 year was a respectable, though not outstanding, 13-10.

On July 20, 1960, then aged 28, Bob replaced Perkinston Junior College Coach Mel Carpenter, who was leaving after four years to accept a position in Florida. Bob's job description was similar to the one at Picayune and has remained the same for nearly four decades. His record, though, got a lot better.

While at Mississippi Southern Bob met and married

1961--Coach Bob Weathers' first pack of Bulldog roundballers, which he dubbed the "Mighty Mites" pose in Wentzell Center. This team finished 12-12 overall and 7-5 in division play. (From left) Coach Bob Weathers, 6'2"; Mack Byrd (6'6" freshman) of Lucedale, Merrill Vitter (6'2" freshman forward) of New Orleans, Bob Tinsley (freshman center) of Gulfport, Donald Ladner (6'1") of Harrison County, Clark Crawley (6' sophomore guard) of Gulfport, Ford Turner (5'11" freshman guard) of Brooklyn, Bill Stigletts (5'7" freshman guard) of Gulfport, Jack Ainsworth (5'10" freshman guard) from Gulfport, John Dickens (5'11" freshman forward) of Saucier, Ogwin Clark (6'1" freshman forward) of Moss Point, Ron Johnson (6'2" freshman forward) of Sturgis, Kentucky, Edward "Boo" Rogers (freshman forward) of Pittsburg, Pennsylvania, Philip Suddeth (6'2" freshman forward) of Moss Point, and Jimmy McArthur (6'4" sophomore forward) of Moss Point, whose grandson showed up to play on the 1993-94 MGCCC football team two generations later. The two managers kneeling with the basketball are Brant Cochran (left) and Daniel Cochran (right) cousins from Janice. Photo from 1961 Perkolator, p. 82.

Tommie Jean Dixon of Laurel, and in his first collegiate game as head coach, he played Southeastern Baptist College in her hometown on Thursday, December 2, 1960. Bob's Bulldogs, composed of only two sophomores and the rest unseasoned freshmen, took the lead in the first few minutes of play and never relinquished it, but they made numerous errors. The Bulldogs prevailed 72-64 and at game's end Coach Weathers allowed he was, "disappointed with his charges but. . . happy with the victory."

The team suffered its first defeat in its second outing against the much taller Tulane Freshmen in New Orleans on December 5. A number of Bulldogs topped six feet and Mack Byrd of Lucedale stood 6'6," but others were in the 5'10"range. Noting their stature, or rather lack of it, but also impressed by their feisty nature, Bob soon christened his first Perk team the "Mighty Mites." Sports writers liked the nickname, and "Mighty Mites" replaced "Bulldogs" as the designation for Bob's team in the newspapers. The nickname appears at least as early as the December 12, 1960, *Daily Herald* in the description of Perk's December 10 victory over Clarke Junior College at Newton. The sports writer said, "Trailing by two points at the half, the "Mighty Mites" of Coach Bobby Weathers ripped the cords at a blistering pace in the final half and won the contest going away." The new appellation achieved such vogue that it appeared in the *1961 Perkolator* yearbook along with the official title of "Bulldogs."

Bob played his first south division game against Perk's perennial rival, Pearl River. In this game played in the Wentzell Center at Perk on Tuesday, January 10, 1961, the Bulldogs stomped the Wildcats 81-55. At that point the season record stood 5-3 overall and 1-0 in division play.

The following Saturday night on the same court the huge Loyola University Freshmen squashed the Mighty Mites 111-55, the worst defeat of Bob's career. Non-division loses continued but so did a string of five division victories--well, until Tuesday, January 24, when the Southwest Bears at Summit in overtime mauled Bob's Dogs with a 72-68 division defeat. Their winning streak broken and momentum shattered, the Bulldogs fell in succession to the Pearl River Wildcats, the Jones Bobcats, the Southwest Bears (again and again in overtime) and the Copiah-Lincoln Wolves. The Dogs rallied for two more victories, and when the smoke cleared at the end of the regular season, the Dogs stood 10-10 overall and 7-5 in division play.

In the south division semi-finals at Raymond on Friday, February 24, 1961, the Dogs went up against the Southwest Bears for the third time that season, and again the game went into overtime, but this time the Dogs triumphed 89-84. On the following night Jones beat Perk 87-84 to clinch the south division title. As runner-up in the south division, the Dogs traveled to the state championship tilt at Decatur on March 6, where they fell 79-60 to the north champion Itawamba Indians.

So ended Bob's first season. With only two experienced sophomores to aid him, he had led his Mighty Mites to the state championship play-offs. They returned with no laurels, but neither did they return in dishonor. And those raw freshmen of '61 would be Bob's seasoned cadre of '62.

It showed. The 1962 Bulldogs won the south division championship and garnered the first men's state basketball trophy in the history of the school. Winning the southern division crown netted a second signal honor for the college. For the first time since 1929, Perkinston was selected to host the Mississippi Junior College State Championship Tournament. State tournament sites were selected on a round-robin basis but the host had to be a contender.

The two-day battle got underway on Friday, March 2, 1962, in Wentzell Center. The Dogs took on north division second-ranked Mississippi Delta and squeaked by 80-79. The north division first-ranked (and defending state champion) Itawamba Indians defeated the number two ranked south division Hinds Eagles 65-56.

The next day the *Daily Herald* billed that night's coming championship tourney thusly: "Favored Itawamba meets upstart Perkinston in the finals of the Mississippi Junior College Conference basketball tournament tonight." The Dogs lost that game to Itawamba that night, but by the close of the 20th century, Bob's players had rampaged the hardwood floors of Mississippi in more than a thousand games, garnering 14 south division titles, nine state championships, and had taken three cracks at the national title.

The triumphant reign of Coach Bob Weathers in the realm of Mississippi junior college basketball was unique in the 20th century. But along with the triumph came tragedy of Biblical proportions. In Wentzell Center at Perkinston Bob instructs his three sons, Raymond Wendell [No. 3] (born August 25, 1957), whose first name commemorated his mother's father killed in an automobile accident when she was aged fifteen; Richard Anthony "Tony" [No. 12] (born May 2, 1959) killed in an automobile accident on March 2, 1986, and Robert Wayne "Little Bob" [No. 50] (born September 6, 1961) killed in an automobile accident on February 4, 1993.

All three of the Weathers boys played on MGCCC state championship teams coached by their father. Little Bob served as a part-time recruiter/assistant coach from 1984 to 1986, and Wendell began service as his full-time assistant coach in 1988. Tony, at the time of his death, was employed at James River Corporation in Wiggins, and Little Bob was an automobile dealer in Wiggins at the time of his death.

Bob had decided to retire and join his son in the automobile business, but Little Bob's death changed that. Said Bob, "With Bob gone nothing else I could do compared to staying on at Perk." Then he added, "I don't believe there is anything worse than losing a child, but friends and family get you through times of tragedy. The worst part was after the wakes when nobody else was coming through the door." Mrs. Weathers summed up her feelings thusly, "I'll never finish dealing with the grief, but my greatest fear is that my sons will be forgotten."

The Biblical adage, "The Lord giveth and the Lord taketh away," was fitting in the Weathers' case. The first child of Wendell and Tammie, born August 27, 1990, was named Ross Anthony in honor of Tony. Tammie was pregnant with twins when Little Bob died. On July 14, 1993, the twins were born. The girl was named Emily and the boy was christened Robert in honor of Little Bob.

A Gallery of Coach Bob Weathers's Championship Teams

1964--Bob's first state championship team and second south division championship team. *The Bulldogs pose with Bob's first state championship trophy immediately following the championship game in which the team defeated Pearl River at Poplarville 60-50 on Saturday night, February 29, 1964. This team finished 20-4 overall.* ***Kneeling*** *(from left) Coach Bob Weathers; Jack Benny Hughes (guard) of Ocean Springs, Louis Holm (forward) of St. Martin.* ***Standing*** *(from left) Eddie Miller (forward) of Gulfport, Mike Noblitt (guard) of Pascagoula, Jimmy Shields (center) of Moss Point, Robin Wilson (forward) of Biloxi, Ronnie Mohr (forward) of Vancleave, Larry Ivey (who later became Bob's assistant coach) (center) of Basin, Jerry Gautier (guard) of Gulfport,Robert Sivills (guard) of Biloxi, Gale Farmer (forward) of Woolmarket (his twin, Dale, also a forward from Woolmarket was on the team but not pictured), and Bobby Bilbo (forward) of Gulfport.*

1966--Bob's second state championship team and third south division championship team. *Bob's Bulldogs celebrate at the conclusion of the 1966 south division championship game. The trophy reads: "M(ississippi) J(unior) C(ollege) A(thletic) A(ssociation) Southern Champions 1965-66, Coach Bob Weathers."* ***First row*** *(from left) Coach Bob Weathers, Johnny Adams (6'2" sophomore Guard) of Gulfport, Mike Felsher (6'3" sophomore forward) of Biloxi, Leslie Breazeale (5'9" freshman guard) of Waynesboro, Donnie Denmark (5'10" freshman guard) of Moss Point, Wayne "Wonderboy" Weathers (Bob's nephew and team manager) of Hattiesburg.* ***Second row*** *(from left) Johnny McPherson (6'2" freshman forward) of Gulfport, Mike Matthews (6'7" freshman center) of Gulfport, Danny James (6'3" freshman center) of Gulfport, Jimmy Gautier (6'3" freshman guard) of Gulfport, Jack Horner (6'5" sophomore center) of Wiggins, Cary Trochesset (6'1" sophomore guard) of Biloxi, Larry Henry (6'1" sophomore guard) of Pascagoula, Charles Kennedy (6'5" freshman forward) of Wiggins, Jimmy Johnson (scorekeeper) of Gulfport, Charles "Cold-Water" Williams (manager) of Hattiesburg.*

On Saturday, February 26, Bob's 1966 team won his second state championship by defeating Pearl River 59-54 at Perkinston. For the first time Bob entered his Bulldogs in the NJCAA Region VII Tournament held March 2-5, 1966, in Madisonville, Tennessee. The Bulldogs made it to the quarterfinals but lost to Cumberland Junior College of Lebanon, Tennessee, ending hopes of a regional title. The Bulldogs finished 20-6 overall for the season.

1969--Bob's perfect regular season resulted in his third state championship and his fifth south division championship. First Row *(from left), Larry Williamson (manager) of Long Beach, Frankie Strohm (No. 35) of Wiggins, Robert Russell (No. 5) of Gulfport, Joe Jenkins (No. 10) of Gulfport, Coach Bob Weathers, Mike Clement (No. 3) Perkinston, Wynn Clark (No. 11) of Pascagoula, Houston Cunningham (No. 4) of Moss Point, Kenneth Goff (manager) of Moss Point.* ***Second row*** *(from left), Kemon Welford (No. 12) of Gulfport, Ronnie Ladner (No. 30) of Pass Christian, Bobby Hope (No. 33) of Biloxi, J. B. Shoemaker (No. 15) of Moss Point, Earthie McMillian (No. 22) of Moss Point, Gary Roberts (No. 20) of Gulfport, and Ronnie Patton (No. 21) of Gulfport. The first black player on Coach Weathers's team was Eugene Vanderbilt in the 1967-68 year. In the 1968-69 season three blacks joined the team--Bobby Hope, a sophomore from Tougaloo, Earthie McMillian, and Houston Cunningham. McMillian and Cunningham were both freshmen from Moss Point. Cunningham became the Bulldogs's first black team captain.*

Bob's 1969 team won all 24 regular season games by an average of 26 points straight through the state championship, but on March 6, 1969, at the NJCAA Region VII tournament in Gulfport, Utica Junior College beat the Bulldogs 65-64. That heartbreaker cost the Bulldogs a shot at the national championship in Hutchinson, Kansas. A generation passed before Bob and his team made it to the nationals.

1990 (Not pictured)-- Bob's Bulldogs lost both the state and south division championships. Ironically, the team then won the NJCAA Region XXIII Championship but lost the bi-regional national play-off to Snead State Community College of Boaz, Alabama.

***Bob's 1991 4th place nationally ranked team poses in the 8,000 seat Hutchinson Sports Arena. Kneeling** (from left), Dale Brown of Moss Point, Nate Barkum of Gulfport, Derrick Gallien of Lake Charles, Louisiana, Tony Jones (manager) of Gulfport, Robert Polk of Gulfport, Doug Stapleton (manager) of Gulfport, and John "Dicky" Foxworth (manager) of Gulfport. **Standing** (from left), Coach Bob Weathers holds the Fourth Place NJCAA Division I National Trophy, Maurice Stephens of Pascagoula, Joe Buxton (No. 12) of Vancleave, Joe Brown (No. 35) of Wiggins, Kendrick Cannon of Baton Rouge, Louisiana, Mark Hubbard (No. 4) of Ocean Springs, Chris Black of Baton Rouge, Louisiana, David Blanco of Venezuela, Tommy Oatis of Gulfport, Pat Hawthorne of New Orleans, Louisiana, assistant Coach Wendell Weathers, and American Legion team host Mike Cristopherson. Photograph courtesy of Bob Weathers.*

1991--This team brought Bob his eighth state championship, his twelfth south division championship, and his second NJCAA Region XXIII Championship in two years. This time, the first time in Bob's career, the Bulldogs went to Hutchinson, Kansas, for a shot at the national title. Hutchinson Junior College and the Lysle Rishel Post, American Legion, began co-sponsorship of the NJCAA championship basketball tournament in 1949. The top 16 teams in the nation vied in the weeklong NJCAA tournament. The play-offs determined the top eight teams, and these were ranked nationally, one to eight. The top four of these eight teams received national trophies. On March 22, 1991, Aquinas Community College of Nashville, Tennessee, defeated the Bulldogs 85-82 and, after a subsequent victory in the championship match, took the NJCAA title. Gulf Coast took fourth place. The team's record for the season was 33-5.

Bob's 1993 5th place nationally ranked team poses in the Hutchinson Sports Arena. *(Kneeling at left), Coach Bob Weathers, Cheerleaders (from left) Candace Payne of Bay St. Louis, Shelli Sims of Long Beach, Tommy Everett of Wiggins, Stacy Jackson of Long Beach, D'Ann Vecchio of Gautier, Tracy Taylor of Gautier. Standing next to Tracy Taylor -- Coach Wendell Weathers, standing behind Coach Bob Weathers wearing jacket--Terrell Holmes, Manager. Players (from left) Quincy Jackson (leaning on Holmes) of Vancleave, Craig Stallings of Long Beach, Albert Graham (No. 30) of St. Martin, Robert Wilkerson of Moss Point, Ike Gamble (No. 40) of Detroit, Michigan, Pat Savoy of Thibodaux, Louisiana, Paul Fleming (No. 35) of Gulfport, Riocus Davis of Wiggins, Sam Bowie of Gulfport, Derrick Oates (No. 5) of Lucedale, Derek Watts of Gulfport, Jeff Davis (Trainer), Ken Ray (manager) of Lucedale, and an unknown spectator "walk-on." Photo courtesy of Bob Weathers.*

1993-This team captured Bob's thirteenth south division trophy, lost the state championship, then turned around and took Bob's third NJCAA Region XXIII Championship in three years. For the second time in two years the Bulldogs went to Hutchinson, Kansas. On Saturday, March 20, 1993, the Bulldogs won a fifth-place national ranking defeating Oklahoma's Rose State College 81-80 in overtime. Team record for the season was 30-5.

Tommie Weathers stands next to her husband as he holds the NJCAA Hall of Fame plaque following presentation ceremonies in Hutchinson, Kansas, on March 19, 1994.

Bob's team did not go back to Hutchinson, Kansas, in 1994, but he did. On March 14, 1994, he was inducted into the NJCAA Hall of Fame. This was the top personal honor in a career that was by no means over. At the close of the 20th century Bob was described as the "Most Winning Active Junior College Basketball Coach in the Nation." Only one other coach in 20th century junior college history had won more games.

As he finished his 40th season at MGCCC in 2000, MGCCC finished its 75th "season," so Bob Weathers had been the basketball coach for more than half the college's existence. In the 20th century the Perkinston institution's men's basketball teams won fourteen south division championships, nine state championships, three Region XXIII titles, one Fourth Place National Trophy, and one Fifth Place National Ranking. Bob Weathers coached all of those teams. No other Perkinston men's basketball coach ever won a collegiate trophy at the state level. In his 20th century career, Bob had one losing season, 10-16 in 1997. The 2000 team finished like old times (19-8) bringing his career record to a stunning 834-314

But Bob's remarkable achievements on the court were by no means his only ones. In summer 1961, he introduced the concept of the "summer basketball" camp in Mississippi. He got the idea by observing such camps while playing summer league basketball in the Catskills of New York in the 1950s, and he patterned his on those. Each summer from 1961 to 1978, Bob ran two separate weeklong camps. One camp was for high school boys becoming sophomores, juniors, and seniors. The other camp was for boys becoming 7th, 8th, and 9th graders. Aside from providing the youngsters with the chance to learn the rules and fundamentals of the game of basketball under the direction of a staff of professionals, Bob gave these boys an unforgettable experience in "going to college." Soon the idea of the summer basketball camp spread to other colleges, some of which still held them in 2000. Bob stopped his camps after 17 years because, in his words:

"Kids who once only played basketball began to play other sports and they wanted to leave my camp to go play something like summer league baseball, and then come back. Well, if I couldn't keep them here to focus them on basketball, then there was no need to hold the camps."

For nearly a decade Bob held a weeklong summer basketball camp gratis for the kids of the Baptist Children's Village in Jackson. Said Bob:

"This was one of the most enjoyable experiences of my life. For the first time I learned the real meaning of "starved for attention." I learned what it is like not to have what the average person has. When I drove in the parking lot there would be eight or ten kids ranging from five or six years old to eighteen waiting for me. They were happy just to sit next to me and listen. In time, changes at the Village, such as raising their own foods and setting up a softball league lessened their need. In the summer of 1979 I was to go to Denmark to teach Danish basketball coaches but Jabo (the Perk mascot at the time) got in a fight. I kicked him trying to break it up and broke my foot. I didn't go to Denmark and I didn't go back to the Children's Village."

Jabo

How the Ball Bounced in Mississippi and MGCCC

In order to provide the layman with a generalized overview of the supra organizations charged with the promotion and governance of Mississippi junior/community college sports, Coach Robert "Bob" Weathers consented to an interview concerning the subject. The information was given from the standpoint of a basketball coach, but much of what he had to say shed light on other sports as well. Additional information obtained from handbooks published by bodies governing Mississippi sports was added by the author.

As the 20th century ended, in basketball, as in other sports, two records were running simultaneously--an "overall record" and more importantly a "division record." The Mississippi Association of Community and Junior Colleges (MACJC) divided major athletic teams (basketball, football, and baseball) into a south division and a north division. Except for East Central all south division community colleges were located south of Interstate 20, which bisected the state east to west. East Central was placed in the south division in order to make an equal number with the seven junior colleges in the north division. In the late 1980s all Mississippi public two-year institutions except Jones adopted the designation "community college." Jones remained a "junior college" in 2000.

South Division
Copiah-Lincoln Community College (Wesson) Wolves
East Central Community College (Decatur) Warriors
Hinds Community College
(Utica Campus) Bulldogs -- basketball
(Raymond Campus) Eagles -- all other sports
Jones Junior College (Ellisville) Bobcats
Mississippi Gulf Coast Community College Bulldogs
Pearl River Community College (Poplarville) Wildcats
Southwest Community College (Summit) Bears

North Division:
Coahoma Community College (Clarksdale) Tigers
East Mississippi Community College (Scooba) Lions
Holmes Community College (Goodman) Bulldogs
Itawamba Community College (Fulton) Indians
Miss. Delta Community College (Moorhead) Trojans
Northeast Community College (Booneville) Tigers
Northwest Community College (Senatobia) Rangers

Each basketball team in each division was required to play "home and home" each season. So each team played twelve division games and a 12-0 division record was perfect. The south division championship record was determined by single elimination until the two teams with the best records met in a showdown, the victor of which became south division (also called south state) champion. Then these two teams met their two counterparts in the north division

Coach Bob Weathers in the Wentzell Center dressing room in 1996.

(number one playing number two in each case) in the state play-offs until one emerged as the final victor--Mississippi state champion. Depending on the breaks, a number two-division team could win the state championship even though it lost its division championship game. (By the same token a team could fail to win a state championship and go on to win in regionals.)

Because the south division contained seven teams, the Bulldogs were required to play only 12 games "home and home" in a regular season. On the other hand, the National Junior College Athletic Association (NJCAA) mandated that no team could play more than 30 games before the Region XXIII play-offs. In Bob's words,

"So I play 25 games per year and save five slots in case I need them to win south division and state because it could take that many to do it. But other states are not organized the same way, so those states' coaches can and do play 30 games and do not have to save any back like I do. You can see how they can rack up games on me so fast that I can never catch them. And I'm not saying any of them choose the weakest teams they can to play out of conference, but I am saying that I don't because I want to test my players against good teams to keep up their edge."

The location of Perkinston within 100 miles of and between New Orleans and Mobile placed Bob in range of many good teams against which his players could test their mettle. Many other isolated community colleges in the state, though, did not have that opportunity. At the MACJC meeting in January 2000, the presidents of Mississippi's community and junior colleges voted to require all south division and all north division teams to compete once in regular season play effective the 2000-2001 season. Beginning that season, therefore, twelve plus seven or 19 games would be required.

The next level above the MACJC state title was the NJCAA regional title. The NJCAA, founded in Fresno, California, in 1938, divided the nation into sixteen regions in 1949. The first sport to have a national title was basketball, and the 1949 NJCAA championship tournament took place in Hutchinson, Kansas, which became the permanent 20th century site of that tournament. From 1949 to the school year 1982-83, NJCAA Region VII included the states of Mississippi, Tennessee, and Kentucky. In the school year 1982-83 Mississippi and Louisiana were combined to form new Region XXIII. The Louisiana teams in Region XXIII were Delgado (New Orleans) Community College, Bossier Parish (Bossier City) Community College, and Southern University Shreveport (Shreveport), which is a junior college. The Mississippi members were the 14 state-supported colleges mentioned earlier plus Mary Holmes College, a private college at West Point, and Meridian Community College.

Meridian Community College, Mississippi's only state-supported municipal community college, withdrew from MACJC (but retained NJCAA membership) in order to elude the severe strictures placed on member institutions by that body. By becoming "independent," Meridian Community College was subject only to the NJCAA rules and regulations. Meridian Community College could practice red-shirting, and it could recruit anywhere in Mississippi or the world. While Meridian could not compete for state athletic titles, it could compete for regional and national titles. Both Meridian and Mary Holmes styled their athletic teams as Eagles.

Once the Mississippi state championship was decided, then all four teams (numbers one and two north division and south division) plus the teams with the next best record from both the north and south divisions went to the NJCAA regional play-offs. After this process of elimination the regional winners then went to Hutchinson, Kansas, for the final play-offs which at last decided the national champion team.

The road to any championship is a hard one. In Bob's words:

"Using Pearl River as an example, first I have to beat them twice 'home and home'. Then if we wind up facing them in the south division play-off I have to beat them again. But no matter which of us wins we both go to the state championship play-offs against the two best north division teams. If we both win against the north teams then we wind up facing one another again for the state title. So I might have to beat Pearl River four times to win the state championship. Then if we both make the Region XXIII play-offs, we face off for a fifth time. I mean--how many times you got to whip somebody to prove you're better? And I don't care how good you are, they are liable to get lucky on you at some point just by the law of averages."

The NJCAA had "divisions," too, but these divisions were not geographical. NJCAA Division I colleges gave full scholarships to athletes, Division II members gave tuition only, and Division III schools gave nothing. To further complicate matters, the same college usually had separate sports in different divisions depending on scholarships. For example, in 2000, MGCCC was Division I in basketball (men's and women's), football, and baseball. But, MGCCC golf, tennis, men's outdoor track and field, and women's slowpitch softball were all Division II.

The scope of aid rendered to student athletes was mandated to member colleges in Division I and Division II by the NJCAA but not the number of scholarships to be granted. Neither did the NJCAA set geographical limits whence recruits could be garnered. Some community colleges gave full scholarships including room, board, and tuition to all the basketball players they wished to recruit, and some recruited not only nationwide but worldwide. The MACJC, though, allowed members only eight basketball scholarships annually, only two of which could be given to out-of-state students, and in-state recruiting was restricted to the district served by any particular community college. In the case of MGCCC, recruiting was restricted to the four counties served by the school--George, Jackson, Stone, and Harrison. These scholarships could be divided into tenths. In this manner the eight could be stretched to serve 13 or 14 athletes on a partial basis.

Relatively few community colleges in the nation fielded football teams in 2000 due to the heavy capital outlay necessary to build a stadium, which then served in no other capacity. On the other hand, most junior colleges had a field house or gymnasium because of the myriad uses offered by such an enclosed structure. Because junior colleges viewed a gymnasium as a necessity and a football stadium as a luxury, 438 (225 were Division I) junior colleges participated in NJCAA basketball while 76 (all were Division I) played NJCAA football, and 379 (191 were Division I) NJCAA members fielded a baseball team.

Coach Bob Weathers's Basketball Championships 1961-2000

Year	South Division	State Championship	NJCAA Tournaments
1961	SD Runner-up	SC Runner-up	
1962	SD		
1963			
1964	SD	SC	
1965	SD Runner-up		
1966	SD	SC	
1967		SC Runner-up	
1968	SD		
1969	SD	SC	
1970	SD	SC	
1971			
1972			
1973	SD Runner-up		
1974			
1975			
1976			
1977	SD		
1978		SC	
1979			
1980	SD		
1981	SD	SC	
1982		SC Runner-up	
1983	SD		NJCAA Region XXIII Runner-up
1984		SC	
1985			
1986	SD Runner-up		
1987	SD		
1988	SD Runner-up	SC Runner-up	
1989			
1990	SD Runner-up		NJCAA Region XXIII Champions
1991	SD	SC	NJCAA Region XXIII Champions NJCAA National Tournament 4th in Nation
1992	SD Runner-up	SC	
1993	SD	SC Runner-up	NJCAA Region XXIII Champions NJCAA National Tournament 5th in Nation
1994			
1995			
1996	SD		
1997			
1998			
1999		SC Runner-up	NJCAA Region XXIII Runner-up
2000	SD Runner-up		NJCAA Region XXIII Runner-up

The year given for a team is the second or spring semester of a college session.

Coach Bob Weathers
Personal Statistics 1955-2000

College:	1,148	834	314
High School:	23	13	10
USM Freshman:	35	30	5
Total Games:	1,206	Won: 877	Lost: 329

SUE ROSS AND THE REVIVAL OF WOMEN'S INTERCOLLEGIATE SPORTS 1960 - 1979

Barbara Ann "Sue" Ross of Gautier began her career at Perkinston in August 1960, when she was hired to teach women's physical education classes. She was an instructor and not a coach because all college women's competitive sports, save tennis, had been eliminated statewide in fall 1955. At Perkinston in 1960, Leonard Sumrall, who was hired at the same time as Ross, among other coaching duties, had charge of the men's and women's tennis teams. When Sumrall resigned in December 1963, Ross succeeded him as men's and women's tennis coach, in addition to her other duties as an instructor. Her women's tennis teams won the Mississippi state championships of 1967 and 1968. But Ross's main contributions to women's junior college sports in Mississippi lay in her efforts to resurrect women's basketball and in the establishment of new areas of women's competition.

Soon after Ross had arrived at Perkinston in 1960, a number of her women students and even some women faculty members who wished to play basketball prevailed on her to sponsor an independent women's team. According to Ross, "The girls could play as long as they had a faculty member coaching or chaperoning the group." By 1962 Ross was sponsoring an independent Perkinston women's team which played a schedule set by an organization called the Amateur Athletic Union (AAU). The AAU had formed a coastal area league made up of teams fielded primarily by businesses but open to any group that wished to participate.

After Ross became the official college tennis coach, she came into contact with other women in the physical education field throughout the state who shared her vision regarding women's junior college sports. Ross and others working through the Mississippi Association of Health, Physical Education, and Recreation professionals (MAHPER) founded a state-wide organization known as the Mississippi Association of Extramural Athletics for College Women (MAEACW). According to Ross, "Since the state had eliminated all intercollegiate women's sports except tennis, we couldn't use the word 'intercollegiate' to describe one college's women's basketball or volleyball team playing another, so we had to find another word. Since the colleges had intramural teams playing one another on their campuses and which I supervised on the Perkinston Campus, we came up with the word 'extramural' to describe play between teams from two different colleges. At Perkinston we financed our MAEACW teams through money earned by holding summer cheerleader clinics which brought in 400 or 500 girls per summer."

With the establishment of MAEACW, junior and senior colleges throughout the state began fielding teams. Ross remembered that Southwest Junior College was one of the first. Other junior colleges participating early on were Hinds, East Central, Co-Lin, Meridian, and Northwest. Senior colleges participating included the University of Southern Mississippi, Mississippi State College for Women, Mississippi College, Belhaven, Blue Mountain, Millsaps, and William Carey.

MGCJC women's basketball players get together with Coach Sue Ross (right) to map out game strategy for the AIAW District III Tournament slated for March 9, 1974. The players are (from left) Daphne Easterling (No. 24) of Long Beach, Debbie Triplett (No. 12) of Saucier, Elizabeth Trussell (No. 11) of Gautier, and Luzenia Cowart (No. 32) of Lucedale.

Ross's MAEACW team played for the first time in the 1967-1968 season, winning five games and losing two. The next season her team posted a 10-1 record with the most memorable victories coming February 27-March 1, 1969, when the MGCJC women hosted the inaugural MAEACW Gulf Coast Tournament and won the tournament trophy. In three days of play the Perk women defeated in succession

Sue Ross's victorious MGCJC women's basketball team with the trophy they won in the inaugural MAEACW Gulf Coast tournament on March 1, 1969, in Wentzell Center. From left, Rita Kalifeh (No. 30) of Mississippi City; Edna (Parker) Bond (No. 32) of Wiggins, Sharon Whatley (No. 40) of Pascagoula, Alice Dalrymple (No. 34) of Wiggins, Karen McKay (No. 44) of Pass Christian , Peggy Richard (No. 24) of Biloxi, Jennifer Ladner (No. 42) of DeLisle, and Laura Murray (No. 52) of Gulfport. Not pictured: Sharon Freret.

Southwest Junior College (55-42), Hinds Junior College (53-45), and the University of Southern Mississippi (50-46). It was only a local tournament and "unofficial" at that, but it and others like it were significant milestones on the road back to state-sanctioned intercollegiate sports for women.

Also in 1969 Ross fielded a women's team in yet another sport--volleyball. In December her volleyball team took the MAEACW state volleyball championship title by defeating Hinds in the state tournament held at USM.

In 1970 Perk hosted a second Gulf Coast Basketball Tournament, but in 1971 the event was billed as "a tournament for the state basketball playoffs." Ross, who was by then the state MAEACW association chairperson, invited fans to attend and "see in practice the new rules adopted for women's basketball just this year." By way of further explanation, she announced, "The women's game is more like the men's game in that they play full-court or five-man basketball and also have a 30-second clock rule." According to Ross, "This 1971 tournament marked the end of the old sextet and the birth of our modern way of playing women's basketball."

In the March 3-6, 1971, state tournament, the MGCJC team defeated East Central 66-39 and Hinds 53-39 to take the junior college division. Then Ross's team defeated MSCW, the winner in the senior college division, to take overall state championship honors.

Florence Jones of Leaf became a member of Ross's basketball team in the 1971-1972 season. She was the first black woman to play for MGCJC in any sport. Photo 1972 Perkolator, p. 145.

The next season, 1971-1972, saw the establishment of a new national women's sports organization called the Association for Intercollegiate Athletics for Women (AIAW). The AIAW aimed to divide the nation into "regions" or "districts" and stage tournaments at that level with the winners of those contests playing for a national championship. The AIAW was not restricted to basketball but also intended to sponsor competition in volleyball, softball, and other sports.

MGCJC affiliated with the AIAW in its first year of existence, and Ross hosted the AIAW Region III championship basketball tournament at Perkinston March 3-4, 1972. In recalling that tournament Ross mused, "We really should have called it the 'District III AIAW Tournament' because that is the official word the AIAW used for geographical divisions, but both 'district' and 'region' mean about the same thing. The National Junior College Athletic Association (NJCAA), which did not sanction women's sports at the time, used the word 'region', so I guess that's why the AIAW used the word 'district'."

AIAW District III included Mississippi, Alabama, Georgia, and Florida, and junior and senior college teams from all four of those states played in the tournament at Perk. According to Ross, "We had won the MAEACW state title that year [1972], and we took the District III Runner-Up trophy at that 1972 tournament. I know the trophy says 'region' on it but it should not have. There was a lot of confusion in trying to set up a new organization."

When asked about the relationship between MAEACW and AIAW, Ross replied, "The MAEACW was to the AIAW exactly what the Mississippi Association of Junior Colleges (MAJC) was to the National Junior College Athletic Association. The one governed the state level, and the other governed district or regional and national level. Since the MAJC wouldn't have us women then the NJCAA couldn't have us. And the NJCAA didn't like it because we were setting up a rival league. So the NJCAA started pressing the states like Mississippi to do something about it. About the same time the federal government through Title 9 started pressing for equal rights for women. Meanwhile we just kept on doing our thing." Ross continued, "After the 1972 season the MAEACW affiliated more closely with the AIAW, so we began to use the acronym 'MAIAW' in order to avoid using 'MAEACWAIAW' to describe our competition at the state level."

The AIAW held "district tournaments" in the 1971-1972 season but did not hold a national junior college tournament. In the 1972-73 season a spokesperson for the organization announced that while AIAW would not hold district competitions that year, it would host a national invitational tournament to determine a national champion.

In August 1972, Ross received a new assistant coach in the person of Doris Ruth "Blackie" Smith, a native of Moselle and a graduate of USM. In addition to assisting in basketball, Smith took charge of the tennis and volleyball teams and began laying the groundwork for a softball team.

Assistant women's coach Doris Smith (left) stands with head women's coach Sue Ross in front of the bulldog painting on the wall of Wentzell Center. Smith became Ross's assistant in August 1972 and succeeded to the head coach's position in 1979 when Ross transferred to the Jackson County Campus.

While the women's basketball team did not win state that year, its 11-5 performance was sufficient to receive an invitation to the inaugural AIAW National Junior College Women's Basketball Tournament slated for March 15-17 at Delta College in Bay City, Michigan. With the blessing of Perkinston Campus Executive Dean C. G. Odom, Ross and Smith set off on the 1,200-mile trek with their ten-member team and equipment packed into a car and a station wagon.

Seventeen women's junior college teams from as far west as Utah and as far north as New York participated in the tournament. The MGCJC team was the only one from Mississippi, and only one other team was from the South. In the opening round on Thursday, March 15, the MGCJC team defeated Bergen Community College of Paramus, New

WHAT A DIFFERENCE A POINT MAKES: THE AIAW NATIONAL WOMEN'S BASKETBALL CHAMPIONSHIP TOURNAMENTS OF 1973 AND 1974.

(Right) The Thrill of Victory! Melody Mixon of Gulfport made the 20-foot jump-shot that won the AIAW national championship of 1973 in Bay City, Michigan, for MGCJC by one point over Anderson (South Carolina) Community College. Photo 1972 Perkolator.

(Far right) The players of the MGCJC basketball team who won the AIAW National Junior College Basketball Tournament in Bay City, Michigan, on March 17, 1973, pose with their trophies in Wentzell Center. ***Kneeling*** *(from left), Daphne Swanier (No. 10) of Pass Christian, Pam Ferrill (No. 14) of Biloxi, Shelia Dees (No. 23) of Biloxi, Elizabeth Trussell (No. 11) of Gautier, and Melody Mixon (No. 20) of Gulfport.* ***Standing*** *(from left), Florence Jones (No. 22) of Leaf, Margaret (Niolet) Scurfield (No. 25) of Pass Christian, Arla Degges (No. 21) of Gulfport, Pat Clark (No. 13) of Sumrall, and Terrie Robinson (No. 15) of Biloxi.*

(Above) The 1974 MAIAW state championship MGCJC basketball team members and coaches pose with their recently won state trophy in Wentzell Center in early March 1974. (From left), Coach Sue Ross; manager Alice Martin of Wiggins, Valerie Swanier (No. 33) of Pass Christian, Debbie Triplett (No. 12) of Saucier, Jane Ann Geil (No. 31) of Gulfport, Luzenia Cowart (No. 32) of Lucedale, Lynn Hammons (No. 14) of Long Beach, Margaret (Niolet) Scurfield (No. 25) of Pass Christian, Daphne Swanier (No. 10) of Pass Christian, Sandy Stiglets (No. 21) of Hattiesburg, Beth Trussell (No. 11) of Gautier, Daphne Easterling (No. 24) of Long Beach, Pam Ferrill (No. 15) of Biloxi, Sheila Dees (No. 23) of Biloxi, and assistant Coach Doris Smith.

(Middle right) The 1974 team took the AIAW District III championship trophy on March 9, 1974, in the tournament at Jefferson Davis Campus. Pam Ferrill (No. 15) holds high the trophy (bottom left) as Beth Trussell (No. 11) (center) steadies Shelia Dees (No. 23) as she cuts the net. This victory gave the MGCJC women a shot at a second national AIAW championship in Bay City, Michigan.

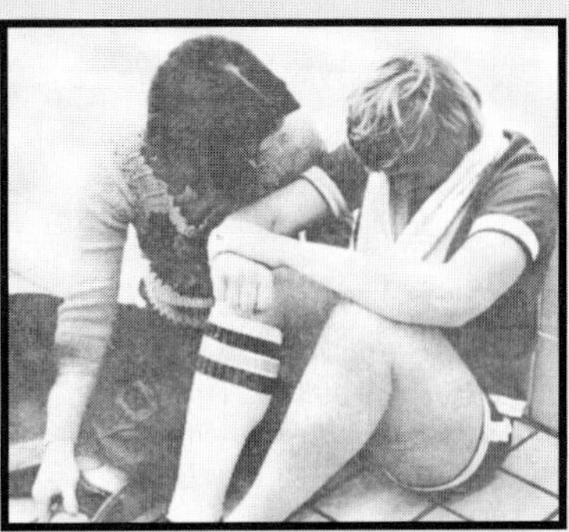

(Bottom right) The Agony of Defeat. An unknown player from Meridian Junior College consoles Jane Ann Geil (No. 31) after the MGCJC team lost the 1974 AIAW national championship to Anderson (South Carolina) Community College by one point in Bay City, Michigan, on March 23.

Jersey, (88-52). The next day the MGCJC women defeated in succession Grand Rapids (Michigan) Junior College (48-40) and Delta College, the host school, (73-35).

On Saturday at 4 p.m. the MGCJC women took the court in the national championship clash against the women's team of Anderson Community College of Anderson, South Carolina, fielded by Coach Annie Tribble. With seven seconds to play Anderson led by one point when Melody Mixon, a 5'3" guard from Gulfport hit a 20-foot jump shot from the top of the key to put MGCJC ahead 37-36 as the buzzer sounded. The AIAW women's basketball national championship of 1973 marked MGCJC's initial entry into the realm of women's sports on the national level.

The 1972-1973 season was a watershed for women's basketball at MGCJC, and the 1973-1974 season was a banner year for all Mississippi junior college women's basketball teams. After a 19-year hiatus, the Mississippi Association of Junior Colleges (MAJC) once again sanctioned women's junior college basketball as a first step to recognizing other women's sports. The impetus for such action was Mississippi's desire to fulfill the requirements of Title 9 of the federal Educational Amendment Act of 1972. Title 9 mandated equal treatment for both sexes in all facets of college life which, of course, included intercollegiate athletics. The 1973-1974 season became the first of two seasons of transition in which women's junior college basketball teams played in two leagues simultaneously and played for two state championships -- the MAIAW title and the MAJC title.

At the MAIAW state championship tournament held in Meridian on February 15, 1974, the MGCJC women's team was trailing by one point in the semi-final game against Meridian. Late in the fourth period with nine seconds to go, Shelia Dees of Biloxi hit the basket putting MGCJC over Meridian 49-48 in a cliffhanger reminiscent of the year before. The next day MGCJC defeated the Hinds Junior College Eaglettes 59-56 to take the MAIAW state championship.

As defending national AIAW champions, the MGCJC women were to host the AIAW District III Junior College Tournament held at MGCJC Jefferson Davis Campus on March 8-9. The winner of that tournament would be eligible to travel to Bay City, Michigan, later in March for a shot at the 1974 AIAW National Junior College crown.

Meanwhile Ross's team traveled to Goodman for the MAJC tournament which would decide that organization's Mississippi state women's junior college championship. The Hinds Eaglettes defeated the MGCJC women and won that state trophy.

On March 8 women's basketball teams from Mississippi, Alabama, Georgia, and Florida gathered at the JD Campus for the AIAW District III Tournament. On the first day MGCJC women defeated the Dekalb (Georgia) Junior College women 51-30. On March 9, MGCJC met the Hinds Eaglettes in the championship tilt. The seesaw battle raged with MGCJC winning the District III trophy by a score of 73-71 in the last minute of the game. As runners-up the Eaglettes also would have been eligible to go to Michigan except that Hinds had not paid its 1974 national dues. Since Meridian junior college had paid its dues, its third-place women's team went instead of Hinds.

The MGCJC and Meridian women shared a bus for the 1,200-mile journey to Bay City, Michigan, to join eleven other teams in the playoffs for the AIAW national title. The MGCJC women took their first victory on March 21 knocking off Brevard (North Carolina) Junior College 56-47. On the next day MGCJC defeated Grand Rapids (Michigan) Junior College 60-44.

On March 24 the MGCJC women again, as the year before, faced Coach Annie Tribble's team from Anderson, South Carolina. Anderson led in the scoring for most of the game, but with 2:22 left to play, the MGCJC women tied the game at 52-52. With 10 seconds to go the MGCJC women, then ahead 58-57, stole the ball but immediately lost possession on a charging foul. With Anderson back in control and six seconds left on the clock, an Anderson player made a lay-up, and the MGCJC women lost the 1974 national championship to the same team from which it had wrested the 1973 national championship and by the same margin -- one point.

At the close of the tournament AIAW officials picked the women of MGCJC and Anderson to meet again for a third time in 1975. That did not happen because the women of Southwest Junior College eliminated Ross's team in the first MAJC south division shoot-out in twenty years. At the MAJC state tournament, north division champion Itawamba wrote an end to the MGCJC season with a victory in the semi-final match. The women of Itawamba Junior College won both the MAIAW and the MAJC state titles that season. The Indianettes also won the District III AIAW trophy and a berth in the AIAW National Tournament in Vincennes, Indiana.

Other developments of that season brought about a situation which ended Mississippi junior college participation in AIAW championship competition. At the end of that season, Perkinston Campus Executive Dean Odom delivered what was the *coup de grace* to the MAIAW when he announced that, "Basketball scholarships for women, equal to those awarded to men, will be given for the 1975-76 fall term." Since MAIAW rules forbade the granting of scholarships, MGCJC would no longer participate in MAIAW-sponsored basketball. MAIAW play continued for the women of Coach Doris Smith's volleyball and softball teams because those sports afforded no scholarships. The MAJC reclaimed women's basketball by granting scholarships to the players, and the NJCAA replaced AIAW in the same fell swoop.

In further explaining compliance with Title 9, Odom explained, "The law requires reasonable expenditure and opportunities for women. Equal expenditure is not a requirement. As a result, our women basketball players will be on scholarship in 1975-76. But we have not gone to scholarships for women in tennis, track, and other sports in which our male players do not receive scholarships."

Odom had three years to comply with Title 9, but he

moved to do so immediately. In March 1975, at the same time he announced women's basketball scholarships, he announced that henceforth men and women would have the same dormitory hours and privileges:

"Students must sign out. The dormitories will be locked at 11 p.m. Women wishing to enter after that time must request a security guard to unlock the doors.

Men will not be permitted in the lobbies of women's dormitories. This regulation is necessary because there are no lobbies in dormitories for men, thus depriving females of equal visitation rights.

Women returning to the campus after 11 p.m. will have their identification cards checked by security guards to make sure they are bonafide residents of the campus."

A single revolutionary proclamation ended more than six decades of cloistering women in the dormitories of Perkinston. Women's liberation had arrived.

Margaret "Peg" Farris
All State 1976 & 1977
All NJCAA Region VII 1977
All NJCAA National Tournament Team 1977

At the awards banquet on April 29, 1975, while the women's basketball team, which turned in a 17-12 season received no honors, Smith's women's tennis team was recognized for taking the MAJC tennis championship. This was to be Smith's only such championship because after that point she no longer coached tennis. After 1975 the tennis team went through a long succession of coaches.

On May 2, 1975, Ross announced five grant-in-aid women's basketball scholarships, the first ever awarded by MGCJC. The first player to sign was Margaret "Peg" Farris, a six footer from Stone High and the daughter of Curly Farris, MGCJC's legendary baseball coach.

The MAIAW acronym disappeared from the 1975-1976 women's basketball schedule, but Smith's volleyball team still played under the aegis of that league. On November 11, Smith's volleyball team, which had been relegated to second place state by the Hinds Eaglettes the year before, took the 1975 state championship after a forfeit by Hinds.

The 1975-1976 MGCJC women's basketball season was unremarkable except in one respect. Ross decided to give the MGCJC women's basketball team a name. Not since the team had been termed "Perkettes" back in the 1950s had there been an official designation for it.

On November 10, 1975, an MGCJC press release announced that Ross's team would be called the "Coeds." That name failed to capture the imagination of sports writers, but on November 19, the *Daily Herald* termed the MGCJC team as the "girl Bulldogs." On November 27 The *North Biloxian* headlined the "Perk Ladies." On December 6 the *Sun Herald* read, "Lady Bulldogs Post Victory." By February

The 1975 women's volleyball state championship team poses with the trophy taken on November 11 due to a forfeit by Hinds. According to Coach Doris Smith (right), she fielded one final volleyball team in 1976. After that volleyball ended at MGCJC as an intercollegiate sport for the 20th century. From left kneeling, Laura Gonzalez (No. 34) of Biloxi, Teresa Gene Pucheu (No. 22) of Long Beach, Randi Bennett (No. 11) of Gulfport, Debbi Higginbotham (No. 13) of Biloxi. From left standing, Ann Wahl (No. 15) of Pass Christian, Brenda Jones (No. ?) of Wiggins, Lynette Havens (No. 24) of Lucedale, Rosemary Moody (No. 32) of Lucedale, Shelia Dellenger (No. 33) of Biloxi, Judy Niolet (No. 21) of Pass Christian, Sandra Palode (No. 12) of Pass Christian, and Glenda Dubuisson (No. 10) of Pass Christian.

1976 the Lady Bulldogs were playing the "Lady Wolves" of Co-Lin, the "Lady Bobcats" of Jones, and the "Lady Bears" of Southwest. The 1975-1976 season marks the point at which most Mississippi junior college women's basketball players became "ladies."

The Lady Bulldogs ended the season 12-4 in south division MAJC play and 14-6 in state MAJC play. Ross's team was still playing in MAIAW senior college invitational tournaments, bringing the whole season record to 15-11. These invitational tournaments, though, were really exhibition matches with no junior college sanction.

The 1976-1977 women's junior college basketball season resulted in an unprecedented three-way tie among MGCJC, Co-Lin, and East Central for best team record on the eve of the south division championship tournament. Mississippi Junior College Conference Executive Director Ray Busby was forced to flip a coin to decide placement of teams in the tournament held at Wesson on February 17-19, 1976.

Once play began, the high scoring trio of Peg Farris, Connie Winstead, and Edna Purvis led the Lady Bulldogs to victory. The three racked up two-thirds of MGCJC's score in the 93-65 defeat of Utica on the first night of play. On the second night against Co-Lin, the trio scored 67 of the Lady Bulldogs' points in the 74-62 win over that team. In the south division championship tilt on February 19, the triumvirate scored 50 of the Lady Bulldog's points in the 65-50 victory over East Central.

That victory gained Perkinston the honor of hosting the women's state championship tournament February 23-25 in

"SOUTH STATE, STATE, REGION SEVEN, AND SEVENTH NATIONALLY IN SEVENTY SEVEN." -- *SUE ROSS*

(Left) On February 24, 1977, in Wentzell Center, MAJC Athletic Commissioner Ray Busby presents the state women's basketball trophy to Marylyne Powe (No. 25) (right) while Angie Wade is held high by Peg Farris (left) and Connie Winstead (center).

(Left) Edna Purvis cuts the net after the Lady Bulldogs defeated East Central for the 1977 state championship. The 5'9" freshman from Lucedale was named All State, All NJCAA Region VII, and All NJCAA National Tournament Team. On March 18, 1977, at the NJCAA Women's National Basketball Tournament in Overland Park, Kansas, Purvis set a new NJCAA record for free throws by making 14 of 16 attempted.

(Above) Connie Winstead scored 42 points in the state championship elimination match against Coahoma on February 23, 1977, the record for points made by a player in a single game during the Ross era. The 6' sophomore from Pass Christian, was named All State in 1976 and 1977. In 1977 she was named All NJCAA Region VII, Most Valuable Player in the NJCAA Region VII Tournament, and NJCAA All American Second Team.

(Right) The 1977 Lady Bulldogs posing in Wentzell Center won the south division, state, and NJCAA Region VII championships, and took a seventh place trophy in the NJCAA National Women's Basketball Championship Tournament held in Overland Park, Kansas March 14-18. This team turned in the best MGCJC women's sports performance in MAJC and NJCAA play in the 20th century. From left, Brenda Clark (No. 24) of Hurley, Debbie Webb (No. 15) of Hurley, Meg Taylor (No. 23) of Gulfport, Sissy Freeman (No. 52) of Lucedale, Cheri McCook (No. 33) of Long Beach, Peg Farris (No. 55) of Perkinston, Patricia O'Neal (No. 20) of Perkinston, Helen Meaut (No. 35) of Ocean Springs, Connie Winstead (No. 11) of Pass Christian, Marylyne Powe, No. 25) of Ocean Springs, Edna Purvis (No. 14) of Lucedale, Robin Williams (No. 12) of Gulfport, Angie Wade (No. 18) of New Iberia, Louisiana, and Valerie Meaut (manager) of Ocean Springs.

Wentzell Center. In the opening game the Lady Bulldogs destroyed runner-up north division Coahoma 105-67 with Winstead alone accounting for 42 points, the record for points scored in a single game by a player in Ross's career. In the next game, runner-up south division East Central defeated the north division champion East Mississippi. That meant that the Lady Bulldogs, having lost one and won one in regular season play against East Central and then having played East Central again to take the south division crown, would have to face the Lady Warriors a fourth time in the same season.

It was touch and go when both Winstead and Purvis fouled out in the fourth period, but in Ross's words, "The bench came through." The Lady Bulldogs defeated the Lady Warriors 76-64 to take the first state-sanctioned Mississippi junior college state championship in the history of the school since its founding in 1911.

MAJC membership brought with it membership in the NJCAA, so the team's next stop was the NJCAA Region VII Tournament for teams from Mississippi, Tennessee, and Kentucky held March 1-5, 1977 in Cleveland, Tennessee. Actually the team made three unscheduled stops due to bus breakdowns enroute to Cleveland, where the bus went into the repair shop.

On Thursday afternoon March 3, the Lady Bulldogs defeated Chattanooga (Tennessee) State Technical College 85-55. That night the MGCJC team hitched a ride on the East Mississippi Junior College bus to the Cleveland State Community College fieldhouse where the Lady Bulldogs repaid the Lady Lions for their courtesy by taking them for a 75-59 ride on the court. On Saturday night the Lady Bulldogs triumphed 68-51 over the Lady Cougars of Cleveland State Community College to take the 1977 NJCAA Region VII championship. The victorious team's next stop was to be Perkinston to get ready for the Third National NJCAA National Women's Basketball Championship Tournament set to begin March 14 in Overland Park, Kansas. Actually the next stop came late the next night enroute to Perkinston when the MGCJC bus broke down yet again.

On the eve of departure for Kansas, the Lady Bulldogs' season record stood at 24-11 with a 13-game winning streak. Ross confessed she felt a bit of triskadiskaphobia, and then she added, "We'll be taking the new bus this time."

The Lady Bulldogs arrived at the Johnson County Community College Campus in Overland Park four victories away from a national crown. In their first game on March 15, they took on unranked Temple (Texas) Junior College and lost 78-59. That loss snapped their winning streak at 13 games, knocked them into the consolation bracket, and put the team in the position of having to win four games in succession merely to take seventh in the nation.

The Lady Bulldogs won four games in a row, defeating Northeast (Norfolk, Nebraska) Community College (88-42), Meramac (St. Louis, Missouri) Community College (64-55), Essex (Baltimore, Maryland) Community College (76-53), and St. Claire (Port Huron, Michigan) Community College (71-62). In the game against Essex on March 18, Edna Purvis set a new NJCAA free throw record of 14 of 16 attempted.

Ross put her 1977 team's accomplishments succinctly, "South state, state, Region Seven, and seventh nationally in seventy-seven." This was destined to be the high water mark of MGCJC women's NJCAA play in the 20th century.

Ross coached the Lady Bulldogs for two more seasons. By the close of the 1978-1979 season her overall record in coaching basketball for the twelve years beginning with the 1967-1968 season stood at 184 wins and 81 losses. In August 1979 she transferred to Jackson County Campus, located in her hometown of Gautier, where she served as the intramural director and as a physical education instructor until her retirement in May 1991.

Ross made a significant contribution in the realm of the re-establishment of state-sanctioned women's competitive sports in Mississippi. In the specific case of MGCJC women's basketball, she re-established the sport. In a dozen years she led her basketball teams from the extra-mural fringe back into full recognition by the Mississippi Association of Junior Colleges, which by the time she accomplished that aim, included membership in the NJCAA. During those 12 years her teams had won trophies at every level of competition in every field of contention. Since she was in a class by herself in what she needed to do and what she did, the only word that can describe her contribution is the adjective "unique."

Sue Ross's Women's Basketball Record 1968-1979

Year	Won	Lost
1967-1968	5	2
1968-1969	10	1
1969-1970	14	5
1970-1971	14	4
1971-1972	15	5
1972-1973	15	5
1973-1974	21	8
1974-1975	17	12
1975-1976	15	11
1976-1977	28	12
1977-1978	16	8
1978-1979	14	8
Totals	**184**	**81**

Sue Ross (left) discusses some of the finer points of basketball with Jackson County students Victor Bailey (center) and Rickey Wolverton. Ross transferred to the Jackson County Campus in her hometown of Gautier in fall 1979 to become the director of intramural sports and a physical education teacher. She retired in May 1991.

WOMEN'S SPORTS 1979 - 2000

Sue Ross passed her mantle to her assistant coach, Doris Smith, who had been with her since 1972 and who had shared in her greatest triumphs in the years 1973 through 1977. In thirteen seasons of coaching the Lady Bulldogs, beginning with 1979-1980 and ending 1991-1992, Smith turned out some strong teams but won only one first place state championship--the south division title of 1988. Though her team did not win the 1988 state title and took only the runner-up trophy at the NJCAA Region XXIII Tournament, Smith was selected by her peers as the Mississippi Junior/Community College Women's Basketball Coach of the Year. The honor represented a departure from tradition, only coaches who had won the overall state title had received such recognition in the past.

The 1984 state championship softball team poses with their trophy in the Perkinston Campus Quadrangle with the Old Gym in the background. ***Front*** *(from left) Gaye Reynolds of Lucedale, Kathy White of Ocean Springs, Dina Fountain of Biloxi, Cindy Gibson of Lucedale, Melonda Peters of Pascagoula, Deborah Linda Burts of Pascagoula.* ***Back*** *(from left), Tracey Mattina of Biloxi, Angela Wolfe of D'Iberville, Nina Monroe of Pascagoula, Tracy Neal of Vancleave, Tammie Dedeaux of Pass Christian, Melinda Webb of Ocean Springs, and coach Doris Smith.*

Glenda Jones accepts the 1988 south division championship trophy for the Lady Bulldogs at Decatur. ***Front*** *(from left), Tina Pipkins of Lucedale, Clara James of Wiggins, Hope Bonne of Pass Christian, coach Doris Smith, Glenda Jones of Wiggins.* ***Back*** *(from left), Tisha Langfitt of Lucedale, Camilla Jackson of Pascagoula, Alyce Lawrence of Lucedale, Rhonda Norwood of Gulfport, Mona Yates of Wiggins, assistant coach Brenda Shotts, and Christy Bartholomew of New Iberia, Louisiana.*

If Smith's attainments in the realm of basketball were not as great as those of others, few could match her abilities as a softball coach. In 1972, her first year at MGCJC, Smith fielded a softball team. For the next two years, though, her energies in the spring were directed to tennis. With tennis in other hands after 1975, she set about making softball a serious spring sport.

Because no scholarships were given in softball, that sport remained under the aegis of the MAIAW for years after women's basketball rejoined the fold of the MAJC. Smith's team took the 1977 MAIAW Mississippi Softball Championship and followed that with three second-place state showings in a row.

By the opening of the 1981 softball season, the sport had been sanctioned by the MAJC, and Smith's team posted a 24 win, 2 loss record to take the initial state trophy. In 1984 the Lady Bulldog softballers won the state trophy again and also the NJCAA Region XXIII title. Smith's team then journeyed to the NJCAA Women's Slowpitch Softball National Championship Tournament hosted by Wallace State Community College in Hanceville, Alabama, where the team tied for seventh place in the nation.

In 1986 the Lady Bulldogs had their best year, winning both the state and Region XXIII championships and posting fifth in the nation at the NJCAA National Tournament. For her 1986 performance Smith was named Softball Coach of the Year by the Mississippi Junior College Athletic Association and by the National Junior College Athletic Association Region XXIII.

Smith led the Lady Bulldog softballers to a south division championship in 1988 and the following year took the trophies for second-place state and NJCAA Region XXIII runner-up. In 1991, Smith's assistant coach, Doug Borries, led the team to the south division crown, the final championship of Smith's tenure. Smith retired in May 1992 after a 20-year career at MGCCC. She pegged her MGCCC basketball record at 129-141 and her softball record at 150-69.

Greg Holmes
Lady Bulldog Basketball Coach 1992-

Greg Holmes, a 41-year-old native of Terry, replaced Smith as coach of the Lady Bulldogs in August 1992. Holmes had attended Hinds Junior College, earned his bachelor's degree at the University of Southern Mississippi and his master's degree in physical education from Jackson State

Coach Greg Holmes's Lady Bulldogs took their first trophy with a south division win against Co-Lin's Lady Wolves in 1997. Keisha Nelson (center) of Wiggins, celebrates the victory. Photo from 1997 Perkolator, p. 130.

University. His previous positions included eight years coaching both boys' and girls' basketball at Utica High School and eleven years as head mentor for the girls' basketball team at Harrison Central High School. His overall coaching record at the time he came to MGCCC stood at 552-75 with four state championships for girls and 158-57 and two state championships for boys. Holmes added his first trophy to the MGCCC Lady Bulldogs' collection by taking the 1997 south division championship and an NJCAA Region XXIII runner-up spot.

In fall 1997 Holmes received aid for his program in the person of Carolyn Patterson, who signed on as assistant coach of the Lady Bulldogs basketball team and coach of the softball team. Patterson, a graduate of South Jones High School in Ellisville, had earned her bachelor's degree from Anderson (South Carolina) College and her master's degree at the University of Southern Mississippi. She had been assistant basketball coach and softball coach at Jones Junior College for one year when she accepted a similar position at MGCCC.

The Holmes-Patterson duo closed the 20th century at MGCCC in grand style. Each of them won a state championship.

The Lady Bulldog basketball team faced the East Central Lady Warriors four times in the 1999-2000 season. The MGCCC women lost both regular season games to East Central but then turned around and defeated Decatur twice in championship matches. On February 17, by a score of 101-91 in the playoffs at Utica, the Lady Bulldogs took the south division crown, and on February 22 at Booneville by a score of 71-64 the state crown as well. Coach Holmes's south division and state championship triumphs of 2000 are eerily reminiscent of Coach Sue Ross's similar victories in 1977. In the history of the institution since its establishment at Perkinston in 1911, only twice had its women's basketball team won both south division and the state titles in state sanctioned play in the same year. In each case, Holmes's team and Ross's team played East Central four times, and in each case Holmes's women and Ross's women defeated the Lady Warriors of Decatur for both trophies.

Coach Greg Holmes's Lady Bulldogs took both the south division and state championships of 2000 defeating East Central to win each title. The Lady Bulldogs were eliminated in the Region XXIII play-offs at Clinton. ***Sitting*** *(from left), Dinesha James (manager) of Alexandria, Louisiana, Reshonda Whiten (No. 12) of Baton Rouge, Louisiana, Shanel Handy (No. 11) of DeRidder, Louisiana, Lacresia Anderson (No. 20) of Gulfport, Yennette Smith (No. 33) of St. Martin, and Miriam Mason (trainer) of Waynesboro.* ***Kneeling*** *(from left), Jennifer Underwood (No. 35) of St. Martin, Felicia Hayes (No. 23) of Gulfport, Robin Collier (No. 32) of St. Martin, and Robyn Lewis (No. 10) of St. Martin.* ***Standing*** *(from left), Kendra Lindsey (manager) of Alexandria, Louisiana, Raina Robinson (No. 15) of Vancleave, Sheila Fairley (No. 40) of Lucedale, Pendra Lindsey (No. 55) of Alexandria, Louisiana, Felicia Gray (No. 21) of Baton Rouge, Louisiana, head coach Greg Holmes, and assistant basketball coach Carolyn Patterson.*

Felicia Hayes holds high the 2000 state women's championship basketball trophy after the Lady Bulldogs sent East Central to defeat at Booneville on February 22.

Patterson's Lady Bulldog Softball team won both the south division championship and the state championship as well. With state honors also came the NJCAA Region XXIII trophy since no other state in Region XXIII fielded a slowpitch softball team in 2000. These last softball trophies of the 20th century won by the Lady Bulldogs were especially historic because they are the final slowpitch trophies in Mississippi junior college history. By common agreement the 2000 season was the last to feature slowpitch softball. The junior/community college presidents voted to replace it with the fastpitch variety thereafter.

THE FIRST AND THE LAST

Seven members of Doris Smith's 1981 state champion slowpitch softball team (right) stand in front of the trophy case in Wentzell Center. This team won the first MAJC slowpitch softball championship in Mississippi junior college history.

Carolyn Patterson's 2000 state champion slowpitch softball team (below) won the last slowpitch softball state trophy in Mississippi junior college history.

The 1981 state championship softball team, the first to take an MAJC state-sanctioned title, consisted of (from left), Shawn Stewart of Biloxi, Pamela Slade of Brooklyn, Jill Pisarich of Biloxi, Dierdre Holden of Vancleave, Karen Johnson of Long Beach, Nancy Lee of Gulfport, and Kathy Brockway of Lucedale. Not pictured -- Evelyn Jackson of Wiggins, Courtney Cook of Pass Christian, Belinda Williams of Pascagoula, Cynthia King of Gulfport, Kelly Fore of Gulfport, Kelly Moak of Gulfport, Melanie Howell of Lucedale, Rina Sweatman of Biloxi, Becky Endt of Lucedale, Dawn Harry of Lucedale, Connie Baker of Brooklyn, Sine Turnage of Lucedale, and Jan Smith of Lucedale. Photo from 1982 Perkolator, p. 83.

The 2000 Lady Bulldogs softball team took south division honors and won the state/ NJCAA Region XXIII slowpitch softball title in the tournament at New Albany on April 28 and 29, 2000. The team finally met defeat on May 6, 2000, in Decatur, Alabama, at the NJCAA National Slowpitch Championship Tournament. ***Front*** *(from left), Nicole Holmes (sitting) of Long Beach, Rachael Bolden of Long Beach, Mandy Theobald of Pass Christian, Catherine Wood of Long Beach, Roni Tops of Pass Christian, Shanika Wells of Moss Point (holding NJCAA Region XXIII circular trophy plaque), Adrianne Parker of Ocean Springs, Takisha Meeks of Moss Point (holding the MAJC rectangular state trophy plaque), Jennifer Underwood of St. Martin, Christy Warren (sitting) of Vancleave.* ***Standing*** *(from left), Miriam Mason (manager) of Waynesboro, Dinesha James of Alexandria, Louisiana, Rachel Allen of Long Beach, Laquitta Smith (student assistant) of Wiggins, head softball Coach Carolyn Patterson of Moselle, Robyn Lewis of St. Martin, Timmy Smith (manager) of Natchez, Robin Collier of St. Martin, Yennette Smith of St. Martin, Brandi Myrick of Hurley, and Lisa English (student assistant) of Laurel.*

Sophomore Shanika Wells (two year All Region, 2000 All American) of Moss Point, holds the MJCAA Region XXIII circular trophy plaque after the victory at New Albany.

TRACK
1927 - 1960

Head coach William C. "Bill" Denson and women's coach Frances Rednick fielded Perk's first intercollegiate team to engage in state competition. At the Mississippi Association of Junior Colleges Field Meet held at Raymond on April 15, 1927, Perkinston men and women achieved several first place and several second place standings in various events.

Lee Roy Weeks fielded a full men's track team in fourteen categories of track competition in session 1929-1930, his first year as head coach at Perkinston. In 1931 assistant coach Ed Gully had charge of the Perkinston cindermen, and one of his best high jumpers was Obie Brown of Big Level. By the end of the decade Brown would himself be the track coach at Perkinston.

The *Daily Herald* March 16, 1932, noted that work had begun at Perkinston on a new track to encircle the Old Athletic Field. The track, however, would not be ready for some time. Until it was finished, the track team would travel with the baseball team and compete on tracks at other schools.

The *Daily Herald* March 20, 1933, named Elizabeth Kerr of Long Beach as "one of the Perkinston track men." Eleven

Richard Kopp photo

(Above) The oldest track trophy in the MGCCC Archives collection in 2000 was a first place loving cup for men's relay won at the MAJC State Field Meet at Raymond on April 15, 1927. The runners were Sherman Wright of Ocean Springs, Andrew Gray of Gulfport, Clyde Richmond of McComb, and Horace Watson of Gautier.

Perkinston Men's and Women's State Championship Track Team 1935. *Photo Courtesy of Joel Simpson.*
Standing *(from left) Robert Cowan (Manager) of Gulfport, J. B. Waterer of Gulfport, Foy Martin of Leland, Theron Fletcher of Vancleave, Jack Jermyn of Gulfport, Burton Hosch of Gulfport, Alfred Sandman of Laurel, John Reilly of New York, New York, Pat Crewes of Gulfport, Arnold Hebert of Houston, Texas, Luther Patton of Saucier, and Coach D. D. O'Neal.* ***Kneeling*** *(from left) Merrill "Red" True of Mississippi City, Jack Simpson of Wiggins, Oliver Smith of Gulfport, Louis Frederick of Pascagoula, Colle Larsen of Pascagoula, Emil Panero of New York, New York, Emmitt Rameriz of Tela, Honduras, and Sherwood Young of Tela, Honduras.* ***Sitting*** *(from left) Walter Hirsch of New York, New York, Helen Gray of Gulfport, Marie Hengen of Biloxi, Stella Turcotte of Waveland, Marguerite Gautier of Biloxi, and Oscar Cassibry of Gulfport.*

1936 Men's State Championship Track Team.
***Front row** (from left) Claude Campbell of Woolmarket, Arthell Kelley of Lyman, Russell Wilson of Vancleave, J. J. Pulliam of Gulfport, Holcomb Rutledge, Eugene Leuba of Moss Point, Billie Krebs of Gulfport, and coach D. D. O'Neal. **Back row** (from left) Evans Spiceland of Lucedale, Harley Baker of Hodges, Alabama, G. C. Golden of Florence, James Land of Kosciusko, Mannie Paine of Donner, Louisiana, Ike Lowery of Gulfport, John Reilly of New York, New York, and James Sasser of Gulfport. Photo Courtesy of G.C. Golden.*

The seven members of the 1936 Women's State Championship Track Team. Photos from 1936 Perkolator.

Frances Miller of Pascagoula

Helen Gray of Gulfport

Irma Lee Shattles of Perkinston

Margaret Fickes of Biloxi

Julia Russum of Perkinston

Stella Turcotte of Waveland

days later in another article the *Daily Herald* reported that Lawson "Caveman" Evans of Pascagoula had been named captain of the track team with Bess Miller of Moss Point as his alternate captain. Perkinston had only one team, and the women's names were mingled with the men's without distinction. Of course, at the contests the sexes competed separately.

Dowey D. O'Neal became the track coach in 1933. That first year only his shot putter, Buster Bosarge of Pascagoula, took first place at the Mississippi state junior college track and field meet, but that was only the beginning.

On March 24, 1934, Coach O'Neal hosted the Jones County Junior College Golden Devils at the inaugural meet on Perkinston's new cinder track. In this contest the women's track team was spoken of as separate from the men's for the first time. Both of the Perkinston teams defeated their Jones County rivals.

A month later at the state track and field meet at Wesson, the Perkinston tracksters came in third over-all, only one-half point from taking second. Perkinston took four first places--440 yard dash, broad jump, javelin, and baseball throw. In this last, Marie Hengen of Biloxi set a new state

Hazel Stone of Gulfport

Richard Kopp photo

Mississippi Junior College Association trophies of 1936. (Left) "MJCA Boys Track and Field Champions 1936" --22 inches tall. (Middle) "MJCA Boys Relay, 1936"-- 10 inches tall. (Right), The base of the women's trophy is broken off, but it read "MJCA Girls Track and Field Champions 1936."

record with a toss of 205 feet, five inches.

In 1935 O'Neal's Perkinston track and field team went undefeated, winning the men's and women's Mississippi junior college championship at Ellisville on April 20. On April 28, 1936, at Raymond, the men's and women's teams reprised their performance of the previous year to take once again both state titles in track and field.

Coach O'Neal resigned his position at Perkinston in 1939 to become Stone County superintendent of education. Coach James Obie Brown stepped into his slot. Apparently women's competition in track ended with the departure of O'Neal.

In 1940 Perkinston took only one first place slot in the state championship track meet held that year in Ellisville. Julius J. Hayden of Pass Christian, later destined to lead the college as president from 1953 to 1986, triumphed in the mile race with a time of 4:42.

On May 3, 1941, the Perkinston track team placed second behind Jones Junior College at the state track meet in Moorhead. That meet was the last one for five years due to World War II.

When intercollegiate track competition resumed in 1946, Perkinston hosted the first post-war state track meet on May 7. While Perk tracksters placed first in five categories, the Hinds Eagles relegated the Bulldogs to second-place overall.

With the completion of Perkinston Stadium in 1949, Perkinston soon became a favored site for the annual state championship track meet. For three years in a row (1951, 1952, and 1953) the state thinclads competed at Perk.

In 1953, for the first time since 1936, the Bulldogs won the state championship. Coach J. V. Shiel's cindermen racked up 60 total points. Holland R. "Dutch" Schatz of Moss Point garnered 15 of those points alone for placing first in 120-yard high hurdles, pole vault, and high jump.

After 1953 Perk did not win another state track championship until George Sekul became the track mentor. During Sekul's 30-year tenure from 1961 to 1991, the Bulldog track team would become not only a state contender but a national contender as well.

1953 State track champions. The four men at top placed first in the mile relay with a time of 3:37. Photos from 1953 Perkolator p. 95 and 1954 Perkolator p. 96.

Cary E. "Buddy" Floore of Pascagoula

John Q. Pipkins Jr. of Leaf

Lee A. Jackson of Gulfport

Albert Reinschmidt of Pensacola, Florida. First in 440 yard dash (time: 52.8).

(Left) "State Track Champion Mile Relay 52-53"-- 13 inches tall.

(Right) "State Track Champions 52-53" --16 inches tall.

John W. Youmans of New Orleans, Louisiana. First in low hurdles (time: 26.5) and First in broad jump (distance 20' 5 ¾")

FOOTBALL 1929 - 1961 AND HOMECOMING 1929 - 2000

The Board of Trustees on September 5, 1929, hired Lee Roy Weeks as head coach and physics teacher to replace Bill Denson. Weeks, a former Mississippi State Agricultural and Mechanical College star, came to Perkinston from Pontchatoula, Louisiana.

Weeks's Bulldogs took the field in 1929 outfitted with yellow jerseys and tan moleskins and attended by a 20-piece band-orchestra and cheerleaders. The last game of the 1929 season, played against Hinds Junior College on Saturday afternoon, November 23, was Perk's first homecoming day contest. On the fourth play of the game an Eagle intercepted a Bulldog pass to make Hinds's only score of the day. Perk won the game 20-6 and finished the season with six wins and three losses.

Chemistry teacher and assistant superintendent Clarence O. Hinton had conceived the idea of inviting the institution's former high school and college graduates to return to their alma mater for this occasion. Seventy-five alumni showed up, despite the inclemency of the weather, and a tradition was born.

Those who chose to brave the elements after the football game toured the nearly completed Denson Administration Building and then gathered at the cafeteria for a banquet during which they were entertained by the orchestra and glee club. After the banquet, Hinton called the alumni together for the first meeting of the Alumni and Former Students Association. Those present elected Noll P. Davis of Wiggins as president and Carleton Sparks of McHenry as secretary-treasurer. The assemblage voted to have the next homecoming day in conjunction with graduation the following spring. All present were to make an effort to contact all former teachers and all former students, whether graduates or not, for the purpose of issuing invitations.

One thousand invitations went out for the gathering set for Friday, May 30, 1930. The regional newspapers carried blanket invitations to all persons formerly associated with the school whether they had received a personal note or not.

The festivities began at 10 a.m. with a musical presentation for the alumni followed by lunch at 1 p.m. in the dining hall. At 5 p.m. diplomas were awarded to 15 college sophomores clad in black caps and gowns and 37 high school seniors dressed in dark gray caps and gowns.

One might infer from the hype in the newspapers before this "graduation homecoming" and then from the dearth of coverage afterwards that it was less than a success. One thing is certain. It never happened again. For a few years this odd homecoming was counted in the total number of homecomings and then even that disappeared.

Clarence Olen Hinton organized Perk's first homecoming celebration on November 23, 1929. Hinton taught chemistry at the school from September 1924, until his resignation on August 11, 1943, to pursue a career as a pharmacist. Hinton died September 24, 1967, and was buried in the Perkinston Cemetery. Photo courtesy of Hazel (Bridge) Necaise.

The 1930 Bulldogs appeared on the gridiron that fall clad in new uniforms of black and gold. An all-male cheerleader squad composed of Francis "Red" Meeks of Macon, Frasier Phelps of Pensacola, Florida, and Herbert Burpee of Pensacola, Florida, pepped up the fans from the sidelines.

By the time the homecoming game rolled around on November 15, 1930, the Bulldogs had won only one game all season. But a win in this game, because it pitted Perkinston against Pearl River, offered redemption. In the words of a *Daily Herald* reporter on November 6, "A victory over Poplarville alone would more than balance the defeats the team has suffered so far this season."

The notices in the regional papers to the alumni promised a battle royal on the football field and a strictly informal day. In Superintendent Cooper J. Darby's words, "No more remarks than necessary will be made." Approximately 100 alumni appeared for the banquet at noon in the dining hall. Dr. Searcy H. Davis, then a Gulfport veterinarian and son of R. N. and Jerusha Davis of Perkinston, was elected as the new alumni president.

After the banquet the alumni stood in the rain with 200 other Perk supporters and watched the Pearl River Wildcats batter the bulldogs 12-0 on a muddy field. This second homecoming game marked the fifth defeat at the hands of Poplarville suffered by Perkinston in the five years the two schools had played college ball.

Despite the dampening effect of rain and defeat, the alumni meeting was counted a success. The festivities closed that night with a ball given by the ladies of Wiggins at the Community Club House in that city.

The miserable 1930 football season closed in a final defeat at Raymond on November 24. The final season tally stood at one win, five losses, and three ties. The loss to Jones, though, was ruled out of the records. The *Daily Herald*, October 17, 1930, did not give the reason why that game was scrubbed.

Despite the defeat of the year before, Hinton announced in the *Daily Herald*, November 14, 1931, that the Perkinston Alumni Association then counted "several hundred members." On November 21 Hinds treated the Bulldog fans to a second homecoming defeat in a row. The Eagles triumphed 7-6. Perk's season that year ended with a tally of three wins, four losses, and one tie.

In advertising the events to be held on homecoming day, November 12, 1932, the Alumni Association announced that a dance would be held in Biloxi following the game with Pearl River. The Wildcats won the game 13-0. One week later a final defeat yielded a final season tally of one win, six losses, and two ties.

At the beginning of the 1933-34 school year, Weeks took the position of athletic director of the college, and C. B. "Pluck" Berry assumed the duties of head coach. Berry, a former star three-letter man at Mississippi College, came to Perkinston from Drew.

In early October the Perkinston student body elected a two-man, two-woman cheerleader squad for the year. Steve Pitalo of Biloxi and Bob Newton were the two men. The two women were Vivian Ezell of Pascagoula and Marguerite Gautier of Biloxi. One week later by a nickel-a-vote system, Ezell became the school's first "Football Queen" and Gautier was elected her runner-up. The proceeds benefited the treasury of the sophomore class.

Homecoming 1933 fell on October 28, and the surviving records reveal some new or at least previously unknown elements in addition to the now familiar pattern of luncheon, alumni meeting, football game, and dance. For the first time

The 1934 "P" Club poses in front of the Old Gym. Organized at least as early as 1928 the "P" Club took its name from the "P" (for Perkinston) awarded to its members. At first the "P" was awarded to both men and women for academic achievement as well as for sports. By 1937 apparently the recognition had been restricted to sports alone. The letters worn by the men in the photograph are black. By 1936 some letters were gold while others were black, and both men and women wore both colors. In 1938 a woman had to play 24 quarters of intercollegiate basketball or make either the tennis or track team to qualify for membership in the "P" Club. The exact qualifications for men were not given in any document in the MGCCC Archives in 2000. Women "P" Club members were last pictured in the 1940 Perkolator. Men "P" Club members were last pictured in 1958. Exactly when the school changed its colors from black and gold to blue and gold was not known to this author in 2000, but the change had occurred by fall 1948. Photo courtesy of Steve Pitalo.

***Front row** (from left) Foy Martin of Leland, Marvin Waters of Perkinston, Brewer Hickman of Perkinston, Warren "Talla" Jones of Biloxi, Keble Ramsay of Vancleave, Etheridge Hudson of Purvis, Jack Jermyn of Mississippi City, Emery Davis of Wichita Falls, Texas, Tony Rosetti of Biloxi, and Buster Bosarge of Pascagoula.*

***Second row** (from left) Cooper Roberts of Ocean Springs, Tom Day of Quincey, Florida, Merrill "Red" True of Gulfport, "Scotty" Moore of Gulfport, A.J. McDonald of Gulfport, Hammond "Tom" Davis of Wiggins, Steve "Chick" Pitalo of Biloxi, Harold "Dilly" Easterling of Lyman, L. D. "Chief" Byrd of Biloxi, and Posey Godard of McHenry*

***Third row** (from left) Ibert Fletcher of Vancleave, J. V. Bontemps of Bay St. Louis, Clyde Wilson, Arthur "Jew" Levine, Jim Shepherd of Gulfport, L. E. Smith of Perkinston, A.P. Francis Jr. of D'Lo, Herman Colle Larsen of Pascagoula, Francis Barthes Jr., and Coach C. B. "Pluck" Berry.*

a particular class, the class of 1924, had a separate convocation. A special homecoming edition of a new school paper called *Hill Top Prints* was issued. For the first time a parade preceded the game. According to the *Daily Herald* of October 21, this parade was to take place between 2 p.m. and game time at 2:30 "featuring the freshmen in pajamas." Precisely what that enigmatic reference meant was not explained nor was any further description given.

A very important "second" occurred as well. For the second time in five attempts, the Perkinston Bulldogs won a homecoming football game. Berry's Bulldogs beat the Millsaps College freshmen 33 to 12. For the first time students, as well as alumni, were invited to the homecoming dance, which followed the game at the Edgewater Hotel in Biloxi.

For their second game in the 1934 season, the Bulldogs journeyed to Ellisville to take part in the first night game in Mississippi junior college history. Superintendent Darby chartered buses for those of the student body who wished to attend at a dollar a head. The Jones County Golden Devils defeated Perkinston 19-6 in this first illuminated game in their new stadium.

In mid-October 1934 the student body elected its second football queen. Sophomore Ruth Nell McDonald of Gulfport attained that title. At the beginning of the football dance, she was crowned and honored with a grand march.

The selection for the third time of Poplarville as the Bulldog's opponent in a homecoming clash resulted in hundreds of alumni pouring into Perkinston on November 10. So great was the throng that Darby substituted an old fashioned barbecue for the usual banquet in the dining hall. The newly organized marching band under the direction of Harmon Longmire was on hand for a concert. Once again a pajama parade led the way to the Old Athletic Field.

Anticipation of breaking the eight-year Pearl River jinx gripped the Perkinston fans as the favored-to-win Bulldogs ran onto the field. The bitter rivals went at it tooth and nail--literally. In the fourth quarter a Wildcat lineman and a Bulldog back had at it one on one. Officials stopped the game until the two gladiators could be separated and ejected from the field. Despite a valiant effort Perkinston went down 19-12 to Poplarville in its ninth defeat in nine meetings with the Wildcats.

In 1935 the tradition of honoring former students and teachers was expanded to include parents of students currently enrolled. Homecoming and Parent's Day was set for November 2. The program was expanded to include a play, "Poor Old Jim," at 10:30 a.m. After the play the crowd was to partake of a barbecue underneath the trees and then gather at the Old Athletic Field for a battle of the Bulldogs--Perkinston vs. Holmes. According to the *Daily Herald* of October 31, popularly elected "football queen," Mary Ellen Gates, a freshman student from Gulfport, was to be "especially honored at the game." The festivities were to culminate that night in an Alumni Association sponsored dance at the Hotel Markham roof in Gulfport.

Since the tentative program for homecoming 1935 was the first to mention a ceremony involving the football queen at the homecoming game, a description of that ceremony would have been most interesting. But none of the planned activities except the dance took place because of the death of 22-year-old Perkinston student Gordon Maki of Big Point in Jackson County.

The day before homecoming, Maki and three other Perkinston students were in the school truck enroute to Gulfport to pick up additional seats for the football game when a Civilian Conservation Camp truck veered into their lane on U. S. Highway 49 north of McHenry. The trucks collided head-on. None of the men in either truck were seriously hurt except Maki, who died later that night in Kings Daughters' hospital in Gulfport. All homecoming day exercises were cancelled on account of the tragedy. Perkinston students served as pallbearers at Maki's burial in the Therrill Cemetery in Escatawpa the next day.

"Pluck" Berry's Bulldogs made up for their cancelled homecoming by ruining the Wildcats' homecoming a week later. On November 8, 1935, for the first time in history, Perkinston defeated Poplarville in a football game. The band and practically the whole Perkinston student body had journeyed by bus to Poplarville to view this homecoming day massacre. In the first quarter Bulldog halfback Jimmy Sasser of Gulfport threw a ten-yard, end-zone pass to G. C. Golden of Florence. Joe Corolla of Leland booted the extra

The earliest photograph of cheerleaders held in the MGCCC Archives collection in 2000 is that of the squad of 1935. (From top left) Eugene Auerbach of Chicago, Illinois, Margaret Fickes of Biloxi, and Jimmy Hosch of Mississippi City. Photos from <u>*1936 Perkolator*</u>*, p. 76.*

1936 State Champion Football Team poses in front of the Old Gym at Perkinston.
***Front row** (from left) Frank Foster of Nashville, Tennessee, Frank "Red" Pfieffer of Henderson, Kentucky, Aubrey Gatlin of Houston, Texas, Jimmie Sarros of Gulfport, Harvey "Foots" Johnson of Sheffield, Alabama, Richmond "Rudy" Morris of Hattiesburg (Captain), Paul McCardle of Brooklyn, Clovis "Sparky" Adams of Glasgow, Kentucky, Thurlow Walker of Daisy-Vestry, Moe Shapiro of New York, New York, Joe Rester of New Hebron, and Wick Wallace of Florence.*
***Second row** (from left) Bowen Bright of Ashland, Blair Bright of Ashland, Claude "Cotton" Campbell of Woolmarket, Robert Watts of New York, New York, Glen Estes of Franklin, Louisiana, Roy Sutton of Sheffield, Alabama, Johnnie Green of Pascagoula, Warren Oliver of Pensacola, Florida, Pat D'Auria of New York, New York, Tom Ramsay of Daisy-Vestry, and Peter Kuljis of Biloxi. **Third row** (from left) Coach S. M. Walker, James Land of Kosciusko (Trainer), Lyonell Walker of Coahoma, R. L. "Tex" McGilvray of Houston, Texas, Monroe Calcote of McCall Creek, Bryce McMahan of Hattiesburg, Walter Ewing of Biloxi, Calhoun Roberts of Pascagoula, Richard May of Marks, Mannie Paine of Donner, Louisiana, Ben Oliver of Panama City, Florida, J. C. White of Florence, Webster Strickland of Brooklyn, Garland Simpson (Manager), and Coach C. B. "Pluck" Berry. Photo courtesy of Hazel (Bridge) Necaise.*

point. In the second quarter Sasser hit Golden with a four-yard, end-zone pass, and Corolla kicked the pigskin through the uprights again. After that the Bulldogs dug in and held. The game ended 14-7.

The Bulldogs finished the season undefeated (with one tie). But, due to the cancelled game with Holmes, the state athletic association ruled Perkinston ineligible for the state title because the school had played too few conference games. Holmes took the 1935 state crown.

On homecoming day, November 21, 1936, after the Alumni Association luncheon in the Stone Hall dining room, the celebrants gathered at the Old Athletic Field to view the conclusion of a Perkinston-Jones cross-country track meet. Perkinston won the track meet and then prepared to take on Pearl River in the football clash.

Bleachers to seat hundreds had been borrowed from Gulfport High School to augment those owned by Perkinston. Still, many of the record 1,500-person crowd had to stand on the sidelines. The contest went on despite the receipt of the news that 27 Pearl River students and faculty had suffered injury, some serious, in the overturning of a bus enroute to the game.

Mary Ellen Gates, once again elected Football Queen, at last participated in the ceremony called off the year before. For the first time a queen and her court ruled over the Perkinston homecoming activities. She and her four maids, Theola Brander of Biloxi, Mary Eleanor Murray of Wiggins, Frances Ramsay of Perkinston, and Jane Hill of New Orleans, Louisiana, sat on the bench with the football squad. At the half, to the accompaniment of the band, Gates and her court marched down the field to the front of the Perkinston stands where all four women were presented with a bouquet, and Queen Mary Ellen was crowned.

In the game the Bulldogs pounded the Wildcats 27-6 to take their second win in two years. Pearl River scored only once against the Bulldog second-string on the last play of the game.

That night Queen Mary Ellen and the maids of her court reigned at the Homecoming Ball held on the Markham roof from 10 p.m. to 2 a.m. Longmire's Swing Barons, a dance orchestra composed primarily of selected Perkinston band members, furnished the music.

If the extent of the injuries to 17-year-old Helen Ladner of Dedeaux, a student aboard that wrecked Pearl River Junior College bus, had been known, the homecoming game of 1936 would have been cancelled. She died the next day. One of her brothers, Berlin Ladner, who attended Perk in 1942, was killed-in-action against the Germans and became one of those memorialized in Gregory War Memorial Chapel.

Perkinston ended the 1936 season with an overall record of 6 wins, 1 loss, and 1 tie. The undefeated Holmes County

PERKINSTON JUNIOR COLLEGE
HOMECOMING DAY
November 21, 1936 -:- Perkinston, Miss.

PERKINSTON BULLDOGS VS POPLARVILLE WILDCATS

1936 FOOTBALL QUEEN & COURT
Upper Left, Jane Hill; Upper Right, Theola Brander; Center (Queen) Mary Ellen Gates; Lower Left, Mary Eleanor Murray; Lower Right, Frances Ramsay.

Compliments Of
TRENTON SUPPLY COMPANY
—and—
TRENTON STORES
WIGGINS, -:- MISSISSIPPI

The program cover of the 1936 homecoming football game against Pearl River. For the second time in history and for the second time in a row, the Bulldogs triumphed over the Wildcats. On this cover the institution is termed "Perkinston Junior College" six years before that name became official on July 15, 1942. In popular parlance the institution was usually referred to as Perkinston Junior College rather than by its ungainly official name of Harrison-Stone-Jackson Junior College.

Bulldogs, who had inflicted Perkinston's only defeat, were declared state champions for the second time in a row. But in mid-January 1937 the Mississippi Junior College Athletic Association disqualified two Holmes County players as having been ineligible to participate. This action resulted in the 1936 Holmes-Perkinston game being forfeited to Perkinston. The association then named "Pluck" Berry's Bulldogs as the new state champions of 1936.

At the close of the 1935-1936 year Berry gave up coaching to enter the oil business, and the Board hired Albert I. "Rex" Rexinger, Perkinston class of 1928, as head coach and history teacher on August 1, 1937.

The high point of the 1937 Homecoming and Parent's Day festivities held on October 30 was the dedication of the new girls' dormitory, Harrison Hall, at 11:45 a.m. After a picnic lunch and a band concert, tours of the new facility were conducted until game time at 2:45. Perkinston lost the game to Holmes 34-0. The dance that year was held at the Edgewater Hotel. Inez Ramsay of Ramsay Springs reigned as football queen.

Rexinger's Bulldogs met the Wildcats in Poplarville on November 19, 1937, in the first night game between the traditional adversaries. Pearl River won the close game on a pass with only three minutes left to play. In giving notice of the game the day before, the *Daily Herald* noted that the Perkinston band and pep squad was expected to attend. This was the first reference to the school's new women's drill and cheering squad. Within a year the pep squad under the direction of Miss Elton Dalier, women's physical education instructor, consisted of more than 30 women. This pep squad was led by a woman drum major and was the first step in the evolutionary process that led 15 years later to the Perkettes.

The Alumni Association decided to make Homecoming and Parent's Day, November 19, 1938, the largest celebration ever. A group of alumni meeting in the Hotel Markham seized on the idea of celebrating the 25th anniversary of the college. One of those present pointed out that 1938-1939 was actually the 27th session since the beginning of the agricultural high school and marked only the 14th session of the college. Undeterred by these facts, the majority decided to celebrate the 25th anniversary of the college anyway.

A motorcade led by Gene Dees and Searcy Davis and escorted by Mississippi state highway patrolmen departed from Gulfport City Hall at 9 a.m. on November 19. The procession arrived at Perkinston shortly after 10 a.m. Following lunch, the crowd, conservatively estimated at 2,500, adjourned to the Old Athletic Field to watch the Bulldogs take on the Wildcats.

That year, for the first time, the designation "Homecoming Queen and Court" was used to describe the royal ladies of the gridiron. Queen Sara Aimee "Sally" Jane of Pascagoula and her maids, Dorothy Covington of Wiggins, Inez Ramsay of Ramsay Springs, Mattie Lou Lyons of Gulfport, and Wilma Proffitt of Biloxi, took the field in pre-game ceremonies. Bulldog captain Reginald Switzer of Gulfport escorted Queen Sally to the middle of the field to meet their Pearl River counterparts whereupon Jane presented a bouquet to her rival. Switzer then officially crowned his queen and the game began. The coronation had to be moved to pre-game because at the half the queen had to perform in her role as combination drum major and star twirler with the band and pep squad then under the direction of Stanley C. Beers.

Pearl River beat Perkinston 19-0. The motorcade returned to Gulfport for the dance at the Markham roof.

In August 1939, Darby, in what was an uncharacteristic move for him, since he did not like to spend money, ordered $1,900 spent to illuminate the Old Athletic Field. It was fitting that Perkinston's opponent in the first battle under the

Perkinston Homecoming Queen Sally Jane (front) and three of her maids walk on the Old Athletic Field for pre-game ceremonies on November 19, 1938.

Perkinston Homecoming Queen Sally Jane (hidden) is escorted to the center of the Old Athletic Field by Reginald Switzer (right). Jane is presenting a bouqet of flowers to the Pearl River homecoming queen who is escorted by a Wildcat (left). Photos from 1939 Perkolator, p. 80.

The 1938 Bulldogs run onto the Old Athletic Field at Perkinston. Photo from 1939 Perkolator, p. 83.

The 1938 football team poses beside the "Black Maria," which is parked in front of the Old Gym.
First row *(from left) Cliett Kemp of Biloxi, James B. George of Pascagoula, William Blakely of Hattiesburg, Wilfred Gallotte of Biloxi, Shannon Pickich of Biloxi, Beaumont Meaut of Biloxi, Thurlow Walker of Perkinston, Solon Ethridge of Town Creek, Alabama, Frank "Stumpy" Hodges of Kosciusko, Holley Stone "Pat" Reeves of Gulfport, Frank Moore of Buford, Georgia, Jefferson Webb of Chipley, Florida, Alvin Malley of Biloxi, and Kenneth "Zip" Vance of Lawrenceburg, Tennessee.*
Second row *(from left) L. J. Stringer of Hattiesburg, James "Pickle" Forte of Pensacola, Florida, Elmer Frank Fillingim of Long Beach, John Denning of Saucier, Frank Davis of Ocean Springs, V. W. Yeager of Wiggins, Sardin Roberts of Ocean Springs, Victor Royal of Buford, Georgia, J. J. Hayden of Pass Christian, Dent O'Neal of Wiggins, William Jorgensen of Chicago, Illinois, Melvin Kenneth of Greenwood, John "Poo Doo" Williams of Buford, Georgia, and James Sprinkle of Pass Christian.*
Third row *(from left) Coach A.I. Rexinger, Joe Thompson of Orange Grove, Manager Terrell Wise of Pensacola, Florida, Reginald Switzer of Gulfport, Captain Emory O. Cunningham of Kansas, Alabama, Hilary Horne of Kosciusko, F. J. Haynes of Mendenhall, Charles T. Manley of Town Creek, Alabama, John Norwood of Bunkie, Louisiana, Thomas Glass of Gulfport, J.T. "Duner" Coffman of Elkmont, Arkansas, Robert Boyd of Amite, Louisiana, Walter Keith of Nashville, Tennessee, and science instructor Travis "Doc" Brasfield. Photo courtesy of Terrell Wise.*

(Left) J. J. Hayden, a young Bulldog in 1938 and 1939, recalled a three-day sortie (October 13-15, 1939) to Scooba to do battle against the Lions. The following is an excerpt from a speech Hayden gave on November 15, 1965, recalling that trip.

"I remember a trip I made to East Mississippi Junior College in Scooba in 1939 while a member of the football team at Perk. Of course, in 1939 very few of us from the Coast had traveled any further north than Hattiesburg or certainly Jackson so to make a trip north of Meridian was a long way. Our ball game was scheduled for Saturday night so we left the campus at Perkinston in our 1930 model bus early Friday morning, loaded down with all the players, uniforms and two 55 gallon drums of water for drinking purposes, as the coaches had learned that the water at Scooba had an extreme laxative effect upon newcomers to that area. We trudged along almost all day Friday stopping in Meridian for our meal and finally arrived at Scooba sometime in the early part of the night. We were housed in bunks and cots placed in the visitors dressing rooms in an old wooden gymnasium. I remember that it got quite cool that night and most of us had forgotten to take a blanket so we ended up sleeping with our clothes on and maybe our jerseys that we had packed with our uniforms. The next day we played the ballgame on a field that looked like it was meant more for the planting of corn than the playing of ball and the grass was about knee high on the field. I have forgotten whether we won or lost the ball game [author's note: Perk won 7-0], but I do remember that there were always several fights involved during the game. Our coach at Perk at that time was A. I. Rexinger who now lives in Natchez and he quite often inspired his players so much that it was easy to get into a fight. On Sunday we started home from Scooba and we made it to Meridian without too much trouble. We had an early lunch and started from Meridian to Laurel and it seems like every twenty miles we had a flat tire. Finally we made Hattiesburg just before dark on Sunday evening and four tires were flat on the bus. The Coach offered us the choice of staying on the bus until he could get the tires repaired or replaced or hitchhiking on to Perk. Most of us chose the latter and made it to Perkinston before lights were out at nine o'clock."

arcs was Jones County since the Bulldogs had battled the Golden Devils five years earlier at Ellisville in the first illuminated game in Mississippi junior college history. By 1939, styling themselves as Bobcats rather than Golden Devils, the Jones team members fought Perkinston to a 6-6 tie on Friday night, September 29. All the home games except homecoming were designated night games in the 1939 season.

Except for the absence of a motorcade, the homecoming festivities of October 28, 1939, were a virtual repeat of the year before, including the fact that the Bulldogs lost the game. Holmes County defeated Perkinston 18-7, bringing Rexinger's career record on homecoming games to three losses. By way of atonement, Rexinger's charges went over to Poplarville on November 17 and whipped the Wildcats at their homecoming.

By 1940 Perkinston's homecoming celebration had settled into the pattern of an Alumni Association meeting and luncheon followed by a football game featuring a queen and court with a dance at a Coast hotel afterward. In a welcome change on that October 19, Rexinger won his first homecoming game, defeating the Southwest Junior College Pilots 39-12 in the last homecoming of the Darby Era.

When Darby resigned to become Harrison County Chancery Clerk in fall 1941, Albert Louis May replaced him as chief executive officer at Perkinston. May's first homecoming followed the pattern set in the Darby era except that as in 1933 a special class was honored. The members of the Class of 1931 were singled out for a ten-year reunion. Likely the idea of a ten-year reunion would have become a feature of future homecomings at that time, but it did not happen due to the entry of the United States into the Second World War on December 7, 1941.

Every homecoming since the first one in 1929 had been held on Saturday. Homecoming 1942 was held on Friday,

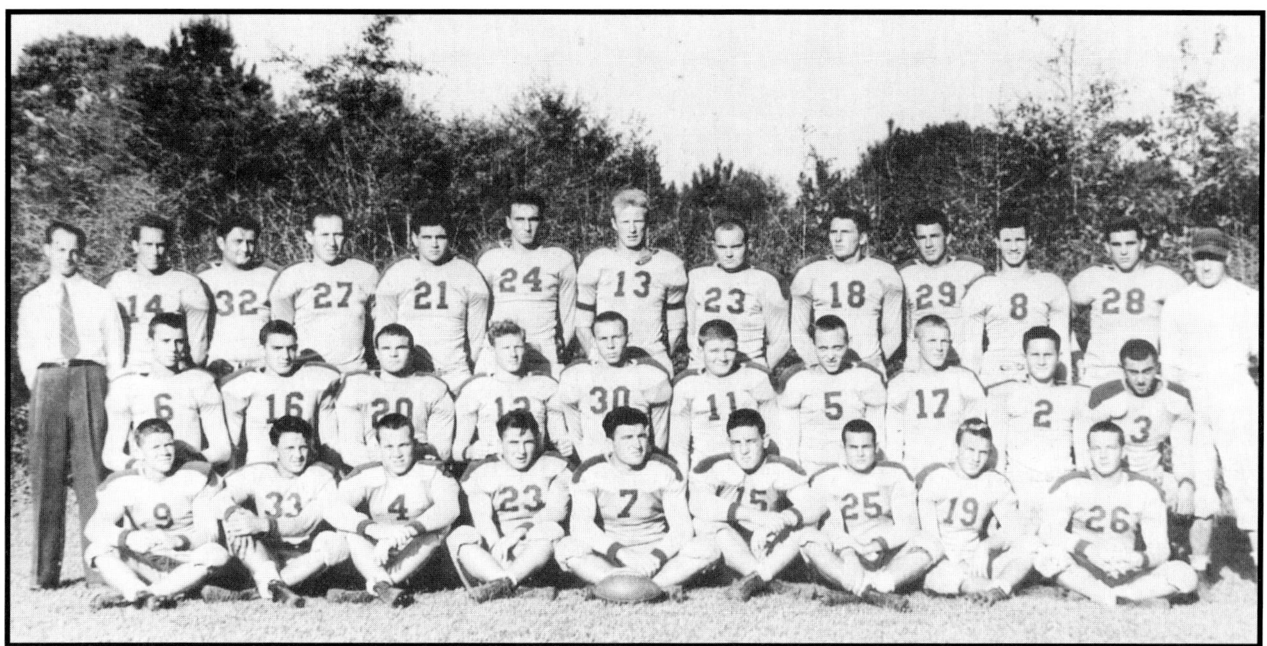

1942 State Championship Football team.
First row *(from left) Tom Havard of Lucedale, Hayes Allen of Wiggins, John Davis of Moss Point, Jimmie Haynes of Pensacola, Florida, James Baughn of Greenwood, Pat Donohoe of Hattiesburg, Ned Driggers of Selma, Alabama, Burns Dews of Hattiesburg, and Edwin Simpson of Pensacola, Florida.*
Second row *(from left) William Allen Nix of Wiggins, Hervey Hinson of Lucedale, Leroy Yeager of Wiggins, Bill Jones of Pensacola, Florida, Charlie Cain of Pensacola, Florida, John Rollins of Norwood, Louisiana, Ross Gatlin of Gulfport, Lee Roy James of Gulfport, Wren Firth of Lyman, and Jimmie Daggett of Pensacola, Florida.*
Third row *(from left) Head Coach George Westerfield, E. T. Whittington of New Orleans, Louisiana, Charles Falkenberry of Monroeville, Alabama, L. A. Krohn of Wiggins, John Jackson of Norco, Louisiana, Kenneth Tarzetti of DeLisle, Jimmie Still of Pensacola, Florida, Robert Buffum of Gulfport, Elroy Scott of New Orleans, Louisiana, Walter Whittington of New Orleans, Louisiana, Harold Wesson of Corinth, Harold White of Big Level, and assistant coach Art VanTone. Not pictured-Davis Perkins of Bond, Manager. Photo courtesy of Wilton "Red" Brown.*

October 30, and was a mere shadow of the homecomings of the past. Parents and alumni were invited to the school for the evening meal, which was followed by a short business meeting and a game against East Central Junior College at 8 p.m. The P-Club did select and crown a queen, but no dance followed the game due to war-related transportation problems. The U. S. Army had ordered U. S. Highway 90 along the beach dimmed out from dark to sunrise due to the German U-boat peril. A reduction in the national speed limit to 35 miles per hour together with gasoline rationing had been ordered and was about to be enforced.

All that and the Bulldogs were having the best football season in the institution's history. When Coach George B. Westerfield, who had replaced Rexinger that season, led his charges against Decatur that homecoming night, the 1942 record consisted of a 0-0 tie against Jones in the first game and three straight victories thereafter. The 10-6 defeat of Decatur made it four victories in a row. Apparently the new "T" formation Westerfield had introduced was having its effect. And all these victories were conference games. Alas, Pearl River and Sunflower, both of which were on the Bulldog schedule and not yet played, had served notice the week before Perk's homecoming that they were withdrawing from intercollegiate competition due to the war emergency. On November 6, Perk met Scooba at Macon and thrashed the Lions 27-0. With no more Mississippi junior conference teams to play, the Bulldogs invited the men of Hattiesburg Air Base down to Perk on November 13 and pulverized them 45-0.

The Bulldogs' 6-0-1 record gained Perk the 1942 Mississippi junior college football state championship. Representatives of the Mississippi Junior College Athletic Association awarded the trophy to the team on December 15, 1942, in the Stone Hall dining room. Six weeks later Westerfield joined the U. S. Army Air Corps. Many of his players soon joined various branches of the military. Within a few months of leaving the playing field at Perk, the Bulldogs of 1942 were fighting on foreign fields.

There were no Perkinston Junior College Bulldogs of 1943. There were no homecoming festivities in 1943. According to the *Daily Herald*, October 28, 1943, Alumni Association President Otis Singletary stated that the usual activities of the alumni would be cancelled and instead a campaign would be carried on to raise funds for a War Memorial Chapel to be erected on the campus.

If there were no Perkinston Junior College Bulldogs in 1943, there were Perkinston Agricultural High School "Bulldogs." Normally styled "Bullpups," the high school boys assumed the title of the college men while the men were away at war. Their 1943 record was five wins, one loss, and one tie. (To avoid confusion the archivist listed the 1943 teams as "Bullpups" in the Higginbotham Report of college and AHS scores printed in this work.)

Perkinston resumed intercollegiate football play in 1944,

but the team played no school north of Jackson, and it played only six games. Two of the games were with Jones and two were with Pearl River. The Bulldogs tied one of the games with the Wildcats, won the other, and lost all the rest. Copiah-Lincoln defeated Perk 19-7 in the homecoming game. The 1944 homecoming was another short Friday night observance like that of 1942 with the only difference being that the proceeds of the homecoming game were donated to the War Memorial Chapel fund.

World War II ended with the Japanese surrender on September 2, 1945, and that fall all Mississippi junior colleges resumed full intercollegiate football championship competition. For some reason Perk played Poplarville twice again that year and best of all beat the Wildcats both times--32-6 on October 11 and 6-0 on November 9.

On October 17 the school celebrated homecoming once again and for the final time on Friday, and once again dedicated the event to the War Memorial Chapel fund. That afternoon members of the Memorial Chapel Fund Committee were stationed by the War Memorial Plaque in Denson Hall to record the names of those who had served and those who had died.

On January 1, 1946, three years after his departure for the war, George Westerfield returned as head coach. That fall an estimated 50 of the 80 candidates for the football team were also veterans.

In many ways 1946 represented a true return to "normalcy." The Bulldogs lost to the Wildcats. Homecoming went back to Saturday with a full day of festivities including an afternoon football game, the crowning of a queen and court, and a dance on the Coast.

In other ways things were not so normal. The team lost seven of ten games. Westerfield became athletic director, and Marvin "Red" Campbell of New Albany replaced him as head coach.

On November 13, Campbell's Bulldogs lost to Pearl River by a heartbreaking 2-0. But, on December 5, in Perk's first and only Tung Bowl appearance in Picayune, the Bulldogs smashed the Wildcats 25-6. Campbell's first season ended with eight wins and only three losses.

The fine record of 1947 proved to be a prologue to excellence. The superb record of Campbell's 1948 team enshrined it in the Bulldog Football Valhalla along with George Sekul's 1971 and 1984 teams.

The Bulldog team of 1948 mowed down its first seven opponents (all of which were conference foes) with an astonishing total of 158 points to 40. Every Bulldog score was double digit. No opponent scored more than seven points, and one failed to score at all.

The homecoming game that year fell on November 6, with Pearl River as the opponent. Legendary coach Dobie Holden commanded the Wildcats that year, and his team held the number two Mississippi conference ranking just behind the Bulldogs. The largest crowd in the history of football at Perkinston filled the bleachers at the Old Athletic Field, and the standing room only throng surrounded both end zones.

In the first quarter Bulldog halfback Bobby Holmes of Tallassee, Alabama, hit halfback Davis Melton of Tallassee, Alabama, with a 21-yard pass to put the ball on the Wildcat 16-yard-line. Holmes followed that with an eight-yard pass to left end Ed Evans of Perkinston. In two line plunges fullback Lindy Stewart of Lakeland, Florida, put the ball within four yards of the goal line. Melton then climaxed the 37-yard drive with a dash around left end for the touchdown. Slyton Cole of Pascagoula kicked the extra point.

After that the Wildcats went wild. At the beginning of the fourth quarter, they had the Bulldogs down 19-7. On the third play of the fourth quarter the Bulldogs came back alive. In four plays the Holmes-Melton combo put the ball on the Pearl River three-yard line, and Nimrod Ellis of Columbus took it in. Cole again kicked the point making the score 19-14.

A few minutes later the Bulldogs drove 49 yards to the Pearl River one-yard line before being stopped by a Wildcat last-ditch stand and a penalty, which put the ball in Pearl River's hands on the seven. As the Wildcats tried to fight out of the hole, a blocked punt turned over the ball at the 19-yard line.

In the words of the *Daily Herald* reporter covering the game, "Holmes lost a yard, then dashed to the 11. He lost another yard and on fourth down gave a hand-off to Melton who propelled around right end for the touchdown that put the Bulldogs ahead." The Bulldogs won the razor-edged thriller 20-19.

On November 11, Perk played its only non-conference game of the year, defeating the Tulane University Freshmen in an Armistice Day feature in the inaugural game at Pascagoula's War Memorial Stadium. After that the Bulldogs

At homecoming November 6, 1948, late in the fourth quarter on a fourth down play, Davis Melton eludes a Wildcat tackle to carry the ball in for the touchdown that defeated Pearl River 20-19. Photograph courtesy of Davis Melton.

1948 Co-National Championship Football Team Snapshots

A photograph of this team did not exist in the MGCCC Archives Collection of 2000. The snapshots published here are courtesy of Davis Melton.

Davis Melton (Wingback) of Tallassee, Alabama

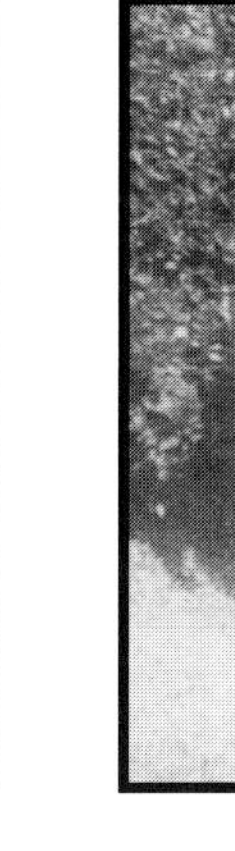

Douglas Boone (Guard) of Mobile, Alabama

Charlie Wing (Blockingback) of Pensacola, Florida

Samuel B. McGowan (Tailback) of Wetumpka, Alabama

Bobby Evans (Center) of Seminole, Alabama

Ed Evans (End) of Perkinston

James Paul Moyer (Tackle) of Columbus

Edwin L. "Cotton" Pearce (Tackle) of Anguilla

Nimrod Ellis (Fullback) of Columbus

William A. "Pickett" Randall (End) of Gulfport

The names of the members of the 1948 Co-National Championship Football Team were engraved on a bronze plaque affixed to the Football Monument in the Perkinston Campus Quadrangle. Edwin L. "Cotton" Pearce was inadvertently placed on the plaque twice--once as "E. Pierce" and again as "C. Pearce." William C. Oakes's name was rendered on the monument as "W. Oates." The mistakes came about because Pearce was listed twice in the 1949 Perkolator under two spellings, and Oakes's name was misspelled in the Perkolator. Members of the team attended the dedication of the plaque on homecoming day, October 30, 1999.

*Fred Cruger (left) (Tackle) of Baldwin, Long Island, New York
Bobby Holmes (right) (Tailback) of Tallassee, Alabama
1948 All-Americans*

Not pictured:
Herbert Adams (Tailback) of Mobile, Alabama
Patrick Allen (End) of Long Beach
Clinton Arnold (Lineback) of Pensacola, Florida
Clarence E. Banks (Back) of Griffin, Georgia
Noel Blackwell (Guard) of Saucier
Travis Blackwell (Guard) of Pascagoula
Victor Blair Jr. (End) of Wiggins
Arthur Bogdahn (Guard) of Pascagoula
Charles Carolla (Blockingback) of Leland
James Sylton Cole (Guard) of Pascagoula
Tommy Comer (Tailback) of Mobile, Alabama
Edward Farragut (Fullback) of Moss Point
James Garner (Guard) of Loxley, Alabama
Kirby King Jr. (Center) of Pascagoula
C. J. Landry Jr. (End) of Biloxi
James Max McCool (Tackle) of Kreole
Alex Louis Pitalo (Center) of Biloxi
Burr Ramage Reeves (End) of Wetumpka, Alabama
Paul Ryan (Back) of Pascagoula
Otis Shattles Jr. (Tackle) of Moss Point
Walter Sherer (Guard) of Jasper, Alabama
Charles Lindy Stewart (Fullback) of Lakeland, Florida
Managers
William C. Oakes of New Albany
Charles "Dixie" Hollis of Biloxi
***Head Coach** Marvin "Red" Campbell*
***Assistant Coach** George Westerfield*
***Assistant Coach** Joe Saia*

Ed Evans catches a 20-yard touchdown pass from Bobby Holmes in the second quarter of the Laurel Lions Bowl on Saturday, December 4, 1948. Perkinston defeated Jones Junior College 27-13. This was the 12th and final victory in the Bulldogs' undefeated and untied 1948 season. Photo courtesy of Ed Evans.

Richard Kopp photo

Trophy reads "Laurel Lions Club Junior College Bowl, 1948."-- 18 inches tall with 14 inch base.

returned to their pre-Pearl River mode of double digit scores to seven or less for the opponent. Sunflower fell 27-6 on November 19, and East Central went down 26-7 on November 23.

Perk students and fans watching the Bulldogs defeat the Warriors on the cold, rain-swept Old Athletic Field on November 23, began singing "California Here I Come." For some time rumors of an invitation to the Little Rose Bowl in Pasadena had been circulating. A few minutes before the game ended, President May announced that the school had indeed received a tentative feeler from the Little Rose Bowl Committee. He further stated that the school had officially notified the committee that such an invitation would be accepted.

The Little Rose Bowl Committee had contacted May because the Williamson Football Rating bureau of New Orleans had rated Perk's team as the number one junior college team in the nation. However, on Sunday, November 28, May received the following message from the chairman of the Little Rose Bowl Committee:

"The board of management of the Little Rose Bowl today voted to select Duluth Junior College to oppose Compton (Cal.) Junior College in the December 11 game. . . . The decision was most hard to reach. . . ."

Despite the foregoing, the three members of the 1948 team personally interviewed by this author were adamant in their belief that school officials either did not or could not pay for the team's trip to the Little Rose Bowl. They likely were correct in their assessment. In a speech on junior college football made by MGCJC President J. J. Hayden on November 15, 1965, Hayden stated, "Perk had an invitation to attend the Little Rose Bowl in 1948 but could not raise the funds for the cost of transportation."

On November 29, President May accepted the invitation of the Laurel Lions Club to play against Jones Junior College, Mississippi's second-ranked 1948 team, in the Fourth Annual Laurel Lion's Bowl on December 4. The Bulldogs had beaten the Bobcats in the first game of the season 19-7, and the Bulldogs beat them again in the Laurel Lion's Bowl 27-13. So ended Perkinston's first undefeated and untied season.

On December 11 in Pasadena, Compton defeated Duluth so handily that the game was scarcely a contest. On December 15, 1948, Paul Williamson of the Williamson Football Rating Bureau sent President May a telegram naming Perkinston Junior College and Compton Junior College as co-champions of the nation for the year of 1948. Williamson released his picks for his All-American junior college squad on December 30, 1948. Williamson named halfback Bobby Holmes of Perkinston Junior College as First Team All-American and tackle Freddy Cruger of Perkinston Junior College as Third Team All-American.

Coach Nolan E. Tollett of Hope, Arkansas, replaced Campbell as head football mentor in March 1949. On September 17, Tollett's Bulldogs took the field against the Jones Bobcats and defeated them 20-7. The game was the first to be played on the field of the newly completed Perkinston Football Stadium.

On homecoming day, October 29, 1949, a crowd of 5,000, the largest in the school's history, attended the dedication ceremonies for Perkinston Football Stadium, which began at 1:45 p.m. At 2:30 the Bulldogs took the field against the Co-Lin Wolves and beat them 21-6. While the 1949 Bulldogs won no state laurels, they did defeat East Central on December 10 for the Laurel Lions Bowl trophy.

From 1950 until 1966, when George Sekul took over as head coach, only two football trophies were added to the Perkinston collection. On December 5, 1953, the Bulldogs were awarded a trophy for tying the Copiah-Lincoln Wolves 6 to 6 in the Laurel Lions Bowl. The other trophy, one of the largest and most ornate in the MGCCC Archives collection in 2000, was acquired by virtue of a 3 to 0 loss suffered by the Bulldogs at the hands of Navarro (Texas) Junior College in the Hospitality Bowl held in Gulfport on November 22, 1962.

The inside front cover of the 1953 Homecoming Football Program shows deceased president A. L. May's face superimposed over May Field with A. L. May Memorial Stadium in the background. During ceremonies that day (October 10, 1953) the then three-year-old facility received the name it bore in 2000.

Richard Kopp photo

The 1953 Bulldogs took the above Laurel Lions Bowl trophy for tying the Copiah-Lincoln Wolves 6-6. The trophy vanished from Perkinston Campus for decades until returned on August 4, 1999, by an alumnus. The 8-inch by 11-inch trophy is the only football trophy in the MGCCC Archives Collection, which bears the names of the team members who won it. The engraved names read: Harold Scott, John Pipkins, Barry Kunz, John Ruth, Clerfet Vicknair, Buddy Floore, Joe McCool, Bill Dooley, Ken Trawick, Carl Lizana, Don Dacus, Maggie Hammond, Davis Mortensen, Don Massengale, Ignacio Gonzales, Elton Barrilleaux, Kenneth Bramlett, Reginald Howell, Jimmy Thomas, Clyde Perrere, Norman Wells, Earl Hubley, Pat Gardner, Jerry Gardner, Robert Elam, R. J. Murrah, Willie Davis, Gary Kunz, Buddy Sellers, Son Rhodes, and Jerry McCool. Photos at right from 1954 Perkolator, pps. 79-80.

Bill Dooley of Mobile, Alabama

Davis Mortensen of Moss Point

Jerry Gardner of Moss Point

Don Massengale of Pascagoula

Homecoming Highlights 1950-2000

In the last half of the 20th century one homecoming ritual established in the 1929-1949 era continued. A homecoming queen and homecoming court was always chosen and presented at the homecoming football game. In 1965, the first homecoming after the establishment of the three campuses, the queen came from Perkinston Campus--Jefferson Davis Campus and Jackson County Campus sent maids to her court. Beginning in 1966 each campus chose its own queen and court.

The tradition of a homecoming dance continued intermittently. After the establishment of the three campuses, one campus or another sponsored separate dances for a few years until the dances disappeared altogether due to lack of attendance. Tri-campus homecoming dances began again in 1995.

In 1950 the homecoming football game returned to nighttime play. In 1951 the game was once again slated for the afternoon, but two weeks before the game the *Stone County Enterprise*, September 28, 1951, announced that the game would be at 8 p.m. The reporter gave as the reason for the change that the "Alumni Association contended that a larger and more representative crowd of Perkinston Alumni will be able to be present for the football game." The game remained at night until returned to the afternoon on homecoming day, October 27, 1985. After that the homecoming game continued to be played in the afternoon until the end of the 20th century.

Before 1950, homecoming had been a general gathering of persons associated with the institution. Only occasionally had a specific class been advertised has having a reunion. After 1950 nearly every homecoming was associated with the reunion of a specific class or group of classes.

At homecoming 1953 those assembled were urged to begin drawing up rolls of specific classes. With those rolls in hand homecoming 1954 was advertised as a reunion of the classes of 1915, 1920, 1925, 1930, 1935, 1940, 1945, and 1950. Members of all eight of those classes were to be recognized at the afternoon program, and according to the *Stone County Enterprise*, October 21, 1954, together honored with "officials of the past who had a large share in developing the school." That meant that all surviving superintendents, registrars, deans, dieticians, faculty, and more would be honored. After the program all of the honorees were to adjourn to the school grill for an hour followed by a barbecue supper. One might wonder when and how long guest speaker U. S. Representative William D. Colmer spoke.

The tradition of honoring eight classes in increments of five years ending successively in 0 and 5, 1 and 6, 2 and 7, 3 and 8, 4 and 9, continued through 1960. The homecomings of 1961 and 1962 were declared "The Golden Year" (50th anniversary of the institution), and everyone ever associated with the institution was invited.

Beginning with homecoming 1963, the five-year increments were abandoned in favor of ten-year groupings. Thus the classes of 1914, 1924, 1934, 1944, and 1954 (with the one of 50 years prior given special "Golden Anniversary" recognition) were invited as honorees. The situation whereby the classes ending in "four" were invited in 1963 and the classes ending in "five" were invited in 1964 and so on ended on homecoming day November 5, 1995, with the honoring of the classes ending in "six."

The perils of "politically correctly" describing the first tri-campus queen or queens or one queen in three persons overwhelmed the scribe who penned the following in the 1967 Perkolator related to homecoming 1966, "Reigning as queen of the 1966 Perkinston Homecoming are (from left) Martha Perry, JC, Wanda Fodrin, JD, and Sally Maddox, Perk. Representing the student body of each college, these three co-eds shared the honor of queen to furthur (sic) unify the three district junior colleges."

The split academic year was the source of much confusion. The class of 1946 had attended Perk during its sophomore year, 1945-1946. The fiftieth anniversary of its graduation was May 1996, but the 50th anniversary of its sophomore year's homecoming was fall 1995. If the school held homecoming at graduation, the off-stepped year problem would never have been a problem. Actually the school had held homecoming at graduation in 1930 and had encountered the problem that almost no one came. By 1995 the problem was that many alumni were missing their reunions due to the confusion of the off-stepped year.

In order to end the confusion Alumni Association officials decided to rectify the situation. At homecoming 1996 no specific year class reunion was held. Instead the school held a special reunion for 25 years of Sam Jones's Perkettes and band members (1952-1978) and a special reunion of George Sekul's 1971 National Championship football team.

In 1997 all classes ending in "seven" were invited for reunions. Thus, beginning in 1997 the school honored its reunion classes one-half year too late rather than one half year too early.

The practice of honoring five classes spaced a decade apart, with the "Golden Class" or 50th anniversary class being the especially honored one, which had begun in 1963, was extended to six classes by 1984. In 2000 the Alumni Association created another reunion group called "Golden Plus." Any former student who had celebrated his or her 50th class reunion could return any year thereafter to be honored as a member of the "Golden Plus" group without regard to a specific class year.

After the inauguration of the Alumni Association Hall of Fame on homecoming day, November 7, 1970, it became customary to hold a special reunion of the class of the honoree in addition to the "regular" class reunions. In the 20th century that tradition was generally observed, except in the case of Otis Singletary in 1974 and in the case of Eddie Khayat in 1975. Singletary's duties as president of the University of Kentucky prevented his attendance at homecoming 1974, so he was honored in conjunction with the dedication of Weeks Hall on February 22, 1975. Khayat's duties as a defensive line coach for the Atlanta Falcons Football Club prevented his attendance at homecoming 1975, so he was honored at the Alumni Association Spring Banquet on April 3, 1976.

The October 28, 1999, inauguration of the Alumni Association Athletic Hall of Fame at a banquet held the Thursday night before homecoming added yet another element to the homecoming festivities. The 15 inaugural members joined those on the list to be honored. The five new members inducted at the Thursday night banquet before homecoming 2000 were similarly recognized.

In addition to the "regular" class reunions, which followed a formula, certain special reunions of various classes or groups associated with the school were held periodically. And, from the beginning, homecoming, being the institution's special day, had been the occasion for dedicating buildings, naming buildings, celebrating anniversaries of the institution, or creating special exhibits. A few of the more salient examples of such homecomings in the last half of the 20th century follow: (The reader is reminded that the Harrison County School Board established the institution on September 5, 1911. The first classes began on September 17, 1912. The junior college division began operation in September 1925. The institution celebrated anniversaries counted from all three of those dates.)

Homecoming Annals

October 18, 1952 40th Anniversary of the beginning of classes at the institution. Homecoming dedicated to James Andrew "Daddy" Huff and Huff Hall named in his honor.

October 10, 1953 Perkinston Football Stadium renamed A. L. May Memorial Stadium in honor of President Albert Louis May, who died July 8, 1953.

October 23, 1954 U. S. Representative William D. Colmer spoke. Blue and Gold Service Pins presented to faculty, staff, and administrators who had helped to establish the school or who had rendered long service.

October 8, 1955 Special reunion of 1948 Co-National Championship Football Team.

October 13, 1956 Stone Hall, Jackson Hall, and George Hall named. Homecoming dedicated to alumni, faculty, and administrators who had become public officials. First Sam Owen Trophy awarded to C. E. Dees Jr. (Gene Dees).

October 5, 1957 Mississippi Lieutenant Governor Carroll Gartin dedicated the New Gym.

October 11, 1958 All Perkettes since the founding of the dance-drill team in 1952 were honored.

October 24, 1959 Five years of homecoming queens honored.

October 29, 1960 Declared "Sam Jones Day." Former band members recognized.

November 11, 1961 The Golden Year (50th anniversary of the establishment of the institution).

October 13, 1962 The Golden Year (50th anniversary of the first classes)

October 26, 1963 Showing of the 18-minute color film "Catalyst" celebrating the institution's Golden Year. Also, a special reunion of all past lettermen and letterwomen of the junior college and the agricultural high school in football, basketball, baseball, track, tennis, boxing, and cheerleading.

October 23, 1964 U. S. Senator John C. Stennis spoke.

October 9, 1965 First tri-campus homecoming.

October 22, 1966 First homecoming with the three queens.

October 25, 1969 Homecoming dedicated to the memory of Sam Owen, an enthusiastic supporter of the institution, who died in Hurricane Camille.

November 7, 1970 Alumni Association Hall of Fame established with Astronaut Fred Haise as recipient.

November 9, 1974 Began Golden Year (50th anniversary) celebration of the existence of the junior college division.

October 25, 1975 Special reunion of Football State Champion Teams of 1928, 1942, 1948, 1966, 1967, 1971, 1974. (Author's note: the 1928 team did not win the state championship. The 1927 team did win the state championship, but the trophy erroneously reads "1928").

November 5, 1977 Special reunion of the 1927 State Champion Football Team on their 50th anniversary.

October 31, 1981 Special reunion of the 1971-1973 classmates of the 1971 National Football Championship Team and cheerleaders.

October 27, 1985 Homecoming football game returned to the afternoon for the first time since 1949.

October 24, 1987 75th anniversary celebration of the first classes.

November 2, 1991 Special reunion of 1931 and 1932 State Championship Baseball Teams.

October 23, 1993 First involvement of the MGCCC Archives with homecoming began with a reception in the Archives room in Dees Hall.

November 5, 1994 First MGCCC Archives Homecoming Exhibit in Heidelberg Hall. Back room of the exhibit for showing of 1984 National Championship Football Game film to special reunion of the 1984 team.

October 21, 1995 MGCCC Archives Exhibit commemorating MGCCC Gold Star students and faculty and the 50th anniversary of the end of World War II. World War II artifacts and exhibit courtesy of Doug Mansfield of Jackson County Campus.

October 19, 1996 Special reunion of Sam Jones's band members and Perkettes (1952-1978) and special reunion of the 1971 National Championship Football Team. Archives Exhibit featuring the band and Perkettes and 1971 team in Heidelberg Hall exhibit area front room and special showing of 1971 football film in back room.

November 1, 1997 Special MGCCC Archives Piney Woods Exhibit featuring artifacts and photographs of piney woods life in the early to mid 20th century. Also exhibit on reunion classes ending in seven.

October 10, 1998 Special reunions of the 1948 Co-National Championship Football Team and special reunion of Ken "Curly" Farris's baseball teams 1962-1989. Heidelberg Hall MGCCC Archives Exhibit on reunion years ending in eight in front room with special emphasis on the 1948 football team. Piney Woods exhibit was continued. Exhibit on Curly Farris's baseball teams in back room.

October 30, 1999 Special reunion of the football teams of George Sekul's career, 1961-1991. Both MGCCC Archives exhibit rooms in Heidelberg Hall devoted to Sekul's teams. In addition artifacts related to reunion classes ending in nine and a special exhibit devoted to the 15 inaugural inductees of the MGCCC Athletic Hall of Fame placed in front room. New plaque placed on the football monument in the Perkinston Quadrangle naming the members of the 1948 Co-National Championship Football Team.

October 21, 2000 George Sekul named to Alumni Association Hall of Fame, so MGCCC Archives Exhibit remained as the year before but with the addition of an exhibit devoted to the five 2000 inductees into the Alumni Association Athletic Hall of Fame and reunion classes ending in zero.

THE SAM OWEN TROPHY

Sam Owen stands to the right of the Sam Owen Trophy on the night of its first awarding, homecoming October 13, 1956. The first recipient, Calvin Eugene Dees, stands at the left of the trophy holding the plaque upon which his and subsequent Sam Owen Trophy winners' names would be inscribed.

A unique feature of homecoming, which had nothing to do with reunions or any of the other usual elements of the day, began on homecoming night 1956, with the awarding of the first Sam Owen Trophy.

Sam Owen, scion of a Lebanese immigrant family, attended Harrison-Stone-Jackson Agricultural High School at Perkinston during session 1927-1928. Later Owen became a successful Gulfport realtor and took an enthusiastic interest in the welfare of the Perkinston school. To encourage others to share his interest, he developed the idea of awarding a trophy each year to a person or persons who had rendered distinguished service to the institution. Owen personally awarded the first trophy to Calvin Eugene Dees, proprietor of Dees General Store in Perkinston. The ceremony took place in A. L. May Memorial Stadium at the half during the homecoming game against Pearl River on October 13, 1956.

Owen continued to personally give the trophy until he and his wife, Genevieve, died as victims of Hurricane Camille on the night of August 17-18, 1969. College officials dedicated homecoming 1969 to Owen's memory and named him the Sam Owen Trophy recipient of October 25, 1969. In 1972 Owen Hall on the Perkinston Campus was named in his honor. The Sam Owen Trophy remained in 2000 the college's premiere award for service.

THE PERKINSTON AGRICULTURAL HIGH SCHOOL BULLPUPS 1952-1961

No rendition of the Perkinston institution's football and homecoming history would be complete without mention of the school's other football team and other homecoming. From fall 1952 through fall 1961 the Perkinston Agricultural High School fielded a team known as the "Bullpups." Beginning on November 5, 1954, the PAHS staged a homecoming complete with a queen separate from that of the junior college division and on a different day.

Of the Bullpup's ten seasons the most successful was that of 1955, when Bullpup coach J. V. Shiel led his charges to an outstanding season record of nine victories and one loss. The finale of the season came on December 1, when the Bullpups defeated Notre Dame High School of Biloxi for the Dairy Bowl trophy in A. L. May Memorial Stadium.

The Perkinston institution had originated with the establishment of the Agricultural High School in 1911. The AHS had remained a vital part of the institution for decades after the college division was established in 1925, but by 1950 AHS enrollment had eroded to a low of 55.

The closure of smaller high schools in North Harrison county and Stone County and the busing of their former students to the AHS resulted in renewed growth in the early 1950s. In fall 1952 the high school students of Perkinston Consolidated High School were sent "across the road" to the AHS and the consequent revitalization of the AHS resulted in the establishment of a complete high school program including sports. When the PAHS was closed in May 1962, it had an enrollment of 281, the highest in the history of the AHS.

The PAHS former students of the decade 1952-1962, because of their unique experience, shared a kinship and tended to hold separate reunions that were not a part of the MGCCC homecoming. In summer 1995 the PAHS decade 1953-1962 graduates held a reunion at the Broadwater Beach Resort Hotel in Biloxi. More than 300 persons from 13 states attended the reunion, which was imbued with a special poignancy since the institution, the memory of which they shared, had long ceased to exist.

On December 1, 1955, Perkinston Agricultural High School Bullpup co-captains Leroy Coker (No. 25) and Fred Gill (No.20) accept the congratulations of Perkinston Junior College Athletic Director Harold White. Coach J. V. Shiel (right) holds the Dairy Bowl trophy. Photo from 1955 Perkolator, p. 131.

The 1955 Dairy Bowl trophy (18 inches tall), a momento of the Bullpups most successful season.

Football and Track 1961 - 1991
THE SEKUL LEGACY

Steven George Sekul was born October 5, 1937, in Biloxi. A scion of one of Point Cadet's famed Yugoslavian seafood families, Sekul excelled early in sports. He was an All Gulf Coast Conference quarterback in both his junior and senior year at Notre Dame High School in Biloxi and a three-year letterman in basketball. Although Notre Dame had no other sports program, Sekul played four years of American Legion baseball.

Following graduation from high school in 1955, he attended Perkinston Junior College, where he signed on as a quarterback under head coach Harold White. The 1955 Bulldogs played the toughest schedule in the history of the college, and it showed. They lost the first seven games in a row. Arch rival Pearl River beat Perk 13-6, the only Bulldog score coming when Sekul hit halfback Iggy Gonzalez with a long pass on the Wildcat 25, and Gonzalez took it all the way.

By Saturday, November 5, in the game against Copiah-Lincoln, the Bulldogs had suffered so much attrition due to injury that the only original member of the backfield still standing was George Sekul. But a four-yard plunge by Sekul in the second period and an eleven yard run by Godfrey Hebert in the fourth brought home Perk's first victory of the year 12-7. On the following Thursday night in A. L. May Memorial Stadium, Perk beat Itawamba 25-0. Sekul's six-point contribution to that score is described thusly in the November 11, 1955, *Daily Herald:*

George Sekul prepares to throw a pass in Perkinston's A. L. May Memorial Stadium in 1956. Photo from 1957 Perkolator, p. 113.

"On the seventh play Sekul executed his swivel-hip prance that brought the slim assembly to its collective feet. Sekul faded to pass but found his intended receivers covered and himself being rushed from all sides. The 160-pound ex-Notre Dame Rebel took matters into his own hands, squeezed through the emerging Indians, flirted with the sidelines for 20 yards, and scored."

At the beginning of the 1956 season, 25-year-old Perkinston native Ed Evans was hired as end coach of the college team and as coach of the agricultural high school team. The friendship which developed that year between Evans, a member of Perk's 1948 championship football team, and the 19-year-old Biloxi quarterback would later prove very beneficial to Sekul's career.

Sekul, with a Bulldog escort, carries the 1986 East Bowl trophy off the field in Boone, North Carolina, on November 23, 1986. This was the final championship trophy of Sekul's career and the last for MGCJC in the 20th century.

While the 1956 team garnered no laurels, Sekul's skilled quarterbacking abilities shined in nearly every game--won or lost. He seemed to be particularly deadly when facing Texans--well, two out of three times anyway.

In the game against Texarkana Junior College played in Texarkana on Saturday, September 29, Sekul scored two touchdowns himself and passed for two more in the 35-7 win. On Thursday, October 19, the Kilgore (Texas) Rangers played Perkinston at Joseph W. Milner Stadium in Gulfport and lost 12-0. The first Perkinston touchdown came in the first quarter when 205-pound Talbot J. "Tank" Pennison of Houma, Louisiana, bulled his way for nine yards into the end zone carrying two Kilgore tacklers in with him. Sekul passed to halfback Paul Smith for the second touchdown in the second quarter.

Bulldog Talbot J. "Tank" Pennison came off the bench on October 25, 1956, in Tyler, Texas, to tackle Tyler Apache Ottis Hargett, who was running unopposed toward the end zone. Photo 1957 Perkolator, p. 114.

On Thursday, October 25, the Bulldogs went to Tyler, Texas, to take on the Tyler Apaches and got scalped 39-0. Sekul did not even make the dispatches that night, but his teammate, Tank Pennison, certainly did. Outraged by the lopsided scoring, Tank came off the bench to drop Tyler's Ottis Hargett, who was running wide-open to an unopposed touchdown. Of course, Tank's efforts were all for naught, and the officials ruled the interrupted run a Tyler touchdown. Sekul remembered, "The only man that got hit harder that night than Ottis Hargett was Tank when Coach White hit him for hitting Hargett."

The 1956 season ended 4-6 overall. One of those losses was a 21-0 shutout by the Pearl River Wildcats in A. L. May Memorial Stadium at Homecoming. Sekul would particularly remember that loss for adjustment later. Despite a losing season Sekul made First Team Mississippi Junior College All-State and Honorable Mention Junior College All-American.

Sekul transferred to Mississippi Southern College at Hattiesburg in January 1957, and in 1958, under the tutelage of legendary coach Thad "Pie" Vann, he quarterbacked Southern's only undefeated and untied season. In the wake of his unique performance, Sekul was selected to play in the prestigious North-South Senior Bowl in Mobile. Sekul played for the South, which won 14-7.

Sekul graduated from Mississippi Southern in May 1959, and over the course of the next two years, he coached both the 1959 and the 1960 Mississippi Southern freshmen team while trying-out for the Canadian Football League and Boston Patriots. He earned his master's degree in educational administration at Mississippi Southern in May 1961.

In summer 1961, head coach Ed Evans offered Sekul the position of backfield coach at Perkinston Junior College. He accepted the position and began work on August 1, 1961.

In their first outing of the 1961 season, the Bulldogs suffered a narrow 14-13 loss to Mississippi Delta. They won the next game against Copiah-Lincoln 12-6. On Thursday, September 21, Perk took on Holmes and lost 14-0. According to the September 23 *Daily Herald*, Ode Burrell of Durant "was the backbone of Holmes' attack and, more than any other one man, was the cause of Perkinston's downfall in the contest." Thirty years later Ode Burrell would become assistant football coach at MGCCC.

On Thursday, September 28, 1961, Perk defeated the Tulane Baby Billow (freshmen) 14-13 at A. L. May

Head Coach Ed Evans hired George Sekul as the new backfield coach for the Bulldogs when Bobby Holmes left after the 1960-61 season.

Memorial Stadium. It had been a different story the year before at Sugar Bowl Stadium when the Baby Billow rolled over the Bulldogs 32-0. The first two touchdowns of the night were inflicted on Perk by Clement "Clem" Dellenger of Biloxi, who later became assistant coach under George Sekul for twenty-five years.

Perk lost the next seven games of the 1961 season. Some of the "lowlites" of this terrible series of defeats follow. On October 7, the Scooba Lions mauled the Dawgs 40-9. A week later Perk's leading ground gainer, William (Hobo) Jones, fell victim to Russian imperialism when the United States activated his reserve unit in response to the Berlin Crisis. On November 2, a "sure" victory over East Central at Decatur went aglimmering with a bad call. The score was 7-6 in Perk's favor with the Warriors halted on the one-foot mark. With the players of both teams gathered in a confused muddle as the clock ticked to zero, East Central quarterback Phil Troutman took the ball from the center and dived over the goal. The officials ruled this crazy travesty a touchdown and gave East Central a 13-7 victory.

But these were small matters compared to what happened on November 11, 1961. This homecoming game, touted as the gala climax of "The Golden Year" celebration of 50 years of Perk's existence, also happened to fall on the forty-third anniversary of the end of World War I. In view of the outcome the day was more reminiscent of the latter than the former. The Pearl River Wildcats under Coach Dobie Holden came onto the field determined to get 32 points to upset Hinds's 1951 Mississippi State Junior College record for the most points scored in a single season. When the smoke cleared, Holden's cats had clawed 60 points out of the Bulldogs, and the Bulldogs had six points. This "cat-astrophe" set a new state record and another one as well. "The Armistice Day Slaughter of 1961" still remains the most lopsided score in Perk-Pearl River history and, by the way, marked the thirteenth successive defeat of the Dawgs by the Cats. The 43-12 defeat suffered at the paws of the Southwest Bears the next week brought the 2-9 season to a close.

The disastrous 1961 football season gave way in the spring of that school year to a shining track effort. In the nineteen-year history of the Magnolia State Track Meet, Perk had won only once—1953. In spring 1962, with Sekul as the new head track coach, Perk took the state track crown once again.

In May 1962, as the Mississippi Gulf Coast Junior College was established, Ed Evans resigned his coaching duties to go into Perkinston Campus administration, beginning a career which, in time, would have an impact on vocational-technical education throughout the state of Mississippi. Into his head coaching job stepped Harold Wesson of Corinth. Wesson, a member of the Perkinston Junior College Class of 1943, had been the halfback on the 1942 state championship team. Sekul remained his backfield coach, and Wesson hired Ken "Curly" Farris as line coach.

The record of the 1962 season totaled seven wins and only four losses, but one loss was a 20-22 loss to Pearl River, a respectable score in terms of the year before, but still, the

(From left) Line coach Ken "Curly" Farris, head coach Harold Wesson, and backfield coach, George Sekul in 1964

fourteenth loss in a row to the Wildcats. There was one horrendous score in the 1962 season, 77 to 6; this time the right way—Bulldogs over the Southwest Bears. This score still stands as the record defeat of a team by Gulf Coast.

The 1962 season closed with the Bulldogs playing for the first time in the eight-year-old Hospitality Bowl. The Hospitality Bowl was designed to pit a Texas team against a Mississippi team, because those were the only two states in the Deep South fielding appreciable numbers of junior college football teams. In the game, played in Milner Stadium in Gulfport, Navarro Junior College of Corsicana, Texas, beat the Bulldogs 3-0.

The 1963 season ended 7 wins and 4 losses, but one of those losses was 24-20 to Pearl River. The 1964 season ended 6 wins and 4 losses, and one of those losses was 30-0 to Pearl River. The 1965 season ended 6 wins and 4 losses, and one of those losses was 20-6 to Pearl River. At that point

"Super-Bulldog" Buck Eure of Pascagoula demonstrates the "flying guard position" in A. L. May Memorial Stadium at Perkinston in fall 1964.

Pearl River held seventeen successive wins over Gulf Coast. As the 1965-66 academic year came to a close, Coach Harold Wesson, an eighteen year veteran of the gridiron with four winning seasons at Gulf Coast, decided to accept the job of administrative assistant for instructional affairs.

According to Dick Lightsey, *Daily Herald* sports editor, the only reason Sekul had not been offered the post of head coach four years prior was lack of experience. Now with four years of experience under Wesson, MGCJC President J. J. Hayden and the Board of Trustees felt he was ready, and he got the job. Ken "Curly" Farris, head baseball coach, remained as line coach for the football squad, and Clement "Clem" Dellenger became assistant football coach.

Dellenger, like Sekul, was a Biloxian and a graduate of Notre Dame High School. An All-Southeastern-Conference

George Sekul (center), named head coach of the Bulldogs in 1966, is flanked by his two assistants, Ken "Curly" Farris (left) and Clem Dellenger.

end at Tulane, Dellenger had been teaching for the past two years at John Curtis High School in New Orleans. With the formation of the team of Sekul, Farris, and Dellenger, a new day dawned in Mississippi junior college football.

As soon as he took over as head coach, Sekul saw to it that Gulf Coast affiliated with the National Junior College Athletic Association because only in that way could the MGCJC team hope to participate in the NJCAA Championship Shrine Bowl Game in Savannah, Georgia. For years Gulf Coast remained the only Mississippi junior college in the NJCAA because the rules required that football players maintain a 1.5 grade point average in ten hours of college work in order to be eligible to play. Coaches at the other Mississippi schools considered that requirement too great a risk.

The 1966 Bulldogs came out of the starting gate pulverizing six opponents in a row--East Central, Hinds, East Mississippi, Co-Lin, Mississippi Delta, and Southwest. Then, inexplicably, they lost two in a row by only one point each to Itawamba and Holmes.

Next on the agenda was Pearl River, whose team was known to its admirers as "Wildcats" and to its detractors, namely those associated with MGCJC, as "River Rats."

Precisely where this appellation was first applied is not known, but seventeen years of defeat followed by defeat followed by impending defeat had stored up high potential for the epidemic of "ratophobia," which burst forth with a vengeance in huge pep rallies held at all three MGCJC campuses. David Curry, a Jackson County Campus contributor to the *Bulldog Barks*, stated his unequivocal views in the November 4 issue under the heading "Flash—The River Rats are coming!"

"Beware, dedicated students of Gulf Coast Junior College District! A vast horde of river rats will soon descend upon your lands!

Annually these loathsome creatures migrate to your area and in the manner of an ancient pestilence to scourge and pillage your lands! For eighteen long and grueling years you have been victimized by these accursed vermin with no means of preventing their inhuman devastation.

But hearken, all is not yet lost! It seems that the villains can be put to rout by large amounts of school spirit and cheering noises."

There was no lack of "spirit and cheering noises" on game night, Saturday, November 12, 1966, at Gulfport's Milner Stadium, which was packed for the occasion. A great roar swelled as the brand new Bulldog mascot, Maxine, pranced in with her team. Bulldog Tommy Boutwell took the opening kickoff and stormed over the Rats for 75 yards and the game's first touchdown. In all, the Bulldogs crossed the Pearl River goal line seven times and kicked three extra points, but two touchdowns were called back. Pearl River never drew blood. At the end, as the crowd counted down the 33-0 victory, President Hayden took the microphone in the press box and declared the following Monday a "Victory Over Pearl River Holiday." The crowd went wild again.

The breaking of the "River Rat Jinx" marked the beginning of the Sekul legend. The next Saturday night the Bulldogs defeated Jones 21-14 at Ellisville to capture Gulf Coast's first Mississippi state football championship since 1948.

On December 3, the Bulldogs journeyed to Shreveport, Louisiana, to play Navarro Junior College of Corsicana, Texas, in the Second Annual Shrine Bowl. By a score of 21 to 7, they avenged the defeat inflicted upon them by this team in the Hospitality Bowl four years earlier. This Shrine Bowl was a local event not to be confused with the NJCAA Shrine Bowl in Savannah, Georgia.

Mississippi State Junior College Football Champions 1966

First row *(from left), Ken Borries (No. 25) of Vancleave, Larry Grimes (No. 23) of Pascagoula, James Taylor (No. 41) of Pascagoula, Kirby Carlisle (No. 89) of Gulfport, Billy Burke (No. 84) of Gulfport, Don Moore (No. 74) of St. Martin*

Second row
Ronnie Seymour (No. 65) of St. Martin, Don Fountain (No. 24) of Biloxi, Clovis Rushing (No. 87) of Pascagoula, Tommy Boutwell (No. 11) of Gulfport, Eddie Gifford (No. 88) of Biloxi, Billy Culpepper (No. 83) of Gulfport, Felix Bertucci (No. 80) of Gulfport

Third row
Bob Carmack (No. 62) of Gulfport, Butch Oustalet (No. 52) of Pass Christian, Richard Daniels (No. 27) of Long Beach, Robert Hincks (No. 30) of Pass Christian, Pat Griggs (No. 71) of Ocean Springs, Woodie Hudson (No. 35) of Biloxi, Joe Allen (No. 51) of Biloxi, B. L. "Sonny" Fletcher (No. 43) of Pascagoula

Fourth row
Gene Bass (No. 60) of Long Beach, Jimmy Shotts (No. 66) of Gulfport, Jerry Moorehead (No. 40) of Pascagoula, Charles McLendon (No. 18) of Lucedale, Billy Graham (No. 31) of Pascagoula, Fred Hornsby (No. 63) of Biloxi, David Ables (No. 77) of Lucedale

Fifth row
Nebo Carter (No. 70) of Vancleave, Frank Beckman (No. 72) of Moss Point, Virgil Prather (No. 82) of Gulfport, Clell Rosetti (No. 10) of Biloxi, Joe Fountain (No. 20) of Biloxi, Glenn "Sonny" Pisarich (No. 81) of Biloxi, Larry Strohm (No. 42) of Wiggins

Sixth row
Coach Ken Farris, Coach Clem Dellenger, Lewis Catrett (No. 76) of Escatawpa, Chuck Johnson (No. 55) of St. Martin, Donnie Holloway (No. 61) of Biloxi, Danny Parker (No. 67) of Biloxi, James Ray Smith (No. 79) of Biloxi, Coach George Sekul

Below: George Sekul, in his first year as head coach of the MGCJC football team, stands at the goal post in A. L. May Memorial Stadium while putting Richard "Red" Daniels (left) of Long Beach and Don Fountain of St. Martin through their paces. Sekul's 1966 team garnered his first state championship in football.

The glorious 1966 season then ended for all the Bulldogs except the six whom accompanied Sekul, Farris, and Dellenger to the First Annual Junior College All-Star Football game played in Jackson's Mississippi Memorial Stadium on December 10. In his first season Sekul had delivered a performance exceeded only by the Bulldogs of 1948.

Sekul turned the 1967 season into a virtual instant replay of 1966. Once again the Wildcats (or Rats) howled (or squeaked) to their deaths, this time 27-7. Once again the season record stood at 9 wins and 2 losses. Once again the Bulldogs won the state championship crown. Once again Sekul and company coached the South, this time to a 27-17 victory over the North, in the Second Annual Junior College All-Star game at Mississippi Memorial Stadium in Jackson. However, the Bulldogs did not go to the Shrine Bowl in Shreveport because it, like its Hospitality Bowl predecessor, died due to lack of spectator support in the host city.

To close out the 1967-1968 year, Sekul's 1968 thinclads

MISSISSIPPI STATE JUNIOR COLLEGE FOOTBALL CHAMPIONS 1967

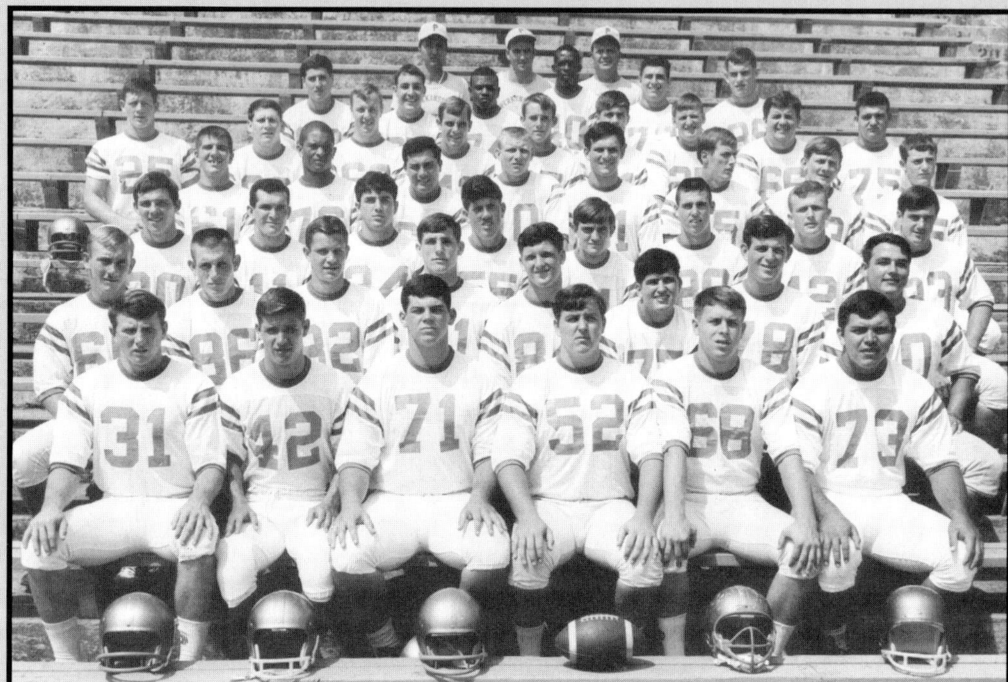

First row (from left) Jim Ryan (No. 31) of Ocean Springs, David Jalanivich (No. 42) of Ocean Springs, Dana Saia (No. 71) of Wiggins, Jay Fletcher (No. 52) of Pascagoula, Clyde Freeman (No. 68) of Mobile, Joe Gazzo (No. 73) of Biloxi

Second row
Richard Huff, (No. 60) of Moss Point, Marshall Reed (No. 86) of Gulfport, Danny Smith (No. 82) of St. Martin, Wade Wilkes (No. 41) of Biloxi, Kim Stewart (No. 84) of Gulfport, Johnny Seymour (No.77) of Ocean Springs, David Ables (No. 78) of Lucedale, David Mohr (No. ?)

Third row
Jim Miller (No. 30) of Moss Point, James Connard (No. 11) of Biloxi, Larry Strohm (No. 34) of Wiggins, Tommy Huntsman (No.55) of St. Martin, Rodney Nourse (No. 51) of Biloxi, Mike Carter (No. 80) of Wiggins, Doug Hassel (No. 12) of Moss Point, Terry Hathcock (No. 83) of Lucedale

Fourth row
Lloyd Seymour (No. 61) of Biloxi, Morris Richardson (No. 76) of Pascagoula, Joe Fountain (No. 20) of Biloxi, Clell Rosetti (No. 10) of Biloxi, Glenn "Sonny" Pisarich (No. 81) of Biloxi, John Hale (No. 15) of Lucedale, Harry Roberts (No. 23) Moss Point, Jerry Moorehead (No. 35) of Pascagoula

Fifth row
Ken Borries (No. 25) of Vancleave, Eddie Gifford (No. 88) of Biloxi, Bob Carmack (No. 62) of Gulfport, B. L. "Sonny" Fletcher (No. 43) of Pascagoula, Larry Bogard (No. 87) of Biloxi, Larry Grimes (No. 65) of Pascagoula, Robert Hincks (No. 27) of Pass Christian, Jimmy Shotts (No. 66) of Gulfport, Mike Gavin (No. 75) of D'Iberville

Sixth row
Billy Culpepper (No. 63) of Gulfport, Bob Johnson (No. 67) of Biloxi, Josh Wells (No. 74) of Pascagoula, Glen Larkin (No. 40) of Pascagoula, James Ray Smith (No. 72) of Biloxi, and John Clay (No. 89)of Moss Point

Seventh row
Coach George Sekul, Coach Clem Dellenger, Coach Ken Farris

The 1967 state championship set a 20th century MGCJC record. It was the only time an MGCJC football team won a second state crown in a row. Three members of the 1967 team also set a precedent. According to Sekul, his recruiting of Josh Wells, Glen Larkin, and Morris Richardson, all of Pascagoula, represented the first time in Mississippi history that black men played for a previously all-white state college. Sekul said, "I don't mean just junior colleges. I mean all state colleges--senior colleges, universities--all of them." He continued, "Josh Wells made All-State that year. In 1968 Josh made it again, and Glen Larkin made it, too. In addition, Larkin picked up the junior college 100 and 220 yard dash records in the spring of 1968. It didn't take long with what we were doing to teams with these guys for the other junior colleges to get black players, too."

Morris Richardson returned to Perk in Fall 1997 after a career in the U. S. Army. In Richardson's words, "After deciding to return to school, I chose MGCCC because of the good memories from thirty years prior." In three years at Perk, Richardson earned a degree in pre-physical therapy. In August 2000 he was hired as supervisor of Harrison Hall and began commuting to USM to work on a degree in kinesiotherapy.

Glenn Larkin

Morris Richardson

Josh Wells

took the state championship in track. As the trophy cases filled, Gulf Coast began to attract state and national attention as a Mississippi junior college powerhouse.

From left: Marshall Reed, John Hale, Glenn Larkin, and Harry Roberts, 1968 Track Champions-- State and MGCJC Record Holders 880 Yard Relay 1:30.0

In the next three years Sekul's players won no trophies, but their won-loss record remained high. Of the ten games of the 1968 season, Sekul lost only one game, but he lost it to a new kind of cat, a Bobcat, which cost him the state title. After that, the Jones Bobcats began to rival the Pearl River Wildcats as a Gulf Coast nemesis.

From left: Dr. J. J. Hayden, Cheerleader Christa Tanner of Wiggins, and Sam Owen show off the No. 1 Grid-Wire trophy in A. L. May Memorial Stadium. The J. C. Grid-Wire of October 29, 1968, naming the Bulldogs No. 1 in the nation, prompted Mayor R. B. Meadows of Gulfport to send the trophy to Hayden celebrating this honor.

In 1969, the worst year to date of his career, Sekul still turned in a very respectable seven and four record. He beat Jones that year, but the Pearl River Wildcats slaughtered his Bulldogs 35-0, a score reminiscent of the bad old days, and the Wildcats went on to win the state title. In spring 1970, though, Sekul's thinclads garnered another state championship in track.

In 1970 changes in Mississippi Junior College Conference football rules resulted in the state being divided into a south division and a north division with the winner of each division being pitted in a play-off for state champion. In former times the team with the best overall conference record had been automatically awarded the state crown. Jones tied Gulf Coast 0-0 on September 26, and Pearl River beat the Bulldogs 12-0 on October 3. Gulf Coast ended the season 8-1- 1, the best record in the state. Pearl River ended 8-2. But in south division play Gulf Coast stood 3-1-1 and Pearl River 4-1-0; that translates as one-half game better. Caught in a crunch between the Bobcats and the Wildcats, the Bulldogs had lost it all. Pearl River took the 1970 state football title.

Nobody knew it at the time, but that October 3, 1970, Wildcat victory was to be Sekul's last defeat for two calendar years. The United States was about to learn the location of Mississippi Gulf Coast Junior College as the Bulldogs went over the top and entered the National Junior College Athletic Association Valhalla. Before this astonishing twenty-two game blitzkrieg ended, the names of the Bulldogs of 1971 would be enshrined in stone and bronze in the Perkinston Campus Quadrangle.

In retrospect the most important name on the bronze plaque was that of James "Dinky" McKay of Long Beach. The 6'1", 170 pounder took over as starting quarterback the week after the October 3 loss to Pearl River, and the Bulldogs neither lost nor tied another game in that season or the next.

The 1971 season opened on September 4 with a 28-21 victory over Itawamba. Copiah-Lincoln fell 30-7 on September 11.

On Thursday, September 18, Jones came to battle Gulf Coast on home ground. The Bulldogs took the Bobcat kickoff and began a 63-yard march to the Jones goal line. Dinky McKay went around the right side from the 15-yard-line for the touchdown. Jim Beck, a six foot, 206-pound kicker from Ocean Springs, made the extra point. With the score at 26 to 6 in the third quarter, McKay hit Eugene Ganucheau, 6'1", 217-pound tight end from Biloxi, at the Jones 20-yard line, and Ganucheau went in for the touchdown. Beck again kicked the conversion. Johnny O'Brien of Pascagoula made the final score of the game with a 24 yard run. Beck missed the extra point and the game ended 27-8.

The Bobcat tie and the Wildcat loss of the previous year had cost Gulf Coast the state crown by giving Pearl River a half-game edge. The Bulldogs had just wreaked vengeance on Jones, and it was about to be payback time for Pearl River.

When the Bulldogs waded into the Wildcats at Biloxi's

Municipal Stadium on September 25, both teams, for the first time in history, were undefeated in season play . From the beginning Pearl River and Gulf Coast had fought, well, like cats and dogs, but the clash of 1971 was to be a real grudge match fought only blocks from Sekul's boyhood home. Before the game, Sekul told a reporter, "We feel like we had the best team last year, and we think we have the best team again. Now it's a matter of proving it."

Prove it they did. The Wildcats drew first blood, but McKay went in to score and then threw a two-point conversion to make the score 8-7 at the half. In the third quarter McKay ran in for another touchdown, and Jimmy Beck booted the extra point. The Cats came back with another score but missed the conversion, and the score stood at 15-13. Then McKay connected with Don Fredericks of Gulfport. Fredericks fumbled the ball at the Pearl River 48-yard-line, but Larry Benefield of Gulfport recovered and went all the way for a touchdown. Beck's kick made the score 22-13. At game's end the Dawgs had mauled the Wildcats 37-21 and stood in sole possession of first place in the south division.

Bulldog Levorne Hawthorne (No. 37) catches the ball for the touchdown that tied the game 27-27 against East Central on October 2, 1971 at War Memorial Stadium in Pascagoula.

On October 2, the Bulldogs took on undefeated north division champion East Central at War Memorial Stadium in Pascagoula in what turned out to be the most dangerous encounter of the season. With the clock ticking, Levorne Hawthorne of Gulfport caught a seven-yard McKay pass in the end zone to tie the game 27-27. With nine seconds to go, Jimmy Beck prepared to kick the extra point. He kicked the football through the uprights and made Mississippi junior college history. A loss or a tie at that point in the 1971 season would have cost Gulf Coast any hope at a national championship berth.

On October 2, 1971, with dreams of national glory hanging in the balance at War Memorial Stadium in Pascagoula, Sekul and the Bulldogs on the sideline stare transfixed at the action. Dellenger bites his nails, while Farris exhorts the Bulldogs on the field. A McKay to Hawthorne touchdown pass followed by a Beck point after touchdown brought victory and a shot at the national crown.

In the wake of the victory over the East Central Warriors, the Bulldogs were ranked No. 1 by the Junior College Grid-Wire, publishers of the national junior college football ratings with headquarters in Santa Ana, California. When the news of this signal recognition reached the office of MGCJC President Hayden, it put him on cloud nine. This news, coupled with his boys beating the stuffing out of Holmes at Goodman 36-7 on Thursday of that same week, resulted in his declaring Friday of that week a holiday. Actually one of the boys on the Bulldog team was one of his own--Glover, his youngest son.

Now really foaming at the mouth, the Bulldog pack ate up the Scooba Lions 33-13 on October 16. On October 28 they devoured the Southwest Bears 36-8.

The Bulldogs annihilated Hinds at Homecoming on November 6. When Glover Hayden kicked the final extra point at A. L. May Memorial Stadium, the Eagles had lost 62-7, and Gulf Coast had the 1971 south division trophy.

The Bulldogs had been slated to play the Mississippi Delta Trojans in their final regular season game at Moorhead on November 11. However, since Delta had emerged as the north division champion and Gulf Coast was the south division contender, the decision was made to move the game up to November 20 and make it the State Championship tilt.

With the invitation to the National Junior College Championship Shrine Bowl game at Savannah, Georgia, already in hand, Gulf Coast could not have been eliminated from national contention by a loss to Delta, but it would have been disastrous to Bulldog morale and would have been reflected in the national polls. The Junior College Grid-Wire Poll still carried Gulf Coast as Number One, but the NJCAA Poll touted Fort Scott (Kansas) Community College in that position.

In the game played in Biloxi's Municipal Stadium on Saturday, November 20, the score stood at 7-6 Delta's way just before the half. All of Gulf Coast's points were from Beck field goals. In the closing seconds of the half, Beck tried a 36-yard field goal, but the ball sailed wide to the right.

In the second half the Dawgs got it together. Jerald Thomas, a 6', 177-pound running back from Pascagoula, emerged as the Bulldog hero in the third quarter. Thomas put the Dawgs out front with a seven-yard run to make the score 12-7. Beck missed his target on the conversion pass. Still in the third quarter, Thomas scored again, and Beck kicked the point for a 19-7 Gulf Coast lead. Delta put seven more points on the board in the fourth quarter, but then a McKay touchdown and a Beck extra point matched that. The game ended 26-14 with team captain Dinky McKay, on the shoulders of his team mates, holding high the gleaming 1971 Mississippi state championship trophy.

But the unsung heroes of this state championship game (and all the others) were the hard-hitting defensive strong men who held the Delta offense to only 63 yards for the night. Defensive stand-outs in this game were William "Skip" Holland of Lucedale, Jerry Brown of Moss Point, Shed Foxworth of Gulfport, Ken Boynick of Gulfport, and John McDougle of Moss Point, who was also co-captain of the team. The talents of these men, and those of linebackers Kenny Wayne Larsen of Pascagoula and Gerald Pickich of Biloxi were to be put to the supreme test on December 3, 1971, in Savannah, Georgia.

Bulldog quarterback James "Dinky" McKay of Long Beach is surrounded by teammates as he hoists the 1971 Mississippi junior college championship trophy following the November 20, 1971, 26-14 victory over Mississippi Delta Junior College at Biloxi.

Hayden, Perkinston Campus Executive Dean C. G. Odom, Prof. Sam Jones, his fifty-member-band and forty Perkettes, along with an unknown number of supporters went with their Bulldogs to Georgia. Fort Scott's counterparts to all these journeyed also to the city by the sea for the great contest. Of course, the Kansas fans had seen it all only a year before when the second-ranked Fort Scott Greyhounds had bested first-ranked Mesa (Arizona) Community College 41-20. The two Fort Scott stars of that game were back to do it all again to NJCAA poll second-ranked Mississippi Gulf Coast.

Kurt Nieman, Greyhound quarterback from Topeka, Kansas, and Greyhound running back Tommy Reaman of Newport News, Virginia, had been freshmen in their record-shattering defeat of Mesa College in 1971. Now sophomore leaders of a team able to recruit from the whole nation and boasting members from six states and the District of Columbia, they did not expect any problems with a team restricted to recruiting from seventeen high schools in four

National Junior College Athletic Association Football Champions, 1971

***First row** (from left)*
Jim Beck (No. 2) of Ocean Springs, Glover Hayden (No. 3) of Perkinston, Ken Boynick (No. 10) of Gulfport, Gilbert Pyron (No. 11) of Biloxi, Gary Jackson (No. 15) of Biloxi, James "Dinky" McKay (No. 18) of Long Beach, Willie Lee Sims (No. 20) of Moss Point, Charles Sims (No. 23) of Moss Point, Bennie Williams (No. 25) of Vancleave, Don Fredericks (No. 26) of Gulfport, Mike Borden (No. 87) of Biloxi

Second row
Jerald Thomas (No. 30) of Pascagoula, Wayne Patrick (No. 31) of Pascagoula, Melvin Morgan (No. 32) of Gulfport, Tommy Robison (No. 33) of Gulfport, Larry Benefield (No. 34) of Gulfport, Ronnie Miller (No. 35) of Moss Point, Johnny O'Brien (No. 36) of Pascagoula, Levorne Hawthorne (No. 37) of Gulfport, Kenny Larsen (No. 43) of Pascagoula, Mike Jenner (No. 51) of Gulfport

Third row
Ronnie Oustalet (No. 27) of Pass Christian, Charles Driskel (No. 52) of Lucedale, Terry Helms (No. 53) of Gulfport, David Taranto (No. 55) of Biloxi, Bobby Saucier (No. 60) of Biloxi, Jimmy Stork (No.61) of Moss Point, Gerald Pickich (No. 64) of Biloxi, Butch Nobles (No. 66) of Biloxi, Larry Campbell (No. 67) of Wade, Harold Holton (No. 68) of Gulfport, Shed Foxworth (No. 70) of Gulfport

Fourth row
John Jalanivich (No. 71) of Ocean Springs, Skip Holland (No. 72) of Lucedale, Ronnie Thomas (No. 74) of Pascagoula, Jerry Brown (No. 75) of Moss Point, Kerry Neal (No. 76) of Moss Point, Vernon Mallett (No. 78) of Biloxi, John McDougle (No. 79) of Moss Point, Tom Garcia (No. 81) of Biloxi, Tom Ferrill (No. 82) of Biloxi, Eugene Ganucheau (No. 83) of Biloxi, William Holloway (No. 88) of Moss point, Rocky Johnson (No. 89) of Biloxi, and Percy Fournier (No. 85) of Biloxi.

Players not pictured: Rikkie Autmon (No. 40), Mike Niolet (No. 41) of Pass Christian, Glen Lamas (No. 77) of Biloxi.

Jimmy DuBuisson
Long Beach
Student Trainer

Cooper Farris
Perkinston
Manager

Stuart Hodges
Gulfport
Manager

The 1971 National Championship Football Cheerleaders pose in Wentzell Center at Perkinston. Bottom row, from left: Marilyn Skellie, Marcia Randall, and Darlene Kapp all of Long Beach. Back row, from left: Kathy Sarris, George Krebs, and Tommy Perry of Biloxi and Patty Backus of St. Martin. Barbara Ann "Sue" Ross (not pictured) was the cheerleader sponsor.

From left: Bulldogs John McDougal (No. 37) and Dinky McKay (No. 18) together with Greyhounds Kurt Nieman (No. 14) and Jerone Hodges (No. 76) have their eyes on the prize the morning of the NJCAA Shrine Bowl championship game in Savannah.

counties in South Mississippi. Reaman alone in 1970 had broken four Shrine Bowl records.

The Bulldog-Greyhound clash would be the Fifteenth Alee Temple Shrine Bowl and the eighth NJCAA national championship game. Born as a fundraiser for the Shriner's Hospital for Crippled Children in Greenville, South Carolina, the game had languished until the Shriners had contracted with the NJCAA to turn the event into the National Junior College Championship Game in 1964. Attendance had grown over the years until 15,000 were expected to fill Savannah's Bacon Park Memorial Stadium in 1971. That might have happened if the weather had cooperated.

Both Fort Scott and Gulf Coast came to the bowl with 10-0 records, but that is where the similarity ended. The Greyhounds were on a 27-game winning streak and were defending National Champions ranked No. 1 by the NJCAA poll to do it again. The Bulldogs were on a 17-game winning streak ranked No. 2 in the NJCAA Poll (but still No. 1 in the JC Grid-Wire Poll), and neither they, nor any other Mississippi football team or NJCAA Region VII team, for that matter, had ever been to any national NJCAA event.

In their current 10-0 season the Greyhounds had scored 420 total points and had given up 137. Gulf Coast had scored 343 total points and given up 119.

Four thousand die-hard fans huddled in Bacon Park Stadium on that blustery, rainy December 3rd, awaiting the 8:00 p.m. kick-off. Gulf Coast scored after only three plays. Runningback Jerald Thomas bolted from the line of scrimmage, and as the Gulf Coast fans rose and screamed, he ran 64 yards for the initial touchdown of the game. Jimmy Beck kicked the extra point to make it 7-0. As the second quarter opened, McKay hit Thomas with a 33-yard scoring pass. The Bulldog fans chanting, "Hotty totty, gosh-a-mighty. Who the hell are we? We're No. 1, second to none!" scarcely noticed when the Greyhounds blocked Beck's point after. The score then stood 13-0.

A few minutes later the Kansans came to their feet and Gulf Coast moaned as Greyhound running star, Tommy Reamon, took a handoff from Kurt Neiman, turned the left corner and outran eleven Bulldogs for 63 yards to score. Kenny Larsen, Skip Holland, Jerry Brown, and John McDougle saw to it that Reamon did not get loose again that night. With the point after, the score stood at 13-7 at the half.

Prof. Jones's Band and Perkettes performed in the icy mist and so did the Greyhound band. The mist turned into a steady freezing drizzle as the second half began.

On the third play of the national championship game in Savannah on December 3, 1971, Bulldog Jerald Thomas (No. 30) of Pascagoula runs for a 64-yard touchdown to draw first blood in the battle against the Greyhounds of Kansas..

Gulf Coast took the kickoff and fought an eight-play battle down into Greyhound territory capped by a pass from McKay to Ganucheau. As Ganucheau raced for 40 yards down the rain-soaked field, Marcus Holland, Executive Sports Editor of the *Savannah Morning News* was moved to

In the third quarter of the national championship game at Savannah on December 3, 1971, Bulldog Eugene Ganucheau (No. 23) of Biloxi (left) smashes into five Greyhounds as he heads for a touchdown.

write:

"Ganucheau's touchdown run in the third period was one of the most determined anybody will witness. After pulling in McKay's pass, Ganucheau cut toward the sidelines, turned back toward the middle, bounced off five tacklers, and sped into the end zone."

The Mississippians' reaction to this was positively tornadic—something between a low-pitched scream and a high-pitched roar. Sports writer, Ray Robson of the Gulfport-Biloxi *Daily Herald*, who was present, noted that the Gulf Coast fans seemed not to notice the sleet and gusty winds acting instead as if "it was sunny and bright." With the failure of the extra point after Gancheau's run, the score stood at 19- 7.

Fort Scott struck back with a 12-play march and Neiman scored. A bad snap cost the Greyhounds the extra point, and the score then tallied at 19-13.

In the final quarter, with the Kansans in range of a tie or even a one-point lead, the crowd noise became a constant roar. The Dawgs settled down into fighting for ground and eating up the clock. This strategy had the salutary effect of keeping Reamon on the bench where he could not get into mischief. Gulf Coast ground out 56 yards in eighteen plays to the point from which Beck booted a 36-yard field goal to remove the one-touchdown Fort Scott threat. That 22-13 score was shortly thereafter embossed in bronze on an MGCJC football monument dedicated to the memory of that special night in Georgia.

As the crowd counted down -- "7, 6, 5, 4, 3, 2, 1"-- a reporter asked Sekul for his reaction. Sekul replied, "I've never been so happy in my life." When the Gulf Coast players returned to the dressing room, they knelt in their muddy uniforms and offered not one but two repetitions of the Lord's Prayer. Georgia Representative Elliot Hagan, who had come from Washington, D. C., with William "Fishbait" Miller to view the game, described this scene in the *Congressional Record* on December 7, 1971. Miller, United States House of Representatives Doorkeeper and Perkinston Junior College alumnus of 1932, had just entered the MGCJC Alumni Hall of Fame.

The Fort Scott Greyhounds from whom the Bulldogs had been delivered were quite subdued. They faced a thousand-mile flight home in defeat. In the words of one mud-caked Bulldog in the dressing room after the game, "We beat 'em. Four little old South Mississippi counties beat the whole United States of America."

A Shriner congratulates Sekul and prepares to present the NJCAA national trophy after the December 3, 1971, victory in Savannah.

Mississippi Governor John Bell Williams (center) proclaims December 1971 as Mississippi Gulf Coast Junior College month in honor of Coach George Sekul's victory at the Shrine Bowl in Savannah, Georgia, while MGCJC President J. J. Hayden (left) looks on.

MGCJC LED THE WAY TO THE NJCAA

Soon after Sekul had become head coach at MGCJC in 1966, Hayden had backed him in affiliating with the National Junior College Athletic Association (NJCAA). Undaunted by the NJCAA rule that required an athlete to pass 9 hours with a 1.5 grade average, MGCJC became the first, and for years, the only Mississippi NJCAA member. Recalling those days in an interview in 1999, Sekul remembered that, "It is like a C- or D+. If they can't do that they shouldn't be playing. Anyway, to make a long story short, when we won the national championship in 1971 it woke everybody up because we got a lot of prestige throughout the country and we invited the [NJCAA] director to speak to the junior college presidents and coaches about the importance of being members of the national organization. From then on, you know, not all of them at one time, but they began to join the national association. Now it is mandatory."

The 1971 cheerleaders ride atop a decorated station wagon as it passes in front of the Mississippi Governor's Mansion in Jackson. Photo courtesy of Larry Hogue.

The participants in the 1971 NJCAA championship victory were honored on May 25, 1972, at a banquet at the Buena Vista Hotel in Biloxi. Coaches Sekul, Farris, and Dellenger, the members of the 1971 championship team, and cheerleaders were honored with the presentation of championship rings. Also on this occasion Biloxi Mayor Danny Guice informed the assemblage that a stone monument would be erected in the quadrangle of the Perkinston Campus to which would be affixed a bronze plaque bearing the names of the 1971 coaches and team members. Private donations, banquet ticket sales, and district county officials raised the funds for the rings and the monument. The monument, in anticipation of the future, contained room for two more bronze plaques.

Several of the stalwarts of the 1971 team returned to play for Sekul in 1972, but superstar Dinky McKay was not among them. Sekul's twenty-two game winning streak, which had begun after the loss to Pearl River of October 3, 1970, ended with the Wildcat defeat of the Bulldogs on September 30, 1972. One month later the Jones Bobcats beat the Bulldogs as well, and the 1972 season ended with a respectable 8-2 record but no laurels.

The Bulldogs outscored all other Mississippi teams in 1973, ending the season at 9-1, and ranked eighth nationally in the JC Grid-Wire poll. But the one game they lost was to tenth-ranked Pearl River, which cost them the south state title and knocked them out of contention for the state championship. To finish out the near-miss season Sekul's track team won south division only to lose the state trophy by one point.

But the next year the Bulldogs found that the vagaries of the system worked both ways. It was okay to lose so long as one lost wisely. In the worst season of his career to date Sekul lost five games, three of them in a row, but four of the losses were to north division teams. So Sekul with a 5-5 record took the south state crown and went against 8-2 Itawamba at Fulton, beat the Indians 10-6, and took the state championship.

From January 1975 through January 1979, though Sekul's football teams had respectable win-loss records, Gulf Coast took only one trophy—the south division crown of 1975. In that same period his thinclads took two trophies—the south division crowns of 1975 and 1976.

But Sekul's luck began to change for the better in the spring of 1979, when he experienced the finest track season of his career. His tracksters took both the south division and the state championship and, in the process, broke three state records and tied another. Assistant coaches Clem Dellenger and Mike Nelson loaded eight members of this super team in a van and drove 2,700 miles to Eugene, Oregon, for the NJCAA Track and Field Meet. For the first time a Gulf Coast track team competed nationally. At the meet the 440-meter relay team composed of Otis Ashford, Robert Booker, Howard Galloway, and Sherman Robinson made it to the finals and placed fourth in the nation in that event. All four members of the 440-meter relay team were named NJCAA All-Americans.

The 1979 state championship track team. First row *(from left), George Redeemer, Donald Buckley, Otis Ashford, Ronald Buckly, Robert Payton.* ***Second row,*** *Gene Rogers, Pat McCowin, Steve Bodin, Myron Cook, Walter Thornton.* ***Third row,*** *"Salt" Galloway, Charles Chapman, Michael Graham, Frank Sabatini, Michael Davison, Robert Booker, and Vincent Pleasant.*

That fall Sekul led his football team to another first made possible by changes in the Mississippi Association of Junior College (MAJC) rules. The new play-off rules called for the number one team from the North Division to play the number two team from the south division and the number one south to play the number two north. The winners of each game would then play for the state crown. The number one team of each division would host its game, and in the event the winners of the first two games were of the same division, the highest rated team would host the championship battle. MAJC director, Ray Busby, said one reason for the new rules was "to get the teams with the best records into state championship."

Sekul applauded the changes. In 1973 a single defeat by Pearl River had knocked him out of state contention though he had a 9-1 record. Recalling 1977 Sekul averred, "Late in the season we beat Itawamba, later the North division winner. But Jones (7-6) defeated us for the south title. In the state championship, Jones lost to Itawamba." In 1978 both Gulf Coast and Jones finished the regular season 9-1. But Gulf Coast's only loss had been once again to Jones, once again by a score of 7-6, which had once again cost Gulf Coast the south title and with it, a shot at the state trophy.

Gulf Coast launched its 1979 season with two victories, and then Hurricane Frederic blew away the third game that had been slated for September 15 with Southwest. The Bulldogs then lost one, won two, and went up against Jones. This time the score was higher than the two previous years but still the wrong way 24-20.

Jones went on to seal the south division title, while Gulf Coast lost two more games before winning the last regularly scheduled game of the season. On November 8, the hurricane-cancelled game against Southwest was played in Summit. The Bulldogs' victory in that contest earned Gulf Coast the second spot in the south and the first play-off ticket to take on the north champion team—Itawamba.

Gulf Coast had defeated Itawamba 9-7 in the first game of the 1979 season, and in the play-off game at Fulton on November 17, the Dogs beat the Indians again, this time 7-0 on a 61-yard touchdown pass from quarterback Vincent Pleasant to wide receiver Robert Booker. In the other north-south shoot-out, Jones defeated Northeast, so the first championship game under the new MAJC rules would be a south-south duel.

Both Jones and Gulf Coast had 6-4 records going into the deciding game, but Jones, by virtue of its earlier season victory over Gulf Coast, was awarded first place status, which carried the right to choose the field of play. Due to damages wrought by Hurricane Frederic on the Jones Campus, the Bobcats elected to host the championship game at Watkins Field in Laurel on November 24. On that rain-lashed Saturday night, the Bobcats clawed the Bulldogs down in a sea of mud and shut them out 12-0. Thus, Gulf Coast "won" the MAJC's first "second-place" state championship trophy.

The Thanksgiving week shutout of 1979 coming on top of years of indignities suffered by Gulf Coast at the hands of Jones caused a shift in south Mississippi rivalries. Bulldogs began to love to hate Bobcats even more than Wildcats.

In the spring of the 1979-1980 session Sekul's track team nearly reprised its performance of the previous year. Once again the Bulldog thinclads took the south division and state championships and again attended the NJCAA track meet. None of Sekul's tracksters made it to the finals in San Angelo, Texas, but it was the second time they had achieved the signal honor of securing a berth at nationals. The 1980 season marked the high-tide of Sekul's track coaching career. He continued to coach track for another decade, and some individuals under his tutelage set state records. One of them, Anthony Guy, attended a national track meet in

1987. But never again would a Sekul track team win a south division or state championship. The state track championships of 1980 were the last of the 20th Century for Gulf Coast.

The 1980 track team again won the state championship and again went to the NJCAA National Track and Field Meet held that year in San Angelo, Texas. ***First row,*** *(from left), "Salt" Galloway, Otis Ashford, Robert Payton.* ***Second row,*** *(from left), Michael Daviis, David Holder, Keith Warren.* ***Third row*** *(from left), Steven Bodin, Larry Matthews, Sherman Robinson, Charles Pierce, Darrel Stanley.* ***Fourth row*** *(from left), Bubba Diaz, Kenny Leggett, Danny Spreitler, John Logan.*

If his track star had begun to fade, Sekul's football sun was about to shine more brilliantly than ever. In the seven seasons inclusive of 1980-1986, his record would become an incredible 70-13-1. In that short span his teams won four state championships (1982 as co-champion) and one national championship. In Sekul's other 19 seasons his teams won four state championships and one national championship. This record is rendered more remarkable by the fact that one of the years in the magic seven was not magic. The 1981 season yielded no championship of any kind.

In 1980, in sweet revenge, the Bulldogs quite literally stomped the Bobcats into the mud twice. The first time was 36-13 on October 18 on a soggy field at Ellisville. The second time was 18-14 in Pascagoula for the state championship. In an ironic and nearly exact reversal of roles from the year before, the Bulldogs were the south division champions and the Bobcats the runners-up. A Jones victory over the northern number one team pitted the Bobcats against the Bulldogs as undercats, and they lost on the rainy field just as Gulf Coast had done the year before.

The 1981 season was a 6-4 sputter in which the Wildcats and the Bobcats both beat the Bulldogs. But then Sekul revved up for the most glorious five-year segment of his 26-year career. In the next five years Sekul would win 52 games, lose eight, and tie one. The Wildcats were to go down five times in succession to the Bulldog blitz. The Bobcats would fall six times but rise to deliver a stunning defeat, once.

Cats did not even figure in Sekul's 1982 season. The Bulldogs flattened both Jones and Pearl River in a nine-game streak that garnered the south division crown. In the north the Northwest Rangers sported the same 9-0 record and its respective division crown. Both teams were nationally ranked—Northwest at No. 2; Gulf Coast at No. 4. And so the stage was set for a collision unique in Magnolia State history. The winner was almost certain to be a national championship game contender. This November 3 game at Senatobia turned out to be unique in another way. Gulf Coast lost by the lowest score possible in a football game where both teams score—3-2.

After dispatching their respective second place challengers in the north-south play-offs, Gulf Coast and Northwest faced one another again on the field at Senatobia on November 20. In the battle of attrition that ensued, the Bulldogs and the Rangers fought to a 7-7 tie. At game's end the two teams were declared state co-champions, but Northwest's superior ranking secured for the Rangers a national junior college bowl bid. The Rangers won the bowl game and ascended into the national football championship Valhalla, while the Bulldogs sat at Perkinston and waited for next year.

In 1983 the Bulldogs lost only one game in regular season play—to the East Central Warriors on September 2. Taking the south division crown Gulf Coast easily brushed aside the north division second place contender. But Jones, in second-place south division, beat the first-place north team, so once again as in 1979, the Bulldogs faced the Bobcats in Pascagoula's storm-clouded War Memorial Stadium. With 40 seconds left in the game and the score 17-12 the wrong way, the Dogs were fourth down with eight yards to go at the Jones 13 yard line. At that critical moment Bulldog Jeff Loftus hit Teddy Weathersby for a game-winning touchdown on the right side of the end zone. As Weathersby went high and snagged the ball, a Bobcat defensive back struck him while he was still

Craig Havard shows off the Region XXIII trophy following the 1982 Gulf Coast --Northwest game which ended in a tie for the state and regional championship.

NATIONAL JUNIOR COLLEGE ATHLETIC ASSOCIATION FOOTBALL CHAMPIONS 1984

This early 1984 team photograph, which became the "official" 1984 team image, was framed together with a team roster from later in that season. By then some men were off the team and others had changed numbers. David Russell (number 31 in the photograph), head football coach at D'Iberville High School in 2000, corrected the errors. Rob Harris and Tony Bennett may be two of the three "unknowns" in the photograph.

First row *(from left), Norman Mims (No. 2) of Moss Point, Philip Anderson (No. 3) of Pascagoula, Ryan Triplett (No. 4) of Moss Point, Darrell Hurst (No. 7) of Moss Point, Anthony Harris (No. 10) of Wiggins, Philip McMillian (No. 11) of Vancleave, Jeff Renshaw (No. 12) of St. Martin, Randy Geiger (No. 14) of Wiggins, David Picard (No. 15) of Biloxi, Gary Jones (No. 16) of Gulfport, Danny Kelley (No. 18) of Biloxi, Carl Croon (No. 19) of Moss Point, Randy Pembrook (No. 20) of Jefferson, Louisiana, Lee Perkins (No. 21) of Pascagoula, Troy Kimmes (No. 22) of Long Beach, Ken Melvin (No. 23) of Biloxi, Sean Logan (No. 24) of Pass Christian, Rodney Buford (No. 25) of Gulfport, Brad Canaan (No. 26) of Biloxi*

Second row
Larry Byrd (No. 28) of Biloxi, Ivan Fairley (No. 29) of Leaf, Ken Willis (No. 30) of Pascagoula, David Russell (No. 31) of Biloxi, Patterson Lowery (No. 32) of Gulfport, Unknown (No. 33), Edward Poindexter (No. 34) of Moss Point, James Evans (No. 35) of Biloxi, Allen Williams (No. 36) of Ocean Springs, Pat Jackson (No. 37) of Vancleave, Barrett Lewis (No. 38) of Lucedale, Darrien Thomas (No. 39) of Pascagoula, Allen Montgomery (No. 40) of Gulfport, Ricky Anglanda (No. 41) of Biloxi, Ike Wells (No. 43) of Pascagoula, Darrell Jones (No. 44) of Pascagoula, Chad Encalade (No. 45) of Westwego, Louisiana, Danny Henry (No. 46) of Pascagoula, Robert Ogle (No. 47) of Pascagoula

Third row
Frank Skinner (No. 52) of Biloxi, Darrell Pickich (No. 53) of Biloxi, Robert Parker (No. 55) of Wiggins, Tony Formica (No. 57) of Pascagoula, Ed Jackson (No. 60) of Wiggins, Gary Stanford (No. 61) of Gulfport, Charlie Williamson (No. 62) of Pascagoula, Mike Herfurth (No. 63) of Long Beach, Chris Frigo (No. 64) of Metairie, Louisiana, Curtis Pettigrew (No. 65) of Gretna, Louisiana, Miguel Gonzalez (No. 66) of Biloxi, Steve Evans (No. 67) of Wiggins, Joe Jackson (No. 68) of Gulfport, Albert Wells (No. 70) of Gulfport, Danny Fore (No. 71) of Wiggins, Danny Walker (No. 72) of Metairie, Louisiana, Jody Theobald (No. 73) of Jefferson, Louisiana, Bob Waldrip (No. 74) of Wildwood, Florida, Eric Conner (No. 75) of Gulfport, Connie Daniels (No. 76) of Gulfport

Fourth row
Gary Taylor (No. 80) of Long Beach, LeMonte Brown (No. 51) of Charleston, South Carolina, Casey Wittman (No. 81) of Pass Christian, Don Merrit (No. 82), of Lucedale, Raymond Johnson (No. 83) of Wiggins, Tim Magandy (No. 84) of Long Beach, Kevin Triplett (No. 85) of Moss Point, Harold Tillman (No. 86) of Wiggins, David Mills (No. 87) of Wildwood, Florida, Joey Anderson (No. 88) of Memphis, Tennessee, Mike Blakney (No. 89) of Gulfport, Ernest Stennis (No. 90) of Pascagoula, Unknown, Rodney Thompson (No. 92) of Gulfport, John McNeil (No. 93) of Gulfport, Shane Schurb (No. 95) of Wiggins, Dwayne Scott (No. 78) of New Orleans, Louisiana, Shannon Page (No. 48) of Long Beach, Unknown, and Frank Rosetti (No. 77) of Biloxi.

The 1984 National Championship Football Cheerleaders. ***Front row*** *(from left), Debbie Wildman of Pascagoula, Stacy Broussard of Biloxi, and Terri Church of D'Iberville.* ***Back row*** *(from left), Lynn Read of Gautier, Geno White of Ocean Springs, Karen Lorona of Biloxi, Ric Williams of Wiggins, Steve Beckham of Wiggins, Donna Colwart of Wiggins, Jonathan Nall of Wiggins, and Tina Shivers of Ocean Springs.*

The 1984 National Championship Football Managers (not pictured) were Charles Fairley, Read McQuagge, Chris James, Jimmy Fields, Jerry McKinney, and Jeff Renshaw.

airborne and knocked him out of bounds. In a call no Bulldog fan will ever rate fair, a referee negated the score and sealed Gulf Coast's fate. As Jones ran out the clock, torrential rains, which seem to be a hallmark of Gulf Coast-Jones games, swept the stadium.

The winner of this game was to host the East Bowl in early December to take on first-ranked Harford Community College of Bel Air, Maryland. That year Ellisville hosted the East Bowl and Jones won. The Bulldogs sat in Perkinston and waited for next year, but this time they stored up a tremendous potential.

And what a year it was--another year like 1971. In succession the Bulldog juggernaut rolled over the Delta Trojans, the Southwest Bears, the Coahoma Tigers, the East Central Warriors, the Northeast Tigers, the Jones Bobcats, the Pearl River Wildcats, the Itawamba Indians, the Co-Lin Wolves, and the Hinds Eagles. In regular season play the Bulldogs amassed 226 points while giving up only 118. Only one team, Co-Lin even came within a one-touchdown threat of a tie by the end of a game.

In the playoff against the second team north, the Bulldogs slaughtered the East Mississippi Lions 50-7 in Biloxi on November 10 and took No. 1 ranking in the nation in the polls. Then once again, with what had become nauseating regularity, along came Jones. Having been beaten by Gulf Coast earlier in the season, Jones had again defeated the first team north to do battle against Gulf Coast for the state championship. Once again the winner of the game would face the team of Harford Community College in the East Bowl.

The November 17 state championship Gulf Coast-Jones battle at A. L. May Memorial Stadium, for once fought under clear skies, was described by one correspondent as a "real barn burner." Bulldog and Bobcat fought tooth and claw through a scoreless first half. In the third quarter the Bulldogs put 17 points on the board, and the Bobcats retaliated in the fourth quarter with 16. With 1:14 to play, the Bobcats fought to the position of third down and goal from the three-yard line. On the next play Bobcat Antonio Prewitt scratched his way inside the one-yard line. Then it was fourth down and goal with inches separating Bulldog national aspirations from a second disaster at the hands of Jones in a year. "I reached in my pocket, grabbed my rosary and prayed," said Sekul. Then the players went into motion. The exhausted Bulldog defenders lurched northward as the Bobcat line crashed inexorably southward. As Prewitt came over the top, Bulldog freshman linebacker, Joe Jackson of Gulfport, stood like a stone wall with every ounce of potential energy his 6'3", 220-pound, frame could muster. It was like an object that could not be moved meeting an object that could not be stopped. Bobcat fans think Jackson moved. Bulldog fans think Prewitt was stopped. One disinterested newspaper correspondent maintained that Prewitt's torso crossed the goal line. But the actual physics of the situation did not matter because no referee called a touchdown. It was a non-call that no Bobcat fan will ever rate fair.

And so the Gulf Coast Bulldogs, cheerleaders, Band of Gold, and Perkettes prepared to journey 1,100 miles to Bel Air, Maryland, to take on the Harford Fighting Owls in the East Bowl in the hopes of being named the number one junior college team by a vote of the NJCAA regional directors. These regional directors function in much the same way, as do the members of the Electoral College in an American presidential election. Just as it is possible (and it has happened) for a presidential aspirant to win the popular vote for president and yet lose the election in the Electoral College, so it is possible to win a junior college bowl game and not be named number one in the NJCAA. The East Bowl was only one of seven junior college bowl games sanctioned by NJCAA and was a post-season contest between the Mississippi state junior college championship team and the winner of NJCAA Atlantic Coastal Conference. In Sekul's words, "If you are down in the polls and win [a bowl game] that doesn't mean you'll be ranked No. 1. But if you are No. 1 and win, from my experiences, you will be No. 1. [If] the team on top wins, [it] stays on top." Gulf Coast on the eve of the 1984 East Bowl stood at No. 1 in the polls; Harford at No. 4.

Jones' victory over highly-ranked Harford in 1983 at the East Bowl in Ellisville did not secure the No. 1 crown for lower-ranked Jones, but it very likely cost Harford that accolade. In the wake of Harford's defeat by Jones and in light of the Coffeeville Community College victory in the Kansas Jayhawker Bowl, that college was named the 1983 junior college champion.

Revenge may be sweet, but it can be quirky, and 1984's vengeance milieu was positively Byzantine. On the eve of the impending December 1 East Bowl battle in Bel Air, Harford Fighting Owl coach Dick Fordyce, riding a 39-game regular season winning streak blemished by the Bobcat defeat of his team in the 1983 East Bowl, announced that he intended to defeat Gulf Coast to avenge what Jones had done to him in that game. So the Bulldogs, who had recently exacted revenge on Jones by virtue of a controversial call, traveled to Maryland to face Bobcat-fueled Owl anger.

The 1984 National Football Championship coaches. (From left), Head coach George Sekul, and assistant coaches Clem Dellenger and Mike Nelson.

In the first quarter Bulldog Ike Wells recovered an Owl

NJCAA 6th Annual East Bowl Game
Bel Air, Maryland, December 1, 1984

5'9", 180 pound Bulldog Robert Ogle (No. 47) pauses before his impending collision with two 6' Harford Owls totaling 377 pounds.

6'1", 210 pound Bulldog running back Allen Williams (No. 36) goes for more yardage.

Perkinston Campus Vice President Clyde Strickland (left) and Perkinston Campus Dean of Business Services L. D. "Buster" Stringfellow watch the Bel Air Owl and Bulldog ballet. Gary Taylor (No. 80) holds onto the pass thrown by quarterback Anthony "Shake and Fake" Harris to go in for a touchdown making the score 21-0 in favor of the Bulldogs.

Bulldog team captains Allen Montgomery (No. 40) and Allen Williams (No. 36) proudly display the 6th annual East Bowl trophy after defeating the Harford Owls 21-7.

fumble on the Harford 24-yard line to set up Gulf Coast's first score. Five plays later James Evans of D'Iberville went in for the touchdown and then added a 2-point conversion run for an 8-0 lead. Late in the first quarter and again in the second, Bulldog quarterback Anthony "Shake and Fake" Harris of Wiggins hit tight end Gary Taylor of Long Beach for touchdown passes. At halftime the score stood at 21-0. The Owls scored once in the second half, and the game ended 21-7. Thus Sekul's Bulldogs completed a perfect 13-0 season and celebrated their second NJCAA Championship in 13 years. Though the regional directors had not yet voted, the results were assured. If No. 1 won, No. 1 it remained. Confirmation of the title was announced the following Tuesday in a near unanimous regional directors' vote for Gulf Coast.

In January 1985 assistant coach Mike Nelson accepted the position of head coach at Pearl River, replacing J. C. Arban, who had coached the Wildcats for a decade. Into Nelson's spot at Gulf Coast stepped Joe Allen of Biloxi High School, who had served as center on Sekul's first two championship teams (1966 and 1967).

In February the MGCJC Board announced plans to construct, adjacent to A. L. May Memorial Stadium, a Bulldog Field House for the use of football and baseball teams. This building, long overdue, was predicted for completion by the fall of 1986. For one more season the Bulldogs would have

The $274,000 Field House located behind the goal at the east end of A. L. May Memorial Stadium contained coaches offices, a weight room, and dressing rooms for both the football and baseball teams. The facility began service in August 1986.

On Homecoming Day October 21, 2000, in ceremonies before the 3 p.m. football game, the field house was officially named the S. George Sekul Field House. The Bulldogs won the game against Pearl River 36-7.

Photo by Richard Kopp.

THE S. GEORGE SEKUL FIELD HOUSE

COMPLETED AUGUST 1986

DEDICATED OCTOBER 21, 2000

to make do with what one newspaper reporter termed, "antiquated, deteriorated facilities . . . with shoddy dressing rooms, showers, and training facilities that would be an embarrassment to the smallest high school in the country."

At the Mississippi Coast Coliseum on March 29, coaches Sekul, Dellenger, and Nelson, together with the NJCAA National Champion Bulldogs and Cheerleaders, were honored with a banquet and presented with national championship rings. As in 1971, the funds for the banquet, rings, and new championship plaque for the football monument in the quadrangle on the Perkinston Campus came from private donations and banquet ticket sales.

The approach of Hurricane Elena resulted in the Delta Trojans canceling the opening game of the 1985 season set for August 31 at Perkinston. On the following Thursday night in Summit, the Bears ended a 19-game Bulldog winning streak by a score of 12-7. But the Dogs rebounded by defeating their next five opponents who included the Bobcats and the Wildcats. Then on October 17 on a rain-drenched field in Fulton, the Itawamba Indians defeated Gulf Coast 14-10. In yet another rebound the Dogs then defeated Co-Lin and Hinds. The Hinds victory netted Gulf Coast the south division crown. Meanwhile, Co-Lin, second south, defeated first north Itawamba to face Gulf Coast for the state title.

On the eve of the 1985 state championship game against Co-Lin set for November 16 at War Memorial Stadium in Pascagoula, Gulf Coast stood at No. 5 in the NJCAA poll. The winner of the game would host the East Bowl against Nassau Community College of New York. If Gulf Coast won the state championship and the East Bowl, the Bulldogs had a chance at a third NJCAA championship. But it evaporated when Gulf Coast managed to snatch defeat from the jaws of victory by one point, giving Co-Lin its first state championship in 47 years. Sekul's succinct assessment of the game said it all. "In 23 years of coaching, I've never seen anything like this game. Our guys played hard but they played stupid."

Still, Gulf Coast's record was good enough to secure a berth in the inaugural Texas Junior College Bowl to be played in Rose Stadium at Tyler. The only bright spot in that disastrous engagement was the standing ovation given the Band of Gold and Perkettes by the 6,000 spectators present. As for the game itself, the Tyler Junior College Apaches scalped the Dogs 31-0.

In a fitting beginning to Sekul's last great season, the Bulldog Field House with its fine facilities was ready for use in the fall of 1986. The Bulldogs won the first three games and then dropped two in a row by the same score 20-10. Then the Dogs defeated the Bobcats, the Wildcats, and the Hinds Eagles in succession. On October 25 the nightmare of the previous year made another visitation when Co-Lin smashed Gulf Coast 27-0. With a victory over Holmes in the last regular season game on November 1, the Dogs wound up second in the south, barely winning a slot in the state playoffs.

The Tyrone Jones (above) - Danny Kelley (No. 16) - "Sock" Chanthavane (No. 3) combination of 1986 garnered Sekul's last state championship trophy on November 15 at Senatobia with a TD pass and PAT. On November 23 at Boone, North Carolina, the Jones-Kelley-Chanthavane combo repeated their previous week's performance to win the East Bowl trophy with a TD pass and PAT.

Quarterback Danny Kelley (No. 16) throws the pass to wide receiver Tyrone Jones, who came out of the end zone to catch the pass and take it back in for the touchdown. This TD tied up the 1986 East Bowl game between Gulf Coast and Lees-McRae College with a score of 13-13. A few moments later Adethsack "Sock" Chanthavane kicked the extra point and the game ended 14-13 in a Bulldog victory. The words "Kelley did it!" written in red on the photograph were placed there by George Sekul when the photograph was given to him back at Perkinston.

Then, for the last time, Dame Fortune smiled on the Gulf Coast coach. On November 8 the Bulldogs defeated Itawamba at Fulton, while the second north Rangers defeated the Wolves at Wesson. The Rangers having lost only one game were ranked No. 6 in the nation on the eve of the November 15 state championship game at Senatobia. Gulf Coast, with three losses was unranked.

In the third period, with the Rangers out in front 13-7, Bulldog quarterback Danny Kelley of D'Iberville hit wide receiver Tyrone Jones of Ruston, Louisiana, with a 14-yard touchdown pass to tie the game. Sekul then sent in 5' 6", 130 pound Adethsack "Sock" Chanthavane, a Laotian anti-Communist refugee whose family had been resettled in Mobile, Alabama. He was called "Sock" because of the soccer style of kicking he had learned in his homeland, and he was the 1986 Bulldog field goal and point after touchdown (PAT) kicker. In Senatobia that day Sock's PAT assured Gulf Coast a state championship trophy and a consequent invitation to the East Bowl.

When the Bulldogs arrived at Conrad Stadium in Boone, North Carolina, on November 23 to do battle against the Bobcats of undefeated fourth-ranked Lees-McRae College of Banner Elk, they were still unranked. However, one imaginative journalist had dubbed the Bulldogs a "Cinderella team" with Sekul as their "royal coach." But he warned that the Lees-McRae Bobcats had been "changing coaches into pumpkins all season." Certainly none of the nearly 2,000 North Carolinians present expected the upstarts from the Mississippi Gulf Coast to shoot down their team's national championship aspirations.

At the end of the fourth quarter, with the clock running down, Lees-McRae had the Bulldogs down 13-7. But the Bulldogs were third and ten at the Bobcat 15-yard line. Wide receiver Jones sprinted into the end zone as quarterback Kelley faded to pass. Said Kelley later, "I saw them [Bobcats] blitzing and I knew I had to get rid of it fast. They hit me just as I released it and I knew it was going to be a little short." Jones, then in the end zone, later remembered, "I saw the ball was going to fall short so I came back out across the line for it. I knew I had to get [back] in so when those guys grabbed me, I used all my strength to break the plane of the goal line."

With the score then tied 13-13 and with 34 seconds to play, Sekul sent in Sock. With the game riding on his shoulders, Sock kicked the ball straight through the uprights. In an incredible reprise of its performance at Senatobia eight days earlier the Kelley-Jones-Chanthavane combination had won a bowl game. Sekul's reaction: "I feel like I'm in a state of shock."

The mountains of North Carolina echoed to the screams and cheers of excited Gulf Coast fans. And then the cheering stopped. The East Bowl trophy of 1986 was the final football trophy of the 20th Century for Gulf Coast. In the aftermath of the East Bowl, the NJCAA gave Gulf Coast a No. 9 national ranking—the college's last top ten football ranking of the 20th century.

Erin Cook, Miss River Rat of 1991, prepares to reign at the MGCCC-PRCC football game on October 6. Not since 1962 had the Cats and Dogs fought in A. L. May Memorial Stadium, so a panel of Perk judges including Diane Sekul selected Queen Erin to preside over the River's return to break the nearly three decade drought. The River drowned the Dogs and Miss River Rat 13-6. Photo from 1992 Perkolator, p. 14.

J.C. Arban, (left) stands with George Sekul on the field at A.L. May Memorial Stadium shortly after becoming an assistant football coach in fall 1991. Arban and Sekul had been friends since their college days at Mississippi Southern College in the 1950's.

In 1987 Sekul experienced the first losing season of his career--two wins, eight losses. In 1988 he managed to break even at 5-5, but in 1989 his team posted yet another 2-8 season record.

By 1990, with 198 career wins, Sekul at least looked forward to setting the NJCAA record as the first junior college coach to achieve 200 wins. On September 1 the Bulldogs defeated the Coahoma Tigers 21-0 at Clarksdale and expectation of breaking the 200-win mark rose to a fever pitch. On September 6 the Bulldogs and the Northeast Tigers fought to a 24-24 tie.

So Sekul prepared to wrest the magic 200th win from the East Central Warriors on September 14. On the eve of that game the story broke in the newspapers that the MAJC had ordered that the Gulf Coast victory over Coahoma be forfeited and counted as a loss. According to MAJC officials, Sekul had fielded three ineligible players in that game. Ironically Coahoma, which had likewise fielded ineligible players in the game, also had to count it as a loss and continue a 50-game losing streak.

According to Sekul, this forfeiture destroyed Bulldog morale for the rest of the season that marked his nadir. The 1990 season, which ended in a record of 1-8-1, was not only the worst in Sekul's career, but also the worst in the history of the institution he served. Until 1990, the college's poorest football showing had been the 1-7-1 season of 1928.

On May 15, 1991, Sekul announced that he would retire in December after one final season as MGCCC head coach.

The first game of the 1991 season was, as the season before, against the Coahoma Tigers, but this time it was played at Perkinston. The Bulldogs won the game 36-12 and this time it stuck. At last on August 29, 1991, Sekul entered the NJCAA record book as the first junior college coach in the nation to win 200 games. Once more, for the last time, Sekul's Bulldogs hoisted him to their shoulders and carried him about a field of victory. This last season ended in a 5-5 draw with a loss to Itawamba in the final game. Yet, Sekul coached one more game, and it ended in victory, a fact much appreciated by Sekul. He led the South to victory over the North in the 1991 All Star Classic held at Keenum Stadium at Booneville on December 7.

It took Gulf Coast coach George Sekul five years to win the 11 games he needed to achieve his 200th victory and a spot in the record books. "It was a long time coming," said Sekul after his Bulldogs defeated Coahoma 36-12 on August 29, 1991, to make him the winningest active coach in community college football and the only one at that time with 200 victories.

With his retirement at the end of 1991, Sekul ended 31 seasons of service to Gulf Coast--five seasons as an assistant coach and 26 seasons as head coach. His final tally of 204 wins, 77 losses and 5 ties still topped the list of NJCAA football coaches' records as the 20th century closed.

In 1996 officials of the NJCAA named Sekul to the association's Hall of Fame. On October 5, Sekul and three other MGCCC coaches who previously had been named to the NJCAA Hall of Fame were honored for their achievement at halftime ceremonies during the Gulf Coast-Southwest football game. On this occasion, then head coach Steve Wright, invited Sekul into the Field House to speak to the 1996 edition of the MGCCC Bulldogs. For the first time since his retirement Sekul addressed a Bulldog team. At this poignant meeting the Bulldogs cheered and applauded, and the team captains presented him with a current coach's sweater.

In the pre-Sekul era from 1926 through 1965, the football

coaches of this institution produced just four state championship teams and one team that was named co-national champion. At the close of the 2000 season his successors had produced no championships of any type. Sekul took seven state championship trophies, one state co-championship trophy, and two national championship trophies.

With the exception of 1943, when the Second World War resulted in the cancellation of junior college football in Mississippi for a season, this institution fielded a football team each year from 1926 through 2000 for a total of 74 seasons.

The 74 teams, which served under a total of 17 head coaches, won 417 games, lost 289, and tied 36. Sekul's 14 predecessors and two successors in 48 seasons of play established a record of 213-212-31. Sekul's record for just 26 seasons totaled 204-77-5. So, in 48 seasons, all the other coaches of this institution combined won only nine more games than Sekul did in 26 seasons.

Sekul's record of games won and lost, unmatched in 20th century American junior college football history, now graces the cold realm of statistics, but his legacy transcends mere figures on paper. The Sekul legacy included the lives he influenced in one degree or another—hundreds of athletes, thousands of Gulf Coast students, and tens of thousands of football fans.

George Sekul's Championships

FOOTBALL

National Championships

1971 1984

State Championships

1966 1980
1967 1982 (Co-Champions)
1971 1984
1974 1986

Second Place State Championships

1979 1983 1985

South Division Championships

1971 1975 1982 1984
1974 1980 1983 1985

Bowl Game Victories

1966 Shrine Bowl (Shreveport, Louisiana)
1971 Shrine Bowl (Savannah, Georgia)
1984 East Bowl (Harford, Maryland)
1986 East Bowl (Boone, North Carolina)

TRACK

State Championships

1962 1979
1968 1980
1970

South Division Championships

1974
1975
1976
1979
1980

On March 17, 1962, Sekul married the former Diane Poulos of Biloxi. In time they would have three daughters: Gia, Kari, and Michelle. Diane (left) scans the field for an action photo at a Bulldog football game. She worked as a Perkinston Campus secretary and served as the football cheerleader sponsor during the latter years of her husband's tenure.

Michelle Sekul cheered Perkinston Campus football from the age of six (below left) to the age of 19 (below).

FOOTBALL & TRACK 1992-2000

Jackson C. "J.C." Arban joined George Sekul's coaching staff for Sekul's final season at MGCCC. Sekul retired in December 1991 and Arban became MGCCC head football coach/athletic director in January 1992.

Born December 5, 1932, in Athens, Alabama, Arban earned his bachelor's at the University of Southern Mississippi in 1959. Arban's friendship with Sekul began at USM where the two were teammates.

Before coming to MGCCC Arban had served as an assistant coach at three high schools and at USM. His junior/community college experience included stints as assistant coach at Pearl River and East Central. He had served as head coach at Pearl River (1975-1984) and as head coach/athletic director at East Mississippi (1988-1990).

In his four years as MGCCC head football coach, Arban posted an even 1992 season (5-5); a 4-6 record in both 1993 and 1994; and a 2-8 win-loss record in 1995. In 1994, for the first time in four years, MGCCC fielded a track team. The track team, coached by two of Arban's assistants--Ode Burrell and Chris Calcote--finished number three in the state. In 1995 the track team finished at second place in the state.

When Arban retired in November 1995, his former responsibilities as athletic director and head football coach were divided. Chris Calcote became the new athletic director. Steve Wright, a 39 year-old native of Jefferson City, Tennessee, began the first head coach's job of his career when he took control of the Bulldog football team on January 1, 1996.

Wright, who had earned his bachelor's at Maryville (Tennessee) College and his master's at the University of Tennessee, came to MGCCC after four years as assistant head coach and offensive coordinator at Jones County Junior College. Prior to that Wright had served in senior colleges as an assistant coach in Virginia at the University of Richmond and at the University of Texas in El Paso. In prior junior college experience he had served as assistant head coach at Navarro Junior College in Corsicana, Texas, from 1986 to 1992. During his time in Corsicana, the Navarro football team made four bowl appearances and won the 1989 National Junior College Athletic Association championship. In speaking of the new head coach's credentials MGCCC President Barry L. Mellinger said, "Coach Wright has the combination of an education first philosophy and a proven record which we think will make our players winners in the classroom and on the football field."

The MGCCC football coaching staff in August 1992 included (from left) sports injury manager Jeff Davis, assistant coach Ode Burrell, head coach J.C. Arban (seated), assistant coach Steve Nagy, and assistant coach Chris Calcote. The NJCAA inducted Arban into its Football Hall of Fame in 1998.

Wright's 1996 team had a 3-7 record and the 1997 team had a record of 2-8. Wright's 1998 team, though, posted a 6-4 winning season, and the Bulldog's 1999 record of 7-3 was the best since 1986, Sekul's last great year.

Calcote continued in charge of the track team in spring 1996. On April 23, 1996, during the state championship track meet at Hinds Community College, Bulldog Cedric Smith broke the Mississippi Community/Junior College Athletic Association pole vaulting record with a jump of 15 feet, one inch. In June 1996, Wright appointed Kelvin Lyon, one of his assistant football coaches, as track coach. Lyon's track teams in 1997, 1998, and 1999 took third place in the state and in 2000 took second place. Due to budget cuts mandated by the legislature MGCCC suspended track indefinitely at the end of the 2000 season.

The MGCCC football coaching staff in August 1999 included (from left) head coach Steve Wright and assistant coaches Kelvin Lyon, Mike Gavin, Mike Beagle and athletic trainer Jerry Sharp.

MEN'S AND WOMEN'S TENNIS 1927 - 2000

Head coach William C. "Bill" Denson, whose career at Perkinston began in July, 1925, and Frances Rednick, a graduate of Texas Industrial and Arts College (Benton, Texas), who joined the faculty in fall 1926 as a teacher of commercial subjects and director of women's athletics, together inaugurated tennis as a sport at Perkinston. On March 21, 1927, the *Stone County Enterprise* reported that the men and women at Perk were "now enjoying the pleasures of an up-to-date tennis court." The new court was constructed on the site of "last year's baseball field" and enjoyed such vogue that Coach Denson had designated certain days for women to practice and certain days for men. The men's and women's tennis teams placed second in the state junior college field meet at Raymond on April 15, 1927.

The November 5, 1927, *Daily Herald* reported a further development in the coming tennis program. It was stated that on October 13 a tennis club had been organized under the sponsorship of Miss Winnie J. Hood, the new home economics teacher. The purpose of the club was stated as making tennis a competitive sport on par with "the other athletic sports in this institution." The Perkinston Tennis Club made use of the clay courts on the campus and occasionally invited the Wiggins Tennis Club down for a match, but apparently nearly seven years passed before a sustained program of intercollegiate tennis competition began.

In September 1929 Lee Roy Weeks replaced Denson as head coach, a position Weeks retained until fall 1933, when he became athletic director. Weeks, then free of year-round, multi-sport coaching responsibilities, chose to develop tennis as an intercollegiate sport at Perkinston.

The *Daily Herald* carried an account of an early intercollegiate tennis competition held March 26, 1934, at Perk. In this "spring athletic carnival" the Perkinston netmen defeated the Jones Junior College players in all matches. One month later the Perkinston men's team reprised its previous effort winning all matches against Pearl River Junior College at Poplarville. But, at the Mississippi state championship meet at Wesson on April 30, Perkinston lost to Copiah-Lincoln Junior College.

On May 29, 1934, the college men's team won four out of five matches with the Mississippi State Teachers' College in the first match played on the new concrete tennis courts at Perkinston. These courts, constructed north of the Power House on the Quadrangle, were the result of five months of effort by workers of the Civil Works Administration (CWA).

Apparently the women's collegiate tennis team made its debut at Perkinston in the 1934-1935 year. On April 13, 1935, at Ellisville, Barbara Peugh and Helen Gray of the Perkinston women's team defeated the Sunflower Junior College doubles team to take the state "doubles crown" trophy in tennis. The next year on May 2, 1936, at Ellisville, Helen Gray and Sophie Wentzell defeated the Hinds County Junior College team to win the women's state doubles championship.

FIRST TENNIS CHAMPS OF THE HARRISON-STONE-JACKSON JUNIOR COLLEGE

Helen Gray of Mississippi City

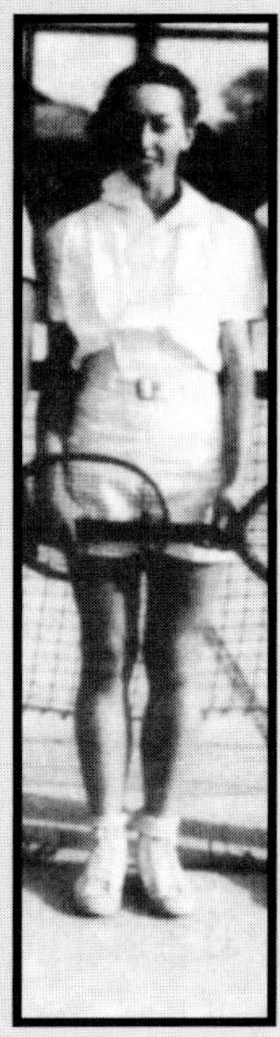

Barbara Peugh of Gulfport

Sophie Wentzell of Biloxi

Richard Kopp photo

1936 Trophy

Peugh and Gray won state doubles in 1935. Gray and Wentzell won state doubles in 1936.

The foot tall bronze trophy marked "M(ississippi) J(unior) C(ollege) A(ssociation) -- 1936," is the only tennis trophy surviving from the 1930s included in the MGCCC Archives Collection in 2000. This trophy was awarded to Helen Gray and Sophie Wentzell for their doubles victory at Ellisville on May 2, 1936.

Gray and Peugh photos from 1936 Perkolator, p. 47 and p. 83. Wentzell photo from 1937 Perkolator, p. 92.

Hinds County Junior College hosted the state junior college tennis tournament the next year. On May 6, 1937, according to the *Herald,* "for the first time in junior college history, a single school took three places." Lawrence Kenneth defeated his Hinds County opponent to take the laurels in men's singles; Eleanor Strowd defeated the Southwest player to win women's singles; Johnny Green and William Goff took the state title in men's doubles from Sunflower. The only title not won by Perkinston at this tournament was women's doubles. Apparently the victories of 1937 were the last for the tennis teams in the decade of the 1930s. In any case, no further tennis titles were mentioned in the available documents.

Weeks continued to coach tennis until he became dean of men in fall 1940. No tennis coach was listed in available documents related to spring 1941, but the school fielded both

THE HARRISON-STONE-JACKSON JUNIOR COLLEGE TRIPLE EVENT CHAMPS (MEN'S SINGLES, WOMEN'S SINGLES AND MEN'S DOUBLES)

Men's tennis 1937 (left to right), Lawrence Kenneth of Gulfport, Captain; William Goff of Gulfport; Johnnie Green of Pascagoula; Tom Leatherbury of Pascagoula; Woodrow Cox of Perkinston; Coach Lee Roy Weeks.

Women's Tennis (left to right), Sophie Wentzell of Biloxi, Captain; Orlene Smith of Wiggins; Frances Gunn of Biloxi; Eleanor Strowd of Gulfport; Julia Hanson of Pass Christian; Mary Hoffman of Pass Christian; Coach Lee Roy Weeks. Photo from 1937 Perkolator, p. 93.

Harrison-Stone-Jackson Junior College 1937 men's and women's championship tennis teams pose with their coach on the concrete courts finished by the Civil Works Administration in May 1934. The campus Power House and its smokestack are visible in the background. The teams pictured here were the first in Mississippi junior college history to take three of the four trophies awarded annually for tennis.

In regard to the May 6, 1937 singles victories of Eleanor Strowd and Lawrence Kenneth at Raymond, the *Clarion Ledger* noted that both of them would be awarded "medals for individual honors . . . at the finals of the track events Saturday at Ellisville." Oddly enough nothing was said about any kind of an award for Johnny Green and William Goff, who won doubles for Perk on the same day. In further reference to the upcoming Ellisville track meet, the *Clarion Ledger* declared that, in the state championship tennis matches, Perkinston had earned 20 points, Summit 9, Goodman 10, Moorhead 6, and Hinds 3. The *Herald* explained further that the three titles (men's and women's singles and men's doubles) "gave Perkinston 20 points toward the general sweepstakes title, the winner to be determined at Ellisville." The prize at Ellisville was the rotating Mississippi State Junior College Loving Cup, which traveled from one institution to another based on total points racked up by each school in many competitions throughout the year. On May 8, according to the *Jackson Daily News,* the Copiah-Lincoln Junior College "track team, by scoring a smashing victory at Ellisville, not only clinched the cup for Co-Lin, but won the track championship for the state, it being the first time in three years it [the big loving cup] had left Perkinston."

From the evidence it appears that junior college tennis (at least until 1937) was considered an adjunct to track. Furthermore, each of the four tennis competitions (men's singles, women's singles, men's doubles, and women's doubles) was considered to be a separate championship with the individual player being awarded a trophy or a medal. Apparently no overall state tennis trophy was awarded. The points earned by individual tennis players were added in the total in taking the State Loving Cup. Track, however, did result in an overall state championship trophy, and the points earned also went toward the State Loving Cup.

a men's and a women's team. In the 1941 state meet, Bobby Thompson of Gulfport was runner-up in men's singles. Frank Russum, son of Perkinston instructor B. P. Russum, and Lee Roy Weeks Jr., son of the former tennis coach, were runners-up in men's doubles.

In spring 1942, ten men, including Thompson, Russum, and Weeks, and five women reported for practice. On April 18 at Summit, Francis Jones of Gulfport won men's singles, and Charles Goff of Mexico, in league with Bobby Thompson, won men's doubles in the only "southern division tennis tournament" mentioned in the annals of Perkinston tennis play from the beginning to the year 2000. In the state meet held in Jackson on April 24, the north division champion players from Goodman defeated all the Perk men.

After 1942 women's intercollegiate tennis became a casualty of war as the college moved to substitute physical education in lieu of women's intercollegiate sports. Men's intercollegiate tennis went into abeyance as the men went into military service.

By spring 1945 intramural tennis was being played on the campus. In December both men and women of Perkinston played in a tournament in Hattiesburg against the Mississippi Southern College team. In spring 1946 Perk hosted a tournament in which its players (both men and women) defeated those of Jones Junior College.

In spring 1947 full-fledged men's and women's junior college tennis intercollegiate play resumed at Perk with social studies instructor Joe Stroud as coach. Stroud of Taylorsville, who had begun teaching at the college in fall 1944, led his teams to an unprecedented clean sweep of championship laurels in the state tennis tournament at Raymond on May 8-9, 1947. Carmen Tarzetti of DeLisle took the women's singles title; Billy Jean Sepich of Mississippi City and Doris Hawley of Vancleave, women's

1941 women's tennis team (from left), Elizabeth Dambrink of Pass Christian; Wilma Proffitt of Biloxi; Marjorie Ann Shepard of Saucier, and Delores (McHenry) Mauldin of McHenry. At Homecoming October 21, 2000, when Mauldin was asked, "Who coached the women's tennis team of 1941?" she answered, "I did." Photo from 1941 Perkolator, p. 94.

1941 men's tennis team.
Lee Roy Weeks Jr. of Perkinston, son of the former tennis coach, likely "coached" the team in 1941; Stewart Trautman of Gulfport; Frank Russum of Perkinston; Bobby Thompson of Gulfport; Robert "Bobbie" Sims of Gulfport. The men's and women's tennis teams of 1941 are the last such teams pictured in the Perkolator for ten years. Photo from 1941 Perkolator, p. 95.

1947 State Championship Tennis Team individual photos: Stroud, 1945 Perkolator, p. 12; McDonald, 1946 Perkolator, p. 23; Alexander, 1947 Perkolator, p. 26; Lightsey, 1948 Perkolator, p. 40; Hawley, 1946 Perkolator, p. 22; Tarzetti, 1948 Perkolator, p. 45; Sepich, 1946 Perkolator, p. 89.

THE 1947 PERKINSTON JUNIOR COLLEGE TENNIS CLEAN SWEEP CHAMPS (MEN'S SINGLES, WOMEN'S SINGLES, MEN'S DOUBLES AND WOMEN'S DOUBLES)

Joe W. Stroud, coach

Billy McDonald

Clark Alexander

Dick Lightsey

Doris Hawley

Carmen Tarzetti

Billie Jean Sepich

doubles; Clark Alexander of Perkinston and William Emmett "Billy" McDonald of Gulfport, men's doubles; and Richard "Dick" Lightsey of Biloxi won men's singles.

On May 7-8, 1948, Stroud led his charges back to Raymond where Carmen Tarzetti once again won the women's singles state championship. None of the other Perk tennis players reached the finals.

Stroud resigned his position at Perk at the close of the first semester of 1948-1949. With Stroud's departure tennis languished at Perk for two years. The teams continued to play but garnered no laurels. In September 1950 Curtis Davis, Perkinston vocational instructor in mechanical drawing and wood manufacture, took over as tennis coach and began the process of turning the 1950s into the Perkinston tennis decade.

Davis and his childhood friends had built dirt tennis courts and played the game while they were growing up in his hometown of Vancleave. In 1949, while attending Mississippi State University, his wife Helen was working for the history department. When Davis learned from her that one of the history instructors was the tennis coach and needed players, he joined the team. That year Davis made it to the semi-finals in the university tournament at Vanderbilt, the farthest any Mississippi State tennis player had gone to that time. Davis graduated from Mississippi State with his bachelor's degree May 28, 1950, and began his career at Perk four days later. Four months after that, President A. L. May named him the tennis coach for the college.

Curtis L. Davis, tennis coach

In summing up his nine spring seasons of coaching inclusive of 1951 to 1959, Davis put his record succinctly, "We won 72 conference matches, lost two, and tied two. In doing that we won seven state championships, five of which were in a row." He remembered that both losses were to Jones Junior College in the same year (1957) and Jones accounted for one of the ties. The 5 to 5 tie with Jones on April 25, 1955, at Ellisville was the first time Davis's teams had not won since he had begun coaching in 1951.

Precisely what constituted an overall state tennis championship (if indeed such existed) in the 1950s is unclear. One thing is certain. No team trophy designating Perkinston Junior College as the Mississippi Junior College Association Champion for any particular year was awarded. Davis's team members who won in specific categories--men's and women's singles and men's and women's doubles--were given trophies. So four trophies were given at each state tournament in the 1950s. Davis's teams won 18 of these trophies, seven of which are in the collection of the MGCCC Archives in 2000.

Joan Tarzetti of DeLisle and Joyce Saucier of Saucier shake hands across the net on the Perkinston tennis court in 1951. The Old Denson Building stands in the background. Photo from 1951 Perkolator, p. 55.

In his first four seasons 1951, 1952, 1953, and 1954, Davis's teams won in three out of four categories, losing in a different category each time.

At the state tournament at Summit on Saturday, May 12, 1951, Merrie Ann Nixon of Pascagoula won women's singles. Joan Tarzetti of DeLisle and Joyce Saucier of Saucier won women's doubles. Jerry Perry of Gulfport and Dick Chapin of Gulfport won men's doubles. Micky Conery of Pass Christian lost men's singles.

At the state tournament at Perkinston on Saturday, May 3, 1952, Joan Tarzetti won women's singles. Katherine Gangloff of Gulfport and Joyce Saucier lost women's doubles. Jerry Perry and Clinton Gill of Saucier won men's doubles. Vincent Scoper of Pass Christian won men's singles.

At the state tournament at Perkinston on Saturday, May 2, 1953, Ellen Pearce of Brooklyn won women's singles. Roxie Branager of Mississippi City and Katherine Gangloff won women's doubles. Max Patterson of Decatur, Alabama, and Clinton Gill lost men's doubles. Jerry Bates of Pass Christian won men's singles.

At the state tournament at Ellisville on Saturday, May 1, 1954, Pat Dick of Biloxi lost women's singles. Ellen Pearce and Roxie Branager won women's doubles. Max Patterson

A Davis-Era Tennis Portfolio 1951-1959

Jerry Perry (1952)

Vincent Scoper (1952)

Ellen Pearce (1954)

1953 Women's team (from left), Pat Dick, Roxie Branager, Mary Ruth Overstreet, Katherine Gangloff, and Ellen Pearce (not pictured.)

Joe McAnulty (1957)

Gordon Scoper (1954)

1953 men's team (from left), Clinton Gill, Jerry Bates, Max Patterson, David Rowe, and Albert Reinschmidt.

Isabelle Rosetti (1959)

Gayle Longbine (1959)

and Leonard Sumrall of Gulfport won men's doubles. Gordon Scoper of Pass Christian won men's singles.

At the state tournament at Moorhead on April 29-30, 1955, Davis's teams won first place in only one category. Leonard Sumrall took the men's singles trophy. But, according to the *Bulldog Barks,* May 11, 1955, Perk "took the state junior college championship . . . [because] by reaching the finals in two other contests, the points added up in favor of Perkinston." Apparently the team gaining the most points was named the state champion although no state championship trophy was awarded.

In 1956 Davis's teams entered the state tournament on April 28 at Raymond with an unblemished season record but then lost in all four categories. 1956 was the first and only year in which Davis's teams failed to place in state championship play.

In 1957 in the state tournament at Wesson on May 11, Joe McAnulty of Albermarle, North Carolina, took men's singles, but none of Davis's other players even made it to the finals contention. Three different junior colleges won in the other three categories. Perhaps once again Perkinston took the mythical overall state championship by points because on April 5, 1958, on the eve of the next season the *Daily Herald* published Perkinston as the "defending Mississippi Junior College Conference champion . . . in tennis."

The 1958 state tournament at Raymond on May 3, was a virtual replay of Wesson in 1957. Once again different junior colleges won in each of the four categories with McAnulty again taking men's singles for Perk. Apparently that time Perk did not take the state championship.

On May 9, 1959, at the state tennis tournament in Raymond, Davis's teams won in three categories. Gayle Longbine of Biloxi and Isabelle Rosetti of Handsboro won women's doubles, D. G. Boyd of Gulfport and Bill Branager of Mississippi City won men's doubles, and Nick Cefalu of Biloxi took men's singles. The *Clarion Ledger* of May 10 gave a more detailed account of this tournament than any other newspaper of the Davis years. The *Clarion Ledger* reporter stated, "Perkinston wrapped up the state junior college tennis championship here yesterday afternoon and also laid claim to three individual titles." For the first time a clear distinction between a state championship title and an individual category victory was given. The reporter also stated, "Perkinston finished the tournament with six points, followed by East Central and Southwest with three. East Mississippi and host Hinds finished with one point each."

On the basis of such a point system Davis's teams certainly won the Mississippi State tennis championships of 1951, 1952, 1953, 1954, 1955, and 1959. Davis remembered winning the state championship seven times, so the other time must have been 1957, since the *Daily Herald* supported his claim. This point system had been mentioned in relation to Perk's tennis victory of 1937 but specifically in regard to winning the big "State Loving Cup." References to that cup disappeared during World War II, so apparently in the postwar era the points were added to determine the state championship in tennis.

Davis era player Leonard Sumrall (1954, above) succeeded Davis as tennis coach in the 1961 season at Perkinston Junior College. Davis-era player Barbara Ann "Sue" Ross (1955, right) succeeded Sumrall as tennis coach at MGCJC in the 1964 season.

For nine years Davis had served gratis as the institution's tennis coach, establishing the 20th century record for both longevity of service and numbers of championships and trophies won in the sport. After the 1959 season Davis gave up coaching tennis in order to work on advanced degrees at Mississippi Southern College and to carry out President J. J. Hayden's imperative to establish centers on the Coast.

The obvious successor to Davis was Leonard Sumrall, who since fall 1958 had been a social studies teacher and coach in the high school department at Perk. Sumrall, an ace tennis player for Davis in 1953 and 1954, had never lost a junior college match in his two years of play at Perk. In 1953 he had won the state doubles championship together with teammate Max Patterson, and he had won the 1955 men's singles trophy. Sumrall had to forego the job as tennis coach in spring 1960 in order to serve a six months tour of duty in the armed services, but he returned to take the position the following year.

The *Bulldog Barks* of May 17, 1961, reported that on May 6, Perk's men's and women's tennis teams at Raymond had "swept through the Mississippi Junior College Conference tennis tournament to emerge with the state crown." Doonie Johnson of Ocean Springs took the women's singles title, and Roy Baker and John Bond, both of Ocean Springs, took the men's doubles. According to the *Daily Herald* account of this tournament, "This was the first time for the junior college tennis tournament to be played on a team basis. Each match won by a team entitled it to one point." Perhaps this point system was new only to the reporter since points had been awarded since the 1930s.

In any case, according to the *Bulldog Barks* at least, the Perkinston men and women tennis players of 1961 constituted one team, which won the "state crown." Whether or not their victories resulted in a single state trophy or individual trophies for women's singles and men's doubles or both remains a mystery, since none of the trophies of this era were in the collection of the MGCCC Archives in 2000.

Apparently things changed again a year later because in the *Bulldog Barks* report on the May 5, 1962, state tournament at Raymond, the Perk men's team and the Perk women's team were competing separately against men's and women's teams of other junior colleges for separate men's and women's state titles. The *Bulldog Barks* stated that Doonie Johnson and Janice Murray of Biloxi "captured first place points" by winning women's doubles thus forcing "Jones Junior College lasses into a tie for the girl's title." The report further averred that Jones's men's team captured the men's title. The *Daily Herald* of May 8, 1962, stated that in the men's division Jones had ten points, Hinds and Delta five each, Perkinston three, and Southwest one. In the women's division Perk and Jones each had eight points, Hinds six, while Southwest and East Central each had three. Whatever titles or trophies the men and women of 1962 won on May 5, these were the last for Perkinston Junior College, because five days after the tournament the institution became Mississippi Gulf Coast Junior College (MGCJC).

Sumrall remained at MGCJC one more season, passing his mantle to Barbara Ann "Sue" Ross in late 1963. Ross's 1966 men's team finished second in the state. On June 6-10 she took two of her men's team members, George Beemon of Gulfport and James Misner of Biloxi, to the National Junior College Athletic Association (NJCAA) National Tennis Tournament held at Central Florida Junior College in Ocala, Florida, where they placed eighth in the nation. Melvin Carpenter, the chairman of the tournament, had issued a special invitation to Ross's Perk netmen because he had been a coach at Perkinston from 1956 to 1960. This was the first time that MGCJC students competed in a national tennis tournament. No women players were invited because the NJCAA did not sanction women's sports at that time.

The issue of whether or not men's and women's tennis teams received overall state trophies in separate divisions was solved so far as MGCJC was concerned in 1967. Ross's women's team won the state trophy in the Mississippi Junior College Conference tennis tournament at Hinds Junior College on Saturday, May 13, 1967. Kay James and Nancy Vogle, both of Gulfport, took No. 1 doubles for MGCJC and Chris Bell of Pass Christian, won No. 1 singles. In the finals, Nancy Goff of Ocean Springs lost No. 2 singles, and Cheryl Goff of Ocean Springs and Linda Mizell of Gulfport lost No. 2 doubles. But the MGCJC women had reached the finals in all four divisions, racking up 10 points to take the title. Hinds finished second with seven points, Southwest scored six, Jones and Delta took three points each, Northwest one,

*The 1961 championship team. **Kneeling** (from left), Pattye Carol Harris of Vancleave, Doonie Johnson of Ocean Springs, Janice Murray of Biloxi, Joan Cubbison of Biloxi, Rita Sue Ranager of Moss Point, and Susie Wetta of New Orleans (not pictured). **Standing** (order unknown)Roy Baker of Ocean Springs, John Bond of Ocean Springs, Bernie Gordon of Orange Grove, James King of Brooklyn, Sonny Walker of Pascagoula, and Carl Welch of Biloxi. Photo from Bulldog Barks, May 17, 1961.*

MGCJC's FIRST NJCAA TENNIS CONTENDERS 1966

James Misner

George Beemon

Photos from 1966 Perkolator, p. 136.

COACH SUE ROSS'S CONSECUTIVE WOMEN'S TENNIS STATE CHAMPIONSHIPS 1967 & 1968

Susanne Dees

Suzanne Reese

Photos from 1968 Perkolator, pps. 94-95.

Front row(from left), George Beemon, Nancy Vogle, Chris Bell, and Cheryl Goff. Back row (from left), Linda Mizell, Nancy Goff, Kay James,Cheryl Rose, and Billie Gwin. Photo from 1967 Perkolator, p. 112.

and East Central failed to place. The Hinds men took the state title with ten points. The MGCJC men and the Holmes men tied for second with nine points each.

The following year on May 11, 1968, at Battlefield Park in Jackson, Ross's women's team won the state trophy again. Both MGCJC doubles teams Nancy Goff and Nancy Vogle and Susanne Dees of Wiggins and Suzanne Reese of Gulfport won their final matches. Chris Bell reached finals but lost. The women total stood at nine points with Jones Junior College placing second with eight. The MGCJC men totaled three to tie for fifth place with East Central. After her twin titles of 1967 and 1968, Ross gave up coaching tennis in order to devote more time to other women's sports and particularly to basketball.

Assistant basketball coach Larry Ivey took charge of the tennis team and in spring 1970 coached the MGCJC women to victory in the state championship tournament on May 8, in Jackson. As in 1968 the MGCJC women placed first, and the Gulf Coast men placed fifth.

After 1970 tennis became an MGCJC college-wide effort with players from Jefferson Davis Campus (JD) and Jackson County Campus (JC) participating along side those from the

1970 WOMEN'S STATE TENNIS CHAMPIONS

Four members of the 1970 womens state championship women's team. (From left), Mary Ellerman, Jenny Ladner, Jean O'Neal, and Jo Wilson (above). 1971 Perkolator, p. 59 and p. 85.

Larry Ivey, coach of the 1970 women's tennis championship team. Photo from 1970 Perkolator, p. 106.

TRI-CAMPUS TENNIS BEGAN IN THE EARLY 1970s

Assistant basketball coach William Lewis coached the men's tri-campus tennis team in 1973 and 1974. He became president of Pearl River Community College in summer 2000. Photo from 1974 Perkolator, p. 72.

Perkinston Campus. Jackson County Executive Dean Curtis Davis, with his tennis coaching background, was particularly interested in JC students garnering laurels in that sport. By the mid-1970s both JC and JD students had achieved high profile recognition in tennis.

At Meridian on April 24, 1975, then assistant women's basketball and women's tennis coach Doris Smith's MGCJC women's team won the state championship. This was the first women's championship team whose players came from all three campuses. Four members of that team were JC students, two were JD students, and two were Perk students.

Assistant basketball coach Bryan Hoda, who had coached the men's tennis team in 1975, took charge of both the tri-campus men's and women's tennis teams in spring 1976. William Therrell, JD social studies department instructor, and Charles Keith, JC physical education department chairman, assisted him. In April at Meridian, Hoda's men's tennis team won the state championship trophy, and the women's

THE 1975 MGCJC TRI-CAMPUS WOMEN'S TENNIS STATE CHAMPIONS

Doris Smith (right), assistant basketball coach and head women's tennis coach of Perk Campus, aided by Charles Keith and Rose Schlie of the JC physical education department coached the team to victory.

Perk player Cheryl Bradley

Perk player Jo Ann Peralta

JD player Helen Pappadakis was undefeated "B" team singles player of 1975.

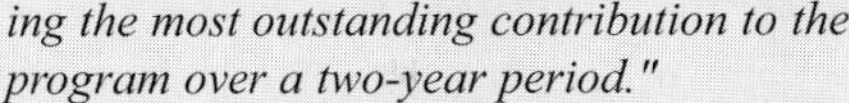

Coach Smith named JD's Gina Davis "the woman player making the most outstanding contribution to the program over a two-year period."

JC player Debbie Sandifer helped the college to win a state crown in 1975 and also won one of her own--the Jackson County Campus beauty pageant crown.

JC player Sherry Wilson displays her form on the court.

JC players Amy Ou (left) and Glenda Alford took state doubles.

Peralta and Davis, 1975 Perkolator, p. 19 and p. 109; Pappadakis, 1975 Beauvoir, p. 19; Sandifer, Wilson, Ou and Alford, 1975 Phases, p. 42; Bradley, 1976 Perkolator, p. 67.

BRYAN HODA'S TRI-CAMPUS TENNIS CHAMPIONSHIPS 1976 AND 1977

The men's tennis team of Coach Bryan Hoda won the 1976 state championship. Hoda stands at rear while members of his men's tennis state championship team hold the state trophy.

(From left), Chester Richey, Doug DeGroot, Steve Sims, Russell Miller, and tournament director James Cameron of Meridian Junior College.

According to the 1977 Perkolator page 128, the rest of "the squad is not pictured because the student photographer lost the negative."

In 1977 both the men's and the women's MGCJC tri-campus tennis teams won the state championship, and for the first time both teams played in the National Junior College Region VII Tennis Tournament. The women's team won the Region VII trophy.

(From left), standing in the Perkinston cafeteria, the team members are: Tom Holder (Perk), Rhonda Balius (JC), Keith Pope (JC), Tim May (JC), Veria McMillian (JC), Ricky Smith (JD), Kim Ferrill (Perk), Russell Miller (Perk), and Cathy Betts (JC). Photo from 1978 Perkolator, p. 134.

team posted third in the state.

Hoda remained head tennis coach in the 1977 spring season, and Therrell remained as assistant at JD, while Rose Schlie, JC physical education instructor, took Keith's place. On April 29 at Meridian both the MGCJC men's and women's teams captured a state championship trophy. The women then went on to win the 1977 Region VII championship at Pulaski, Tennessee, on May 13.

The NJCAA had formed a Women's Division in 1975, approving national competition for women in volleyball, basketball, and tennis. In 1977 the MGCJC women not only won the NJCAA Region VII championship in tennis, but in March, the MGCJC women had also taken the NJCAA Region VII trophy in basketball.

In August 1977 Hoda left MGCJC, and Perkinston campus social studies instructor Jon Lewis took over as head men's and women's tennis coach with Rose Schlie of JC as assistant coach. Lewis's 1978 women's team won the state championship and posted runner-up status in the NJCAA Region VII tournament in Pulaski, Tennessee. In 1979 Lewis led the MGCJC women to yet another state crown and yet another runner-up standing in the NJCAA Region VII competition in Pulaski. Lewis's men's team placed second in the state in 1979. In 1980 Schlie became head tennis

TRI-CAMPUS TENNIS 1977-1984

Rose Schlie (seated) and Charles Keith pose in front of the trophy case in the Physical Education and Health Building at JC Campus. Both had served as MGCJC assistant coaches in the past, but in 1980 Schlie became the first head coach of an MGCJC sport who was not based at the Perkinston Campus. Photo from 1982 Phases, p. 85.

*1984 Tri-Campus State/Region XXIII Championship Team: **Kneeling** (from left), Jon Lewis, coach, Jill Treadway of Ocean Springs (JC), Melody Lane of Ocean Springs (JC), Shelly Martin of Gautier (JC), Sally Miller of Gautier (JC), and Robert Rominger, assistant coach. **Standing** (from left), Robert Stoebe of Biloxi (JD), Bill Briggs of Moss Point (JC), Jimmy Audoyan of Gulfport (JD), Don Fletcher of Gulfport (JD), and Myron Seaton of Moss Point (JC).*

The men's team was undefeated in regular season play and captured three singles and both doubles titles at the state and regional tournaments. All five men were named to the All-State team.

coach and her men's team tied with Mississippi Delta to take a co-state championship. In 1983, the year the NJCAA placed Mississippi in new Region XXIII, Schlie's men's team took second place in State/Region XXIII.

When Schlie left MGCJC after the 1983 season, Jon Lewis resumed his former position as head tennis coach with Robert Rominger, Perkinston Campus social studies instructor, as assistant. On April 26, 1984, at Meridian, Lewis's men's team won State/NJCAA Region XXIII later placing 25th in the nation at the NJCAA National Junior College Tennis Tournament held May 21-26 at Ocala, Florida. Lewis's 1985 men's team took second place State/Region XXIII.

Rominger took over as head tennis coach in 1987. In his first year both his men's and women's teams placed second in State/Region XXIII. In 1988 his men's team once again placed second. Rominger relinquished the position of tennis coach before the 1989 season. Bruce Layton, Perkinston Campus science instructor, took over tennis coaching duties from 1989-1993.

JD science instructor Charles Spence was named tennis coach beginning in spring 1994. Spence, a native of Arkansas and an avid tennis player since 1967, managed to eke out a men's team fourth place state finish in his first season. In 1995 he resurrected the women's team, moribund since 1990, and his men's team finished second in State/Region XXIII. Spence took seven of his 1995 netmen to Corpus Christi, Texas, for the NJCAA national tournament. Six of them lost in the first round but 37-year-old Tom Friscia, whom Spence termed "a second coach," made it to the semi-finals before an ankle injury knocked him out of contention.

Beginning in 1996 Spence's men's team went on a winning spree reminiscent of the days of Curtis Davis. Spence even outdid Davis because regionals and nationals had not existed when Davis coached.

On April 27, 1996, Spence's men, by one point, broke a five-year Hinds Community College lock on the State/Region XXIII championship. Spence then took the men's team to the nationals in Corpus Christi, where the team made it to the second round before being eliminated and wound up ranked 15th in the nation. Spence's 1996 women's team broke even with a 4-4 record.

In spring 1997 Spence's men took the State/Region XXIII championship for the second year in a row, and the women ended up third in the State/Region XXIII, missing by one point the opportunity to accompany the men to nationals. In November 1997 Spence's men's team was ranked fifth in the nation--the highest tennis team ranking in the history of the institution to 2000. One of Spence's players, Johan Lonner of Vasteras, Sweden, finished ranked No. 1 nationally in singles.

In spring 1998 Spence's men took the State/Region XXIII championship for the third consecutive year. At the national

JD'S CHARLES SPENCE TOOK MGCCC'S TENNIS PROGRAM TO THE TOP

Charles Spence

Tom Friscia on the court after Coach Charles Spence recruited him for the JD campus so that Friscia could play on Spence's inaugural MGCCC tennis team in spring 1994. Friscia, then a 37-year-old former U. S. Navy SEAL, was almost twice the age of any of his opponents on the court. In the words of Sun/Herald reporter Kamon Simpson, published May 21, 1995, he was also usually "almost twice as good."

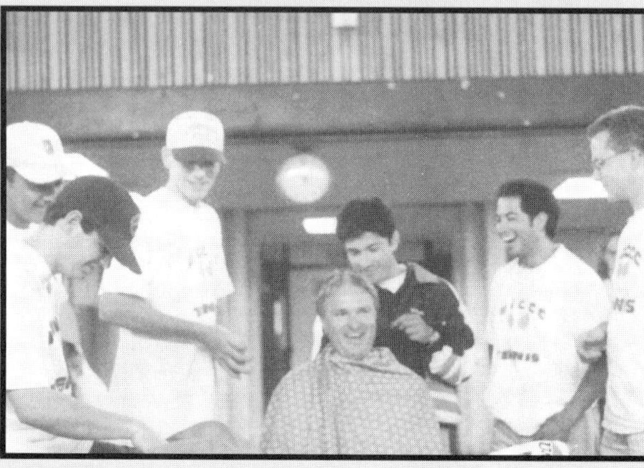

The men's tennis team shaves Spence at JD in March 1996. Spence told his 1996 team members that they could shave his head if they would defeat his nemesis--Hinds County Community College. The team beat Hinds and shaved Spence in March. In April the men shaved Hinds by one point to take Spence's first State/Region XXIII tennis championship.

The 1998 MGCCC men's tennis team won more trophies and garnered more laurels than any other tennis team in the history of the institution. The team won state/Region XXIII honors and went on to place 8th in the nation with Johan Lonner taking the No. 1 singles position in the nation.

***First row** (from left), Johan Lonner of Vasteras, Sweden, Jeff Davis of Biloxi, and Jeff Auberson of Geneva, Switzerland. **Second row** (from left), Josh Weaver of Long Beach and Felipe Monsalve of Bogata, Columbia. Rear, Coach Charles Spence.*

tournament in Corpus Christi the men's team scored 13 points to achieve a No. 8 ranking nationally.

In 1998 Charles Serpente, a counselor at JD's West Harrison County Occupational Training Center, replaced Spence as tennis coach. Serpente knew that following in the footsteps of Spence would be a daunting task. Like Spence had done before him, Serpente used his first season to build a team. In the 2000 season his men's team tied Pearl River Junior College to take the Co-State/NJCAA Region XXIII championship.

*The 2000 MGCCC State/Region XXIII co-champion tennis team displays its trophies. **First row** (from left), Bo Bowman of Pascagoula, Coach Charles Serpente of West Harrison County Occupational Training Center, Kai Thrash of Perkinston, and Henry Cespedes of Bogota, Columbia. **Second row** (from left), Charles Boggs of Wiggins, Cameron Kershaw of Gulfport, Christian Ladner of Diamondhead, Sheldon Baker of Johannesburg, South Africa, and Brian Fairley of Lucedale.*

Tennis Record
1935-2000

1935	State Champion in Women's Doubles
1936	State Champion in Women's Doubles
1937*	State Champion in Men's Singles, Women's Singles, and Women's Doubles
1941	State Runner-up in Men's Singles and Men's Doubles
1942	South Division Champion in Men's Singles and Men's Doubles
1947*	State Champion in Women's Singles, Women's Doubles, Men's Singles, and Men's Doubles
1948	State Champion in Women's Singles
1951*	State Champion in Women's Singles, Women's Doubles, and Men's Doubles
1952*	State Champion in Women's Singles, Men's Doubles, and Men's Singles
1953*	State Champion in Women's Singles, Women's Doubles, and Men's Singles
1954*	State Champion in Women's Doubles, Men's Doubles, and Men's Singles
1955*	State Champion in Men's Singles
1957*	State Champion in Men's Singles
1958	State Champion in Men's Singles
1959*	State Champion in Women's Doubles, Men's Doubles, and Men's Singles
1961*	State Champion in Women's Singles, and Men's Doubles
1962	Women's Team Co-State Champions with Jones
1966	George Beemon and James Misner placed 8th in nationals
1967	Women's Team State Champion
1968	Women's Team State Champion
1970	Women's Team State Champion
1975	Women's Team State Champion
1976	Men's Team State Champion
1977	Men's Team State Champion
	Women's Team State Champion and NJCAA Region VII Champion
1978	Women's Team State Champion and NJCAA Region VII Runner-Up
1979	Women's Team State Champion and NJCAA Region VII Runner-Up
1980	Men's Team Co-State Champions with Miss. Delta
1984	Men's Team State/NJCAA Region XXIII Champion and 25th in nationals
1985	Men's Team State/NJCAA Region XXIII Runner-Up
1987	Men's Team State/NJCAA Region XXIII Runner-Up
	Women's Team State/NJCAA Region XXIII Runner-Up
1988	Men's Team State/NJCAA Region XXIII Runner-Up
1995	Men's State/NJCAA Region XXIII Runner-Up
1996	Men's Team State/NJCAA Region XXIII Champion and 15th in nationals
1997	Men's Team State/NJCAA Region XXIII Champion (Ranked 5th in the nation)
1998	Men's Team State/NJCAA Region XXIII Champion and 8th in nationals
2000	Men's Team Co-State/Region XXIII Champions with Pearl River

*Apparently no tennis state championship trophy was awarded in these years, but Perk's record on the basis of total points earned, evidently entitled the school to claim the overall state title.

BOXING 1930 - 1940

Coach Lee Roy Weeks announced in the *Daily Herald* of July 26, 1930, that an athletic show including boxing, wrestling, and trapeze work would be held in the college gym on August 1. This athletic show would, according to Weeks, "inaugurate the boxing sport into the regular routine of college athletics." The bouts were to be held in a ring erected inside the gym.

Apparently, though, organized boxing at Perkinston did not become a reality for three years. The *Daily Herald* reported that the first boxing tournament occurred in the Perkinston gym on Friday night, December 14, 1933. In the series of bouts that night, student coach Elmer "Bull" Watjus pitted his squad against a team of amateurs from Moss Point and Pascagoula, and the Perkinston fighters won six of the nine fights. In coverage of the contest the *Daily Herald* reported that "school officials" predicted that the junior colleges of the state would soon hold regular boxing tournaments. This prediction came true less than a month later.

The first intercollegiate boxing tournament to be held at Perkinston took place on Friday night, January 19, 1934, when the Perkinston mittmen met the boxers of Mississippi State Teachers' College in a ten-bout battle.

According to the *Daily Herald* of January 20, 600 spectators witnessed the event. In the words of the *Daily Herald* reporter, "To start the card, five blindfolded warriors with one hand tied behind them fought for five minutes. All the punches that were ever originated or probably ever will be used were exhibited in that battle royal." The Perkinston boxers took the tournament honors by winning five bouts and fighting to a draw in a sixth. Ironically, one of the four State Teachers' College victories went to Obie Brown, a former Perkinston star athlete, who defeated Steve Pitalo of Biloxi.

On January 8, 1935, the *Daily Herald* reported that boxers from the "high school department of the Harrison-Stone-Jackson Junior College" were scheduled to fight later in the week against pugilists from Coast high schools at the Gulfport Fairgrounds. This author encountered no other references to high school boxers from Perkinston.

From the records available, it appeared that in the 1930s

The 1933-1934 Harrison-Stone-Jackson Junior College boxing team poses in front of the Old Gym. Photo courtesy of Merrill "Red" True. ***First row*** *(from left) student coach Elmer "Bull" Watjus of Kreole, Jay P. "Jake" Hatten of Perkinston,George "Hinky" Bryant of Tela, Honduras, Jimmie Davis of Gulfport,Tony Rosetti of Biloxi, and team manager Unknown.* ***Second row*** *(from left), Unknown, Steve Pitalo of Biloxi, Johnny Cook of Wiggins, and Richard "Dick" Davis of Gulfport.* ***Third row*** *(from left) Merrill "Red" True of Mississippi City, Boyd Stark of Gulfport, and Joe Corollo of Leland.*

The 1935-1936 Harrison-Stone-Jackson Junior College boxing team poses in front of the Old Gym. The photograph was made between January 27 and March 6, 1936. Photo courtesy of Hazel (Bridge) Necaise.

***First row** (from left), Milton "Mickey" McIntosh of Gulfport, Emile Panero of New York, New York, Harold Ervin of Long Beach, Lucien Kidd of Puerto Castilla, Honduras, and W. A. "Sam" Maxwell of Long Beach*
***Second row** (from left), Richard "Dick" Davis of Gulfport, George Butler of Progresso, Honduras, George "Hinky" Bryant of Tela, Honduras, James Desporte of Biloxi, Jimmie Hosch of Mississippi City, and Tom Leatherbury of Pascagoula.*
***Third row** (from left) William A. "Bill" Cowart of Middleton, Tennessee, Rene Trochesset of Biloxi, Ralph Burns of Gulfport, Glenn Fayard of Gulfport, Edward Estes of Gulfport, Elman Price of Wiggins, and James Simpson of Brooklyn.*

only four junior colleges fielded full teams in all eight weight divisions ranging from bantam to heavy. These were Perkinston, Pearl River, East Mississippi, and Southwest. In March 1936, the state junior college boxing championship was held at Scooba. Rene Trochesset of Biloxi won Perkinston's only state boxing title for that year by defeating the heavy weight boxer from East Mississippi in the elimination bout and the Southwest heavyweight in the titular bout.

On March 27, 1937, Perkinston hosted the state junior college boxing championship. Once again Perkinston took only the heavy weight crown. Once again Rene Trochesset, by then captain and student coach of the team, was the victor. But this time he had to beat Bryce "Mac" McMahan, one of his own team members, for the title.

In the 1938 state junior college boxing championship tournament held in Poplarville, the Perkinston team turned in the best performance in the history of the college, winning four state crowns--Bryce McMahan, heavyweight; Robert Corrales, bantam weight; R. L. McArthur, welterweight; and Dallas "Cannonball" Smith, middleweight. Each of the four Perkinston fighters defeated a Pearl River boxer for the title.

According to the *1939 Perkolator* yearbook, Pearl River struck back the following year, sending that season's Perkinston boxers to defeat. The *Daily Herald,* December 8, 1939, announced a new boxing season for 1940, but the *1940 Perkolator* yearbook carried no picture of a team, and this author encountered no further information from any other sources. Apparently boxing at Perkinston fizzled out on the eve of the Second World War.

The 1938 Harrison-Stone-Jackson Junior College boxing team poses in front of the Old Gym. Four members of this team won state championship laurels. Photo from 1938 Perkolator, p. 76

***First row** (from left), Roberto Corrales of Progresso, Honduras, Bill Weaver of Gulfport, James Palencia of Puerto Castilla, Honduras, Arthur Wood of Puerto Castilla, Honduras, and Jack Cook of Kingsville, Texas.*
***Second row** (from left), student coach Richard "Bud" Lewis of Gulfport, Victor Royal of Buford, Georgia, Bryce McMahan of Hattiesburg, R. L. McArthur of Gulfport, Dallas "Cannonball" Smith of Hattiesburg, and manager James Hopper of Meridian.*

GOLF
1938 - 2000

Merrill "Red" True of Mississippi City was a member of the 10-cent-per-hour student labor gang at Perk from September 1930 to January 1936. True remembered "grubbing a lot of stumps" for various reasons, but at the end of his tenure, stumps on the north side of the campus behind the barn and Bennett Hall (the site of Dees Hall in 2000) were being removed to build a nine-hole golf course.

In spring 1938 the *Perkolator* (yearbook) staff announced that Coach S. M. Walker had founded "an infant organization of golfers on the campus" called the "Country Club." Walker, according to the *Perkolator*, had molded the Country Club into a group dedicated to the study of the history and value of golf and the "big job of keeping the golf course in condition."

In spring 1939 the 13 member (seven women and six men) Country Club was pictured in the *Perkolator* along with science teacher Linwood P. Ingram as sponsor. In extolling the achievement of the Country Club, the *Perkolator* recorded that, "The club has had as its purpose this year the improvement of the fairways and greens. Due to the efforts of the members this purpose has been realized. Three holes, useless at the beginning of the year, were put into playing condition by early spring."

More than any other sport at Perk, golf was a casualty of World War II in a very literal sense. Both Country Club sponsor Ingram and club member Glen Sletten joined the U.S. Army Air Corps, and both died in action in the Pacific. The golf course, cut by a road and partially covered by building sites, disappeared.

In 1974 the State Junior College Activities Association established golf as an intercollegiate sport. In spring 1975 MGCJC fielded two golf teams—a Perkinston Campus team coached by Charles Cooper and a Jackson County Campus team coached by Dr. Bobby Garvin, director of instruction. The two teams competed separately in the regular season but then combined into one entity for the state golf tournament at Hinds, where the MGCJC team placed third.

Cooper and Garvin collaborated again in the 1976 season. The MGCJC team took third in the state once again and placed eighth in the National Junior College Athletic Association (NJCAA) Region VII Golf Tournament.

Cooper, born in Hattiesburg in 1946, was the third of eight sons born to Albert and Clara Cooper. After graduation from Forrest County's Earl Travillion Attendance Center in 1964, Cooper attended Coahoma Junior College. After graduating from Coahoma in 1966, he earned a bachelor's degree in elementary education at William Carey College in 1969. He taught in the Stone County School System as an elementary teacher from 1970 to 1974, when he joined the staff of Perkinston Campus as assistant director of housing. In the spring of his first year at Perk, Cooper began his golf coaching career. In addition to his duties at MGCJC Cooper continued his education. He received his master's in educational

S. M. Walker, a science teacher and assistant coach at Perkinston since September 1934, founded the Country Club as Perk's first official golf organization in spring 1938. Walker, who went to Louisiana State University in fall 1938 to work on his doctorate, left the fledgling group in the hands of fellow science instructor, L. P. Ingram. Photo from 1938 Perkolator, p. 68.

COUNTRY CLUB

***Top row** (from left): Jimmie Balthrope, Sally Core, Uloa Curren, Nettie Davis, and Sara Frances Eldridge. **Middle row**: "Buddy" Gillis, Joyce Holland, Ollian Netherland, "Glen" Sletten, and Mary Edna Taltavull. **Bottom row**: "Jeff" Webb, Sam Wilson, Alice Worthington, and L. P. Ingram, club sponsor. Photo from 1939 Perkolator, p. 79.*

Four members of the1975 MGCJC golf team stand with their coach in front of Gregory War Memorial Chapel on the Perkinston Campus. (From left): Bill Baggett, Monty Stevens, Coach Charles Cooper, Jeff Wilson, and Daryl Ladner. Not pictured: Bart Madden. Photo from 1975 Perkolator, p. 53.

MGCJC'S FIRST INTERCOLLEGIATE GOLFERS 1975

Jackson County Campus Director of Instruction and golf coach Bobby Garvin (right) confers with Copiah-Lincoln Junior College golf coach Walter Angeloff. Garvin became president of Mississippi Delta Community College in July of 1992. Photo from 1975 Phases, p. 43.

Charles Powers, a Jackson County Campus team member, held the best score on the golf team with a low of 77. Photo from 1975 Phases, p. 43.

administration from William Carey in 1977, rising immediately to the position of counselor and later to the position of director of admissions at Perkinston Campus.

By 1979 Cooper was head MGCJC golf coach, and that spring his charges won for MGCJC its first state championship trophy in golf. Also at the state tournament, held in late April in Biloxi, Mike Smith took state medallist honors, yet another first for MGCJC. The MGCJC team traveled to Henry Horton State Park in Pulaski, Tennessee, and placed fourth in the NJCAA Region VII tournament held May 7-8. The 1979 season closed with still another first. Smith, who had been named All-Region at Pulaski, represented MGCJC for the first time in the NJCAA National Golf Tournament held that year in Odessa, Texas. According to Charles Cooper, "The act of an individual player being named All-Region qualified him for competition in an NJCAA national golf tournament. In order for a whole team to go the team had to win the regional tournament. That is why Smith went to national and the rest of the team did not."

In 1981, though his team placed second in the state, Cooper produced another state medallist in the person of Kenny Hughes, a Jefferson Davis Campus golfer from Biloxi. In 1982 Hughes returned and though the MGCJC team placed only third in the state championship tournament, the team took the runner-up trophy in the NJCAA Region VII tournament at Chapel Hill, Tennessee. In Cooper's words, "I

MGCJC Golf Champions 1979-1986

In 1979 Jackson County Campus player Mike Smith of Ocean Springs became MGCJC's first state medallist in golf and the first to compete in a NJCAA tournament.

In 1982 Jefferson Davis player Kenny Hughes of Biloxi became MGCJC's second state medallist in golf. In 1982 Hughes was a member of the team that took the NJCAA Region VII Runner-up trophy and was one of three MGCJC golfers to compete in the NJCAA national tournament.

Richard Kopp photo

The golf trophy bearing the inscription "Mississippi Jr. College Association 1979 State Champions" is the first won by an MGCJC team.

1986 state championship team. (From left) Mitch McDowell (JD); Bob Campbell (JD); Mike McMahon (JD), Stan Gill (Perk), and Richard Smith (JC). Richard Smith was the brother of Mike Smith of 1979 MGCJC golf team fame. Mike had been a member of Cooper's first state championship team, and Richard was a member of the second. And, like his brother before him, Richard played in the NJCAA national tournament.

In session 1982-83 the NJCAA placed Mississippi together with Louisiana in new Region XXIII. Since Louisiana had only three community colleges, only one of which had a golf team, the competition in golf was cut considerably. In the case of golf in Mississippi, the state championship and the NJCAA Region XXIII championship were decided by the same game. On the other hand Meridian Junior College, usually won regional championships in golf because in the mid-1980s Meridian had seceded from the Mississippi Association of Junior Colleges Athletic Association (MAJCAA). As a member of the NJCAA but not the MAJCAA, Meridian was not subject to the MAJCAA area strictures on recruiting. The NJCAA placed no area recruiting strictures on its members, so Meridian could recruit worldwide. When Meridian won a State/Region XXIII championship tournament, the state trophy went to the defeated MAJCAA member college because Meridian was not a member of MAJCAA, but the Region XXIII trophy went to Meridian. Bossier City (Louisiana) Community College, Louisiana's only golf contender, occupied a position somewhat analogous to that of Meridian vis-a-vis the other Mississippi junior colleges. Bossier City could win Region XXIII, but obviously not the Mississippi championship, since Bossier City is in Louisiana.

was very proud of that runner-up trophy because Region VII included all of Mississippi, Tennessee, and Kentucky. It meant a lot to take a trophy, even second place, from an area that large." After regionals, Hughes and two other teammates from JD Campus, Woody Cowart of Ocean Springs and Harold Danford of Long Beach, went on to compete in the national tournament in Scottsdale, Arizona.

In 1986 the MGCJC team was awarded the state championship in golf for the second time in Cooper's career but came in second in NJCAA Region XXIII behind Bossier City (Louisiana) Community College. Two of the Gulf Coast team members, Perk Campus student Stan Gill of Lucedale and JC Campus student Richard Smith of Ocean Springs, went on to compete in the NJCAA national tournament held that year at San Jacinto (Texas) Junior College.

At the beginning of the 1990 season the NJCAA went to

1990 CHAMPIONSHIP GOLF TEAM

(From left) Coach Charles Cooper, Todd Donhaiser of Gulfport, David Lee of Long Beach, Wyatt Boyett of Wiggins, John Boothby of Gulfport, and Steve Wilson of Biloxi. Boyett holds the Hinds Community College Invitational Golf Tournament Trophy won April 3, 1990.

Richard Kopp photo

Mississippi Junior College Commissioner of Athletics R. L. "Mac" McClellan (left) shakes hands with Cooper as he hands him the 1990 NJCAA Region XXIII trophy in front of Dees Hall at Perkinston while Perkinston Campus Vice President Clyde Strickland holds the 1990 state trophy. McClellan delivered the trophies to Perkinston after the April 1990 State/Region XXIII victory of Northwest over MGCCC was overturned due to Northwest's fielding of ineligible players. Cooper's 1990 team then took fifth place in the nation at the NJCAA (Division III) Golf Tournament in Scottsdale, Arizona. The fifth place trophy (above right), was the last fifth place trophy awarded by the NJCAA.

Division I (full scholarship), Division II (tuition only), and Division III (no student aid) play. All nine MAJCAA golf contenders agreed to place their golf teams in Division III. That action leveled the playing field by eliminating both Meridian Community College and Bossier City, since each of them elected to contend in other divisions. At that point a Division III State Tournament victory brought both state and Region XXIII honors.

MGCCC hosted the 1990 State/Region XXIII (Division III) tournament in late April at Hickory Hills Country Club in Gautier. Northwest Community College of Senatobia swept the tournament with Cooper's team in second place. A month later the NJCAA disqualified Northwest and named the MGCCC team as the State/Region XXIII (Division III) champion. The NJCAA took the action because four of the five Northwest golfers were receiving scholarships to play, in violation of Division III rules. When he received the news, Cooper exclaimed, "I'm stunned, excited, elated and anything else you can think of. But mostly I'm happy for the kids . . . [and] . . . to be honest, I was getting tired of finishing second."

In the past Cooper had taken one to three players who had qualified by making All-Region to national tournaments on seven occasions. But in 1990, for the first time his team won the regional title, which qualified the team to compete as a team. At the NJCAA national (Division III) Golf Tournament

The MGCCC 1993 golf team stands on the golf course at St. Simons Island, Georgia. (From left) Robert Snelling (JC) of Moss Point, Ronnie Seymour (Perk) of Biloxi, Blake Watts (Perk) of Baton Rouge, Louisiana, Joe Bannister (JC) of Ocean Springs, Todd Moody (JC) of Lucedale, and Coach Charles Cooper. This team with its fourth place national finish attained the highest level of an MGCCC golf team in the 20th century.

Charles Cooper (left) coaches Randon Heim, "the world's next Tiger Woods" in November 2000. Photo courtesy of Marie Heim.

held in Scottsdale, Arizona, June 5-8, the MGCCC golfers took the trophy for fifth in the nation. This 1990 fifth-place trophy was unique because beginning the following year the NJCAA restricted golf trophies to first, second, and third places. Also at Scottsdale two team members, Perk Campus player Steve Wilson of Biloxi and JD Campus player David Lee of Long Beach, were named respectively Second Team Junior College All-American and Third Team Junior College All-American.

The 1991 season proved to be, in Cooper's words, "a nightmare." His team came in fifth in the state with only Perk Campus player Wyatt Boyett of Wiggins qualifying to compete at the national tournament held in Midland, Texas. Two "dream teams," though, followed the 1991 nightmare.

Cooper's 1992 team swept the State/Region XXIII (Division III) Championship Golf Tournament at Millbrook Country Club in Picayune, April 21-22. Perk Campus player Brannon Besse of Shawnee, Oklahoma, took State/Region XXIII (Division III) medallist honors. In June at the NJCAA National (Division III) Golf Tournament at Jekyll Island, Georgia, the team posted seventh in the nation with Besse being named Third Team Junior College All-American.

Cooper's 1993 team swept the State/Region XXIII (Division III) Championship Golf Tournament held at Millbrook Country Club in Picayune, April 20-21. JC Campus player Joe Bannister of Ocean Springs, took State/Region XXIII (Division III) medallist honors. In June at the NJCAA National (Division III) Golf Tournament at St. Simons Island, Georgia, the team posted fourth in the nation with Bannister being named Third Team Junior College all-American.

At the close of the 1993 season MGCCC moved from Division III to Division II, which meant that Cooper could award four tuition scholarships to players. His 1994 team came within three strokes of winning the State/Region XXIII (Division II) championship but had to be satisfied with second place behind Hinds. Even so three players, Biloxi's Greg Nordstrom and Ronnie Seymour and Wiggins's Jason Seal, went to the NJCAA National (Division II) Golf Tournament in Greensboro, North Carolina in June.

Cooper retired as director of admissions in July 1994 but remained as MGCCC golf coach for one more season. His last team finished fourth in State/Region XXIII (Division II), but Nordstrom once again qualified for the national tournament held again in Greensboro. Nordstrom finished eleventh in the nation and was named Second Team Junior College All-American.

In 21 seasons (1975-1995) Cooper won five state championships, three NJCAA Region XXIII (Division III) championships, and an NJCAA Region VII runner-up trophy. His teams took a fifth place national trophy and placed seventh and fourth in the nation on two other occasions. He coached two state medallists and two State/Region XXIII (Division III) medallists. More than 30 of his players were named All-State and/or All-Region, and six were selected as Junior College All-Americans. He was selected Mississippi Association of Community and Junior Colleges Coach of the Year in 1979, 1986, 1990, 1992, and 1993. He was selected NJCAA Region XXIII Coach of the Year in 1990, 1992, and 1993. In 1996 the National Junior College Athletic Association inducted Cooper into the NJCAA Hall of Fame—the first and the only Mississippi junior college golf coach accorded that honor in the 20th century. On October 28, 1999, he was inducted into MGCCC's inaugural Athletic Hall of Fame.

After Cooper retired to his home in McHenry, he continued to coach golf for a selected client. In 1997 he began instruction for Randon Heim, the one year-old son of MGCCC Perkinston Campus Developmental Studies Department Chairperson Marie Heim. In Cooper's words, "This kid will be the world's next Tiger Woods."

Chris Calcote succeeded Cooper as golf coach. Calcote, a native of McCall Creek, attended Copiah-Lincoln Junior College and earned his bachelor's and master's at Delta State University. Prior to becoming an assistant football coach at MGCCC in August 1992, he had held coaching jobs at Natchez, Laurel, and Wiggins. Calcote became MGCCC athletic director and golf coach on February 1, 1996.

In his five-year stint as golf coach, Calcote sent two of his players to national tournaments, one of whom went twice. Perk Campus player Matt Driskell of Vancleave, who missed being state medallist on a scorecard playoff, went to the 1997 NJCAA (Division II) National Golf Tournament at Vass, North Carolina, where he finished in the top third of the nation. Perk Campus player E. J. Hamrick of Hurley went to the NJCAA (Division II) National Golf Tournament at Vass in 1998 and to the national tournament at Clayton, North Carolina, in 1999. He finished 66th out of a field of 108 at Vass and 43rd out of 109 at Clayton.

Chris Calcote

Calcote's 2000 team took the state runner-up trophy at the State/Region XXIII (Division II) Championship Golf Tournament held April 17-19 at the Natchez Trace Country Club in Tupelo. The team likewise placed third in NJCAA Region XXIII (Division II) behind first place Hinds and second place Meridian.

In late June 2000, MGCCC President Willis H. Lott announced the hiring of Tommy Snell as the college's new golf coach. According to Athletic Director Calcote, MGCCC had been trying to hire Snell for "at least three years."

A fund-raising effort on the part of MGCCC booster and golf enthusiast Webb Lee, combined with the opening of an instructor of English position at Perkinston Campus, finally made the desire to secure Snell a reality.

The 48-year-old Snell earned his bachelor's degree in English with highest honors at the University of Southern Mississippi and took his master's degree in education with a concentration in English at William Carey College. He was a professional golfer from 1971 to 1980. From 1980-1987 Snell was director of golf at Shady Valley Golf Club in Arlington, Texas. Snell then served as a gaming consultant in Las Vegas, Nevada, from 1987 to 1993. In 1994 he took a position as an English teacher and golf coach at St. John High School in Gulfport. At St. John he coached his teams to five consecutive state championships in 1996, 1997, 1998, 1999, and 2000—a state record. Snell helped organize and also played in the 1996 NIKE Mississippi Gulf Coast Classic and served as director of other Coast golf tournaments. In 2000 he was president of Gulfport's Great Southern Golf Club, Inc.

Tommy Snell

According to President Lott, "The addition of Snell to Gulf Coast is the first step in the college's long range strategic plan to boost its golf program." That plan included the construction of an 18-hole golf course at Perkinston Campus. As for Webb Lee's fund-raising efforts to pay Snell's salary and build the golf course, Lott further stated, "Part of our strategic plan is to seek outside funding to support the operation and improve what we're able to do at the college. This is just one example of how private support will improve what we're doing."

Lee envisioned the golf program as "world class" in scope. He touted the program as both a magnet for talented players and as a spotlight illuminating the college and its programs. Lee stated his aim succinctly, "If all the alumni and businesses will chip in and help us with this proposal, I think we can build a nice [golf] course and program."

Perkinston Campus Vice President Mary Graham pointed out that the new plans would aid a pre-existing program at Perk. She said, "We have a growing Golf Recreational Turf Management program already in place in response to the booming golf industry on the Coast. A golf course at Perk would not only enhance the college's athletic program but also the instructional programs in golf turf management and horticulture."

On inheriting a golf program with a quarter century history punctuated by state and regional championships and placement in national tournaments, Snell stated his aim precisely, "Our goal is to win a national championship." Calcote seconded Snell's motion. "These are exciting times for Gulf Coast golf. With the addition of Coach Snell and the college's future plans, we have a chance to put our program in national prominence."

The college's golf program began with "Red" True and other students digging up huge pine stumps by hand to make a nine-hole golf course at Perkinston. Their efforts succeeded only to be nullified in the rush to defend the nation in the Second World War. On the eve of a new millennium the college moved to resurrect a project completed and then abandoned six decades before.

Golf Record 1975-2000			
1975	3rd in state		
1976	3rd in state	8th in Region VII	
1977	3rd in state		
1978	2nd in state		
1979	State Champions	4th in Region VII	Mark Smith to nationals
1980	2nd in state	Gordon Fryfogle and George Birdrow to Region VII	
1981	2nd in state Kenny Hughes State Medallist	Kenny Hughes and Paul Curtis to Region VII	Kenny Hughes to nationals
1982	3rd in state	2nd in Region VII	Kenny Hughes, Harold Danford, and Woody Cowart to nationals
1983	3rd in state	3rd in Region XXIII	
1984	4th in state	4th in Region XXIII	George Byrd and Gary Taylor to nationals
1985	2nd in state	3rd in Region XXIII	George Byrd to nationals
1986	State Champions	2nd in Region XXIII	Stan Gill and Richard Smith to nationals
1987	4th in state	5th in Region XXIII	
1988	3rd in state	4th in Region XXIII	
1989	4th in state	5th in Region XXIII	
1990	State Champions	Region XXIII (Division III) Champions	5th place in nationals Steve Wilson – Second Team All-American David Lee – Third Team All-American
1991	5th in state	6th in Region XXIII (Division III)	Wyatt Boyett to nationals
1992	State Champions Brannon Besse State/Region Medallist	Region XXIII (Division III) Champions	7th place in nationals Brannon Besse – Third Team All-American
1993	State Champions Joe Bannister State/Region Medallist	Region XXIII (Division III) Champions	4th place in nationals Joe Bannister – Third Team All-American
1994	2nd in state	2nd in Region XXIII (Division II)	Ronnie Seymour, Greg Nordstrom, and Jason Seal to nationals
1995	4th in state	4th in Region XXIII (Division II)	Greg Nordstrom to nationals, Greg Nordstrom – Second Team All-American
1996	7th in state	8th in Region XXIII (Division II)	
1997	4th in state	5th in Region XXIII (Division II)	Matt Driskell to nationals
1998	5th in state	6th in Region XXIII (Division II)	E. J. Hamrick to nationals
1999			E. J. Hamrick to nationals
2000	2nd in state	3rd in Region XXIII (Division II)	

MEN'S AND WOMEN'S SOCCER 1940 - 2000

The *Stone County Enterprise* of August 26, 1998, carried an article with the headline, "Bulldogs field soccer teams for first time ever in school history." The "school" referred to was MGCCC. The report was in error because a women's intramural soccer team had been fielded at Perkinston at least 58 years earlier.

The *Stone County Enterprise* of March 7, 1940, carried an article with the headline, "Letters Awarded at Junior College." The "junior college" referred to was the Harrison-Stone-Jackson Junior College which later evolved into MGCCC. The 1940 article avowed that:

> "The following girls were awarded letters for playing on the girls' soccer squad: Mildred Russum, captain, Perkinston; Jewell Simmons, Pass Christian; Madeline Kuljis, Biloxi; Jeannie Mills, Lyman; Kathleen Colle, Pascagoula; Clare Sekul, Biloxi; Bonnye Broadus, Chunkey; Thelma Dale, Ocean Springs; Annie Ruth Fairley, Lucedale; and Peggy Cherry, Wiggins."

The letters awarded by "A. I. Rexinger, head coach, and Miss Elton Dalier, head of the girl's physical education department," were intramural rather than intercollegiate in nature.

The *Bulldog Barks* of April 14, 1948, carried an account of an intramural soccer tournament in which, "Helen Bond captained her team to an easy 10-0 victory over the team led by Flo Shepard. Bond made four field goals for eight points. Penton made the other field goal to make the total."

Available records indicate that only women played soccer at Perkinston solely as an intramural sport from at least 1940

Bulldog Eric Fisher of St. Martin (center) battles two Itawamba Indians in A. L. May Memorial Stadium on October 21, 1998. Seven weeks earlier in the same stadium Fisher had made the only goal in MGCCC's first intercollegiate soccer game to defeat Hinds 1-0.

until at least 1950. The women played the game on the Old Athletic Field and in front of the Old Gym. The fielding of a men's soccer team and a women's soccer team by MGCCC in fall 1998 was the first time in its history that the college had participated in soccer at the intercollegiate level.

In July 1998 Perkinston Campus drafting and design instructor Bary Thrash was appointed head soccer coach with Swedish-born Salomon Kidane as his assistant. With authorization to offer 20 two-year scholarships (ten for men and ten for women) Thrash and Kidane held soccer try-outs at Espy Field in Long Beach on July 24, 1998. Fifty players, only ten

The 1943-1944 women's intramural soccer teams play the game on the Old Athletic field. The Daily Herald, December 1, 1943, reported four women's teams engaging in competition--the Yellow Jackets, the Amazons, the Blue Panthers, and the Sugar Blues. Photo from 1944 Perkolator, p. 55.

The 1944-1945 women's intramural soccer teams at play in front of the Old Gym. Photo from 1945 Perkolator, p. 49.

MGCCC's 1998 Inaugural men's soccer team are: **First row** (from left), Anthony VanCourt of Long Beach, Kai Thrash of Perkinston, Trey Turner of Vancleave, and Nhan Nguyen of Long Beach. **Second row** (from left), Joel Johnson of Harrison Central, Chris Fairley of Harrison Central, Donnie Virgillo of Harrison Central, Paul Fayard of Biloxi, and Chris Fayard of St. Martin. **Third row** (from left), assistant coach Salomon Kidane, Chris Chambers of D'Iberville, Chris Suckow of Harrison Central, Ryan Webb of Gulfport, Jason Poole of Pascagoula, and head coach Bary Thrash. Fourth row (from left) manager Joshua Ladnier of Bay St. Louis, Michael Wyatt of Ocean Springs, Kevin Kostmayer of Biloxi, Erik Snyder of Lucedale, Michael Hendon of Long Beach, and Eric Fisher of St. Martin. Not pictured is assistant coach Charlie McEwan of the Republic of South Africa.

Kai Thrash (front row, second from left) was the son of Kathy and head soccer coach Bary Thrash. Despite a life-long battle with cystic fibrosis, Kai was an avid soccer and tennis player. He received a double-lung transplant in September 1997, and another double-lung transplant in September 1999. When he grew too ill to play, his No. 23 soccer jersey was retired. Kai died September 21, 2000.

of whom were women, showed up to compete for the scholarships. Thus the lack of women players, the first year's worst problem, was apparent from the beginning.

On Saturday, August 29, 1998, in A. L. May Memorial Stadium at Perkinston, the men and women of MGCCC met the men and women of Hinds Community College in the first intercollegiate soccer contests in MGCCC history. At 6 p.m. eleven Lady Bulldogs took the field against the Hinds Eaglettes, and the same eleven Lady Bulldogs played the entire game since none were on the bench. The Eaglettes, not surprisingly, triumphed 9-0.

At 8 p.m. the Bulldogs faced the Eagles. Midway through the first period Bulldog freshman Eric Fisher of St. Martin kicked MGCCC's first and the game's only goal and thus netted MGCCC's first intercollegiate soccer victory.

In 1998 seven other Mississippi Community Colleges fielded men's soccer teams--Copiah-Lincoln, Mississippi Delta, Hinds, East Mississippi, Itawamba, Meridian, and Holmes. Holmes, however, fielded two separate teams--Holmes Ridgeland and Holmes Grenada (replaced by Holmes Goodman after 1998). The 1998 Bulldogs played all eight of the other Mississippi teams, ending the season with a 12-6 record and finishing second in the state and third in the National Junior College Athletic Association (NJCAA) Region XXIII.

In 1998 three other Mississippi community colleges fielded women's soccer teams--Copiah-Lincoln, Hinds, and Holmes Grenada. The 1998 Lady Bulldogs played all three of the other Mississippi teams and also Shelton State of Tuscaloosa, Alabama (a team from NJCAA Region XXI). The Lady Bulldogs ended their first season with a 5-5 record winding up second in the state and second in NJCAA Region XXIII.

Division play in men's soccer was inaugurated in the 1999 season, and MGCCC took the first south division title. The team finished with a 14-1-1 season record. The 1999 women's team finished 13-2 and came in second in state and second in NJCAA Region XXIII.

Women's division play was added in the 2000 season, and the Lady Bulldogs came in second in the south division finishing the season 8-5-2. The men's team came in second in south division as well finishing the season with a 11-4-1 record.

1998 Women's Soccer Team
First row (from left) Rebecca Dupuy of Bay St. Louis, and Sindi Rogers of St. Martin. **Second row** (from left) Rhonda Mitchell of Ocean Springs, Alicia Hoda of Harrison Central, Jaclyn Rockco of D'Iberville, Mea Bordes of Bay St. Louis, Tashia Deshazo of D'Iberville, and Niki Woods of Harrison Central. **Third row** (from left) assistant coach Charlie McEwan, Angie Neumann of Ocean Springs, Rabiotha Brown of George County, Robin Terrell of Ocean Springs, Carmen Dixon of George County, Jennifer Anderson of Gulfport, Jennifer Storey of Bay St. Louis, Valerie Dean of Harrison Central, and head coach Bary Thrash. **Fourth row** (standing) manager Joshua Lanier of Bay St. Louis.

MASCOTS: A PHOTOGRAPHIC ALBUM
1924 - 2000

(Right) In spring 1924 Old Bob poses in front of Bennett Hall with Superintendent J. L. Denson's children and other denizens of the Harrison-Stone Agricultural High School. According to the Daily Herald, an unknown gunman on Tuesday night, September 22, 1925, killed "Old Bob, the large white bulldog that belonged to the A.H.S. . . ." By November in that same football season the Hattiesburg American and the Daily Herald were referring to the school football team as "bulldogs." At Perkinston the mascot named the team.

(Below) The unknown bulldog of session 1946-1947. This author examined thousands of documents and hundreds of photographs related to the school in the two decades following the death of Old Bob. In all that material not one reference to or photograph of a bulldog surfaced. Then on page 52 of the 1947 Perkolator an unknown bulldog appeared. Likely the dog was the school mascot. In any case it was an English bulldog, and all the ones who followed were of that breed.

In 1949, coincident with the completion of A. L. May Memorial Stadium, the school acquired a mascot named Duke. Duke appears above next to the 30-yard-line marker in the stadium with a majorette. Apparently Duke did not last long because the Bulldog Barks, October 8, 1952, under the heading, "Yea, Bulldog!" announced that guidance counselor Robert Lambuth was spearheading the drive to collect the money for a new mascot. "After all," said the writer of the article, "If Southwest has been able to obtain and support a real live bear, why can't we do the same with a bulldog." Photograph from 1950 Perkolator, p. 112.

Perkette Kathryn Mallette [later Floore] of Lucedale and Buck, the PJC mascot, in A. L. May Memorial Stadium in fall 1953. Counselor Robert Lambuth's bulldog fund drive launched in October 1952, netted only $6.50 over the following 14 months. In February 1953, the college sophomore class stepped in and bought the dog with money from the class treasury. Buck, son of "Grand Champion of Jackson," cost $50.00. Buck arrived on campus by April, and Sophomore Class president Albert Reinschmidt of Pensacola, Florida, officially presented the mascot to the school at Awards Day ceremonies on May 14, 1953. By September 1953, Buck had received enough education to pen a column called "Buck Barks" in the Bulldog Barks. On October 23, he wrote, "As I stood barking furiously at what I thought was a man from Mars yesterday some cat informed me that it was only Russ Hackman, a Biloxi Freshman, and his extremely loud shirt. Give us a break, Russ, our eyes can stand only so much." Buck always signed off "I'll be chasing you."

The Daily Herald, November 5, 1953, in advertising the Perk-Itawamba football game set for that night in A. L. May Memorial Stadium, stated that, "The Perkettes are planning a special show and the cheerleaders and the Perkinston mascot, Buck, will add color to the event. . . ." The above photograph was very likely taken that day. In any case, stadium caretaker George Nelson snapped the picture. His daughter, Mary Nelson, who worked in the Perkinston Campus Student Grill in 2000 gave the photograph to the MGCCC Archives.

The archivist placed the above photograph in the spring 1998 Alumni Action magazine seeking the name of the Perkette and the name of the dog. Phone calls and letters on a line from Seminole, Florida, to Beaumont, Texas, poured in. Not only did the archivist learn the names of the Perkette and the mascot but also learned of Buck's eventual fate. George Sherer (PJC Class of 1958) wrote the following in a letter from Seminole, Florida, postmarked June 6, 1998:

> *"The bulldog's name in the picture is 'Buck,' the college mascot. He passed away in the fall semester of 1956. His remains are probably still where he died under Rodney Mansfield's room of the old Jackson Hall dormitory. . . . Rodney Mansfield's room was the second from the north end of the building . . . on the east side. . . . The odor was terrible. I had told the college administration office about the dog dying, that he should be buried, but the college never did anything. Now forty-one years later I want to ask a favor from you. Will you bury Buck's remains for me? It would be deeply appreciated."*

In 2000 during the renovation of Jackson Hall the workmen tearing out the floor were instructed to look for Buck's remains. Alas, no bones were found so there could be no funeral. However, the archivist was assured by Associate Vice President for Institutional Relations Colleen Hartfield, that the photograph of Kathryn Mallette and Buck would be suitably framed and placed on the wall of the renovated Jackson Hall in memory of the departed mascot.

Apparently the school did not find a replacement for Buck until 1959 when nine-year old Mack took the field. On March 8, 1961, the editor of the Bulldog Barks noted Mack's departure:

"To Mack . . . . Farewell

"It is with a feeling of remorse . . . remorse that cannot be expressed adequately by words that we must bid a last farewell to "Mack."

"Mack, who faithfully served for the last two years of his long illustrious life as mascot for Perkinston Junior College. Mack, who suffered miserably when the tide of defeat occasionally swept over our teams and who experienced, along with the rest of us that unexplainable feeling of profound ecstasy when victory was our game. Often it seemed he loved victory even more than we did.

"Eleven years is a long life for a dog but if recognition were given to "Outstanding Dog of the Year" we know Mack would have captured the honor until the end. He served us well and will be deeply missed.

"Now we are without an official mascot. Even though those of the caliber of Mack are hard to find, we feel the need is apparent for another replacement to the long heritage of "Perk Mascots.'"

Photograph from 1961 Perkolator p. 69.

(Above left) Maxine, born August 28, 1966, in New Braunfels, Texas, is greeted by Perkinston Campus students at a pep rally honoring her arrival on November 10, 1966. As a tri-campus bulldog she received accolades and monetary support from Jefferson Davis Campus and Jackson County Campus as well. (Above right) Two days after her arrival, Maxine tore into a giant paper River Rat at A. L. May Memorial Stadium as her fellow Bulldogs tore into the real River Rats defeating them 33 to 0. Alas, Maxine's aggressiveness faded as she grew older. The Bulldog Barks editor on November 17, 1967, noted that "Perky Maxine dislikes bombs. She doesn't go to all the games because when she hears the bombs explode after our touchdowns she explodes and takes off running!" Coach [Bob] Weathers and his wife keep Maxine at their house across the street from Jackson Hall. She sun-bathes in their backyard everyday, so stop by and see her."

Like her predecessor, Buck, Maxine became a writer for the Bulldog Barks. At least as early as November 14, 1968, she was answering students "most searching questions" in an advice column called "Dear Maxine." In a reply to a student distressed over a roommate's demands that her worn twelve-year-old teddy bear be sent home, Maxine showed her fangs. "Dear Distressed" she wrote, "Keep the bear! Your roommate is obviously an animal hater. Turn her name over to the SPCA and perhaps they will send her home. You'll be losing a roommate but gaining a separate bed for your teddy bear." Photograph from 1967 Perkolator, p. 145.

(From left) Perkinston Campus Dean C. G. Odom, Coach Bob Weathers, counselor Margie Rabby, Student Services Director Tom Hilbun, Student Housing Director L. D. "Buster" Stringfellow, and Financial Director John Putnam check out Maxine's brood in the back yard of the Weather's residence in Perkinston in October 1969. The administrators chose two--Max and Jabo--for future Perk mascots. They gave one to the owner of the male, sold one to a sporting goods salesman, and sold the last one to Vancleave High School. Sales proceeds went to fund a scholarship for a Vancleave student. Max died two years later, and Jabo succeeded his brother as Perk Mascot. According to Tommie Weathers, Jabo earned his name by "barking and talking all the time as a puppy. . . . We would have named him 'Jabber' but that was the name of the next door neighbor's cat. So we called him Jabo."

"Little Max," son of Maxine, poses with MGCJC cheerleader Mary Ann Smith circa 1970. Little Max died at age two and his brother Jabo succeeded him as Perk Mascot. Mary Ann (Smith) Davis Bond became Perkinston Campus choir director from Sept. 1988-Dec. 1990.

Jabo, Bicentennial Bulldog, poses behind Denson Hall in 1976.

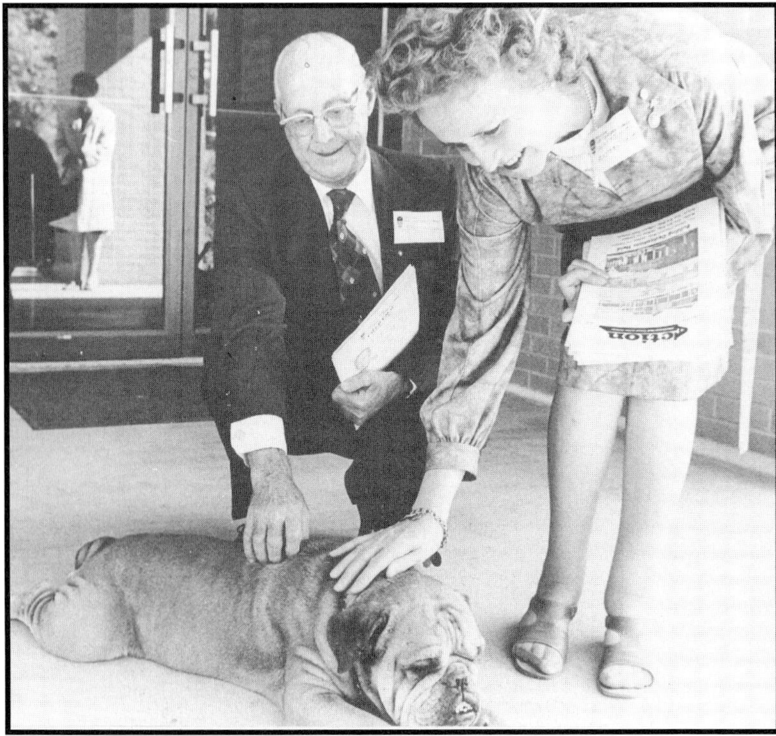

On homecoming day, November 6, 1977, Hersel and Sally McDaniel pet Jabo in front of the cafeteria. Hersel McDaniel had been the institution's first college graduate and the only college graduate of 1927.

In 1980, J. Edgar Hoover, ensconced in MGCJC President J. J. Hayden's chair, sees to college affairs. Gulf National Bank President Chun Sneed of Gulfport presented the one-year-old Hoover to the college in early December 1977, shortly after the death of Jabo. Hoover served as mascot until his death by automobile on April 30, 1984.

In fall 1985, one and one-half-years after Hoover's death, a new type of bulldog mascot appeared on the campus--a student in a bulldog suit. Six football cheerleaders surround Clark Hennigan, the first student Bulldog Mascot. Later the same year Gene Stanley performed as the Bulldog Mascot with the basketball cheerleaders. (From September 1979 until May 1991, the school fielded two sets of cheerleaders, one for football and one for basketball.) Photograph from <u>1986 Perkolator</u>, p. 55.

During the 1990 football season, student Bulldog Mascot Patrick Mithias sits astride fiberglass mascot Maxine in A. L. May Memorial Stadium. The fiberglass Maxine, which had stood guard atop Wentzell Center for many years, had suffered damage to its paws and ears during Hurricane Elena in September 1986. Removed to the stadium to await repairs which were never made, fiberglass Maxine became a fixture on the field and also a target for malefactors. On the night of September 29, 1992, two Perk students spotted masked intruders dressed in black entering A. L. May Memorial Stadium. The next morning Maxine was gone. The students said they "smelled a Rat." By whatever means the return of Maxine was effected. Two years later, fiberglass Maxine was removed to Weeks Hall for repair. In December 2000, she was still awaiting repair in Weeks Hall.

Moreover Carter Stewart, "Mo" for short, born July 7, 1991, reads the *Athletic Review* *at Perk shortly after becoming the college's first real bulldog mascot in nearly eight years. Alas, Mo moved to Moorhead and began rooting for the Trojans when Perkinston Campus Vice President Bobby Garvin became president of Mississippi Delta Junior College in summer 1992.*

Student Bulldog Mascot Dallas Crosby leads "Killer" who replaced Mo in 1995, along the track in A. L. May Memorial Stadium during a football game in fall 1996. Killer died in summer 1999. Photograph from *1997 Perkolator, p. 105.*

Mac at age three months. In October 2000 MGCCC Trustee Pat Descher and her son Greg presented the college with a three-month old English bulldog as its new official mascot. The new MGCCC mascot came from the same litter as "Bully," the new official mascot of Mississippi State University. Since the Deschers owned McDonald's franchises, the bulldog was, of course, christened "Mac." In 2000, the students referred to him as "Little Mac." If one might hazard a prediction, the dog will in time be called "Big Mac."

HIGGINBOTHAM REPORT: JUNIOR COLLEGE FOOTBALL SCORES 1926 - 2000

Gary Higginbotham, MGCJC Class of 1965, compiled the scores of the Perkinston institution's junior college football games from 1926 to 2000. He graciously consented to the use of this report for this work. The MGCCC archivist verified the junior college scores with the information at his disposal, which amounted to about 80 percent of the games. In many cases different newspapers gave conflicting scores for the same game. In some cases the same newspaper in different articles gave conflicting scores for the same game. In a few cases the same newspaper article gave two different scores for the same game. With that in mind, Higginbotham and the archivist agree that the following scores are complete and are as accurate as possible. The Higginbotham Report (related to junior college games) was first printed in the *MGCCC Athletic Review* in August 1998. That list was revised in 1999 and in 2000. The lists contained in those three *MGCCC Athletic Reviews* are incorrect and should not be used for reference. The name of the Perkinston institution changed several times from 1926 to 2000 with the term "Gulf Coast" achieving widespread use only after 1962. But in identifying the Bulldog scores in the Higginbotham Report the archivist elected to use the initials "GC" throughout. In the lists, homecoming games are identified by bold print.

Junior College	**Town**	**Team Name**
Hinds County	Raymond	Eagles
Itawamba County	Fulton	Indians
East Central	Decatur	Warriors
Sunflower County*(Miss. Delta)*	Moorhead	Trojans
Northeast	Booneville	Tigers
Pearl River	Poplarville	Wildcats
Jones County	Ellisville	Golden Devils/Bears
Copiah-Lincoln	Wesson	Wolves
Coahoma County	Clarksdale	Tigers
Tate County*(Northwest)*	Senatobia	Rangers
East Mississippi	Scooba	Lions
Southwest	Summit	Pilots/Bears
Holmes County	Goodman	Bulldogs
Leake County*(Defunct)*	Carthage	Unknown
Clarke*(Baptist Jr. Col.)(Defunct)*	Newton	Panthers

1926

Date		GC	Opponent	Opp.
Sept. 24	GC	32	Miss. Industrial Training School	0
Oct. 1	GC	69	Chamberlain Hunt Military Academy	0
Oct. 9	GC	0	Gulf Coast Military Academy	6
Oct. 15	GC	19	Jesuit High School(New Orleans)	7
Oct. 22	GC	3	Miss. State Teacher's College Varsity	26
Oct. 30	GC	0	Spring Hill High School(Mobile)	0
Nov. 5	GC	0	Pearl River Junior College	6
Nov. 13	GC	0	Clarke Junior College	17
Nov. 19	GC	6	Hinds County Junior College	3

Season Record: 4 wins - 4 losses - 1 tie Coach: W. C. "Bill" Denson

1927 State Champions

Date		GC	Opponent	Opp.
Oct. 1	GC	0	Miss. State Teacher's College Varsity	0
Oct. 8	GC	31	Holmes County Junior College	0
Oct. 17	GC	31	Mississippi College Freshmen	7
Oct. 29	GC	13	St. Stanislaus College	6
Nov. 5	GC	0	Pearl River Junior College	13
Nov. 12	GC	6	Clarke Junior College	6
Nov. 19	GC	25	Hinds County Junior College	0

Season record: 4 wins - 1 loss - 2 ties Coach: W. C. "Bill" Denson

1928

Date		GC	Opponent	Opp.
Oct. 5	GC	2	Miss. State Teacher's College Varsity	12
Oct. 13	GC	0	Copiah-Lincoln Junior College	19
Oct. 20	GC	6	Leake County Junior College	0
Oct. 27	GC	0	Clarke Junior College	37
Nov. 3	GC	13	Millsaps College Freshmen	13
Nov. 9	GC	0	Holmes County Junior College	12
Nov. 12	GC	0	Marion(Alabama) Institute	97
Nov. 17	GC	6	Pearl River Junior College	7
Nov. 24	GC	0	Hinds County Junior College	6

Season Record: 1 win - 7 losses - 1 tie Coach: W. C. "Bill" Denson

1929

Date		GC	Opponent	Opp.
Sept. 28	GC	27	Tate County Junior College	0
Oct. 5	GC	38	Jones County Junior College	0
Oct. 11	GC	0	Copiah-Lincoln Junior College	27
Oct. 19	GC	19	East Mississippi Junior College	13
Oct. 26	GC	7	Sunflower County Junior College	0
Nov. 2	GC	12	Leake County Junior College	6
Nov. 9	GC	7	Holmes County Junior College	12
Nov. 16	GC	0	Pearl River Junior College	20
Nov. 23	**GC**	**20**	**Hinds County Junior College**	**6**

Season Record: 6 wins - 3 losses - 0 ties Coach: Lee Roy Weeks

1930

Date		GC	Opponent	Opp.
Sept. 26	GC	7	Tate County Junior College	0
Oct. 3	GC	*0	Jones County Junior College (*Ruled out of the records)--not counted.*	*18
Oct. 10	GC	0	Copiah-Lincoln Junior College	34
Oct. 18	GC	0	East Mississippi Junior College	0
Oct. 25	GC	7	Sunflower County Junior College	33
Oct. 31	GC	13	Millsaps College Freshmen	13
Nov. 8	GC	6	Holmes County Junior College	6
Nov. 15	**GC**	**0**	**Pearl River Junior College**	**12**
Nov. 22	GC	0	Hinds County Junior College	19

Season Record: 1 win - 4 losses - 3 ties Coach: Lee Roy Weeks

1931

Date		GC	Opponent	Opp.
Sept. 26	GC	0	East Mississippi Junior College	12
Oct. 3	GC	6	Jones County Junior College	7
Oct. 9	GC	24	Clarke Junior College	0
Oct. 15	GC	13	Southwest Mississippi Junior College	6
Oct. 24	GC	0	East Central Mississippi Junior College	18
Oct. 30	GC	12	Miss. State Teacher's College Freshmen	6
Nov. 7	GC	0	Holmes County Junior College	13
Nov. 14	GC	7	Pearl River Junior College	37
Nov. 21	**GC**	**6**	**Hinds County Junior College**	**7**

Season Record: 3 wins - 6 losses - 0 ties Coach: Lee Roy Weeks

1932

Date		GC	Opponent	Opp.
Sept. 24	GC	0	East Mississippi Junior College	7
Oct. 1	GC	0	Jones County Junior College	0
Oct. 8	GC	19	Clarke Junior College	0
Oct. 15	GC	0	Southwest Mississippi Junior College	6
Oct. 22	GC	0	East Central Mississippi Junior College	42
Oct. 28	GC	0	Miss. State Teacher's College Freshmen	0
Nov. 5	GC	0	Holmes County Junior College	33
Nov. 12	**GC**	**0**	**Pearl River Junior College**	**13**
Nov. 19	GC	6	Spring Hill College Freshmen	33

Season Record: 1 win - 6 losses - 2 ties Coach: Lee Roy Weeks

1933

Date		GC	Opponent	Opp.
Sept. 23	GC	12	East Mississippi Junior College	18
Sept. 30	GC	0	Jones County Junior College	6
Oct. 7	GC	35	Clarke Junior College	0
Oct. 14	GC	6	Southwest Mississippi Junior College	6
Oct. 21	GC	0	East Central Mississippi Junior College	12
Oct. 28	**GC**	**33**	**Millsaps College Freshmen**	**12**
Nov. 4	GC	21	Holmes County Junior College	20
Nov. 11	GC	0	Pearl River Junior College	28
Nov. 17	GC	6	Spring Hill College Freshmen(Mobile)	6

Season Record: 3 wins - 4 losses - 2 ties Coach: C. B. "Pluck" Berry

1934

Date		GC	Opponent	Opp.
Sept. 22	GC	7	East Mississippi Junior College	7
Sept. 28	GC	6	Jones County Junior College	19
Oct. 6	GC	26	Clarke Junior College	0
Oct. 11	GC	38	Southwest Mississippi Junior College	6
Oct. 20	GC	7	Mississippi College Freshmen	14
Oct. 26	GC	7	Miss. State Teacher's College Freshmen	0
Nov. 2	GC	7	Holmes County Junior College	19
Nov. 10	**GC**	**12**	**Pearl River Junior College**	**19**
Nov. 16	GC	31	Spring Hill College Freshmen	0

Season Record: 4 wins - 4 losses - 1 tie Coach: C. B. "Pluck" Berry

1935

Date		GC	Opponent	Opp.
Sept. 28	GC	6	Jones County Junior College	0
Oct. 4	GC	7	Southwest Mississippi Junior College	7
Oct. 12	GC	26	Mississippi College Reserves	0
Oct. 19	GC	40	East Mississippi Junior College	6
Oct. 26	GC	18	Mississippi College Freshmen	0
Nov. 2	**--**		**Holmes County Junior College (Game cancelled)**	
Nov. 9	GC	14	Pearl River Junior College	0

Season Record: 5 wins - 0 losses - 1 tie Coach: C. B. "Pluck" Berry

1936 State Champions *(*Championship stripped from Holmes for fielding ineligible players. The October 30 game counted as a win for Perkinston.)*

Date		GC	Opponent	Opp
Sept. 25	GC	12	Jones County Junior College	0
Oct. 3	GC	13	Southwest Mississippi Junior College	12
Oct. 10	GC	7	Spring Hill College Freshmen	6
Oct. 17	GC	6	East Mississippi Junior College	6
Oct. 24	GC	12	Millsaps College Freshmen	7
Oct. 30	GC	*12	Holmes County Junior College	*19
Nov. 7	GC	33	Mississippi College Freshmen	18
Nov. 21	GC	**27**	**Pearl River Junior College**	**6**

Season Record: 7 wins - 0 loss - 1 tie Coach: C.B. "Pluck" Berry

1937

Date		GC	Opponent	Opp
Sept. 25	GC	7	Jones County Junior College	7
Oct. 4	GC	7	Southwest Mississippi Junior College	0
Oct. 9	GC	14	Spring Hill College Freshmen	0
Oct. 16	GC	13	East Mississippi Junior College	6
Oct. 23	GC	6	Millsaps College Freshmen	0
Oct. 30	**GC**	**0**	**Holmes County Junior College**	**34**
Nov. 6	GC	0	Mississippi College Freshmen	25
Nov. 19	GC	0	Pearl River Junior College	6

Season Record: 4 wins - 3 losses - 1 tie Coach: Albert I. "Rex" Rexinger

1938

Date		GC	Opponent	Opp
Sept. 24	GC	0	Jones County Junior College	3
Oct. 1	GC	25	Southwest Mississippi Junior College	0
Oct. 7	GC	0	Millsaps College Freshmen	7
Oct. 15	GC	31	East Mississippi Junior College	0
Oct. 22	GC	14	Spring Hill College Freshmen	0
Oct. 28	GC	12	Holmes County Junior College	6
Nov. 4	GC	49	Mississippi College Freshmen	0
Nov. 19	GC	**0**	**Pearl River Junior College**	**19**

Season Record: 5 wins - 3 losses - 0 ties Coach: Albert I. "Rex" Rexinger

1939

Date		GC	Opponent	Opp
Sept. 22	GC	13	Southwest Mississippi Junior College	0
Sept. 29	GC	6	Jones County Junior College	6
Oct. 5	GC	0	Millsaps College Freshmen	12
Oct. 14	GC	7	East Mississippi Junior College	0
Oct. 20	GC	0	Southeastern Louisiana College Freshmen	12
Oct. 28	GC	**7**	**Holmes County Junior College**	**18**
Nov. 4	GC	27	Mississippi College Freshmen	0
Nov. 10	GC	27	Spring Hill College Freshmen	6
Nov. 17	GC	7	Pearl River Junior College	0

Season Record: 5 wins - 3 losses - 1 tie Coach: Albert I. "Rex" Rexinger

1940

Date		GC	Opponent	Opp
Sept. 20	GC	24	Mississippi College Freshmen	0
Sept. 28	GC	6	Jones County Junior College	13
Oct. 4	GC	6	Southeastern Louisiana College Freshmen	12
Oct. 12	GC	0	East Mississippi Junior College	13
Oct. 19	GC	**39**	**Southwest Mississippi Junior College**	**12**
Oct. 25	GC	6	Copiah-Lincoln Junior College	12
Nov. 1	GC	0	Holmes County Junior College	26
Nov. 8	GC	27	Spring Hill College Freshmen	6
Nov. 15	GC	0	Pearl River Junior College	14

Season Record: 3 wins - 6 losses - 0 ties Coach: Albert I. "Rex" Rexinger

1941

Date		GC	Opponent	Opp
Sept. 19	GC	13	Mississippi College Freshmen	6
Sept. 26	GC	6	Jones County Junior College	24
Oct. 3	GC	19	Southeastern Louisiana College Freshmen	14
Oct. 11	GC	6	East Mississippi Junior College	6
Oct. 16	GC	14	Southwest Mississippi Junior College	6
Oct. 25	GC	**6**	**Copiah-Lincoln Junior College**	**51**
Oct. 31	GC	0	Holmes County Junior College	0
Nov. 14	GC	20	Pearl River Junior College	29
Nov. 28	GC	38	166th Field Artillery (Camp Shelby)	0

Season Record: 4 wins - 3 losses - 2 ties Coach: Albert I. "Rex" Rexinger

1942 State Champions

Date		GC	Opponent	Opp
Sept. 26	GC	0	Jones County Junior College	0
Oct. 2	GC	12	Holmes County Junior College	6
Oct. 9	GC	30	Hinds County College	6
Oct. 23	GC	31	Copiah-Lincoln Junior College	6
Oct. 30	GC	**20**	**East Central Mississippi Junior College**	**6**
Nov. 6	GC	27	East Mississippi Junior College	0
Nov. 13	GC	45	Hattiesburg Air Base	0

Season Record: 6 wins - 0 losses - 1 tie Coach: George B. Westerfield

1943

Perkinston Junior College did not field a football team for the 1943 football season. Lack of player manpower, travel restrictions, limitation of playing time to day games and so on all played a part in the decision not to field a football team.

1944

Date		GC	Opponent	Opp
Oct. 6	GC	8	Jones County Junior College	19
Oct. 13	GC	13	Pearl River Junior College	6
Oct. 20	GC	0	Hinds County Junior College	27
Nov. 3	GC	**7**	**Copiah-Lincoln Junior College**	**19**
Nov. 10	GC	6	Jones County Junior College	13
Nov. 17	GC	7	Pearl River Junior College	7

Season Record: 1 win - 4 losses - 1 tie Coach: R. T. Walker

1945

Date		GC	Opponent	Opp
Unknown	GC	0	Merchant Marine Base	0
Sept. 28	GC	12	East Central Mississippi Junior College	0
Oct. 5	GC	0	Copiah-Lincoln Junior College	0
Oct. 11	GC	32	Pearl River Junior College	6
Oct. 19	**GC**	**0**	**Hinds County Junior College**	**31**
Oct. 26	GC	6	Holmes County Junior College	24
Nov. 3	GC	13	Merchant Marine Base	13
Nov. 9	GC	6	Pearl River Junior College	0
Nov. 16	GC	0	Jones County Junior College	14

Season Record: 3 wins - 3 losses - 3 ties Coach: Louis D. Megehee

1946

Date		GC	Opponent	Opp
Sept. 20	GC	6	Sunflower County Junior College	0
Sept. 27	GC	2	East Central Mississippi Junior College	6
Oct. 4	GC	0	Jones County Junior College	12
Oct. 11	GC	0	Holmes County Junior College	20
Oct. 18	GC	0	Southwest Mississippi Junior College	14
Oct. 26	**GC**	**13**	**Hinds County Junior College**	**20**
Nov. 1	GC	18	East Mississippi Junior College	0
Nov. 8	GC	13	Northwest Mississippi Junior College	0
Nov. 16	GC	7	Copiah-Lincoln Junior College	25
Nov. 22	GC	6	Pearl River Junior College	7

Season Record: 3 wins - 7 losses - 0 ties Coach: George B. Westerfield

1947

Date		GC	Opponent	Opp
Sept. 18	GC	18	East Central Mississippi Junior College	0
Sept. 26	GC	0	Jones County Junior College	27
Oct. 4	GC	27	Holmes County Junior College	7
Oct. 11	GC	42	Southwest Mississippi Junior College	6
Oct. 18	GC	21	Hinds County Junior College	34
Oct. 25	**GC**	**20**	**East Mississippi Junior College**	**0**
Oct. 30	GC	13	Northwest Mississippi Junior College	0
Nov. 6	GC	13	Copiah-Lincoln Jr. College	0
Nov. 13	GC	0	Pearl River Junior College	2
Nov. 25	GC	26	Sunflower County Junior College	14
Dec. 5	GC	25	Pearl River Junior College (Tung Bowl)	6

Season Record: 8 wins - 3 losses - 0 ties Coach: Marvin "Red" Campbell

1948 State Champions and Co-National Champions

Date		GC	Opponent	Opp
Sept. 18	GC	19	Jones County Junior College	7
Sept. 24	GC	14	Holmes County Junior College	7
Oct. 2	GC	33	Southwest Mississippi Junior College	7
Oct. 8	GC	21	Hinds County Junior College	6
Oct. 14	GC	13	East Mississippi Junior College	6
Oct. 22	GC	39	Northwest Mississippi Junior College	7
Oct. 29	GC	19	Copiah-Lincoln Junior College	0
Nov. 6	**GC**	**20**	**Pearl River Junior College**	**19**
Nov. 11	GC	34	Tulane University Freshmen(New Orleans)	20
Nov. 19	GC	27	Sunflower County Junior College	6
Nov. 23	GC	26	East Central Mississippi Junior College	7
Dec. 4	GC	27	Jones County Junior College (Laurel Lions Bowl)	13

Season Record: 12 wins - 0 losses - 0 ties Coach: Marvin "Red" Campbell

1949

Date		GC	Opponent	Opp
Sept. 17	GC	20	Jones County Junior College	7
Sept. 22	GC	7	Holmes County Junior College	27
Oct. 1	GC	13	Southwest Mississippi Junior College	13
Oct. 7	GC	14	Hinds County Junior College	13
Oct. 15	GC	27	East Mississippi Junior College	6
Oct. 21	GC	12	Northwest Mississippi Junior College	0
Oct. 29	GC	**21**	**Copiah-Lincoln Junior College**	**6**
Nov. 5	GC	7	Pearl River Junior College	20
Nov. 12	GC	40	Northeast Mississippi Junior College	15
Nov. 18	GC	20	Sunflower County Junior College	0
Nov. 23	GC	21	East Central Mississippi Junior College	19
Dec. 10	GC	14	East Central Miss. Jr. College (Laurel Lions Bowl)	12

Season Record: 9 wins - 2 losses - 1 tie Coach: Nolan E. Tollett

1950

Date		GC	Opponent	Opp
Sept. 16	GC	0	Jones County Junior College	12
Sept. 23	GC	0	Holmes County Junior College	27
Sept. 30	GC	6	Southwest Mississippi Junior College	25
Oct. 7	GC	18	Hinds County Junior College	18
Oct. 13	GC	21	East Mississippi Junior College	61
Oct. 21	**GC**	**13**	**Francis T. Nicholls Junior College (Thibodaux, Louisiana)**	**6**
Oct. 28	GC	27	Copiah-Lincoln Junior College	6
Nov. 4	GC	0	Pearl River Junior College	33
Nov. 11	GC	20	Northeast Mississippi Junior College	20
Nov. 22	GC	7	East Central Mississippi Junior College	46

Season Record: 2 wins - 6 losses - 2 ties Coach: Nolan E. Tollett

1951

Date		GC	Opponent	Opp
Sept. 15	GC	6	Jones County Junior College	33
Sept. 20	GC	7	Holmes County Junior College	10
Sept. 29	GC	20	Southwest Mississippi Junior College	13
Oct. 6	GC	0	Hinds County Junior College	41
Oct. 13	**GC**	**31**	**East Mississippi Junior College**	**7**
Oct. 20	GC	7	Northeast Mississippi Junior College	19
Oct. 27	GC	7	Copiah-Lincoln Junior College	20
Nov. 3	GC	0	Pearl River Junior College	46
Nov. 13	GC	24	Biloxi Athletic Club ("Galloping Gaels")	13
Nov. 20	GC	0	East Central Mississippi Junior College	14

Season Record: 3 wins - 7 losses - 0 ties Coach: Robert Whitman

1952

Date		GC	Opponent	Opp.
Sept. 13	GC	9	Jones County Junior College	0
Sept. 20	GC	12	Holmes County Junior College	7
Sept. 27	GC	6	Southwest Mississippi Junior College	12
Oct. 4	GC	13	Hinds County Junior College	7
Oct. 11	GC	19	East Mississippi Junior College	7
Oct. 18	**GC**	**41**	**Northeast Mississippi Junior College**	**13**
Oct. 25	GC	14	Copiah-Lincoln Junior College	25
Nov. 1	GC	6	Pearl River Junior College	38
Nov. 7	GC	26	Itawamba Junior College	13
Nov. 22	GC	13	East Central Mississippi Junior College	6

Season Record: 7 wins - 3 losses - 0 ties Coach: Harold White

1953

Date		GC	Opponent	Opp.
Sept. 12	GC	22	Jones County Junior College	13
Sept. 17	GC	31	Holmes County Junior College	12
Sept. 26	GC	20	Southwest Mississippi Junior College	25
Oct. 3	GC	6	Hinds County Junior College	21
Oct. 10	**GC**	**35**	**East Mississippi Junior College**	**13**
Oct. 17	GC	17	Northeast Mississippi Junior College	0
Oct. 24	GC	14	Copiah-Lincoln Junior College	0
Oct. 31	GC	0	Pearl River Junior College	22
Nov. 5	GC	32	Itawamba Junior College	13
Nov. 20	GC	23	East Central Mississippi Junior College	6
Dec. 5	GC	6	Co-Lin Junior College (Laurel Lions Bowl	6

Season record: 7 wins - 3 losses - 1 ties Coach: Harold White

1954

Date		GC	Opponent	Opp.
Sept. 11	GC	7	Jones County Junior College	20
Sept. 25	GC	20	Hinds County Junior College	31
Oct. 2	GC	18	Tulane University Freshmen	19
Oct. 9	GC	8	Southwest Mississippi Junior College	0
Oct. 16	GC	7	Pearl River Junior College	12
Oct. 23	**GC**	**13**	**Holmes County Junior College**	**12**
Oct. 28	GC	6	Tyler (Texas) Junior College	6
Nov. 6	GC	13	Copiah-Lincoln Junior College	0
Nov. 11	GC	12	Itawamba Junior College	6

Season Record: 4 wins - 4 losses - 1 tie Coach: Harold White

1955

Date		GC	Opponent	Opp.
Sept. 10	GC	0	Jones County Junior College	32
Sept. 16	GC	6	Little Rock(Arkansas) College	33
Sept. 24	GC	7	Hinds County Junior College	14
Oct. 8	**GC**	**6**	**Southwest Mississippi Junior College**	**27**
Oct. 15	GC	6	Pearl River Junior College	13
Oct. 22	GC	12	Holmes County Junior College	14
Oct. 27	GC	13	Tyler (Texas) Junior College	26
Nov. 5	GC	12	Copiah-Lincoln Junior College	7
Nov. 10	GC	25	Itawamba Junior College	0

Season Record: 2 wins - 7 losses - 0 ties Coach: Harold White

1956

Date		GC	Opponent	Opp.
Sept. 8	GC	6	Jones County Junior College	19
Sept. 15	GC	45	Holmes County Junior College	7
Sept. 22	GC	7	Hinds County Junior College	12
Sept. 29	GC	35	Texarkana (Texas) Junior College	7
Oct. 6	GC	13	Southwest Mississippi Junior College	7
Oct. 13	**GC**	**0**	**Pearl River Junior College**	**21**
Oct. 18	GC	12	Kilgore (Texas) Junior College	0
Oct. 25	GC	0	Tyler (Texas) Junior College	39
Nov. 3	GC	13	Copiah-Lincoln Junior College	21
Nov. 10	GC	19	Itawamba Junior College	20

Season Record: 4 wins - 6 losses - 0 ties Coach: Harold White

1957

Date		GC	Opponent	Opp.
Sept. 7	GC	7	Jones County Junior College	7
Sept. 12	GC	6	Holmes County Junior College	13
Sept. 21	GC	0	Hinds County Junior College	27
Sept. 26	GC	7	Texarkana (Texas) Junior College	12
Oct. 5	**GC**	**19**	**Southwest Mississippi Junior College**	**0**
Oct. 12	GC	13	Pearl River Junior College	26
Oct. 17	GC	0	Kilgore (Texas) Junior College	22
Oct. 24	GC	6	Tyler (Texas) Junior College	20
Nov. 2	GC	12	Copiah-Lincoln Junior College	14
Nov. 7	GC	20	Itawamba Junior College	20

Season Record: 1 win - 7 losses - 2 ties Coach: Leo P. Jones

1958

Date		GC	Opponent	Opp.
Sept. 6	GC	13	Jones County Junior College	8
Sept. 13	GC	14	Holmes County Junior College	6
Sept. 20	GC	13	Hinds County Junior College	0
Sept. 25	GC	0	Kilgore (Texas) Junior College	14
Oct. 4	GC	0	Southwest Mississippi Junior College	6
Oct. 11	**GC**	**6**	**Pearl River Junior College**	**12**
Oct. 18	GC	22	Itawamba Junior College	12
Oct. 25	GC	21	Northwest Mississippi Junior. College	8
Nov. 1	GC	30	Copiah-Lincoln Junior College	7
Nov. 8	GC	30	Sunflower County Junior College	12

Season Record: 7 wins - 3 losses - 0 ties Coach: Leo P. Jones

1959

Date		GC	Opponent	Opp.
Sept. 5	GC	0	Jones County Junior College	10
Sept. 10	GC	0	Holmes County Junior College	22
Sept. 19	GC	18	Hinds County Junior College	12
Sept. 26	GC	18	Kilgore (Texas) Junior College	20
Oct. 1	GC	29	Southwest Mississippi Junior College	6
Oct. 10	GC	7	Pearl River Junior College	24
Oct. 17	GC	6	Texarkana (Texas) Junior College	21
Oct. 24	**GC**	**32**	**Northwest Mississippi Junior College**	**6**
Oct. 29	GC	7	Copiah-Lincoln Junior College	6
Nov. 5	GC	36	Sunflower County Junior College	14

Season Record: 5 wins - 5 losses - 0 ties Coach: Ed Evans

1960

Date		GC	Opponent	Opp.
Sept. 10	GC	7	Mississippi Delta Junior College	16
Sept. 17	GC	6	Copiah-Lincoln Junior College	22
Sept. 22	GC	13	Holmes County Junior College	12
Sept. 30	GC	0	Tulane University Freshmen	32
Oct. 8	GC	8	East Mississippi Junior College	35
Oct. 15	GC	8	Jones County Junior College	15
Oct. 22	GC	12	Northwest Mississippi Junior College	22
Oct. 29	**GC**	**6**	**Hinds County Junior College**	**7**
Nov. 5	GC	6	East Central Mississippi Junior College	6
Nov. 12	GC	12	Pearl River Junior College	32
Nov. 19	GC	6	Southwest Mississippi Junior College	0

Season Record: 2 wins - 8 losses - 1 tie Coach: Ed Evans

1961

Date		GC	Opponent	Opp.
Sept. 9	GC	13	Mississippi Delta Junior College	14
Sept. 16	GC	12	Copiah-Lincoln Junior College	6
Sept. 21	GC	0	Holmes County Junior College	14
Sept. 28	GC	14	Tulane University Freshmen	13
Oct. 7	GC	0	East Mississippi Junior College	49
Oct. 14	GC	0	Jones County Junior College	6
Oct. 21	GC	6	Northwest Mississippi Junior College	20
Oct. 28	GC	6	Hinds County Junior College	20
Nov. 2	GC	7	East Central Mississippi Junior College	12
Nov. 11	**GC**	**6**	**Pearl River Junior College**	**60**
Nov. 16	GC	12	Southwest Mississippi Junior College	43

Season Record: 2 wins - 9 losses - 0 ties Coach: Ed Evans

1962

Date		GC	Opponent	Opp.
Sept. 6	GC	18	Holmes County Junior College	6
Sept. 15	GC	42	Hinds County Junior College	6
Sept. 22	GC	29	Northwest Mississippi Junior College	14
Sept. 29	GC	20	Pearl River Junior College	22
Oct. 6	GC	27	East Central Mississippi Junior College	6
Oct. 13	**GC**	**27**	**Itawamba Junior College**	**6**
Oct. 27	GC	7	Copiah-Lincoln Junior College	28
Nov. 1	GC	13	East Mississippi Junior College	8
Nov. 10	GC	7	Jones County Junior College	18
Nov. 15	GC	77	Southwest Mississippi Junior College	6
Nov. 22	GC	0	Navarro(Texas) Junior College (Hospitality Bowl)	3

Season Record: 7 wins - 4 losses - 0 ties Coach: Harold Wesson

1963

Date		GC	Opponent	Opp.
Sept. 7	GC	27	Holmes County Junior College	7
Sept. 12	GC	27	Hinds County Junior College	12
Sept. 19	GC	6	Northwest Mississippi Junior College	21
Sept. 28	GC	20	Pearl River Junior College	24
Oct. 5	GC	7	East Central Mississippi Junior College	6
Oct. 12	GC	21	Itawamba Junior College	26
Oct. 17	GC	21	University of Southern Mississippi Freshmen	13
Oct. 26	**GC**	**7**	**Copiah-Lincoln Junior College**	**0**
Nov. 2	GC	47	East Mississippi Junior College	18
Nov. 9	GC	6	Jones County Junior College	20
Nov. 14	GC	27	Southwest Mississippi Junior College	8

Season Record: 7 wins - 4 losses - 0 ties Coach: Harold Wesson

1964

Date		GC	Opponent	Opp.
Sept. 12	GC	13	Mississippi Delta Junior College	0
Sept. 19	GC	28	Copiah-Lincoln Junior College	16
Sept. 24	GC	14	East Mississippi Junior College	34
Oct. 3	GC	10	Hinds County Junior College	7
Oct. 10	GC	41	East Central Mississippi Junior College	0
Oct. 24	GC	27	Itawamba Junior College	8
Oct. 31	GC	0	Pearl River Junior College	30
Nov. 7	**GC**	**0**	**Northwest Mississippi Junior College**	**27**
Nov. 14	GC	32	Southwest Mississippi Junior College	28
Nov. 21	GC	6	Jones County Junior College	14

Season Record: 6 wins - 4 losses - 0 ties Coach: Harold Wesson

1965

Date		GC	Opponent	Opp.
Sept. 11	GC	14	Mississippi Delta Junior College	0
Sept. 18	GC	7	Copiah-Lincoln Junior College	10
Sept. 25	GC	35	East Mississippi Junior College	7
Oct. 2	GC	23	Hinds County Junior College	0
Oct. 9	**GC**	**18**	**East Central Junior College**	**14**
Oct. 23	GC	21	Itawamba Junior College	14
Oct. 28	GC	6	Pearl River Junior College	20
Nov. 6	GC	14	Northwest Mississippi Junior College	27
Nov. 13	GC	12	Southwest Mississippi Junior College	7
Nov. 20	GC	6	Jones County Junior College	8

Season Record: 6 wins - 4 losses - 0 ties Coach: Harold Wesson

1966 State Champions

Aug. 27	GC	14	Pas-Point "Steelers" (Semi Pro Team of Pascagoula, Moss Point)	6
Sept. 10	GC	33	East Central Mississippi Junior College	20
Sept. 15	GC	50	Hinds County Junior College	28
Sept. 22	GC	14	East Mississippi Junior College	10
Oct. 1	GC	14	Copiah-Lincoln Junior College	6
Oct. 8	GC	40	Mississippi Delta Junior College	13
Oct. 15	GC	34	Southwest Mississippi Junior College	7
Oct. 22	**GC**	**14**	**Itawamba Junior College**	**15**
Nov. 3	GC	9	Holmes County Junior College	10
Nov. 12	GC	33	Pearl River Junior College	0
Nov. 19	GC	21	Jones County Junior College	14
Dec. 3	GC	21	Navarro Junior College (Shrine Bowl)	7

Season Record: 10 wins - 2 losses - 0 ties Coach: George Sekul

1967 State Champions

Sept. 9	GC	54	East Central Mississippi Junior College	17
Sept. 16	GC	33	Hinds County Junior College	0
Sept. 23	GC	13	East Mississippi Junior College	14
Sept. 28	GC	41	Copiah-Lincoln Junior College	20
Oct. 7	GC	22	Mississippi Delta Junior College	14
Oct. 14	**GC**	**22**	**Southwest Mississippi Junior College**	**7**
Oct. 21	GC	59	Itawamba Junior College	34
Oct. 26	GC	14	Marion Institute	26
Nov. 4	GC	36	Holmes County Junior College	7
Nov. 11	GC	27	Pearl River Junior College	7
Nov. 18	GC	39	Jones County Junior College	21

Season Record: 9 wins - 2 losses - 0 ties Coach: George Sekul

1968

Sept. 14	GC	31	East Mississippi Junior College	12
Sept. 21	GC	28	Itawamba Junior College	0
Sept. 28	GC	51	Hinds County Junior College	6
Oct. 5	GC	7	Pearl River Junior College	6
Oct. 12	**GC**	**24**	**Southwest Mississippi Junior College**	**0**
Oct. 17	GC	28	Marion Institute	16
Oct. 26	GC	14	Mississippi Delta Junior College	0
Nov. 2	GC	44	Copiah-Lincoln Junior College	0
Nov. 9	GC	7	Jones County Junior College	28
Nov. 14	GC	43	Northeast Mississippi Junior College	7

Season Record: 9 wins - 1 loss - 0 ties Coach: George Sekul

1969

Sept. 13	GC	7	East Mississippi Junior College	10
Sept. 20	GC	14	Itawamba Junior College	0
Sept. 25	GC	38	Hinds County Junior College	22
Oct. 4	GC	0	Pearl River Junior College	35
Oct. 9	GC	21	Southwest Mississippi Junior College	6
Oct. 18	GC	17	Marion Institute	14
Oct. 25	**GC**	**21**	**Mississippi Delta Junior College**	**37**
Oct. 30	GC	26	Copiah-Lincoln Junior College	10
Nov. 8	GC	14	Jones County Junior College	3
Nov. 13	GC	14	Northeast Mississippi Junior College	28
Nov. 21	GC	31	University of Southern Mississippi Freshmen	20

Season Record: 7 wins - 4 losses - 0 ties Coach: George Sekul

1970

Sept. 5	GC	0	Marion Institute	14
Sept. 10	GC	33	Itawamba Junior College	13
Sept. 19	GC	30	Copiah-Lincoln Junior College	6
Sept. 26	GC	0	Jones County Junior College	0
Oct. 3	GC	0	Pearl River Junior College	12
Oct. 8	GC	31	East Central Mississippi Junior College	3
Oct. 17	GC	28	Holmes County Junior College	25
Oct. 24	GC	23	East Mississippi Junior College	0
Oct. 31	GC	52	University of Southern Mississippi Freshmen	14
Nov. 7	**GC**	**28**	**Southwest Mississippi Junior College**	**21**
Nov. 14	GC	21	Hinds County Junior College	9
Nov. 21	GC	24	Mississippi Delta Junior College	7

Season Record: 9 wins - 2 losses - 1 tie Coach: George Sekul

1971 State Champions and National Champions

Sept. 4	GC	28	Itawamba Junior College	21
Sept. 11	GC	30	Copiah-Lincoln Junior College	7
Sept. 18	GC	27	Jones County Junior College	8
Sept. 25	GC	37	Pearl River Junior College	21
Oct. 2	GC	28	East Central Mississippi Junior College	27
Oct. 7	GC	36	Holmes County Junior College	7
Oct. 16	GC	33	East Mississippi Junior College	13
Oct. 28	GC	36	Southwest Mississippi Junior College	8
Nov. 6	GC	**62**	**Hinds County Junior College**	**7**
Nov. 20	GC	26	Miss. Delta Jr. College (State Championship Game)	14
Dec. 3	GC	22	Ft. Scott (Kansas) Jr. College (Shrine Bowl)	13

Season Record: 11 wins - 0 losses - 0 ties Coach: George Sekul

1972

Sept. 2	GC	35	Northeast Mississippi Junior College	24
Sept. 7	GC	24	Southwest Mississippi Junior College	0
Sept. 15	GC	27	East Mississippi Junior College	7
Sept. 23	GC	24	Copiah-Lincoln Junior College	9
Sept. 30	GC	21	Pearl River Junior College	22
Oct. 14	GC	43	East Central Mississippi Junior College	9
Oct. 21	**GC**	**29**	**Hinds County Junior College**	**13**
Oct. 28	GC	9	Jones County Junior College	14
Nov. 4	GC	41	Marion Institute	28
Nov. 11	GC	14	Itawamba Junior College	13

Season Record: 8 wins - 2 losses - 0 ties Coach: George Sekul

1973

Sept. 1	GC	34	Northeast Mississippi Junior College	6
Sept. 8	GC	34	Southwest Mississippi Junior College	0
Sept. 15	GC	28	East Mississippi Junior College	7
Sept. 20	GC	14	Copiah-Lincoln Junior College	0
Sept. 29	GC	3	Pearl River Junior College	10
Oct. 11	GC	41	East Central Mississippi Junior College	0
Oct. 20	GC	17	Hinds County Junior College	7
Oct. 27	GC	29	Jones County Junior College	10
Nov. 3	GC	28	Marion Institute	14
Nov. 10	**GC**	**62**	**Itawamba Junior College**	**7**

Season Record: 9 wins - 1 loss - 0 ties Coach: George Sekul

1974 State Champions

Sept. 7	GC	21	Holmes County Junior College	0
Sept. 14	GC	14	Jones County Junior College	0
Sept. 21	GC	7	East Mississippi Junior College	14
Sept. 28	GC	10	Hinds County Junior College	16
Oct. 5	GC	10	Mississippi Delta Junior College	13
Oct. 12	GC	21	Pearl River Junior College	0
Oct. 19	GC	20	Southwest Mississippi Junior College	10
Oct. 26	GC	6	Northwest Mississippi Junior College	13
Nov. 9	**GC**	**28**	**Copiah-Lincoln Junior College**	**13**
Nov. 14	GC	13	East Central Mississippi Junior College	30
Nov. 22	GC	10	Itawamba Jr. College (State Championship Game)	6

Season Record: 6 wins - 5 losses - 0 ties Coach: George Sekul

1975

Sept. 6	GC	7	Holmes County Junior College	0
Sept. 13	GC	25	Jones County Junior College	7
Sept. 20	GC	21	East Mississippi Junior College	0
Sept. 25	GC	40	Hinds County Junior College	6
Oct. 4	GC	47	Mississippi Delta Junior. College	0
Oct. 11	GC	36	Pearl River Junior College	29
Oct. 18	GC	14	Southwest Mississippi Junior College	0
Oct. 25	**GC**	**18**	**Northwest Mississippi Junior College**	**6**
Nov. 1	GC	35	Coahoma County Junior College	0
Nov. 6	GC	6	Copiah-Lincoln Junior College	9
Nov. 13	GC	28	East Central Mississippi Junior College	12
Nov. 21	GC	12	Itawamba Jr. College (State Championship Game)	21

Season Record: 10 wins - 2 losses - 0 ties Coach: George Sekul

1976

Sept. 11	GC	35	Coahoma Junior College	0
Sept. 18	GC	24	Northeast Mississippi Junior College	6
Sept. 25	GC	0	East Central Mississippi Junior College	0
Oct. 2	GC	17	Southwest Mississippi Junior College	7
Oct. 9	GC	0	Northwest Mississippi Junior College	10
Oct. 16	GC	3	Pearl River Junior College	14
Oct. 21	GC	10	Jones County Junior College	7
Oct. 30	GC	27	Copiah-Lincoln Junior College	13
Nov. 6	**GC**	**27**	**Hinds County Junior College**	**6**
Nov. 13	GC	17	Itawamba Junior College	18

Season Record: 6 wins - 3 losses - 1 tie Coach: George Sekul

1977

Sept. 3	GC	27	Coahoma County Junior College	0
Sept. 10	GC	7	Northeast Mississippi Junior College	32
Sept. 17	GC	10	East Central Mississippi Junior College	0
Sept. 24	GC	9	Southwest Mississippi Junior College	0
Sept. 29	GC	7	Northwest Mississippi Junior College	7
Oct. 8	GC	21	Pearl River Junior College	20
Oct. 15	GC	6	Jones County Junior College	7
Oct. 22	GC	3	Copiah-Lincoln Junior College	0
Oct. 27	GC	17	Hinds County Junior College	6
Nov. 5	**GC**	**17**	**Itawamba Junior College**	**6**

Season Record: 7 wins - 2 losses - 1 tie Coach: George Sekul

1978

Sept. 2	GC	19	Itawamba Junior College	7
Sept. 9	GC	26	East Central Mississippi Junior College	16
Sept. 16	GC	21	Southwest Mississippi Junior College	12
Sept. 23	GC	24	Mississippi Delta Junior College	10
Sept. 28	GC	10	Northeast Mississippi Junior College	6
Oct. 7	GC	21	Pearl River Junior College	6
Oct. 14	GC	6	Jones County Junior College	7
Oct. 21	GC	29	Hinds County Junior College	0
Oct. 28	GC	**17**	**Copiah-Lincoln Junior College**	**10**
Nov. 4	GC	40	Coahoma County Junior College	7

Season Record: 9 wins - 1 loss - 0 ties Coach: George Sekul

1979

Sept. 1	GC	9	Itawamba Junior College .7
Sept. 8	GC	14	East Central Mississippi Junior College 9
Sept. 15	--		Southwest Mississippi Junior College (Game Cancelled)
Sept. 22	GC	0	Mississippi Delta Junior College 10
Sept. 29	GC	27	Northeast Mississippi Junior College 9
Oct. 6	GC	28	Pearl River Junior College 23
Oct. 13	GC	20	Jones County Junior College 24
Oct. 20	GC	7	Hinds County Junior College 17
Oct. 27	GC	21	Copiah-Lincoln Junior College 28
Nov. 3	**GC**	**40**	**Coahoma County Junior College 10**
Nov. 8	GC	14	Southwest Mississippi Jr. College (Rescheduled) . .0
Nov. 17	GC	7	Itawamba Jr. College (Play-off Game) 0
Nov. 24	GC	0	Jones County Jr. College (State Champ. Game) . . .12

Season Record: 7 wins - 5 losses - 0 ties Coach: George Sekul

1980 State Champions

Sept. 4	GC	33	Northwest Mississippi Junior College 17
Sept. 13	GC	3	Southwest Mississippi Junior College 7
Sept. 20	GC	15	East Mississippi Junior College 7
Sept. 27	GC	31	East Central Mississippi Junior College 6
Oct. 4	GC	35	Mississippi Delta Junior College 6
Oct. 11	GC	28	Pearl River Junior College 10
Oct. 18	GC	36	Jones County Junior College 13
Oct. 25	GC	24	Hinds County Junior College 14
Oct. 30	GC	27	Holmes County Junior College 7
Nov. 8	**GC**	**35**	**Copiah-Lincoln Junior College 30**
Nov. 14	GC	10	Holmes County Junior College (Play-off Game) . . .9
Nov. 21	GC	18	Jones County Jr. College (State Champ. Game) . . .14

Season Record: 11 wins - 1 loss - 0 ties Coach: George Sekul

1981

Sept. 5	GC	7	Northwest Mississippi Junior College 6
Sept. 10	GC	10	Southwest Mississippi Junior College 7
Sept. 19	GC	23	East Mississippi Junior College 3
Sept. 26	GC	24	East Central Mississippi Junior College 14
Oct. 3	GC	21	Mississippi Delta Junior College 25
Oct. 10	GC	10	Pearl River Junior College 14
Oct. 17	GC	23	Jones County Junior College 28
Oct. 24	GC	27	Hinds County Junior College 13
Oct. 31	**GC**	**29**	**Holmes County Junior College 21**
Nov. 7	GC	14	Copiah-Lincoln Jr. College 41

Season Record: 6 wins - 4 losses - 0 ties Coach: George Sekul

1982 State Co-Champions

Sept. 2	GC	31	Northeast Mississippi Junior College 0
Sept. 11	GC	17	East Central Mississippi Junior College 14
Sept. 18	GC	16	Holmes County Junior College 0
Sept. 25	GC	35	Southwest Mississippi Junior College 0
Oct. 2	GC	24	Jones County Junior College 13
Oct. 9	GC	21	East Mississippi Junior College 0
Oct. 16	GC	17	Pearl River Junior College 14
Oct. 23	**GC**	**14**	**Copiah-Lincoln Junior College 7**
Oct. 28	GC	19	Hinds County Junior College 10
Nov. 6	GC	2	Northwest Mississippi Junior College 3
Nov. 13	GC	48	Itawamba Junior College (Play-off Game) 0
Nov. 20	GC	7	Northwest Miss.i Jr. College (State Champ. Game) 7

Season Record: 10 wins - 1 loss - 1 tie Coach: George Sekul

1983

Sept. 3	GC	33	Northeast Mississippi Junior College 0
Sept. 10	GC	2	East Central Mississippi Junior College 13
Sept. 15	GC	44	Holmes County Junior College 3
Sept. 22	GC	32	Southwest Mississippi Junior College 0
Oct. 1	GC	17	Jones County Junior College 15
Oct. 8	GC	55	East Mississippi Junior College 0
Oct. 15	GC	28	Pearl River Junior College 7
Oct. 22	GC	28	Copiah-Lincoln Junior College 10
Oct. 29	GC	35	Hinds County Junior College 2
Nov. 5	**GC**	**28**	**Northwest Mississippi Junior College 20**
Nov. 12	GC	42	Northeast Mississippi Jr. College (Play-off Game) .0
Nov. 19	GC	12	Jones County Jr. College (State Champ. Game) . . .17

Season Record: 10 wins - 2 losses - 0 ties Coach: George Sekul

1984 State Champions and National Champions

Aug. 30	GC	27	Mississippi Delta Junior College 0
Sept. 8	GC	16	Southwest Mississippi Junior College 7
Sept. 15	GC	28	Coahoma County Junior College 13
Sept. 22	GC	16	East Central Mississippi Junior College 6
Sept. 29	GC	33	Northeast Mississippi Junior College 3
Oct. 6	GC	21	Jones County Junior College 12
Oct. 13	GC	24	Pearl River Junior College 14
Oct. 20	GC	30	Itawamba Junior College .21
Oct. 27	GC	**28**	**Copiah-Lincoln Junior College 21**
Nov. 3	GC	30	Hinds County Junior College 21
Nov. 10	GC	50	East Mississippi Junior College (Play-off Game) . .7
Nov. 17	GC	17	Jones County Jr. College (State Champ. Game) . . .16
Dec. 1	GC	21	Harford Community College(Maryland) . . . . .7 (National Championship Game)

Season Record: 13 wins - 0 losses - 0 ties Coach: George Sekul

1985

Aug. 31	--		Mississippi Delta Junior College (Game Cancelled)
Sept. 5	GC	12	Southwest Mississippi Junior College 7
Sept. 14	GC	61	Coahoma County Junior College 0
Sept. 21	GC	45	East Central Mississippi Junior College 6
Sept. 28	GC	19	Northeast Mississippi Junior College 3
Oct. 5	GC	17	Jones County Junior College 7
Oct. 12	GC	10	Pearl River Junior College 6
Oct. 17	GC	10	Itawamba Junior College .14
Oct. 26	GC	24	Copiah-Lincoln Junior College 7
Nov. 2	**GC**	**20**	**Hinds County Junior College 0**
Nov. 9	GC	17	Northwest Miss. Jr. College (Play-off Game) 13
Nov. 16	GC	23	Copiah-Lincoln Jr. College (State Champ. Game) .24
Dec. 7	GC	0	Tyler Junior College (Texas Jr. College Bowl) 31

Season Record: 9 wins - 3 losses - 0 ties Coach: George Sekul

1986 State Champions

Aug. 30	GC	19	East Mississippi Junior College 7
Sept. 6	GC	10	East Central Mississippi Junior College 6
Sept. 11	GC	9	Itawamba Junior College .7
Sept. 20	GC	10	Southwest Mississippi Junior College 20
Sept. 25	GC	10	Northeast Mississippi Junior College 20
Oct. 4	GC	26	Jones County Junior College 9
Oct. 11	GC	9	Pearl River Junior College 7
Oct. 18	GC	17	Hinds County Junior College 12
Oct. 25	GC	9	Copiah-Lincoln Junior College 27
Nov. 1	**GC**	**59**	**Holmes County Junior College 28**
Nov. 8	GC	20	Itawamba Junior College (Play-off Game) 16
Nov. 15	GC	14	Northwest Miss. Jr. College (State Champ. Game) .13
Nov. 23	GC	14	Lees-McRae Com. College (East Bowl) 13

Season Record: 10 wins - 3 losses - 0 ties Coach: George Sekul

1987

Sept. 3	GC	0	East Mississippi Junior College 12
Sept. 12	GC	7	East Central Mississippi Junior College 0
Sept. 19	GC	17	Itawamba Junior College .28
Sept. 26	GC	14	Southwest Mississippi Junior College 17
Oct. 1	GC	7	Northeast Mississippi Community College 24
Oct. 10	GC	3	Jones County Junior College 13
Oct. 17	GC	7	Pearl River Junior College 33
Oct. 24	**GC**	**12**	**Hinds County Junior College 42**
Oct. 31	GC	24	Copiah-Lincoln Junior College 17
Nov. 5	GC	10	Holmes County Junior College 28

Season Record: 2 wins - 8 losses - 0 ties Coach: George Sekul

1988

Sept. 1	GC	7	Holmes County Junior College 12
Sept. 8	GC	26	Southwest Mississippi Community College 23
Sept. 15	GC	20	Northwest Mississippi Community College 35
Sept. 24	GC	21	East Central Mississippi Community College 0
Oct. 1	GC	14	Pearl River Community College 21
Oct. 8	GC	31	Jones County Junior College 6
Oct. 15	GC	48	Itawamba Community College 9
Oct. 22	GC	27	Copiah-Lincoln Community College 10
Oct. 29	GC	6	Hinds Community College 35
Nov. 5	**GC**	**28**	**East Mississippi Community College 31**

Season Record: 5 wins - 5 losses - 0 ties Coach: George Sekul

1989

Aug. 31	GC	21	Holmes Community College 7
Sept. 7	GC	17	Southwest Mississippi Community College 20
Sept. 16	GC	17	Northwest Mississippi Community College 21
Sept. 23	GC	28	East Central Mississippi Community College 13
Sept. 30	GC	19	Pearl River Community College 22
Oct. 7	GC	43	Jones County Junior College 45
Oct. 14	GC	14	Itawamba Community College 15
Oct. 21	GC	11	Copiah-Lincoln Community College 38
Oct. 28	**GC**	**15**	**Hinds Community College 28**
Nov. 4	GC	21	East Mississippi Community College 23

Season Record: 2 wins - 8 losses - 0 ties Coach: George Sekul

1990

Sept. 1	GC	*21	Coahoma Community College . . . .*0 *(*Game counted as a loss for both teams. Both fielded ineligible players.)*
Sept. 6	GC	24	Northeast Mississippi Community College 24
Sept. 15	GC	7	East Central Mississippi Community College 20
Sept. 20	GC	49	Southwest Mississippi Community College 9
Sept. 29	GC	13	Northwest Mississippi Community College 38
Oct. 6	GC	0	Pearl River Community College 27
Oct. 13	GC	20	Jones County Junior College 36
Oct. 20	GC	7	Copiah-Lincoln Community College 15
Oct. 27	GC	**17**	**Hinds Community College 40**
Nov. 3	GC	6	Itawamba Community College 38

Season Record: 1 win - 8 losses - 1 tie Coach: George Sekul

1991
Aug. 29 GC 36 Coahoma Community College 12
Sept. 5 GC 14 Northeast Mississippi Community College 28
Sept. 14 GC 21 East Central Mississippi Community College 19
Sept. 19 GC 19 Southwest Mississippi Community College 16
Sept. 26 GC 14 Northwest Mississippi Community College 56
Oct. 5 GC 6 Pearl River Community College 13
Oct. 12 GC 28 Jones County Junior College 0
Oct. 19 GC 30 Copiah-Lincoln Community College 12
Oct. 26 GC 10 Hinds Community College 13
Nov. 2 GC 0 Itawamba Community College 19
Season Record: 5 wins - 5 losses - 0 ties Coach: George Sekul

1992
Sept. 3 GC 20 Itawamba Community College 34
Sept. 10 GC 42 East Central Mississippi Community College 6
Sept. 19 GC 21 Southwest Mississippi Community College 2
Sept. 26 GC 26 Mississippi Delta Community College 13
Oct. 1 GC 24 Northeast Mississippi Community College 28
Oct. 10 GC 13 Pearl River Community College 16
Oct. 17 GC 20 Jones County Junior College 10
Oct. 22 GC 0 Hinds Community College 15
Oct. 31 GC 37 Copiah-Lincoln Community College 18
Nov. 5 GC 35 Coahoma Community College 12
Season Record: 6 wins - 4 losses - 0 ties Coach: J. C. Arban

1993
Sept. 2 GC 27 Itawamba Community College 28
Sept. 9 GC 20 East Central Mississippi Community College 6
Sept. 16 GC 34 Southwest Mississippi Community College 0
Sept. 23 GC 7 Mississippi Delta Community College 49
Sept. 30 GC 20 Northeast Mississippi Community College 21
Oct. 9 GC 20 Pearl River Community College 64
Oct. 16 GC 7 Jones County Junior College 32
Oct. 23 GC 13 Hinds Community College 22
Oct. 30 GC 22 Copiah-Lincoln Community College 7
Nov. 6 GC 44 Coahoma Community College 20
Season Record: 4 wins - 6 losses - 0 ties Coach: J. C. Arban

1994
Sept. 1 GC 21 Northwest Mississippi Community College 38
Sept. 8 GC 36 Southwest Mississippi Community College 20
Sept. 15 GC 14 East Mississippi Community College 24
Sept. 22 GC 28 East Central Mississippi Community College 12
Sept. 29 GC 23 Mississippi Delta Community College 31
Oct. 8 GC 25 Pearl River Community College 14
Oct. 15 GC 21 Jones County Junior College 38
Oct. 20 GC 0 Hinds Community College 24
Oct. 27 GC 17 Holmes Community College 34
Nov. 5 GC 15 Copiah-Lincoln Community College 14
Season Record: 4 wins - 6 losses - 0 ties Coach: J. C. Arban

1995
Aug. 31 GC 16 Northwest Mississippi Community College 44
Sept. 7 GC 36 Southwest Mississippi Community College 37
Sept. 14 GC 14 East Mississippi Community College 39
Sept. 21 GC 43 East Central Mississippi Community College 18
Sept. 28 GC 7 Mississippi Delta Community College 19
Oct. 7 GC 14 Pearl River Community College 21
Oct. 15 GC 24 Jones County Junior College 23
Oct. 21 GC 0 Hinds Community College 55
Oct. 28 GC 27 Holmes Community College 51
Nov. 2 GC 10 Copiah-Lincoln Community College 27
Season Record: 2 wins - 8 losses - 0 ties Coach: J. C. Arban

1996
Sept. 5 GC 7 Itawamba Community College 45
Sept. 12 GC 35 East Mississippi Community College 45
Sept. 19 GC 21 Mississippi Delta Community College 28
Sept. 28 GC 21 Jones County Junior College 16
Oct. 5 GC 21 Southwest Mississippi Community College 25
Oct. 12 GC 27 Pearl River Community College 23
Oct. 19 GC 23 East Central Mississippi Community College 28
Oct. 26 GC 9 Copiah-Lincoln Community College 12
Oct. 31 GC 28 Coahoma Community College 6
Nov. 9 GC 28 Hinds Community College 38
Season Record: 3 wins - 7 losses - 0 ties Coach: Steve Wright

1997
Sept. 4 GC 12 Itawamba Community College 34
Sept. 11 GC 22 East Mississippi Community College 27
Sept. 18 GC 14 Mississippi Delta Community College 20
Sept. 27 GC 25 Jones County Junior College 21
Oct. 2 GC 10 Southwest Mississippi Community College 28
Oct. 11 GC 55 Pearl River Community College 61
Oct. 18 GC 21 East Central Mississippi Community College 24
Oct. 25 GC 18 Copiah-Lincoln Community College 20
Nov. 1 GC 45 Coahoma Community College 0
Nov. 8 GC 27 Hinds Community College 47
Season Record: 2 wins - 8 losses - 0 ties Coach: Steve Wright

1998
Sept. 3 GC 7 Mississippi Delta Community College 35
Sept. 12 GC 16 Coahoma Community College 0
Sept. 17 GC 20 Holmes Community College 43
Sept. 26 GC 30 Hinds Community College 21
Oct. 3 GC 10 Jones County Junior College 33
Oct. 10 GC 48 Northeast Mississippi Community College 14
Oct. 17 GC 34 Pearl River Community College 13
Oct. 22 GC 7 Southwest Mississippi Community College 16
Oct. 31 GC 21 Copiah-Lincoln Community College 14
Nov. 5 GC 17 East Central Mississippi Community College 14
Season Record: 6 wins - 4 losses - 0 ties Coach: Steve Wright

1999
Sept. 2 GC 53 Mississippi Delta Community College 47
Sept. 9 GC 35 Coahoma Community College 0
Sept. 16 GC 24 Holmes Community College 3
Sept. 23 GC 24 Hinds Community College 29
Oct. 2 GC 52 Jones County Junior College 21
Oct. 7 GC 35 Northeast Mississippi Community College 0
Oct. 16 GC 48 Pearl River Community College 16
Oct. 23 GC 14 Southwest Mississippi Community College 19
Oct. 30 GC 38 Copiah-Lincoln Community College 7
Nov. 4 GC 12 East Central Mississippi Community College 50
Season Record: 7 wins - 3 losses - 0 ties Coach: Steve Wright

2000
Aug. 31 GC 7 Holmes Community College 26
Sept. 7 GC 32 Northeast Mississippi Community College 6
Sept. 16 GC 34 Northwest Mississippi Community College 79
Sept. 21 GC 47 East Central Mississippi Community College 41
Sept. 28 GC 28 Hinds Community College 31
Oct. 5 GC 27 Jones County Junior College 13
Oct. 14 GC 19 Southwest Mississippi Community College 55
Oct. 21 GC 36 Pearl River Community College 7
Oct. 26 GC 28 Copiah-Lincoln Community College 6
Nov. 2 GC 20 Itawamba Community College 23
Season Record: 5 wins - 5 losses Coach: Steve Wright

HIGGINBOTHAM REPORT: AGRICULTURAL HIGH SCHOOL "AGGIE" AND "BULLPUP" FOOTBALL SCORES 1914 - 1961

Gary Higginbotham, MGCJC Class of 1965, compiled the scores of the Perkinston institution's high school football games from 1914 to 1961. He graciously consented to the use of this report for this work. The Perkinston institution underwent several name changes between 1912 and 1925, but the football team retained the name "Aggies" until midseason 1925. The Agricultural High School at Perkinston fielded its first "Aggie" team in fall 1914. The Higginbotham Report AHS scores are incomplete due to fragmentary records.

1914

Oct. 24	"Aggies"	0	Gulf Coast Military Academy	32
Nov. 7	"Aggies"	?	Mississippi Normal College	?
Nov. 21	"Aggies"	82	Gulfport High School	6
Nov. 26	"Aggies"	0	Pearl River AHS	51

Coach: G. N. McIlhenny

1915

Oct. 23	"Aggies"	25	Gulfport High School	0
Oct. 30	"Aggies"	0	Mississippi Normal College	26
Nov. 13	"Aggies"	19	Gulfport Athletic Association	0
Nov. 20	"Aggies"	?	Pearl River AHS	?

1916

Oct.14	"Aggies"	36	Gulfport High School	0
Oct. 21	"Aggies"	Lost	Pearl River AHS	Won
Nov. 10	"Aggies"	Won	Wiggins	Lost (0)
Nov. 18	"Aggies"	Won	Biloxi High School	Lost
Nov. 25	"Aggies"	6	Gulf Coast Military Academy	26

1917

Nov. 10	"Aggies"	0	Springhill College	47
Nov. 17	"Aggies"	?	Gulfport High School	?

Coach: R. H. Harmon

1918

No team fielded due to World War I and outbreak of Spanish Influenza Epidemic.

1919

Oct. 4	"Aggies"	0	Mississippi Normal College	12
Oct. 11	"Aggies"	0	Gulf Coast Military Academy	20

1920

?	"Aggies"	Lost	Laurel High School	Won
Oct. 2	"Aggies"	0	Mississippi Normal College	65
Oct. 9	"Aggies"	0	Gulf Coast Military Academy	117
Oct. 30	"Aggies"	Won	Biloxi High School	Lost
Nov. 5	"Aggies"	7	Gulfport High School	7

Coach: R. J. Koonce

1921

Oct. 8	"Aggies"	0	Gulfport High School	32
Oct. 28	"Aggies"	0	Hattiesburg High School	25
Nov. 5	"Aggies"	0	Biloxi High School	0
Nov. 11	"Aggies"	0	Lamar County AHS	48
Nov. 12	"Aggies"	53	Methodist Seashore Campground School	0
Nov. 15	"Aggies"	27	Biloxi High School	13
Nov. 19	"Aggies"	0	Pascagoula High School	3
Dec. 3	"Aggies"	7	Biloxi High School	39

1922

Sept. 30	"Aggies"	0	Laurel High School	37
Oct. 6	"Aggies"	6	Jones County AHS	6
Oct. 14	"Aggies"	0	Pascagoula High School	6
Oct. 20	"Aggies"	0	Hattiesburg High School	44
Oct. 28	"Aggies"	?	Miss. Industrial Training School	?
Nov. 4	"Aggies"	0	Gulfport High School	14
Nov. 11	"Aggies"	0	Lamar County AHS	48
Nov. 18	"Aggies"	47	Meth. Seashore Campground School	0
Nov. 24	"Aggies"	20	Forrest County AHS	0

Coach: M. G. Evans

1923

Sept. 21	"Aggies"	6	Picayune High School	19
Sept. 26	"Aggies"	6	Forrest County AHS	0
Oct. 6	"Aggies"	0	Gulf Coast Military Academy	42
Oct. 13	"Aggies"	31	Gulfport High School	0
Oct. 19	"Aggies"	0	Meth. Seashore Campground School	19
Nov. 10	"Aggies"	0	Pascagoula High School	25

Coach: B. P. Webb

1924

Oct. 17	"Aggies"	7	Gulfport High School	12
Nov. 1	"Aggies"	0	Miss. Industrial Training School	6
Nov. 8	"Aggies"	0	Lamar County AHS	44
Nov. 22	"Aggies"	40	Forrest County AHS	0
Nov. 27	"Aggies"	0	Biloxi High School	20

Coach: William "Billy" Wood

1925

Oct. 3	"Aggies"	7	Varnado (Louisiana) High School	13
Oct. 10	"Aggies"	6	Spring Hill High School (Mobile)	0
Oct. 16	"Aggies"	20	Gulfport High School	0
Oct. 23	"Aggies"	0	Jesuit High School (New Orleans)	8
Oct. 31	"Aggies"	Won	Pascagoula High School	Lost
Nov. 7	"Bulldogs"	6	Lamar County AHS	0
Nov. 19	"Bulldogs"	14	Biloxi High School	6

In the 1925 season the school also began fielding a junior varsity or "scrub" or "second-string" team known as the "Bullpups." In the 1926 season, with the fielding of a junior college team, the "Bullpups" became the high school team. The purpose of the "Bullpup" team was to train "Bulldogs." So far as can be ascertained, the "Bullpups" played only one or two games a year from 1925 to 1931. From 1925 through 1928 Coach W. C. "Bill" Denson had charge of the "Bullpups" as well as the "Bulldogs." In 1930 Coach Lee Roy Weeks served in Denson's former role.

Nov. 6	"Bullpups"	20	Wiggins High School	0

1926

Nov. 13	"Bullpups"	0	Forrest County AHS	7

1927

Sept. 23	"Bullpups"	45	Lyman High School	0
Oct. 22	"Bullpups"	6	Gulf Coast Military Academy	6

1928

Sept. 29	"Bullpups"	0	Gulfport High School	50
Oct. 17	"Bullpups"	18	Lyman High School	0

1930

Oct. 15	"Bullpups"	7	Wiggins High School	0

1943

Only the high school fielded a team in 1943. The junior college team did not play due to travel restrictions accompanying World War II rationing and because most of the men went into the service. The Perkinston Agricultural High School team styled itself the "Bulldogs" in 1943, so in this listing the team will be styled "Bulldogs AHS."

Oct. 8	"Bulldogs AHS"	0	Petal High School	52
Oct. 15	"Bulldogs AHS"	7	Lumberton High School	6
Oct. 22	"Bulldogs AHS"	20	Hattiesburg High School	0
Oct. 29	"Bulldogs AHS"	13	Pearl River AHS	0
Nov. 5	"Bulldogs AHS"	0	Pearl River AHS	0
Nov. 12	"Bulldogs AHS"	7	Richton High School	6
Nov. 19	"Bulldogs AHS"	31	Lumberton High School	0

Coach: R. T. Walker

1944

	"Bullpups"	7	Forrest County AHS	0
Sept. 22	"Bullpups"	33	Lumberton High School	7
	"Bullpups"	13	Lumberton High School	0
	"Bullpups"	13	Notre Dame High School (Biloxi)	7

Coach: R. T. Walker

"Little Perk"
Perkinston Consolidated High School "Eagles"
1948-1951

1948

In fall 1948 Perkinston Consolidated School, also known as "Little Perk," added the 11th and 12th grades becoming Perkinston Consolidated High School. The PCHS fielded a football team known as the "Eagles." Because of the symbiotic relationship between "Little Perk" and "Big Perk," the "Eagles" scores were included herein. Homecoming games are identified by bold print.

Sept. 10	"Eagles"	0	Lucedale High School	12
Sept. 17	"Eagles"	7	Ocean Springs High School	13
Sept. 23	"Eagles"	14	Wiggins High School	0
Oct. 1	"Eagles"	13	Bay St. Louis High School	34
Oct. 8	"Eagles"	0	Hattiesburg High School "B" Team	6
Oct. 21	"Eagles"	6	Pass Christian High School	27
Oct. 28	"Eagles"	6	Long Beach High School	20
Nov. 9	"Eagles"	?	Wiggins High School	?

Coach: Harold White

1949

Sept. 9	"Eagles"	27	Leakesville High School	13
Sept. 24	"Eagles"	26	Our Lady of Victories High School (Pascagoula)	6
Sept. 30	"Eagles"	13	Bay St. Louis High School	26
Oct. (?)	"Eagles"	Tied	Poplarville High School	Tied
Oct. 7	"Eagles"	26	Ocean Springs High School	6
Oct. 21	"Eagles"	39	Pass Christian High School	19
Oct. 28	"Eagles"	27	Eatonville High School	6
Nov. 4	"Eagles"	27	Wiggins High School	7
Nov. 11	"Eagles"	13	Ocean Springs High School	14
Nov. 25	"Eagles"	39	Mt. Olive High School	0
Dec. 2	"Eagles"	13	Crosby High School	19

Coach: Harold White

1950

Sept. 8	"Eagles"	48	Carriere High School	0
Sept. 15	"Eagles"	13	Poplarville High School	6
Sept. 29	"Eagles"	41	Bay St. Louis High School	6
Oct. 6	"Eagles"	27	Decatur High School	0
Oct. 13	"Eagles"	27	Petal High School	0
Oct. 20	"Eagles"	52	Pass Christian High School	0
Oct. 27	"Eagles"	35	Prentiss High School	7
Nov. 3	"Eagles"	49	Our Lady of Victories High School	0
Nov. 30	"Eagles"	48	Lucedale High School (Dairy Bowl)	7

Coach: Harold White

1951

Sept. 7	"Eagles"	33	Carriere High School	0
Sept. 14	"Eagles"	0	Poplarville High School	39
Sept. 20	"Eagles"	Lost	Demonstration High School (Hattiesburg)	Won
Sept. 27	"Eagles"	6	Bay St. Louis High School	0
Oct. 5	"Eagles"	6	Decatur High School	13
Oct. 12	"Eagles"	19	Petal High School	20
Oct. 19	"Eagles"	25	Pass Christian High School	0
Oct. 26	"Eagles"	22	Tylertown High School	7
Nov. 9	"Eagles"	37	Flora High School	0
Nov. 16	**"Eagles"**	**0**	**Forrest County AHS**	**0**

Coach: Joe Blaylock

Perkinston Agricultural High School and Junior College "Bullpups" 1952-1961

1952

In fall 1952 the high school students of Perkinston Consolidated High School joined with those of Perkinston Agricultural High School, and the "Eagles" became "Bullpups."

Sept. 12	"Bullpups"	23	Columbia Industrial School	0
Sept. 18	"Bullpups"	20	Carriere High School	12
Sept. 26	"Bullpups"	6	Pass Christian High School	6
Oct. 2	"Bullpups"	38	Our Lady of Victories High School	0
Oct. 9	"Bullpups"	7	Bay St. Louis High School	20
Oct. 24	"Bullpups"	26	Copiah-Lincoln AHS	0
Oct. 31	"Bullpups"	27	McLain High School	6
Nov. 14	"Bullpups"	0	Forrest County AHS	20

Coach: J. V. Shiel

1953

Sept. 10	"Bullpups"	0	Long Beach High School	6
Sept. 18	"Bullpups"	0	Carriere High School	0
Sept. 25	"Bullpups"	12	Pass Christian High School	33
Oct. 2	"Bullpups"	26	Our Lady of Victories High School	0
Oct. 9	"Bullpups"	14	Bay St. Louis High School	12
Oct. 23	"Bullpups"	24	Copiah-Lincoln AHS	7
Oct. 30	"Bullpups"	45	McLain High School	14
Nov. 13	"Bullpups"	13	Forrest County AHS	13

Coach: J. V. Shiel

1954

Sept. 10	"Bullpups"	20	Our Lady of Victories High School	33
Sept. 17	"Bullpups"	26	Carriere High School	19
Sept. 23	"Bullpups"	13	Long Beach High School	40
Oct. 1	"Bullpups"	6	Leakesville High School	18
Oct. 8	"Bullpups"	6	Bay St. Louis High School	51
Oct. 14	"Bullpups"	13	Purvis High School	25
Oct. 29	"Bullpups"	13	Ocean Springs High School	55
Nov. 5	**"Bullpups"**	**47**	**Pass Christian High School**	**13**

Coach: J. V. Shiel

1955

Sept.8	"Bullpups"	26	Our Lady of Victories High School	8
Sept. 15	"Bullpups"	14	Carriere High School	25
Sept. 23	"Bullpups"	7	Long Beach High School	6
Sept. 30	"Bullpups"	22	Leakesville High School	19
Oct. 7	"Bullpups"	26	Bay St. Louis High School	6
Oct. 14	**"Bullpups"**	**33**	**Purvis High School**	**0**
Oct. 20	"Bullpups"	13	Ocean Springs High School	12
Oct. 29	"Bullpups"	26	Lumberton High School	19
Nov. 4	"Bullpups"	46	Pass Christian High School	7
Dec. 1	"Bullpups"	39	Notre Dame H.S. (Dairy Bowl)	12

Coach: J. V. Shiel

1956

Sept. 13	"Bullpups"	13	Carriere High School	14
Sept. 20	"Bullpups"	0	Long Beach High School	38
Oct. 4	"Bullpups"	0	Bay St. Louis High School	43
Oct. 11	"Bullpups"	0	Ellisville High School	34
Oct. 25	"Bullpups"	8	Lumberton High School	13
Nov. 1	**"Bullpups"**	**0**	**Pass Christian High School**	**7**

Coach: Ed Evans

1957

Sept. 6	"Bullpups"	6	Rocky Creek High School	0
Sept. 14	"Bullpups"	20	Carriere High School	13
Sept. 20	"Bullpups"	0	Long Beach High School	7
Sept. 27	"Bullpups"	7	D'Iberville High School	13
Oct. 10	"Bullpups"	0	Ellisville High School	19
Oct. 19	"Bullpups"	7	Pass Christian High School	7
Oct. 25	"Bullpups"	14	Lumberton High School	7
Nov. 5	**"Bullpups"**		**St. John High School**	

Homecoming game not played in 1957 due to flu epidemic so said team member James M. Rutledge.

Coach: Mel Carpenter

1958

Sept. 5	"Bullpups"	0	Rocky Creek High School	19
Sept. 11	"Bullpups"	6	Carriere High School	14
Sept. 19	"Bullpups"	12	Long Beach High School	25
Sept. 26	"Bullpups"	12	D'Iberville High School	6
Oct. 3	"Bullpups"	18	Harrison Central High School	7
Oct. 9	"Bullpups"	34	St. Martin High School	0
Oct. 16	**"Bullpups"**	**12**	**Pass Christian High School**	**28**

Coach: Leonard Sumrall

1959

Sept. 11	"Bullpups"	0	Notre Dame High School	50
Sept. 18	"Bullpups"	19	Harrison Central High School	13
Sept. 24	"Bullpups"	20	D'Iberville High School	12
Oct. 2	"Bullpups"	0	Long Beach High School	7
Oct. 16	"Bullpups"	25	Pass Christian High School	0
Oct. 23	"Bullpups"	0	Bay St. Louis High School	19
Oct. 30	"Bullpups"	25	Vancleave High School	0
Nov. 6	**"Bullpups"**	**6**	**St. John High School**	**13**

Coach: Leonard Sumrall

1960

Sept. 9	"Bullpups"	0	Notre Dame High School	33
Sept. 16	"Bullpups"	20	Harrison Central High School	12
Oct. 1	"Bullpups"	6	Long Beach High School	24
Oct. 7	"Bullpups"	0	Ocean Springs High School	20
Oct. 14	"Bullpups"	26	Pass Christian High School	7
Oct. 21	"Bullpups"	7	Bay St. Louis High School	14
Oct. 27	**"Bullpups"**	**37**	**Hancock North Central H.S.**	**19**
Nov. 4	"Bullpups"	19	St. John High School	13

Coach: Leonard Sumrall

1961

This was the final season for the "Bullpups" because Perkinston Agricultural High School was eliminated in May 1962.

Sept. 1	"Bullpups"	0	Rocky Creek High School	26
Sept. 7	"Bullpups"	19	St. John High School	7
Sept. 15	"Bullpups"	20	St. Martin High School	0
Sept. 22	"Bullpups"	14	Harrison Central High School	0
Oct. 6	"Bullpups"	7	Long Beach High School	32
Oct. 12	"Bullpups"	6	Ocean Springs High School	19
Oct. 20	"Bullpups"	6	Pass Christian High School	7
Oct. 27	"Bullpups"	0	Bay St. Louis High School	33
Nov. 3	**"Bullpups"**	**19**	**Hancock North Central H.S.**	**6**

Coach: Leonard Sumrall

BOOK III

Performing Arts, Clubs, and Student Life

MUSIC: A PHOTOGRAPHIC ESSAY 1913 - 2000

Musical Beginnings: September 1913 to July 1927

The Harrison County Agricultural High School introduced the study of music into its offerings during its second session, 1913-1914. Courses in instrumental music and voice were extra-curricular in that they cost "extra" and carried no credit. By 1920 music instruction still cost extra, but the AHS awarded a diploma in the subject.

The first musical performance at the AHS not specifically related to coursework in music took place in late November 1922 with the staging of a Harrison-Stone AHS "Glee Club" performance in Bennett Hall Auditorium. So the Glee Club, renamed the "choir" in 1949, made its appearance during the superintendency of J. H. Forbis. As school started in September 1923, Forbis announced his intention to form a "Brass Band" within a month. Forbis did not follow through on his intention, but his successor, Jefferson Lee Denson, ordered the formation of an orchestra.

Also, shortly after Denson took over as superintendent of the institution in fall 1924, he announced the impending reorganization of the Glee Club and the formation of a boys' quartette. The Glee Club and the boys' quartette performed during Denson's first session. Music director Mary Lillian Peters had charge of these singing groups.

First row *(from left), Mesker Bond of McHenry, music teacher Mary Lillian Peters, Aubry McIntosh of Jackson, Alabama.* ***Second row*** *(from left), Jessie Cooke of Wiggins, and Morris "Babe" Baker of Ocean Springs. On April 11, 1925, at the Gulf Coast Schoolmaster's Club Regional Field Meet held at Gulfport High School, the Harrison-Stone AHS Boys' Quartette took the five-inch tall first-place silver loving cup (below). In late April, Peters took the boys to the Mississippi State Field Meet held at the Agricultural and Mechanical College in Starkville where the quartette took third-place honors. Photograph of the 1925 Boys' Quartette from Harrison-Stone AHS and JC Bulletin of 1925, p. 17*

Richard Kopp photo

Richard Kopp photo

1925-1926 Glee Club

(Above) Music director Mary Lillian Peters stands in the center of this photograph of the Harrison-Stone-Jackson Agricultural High School and Junior College Glee Club taken on the stage of Bennett Hall auditorium during session 1925-1926. One of the students in the photograph, Irene Flurry, (second from left, third row) was one of the ten junior college students enrolled for the first time that session. All the rest of the singers in the Glee Club were AHS students. Of the AHS girls on the first row (from left) the first is unknown but the other three are Emma Clara Deane of Brooklyn, Lois Ramsay of Saucier, and Goldie Hatten of Gulfport. At the far left third row is Bea Brown of Barth. At far right, third row is Alfreda Von Seutter of Mississippi City. Photograph from 1925-1926 Catalogue, photo section.

Music director Mary Lillian Peters placed her assistant, Dorothy Daughdrill, in charge of the band-orchestra while she retained responsibility for the Glee Club and the various quartettes. In mid-April 1927, the mixed quartette composed of Virginia Gardner of Biloxi, Lois Ramsey of Saucier, Stanford Caraway of Perkinston, and Holly Bond of Perkinston won the seven-inch tall state trophy (above right), for their performance at the Mississippi Junior College Association Field Meet held at Raymond.

Orchestra director Dorothy Daughdrill, assistant in music to Mary Lillian Peters, began organizing an orchestra for the institution in session 1925-1926. The photograph above, published in the 1926-1927 Catalogue shows the orchestra seated on the stage of Bennett Hall auditorium. The students are unknown, but music director Mary Lillian Peters is seated sixth from the left.

In fall 1923, J. H. Forbis had announced his intention to form a brass band, but did not do it. In fall 1925, J. L. Denson announced his intention to form an orchestra. But, did he? According to David Dueitt, director of the Band of Gold in 2000, a band and an orchestra differ in several important respects. An orchestra specializes in instruments of the viol or "string" class and generally performs on a stage. A band specializes in wind and percussion and, when associated with a school, generally performs at athletic events. A band may perform on stage or in stands, but it also marches. Furthermore, members of an orchestra generally dress with uniformity while a band always does, and, moreover, almost always wears a military-style uniform.

The "orchestra" formed at Perkinston in 1925 remained the college's primary musical component for the following nine years. It performed on stage and in the bleachers or standing on the sidelines at athletic events. There is every indication that upon occasion it marched. On the other hand, there is no indication that its members ever dressed with uniformity, and the members definitely never wore uniforms. By 1927 the area newspapers were referring to this strange amalgamation as a "band-orchestra" because that was the only descriptive term approximating reality. The Perkinston institution's musical entity possessed most of the attributes of both a band and an orchestra except that the members did not dress alike.

Music: The Zenobia Ruth (Denson) Houston Era, July 1927 to May 1932

Zenobia Ruth (Denson) Houston, born December 24, 1901, graduated from high school at Bay Springs in 1920. Noby Ruth, as she was called, taught for a short time at a country school near Progress in Perry County and then entered Mississippi Women's College in Hattiesburg. In 1924 she graduated from Mississippi Women's College, then a Baptist institution solely for women, which later evolved into co-educational William Carey College.

After college, Noby Ruth taught one year at Magnolia Consolidated School ten miles west of Perkinston in Stone County, and then she taught for two years at Piave, a sawmill town in Greene County. She was at Piave when her cousin, Superintendent Lee Denson, recruited her to come to Perkinston. At Perkinston Noby Ruth taught violin, music history, music theory, and public school music in addition to directing the band-orchestra and coaching women's basketball. In 1927 and again in 1932, she also directed the Glee Club.

When Noby Ruth came to Perkinston, her younger brother, Joe Blankinship Denson, born March 23, 1911, came also. Noby Ruth taught at Perkinston for five years from July 1927 to May 1932, and her brother attended high school and college for that same period. Joe played the banjo in Noby Ruth's band-orchestra, sang in the Glee Club and the men's quartette, and aided his sister in managing the girls' basketball team. In addition, Joe played sports, particularly baseball, and was a member of both the 1931 and the 1932 state championship baseball teams.

In addition to all the other activities, Noby Ruth and Joe functioned as the "publicity department" for the school. The order would come down to set up publicity shots for college publications, so Noby Ruth and Joe set them up--and often appeared in the pictures themselves as "actors." Both of them appeared in photographs holding instruments they did not play as well as those they did play. If she could not find the "correct" students for a photograph session, Noby Ruth pressed into service any student in the vicinity at the time. In an interview at her home in Bay Springs on December 27, 1997, Noby Ruth said, "The object was to show prospective students how great everything was at Perkinston so they would come."

(Above) The Perkinston Band-Orchestra is pictured in front of Huff Hall in October 1927, four months after Noby Ruth Denson became its director. Noby Ruth, dressed in black, stands near the center of the group. Her brother Joe (far left at rear) holds a banjo, an instrument not normally found in a band or an orchestra. Photograph courtesy of Dixie Press of Gulfport.

After Noby Ruth took charge of the band-orchestra, its activities increased and so did the descriptions of those activities. A *Daily Herald* article describing the Perkinston-Poplarville football game of November 5, 1927, placed the members of the band-orchestra on the sidelines without even a place to sit and playing until their lips were "swollen and blistered." On February 6, 1928, the *Daily Herald* reported the band-orchestra playing at a Perkinston girls' AHS basketball game in McLaurin. Another *Daily Herald* article, January 28, 1929, described Perkinston's band-orchestra as one of the best in Mississippi and stated that it was "in use for entertainments and for pep work at the games." From time to time the papers carried notices that Noby Ruth intended the formation of a proper brass band, but she did not do so.

Members and "pretend members" of Noby Ruth Denson's Band-Orchestra "pretend to play" in session 1928-1929. Photograph from 1929 Department of Music Catalog.

Richard Kopp photo

Members of Noby Ruth's band-orchestra won the 10-inch tall "Piano Ensemble, Junior College, 1929" trophy.

Noby Ruth created an ensemble group from the band-orchestra which specialized in minstrel shows and became known as the Jazz Orchestra. The Perkinston "Jazz Orchestra" was highlighted in the May 5, 1930, Perkolator newspaper. The publicity shot (above) contains both "real" and "pretend" musicians. (From left) Wilma Wallace of Moorhead who did not play the drums, Laverne "Jane" Denson, daughter of Superintendent Lee Denson, who did not play the trombone, Joe B. Denson of Bay Springs who did play the banjo, Jessie Lee Holleman of Wiggins who did play the piano, Lucille Dosset of Hattiesburg who did play the violin, and Noby Ruth Denson, the orchestra director, who did not play the trumpet. Photograph courtesy Noby Ruth (Denson) Houston.

In 1929 Noby Ruth and her music department colleague, Corinne Holleman, published a unique *Harrison-Stone-Jackson Agricultural High School and Junior College Department of Music Catalog.* This illustrated 26-page pamphlet, containing photographs of the session 1928-1929 performances, depicted the various elements of the musical offerings of the college: the band-orchestra, a men's quartette, a mixed sextet, a piano ensemble, and a violin sextet. Some of these elements had been merged to produce a ballet, several scenes from which were pictured in the catalog.

SCENES FROM THE 1929 MUSIC CATALOG

(Left) "Violin Sextet"

(Below) "Spanish Tango"

(Above) Sextet from Schubert's "Blossom Time"

(Right) "Ballet--Finale from Schubert Scene." The log structure in the background is the "Y-Hut" or "Dorothy Hinton Hut." A portion of Bennett Hall is visible at the far right behind the tree.

The actors in the fall 1930 Glee Club production of the Japanese fantasio "Miss Cherry Blossom," pose at the west entrance of Fahnestock Hall. The cast consisted of two main characters "Kokemo" (Curtis Parker) and "Cherry Blossom" (Williard Eubanks) and a Geisha Girl chorus. (From left) Kearney Ramsay of Saucier, Maude Black of Piave, Evelyn Ramsay of Saucier, Mary Alice Ross of Gulfport, Bobbie Cockrell of Lucedale, Curtis Parker of McHenry, Williard Eubanks of Lucedale, Adeline Horn of Bay Springs, Bell McMullan of Sylvarena and Ted Black of Leaf.

The cast members of the fall 1930 Glee Club production of the one-act operetta "Rose of Castille," pose for a publicity photograph. (From left) Senorita Marita (Imogene Anthony of Enid, Oklahoma) in love with Enrico; Don Enrico (Hammond "Tom" Davis of Wiggins), a matador; Don Eduardo (Len Blackwell of McHenry), Enrico's rival; and Donna Teresa (Velma Hill of Soso), Marita's mother.

Members of the 1930 Harrison-Stone-Jackson Junior College Men's Quartette pose with accompanist Corinne Holleman of the Perkinston music department. (From left) first tenor Joe B. Denson of Bay Springs, second tenor Hammond "Tom" Davis of Wiggins, first bass F. Howell McDonald of Petal and second bass Obry Breland of Wiggins. This quartette, with a stand-in for F.H. McDonald who died of appendicitis in April 1930, took first place in the state junior college competition in May 1930.

The members of the Jazz Orchestra warm-up on the stage in Denson Hall circa 1932. Joe B. "Smoky Joe" Denson (third from left), is holding a tuba and a banjo. Photograph courtesy of Noby Ruth (Denson) Houston.

As graduation approached in 1932 the various elements of the music department gave a number of performances as usual. On graduation night, May 28, though, something unusual happened. After Superintendent Cooper J. Darby gave out the diplomas, Noby Ruth, seated at a piano on stage, played the Perkinston Alma Mater while the assemblage sang the words. This was the first instance in any document held in the MGCCC Archives collection in 2000 of the singing of the alma mater. The words follow:

Way down south there's a school that we all know,
Where the wind from the Gulf doth ever blow,
'Mong the pines so stately and so tall,
We listen to your call,
We love you best of all;
Fame was thine in the years of thy past,
And we know thy name shall ever last,
Thou art noble, proud and true,
Oh! Perkinston, we all love you.

Robert Young

Sixty-six years later at the graduation reception at Jackson County Campus, Annie C. (Wilkerson) Young Ward of Moss Point told then MGCCC President Barry L. Mellinger that her deceased husband, Robert Young of Saucier, had written the words to the alma mater. She further stated that Noby Ruth (Denson) Houston had written the music for the song. A query to Noby Ruth in Bay Springs in May 1998, revealed that she had adopted a "well-known march of the time" to fit Robert Young's words. She did not remember which march. Extant records related to Robert Young revealed that he graduated from the AHS in May 1928 and attended the college for at least one more year. Young's words and Noby Ruth's tune came together by May 28, 1932. In February 2001, MGCCC Assistant Band Director Cliff Taylor found both the words and the music of the alma mater in a folder in the Sam P. Jones Band Hall at the Perkinston Campus. After much research he concluded that Noby Ruth had set the words of the Perkinston Alma Mater to the trio of John Philip Sousa's *Liberty Bell March*.

In any case the alma mater rendition of 1932 was Noby Ruth's swan song. Her brother, Joe, graduated from the college that night, and she resigned to marry Rueben Kidd Houston of Sylvarena in June.

(Right) Noby Ruth Denson sits on the stage in Denson Hall as her 1932 Glee Club stands behind her. The HSJ on the stage curtain stands for Harrison-Stone-Jackson, the three counties supporting the school.

In 1929, Noby Ruth began a spring tour featuring the Glee Club and the band-orchestra. By 1932, the tour dates extended from April 18 to May 6 and included, in succession, performances at Pascagoula High School, Lucedale High School, Moss Point High School, Pass Christian High School, Mississippi Women's College at Hattiesburg, Bay Springs High School, State Teacher's College in Hattiesburg, Jones County Junior College in Ellisville and lastly Ponchatoula (Louisiana) High School.

Most of the photographs in the Noby Ruth Denson era, including the one at right, were made to illustrate large posters advertising spring tours. The actual glossy photographs were pasted to the posters. Admission was 15 cents and 25 cents. Spring tour programs often reprised productions presented on campus the previous fall. Photograph courtesy of Noby Ruth (Denson) Houston.

Music: The Glee Club and the formation of the Harrison-Stone-Jackson Agricultural High School and Junior College Brass Band and the formation of the Swing Barons Orchestra, September 1932 to May 1937

Lillian Leggett of Laurel replaced Noby Ruth Denson in session 1932-1933 and continued her policies. The Glee Club, the band-orchestra, and the other musical elements of the college remained closely united with the 1933 annual spring tour going on as usual. For the first time, though, the band-orchestra was given a name--the "Collegians."

Leggett remained only one year giving way in September 1933 to Elizabeth Davis, a native of Mendenhall and a graduate of Mississippi Women's College in Hattiesburg. Davis followed the framework of her two predecessors, but in her first year the band-orchestra assumed a new role on campus--playing for student dances.

Superintendent Cooper J. Darby remembering the issue of student dancing forty years later recalled:

"It required three years for me to persuade the trustees that we should have supervised dances on the campus. One parent remarked that he would rather see his daughter dead than see her dancing on a ballroom floor. I could not dance myself because I was reared to look upon dancing as an evil, but I saw the need for change."

A Perkinston student council petition sent to the Board of Trustees for consideration at their December 1933 meeting finally broke the impasse over campus dances. In the petition the student council stated the problem succinctly, "Our social activities here at the college are very limited, and the parties that we do have are entirely too childish for college students." The petition further stated that the college had a good orchestra and a good dance floor (the Old Gym), and the students wanted weekend faculty-chaperoned dances to which no outsiders would be admitted. The board voted six to four for the proposition. The school orchestra played for the first Perkinston Campus dance on Friday night, January 6, 1934, from 7:30 to 10:30. Attendance was restricted to current students, their parents, and college faculty and administration. Despite a heavy rain, students packed the Old Gym in what was the first such event in Mississippi junior college history.

That same year, music director Davis also organized Perkinston's first uniformed marching brass and percussion band. She made her point to the superintendent and the Board by the not so subtle method of taking her Glee Club and band-orchestra to Gulfport in March 1934 to stage a benefit to raise money for new uniforms for the Gulfport High School Band. Davis's efforts resulted in much publicity in regional newspapers, and Darby and the Board got the point. Their music director was raising money to outfit the band of a school served by their junior college, which had no such organization itself. Other tri-county high schools also had bands and so did Pearl River Junior College.

Accordingly, at their August 1934 meeting, the Trustees hired, at $50 per month and board, an assistant for Davis. Thus, Utica native Roy Harmon Longmire, a recent graduate of Mississippi College, became the institution's first band director. Longmire also took over the orchestra and coached the men's Glee Club and the men's quartette.

Longmire recruited about 35 band members in his first year, most of whom had never played a note before. The announcement of the activities for homecoming to be held November 10, 1934, included notice of "possibly a semi-concert by the recently organized college band . . . ." Whether or not the semi-concert happened was not mentioned in extant reports issued afterward.

The first Harrison-Stone-Jackson Agricultural High School and Junior College Band session 1934-1935 poses in front of the Old Gym during session 1934-1935. Robert Harmon Longmire, the institution's first band director, stands in the midst of the band dressed in a white uniform. Base Drum - W. A. "Sam" Maxwell of Long Beach, Saxaphone - Frederick Brewer of Kosciusko, Clarinet - Lewis Blackman of Perkinston, Clarinet - Jack Simpson of Wiggins, Clarinet - Frank Doubleday of Tela, Honduras, Clarinet - Lee Roy Weeks Jr. of Perkinston, Horn - Ben Huston of Lyman, Horn - Helen Hudgens of Grand Bay Alabama, Bass Baritone - Lionel Gardner of Biloxi, Trombone - Sherwood Young of Tela, Honduras, Trombone - Cassie Breland of Perkinston, Trombone - Glenn Breland of Wiggins, Trombone - Nell Bass of Lumberton, Trombone - Mildred Russum of Perkinston, Trumpet - Oliver Smith of Gulfport, Trumpet - H. Emmitt Ramirez of Tela, Honduras, Trumpet - Arlington Evans of Perkinston, Trumpet - Zettie Bond of Perkinston, Trumpet - Frank Russum of Perkinston, Cymbals - Bill Clardy of Howison, Cornet - James Simpson of Wiggins, Cornet - Arthur Doubleday of Tela, Honduras, Snare Drum - Mickey McIntosh of Gulfport. Photograph courtesy of Cassie (Breland) Batson.

In the session 1935-1936, the band improved, and reports of its activities became more frequent. Whatever plans were made for the band at homecoming 1935 certainly never occurred because the campus events were scrubbed due to the death of Perkinston student Gordon Maki. However, the band traveled by bus to the Perkinston-Pearl River game on November 9, 1935, for the college's first football victory over that school.

In February 1936, the band presented a concert at the Civilian Conservation Corps Camp at Ramsay Springs. After that, accounts of such concerts delivered at neighboring CCC camps and other installations became fairly common. On April 11, 1936, for the first time, the band participated in the Annual Band Contest for Junior Colleges held that year at Goodman. The band placed fourth.

By session 1935-1936 Longmire had recruited selected members of his new band as members of his orchestra which he dubbed the "Swing Barons." The Swing Barons embarked on the 1936 spring tour with the Glee Club. In the words of Cleve Huggins, a member of the orchestra at the time, "We brought the house down everywhere we played."

1935-1936 Swing Barons Orchestra. ***First row*** *(from left) Cleve Huggins of Biloxi, George Prewett of Birmingham, Alabama, and Harold Ervin of Long Beach.* ***Second row*** *(from left) B. C. Cox of Gulfport, John Pulliam of Gulfport, Vernon Gilly of Biloxi, Emmitt Ramirez of Tela, Honduras, George Davis of Gulfport, and Freda Stuart of Biloxi, Accompanist.*

1935-1936 Boys' Quartette (from left) Perkinston Music Department Director Elizabeth Davis, Elliott Anderson of Gulfport, James Simpson of Wiggins, J. J. Pulliam of Gulfport, and Ralph Burns of Gulfport.

1935-1936 Glee Club ***Front row*** *(from left) Doris Walker of Picayune, Lessie Hudson of New Orleans, Louisiana, Nell Bass of Lumberton, Cassie Breland of Perkinston, Vivian King of Hurley, Edith Woodward of Gulfport, Annie L. Simpson of Wiggins, Glee Club Director Elizabeth Davis, Elizabeth Lightsey of Biloxi, Florence McCorkle of Gulfport, Louise Curtis of Biloxi, Glenvol McBryde of Sumrall, Mary Hoffman of Pass Christian, Marie Covington of Wiggins, and Bonnie Colle of Pascagoula.* ***Back row*** *(from left) Julia Russum of Perkinston, Bessie Ladner of Biloxi, J. J. Pulliam of Gulfport, W. A. "Sam" Maxwell of Long Beach, Claude Campbell of Ocean Springs, Michael Eubanks of Perkinston, Ralph Burns of Gulfport, James Simpson of Wiggins, Rene Trochesset of Biloxi, Earl Heiderhoff of Gulfport, Eugene Pollack of New Orleans, Louisiana, Elliott Anderson of Gulfport, Edward Estes of Gulfport, Betsey Mae Bayley of Biloxi and Bill Clardy of Howison, and Accompanist Freda Stuart.*

Scene from Light Opera, "Martha," staged by the Perkinston department of music. Pictured are, from left, Elliott Anderson of Gulfport, Julia Russum of Perkinston, Elizabeth Lightsey of Biloxi, and band director Harmon Longmire. The production was part of the department's 1936 spring tour.

The Swing Barons played for the students' campus dances at least once a month. In late spring 1936 the Swing Barons, with school permission, began to accept off-campus engagements. By the next fall the Swing Barons were playing at the first-class hotels on the coast such as the Gray Castle in Pass Christian, the Markham in Gulfport, and the White House and Buena Vista in Biloxi. The orchestra also played at town community centers and area colleges such as Gulf Park at Long Beach. Saxophonist Huggins remembered, "We set about sprucing ourselves up. More jackets were purchased, attractive music stands were made by the members, and a new device called a portable amplifier was purchased to give us greater depth, or should I say, loudness?"

The fame of the Swing Barons became so great, said Huggins, that the Swing Barons toured with the Glee Club in spring 1937, and the orchestra played to sell-out crowds in every auditorium visited. The major contribution of the Swing Barons to the college, according to Huggins, was that this orchestra "helped enrollment at the school because dancing and a dance band on campus of a junior college was unheard of back in those days."

The session 1936-1937 edition of the Swing Barons Orchestra projects a new "professional" look on the stage of Denson Hall. ***First row*** *(from left) Walter Trautman of Gulfport, orchestra director Harmon Longmire, Bobby Ehlers of Moss Point, Ulysses Fayard of Bay St. Louis, George Prewett of Birmingham, Alabama, and Cleve Huggins of Biloxi.* ***Second row*** *(from left) John W. Starliper of New Orleans, Louisiana, Vernon Gilly of Biloxi, and J. J. Pulliam of Gulfport.* ***Third row*** *(from left) Gordon Dacey of Biloxi and George Davis of Pass Christian. Photograph courtesy of Elizabeth Brash of Gulfport Printing Company.*

Music: Band and Orchestra September 1937 - December 2000

Session 1937-1938 brought change to the music department. Elizabeth Davis, the music department director, took a leave of absence to attend Louisiana State University, and Lorraine Godbold of Baton Rouge replaced her. Band director Longmire resigned, and Stanley C. Beers of Pine Bluff, Arkansas, replaced him. But whereas Longmire had been an "assistant" to Davis, Beers was not subservient to Godbold. Thus the band began evolving into an autonomous entity with its director on an equal basis with the Glee Club director.

In Beers's first session, 1937-1938, he did not precipitously increase the number of bandsmen, but he added in other areas. Beers fielded two women drum majors in addition to Longmire's one man, and, moreover, created a new women's band auxiliary corps called the "Pep Squad."

Little was said of this new unit in its first year, but it was composed of a number of young women organized for the purpose of entertaining at games and also for the purpose of aiding the cheerleaders by acting as a cheering section in the stands. Whether or not the women wore uniforms or drilled at the football games in fall 1937 was not stated, but they certainly did so in fall 1938.

The top panoramic photograph shows the band and Pep Squad marching on the Old Athletic Field at half-time during the homecoming game of November 19, 1938. In both panoramas the 30 Pep Squad women are intermixed with the band members both marching and standing one on one. "Pep Squad Leader" Mabeline Bogdahn of Pascagoula, wears a "Bearskin-type" hat and marches at front in the top panorama. The three drum majors are out front in the bottom panorama. The Pep Squad women wear white shoes, white socks, white skirts, dark jackets and dark garrison caps set at a rakish angle. The uniforms never varied in the 10-year existence of the Pep Squad. Photograph from 1938 Perkolator, p. 80.

Stanley Beers (far left) stands at attention with his band in the Perkinston Quadrangle in 1938. Drum major Randall Burke of Gulfport stands out front. The two women drum majors flanking him are Sally Jane of Pascagoula and Lorraine Patterson of Gulfport. Photograph from 1938 Brochure.

The 1939-1940 Harrison-Stone-Jackson Agricultural High School and Junior College Band poses on the steps of Denson Hall. The drum in the foreground advertises the unit as the "Perkinston Junior College" Band two years before that name became official on July 15, 1942. The members wear new uniforms that arrived in time for homecoming, October 28, 1939.

***First row** (from left) Jewell Sims of Pass Christian, Wilma Proffitt of Johnson City, Tennessee, Otis Singletary of Gulfport, Frank Russum of Perkinston, Mildred Russum of Perkinston, Sybil McBay of Lucedale, James Finley of Gulfport, Sam Wilson of Gulfport, Corry DeWitt "Jimmy" Blount of Gulfport, Ewell Singleton of Handsboro, Hazel Ramsay of Ocean Springs, Curtis Parker of McHenry, Glen Sletten of Gulfport, John Dambrick of Pass Christian, Ann Elma Beckham of Pascagoula, Stewart Trautman of Gulfport, James Estes of Moss Point, and Mary Elaine Batson of Wiggins. **Second row** (from left), Charles B. Meyers of Gulfport, Lee Roy Weeks of Perkinston, Richard "Dick" Harrison of Biloxi, Bessie Black of Purvis, Ray Dubuisson of Long Beach, Dora Ellen Hanson of Pass Christian, Charles McNamee of Jackson, Glen Kemp of Biloxi, Jack Boyer of Biloxi, William Stapp of Gulfport, and Max Telhiard of Biloxi. **Third row** (from left), Marjorie Shepard of Saucier, Zettie Bond of Perkinston, Delores McHenry of McHenry, Fred Schwann of Biloxi, Elwood Collins of Biloxi, William Newsum of Biloxi, Albert Mangin of Biloxi, Emilie Marie Stapp of Wiggins, John Welch of Biloxi, Albert Saucier of Mississippi City, and band director Stanley Beers. **Fourth row** (from left), Philip Brandt of Pass Christian, William Elam of Gulfport, Millard Bond of Perkinston, Joseph J. Hartman of Biloxi, and Mattie Lou Lyons of Gulfport.*

Photo by Richard Kopp

On April 13, 1940, at the State Junior College Band Contest held that year in Jackson, the "PJC" band triumphed over Copiah-Lincoln, Hinds, Sunflower, and Holmes to take the state prize. One newspaper account of its victory march from the Illinois Central Depot up Capitol Street to the Old Capitol acclaimed the Perkinston band as "one of the most outstanding units ever to parade in Jackson." In 1940, Perkinston claimed its first and only state junior college band championship trophy (right) because that was the last year such contests were held.

The session 1939-1940 combined PJC Band-Glee Club production of Trial by Jury apparently marked the end of such collaborations by the two entities. Apparently the Band-Glee Club spring tour, a tradition since 1929, ended at the close of this session (as did so many other traditions) due to the dislocations occasioned by the American Preparedness Program and the subsequent outbreak of World War II. Ironically, though, Trial by Jury did play at Perk one more time in the 20th century on April 28, 1987, in Malone Hall. Then choir director John Jenkins described the production as "a choral presentation in costume" rather than an "operetta" and noted that it had been first performed in London in 1875. Photograph from the 1940 Perkolator, p. 81.

The PJC Pep Squad and cheerleaders pose for the camera in November 1940. Costa Rican twins Alvaro (left) and Mario Facio flank the other cheerleaders on the front row. The other cheerleaders (from left) are Hubert Manning of New Orleans, Louisiana, Anne Broadus of Perkinston, Dorothy Moore of Grand Bay, Alabama, and Howard Pollock of New Orleans, Louisiana.

*The Pep Squad members are **Second row** (from left) Head Pep Squad Major Betty Thompson of Gulfport, Gloria Keller of Biloxi, Ione Roberts of Big Point, Gertrude Highsmith of Long Beach, Betty Campbell of Biloxi, Freda Long of Biloxi, Maryanne Passmore of Dallas, Texas, Agatha Juaice Tanner of Wilmer, Alabama, Helen Moore of Wiggins, and Squad Major Dorothy Bleuer of Biloxi. **Third row** (from left), Muriel "Peg" Hutchins of Covington, Kentucky, Jean Saunders of Gulfport, Corinna Boone of Mobile, Alabama, Beth Bailey of Lucedale, Ersi Bates of Wiggins, and Virginia French of Rose Hill. **Fourth row** (from left), Helen Beasley of Lucedale, Annie Ruth Fairley of Lucedale, Dorothy Roberts of Moss Point, Beulah Smith of Lumberton, and Patricia Kinch of Lucedale. **Fifth row** (from left), Sybil Johnson of Saucier, Irline Sapp of Perkinston, Hazel Hobby of Merrill, Lois Franke of Gulfport, and Walline Ladner of Perkinson. **Sixth row** (from left), Mary Daniels of Wiggins, Nettie Sapp of Perkinston, Hilda Gracias of Guatemala City, Guatemala, Walline Cowart of Perkinston, and Bernice Carter of Escatawpa. **Seventh row** (from left), Jean Graves of Hazlehurst, Marjorie Ann Moore of Biloxi, Helen Cain of Mississippi City, and Louise Allen of Bexley, Alabama. **Eighth row** (from left), Sallie Welch of Biloxi, Miriam Freridge of Mississippi City, and Dorothy Fairley of Lucedale. Photograph from 1940 Homecoming Program.*

The session 1941-1942 Pep Squad members stand at attention on the campus in November 1941.

Rows beginning with the left (front to back), **First row**, *Lois Blackledge of Staten Island, New York, Maurine Easterling of Merrill, Betty Jackson of Biloxi, Dorothy Cook of Wiggins, Vivian Davis of Panama City, Florida, Margie Cunningham of Pass Christian, Babette Rhodes of Washington, D. C., and Dorothy O'Neal of Saucier.* **Second row** *(front to back), Janis Pitcher of Biloxi, Marjorie Cook of Pensacola, Florida, La Nora Byrd of Howison, Annie Belle Winters of McHenry, Alma Cowart of Lucedale, Alberta Ann Scott of Gulfport, Lora Ladner of Saucier, and Helen Redmond of Perkinston.* **Third row** *(front to back), Gloria Keller of Biloxi, June Sneden of Sulphur Springs, Texas, Melionee Allen of Lucedale, Nettie Mae Hickman of Wiggins, Vera Stewart of Isola, Colleen Hamilton of Gulfport, and Catherine Ramsey of Wiggins.* **Fourth row** *(front to back), Alice Evans of Gulfport, Mary Devore of Mobile, Alabama, Helen Gollotte of Biloxi, Barbara Crecelius of Hattiesburg, Mary Havard of Lucedale, Joan Dunlap of Belle Plaine, Iowa, Mina Saunders of Gulfport, and Geraldine Roberts of Perkinston.* **Fifth row** *(front to back), Gloria Thornton of Winterville, Hope Abbott of New Orleans, Louisiana, Elise Bayless of Bay Springs, Alga Ladner of Perkinston, Willie Pearl Bennett of Gulfport, Bernice Saucier of Saucier, Dorothy Clemens of Gulfport, and Dorothea Travis of Hattiesburg. Pep Squad leader Dorothy Bleuer of Biloxi. Photograph from 1942 Perkolator p. 60.*

The Swing Barons of session 1941-1942. **First row** *(from left), James Raley of Biloxi, Sam Readman of Gulfport, and George Saab of Canton.* **Second row** *(from left), Glenn Kemp of Biloxi and orchestra director Stanley Beers. Drummer at rear is Bill "Jug" Raborn of Mobile, Alabama. Pianist is Elise Bayless of Bay Springs. At right on bass fiddle is Charles Goff of Merida, Mexico. Photograph courtesy of Mr. and Mrs. William S. Raborn*

Stanley Beers resigned June 20, 1945. In August, Virginia Mae McCall, holder of a master's degree in music from Converse College, signed on to teach piano and to take charge of the band and the orchestra. McCall stayed only one year, being replaced by James Orian Ware Jr. on June 1, 1946.

On the eve of his first session as band director, Ware received a recruitment tool that none of his predecessors had possessed. On August 21, 1946, the Board voted to award tuition scholarships to "band students and others beneficial to the school."

Ware gave the band a new name--the "Bull-Dog Band." He retained the name Swing Barons for the orchestra until September 1950, changing the name at that time to the "Stardusters." The Pep Squad apparently disappeared after Ware's first year because the last photograph of it appeared in the *1947 Perkolator*.

1946-1947 Pep Squad. ***First row*** *(from left) Jimmie Earle Hoven of Lucedale, Ellene Cooley of Lucedale, Maryon Ruth Roberts of Vancleave, majorette Vivian Ward of Lucedale, Edith Fae Coker of Perkinston, and Betty Lois Overton of Gulfport.* ***Second row*** *(from left), Dorothy Jane Pilgrim of Lucedale, Betty Ann Thames of Lyman, Iris Guillen of Izbal, Guatemala, Jeanne Fern Tanet of Clermont Harbor, and Margaret David of Perkinston.* ***Third row*** *(from left), Lula Mae Solomon of Lucedale, Lorette Rouse of Saucier, Faye Pope of Lucedale, Zada Griffie Ludlow of Biloxi, and Ann Immogene Laird of Lyman.* ***Fourth row*** *(from left), Gladys Pearl Harwell of Quitman, Helen Griffin of Ocean Springs, Mary Carolyn Ludlow of Biloxi, and La Joyce Bilbo of Gulfport. Photograph from 1947 Perkolator p. 69.*

1947-1948 Swing Barons Orchestra.
First row *(from left), Pianist Betty Mae Pickard of Biloxi, Vocalist Betty Jean Lavender of Pensacola, Florida, Orchestra Director J. O. Ware, Herman Emil Rolfs of Pensacola, Florida, Grady Parker of Bay St. Louis, Alfred Wright of Gulfport, Jimmy Charles Campbell of Pascagoula, and Charles "Duke" Davis of Ocean Springs.* ***Second row*** *(from left) Blanche Simmons of Moss Point, William Joe Goff of Gulfport, Clarence Thomas Frentz of Biloxi, Laverl Sherell of Biloxi, Jack McGee of Pensacola, Florida, Donald Dubuisson of Gulfport, and John Wise of Biloxi.* ***Third row*** *(from left) Drummer Raymond Rape of Gulfport, and Bass player Sterling A. "Buddy" Dees of Biloxi.*

J. O. Ware's last "Bull-Dog Band," session 1951-1952. The Majorettes are (from left), Bettye Brown of Lucedale, June Cox of Perkinston, Joyce Lyons of Saucier, head majorette Joyce Burgess Garner of Biloxi, assistant majorette Janice "Ci" Felsher of Biloxi and Ann Mathieu of Pascagoula. Ware had promised Janice Felsher the position of head majorette in the coming season. When Sam Jones replaced Ware, Felsher had to try out for the top spot all over again. Jones, impressed with her abilities, made her the institution's first head Perkette.

Sam Jones's first band, session 1952-1953. ***First row*** *(from left), Barbara Varnadore of Lucedale, Verna Mae Read of Lucedale, E. Jean Burnham of Perkinston, Louise Diamond of Howison, Nell Summers of Saucier, Frances Thompson of Prichard, Alabama, Robert Payne of Biloxi, Dean Randall of Ocean Springs, Andrew Scafidi of Bay St. Louis, and Doris Kornman of Biloxi.* ***Second row*** *(from left), Linnell Malone of Saucier, William "Bill" Mixon of Prichard, James Plaisance of Biloxi, Aubrey Vernon Bannister of Perkinston, Gary Gollotte of Biloxi, Baldwin Bunkley of Opp, Alabama, Mary Gail Whitaker of Perkinston, Bert Byrd of Biloxi, and Kerby Ladner of Saucier.* ***Third row*** *(from left) Carroll Moore of Eight Mile, Alabama, Lonnie George of Biloxi, Karl Hatten of Perkinston, Robert Weimorts of Eight Mile, Alabama, James Burch of Prichard, Alabama, Pat Dick of Biloxi, Betty Jo Gill of Biloxi, Ann Peterson of Biloxi, Harve Hagerty of Gulfport, and Carmelite Ann Pisarich of Biloxi.* ***Fourth row*** *(from left), Wiley Wedgeworth of Saucier, Russ Hackman of Biloxi, John L. Walker of Lucedale, Conrad Bowman of Pascagoula, Kirk Middleton of Yazoo City, Elva Ware of Vancleave, Verne "Twink" Humble of Mobile, Alabama, Annette Berrey of Saraland, Alabama, Pat Cate of Prichard, Alabama, Muriel Oehler of Biloxi, and Walter Correjolles of Mississippi City.*

Prof. Jones and the Perkettes

Sam Jones, Band director, 1956 Perkolator p. 92.

Sam Porter Jones Jr. was born February 20, 1920 in Pontchatoula, Louisiana, but spent most of his childhood and youth in Kentwood, another Tangipahoa Parish town. Following his graduation from Kentwood High School, he attended Southeastern Louisiana College in Hammond. At Southeastern he met his future wife Marguerite, and he earned his bachelor's degree in music in 1941. After a short stint as band director at Hammond High School, Jones joined the United States Army Air Corps in 1942 and served as a bandsman for three and one-half years, including one year in India.

After World War II, Jones taught elementary and high school band in Meadville for six years. In summer 1952, when he heard that PJC Band Director J. O. Ware had taken a position in Louisville, Jones applied at Perkinston. On June 19, 1952, President A. L. May notified him of his selection as Ware's replacement effective July 1. So "Prof. "Jones, his wife, and their seven year old daughter Carol moved to Perkinston.

The band that Jones inherited from Ware had fielded six majorettes, one of them styled a head majorette. Immediately after his arrival at Perk, Jones decided to expand the band's women's auxiliary group by creating a dance and drill team. To head this new squad he chose Janice Felsher who had been Ware's assistant head majorette the previous year. And Felsher was a "Perkette"--that is--she played on the college's women's basketball team the members of which had been known as "Perkettes" since fall 1950.

This author spoke with Janice (Felsher) Seymour on several occasions from 1996 to 2001, and she steadfastly maintained that she never knew that the basketball team was called the Perkettes. Others who played on Perkette basketball teams from 1950 through 1955 said they did not remember the designation either. This "Perkette" question was considered at length in the section in this work entitled "Basketball: Junior College and Agricultural High School 1929-1960." Suffice it to say, every newspaper in south Mississippi, including the *Bulldog Barks* used the name in reference to the women's basketball team. Janice Felsher, Jones's first Head Perkette, was a member of the Perkette basketball team. For whatever reason Jones thought the term "Perkette" applied to the majorettes, and thus he used the name for his new dance/drill team. He never claimed to have originated the name and, in fact, said he did not.

Jones did not originate the idea of a women's drill team at Perkinston either. His predecessor Stanley Beers had organized the Pep Squad in 1937, but the Pep Squad had disappeared several years before Jones's arrival at Perkinston. By all accounts, though, the Pep Squad was only a drill and cheering squad. Apparently Pep Squad performances did not include dancing.

By adding dance to the repertoire of his drill team, Jones did create something new at Perkinston. To choreograph the Perkette dance numbers, Jones enlisted the aid of Frances Hemeter of Wiggins. Hemeter served for 22 years until her retirement in 1974. Mary Jane (Reddell) James, also of Wiggins and the former Head Perkette of session 1969-1970, served as choreographer until Jones's retirement in May 1978.

Sam Jones presents a trophy to Frances Hemeter at the time of her retirement in 1974 in appreciation for her 22 years as the choreographer for the Perkette dance team. (Left) Mary Jane (Reddell) James, replaced Hemeter as choreographer.

Jones devoted his 26-year career at Perk in his words to "turning out bands that play good music." He certainly did that, but so had his predecessors. Jones's greatest contribution to the institution was the formation of the Perkettes. Through his efforts and those of Hemeter and James the Perkettes became one of the most acclaimed junior college dance teams of the Deep South.

Perkettes of 1952 (from left), Janet Ellsberry of Perkinston, Nancy Stringer of Pascagoula, Carlyn K. Cox of Perkinston, Harriet Davis of Pascagoula, June Cox of Perkinston, Elizabeth Jackson of Alexander City, Alabama, Lynn Gentry of New Orleans, Louisiana, Geraldine "Jerry" Jordan of Perkinston, Bettye Lewis of Gulfport, Lorna Doone "Doonie" Carr of Ocean Springs, Roxie Branager of Mississippi City, Margaret Wallsmith of Lucedale, Bettye Brown of Lucedale, Joye Ingram of Hattiesburg, Dorothy Johnston of Lucedale and Head Perkette Janice "Ci" Felsher of Biloxi.

Janice Felsher (front) leads the Perkettes in practice in A.L. May Memorial Stadium in fall 1952. According to Janice (Felsher) Seymour, the hats and canes were gold. Made by the Perkinston home economics department, the uniforms consisted of a sleeveless white satin top with a Mandarin collar and a full white satin circular skirt lined with gold satin. One of the numbers they danced to the first year was "I Don't Care if the Sun Don't Shine" choreographed by Frances Hemeter.

(Above) Janice Felsher leads the Perkettes in a parade down First Street in Wiggins. Photograph courtesy of Janice (Felsher) Seymour. (Right) Janice "Ci" Felsher, billed as the "High-stepping Head Perkette," is pictured in the Bulldog Barks November 19, 1952. According to Janice (Felsher) Seymour, her nickname "Ci" was short for the fast-stepping racehorse, Citation.

1953-1954 Perkettes pose on the steps of Harrison Hall. (From left), Norma Dease of Gulfport, Iva Ann Moore of Pascagoula, Harriet Davis of Pascagoula, Sory M. Shearer of Gulfport, Maria Marta Cabus of San Pedro Sula, Honduras, Lorna Doone "Doonie" Carr of Ocean Springs, Kathryn Mallette of Lucedale, Roxie Branager of Mississippi City, Head Perkette Janie Morris of Gulfport, Jane Page of Mississippi City, Joye Ingram of Hattiesburg, Millie Webb of Long Beach, Peggy Hicks of Gulfport, Geraldine "Jerry" Jordan of Perkinston, June Cox of Perkinston, Janet Ellsberry of Perkinston, Ruth Steele of Gulf Shores, Alabama, Nancy Stringer of Pascagoula. Photograph from 1954 Perkolator, p. 116.

Head Perkette Janie Morris, session 1953-1954. Photograph from 1954 Perkolator, p. 116.

Head Perkette Janie Morris, session 1954-1955. Photograph from 1955 Perkolator, p. 123.

Janie Morris, a former state champion twirler and drum major at Gulfport High School, attended the twirling and drum majoring school at Huntsville, Texas, the summer after her high school graduation. At Huntsville she won the title "Fire Baton Champion of the Middle West." Sam Jones went to her home in Gulfport in summer 1953 and recruited Morris to lead the Perkettes that coming fall. She was the first freshman Head Perkette of Jones's career and only one of two women who served two years as Head Perkette. The other was Audrey McInnis of Wiggins who served as Head Perkette in session 1957-1958 and in session 1958-1959.

The Perkinston Junior College Orchestra poses in the Old Gym during the 1958 Prom. **Front Row** (from left), George P. Scherer of Seminole, Florida, Frank Mahoney of Pensacola, Florida, and Clarence Bauer of Foley, Alabama. **Back Row** (from left), Ronnie Sanders of Milton, Florida, James David Broome of Gulfport, Robert Hermetz of Foley, Alabama, and Jimmy Tom Savage of Moss Point. Photo courtesy of George P. Scherer.

The PJC orchestra, which had been named the Stardusters under J. O. Ware, became the Star Lighters under Sam Jones. In 1955, Jones himself played the piano for the group. By 1956 the orchestra had taken the name Rhythm Kings. By 1957 the group sported music stands reading "Frank Mahoney." According to George Scherer, who played the saxophone in the orchestra, "The music stands say 'Frank Mahoney' because Frank brought them to Perk." Going further in his letter to the MGCCC Archivist of August 12, 1998, Scherer explained, "Mahoney also had a plaid coat so the rest of us had to buy a plaid coat. Mine cost me 150 work hours." Scherer, Mahoney, and most, if not all the orchestra members, were also members of Jones's band. In recalling Jones, Scherer remembered him as "a very good teacher, not only in music but in leadership and guidance." In spring 1962 another dance orchestra called the Mystics flourished for a few months and was the last campus dance orchestra known to this author in 2000. Apparently the importance of campus dance orchestras lessened as students achieved greater mobility and freedom, and performance orchestras or "stage bands" replaced them. Jones aided band students in forming orchestras throughout his career. Once a group had been formed, it became a student organization, which usually lasted only a year or two, disappearing when the group graduated or departed. For example--The Gulfport Pictorial Review newspaper carried notice on December 12, 1968, of the first performance of "a new stage band" trained by Jones. The newspaper, though, quoted Jones as saying "hereafter the group will be on its own as a student organization."

The Golden Anniversary of the founding of the institution in 1911 coincided with the centennial of the outbreak of the American Civil War in 1861. The institution celebrated its 50th anniversary from homecoming 1961 through homecoming 1962. Former Head Perkette Carol (Jones) Taylor identified the above photograph of the band and Perkettes practicing the formation of a Beauregard Battle Flag in A. L. May Memorial Stadium and dated it as fall 1962. Head Perkette Carol (Jones) Taylor is at the center of the flag. She wears a Confederate officer's wide-brimmed hat and the other Perkettes wear Confederate kepis.

1962-1963 Perkettes
First row *(from left), Nancy L. Napier of Milner, Georgia, Frances Ball of Cleveland, Tennessee, Karen White of Wiggins, Sue Allen of Ocean Springs, Head Perkette Carol Jones of Perkinston (daughter of Sam Jones), Marsha Brewer of Lucedale, Barbara Davis of Vancleave, Elizabeth Ainsworth of Gulfport, and Gladyne Breland of Lucedale.* ***Second row*** *(from left), Myrna Jo McGowen of Pascagoula, Warrene Watts of Wiggins, Sherry Watts of Kreole, Cappie Dee Fike of McLain, Brenda Morris of Ocean Springs, Carleen Hateley of Moss Point, Penny Walker of Pascagoula, and Tana M. Butera of Biloxi.* ***Third row*** *(from left), June Ladner of Gulfport, Joan Faye Murray of Gulfport, Helen Entrekin of Vancleave, Michelle Moore of Pascagoula, Evelyn Broderick of Biloxi, Rita M. Kates of Biloxi, Jean Moran of Biloxi, Kay Gunn of Moss Point, and Dwynelle Broadus of Moss Point.*

Carol Jones, as her father's "littlest Perkette" of 1953, poses on the steps of Harrison Hall. A decade later she became Head Perkette. Photograph courtesy of Jaclyn Moffett.

Page J.J. Hayden III and maid Carol Jones at the Annual Ball of 1953. Photograph from 1953 Perkolator, p. 67.

The session 1964-1965 band and Perkettes, in a December 1964 parade in Gulfport, escort Miss America Vonda Kay Van Dyke of Phoenix, Arizona. The Perkette blocking the sign on the convertible is Nellie Ruth "Nell" (O'Neal) Murray.

Karla Hager (left) and David Reeves, both of Long Beach, model the new uniforms of the "Pride of Prof. Jones Band." The band marched into A. L. May Memorial Stadium attired in the new uniforms for the first time during the half of the MGCJC game against Itawamba on September 4, 1971. The Bulldogs won the game 28-21 and then won the next ten games. The band and Perkettes accompanied with the Bulldogs to Savannah, Georgia, and national football championship glory. These uniforms lasted through the balance of the Jones era and one year beyond.

Rita Pearl Baker

The Head Perkettes of Prof. Jones

1952-1953	Janice Felsher of Biloxi
1953-1954	Janie Morris of Gulfport
1954-1955	Janie Morris of Gulfport
1955-1956	June Cox of Perkinston
1956-1957	Mona Khayat of Moss Point
1957-1958	Joanne Eklund of Moss Point
1958-1959	Audrey Mae McInnis of Wiggins
1959-1960	Audrey Mae McInnis of Wiggins
1960-1961	Kathryn Nell Henley of Lucedale
1961-1962	Rebecca Ford of Wiggins
1962-1963	Carol Jones of Perkinston
1963-1964	Evelyn Broderick of Biloxi
1964-1965	Michael Lee Annis of Wiggins
1965-1966	Rita Pearl Baker of Wiggins
1966-1967	Mary Diane Still of Wiggins
1967-1968	Ann Marie Bobinger of Long Beach
1968-1969	Susanne Dees of Wiggins
1969-1970	Mary Jane Reddell of Wiggins
1970-1971	Elizabeth Butterfield of Biloxi
1971-1972	Cynthia Ann Scarbrough of Ocean Springs
1972-1973	Ginger Seymour of Ocean Springs
1973-1974	Jenny Hilton of Biloxi
1974-1975	Charlotte Walton of Ocean Springs
1975-1976	Rae Hermes of Biloxi
1976-1977	Cindy Easterling of Pass Christian
1977-1978	Debbie Triplett of Ocean Springs

Michael Lee Annis

Audrey Mae McInnis

Susanne Dees

Evelyn Broderick

Rae Hermes

Elizabeth Butterfield

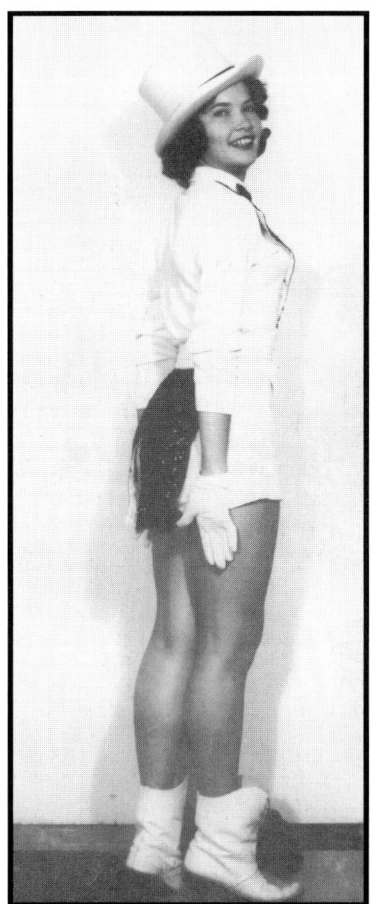

Rebecca Ford

Kathryn Nell Henley

Ginger Seymour

On Navy Day in session 1955-1956 the Perkettes performed a routine featuring that venerable mascot of the U. S. Navy--a goat. The Perkettes are (from left) Mona Khayat of Moss Point, Inell Whorton of Biloxi, Sue Ellen Mattina of Biloxi, and Genevieve (Hinkle) Peyregne of Moss Point. Her daughter, Debbie Peyregne, is third from left, top row in the 1977-1978 Perkette squad in the photograph at the bottom of this page.

Session 1977-1978 was to be Jones's last year as PJC band director. Early in that session in the Dees Hall coffee lounge, Jones stared morosely into his coffee cup and announced to those present, "I have a legacy. I may have had one before, but I know it now." When asked the definition of a "legacy" Jones replied, "The child of a student." Then he concluded, "It's time to go when you start getting a second generation." 1977-1978 Perkette Debbie Peyregne was the daughter of session 1955-1957 Perkette Genevieve (Hinkle) Peyregne of Moss Point.

Jones retired in May 1978. By his estimate his band members and Perkettes had delivered over 500 performances in south Mississippi in 26 years.

1977-1978 Perkettes--Prof. Jones's last group. Photo from 1978 Perkolator, p. 49.

Perkette choreographer Delta De La Fuente (near) and MGCJC Band Director John Jenkins observe a performance of their charges in A. L. May Memorial Stadium circa 1982.

Dr. John Edward Jenkins succeeded Sam Jones on July 1, 1978. A native of Ruston, Louisiana, Jenkins had directed the bands of Natchez High School and West Jefferson (Louisiana) High School. He held a bachelor of music degree from Louisiana Tech University and his master's and doctoral degrees from the University of Southern Mississippi. His wife, Eva, took charge of the Perkettes.

In his first year Jenkins added a rifle corps, feature twirlers, and increased the number of flag corps members. And, for the last time the Perkettes were lead by a Head Perkette--Cindy Cox of Ocean Springs. The following year two women, Jamie Lloyd and Carol Gray both of Ocean Springs, were named co-head Perkettes.

On June 10, 1980, a press release announced that MGCJC would field a "precision drill team" composed of women from all three campuses. The college hired Delta De La Fuente as choreographer and team director and charged her with training a 20-woman squad on each campus. The Perkinston Campus squad retained the name "Perkettes," but the term "Head Perkette" disappeared as each of the three squads was to have a "captain." Individual squads were to perform at their respective campuses, but all three squads were to combine for parades and football games.

A year later in June 1981, another press release announced that students at the Jefferson Davis Campus and the Jackson County Campus would be eligible to join the MGCJC band in the coming 1981-1982 school session. As in the case of the Woman's Precision Drill Team, the three sections of the band would rehearse and perform on their respective campuses and unify for parades and football games. Band scholarships, offered at Perk since August 21, 1946, were made available to students on all three campuses.

On June 9, 1981, Jenkins told a *Daily Herald* reporter regarding the new tri-campus band, "Now that students at all the campuses can participate we hope to build a bigger, better organization, something that should go a long way in promoting college-wide school spirit."

Thirteen months later in August 1982, Delta De La Fuente announced that for the first time "Perkettes" [read "Precision Drill Team" members] would receive scholarships. Like Jenkins, De La Fuente lauded the unifying effect of tri-campus organization.

There was, of course, one problem facing the band director and the choreographer. Traveling among three campuses for the purpose of training sections of teams located in three counties that were supposed to perform with precision was a logistical nightmare. The band being larger, Jenkins's problem was greater. Consequently in summer 1983, Virgel Fulcher, former

In late April 1985, Perkette Choreographer Delta De La Fuente (far left) works with her Perkette captain and co-captains who will help her in training the other members of the dance team. The Perkettes are (from left) co-captain Andre Johnson of Wiggins, co-captain Kim Jacobs of Wiggins, captain Sherri Sanders of Wiggins, and co-captain Angela Thibodeaux of Ocean Springs.

Stone High School band director, hired on to take charge of the marching section of the MGCJC band, while Jenkins handled the MGCJC concert band.

Just before the Board hired Fulcher, new band uniforms had been ordered. The hats were of the "Aussie" style [one side pinned up] and sported a gold feather. The uniform pants were blue, the shirts were gold. So Jenkins had "gold" on his mind when Perkinston Campus Vice President Clyde Strickland informed him that Fulcher's employment was another manifestation of MGCJC President J. J. Hayden's determination to forge a more perfect "marriage" among the three campuses. Jenkins, always quick with a quip, replied to Strickland, "Then why don't you name our band the "Band of Gold?" Strickland liked the idea and so did Hayden. Thus the MGCJC Band of Gold marched onto the field for the first time in fall 1983.

Band of Gold Director Virgel Fulcher. From 1988 Perkolator, p. 272.

By spring 1985 the "Precision Dance Team" experiment was at an end. On April 25, 1985, Delta De La Fuente told a *South Mississippi Sun* reporter, "We tried having members from the other campuses, but it was too hard to get a cohesive unit. Now all the girls are required to live in dormitories." De La Fuente left in summer 1987, and Kathy Braun replaced her as Perkette choreographer. Braun remained in that position in 2000.

Perkette choreographer Kathleen "Kathy" Braun. Photo from 1989 Perkolator, p. 152.

The members of the 1983-1984 original Band of Gold guard (flags and rifles) pose behind Malone Hall. According to Band of Gold Director Virgel Fulcher, the students in the photograph represent all three MGCJC campuses. The gold plumed hats and gold uniform blouses introduced in session 1983-1984, together with MGCJC President J. J. Hayden's desire for a "tri-campus marriage," inspired MGCJC Director of Bands John E. Jenkins to name the institution's band "The Band of Gold." According to Band of Gold Director Virgel Fulcher, "The first Band of Gold practice had a total of 72 people, including musicians, dancers, twirlers, and guard members. Before the first performance we had expanded to a total of 85 or so. We ended the first marching season with 115 members. The first performance of the Band of Gold took place at Perkinston Stadium. . . . The first show was so well received the Band of Gold actually received a standing ovation from the fans. . . . The program continued to grow to approximately 150 by the end of the fourth year."

Virgel Fulcher ran for the office of Stone County Superintendent of Education in fall 1987 and won. In January 1988 David P. Dueitt, a native of Tuscaloosa, Alabama, took Fulcher's place as director of the Band of Gold.

Dueitt had served as band director of Fayette (Alabama) High School, 1978-1980, and as band director of John S. Shaw High School in Mobile, Alabama, 1980-1986. At the time he was hired to direct the Band of Gold, Dueitt was a graduate assistant at the University of Alabama, having recently completed his master's degree in music.

Over the next decade Dueitt dramatically increased the number of band members, peaking at about 160 members. Also, in his words, "We started a jazz band, a percussion ensemble, a brass ensemble, and a woodwind ensemble in addition to the concert and marching bands. We later added a clarinet choir, flute choir, and a mallet ensemble, an indoor drum line and a winter guard to our list of performing groups. Some of these groups had been part of the curriculum years before, but were not currently active."

The addition of the new elements of the Band of Gold together with the movement to play junior college football games on Thursday nights ended the days of the itinerant band director traveling among the campuses. Interested JD and JC students were, for a time, bussed to Perkinston Campus. The busing stopped when numbers fell below the level deemed economical for transport. "But," said Dueitt, "ten or fifteen JD and JC students commute on their own every year, and they get a scholarship equal to the Perk members. So the Band of Gold is a tri-campus organization."

Several assistant band directors worked with Dueitt during his first decade, but in light of Perkinston history, he received a very special assistant in July 1997. Clifton D. Taylor Jr., grandson of legendary band director Sam Jones, left his position at Sam Houston High School in Lake Charles, Louisiana, to come to Perk.

In speaking of Jones and his grandson, Dueitt said, "We are proud of our band heritage and those who brought us to where we are today. Professor Sam Jones's contributions can not be overestimated. The directors who followed him had big shoes to fill. I am pleased to be partially responsible for hiring his grandson as assistant director who teaches theory and jazz studies. The future of the Band of Gold is secure with such a competent musician who is so familiar with our history ready to take the reins when I decide to retire."

Band of Gold Director David Dueitt.

1994-1995 Band of Gold. ***First row*** *(from left) Chad Parks (drum major) Angie Richards (feature twirler), Menya Jefferson and Kim Miller (Perkette captains), Hayley Guillot (feature twirler), and Darlene Gray (drum major).* ***Second row*** *(from left) Lana Coley, Melissa Paffe, Andrea Simpson, Kelli Newman, Erin Brown, Hildie Syverson, Missy Belcher, Michelle Hewtty, Sylvia Goudy, Donna Cravens, Katie Spiller, Melissa Rouse, Heather Hadley, Mandy Farve, Wendelin Hunter, Jennifer Ausborn, and Katy Stallings.* ***Third row*** *(from left) Christina Murray, Alvin Bjorensen, Robin Walters, Marshall Crutchfield, Christina Basilio, Donna Holland, Shannon Connar, Tonya Ost, Alicia Everett, Joe Abston, Tammy Burger, and Sherry Peckens.* ***Fourth row*** *(from left) Chantel Thompson, Kevin D. Green, Christopher Swindell, Amanda C. Taylor, Tim Clarest, Katie McMahan, Jason Morgan, Nikol Willis, Michelle Judge, Greg Sonoff, Kimberly Memitt, Jennifer Gates, Shawan du Paschall, and Antonia M. Harper.* ***Fifth row*** *(from left) Katrina D. Howard, Lynn Breland, Shane Smith, Steven Humphrey, Jonas Cockson, Ryan Alexander, Renee Richard, Kelly Holland, Gena Miller, Dennis A. Wright, Andrew Penrow III, Brian Harris, and Greg Woods.* ***Sixth row*** *(from left) Tremayne Martin, Jason Walker, Norris B. Thompson, Jeremy Morgan, Glen Agustin, Matt Coburger, Chris Newton, Jack Lastorka, Nathan Ladner, Ronnie Dennis, Brian G. Davis, April Johnson, and Myka Hale.* ***Seventh row*** *(from left) Jana Fulmer, Brian Stewart, Bryant Johnson, C. J. Hilborn, Randall Albert, Stacy Grooden, Patrick Halstead, Colt Hall, Mike Tremaine, James Hamilton, Adam Mason, Sheldon Deloach, and Becky Edwards.* ***Eighth row*** *(from left) Amber Leatherwood, Dolive Sasser, Yolanda Ashley, Felisha Thompson, David Gatto, Brad Graham, Tim Parkman, Gary Griffin, Geoff Whetstone, John Davis, Daron Richburg, Briley Richmond, and Amy Strength.* ***Ninth row*** *(from left) Tony Geringer, Jeremy Bailey, Trendell Edwards, Jason Hise, Alexander Dott, Jessie C. Howell, and Joey Boyd.* ***Tenth row*** *(from left) Don Green, Derek Simmons, Byron Cobern, Sean Westmoreland, Justin Richards, Chris Vest, and Charles Davis, Jr.*

The MGCCC Alumni Association dedicated Homecoming Day, October 19, 1996, as a salute to Sam Jones and to the band members and Perkettes that he taught in his 26-year career. (Above) Jones holds his scrapbook of memories as he sits with a new generation of Perkettes in A. L. May Memorial Stadium during the homecoming game. His former Head Perkette of session 1965-1966, Rita Pearl (Baker) Sheffield Hester was inducted into the MGCCC Alumni Association Hall of Fame at the luncheon that day.

The groundbreaking for the $900,000 Sam P. Jones Jr. Band Hall took place in May 1997. (From left) Sam Jones, Band of Gold Director David Dueitt, former Perkinston Campus Vice President Clyde Strickland, and Perkinston Campus Fine Arts Department Chairperson Kathryn Lewis.

The building inspectors declared the building ready for occupancy at 11:30 a.m. on March 24, 1998. The members of the Band of Gold entered the structure at 1:15 p.m. on that day. According to band student Carrie Price, "The moving was concluded around 2:30 p.m. At that time the conductor's podium and concert set was assembled. Shortly thereafter, Mr. Dueitt called the band to order and playing position. Russell Wiley, first chair trumpet player, was the first to actually play a note in the new room."

A FAREWELL TO PROF. JONES

The Jones-Taylor musical family poses inside the Sam P. Jones Jr. Band Hall on dedication Day October 9, 1998.
***First row** (from left) Carol (Jones) Taylor, Sam Jones, and Clifton D. Taylor Jr. **Second row** (from left) Clifton M. Taylor, Clifton D. "Donnie" Taylor Sr., James M. Taylor, John C. Taylor, Stacy (Stewart) Taylor [John's wife], Evelyn D. Taylor, and Charlotte (Wise) Taylor [Clifton Jr.'s wife].*

All five of the men in the photo were then or had been professional musicians. Donnie Taylor, husband of Sam Jones's daughter, Carol, and vice president of the MGCCC Jefferson Davis Campus, had been director of both the JD and JC campus choirs in session 1965-1966 and of the JD choir alone until 1969. Clifton Jr. was then MGCCC Band of Gold assistant director. Clifton Jr.'s son Clifton M. and his daughter Evelyn, auger for a fourth generation of Jones-Taylor musicians. Sam Jones last visited Perk for the dedication of the band hall and its naming in his honor. He died November 19, 1999.

Music: Glee Club/Choir, September 1937-December 2000

In fall 1937 Lorraine Godbold of Baton Rouge, Louisiana, replaced Perkinston Music Director Elizabeth Davis for a year while the latter took leave to attend the Louisiana State University school of music. Simultaneously, Stanley Beers of Pine Bluff, Arkansas, replaced Harmon Longmire as band director. For the institution's tenth annual spring tour in 1938, Godbold's Glee Club and Beer's orchestra teamed up to present *Cleopatra*, a burlesque opera.

Scene from the spring 1938 production of the burlesque opera, Cleopatra. The Glee Club men's chorus performed the opera with Curtis Parker of McHenry in the starring role of Cleopatra, who was described as a "modernized Egyptian co-ed." Photo from 1938 Perkolator, p. 57.

Davis returned to her job as Perkinston music director in fall 1938, but left permanently in spring 1939. Harriet Fulton of Jamestown, North Dakota, replaced Davis in fall 1939. In spring 1940 the orchestra and glee club teamed up for the institution's last spring tour.

All the programs at Perkinston were disrupted by America's preparation for and subsequent participation in the Second World War but none more than the music program. After Fulton left in spring 1942, she was followed by five glee club sponsors in eight years.

Perkinston Campus Choir Director Eugene Clement warming up the choir before a performance in Wilkes-Barre, Pennsylvania, in December 1972.

On September 1, 1949, the Perkinston Board of Trustees hired Eugene Clement as the first man to direct the Glee Club at the institution. He remained in that position for the next 37 years. A native of Hattiesburg, Clement had first studied for the ministry at Mississippi College. In his junior year he had changed his major to music and started over as a freshman. When he arrived in Perkinston at age 25, he held the bachelor's degree in music from Mississippi Southern College.

After Clement's arrival at Perk in September 1949, no more was heard of the designation, "Glee Club." Clement called his singing group a "choir." Less than a year later on July 8, 1950, a large advertisement in the *Daily Herald* trumpeted PJC's offerings in "fine arts" which were described as "music, dramatics, writing, and painting." Though MGCJC did not officially use the term "fine arts" until the publication of the *1970-1971 Catalog*, Clement began popularizing the designation 20 years earlier.

So far as his music was concerned, Clement's choir performed annually throughout south Mississippi, but performances in other regions of the state were not rare. Occasionally a Clement choir performed in a distant state.

Perhaps Clement's most famous distant choir performance took place in Wilkes-Barre, Pennsylvania, on the afternoon of December 2, 1972. Wilkes-Barre and other towns in Pennsylvania's Wyoming Valley had been heavily damaged by floods unleashed by Hurricane Agnes on June 23, 1972. In the aftermath of the disaster, a "sister city" connection had been forged between Wilkes-Barre and the Camille-ravaged towns of the Mississippi Gulf Coast.

Coast businessmen, remembering Clement's Christmas-time choir performance of 1969 in the virtually destroyed town of Pass Christian, persuaded Southern Airways to fly the 42-member Perkinston Campus choir to Wilkes-Barre. The most poignant moment in the performance in the Luzerne County Courthouse came when the Perkinston Choir sang "The Battle Hymn of the Republic."

In regard to his teaching Clement felt that he had been "called" to teach music "just as any preacher who is called to preach." "In fact," he continued "I've touched lives as a teacher that I'd never have been able to touch as a preacher." While his choirs sang a great deal of secular music, his most memorable choir performances came at Easter and at Christmas.

In May 1986, just before the close of his 37-year tenure at Perkinston, Clement summed up his thoughts on what was then the longest period of service by an employee in the history of the institution. He said, "I wouldn't trade my career for any other in the world. I would do it over again at the drop of a hat--in fact, I don't think I could have done anything else."

After Clement retired in May 1986, John Jenkins took charge of the choir until September 1988 when Mary Ann Bond succeeded him. In December 1990 Marilyn (Porter) Smith [later Lott] replaced Bond.

Lott, a Long Beach native and a Perkinston Campus graduate (class of 1974), had been a student of Clement's. She was still the choir director when the 20th century ended.

On December 2, 1972 the MGCJC Perkinston Campus choir, under the direction of Eugene Clement, sings on the steps of the Luzerne County Courthouse in Wilkes-Barre, Pennsylvania. Standing at the piano is Francis Wysner, seated is Cheryl Blackwell. First row, from left, Paulene Dedeaux, Cindy Guild, Cathy Moore, Susan Ezell, Laura Padgett, and Michela Vizzini. Second row, unknown, Johnnie Overstreet, Brenda Davis, Eve Reed, Diane Buxton, Priscilla Reeves, and Maria Vizzini. Third row, Myra Taylor, Toni Smith, Debo Kennedy, Kandi Broome, and Cathy Ball. Fourth row, Sharon Reynolds, Myrtle Potter, Rhonda Gibson, Anita Wesson, Kathleen George, and Kay Ruffin. Fifth row, Bill Wesson, Robert Stroup, Johnny Lewis, Bob Innes and Jimmy McFarland. Sixth row, Kenny Goff, Wade Ivey, Mark Reed, and Virgel Fulcher. Seventh row, Robert Hilbun, Nick Vizzini, Hugh Griffon, Milton Walker and Maurice Gary. Eighth row, Bruce Dethfloff, Ronnie Slater, John Landers, Joel Slayter and Bill Ford. Photo identified by Virgel Fulcher.

In addition to directing the choir, Marilyn [Smith] Lott acted in several drama productions in the 1990's and even directed The Music Man in 1996. (Above) Lott portrays the lead role in Peter Pan on Malone Hall stage in April 1993. The children are (from left) Christa Mellinger, Ryan Chotto, and Matthew Altman.

The Perkinston Campus choir ensemble known as Mississippi Sound began in 1979 under Eugene Clement as the "Kids of Note." (Right) Mississippi Sound performs in 1991 under the direction of choir director Marilyn [Smith] Lott. ***Front row*** *(from left) Catherine Guess, Richard Wales, Anthony Barnes, and Lori Wales.* ***Second row*** *(from left) Jeremy Morgan, Kristi Evans, director Marilyn Smith, Melanie Rawls, and John Jones. Photo courtesy of Marilyn Lott.*

Music: A Case of "Musical Choir Directors"
The Jefferson Davis Singers and the Jackson County Singers

With the opening of the two Coast campuses in September 1965, Clifton D. "Donnie" Taylor directed the choirs of both JD Campus and JC Campus for the session 1965-1966. Beginning in fall 1966 Taylor directed only the JD choir, and Joe Ello took charge of the JC choir.

In fall 1969, as Taylor embarked upon an administrative career that eventually led to his becoming vice president of the JD Campus, Adam Ortiz succeeded him as choir director. Ortiz named the choir the Jefferson Davis Singers and remained as its director for 20 years.

In 1972 JC Fine Arts Department Chairman Joe Ello put Martha (Moore) Richardson in charge of the JC choir, which she renamed the JC Singers. When she succeeded Ello as department chairperson in 1981, Richardson placed direction of the JC Singers in the hands of Rhonda (Fisher) Hood. Leon Gray succeeded Hood at JC in fall 1987. But then Hood succeeded Ortiz at JD in fall 1989.

In 1992 Hood left JD. Retired Biloxi High School choral director Hilda Barnes filled in until Dr. David Knowles took charge in fall 1993. Knowles remained JD choir director in 2000.

In 1999 Dr. Rhonda Fisher [formerly Hood] returned to JC. According to Fisher, Leon Gray was still leading the JC Singers when she re-arrived, but the JC Singers, which used to be the whole choir was by then an ensemble. So Fisher resurrected the choir and Gray retained the JC Singers. In fall 2000 Gray gave Fisher the JC Singers, too. She then re-merged all the singers and renamed the amalgamation the Jackson County Choir.

Both Fisher and Knowles, when interviewed by this author, mentioned that they were pleased with the spirit of unity among the three campus choirs. On several occasions their choirs, together with Marilyn Lott's Perkinston Campus choir, had performed as one body. The tradition of tri-campus choir performances began at least as early as November 6, 1971. On that day at Perkinston, Eugene Clement, Adam Ortiz, and Joe Ello combined their choirs to sing for the assemblage at homecoming.

Adam Ortiz leads an element of the JD Singers in practice circa 1973. Ortiz directed the JC Choir from fall 1969 to spring 1989.

Dr. Rhonda [Hood] Fisher, two-campus [two times JC] choir director.

Jackson County Campus Choir Director Martha (Moore) Richardson sits at the piano during a JC Singers performance. The JC Singers are (from left) Joe Lohfink, Pat Beldin, Dannie Edwards, Jean Derrick, Jack Busby, Merry Limehouse, James Bowers, and Jerilyn Bridges. Photograph from 1980 Phases, p. 81.

DRAMA: A PHOTOGRAPHIC ESSAY 1914 - 2000

Drama at Perkinston

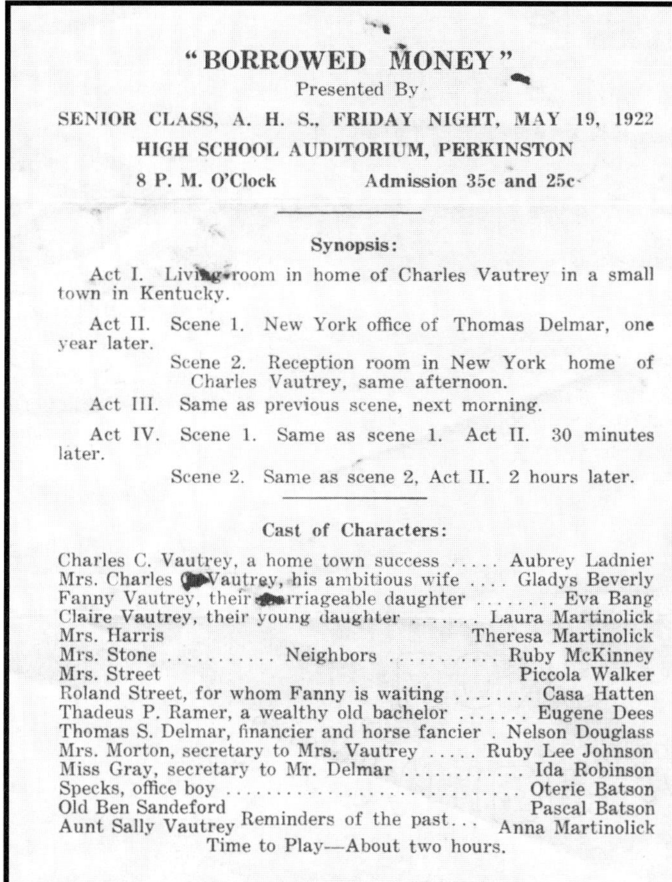

"BORROWED MONEY"

Presented By

SENIOR CLASS, A. H. S., FRIDAY NIGHT, MAY 19, 1922

HIGH SCHOOL AUDITORIUM, PERKINSTON

8 P. M. O'Clock Admission 35c and 25c

Synopsis:

Act I. Living-room in home of Charles Vautrey in a small town in Kentucky.

Act II. Scene 1. New York office of Thomas Delmar, one year later.

Scene 2. Reception room in New York home of Charles Vautrey, same afternoon.

Act III. Same as previous scene, next morning.

Act IV. Scene 1. Same as scene 1. Act II. 30 minutes later.

Scene 2. Same as scene 2, Act II. 2 hours later.

Cast of Characters:

Charles C. Vautrey, a home town success ..... Aubrey Ladnier
Mrs. Charles C. Vautrey, his ambitious wife .... Gladys Beverly
Fanny Vautrey, their marriageable daughter .... Eva Bang
Claire Vautrey, their young daughter .... Laura Martinolick
Mrs. Harris ... Theresa Martinolick
Mrs. Stone .... Neighbors .... Ruby McKinney
Mrs. Street ... Piccola Walker
Roland Street, for whom Fanny is waiting .... Casa Hatten
Thadeus P. Ramer, a wealthy old bachelor .... Eugene Dees
Thomas S. Delmar, financier and horse fancier . Nelson Douglass
Mrs. Morton, secretary to Mrs. Vautrey ..... Ruby Lee Johnson
Miss Gray, secretary to Mr. Delmar .... Ida Robinson
Specks, office boy .... Oterie Batson
Old Ben Sandeford ... Reminders of the past... Pascal Batson
Aunt Sally Vautrey ... Reminders of the past... Anna Martinolick

Time to Play—About two hours.

(Above) The Harrison-Stone Agricultural High School graduating class of 1923 performed The Rose O'Plymouth Train at 8 p.m. on Saturday, May 19, 1923, as the first event in commencement week. The cast members pose outside Bennett Hall before the performance. The earliest dramatic presentations at the Agricultural High School (AHS) at Perkinston were senior class plays usually presented annually during commencement week.

(Left) The earliest playbill held in the MGCCC Archives in 2000 was found among the souvenirs of Casa Hatten by his son Clyde, who placed the document on loan.

Drama production began at Perkinston on May 21, 1914 with the staging of the senior class play titled *The Junior* during the institution's first commencement week. From that first high school graduation until the last one in May 1962, the high school seniors usually presented a play near the end of the school session.

Most of the plays before 1929 were put on by one or another of the high school classes and almost always in the spring. The establishment of the junior college division in September 1925, gave impetus to the idea of collecting the most talented actors at the school into a troupe for the purpose of presenting fine plays. Why? Because the Mississippi Association of Junior Colleges (MAJC) sponsored a Little Theatre contest and gave a trophy to the school producing the winner.

On May 10, 1929, at Moorhead, the Perkinston Little Theatre group won the state championship in drama under the direction of history instructor Zola Emerson and English instructor Minnie Kay Pearson. Emerson was still chortling over that singular victory forty years later. She wrote, "Miss Pearson and I were pleased with our success with our Little Theatre program. Perk got first place over mighty Hinds Junior College. . . ."

In October 1929, with the completion of Denson Hall, the great curtain emblazoned HSJ (for Harrison-Stone-Jackson) rose for the first time in the 500-seat auditorium on the third floor. The Emerson-Pearson team set about training fledgling thespians for yet another crack at the state title. Not only did the Perk actors triumph, but they did in it in the "Eagles nest."

The 1930 victory came on March 28 at Raymond for a 30-minute fantasy entitled "Maker of Dreams." Mosley "Fishbait" Miller of Pascagoula served as stage manager for this production which featured three characters--F. H. "Mac" McDonald of Petal, Edwina Lassiter of McHenry, and Fred Reeves of Gulfport. In a tragic postscript to this drama, McDonald, who also had been a member of Perkinston's prize-winning state championship debate team three weeks before the play, died two weeks after the play of appendicitis.

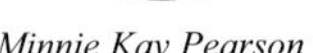

Minnie Kay Pearson

Zola Emerson

(From left) The Mississippi Association Junior Colleges (MAJC) Little Theatre championship trophies of 1929(10 inches tall), 1930, and 1934 won by Harrison-Stone-Jackson Junior College actors directed by Emerson and Pearson.

(Far Left) F. H. "Mac" McDonald and Edwina Lassiter appear in their costumes for the fantasy Maker of Dreams, which won the MAJC 1930 Little Theatre championship. Photograph courtesy of Jane (Denson) Covington.

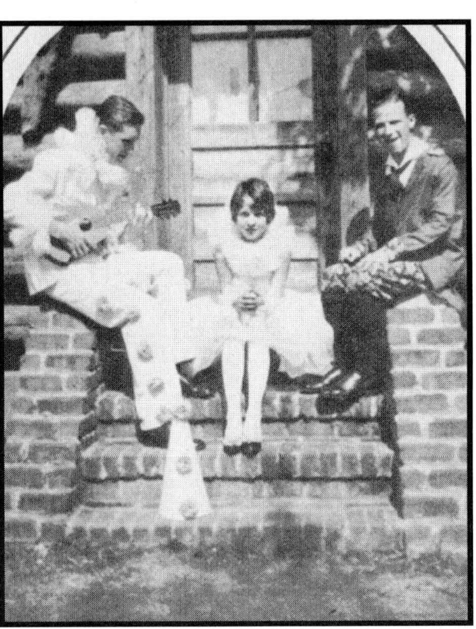

(From left) F. H. "Mac" McDonald as Pierrot, Edwina Lassiter as Pierret, and Fred Reeves as the "Maker of Dreams" pose on the steps of the Dorothy Hinton Hut (or "Y-Hut") at Perkinston in May 1930. Photograph from an unnamed newspaper (probably the Times Picayune) courtesy of Margurite (Callahan) Boswell.

Perkinston's aspiring actors of the early 1930s belonged to the "Literary Club," but in session 1932-1933, that rather nondescript designation improved dramatically. Emerson and Pearson christened it the "Dramatic Club" and stated the association's purpose as that of training students in public speaking, dramatics, and debate. On April 5, 1934, the Perkinston Dramatic Club hosted the MAJC Little theatre Tournament, and the Emerson-Pearson directorial team garnered for Perk a third state trophy.

The 1934 championship play, titled *The Valiant*, starred Merrill "Red" True as a Georgia convict scheduled to die in the electric chair. The 30-minute drama featured a loudly ticking clock, which counted down the final 30-minutes before the inmate's impending execution.

With eight schools competing that night in Denson Auditorium, the clock ticked from Thursday, April 5 into the wee hours of Friday, April 6. Consequently, in 1935 the MAJC divided the state into two Little Theatre divisions with Perk hosting the south division and Hinds hosting the north. On March 15, 1935, Perk won south division with *Trifles*, a light tragedy adapted from *A Jury of Her Peers*. Unfortunately the next week at Raymond, Perk lost in the state "play-offs."

In the seven years that Emerson and Pearson directed theatre at Perkinston, the college never failed to place in the state tournament. When they departed for government careers in Washington, D. C., in May 1935, they left behind a record of three first places, two second places (one a south division championship), and two third places.

English instructor Martha Louise Hudson took charge of the Dramatic Club during session 1935-1936. Hudson patterned the Perkinston Dramatic Club on Little Theatres of America, dividing the club members into five departments--acting, make-up, electrical, stage managing, and costume. The club prepared *Mansions* as its 1936 effort in the MAJC Little Theatre contest but forfeited only a few days before the contest due to a flu epidemic at Perk. The next year Hudson's troupe took third place in the state contest at Goodman for *The Monkey's Paw*.

In session 1937-1938 English instructor Dorothy Brown led her charges in tying for third place in the state at the MAJC contest. The next year home economics instructor Mary Eleanor Johnston's actors failed to place in the state contest, but their production of *Spring Fever* enjoyed the distinction of being the first photographed for the *Perkolator* yearbook. In session

The session 1938-1939 production of Spring Fever took place in Denson Hall auditorium. The actors are (from left) standing: Mattie Lou Lyons of Gulfport, Elva Downing of Perkinston, Alvin Malley of Gulfport, Jean Parker of Biloxi, and Victor Royal of Buford, Georgia. Kneeling (from left) William Jorgensen of Chicago, Illinois, and William Jackson "Jack" Anders of Biloxi. Lying is Lorraine Patterson of Gulfport. Sitting (from left) Hazel Ramsay of Vancleave, John Williams of Buford, Georgia, and Sara Joyce Holland of Camden, Arkansas. The HSJ monogram on the curtain stands for Harrison-Stone-Jackson. Photograph from 1939 Perkolator, p. 73.

The cast of The Importance of Being Earnest pose on the stage in Denson Hall in session 1939-1940. (From left), the actors are Lois Lawrence of New Orleans, Louisiana, Wyeth Ramsay of Vancleave, Samuel Wilson of Gulfport, Aimee Ros of Pascagoula, Jean Parker of Biloxi, Edward Hudgens of Theodore, Alabama, James Byrd of Gulfport, and Mattie Lou Lyons of Gulfport. Harriet Fulton (right), the first instructor hired specifically to teach a drama class, directed the play. Photograph 1941 Perkolator, p. 16.

Harriet Fulton

1939-1940 the school ratcheted up its commitment to drama by adding a new elective dubbed "English 14-15--Play Production." The course met two hours per week for two semesters and carried a total of four semester hours credit. The course description declared that:

> "The aims of this course are to arouse appreciation of dramatic art and to familiarize students with practical dramatic production. Theory and practical play production are combined. Some study will be devoted to the principles and methods of acting, directing plays, and to arranging stage scenery, and properties. Attention will be given to analysis of plays, characterization, conduction of rehearsals, etc."

The 16" tall 1946-1947 MAJC Little Theatre championship trophy won by Perkinston Junior College for its production of Raw Men.

To teach the new course the Board of Trustees hired Harriet Fulton of Jamestown, North Dakota. Her job description advertised her as instructor in "voice and dramatics."

So in September 1939, coincident with the German invasion of Poland which detonated World War II, Perkinston added credit in drama and hired a teacher specifically to teach drama. The greater drama in Europe had an impact on the conduct of the affairs of the MAJC and consequently on Fulton's program. Though America was not yet in the war, the dislocation occasioned by the American Preparedness Program caused MAJC officials to begin suspending intercollegiate competition in area after area. Apparently one of the first to go was the Little Theatre contest, which became a "festival" rather than a competition for a trophy.

Music department instructor Gertrude Sandrock took Fulton's place as second semester 1943 began. Two years later Joe Stroud of Taylorsville hired on as a social studies teacher and instructor in play production.

On April 7, 1947, Stroud's actors took the MAJC state championship trophy for their rendition of *Raw Men*, a tale of the north woods. The 1947 contest, apparently the first since the end of the Second World War, may have been the last Little Theatre competition in Mississippi junior college history. Perk hosted the contest. Only one other school, Meridian Junior College, sent a troupe. The judges rated Perk's performance at 89.6 and Meridian's at 88.8, so by a razor-thin margin Perk took the prize.

Perk Players sponsor Myrah Riley (left at lectern) poses with the charter members of Delta Psi Omega National Honorary Dramatic Society in the War Memorial Chapel in May 1955. The charter members are (from left) Robert Murrah of Moss Point, Nancy Mabry of Wiggins, Kerby Ladner of Saucier, Robert Kirkconnell of La Lima, Honduras, Janette Jones of Gulfport, Charles Huthmaker of Biloxi, Myrta Faye Higginbotham of Biloxi, Landy Avant of Georgetown, South Carolina, and Obra Quave of Gulfport. Photograph from 1956 Perkolator, p. 80.

Natalie Watson of Blue Mountain, who was already on contract as an English teacher, succeeded Joe Stroud as Dramatic Club sponsor and play production instructor in January 1949. Watson renamed the Dramatic Club the "Mask and Scroll" and set about producing plays, the proceeds of which were directed toward improving the facilities in Denson Hall Auditorium. In October 1950 the old "HSJ" curtain in Denson Hall fell for the last time and was replaced by a "Saluda Velour blue curtain with gold valence and gold letter P." It was about time since the school's name had been changed from Harrison-Stone-Jackson Junior College to Perkinston Junior College eight years before. Watson then announced that, "The main goal of the Mask and Scroll . . . is to buy a background drop for the stage to replace the burlap which is now used."

In September 1952, Myrah N. Riley of Hattiesburg, holder of a bachelor's and master's degree in English from Mississippi Southern College, took charge of Perkinston drama. Riley eliminated the name "Mask and Scroll" in favor of its generic predecessor "Dramatic Club." But then in a *Daily Herald* article of Friday, November 5, 1954, a new name for Riley's drama students appeared. The article stated that, "The talent show sponsored by the Perk Players of Perkinston Junior College was presented Tuesday night." After November 1954 the name "Perk Players" became the name used to describe the drama students at Perkinston.

Joseph C. Feduccia

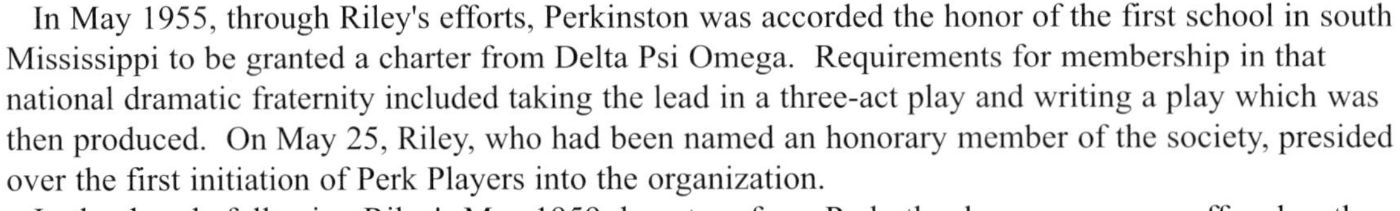

In May 1955, through Riley's efforts, Perkinston was accorded the honor of the first school in south Mississippi to be granted a charter from Delta Psi Omega. Requirements for membership in that national dramatic fraternity included taking the lead in a three-act play and writing a play which was then produced. On May 25, Riley, who had been named an honorary member of the society, presided over the first initiation of Perk Players into the organization.

In the decade following Riley's May 1959 departure from Perk, the drama program suffered as the institution passed through the upheaval attending the formation of the two Coast campuses. At least four drama instructors served during that decade. Philip Lisotta, who had charge of the Perk Players from 1962 to 1965, was in the process of building a strong program, but he left Perk to teach at Jefferson Davis Campus when it opened in September 1965.

Joseph Feduccia, who took charge of drama in September 1966, was the last instructor to teach the two-hour play production course instituted in 1939. In September 1967 the institution replaced that course with a three-hour theatre appreciation course. The reason for the change, according to the *Bulldog Barks*, March 16, 1968, was that the old course focused only on producing a play and involved no academic study. The new theatre appreciation course did involve

(Above) On Denson Hall stage in fall 1969 Kathryn (Schledwitz) Lewis (center) directs her first Perk Players in practice for The Sandbox. The one-act play together with another one-act play, titled The Lottery, constituted Lewis's first production. The Perk Players are (from left) Mike Murphy of Gulfport, Becky Sloan of Columbus, and Jane Hill of Biloxi.

(Above) The stoning of Stephanie Jane "Stevie" Siler of Ocean Springs by the villagers in the climatic ending of The Lottery. Photos from 1970 Perkolator, p 44-45.

academic study and thus fulfilled requirements for fine arts credit. Feduccia departed after only three years, but his replacement stayed ten times that long, directing the Perk Players throughout the balance of the 20th century.

Kathryn Ann Schledwitz [later Lewis], a native of Memphis, Tennessee, earned her bachelor's degree and her master's degree with a major in speech and a minor in theatre at the University of Southern Mississippi. In summer 1969 at the age of 20, while still in graduate school, she went job-hunting. She had tentatively accepted a job as a remedial reading instructor at Holmes Junior College when on July 23 the Board of Trustees of MGCJC offered her the position of instructor of "Speech and Debate, salary of $6,250 for 9 months, effective September 1."

Lewis accepted. On her arrival at Perk, she set about teaching a full load of speech classes and began searching for debaters. She found four. One was a football player who could not travel on tour with a debate team and, in her words, "One got kicked out of school."

Since theatre had lapsed with Joe Feduccia's departure, she requested that the Board of Trustees allow her to teach theatre instead of debate. The Board granted her request and she resurrected the Perk Players with a vengeance. In her first year Lewis demonstrated the high-powered frenetic pace of play production and teaching that she sustained for the next 32 years.

On December 11 and 12, 1969, Lewis's first troupe of Perk Players took the stage in the Denson Hall Auditorium for a performance of two one-act plays--*The Lottery* and *The Sandbox*. On April 8, 1971, she oversaw the Perk Players' presentation of *A Night of One-Acts*. All four of the one-act plays presented that night had been written, produced, and directed by Perkinston Campus students. Lewis's actors then capped the year on May 5 with the dramatization of a current best-selling book titled, *Up the Down Staircase*.

In fall 1970, the Perk Players on November 18 staged a comedic satire titled *The American Dream*. On December 15 they "brought the house down" with *Charley*, an adaptation of the book *Flowers for Algernon*. Lewis and cast then departed for Christmas vacation, and while they were gone, the house really did go down. A section of the ceiling of Old Denson Hall fell, crushing the foreign language lab beneath the auditorium.

When Lewis and the Perk Players came back in January, they had to find new quarters. The Perk Players' spring 1971 production of *O Dad, Poor Dad* debuted the last week of March in Heidelberg Hall Cafeteria. Thereafter Gregory War Memorial Chapel with a seating capacity one-fifth that of Denson Hall became the Perk Players Playhouse.

Since cramped facilities then restricted the size of the audience that she could entertain on the campus, Lewis decided to take the Perk Players on the road to serve a very special audience--elementary school children. Serve them they did--both theatrically and literally. The first week in April 1971, Lewis's inaugural Perk Players Children's Touring Company traveled among nine Coast elementary schools performing *The King of Ice Cream Mountain*. David Byrd as Zeno, Lynn Glaze as King Bumpygruff, Jane Hill as Princess Happy, and Johnny McKinney as Muffles ended each performance by serving the children cups of ice cream. The kids ate it up!

Lewis's second children's tour lasted from March 15 to April 5, 1972. The Perk Players performed *Snow White and Rose Red* at 14 elementary schools located from Richton in the north to the Seabee Base in the south, from Hancock North Central to Lucedale. On the heaviest day of that itinerary they performed five times.

The Perk Players' third annual children's tour troupe hit the road in December 1972, performing *The Mouse Who Didn't Believe in Santa*. The plot of the play was built around a mouse named Squeaknibble who did not believe in Santa Claus until she was captured by Pete the Cat and saved by Saint Nick on Christmas Eve. The itinerary included 20 schools with multiple performances on several days.

Lewis and the Perk Players in full costume left campus in two cars bound for two morning performances at two different schools in Biloxi. Lewis drove Santa in her vehicle to the school of the earliest performance, and the mice and the cat in the other car went to the other one. When the driver at the wrong school realized her error, she drove to the nearest Burger King to use the phone to call Lewis at the right school to tell her they were on the way.

Meanwhile Lewis, having figured out what must have happened to her errant troupers, drove toward the wrong school and chanced upon what she described as a scene from the television show "Cops"--her mice and her feline being frisked.

The immediate background to that scene had involved frantic mice and one cat (which the employees of the not-yet-open-for-business Burger King had interpreted as panicky bandits) holding notes up to the window (which the Burger King workers interpreted as give-us-all-your-money demands) asking to use the phone. The Burger Kingers had dialed 911. The police had responded, and therein lay the tale. Lewis finally saved her troupers from the Biloxi police, and thereafter those malefactors certainly believed more fervently in Lewis's itineraries. If the plot of this farce was not an exact case of "life imitating art," it was, in the words of the WPA workers of the 1930s, "Close enough for government work."

In a tragic postscript to the Burger King Drama, the Santa Claus show did not go on that morning at the first school because the mice and the cat were up against the wall. That, of course, much to the disappointment of 600 school children. But the tragedy had a final act with a fairy tale ending. Lewis rescheduled the school. Santa took candy for the kids and in Lewis's words, "They lived happily ever after." Thereafter when the troupe traveled, Lewis went into eating establishments first to prepare the workers for the "things" that were coming.

The cast of The Mouse Who didn't Believe in Santa prepare for a performance in December 1972. Santa is David Dearman of Lucedale. From left, mouse Deanne Stephens of Biloxi, mouse Wendy Herbert of Biloxi, cat Robert Hilbun of Laurel, mouse Kandi Broome of Hurley, and mouse Maria Vizzini of Long Beach. Not pictured--Kathy Graham as Squeaknibble and Maurice Gerry as Grandfather Clock. Photograph from 1973 Perkolator, p. 77.

The Perk Players Children's Touring Company continued to entertain thousands of children each year with productions such as *Hansel and Gretel* and *Alice in Wonderland.* Then in an epiphany experienced at a theatrical conference, Lewis changed her whole approach to children's educational theatre.

At that conference Lewis saw a performance of *Hugs and Kisses*, a sex abuse prevention and awareness program. In order to perform the show Lewis was required by contract with the licensing agency to provide counseling to the children seeing the show during the Perk Players Children's Tour of 1987. In Lewis's words, "We did 65-plus performances of this show. We'd travel from school to school, and after each performance, we'd leave volunteers from the social service agencies there to talk with the children. More than 600 children were counseled through this. . . . I knew I could make a change, and I became committed to doing that."

For the 1988 Perk Player's Children's Tour, Lewis began production of *The Kids on the Block.* This program had been created by a Washington, D. C. education teacher in response to the 1972 "mainstreaming law" (U. S. Public Law 94-142), which placed disabled children in classrooms with their non-disabled peers. By means of puppets representing both disabled and non-disabled children, the show aimed to create honest communication and understanding between the two groups. Among the disabled puppets, each of which was "worked" by a Perk Player, one was deaf, one had cerebral palsy, and another had spina bifida. The puppets achieved life through a Japanese technique called "Bunraku." The puppeteers were visible, but their dark clothing caused them to fade into the background.

The Kids on the Block ran for ten seasons, but puppets and themes changed with each new tour season. For example, to show her audience that even physically healthy children often had to cope with debilitating circumstances, Lewis, in 1989, added Brenda, a puppet child whose parents were divorced.

Kathryn "Lewy" Lewis poses with four of her puppets in October 1994.

If her Perk Players Children's Touring Company, unique in both scope and longevity among colleges in Mississippi, became Lewis's most famous achieve-

Tevye (Charles Bosworth), his wife Golda (MGCCC Perkinston Campus Choir Director Marilyn Lott), and their five daughters from Fiddler on the Roof presented in mid-April 1999 in the Malone Hall Auditorium. (From left, seated) Brooke Quinn, Julie Alexander, and Reagan Belton, all of Wiggins. (From left, standing) Amber Johnson of Biloxi, Marilyn Lott of Perkinston, Charles Bosworth of Wiggins, and Patricia Warden of Hurley.

Ronny Blum of Amsterdam, Netherlands, and Sarah Johnson of Lucedale perform in fall 2000 in I Never Saw Another Butterfly, a play based on the Holocaust. I Never Saw Another Butterfly was the last play directed by Kathryn Lewis, and it was also the last Perk Players Children's Tour presentation of the Lewis era.

ment, it was no more than one facet of her career. After the condemnation of Denson Hall in January 1971, Lewis's Perk Players performed in Heidelberg Hall, Gregory War Memorial Chapel, and in the Old Gym until the completion of Malone Hall in November 1972. After two years the Perk Players had a new home with a 468 seat auditorium. On April 16 and 17, 1973, Lewis and the Perk Players teamed up with Gene Clement's choir and the rest of the fine arts department to present the first musical of Lewis's career--*Oklahoma!* Thereafter at intervals of approximately two years, Lewis directed a musical, ending with *Fiddler on the Roof* in spring 1999.

The production of *Fiddler on the Roof* led to the presentation of three interactive theatre pieces on the Holocaust in 2000. These were *Echoes of the Holocaust*, *And Then They Came for Me*, and *I Never Saw Another Butterfly*. That last piece was slated as Lewis's final Perk Players Children's Touring company production. Lewis announced in fall 2000 that she would retire in July 2001.

In December 2000, the cutoff point for this work, the archivist asked Lewis to sum up her career:

> "I feel that my greatest contribution has been in the realm of children's theatre. I began the tours in April 1971, which means to this point I have run thirty tours. The Perk Players did far more shows per tour later than we did at the beginning. I estimate we averaged 30 shows a year for 30 years. That is 900 shows we performed for as many as 600 kids a show and as few as 100, but we certainly reached over 100,000 of them. In addition to the children's theatre tours, I began a series of summer performance arts workshops for children in 1990 which still continues.
>
> "I believe the musicals we produced every second year were our most popular productions for the general public. One purpose of theatre is to entertain, but it certainly is not the only purpose or even the major purpose.
>
> "Since its invention by the Greeks more than 2,500 years ago, the theatre has been an instrument of social change both through use of satire and through clear unadorned statements. Theatre mirrors life. Life is certainly not always entertaining and neither is theatre.
>
> "In addition to musicals the Perk Players season included comedies and dramas. Some highlights were the 1995 production of *The Miracle Worker* directed by Daisha Walker, newly hired speech/drama instructor. The production included shadow signers and an appearance by the current Miss America Heather Whitestone, who was deaf. I directed *Boys Next Door* on two different occasions with the cast working closely with mentally challenged residents on the coast. Daisha also directed *The Yellow Boat* about the playwright's son Benjamin who died of AIDS. Attending the performance were the playwright and the current Miss America, Kate Shindle, who is an AIDS activist.

"My fondest memory is the week of "The Wall" in April 1996. The Easter sunrise service opened the Vietnam Memorial Moving Wall--a week of *Taps*, 24 hour vigils, candle light services and performances of *A Piece of My Heart* (nurses in Vietnam) directed by Daisha Walker. An estimated 8,000 people visited the Perkinston Campus to view the Wall. I saw the Wall as a memorial to all the students and employees of MGCCC who fought in all wars. I also thought of it as a fitting memorial to my father, who fought in World War II and Korea. Theatre does mirror life. I am very proud that I brought the Wall to Perk.

"We were bringing the Anne Frank exhibit to Malone Hall, so the last children's touring show I directed was *I Never Saw Another Butterfly*. In addition to the touring, hundreds of school children viewed the exhibit and the performance at the Malone Fine Arts Building.

"I have been a speech/theatre instructor here for 32 years, and chairperson of the fine arts department since 1987. The theatre curriculum has grown from one course to ten. The Perk Players performed twice at the Southeastern Theatre Conference, the New Orleans Word's Fair, and showcased at the Regional American College Theatre Festival. I am most proud of the fact that the drama program meets the needs of the community and fulfills the college's mission to develop the cultural resources of the people of the area. I am confident that former Perk Player Daisha Walker will carry the traditions of the Perk Players into the next century."

On October 21, 1995 Heather Whitestone, Miss America 1995-1996, and The Miracle Worker cast pose backstage in Malone Hall Auditorium. Speech and drama instructor Daisha Walker (second row, standing, fourth from left) poses next to Miss America Heather Whitestone (second row, standing, fifth from left). Walker played the role of Annie Sullivan and also directed the play.

On October 20, 1998 Kate Shindle, Miss America 1998-1999 and AIDS activist, speaks prior to a performance of The Yellow Boat in Malone Hall Auditorium. Behind her on the wall of Malone Gallery is a portion of the AIDS Quilt.

Kathryn Lewis and Daisha Walker celebrate Elvis's birthday on January 8, 2000 with a performance of Graceland in the Black Box Theatre in Malone Hall. Photograph from 2000 Perkolator, p. 286.

A Day on a Perk Players Children's Tour with Isaac the Rooster

Monday, 5:30 a.m. It's time to get up and drag my tired body to the makeup room to transform from a college student to Isaac the Rooster in preparation for another day of touring with the "Perk Players." I'm joined by Pigletta Pig, Bagel Beagle, Henrietta the Cat, and Mrs. Greenthumb.

6:30 a.m. The makeup is almost finished and not only do I look like a rooster but I feel like one! It takes about one and a half hours to make the transformation complete.

7:00 a.m. Our director Kathryn Lewis, whom we fondly call "Lewy," arrives with the school van. The entire cast and stage managers pitch in to load the props into the vehicle. In this company everybody pulls their own weight--or nearly. That means Henrietta, a scant 100 pounds, has to carry a speaker weighing 30 pounds. We grab our morning "treats" from the cafeteria--homemade sweet rolls and juice. We stuff ourselves into the van, five to a seat, and are on our way south. Vocal warm-ups are the next order of business and the van reverberates with our efforts.

8:15 a.m. We arrive at WLOX for a taping of one of the segments of the show for Good Morning South Mississippi. A little taste of Hollywood right here in Biloxi!

10:00 a.m. One show for about 250 kindergarten children at Keesler, AFB is next. We are welcomed on base by a large sign, "Welcome Perk Players." It really makes the ole rooster remember why he performs. It's those excited little faces anxiously awaiting our every line.

10:35 a.m. The show is over. Now we will take time to meet the children--let them pull the dog's tail, pinch the pig's nose, and they love to hug the cat!

12:00 noon. Our second show is at Vancleave Elementary. This time there are about 500 children, and Henrietta is especially excited about this performance because she went to school here. And she doesn't waste any time in waddling out of the van and into the school to look for former teachers.

12:45 p.m. It's time to load the van again and hit the road. We make a quick stop at Wendy's for burgers and a coke. Today we have to eat in the van on the way to the next show. I'm a two-burger rooster with fries, lots of ketchup, and a shake. Touring is hard work. Sometimes I think Lewy was a drill sergeant in her other life, "load the van--start the show--eat fast--project your lines." Anyway, you get the picture.

2:00 p.m. It's our last show of the day at St. James Elementary in Gulfport. And this ole bird is really tired, but then I remember a recent letter we received after a performance:

'Dear Perk Players,

I really enjoyed your play. It was funny. Thank you for coming to our school. I hope other children like your play and think it is funny. I hope I see you again. You could really cheer up someone if they were sad.

Your friend,
Michelle Sanders
St. Thomas, 3rd grade
Mrs. Sheridan's class.'

And again I realize just why I perform.

3:15 p.m. We're on our way home. I want to sleep but I'm too excited. It's been a good day.

4:00 p.m. Unload the van, take off what makeup is left, hang the costumes and get ready for tomorrow--three more performances, two in Stone County and one in Biloxi.

Tuesday, 5:30 a.m. It's time to get up and drag my tired body. . . . Guess what! It's raining. That means I'll be a wet rooster all day.

[Jimmie Milling of Ocean Springs and Marc Micele of Long Beach both played Isaac the Rooster in October, 1986. According to Lewy, Milling penned the adventures of a day on tour.]

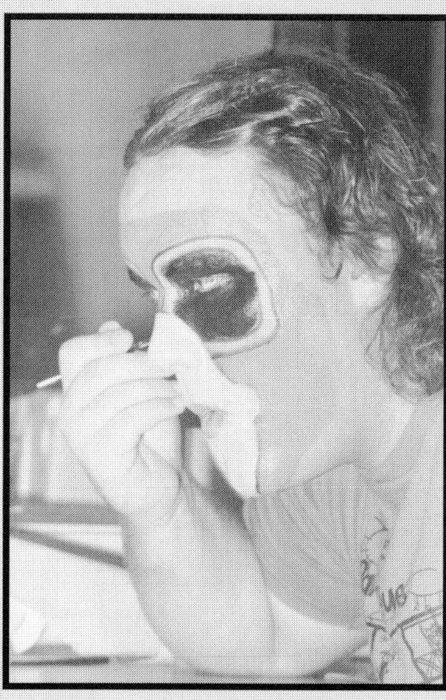

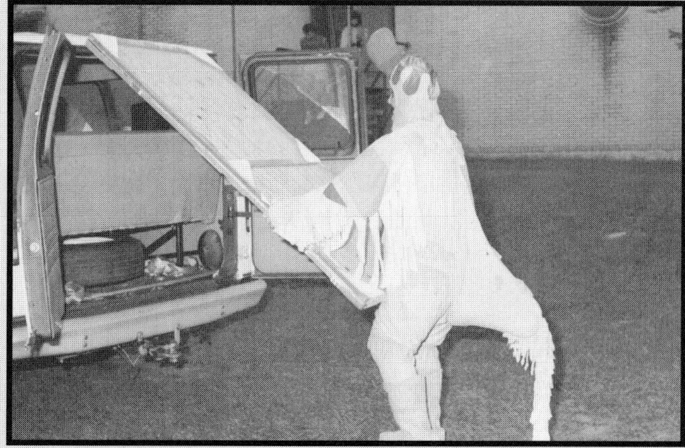

Jimmie Milling (above) in the process of transforming himself into Isaac the Rooster. (Above, right) Marc Micele as Isaac the Rooster and Caroline Brenke of Vancleave as Henrietta the Cat in the midst of a performance. (Right) Isaac the Rooster handling the props for Barnyard Blues at Stone Elementary School.

Drama at Jefferson Davis Campus
September 1965-December 2000

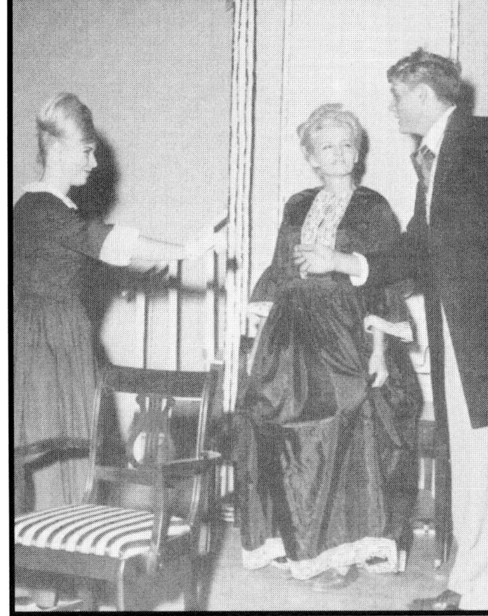

Members of the first Jefferson Davis Drama Club stand in front of the JD flagpole in session 1965-1966. (From left) Sharon Lang of Biloxi, John Bechard of Gulfport, Iva McBride of Biloxi, Richard Winterstein of Biloxi, Eileen Patterson of Long Beach, Jesse Kanode of Biloxi, and Shirley Mitchell of Handsboro. Dramatic presentations at Jefferson Davis Campus began the semester the campus opened and continued throughout the 20th century. Photograph from 1966 Perkolator, p. 87.

(Far left) Philip Lisotta (standing at right) instructs Jefferson Davis drama students in 1967. Photograph from 1968 Perkolator, p 113.

(Right) Members of the Jefferson Davis Campus drama club perform The Heiress, December 1965.

Lucas Philip Lisotta, who began as an instructor of speech and drama at Perk in September 1962, became one of six faculty members delegated to teach at both Coast Campuses in September 1965. Apparently he taught speech at both campuses but staged dramas only at the Jefferson Davis Campus. On October 20, 1965, the Board of Trustees authorized Lisotta a payment of $300 for "play production" at JD, but no mention was made of play production at the Jackson County Campus.

On November 5, 1965, Lisotta announced the casting of JD's first drama--*The Heiress*. According to the *Bulldog Barks*, *The Heiress* was slated "for production in early December to be presented in the Biloxi High auditorium."

On November 16, 1966, the Jeff Davis Drama Club presented two one-act plays--*Portrait of a Madonna* and *Suppressed Desires*. These plays began at 8 p.m. in the JD Student Center.

Since JD did not yet have an auditorium, Lisotta had used the Biloxi High stage for his 1965 production, and the next year he had opted for the JD Student Center. The lack of facilities may have accounted for the lack of student participation more than the charge of student "apathy" alleged by the December 15, 1967, *Bulldog Barks*:

Donald Moore as he appeared in 1969, when he became a speech instructor at JD.

"Due to the apathy of many Jefferson Davis Students, the Drama Club has cancelled the proposed melodrama, *Caught in the Villain's Web*.

"This same play, scheduled for the '66 term was postponed and finally cancelled. It was replanned for the '67 term, postponed, and cancelled again.

"The reason for the cancellation is the lack of participation; the fact that few of the students ever went to rehearsals.

"If the Jefferson Davis students want extra-curricular activities, they are the ones that will have to do something about it. They had had their chance time and time again and have not taken advantage of it."

Despite lack of facilities and/or "apathy" Lisotta persevered. The plays, though few and far between, continued to be held in the Student Center.

In September 1969, Lisotta received some much needed aid. Meridian native Donald Earl Moore, armed with a master's degree in theatre from the University of Southern Mississippi, joined the JD fine arts department. Shortly after Moore's arrival the name "Jefferson Davis Players" replaced the more prosaic "Jefferson Davis Drama Club." Soon, too, Moore shared billing with Lisotta as sponsor of the troupe.

Productions became more frequent and more complex. In November 1973 the Lisotta-Moore team presented the musical *South Pacific*.

In October 1974, following the production of *Blithe Spirit*, Lisotta and Moore announced that the Jefferson Davis Players would be performing their spring offerings--*The Bat* and *Pajama Game*--in far finer surroundings. The new 30,145 square-foot JD Fine Arts Building, which opened in March 1975, provided among other things a 485-seat auditorium.

Lisotta and Moore continued to work as a team until Moore accepted the position of Learning Resources Coordinator in July 1977. After that, speech instructor Cheryl Welch teamed up with Lisotta in sponsoring the Jefferson Davis Players.

In 1981, when illness resulted in Lisotta's retirement, Moore returned to the fine arts department. Moore and (by then) Cheryl (Welch) Larsen became co-sponsors of the Jefferson Davis Players.

With the retirement of James Mathis on June 10, 1986, Moore became fine arts department chairman. Moore's death the following July delivered a stunning blow to the department.

Moore's successor, Wayne Catlett, had much in common with him. Both men were Meridian natives, and both held their master's degrees from the University of Southern Mississippi. Cheryl Larsen, who had worked closely with Moore, aided Catlett as well.

In December 2000, the archivist requested that Catlett provide a synopsis of JD drama development in the final 13 years of the 20th century. Catlett's reply follows:

"The Jefferson Davis Campus has built a statewide reputation for excellence in college-level theatre. Beginning as a two production per year program (two performances per production), the season has expanded to three or four productions per year (depending on calendar and demands), with each production running three to five performances, resulting in the exposure of over 3,000 audience members to MGCCC-JD productions annually. Productions for each season vary and include theatre classics, newer cutting edge plays, and musicals, giving students and patrons from the community the opportunity to experience all types of theatre.

"The theatre curriculum has grown as well. Originally, the only academic theatre course offering was one section of theatre appreciation. Currently, the course offerings are the widest in the state for a community college and include Theatre Appreciation, Fundamentals of Acting, Movement for the Actor, Stagecraft, Theatrical Make Up,

On January 27, 1995, Dori Garziano of Pass Christian and Justin Tisdale of Biloxi appear in The Voice of the Prairie on the stage of the JD Fine Arts Auditorium. Wayne Catlett first directed the Jefferson Davis Players in this production in October 1994. Photograph from 1995 Beauvoir, p. 97.

Fundamentals of Directing, and Drama Production. This varied curriculum stresses broad-based theatre education and prepares students for further study or work as performers or designers/technicians.

"In recent years the campus has been recognized not only by the state, but regionally as well. In 1994-95 the JD production of John Olive's *The Voice of the Prairie* was honored by the Kennedy Center/American College Theatre Festival by its inclusion as one of six productions from the ten-state southeast region to be presented at the Regional Festival at the University of North Carolina at Greensboro. The show received additional honors with its recognition for Artistic Achievement by the Kennedy Center. MGCCC-JD was the only two-year college represented at the regional festival.

"In fall of 2000 the campus opened its new arena theatre complex, a 14,600 square foot facility. The new state-of-the-art arena with computerized lighting and sound is a custom designed theatre and the only permanent arena in the state. The inaugural production was *All in the Timing* by David Ives, October 25-28, 2000. This production, adjudicated by an American Theatre College Festival respondent, resulted in performance and design honors for one of the company members. Carrie Ferguson-Bellew was nominated for an Irene Ryan Acting Award Scholarship for her performance. She auditioned along with some 160 other nominees at the regional festival at USM in Hattiesburg, and she and her scene partner, Werner DuPlessis, were among forty-one semi-finalists selected.

"Carrie also served as scenic designer for the production. Her designs were entered in the design competition at Southeastern Theatre Conference Convention, the world's largest theatre organization, March 15-18 in Jacksonville, Florida. New York Tony Award-nominated designer Scott Bradley served as design adjudicator. Of the eighty-nine designs entered, four scenic designs were selected for award recognition--a first, a second, and two honorable mentions. Carrie's design was one of those to receive an honorable mention, and was the only design in the entire competition representing a two-year institution, many of the others being graduate entries, which gives testimony to the success of JD's philosophy of broad-based theatre training."

The cast of All in the Timing, the first production in the new Jefferson Davis Campus Arena Theatre, pose on the set in October 2000. Clockwise from II: Jesse Graves of Long Beach, George Tipton of Gulfport, Melissa Hall of Biloxi, Keri Mills of Biloxi, Carrie Ferguson-Bellew of Long Beach, Dustin Mosko of Biloxi, and Travis Baum of Diamondhead. Photograph from the 2001 Trident p. 85.

Jefferson Davis Campus Fine Arts Department Chairman Wayne Catlett stands behind the department members during the October 4, 2000, dedication ceremony for the JD Campus Arena Theatre. The JD fine arts department members are (from left) Dr. David Knowles, Cheryl (Welch) Larsen, Pat West, and Tim Davis.

Drama at Jackson County Campus September 1965- December 2000

Drama at Jackson County began as a part of that campus's vocational television program, which was designed to train television production engineers. Electronics instructor Theo Cowsert had charge of the program, which was the only one in a southern junior college when JC opened in September 1965. The $75,000 television studio deep in the bowels of Building A furnished closed circuit television to all the classrooms on the campus and lacked only a transmitting tower to operate as a television station.

Philip Lisotta, who was listed in the 1965-1966 rolls of the college as a teacher of speech at both JD and JC, joined with Cowsert to work out plans to televise speech and drama classes. The *Bulldog Barks*, October 8, 1965, carried the statement that, "Mr. Cowsert believes that work with live subjects such as these will help both his TV production students and Mr. Lisotta's speech and drama groups."

The *Pascagoula Chronicle*, November 8, 1965, noted that Lisotta's "drama students are preparing to produce some one-act plays. The class will cooperate with Jackson County College television department in staging these performances." The records of the MGCCC Archives contained nothing more in 2000 about the Lisotta-Cowsert connection. One might wonder, though, if the two men could have done much work along these lines at JC. Lisotta was commuting between two campuses located 30 miles apart, teaching speech at both, and presenting stage plays at JD. Cowsert was a member of a three-man team teaching 15 electronics courses in addition to television production. And, according to Doug Mansfield, who later became the television production technician at JC, "The TV system had problems that first year. They taped the dedication of the campus [October 22, 1965], and when they played the tape--nothing was on it."

Lisotta appeared again on the rolls the next session, 1966-1967, as a speech teacher at both JD and JC. He may have in fact taught at both campuses, but since Bruce Fisher hired on as a speech teacher at JC in September 1966, Lisotta may have taught only at JD that session.

On March 10, 1967, the *Bulldog Barks* announced the organization of a chapter of Delta Psi Omega honorary drama society under the sponsorship of English instructor Francesca Howard. Among the names of a dozen new members was that of Tommy Wixon, president. The article further stated that "plans were being made to present a production in the spring." Considering the stringent previous stage experience required for membership in Delta Psi Omega, one might be forgiven for wondering how any students at JC at that time could have fulfilled those requirements. When queried about the 34-year-old article, Tommy Wixon vaguely remembered the incident. He said, "I recognize many of the names in the article. Some of them had been in plays with me in high school, but none of us were in any plays at JC before the article. And we certainly did not produce a play that spring. I left JC that May and so did most of the others."

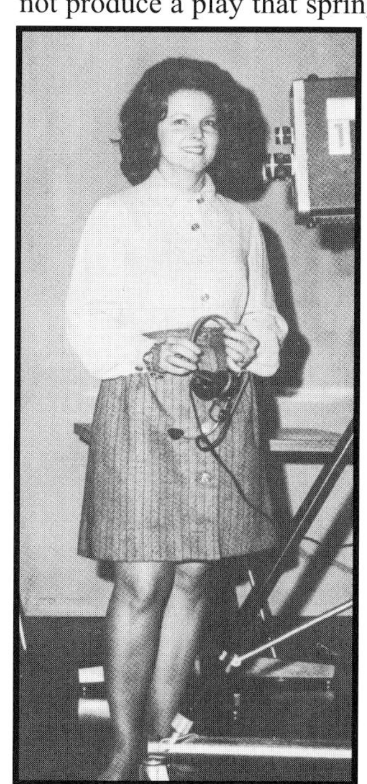

Betty Oswald prepares for a shoot in the Jackson County Campus television studio circa 1971. Photo from 1972 Phases, p. 346.

In September 1967 John McRaven, formerly head producer at Station KARK-TV in Little Rock, Arkansas, joined the staff of JC as director of television production. In addition to taking charge of campus programming and teaching the nine-month vocational TV production course, McRaven announced plans to originate programs for the Mississippi Educational Television Network.

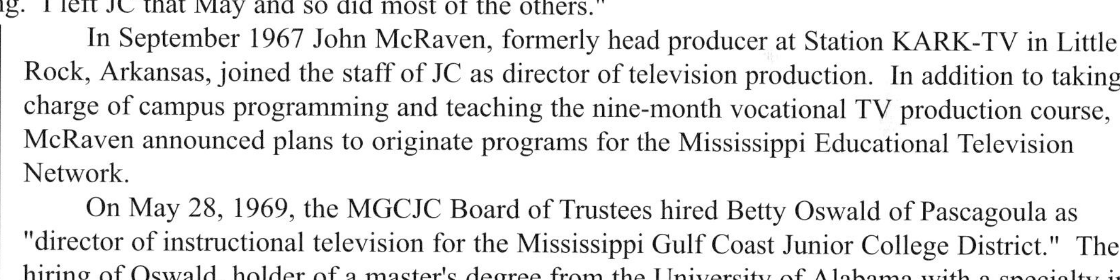

On May 28, 1969, the MGCJC Board of Trustees hired Betty Oswald of Pascagoula as "director of instructional television for the Mississippi Gulf Coast Junior College District." The hiring of Oswald, holder of a master's degree from the University of Alabama with a specialty in educational television, marked the beginning of drama production at JC.

In August 1969, Doug Mansfield, then a high school student, signed up for McRaven's nine-month vocational television course. He attended Pascagoula High School in the mornings and JC in the afternoons. Mansfield's on-the-job training included working the TV camera for Oswald's course in television communications. The course, which carried three hours of academic credit in the area of speech and drama, involved weekly telecasts patterned on a commercial television format.

The productions were aired on Wednesdays over the closed circuit system and began thusly: "This is WJC-TV, Channel 4 with studios in the center of the Jackson County Campus of the Mississippi Gulf Coast Junior College in beautiful downtown Gautier. . . ." Programming included news and weather, sports, interviews, and, of course, commercials. Television drama debuted as a soap opera with a hillbilly theme titled, *The Belles of Horsefly Gulch.*

That first year, Oswald expanded her efforts to all three campuses by convincing Ray Butterfield of WLOX-TV in Biloxi to provide time for a weekly television series titled *Mississippi Gulf Coast Junior College Presents . . .* Each 15-minute production aired early on Monday morning. The series allowed students and faculty to showcase college activities and

(From left), MGCJC Instructional Television Director Betty Oswald, Pascagoula High School drama instructor Martha Gautier, and Jackson County Campus Executive Dean Curtis Davis confer regarding the video-taping of Gautier's production of Pinocchio in the JC TV studio in 1969. Gautier later presented the drama, Our Town, on the JC Campus in 1976.

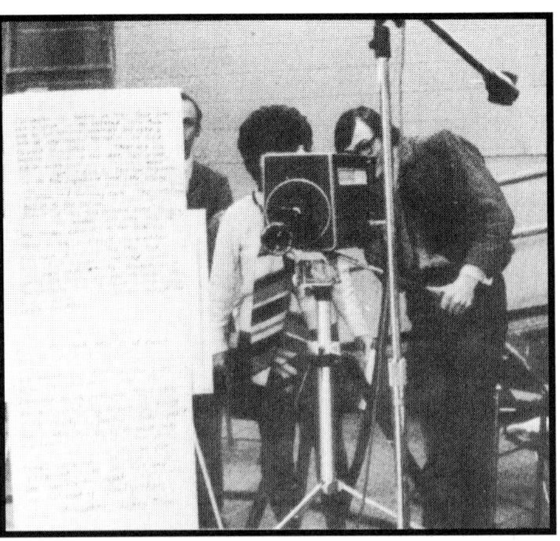

MGCJC ITV Director Betty Oswald and MGCJC Director of Television Production Instructor John McRaven both stare into the camera in the Jackson County Campus television studio in 1969. Note primitive cue cards at left.

Larry Thomas with the WJC-TV weather forecast in 1969. The umbrella and sunflowers to the left on the floor were visual aids.

produce dramas. According to Doug Mansfield, "We could not produce these shows at JC because we had only black and white capability at the time. WLOX had color."

In summing up her first-year efforts, Oswald projected her hopes for the future. She said, "With statewide ETV now a reality, we hope to become the southern part of the network. When classroom television teaching comes of age in Mississippi, Jackson County Campus will have a head start."

At the end of that year Mansfield graduated from high school. He enlisted in the U.S. Army, remaining in the service for three years.

Oswald continued her closed circuit Jackson County television production and the show on WLOX. In 1971 WLOX moved *MGCJC Presents . . .* to an early evening time slot, resulting in a far wider audience.

Also in 1971 Oswald began live drama presentations at JC. In April, students under her direction presented *You, the Jury* in the college cafeteria.

The following year Oswald presented *Lil Abner*, JC's first musical. That production was "staged" in the Gautier Junior High School auditorium because JC as yet had no stage. Martha (Moore) Richardson directed the JC choir, and Eugene Clement of Perkinston Campus conducted the orchestra.

In January 1973, Doug Mansfield returned to JC to attend academic classes on the GI Bill. Since John McRaven did not return after Christmas holidays, Executive Dean Curtis Davis sought out Mansfield on the campus in April and asked him to take the job of television production technician for the college. Mansfield accepted the position in May and finished the 20th century in that position.

Mansfield resumed working with Betty Oswald. A year later she resigned to work in her husband's law office.

Early in second semester 1976, workmen completed the 19,700 square foot JC Fine Arts Building, which contained a 472-seat auditorium. The *Mississippi Press Register*, April 25, 1976, carried the announcement that on the following Friday and Saturday nights at 8 p.m. the Fine Arts Auditorium would be the scene for, "the opening production of the new Jackson County Junior College drama class." Martha Gautier, instructor of that first JC theatre appreciation class, directed her students in staging *Our Town*. Gautier, who had taught speech and drama in Coast schools for several years, was at the time Jackson County Coordinator for Volunteer Services.

Apparently the production of *Our Town* was the last for nearly two-and-one-half years. In December 1978, a JC Campus press release announced the "first performance for the newly organized drama group at Jackson County Campus." The press release gave the name of the December 8 production as *Christmas Coast to Coast* and gave the name of the director--Betty Oswald. The return of Oswald to the JC Campus in session 1978-1979 marked the beginning of an unbroken line of drama production throughout the balance of the 20th century.

Oswald's repertoire ran the gamut of theatrical production. In March 1980, she produced *Kiss Me Kate*, JC Campus's first musical since her *Lil Abner* eight years before. She followed that in November 1980, with the tragic *Black Elk Speaks*. Next came a children's classic, *Heidi,* in October 1981, and in March 1981, Oswald presented the Woody Allen comedy hit, *Don't Drink the Water*.

These productions provided the cadre of experienced actors necessary for membership in Delta Psi Omega. On April 29, 1981, Oswald presided at the banquet at which that national theatre society's charter (dated December 8, 1980) was presented to JC Campus.

JC drama student George Shrout brings down the house with his portrayal of a politician "stumping" the Neshoba County Fair in Its Yours in Mississippi in 1983. Photos courtesy of Betty Oswald.

The It's Yours in Mississippi singers and dancers Debbie Davis (kneeling) and (left-right), Page Davis, Candy Walker, Hamilton Holiman, Carolyn Watts, and Sheri Barlow.

In 1983, not satisfied with mere direction, Oswald decided to write and produce a show of her own. *It's Yours in Mississippi* was a whirlwind time machine bus tour of the regions of Mississippi through song, dance, dialogue, and 400 slides. The show involved the talent and expertise of the JC Campus Fine Arts Department and others in the community.

The one-and-one-half hour production went on stage at the JC Fine Arts Auditorium on May 10, 1983. In July, Oswald presented the show to 1,000 teachers gathered for the Delta Kappa Gamma International teachers' society conference in the Mississippi Coast coliseum. Portions of the show were performed by JC students at the Louisiana World Exposition of 1984. The production played yet again at the Jackson County Fair on October 23, 1990.

In May 1992 Oswald relinquished JC Campus drama production to her colleague, Wanda Stewart. Stewart carried the tradition of drama production established by Oswald at JC Campus on to the end of the century.

Wanda Stewart hands out scripts to Marcel Welch and James Bolon for the upcoming production of If a Man Answers to be presented November 20-21, 1992. Photograph from 1993 Phases, p. 34.

Doug Mansfield and the Jackson County Campus Television Studio

Doug Mansfield, as a student trainee, had been involved in the origin of drama at JC practically from its beginning. In May 1973 he became a full-time employee and worked with successive JC drama instructors and with the drama instructors in area high schools as well. He filmed their practice sessions, which served as training films, and he filmed performances. He also taught photography and television production and presided over the conversion of the JC television studio from black and white to color in summer 1978.

From 1988 to 1992 Mansfield was involved in the production of docudramas. He wove this author's words together with Central Office Publicity Director Winfred Moncrief's video tape to produce MGCCC's *Magnolia Series* of Mississippi history video documentaries. The productions were: *Henry Jetton Tudury: Mississippi's Most Decorated Doughboy of World War I* (1988), *Gathering at the River: Methodist Campmeetings in South Mississippi* (1990), *Beauvoir: Memorial to the Lost Cause* (1991), *No Greater Love: Roy Wheat in Vietnam* (1992), and *The Green Fields of France* (1992) Not only did Mansfield display the technical wizardry gained from a quarter century of television production but considerable directorial ability as well. For his work on the *Magnolia Series*, Mansfield received the Mississippi Historical Society's Award of Merit in 1992.

Doug Mansfield, at camera, tapes a Pascagoula High School drama class production of Pinocchio in 1969.

Mansfield poses between two cameras in the Jackson County Campus television studio in 1977. Photo from 1977 Phases, p. 68.

During school session 1985-1986, Mansfield instructs two JC Campus students during field training exercises at the U.S. Army School at Eglin Air Force Base, Florida. From 1985 to 1988 Mansfield was the ROTC Ranger instructor for recruits at Jackson County Campus. Photo from 1986 Phases, p. 40.

Mansfield at the editing console at the Jackson County Campus television studio in 1997. Photo from 1997 Phases, p. 102.

STUDENT CLUBS AND ORGANIZATIONS 1912 - 2000

The fragmentary evidence remaining from the 1912-1922 period indicated that the institution's first two clubs were the Boy's Literary Society and the Girl's Literary Society, both of which were in operation by fall 1913. Other than those, virtually the only school sponsored "clubs" were the various "classes"--freshman, sophomore, junior and senior. County organizations, such as the Tomato and Canning Clubs for girls and the Corn and Pig Clubs for boys, operated on the campus particularly in the summers. Many of Perk's students belonged to these organizations, but these groups were sponsored by Harrison County and Stone County and not by the Perkinston institution.

School-sponsored organizations such as the AHS Corps, devoted to marching and drilling, and the Boy's Working Reserve, aimed at increasing food production, were temporary phenomena spawned by American entry into the First World War. The AHS Corps disbanded at the close of the war, and the Boys Working Reserve disappeared by 1921.

The *Daily Herald*, September 13, 1921, recorded the doings of Perk students related to the Baptist Young People's Union (BYPU). However, this organization seemed to be under the sponsorship of the Perkinston Baptist Church and was not a campus organization.

The real beginning of student clubs and organizations came with the selection of J. H. Forbis as superintendent. In the *Harrison-Stone Bi-County Agricultural High School, Perkinston, Mississippi, Announcement for Session Beginning September 11, 1922*, Forbis wrote, "Each student must be a member of one of the Literary Societies and help in the making and rendering of programs every week."

The *Stone County Enterprise*, November 23, 1922, recorded the operation of a Glee Club at Perk. This organization, renamed the "Choir" in 1949, continued to function on the Perkinston Campus in 2000.

The *Daily Herald*, February 16, 1924, announced that a Girls' Hiking Club, specializing in three to five mile hikes, and a Girls' Prayer Meeting, set for Wednesday nights, had been organized. Neither of these organizations lasted, but that same article gave the names of the two "Literary Societies" formed two years prior. One bore the name Wilsonian Society, in honor of former United States President Woodrow Wilson, and the other was called the "Utopian Society." Members of these two societies were to compete against one another in debate, and each society was pledged to sponsor social events. When Superintendent J. L. Denson replaced Forbis in 1924, the Utopian Society was renamed the Densonian Society in honor of Denson himself.

The *1924-1925 Catalogue*, written by Denson, noted that "two religious organizations are maintained in the school. The Hi-Y Club for boys and the Girl Reserve Club for girls. . . ." Apparently Forbis had organized the Girl Reserve as early as the 1922-1923 session because the *Daily Herald*, September 27, 1924, noted that, "Owing to the inactivity of the Girl Reserve club last year a complete reorganization was necessary." Be that as it may, in composing the following chart this author dated both the Girl Reserve Club and the Boys' Hi-Y Club as having begun in 1924. The Girl Reserve Club was the high school division of the Young Women's Christian Association (YWCA). The Boys' Hi-Y was the high school division of the Young Men's Christian Association (YMCA). As the Perkinston institution evolved from a high school into a junior college, the Girl Reserve evolved into the YWCA and the Boys' Hi-Y evolved into the YMCA. During the period of transition both the high school and the college organizations of both sexes existed side-by-side, or at least the names were used interchangeably in school documents until about 1930. Therefore this author will list these organizations in the following chart thusly, YWCA (formerly Girl Reserve) and YMCA (formerly Boys' Hi-Y).

The following charts entitled "Clubs and Organizations" are inaccurate. Prior to session 1935-1936, the main sources for the existence of clubs and organizations of the earlier period were the institution's catalogs and contemporary newspaper articles. The catalogs for six sessions in a row (1914-1920) together with those for sessions 1921-1922, 1923-1924, and 1926-1927 were not in the MGCCC Archives Collection in 2000. Apparently the catalogs for sessions 1933-1934 and 1935-1936 were never published, probably as a money saving measure during the Great Depression.

The institution began publication of a yearbook in session 1935-1936. The yearbook continued to be published in an unbroken line through 2000. Eleven times after the institution split into three campuses in 1965, one single yearbook divided into three sections was published. Thus 124 yearbook volumes illustrated a total of 135 "years" (65 for Perk and 35 each for JD and JC).

At first the author attempted to merge the information contained in the yearbooks with that contained in the catalogs. That proved impossible. Clubs remained in the catalog lists sometimes for decades after photographs disappeared from the yearbook. Apparently proud new sponsors informed the person in charge of the catalog to put his or her new club on the lists but never informed the cataloger to take them out when the clubs went defunct. Two clubs listed in the *2000 Catalog* had not been pictured in any yearbook for 30 years.

Many clubs and organizations that appeared in the yearbooks were never listed in the catalogs. On the other hand, organizations, the existence of which this author was never able to confirm in a yearbook or anywhere else, were listed in the catalogs. For example an organization called "The

Watcher Society" was listed in every catalog from 1976 to 1985 as "active on only one campus." This author was never able to determine upon which campus "The Watchers" watched nor what nor why nor whom they were watching.

In the surprisingly numerous cases when a yearbook pictured a club with no explanation for its existence, the catalog sometimes yielded a description. In the case of Jefferson Davis Campus's "Junior (the junior was not in the yearbook) Food Service Executives Association," the catalog really came through. The session *1975-1976 Catalog* contained the following statement of purpose pertaining to that world-class organization: "To upgrade food service standards, enact sound legislation, find solutions to international nutritional needs and expand food research are only a few of the goals of the FSEA . . . [which] also strives to promote education, good fellowship and humanitarianism among its membership and with people everywhere." In view of this ambitious club's "few" stated goals, one could only marvel at what the unpublished goals might have been. This club showed up in the yearbook from 1975 to 1977 but remained in the catalog through session 1984-1985 after which one might suppose it merged with the United Nations.

The dates given in the following lists after 1936 were usually the years during which the club or organization was pictured in the yearbooks. The club or organization may have and likely did exist both before and after the dates given, but it certainly did exist in the years given because it was pictured. In a few cases where more accurate information was available from other primary sources, the more certain dates were used.

In cases where a club disappeared from the yearbook pictures for a year or two, that was not noted. When a club disappeared from the yearbook for several years, that information was noted since the club may have gone defunct and then been rejuvenated. Instances arose in making these lists where clubs disappeared and then were resurrected by later sponsors who obviously did not know the club had had an earlier incarnation. In such a case, if this author knew that that had happened, the club was listed more than once.

A yearbook covers a school session composed of the fall of one calendar year and the spring of another calendar year. Therefore, in the absence of other information, this author assumed the establishment of a club or organization to have occurred in the fall of a session and its dissolution to have occurred in the spring of a session.

In the case of Jefferson Davis Campus, information related to clubs and organizations contained in the yearbook became intermittent in the early 1990s and disappeared altogether in the session 1998-1999 yearbook. JD student activities counselor Denise Daniel, supplied the information pertaining to JD contained in the list in the 1990s.

Perkinston Campus secretary to the dean of student services Sylvia Davis corrected the late 1990s lists for Perk. JC student activities counselor Sheri Stanford corrected the late 1990s lists for JC.

Student Newspapers

The most accurate descriptions of club activities were found in the pages of student newspapers. Unfortunately, comparatively few issues of such publications were in the MGCCC Archives Collection in 2000.

Apparently the institution's first newspaper was the *Agricultural High School News*, which was reprinted in both the *Stone County Enterprise* and the *Daily Herald* during the World War I era. A single issue of the *Perkinston Aggie*, circa April 1921, remained in 2000, together with scattered issues of the *Perkolator* newspaper 1928 to 1930.

When publication of the yearbook began in session 1935-1936, the yearbook was christened the *Perkolator*, so obviously the newspaper had to be given another name. Consequently, the *Bulldog Barks* began publication on February 10, 1945. When the institution divided into three campuses in September 1965, the *Bulldog Barks*, published at Perkinston, continued to be the organ of the institution with each campus having an editor and reporters.

In fall 1969 the name of the Jefferson Davis Campus paper was changed to the *Mississippi Sound.* Publication of the *Mississippi Sound* ceased after spring 1994. By fall 1997 the *JD Current* was being published but apparently ceased within a year.

In fall 1968, Jackson County Campus began publishing its own newspaper--the *Gulf Coast Communique*. This paper was published at least until spring 1971. By fall 1978, according to the JC Campus yearbook, another JC Campus paper was being published. Since the yearbook editor referred to it simply as "the paper," this author could not ascertain its name. By fall 1981 "the paper" was being referred to as *Insight*. By fall 1984 *Coastliner* had replaced *Insight*. In fall 1986, when budget cuts eliminated the funding necessary to publish *Coastliner*, Terry (Price) Fountain prevailed upon the *Mississippi Press* newspaper to publish the JC campus paper on a special page. Thus the JC Campus paper went into 40,000 homes every two weeks and more importantly into the microfilmed archives of the *Mississippi Press*. This symbiotic relationship ceased in 1995. Fountain continued to publish the paper until she retired in May 1998 at which time the paper ceased publication. In 1999 Pat West resurrected the paper, but it ceased publication once again when she transferred to the JD Campus in May 2000. On November 8, 1973, the *Bulldog Barks* was renamed the *Perkinston Campus Bulldog*. The *Perkinston Campus Bulldog* went defunct in May 1980. The Perk Campus paper was resurrected at least as early as October 1988 as, once again, the *Bulldog Barks*. The *Bulldog Barks* ceased publication in late 1995.

Perkinston Campus Student Clubs and Organizations 1913-2000

The beginning and ending dates given in the chart below should be regarded as approximate dates. These dates were the best available to the archivist from photographs and documents in the MGCCC archives collection in 2000. Since this present work extended through the close of the year 2000, an ending date of 2000 was assigned to clubs and organizations existing when the study ended. In rare cases that date may have been the actual club's dissolution date, but that fact could not be confirmed at the time this present study ended.

Began	Name of Club or Organization	Ended
1913	Boy's Literary Society and Girl's Literary Society	1920
1917	Agricultural High School Corps (Paramilitary group)	1918
1919	Boys Working Reserve (Paramilitary group)	1921
1922	Glee Club (Name changed to Choir in fall 1949) (Some of the various units of this organization: Girls Ensemble 1945-1965; Boys Quartet 1957-1959; Kids of Note (renamed Mississippi Sound in 1988), a mixed song and dance show group, 1979-2000; Soundwaves, a men's ensemble, 1991-1998; Soundsations, a women's ensemble, 1996-1999)	2000
1922	Utopian Society (Debate and social) Renamed Densonian Society in September 1924 in honor of Superintendent J. L. Denson)	1929
1922	Wilsonian Society (Debate and social) (Named for U. S. President Woodrow Wilson)	1929
1924	Girls Hiking Club	1924
1924	Girls Prayer Meeting	1924
1924	Young Women's Christian Association (YWCA) (Formerly Girl Reserve)	1959
1924	Young Men's Christian Association (YMCA) (Formerly Boy's Hi-Y)	1958
1926	College Club (Organized for the institution's initial college students)	1928
1927	Orchestra (Intermittent) (Known as the Swing Barons from 1935 to 1949) (Known as Star Dusters 1950-1952) (Known as the Rhythm Kings 1956 to 1957)	1957
1928	Spanish Club (Intermittent)	1943
1928	Home Economics Club (Founded December 1928) (Known as Social Arts Club 1941 to 1947 after which reverted to original name)	1982
1928	P-Club (Men and women who excelled in sports and academics were awarded a letter "P" for Perkinston to wear on a sweater or jacket. In time the P-Club was restricted to sports and after 1945 for men only. The first letters were black. The later ones were gold)	1958
1929	Dramatic Club (Originally called the "Literary Society") The name "Dramatic Club" was adopted in 1932. The 1951 and the 1952 *Perkolators* published the club as "Mask and Scroll." The *Daily Herald*, November 5, 1954 referred to the Perkinston thespians as "Perk Players." That designation continued in 2000.	2000
1929	Epworth League (Methodist)	1930
1929	Philomathean Literary Society	1930
1930	Chemistry Club (C. O. Hinton organized it March 18, 1930). Since no photo appeared after the *Perkolator* began publication in session 1935-1936, the arbitrary date of 1934 was assigned for its demise though it likely lasted much longer.	1934
1934	Band (Renamed Band of Gold in 1984.) (Some of the various units of this organization: Jazz Band 1990-2000 and Color Guard 1983-2000.)	2000
1935	Commercial Club (Also known as Business Education Club)	1957
1935	French Club	1943
1935	Education Club	1937
1935	Zoo Zoo Club (Social)	1936
1935	Debate	1938
1936	Student Council	2000
1936	Beta Perk COs	1938
1937	Phi Theta Kappa (Gamma Nu Chapter chartered January 15, 1937)	2000
1936	International Relations Club	1955
1936	Newman Club (Catholic) (Intermittent) (Not pictured 1974-1977)	1981
1937	Language Club	1938
1937	Baptist Student Union	2000

1937	Wesley Foundation (Methodist) (Intermittent) (Not pictured 1987-1998)	2000
1937	Pep Squad (Women's drill team)	1947
1938	College Women's Athletic Association	1940
1938	Country Club (Golf)	1940
1938	Agriculture Club (Not pictured from 1963 to 1968)	1975
1939	Presbyterian Club	1943
1939	Social Recreation Club	1943
1940	Episcopal Club	1942
1941	Men's Home Guard (Four paramilitary platoons)	1943
1941	Girl's Home Guard (Five paramilitary platoons)	1943
1941	Future Teachers of America (Chartered October 27, 1941)	1957
1941	Camera Club	1955
1942	Christian Council (Organized October 17, 1942) (Composed of representatives from all Christian groups on campus)	1981
1943	Athletic Board (Women's intramurals) (Renamed Women's Intramural Association in 1949) (Renamed Girls Athletic Association in 1953)	1957
1944	Language Club	1951
1944	Junior State Guard (PJC National Guard unit)	1946
1945	The Sharp and the Flat Club (A club for singers)	1946
1945	Veterans Club (Organized December 1945)	1948
1945	Music Club	1946
1946	Gershwin Club (A club for musicians, singers, and music majors)	1957
1948	Art Club	1950
1951	Canterbury Club (Episcopal)	1962
1952	Future Homemakers of America (High school girls home economics)	1962
1952	Future Farmers of America (High school boys agriculture club)	1958
1952	Perkinston Junior College Fire Department (Student volunteer fire department)	1955
1952	Debate Club	1961
1952	Perkettes	2000
1953	4-H Club (High school farm club)	1955
1954	Circle K (College-age Kiwanis chartered February 23, 1954) (First in Mississippi)	1970
1955	Delta Psi Omega Honorary Dramatic Society (Organized May 19, 1955) (Intermittent)	2000
1956	Veterans Club	1960
1957	Student Education Association (Replaced Future Teachers of America)	1964
1957	Practical Nurses	1958
1957	Perkinston Classical Music Club (A music appreciation club)	1974
1958	Westminster Fellowship (Intermittent) (A fellowship of Presbyterian, Episcopalians, and Lutherans)	1971
1958	Math and Science Club	1961
1958	Future Business Leaders of America (Chartered November 5, 1958) (A high school club)	1962
1959	Youth Congress (A mock legislature)	1964
1960	Phi Beta Lambda (Alpha Omega Chapter) (National fraternity for business majors) (The collegiate counterpart of Future Business Leaders of America)	2000
1960	Key Club (High school Kiwanis)	1962
1960	Beta Club (High school boys and girls honor society)	1962
1961	Junior Engineering Technical Society (High school boys)	1962
1961	Nurses	1962
1962	Young Scientists of America	1964
1963	WPJC (Campus-wide radio station)	1964
1965	Delta Club (National Society of Engineers fraternity)	1969
1965	Perk Debate Team	1968
1966	Youth for Christ	1967
1968	PJC Volunteer Fire Department (Student firemen)	1969
1970	Women's Recreation Association (Organization for women majoring in physical education)	1974
1971	Young Republicans (Intermittent) (Not pictured 1975-1980)	1982
1971	Black Cultural Society	1978

1972	Debate Club	1974
1973	Reserve Officers Training Corps (ROTC)	1985
1974	Foreign Students	1977
1974	Vocational Industrial Clubs of America (VICA) chartered April 18, 1974 (Name changed to Skills USA-VICA in 1998)	2000
1974	Gulf Coast Modeling Squad	1996
1975	Collegiate Civitan	1978
1975	Horticulture Club (Renamed the Horticulture and Turf Club in 2000 to reflect the membership of Golf Turf Management students)	2000
1977	Fellowship of Christian Athletes	1978
1978	Rotaract (Chartered January 2, 1978) (College division of Rotary International)	1989
1978	Youth Congress	1979
1979	Science Club	1981
1983	Reflections Team (MGCJC recruiting and hospitality team)	2000
1983	Forestry Club	1985
1984	Delta Phi Omega (Also known as Delta Pi Omega) (Renamed Delta Pi Epsilon in 1993). (A club for math, engineering and computer majors)	
1985	Students Against Drunk Driving	1986
1985	Association of Baptist Students	1988
1986	Association of Diverse and Unique Leaders of Today (ADULT) (A club for the returning student)	1987
1987	Perk Ad Club (Club for students majoring in commercial art and advertising)	2000
1987	Honors Program	2000
1990	Minority Leadership (An African-American leadership club)	1992
1992	Interclub Council	2000
1992	Adult Support Group (For non-traditional students)	1994
1993	Students in Free Enterprise (An economics club)	1996
1995	Running Club	1997
1995	Scholars Bowl (Student members competed annually at the University of Mississippi for the state junior college championship)	2000
1995	Literary Society	1997
1997	Adult Student Association/New Horizons	1999
1997	MGCCC Rodeo Team	2000
1997	International Student Association	2000
1997	Circle of Believers (An interdenominational prayer club)	2000
1998	Catholic Student Association	2000
1999	Frisbee Golf Club	2000
2000	Environmental Science Club	2000
2000	Medical Club	2000

George County Occupational Training Center Student Clubs and Organizations 1973-2000

1973	Phi Beta Lambda (National fraternity for business majors) (Post-secondary)	2000
1974	Vocational Industrial Clubs of America (VICA) (Clubs for both high school and post-secondary divisions) (Name changed to Skills USA-VICA in 1998)	2000
1993	Health Occupations Students of America (HOSA) (Club for licensed practical nurses, allied health students, and surgical technology students)	2000

Jefferson Davis Campus Student Clubs and Organizations 1965-2000

The beginning and ending dates given in the chart below should be regarded as approximate dates. These dates were the best available to the archivist from photographs and documents in the MGCCC archives collection in 2000. Since this present work extended through the close of the year 2000, an ending date of 2000 was assigned to clubs and organizations existing when the study ended. In rare cases that date may have been the actual ending date, but that fact could not be confirmed at the time this present study ended.

Began	Name of Club or Organization	Ended
1965	Phi Beta Lambda (National fraternity for business majors)	2000
1965	Student Council	2000
1965	Jefferson Davis Junior College Choir (Renamed Jefferson Davis Singers in 1969)	2000
1965	Jeff Davis Drama Club (Renamed Jeff Davis Players in 1969)	2000
1965	Student Nurses Club (Renamed Student Nursing Association in 1969) (Renamed Student Nurse Organization in 1997)	2000
1965	Newman Club (Catholic)	1971
1966	Phi Theta Kappa (Omicron Alpha Chapter chartered March 31, 1966)	2000
1966	Baptist Student Union	2000
1966	Wesley Foundation (Methodist)	1968
1967	Hotel-Motel-Restaurant Club	1992
1967	Student Education Association (Renamed Student Mississippi Association of Education in 1976) (Apparently defunct 1987-1996) (Reappeared at least as early as 1996 as Student Educational Association)	2000
1967	Circle K (College Kiwanis) (Chartered February 10, 1967)	1978
1967	Beam-in-Balance (Pre-Law) (Apparently renamed Law Club in 1971)	1972
1968	Debate Club	1969
1970	Mid-Management Association	1972
1971	Black Cultural Society (Renamed Afro-American Club in 1979)	1980
1972	Polygolians	1973
1974	Mississippi Youth Congress	1979
1975	Food Service Executives Association	1977
1976	Jeff Davis Science Association	1978
1977	Jefferson Davis Jaycees (Chapter 0364 of U. S. Jaycees organized October 1977)	1979
1978	Distributive Education Clubs of America (DECA, a high school club, was replaced by Delta Epsilon Chi (DEX), DECA's collegiate counterpart organization in 1982)	2000
1978	Muslim Students Association	1979
1979	Chi Alpha Non-Denominational Christian Fellowship	1980
1981	Art Club (also known as Art Dimensions)	2000
1982	Harrison County Occupational Training Center VICA	1983
1983	Reflections Team (MGCJC recruiting and hospitality team)	2000
1985	Science Club (also known as the Science Association)	2000
1985	Young Democrats	2000
1987	Delta Psi Omega National Honorary Theatre Fraternity	2000
1988	College Republicans	2000
1989	Vocational Industrial Clubs of America (VICA) (Name changed to Skills USA-VICA in 1998)	2000
1989	Honors program	2000
1989	New Horizons (For returning students)	1998
1989	Students Against Driving Drunk	1990
1989	Students In Free Enterprise	1991
1989	WJDC Radio	1992
1991	Student Paralegal Association	2000
1992	Scholars Bowl	2000
1993	Debate Team	2000
1993	Health Occupations Students of America (HOSA) (Club for licensed practical nurses)	2000
1994	Coastal Vibrations Vocal Jazz Group (an ensemble of the Jeff Davis Singers formed Homecoming Day, 1994)	2000

1995	Science Demonstration Squad	2000
1996	Catholic Student Association	2000
1996	Student Court Reporters Association	2000
1996	Criminal Justice Association	2000
1997	Connections (Student tutors)	2000

West Harrison County Occupational Training Center Clubs and Organizations 1985-2000

1985	Phi Beta Lambda (National fraternity for business majors) (Post-secondary)	2000
1985	Future Business Leaders of America (High school counterpart of PBL)	1998
1985	Vocational Industrial Clubs of America (VICA) (Clubs for both high school and post-secondary divisions) (Name changed to Skills USA-VICA in 1998)	2000
1985	Health Occupations Students of America (HOSA) (Club for high school allied health classes)	2000
1985	Technology Club (Club for high school diversified technology classes)	2000
1995	Future Farmers of America (Clubs for both high school and post-secondary aquaculture students)	2000

Jackson County Campus Student Clubs and Organizations 1965-2000

The beginning and ending dates given in the chart below should be regarded as approximate dates. These dates were the best available to the archivist from photographs and documents in the MGCCC archives collection in 2000. Since this present work extended through the close of the year 2000, an ending date of 2000 was assigned to clubs and organizations extant when the study ended. In rare cases that date may have been the actual ending date, but that fact could not be confirmed at the time this present study ended.

Began	Name of Club or Organization	Ended
1965	Phi Beta Lambda (National fraternity for business majors) (not pictured 1976-1983)	2000
1965	Student Council	2000
1965	J. C. Choir (Apparently defunct 1967-1972 and 1975-1977) (renamed JC Singers 1977-1996) (Apparently defunct 1997-1999) (Reorganized as JC Choir in 1999)	2000
1965	Christian Council	1966
1965	Circle K (College Kiwanis) (Intermittent) (Dean Curtis Davis announced in the newspaper that this club was organized in 1965, but it was not pictured until 1971)	1979
1966	Baptist Student Union (Apparently intermittent in 1970s)	2000
1966	Wesley Foundation (Methodist)	1967
1966	Westminister Fellowship (Presbyterian) (defunct 1967-1999) Reactivated in 1999.	2000
1966	Newman Club (Catholic)	1969
1967	Student Nurses Club (Renamed Student Nursing Association in 1969) (Renamed Student Nurse Organization in 1997)	2000
1967	Phi Theta Kappa (Pi Epsilon Chapter chartered February 8, 1967)	2000
1967	Drama Club (apparently defunct 1968-1974)	2000
1967	Beam-in-Balance (Pre-Law)	1968
1968	Samonthrace Club (A social and service organization for college women. Men were admitted in 1974)	1975
1968	Canterbury Club (Episcopal)	1969
1968	Bridge and Chess club	1969
1968	Student Education Association (Renamed Student Mississippi Education Association in 1971)	1976
1969	The House (A student group to promote campus activities and school spirit)	1970
1969	Projects Club (A student volunteer work group)	1970
1969	Youth Congress	1976
1970	Technical Education Majors Association	1971
1970	Art Guild (An organization designed to promote art on the campus and in the community) (Apparently defunct 1989-1995)	2000

1972	Speech Potpourri and Phi Rho Pi (Honorary Speech Fraternity)	1976
1974	Reserve Officers Training Corps (See also 1982)	1975
1975	Distributive Education Clubs of America (DECA, a high school club, was replaced by Delta Epsilon Chi (DEX), DECA's collegiate counterpart organization in 1982)	2000
1975	Vocational Industrial Clubs of America (Renamed Skills USA-VICA in 1998)	2000
1975	VICA (High school division)	1976
1977	Student Licensed Practical Nurses Club (Renamed Student LPN Association in 1980) (See HOSA in 1993)	1993
1977	Alternatives Club (Organization for returning students)	1978
1978	JC Dancers	1979
1980	Black Cultural Society	1983
1980	Delta Psi Omega National Honorary Theatre Fraternity (Chartered December 8, 1980)	2000
1980	New Images (A club for single parents/displaced homemakers) (Renamed New Images/New Choices in 1991) (Name changed to New Horizons in 1993) (Name changed to Vocational-Technical Support Services in 1999)	2000
1981	MGCJC Band (JC section)	1985
1982	Respiratory Therapy Club (Not pictured 1989-1994)	1997
1982	Reserve Officers Training Corps (ROTC)	1985
1983	Student Tutors	1988
1983	Reflections Team (MGCJC recruiting and hospitality team)	2000
1984	Human Services Club	2000
1985	United Ministries Christian Fellowship	1986
1985	Medical Laboratory Technicians Club	2000
1986	Medical Unit Managers Club (Not pictured 1987-1990) (Renamed Health Unit Co-ordinators Club in 1995)	1997
1986	American Welding Society	2000
1987	Honors program	2000
1987	Radiological Technology Club	1988
1988	Student Association of Educators	1989
1989	Abilities Unlimited (A club for handicapped students)	1993
1992	Students Against Drug Abuse	1993
1993	Jackson County Computing Association	2000
1993	Country Club (A dance club)	1994
1993	Health Occupation Students of America (HOSA) (The licensed practical nurses joined HOSA in 1993)	2000
1994	Math Club	1997
1994	International Students Club	1995
1995	Students for Environmental Action	2000
1996	College Republicans	1998
1996	College Bowl (Renamed Scholars Bowl in 1997)	2000
1997	Alpha Beta Gamma (International Business Honor Society)	2000
1998	Post Secondary Association of Student Teacher Educators (PASTE) (an organization for those interested in home economics and child care)	2000
1999	Next Step Dance Club	2000
2000	Wesley Foundation	2000

Phi Theta Kappa

Phi Theta Kappa was established in 1918 by the presidents of Missouri's two-year colleges for women for the purpose of encouraging scholarship. In the course of the next decade Phi Theta Kappa spread beyond the borders of Missouri and began organizing chapters in co-educational two-year colleges as well. In 1929 the American Association of Junior Colleges in its national meeting at Atlantic City, New Jersey, recognized Phi Theta Kappa as the two-year or junior college counterpart of Phi Beta Kappa, the national senior college honor society.

In 1929 two private women's colleges in Mississippi, Gulf Park College in Gulfport and Whitworth College in Brookhaven, established Phi Theta Kappa chapters. In 1930 Margaret James (later Mosal) of Canton became Phi Theta Kappa's first elected student national president.

From 1935 to 1985 Mosal served as Phi Theta Kappa's executive director, the society's only full time employee. For nearly 30 years her home in Canton was the national headquarters of the organization. Beginning in 1964, several progressively larger structures in the town served as headquarters buildings. In March 1990, Phi Theta Kappa operations were removed to an interim facility in Jackson until the new headquarters facility could be completed. The Phi Theta Kappa Center for Excellence was completed in the Mississippi Education and Research Center and dedicated on October 18, 1997. In the last decade of the 20th century Phi Theta Kappa established its thousandth chapter, inducted its millionth member, and went international with chapters in Canada, Europe, and Asia.

Gamma Nu Chapter of Phi Theta Kappa
Perkinston Campus
Chartered January 15, 1937

Hinds Junior College at Raymond chartered the first Mississippi public junior college chapter of Phi Theta Kappa on May 15, 1936. A few months later on January 15, 1937, Harrison-Stone-Jackson Junior College chartered the second--Gamma Nu.

Membership was by invitation and open to students "of good moral character" and possessed of "recognized qualities of citizenship as judged by the faculty." Prospective members had to complete one semester of college work "within the upper scholastic ten percent of the regularly enrolled student body of the college division." By the close of the 20th century membership had been extended to vocational-technical students and part-time students meeting the requirement of a 3.5 average in 12 hours of work and subsequent maintenance of a 3 point average.

Charter Members of Gamma Nu Chapter

Beginning at top, (read left to right) science instructor and sponsor S. M. Walker and members Marie Covington, Cyril Carvin, Bonnie Colle, Olin Davis, Vernon Gilly, Claude Campbell, Anita Roberts, Edna M. Delacruz, Elizabeth Lightsey, Betsey Mae Bayley, Clovis Adams, and Francis O'Neal. Photos from 1937 Perkolator, p. 60.

National Officers of Gamma Nu Chapter

Until the early 1960s the constitution of Phi Theta Kappa specified the election of four national officers by majority vote of the delegates assembled in the annual national convention. These officers were president, vice president, second vice president, and historian. The president was to sign charters and "order all disbursement." The vice president was to "act for the president in his absence" and to "formulate a national study program." The second vice president was to serve in the absence of the vice president and "interest himself in the ritualistic work of the society and give advice to local chapters for activities." The historian was to write the "minutes and chapter reports of the convention into an official history."

Gamma Nu Chapter set the 20th century record for national presidents by having five of its members elected to that post. Four of the national presidents were elected in a single decade, 1960-1970. In addition, Gamma Nu contributed three national vice presidents, one national second vice president, and three national historians. No other of the thousand chapters of Phi Theta Kappa in 2000 could equal the record of a member elected to each of the four national offices, not to mention multiples in two.

Howard Pollock of New Orleans, Louisiana 1940-1941 National President Photo 1941 Perkolator, p. 75.

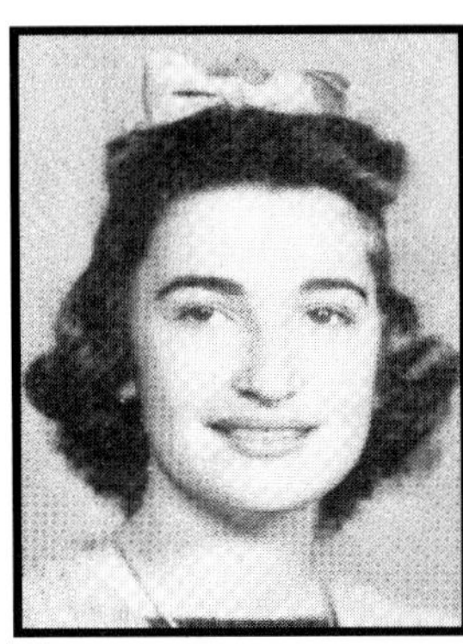

Maryanne Passmore of Dallas, Texas 1941-1942 National Historian Photo 1941 Perkolator, p. 44.

Margaret Ann Dantagnan of New Orleans, Louisiana 1948-1949 National Historian Photo 1948 Perkolator, p. 107.

Russell R. Beaulieu of Hightstown, New Jersey 1950-1951 National Vice President Photo 1951 Perkolator, p. 102.

Carol Horton (center) was elected national second vice president at the national convention in Houston, Texas, in April 1955. Carol (Horton) Daniels returned to school for the first semester following her marriage but departed in January 1956 before second semester began. In March, the national president appointed then current Gamma Nu chapter president Dora Nell McLeod (far right) to fill the new Mrs. Daniels's unexpired term. Consequently, McLeod attended the 1956 national convention in Columbia, Missouri, in Daniels's place. In the photograph taken in the lobby of Harrison Hall in late 1955, members of Gamma Nu Chapter, prepare for initiation of new members. (From left), Nell (Mrs. Gene) Clement, Gamma Nu sponsor Miss Susie Cooley, Mrs. Eileen Brockway, Tina (Mrs. William P.) Lipscomb, Carol (Horton) Daniels, Bill Felsher, Delores Cumbest, Camelia Ann Parrish, and Dora Nell McLeod. Miss Susie Cooley, (second from left) instructor in English, French, and Spanish, served as sponsor of Gamma Nu Chapter from 1948 to 1964. During that period six members of Gamma Nu were elected to Phi Theta Kappa national office--one president, two vice presidents, one second vice president, and two historians. When Cooley retired in May 1964, she had served 43 years as an educator, the last 20 years at Perk.

Sue Beeson of
Long Beach
1959-1960
National Historian
Photo 1959 Perkolator, p. 19.

Leonard A. Blackwell of
Lucedale
1960-1961
National President
Photo 1961 Perkolator, p. 198.

James B. Pennebaker of
Lucedale
1962-1963
National Vice President
Photo 1963 Perkolator, p. 120.

Tola Burton Moffett of
Rocky Creek
1965-1966
National Vice President
Photo 1966 Perkolator, p. 151.

Karl C. Mertz of
Long Beach
1966-1967
National President

Gary Lee Roberts of
Gulfport
1968-1969
National President

MGCJC President J. J. Hayden (left) congratulates Gary Roberts on his election as national Phi Theta Kappa president at the Fiftieth Anniversary Convention of the scholastic fraternity held in Houston, Texas, April 8-11, 1968. While at the convention Hayden was presented with a certificate naming him a national honorary member of Phi Theta Kappa. Alaskan Congressman Howard Pollock, Gamma Nu's first member to gain the fraternity's top slot in 1940-1941, delivered the keynote address to the convention. Accompanying Pollock was his wife, the former Maryanne Passmore, Gamma Nu's first member to attain the position of Phi Theta Kappa national historian (1941-1942). Also attending the national convention with MGCJC's 22-member delegation was Tola Moffett, Gamma Nu's 1965-1966 national first vice president. Photo from Bulldog Barks May 10, 1968.

Billy Zane Gordon of
Wiggins
1970-1971
National President

(From left) MGCCC President J. J. Hayden, newly elected National Phi Theta Kappa President Billy Zane Gordon, and Alaskan congressman Howard Pollock stand together on March 24, 1970, at the National Phi Theta Kappa Convention held in Panama City, Florida. At the convention, the members of Gamma Nu, unable to decide between Pollock and astronaut Fred Haise as their nominee for the society's initial National Alumnus of the Year, nominated both. Both won. But the year 1970-1971 marked the close of Gamma Nu's national Phi Theta Kappa accolades in the 20th century. Photo from Phi Theta Kappa Newsletter, April 1970, p. 14.

Omicron Alpha Chapter of Phi Theta Kappa
Jefferson Davis Campus
Chartered March 31, 1966

Present at JD Campus for the installation of Omicron Alpha Chapter are (from left) MGCJC President J. J. Hayden, Perk Campus Gamma Nu sponsor Earline Hart, Past Gamma Nu Chapter President James C. Moore, JD Campus English teacher and Omicron Alpha sponsor Betty Malone, Past National Vice President Tola Moffett, and JD Campus Dean William P. Lipscomb. Omicron Alpha Chapter President Nancy Broom presented Lipscomb with an honorary Phi Theta Kappa membership during the ceremonies that night. Photo Bulldog Barks, September 8, 1966

Charter Members

Nancy Broom of Biloxi
Raymond Cox of Biloxi
Sandra Frey of Biloxi
Michael Fulcher of Long Beach
Paulette Jordan of Gulfport
John Langford of Biloxi
Claudia Lewis of Gulfport
Barbara Loper of Handsboro
Sherrie Mitchell of Biloxi
Vincent Perrone of Pass Christian
Brenda Plaisance of Biloxi
Stuart Sims of Gulfport
Laura Sweeting of Long Beach
Virginia Thomas of Gulfport
Sarah Varnado of Biloxi
Jack Vice of Long Beach
Richard Wink of Gulfport
Freda Wise of Gulfport

Then Phi Theta Kappa National President Karl Mertz of Gamma Nu (left) and 1960-1961 Past National President Len Blackwell of Gamma Nu assist Omicron Alpha Chapter President Nancy Broom during JD Campus's third initiation on February 9, 1967. Photo from 1967 JCD Perkolator p. 77

Five Omicron Alpha Chapter charter members pose in the JD Campus library circa 1967. (From left) Virginia Thomas, Jack Vice, Nancy Broom, Sherrie Mitchell, and Mike Fulcher. Photo from 1967 JCD Perkolator, p. 35.

Pi Epsilon Chapter of Phi Theta Kappa
Jackson County Campus
Chartered February 8, 1967

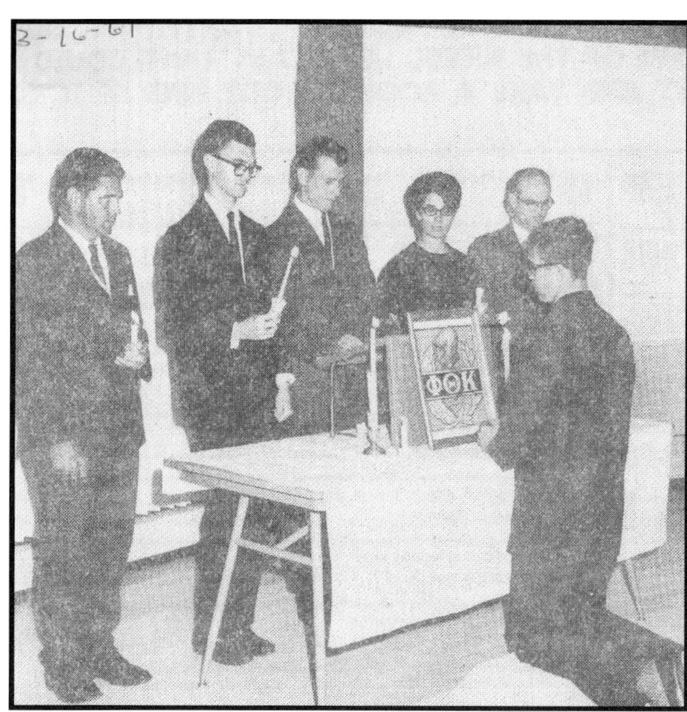

Standing are the five charter members of Pi Epsilon Chapter at Jackson County Campus. These five had been installed and the charter presented by National Phi Theta Kappa President Karl Mertz on February 8, 1967. In the photograph, taken March 13, 1967, the charter members are conducting the second initiation of Pi Epsilon Chapter. Standing (from left) are Treasurer Farrell Parker, President Richard Williams, Secretary Pat Owens, and Councilor Jerry Beeson. Kneeling to be initiated is David Allen. Photo from Mississippi Press, March 16, 1967

Charter members

Jerry Beeson of Moss Point
Patricia Owens of Ocean Springs
Farrell Parker of Pascagoula
David Walker of Escatawpa
Richard Williams of Vancleave

Members of Pi Epsilon Chapter in session 1967-1968 at Jackson County Campus pose with their Phi Theta Kappa emblem, charter, and sponsor. Sitting (from left) are Lauren Coats, Myrna Pittman, Nora Stanley, and Don Forsman. Standing (from left) are Kathy Jahnke, Terry Price (later Fountain), English instructor and sponsor Francesca Howard, and David Allen. 1968 JCD Perkolator p. 103

Pi Epsilon Chapter member Lynn Zimmerman was one of 20 community college students in the nation named to the All-USA Academic First Team by USA Today newspaper and Phi Theta Kappa in 1997. She was featured in USA Today on April 14, 1997, and was honored by the American Association of Community Colleges in Anaheim, California. She is shown with USA Today president and publisher Tom Curley (left) and MGCCC President Barry L. Mellinger. Photo from 1997 Trident, p. 75

Pi Epsilon Chapter member Melissa Leigh Hanna was one of 20 community college students in the nation named to the all-USA Academic First Team by USA Today newspaper and Phi Theta Kappa in 1998. She was featured in USA Today on April 27, 1998, and was honored at the American Association of Community Colleges Annual Convention in Miami, Florida. Hanna (center) was accompanied to the AACC Convention by (from left) MGCCC President Barry L. Mellinger, Pi Epsilon Chapter sponsor Kay Sims, Dorothy Hanna (her mother), and JC Campus vice president Houshang Moradmand. Photo from 1998 Trident, p. 74

Vocational Industrial Clubs of America VICA

VICA was established in 1965 as the national student organization for secondary and post-secondary trade, technical, industrial, and health occupations students. By session 1973-1974 the organization boasted 180,000 members in 44 states, Puerto Rico, and the Virgin Islands.

Membership cards were issued to the provisional members of the Perkinston Campus Chapter of VICA on November 11, 1973. The club received its charter on April 18, 1974, at the State Skill Olympics at Hinds Junior College. At that initial meet, members won three gold and two silver medals. Also at Raymond the Perkinston Campus Club was named Mississippi's Most Outstanding Chapter.

In June 1974 at the VICA United States Skill Olympics at San Antonio, Texas, the Perkinston Campus Chapter received the trophy as the nation's most outstanding post-secondary club. Club member Don Harden of Gulfport was elected national treasurer.

In school session 1974-1975 Perkinston Campus VICA members assisted students at Jefferson Davis Campus, Jackson County Campus, and George County Occupational Training Center (a Perkinston Campus branch) in establishing VICA clubs. In 2000 every MGCCC campus and center had an active VICA club.

At the 1975 Mississippi Skill Olympics in Raymond, the Perkinston VICA Club was once again named the state's most outstanding chapter, and once again members won gold and silver. At the VICA United States Skill Olympics held in Washington, D. C., in June 1975, the Perkinston VICA Club was named the nation's third most outstanding club. Also at the Washington meet, Melvin Lester of the George County Occupational Training Center placed third in the nation in the category of job interview.

In the last 25 years of the 20th century, the various VICA chapters of MGCCC won so many awards at the state level that the archivist decided not to attempt a state level listing. However, in the following section an attempt was made to catalog the national and international awards. Suffice it to say that the prerequisite for national competition was winning gold at the state level.

First officers of Perkinston Campus VICA Chapter. ***Front row*** *(from left), President Peter Blake of Gulfport, Secretary Willie Mae Holland of Lucedale, Parliamentarian Steve Pickich of Pass Christian, Historian Keith Saucier of Biloxi.* ***Back row****, Vice President Howard Jones of Puerto Armuelles, Panama, Treasurer Don Harden of Gulfport , Reporter, and John Long of Hattiesburg. Sponsor George L. Mathis is not pictured.*

The president of the second slate of officers of the Perkinston Campus VICA Chapter holds the trophy awarded to the club at the VICA United States Skill Olympics in June 1974, as the most outstanding post-secondary club in the nation. (Seated from left), Club Artist Donnie Rayburn of Wiggins, Reporter Kelly Castiglia of Gulfport, Secretary Willie Mae Holland of Lucedale, Treasurer Seren Ainsworth of Lucedale . (Standing from left), Parlaimentarian Ronnie Rayburn of Wiggins, President Henry Fox of Pascagoula, and Vice President Charles Long of Gretna, Louisiana.

June 1980-June 1981 -- 1980 VICA United States Skill Olympics and the 1981 International Skill Olympics in Atlanta, Georgia.

Linda Kay Triplett of Saucier, a member of the Perkinston Campus VICA Chapter, competed in June 1980 at the VICA United States Skill Olympics in Atlanta, Georgia, and won the national gold medal in machine drafting (mechanical drawing). At the VICA skill trials held October 26 - November 1, 1980, at Wilmington, Ohio, Triplett was selected as one of 16 members of the United States VICA International Skill Olympics Team destined to compete at Atlanta in June 1981.

The International Skill Olympics, modeled on the more famous Olympic Games, had been conducted since 1950 with the United States competing since 1975. The International Skill Olympics set for Atlanta in 1981 marked America's first time to host the competition. The United States relied on VICA and technical schools to provide the U.S. team members.

Triplett was the first Mississippian to compete in the international event and the first American woman to represent the United States in the category of machine drafting. At the International Skill Olympics at Atlanta, June 11-20, 1981, she placed sixth in a field of contenders representing eleven nations. Triplett was the only MGCCC student to compete and place in an international event in the 20th century.

VICA sponsor and drafting instructor Roney Walker stands beside Linda Triplett at her drafting table in Weeks Hall in 1980.

Roney Walker (left) and Linda Triplett display the gold medals awarded to them in June 1980 at the VICA United States Skill Olympics in Atlanta, Georgia.

Linda Triplett at her drafting table in Weeks Hall. She is dressed in her VICA blazer with the VICA emblem visible on her pocket.

(From left) Mississippi State Superintendent of Education Charles Holladay, Perkinston Campus Executive Dean Clyde Strickland, Perkinston Campus VICA sponsor Roney Walker, Linda Triplett, and Mississippi Governor William Winter pose in the governor's office in Jackson in May 1981, two weeks before the International Skill Olympics in Atlanta. Photo courtesy of Roney Walker.

National Vica Awards 1983-2000

June 1983 -- VICA United States Skill Olympics in Louisville, Kentucky

The Perkinston Campus VICA Chapter placed second in the nation in opening and closing ceremonies. This was the first time any Mississippi team had placed in that category. The members of the national second-place team were Kerry O'Neal and Glenda Sumrall both of Benndale, Lee Hancock of Lucedale, Marcus Jones, and Greg VanCourt, both of Ocean Springs, Debra Taylor of Saucier, and Patricia Faciana of Bay St. Louis. In addition, at Louisville, Perkinston Campus VICA member Marcus Jones of Ocean Springs placed fourth in the nation in machine drafting.

April 1984 -- Perkinston Campus drafting instructor Roney Walker announced that VICA member Floyd Waltman of Wade had won first place in the American Institute for Drafting and Design National Contest. Waltman's drawing was displayed at the AIDD Exposition in Anaheim, California, on April 10-12, 1984.

May 1985 -- Perkinston Campus VICA member Ron Northrop of Saucier won first place in the American Institute for Drafting and Design National Contest in machine drafting. Perkinston Campus VICA member Mark A. Mauldin of Lucedale won first place in the AIDD National Contest in the piping category. Both men's drawings were exhibited at the Albert Thomas Convention Center in Houston, Texas, during the 1985 AIDD National Convention. Both were drafting students of Roney Walker.

June 1985 -- VICA United States Skill Olympics in Phoenix, Arizona. A seven-member VICA team became the first Mississippi team to win gold medals in the National Skill Olympics opening and closing ceremonies category. All were drafting students of Perkinston instructor Roney Walker. According to Walker each member was judged on stage presence, speaking, poise, and team work in opening the meeting, presenting the parts of the emblem that symbolized VICA, and in closing the meeting with the organization's pledge. Seven thousand students from junior colleges in all states except Wyoming and Maine participated in the National VICA Skill Olympics at Phoenix.

June 1991 -- VICA United States Skill Olympics at Louisville, Kentucky. Jean Whitney of Ocean Springs, Jefferson Davis Campus VICA member and graduate of JD Campus's Teacher's Assistant Program, took first place in Job Skills for her six-minute demonstration in the use of puppets made from cardboard and paper to tell children's stories. Whitney's instructor, Sandra Weinberg, accompanied her to Louisville.

June 1992 -- VICA United States Skill Olympics at Louisville, Kentucky. Jefferson Davis Campus VICA students won the gold medal in the category of display bulletin board.

June 1993 -- VICA United States Skill Olympics at Louisville, Kentucky. A five member team from Perkinston Campus took a fifth place in the National VICA Quiz Bowl.

June 1996 -- VICA United States Skill Olympics at Kansas City, Missouri. Jefferson Davis Campus VICA students won second place in promotional bulletin board.

June 1997 -- Skills USA-VICA Championship in Kansas City, Missouri. Jim Salley, a native of Miami, Florida, and a Perkinston resident, won the gold medal in Extemporaneous Speaking. One of those rare individuals who excelled in both

The seven gold medal members of the state and national opening and closing exercises competition pose between Weeks Hall and A. L. May Memorial Stadium on Perkinston Campus in April 1984 with their state gold medals. (From left) Chris Bond of Perkinston, Mark Mauldin of Lucedale, Harry Hartlee of Brooklyn, Mike Leonard of Gulfport, Floyd Waltman of Wade, Linda Sullivan of Wiggins, and Robin Morgan of Theodore, Alabama.

a vocational-technical program and in academics, Salley took welding from 7 a.m. to 1 p.m. and academics in the afternoon twice making the President's List. Sometimes he arrived at his history class with his clothes still smoking from the welding torch. At Perkinston in 1997 his abilities in both areas resulted in an unprecedented occurrence. At the Awards Dinner he took the History Award, the Ancient Literature Award, and the Welding Award. Salley, who termed himself a "Renaissance welder," credited his unique blend of "techno-academic" knowledge for his ability to deliver his state and his national gold medal speeches.

Summer 1998 -- Skills USA-VICA Championship Kansas City, Missouri. Jefferson Davis Campus VICA sponsor Sandra Weinberg's four-member all Biloxian Quiz Bowl Team won gold medals for their knowledge of VICA affairs, current events, math, science, history, geography, and fine arts. The team consisted of Lisa Thomas, Bryan Perkins, and Bobby Steele of JD and George Ashbaugh of Mississippi Gulf Coast Applied Technology and Development Center. In addition, JD VICA member Caprice Smith of Waveland took second place in the job skills demonstration category.

Summer 1999 -- Skills USA-VICA Championship at Kansas City, Missouri. Jefferson Davis Campus VICA member Colton Hall won second place in Architectural Drafting. Jefferson Davis Campus VICA member Hai Tran took a third place in Heating, Air Conditioning, and Refrigeration.

Perkinston Campus student Jim Salley,1997 VICA national gold medal winner in extemporaneous speaking.

National Achievements of Students in Specialized Clubs: A Partial List

The following fragmentary list of the national achievements of students in specialized clubs to December 2000 resulted from a combination of the sparse information on the subject held by the MGCCC Archives together with information garnered by the archivist from then current sponsors of specialized clubs. Listings were restricted to first through fifth placement at national conferences.

Distributive Education Clubs of America (DECA)--national organization for students seeking careers in marketing, merchandising, and management.

Renee Alexander, of JC Campus, placed first in Food Marketing--1978

Noel Aucoin, of JC Campus, placed third in food Marketing--1978

Rhonda Bloom, of JC Campus, placed second in Fashion Merchandising--1978

Phi Beta Lambda (PBL)--national professional association for students pursuing business careers.

Chris Tillman, of JC Campus, placed first in Economics--1990

Tommie Staten, of JD Campus, placed first in Job Interview--1995

Nicole Goff, of JC Campus, placed first in Impromptu Speaking--1999

Health Occupations Students of America (HOSA)--an association composed primarily of Licensed Practical Nursing students.

Lisa Tilley, Lorraine Dempsey, Cynthia Lawrence, Christie Dufrene, all of George County Occupational Training Center, placed first in Community Awareness Project--1993.

Delta Epsilon Chi--national association for marketing majors.

Dee Williams, of JC Campus, placed first in Sales Promotion Plan--1995

Josh Tolleson, Tim Wall, Phillip Drake, all of JC Campus, placed first in Advertising Campaign--1999

Beth Scamardo, of JC Campus, placed third in Sales Promotion Plan--1999

Emile Scamardo, of JC Campus, placed third in Human Resource Management--1999

Phillip Drake, of JC Campus, placed second in Design presentation--2000

GRADUATION, DIPLOMAS, CERTIFICATES, AND DEGREES 1912 - 2000

The Harrison County Agricultural High School (HCAHS) *Announcement* of 1912 contained no statement regarding graduation. The HCAHS *Second Annual Catalogue* published in summer 1913 contained specific requirements for graduation in terms of units. A unit was defined as a full session's work (nine months) in any particular subject. The boys had to have four units of agriculture, and the girls had to have four units of Home Science. In order to graduate a student had to complete four units of English, three of mathematics, two and one fifth of history, and three and four fifths of elective studies, "making in all sixteen units of work, fifteen of which are required for graduation" (the total was not added correctly--the total was seventeen). Elective studies included all subjects not listed as "required." Examples of electives were Latin, manual training, more history, more math, and pedagogy. Girls could take agriculture as an elective, and boys could elect "certain phases" of home science. Apparently Grace Ruble's "classes in Instrumental Music, Voice and Expression" carried no credit. All students wishing to take those had to pay $3.00 per class per month.

The HCAHS opened on September 17, 1912. Apparently no one graduated in the session 1912-1913, but two students did graduate at the close of the 1913-1914 session.

Beginning Sunday, May 17, 1914, the school staged a "commencement week" which set the pattern for those of the future. At 8 p.m. that Sunday night the Rev. L. A. Darsey preached the baccalaureate or "bachelor of arts" sermon. On Wednesday night students in all classes participated in a music and expression recital. At 11 a.m. on Friday, May 21, attorney R. C. Cowan of Gulfport delivered the commencement address after which Tom Ford Ruble and Leo Singleton Tisdale, both of McHenry, received their diplomas. The exercises closed with the presentation of the class play entitled "The Junior."

In what must set the record for the shortest time for

Students of the Harrison County Agricultural High School standing on the portico of the Bennett Building circa 1914: ***First row*** *(from left) Flora Baxter of Perkinston, Leo Singleton Tisdale of McHenry, and Ruby Daffin of Wiggins.* ***Second Row*** *(from left) Tom Ford Ruble, Harrison "Red" Sloane, and Howard Bond all of McHenry.*

Tom Ruble and Leo Tisdale are the first known graduates of the Harrison County Agricultural High School. It would have been possible, but unlikely, that anyone would have graduated from the school in 1913. The Daily Herald published two articles, one on May 12, 1914, announcing the commencement exercises, and another on May 22, 1914, describing the exercises. The two articles were worded such that no inference could be made as to there having been a previous graduation ceremony or not. A diligent search of all surviving records of every type failed to turn up any account of commencement exercises in 1913.

On Monday, May 31, 1915, the Daily Herald reported that five students had graduated from the Harrison County Agricultural High School the previous Thursday night. Three of them--Harrison Sloane, Ruby Daffin, and Howard Bond--are in this picture. The other two were Kathleen McKnight and Searcy Davis. The author of the 1915 article averred, "Last year there were only two graduates and this year there were five and next year it is expected there will be still more."

Though it is not stated, the opportunity was there to give the number of graduates in 1913 if there had been any. The article originated in Perkinston as a "Special to the Herald," so presumably the author would have known if anyone had graduated in 1913. Of the six people in the photo only Harrison Sloane was not on the original 1912-1913 roll of the AHS. Of the six people in the photo only Flora Baxter was not listed among the graduates of 1914 or 1915. Of the two 1915 graduates not pictured, Kathleen McKnight was not on the original roll.

At the conclusion of what Mississippi Gulf Coast Junior College President J. J. Hayden termed the "Golden Year," the five AHS graduates of 1915 graduated again. During commencement exercises on May 20, 1962, Hayden conferred honorary junior college degrees on Howard H. Bond, Kathleen (McKnight) Clark, Searcy "Doc" Davis, Ruby (Daffin) Harvey, and Harrison Sloane. College press releases deemed the five as the "graduates from the first high school graduating class." Apparently the college had by then forgotten Tom Ruble and Leo Tisdale, the two graduates of 1914. Ironically, though, the five 1915 graduates received their honorary degrees with the final AHS graduates of the school as the AHS was terminated that day. Photo courtesy of Edna Bishop.

a reunion, exactly half the known alumni of the school in the person of Tom Ruble returned for a reunion picnic of past and present students on June 19. However, the death of Mrs. T. T. Garner, the wife of one of Perkinston's earliest settlers, cast a pall over the proceedings, and the day was passed quietly in the dormitory.

The events of commencement week 1915 duplicated 1914 with the exception that the five graduates received their diplomas from the hands of Harrison County Superintendent of Education John Jefferson Dawsey on Thursday night, May 27. The five graduates that year were Harrison "Red" Sloane and Howard Bond of McHenry, Kathleen McKnight and Ruby Daffin of Wiggins, and Searcy Davis of Perkinston.

The elements of commencement week--a baccalaureate sermon, student recitals, class plays, a commencement address, the awarding of diplomas--not surprisingly tended to remain the same. The order, though, of these ceremonies tended to change with the exception that the baccalaureate sermon fell almost always on Sunday, and the graduation ceremony soon became the last event. The person actually giving the diplomas to the graduates during the AHS era alternated among three officials seemingly at whim--the Harrison County superintendent of education, the president of the AHS Board of Trustees, or the AHS principal (or AHS superintendent as he was termed by 1919).

The twelve diplomas given out on May 18, 1916, were the last to bear the name "Harrison County Agricultural High School." The diplomas were awarded to W. Merritt Davis, Harry Eddy, Ruth A. Gilkey, Eleanor M. Kelly, H. Eugene Krohn, Lois E. Morehead, Houston L. Murray, Hattie E. McLeod, W. F. Wilson, Leah Ruble, Kathryn B. Swetman, and Leo Taylor. The birth of Stone County the next month resulted in the name of the school being changed to Harrison-Stone Agricultural High School.

In both 1917 and 1918 the events of commencement week were compressed because the AHS closed two weeks early both years the United States fought in World War I. The board authorized the early closings to allow the students to engage in war work in factories and on farms.

In the *Daily Herald*, May 15, 1917, HSAHS Principal J. A. Huff stated that, "our graduating exercises will be held May 18 at 8 p.m. Prof. G. G. Hurst of Mississippi Normal College (by 2000 called the University of Southern Mississippi) will deliver the

Harrison-Stone Agricultural High School

This Certifies That Lydia Mae Cruthirds has honorably completed the Literary Course of Study as prescribed by this Institution and by intellectual attainments and correct deportment is entitled to receive this

DIPLOMA

In Witness Whereof Our signatures are hereunto affixed this 25th day of May A.D. 1920

Principal

The graduates of the class of 1920 earned either a "Literary Diploma" or a "Music Diploma" or both. Lydia Mae Cruthirds of Lyman received this 22" x 17" Literary Diploma, which is signed by W. F. Gorenflo, President of the Board of Trustees of Harrison-Stone Agricultural High School, and HSAHS Superintendent Claude Bennett. This diploma was donated to the MGCCC Archives by Andrea Ladner in 1997.

(From left) William M. Cruthirds, his wife, Lota, and his daughter, Lydia Mae, pose with their automobile at Lyman circa 1920 about the time Lydia Mae graduated from the Harrison-Stone Agricultural High School. Photo courtesy of Andrea Ladner.

address and W. E. Gorenflo, president of our Board of Trustees, will deliver diplomas to six young ladies and fourteen young men. We extend a cordial invitation to the public to visit their school on this occasion." The last *HSAHS News* of the session, dated May 17, noted that, "The student body spent Thursday afternoon on the banks of old Red Creek." Then the editors bid adieu to friends and patrons without giving the names of the next day's graduates.

Two known graduates of the AHS Class of 1917 were Glen Swetman and John C. Lamey. On the morning after graduation Lamey married AHS student, Kate Bond, daughter of Mr. and Mrs. Rankin Bond. Andrew Wiggins Bond, president of the Stone County Board of Supervisors and "Father of Stone County," performed the nuptials.

In 1918 graduation day was advertised as May 14. Once again no names were published, and for the only time in the history of the institution not even the number of graduates was given. The only student known to have graduated was Clio Louise Ruble of McHenry.

The 1919 commencement exercises began at 8:30 on Thursday evening, May 22, with a student recital. Miss Vivian Davis gave a recital in music and expression on the following night. On Sunday at 11 a.m., Dr. B. G. Lowery delivered the commencement sermon, and that night at 8:30 a "sacred concert" was held. On Monday evening at 8:30 p.m. State Superintendent of Education Willard F. Bond delivered the baccalaureate address. Following Bond's speech, Harrison County Superintendent of Education W. H. Wood conferred 16 diplomas.

In 1920, commencement exercises lasted from Wednesday, May 19, until Tuesday, May 25. On May 25, for the first time, the diplomas awarded by the HSAHS were divided into two groups--literary and music. The 29 students who graduated that night took home 34 diplomas because five of the girls on the literary list also claimed all but two of the music diplomas. Music courses were not part of the required curriculum of the HSAHS, and the school charged tuition for them. Hence, music instruction carried a separate diploma. The class of 1921 was awarded 19 literary and four music diplomas, and the class of 1922 claimed 15 literary and three music diplomas, but in neither year did anyone earn both.

Ruby Lee (Johnson) Probst Strong received a "Music Diploma" from the HSAHS in 1922. In an interview conducted with her at homecoming, October 19, 1996, Strong stated that this diploma qualified her to teach in the public schools of Mississippi without taking an examination. By a Legislative Act of 1918

***Photo left**, (from left), Ruby Lee Johnson, unknown, and Gladys Beverly stand beside the steps of Bennett Hall at the time of their 1922 graduation from Harrison-Stone Agricultural High School. **Photo center,**(from left), Ruby Lee (Johnson) Probst Strong of Purvis and Gladys (Beverly) Powe of Winchester, ca. 1995. **Photo right**, Charlie Probst as he appeared in 1962, when he was the last principal of the Perkinston Agricultural High School. After her graduation from HSAHS in 1922, Ruby Lee Johnson married William Probst. After his death she married Madison Strong in 1958. In the course of an interview conducted with Ruby Lee (Johnson) Probst Strong at homecoming on October 19, 1996, she remarked, "I graduated from the AHS in 1922, and my son, Charlie, closed it 40 years later in 1962." After the closure of the AHS in 1962, the school's students were dispersed to Wiggins High School and Harrison Central High School. Photos courtesy of Charlie Probst.*

Agricultural High School

Perkinston, Mississippi

This Certifies That Ruby Lee Johnson having honorably completed Music Course of Study as prescribed by the Board of Trustees is a Graduate of this Institution and is therefore awarded this

DIPLOMA

In Witness Whereof our signatures are hereunto affixed at Perkinston, Mississippi, this Twenty second day of May A.D. 1922

Thos I Cook SUPERINTENDENT

[illegible] PRESIDENT

C. C. Swetman SECRETARY

The 17" x 13 3/4" music diploma awarded to Ruby Lee (Johnson) Probst Strong in 1922 carries a picture of the Bennett Building that contained the top-story auditorium wherein she received it. Only 14 music diplomas were known to have been awarded in the history of the Perkinston institution. Diploma courtesy Ruby Lee (Johnson) Probst Strong.

any AHS graduate in the State of Mississippi was granted a teacher's license provided two of the 15 Carnegie units required for graduation were educational electives and furthermore that the licensee attended a summer normal of not less than 25 days duration. After 1922 the distinction between a literary and a music diploma was no longer noted in the lists of candidates for graduation from the HSAHS.

By 1923 sixteen Carnegie units were required for "diploma graduation." These units, as before, included four required in agriculture for boys and four required in home economics for girls. The balance could be accrued from four units of English, four units of electives, three units of math, five units of science, and two units of history. What it amounted to was that a student had to take one elective but could take more electives. In lieu of a high school diploma, the school offered a high school "certificate." This certificate also required 16 units of work but could be had with only two years in agriculture or home economics.

The accounts of the graduation ceremonies held May 25, 1923, mentioned the terms "salutatorian" and "valedictorian" for the first time. The salutatorian, the second highest-ranking student in grades, saluted or greeted those assembled for commencement. The highest ranked scholar gave the valedictory oration or farewell address. The crowd apparently received two greetings that Friday night because both Sybil Bowden of McHenry and Mary Forbis, daughter of the then current HSAHS superintendent, were listed as salutatorians. William Easley of Lumberton gave the valedictory speech.

On June 1, 1923, HSAHS Superintendent J. H. Forbis in the *Daily Herald* stated that no more students would be awarded diplomas for "only three years of high school work," nor would any more students be allowed to transfer from another school bringing in more credits than the State Accrediting Commission allowed.

At Forbis's last graduation, May 23, 1924, more students joined the ranks of the speakers at the occasion. Hazel Davis of Perkinston read the class history. Mason Thompson of Biloxi, in his role as seer, prophesied the future. Margaret O'Neal of Saucier waxed lyrical as class poet. Clarence Flurry of Hattiesburg read the list of bequests from the lofty senior class to the lowly juniors.

HSAHS Superintendent Jefferson Lee Denson presented 24 diplomas on his first graduation night, May 23, 1925. Nine of those graduates formed the nucleus for the first junior college freshman class in the coming fall.

Two days after that 1925 graduation, the first fully accredited summer school in the institution's history began. At the close of the summer term on August 14. Denson held an abbreviated commencement exercise in Bennett Hall Auditorium for six graduates. Harrison County Superintendent of Education Cooper J. Darby, delivered the commencement address, and Denson presented the diplomas. This first summer graduation

The diploma of William Albert Frantzen, awarded May 23, 1924, consisted of a 13 3/8" x 10 3/8" document folded inside a black velvet cover of slightly larger dimensions. The legend, "Harrison-Stone Agricultural High School, William Albert Frantzen, Class of 1924," was embossed in gold letters on a leatherette oval set on the front of the velvet cover. Why Frantzen was spelled with a "z" on the cover and with an "x" on the document was unknown to Frantzen himself, but he mentioned that anomaly when he presented the item to the MGCCC Archives.

Harrison-Stone Agricultural

High School

This Certifies that

William Albert Frantxen

has satisfactorily completed the Course of Study prescribed by the Board of Education for the High School Department and is therefore entitled to this

DIPLOMA

Given under our hands at Perkinston, Mississippi, this 23rd day of May 1924

SUPERINTENDENT

PRESIDENT

SECRETARY

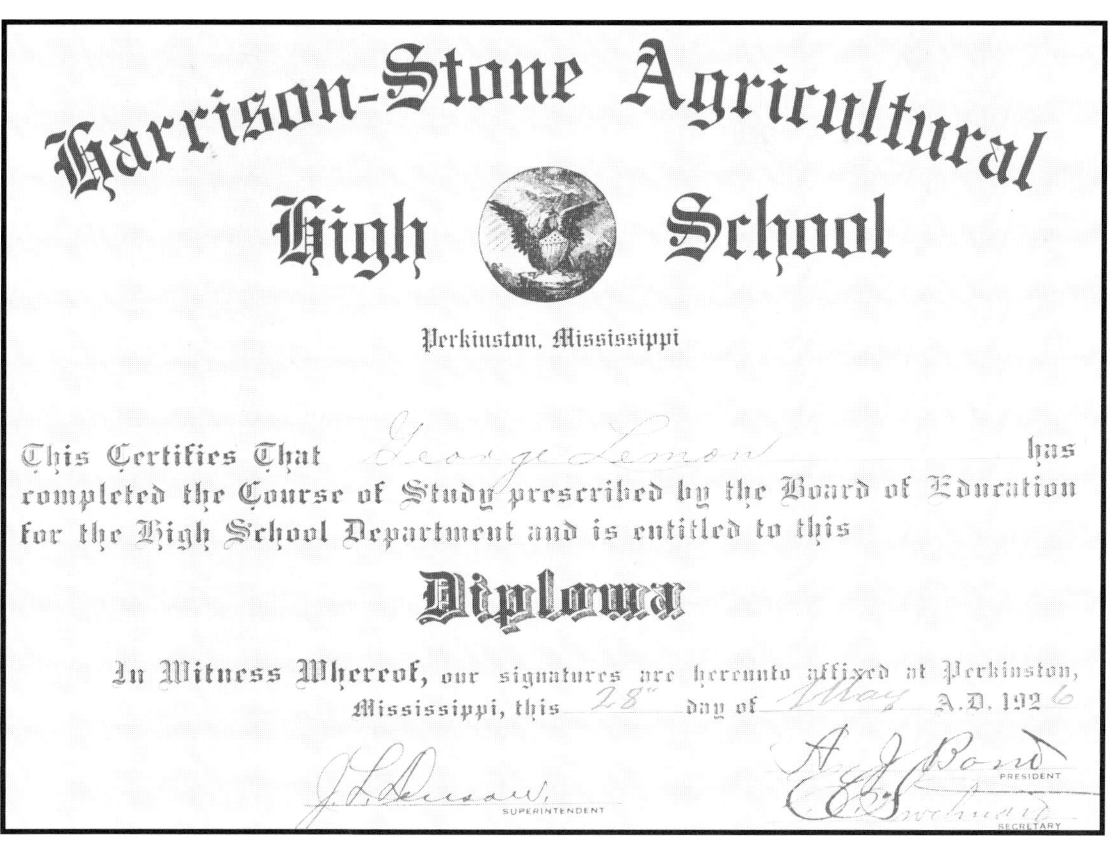

Harrison-Stone Agricultural High School

Perkinston, Mississippi

This Certifies That George Lemon has completed the Course of Study prescribed by the Board of Education for the High School Department and is entitled to this

Diploma

In Witness Whereof, our signatures are hereunto affixed at Perkinston, Mississippi, this 28th day of May A.D. 1926

SUPERINTENDENT

PRESIDENT

SECRETARY

Harrison-Stone Agricultural High School became Harrison-Stone-Jackson Agricultural High School and Junior College on September 9, 1925. George Lemon's May 28, 1926, diploma does not reflect that change because it still reads Harrison-Stone AHS.

would be the last until World War II. From 1926 until 1937 those students expected to finish in summer school were allowed to take part in the regular session commencement exercises with the exception that they did not receive their diplomas until the units or credits were earned. Summer school was eliminated in 1938, 1939, 1940, and 1941. Summer school was resumed in 1942, but summer school graduation was not resumed until the following summer. Beginning in 1943, summer graduations were held each summer until 1970. From 1971 to 2000 diplomas and degrees continued to be awarded in the summer, but summer ceremonies were held only occasionally.

The specifics of the graduations of the Harrison-Stone-Jackson Agricultural High School and Junior College (HSJAHS & JC) classes of 1926, 1927, and 1928, due to their bearing on the establishment of the junior college, are contained herein in the chapter entitled "Denson and the Junior College."

A tradition that began in 1928 lasted until 1937. The salutatorian, Sheppard Walker of Ramsay Springs came from the HSJAHS class. The valedictorian, Laverna Ladner of Perkinston, came from the HSJJC class. In May 1937, a salutatorian and a valedictorian were named for the last time, and special honor graduates and honor graduates were named for the first time.

No student speakers were noted from 1938 through 1941. In May 1942, the president of the high school senior class and the president of the sophomore junior college class addressed the assemblage at graduation. The tradition of the two class presidents speaking lasted until the demise of the AHS in May 1962.

The *Session 1928-1929 Announcement* gave the "Requirement for certificate of completion of Junior College work" in terms of semester hours. The *Announcement* stated, "Junior Colleges cannot grant degrees, but a certificate will be issued at the regular graduation exercises showing completion of work, provided the student shall have finished sixty semester hours of work as follows:

Mathematics	6 semester hours
English	12 semester hours
History	6 semester hours
Science	6 semester hours
Electives	30 semester hours

Denson's last graduation, which took place on May 31, 1929, was billed as the largest graduating class in the history of the school. Denson had claimed that distinction successively each of the five years of his tenure, and each year the claim had been true if those predicted to finish each summer actually did finish.

According to the *Daily Herald* of May 24, 1929, "Forty-eight students will receive high school diplomas, twenty-eight will receive junior college certificates and one a certificate of graduation in music." The reporter used this phraseology because somebody at the school told him to do so. By state law the term "degree" was reserved for four-year colleges and uni-

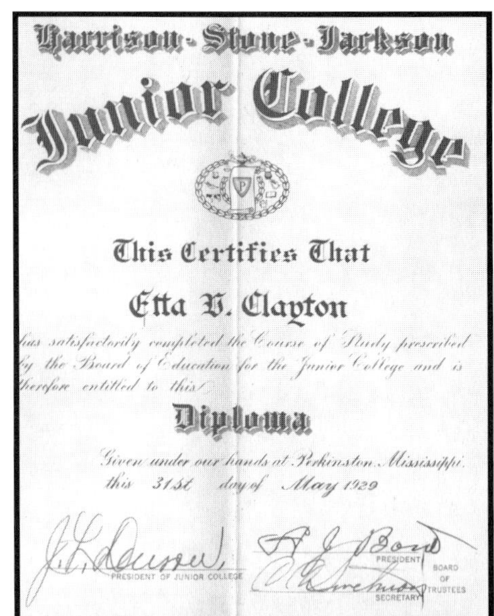

Harrison-Stone-Jackson
Junior College
This Certifies That
Etta V. Clayton
has satisfactorily completed the Course of Study prescribed by the Board of Education for the Junior College and is therefore entitled to this
Diploma
Given under our hands at Perkinston, Mississippi, this 31st day of May 1929
PRESIDENT OF JUNIOR COLLEGE
PRESIDENT
SECRETARY
BOARD OF TRUSTEES

(Left) The earliest junior college graduation instrument in the collection of the MGCCC Archives in 2000 was that of Etta V. Clayton, Class of 1929. The 8 1/2" by 7" document was folded into a slightly larger black velvet cover with the words, " Harrison-Stone-Jackson Agricultural High School and Junior College, Etta V. Clayton, Class of 1929, " embossed in gold on a leatherette oval set in the front of the cover. The cover of the AHS graduation instrument of John Pickering (right) for the same year was identical to Clayton's in every respect, but the document inside differed in two important respects. In the first case, where the Clayton document read "Junior College," Pickering's read "High School." In the second case, J. L. Denson signed Clayton's document above a line reading "President of Junior College," while he signed Pickering's document above a line reading, "Superintendent of High School." Yet, in no other document, and never in the press, was Denson referred to as a "president." The chief executive officer of the Perkinston institution was not officially termed "president" until November 7, 1941. The two "diplomas" of 1929 highlighted yet another inconsistency. The institution exerted a great deal of effort in the press and in official documents distinguishing between a high school "diploma" and a junior college "certificate." Yet both 1929 graduation documents carried the term "diploma." The size and style of the AHS graduation instrument remained the same as Pickering's 1929 instrument through May 1942, with the exception that beginning in May 1937, the legend embossed on the front no longer contained the words "Junior College."

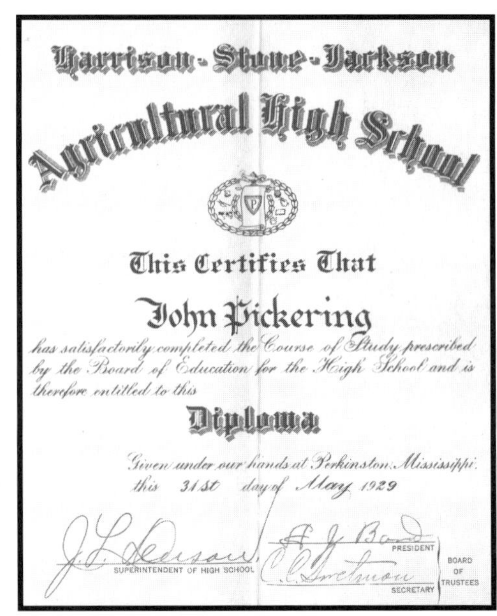

Harrison-Stone-Jackson
Agricultural High School
This Certifies That
John Pickering
has satisfactorily completed the Course of Study prescribed by the Board of Education for the High School and is therefore entitled to this
Diploma
Given under our hands at Perkinston, Mississippi, this 31st day of May 1929
SUPERINTENDENT OF HIGH SCHOOL
PRESIDENT
SECRETARY
BOARD OF TRUSTEES

Harrison-Stone-Jackson
Agricultural High School
and Junior College
John Pickering
Class of 1929

versities. The high schools of the state granted a diploma and the junior colleges granted a "certificate of completion." The *Session 1928-1929 Announcement* set the requirement for a high school diploma at 16 units and the requirements for a junior college certificate at 60 semester hours.

C. J. Darby's first graduation ushered in a new tradition and failed to start another. Caps and gowns came to stay, and Darby found out that alumni preferred to cheer for the football team rather than attend a graduation ceremony at homecoming.

Commencement week began as usual with the baccalaureate sermon in the college auditorium, but that was all that was usual about Sunday evening, May 25, 1930. This time the auditorium was not the one in Bennett Hall. Reverend E. N. DeMiller of Biloxi preached in the new 500 seat auditorium of the Denson Administration building. The 53 candidates for graduation assembled for the sermon dressed in caps and gowns. The 16 junior college sophomores wore black. The 37 AHS seniors wore gray.

The usual plays, recitals, and banquets dominated the week until Friday, which had been set aside as homecoming day. The Alumni Association, founded the previous fall, had decided to hold homecoming in conjunction with graduation instead of a football game. Consequently the plans for Friday called for a 10 a.m. glee club and orchestra musical program followed by a luncheon. Graduation was to follow at 4 p.m. so that the expected throngs of alumni could gather on the banks of Red Creek for a gala picnic. Apparently all that happened, but equally apparently the expected homecoming crowd failed to materialize. 1930 was the only graduation homecoming.

At the baccalaureate sermon on May 24, 1931, the orchestra played as the 63 candidates for graduation marched into Denson Hall Auditorium and took seats reserved for them on the front rows. The junior college sophomores wore black and the high school seniors once again wore gray, more fully described as "national high school gray caps and gowns."

For the first time in the history of the institution the candidates for graduation held a class night on the Thursday before the Friday night graduation. Obviously the intent was to perform a number of the ceremonies usually reserved for graduation night in order to shorten the program. So on class night the salutatorian and the valedictorian spoke and the wills, histories, prophecies, and poems were read. Class night ended with the college sophomores and the high school seniors handing down candles of learning to their successors. This candle service may have occurred in previous years, but 1931 was the first time it was mentioned.

Photo courtesy of Randle Dedeaux.

Richard Kopp Photo

(Far left) Charles Clay Swetman

(Left) The bronze plaque on the fountain reads: "Dedicated to Uncle Charlie Swetman for faithful and active service to this school from its establishment in 1912 to his death in May 1934."

For the first time in the session 1931-1932, junior college enrollment was greater than that of the high school, and that change was particularly apparent on graduation night, May 27, 1932. Junior college candidates for graduation, seated on the stage that night in Denson Hall Auditorium, outnumbered their high school counterparts 43 to 15. Darby gave three new awards that night. The first two service medals for highest contributions to the school in the realm of student labor went to Mary Parsons of Perkinston and Paul Runnels of Hattiesburg. Wayne McHenry took the medal for the best progress in piano.

The 1932 commencement speaker, Claude Bennett, president of State Teachers College at Hattiesburg, had been superintendent of the Harrison-Stone Agricultural High School from 1917-1919. The proceedings closed that night with the singing of the alma mater, which was the first time that activity was mentioned in print.

Bennett's participation in the 1932 graduation ceremonies had added a note of nostalgia to those proceedings, but graduation day May 31, 1935, was a veritable time trip. At 4 p.m. that Friday afternoon the students, faculty, staff of the school, and many people from the community gathered to dedicate the Swetman Memorial Fountain to the memory of "Uncle Charlie Swetman," who had died a year earlier on May 23, 1934.

Swetman on September 3, 1910, had made Perkinston's initial offer to become the site of the Harrison County AHS to the Harrison County school board. He had served as secretary of the Board of Trustees from its inception until near the time of his death. He had served the school in general as postmaster of the community, and his mercantile establishment had been the bookstore for the school from the beginning. The two-thirds of the school quadrangle from the railroad up to the base of the hill had been his land. The fountain being dedicated that graduation day next to the superintendent's home (the Alumni House of 2000) stood on a portion of that land. The camellias planted about the fountain on that dedication day had been his, too. He had given a camellia bush to each faculty member before his death, and they had arranged them in a garden about the fountain. At the dedication ceremony E. J. Adams of Pass Christian, who had served on the first Board of Trustees with Swetman, eulogized him. A student recited Tenneyson's "Crossing the Bar." The school's newly organized marching band played memorial music.

Judge J. L. Taylor, the commencement speaker that night, had been the Chairman of the Agricultural High School Committee of the Gulfport Commercial Union in 1910. He had worked closely with Swetman to locate the school at Perkinston and had been with him the morning of Sept. 3, 1910, when that effort began.

After Taylor's speech, Board of Trustees President W. Leach awarded the diplomas. Darby awarded the usual medals and several new ones. Jack Jermyn of Gulfport, the first five-letter man of the school, received the men's medal as best all-around athlete. Helen Gray of Gulfport took the counterpart medal in the women's category. The Wiggins Rotary Club medal for high school girl with the best scholastic average went to Lydia Douglas of Tuscaloosa, Alabama. The Newman Warnell Memorial Medal for outstanding service to the junior college in the current year could be given to a current student or a former student. The initial award went to Vonceil Moffett of Shipman. This medal, donated yearly by campus engineer Newman A. Warnell, was given in honor of his son, Newman Bradley Warnell.

At the 1936 graduation on May 29, Darby awarded the first A. J. Price Medal to Alice Emily Hague of Pascagoula. Dr. A. J. Price of Gulfport supplied this gold medal to be given to the student "voted to have most effectively practiced the Golden Rule during the year."

At the 1936 graduation the high school graduates

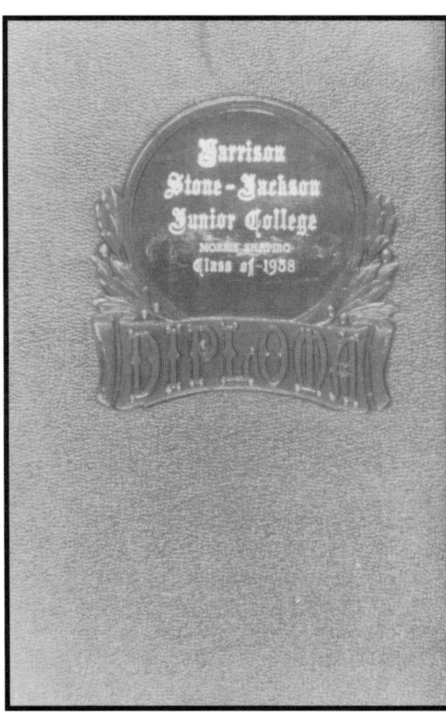

As Wick Wallace's 1937 AHS graduation instrument cover attests (left), the words "Junior College" have disappeared leaving only the legend "Harrison-Stone-Jackson Agricultural High School." The MGCCC Archives in 2000 had no 1937 junior college graduation cover, but the 1937 cover almost certainly matched Morris Schapiro's of 1938 (center). In 1939, as attested by Evelyn Rebecca McQuagge's junior college graduation instrument cover (right), the façade of the New Capitol in Jackson was embossed on Perkinston covers for the first time. All three graduation instruments (above) were black with gold lettering on front and gold backing inside. All three documents read "diploma" and the word was actually embossed beneath the gold lettering on Schapiro's cover. But Schapiro's and McQuagge's covers were of leather and not velvet as was Wallace's. Both the 1938 and the 1939 covers measured 5 3/4" x 8 5/8" while the Wallace AHS cover measured 4" x 8 5/8".

continued to wear national high school gray caps and gowns, but the colors worn by the junior college graduates changed from black to blue. In reporting the baccalaureate sermon on May 24, the *Daily Herald* stated that, "the junior college graduates wore the navy blue caps and gown, the uniform which has been selected for junior colleges throughout America." MGCCC graduates still wore navy blue in 2000.

For the first time in the session 1936-1937, junior college enrollment doubled that of the high school. The number of total graduates grew so large at 89 that "open-air graduating exercises" were held on the campus that May 28. Darby gave out the diplomas that year, and Board Vice President H. P. Heidelberg of Pascagoula gave the awards. As usual, some high school and college candidates were listed as expected to receive their diplomas at the end of summer school, but for the first time, summer school was announced to be restricted only to junior college courses.

In session 1937-1938 enrollment rose but the number of graduates fell, so the graduation exercises of June 3, 1938, were once again held in Denson Hall Auditorium. As usual the names of those taking part in the exercises but finishing in the summer were listed. Most unusual, however, was the fact that Darby announced that there would be no summer school at Perkinston that coming summer.

The graduation exercises of May 26, 1939, took place in the Denson Hall Auditorium, but that was the last time that happened in the Darby Era. The crowd which gathered to witness the exercises for 77 graduates (54 junior college and 20 AHS) taxed that facility to its limits. One should also consider that this was the pre-air conditioning age.

Enrollment in the session 1939-1940 rose to an all time high of 488, a record that would stand until the year after the end of World War II. The total graduation figure for 1940 broke the 100 mark for the first time with 85 from the junior college and 18 from the AHS. The exercises on Monday night, June 3, were held on the Athletic Field, which had been illuminated the previous fall.

Enrollment fell by nearly 100 in the session 1940-1941 because of the elimination of the 9th and 10th grades of the AHS in September 1940. Yet the number of graduates actually climbed slightly to set a new record, five higher than the previous year.

As the crowd filled the bleachers under the arcs at the Athletic field on Monday night, June 2, 1941, nobody, Darby included, knew that he would be dis-

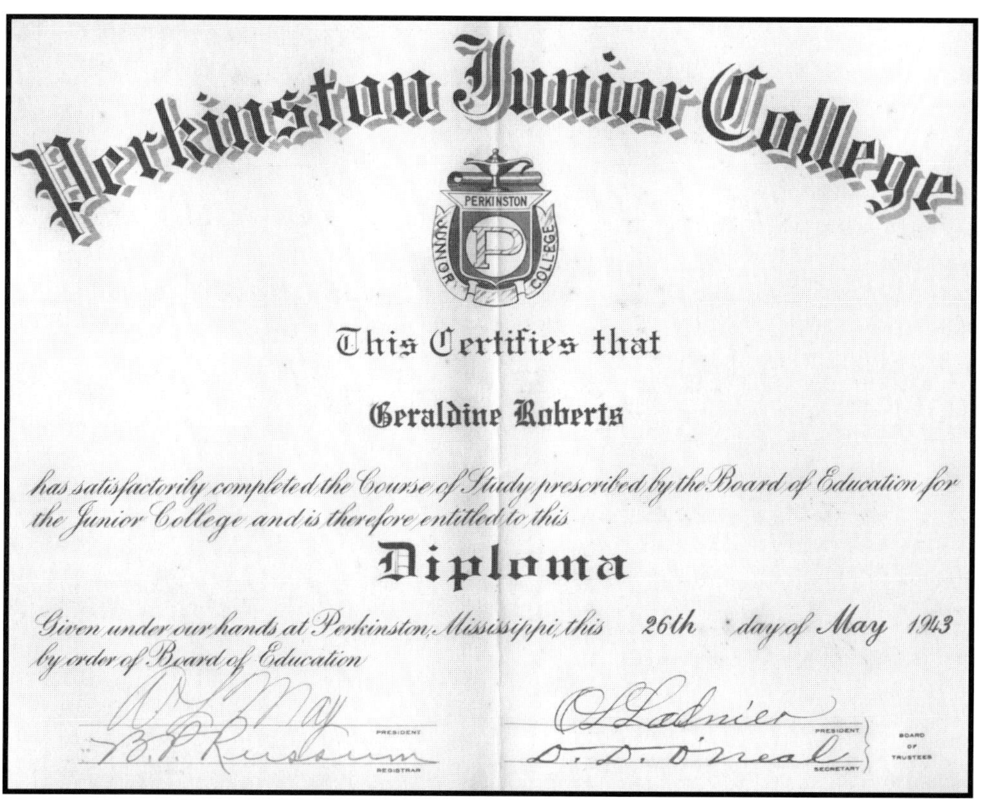

Perkinston Junior College

PERKINSTON JUNIOR COLLEGE

This Certifies that

Geraldine Roberts

has satisfactorily completed the Course of Study prescribed by the Board of Education for the Junior College and is therefore entitled to this

Diploma

Given under our hands at Perkinston, Mississippi, this 26th day of May 1943 by order of Board of Education

PRESIDENT | PRESIDENT
REGISTRAR | SECRETARY
BOARD OF TRUSTEES

(Left) On July 15, 1942, the name of the institution officially became Perkinston Agricultural High School and Junior College. Thus on May 26, 1943, Geraldine Roberts was the recipient of one of the first junior college diplomas to bear the inscription "Perkinston Junior College." For the first time the cover was blue (instead of black) leather embossed with gold.

(Above) Only one high school graduation instrument cover of the period 1943 to 1962 remained in the MGCCC Archives in 2000. It was the same size as the junior college cover, 5 3/4" x 8 5/8". Like the junior college cover, the AHS cover was blue and gold but carried a ribbon of gold inset on its left side. It bore the legend "Perkinston High School" (the word "agricultural" not having been included--reason unknown.) The date of this high school diploma cover was unknown because the document was not inside.

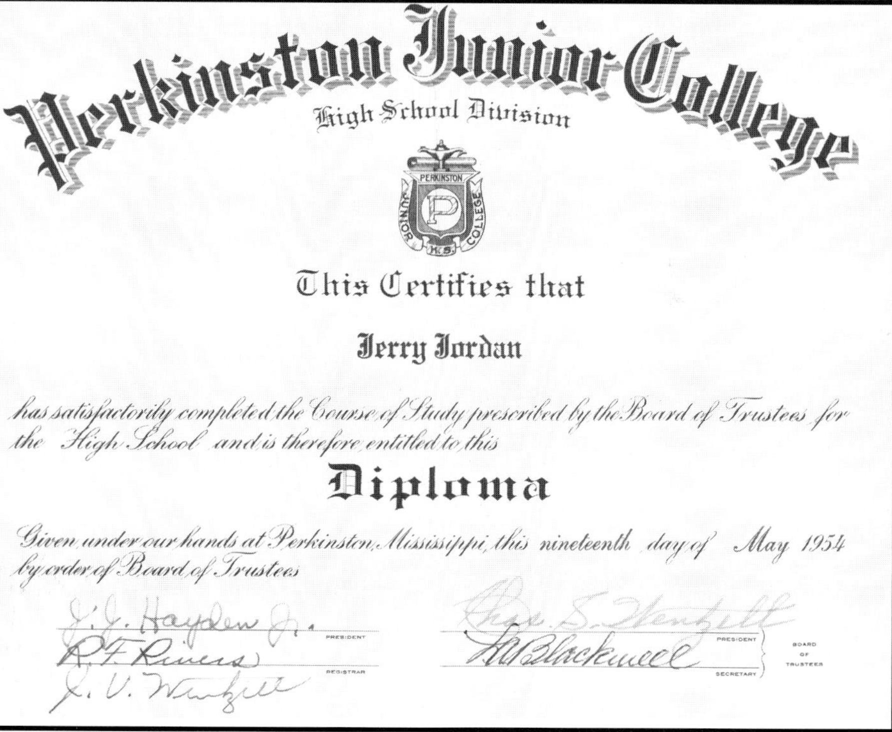

Perkinston Junior College

High School Division

PERKINSTON JUNIOR COLLEGE

This Certifies that

Jerry Jordan

has satisfactorily completed the Course of Study prescribed by the Board of Trustees for the High School and is therefore entitled to this

Diploma

Given under our hands at Perkinston, Mississippi, this nineteenth day of May 1954 by order of Board of Trustees

PRESIDENT | PRESIDENT
REGISTRAR | SECRETARY
BOARD OF TRUSTEES

(Above) The High School diploma of Geraldine "Jerry" Jordan, who graduated May 19, 1954, did not carry the word "Agricultural" either but rather the legend "Perkinston Junior College, High School Division."

The style of the high school diploma almost certainly remained the same from 1943 until the AHS was closed in May 1962. Certainly the style of the junior college graduation instrument was the same in 1952 and in 1963 because instruments from those years remained in the MGCCC Archives in 2000. However, the student who graduated in 1952 received a junior college "diploma" in a two-year terminal vocational-technical program, and the 1963 graduate received the "Degree of Associate in Science." After 1950, by legislative fiat, junior colleges were empowered to give diplomas for junior college level work in vocational-technical programs and to award "degrees" for university preparatory work.

tributing diplomas for the last time. The commencement speaker, former Mississippi State Senator George R. Smith of Pass Christian, urged the 87 junior college and 21 AHS graduates present to assume a position of leadership in the world. This was necessary, Smith said, because the failure of the present leaders had resulted in a "virtually world-wide war."

During the session 1940-1941, at least 12 students and three teachers had enlisted or been drafted into military service. On December 7, just over six months after that last peacetime graduation, the Japanese would bomb the United States into the Second World War. Many of the graduates listening to Smith that June night would serve in combat. Four of them and one of the teachers present would die in the war.

As the proceedings came to a close, all present sang the Perkinston Alma Mater. Winston O'Neal, a fresh junior college honor graduate from Saucier, pronounced the benediction. The Perkinston band played "Pomp and Chivalry" as the graduates marched away.

On January 22, 1942, six weeks after Pearl Harbor, the *Stone County Enterprise* carried notice that a number of new courses would be offered second semester as part of the junior college's effort in the Defense Program. Among these were Military Spanish, Navigation Mathematics, and Welding. On February 11, 1942, the Board of Trustees adopted a "Resolution approving Application of Harrison-Stone-Jackson Junior College to carry on Vocational Training Courses in Cooperation with the Mississippi State Vocational Board." One month later the Board authorized President A. L. May to incorporate industrial education as a part of the institution's offerings. Summer school, eliminated in 1938, was re-instituted in the summer of 1942 in order to allow students, particularly near-draft-age young men, to complete junior college in two summers flanking one regular session. The object was to prepare the young men to enter the military or defense industries quickly. The trade and industrial courses already introduced were expanded to include automotive mechanics and metal work. Thus began the vocational-technical role of Perkinston Junior College. This role expanded throughout the war years and grew even greater in the years following the conflict as returning veterans sought to take advantage of the educational benefits granted to them by the G. I. Bill.

These "vo-tech" programs were something new in the junior college curriculum. The diplomas and certificates heretofore granted to the graduates respectively of the AHS and the junior college were based on academic offerings, and no machinery existed to issue any kind of counterpart document to a student who completed a course in a vocational or technical field. Consequently in 1950, the Mississippi state legislature greatly expanded the power of junior colleges to grant documentary recognition to various types of graduates. The 1950 law smashed the senior colleges' monopoly on the term "degree," changed the meaning of the word "diploma," and legalized the appellation "certificate."

On August 3, 1951, President May at summer graduation awarded a diploma to Edna Ray Taquino of Handsboro, the only AHS graduate. But he awarded Associate of Arts degrees to three junior college graduates--Shirley Batson of Wiggins, Marvin F. Pilgrim of Columbus, and Joe Bennett Rouse of Gulfport. According to the *Announcements Session 1950-1951* (though there is no indication that he did it in either the May or the August graduation ceremonies), President May, for the first time, had the power to confer a two-year terminal junior college diploma in a vocational-technical program.

The *Announcements for Session 1951-1952* spelled out all the new degree, diploma, and certificate granting powers of the President and Board of the Perkinston Agricultural High School and Junior College. The author of this remarkable document must have possessed the I.Q. of Albert Einstein and a Ph.D. in Sanskrit because such qualifications would be necessary to decipher it and understand it. This author, sadly lacking in both qualifications, shall endeavor to give the reader the gist of it:

1. The Plan A Associate of Arts Degree was the typical first two years of a senior college degree.
2. The Plan B Associate of Science Degree was oriented to a career in business, engineering, medicine, or teaching. This degree was designed to be either terminal or to serve as a stepping stone toward a four-year degree at selected senior colleges that offered further study in the selected field.
3. The Plan C Diploma required 60 semester hours of academic credit with a C average and specified at least three courses in English, two courses in science, two courses in social studies, four hours in physical education, and one hour in library science. Eighteen of these hours had to be of "sophomore rank."
4. The Plan D Certificate of Graduation required 60 semester hours of academic credit with a C average also but specified only that two courses be in English, four hours be in P.E. and one hour in library science.
5. The Plan E Vocational-Technical Certificate was awarded for 24 months in auto-mechanics or wood manufacture or for 36 months in radio mechanics.
6. Hidden 17 pages away was yet another way to go which bore no plan or letter. The Two-Year Terminal Junior College Diploma was awarded for a mixture of vocational-technical and academic courses broken down into two programs--one for "boys" and one for "girls." Every course was specified. There were no electives. Yet this program was wonderfully con-

structed to suit a "boy" to build and equip a house and shop and run a farm. Likewise it was geared to fit a "girl" to run a home, rear children, and serve in the local church.

At least this plethora of degrees, diplomas, and certificates, running the gamut from the most stringent control to "have it your way," did offer something for everybody. And, with all these choices, just about any student who applied himself ought to have been able to come up with some kind of a "sheepskin" to show for two years of work.

A comparison of the degrees, diplomas, and certificates of Session 1951-1952 with those of Session 1999-2000 revealed remarkable similarities and striking differences. In 1999-2000 MGCCC offered three degrees, a diploma, and a certificate of completion.

All three degrees required the completion of 64 hours with a C average. The Associate of Arts Degree remained what it had been from its beginning--the first two years of a liberal arts senior college degree. The Associate of Applied Science Degree was a two-year terminal technical degree designed to prepare a student for a career in one of many different fields. Among those fields were medicine, business, law enforcement, drafting, electronics, and tourism.

In the years since 1952, a division between the term "technical" and the term "vocational" had occurred. One major basic difference between the two terms was the amount of time invested in securing one or the other. A technical degree required two years of effort. A vocational diploma required usually one year and sometimes less. For example, registered nurses took two years of work, and that is why the RN program was termed "Associate Degree Nursing." Licensed Practical Nurses took one year of work, so the LPN program was classified as vocational.

A diploma was awarded at the successful completion of a vocational program and also to those who completed an apprenticeship program. Those students who earned a diploma or who completed 36 semester hours in a vocational program might, by taking an additional 36 hours of mainly academic courses, receive the Associate of Applied Science Degree in Occupational Education (AASOE).

Certificates of completion were granted on request to students completing an adult vocational course or a continuing education course. The "certificate" of 1999-2000 had no counterpart in the 1950s, but the certificates of the 1950s were somewhat analogous to the Associate of Applied Science of 1999-2000.

On June 1, 1955, the *Daily Herald* noted that Charles D. Rich of Biloxi received a certificate as the first student to finish the two-year full-time vocational course for radio and television repairmen. No account of any ceremony was given. Not even who gave Rich the certificate was recorded, although it was likely the instructor of the course, Richard Baldwin. The name of Charles D. Rich was not recorded in the lists of graduates published by Perkinston Junior College in August 1955. This situation continued in 2000. No accurate count of MGCCC's graduates will ever be possible because of the thousands of vocational students who never appeared on the lists.

On Sunday, May 18, 1958, for the first time, all graduation-related ceremonies were held on the same day. Rev. Dr. J. D. Gray of New Orleans preached the baccalaureate sermon at 11 a.m. in the Wentzell Center. Perkinston Junior College President J. J. Hayden presented degrees or diplomas to 83 college graduates and diplomas to 42 AHS graduates in commencement exercises which began at 6 p.m. in A. L. May Memorial Stadium. On Sunday, May 20, 1962, for the last time, high school students received a diploma at Perkinston. That graduation, the final event in the Golden Year celebration of the 50th anniversary of the founding of the institution, marked the demise of the AHS.

Ten days before that Golden Year graduation, Mississippi Governor Ross Barnett had signed the bill creating the Mississippi Gulf Coast Junior College District. Due to insufficient time to change the wording on the junior college documents, the junior college graduation instruments of 1962 read "Perkinston Junior College." They read the same in 1963, too. Not until May 1964, did the documents carry the legend "Mississippi Gulf Coast Junior College District."

On Sunday, May 22, 1966, for the first time, there was no baccalaureate sermon at Perkinston because Perkinston had become only one of three Mississippi Gulf Coast Junior College campuses. At 6 p.m. that day in A. L. May Memorial Stadium, Hayden presided over the first MGCJC unified tri-campus graduation. He conferred degrees on 137 graduates from the "Perkinston College," 56 from "Jefferson Davis Junior College," and 16 from "Jackson County Junior College."

On Friday, August 12, 1966, at 10 a.m. in Denson Hall Auditorium on the Perkinston Campus, Hayden presided over the first unified tri-campus MGCJC summer graduation. He conferred degrees on eight from Perk, seven from JD, and four from JC. Two days later Hayden attended another graduation where he was on the receiving end. He was awarded his doctoral degree at USM.

Tri-campus unified regular session graduations continued to be held at Perkinston for two more years. In May 1969, in response to student requests on the coast campuses, each campus was allowed to hold a separate graduation. For the next 30 years Hayden, or his designate, and his successor, President Barry L.

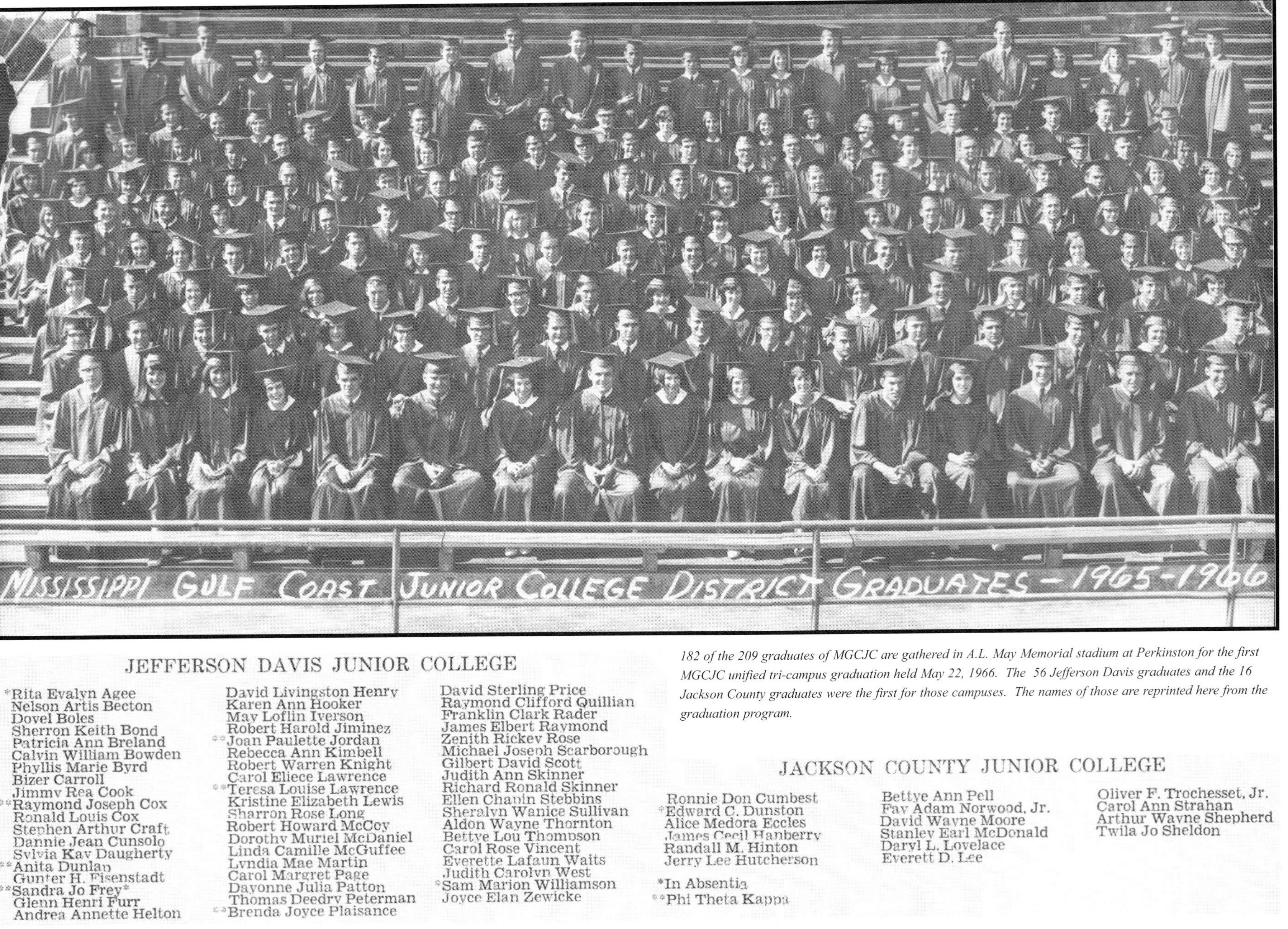

182 of the 209 graduates of MGCJC are gathered in A.L. May Memorial stadium at Perkinston for the first MGCJC unified tri-campus graduation held May 22, 1966. The 56 Jefferson Davis graduates and the 16 Jackson County graduates were the first for those campuses. The names of those are reprinted here from the graduation program.

JEFFERSON DAVIS JUNIOR COLLEGE

*Rita Evalyn Agee
Nelson Artis Becton
Dovel Boles
Sherron Keith Bond
Patricia Ann Breland
Calvin William Bowden
Phyllis Marie Byrd
Bizer Carroll
Jimmy Rea Cook
**Raymond Joseph Cox
Ronald Louis Cox
Stephen Arthur Craft
Dannie Jean Cunsolo
Sylvia Kay Daugherty
**Anita Dunlap
Gunter H. Eisenstadt
**Sandra Jo Frey*
Glenn Henri Furr
Andrea Annette Helton
David Livingston Henry
Karen Ann Hooker
May Loflin Iverson
Robert Harold Jiminez
**Joan Paulette Jordan
Rebecca Ann Kimbell
Robert Warren Knight
Carol Eliece Lawrence
**Teresa Louise Lawrence
Kristine Elizabeth Lewis
Sharron Rose Long
Robert Howard McCoy
Dorothy Muriel McDaniel
Linda Camille McGuffee
Lyndia Mae Martin
Carol Margret Page
Dayonne Julia Patton
Thomas Deedry Peterman
**Brenda Joyce Plaisance
David Sterling Price
Raymond Clifford Quillian
Franklin Clark Rader
James Elbert Raymond
Zenith Rickey Rose
Michael Joseph Scarborough
Gilbert David Scott
Judith Ann Skinner
Richard Ronald Skinner
Ellen Chapin Stebbins
Sheralyn Wanice Sullivan
Aldon Wayne Thornton
Bettye Lou Thompson
Carol Rose Vincent
Everette Lafaun Waits
Judith Carolyn West
*Sam Marion Williamson
Joyce Elan Zewicke

JACKSON COUNTY JUNIOR COLLEGE

Ronnie Don Cumbest
*Edward C. Dunston
Alice Medora Eccles
James Cecil Hanberry
Randall M. Hinton
Jerry Lee Hutcherson
Bettye Ann Pell
Fay Adam Norwood, Jr.
David Wayne Moore
Stanley Earl McDonald
Daryl L. Lovelace
Everett D. Lee
Oliver F. Trochesset, Jr.
Carol Ann Strahan
Arthur Wayne Shepherd
Twila Jo Sheldon

*In Absentia
**Phi Theta Kappa

(Left), Blue and gold graduation instrument cover measuring 8 7/8" x 6 7/8" for Stephen Arthur Craft, a graduate of the Mississippi Gulf Coast Junior College District. Craft, who had attended "Jefferson Davis Junior College," was one of 209 students who were awarded their degrees on the campus of "Perkinston College" on May 22, 1966, in the "District's" first unified tri-campus graduation ceremony. On April 23, 1969, the Board of Trustees ordered the word "District" stricken from all documents and Perkinston College, Jefferson Davis Junior College, and Jackson County Junior College to be styled "campuses." Obviously that order came too late to change the 1969 covers, but "District" was dropped from the covers as soon as possible. On October 1, 1987, the college changed its name to Mississippi Gulf Coast Community College, and the graduation covers reflected that change as soon as possible.

Mellinger, traveled among the three campuses each May to confer the degrees. Then on Monday, May 10, 1999, at 6:30 p.m. President Willis Lott's initial graduation ceremony, held in the Mississippi Coast Coliseum, became the first tri-campus unified regular session graduation in three decades. On Wednesday, May 10, 2000, at 6:30 p.m. Lott presided over his second tri-campus unified regular session graduation. A new tradition had begun.

Members of the 1999 graduation platform of speakers at the Mississippi Coast Coliseum were from left, MGCCC President Willis H. Lott, MGCCC Board Chairperson Jean Peden, and U. S. Senate Majority Leader Trent Lott.

May 2000, MGCCC graduates, seated inside the Mississippi Coast Coliseum, show their elation after receiving their diplomas and degrees.

Enrollment and Graduation Statistics 1912-1924

Harrison County Agricultural High School 1912-1916
Harrison-Stone Agricultural High School 1916-1924

Year	AHS Enrollment	AHS Graduates
1912-1913	63	0
1913-1914	Unknown	2
1914-1915	Unknown	5
1915-1916	[a]140	12
1916-1917	[b]100	20
1917-1918	[c]105	Unknown
1918-1919	125	16
1919-1920	Unknown	29
1920-1921	100	23
1921-1922	Unknown	18
1922-1923	95	21
1923-1924	140	26
Total		172

The graduation figures were stated precisely in the newspapers and most were verifiable by name count. On the other hand, only the 1912-1913 enrollment figures were verifiable by name count. All other enrollment figures were estimates extracted from newspapers. The enrollment total for sessions 1915-1916 and 1918-1919 both contained 15 day students. Whether or not the other figures include both boarding and day students was not known to this author.

[a]Enrollment rose due to the completion of Stone Hall (girls' dormitory).
[b]Enrollment fell due to the uncertainty and late opening resulting from the formation of Stone County.
[c]The outbreak of World War I caused a decline in enrollment due to enlistments and due to rural students remaining at home to grow crops for the war effort. The AHS closed two weeks early in both sessions 1916-1917 and 1917-1918 for students to return home early to grow "victory gardens." No evidence of a 1918 graduation ceremony had been found by this author in 2000.

Denson and Darby Era Enrollment and Graduation Statistics 1924-1941

Harrison-Stone Agricultural High School 1924-1925
Harrison-Stone-Jackson Agricultural High School and Junior College 1925-1941

Session	Total High School	College Freshmen	College Sophomores	Total Enrollment	AHS Graduates	College Graduates
1924-1925[a]	205	0	0	205	30	0
1925-1926	233	9	0	242	40	0
1926-1927	236	36	3	275	37	1
1927-1928	206	66	18	290	53	10
1928-1929[b,c]	229	69	33	331	48	28
1929-1930	192	56	31	279	27	16
1930-1931	161	115	39	315	40	23
1931-1932[d]	125	128	82	335	15	43
1932-1933	130	123	94	347	19	55
1933-1934	120	119	102	341	22	46
1934-1935	120	149	91	360	18	65
1935-1936	Unknown	Unknown	Unknown	355	20	67
1936-1937[e]	115	230		345	16	73
1937-1938	144	214		358	26	53
1938-1939	147	284		431	20	54
1939-1940	148	340		488	18	85
1940-1941[f]	76	317		393	21	87
Total					470	706

[a] From session 1924-1925 until at least session 1934-1935 a category of students termed "special" and another termed "irregular" were included in the catalogs. Special students were persons over age 21 without a high school diploma who wished training in a special field. Irregular students were those taking less than the minimum 12 credit hours. Special and irregular students usually totaled about ten students per year. Sometimes there were added in the total enrollment figures and sometimes not.

[b] Beginning with the session of 1928-1929, summer school 1928 enrollment was added to the 1928-1929 total figures. This continued until the elimination of summer school in the summer of 1938, so the session 1937-1938 was the last in the Darby era to contain summer school figures.

[c] The ninth grade was eliminated in May 1928.

[d] The ninth grade was reinstated in September 1931.

[e] Beginning with session 1936-1937, enrollment for college students was given as a total with no differentiation between freshmen and sophomores.

[f] The ninth and tenth grades were eliminated in September 1941.

The far right column of numbers on this chart includes those graduates who were awarded diplomas at the end of the session in May or June and also the students slated to graduate in the coming summer school. On Friday, August 14, 1925, Denson held a graduation ceremony in Bennett Auditorium for seven summer graduates. C. J. Darby was the speaker for the occasion. This summer graduation appears to be the only one of the Denson-Darby era. Thereafter, those students predicted to graduate in the coming summer participated in all the exercises at the close the regular session with the exception that they received no diploma. Apparently they received it at the end of the summer with no further ceremony. This practice ended in 1938 when summer school ended for the balance of the Darby Era. The numbers of graduates given from 1924-1938 should be more accurately styled as "candidates for graduation." In some cases, those predicted to graduate may not have done so.

AGRICULTURAL HIGH SCHOOL AND JUNIOR COLLEGE ENROLLMENT AND GRADUATION STATISTICS
Session 1941-1942 through Session 1958-1959

	Regular Session Enrollment						Graduates		Summer Enrollment					Graduates	
Session	AHS	Junior College Regular	Junior College Night	Farm Trainees	Vo-Tech	Total	AHS	JC	AHS	Junior College Regular	Junior College Night	Vo-Tech	Total	AHS	JC
1941-1942	82	194				276	23	42	[a]28	25			53		
1942-1943	100	199				299	38	43	98	29			127	24	3
1943-1944	85	118				203	27	16	154	35			189	40	3
1944-1945	[b]117	105				222	47	22	135	46			181	23	5
1945-1946	[c]174	201				375	48	19	103	112			215	43	3
1946-1947[d]	102	415				517	36	53	44	73		12	129	4	6
1947-1948	79	332			47	458	38	84	33	55		67	155	5	14
1948-1949	82	289			242	613	26	65	23	78		192	293	1	13
1949-1950	55	306	9	28	235	633	27	73	14	64	8	164	250	1	9
1950-1951[e]	95	296	12	25	139	567	20	61	20	47	19	102	188	1	4
1951-1952	109	222	41	19	72	463	25	51	23	24	16	23	86	3	5
1952-1953	174	272	46	6	21	519	38	58	38	39	22	19	118	1	7
1953-1954	188	316	44	5	30	583	48	65	31	53	38	29	151	6	14
1954-1955	217	351	27		45	640	43	84	33	49		31	113	4	4
1955-1956	221	407	18		31	677	43	78	40	60		10	110	2	11
1956-1957	235	454	22		16	727	44	89	43	50		30	123	2	6
1957-1958	229	448	23		50	750	42	84	30	45		31	106	2	5
1958-1959	274	508	27		54	863	57	83	44	83			127	2	8

AGRICULTURAL HIGH SCHOOL ENROLLMENT AND GRADUATION STATISTICS
Final Three Sessions (1959-1962)

Due to changes in the junior college offerings which presaged the demise of the AHS, Session 1958-1959 is the last year that the format of the above chart could be used. The format of the chart has been continued to show the demise of the AHS.

1959-1960	237						52	33						6	
1960-1961	247						47	35						4	
1961-1962	281						50								

a This figure included five special students defined as students over 21 who did not possess documentation of 15 units of high school work but who desired special training in certain courses. All five of these students were Central Americans.

b This figure included 26 special students, only 11 of which were listed with Central American addresses. Most of the other 15 were a new kind of special student--Vocational Technical students. One of these was Ed Evans, who in a personal interview, confirmed that he was not then over 21 years of age, and he was taking one vocational course in order to play football. Apparently the school was adapting a pre-existing term to describe a new kind of student.

c Eighty students in this total of 174 were designated "special." The explanation given on page 88 of the *1945-1946 Catalog* stated that these 80 students included "full-time Vocational and full-time Technical students and 14 Veterans who graduated as a result of the General Educational Development Test." This was the first time in the official documents of this institution that this new type of "special" student was designated as a vo-tech student. In summer 1946, the college listed 23 "specials" and the AHS listed seven "specials" with no reference as to whether they were vo-tech or not.

d In the regular session 1946-1947 the college listed 16 "specials" and the AHS listed seven "specials" with no reference to vo-tech. Beginning in the summer of 1947 the college created a new reporting category called "Vocational and Technical Special" and listed 12 students. Once the new category was established the term "special student" reverted back to its original meaning and was included in the respective totals of the college and AHS in this chart.

e In September 1950, the AHS 9th and 10th grades, eliminated in September 1941, were re-instituted.

Junior college night classes, inaugurated during regular session 1949-1950, began with nine students. Enrollment rose to 41 in session 1951-1952 with the addition of a class for 20 Keesler Air Force Base airmen. Nine airmen enrolled for night classes the following year after which attendance by airmen became sporadic and individual. This was, though, the beginning of this institution's educational alliance with Keesler.

Perkinston Junior College and MGCJC Graduates 1960-1965 and Tri-Campus (Perkinston, Jefferson Davis, and Jackson County) Graduates 1966-2000

Year	Perk Regular Session	Perk Summer Session	JD Regular Session	JD Summer Session	JC Regular Session	JC Summer Session	Total
1959-1960	98	2					100
1960-1961	86	7					93
1961-1962	162	22					184
1962-1963	183	7					190
1963-1964	167	15					182
1964-1965	195	18					213
1965-1966	137	8	56	7	16	4	228
1966-1967	120	2	68	7	74	8	279
1967-1968	113	3	88	14	51	15	284
1968-1969	127	10	95	20	95	23	370
1969-1970	143	4	107	16	81	10	361
1970-1971	133	3	117	19	98	24	394
1971-1972	130	4	117	16	112	12	391
1972-1973	164		137	15	124	15	455
1973-1974	154		110	27	109	10	410
1974-1975	176	6	146	80	137	23	568
1975-1976	206		187	107	184	46	730
1976-1977	178		237	82	198	19	714
1977-1978	175		207	82	179	17	660
1978-1979	204		244	82	183	21	734
1979-1980	187	5	209	104	204	27	736
1980-1981	206		227	110	228	41	812
1981-1982	205	12	256	50	189	40	752
1982-1983	199		248	48	211	28	734
1983-1984	215	16	262	57	222	33	805
1984-1985	236		202	66	224	44	772
1985-1986	157		255	61	181	37	691
1986-1987	217		201	56	215	28	717
1987-1988	176		195	66	239	40	716
1988-1989	177		257	60	224	53	771
1989-1990	181		216	62	257	43	759
1990-1991	201		310	63	232	86	892
1991-1992	190		316	83	261	83	933
1992-1993	197		343	78	335	81	1,034
1993-1994	189		382	73	320	64	1,028
1994-1995	208		330	65	323	103	1,029
1995-1996	232		339	84	327	77	1,059
1996-1997	219		332	63	321	116	1,051
1997-1998	222		404	70	302	112	1,110
1998-1999	228	12	365	91	347	121	1,164
1999-2000	257	12	394	77	346	95	1,181
Total	7,350	168	7,959	2,061	7,149	1,599	26,286
	7,518		1,020		8,748		26,286

1927-1941	Junior College Graduates	706
1942-1959	Junior College Graduates	1,190
1960-2000	Junior College Graduates	26,286
	Junior College total	28,182
1914-1962	AHS Graduates	1,636

Grand Total all 20th Century Graduates 29,818

THE INSTITUTION'S GRADUATES BY SESSION 1914-2000

Harrison County Agricultural High School (September 17, 1912 - June 5, 1916)		
Session	AHS Graduates	College Graduates
1912-1913		
1913-1914	2	
1914-1915	5	
1915-1916	12	
Harrison-Stone Agricultural High School (June 5, 1916 - May 23, 1925)		
1916-1917	20	
1917-1918a	Unknown	
1918-1919	16	
1919-1920	29	
1920-1921	23	
1921-1922	18	
1922-1923	21	
1923-1924	26	
1924-1925	30	
Harrison-Stone Agricultural High School and Junior College (May 23, 1925- September 9, 1925) Harrison-Stone-Jackson Agricultural High School and Junior College (September 9, 1925 - July 15, 1942)		
1925-1926	40	
1926-1927	37	1
1927-1928	53	10
1928-1929	48	28
1929-1930	27	16
1930-1931	40	23
1931-1932	15	43
1932-1933	19	55
1933-1934	22	46
1934-1935	18	65
1935-1936	20	67
1936-1937	16	73
1937-1938	26	53
1938-1939	20	54
1939-1940	18	85
1940-1941	21	87
1941-1942	23	42
Perkinston Agricultural High School and Junior College July 15, 1942 - May 10, 1962		
1942-1943	62	46
1943-1944	67	19
1944-1945	70	27
1945-1946	91	22
1946-1947	40	59
1947-1948	43	98
1948-1949	27	78
1949-1950	28	82
1950-1951	21	65
1951-1952	28	56
1952-1953	40	65
1953-1954	54	79
1954-1955	47	88
1955-1956	45	89
1956-1957	46	95
1957-1958	44	89
1958-1959	59	91
1959-1960	58	100
1960-1961	51	93
1961-1962b	50	184
TOTAL	1,636	continued

[a]The AHS closed two weeks early in Session 1917-1918 so that students could return home to grow "Victory Gardens" to aid America's effort in World War I. No account of the 1918 graduation had been found by this author in 2000.
[b]The AHS was discontinued in May 1962.

Mississippi Gulf Coast Junior College (May 10, 1962 - October 1, 1987)		
1962-1963		190
1963-1964		182
1964-1965		213
1965-1966		228
1966-1967		279
1967-1968		284
1968-1969		370
1969-1970		361
1970-1971		394
1971-1972		391
1972-1973		455
1973-1974		410
1974-1975		568
1975-1976		730
1976-1977		714
1977-1978		660
1978-1979		734
1979-1980		736
1980-1981		812
1981-1982		752
1982-1983		734
1983-1984		805
1984-1985		772
1985-1986		691
1986-1987		717
Mississippi Gulf Coast Community College (October 1, 1987 to August 2000 chart cutoff)		
1987-1988		716
1988-1989		771
1989-1990		759
1990-1991		892
1991-1992		933
1992-1993		1,034
1993-1994		1,028
1994-1995		1,029
1995-1996		1,059
1996-1997		1,051
1997-1998		1,110
1998-1999		1,164
1999-2000		1,181
Total	Total Junior College	28,182
	Total AHS	1,636
	Grand Total	29,818

The two Coast campuses of the Mississippi Gulf Coast Junior College began service in September 1965. On May 22, 1966, the first united tri-campus graduation was held at A. L. May stadium on the Perkinston Campus. United tri-campus regular graduations continued for two more years, and united tri-campus summer graduations continued until at least 1970. Beginning in May 1969, each of the three campuses held separate regular graduations until May 10, 1999, when the Mississippi Coast Coliseum became the site of the first united tri-campus regular graduation in 30 years.

The figures given in the graduates chart are accurate until the establishment of the three campuses in 1965. The establishment of a multitude of vocational-technical programs beyond that point which held miniature graduations at odd times of the year together with open-entry, open-exit programs in which the student was given a certificate of completion with no attendant ceremony made a comprehensive count of graduates impossible.

Counting the names on the regular graduation programs and lists of summer graduates yielded the figures that appear in the chart for the years after 1965. The figures therefore contain all the academic graduates, most of the technical graduates, but very few of the vocational graduates until about 1990.

Fragmentary evidence available from Mississippi Public Junior College Statistical Data Reports in the 1970s indicates that the figures on this chart were averaging 150 graduates per year less than the number being reported to the Junior College Commission. Therefore, a very conservative estimate of "lost vocational-technical graduates" would total at least 3,000. The actual total was likely far greater. In any case, the graduates of this institution both junior college and AHS easily aggregated in excess of 30,000 in the 20th century.

GREGORY WAR MEMORIAL CHAPEL

Gregory War Memorial Chapel was removed from Gulfport Army Air Corps Base to the campus of Perkinston Junior College after World War II. The Chapel was erected to honor those of the institution who served and to memorialize those of the institution who died in the Second World War.

During World War II families with members in the service displayed in their front window a banner composed of a white field bordered in red with a blue star sewn on to represent each serving family member. In the case of a death of a family member a gold star was sewn atop the blue star. The banner at right is from the collection of Jackson County Campus Television Technician Doug Mansfield. According to Mansfield, the banner is from a family who had three sons serving. One of them, an infantryman, was killed in the first 30 minutes of the D-Day invasion of Normandy on June 6, 1944. At 4:30 p.m. that afternoon, his brother who was in the Coast Guard, was serving on the boat that picked up the floating body of his brother. One of the Perkinston dead, Warren Moran, a Coast Guardsman, was killed in action in the D-Day invasion.

Since the Gold Star was the national emblem denoting death in the service, the Perkinston Junior College Board of Trustees ordered that emblem attached to the nameplate of each of the dead on the War Memorial Plaque in the War Memorial Chapel. The War Memorial Plaque in 2000 contained the names of 705 students and 13 faculty members who served. Gold Stars were affixed to the nameplates of the 23 students and one faculty member known to have died. The following photographic section contains the photographs of 31 students known by 2000 to have died in addition to that of the faculty member.

The original school colors for the institution at Perkinston were black and gold. On May 26, 1943, the institution issued its first diplomas bearing the name Perkinston Junior College. For the first time the diploma covers were blue while the lettering remained gold. From that time until 2000 the school colors were blue and gold. This author was unable to discover the reason in any document why the change was made, but the change coming at the time that the students at Perkinston were dealing with banners embossed with blue and gold stars and placing gold stars on the War Memorial Plaque may have been a factor.

GOLD STAR FACULTY AND STUDENTS

Key to Perkinston Institutional Abbreviations

The official name of the Perkinston institution at the time the nation entered the Second World War on December 7, 1941, was Harrison-Stone-Jackson Agricultural High School and Junior College. On July 15, 1942, the official name was changed to Perkinston Agricultural High School and Junior College. Some of the former students who died in World War II had enrolled in the agricultural high school department without ever having attended the junior college department and vice versa. Some had attended both. Therefore, the abbreviations used were,

HSJAHS
HSJJC
HSJAHS&JC
PAHS
PJC
PAHS&JC

The abbreviation in vogue at the time of the departure or graduation of the student was the one given under his or her photograph. The dates given were of attendance. From 1912 to 2000, alumni status was conferred by the institution on the basis of enrollment and attendance and not by graduation or even by length of attendance. For example: Berlin John Ladner entered PJC on September 9, 1942, and withdrew to enter the service on October 12, 1942, having attended only a little more than a month.

Cause of Death or Type of Casualty

In this work, cause of death was given as specifically as possible related to available information. In cases where specifics were not available, the military designation for type of casualty was used. The U.S. Army designation for personnel lost in engagements with the enemy in World War II was "Killed In Action" (KIA). The Navy, Marines, and Coast Guard reported KIAs together with those who "Died of Wounds" or "Lost Lives as Result of Operational Movements in War Zones." Such casualties were combined herein under the designation "Combat." All services used the designation "Missing in Action" (MIA). By the provisions of Public Law 490, 77th Congress, approved March 7, 1942, service personnel who remained MIA for 12 months without "receipt of evidence to support a continued presumption of survival" were to be declared dead on the basis of "presumptive finding of death" (FOD). For whatever reason this author encountered some records in this study and many in the course of researching *Valor Remembered* which still carried the designation MIA. This author did not presume to change that designation unless unimpeachable evidence of death was available.

Linwood Permenter Ingram
Cleveland
Instructor of Science and Mathematics
Harrison Stone Jackson Agricultural High School and Junior College at Perkinston
1938-1942
US Army Air Corps
1st Lieutenant
Killed in Action
Biak Island
May 28, 1944

William Martin Anderson
Gulfport
HSJJC 1940-1941
US Army Air Corps
1st Lieutenant
Killed in Action
St. Nazaire, France
January 3, 1943

Philip Bellew
Success
HSJJC 1939-1941
US Marine Corps
Lieutenant
Pneumonia
San Diego, Cal.
April 2, 1943

John Douglas Clark
Gulfport
HSJJC 1938-1941
US Army Air Corps
1st Lieutenant
Airplane Crash
India
January 25, 1944

Charles F. DeMetz Jr.
Pass Christian
HSJAHS&JC1937-41
US Army
Private 1st Class
Died of Wounds
Kawajalein Atoll
February 4, 1944

David Huffman Denning
Saucier
PJC 1942-1943
US Army Air Corps
Sergeant
Killed in Action
Germany
March 25, 1945

Harold Welch Ervin
Long Beach
HSJJC 1935-1936
US Army Air Corps
1st Lieutenant
Killed in Action
South Pacific
February 7, 1943

Stova Wilbern Firth
Pascagoula
HSJJC 1939-1941
US Naval Reserve
Ensign
Training Crash
San Diego, Calif.
July 21, 1942

James William Forte Jr.
Pensacola, Florida
HSJJC 1937-1939
US Army Air Corps
1st Lieutenant
Killed in Action
Mediterranean
March 22, 1943

Douglas Kell Hague
Pascagoula
HSJJC 1938-1940
US Naval Reserve
Lieutenant (jg)
Killed in Action
New Hebrides
March 1, 1943

Josh Oden Haney
Gulfport
PAHS 1944
US Marine Corps
Private 1st Class
Combat
Okinawa
May 20, 1945

Judson B. Johnson
Saucier
HSJJC 1939-1942
US Army
Private 1st Class
Killed in Action
Anzio
January 26, 1944

Andrew J. Ladner
Lizana
HSJJC 1936-1939
US Army
Private
Killed in Action
Southwest Pacific
November 30, 1942

Berlin John Ladner
Dedeaux
PJC 1942
US Army
Staff Sergeant
Killed in Action
Belgium
November 23, 1944

Toxie Howard McBryde
Sumrall
HSJJC 1932-1934
US Army Air Corps
1st Lieutenant
Training Crash
Ft. Knox, Kentucky
November 11, 1943

Carlos Reese McKee Jr.
Hazelhurst
HSJJC 1938-1939
US Navy
Lieutenant
Carrier Crash
Hawaiian Islands
August 17, 1944

Madison Kent "Jack" Moorman
Biloxi
HSJJC 1935-1936
US Navy
Ensign
Killed in Action
Mediterranean
May 31, 1944

Warren Joseph Moran
Pass Christian
HSJJC 1939-1941
US Coast Guard
Coxswain
Combat
Normandy
June 6, 1944

Clifford Winford Murphy
Vancleave
HSJJC 1938-1940
US Army
Private
Drowned in Invasion
Sicily
July 15, 1943

Leslie Francis Myers
Brandon
HSJJC 1936-1937
US Army Air Corps
1st Lieutenant
Killed in Action
China
January 12, 1943

William Paul Newsum
Biloxi
HSJJC 1938-1941
US Naval Reserve
Ensign
Airplane Crash
Corpus Christi, Texas
May 15, 1943

Fred Roy Rainey Jr.
Pensacola, Florida
PJC 1941-1943
US Army Air Corps
Staff Sergeant
Killed in Action
Dulag, Philippines
November 12, 1944

Holley Stone "Pat" Reeves
Gulfport
HSJJC 1938-1939
US Navy
Seaman 2nd Class
Death by Lightning
Pensacola, Florida
April 9, 1942

Otts Bernard Reeves
Gulfport
HSJJC 1936-1937
US Army Air Corps
2nd Lieutenant
Killed in Action
North Africa
September 14, 1942

Woodrow Wilson Reeves
Perkinston
HSJJC 1936-1937
US Army
Staff Sergeant
Killed in Action
Belgium
December 18, 1944

James Douglas Sasser
Gulfport
HSJJC 1934-1936
US Army Air Corps
1st Lieutenant
Test Flight Crash
England
July 19, 1944

David Edward Shattles
Pascagoula
HSJJC 1940-1942
US Naval Reserve
Seaman 1st Class
Combat
Mediterranean
December 3, 1943

Glen Edward Sletten
Gulfport
HSJJC 1938-1940
US Army Air Corps
Staff Sergeant
Killed in Action
New Guinea
July 11, 1943

Marjorie Lucille Stallings
Gulfport
HSJAHS 1936-1937
US Marine Corps
Enlistee
Accidental Death
Washington, D.C.
July 8, 1943

William Bradley Stribling Jr.
Gulfport
HSJJC 1939 - 1940
US Naval Reserve
Lieutenant (jg)
Carrier Crash
Quonset Point, R.I.
May 12, 1945

Jack Taylor
Mobile, Alabama
HSJJC 1938-1940
US Naval Reserve
Ensign
Training Crash
Metairie, La.
May 20, 1942

Leslie Arthur Wood
Puerto Castilla, Hon.
HSJAHS 1937-1938
Canadian Air Force
Pilot Officer
Killed in Action
Dieppe, France
July 18, 1943

Gold Star Faculty and Students Research Data

Due to the importance of the information concerning the 32 known dead of the Perkinston institution in World War II, this research data section has been appended. The attempt to assemble the eight pieces of information concerning each of the dead listed under each photograph proved to be a daunting task, which lasted intermittently for nearly a decade. If a database of documents and news clippings was established regarding the dead during the war by W. G. Gregory and those who aided him, such database was not to be found in any file available to the archivist when the MGCCC Archives was founded in 1992. The small body of information that did exist was at best incomplete and at worst erroneous and misleading.

The Mississippi Gulf Coast Community College Press in 1996 published a monograph titled, *Valor Remembered: War Dead of the State of Mississippi--Lists by County of Mississippians Who Died in the Service of the Nation in the Major Wars of the 20th Century: World War I, World War II, Korea and Vietnam* (hereinafter cited as *Valor Remembered*). This work by MGCCC Archivist Charles L. Sullivan and honors student Bourbon Hughes was dedicated to the 28 Gold Star students and faculty of the institution known in 1996.

In the course of this present work, the archivist discov-

Alumni and Faculty of the Perkinston Institution who Died in the Service in World War II

1944 "In Memoriam" List	**1946 *Bulldog Barks* List***	**Names on Neither List**
William Martin Anderson	William Martin Anderson	
Phillip Bellew	Phillip Bellew	
John Douglas Clark		
		David Huffman "Buck" Denning
Charles F. DeMetz Jr.	Charles F. DeMetz Jr.	
Harold Welch Ervin	Harold Welch Ervin	
Stova W. Firth	Stova W. Firth	
James W. Forte Jr.		
Douglas Kell Hague	Douglas Kell Hague	
		Josh Oden Haney
Linwood P. Ingram	Linwood P. Ingram	
Judson B. Johnson	Judson B. Johnson	
Andrew J. Ladner	Andrew J. Ladner	
	Berlin John Ladner	
Toxie Howard McBryde	Toxie Howard McBryde	
Carlos Reese McKee Jr.	Carlos Reese McKee Jr.	
	Madison Kent "Jack" Moorman	
Warren Joseph Moran	Warren Joseph Moran	
Clifford Winford Murphy	Clifford Winford Murphy	
Leslie Francis Myers	Leslie Francis Myers	
William Paul Newsum	William Paul Newsum	
	Fred Roy Rainey	
Holley Stone "Pat" Reeves	Holley Stone "Pat" Reeves	
Otts Bernard Reeves		
		Woodrow Wilson Reeves
James Douglas Sasser		
David Edward Shattles	David Edward Shattles	
Glen Edward Sletten	Glen Edward Sletten	
Marjorie Lucille Stallings	Marjorie Lucille Stallings	
		William Bradley Stribling Jr.
Jack Taylor	Jack Taylor	
Leslie Arthur Wood	Leslie Arthur Wood	

*Only the 24 individuals listed on the 1946 *Bulldog Barks* list had a Gold Star affixed to their names on the War Memorial Plaque in 2000. None of the four individuals on the 1944 "In Memoriam" list who were not duplicated on the 1946 *Bulldog Barks* list had a Gold Star and neither did the four that appeared on neither list.

ered that A. B. "Basil" Byrd of McHenry, who was included on the dedication list of *Valor Remembered*, never attended the Perkinston institution. That mistake came about because Byrd's obituary contained the claim that he had attended Perkinston Junior College. The claim was mistaken, and family members confirmed that the information was in error on the part of the newspaper reporter. Byrd's name appeared on no records of the institution, and his name was not on the War Memorial Chapel Plaque. On the other hand this present study revealed the names of four other students who died in the war and whose names were on the Memorial Plaque but none of which were marked by a Gold Star.

Only two contemporary lists of the dead surfaced in this author's research. One of these lists appeared in the *1944 Perkolator* dedication page entitled "In Memoriam," and the 27 names were presented with the claim, "They gave their lives that Freedom should not perish." Obviously, whoever put that list in the *Perkolator* contended that all 27 died in the war. The other list containing 24 names appeared in the October 25, 1946, *Bulldog Barks*.

The *1944 Perkolator* "In Memoriam" list contained two names not placed in the foregoing chart because they did not die in the war. These were given as "Lt. Donald Collins ('39-'40)--Biloxi" and "Sgt. Autley Smith ('36-'37)--Perkinston."

The Perk years following Collins's name were actually those for Elwood Collins of Biloxi. Donald Collins, who also hailed from Biloxi, graduated from HSJJC in 1935. Elwood Collins served in World War II and died in Biloxi on March 17, 1994. According to the May 26, 1945, *Daily Herald*, First Lieutenant Donald Collins, U. S. Army Air Corps, was shot down over Germany in 1944 and spent 10 months as a prisoner of war at Stalag 7-A in Mooseburg before being liberated on April 29, 1945, by General George Patton's army. The June 5, 1945, *Daily Herald* noted his impending arrival home.

The *Stone County Enterprise*, June 15, 1944, noted that Sgt. Autley Smith had been reported "missing in action." The *Stone County Enterprise*, April 4, 1945, reported that Smith, his wife, and baby had returned to California following a visit to Wiggins.

Apparently whoever put the names on the 1944 "In Memoriam" list believed both Donald Collins and Autley Smith to be dead. That mistake coupled with the gratuitous entangling of the two different Collins furnished the archivist with many hours of grueling research a half century later. It also had the salutary effect of making the archivist mistrustful of both lists bequeathed to him from the past, and that resulted in weeks of even more grueling research. Why? Because the archivist was determined not to publish a list of the dead and have someone who did not die communicate that joyous information to him.

The two lists from the past did more than that. The archivist spent more hours wondering why if the listers believed the men dead in 1944, that they did not still believe them dead in 1946. In the case of Smith and Collins the information was readily available that they were MIAs who had returned. But not only were Smith and Collins not given a Gold Star, neither were Clark, Forte, Barney Reeves, or Sasser. Apparently the explanation for Denning, Haney, Woodrow Reeves, and Stribling not being given a Gold Star resulted from their deaths coming late in the war.

Apparently no one who died after August 1944 got a star except Fred Roy Rainey. That likely happened because his sister, Emogene, was still in school at the Perkinston AHS at the time of her brother's death.

For whatever reason, only 24 of the dead were given a star. Yet when the *Stone County Enterprise*, March 3, 1949, advertised the dedication of the chapel for March 6, the reporter stated that, "the records indicate that thirty-seven young men who were alumni of Perkinston Junior College lost their lives in the service of their country." No list was published. That may have been a blessing.

In writing *Valor Remembered* the archivist and Bourbon Hughes proved the deaths of Stribling, Haney, Denning, and Woodrow Reeves. In completing this present work the archivist proved that Clark, Forte, Sasser, and Barney Reeves also died. Thus in 2000 the total stood at 32. That total was very likely incorrect.

Two major U. S. government lists were used in the information published about Mississippi war dead in *Valor Remembered.* The list for the U. S. Army: "The Honor List of Dead and Missing of the Military Personnel for the State of Mississippi in World War II," *Congressional Record* (Proceedings and Debates of the 81st Congress, First Session), July 28, 1949. The list for the U. S. Navy, Marines, and Coast Guard: "Summary of Mississippi War Casualties--Navy, Marine Corps, and Coast Guard," *Congressional Record* (Proceedings and Debates of the 81st Congress, First Session), October 3, 1949. Most serial numbers included in the following came from those lists.

Jane Sullivan, in the course of this study, located the web site for the American Battle Monuments Commission. She checked that site for all thirty-two names of the dead and found seven of them.

In mid-May 2001, in a last ditch effort to locate the desired information still missing on several of the dead, the archivist contacted the *Sun Herald* newspaper in Gulfport, and the *Pensacola News Journal* in Pensacola, Florida. On May 28, 2001, the *Sun Herald* published a comprehensive article about the MGCCC war dead and published all 32 photographs. On June 15, 2001, the *Pensacola News Journal* published an article specifically asking for information on the two Pensacola KIAs.

Final victory in the long battle to determine the fate of the final Gold Star students came through the twin broadsides published by the *Sun Herald* and the *Pensacola News Journal* and the aid of Mitchell Cirlot, a military researcher from Ocean Springs. Cirlot, who called the archivist to volunteer his services in September 2001, answered all remaining questions by March 12, 2002.

Ingram, Linwood Permenter. Photo: *1942 Perkolator* Dedication Page.

1. War Memorial Plaque in Gregory War Memorial Chapel: (Far right panel listed with twelve other faculty members) Ingram, L. P. (Gold Star)Army
2. The Honor List of Dead and Missing of the Military Personnel for the State of Mississippi in World War II (U. S. Army). Reprinted in *Valor Remembered*, p. 70: Bolivar County--Ingram, Linwood P./O-676623/1LT/Killed in Action
3. *Daily Herald*, April 16, 1942. The article noted that Ingram would enter the U.S. Army Air Corps "at the close of the present school term."
4. *Dixie Guide* newspaper, June, 1944. Excerpt follows:

   "The War Department notified Mr. and Mrs. G. C. Ingram Wednesday, May 7, (sic-- June 7) that their son, Lieutenant Linwood Ingram of the Army Air Corps, had been killed in action in the Pacific Sunday, May 28.

   "Lieutenant Ingram, a graduate of the Cleveland High School and the Delta State Teachers College, taught at the Harrison-Stone-Jackson Junior College at Perkinston between the time of his graduation from the Delta State teachers College and his enlistment in the Army Air Corps. "Lieutenant Ingram trained at Randolph Field and Brooks Field in Texas and at Laurel. . . ."
5. The *Sun Herald* Memorial Day (May 28, 2001) article asking for information concerning the MGCCC war dead elicited the following response from Linwood Ingram's sister, Dorothy (Ingram) Nunnery of Clinton by letter postmarked June 16, 2001:

   "My information is based upon War Department contacts with my parents, including the telegram first notifying them that Linwood had been lost during a reconnaissance mission over Biak Island on May 28, 1944. On that date he was acting as the co-pilot of a B-25 "Mitchell" medium bomber which had been 'stripped' to fit it for photography and other reconnaissance purposes. His flight was fatally struck by anti-aircraft fire, apparently of a railroad or other mobile source, since intelligence at his New Guinea base showed no 'flak' in that area on the date of the May 28 mission. Lt. Ingram's remains were recovered, and in 1948, at the election of my parents, were returned to their home in Cleveland, Mississippi. One of the newspaper articles which I dispatch to you by mail this date recounts the funeral services in Cleveland and the fact that his remains are interred in a family plot in Cleveland municipal cemetery."
6. *Memphis Commercial Appeal*, undated article dated by Dorothy (Ingram) Nunnery as 1948. Excerpt follows:

   "Full military honors were held at the grave, and a flight of planes from the Jackson Airport flew over the cemetery in tribute to their fellow countryman . . . ."

Anderson, William Martin. Photo: *1941 Perkolator* p. 20.

1. War Memorial Plaque in Gregory War Memorial Chapel: Anderson, William (Gold Star) Army
2. The Honor List of Dead and Missing of the Military Personnel for the State Of Mississippi in World War II (U. S. Army). Reprinted in *Valor Remembered*, p. 72: Harrison County--Anderson, William M./O-789362/1LT/Killed in Action
3. *Daily Herald*, September 23, 1942. Notice given of Anderson's promotion to first lieutenant. Article further stated that he had been commissioned as a "flying officer in the U. S. Army Air Forces, Columbus, Miss., Flying School." Parents given as Mr. and Mrs. Albert A. Anderson of 1415 22nd Avenue, Gulfport.
4. On June 4, 2001, the archivist received by fax from Myrtis Franke of United States Senator Trent Lott's office in Gulfport a copy of a letter dated May 24, 2001, sent to the senator from the National Personnel Records Center in St. Louis, Missouri. The letter read in part:

   "The following information is provided under Freedom of Information Act.
   Date of Death: January 3, 1943
   Place of Death: European Area
   Place of Burial: Not shown in record
   Cause of Death: Killed in Action
   Medals and Awards: Air Medal, American Defense Service Medal, Good Conduct Medal, European-African-Middle Eastern Campaign Medal, WWII Victory Medal and Honorable Service Lapel Button WWII"
5. No obituary for William Martin Anderson was located in a search of *Daily Herald* microfilm following his date of death. However, an article was found dated June 24, 1944, regarding his brother, Joe, who graduated from Harrison-Stone-Jackson Agricultural High School on June 1, 1942. Joe Anderson's name was listed on the War Memorial Plaque as having served during World War II. Excerpt follows:

   "Ensign Joe Anderson . . . son of Mr. And Mrs. A. G. Anderson of 43 Harrison Court, Biloxi, formerly of 1415 22 Avenue, Gulfport, was commissioned as an ensign at the Naval Air Training Center, Pensacola, Fla., June 6, and given the wings of a Navy pilot . . . ."
6. Mitchell Cirlot of Ocean Springs received the following e-mail from Rusty Bloxom, Chief Historian of the 8th Air Force, dated August 23, 2001. "According to a condensed Missing Air Crew Report (MACR) in our collections, and a brief entry in a unit history, 1st Lt. William M. Anderson was a member of the 91st Bomb Group's 323rd Bomb Squadron when he was shot down on 3 January 1943. He was flying on B-17 42-5084 "Panhandle Dogie" during a raid on the French port city of St. Nazaire when he went down."
7. Cirlot then via Internet located Anderson's grave as No. 17567 in Plot W, Vicksburg National Cemetery in Vicksburg National Military Park.

Bellew, Philip. Photo: *1941 Perkolator* p. 20.

1. War Memorial Plaque in Gregory War Memorial Chapel: Bellew, Philip (Gold Star) Marines
2. Bellew was not placed on the U. S. Marine Corps Mississippi Noncombat casualty list--reason unknown.
   The authors of *Valor Remembered* placed him on p. 93 as: Harrison County--Bellew, Philip/Saucier/USMC/Lieutenant/Cause of death--unknown
3. *Daily Herald,* April 17, 1944. The article was accompanied by a photo of Bellew in a U. S. Marine lieutenant's uniform.
   The article noted that Bellew died in the Naval Hospital in San Diego, California, and that he was married to the former Mary Pittman of Collins.
4. Undated newspaper clipping (certainly 1944), probably *Daily Herald* (carrying the same photo as the April 17 article noted above) donated to the MGCCC Archives by Jaclyn Moffett of Saucier read in part:

   "DIED--Lt. Phillip Bellew, son of Mr. and Mrs. Edgar Bellew of Saucier, died April 2nd in San Diego, Calif., as a result of a severe attack of pneumonia. Lieutenant Bellew, a graduate of Perkinston Jr. College entered the Naval Air Corps in Pensacola, Florida, in 1942. Shortly before receiving his wings, he transferred to the Marines."
5. Jaclyn Moffett donated three photos of Bellew (two of which included his wife), and informed the archivist that Bellew had been buried in the Poplarhead Methodist Church Cemetery on Highway 67 near Saucier.

Clark, John Douglas. Photo: *1941 Perkolator* p. 21.

1. War Memorial Plaque in Gregory War Memorial Chapel: Clark, John D. (His name was not starred in 2000) Army
2. Clark was not listed in *Valor Remembered.* His mother lived in New Orleans at the time of his death, thus he probably appeared on the Louisiana lists.
3. *Daily Herald*, February 12, 1944. Clark was reported missing in action as of January 25, 1944.
4. *Daily Herald*, March 3, 1944. The article was accompanied by a photo of Clark in the uniform of a U. S. Army Air Corps officer. Clark had been

promoted to First Lieutenant while still missing. He had received the Air Medal on August 14, 1943. Posted to the China-Burma-India (CBI) Theater, he crashed while "Flying the Hump" (the Himalayas). The article contained the following:

"An unusual incident has been told in connection with the report of Lt. Clark's last flight on January 25, and officials thought enough of the fact to calculate time and flying speed and wire particulars to the searching parties. Mrs. Clark, mother of the missing flyer, told officers that on the night of January 25, before she received word that her son was missing, she felt as though she had been plunged into ice water from her waist to her feet and that she remained in that condition for a number of days. Upon regaining her normal feeling, she stated that she desired only hot drinks and food. Officials in contact with Mrs. Clark asked the exact time of this reaction and estimating the time in India and the speed of the plane, an approximate location of where the crash occurred was mapped out and the information wired to India. The explanation given was that in all possibility the flyer, as the plane plunged into the ice and snow, was thinking of his mother and she received his thoughts."

5. According to a missing air crew report obtained by Mitchell Cirlot of Ocean Springs, Clark (Serial No. 0794529) was the co-pilot of a B-24 which crashed in the vicinity of Chabua, India, in the foothills of the Himalayas. The plane was located a year later, and Clark's body was interred along with others of the crew on November 10, 1949, in Group Burial 4914 CG-425 in the Jefferson Barracks National Cemetery in St. Louis, Missouri.

DeMetz, Charles F. Jr. Photo: *1941 Perkolator* p. 22.

1. War Memorial Plaque in Gregory War Memorial Chapel: DeMetz, Charles (Gold Star)Army
2 The Honor List of Dead and Missing of the Military Personnel for the State Of Mississippi in World War II (U. S. Army). Reprinted in *Valor Remembered*, p. 72: Harrison County--DeMetz, Charles F., Jr./34479404/PFC/Died of Wounds
3. Captain Donald DeMetz of Pass Christian informed the archivist by phone on August 16, 2000, that Charles F. DeMetz died on the hospital ship *Constellation* on February 4, 1944, after being wounded in the Battle of Kawajalein Atoll. He was buried first in Hawaii and then at Arlington National Cemetery.
4. According to Mitchell Cirlot of Ocean Springs, DeMetz was interred at Arlington National Cemetery on October 14, 1949, in Section 17 Grave No. 18319-64.

Denning, David Huffman "Buck." Photo courtesy of Sara Lana Denning, wife of Buck Denning's nephew.

1. War Memorial Plaque in Gregory War Memorial Chapel: Denning, David (His name was not starred in 2000) Army
2. The Honor List of Dead and Missing of the Military Personnel for the State Of Mississippi in World War II (U. S. Army). Reprinted in *Valor Remembered* p. 72: Harrison County--Denning, David/34870892/SGT/Finding of Death (declared dead after a year)
3. *Daily Herald*, May 16, 1945.
Denning, a nose gunner and assistant radioman on a B-24 Liberator bomber flying out of England, was reported missing on March 25, 1945.
4. Denning letter courtesy of Sara Lana Denning, a Perkinston Campus history student in fall 1996. The letter bore no date and apparently was sent home with his effects. The letter read in full:

"My Dear Family,

"It is difficult for me to write this letter. But I feel that in case my crew should get forced down over the Reich, you would like to know how I felt about everything.

"There is no use thinking that I might have parachuted to safety and am now a prisoner of war at this stage of the game. You know the Germans are killing all airmen they get a hold of. On every mission I carry my .45 automatic Colt pistol, two clips and a pocket full of cartridges. If I am not fortunate enough to be able to work my way through the lines, I intend to shoot any Nazi, soldier or civilian who tries to stop me. This one man stand will last until I am dead. It is not that I am afraid of the Nazis that I say this. But I can't stand the idea of being tortured, or shot before one of their firing squads without a chance to fight back. I am a soldier of the U.S. Air Forces and I'll fight to the end of the war, or me, whichever comes first.

"I am probably gone now. My flying has not been a time of fear. Fortunately, I have been able to pray much, and have the firm conviction that I may look forward to a death in Christ. It isn't so terrible, after all, death takes only a few seconds, and then I shall be with God, no more of the miseries and sadness of this earth shall befall me. Is that, after all, such a dreadful transition?

"On the contrary; it is beautiful to be in God's strength. Every time, before each briefing and mission, I have prayed a short and strengthening prayer. God has told us He will not forget us if only we pray to him for support. I feel so strongly my nearness to God I am fully prepared to die. I hope that will be a consolation to you. I know quite well that it is horrible. We are all so young. But God knows best, and that our cause was a just one. I think it worse for you than me because I know that I have confessed all my sins to Him and have become very calm. Therefore please do not mourn my leaving too much, but pray for strength and trust in God. Mother, Dear Mother, let me embrace you. Forgive me any wrongs I may have done. Do not cry, Darling. Be courageous, you still have children left. I know I will see you again. One last tender kiss from your son, Buck.

"Father, forgive me too. Be strong in your belief which I know you have like Mother. Do not mourn, but thank God that we may have the certainty of His grace. Do not say, 'Because you are gone peace can be no joy for us anymore.' Because after all, I am giving my life for my country as so many other Yanks are doing at this time. Give me a firm handshake. God's will be done.

"Many kisses to my brothers and little sister from me, Buck. Maybe they won't understand it so well, but teach them too, to believe.

"Greet everybody for me. My sincere thanks for everything they ever did for me.

"Use the money I left to you Mother, toward giving my brothers and sister a good education and making the family more comfortable.

"Be courageous. They can only take my life and body. My soul is in God's hands. Until we meet again in a reunion which will be so much happier. Good-bye

Your Loving Son,
Buck"

5. Major General Edward F. Whitsell's letter courtesy of Sara Lana Denning.
On March 26, 1946, one year and one day after he was reported missing, Denning's mother received a letter from Major General Edward F. Whitsell informing her that her son's plane, while enroute to bomb Buchen, Germany, had encountered enemy fighters near Domitz, Germany. The heavily damaged Liberator was last seen at 10:17 a.m. going into a dive. Since a year had passed, continued the general, "without the receipt of evidence to support a continued presumption of survival, the War Department must terminate such absence by a presumptive finding of death."
6. Untitled military document from Sara Lana Denning: The document stated that a group burial composed of "6 Remains in 3 Caskets" took place on April 15, 1952, at 10:30 a.m. Buck Denning's name was on the list of the six men in the group burial. Apparently this document was an enclosure in a letter sent to the family seven years after the war.
7. On June 28, 2001, at the Alumni House on the Perkinston Campus, the archivist met Carol McReedy of Saucier, who was on the campus preparing for a high school class reunion. Since she was from Saucier, the archivist inquired if she knew the Denning family. One week later McReedy brought a letter to the archivist. Superintendent Frank A. Lockwood of the Jefferson Barracks National Cemetery in St. Louis, Missouri, had sent the letter to Mr. and Mrs. Joseph H. Denning of Route 1, Perkinston. The letter, dated April 18, 1952, follows:

"On Tuesday morning the 15th of April 1952, the remains of the late Sgt. David H. Denning were permanently buried in Section 85, Graves 77, 78, 79 of this National Cemetery, together with the remains of those other decedents comprising the group which could not be separated because of the circumstances under which their deaths occurred. Customary military funeral services were conducted and full military honors were rendered.

"An appropriate headstone will be erected and maintained by the Government to perpetually mark the common graves of these fallen heroes.

"With the thought that it will prove to be of sentimental value to you, this United States flag is forwarded to you by the Government as a token of appreciation and sympathy of a grateful nation."

Ervin, Harold Welch. Photo: *1936 Perkolator* p. 29.

1. War Memorial Plaque in Gregory War Memorial Chapel: Ervin, Harold W. (Gold Star) Army
2. The Honor List of Dead and Missing of the Military Personnel for the State Of Mississippi in World War II (U. S. Army). Reprinted in *Valor Remembered*, p. 72: Harrison County--Ervin, Harold/O-854304/1LT/Death Non Battle
   (The "Death Non Battle" was obviously an error as all other information pointed to Killed in Action.)
3. American Battle Monuments Commission. The World War II Honor Roll:
   Harold W. Ervin
   First Lieutenant, U.S. Army Air Forces
   O-854304
   17th Photographic Squadron, 4th Reconnaissance Group
   Entered the Service from: Mississippi
   Died: February 7, 1943
   Missing in Action or Buried at Sea
   Tablets of the Missing at Honolulu Memorial
   Honolulu, Hawaii
4. *Daily Herald*, February 11, 1945. The article read in full:
   "First Lieut. Harold W. Ervin, 24, son of Mr. and Mrs. William Luther Ervin of Long Beach, was killed in action Sunday, February 7, in the Pacific war zone, according to telegram received Wednesday by his family from the War Department. Lieutenant Ervin, Army Air Corps, was in the photography division."
5. *Daily Herald*, February 17, 1945
   The article, accompanied by a photo of Ervin in U.S. Army Air Corps officer's uniform, contained a detailed biography of Ervin.

Firth, Stova Wilbern. Photo: *1941 Perkolator* p. 22

1. War Memorial Plaque in Gregory War Memorial Chapel: Firth, Stova (Gold Star) Navy
2. Firth did not appear on the U. S. Navy list for Mississippi Noncombat Casualty list.
3. The Friday, July 24, 1942, *Chronicle* (Pascagoula) carried an account of Firth's death "in an airplane crash in San Diego, Calif., Tuesday." The *Daily Herald*, Tuesday, July 28, 1942, carried an account of his burial in Macpelah Cemetery in Pascagoula that day. The July 30, 1942, *Daily Herald* carried another account of his funeral under a photo of Firth in a U.S. Navy officer's dress uniform.
4. According to information supplied by Mitchell Cirlot of Ocean Springs, Firth, while on a training mission in an F4F-4 Wildcat fighter, went into a spin and crashed one mile west of Sweet Water lake in San Diego County on July 21, 1942.

Forte, James William Jr. Photo: *1939 Perkolator* p. 34.

1. War Memorial Plaque in Gregory War Memorial Chapel: Forte, James (His name was not starred in 2000) Army
2. Forte was not listed in *Valor Remembered* because he was from Florida.
3. American Battle Monuments Commission. The World War II Honor Roll:
   James W. Forte, Jr.
   First lieutenant, U. S. Army Air Forces
   O-726893
   37th Bomber Squadron, 17th Bomber Group, Medium
   Entered the Service from: Florida
   Died: March 22, 1943
   Missing in Action or Buried at Sea
   Tablets of the Missing at North Africa American Cemetery
   Carthage, Tunisia
   Awards: Air Medal, Purple Heart
4. On June 15, 2001, the *Pensacola News Journal*, at the request of the archivist, published an article requesting information related to MGCCC's two Pensacola KIAs. In response to this article, Penny Yadrick of Dothan, Alabama, called with the information that a tombstone in the Fort Barrancas National Cemetery in Pensacola read: "James William Forte, born 5-14-1919, died 3-22-1943, at Plot MA 033-B." The archivist telephoned the cemetery and was told the "MA" section is the "memorial section." The stone was placed there by request of a family member or a friend on May 11, 1990.
5. On March 12, 2002, Mitchell Cirlot of Ocean Springs delivered to the MGCCC Archivist a copy of a letter sent from the Department of the Army to Forte's father on April 29, 1948. The letter read in part: "The records of the Department of the Army disclose that your son was a crew member on board plane number A/C/ B26-B2 41-17883, that was lost as a result of enemy action over the Mediterranean, north of Cape Bizerte, Tunisia on 22 March 1943. The American Graves Registration Search and Recovery Teams have operated in this probable area with negative results. The circumstances surrounding his death have been thoroughly reviewed and after a detailed study of all records and reports, the Department of the Army has been forced to conclude that the remains are not recoverable."

Hague, Douglas Kell. Photo: *1940 Perkolator* p. 59.

1. War Memorial Plaque in Gregory War Memorial Chapel: Hague, Douglas (Gold Star) Navy
2. Summary of Mississippi War Casualties--Navy, Marine Corps, and Coast Guard (October 3, 1949). Reprinted in *Valor Remembered*, p. 190.
   Killed in Action, Died of Wounds, or Lost Lives as Results of Operational Movements in War Zones. Hague, Douglas Kell, Ensign, USNR. Mother, Mrs. Pearl Rose Gautier Hague, Box 36, Pascagoula.
3. American Battle Monuments Commission. The World War II Honor Roll:

Douglas K. Hague
Lieutenant Junior Grade, U.S. Navy
O-112679
United States Naval Reserve
Entered the Service from: Mississippi
Died: March 1, 1943
Missing in Action or Buried at Sea
Tablets of the Missing at Honolulu Memorial
Honolulu, Hawaii

4. *Daily Herald*, Wednesday, March 10, 1943. Article read in part:
"Mr. and Mrs. George B. Hague of Pascagoula received a cablegram Saturday morning from Rear Admiral Randall Jacobs, chief of the Navy Personnel, advising them that their son, Ensign Douglas Kell Hague, had been killed in action.
"The cablegram read, 'We regret to advise you that your son, Ensign Douglas Kell Hague of the Naval Air Corps Reserve, has been killed in the performance of his duty and in the service of his country and that his body has not been found. We extend our sympathy to you for your great loss.'
"Ensign Hague would have been 23 years old March 16 and enlisted in the Naval Air Corps two years ago, having his father sign the necessary papers to enter the service. He enlisted at Mobile in March 1941, and was called into the service in May of the same year. He received his basic training at Miami, Fla., and received his advance flying and his silver wings at Jacksonville, Fla., in April 1942.
"Upon completion of his training course and receiving his wings he was granted a 15-day furlough which he spent in Pascagoula with his parents.
"He reported back to duty at Norfolk Naval Base, where he received his bombing training. He was among the pilots taking part in the invasion of Africa, and again returned to the United States. His mother talked to him by phone in December following his return home and shortly after he left for active duty in the Pacific war zone where he was killed. . . ."
5. *Daily Herald*, Saturday, March 13, 1943. The article was accompanied by a photo of Hague in U. S. Navy officer's dress uniform.
6. Mitchell Cirlot of Ocean Springs received a letter from the Department of the Navy dated September 13, 2001, stating that Hague, who was attached to the *USS Sangamon,* died when his plane went into a spin and crashed into the sea near the city of Vila on Efate, an island in the New Hebrides.

Haney, Josh Oden. Photo: *1944 Perkolator* p. 33.
1. War Memorial Plaque in Gregory War Memorial Chapel: Haney, Josh (His name was not starred in 2000) Marines
2. Summary of Mississippi War Casualties--Navy, Marine Corps, and Coast Guard (October 3, 1949). Reprinted in *Valor Remembered*, p. 190.
Killed in Action, Died of Wounds, or Lost Lives as Results of Operational Movements in War Zones. Haney, Josh Oden, Pvt., USMCR. Parents, Mr. and Mrs. Joseph S. Haney, 807 Thirty-eighth Avenue, Gulfport.
3. *Daily Herald* June 7, 1945, excerpt follows:
"Pfc. Josh Oden Haney, 19 son of Mr. and Mrs. Joe S. Haney of 807 38th Avenue Gulfport was killed in action May 20 on Okinawa with the Fifth Marines according to a telegram received Wednesday evening by his parents. Young Haney, born in Prentiss May 8, 1926, entered the Marine Corps nine months ago and received training at Parris Island . . . . He was sent overseas in September with a replacement group. . . ."
4. Telephone notification by personnel of Evergreen Cemetery. Haney was buried in the Evergreen Cemetery in Gulfport at Block 45, Lot 21, Space 3.
5. Letter postmarked June 1, 2001, from Charles H. Iversen of Biloxi in response to the May 28, 2001, *Sun Herald* Memorial Day article requesting information about MGCCC War Dead.
"Information concerning death of PFC Josh Oden Haney, U. S. Marine Corps, Killed In Action, Okinawa, May 20, 1945. Josh was one of my best friends in school and out of school. We--about seven boys--always did things together. As a group we called ourselves 'The Boys.'
"Josh and myself wanted to join the Marines. We went to New Orleans to enlist. Josh was accepted and I was rejected (I was 16 and my alteration of the Birth Certificate failed to pass the recruiter's inspection). I guess the reason to join the Marines was partly patriotic, but the driving reason was to kill Japs (a popular feeling during WWII). We wanted to be with the best, the Marines. When Josh went off to Parris Island the next morning I went with him to the train and I came back to Gulfport.
"When Josh came home on Boot Leave, I went with him up to Perk to visit one of his teachers and a friend. After leave he was sent to the Pacific on a replacement draft, where he was assigned to the Fifth Marines of the First Marine Division. He was in a rifle company in the third Battalion of the Fifth Marines. At last he said he was in the best of the best.
"A Marine from Gulfport, Robert Attya, one of our mutual friends from school told me he had been on the lookout for Josh. He had not seen him since before the landing (twenty days earlier). His unit was passing up into the assault, he saw Josh laid out with the dead. He was killed in the assault on Shuri Castle (the anchor of the main Jap defensive line). He said Josh was killed by rifle or machine gun fire. He was not all messed up as with artillery fire. I enlisted on May 1st, 1945, the day of the Okinawa landing . . . . I had several letters from Josh while he was in training and one from him while he was on Okinawa. The picture of the two Jap soldiers, the woman, and the money was in his last letter to me."

Johnson, Judson B. Photo: *1941 Perkolator* p. 24.
1. War Memorial Plaque in Gregory War Memorial Chapel: Johnson, Judson (Gold Star) Army
2. The Honor List of Dead and Missing of the Military Personnel for the State Of Mississippi in World War II (U. S. Army). Reprinted in *Valor Remembered*, p. 77: Oktibbeha County--Johnson, Judson B./34426199/PFC/ Killed in Action
(The archivist in researching *Valor Remembered* accidentally discovered Johnson's name on the Oktibbeha County list. Years later the reason for Johnson's name being on that list surfaced. He had been attending Mississippi State College at Starkville when he enlisted.)
3. *Stone County Enterprise*, March 2, 1944. The article reported Johnson missing in action as of January 26, 1944. The article stated, "Private Johnson has been overseas since May, 1943, and prior to that he was stationed at Camp Gordon, Ga. He was in the Sicilian invasion and went into Italy about November 1."
4. Letter dated January 12, 2001 from Walline Vogle of Corpus Christi, Texas to MGCCC Archives.
In response to a query about the World War II dead in *Action* (the MGCCC alumni magazine), Walline Vogle wrote that she and her husband, Thomas, had been Johnson's classmates at Perk. She gave the phone number of her husband's cousin, Richard Vogle of Saucier, and he put the archivist immediately in touch with Glendon Johnson, Judson's brother.
5. Glendon Johnson by telephone conversation on January 17, 2001, informed the archivist that his brother, Judson, was buried in the Blackwell Cemetery on Blackwell Farms Road of Highway 67 in the Success Community of Harrison County. The stone read, "Judson B. Johnson, Born August 6, 1921, Died January 26, 1944, 83rd Chemical Bn., Part of the 5th Army." Millard Bond of Perkinston, who had been with Johnson on an LST, which was anchored off the Anzio Beachhead, told the family what happened. Bond said a mine drifted into the ship at 4:00 a.m. on January 26, 1944. When the mine exploded it ignited the cargo of phosphorous shells, and the ship burned and sank. Bond never saw Judson Johnson again. After the war Johnson's

body was discovered in a grave four miles inland from the beach. Johnson's body was later returned home.

6. *Daily Herald*, August 4, 1944. This article, found two days after the conversation with Glendon Johnson while searching microfilm for an unrelated topic, read in total:

"Pfc. Judson B. Johnson, son of Mr. and Mrs. Willard Johnson of Saucier, Route 2, was killed in action while on a boat in harbor anchored off the Anzio beachhead in Italy, according to a telegram received by his parents from the War Department. Pfc. Johnson, who was with a chemical battalion, was earlier reported missing as of January 26."

Ladner, Andrew J. Photo courtesy of *Sun Herald* -- from *Daily Herald*, February 10, 1943.

1. War Memorial Plaque in Gregory War Memorial Chapel: Ladner, Andrew (Gold Star) Army
2. The Honor List of Dead and Missing of the Military Personnel for the State Of Mississippi in World War II (U. S. Army). Reprinted in *Valor Remembered*, p. 72: Harrison County--Ladner, Andrew J./34133073/PVT/Killed in Action
3. American Battle Monuments Commission. The World War II Honor Roll:
Andrew J. Ladner
Private, U.S. Army
34133073
126th Infantry Regiment, 32nd Infantry Division
Entered the Service from: Mississippi
Died: November 30, 1942
Missing in Action or Buried at Sea
Tablets of the Missing at Manila American Cemetery
Manila, Philippines
Awards: Bronze Star, Purple Heart
4. *Daily Herald*, February 10, 1943. The article was accompanied by a photo of Ladner in the dress uniform of a U. S. Army enlisted man, read, in part:
"Andrew Joseph Ladner, 30, . . . was killed in action in the Southwest Pacific, according to information received a few days ago by relatives in the Lizana community. He had been in the service approximately 14 months. Born at Lizana on November 29, 1912, . . . [he was] . . . the son of Mrs. Mary Laura Ladner and the late Armogen V. Ladner. . . ."

Ladner, Berlin John. Photo courtesy of *Sun Herald* -- from *Daily Herald*, November 4, 1947.

1. War Memorial Plaque in Gregory War Memorial Chapel: Ladner, Berlin J. (Gold Star) Army
2. The Honor List of Dead and Missing of the Military Personnel for the State Of Mississippi in World War II (U. S. Army). Reprinted in *Valor Remembered*, p. 72: Harrison County--Ladner, Berlin J./34478266/SGT/ Killed in Action
3. Two undated newspaper clippings from the scrapbook of June (Ladner) Jefferson. Both clippings are almost certainly from the *Daily Herald*. The first was published between his death on November 23, 1944, and the services held at St. Ann's Church at Dedeaux on December 17. The second clipping accompanied by a photo of Ladner in U.S. Army dress uniform, was published after the December 17 services. The earlier article read in part:
"Staff Sergeant Berlin J. Ladner, 23, son of Mr. and Mrs. F. E. Ladner of Pass Christian, was killed in action in Germany November 23, according to a telegram received Sunday from the War Department. He had been in service two years and overseas for three months.
"Church services will be held for Sergeant Ladner December 17 at 11 o'clock at St. Ann's Church, Dedeaux, with Rev. R. F. Waters officiating."
4. Undated newspaper clipping from the scrapbook of June (Ladner) Jefferson. The article almost certainly from the *Daily Herald* and probably published in 1945, carried a photograph of Berlin Ladner in U.S. Army dress uniform. The article read in total:
"To Award Silver Star Posthumously
"A special service will be held at the Dedeaux Catholic Church in honor of Sgt. Berlin J. Ladner, above, who was killed in Germany last November. The Silver Star Medal will be presented to Sgt. Ladner's parents, Mr. and Mrs. F. E. Ladner, by Colonel Thomas B. Birdsong of Camp Shelby.
"Mr. and Mrs. Ladner received the citation from Major General Edward F. Whitsell. He was cited for gallantry in action on November 19, 1944, when Sergeant Ladner's company came under heavy fire from well-entrenched enemy field fortifications, and suffered many casualties. Sergeant Ladner led a patrol to within 150 yards of the enemy positions at which point it was pinned down by heavy enemy fire which seriously wounded several men. With complete disregard for his personal safety and while under intense enemy machine gun, mortar, and small arms fire, Sergeant Ladner carried wounded men 400 yards across fire-swept terrain to a safe position where they could receive medical aid, the citation said. In one instance he braved enemy fire at point-blank range to rescue a seriously wounded man, and while doing so was fatally wounded."
5. *Daily Herald*, October 28, 1947. The article stated that Ladner's body had been exhumed from a grave in Chappelle, Belgium, and was being returned home for reinterment.
6. *Daily Herald*, Tuesday, November 4, 1947. This article, accompanied by the photo of Ladner in a U.S. Army dress uniform, read in part:
"The body of Berlin J. Ladner, 22, son of Mr. and Mrs. Filman Ladner of the Dedeaux community, north of Pass Christian, who was killed overseas in World War II, will arrive in Gulfport Wednesday afternoon aboard the Illinois Central at 12:20 o'clock.
"The former staff sergeant served in the European theater with Company K, 413th Infantry Regiment, 104th Timberwolf Division. He was killed during fighting between Brussels and Luxembourg on Nov. 23, 1944. He enlisted at Camp Shelby on February 11, 1942, and served at Camp Adair, Oregon, and Camp Carson, Colorado, before shipping overseas. . . .
"Funeral services will be conducted by Father R. F. Waters with high mass at 11 o'clock Thursday morning. Burial will be in the Rotten Bayou Cemetery. . . ."
7. A formal color photo was donated to the MGCCC Archives by Mr. and Mrs. Herman Ladner, Berlin's brother and sister-in-law. His niece, June (Ladner) Jefferson, donated black and white snapshots.

McBryde, Toxie Howard. Photo courtesy of the Archives and Special Collections of the John Davis Williams Library at the University of Mississippi--from the *1936 Ole Miss* yearbook.

1. War Memorial Plaque in Gregory War Memorial Chapel: McBryde, Toxie (Gold Star) Army
2. The Honor List of Dead and Missing of the Military Personnel for the State Of Mississippi in World War II (U. S. Army). Reprinted in *Valor Remembered*, p. 75: Lamar County--McBryde, Toxie H./O-661111/1LT/Death Non Battle
3. Letter from Toxie McBryde's brother, Retired Lt. Col. Claude M. McBryde, of Oakland Park, Florida, dated August 16, 2000.
Lt. Col. McBryde said his brother was born November 20, 1915, in Purvis but that he grew up in Sumrall. After graduation from Perk in 1934, he earned a degree in pharmacy at the University of Mississippi. During World War II he became an Army Air Corps P-38 pilot and was enroute to Europe

when he died steering his plane away from a drill field in Kentucky. He was buried at Highlands Cemetery in Hattiesburg.

4. Lt. Col. Claude McBryde sent with his letter a copy of a March 23, 1944, letter and Distinguished Flying Cross citation sent to his father from Headquarters, Army Air Forces, Washington, D.C. The citation read in total:

"First Lieutenant Toxie H. McBryde, O-661111, Air Corps, United States Army. For heroism while participating in an aerial flight near Godman Field, Fort Knox, Kentucky, on 11 November 1943. Lieutenant McBryde, as pilot of a P-40F airplane, was taking off on a routine ferrying mission to Bowling Green, Kentucky. Before reaching an altitude of 300 feet, Lieutenant McBryde retracted his landing gear and started a turn to the left toward a clearing approximately one (1) mile northwest of Godman Field. Realizing that a crash landing in this clearing would endanger the lives of Army personnel working in this area, Lieutenant McBryde elected to turn left again to avoid this clearing. This action threw the aircraft into a spin which resulted in a crash on the edge of the clearing and the death of Lieutenant McBryde. As a result, of this decision, made at a time of extreme personal danger, Lieutenant McBryde averted endangering the lives of military personnel and the destruction of government property. Lieutenant McBryde's unselfish devotion to duty in placing the safety of others before his own exemplifies the highest tradition of the Army Air Forces.

5. *The Booster* (Purvis) newspaper, November 19, 1943, carried an account of Toxie McBryde's November 15 funeral services at Sumrall Methodist Church followed by interment in Hattiesburg.

McKee, Carlos Reese Jr. Photo: *1939 Perkolator* p. 36.

1. War Memorial Plaque in Gregory War Memorial Chapel: McKee, Carl (Gold Star) Navy
2. McKee did not appear on the U. S. Navy Mississippi Noncombat Casualty list for Mississippi.
3. Paul Cartwright of the Copiah-Jefferson Regional Library in Hazelhurst sent two newspaper articles and a gravestone inscription relating to McKee. The earliest article from the *Hazelhurst Courier*, Thursday, August 24, 1944, contained the following:

"The following telegram was received by Dr. and Mrs. Carlos Reese McKee, Sr., on Monday night of this week:

"The Navy Department deeply regrets to inform you that your son, Lt. Carlos Reese McKee, Jr., USNR, was killed 17 August 1944, in the performance of his duty and in the service of his country. The Department extends to you its sincerest sympathy in your great loss. On account of existing conditions the body cannot be returned at present. If further details are received you will be informed. To prevent possible aid to our enemies please do not divulge the name of his ship or station.

"Lt. McKee enlisted in the navy Air Corps in October of 1941, being graduated and commissioned as an ensign. He was promoted to the rank of Lieut. in June of 1944. He is survived by his wife, the former Barbara Peterson of San Francisco. . . ."

4. The second article likely from the same paper the following week, carried a photo of McKee in U.S. Navy uniform and the following information reprinted in total:

"The sad news of the death of Lt. Carl McKee was received last week.

"On Wednesday of this week it was learned that Lt. McKee and another officer were sitting in the cockpit of their ship on the deck of an airplane carrier, when one of their fellow officers, in making a landing on the flight deck of the carrier, crashed into their plane killing Lt. McKee and the other officer in the plane with him."

5. McKee's gravestone inscription from the Peets Cemetery near Hazelhurst:
"Lt. Carlos Reese McKee, Jr./U.S.N.R./b. July 9, 1920/ d. Aug. 17, 1944/ Buried at sea Lat. 20, 32" N. Long., 159, 48"W., approximately 75 miles south of Honolulu."

6. Since McKee was buried at sea, Jane Sullivan could not understand why she could not find him on the American Battle Monuments Commission Honor Roll. Mitchell Cirlot solved the problem. In typing in a query for any person with "Mc" as part of his last name, a space must be typed after "Mc" and then the rest of the name typed after the space. McKee's World War II Honor Roll information follows:
Carlos R. McKee, Jr.
Lieutenant, U. S. Navy
O-124987
United States Naval Reserve
Entered the Service from: Mississippi
Died: August 17, 1944
Missing in Action or Buried at Sea
Tablets of the Missing at Honolulu Memorial
Honolulu, Hawaii
Awards: Air Medal

Moorman, Madison Kent "Jack." Photo courtesy of Dixie Press of Gulfport--from *Dixie Guide* newspaper, June 1944.

1. War Memorial Plaque in Gregory War Memorial Chapel: Moorman, Jack (Gold Star) Navy
2. Summary of Mississippi War Casualties--Navy, Marine Corps, and Coast Guard (October 3, 1949). Reprinted in *Valor Remembered*, p. 192.
Killed in Action, Died of Wounds, or Lost Lives as Results of Operational Movements in War Zones. Moorman, Madison Kent, Ensign, USNR. Mother, Mrs. Marguerritte Moorman Murphy, Hotel Riviera, Biloxi. [Why his mother's name was given as "Marguerritte" in one article and as "Eda" in another was unknown to this author.]
3. *Dixie Guide* newspaper, September 1943. Caption under a large photo of Moorman in U. S. Naval dress while with the superintendent of the U.S. Naval Academy at Annapolis, Maryland, read in total:

"Madison Kent Moorman, of Gulfport, son of Mrs. Eda Moorman Murphy, Hotel Riviera, Biloxi, graduate of the Naval Reserve Class at the U. S. Naval Academy, is shown receiving a letter of commendation from Rear Admiral J. R. Beardall, Superintendent of the Academy.

"Moorman, Sub-Commander of the reserve Battalion was commended for 'exhibiting officer like qualities and positive naval character to an outstanding degree,' and stood first in a class of 276 midshipmen in officer aptitude.

"Upon being commissioned, he was assigned to the Executive Department of the Naval Academy."

4. *Dixie Guide*, Newspaper, June 1944. Article read in part:

"Ensign Madison Kent 'Jack' Moorman of Gulfport was killed in action on May 31 just three days after writing what became a last letter to his mother. He was serving as a volunteer with an MTB [Motor Torpedo Boat] squadron in the Mediterranean and is known to have participated in at least eight missions. "Ensign Moorman was born July 19, 1918. He graduated from Gulfport High School in 1934, Perkinston Junior College in 1936 and Oregon State College in 1940-41 where he was on the varsity football team. He enlisted in the Naval Reserve in June 1942, and received his commission as ensign at Annapolis in August 1943. He stayed on at Annapolis as an instructor and assistant football coach for the plebs, and then was sent to Rhode Island for PT [Patrol Torpedo] training.

"On Wednesday afternoon, June 14, memorial services were held for Ensign Moorman at St. Peter's-by-the-Sea Episcopal Church in Gulfport.

Ensign Moorman was baptized and confirmed in St. Peter's Church in his early youth."

5. Mitchell Cirlot of Ocean Springs recalled that his father, who served in an MTB Squadron in the Mediterranean Sea in World War II, had told him about being assigned as honor guard of a burial detail at Bastia, Corsica, for the burial of men from his unit. Since the bodies of few MTB squadron men killed in action were recovered and fewer still buried in Bastia, the incident mentioned by Cirlot's father was very likely Moorman's burial. Cirlot obtained Moorman's burial card by letter dated August 31, 2001, from William N. Stafford Jr., Mortuary Affairs Section, Department of the Navy, Bureau of Medicine and Surgery, Military Medical Support Office, P. O. Box 886999, Great Lakes, Illinois 60088-6999. The card contained the following information related to Moorman. A 20-mm shell struck him while on duty as executive officer of USS PT 307 off the coast of Italy on May 31, 1944. He was first interred at the U. S. Military Cemetery at Bastia, Corsica and later reinterred at the U. S. Military Cemetery at Nettuno, Italy. His body was returned to Lang Undertaking Company in Gulfport on July 6, 1948. Cirlot then determined that Moorman's final resting place was Block 5, Lot 9, Space 8, Evergreen Cemetery in Gulfport.

Moran, Warren Joseph. Photo: *1940 Perkolator* p. 68.

1. War Memorial Plaque in Gregory War Memorial Chapel: Moran, Warren (Gold Star) Coast Guard
2. Summary of Mississippi War Casualties--Navy, Marine Corps, and Coast Guard (October 3, 1949). Reprinted in *Valor Remembered*, p. 192. Killed in Action, Died of Wounds, or Lost Lives as Results of Operational Movements in War Zones. Moran, Warren Joseph, Coxswain, USCG. Father, Mr. Damase V. Moran, Rt. 1, Box 856, Pass Christian.
3. Lillian Hayden, wife of former MGCJC President J. J. Hayden, gave the following information by telephone on August 15, 2000:
   "Warren Moran was born April 25, 1921, and was killed in Normandy on D-Day. He is buried in the Malley Cemetery in DeLisle."

Murphy, Clifford Winford. Photo: *1940 Perkolator* p. 73.

1. War Memorial Plaque in Gregory War Memorial Chapel: Murphy, Clifford (Gold Star) Army
2. The Honor List of Dead and Missing of the Military Personnel for the State Of Mississippi in World War II (U. S. Army). Reprinted in *Valor Remembered*, p. 74: Jackson County--Murphy, Clifford W./34612484/PVT/Death Non Battle
3. American Battle Monuments Commission. The World War II Honor Roll:
   Clifford W. Murphy
   Private, U. S. Army
   34612484
   19th Malaria Control Unit
   Entered the Service from: Mississippi
   Died: July 15, 1943
   Buried at: Plot I Row 13 Grave 4
   North Africa American Cemetery
   Carthage, Tunisia
4. Robert G. Cossey, Murphy's brother-in-law, by telephone on August 13, 2000, stated that Murphy drowned in the invasion of Sicily. That invasion was launched from North Africa. Why the U.S. Army classed his death as "Non Battle" was not known to Cossey. A memorial stone was placed in Vancleave Cemetery No. 1 on Jim Ramsey Road with the following inscription: Clifford Murphy/Died in Action in World War II/ 1918-1943.
5. Undated newspaper clipping probably from the *Daily Herald* carrying a photo of Murphy in civilian dress read in total:
   "KILLED IN ACTION--Clifford Murphy, 25, son of Mr. and Mrs. R. N. Murphy, Vancleave, who died in action in North Africa recently. A memorial service will be held for him at Vancleave this week-end. He attended Mississippi State College and later was with the Jackson County health department."
6. *Pascagoula Chronicle-Star*, August 6, 1943. Excerpt follows:
   "The death of . . . Clifford Murphy in the service of his country in North Africa, July 15, is one of several tragedies that have robbed Dr. and Mrs. R. N. Murphy of Vancleave of children within little more than a year as they lost three daughters and a son-in-law in an auto-train collision near Ocean Springs only a little more than 12 months ago. Murphy first enlisted in the Navy and was sent to Notre Dame, where he attained the rank of midshipman before being transferred to the Army." (Robert Cossey told this author that Murphy resigned his commission in the U. S. Navy and joined the U. S. Army because "he didn't want to give orders that might result in the deaths of others.)

Myers, Leslie Francis. Photo courtesy of personnel of Bethel Baptist Church near Brandon.

1. War Memorial Plaque in Gregory War Memorial Chapel: Myers, Leslie Francis (Gold Star) Army
2. The Honor List of Dead and Missing of the Military Personnel for the State Of Mississippi in World War II (U. S. Army). Reprinted in *Valor Remembered*, p. 78: Rankin County--Myers, Leslie F./O-431477/1LT/Death Non Battle
3. *Daily Herald*, January 19, 1943. Article read in total:
   "Jackson, Jan. 19 - (AP) Lieut. Leslie F. Myers, 26, US Army Air Corps, formerly of Brandon, near here, has been killed in action over China, his mother, Mrs. Lula Myers, now of Jackson, was advised today by the War Department.
   "No further details were given.
   "Myers was graduated from Brandon High School and Mississippi State College and enlisted in the Air Corps in April, 1941. Flying a pursuit plane, he had seen action over India and China. He was promoted to first lieutenant after arrival in the Far East."(The archivist was unable to determine why the U.S. Army declared Myers's death "Non Battle" while the newspaper listed him "Killed in Action.")
4. Rankin County Cemetery Records, 1924-1980. Bethel Baptist Church Cemetery (5 miles south of Brandon, east of Hwy 469) in the Mississippi Department of Archives and History. The gravestone read:
   "Myers, Leslie F.
   Miss. 1st Lt. 16 AAF Fighter, SQ WWII
   29 Jan. 1916-12 Jan. 1943"
5. On August 7, 2000, the secretary of Bethel Baptist Church at the request of the archivist, sent the photograph of McKee used in this work.
6. On May 29, 2001, inspired by the *Sun Herald* Memorial Day article of May 28, 2001, Maurice O'Keefe of Long Beach sent a copy of page 140 of *Descendants and Allied Families of Isaac Myers and Gracie Butler Myers* compiled by Nina M. Anderson. The article read in part:
   "He was a casualty of World War II, killed in action over China. . . . He was interred first in a U. S. Military cemetery in China and was later re-interred in Bethel Cemetery. . . . "

Newsum, William Paul. Photo: *1941 Perkolator* p. 34.

1. War Memorial Plaque in Gregory War Memorial Chapel: Newsum, Bill (Gold Star) Navy
2. Summary of Mississippi War Casualties--Navy, Marine Corps, and Coast Guard (October 3, 1949). Reprinted in *Valor Remembered*, p. 206. Noncombat Dead: Newsum, William Paul, Ensign, USNR. Mother, Mrs. H. D. Newsum, U.S.V.A. Nurses Home, Biloxi.
3. *Stone County Enterprise*, June 3, 1943. Article accompanied by a photo of Newsum in khaki U.S. Navy officer's uniform. Excerpts of the article follow:

   "The funeral service for William Paul Newsum, son of Mrs. H. D. Newsum, Veterans Facility, and the late David Keller Newsum, was held from the Methodist Church of Biloxi, of which he was a member, on May 19th. . . . Services were concluded at the National Cemetery on the reservation at the Facility with full military honors. . . .

   "He received his basic training at Athens, Georgia, and Henly Field, Texas, and his advanced training at Corpus Christi, 'University of the Air'. . . .

   "He received his 'Navy Wings of Gold' only two weeks before his death, and had been assigned to duties as an Instructor in Torpedo Squadron at Corpus Christi. His mother and his fiancée, Miss Marion Rockwell, attended the graduation. . . . Ensign Newsum was a passenger on a routine instruction flight in a Voltee type training plane piloted by Ensign Earl Leon Pelley, USNR. The cause of the accident is not known. The crash proved instantly fatal death to both officers. . . ."

Rainey, Fred Roy Jr. Photo: Courtesy of Emogene Rainey.

1. War Memorial Plaque in Gregory War Memorial Chapel: Rainey, Fred (Gold Star) Army
2. Rainey was not listed in *Valor Remembered* because he was from Florida.
3. Rainey was not listed on the *1944 Perkolator* "In Memoriam" list which meant that he was killed after August, 1944.
4. On May 28, 2001, inspired by the *Sun Herald* Memorial Day article of that same day, Jean Williams of Picayune sent an e-mail directing the archivist to a web site listing those interred in Myrtle Grove United Methodist Cemetery located five miles west of Pensacola, Florida. One of those listed was: "Rainey, Fred Roy, Jr. S/Sgt. WWII 1924-2-29 1944-11-12"
5. On June 15, 2001, the *Pensacola News Journal*, at the request of the archivist, published an article requesting information related to MGCCC's two Pensacola KIAs. A relative in Pensacola saw the article and immediately called Fred Roy Rainey's sister, Emogene, in Leesburg, Florida. Emogene called the archivist the same day. She had been a senior at Harrison-Stone-Jackson Agricultural High School at the time her brother was killed, but she recalled, "My family did not receive notification of my brother's death until Christmas Day, 1944." Emogene returned to Perk, graduating from the AHS on May 23, 1945.
6. On July 7, 2001, Emogene Rainey mailed all the documents and photographs in her possession related to her brother to the MGCCC Archives. Among those documents were:

   A. Western Union telegram sent to Fred Roy Rainey's mother, Daisy Rainey, from Washington, D.C., December 23, 1944, at 10 a.m. Full text follows:

   "The Secretary of War desires me to express his deep regret that your son Staff Sergeant Fred R. Rainey Jr. was killed in action on twelve November on Leyte. Letter follows. Dunlop Acting the Adjutant General."

   B. Letter to Daisy Rainey dated November 27, 1944, from Captain Theodore R. Wright of the 498th Bombardment Squadron of the 345th Bombardment Group. Full text follows:

   "In all my experience in the service, I have found that the duty which I am performing now is the most difficult and painful of all. This is to inform you of the death of your son, Fred, who was killed in action on November 12, 1944, as a result of enemy bombing in Dulag Harbor, Leyte Island, in the Philippines.

   "Fred has been in our squadron six months and has seen much action since leaving the states early last summer. Your son was always willing and eager to perform his duties in meeting the enemy wherever and whenever it was possible. His cooperation, with his fellow crew members, and his dependability in performing his duties as a radio-gunner, will always be remembered. His friendliness and personality were unsurpassed. These qualities won him many comrades and friends.

   "It may help you to know that your son suffered no pain in death and has been buried in an American Cemetery in Dulag, Leyte Island, with full military honors. Many of us are serving our country, but Fred is one of those who rendered the supreme sacrifice for the freedom of the nation. Nothing greater could be said of any man, for his deed was as great as that of any hero recorded in the annals of history.

   "Let me impress upon you once again how deeply we feel the loss of your son. You may be certain that we of the squadron who remain will carry on his ideals to the fullest extent. The memories of him will always carry on among those of us who worked with him. Please do not hesitate to call me at any time if I may be of assistance to you. I wish to express again my sincere sympathy on behalf of the entire squadron in your hours of bereavement.

   Theodore R. Wright,
   Captain, Air Corps, Commanding"

Reeves, Holley Stone "Pat." Photo: *1939 Perkolator* p. 41.

1. War Memorial Plaque in Gregory War Memorial Chapel: Reeves, Pat (Gold Star) Coast Guard (An error--he was in the Navy not the Coast Guard) Summary of Mississippi War Casualties--Navy, Marine Corps, and Coast Guard (October 3, 1949). Reprinted in *Valor Remembered*, p. 206 Noncombat Dead: Reeves, Holley Stone, Seaman 2, USNR. Wife, Mrs. H. S. Reeves, 628 Bohn St., Biloxi. The authors of *Valor Remembered* listed him twice on p. 93 under Harrison County as follows: Reeves, Holley Stone/Biloxi/USNR/Seaman 2C/Non Combat Dead and also as Reeves, Pat/Gulfport/USCG/Seaman 2C/Cause of death--unknown The error came about because the authors had the "Summary of Mississippi War Casualties--Navy, Marine Corps, and Coast Guard," which listed Holley Stone Reeves as a U. S. Navy Noncombat casualty whose wife lived in Biloxi. The authors also had the *1944 Perkolator* "In Memoriam" list which gave Reeves's hometown as Gulfport, and they had a copy of Reeves's nameplate on the War Memorial Plaque in the War Memorial Chapel which listed him as a member of the Coast Guard. Only in the course of research for this present work did the archivist discover that "Pat" was Holley Stone Reeves's nickname and that the two were one. Holley Stone "Pat" Reeves's hometown was Gulfport. He was a seaman 2C in the United States Naval Reserve. He never served in the Coast Guard. The *Daily Herald*, April 10, 1942, recorded that Holley Stone "Pat" Reeves had been struck and killed by lightning the day before while on duty in the Gulf of Mexico near Pensacola, Florida. His mother, Mrs. Icham Reeves, lived in Gulfport. His wife, Claire, lived in Biloxi. The funeral was to be held at Coalville Methodist Church with interment at Evergreen Cemetery in Gulfport. The *Daily Herald*, April 13, 1942, carried a photo of Reeves in a U. S. Navy uniform and gave an account of the funeral held at Coalville Methodist Church with interment across the road in Coalville Cemetery. Holley Stone "Pat" Reeves was buried in Coalville Cemetery at Woolmarket and not at Evergreen Cemetery in Gulfport. To be absolutely truthful, the archivist concluded that his body was likely where the stone was. The story of Holley Stone "Pat" Reeves's' death and burial was one of scores of examples of how fragmentary and erroneous information turned a seemingly simple rendition of facts into a researcher's nightmare. Such incidences resulted in this present work, which was to have been completed in three years, expanding to seven years.

Reeves, Otts Bernard. Photo: *1938 Perkolator* p. 21.

1. War Memorial Plaque in Gregory War Memorial Chapel: Reeves, Bernard (His name was not starred in 2000) Army
2. The Honor List of Dead and Missing of the Military Personnel for the State Of Mississippi in World War II (U. S. Army). Reprinted in *Valor Remembered*, p. 72: Harrison County--Reeves, Otts B./O-659590/2LT/Finding of Death (Declared dead after a year)
3. American Battle Monuments Commission. The World War II Honor Roll:
   Otts B. Reeves
   Second Lieutenant, U.S. Army Air Forces
   O-659590
   81st Bomber Squadron, 12th Bomber Group, Medium
   Entered the Service from: Mississippi
   Died: September 14, 1943*
   Missing in Action or Buried at Sea
   Tablets of the Missing at North Africa American Cemetery
   Carthage, Tunisia
   Awards: Air Medal, Purple Heart
   *(This date is in error. Apparently the American Battle Monuments Commission inadvertently listed the date he was "declared dead" instead of the date he actually died. He died September 14, 1942. He was declared dead September 14, 1943. Also, this reference and all military references to Reeves gives his first name as "Otts." His official Harrison-Stone-Jackson Junior College transcript gives his fist name as "Ottis.")
4. *Daily Herald*, May 6, 1942. A photo of Reeves in flight uniform accompanied the article. The article read in part:
   "Otts B. 'Barney' Reeves graduated with the first class of 'Hell from Heaven Men' at one of the world's greatest bombardier colleges at Midland Army Flying School, Texas, and was commissioned a second lieutenant in the US Army Air Force."
5. *Dixie Guide* newspaper, October 1942. The article was accompanied by a photo of Reeves in a flight uniform different from the one in the previous article. The article read in total:
   "Lieut. O. B. (Barney) Reeves, son of Mr. and Mrs. L. I. Reeves, 1002 39th Ave., Gulfport, was reported 'missing' on September 19 as of the 14th. Second lieutenant and bombardier Barney Reeves was on duty in Egypt when the War Department reported him as having not returned from a flight. He graduated from the Gulfport High School in '36, obtained his degree from the University of Mississippi in '40, joined the U. S. Army Air Corps and won his wings soon thereafter."
6. According to information provided by Mitchell Cirlot of Ocean Springs, the Germans shot down Reeves's B-25 over Egypt. The pilot of the plane, Colonel Charles G. Goodrich, survived and was sent to Stalag Luft III in Sagan, Poland.

Reeves, Woodrow Wilson. Photo courtesy Daunton Gibbs of Franklinton, Louisiana.

1. War Memorial Plaque in Gregory War Memorial Chapel: Reeves, Woodrow (His name was not starred in 2000.) Army
2. The Honor List of Dead and Missing of the Military Personnel for the State Of Mississippi in World War II (U. S. Army). Reprinted in *Valor Remembered*, p. 79: Stone County--Reeves, Woodrow W./34137164/SSG/Killed in Action
3. On November 11, 1987, Daunton Gibbs arrived at Taylor's Store in Perkinston asking for directions to the grave of Woodrow Wilson Reeves, who had been his platoon sergeant at Fort Riley, Kansas in 1943. He had a photograph of Reeves's platoon at Fort Riley and a letter dated December 20, 1946, from Reeves's mother bearing a Route A, Perkinston address telling him of her son's death in Belgium during the Battle of the Bulge on December 18, 1944. Gibbs had no idea at the time that a Perkinston address covered an area as large as the nation in which Reeves had died. The personnel of Taylor's Store directed Gibbs to the office of the chairman of the department of social studies at the Perkinston Campus. The chairman, who was five years away from being the MGCCC archivist, directed Gibbs to Reeves's grave location in the Hunt-Whittington Cemetery 15 miles to the east.
   When asked why he wished to see the grave, Gibbs replied, "My opinion of Sgt. Woodrow Reeves has always been that he was about the best advertisement for Mississippi at a time when it was a little short. I recall Sgt. Reeves as the best platoon sergeant that I ever came into contact with." After Fort Riley, Reeves had been sent to Europe and Gibbs had been posted to the Pacific. Only after contacting Reeves's mother following the war had Gibbs learned of his death in battle.
   The *Stone County Enterprise*, May 26, 1988, carried an account of Gibbs's quest, and the chairman wrote another account of the incident in the *Magnolia Series* booklet "Roy Wheat and Willie McBride," which was reprinted in Appendix I of *Valor Remembered.*
   Nearly a decade passed before the chairman, then the MGCCC archivist, saw Woodrow Wilson Reeves's name on the War Memorial Plaque in the War Memorial Chapel. The first thing he realized when the shock wore off was that there was no Gold Star by Reeves's name. The second thing he did was call Daunton Gibbs in Franklinton Louisiana. Though very ill, Gibbs found the Fort Riley platoon photo and mailed it to Perkinston for copying in June 1996. Gibbs died February 12, 1998.
   In researching this present work the archivist located three articles in the *Stone County Enterprise* related to Woodrow Wilson Reeves. An article on January 25, 1945, noted his death. An article of December 4, 1947, informed the public of his burial set for December 6, 1947. An article dated March 29, 1945, described the posthumous awarding to Reeves of the nation's second highest medal for valor--the Distinguished Service Cross. The citation accompanying the medal read,
   "Staff Sergeant Woodrow W. Reeves, 34137164, 18th Cavalry Reconnaissance Squadron, Mechanized United States Army, for extraordinary heroism in action against the enemy on 18 December 1944 in Belgium. Staff Sergeant Reeves was in command of two tanks in support of a dismounted patrol. When the patrol was attacked by a battalion of German infantry and was caught in the crossfire of our machine guns he climbed upon the turret and at great risk, effectively coordinated the fire of the weapons of both tanks. In plain view of the enemy he manned an antiaircraft machine gun atop his tank and inflicted heavy casualties until he was fatally wounded by hostile machine gun fire. Staff Sergeant Reeves's valor and self-sacrificing devotion to duty exemplified the highest traditions of the armed Forces. He entered military service from Mississippi."

Sasser, James Douglas. Photo: *1936 Perkolator* p. 47.

1. War Memorial Plaque in Gregory War Memorial Chapel: Sasser, James D. (His name was not starred in 2000) Army
2. Sasser was not listed in *Valor Remembered* because he enlisted from Tennessee.
3. American Battle Monuments Commission. The World War II Honor Roll:
   James D. Sasser
   First Lieutenant, U.S. Army Air Forces
   O-813786
   412th Bomber Squadron, 95 Bomber Group, Heavy
   Entered the Service from: Tennessee

Died: July 19, 1944
Buried at: Plot F Row 2 Grave 28
Cambridge American Cemetery
Cambridge, England
Awards: Air Medal with 2 Oak Leaf Clusters

4. *Daily Herald*, August 5, 1944. The article read in part:

"1st Lt. James D. Sasser, pilot of a Flying Fortress, has been killed in a practice flight in England with his co-pilot, according to unofficial word received by his wife, Mrs. Fredrika Moore Sasser, Memphis, and his mother, Mrs. E. D. Sasser, 1811 24th Avenue, Gulfport.

"No details of his death are known other than a letter received by his wife from a member of his crew in England saying that he and his co-pilot were killed in a crash, or 'practice flight'. . . . "

"Lieutenant Sasser won his wings October 1, 1943, at Moody Field, Valdosta, Ga., and went overseas March 27, 1944. He received the Air Medal for meritorious achievement, and was recently promoted to first lieutenant and awarded two Oak Leaf Clusters to the Air Medal."

5. *Memphis Commercial Appeal*, August 7, 1944. Article excerpt:

"Lieut. James Douglas Sasser, a graduate of Southwestern and son of Mrs. E. D. Sasser of Gulfport, Miss., was killed in England on July 19, in an accident while on a test flight. Overseas since March he had taken part in 21 missions over the Continent in a B-17 Flying Fortress which he copiloted. He was 29."

Shattles, David Edward. Photo: *1942 Perkolator* p. 23.

1. War Memorial Plaque in Gregory War Memorial Chapel: Shattles, David (Gold Star) Navy
2. Summary of Mississippi War Casualties--Navy, Marine Corps, and Coast Guard (October 3, 1949). Reprinted in *Valor Remembered*, p. 193.
Killed in Action, Died of Wounds, or Lost Lives as Results of Operational Movements in War Zones.
Shattles, David Edward, Seaman 1c, USNR. Parents, Mr. and Mrs. David Solomon Shattles, RFD 2, Box 18-E, Pascagoula.
(Shattles's address on various documents was given as Ocean Springs, Daisy-Vestry, Ramsay Springs, Perkinston, and Pascagoula. Since the U. S. Navy gave his address as Pascagoula, that address was used in this work.)
3. The *Daily Herald*, January 7, 1944, reported Shattles missing in action.
4. The *Daily Herald* of February 5, 1944, contained a letter sent from Commander William J. Cookley to David Shattles's sister, Irma Lee (Shattles) David. In part the letter read:

"Your brother, David Edward Shattles, was a member of a naval gun crew on board an armed merchant vessel which was recently bombed and sunk in foreign waters. I regret that military secrecy, prevents me from giving you the name of the ship and the time and place at which the disaster occurred. Inasmuch as no survivors have been reported as yet, it is believed that all on board perished. . . . "

5. The *Stone County Enterprise*, Thursday, December 2, 1948.The article stated that Shattles's body would arrive in Pascagoula the next day with the funeral slated for Saturday with "Rev. Boone of Moss Point Methodist Church officiating." The article noted that Shattles held the Atlantic Theatre of War Ribbon with two battle stars and the Pacific Theatre of War Ribbon with two battle stars. According to the article, "He was a gunner on an ammunition ship and was 'missing in action' in an encounter with the Germans at Bari, Italy, in which all aboard the *USS Harvey* perished on December 3, 1943. His body was later found where it drifted ashore. He was 22 years old."
6. In response to the *Sun Herald* Memorial Day (May 28, 2001) article asking for information concerning the MGCCC war dead, Bobbie Tolar of Pascagoula e-mailed Kat Bergeron at the *Sun Herald* that Shattles's tombstone in the Griffin Cemetery in Moss Point read, "David Edward Shattles, Naval Reserve Seaman 1st Class, Combat, December 3, 1943." Tolar sent the e-mail at the request of John Lynn of Moss Point, Shattles's nephew.

Sletten, Glen Edward. Photo: *1939 Perkolator* p. 37

1. War Memorial Plaque in Gregory War Memorial Chapel: Sletten, Glen (Gold Star) Army
2. The Honor List of Dead and Missing of the Military Personnel for the State Of Mississippi in World War II (U. S. Army). Reprinted in *Valor Remembered*, p. 72: Harrison County--Sletten, Glen E./14075911/SSG/Killed in Action
3. The *Dixie Guide* newspaper, August 1943, carried a photo of Sletten with the news that he had been a gunner and radio operator on duty "somewhere over the Southwest Pacific area" when killed in action on July 11, 1943. He left a wife and baby.
4. In a letter dated May 1, 1989, James P. "Jim" Estes (HSJJC Class of 1940) in response to a query from Alumni Association Secretary Louise Brown stated: "Glen Sletten: An enlisted man in the Army Air Corps, he died when the bomber on which he was a crewman was shot down over New Guinea on its first combat mission."
5. According to information delivered to the MGCCC Archivist on March 12, 2002, by Mitchell Cirlot of Ocean Springs, Sletten was first buried at Port Moresby, New Guinea; secondly in Ipswich Army Air Corps Cemetery, Brisbane, Australia; and lastly, on March 3, 1948, in Gulfport's Evergreen Cemetery (Block 42, Lot 18, Space 2). Sletten was a Staff Sergeant serving in the 64th Bomb Squadron, 43rd Bomb Group.

Stallings, Marjorie Lucille. Photo: *1937 Perkolator* p. 36.

1. War Memorial Plaque in Gregory War Memorial Chapel: Stallings, Marjorie (Gold Star) Marines
2. Stallings was not placed on the U. S. Marine Corps casualty lists because she had not served 180 days at the time of her death.
3. The *Daily Herald*, Friday, July 9, 1945, carried an article declaring that Marjorie Stallings, "a statistician in Ordinance Personnel of the War Department, Washington, D.C., died of injuries received Thursday afternoon when she was thrown from a horse in a Washington Park. She was riding with her sister, Mrs. J[ames] Slater, when the horse became frightened and threw her. She received a head injury and died about four hours later without regaining consciousness." Stallings had recently been inducted into the U. S. Marine Corps and was slated for officer's training at Hunter College, New York.
4. The *Daily Herald*, July 13, 1943, reported that at her funeral the day before that "as a member of the Marine Corps the casket was draped with an American flag." She was buried in Evergreen Cemetery in Gulfport in Block 10, Lot 7, Space 3.

Stribling, William Bradley Jr. Photo: *1941 Perkolator* p. 75. [U.S. Naval Reserve Serial No. 263790]

1. War Memorial Plaque in Gregory War Memorial Chapel: Stribling, Bradley (His name was not starred in 2000) Navy
2. Summary of Mississippi War Casualties--Navy, Marine Corps, and Coast Guard (October 3, 1949). Reprinted in *Valor Remembered*, p. 206.
Non Combat Dead, Stribling, William Bradley Jr., Lieutenant (jg), USNR. Mother, Mrs. Nancy Vida Stribling, 1520 Kelly St., Gulfport.
3. *Daily Herald*, May 8, 1943. The article carried a photo of Stribling in flight gear and read in part:

"William Bradley Stribling Jr. . . recently graduated from the Naval Air Training Center, Corpus Christi, and was commissioned an Ensign in the Naval Reserve. Ensign Stribling, former student of Perkinston Junior College, volunteered for flight training last June and received preliminary flight instruction at the New Orleans Naval Air Station."

4. *Daily Herald*, February 2, 1944. The article stated that "Ensign Bradley Stribling, Naval Air Corps pilot, is stationed at Kingsville, Texas."
5. Undated newspaper article probably *Daily Herald* accompanied by a photo of Stribling in a U.S. Navy dress uniform. (Enola Broussard of Biloxi cut nearly 1,000 articles from the *Daily Herald* related to Coast men and women serving in World War II, and did not put a date on any of them.) Three different researchers, including the archivist, failed to find the undated article in the *Daily Herald*. The obituary read:

   "Lieutenant (JG) William Bradley Stribling [was] killed May 12 when his F6F crashed off the New England coast.

   "Bradley, 23, received his wings at Corpus Christi, Texas, in April, 1943. He was stationed at Kingsville, Texas, until November when he went to Sanford, Fla. He also received training at Longview, Tex., Chicago, Grossesse Ille, Mich., and Atlantic City before going to Groten, Conn., for operational training prior to being assigned sea duty. Simultaneous memorial services were held for him at the first Presbyterian Church, Gulfport, and at the Naval Chapel, Groten, Conn."

   (If he was in Kingsville, Texas, in February, 1944, (see previous article) and the article above says he remained there until "November," then he must have crashed on May 12, 1945. The First Presbyterian Church had no record of the memorial services for Stribling, but the church archives contained records on all military memorial services conducted in World War II. One might wonder why Stribling, a Methodist, would have been memorialized at a Presbyterian Church. Three calls to the "Naval Chapel, Groten, Conn." bore no fruit.)
6. A letter sent to each Stribling family residing on the Mississippi Gulf Coast in 2001 resulted in the archivist obtaining the phone number of Webb Stribling, brother of Bradley Stribling, then living in Madison. He said he was only a youngster when his brother died, and he did not remember the date. He did, however, remember how his brother died. He was practicing landing on a carrier. His body was not recovered.
7. Webb Stribling gave the archivist the phone number of another brother, Arris, then living in Larkspur, California. On May 1, 2001, the archivist phoned Arris Stribling and learned that he had been an officer in the Army Air Corps stationed in Alaska at the time of Bradley's death. Arris was given leave in 1945 to fly to Gulfport for the memorial service which was held in the Methodist (not Presbyterian) Church in Gulfport. Arris said he was told that Bradley had died in a carrier crash.
8. Mitchell Cirlot of Ocean Springs received a letter from the Department of the Navy dated February 4, 2002, stating that, "Lt.(jg) Stribling was the pilot of the second plane to take off from the *U.S.S. Card* for day qualification landings [May 12, 1945] and the take off was normal in all respects. This plane was then observed to enter a normal carrier approach until on the cross leg where the approach became low. The pilot continued the low approach until almost in the groove where the plane struck the water, left wing first, broke in half, aft of the cockpit and sank with the pilot. The plane guard destroyer escort arrived at the scene of the crash in less than a minute but could find no trace of pilot or plane. Extensive search by destroyer escort and aircraft failed to locate pilot's body. Observers on the destroyer escort plane guard stated that the pilot appeared to be leaning over in the cockpit during his approach as his head was not visible above the cockpit combing. It is the opinion of the trouble board that Lt.(jg) Stribling leaning over making some cockpit adjustment inadvertently eased forward on the stick and was not aware of the dangerous loss of altitude which resulted in the crash."
9. At the time of the crash the *U.S. S. Card* (CVE-11) was conducting carrier training off Quonset Point, Rhode Island. For some unknown reason Stribling's name was not included in the U.S. Navy's missing list. Cirlot announced his intention to ask the Navy to correct that oversight.

Taylor, Jack. Photo: *1940 Perkolator* p. 28.

1. War Memorial Plaque in Gregory War Memorial Chapel: Taylor, Jack (Gold Star) Navy
2. Taylor was not listed in *Valor Remembered* because he was from Alabama.
3. Letter dated May 1, 1989, from James P. "Jim" Estes (HSJAHS class of 1940) posted from Deadwood, Oregon. Excerpt follows:

   "Jack Taylor: A navy pilot, he died in or near New Orleans some time in late 1941 or early '42 when he was instructing and a student froze at the controls and crashed their training plane."
4. Letter received in response to questions by the archivist dated January 16, 2001, from Estes postmarked Deadwood. Excerpt follows: "I can't give you much more information on Jack Taylor. He died in a crash at the New Orleans naval air facility, which I believe was at Moisant Airport, and was buried in a cemetery in Mobile. I don't know which one but I'm sure it was a Protestant cemetery. . . . I've been trying to pinpoint dates from where I was living at the time, but it's a long time ago. I know it was before I went into the Navy, which was in October '42. . . ."
5. City of Mobile Archivist Jay Higginbotham notified the MGCCC Archivist on March 5, 2001, of the following: "Ensign Jack Taylor was born 1920 or 1921, died May 20, 1942, and was buried in lot 33 of section 17 in Pinecrest Cemetery in Mobile."
6. *Times Picayune*, Thursday, May 21, 1942, "Two are killed as Naval Plane Crashed in Yard--Instructor and Pilot Die After Training Ship Falls in Metairie." Taylor and student pilot Richard Eugene Hillman of Warren, Ohio, were fatally injured when their training plane crashed at 2 p.m., May 20, 1942. Both were taken from the crash site in the yard of Dr. and Mrs. Alec Brown on Metairie Road to LaGarde General Hospital. Hillman died at 5:34 p.m. and Taylor died at 5:50 p.m.

Wood, Leslie Arthur. Photo: *1938 Perkolator* p. 31.

1. War Memorial Plaque in Gregory War Memorial Chapel: Wood, Arthur (Gold Star) RAF (An error. He served in the Royal Canadian Air Force--RCAF)
2. The *1944 Perkolator* "In Memoriam" list contained the name of "Arthur Wood, '36-'38. (ANZAC), Puerto Castilla, Honduras, C(entral) A(merica)." He entered HSJAHS as a high school senior in fall 1937 giving his name as "L. Arthur Wood" of Puerto Castilla, Honduras. Later the registrar at Perkinston crossed out "Puerto Castilla" and wrote above it "Progresso." By telephone on August 4, 2000, James Palencia (HSJAHS class of 1939) avowed that he was from Puerto Castilla and so were Arthur and Frazer Wood and that his father and their father worked for United Fruit Company. Both Arthur and Frazer entered Perk together. Both gave out that their previous high school work had been taken at Queen's Park School, Scotland. Both graduated with honors from HSJAHS on July 3, 1938. Why anyone at Perkinston thought Arthur joined the Australia New Zealand Army Corps (ANZAC) is beyond this author's ability to comprehend, but that was what was written in the 1944 "In Memoriam" list. To complicate matters more someone else at Perkinston decided that Arthur Wood died in the Royal Air Force because that was placed under his name on the War Memorial Plaque in the War Memorial Chapel. Thus began a lengthy correspondence with the British Commonwealth War Graves Commission which finally bore fruit by means of a letter sent by that commission to the archivist dated May 27, 1998. Judith Donald of the Enquires Section regretted that while she could find no ANZAC or RAF connection, she had on a whim decided to check the lists of the Royal Canadian Air Force and found the following:
   Casualty: Pilot Officer LESLIE ARTHUR WOOD, J/17041
   Served With: 410 Sqdn. Royal Canadian Air Force
   Died: 18th July 1943
   Commemorated: DIEPPE CANADIAN WAR CEMETERY Seine-Maritime, France, Row H., Grave 58.

   So after having been sent halfway around the world by a mistake in the *1944 Perkolator* and then sent an eighth of the way around the globe by a second mistake on the War Memorial Plaque, a lucky hit by a British researcher finally located Wood. He fought with the RCAF and died in the "Canadian dress rehearsal for the Normandy Invasion"--the Dieppe Raid.

Gregory War Memorial Chapel: A History

The idea of erecting an interdenominational chapel as a memorial to Perkinston alumni serving in the armed services during World War II was first publicly announced on May 29, 1943, during graduation exercises. On that occasion Lee Roy "Sonny" Weeks Jr., president of the junior college graduating class, informed the assemblage that he and his classmates would present to the college a fund for that purpose. A fund-raising committee composed of three faculty members, four alumni, and three members of the 1943 graduating class, one of whom was Weeks, had already been formed. All funds were to be kept in war bonds until needed for actual construction.

By October 13, 1943, the committee had raised $205.52, and on that day the Board of Trustees agreed to grant $1,000 in matching funds as soon as the first $1,000 was raised. Simultaneously the PJC Alumni Association announced that the usual 1943 Alumni Association homecoming activities would be cancelled in favor of a fund-raising campaign for the chapel. Since junior college football had been cancelled for the 1943 season, homecoming would not have been "usual" anyway.

By graduation day, May 25, 1944, the $1,000 mark had been reached, and the Board matched it. By homecoming day, November 3, 1944, the funds held were in excess of $2,000. The game against Copiah-Lincoln that night was dedicated to the "Perkinston War Memorial Chapel."

On December 20, 1944, the Board authorized the purchase of a "War Memorial Plaque" to contain the name and military branch of every known former Perkinston student, staff member, or administrator serving the nation. This plaque was to be displayed in the hall of Denson Administration Building until such time as the War Memorial Chapel could be constructed after the end of the war.

By February 1945, the chapel fund contained $4,000, and Mathematics Department Chairman William G. Gregory had taken over as chairman of the fund-raising committee. On homecoming day, October 19, 1945, the third homecoming in a row dedicated to the chapel fund, Gregory and others stationed themselves at the War Memorial Plaque in Denson Hall to take additional names.

The Second World War formally ended with the Japanese surrender on September 2, 1945, and veterans soon swelled the enrollment at Perkinston. The graduation program published for May 29, 1946, carried notification that the War Memorial Plaque would be expanded "to include our present and future World War II veterans." At that time the chapel fund held $4,554.82 with the promise by the Board to match a third thousand.

The college authorities dedicated homecoming day, October 26, 1946, to those students who had given their lives in the war effort. On the War Memorial Plaque in Denson Hall, gold stars had been affixed to the nameplates of the 23 students and one faculty member known to have died.

Lee Roy "Sonny" Weeks Jr.

Lee Roy Weeks Jr., son of Coach Lee Roy Weeks and dietician Anna Weeks, as president of the junior college graduating class, made the first public call for a War Memorial Chapel at graduation on May 29, 1943. Scarcely two years later on May 23, 1945, Weeks was awarded the Silver Star "For gallantry in action near Matina, Mindanao, Philippine Islands." The citation read: "During an infantry company's attack about 1400 yards north of Matina, it became necessary to secure a hill on the right side of the road to protect the gains of the day's advance. At 1800, the task was assigned to First Lieutenant Weeks, knowing that the morale and physical endurance of his men were low from weeks of arduous fighting, he realized that only aggressive personal leadership could enable his men to secure the vital hill. Exchanging position with the first scout, he led his men in a flanking movement to the rear of the enemy, crawling slowly over approximately 200 yards of ground, taking full advantage of the cover and concealment available. From that position, First Lieutenant Weeks, shouting encouragements to his men leaped to his feet and led his platoon in a charge across the exposed hill top, a distance of 30 yards. The attack was launched so suddenly that three of the enemy were killed and at least twelve others fled from their spider holes and trenches. First Lieutenant Weeks immediately set about the reorganization of the position, and although his men had to work in darkness they dug in and held the position through the night. First Lieutenant Weeks, by his outstanding leadership and courage, transformed his platoon from a group of weary men into a closely knit and efficient fighting force and was the determining factor in the success of a most important mission." A few weeks later Weeks earned the nickname "Banzai" because, according to the Stone County Enterprise, August 16, 1945, "He out Banzaied the Japs." On that occasion in Davao Sector, Mindanao, Philippine Islands, he took command of his company when his company commander was wounded and led an attack against Japanese positions taking two machine guns and killing 14 of the enemy. Photo from 1943 Perkolator p. 23.

Mathematics Department Chairman William G. Gregory as he appeared in 1937. Gregory, a native of Pondville, Tennessee, was born in 1891. He earned his bachelor's degree at Bethel College in Russellville, Kentucky, and his master's degree at George Peabody College in Nashville, Tennessee. Gregory taught at Perk from September 1926, until July 17, 1957. He died October 11, 1967, in Campbellsville, Kentucky, and was buried in the Sulfur Springs Cemetery near Russellville, Kentucky. After a 14-year courtship he married the former Ina Mae Hart, who had begun teaching business and commercial subjects at Perk in September 1928. The couple had one child--Ina Sue. Photo courtesy of Hazel (Bridge) Necaise.

On April 23, 1947, President A. L. May reported to the Board concerning the possibility of securing an "Army Chapel located at the Army Air Base at Gulfport to be used as the War Memorial Chapel." Gulfport Field, like many other World War II bases, had been decommissioned, and the base accoutrements, including structures, had been declared surplus property.

President May and four other members of the War Memorial Chapel Committee including the chairman, W. G. Gregory, traveled to Gulfport Field and chose the particular chapel they wished removed to the campus. The Board minutes of May 21, 1947, contained the following:

"On motion by A. F. Megehee and seconded by C. E. Dees, Jr., the purchase of Chapel building No. T-3101 located at the Gulfport Army Air Field, Gulfport, Mississippi at $1,250 was unanimously authorized and the President of the College

(From left) Perkinston Junior College President A. L. May, English instructor Frances Harrell, Baptist Student Union representative Dorothy (Geiger) Stevens, YWCA and Wesley Foundation representative Reba (Moffett) Counselman, and Mathematics Department Chairman W. G. Gregory. The five members of the War Memorial Chapel Committee, of which Gregory was chairman, stand at one corner of U. S. Army Chapel Building No. T3101 located at Gulfport Field sometime between April 24 and May 20, 1947. The photograph was snapped on the day they chose the chapel as the one to be removed to Perkinston to serve as the institution's War Memorial Chapel. Photo courtesy of Reba (Moffett) Counselman.

and the President of the Board of Trustees were authorized to sign the necessary documents and agreement of purchase for the chapel."

On July 23, 1947, the Board advertised for bids for "the dismantling, transferring and reerecting of Chapel Building T-3101 . . . together with such heating system, plumbing system, electrical wiring and fixtures and toilet facilities that may be attached hereto. . . ." The *Stone County Enterprise* reporter who covered this meeting said that the chapel purchased from the War Assets Administration would be a war memorial "honoring" those who served and "dedicated to those who lost their lives in service."

Harrell Construction Company of Biloxi, the only bidder by the closing date of August 20, submitted a bid of $8,889.99 for the job. The Board rejected the bid by unanimous vote on September 17. On that same day the Board put a cap of $5,000 on dismantling and reerection of the structure. The Board hired N. E. Bell to supervise the work.

At a cost of $300 the elements of the dismantled chapel were transported to Perkinston in early October. The site chosen for its erection lay among four other military structures in the course of erection following their purchase as surplus property from the Gulfport Navy Base (Seabee Base). The "military Perk addition," of which the chapel became the focal point, was located west of or behind Harrison Hall and Fahnestock Hall.

The *Bulldog Barks*, November 26, 1947, noted that the War Memorial Chapel was fast nearing completion and predicted that it would be finished in January. The *Bulldog Barks* further stated that "plans for brick-veneering the building have been set aside for the present, though this will be done in the future. Asbestos shingles will now form the outer covering."

By January 21, 1948, the $3,455.44 raised by the chapel committee since 1943 and the $3,000 given by the Board in matching funds had been spent, and the project was $222.98 in the hole. Therefore, the Board ordered work suspended "until further arrangements can be made for financing the construction."

As work on the chapel languished, the students raised money through baseball game gate receipts and through such novel contests as a "Donkey Basketball Game" in the Old Gym, but those efforts fell short. At last on July 21, 1948, the Board authorized President May to purchase the materials necessary for completion of the inside of the War Memorial Chapel with the "work to be done by the wood manufacturing class of the college." As W. D. Smith's students finished the inside, agriculture instructors James V. Gammage and Milton D. Blakeney directed landscaping for

The War Memorial Chapel being reassembled at Perkinston circa spring 1948. The temporary shed in front of the Chapel is the storage place for tools and furniture. Photo from *1948 Perkolator, p. 119.*

the chapel using equipment loaned by Stone County.

On September 22, 1948, the Board authorized May to "put the roof on the Chapel using the corrugated sheet metal on hand." On November 17, the Board matched $500 raised by the Chapel committee. That final $1,000 did the job. The Board inspected the War Memorial Chapel on February 23, 1949.

Dedication services were set for Sunday evening, March 6, 1949, at 7:30 p.m. Dr. J. N. Brown, pastor of the First Presbyterian Church of Gulfport, delivered the dedicatory address. A *Daily Herald* reporter described the 400-person capacity chapel as "well filled." The War Memorial Plaque, which had been removed to the chapel from its former location in Denson Hall, was flanked by the national and state flags. According to the *Stone County Enterprise*, special seats had been reserved for "Gold Star fathers and mothers and families" in attendance since the chapel was being dedicated to the dead.

The War Memorial Chapel rapidly became the center of campus religious life. In addition to an auditorium, the chapel contained two rooms flanking the foyer and two rooms behind the stage. One of these became a Catholic altar room, and the other three served as offices for the Baptist Student Union, the Newman (Catholic) Club, and the Wesley (Methodist) Foundation. These religious organizations held services each morning at 7:45 on a weekly rotation basis. The War Memorial Chapel also served as the site of YMCA and YWCA initiations, Christmas choir concerts, Easter Sunrise Services, and weddings.

On July 17, 1957, W. G. Gregory resigned after 31 years as a mathematics instructor, and the following May his wife joined him in retirement. On April 20, 1960, the Board, in recognition of his efforts to raise the funds to build the chapel, ordered the structure renamed "Gregory Chapel" and dedicated as such on May 14.

Throughout 1964, Lillian Hayden, wife of then MGCJC President J. J. Hayden, supervised the Christian Council members in renovating the interior of the chapel. The sanctuary was repainted, the altar redecorated, new pews were installed, and acoustical tile was placed in the ceiling. On December 6, 1964, the Gregorys and their daughter were present at the re-dedication ceremonies of the refurbished Gregory Chapel.

At homecoming 1995 the MGCCC Alumni Association announced a fund raising effort to restore the, by then decrepit, Gregory Chapel. At that same time Alumni Association officials formally merged the two former names for the structure designating it as "Gregory War Memorial Chapel." By 1997 Reba (Moffett) Counselman, who had been a member of the committee which had selected the chapel at Gulfport Field fifty years before, was a member of the committee charged with saving it from the ravages of time.

(Left) W.G. Gregory presides over a meeting of the Baptist Student Union Executive Council in school session 1952-53. The War Memorial Plaque is visible in the background. The names of 718 persons associated with the Perkinston institution who served or died in World War II are enshrined on the War Memorial Plaque. Photo from 1953 Perkolator, p. 102.

Members of the Baptist Student Union are seated on the original military pews inside the War Memorial Chapel circa 1958. Photo from 1958 Perkolator p. 53.

(Right) MGCJC President J. J. Hayden (rear) poses with the Gregory family on December 6, 1964, at the reception following the re-dedication of Gregory Chapel after its first renovation. (From left) Ina Mae (Hart) Gregory, W. G. Gregory, and Ina Sue Gregory. The chapel which had been first named War Memorial Chapel had been renamed Gregory Chapel on April 20, 1960. At homecoming, 1995, the chapel was renamed Gregory War Memorial Chapel.

Gregory War Memorial Chapel Weddings

Kathy Strickland and Wentz Batson Jr.
June 2, 1973

(Left to right), Bill Kuzmitz, Melanie (Batson) Kuzmitz, Wentz Batson Sr., Kathy Ladner, Dan Batson, Marge Batson, Wentz Batson Jr., Kathy (Strickland) Batson.
May 12, 1979

Don Rawls and Thelma Brechtel
August 13, 1966

Dave Brockmeyer Sr. and Elaine (Alexander) Stephens
January 18, 1997

GLIMPSES AND VIGNETTES 1912 - 2000

Harrison-Stone-Agricultural High School Yellow Jackets Estelle "Bill" David (left) and Irene Flurry pose in their basketball bloomer uniforms at the front door of Huff Hall in session 1924-1925.

For Whom the Bells Tolled (A Tale of Three Bells)

Most denizens of educational institutions for hundreds of years marched to the sound of a bell defining the divisions of a student's day. In more recent times ear-jangling, raucous buzzers came into use. The auditory assault of the hateful buzzer and the interminable "Voice of Perkinston" announcements which followed, blessedly ended in June 1991, when Rita Spreitler, the last "Voice of Perkinston" departed. The same year, the system broke for the umpteenth time, and nobody wanted to fix it. After that, everyone was ordered to synchronize on Bank of Wiggins time. Sure, some teachers of 2000 held classes beyond the allotted time, but they did that when the buzzers buzzed, too. But real bells once ruled at Perkinston, and for the generations that once thrilled to their bong and clatter, they remained auditory artifacts imbued with love and affection.

Among the treasures on display in the Alumni House at Perkinston in 2000 was a large hand-held school bell. In fact, it was about as large as any person of normal strength would wish to wield, and certainly its rattle was as loud as any normal ringer could stand. Its provenance as the original bell of the Harrison County Agricultural High School in 1912 rested on nothing more than a strong tradition for being such. It was old enough to be such and loud enough to be such, but whether it is or not is a matter of faith. According to Margurite (Callahan) Boswell, that bell was certainly in use in the mid-1920s as a dinner bell before the Posey Howell Dinner Bell arrived circa 1927. In a letter she sent to the MGCCC Archives on October 23, 2000, two days after homecoming, she stated, "When I walked into the Alumni [House], the first thing that caught my eye was the hand bell. Many times, at noon I saw the dietician come out [of Stone Hall dining room] and ring that bell. She had to hold it with both hands to ring it."

The hand-held bell is 12 inches high with a diameter of 7 inches at it's widest.

Both of the other historic bells were heavy and large and were (or are) mounted on the campus on brick pedestals. The shift in verb tense is necessary because one of the bells was still on the Perkinston Campus in 2000 and the other one was not.

THE BENNETT/HUFF BELL from circa 1913 to circa 1969

Photo courtesy of Walter Atchison.

The 1923 Harrison-Stone Agricultural High School football team simulates action on the campus for an advertising brochure. Huff Hall (right) is the boy's dormitory. Bennett Hall (rear) is the administration building. The wire fence behind the team is there to keep out woods cows, which wandered the campus at least as late as 1972. William Albert "Ship Island" Frantzen is standing tall behind the football. In an interview in 1996 he recalled that the cupola or "little rat roost," as he termed it, on top of 1913-era Bennett Hall held a bell. It was not there long, he said, because the boys would pass under it inside the building, reach up and cut the bell rope with pocketknives so no one could ring it. This bell was eventually moved to a pedestal between Huff and Bennett. As the first large bell permanently affixed on the campus, it was likely the same one later mounted on a pedestal by the steps at the lower end of Huff Hall. In any case, the Huff Hall bell remained in place from at least 1936, when the school's first yearbook pictured it there, until at least 1969, when it appeared in a yearbook photo for the last time.

(Left) the Huff Hall bell is visible at the south end of the building ca. 1966. (Below) An unknown student stands next to the Huff Hall bell in 1948.

The Bulldog rings the Huff Hall bell in the 1949 Perkolator.

Wilton "Red" Brown (AHS summer class of 1945 and PJC student in session 1945-1946), one of a long line of bell ringers, recalled that, "I was paid $6 a month to ring that bell. I got out five minutes early from each class to signal when classes would begin and end."

THE HOWELL DINNER BELL from circa 1927 - 2000

(See arrow, right) The Howell Dinner Bell is visible in the front of Stone Hall ca. 1936 in the school's first yearbook (Perkolator). The lower level of Stone Hall was the dining hall for the school from 1915 to 1948. The students entered the dining hall through the arbor on the south end of the building. The students exited through the doors in the middle of the lower level near the location of the bell in this photo.

(*Below right*), Perkinston Superintendent Jefferson Lee Denson stands next to the Howell Dinner Bell circa 1927. (*Below left*), Posey N. Howell of Howison, a forester for Dantzler Lumber Company and a member of the college Board of Trustees, removed the bell from a lumber company locomotive in 1927 and donated it to the school as a dinner bell. As a forester, Howell deplored the Piney Woods tradition of "burning the woods off" to improve cattle grazing because the practice killed the young pines. The bell came with a metal plate (visible in photo) bearing an inscription designed to persuade Perkinston's rural students to influence their families to stop forest fires. The metal plate which has disappeared, carried this inscription:

Posey N. Howell Photo from Mississippi Today (1928), p. 120.

Superintendent Jefferson Lee Denson photo courtesy Noby Ruth (Denson) Houston.

Donated to the Best School in Mississippi
By P. N. Howell

Unless the woods quit burning, this dinner bell will quit ringing. There will be no dinner to ring for.
Fires injure the range, impoverish the government, destroy bird eggs, run the game away, kill young timber.
Make a country and people poor.
Young folks of today will be grown folks of the future.
Young trees of today will be grown trees of the future.
They need you---you will need them.
Forest Protection is an economic necessity
Do your part in this patriotic duty.

Charles L. Sullivan (left), MGCCC archivist, and Margurite (Callahan) Boswell, stand by the Posey Howell Dinner Bell on homecoming day October 21, 2000, in a re-enactment of Boswell's photo of 70 years prior. The bell stands on a pedestal in the Perkinston Agricultural High School Commemorative Bell Garden, but in 1930 it stood on another pedestal in front of Stone Hall. The former site is visible in the extreme upper left of the photograph beyond the outside stairs on the front of Stone Hall. Dees Hall is in the background.

Maggie McManus (left) of Gulfport and Margurite (Callahan) Boswell of Philadelphia stand by the Posey Howell Dinner Bell in 1930 waiting for "Ma Fannie" (Dietician Jane Fahnestock) to ring it. The bell stands on a brick pedestal near the front door of Stone Hall (then called "Girls" Dormitory No. 2 and Dining Hall"). The front of Jackson Hall (Boy's Dormitory No. 2) is visible at left. The facade of Denson Hall (Administration Building) is at the far right. Photo courtesy of Margurite (Callahan) Boswell.

The Posey Howell Dinner Bell (left) was moved to a pedestal behind Harrison Hall near the front of the new Cafeteria and Classroom Building when it opened in 1948 and was used until September1950, when it was replaced with electric bells. When the Cafeteria and Classroom Building burned on January 25, 1958 the old Stone Hall Dining Room was reactivated until Heidelberg Hall could be completed. The bell (below), remained in place for decades until removed for storage.

On April 11, 1997, Sam Tucker (PJC Class of 1941) and Sarajane (Edwards) Smith (AHS Class of 1962) unveil the Howell Dinner Bell in the Perkinston Agricultural High School Commemorative Bell Garden in the middle of the Perkinston Campus Quadrangle.

In summation, it would seem that the hand-held bell “tolled” Perksters when to eat, perhaps from the beginning of the school until the Posey Howell Dinner Bell arrived circa 1927. The Posey Howell Dinner Bell "tolled" Perksters when to eat from 1927 to 1950. The Bennett/Huff Bell apparently "tolled" them when to go to class from 1913 to 1950. At least this was what the archivist had been told about the tolling of bells by December 31, 2000.

From Perkolator to Trident: The Yearbook Through the Years

From 1936 through 1965 the yearbook bore the name *Perkolator* with the exception of 1961 when it bore the name *This is Perk*. The 1966 *Perkolator* was the first to serve the new tri-campus district, but the photos of the students were grouped separately by campus. Both the 1967 and the 1968 *J(unior) C(ollege) D(istrict) Perkolators*, as they were called, carried the photos of the students of all three campuses intermixed. The 1969 yearbook, which was divided into three campus sections, bore a new name, *Gulf Trident*, and carried Neptune's trident as its logo. The 1970 *Trident* followed the pattern of its predecessor, but each campus section was given a new name--*Perkolator* (for Perk), *Beauvoir* (for JD), and *Beachcomber* (for JC). The next four yearbooks continued in that vein. In 1975 the college published its yearbook in three separate volumes--*Trident: Perkolator*, *Trident: Beauvoir*, and *Trident: Phases*. The name of the JC yearbook changed because Terry (Price) Fountain, the JC yearbook sponsor, felt that JC was too far from the beach to have a yearbook called *Beachcomber*. She let the JC students vote, and they selected as the new name--*Phases (*meaning that their time at JC was one of the "phases" of life). The three volumes united into one volume in 1988 and then split again in to three until 2000 when they reunited yet again. In that year the names *Perkolator, Beauvoir*, and *Phases* disappeared, leaving the name *Trident* as the only designation for the MGCCC yearbook.

The title page of the first Perkolator (1936) and the cover of the 1969 Gulf Trident, the first yearbook to bear the name Trident. The title page of the first Perkolator reads "THE PERKOLATOR, Published by the Students of HARRISON-STONE-JACKSON, Agricultural High School and Junior College, With the Kind Support and Co-operation of the FACULTY, Perkinston, Mississippi, 1936."

The 1988 Trident was published as one volume in three sections--Perkolator, Beauvoir, and Phases.

Photos by Richard Kopp

From 1975 through 1999, with the exception of 1988, the yearbooks were published in three volumes, bearing the titles Trident: Perkolator, Trident: Beauvoir, and Trident: Phases.

Hazing and Hell Week

The discipline section of the *1931-1932 Catalog* contained the following admonition for the first time: "No form of hazing will be allowed." The discipline section of the *1932-1933 Catalog* contained the same prohibition, but the statement disappeared from subsequent publications. Apparently hazing of freshmen began at that point. The pre-game homecoming parade on October 28, 1933, featured freshmen in pajamas.

The 1936 Perkolator, the school's first yearbook, contained a drawing (left) by Freda Stuart showing a freshman with a recently shaved head wearing a "Perk" shirt and carrying a skullcap or "beanie."

(Right) Freshman in a "P" beanie at study. Photo from 1942 Perkolator, p. 32.

Subsequent *Perkolators* for more than three decades carried photos of freshmen with shaved heads with and without beanies. Oddly dressed freshmen and freshwomen were depicted bowing to their sophomore betters, and beginning in World War II, they were shown having "hit the dirt" (below) at the cry "Air Raid." The words "Air Raid" were written under the pictures.

(Below) "Air Raid" Photograph from 1943 Perkolator.

By 1944 the fall freshmen ordeal bore the name "Hell Week" and that culminated in "Hell Day." But, according to Wilton "Red" Brown of Wewahitchka, Florida, the hell lasted far longer than a week in fall 1944:

Freshmen in suits which have been turned inside out and backward pose in front of Bennett Hall in fall 1944. Photo courtesy of Wilton "Red" Brown.

"The boys dressed as women one day and the next day we wore our suits wrong side out and backward. The girls also had to dress very crazy. They had to wear their skirts upside down and backward and also the blouses. They had to wear a stocking over their heads and wear tennis shoes and socks. All this went on for weeks. This was after we had been initiated and had our heads shaved in various and sundry fashions and my particular style was that they left a rim right around my head just above my ears, shaved the rest of my head and in the process cut it nine times. We were supposed to leave our heads just as they left them for at least three days before we went anywhere to have it taken care of. Of course, all I could do was have the rest of mine shaved off and being football players most of us found it pretty rough for the next two to three weeks, wearing those helmets with shaved heads, especially with the kind of helmets we had back then."

A campus reporter gave his impression of "Hell Week" in the October 15, 1944, *Bulldog Barks*:

"The freshman, that lowest species of animal life in the college student body, bore the brunt of sophomore sadistic wit.

"Some of the 'sights' on the campus were men dressed as women, maidens strolling about in business suits and tennis shoes, and barefoot boys dressed in pajamas. The Perk girls may not have been in the height of style with dresses slightly above the knee, but all the boys sure greatly appreciated this leg art. In fact, we heard from a very reliable source that some boys until now were uncertain that a woman's leg extended above the knee. The theory that clothes make the man was open to doubt with our freshman boys wearing dresses. It was no more ridiculous however, than the teenage rage of wearing brother's pants and shirt."

Freshmen dressed as women pose on the campus in 1944. Photo from 1945 Perkolator, p. 54.

Three pigtailed freshwomen in "above the knee" attire. Photograph from 1946 Perkolator, p. 30.

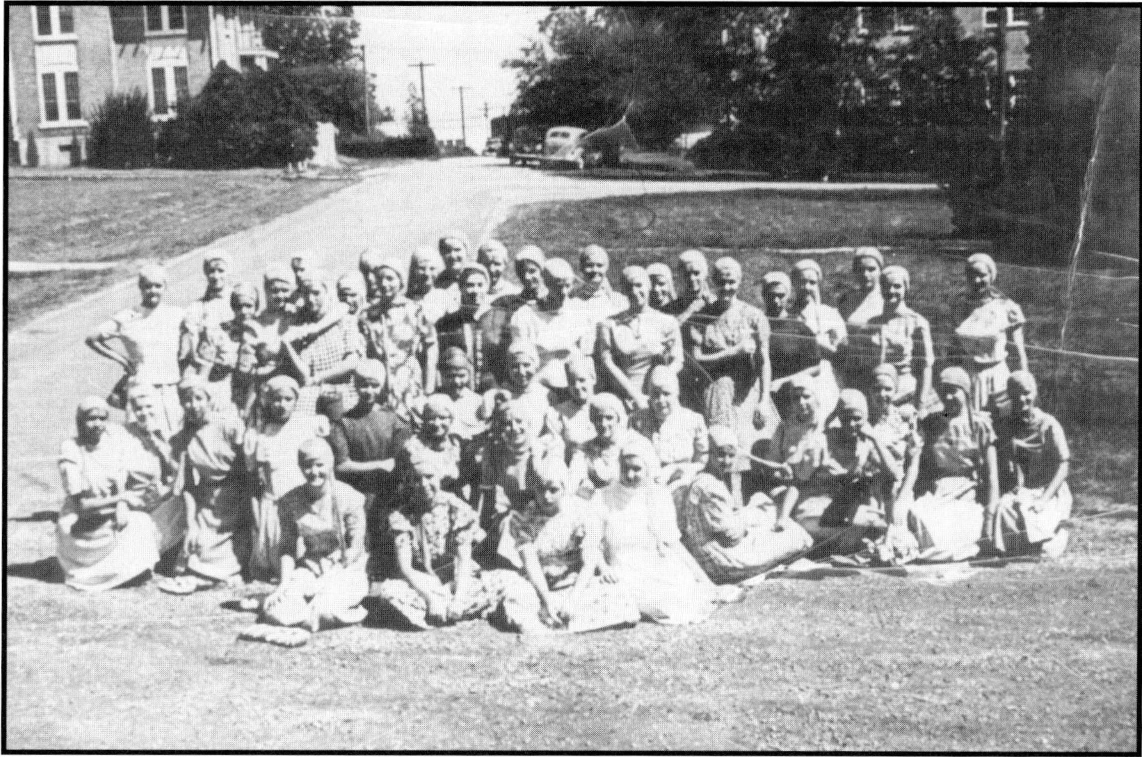

"Freshwomen," their clothing turned inside out and backward, pose with stockings on their heads in front of Harrison Hall in fall 1944. Jackson Hall is at the left in the background, and Old Denson Hall is at right. Photograph courtesy of Emogene Rainey.

Hell Day 1952 fell on September 29. The day began with freshmen carrying their meal tickets to the cafeteria in trunks. At each meal freshmen were required to wait table for the sophomores and serenade them while they ate. All freshmen were required to attend a special dance at the Old Gym during which any sophomore present could yell "Air Raid," and all freshmen had to hit the floor. The festivities ended with sophomores tying all freshmen's shoes together indiscriminately, heaping them in a large pile, and then ordering a charge on the pile by all freshmen to retrieve his or her footwear.

Photographs in the *Perkolator* showing the shenanigans of Hell Week began to lessen in the mid-1960s. Such images disappeared altogether in session 1968-1969. According to former Perkinston Campus Vice President Clyde Strickland, "Increasing roughness and the fact that sophomores were throwing freshman into the swimming pool after hours finally led to a halt in hazing altogether."

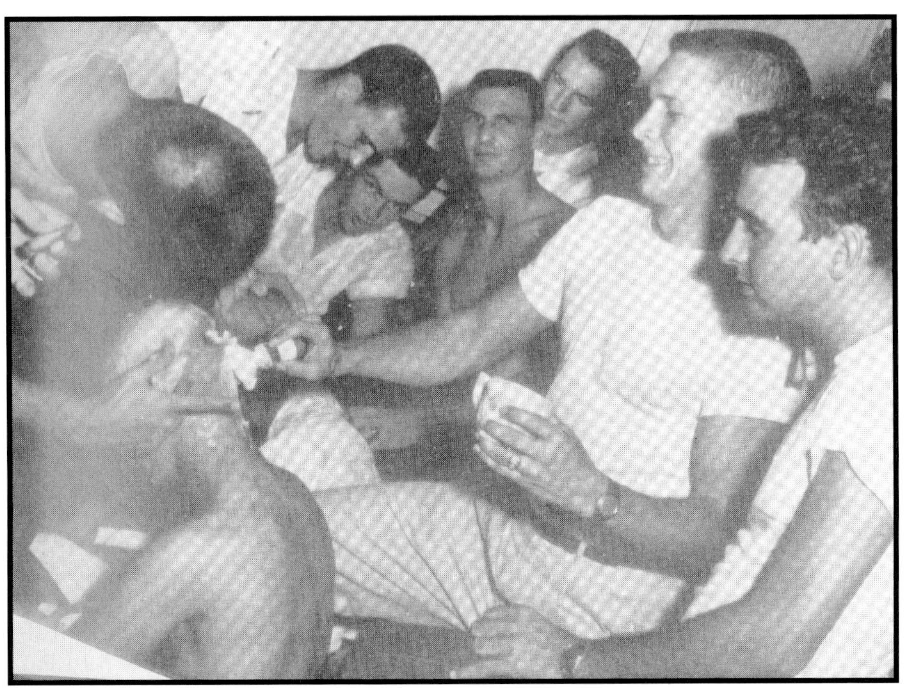

A freshman loses his hair to "barber-ous" sophomores in 1957. Photograph from 1958 Perkolator, p. 9.

The Bulldog Barks, October 3, 1963, noted that the sophomores had launched a campaign of cranial carving to advertise the school. The freshmen from each dormitory would be allowed to keep some of their hair. Only the portion necessary to spell "Perkinston" would be removed. Ten of these lucky men kneel outside Darby Hall with President J. J. Hayden standing behind them.

Red Creek: Perkinston's Playground

Red Creek remained a favorite gathering place for Perk students throughout the 20th century. (Above) Tenting and boating on Red Creek as depicted in the 1913-1914 Catalogue. Since that document was distributed in August 1913, the photograph was taken during the school's first session (1912-1913).

The old U.S. Highway 49 bridge over Red Creek one mile from the campus was a favorite site of campus picnics until the building of the new Red Creek bridge nearer the school about 1937. Photograph from Illinois Central System Farm and Factory Magazine (December 1929), p. 15. The picnickers in the photo are likely students from "Little Perk" or Wiggins.

By May 1984 Perk coeds wore bikinis on Red Creek, and men are present in the pictures.

(Right) Perk coeds pose on Red Creek in bathing suits and shorts circa 1938. Photograph from 1939 Perkolator, p. 54. Such attire was not permitted on campus at the time, and no men are in the picture.

Perkinston students on Red Creek in a photo published in a college brochure circa 1986.

Men Working

Perk students build a dairy barn for the school in October 1927. Photograph courtesy of Sherry Dillard of Dixie Press in Gulfport.

Three student workers pull "kitchen police" duty in the Stone Hall kitchen annex circa 1945. This kitchen annex, which began service on September 5, 1927, was razed circa 1969.

Perk students shear sheep in the barnyard circa 1943. Photo from 1944 Perkolator, p. 42.

(From left), student worker Dempsey Blackwell, student worker Posey Brown, and campus engineer Grady Blackwell (all of Perkinston) take a break on the campus maintenance truck circa 1936. The Blackwell men were brothers. The building at left is Bennett Hall. The building at right down the hill is Jackson Hall. Photograph courtesy of Hazel (Bridge) Necaise.

Home Economics and Agriculture

At first, home economics at Perk was the special province of women. That changed. (Above) Six women (all of Perkinston) show off their canning skills on the front steps of Bennett Hall circa 1929. (At left, from bottom up the steps) Bertie Blackwell, Archie Lindsey, and Sarah Jane Lindsey. (At right, from top down the steps) Cleo Garner, Alvena Rath, and Ruby Lee O'Neal. Photograph courtesy of Tom Brown.

Circa 1980, Kenneth Rafferty of Pass Christian puts a pan of biscuits into the oven in the Megehee Home Economics Building while Jeff Bell of Gulfport holds open the oven door. Both were enrolled in a single living class.

At first, agriculture at Perk was the special province of men. That changed. (Right), Perk students dehorn cattle in the barnyard in 1943. Photograph from 1944 Perkolator, p. 42.

By 1972, two of the officers of the Agriculture Club at Perk were women. The officers are (from left) Bill Breland, treasurer; Kim Casano, historian; JoAnn Guiffria, vice-president; and Barry Lack, president. Photograph from 1973 Perkolator, p. 83.

"Home of the World's Most Delicious Hamburger" or "McDonald's" of Perkinston

Dew Drop Inn

Frigidaire System

Cold Drinks, Sandwiches and Cigars
Fancy Groceries

W. D. McDONALD, Proprietor

Perkinston Mississippi

(Above left) Max Telhiard of Biloxi, Dolores McHenry of McHenry, and Frank Gruich of Biloxi stand in front of Bond's Campus Edge in December 1939. The establishment, variously known as Mack's Corner, the Dew Drop Inn, Bond's Campus Edge, and Reid's Café stood across the Illinois Central Railroad tracks from the campus and near the Old Athletic Field. Old U. S. Highway 49, which made a hairpin turn to the south just west (or right) of the store, had been rendered "old" in 1937 by the opening of "new" U. S. Highway 49, which bypassed Perkinston on the east side. Under its several names the establishment was the main gathering place for Perk students from the mid-1920s until the 1950s. Numerous former students who had frequented the place described it to this author as "the home of the world's most delicious hamburger." Photographs courtesy of Dolores (McHenry) Mauldin. Advertisement from February 10, 1930 Perkolator newspaper.

Perk--A Leader in Reforestation

The Gulfport Commercial Union championed the establishment of the institution at Perkinston in 1910 in order to train farmers to grow truck crops on cutover pine lands. That idea was doomed from the start because piney woods soil was not suitable for such crops. At last in early 1930 the leaders of south Mississippi and the U.S. government realized that piney woods soil was remarkably suited for growing pine trees. The U.S. government chose the Harrison-Stone-Jackson Agricultural High School and Junior College as the site for Mississippi's first Federal Forestry Nursery. Perkinston Agriculture Department Chairman E. B. Colmer and his students began preparing the site for a nursery to grow both pine and hardwood seedlings on the school farm in February 1930. Within a year the nursery had produced 130,000 slash pine seedlings and 20,000 black locust seedlings in addition to other varieties. The pine seedlings were sold at $1.50 per thousand and shipped by rail to all parts of the state. One of the first shipments was a donation of seedlings sent by the school to Jackson for planting on the New Capitol grounds. Colmer left Perk to take charge of the Agriculture Department at Mississippi Agricultural and Mechanical College at Starkville in September 1935, but he stayed in contact with his successors at Perk and aided them in their tree farming efforts. During the 1930s the school supplied hundreds of thousands of pine seedlings to Civilian Conservation Corps (CCC) Camps and individual landowners who reforested thousands of acres of cutover lands. The later pulpwood, post, and pole industries of the state owed much to Perk's efforts.

Perkinston women engage in the log sawing contest held on the afternoon of Saturday, November 2, 1940, as part of the inaugural DeSoto National Forest Day. Dean E. B. Colmer, who rarely left his work at Mississippi State College, broke precedent to travel to Perk to deliver the keynote address at the celebration. Photograph from 1941 Perkolator, p. 84.

PJC forestry instructor Randle Dedeaux teaches a class on the campus circa 1955. Dedeaux taught forestry at the school from September 1949 to May 1958. The forestry course was offered intermittently throughout the balance of the 20th century.

Dean of Women Julia (Brown) Slay

Julia (Brown) Slay painting.

The Board of Trustees employed Julia (Brown) Slay as dean of women on April 1, 1931, and she remained in that position until her retirement in May 1950. Harrison Hall, which opened in November 1937, became her special domain. This author interviewed a number of her former charges. They remembered her as fair but firm, and without exception they recalled her famous "light test." The light was a spotlight of sorts plugged into the wall to one side of her desk. Foye (Dear) Bycofski (PJC Class of 1945) explained how the test worked:

"I remember that whenever we had a formal dance, we had to pass a "light test" for Mrs. Slay in her office to be sure no one could see through our dress. Of course, as far as I can remember, long slips were not available unless someone had one made. So the person who had one would 'loan' it to everyone. One girl would put it on (half slip)--go in Mrs. Slay's office--come out--take it off and hand it to the next girl in line. We were really not trying to be deceptive--we just had no choice.

"I remember my two years at Perk being really good--the students and the faculty were wonderful."

On March 1, 1951, Slay returned to Perk for a special assembly during which former Harrison-Stone-Jackson Junior College Superintendent Cooper J. Darby presented an oil painting of her to the school. The 25-inch by 30-inch painting in a gold leaf frame, commissioned by Perk instructors Mr. and Mrs. W. G. Gregory, was placed on the wall of the Harrison Hall lobby in Slay's honor.

At some point after Harrison Hall became a men's dormitory in 1982, the painting wound up in a closet. Slay's grandson, Wilton "Red" Brown, a summer 1945 graduate of Perk AHS and a Perkinston Junior College student in session 1945-1946, returned to the campus in 1994 and found the then damaged painting in the closet. He took the painting to his home in Panama City, Florida, and had it professionally cleaned and restored. In response to repeated entreaties by the MGCCC archivist, who had not known of the existence of the painting, much less of its mistreatment, Brown returned the painting to the care of the MGCCC Archives. Since 1995 the Slay painting has been accorded a place of honor in each successive homecoming archives exhibit.

The Star Dust Ball of 1940

The Star Dust Ball court is gathered for the Star Dust Ball in the Old Gym on Saturday night, March 9, 1940. The Swing Barons played for the dance. (From left) Maid Dolores McHenry of McHenry, Maid Bessie Clark of Gulfport, Maid Mattie Lou Lyons of Gulfport, Maid Helen James of Gulfport, Maid Doris Rush of Laurel, Maid Madeline Kuljis of Biloxi, Campus King Ruby Johnson of Pensacola, Florida, Campus Queen Marjorie Ann Moore of Biloxi, Duke E. O. Cunningham of Kansas, Alabama, Duke George Wilson of Sheffield, Alabama, Duke Stewart Trautman of Gulfport, Duke Melvin Kenneth of Greenwood, Duke Elwood Collins of Biloxi, and Duke Ewell Singleton of Gulfport. Photograph courtesy of Bobby Underwood and Dolores (McHenry) Mauldin.

PeRkInStON 1946-1947

A Memoir by Willie Eloise (Goff) Rouse

Willie Eloise (Goff) Rouse sits beside the tennis court at Perk in 1947. Photograph courtesy of Willie Eloise (Goff) Rouse.

In response to a request by the archivist through *Action* (Alumni Magazine) for the unvarnished truth about student life, Willie Eloise (Goff) Rouse wrote:

"I enrolled as a sophomore at Perkinston Junior College in the fall of 1946 and graduated in May 1947. My freshman year was completed at Graceland College, Lamoni, Iowa, and upon entering Perkinston Jr. College, I had a bright concept of college life. This concept changed within a couple of weeks. The contrast between the two colleges was unbelievable. At Graceland there was good rapport between administrators and students, but "Perk" seemed to have a negative atmosphere.

"Many students didn't share my opinion of Perkinston Jr. College. Perhaps I could have accepted the rules and regulations, had I never attended Graceland, but having done so, I knew there was a better way. Academically, I believe Perkinston had a good curriculum, though on campus girls were discriminated against, and I was not comfortable with that fact. To give up so many freedoms really vexed me.

"I don't remember all the handbook rules, but by the time I had learned them I had already broken a few. Girls were not allowed on campus (out of dorms) after the lights came on. Girls were not allowed to use the library at night. To attend any of the few campus activities at night, everyone was required to go in a huge group that was chaperoned by a faculty member or members. Girls were not permitted to leave campus during the day. Girls must have written permission from parent or guardian before going home for the weekend; the note had to state when, where, and with whom, otherwise there was no leaving campus. Also sitting on the little bridge over the campus lake was not allowed. Girls were not allowed to wear shorts or long pants except to tennis courts and to some physical education classes. . . .

"Perk campus equipped me with some valuable experiences. I didn't realize, at the time, that being a victim of discrimination, being deprived and scrutinized and by living in an environment similar to a prison, put me in a position to maybe understand how minorities feel. . . .

"Fifty-one years have passed and today I look back at Perkinston Junior College remembering my many friends, and laugh at those silly rules and wonder who made them."

The conditions described by Willie Eloise (Goff) Rouse continued throughout the 1950s. Choir Director Eugene Clement (right) and Sam Jones take a break in the Cafeteria and Classroom Building in 1952. Clement had been on the job for three years and Jones had just arrived. They still "had it all before them." In his retirement interview in May 1986, Clement created a "word picture" of the 1950s era.

"Those were the days of dress codes and strict social behavior. The young men wore dress pants and shirts--and even ties--to class. The women had to wear dresses or skirts and blouses. Why, the men and women weren't allowed to sit on the benches and hold hands. When the sun went down and the outside lights came on, the women had to go into the dormitory not to come out again that evening."

When an evening choir practice was scheduled, Clement said he would go to the women's dorm, line up the choir members, check them out one by one, and march single file to practice. After practice, they were marched back to the dorm and checked in.

"In fact, the students used to take every other letter except one out of the name Perkinston and they would have P-R-I-S-O-N. And that's almost what it was like in those days when the sun went down."

Clement said that in the earlier days there was no need for a discipline committee. Instructors and dorm supervisors handled their own discipline problems.

"I don't recall what kind of punishment the women had, but the men would have to dig up stumps. There were a lot of big tree stumps on campus. The student was given a shovel and an axe and a certain amount of time to get the stump out of the ground. When you saw a fellow digging a stump, you knew he had done something real bad 'cause that was the most severe punishment one could get--other than being sent home. But one thing for sure, it gave him plenty of time to think about what he had done. Most all disciplinary action was in the form of work."

Perk and Fire Fighting

The 1952-1953 Perkinston Junior College Volunteer Fire Department poses with its hose "buggies," axes, and fire extinguishers on the front steps of Old Denson Hall. (From left bottom row) Kerby Ladner of Saucier, Vern Humble of Mobile, Alabama, Eddie Pucheu of Gulfport, Kade Anderson of Panama City, Florida, Elizabeth Jackson of Alexander City, Alabama, Mayo Hans of Pascagoula, Orin Bailey of Pensacola, Florida, and Russ Hackman of Biloxi. Second row (from left) James Bounds of Brooklyn, Paul James of Pass Christian, Albert Crowder of Gulfport, Ralph Coronas of San Jose, Costa Rica, Marion Walker of Gulfport, Luther Conn of Gulfport, and William Whitley of Biloxi. Third row (from left) President A. L. May, Robert Strickler of Pascagoula, John L. Walker of Lucedale, Jack Albritton of Lucedale, and Dean of Students J. J. Hayden. Fourth row (from left) Business Manager L. A. Krohn, Orease Ladner of Perkinston, and Joe Gregg of Taylorsville. Photograph from 1953 Perkolator, p. 107.

Ten days after the December 7, 1941, Japanese attack on Pearl Harbor, President A. L. May ordered student fire-fighting squads organized at Perk as part of the college's Civil Defense program. The next year the school purchased from the Mississippi Surplus Property Commission a red LaFrance fire truck which the denizens of Perk promptly dubbed "Rusty." The student fire-fighting squads were disbanded at the close of World War II, and the Perk maintenance department became the college's fire-fighting unit.

In March 1952, the Board of Trustees purchased new hoses and other equipment for Rusty. In November, administration, instructors, and students combined to form the Perkinston Junior College Volunteer Fire Department. The members of this fire department were pictured in the *Perkolators* of 1953, 1954, and 1955 and then no more.

The volunteers certainly were not on duty in the pre-dawn hours of January 25, 1958, when Perk's greatest fire of the 20th century destroyed the Cafeteria and Classroom Building. Apparently Rusty did not show up either. In the absence of fire plugs the Gulfport pumper truck siphoned water out of the swimming pool for use in battling the blaze. The year after the Cafeteria and Classroom Building fire, the Board of Trustees ordered the installation of fireplugs.

Apparently Rusty continued to rust in a shed behind the Colmer Building until 1967 when Perkinston Campus Dean C. G. Odom decided to revive it. He had the truck upgraded from a six-cylinder engine to an eight-cylinder engine and upped the six-volt firing system to a twelve-volt firing system. According to Odom the reason for changing the firing system was "so you won't have to push it in order to start it." Odom also required faculty members to train on Rusty. This author was one of them, and he can tell you that most of the time Rusty did not crank even if it were pushed. Rusty did not pump water worth a flip, either.

By 1968 the Circle K Club members became campus volunteer firemen serving Rusty. That did not last long because the Circle K Club folded a year later. Rusty vanished sometime in the mid-1970s and was replaced by a newer fire truck, but the campus did not receive good fire protection until September 1989 with the establishment of the Perkinston Volunteer Fire Department. This last was a community fire department under chief Bob Carlin and assistant chief Ronnie Sims, which later raised the funds to construct a firehouse located a half-mile west of the campus.

Nancy Cluff (left) and Vicki Parker pose as firewomen beside Rusty in 1967. Photograph from the Bulldog Barks, October 14, 1967.

Circle K Club members man Rusty in 1968 while campus fire chief Willie Boy Rogers prepares to open the hood and try to crank the truck. Photograph from 1969 Perkolator, p. 53.

"Manless Weddings" and "Womanless Weddings"

(Above left, from left) A. L. May, Helen Davis of Vancleave, Jackie Voivedich of Ocean Springs, Juanita O'Neal of Saucier, Mereline O'Neal of Saucier, Helen Bond (best man) of Saucier, Carmen Tarzetti (groom) of DeLisle, Margaret Dantagnan (bride) of Bay St. Louis, Lorette Rouse of Saucier, Mary Zachow of Lyman, Dorothea Jacobs of Saucier, June Ward of Lucedale, Sybil Hamilton of Gulfport, and Billie Ruth Williams (minister) of Bond. (Above right), The wedding party exits Harrison Hall.

The "Manless Wedding" of Sunday, May 2, 1948, in the lobby of Harrison Hall featured PJC President A. L. May as father of the bride. All the other members of the bridal party were women.

According to the *Stone County Enterprise*, May 6, 1948, the women had been "selected by the YWCA with faculty approval, because of their qualities of character and leadership." The reporter hailed the event as "outstanding among the social events on Perkinston Junior College Campus of widespread interest in this section. . . ." At least 150 guests, many from out of town, attended the reception honoring the wedding party. The YWCA, which existed at Perk from 1924 to 1959, sponsored, by the 1940s, a manless wedding every second year.

The "Womanless Wedding" sponsored by the College Club on December 9, 1926, featured the Bulldog football team. When this author read the description of the wedding in the January 6, 1927, *Stone County Enterprise*, he concluded that the lack of photographs in this case might have been a blessing. Also, he found himself unable to imagine a re-enactment of this singular event by the 2000 Bulldog football team.

For the 1927 Bulldog wedding English instructor Minnie K. Pearson decorated the stage, which was dominated by a white and pink arch from the keystone of which hung a wedding bell. Under that bell, "Vernon Brown, the plunging fullback, became the beautiful bride of Albert Rexinger, the dashing halfback, and handsome groom." As the sweet strains of the wedding march filled the auditorium, James McManus, the weeping mother of the bride, was ushered in by two stalwart Bulldogs. Hersel McDaniel and his wife, Ogden Lott, the proud parents of the groom, were led in by two other footballers. Andrew Gray, well-dressed feminine soloist sang "O Sole Mio," and then Stanford "Cotton" Carraway, similarly attired, rendered, pathetically, "I Love You Truly." The procession moved to the stage lead by pink and black bedecked bridesmaids Carlton Sparks, Everett Davis, Grant Eighmey, and Harold Clendenin. The maid of honor, Posey Godard, was daintily attired in white chiffon. Coach Denson, the ring bearer, was dressed in white satin with a band of dainty white and pink ribbons accentuating his long curly hair. Next came flower girls, Newman "Runt" Warnell, who wore a dress of white georgette, and Sam Lott who wore pink georgette. The blushing bride in white satin trod on the petals of white and pink carnations as she leaned on the arm of her father, Herbert Gasby. Lemonade and cake was served after the ceremony. The newlyweds skipped the honeymoon.

Readers wishing to more fully visualize these unique nuptials are invited to refer to photographs of the 1925-1926 football team and the 1927-1928 football team located in the sports section of this work. Many members of the bridal party are pictured.

The Campus Grill

Coeds in the college grill in 1943. One former student of that era remembered her time at Perk as "the loneliest of her life" because "most of the men were away at war." The grill pictured at left was located on the ground floor of Old Denson Hall and served from circa 1936 through December 1947. Photograph courtesy of Gertrude Sandrock, who wrote on the back, "Mrs. Russum and Frank Russum [are behind] the snack bar."

According to the caption of this photograph from the 1952 Perkolator, p.60, the students pictured are "Campusology Majors." This campus grill, which opened in January 1948, was dubbed the Snack Shack by popular vote in February 1952. The Snack Shack was located on the ground floor of Stone Hall and was fashioned from the 1915-1947 dining hall after food service began in the Cafeteria and Classroom Building. The jukebox in the photograph had virtually played out by May 11, 1955. According to the Bulldog Barks of that date:

"Students are wondering why something can't be done about the grill jukebox. For some time there was a problem concerned with keeping current hits on the machine. Now we have the songs but on a machine not in condition to play them. After putting money in the juke box, it is necessary for a student to jolt the machine to get proper results from a stuck record, thus losing half the playing time and effect of the song.

"We are wondering if it would be possible to have a new juke box in good playing condition which would also carry one hundred recordings instead of the small number our present jukebox holds. Since students spend so much money on the jukebox, aren't we entitled to more music played the way it should be played?"

Trains, Buses, and Automobiles

Perk students waiting for the train at the Perkinston Depot circa 1940. The Illinois Central Railway suspended passenger service between Gulfport and Jackson in 1950 thus ending 38 years of Perkinston student patronage of the line.

Two coeds disembark from a Trailways bus in front of Reid's Café in 1948, the year that Trailways named Reid's Café in downtown Perkinston an official bus stop. In the decade prior to 1948, students faced a half-mile trek to and from new U. S. Highway 49 in order to use the Trailways system. Photograph from 1949 Perkolator, p. 1932.

Day students had commuted to and from the campus in automobiles since the 1920s, but the initial statement related to dormitory students having cars on campus came in the *1936-1937 Catalogue*: "Students who have cars on the campus are not to use them at any time under any circumstances without special permission from the dean or superintendent. Any infraction of this regulation will forfeit the right to keep the car on the campus." That statement remained constant in all subsequent Cooper J. Darby-era catalogs.

The session *1941-1942 Catalog*, the first of the A. L. May era, contained the following terse statement: "Dormitory students are not permitted under any circumstances to keep automobiles on the campus."

In session *1942-1943 Catalog*, President A. L. May added four additional words to his automobile dictum: "or in the vicinity."

The influx of World War II veterans forced President May to reassess his anti-student-automobile stance. The Session *1946-1947 Catalog* stated that, "Dormitory students 20 years and older may be allowed the use of automobiles, but the use will be restricted."

In session 1949-1950 "will be restricted" gave way to "may be restricted." That statement remained in subsequent catalogues until session 1961-1962 after which it vanished.

Nothing more was said about automobiles until in the *1964-1965 Student Handbook*, which contained the statement that, "Students are permitted to have automobiles on the campus for their personal use." Each car had to be registered and registration stickers placed on the windshield. Other than that the main restrictions were that speed limits had to be obeyed and "absolutely no student cars will be moved on the campus after 10:30 p.m." The equal rights amendment erased that last dictum in session 1975-1976. By 2000, finding a parking place on any MGCCC campus during main class hours was a major problem.

Perk students pose with an automobile in front of Harrison Hall circa 1938. Photograph from 1939 Perkolator, p. 54.

Sonny Walker of Pascagoula and Jimmy Jeffries of Gulfport are parked in front of the Old Denson building prior to cruising the campus during session 1960-61. Photo from 1961 Perkolator, p. 63.

Campus Radio Stations--Station WPJC and Station WJDC

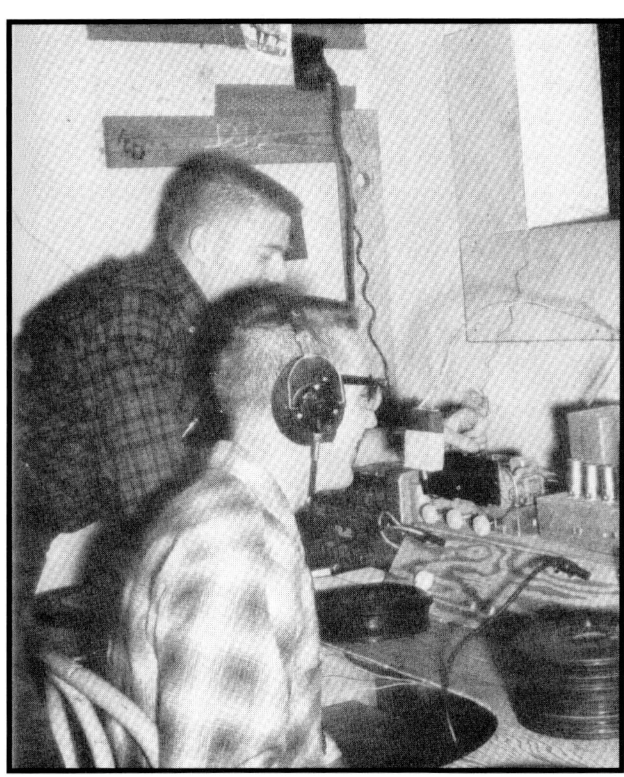

In early 1946 (from left) engineer Jerry Martin and disc jockey P. E. McIntosh spin the platters in Radio Station WPJC operating out of Old Denson Hall. The one milliwatt station broadcasted to receivers within a three-mile radius of Perkinston. Photograph from 1964 Perkolator, p. 65.

Jefferson Davis Campus radio broadcasting instructor Douglas Hendon instructs a fledgling JD DJ in the techniques of her craft. Hendon began a 25-year career at JD in 1967.

The 1991 WJDC broadcast crew included (front, from left) Ken Spelman, Elizabeth White, and Tol Wright. (Back from left) Tom Jones, Dawn Moore, Greg Weems, Steve Galle, and Kyle Curley. WJDC served the JD Campus until its demise circa 1992. Crew photograph from 1992 Beauvoir, p. 8.

The "Old West Florida" Magnolia Marker

On March 21, 1954, the area in the Perkinston quadrangle in front of the Old Denson Building became the site of the dedication of the "Old West Florida" Mississippi magnolia marker. (From left) Eminent Mississippi historians James K. Bettersworth and Cyril E. Cain stand with former history teacher then Perkinston Junior College President J. J. Hayden. After the dedication the marker was removed to a spot on U. S. Highway 49 two miles south of Black Creek Bridge where it stood for 40 years before it vanished.

Television Comes to Perk

Students watch television during session 1956-1957. Photograph from 1957 Perkolator, p. 56. The Daily Herald, October 16, 1952, noted that a television set had been installed in the grill, which was then located on the ground floor of Stone Hall. The same article likewise noted that the P Club had its own television set in the "P" Clubroom in the new dormitory (later named George Hall). On October 10, 1973, the Bulldog Barks noted that color televisions had been ordered for the lobbies of Owen, Moran, and Jackson Halls.

The Miss Junior College District Beauty Contest

Diane Griffin

Terry Price

Margo Ross

Dorothy Wilson

The third event (after homecoming and graduation) to reach tri-campus status was the Miss Junior College District Beauty Pageant. The *Bulldog Barks*, November 18, 1966, carried notice that the annual staff of each campus would jointly sponsor the contest in January 1967, and the winner would be eligible to compete in the Miss Mississippi pageant in Vicksburg the following July. On January 28, five coeds from Perk, and five from JC, and four from JD vied for Miss JCD honors in Biloxi High School auditorium. Dorothy Wilson, a JC student from Ocean Springs was named the District's first queen. JD contestant Diane Griffin of Vancleave was named first runner up. Terry Price and Margo Ross, both JC students from Ocean Springs, were named respectively second and third alternates. The Miss JCD Pageant, renamed the Miss Mississippi Gulf Coast Junior College Pageant after the word "District" fell from favor after 1969, continued until the retirement of Perkinston Campus Dean of Student Services Ed Scarborough in December 1984. According to Scarborough, his successor decided to eliminate the pageant on the Perkinston Campus, and after that JD and JC eliminated it as well. Photographs from *1967 Perkolator*, pps. 13 and 14.

Jackson County Campus Faculty Cheerleaders

(Left) On November 11, 1967, the Jackson County faculty cheerleading squad fires up the denizens of "Gautier Tech" on the eve of the annual pigskin brawl with Pearl River. (From left) Speech instructor Bruce Fisher, physical education instructor Vivian Burkett, social studies instructor Bill Ruddiman, and science department chairman Robert Hollingsworth. (Above) Another view of the same squad this time with the names reading from right. MGCJC triumphed over the "River Rats" the next day for the first time in 17 years. Some attributed that singular 33-0 victory to Bulldog fighting spirit aroused by JC's inspiring demonstration of martial spirit. Photographs from 1967 Perkolator, pps. 144 and 172.

Jackson County Campus MASH Unit

A Licensed Practical Nurse (LPN) class awaits the teacher in Jackson County Campus Building D circa 1971. The cardboard boxes visible at the rear of the photo contain a full Mobile Army Surgical Hospital (MASH) unit. When JC opened in September 1965 the U. S. Civil Defense Department designated the campus as an official fallout shelter. The eventual fate of the MASH unit equipment was not known to this author in 2000.

Liberty, Equality, and the Voice of Perk

The harsh rules governing student conduct numbered 55 in 1936. A student strike resulted in a number of them being rescinded, but as one striker recalled, "So many were left, it really didn't change a thing." In 1945 the students staged another strike. The 1945 strike was triggered by the impending expulsion of a couple who, according to striker Wilton "Red" Brown, had done "little more than holding hands." The administration placed the couple on probation and the crisis passed.

Liberty Leading the People by Eugene Delacroix.

One Thursday night in spring 1971, the students staged a mini-revolution to protest the virtual cloistering of the women on the campus. The revolutionaries poured the powder from several shotgun shells into a tomato can, sealed the can with paraffin, fused it, stuck a burning cigarette on the fuse, and set the bomb in the no man's land between Owen and Moran Halls. At 11 p.m.--"KA-BOOM!" All the teachers and administrators who lived on campus (which was most all of them in those days) and security guards went to the sound of the blast. As they milled about, a man's voice burst from the loudspeakers on the nearest campus light pole setting forth demands for longer dating hours for women. The Dean of Student Services looked at the pole and told a nearby history teacher that he was going to climb the pole and cut the wire to the speaker.

Suddenly the sky lit up in the vicinity of the duck pond, and all the administrators, teachers, and security guards ran to the pond. The revolutionaries had poured a can of gasoline in the pond and set it on fire--an action not appreciated by a number of ducks which were quacking and running about.

The loudspeaker on the pole by the pond carried the same message as the one by the dorms. The Dean of Student Services said, "I guess I'll have to climb two poles." The history teacher replied, "I don't think the tape recorders are on the poles. I think somehow they got into the Dees Building and what we are hearing is coming from the Voice of Perkinston."

The "Voice of Perkinston" consisted of a microphone by means of which an announcer could sit at a desk and reach the inhabitants of Perkinston in every classroom and dormitory and even reach pedestrians on campus by means of speakers on the light poles. The Executive Dean's house, which was on campus, also received all Voice of Perkinston announcements.

The Dean of Student Services said, "Well, there is no way they could have gotten in the Dees building so they must have recorders attached to the poles." Then he proceeded to climb a pole.

The history teacher said to a nearby security guard, "We ought to go up to Dees and check it out anyway." Off they went. When the two arrived at Dees and entered the Voice of Perkinston inner sanctum--there it was. A recorder had been set up to speak endlessly into the microphone, the control button of which had been taped to open position.

The security guard reached under the table, jerked an electric cord out of the socket, and the tape recorder went dead. Then the guard, who was exhausted, leaned over the microphone and said slowly and with great feeling, "We ought to take every one of these little *&%#@ out in the woods, tie 'em to trees and beat 'em with *&%#@ chains."

To this the history teacher who was likewise leaning over the microphone rejoined, "But just look at how they handled it. It was marvelous. They set off a bomb to make us go to one section of the campus while they penetrated the Voice of Perkinston nerve center. The flaming duck pond took us still further away from Dees. Gee Whiz--They must have been listening to my lectures on revolutionary tactics. I always envied vo-tech teachers because they actually get to see their students do what they teach them."

The security guard did not share the history teacher's assessment and was still leaning over the microphone muttering expletives when the telephone rang. The security guard picked up the phone, jumped to attention and said, "Yes, sir! Yes, sir! Yes, sir!" He hung up the phone, fell to his knees, reached up under the table, and that time he jerked the microphone cord out of the socket.

Oh well! For the rest of the semester that security guard tried to avoid the students. The history teacher tried to avoid all administrators.

The stipulations of Title IX of the U. S. Educational Amendments Act of 1972, requiring equal rights for men and women, were effected on Perkinston Campus in spring 1975. Instead of women having to come in at 10 p.m., they (and men as well) were locked out at 11 p.m. Now, that was a real revolution.

Tri-Campus R.O.T.C.

Six months after the outbreak of the Korean War, PJC President A. L. May issued a public call for a Reserve Officer Training Corps unit at Perkinston. The *Daily Herald*, December 19, 1950, quoted May as saying, "Only through getting an educated military force can we gain final victory." May carried his appeal to the Mississippi Association of Colleges meeting in Jackson in March 1951 but to no avail.

The first Perkinston ROTC unit poses on the outside stairs of Denson Hall. Bottom row (from left) Instructor Captain Thomas Raines, Cindy Guild, Eltroy Howell, Terry Armstrong, Mike Bialas, Steve Slyfield, Joey Guiffria, and Richard Blais. Second row (from left up the stairs) Donna Cantrell, Sheree Miller, Jackie Coludrovich, Don Wells, Bob Sawyer, and Bobby Dungan. Third row (by the stairs) Dennis Ladner, Willie Mosely, Wade Ivey, Dwight Holloway, and Bob Firth. Photograph from 1974 Perkolator, p. 81.

Twenty-two years later in September 1973, ROTC came to Perk. By means of a cross enrollment agreement signed by Perkinston Campus Executive Dean C. G. Odom and University of Southern Mississippi President William D. McCain, USM ROTC personnel administered the program at Perk. The ROTC unit formed at Perk was not the first in a Mississippi junior college, but it was the first to admit women. Under the terms of the agreement a student at Perk could earn the scholarships and pay offered by the program for two years and then transfer into the advanced program at USM as a junior.

In fall 1974 both Jackson County Campus and Jefferson Davis Campus joined Perk in offering ROTC. The program ended at MGCJC in May 1988. According to former Jackson County Campus ROTC instructor Doug Mansfield, "In session 1987-1988 the training department of the U. S. Army transferred the administration of ROTC programs to the Department of Defense. Since the Department of Defense officials did not think junior colleges were sending enough ROTC recruits to senior colleges they shut down all ROTC units in all the nation's junior colleges that year. They did it as part of their cost-cutting program."

Jefferson Davis Campus men and women recruits pose with ROTC instructor Captain Tom Calloway in 1975. Photograph from 1976 Beauvoir, p. 49

Jackson County Campus men and women ROTC recruits salute their officer in 1983. Photograph from 1984 Phases, p. 72.

The Irrepressible Word Guild

Dr. Word Guild discos with students on Perk Campus in March 1979.

In the words of Dr. Bilbo Young, Mississippi's teacher licensing agent, Word Guild was the "most 'certificated' teacher in Mississippi." She boasted 13 master's degrees in such divergent fields as foreign languages, history, music, and speech pathology. She attended 14 colleges and universities in five countries on three continents. The countries were the United States, France, Spain, Mexico, and Columbia. In addition to her Ph.D. in foreign languages at the University of Southern Mississippi, she completed the course work for two other terminal degrees at the same institution. She began teaching at Perk in August 1964, and five years later she conducted her first international educational tour. According to Dean C. G. Odom, she, being independently wealthy, did not need her paychecks so she put several years worth of them in her desk drawer and nearly bankrupted the school when she finally cashed them. He had a word with her about that. And no one was ever more aptly named. One afternoon in 1974 this author decided to see how long Word would talk to a willing audience. He knew that her husband George always parked in the west Dees Hall parking lot, so he positioned himself between Word and George, and when she walked by the desk where he was sitting, he engaged her in conversation--no--he merely asked, "What's happening, Word?" At 4:30 she left to go tell George to wait a little longer. At 6 p.m. she went out and told him to wait a little longer still. At 8 p.m. George took her home. A mystery solved--Word would talk for five hours with George waiting for her. How long she would have gone on without him waiting remained a mystery that this author did not want to solve. Of course, it did not matter to George how long he waited because the moment he parked the truck, he switched off his hearing aid and went to sleep sitting behind the wheel. Actually, he kept his hearing aid switched off most of the time. In 1979 at the time the above picture was snapped, Word had been recently notified that she would have to retire at the end of the term because she had reached the then mandatory retirement age of 70. The scuttlebutt on the street at the time had it that she had actually reached retirement age at a somewhat earlier time having been born before birth certificates were filed. However, by 1979, she had surely reached 70 even according to the records she had given to the school. In one of her very few losing battles, she went after the state legislature too late to get a bill through to remove the mandatory retirement age, so she had to retire. Well, she sort of retired. Setting up shop at Phillips Junior College in Gulfport, she became an international educational tour director. After that she was as much in evidence at Perk as she had been before her "retirement." Her international exploits became legendary and her fame grew. When one of her tours was halted by Mexican policemen over some document irregularity of some sort, she somehow personally got to the vice president of Mexico, who, seeking solace from her verbal deluge, personally removed all obstacles to her departure. Word continued her tours almost to the time of her departure from this life on September 16, 1995, an "iron magnolia" to the end.

Jefferson Davis Campus: Scholar's Bowl Star

In the last decade of the 20th Century, JD Campus students compiled an enviable record in state junior/community college Scholar's Bowl competition sponsored by the University of Mississippi and won thousands of dollars in scholarships in the process.

The JD Campus record:

1990 - 2nd place State and 3rd place Regional
1991 - 1st place State and Regional
1993 - 2nd place State
1994 - 1st place Regional
1995 - 2nd place State and Regional
1996 - 1st place State and Regional
1997 - 1st place State and 2nd place Regional
1997 - 1st place State and 2nd place Regional
1998 - 1st place Regional
1999 - 1st place Regional

Homecoming Queens a Half-Century Apart

(Right) 1999 Perkinston Campus Homecoming Queen Irvette James stands in A. L. May Memorial Stadium with 1948 Perkinston Junior College Homecoming Queen Louise (Penton) Pearce. Penton was the last queen to be crowned on the Old Athletic Field. She was crowned November 6, 1948, before the largest homecoming crowd in Perkinston's history to that time as the Bulldogs triumphed over Pearl River 20-19 in the undefeated season which led to co-national championship status. (Above) Louise Penton of Gautier as PJC Homecoming Queen of 1948. Photograph from 1949 Perkolator, p. 120.

Lili Marlene

(Left) Pat Blake of Gulfport and Patricia Napier of Biloxi, voted "Most Fun to Be With" in 1958 sing "Lili Marlene," the most famous song in world history. Photograph from 1958 Perkolator, p. 84.

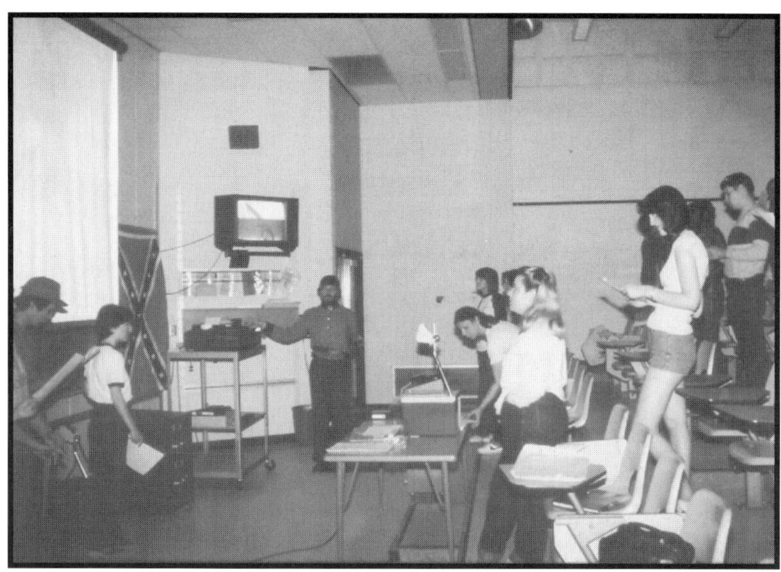

In May 1982 world history students in room 206 Dees Hall sing "Lili Marlene" during the Iron Cross ceremony following their final examination. During the last quarter of the 20th century thousands of Perk Campus history students, who became soldiers in the mythical nations of "Thermopylae" and "Barbarossa," sang this song as their "anthem" twice each semester.

Tri-Campus Harmony Oak

(Above) MGCJC President J.J. Hayden stands at the lectern during the August 6, 1977, Jefferson Davis Campus Harmony Oak Dedication ceremony. From right, JD Campus Dean of Student Services William Vierling, Board of Trustees member Eula Switzer, and (standing behind Switzer), JD Campus Executive Dean William P. Lipscomb. (Right) Hayden and Switzer hold the document dedicating the 300-year-old oak in the background as "Harmony Oak." Switzer, in addition to representing the college as a Trustee, also represented the Switzer family that had originally homesteaded the land where the oak stood. The Harmony Oak symbolized, according to Switzer, "the spirit of brotherhood [among] the three campuses of the junior college and residents who support them."

She came to Study and Returned to Teach

Natchez native Debra (Mize) Smith [later Matthews] enrolled as a student on a grant secured through Jean McCool's Displaced Homemakers Program at Jackson County Campus in 1979. She entered the industrial electricity program and finished with a 4.0 grade point average (that means straight As). She worked at Chevron from 1979 until November 1986 when she returned to JC to teach the courses she had taken seven years before. At the time she was the only woman industrial electrician instructor in the southeastern United States. She earned her Associate Degree of Applied Science in Occupational Education at JC in 1992 and had nearly completed her bachelor's degree in industrial education at the University of Southern Mississippi (JC Campus) when the century ended. In 1999, she was named JC Campus Instructor of the Year. In October 2000 she was named the recipient of the Mississippi Manufacturers Association Award for Excellence in Vocational Education. Matthews had arrived at JC as a 21-year-old divorced mother with no prospects. Her astonishing success was a textbook example of what a person determined to succeed could do with the resources made available by MGCCC and its Two-Plus-Two Program with USM.

Debra Smith at work as a troubleshooting mechanic at Chevron USA's Pascagoula refinery in February 1984. Photograph courtesy of Doug Mansfield.

Lucy Mae (Sumrall) Lee --56-Year Stopout

Lucy Mae Sumrall (fourth from left) stands with her HSJAHS sophomore classmates at Perkinston in 1937. Photograph from 1937 Perkolator, p. 36.

In the educational parlance of the 1990s, a dropout was a student who departed school never to return. A stopout was a student who left and returned later. Lucy Mae (Sumrall) Lee left Perk in 1937 and returned to continue her education in 1993, setting the institution's 20th century stopout record.

Lee was born on September 12, 1919, in three-year-old Stone County and grew up on the Sumrall place located off Sunflower Church Road east of Perkinston. In an interview conducted in 1996 she remembered, "I had to walk practically a mile to catch the school bus." She graduated from Perkinston Grammar School, then located by the railroad tracks in downtown Perkinston, on April 30, 1935. She then attended the Harrison-Stone-Jackson Agricultural High School up the hill. As she finished the 10th grade, her father died, so she went to Brooklyn to live with relatives. At Brooklyn she attended the 11th grade at Forrest County Agricultural High School, after which she married L. V. Lee and lived near Carnes. In Lee's words, "We had five children putting them through high school. Some through college. My youngest son, Randy, finished here at Mississippi Gulf Coast Community College. Anyhow, after I got them all raised . . . and my husband passed away . . . I decided I would come back and get my GED which was a lot of fun." So on November 7, 1993, in the MGCCC Literacy Program's first GED graduation ceremony, Lucy Mae (Sumrall) Lee received her high school diploma after a 56-year hiatus. After receiving her diploma Lee enrolled in the horticultural program. In the interview conducted by this author on January 6, 1996, Lee said, "I have had the most fun down here. This makes my third year I have been down here aggravating everybody. X. Earl McCoy [horticulture instructor] said they weren't going to let me quit--I was an inspiration to the kids." When asked if she intended to graduate from junior college, she said, 'No, I am just taking horticulture . . . [because] . . . I work with the kids at Ashe Nursery in Brooklyn. I carry them through the nature trail when they bring a group in there. Then I carry lunches out to the community center at Brooklyn every Tuesday. Some of the old people and others want food carried at lunch. I have about 40 head of cows to tend to."

Related Education Instructor Roxie Hatten embraces graduate Lucy Mae (Sumrall) Lee at the inaugural GED graduation ceremony in Malone Hall, November 7, 1993.

Lucy Mae (Sumrall) Lee (front row center) stands with her General Education Development (GED) fellow graduates outside Malone Hall at Perkinston on November 7, 1993. She holds a box containing a dozen long stemmed red roses.

The Vietnam Veterans Memorial Moving Wall and the Perkinston Campus Flagpole

Perkinston Campus Speech and Drama Instructor Daisha Walker (left) stands with Perkinston Campus Fine Arts Department Chairperson Kathryn Lewis in front of the Vietnam Memorial Moving Wall in April, 1996.

Lewis read in Parade Magazine that communities desiring to exhibit the Moving Wall should call for information about how to obtain it. She secured the Wall for Perkinston Campus for the week of April 6-12, 1996. The Wall was erected in the Quadrangle in front of Dees Hall.

An estimated 8,000 people visited the Wall while it was on the Perkinston Campus.

(Above) Visitors attending the flagpole dedication observe the 60 crosses bearing the names of those soldiers killed in Vietnam from Harrison, Stone, Jackson, and George counties. The crosses were erected on the site where the Vietnam Veterans Memorial Moving Wall had been located one year prior. (Right) Lieutenant Colonel (ret.) Dick E. Wilson, left, stands with Perkinston Campus Vice President Willis Lott at the Perkinston Campus flagpole on dedication day April 10, 1997. The plaque at the base of the flagpole reads:

THIS FLAGPOLE
erected in honor of the
students, faculty, staff, and administrators
of Perkinston Campus who have served the Nation
in the Armed Services.
Dedicated
April 10, 1997
on the Anniversary
of the
Emplacement at this site
of the
Vietnam Veterans Moving Wall

Ollie Reeves-Super Fan

Ollie Reeves walks the sideline in A.L. May Memorial stadium during a football game in the 1980s.

Ollie Reeves prepares to umpire the umpires from his position behind the wire at homeplate in Ken "Curly" Farris baseball field.

Ollie Reeves set the record as the most devoted fan of MGCCC baseball and football in the 20th century. One of 12 children (six boys and six girls), he was born May 9, 1902, and grew to manhood in George County. Together with his wife, the former Jeanette Flurry, Reeves moved to Perkinston in the early 1930s to take a job in reforestation with the L. N. Dantzler Lumber Company. In 35 and one half years of working for the company he missed one day and that was due to an injury.

At the same time Reeves began working for L. N. Dantzler, he began attending football and baseball games on the Old Athletic field. His record for attending Perk games rivaled that of his work attendance--he seldom missed. He attended the games for nearly 65 years.

In his time Reeves "coached" some 16 head football coaches, and he kept a far greater number of assistant football coaches (who were many times also baseball coaches) on the straight and narrow. He let the basketball coaches fend for themselves. In his words, "I never could make head nar tail outta that game."

Reeves was far more than a fan. He actually helped to keep the fields and stadium up to snuff--or rather up to chewing tobacco, which he used constantly. He stepped up his work commitment to the college after his retirement from L. N. Dantzler Lumber Company in the late 1960s. After the death of his wife in 1974, he became virtually a volunteer employee.

Ken "Curly" Farris, who coached football from 1962-1975 and baseball from 1963-1989, was Reeves's all-time favorite coach. Though he stopped coaching football following the 1975 season, when he became athletic director, Farris continued to line both the football field and the baseball field before every game. "Many times," remembered Farris, "Ollie would be at the field early in the morning waiting to help line the field." Reeves helped him coach, too. He made the initial pep talk to each new freshman baseball team.

Among Farris's memories of Reeves were two jewels--one for football and one for baseball. Reeves loved to walk along the sidelines dressed in his "uniform" of overalls and a brown felt hat constantly exhorting the football players. Farris told him it was dangerous, but, of course, Reeves did not listen. During a game in the early 1970s, Reeves was walking the sideline when a grand sweep play swept out of bounds, and he found himself in the middle of a number of very large fast-moving football players. Farris saw Reeves's hat fly high in the air as he disappeared into the vortex of the melee. Reeves wound up flat on the ground. Though uninjured, he did swallow a large chew of tobacco. After that Reeves stayed several feet from the sideline.

Reeves not only coached coaches--he also umpired umpires. From his position behind the wire at the rear of home plate, he evaluated an umpire's performance. When an umpire made, in his estimation, a bad call against a Bulldog, he would loudly share his opinion of the call, and sometimes he would vocalize his assessment of the umpire. In one instance when a corpulent umpire offended Reeves's sensibilities, he yelled, "Get down on your knees. You're too fat to see over your own belly!"

Ollie continued to attend MGCCC football and baseball games nearly to the end. He died January 21, 1998.

The Pines: Perk's Rathskeller

The follow paean to the Pines Club appeared in the *1978 Perkolator*, p. 96:

"A motorist traveling on Highway 49 any Wednesday night about 9:00 might wonder what is going on inside that gray building called 'The Pines Club.' Looking at all the cars lined up and down the highway, he might guess they're giving away something free in there. Unfamiliar with the area he surely would wonder where all the people came from.

"Over the past 30 years Robert and Martha Grantham have possibly become the biggest fans of the Perk students; especially since they bought the Pines six years ago. With few places for the students to go and with Stone County being dry, there was a need for the Pines. Furnished with a jukebox, pinball machines, pool and foosball tables, the Pines, (just across the county line) is allowed to sell beer to its customers. After remodeling and opening for business, the Granthams set aside Wednesdays as "College Night" and have been successful ever since.

"Known as 'the Home of the Perk Bulldogs' the Pines offers the students a place to get away from the books and have a good time. The Granthams remarked, 'We look forward to Wednesdays. The kids from Perk are excellent, conductwise.'

"On holidays and special occasions, the Granthams have parties especially for Perk students The free draft beers at the 'Welcome Back,' 'Halloween,' 'Christmas,' and 'End of Year' parties are always enjoyed by the students. The Granthams have even held reunions for past students. When asked what has been the most memorable experience, they replied, 'when the former students keep coming back after they've graduated.'"

Martha and Robert Grantham

In the heyday of the Pines only the most foolhardy Perkinston Campus instructor offered a Wednesday night class. The raising of Mississippi's legal drinking age from 18 to 21 on October 1, 1986, sounded the death knell of the "Home of the Bulldogs." The Pines Club was located in Harrison County on the east side of U. S. Highway 49 two miles south of the Stone County line. The structure was razed in the mid 1990s.

The front of the Pines Club (above) in 1980. Photo courtesy of Hanson Breland who took the picture because his father, Houston Breland, painted the sign. A full page advertisement (right) for the Pines Club published in the Fall 1987 Mississippi Gulf Coast Community College Athletic Review contained an interior photograph of the establishment. (from left) Wanda Prehoda, "Rooster" Bosarge, Randy Jones, and owners Linda, and Ronald Bosarge. The ad, which touted such attractions as a "Full-time D.J. with live band on Friday and Saturday nights" and "Turkey shoot and free dinner on Sundays, beginning at 2 p.m." was the only such ad that appeared in MGCCC publications. The college administration, according to the scuttlebutt at the time, "were not amused."

APPENDICES

Appendix I

MISSISSIPPI GULF COAST COMMUNITY COLLEGE ALUMNI ASSOCIATION
HALL OF FAME
AWARD RECIPIENTS
1970 - 2000

The Hall of Fame award was established in 1970 to honor former students who have exhibited exceptional merit and achievement resulting in fame and recognition for themselves and by extension for MGCCC.

1970
Fred W. Haise Jr.
Perkinston Junior College Class of 1952
Astronaut

Fred Haise, born November 30, 1933, graduated from Biloxi High School and entered Perkinston Junior College as a freshman in fall 1950. His work on the Biloxi High School paper and as a part-time reporter for the *Biloxi-Gulfport Daily Herald* won him the position as editor of the *Bulldog Barks*, the college newspaper. Haise seemed destined for a career in journalism until he joined the Navy Air Cadet Program after his graduation from Perk. After winning his wings Haise took his commission in the United States Marine Corps. Discharged in 1956, he continued to fly for the Oklahoma National Guard, while attending the University of Oklahoma where he received a Bachelor of Science degree in aeronautical engineering in 1959. Haise then became a test pilot for the National Aeronautics and Space Administration.

Chosen as one of 19 new astronauts in 1966, the flight of Apollo 13 in April 1969 was his first space mission. Haise was the lunar module pilot for the near-fatal mission. When the craft suffered an internal explosion while 200,000 nautical miles out in space, the original aim of landing on the moon was forgotten in the attempt to bring Haise and the two other Apollo 13 astronauts back to earth alive. In one of the great television news events of history, people of all nations watched as the men safely returned to earth. U. S. President Richard M. Nixon in presenting the presidential Medal of Freedom to the three, summed up the voyage, "The three astronauts did not reach the moon, but they reached the hearts of millions of people in America and in the world."

1971
William Mosley "Fishbait" Miller, L.L.D.
Harrison-Stone-Jackson Junior College Class of 1932
Doorkeeper, United States House of Representatives

"Fishbait" Miller was born July 20, 1909, in Pascagoula. Asked about his nickname, he said as a child he was struck by all types of "chillun" diseases and weighed only 75 pounds at the age of 15. "Being so scrawny, I was nicknamed 'Fishbait.' While still a student at Pascagoula High, Miller first met an up-and-coming Jackson County lawyer named William C. "Bill" Colmer, who in 1929 gave him a scholarship to Perk so that he could attend college. While at Perk, Miller was the stage manager for theater and glee club productions, the athletic manager for the basketball team, and delivered mail on campus. Also while at Perk, Miller volunteered to drive Colmer around the southern congressional district in his race for the U. S. House of Representatives. Colmer won, and as he departed for Washington, D. C., Miller asked Colmer to send for him. Colmer sent for him in 1933.

Beginning with a job delivering mail in the House Office Building, Miller, by 1949 had worked his way up to the position of Doorkeeper of the House of Representatives. At the time of his selection to the MGCJC Hall of Fame, Miller retained that position as an elected officer of the House charged with the supervision of 340 employees. In addition he had served as chief doorkeeper at the 1948, 1952, 1956, 1964, and 1968 Democratic National Conventions. Miller attended George Washington Law School and earned the doctor of laws from Atlanta Law School. In 1971 Miller wrote a book entitled *Fishbait: The Memoirs of the Congressional Doorkeeper*. Miller retired in 1975 and died September 12, 1989, at his home in Greensboro, North Carolina.

1972
Howard W. Pollock
Harrison-Stone-Jackson Agricultural High School Class of 1939
Harrison-Stone-Jackson Junior College Class of 1941
Congressman and Civil Servant

Howard Pollock, born April 11, 1920, in Chicago, grew up in New Orleans. In his seven year attendance at Perkinston he graduated from both the AHS and the junior college. While at Perk, Pollock lettered in boxing and track and served as head cheerleader. In April 1940 he became the first of five 20th century Perk students to be elected National President of Phi Theta Kappa, the national junior college honor society. After graduating from Perk, Pollock enlisted in the navy as an ordinary seaman and rose to the rank of lieutenant commander by the end of World War II.

Following military service, Pollock and his wife, the former Maryanne Passmore of Dallas, Texas, whom he had met at Perk, emigrated to Alaska, where they homesteaded 80 acres. Pollock joined the movement for Alaskan statehood serving in the territorial legislature. He secured a bachelor of law degree at the University of Houston in 1955 and a master's degree in industrial management at the Massachusetts Institute of Technology in 1960.

He served as a member of the Alaskan State Senate from 1960 until 1966, when he was elected as Alaska's sole representative to the United States Congress. In 1970 Pollock resigned as Alaska's congressman to make an unsuccessful Alaskan gubernatorial bid. At the time of his selection to the MGCJC Hall of Fame, he was serving as Deputy Administrator of the National Oceanic Atmospheric Administration.

1973
Emory O. Cunningham
Harrison-Stone-Jackson Junior College Class of 1940
Corporate President and Publisher

Emory Cunningham, born in 1921, grew up in Walker County, Alabama. Following his 1938 graduation from Carbon Hill High School, Carbon Hill, Alabama, he accepted a football scholarship to attend Harrison-Stone-Jackson Junior College in the fall. At Perk he lettered in football and served as president of the "P" Club in his sophomore year. Cunningham also held membership in the Agriculture Club, a noteworthy allegiance since he was to become Perk's stellar contributor to that discipline.

After graduating from Perk in June 1940, he became a U. S. Navy pilot and served in photo reconnaissance in the Pacific. Returning to his home state following World War II, Cunningham graduated from Auburn University with a degree in agriculture in 1948.

He immediately went to work for the Progressive Farmer Company in Birmingham, Alabama, which had produced *The Progressive Farmer Magazine* since 1886. In 1966 he was the key individual in launching the company's second magazine, *Southern Living*, designed to serve the urban and suburban South.

In 1968 Cunningham became president of the parent company and by 1973, when he was named to the MGCJC Alumni Hall of Fame, the circulation of *Southern Living* had matched the one million subscriptions to *Progressive Farmer*.

1974
Otis Arnold Singletary, Ph.D.
Harrison-Stone-Jackson Junior College Class of 1942
University President

Otis Singletary, a native of Gulfport, was born October 31, 1921. He graduated from Gulfport High School in spring 1939 and entered Perk that fall. He was the drum major of the band in 1940, 1941, and 1942, participated in dramatics, and was a member of the annual staff. Singletary, while serving as a naval officer during World War II, exhibited his talent for combining administrative skills with education. He taught history classes aboard *U. S. S. Aldebaran* as the ship made history in the Pacific.

In 1947 Singletary earned his bachelor's degree at Millsaps College and two years later a master's degree at Louisiana State University. Then came another stint in the service during the Korean War, after which he returned to LSU to take a doctorate in history. He taught at the University of Texas from 1954 to 1960, where he won three awards for teaching excellence and authored two books, *Negro Militia and Reconstruction* and *The Mexican War*. The former won the Moncado Award of the American Military Institute for the best military monograph of 1955.

Singletary moved into administration in 1961 as chancellor of the University of North Carolina. In 1964 he took leave from that post to serve for two years as director of the Job Corps, Office of Economic Opportunity, Washington, D. C. From 1966 to 1968 he served as vice president of the American Council of Education. He became the eighth president of the University of Kentucky in 1969, the post he held when named to the MGCJC Alumni Hall of Fame.

1975
Edward Michel Khayat
Perkinston Junior College Class of 1955
Professional Football Coach

Eddie Khayat was born September 14, 1935, in Moss Point. Graduating from Moss Point High in 1953, Khayat spent a year at Millsaps College before going to Perkinston in fall 1954. While at Perk he played under Coach Harold White. In remembering those days, Khayat recalled, "I don't know if you would believe the length of the practices. I never had to do anything as tough since . . . . I've never been in that kind of condition . . . . That's where I became a man." After Perk Khayat continued his education and athletic career at Tulane University where he received a bachelor's degree in sociology in 1959.

After college, Khayat played professional football with the Washington Redskins, the Philadelphia Eagles, and the Boston Patriots. He was a defensive standout when the Eagles won the National Football League Championship in 1960.

In 1967 Khayat began coaching professional football as a defensive line coach for the New Orleans Saints. In 1971 he moved to Philadelphia as defensive line coach and, after three games, was promoted to head coach of the Eagles. At age 35 he was the second youngest head coach in the NFL. Khayat became a defensive line coach for the Detroit Lions in February 1973. In January 1975 he joined the Atlanta Falcons as a defensive line coach, the position he held when selected for the MGCJC Alumni Hall of Fame.

1976
Della Marie (Sims) McCaughan
Perkinston Junior College Class of 1949
Marine Biologist

Della Sims was born April 10, 1928, in Pass Christian. She graduated from Pass Christian High School in spring 1947 and entered Perkinston Junior College in the fall. At Perk she was a member of Phi Theta Kappa, the band, and was vice president of both the Language Club and the International Relations Club.

Upon graduation from Perk in 1949, she entered the University of Southern Mississippi, majoring in biology and general science, and completed her undergraduate work in 1951. She began teaching in the Biloxi Public School System that same year. In 1952 she married Findley McCaughan and continued her education part-time receiving her master's from the University of Southern Mississippi in 1959.

McCaughan's interest in teaching marine biology dated from her earliest days in the classroom, and from the beginning, she felt the best way to make the course "come alive" was to take her students to the beaches and the barrier islands. By 1966 she had attained the position of chairperson of the science department for the Biloxi Secondary Schools and had developed the pilot program in marine biology in secondary schools for the state of Mississippi. Through workshops the principles of the course she pioneered were spread not only to other schools but to many other states. In 1976 she was selected as one of five educators in the nation to receive the National Science Teacher's Association Distinguished Service to Science Citation.

1977
Jesse Boyce Holleman
Harrison-Stone-Jackson Junior College Sept. 1940 - May 1941
Attorney At Law

Boyce Holleman was born February 26, 1924, in Wiggins. Graduating from Wiggins High School in 1940, he matriculated at Perk that fall. Though he stayed only one year, he held membership in the Drama Club, French Club, Y.M.C.A. and worked on the yearbook staff. As a member of the debate team he entered and won the State Junior College Oratorical Contest held at Raymond. In addition, he announced all the football games.

He transferred after his freshman year to the University of Mississippi, where he planned to pursue studies in the field of law, but his plans were interrupted by World War II. In July 1942, he joined the Navy and became a pilot. Flying off the carrier, U. S. S. Gambier Bay, for a bombing attack during the Saipan invasion, his plane was hit by enemy fire, and he suffered severe burns and was hospitalized for almost two years.

Following the war, Holleman returned to Ole Miss and obtained a bachelor's degree and a Juris Doctorate degree. Holleman's political career began at the age of 23 with his election as a member of the Mississippi House of Representatives from Stone County. He served from 1947 to 1953. He became District Attorney for the Second Circuit Court District in 1953 and served until 1972, when he declined to seek re-election and returned to full-time practice in Gulfport as an attorney and counselor-at-law. Regarded as one of Mississippi's great trial lawyers, Holleman served as president of the Mississippi Bar Association and was named Fellow of the American Bar Association.

1978
Charles Bishop "Chuck" Scarborough III
MGCJC (Perkinston Campus) Sept. 1963 - May 1965
MGCJC (Jefferson Davis Campus) Sept.1966 - Jan.1967
Broadcast Journalist

Chuck Scarborough was born November 4, 1943, in Pittsburgh, Pennsylvania. Following high school graduation in 1961, Scarborough joined the United States Air Force and was posted to Keesler Air Force Base. In Scarborough's words, "While I was at Keesler, I was made an instructor of electronic engineering, and all I had was a high school diploma. I felt I needed some sort of college degree and the only place I could get it was Perkinston."

Beginning in 1963, Scarborough began 100-mile daily round trips to Perkinston, while teaching from 3 p.m. to midnight at Keesler. In 1965, his Air Force enlistment at an end, Scarborough went to work as a technician for WLOX-TV in Biloxi and transferred from Perkinston to the newly opened Jefferson Davis Campus of MGCJC. In 1968 he resigned from WLOX and took a job as night reporter at WDAM-TV in Hattiesburg, so that he could pursue full-time his studies of broadcast journalism at the University of Southern Mississippi. He graduated from USM in May 1969.

When Hurricane Camille struck in August 1969, Scarborough video taped the destruction, went to Atlanta, and was hired by WAGA-TV as a general assignment reporter. After two-and-one-half years at WAGA, he moved to WNAC in Boston. In 1974 he accepted the offer of New York's WNBC-TV station to co-anchor its new two-hour early news program, "News Center 4." By 1978, when Scarborough was selected for the MGCJC Alumni Hall of Fame, he had won four Emmy Awards and was reporting the news to ten percent of America's television audience each night.

1979
Frank George Gruich, M.D.

Harrison-Stone-Jackson Junior College Class of 1941
Medical Doctor

Born to Yugoslavian immigrant parents on March 12, 1920, Frank Gruich spent his childhood in Biloxi's Point Cadet, the heart of the Gulf Coast's fishing and seafood industry. After graduating from Biloxi High School in 1937, he spent the next two years working in a seafood factory. In fall 1939 he enrolled at Perkinston for the sole purpose of obtaining enough chemistry hours to qualify to take the civil service examination for the position of shrimp inspector.

At Perk he met two science instructors, T. W. Brasfield and Clarence O. Hinton, who inspired him to set his sights on becoming a medical doctor. Gruich graduated from Perk with special honors in 1941 and entered the University of Mississippi that fall. Receiving a bachelor's degree from Ole Miss in 1943, he then enrolled at Tulane University School of Medicine, obtaining his medical degree in 1945. After a residency at New Orleans Charity Hospital, Gruich served two years as a United States Army Medical Officer rising to the position of Chief of Medicine at Camp Hood, Texas.

Gruich began general practice in Biloxi in 1948, but after further training, he became a specialist in obstetrics and gynecology in 1955. By the time he was named to the MGCJC Alumni Hall of Fame, he had delivered an estimated 6,000 babies. Exactly how many students he had "delivered" to MGCJC was unknown, but the number was considerable. In his words, "I am an ambassador of the junior college because I love the system." Five years before being elevated to the MGCJC Hall of Fame, Gruich was awarded the Sam Owen Trophy for outstanding service to MGCJC.

1980
Walter Greaves Cowan

Harrison-Stone-Jackson Junior College Class of 1932
Newspaperman and Editor

Walter Cowan was born March 24, 1912, in Bond but spent most of his early life in Mississippi City. By the time Cowan graduated from Mississippi City High School in 1930, both his parents were deceased. In Cowan's words, "When I graduated from high school, a long time friend of my father, Cooper J. Darby, who was superintendent of the junior college at Perkinston, offered me an opportunity to continue my education. Cowan was named the college's first student publicity agent at $10.00 per month." With five dollars each month from his half brother, together with the few dollars he could earn as a correspondent from the newspapers in New Orleans and in Mississippi to which he sent news releases, he could afford the $16.50 per month charges at Perk. In that manner Cowan secured a junior college diploma in 1932.

After Perk, Cowan worked his way through the Journalism School of the University of Missouri. Soon after he graduated in 1936, he went to work as a general assignments editor on the *New Orleans Item*. From 1941 to 1945 he worked as a publicity agent for the Gulf, Mobile and Ohio Railroad in Mobile. He then returned to the Crescent City, where he soon became city editor of the *New Orleans States* and later the *States-Item* (after the two newspapers merged in 1958). In 1964 Cowan was promoted to managing editor and five years later to editor. For the next decade Cowan served as editor of the *States-Item* retiring August 1, 1979. Fifteen months after his retirement, he returned to Perk to be honored at the place where his achievements in the newspaper world had begun on a mimeograph machine in C. J. Darby's office.

1981
1971 National Champions
Football Team, Coaches, Cheerleaders, Cheerleader Sponsor

Those honorees among the players and cheerleaders present at halftime at the homecoming game on October 31, 1981 were photographed on the track in A. L. May Memorial Stadium. Those honorees not present for this photograph, including cheerleader sponsor Barbara A. " Sue" Ross, are named and or pictured herein in the chapter titled, " Football andTrack 1961-1991: The Sekul Legacy."

1. Mike Niolet
2. Jimmy Dubuisson (manager)
3. Jimmy Stork
4. Gerald Pickich
5. Marilyn V. (Skellie) VanCourt
6. Ronnie Miller
7. Marcia Lorraine Randall
8. Darlene Ann (Kapp) Wixon
9. Kathleen Ann (Sarris) Elias
10. Wayne Patrick
11. Patricia Michelle Backus
12. Kenny Larsen
13. Larry Benefield
14. Glover Hayden
15. Mike Jenner
16. Ronnie Thomas
17. John McDougle
18. Shed Foxworth
19. Levorne Hawthorne
20. Kenny Boynick
21. Kerry Neal
22. Tommy Robison
23. Mike Borden
24. George Krebs (cheerleader)
25. Harold Holton
26. Skip Holland
27. Bobby Saucier
28. Tommy Perry (cheerleader)
29. Stuart Hodges (manager)
30. Cooper Farris (manager)
31. Charles Driskell
32. Tom Ferrill
33. Don Fredricks
34. Jimmy Beck
35. Dan Taranto
36. John Jalanivich
37. Terry Helms

1982
Clare (Sekul) Hornsby
Harrison-Stone-Jackson Junior College Class of 1941
Attorney At Law

Clare Sekul was born in Biloxi on August 16, 1922. Following her graduation from Biloxi High School in 1939, she went to Perk, where she was a member of the Catholic Club, Spanish Club, and was elected "dean of women" in the student government. In 1941 she entered the University of Mississippi and earned her Juris Doctor degree in 1945. A woman lawyer was an oddity at the time, but so great was the need for lawyers that she remembered, "I received offers from many states, but I knew I would remain in Mississippi." Back home in Biloxi she entered practice with her brother John M. Sekul and soon married Warren Hornsby.

As the only woman lawyer in south Mississippi at the time, Hornsby began a long list of "firsts." In 1946 she became the first woman president of the Perkinston Junior College Alumni Association. In 1959 she became the first woman to receive Perkinston Junior College's Sam Owen Trophy for distinguished service to the institution. In 1970 Hornsby became the first woman president of the Harrison County Bar Association. In 1974 she became the sole woman charter member of the Mississippi Gulf Coast Junior College Foundation. By 1982 she was serving as the first woman president of the Gulf Coast John C. Stennis Chapter of the U. S. Air Force Association, having succeeded a three star general in that post. Hornsby's association with the Air Force had begun early. In her first case in 1945, she successfully defended four Keesler Airmen. In May 1971 she was one of only four women selected to attend a high-level security forum at the invitation of the Air Force. One of the others was then United Nations Ambassador Shirley Temple Black.

1983
John Clifton Dees
Harrison-Stone-Jackson Agricultural High School Class of 1929
Harrison-Stone-Jackson Junior College Class of 1931
Businessman, Supervisor, Bank Board Chairman

John Dees was born July 20, 1912. As one of four sons of Calvin Elias Dees, owner of Dees and Company General Store in Perkinston, he received 14 years of education, elementary through junior college, a stone's throw from his father's store. After graduating from Perk in 1931, Dees attended the Gupton-Jones School of Mortuary Science in Nashville, Tennessee. Graduating with highest honors in 1934, he returned to Perkinston becoming the first licensed mortician to practice in the area. During World War II Dees served 44 months in the U. S. Army of which 33 months were spent in the European Theater. In 1947 he moved to Wiggins, where he established Dees Funeral Home. In addition he owned Dees Building Supply in Wiggins and managed Dees and Company General Store in Perkinston.

In February 1950, Dees became supervisor, Beat 1, Stone County, a position he held until January 1, 1980, claiming that seat in eight consecutive elections in the first primary. During that period, he served as a Trustee of the Board of the junior college at Perkinston, served two terms as the junior college's Alumni Association president, and served as chairman of the board of the Bank of Wiggins. In 1971 Dees was awarded the Sam Owen Trophy for distinguished service to the college. His 1942 marriage to the former Margaret Rose Eubanks of Lucedale produced two daughters, Johnnette and Helen, both of whom graduated from the college. Dees died November 22, 1989. In 1996 the Garden of the Oaks in front of Dees Hall on the Perkinston Campus was dedicated to him, his father, and three brothers.

1984
George Anthony Schloegel
Perkinston Junior College Sept. 1958 - May 1959
Bank Executive Vice President

George Schloegel was born in Gulfport on June 17, 1940. In 1956, as a high school student, he began working for Hancock Bank located in downtown Gulfport. When he graduated from Gulfport High in 1958, he continued to work for 40 hours per week at night while traveling daily to the Perkinston Junior College via the college's commuter bus. Said Schloegel of those days, "I was earning $1 an hour and getting a college education at the same time. It was ideal, just plain and simple."

After a year at Perkinston, Schloegel and his new wife, the former Peggy Harry of Gulfport, moved to New Orleans. Schloegel worked full-time on the night crew at the Whitney Bank and attended year-old Louisiana State University at New Orleans (LSUNO). In 1962, armed with a business administration degree from LSUNO, he returned to Hancock Bank. Two years later at age 24, he was elected assistant cashier, the youngest officer in the history of Hancock Bank. In time Schloegel rose through the ranks to become executive vice president of the bank. He also served as secretary to the board of directors and as president of Hancock Bank Securities Corporation.

Schloegel was named the Mississippi Jaycees' Outstanding Young Man in 1965. He later served as local and state president of the Jaycees and as national vice president. In 1982 MGCJC presented Schloegel with the Sam Owen Trophy for distinguished service to the college.

1985
Dolores (McHenry) Mauldin
Harrison-Stone-Jackson Junior College Class of 1941
Postmaster

Dolores McHenry was born April 8, 1922, in the Stone County town founded by and named for her grandfather, Dr. George A. McHenry. After graduating from Hattiesburg High School, she enrolled at Perk in fall 1939. She was a member of the band, the glee club, the pep squad, and five other organizations on the campus in addition to playing tennis for the college. After graduating from Perk in 1941, she enrolled at the University of Mississippi. On a trip to Tennessee, she met Sonny McWhorter of Waynesboro whom she married. After her husband was killed in action in the Army Air Corps in Europe, she and her baby daughter Vivian returned to McHenry, where she became postmaster in 1945.

In 1947 she married William S. "Bill" Mauldin and the couple had a daughter, Hannah. Perk became a focus of attention not only for Dolores but also for the whole Mauldin family. Both daughters attended the institution, and her husband Bill served 20 years on the college Board of Trustees, including five one-year terms as Chairman of the Board. Dolores served four one-year terms as president of the MGCJC Alumni Association, the 20th century record. In 1976 she was awarded the Sam Owen Trophy in recognition of her distinguished service to MGCJC.

Dolores remained postmaster of McHenry from 1945 to 1973, at which time she transferred to Perkinston and served as postmaster there until her retirement in 1984. As a member of the National Association of Postmasters, she served two years as national vice president.

1986
Julius John Hayden Jr., Ed.D.
Harrison-Stone-Jackson Junior College Class of 1940
Junior College President

J. J. Hayden, born May 19, 1920, in Pass Christian, entered Harrison-Stone-Jackson Junior College in fall 1938 on a six-dollar-a-month football scholarship. In 1939 his childhood sweetheart, Lillian Ruth Aschbacher, matriculated at Perk, in her words, "because J. J. was there." Hayden graduated in 1940 and went into the service, first in the Army Air Corps and then in the Coast Guard. J. J. and Lillian married April 23, 1943. In 1950 the couple returned to Perk. Hayden, who by then held a bachelor's degree and master's degree from Mississippi State University, taught history for two years and in 1952 was appointed dean of men. The following year at the age of 33, he became the ninth chief executive officer (the second to hold the official title of "president") of the institution which was then styled Perkinston Agricultural High School and Junior College. He received a doctorate of education from the University of Southern Mississippi on August 14, 1966. When Hayden retired December 31, 1985, the institution had evolved into Mississippi Gulf Coast Junior College, composed of three campuses and four centers. As the first multi-campus junior college in Mississippi, MGCJC served as a model for the growth of others in the state.

The Haydens retired to their hometown of Pass Christian to live in a house named "America."

1987
Karen Marguerite Yarborough, Ph.D.
Perkinston Junior College Class of 1958
Geneticist and University Vice President

Karen Yarborough was born March 4, 1938, and grew up in her hometown of Tunica. Shortly after her graduation from high school, her family moved to Biloxi, and she entered Perkinston Junior College in fall 1956. At Perk she played in the band, was voted most athletic, and was a member of Phi Theta Kappa.

After Perk she entered Mississippi State University where she earned her bachelor's degree in microbiology and her master's degree in genetics. She then went to North Carolina State University, where she earned her Ph.D. with a major in genetics and a minor in zoology and statistics.

Yarborough's teaching career began in 1967, when she became assistant professor of biology at the University of Southern Mississippi. Four years later she founded the Institute of Genetics at USM and became its first director. In 1982, in addition to that post, she was named to the position of USM's vice president for research and extended services.

Shortly before being named to the MGCCC Hall of Fame, Yarborough was elected president of the Mississippi Academy of Sciences--the first woman to serve in that capacity. Among her many honors she was the recipient of USM's Excellence in Teaching Award.

1988
Lionel Numa Eleuterius, Ph.D.
Perkinston Junior College Class of 1959
Botanist

Lionel Eleuterius was born December 25, 1936, in Biloxi and grew up on Point Cadet, where his father was a boat builder. After his graduation from Biloxi High School in 1956, he entered Perkinston Junior College. He had wanted to be an artist, but as he put it, "In those days men just didn't make their livings being artists." At Perk he entered the program in pre-engineering, turning in a president's list academic performance. After graduating from Perk he went to Mississippi State University, where he decided that he did not want to be an engineer and joined the U. S. Army.

In 1965 he enrolled at the University of Southern Mississippi, where he earned a master's in biology in 1968. He then went to Ocean Springs to set up the botany department in the Gulf Coast Research Laboratory. In addition to his duties at GCRL, he continued his academic studies, receiving his Ph.D. in botany from Mississippi State University in 1974.

Eleuterius's area of specialization was the tidal marsh plants of the Mississippi Gulf Coast. In 1981 he completed a book entitled *An Illustrated Guide to Tidal Marsh Plants of Mississippi.* Not only did he write the book, he illustrated it as well. He dedicated the book to the high school biology teacher who had sparked his interest in the subject, Della McCaughan (1976 inductee in the MGCJC Hall of Fame). The book became a surprise popular hit and resulted in natural beach erosion control through the planting of sea oats on the Gulf Coast littoral.

1989
Doyle Preston Smith, M.D.
Perkinston Junior College Class of 1944
Addictionologist

Doyle Smith was born November 20, 1925, at Stillmore. He graduated from Magnolia High School near Stillmore in 1942 and went to Perk that fall. In 1944, the year he graduated from Perk, Smith joined the U. S. Navy. After the service Smith went to Mississippi State University, where he began the study of medicine. He earned a bachelor's degree in entomology at MSU and entered Tulane Medical School in 1947. Smith began his practice of general medicine in 1952 in Collins, where he remained five years before he moved to Jackson to specialize in anesthesiology. By the mid-1970s Smith had achieved the "American Dream" complete with a great career, a beautiful wife, and two bright children--a boy and a girl. But, said Smith, "I [had] become a full-blown alcoholic." His wife together with some friends convinced him to seek help at a treatment center in Georgia.

After his recovery, Smith began to focus his energies on research, teaching, and practice in the unexplored field of addictionology. He opened an alcohol and drug treatment center at Doctors hospital of Jackson in 1981, where he worked for two years. He then was invited to Hattiesburg to spearhead for Forrest General Hospital a project which resulted in the formation of the Pine Grove Recovery Center. He also became involved in an "impaired professional" program which addressed the widespread problem of alcoholism and drug addiction among those in the medical profession. A true pioneer in the field of addictionology, Smith helped form associations in the new discipline throughout the nation and abroad, particularly in the Soviet Union.

1990
William F. Holmes
MGCJC (Jefferson Davis Campus) Class of 1970
Executive Director, Coliseum and Convention Center

Born September 1, 1946, Bill Holmes's hometown was the United States Navy. In speaking of life with a career Navy father, Holmes remembered, "It was always exciting. I went to 11 different schools in 12 years." He graduated from high school in Ocean City, New Jersey, in 1964 and joined the United States Air Force. He served at Keesler Air Force Base as supervisor of computer operations until 1968.

A few months before his Air Force service ended, he married Sandra Toncrey of D'Iberville and began taking business courses at MGCJC Jefferson Davis Campus. He attended JD while working a full-time night job in the computer department at Gulf National Bank. He graduated from MGCJC in 1970 and, keeping his night job, commuted to the University of Southern Mississippi in Hattiesburg until he earned his bachelor's degree in business administration in May 1972.

Holmes moved his wife and three children to Woodbine, N.J., where his father lived, and took a job as assistant business manager at the Institute of Mental Retardation. Five years later Holmes decided to move his family back to the Gulf Coast due to the illness of his wife's father. In August 1977, three months before the opening of the Mississippi Gulf Coast Coliseum and Convention Center, Holmes was hired as comptroller. Holmes quickly moved to the position of assistant director, and in 1985 he became executive director of the $26 million facility. In 1988 *Performance* magazine named Holmes, then aged 40, one of the top Fifty Facility Directors in the United States.

1991
Gerald J. Miller, Ph.D.
Perkinston Junior College Class of 1962
Ecologist

Gerald Miller, a native of Jersey City, New Jersey, grew up in Gulfport. He graduated from Gulfport High School in 1960 and entered Perkinston Junior College. He graduated first in the Perk Class of 1962 and later married the number one graduate of MGCJC Perkinston Campus Class of 1966--the former Glenda Faye Hunt of Gulfport.

After Perk, Miller went to the University of Southern Mississippi, taking his bachelor's degree in 1964 and master's degree in 1966, both with highest honors. Drafted in 1966 he flew a U. S. Army air ambulance in Vietnam from 1967 to 1969. During his air ambulance career he transported approximately 3,500 wounded servicemen. He was awarded the Distinguished Flying Cross, the Air Medal with eight Oak Leaf Clusters, and the Army Commendation Medal.

Following the service Miller earned a Ph.D. in coastal ecology from the University of Georgia in 1973. Miller then embarked on a career in the United States Government Environmental Protection Agency (EPA).

Based in Atlanta, the region he served included Mississippi. In Miller's words, "I've been to more places in Mississippi than I knew were in Mississippi." As to the Gulf Coast in particular, Miller was involved in site work for rocket testing in Hancock County, and he has done work with the Gulfport Harbor, the Pascagoula Homeport, and the Gulf Islands National Seashore.

1992
James Gregory Hibbard
MGCJC (Perkinston Campus) Class of 1984
Professional Baseball Pitcher

Greg Hibbard, born in New Orleans on September 13, 1964, lived in Florida, Hawaii, New York, and Guam before his father, who was in the U. S. Coast Guard, moved the family to Gulfport in 1977. He lettered in baseball all four years at Harrison Central High School before going to Perk in 1982 to play for Coach Ken "Curly" Farris.

Because Farris had, in his words, "a lot of good pitchers" in the 1982-1983 season, Hibbard posted only three wins and one loss. The next season, though, the southpaw was Gulf Coast's ace pitcher and racked up a 14-4 record. His standout game was the 1984 South Division Championship game against arch rival Pearl River Junior College "He pitched a one-hitter," said Farris.

After Gulf Coast, Hibbard signed a scholarship with the University of Alabama, where he set the university's single season pitching record of 39 games and the career pitching record of 75 games. After two years at Alabama, Hibbard spent a year with the Kansas City Royals before being traded to the Chicago White Sox in 1987.

The White Sox sent him to a Triple A Vancouver team in 1988, and the next year he was called to Chicago as a rookie. In his first full year in the major leagues Hibbard pitched 211 innings and led the White Sox in earned run average (3.16), the eighth best average in the American League.

1993
Davis Kilstolfe Mortensen
Perkinston Junior College Class of 1955
Corporate Executive Vice President

Davis Mortensen was born in Charles City, Iowa, on April 25, 1932, of a Danish immigrant father and a first-generation Danish-American mother. When Mortensen was one year old, his family moved to Harrelston, a Danish community in Jackson County. A few years later the family moved to Moss Point.

Soon after he graduated from Moss Point High School in 1950, Mortensen's National Guard unit was activated for the Korean War and sent to Germany. In Mortensen's words, "When I got out of the Army, I got married about a month later and decided that I needed to work. I worked at Ingalls, and that's when I decided that I probably ought to do something more than work at the shipyard." In September 1953 Mortensen and his wife Ann moved into the Apartment Dorm at Perk. She worked in a bank in Wiggins, while he attended college on the G.I. Bill and played football. His wife, Ann, remembers, "In his second year, he didn't play football. . . . He studied."

After Perk, Mortensen earned a bachelor's degree in industrial engineering at Mississippi State University in 1956. In 1962 he was an industrial engineer for Crossett Lumber Company in Crossett, Arkansas, when Georgia Pacific Corporation acquired the company. Mortensen then began a rapid rise up the Georgia Pacific corporate ladder to the position of executive vice President for building products in 1987. In that position he was responsible for six million acres of timber holdings and 20,000 employees.

1994
Lenwood Stokley Sawyer
MGCJC (Perkinston Campus) Jan. 1963 - Jan. 1964
MGCJC (Jefferson Davis Campus) Sept. 1966 - Jan. 1967
Jan. 1969 - May 1969
Real Estate and Insurance Company President and Owner

Lenny Sawyer was born December 20, 1943, in Gulfport. He graduated from Gulfport High School in 1962 and attended Mississippi College in the fall. In January 1963 he began riding the college commuter bus to the Perkinston Campus, taking classes until January 1964. With the opening of the Jefferson Davis Campus in 1965, he transferred to the new campus, attending for two semesters. Though he did not graduate, his wife Earline (Croncich) Sawyer graduated with the JD Class of 1967.

As a member of a family involved in Gulfport real estate since 1901, Sawyer worked in the family business, and in 1986 he became president and sole owner of Sawyer Real Estate and Insurance, Inc. Success in developing shopping center projects for clients such as Wal-Mart, Winn-Dixie, K-Mart, and Delchamps placed him in the big leagues of Gulf Coast development and prepared Sawyer for new opportunities when the gaming industry located on the Coast. His expertise and success in that industry expanded his territory to anyplace in the nation where gaming was legalized. In 1993 he was named director of real estate and gaming acquisition for Stations Casino in Las Vegas. Though he spent most of his time crisscrossing the nation, his home base remained the Mississippi Gulf Coast.

As for Gulf Coast Community College, not only his wife but also his daughter graduated from the institution, and his brother and sister attended. In testimony of his commitment to MGCCC in 1994 Sawyer volunteered to chair the Harrison County effort in the college's $1.5 million Building on Our Heritage fund-raising campaign.

1995
Paul N. Howell
Harrison-Stone-Jackson Agricultural High School Class of 1936
Harrison-Stone-Jackson Junior College Sept. 1936 - May 1937
Corporation President

Paul Howell was born in 1918 in Howison and entered Harrison-Stone-Jackson Agricultural High School as a senior in 1935. He graduated as valedictorian of his AHS class in 1936 and remained at Perk for his first year of college. Howell then entered Louisiana State University, where he majored in chemical engineering. Shortly after graduating from LSU, he was called to active duty in June 1940 with the U. S. Navy. Howell survived the December 7, 1941, Japanese attack on Pearl Harbor and the four years of Pacific Theater war which followed, gaining seven battle stars and rising to the rank of commander.

Back in civilian life he began work as a chemical engineer at a Baton Rouge, Louisiana, refinery. Five years later he was reactivated due to the Korean War and assigned to the Pentagon. Released once again from the Navy in 1953, he recalled, "I just decided I'd become an independent and not try to regain all those years lost with a major oil company."

By 1955 he had established himself in Houston, Texas. Forty years later Howell's corporate holdings included an oil and gas company, a national trucking company, a specialty chemical company, and a common carrier pipeline. Howell continued his service in the Naval Reserve, retiring as a rear admiral. He chaired the U. S. Navy memorial Foundation, which raised in excess of $20 million to build the U. S. Navy Memorial on Pennsylvania Avenue in Washington, D.C. In 1991 he met with his friend, U. S. President George Bush, at the U.S.S. Arizona Memorial Ceremony at Pearl Harbor.

1996
Rita Pearl (Baker) Sheffield Hester
MGCJC (Perkinston Campus) Sept. 1964 - May 1965
Entertainment Industry Producer/Director

Rita Baker was born December 8, 1946, and grew up in Wiggins. Her mother, Myrtle, who had been a dancer in the 1920s, encouraged her daughter to pursue the art of dance. Rita was head majorette and student conductor of the band at Stone High School in Wiggins. After she graduated from Stone High in 1965, she entered Perk becoming head Perkette in her freshman year, an unusual accomplishment. She performed the task with excellence but left Perk after one year determined to pursue a career in show business.

She transferred to the University of Southern Mississippi, where she majored in fine arts and met Morris "Buddy" Sheffield of Biloxi. They graduated in 1969, married in 1970, and founded the Sheffield Ensemble children's theater group based in Biloxi but which performed throughout the southeast.

The Sheffield Ensemble won critical acclaim at the 1984 Louisiana World's Fair Exposition but suffered financial disaster when the New Orleans based event went bankrupt. Another casualty of the Louisiana Exposition was the Sheffields' marriage. Even though they divorced, they remained business partners. In 1989 the two went to Los Angeles, where they created and produced the Ollie Award winning children's television show "Roundhouse." In the process Rita met Benny Hester, a successful contemporary Christian music artist, and they married in 1993. Rita, Benny, and Buddy formed an entertainment company and were involved in a project for 20th Century Fox Television when Rita was named to the MGCCC Hall of Fame.

1997
Jere William Hess Jr.
MGCJC (Perkinston Campus) Class of 1964
Corporate Director of Public Relations and Education

Jere Hess, a native of Fruitland Park, born August 5, 1944, graduated from Forrest County Agricultural High School in 1962. He entered Perk as an education major and played in the band. As it turned out both of those pursuits furthered his career. While at Perk he met his wife-to-be, the former Jo Etta Spooner of Moss Point, who graduated with him in 1964.

After Perk, Hess went to Mississippi State University. An honors student his senior year, he graduated in 1966 with a bachelor's degree in personnel management. He earned his master's degree the following year and began a career that eventually led to an executive position as Director of Personnel at Meridian-based Peavey Electronics in 1978. Later his duties were extended to include the firm's public relations and educational programs. Hess has been described as "the No.1 spokesman for the nation's No.1 manufacturer of a product line that includes more than 3,000 musical instruments and portable sound equipment with sales in 104 countries." So powerful was the Peavey success mystique in 1991 that U. S. President George Bush paid the company an unprecedented personal visit. Hess in his role as public relations director was there to greet the President and take him on a guided tour.

In his role as education director Hess was appointed in 1982 by Mississippi Governor William Winter to serve on the first lay State Board for Technical and Vocational Education. Also in this role he helped to acquire for Peavey employees a bachelor's of science program in manufacturing technology at MSU Meridian.

1998
Harry Grey Walker
Perkinston Agricultural High School Jan. - Aug. 1944
Chief Justice of Mississippi Supreme Court

Harry Walker, born at Ovette, Jones County, on September 30, 1924, was aged six when his family moved to Gulfport. He dropped out of high school in the 11th grade during World War II to join the United States Coast Guard, where he served as a chemical warfare instructor. While stationed in Florida, he suffered a broken back in a fall from a truck. After a year in the hospital, he was honorably discharged and returned home to Gulfport. He enrolled in the Perkinston Agricultural High School in January 1944, securing enough credits by August to enter the University of Mississippi in the fall.

While at Ole Miss, Walker's back problem worsened, resulting in his confinement to a wheelchair. Undaunted, he graduated from the University of Mississippi School of Law in 1952 and returned to Gulfport to establish a private practice. Elected to the Mississippi House of Representatives in 1963, he resigned in 1964 to accept an appointment as County Court Judge of Harrison County. Walker remained in that position until 1968, when he was appointed judge of the Circuit Court, Second Circuit Court District (Harrison, Hancock, and Stone Counties), a position he held until 1972.

In Walker's words, "In 1972 [I] was elected to the Mississippi State Supreme Court to a term beginning January 1973. [I] served as associate justice from January 1973 to July 1982 . . . as presiding Justice from July 1982 to July 1986 . . . as Chief Justice from July 1, 1986 to October 1, 1987, at which time I retired and moved back from Jackson to Gulfport." Walker died April 15, 2000, in Biloxi.

1999
Barry Lee Mellinger, Ph.D.
Perkinston Junior College Class of 1960
Community College President

Barry Mellinger, a native of Colorado Springs, Colorado, was born December 19, 1939, the eldest child and only son of Paul and Edna Mellinger. His family moved to Mississippi in 1950, and he graduated from Lyman Consolidated High School in 1957. He entered Perkinston Junior College in 1958 and graduated May 15, 1960. After Perk, Mellinger attended Mississippi State University, where he earned a bachelor's degree in industrial education in 1962 and a master's degree in school administration in 1963. In May 1963 he began his career with MGCJC as assistant director of vocational technical education.

In 1966 Mellinger resigned his position at MGCJC to work on his doctorate at Purdue University in West Lafayette, Indiana. Four years later he was awarded the doctorate of philosophy in vocational industrial education. From 1972 to 1977 he served as associate executive secretary of the commission on colleges of the Southern Association of Colleges and Schools, in Atlanta, Georgia. From 1977 to 1979 he was director of the Dekalb Area Technical School and dean of occupational education of Dekalb Community College in Clarkston, Georgia. In 1979 he returned to MGCJC as vice president for instructional affairs. On January 1, 1986, Mellinger became the college's tenth chief executive officer (the third to bear the official title of president) and served in that capacity until his retirement on August 1, 1998.

2000
Steven George Sekul
Perkinston Junior College Sept. 1955 - Jan. 1957
Football and Track Coach

George Sekul, born October 5, 1937, in Biloxi began his coaching career at Perkinston in summer 1961 as an assistant coach. In August 1966, he became head coach, serving until his retirement in December 1991. In 1981 Sekul, together with the other coaches, the team, the cheerleaders, and the cheerleader sponsor of the 1971 National Championship Football Team, were inducted into the MGCCC Alumni Association Hall of Fame. In 1999 Sekul was inducted into the MGCCC Athletic Hall of Fame. On October 21, 2000, Sekul was inducted individually into the MGCCC Alumni Association Hall of Fame, and the S. George Sekul Field House was named for him the same day. As an inductee of both Halls of Fame and as an inductee of one of them twice (as part of a group and as an individual) together with having a building named for him, Sekul earned the designation as MGCCC's most honored alumnus of the 20th century.

For an overview of Sekul's athletic achievements see the entry devoted to him in the next section of this work titled "Athletic Hall of Fame Inaugural Inductees, October 28, 1999." For an indepth biographical treatment see the chapter in the Sports section of this work titled, " Football and Track 1961-1991: The Sekul Legacy."

MISSISSIPPI GULF COAST COMMUNITY COLLEGE ALUMNI ASSOCIATION

ATHLETIC HALL OF FAME INAUGURAL INDUCTEES

OCTOBER 28, 1999

MGCCC President Willis Lott originated the Athletic Hall of Fame in 1999 to recognize the accomplishments of MGCCC's coaches and athletes. Fifteen persons were chosen for the inaugural induction, which took place at a dinner at Heidelberg Hall on the Perkinston Campus on October 28, 1999.

John S. "Johnny" Adams (Gulfport) MGCJC (Perkinston Campus) Class of 1966
Athlete 1964-1966

Adams was a starting guard on Coach Bob Weathers' 1966 south division and state championship basketball team. At the conclusion of that season, he was selected as an All-Region Five player. Adams attended Belhaven College, 1966-68, where he was also a starting guard. While there, he had the highest scholastic average of any Belhaven athlete in 1968 and led the team in assists and free throw percentage (87 percent, third in the National Association of Intercollegiate Athletics). Following graduation from Belhaven, Adams pursued a business career.

James Obie Brown (Big Level) Harrison-Stone-Jackson JC Class of 1932
Athlete 1930-1934, Coach 1934-1951

Brown earned a total of eight varsity letters in football, baseball, basketball, and track. In his first year, he was selected for the State All-Junior College First Team in basketball, and in his second year, he was named the college's Best All-Around Athlete. A member of both the south division and state baseball championship teams of 1931 and 1932, Brown played first base and right field. Brown continued his athletic career at Mississippi State Teacher's College in Hattiesburg and then began a coaching career lasting from 1934-1951. From 1939-1942, he returned to Perkinston, where he was assistant football, basketball, and track coach under head coach Albert I. Rexinger. In his years as head coach at five Mississippi high schools, he never had a losing season in coaching football, basketball, baseball, and track. In 1978, Brown was inducted into the Mississippi Coaches Hall of Fame. From 1951 until his retirement in 1979, Brown served Natchez and Adams County as a school administrator.

Charles Cooper (Hattiesburg)
Coach 1975-1995

A counselor and administrator at Gulf Coast, Cooper also coached golf, 1975-1995. His teams won the Mississippi Association of Community and Junior Colleges (MACJC) state golf championship in 1979, 1986, 1990, 1992, and 1993. In 1983, his golf team was runner-up in National Junior College Athletic Association (NJCAA) in Region VII. His teams were NJCAA Region XXIII (Division III) champions in 1990, 1992, and 1993. His 1990 team placed fifth in the nation, his 1992 team placed seventh in the nation, and his 1993 team placed fourth in the nation. He was NJCAA Region XXIII Coach of the Year in 1990, 1992, and 1993. He was also MACJC Coach of the Year in 1979, 1986, 1990, 1992, and 1993. Cooper retired from MGCCC in 1994, but remained as Golf coach for one final season in 1995. In 1996 he was named to the National Junior College Athletic Association Hall of Fame. Cooper was the only Mississippi junior college golf coach accorded that honor in the 20th century.

Curtis Davis (Vancleave) Perkinston Junior College Class of 1948
Athlete 1946-1948 Coach 1951-1959

Davis learned to play tennis as a youngster on homemade dirt courts in his hometown. He played basketball while attending PJC, 1946-48. At Mississippi State College, 1948-50, Davis played tennis, advancing to the semi-finals in Southeastern Conference play in 1950 - a first for his college. Davis began his work career at Perk in 1950 as a vocational-technical instructor and soon became the tennis coach. In nine seasons, Davis's men and women won 72 matches, lost 2 and tied 2, garnering seven Mississippi junior college state championships. In 1960, he gave up his coaching responsibilities to play an important role in the formation of the Mississippi Gulf Coast Junior College District. He was named dean of the new Jackson County Campus in 1964 and retired in 1991 as JC Campus vice president. Davis's tenure with the college totaled 41 years and seven months--the 20th century record. In late 2000, Davis received word that he would be inducted into the NJCAA Hall of Fame on May 14, 2001.

Edward A. Evans (Perkinston) PAHS Class of 1948, Perkinston Junior College Class of 1950
Athlete 1944-1952, Coach 1956-1962

Evans lettered in football for four years at Perkinston Agricultural High School, and he lettered in football for two years at Perkinston Junior College. He was certainly one of the few players, if not the only player, to letter six years in football at Perk. He also played baseball, basketball, and ran track. He was twice named All-State First Team football. He was a member of Perk's 1948 state and co-national championship football team, and he was co-captain of the 1949 football team. He played first string end for two years on the Mississippi State College football team. After that he played one year of service football at Fort Jackson, South Carolina. Evans returned to Perkinston and began coaching in 1956. In 1959, he became the head football coach and hired Bobby Holmes as backfield coach. When Holmes left in 1961, Evans replaced him with George Sekul. In December 1961 Evans served as line coach of the east squad which defeated the west squad in the All-American Junior College Bowl at Albuquerque, New Mexico. Evans left coaching in 1962 to begin a career as an administrator. Evans retired from MGCCC in 1991. In 1996 the MGCCC Alumni Association awarded Evans the Sam Owen Trophy Award for service to the college.

Kenneth Callie "Curly" Farris (Corinth)
Athlete 1947-1952, Coach 1952-1989, Athletic Director 1976-1988

Farris lettered in football and baseball at Hinds Junior College 1947-1949 and continued to participate in both those sports at Mississippi Southern College in Hattiesburg. Following graduation from Mississippi Southern in 1952, Farris spent the next decade coaching high school football and baseball at Lumberton, Corinth, Tupelo, and Greenville. In 1962, Farris signed on at MGCJC as line coach in football under then head coach, and fellow Corinthian, Harold Wesson. In spring 1963, Farris began the resurrection of baseball, which had been eliminated at Perk three years before. Through Farris's efforts, MGCJC not only re-instituted baseball, but its teams came to dominate the junior college game in the state of Mississippi. Farris's Bulldogs delivered 27 consecutive winning seasons, capturing 20 Mississippi Association of Junior Colleges (MAJC) south division championships and 13 MAJC state championship trophies. Both his 1972 and 1975 teams finished as runner-up in the National Junior College Athletic Association (NJCAA) Eastern District Tournament, and his 1979 team took the NJCAA Region VII Title. Though Curly made the name "Farris" a synonym for "Junior College Baseball" in Mississippi, his first love was football. He was line coach for four MGCJC state football championship teams and for the 1971 NJCAA football championship team. In the realm of awards, Farris received the 1976 NJCAA Athletic Director's Award Region VII. In 1978 the American Association of College Baseball Coaches gave him the "Award for Quarter Century of Leadership and Devotion to College Baseball." In 1983 he was selected to coach in the United States Olympic Committee's National Sports Festival in Colorado Springs, Colorado. The MAJC named him Coach of the Year four times. The Mississippi Association of Coaches named him Coach of the Year three times and in 1986 inducted him into its Hall of Fame. Farris retired July 1, 1989, and was succeeded by his son, Cooper Farris. In 1990, he was named to the NJCAA Hall of Fame.

B. L. "Sonny" Fletcher (Pascagoula) MGCJC (Perkinston Campus) Sept. 1966 - Jan. 1968
Athlete 1966-1970

He was a member of George Sekul's first two state championship football teams, 1966 and 1967. In 1966, he became MGCJC's first freshman All-American. He was named All-State in 1966 and 1967 and played in the 1967 All-Star Football Game. In 1999 Fletcher still held the MGCCC record for the most touchdown passes caught in a season (11 in 1966), and remained tied for the most touchdowns caught in a game (3 in the 1966 Hinds game). After leaving Gulf Coast, Fletcher played football for two years at Southeastern Louisiana University. In 1999, he was project coordinator for Ingalls Shipbuilding.

James Gregory Hibbard (Gulfport) MGCJC (Perkinston Campus) Class of 1984
Athlete 1982-1997

He was a pitcher on Curly Farris' south division championship team of 1983 and the starting pitcher for the south division championship team of 1984. The former Bulldog was named to the 1984 All-State, All-Region, All-Star, and All-American teams. After Gulf Coast, Hibbard played baseball at the University of Alabama. Hibbard began playing for the Chicago White Sox in 1989 and remained for four years. In 1990, his record with the White Sox was 14-9. Hibbard signed with the Chicago Cubs in 1993 and finished the year with a 15-11 record. He closed out his professional career with the Seattle Mariners, playing for that team from 1994-97. In 1992, Hibbard was inducted into the MGCJC Alumni Hall of Fame. His 1999 induction into the MGCCC Athletic Hall of Fame earned him the distinction of being the first person named to both. Hibbard continued his association with MGCCC during the 1990s by conducting off-season baseball camps for boys in collaboration with Cooper Farris, Curly's son and successor as MGCCC baseball coach.

Robert Harold "Bobby" Holmes (Tallassee, Alabama) Perkinston Junior College Class of 1949
Athlete 1947-1951, Coach 1951-1979

Holmes played football, basketball, and baseball at Perk from 1947 to 1949. In 1947 he was the football team co-captain and was named to second team All-State. In 1948, he was captain of Perk's state and co-national championship football team and was named to the All-State and All-American first teams. After leaving Perk, Holmes played football for Mississippi Southern College, where he set the record for most touchdown passes in a game (four) and career passing (58 percent). In 1950, Holmes was named to the first team All-Gulf Coast Conference. He returned to Perk as an assistant coach from 1959 to 1961. His coaching honors included induction into the University of Southern Mississippi Hall of Fame in 1966, induction in 1985 into the Mississippi Coaches Association Hall of Fame, and the 1986 Mississippi Gulf Coast Distinguished American Award. He was coach, athletic director, and assistant principal during a 28-year career in education.

Kenneth Raymond Hughes Jr. (Biloxi) MGCJC (Jefferson Davis Campus) 1980-1982
Athlete 1980-1986, Golf Professional 1986-

He played golf for Gulf Coast from 1980 to 1982 and was named Player of the Year both his freshman and sophomore years. He was named an All-State player in 1981 and 1982. In 1982 he was the Mississippi State Junior College Medalist in Golf. He attended the University of Nebraska on a golf scholarship for a year and then enrolled at the University of Southern Mississippi. In 1985 he was named USM Golf Player of the Year. After graduation from USM in 1986, Hughes became a golf professional. Hughes was named president of the Mississippi Gulf Coast Golf Association in 1997, and served on the board of the Mississippi Gulf Coast Hotel/Motel Association. In 1999 Hughes was director of golf for the President/Broadwater Golf Club.

Barbara Ann "Sue" Ross (Gautier) Perkinston Junior College Class of 1955
Athlete 1953-1957, Coach 1963-1979, Intramural Director 1979-1991

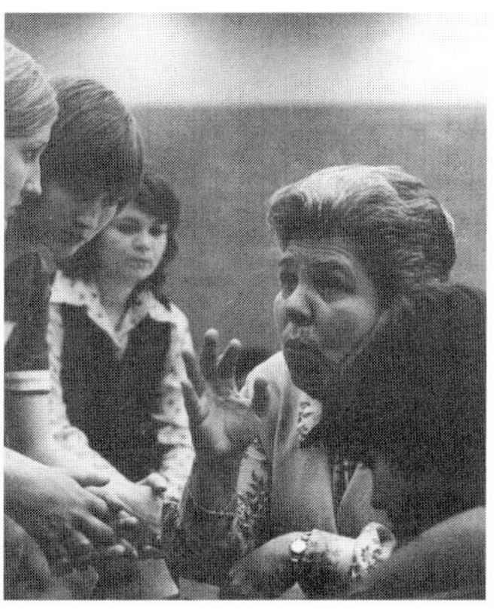

She attended Perk from 1953 to 1955, and in 1954 was named Perk's Most Athletic Woman. During her years at Perk, she played basketball and was a member of the 1955 state championship team in tennis. After Perk she attended Mississippi Southern College, where she received the Women's Overall Intramural Award in 1957. She graduated from Mississippi Southern in 1957 and spent the next two years teaching for the Houston (Texas) Independent School District. In 1960 she returned to Perk as a physical education instructor. At that time, she became involved in the movement to resurrect state level women's competitive sports, which had been eliminated in fall 1955. In 1963, the administration of MGCJC officially named her as a "coach," a title she would retain until 1979. In sixteen years as a coach, Ross's womens' teams won two tennis, one volleyball, and four basketball state championships. In addition, her basketball teams took one national title, one runner-up national spot, a seventh place national ranking, and two regional championships. In addition to her coaching duties, Ross served as the junior college representative to Association of Intercollegiate Athletics for Women District III from 1971 to 1975. She was the only junior college women's basketball coach chosen to serve on the selection committee charged with determining the players and coaches of the 1974 World University Games. In 1976 she was named assistant coach for the Women's South Basketball Team for the First National Sports Festival in Colorado Springs, Colorado. From 1977 to 1986 she served in succession as the National Junior College Athletic Association (NJCAA) women's director for Region VII and Region XXIII. From 1980 to 1984 she served as the NJCAA representative to the American Basketball Association of the United States of America for the purpose of selecting the 1984 Olympics women's basketball team and coaches. In 1979, Ross transferred to the Jackson County Campus of MGCCC and served as the intramural director of that campus until her retirement in May 1991. In mid-December, 2000, NJCAA officials notified Ross that she would be inducted into the NJCAA Hall of Fame on March 19, 2001. She was the first Mississippi community college women's basketball coach selected for that honor.

Margaret (Niolet) Scurfield (Pass Christian) MGCJC (Perkinston Campus) Class of 1974
Athlete 1972-1974

Pass Christian High School retired her jersey number in 1972, as she headed to MGCJC, where she played basketball and volleyball. She was a member of the 1973 Association of Intercollegiate Athletics for Women (AIAW) state and national junior college championship basketball team. She was also a member of the 1974 basketball team which won the Mississippi AIAW (MAIAW) state championship, the AIAW District III championship, and which finished as runner-up in the nation at the AIAW national women's basketball tournament. In 1974 she was named to Outstanding College Athletes of America. After leaving Gulf Coast, Scurfield served as an American Red Cross volunteer, and in 1999 she was the director of counseling for the Navy Family Service Center in Gulfport.

Steven George Sekul (Biloxi) Perkinston Junior College Sept. 1955 - Jan. 1957
Athlete 1955-1961, Coach 1961-1991

Sekul played football and baseball for Perk, 1955-1957. In 1956, he was named First Team Mississippi Junior College All-State and Honorable Mention Junior College All-American. From 1957 to 1961, he played and coached at Mississippi Southern College and earned a master's degree. In summer 1961, he signed on as an assistant football coach and head track coach at Perk. In 1966, he became both head football and track coach. In 31 years as head track coach, his thinclads garnered five south division and five state championships with a few individuals taking national laurels. His 26 years as head football coach yielded two National Junior College Athletic Association (NJCAA) championships (1971 and 1984), eight Mississippi Association of Junior Colleges (MAJC) south division championships, seven state championships, and one state co-championship. In addition, he guided the Bulldogs to three second place state championships and four bowl game victories, including the two that resulted in national titles. Sekul retired in December 1991. In 1999, he held the record as the "Winningest Football Coach in Junior College History" for a career record of 204-77-5. Sekul was named to the University of Southern Mississippi Sports Hall of Fame in 1968. He was chosen as MAJC Coach of the Year twice. He was named MAJC/ NJCAA Region XXIII Coach of the Year four times. In 1996, he was inducted into the NJCAA Hall of Fame. On October 21, 2000, Sekul was named to the MGCCC Alumni Hall of Fame, becoming the second person (after Greg Hibbard) to be inducted into both Halls of Fame.

Robert Wayne "Bobby" Weathers (Oak Grove)
Athlete 1951-1955, Coach 1955-

Weathers played basketball for four years at Mississippi Southern College and coached the freshman team, 1955-1957. He went into the automobile business for one year, 1957-1958, and then returned to coach the Mississippi Southern freshman for the 1958-1959 year. Following the completion of his master's degree in 1959, he coached one year at Picayune and then accepted the position as head basketball coach at Perkinston Junior College. In 1999, he continued in that position at MGCCC. In 40 years, his roundballers had racked-up more than 800 victories gaining 14 Mississippi Association of Community and Junior Colleges (MACJC) south division basketball championships and nine MACJC state basketball championships. His 1990, 1991, and 1993 teams each won the National Junior College Athletic Association (NJCAA) Region XXIII title. Weathers's 1991 team finished fourth in the nation, and his 1993 team finished fifth in the nation. In 1999, he was styled the "Winningest Active Basketball Coach in Junior College History." Also, in 1999, only one coach in American junior college history had won more games than Weathers. He was named MACJC Coach of the Year four times. He was chosen NJCAA Region XXIII Coach of the Year three times. He was inducted into the University of Southern Mississippi Hall of Fame in 1993. In 1994, he was inducted into the NJCAA Hall of Fame, and in 1999 he was inducted into the Mississippi Association of Coaches Hall of Fame.

William Harold Wesson (Corinth) Perkinston Junior College Class of 1943
Athlete 1941-1943, Coach 1948-1966

At Perk he played football, baseball, and basketball. He lettered in football and was a back on the 1942 State Championship Football Team. Following three years of service in the Army Air Corps, Wesson attended Mississippi Southern College in Hattiesburg. After graduation, he coached in various Mississippi high schools from 1948 until 1962, including nine years in his hometown of Corinth. His Kosciusko High School team took the 1949 state championship, and he was named Big Eight Conference Coach of the Year in 1951. On April 18, 1962, the Board of Trustees of Perkinston Junior College approved Wesson for the head coach's position vacated in January that year by Ed Evans. On the same day, at Wesson's urging, the Board hired fellow Corinthian Ken "Curly" Farris as his football line coach. On May 10, 1962, Wesson and Farris, together with George Sekul, whom Wesson had inherited as backfield coach from Evans's regime, became the first complement of football coaches to serve the institution under the appellation "Mississippi Gulf Coast Junior College." In 1966, Wesson joined the central office administration of MGCJC, leaving his head coach job to Sekul. Wesson retired from MGCJC in June 1977 and died September 16, 2000.

MISSISSIPPI GULF COAST COMMUNITY COLLEGE ALUMNI ASSOCIATION

ATHLETIC HALL OF FAME

OCTOBER 19, 2000

William Charles Boone (Biloxi) Perkinston Junior College Class of 1952
Athlete 1950-1954, Coach 1957-1969

"Flopy" Boone, born in Hattiesburg February 4, 1932, graduated from Biloxi High School and entered Perkinston Junior College in fall 1950. In his two years at Perk he played football, basketball, baseball, and ran track. Named "Most Athletic" man in 1952, Boone made his greatest athletic contribution to Perk in the realm of basketball, where he played center position and led the team in scoring both years he played. From Perk, Boone went to Livingston (Alabama) State College, where he played baseball and basketball. As he had at Perk, Boone led the Livingston basketball team in scoring both years. After graduating in 1954, he served two years in the United States Army. Honorably discharged in 1956, he entered Mississippi Southern College in Hattiesburg, earning his master's degree in June 1957. He immediately began his coaching/teaching career at Quitman High School, serving as mentor in all sports for both girls and boys. He was named Choctaw Conference Coach of the Year in several sports. Boone was inducted into the Mississippi Association of Coaches Hall of Fame in 1992. Following his coaching career Boone served as principal at Quitman High School from 1969 to 1981. Elected Clarke County Superintendent of Education, he held that position for a decade until his retirement in 1991. In recognition of his contributions to the athletic, educational, and religious life of his community, he was selected to carry the Olympic Torch in Mississippi in 1996. In 2000, Boone completed 17 years as a member of the Jones County Junior College Board of Trustees.

William Elvin Davis Sr. (Pensacola, Florida) Perkinston Junior College Sept. 1946 - May 1948, Athlete 1946-1955

Bill Davis, born July 17, 1928, in Beulah, Florida, graduated from Catholic High School in Pensacola in May 1946. He entered Perkinston Junior College in the fall where he played two years of football and baseball and lettered in both. As a Bulldog pitcher on the baseball diamond, Davis earned the sobriquets "Doc," "Sweet William," "Fireball," "Wild Bill," and "Iron Man." (This may be a Perk record for the number of nicknames assigned to an individual.) On May 6, 1947, David pitched the Bulldogs to a south division victory over the Southwest Junior College Pilots. On May 14 he won both games in a double header against the Northwest Junior College Rangers to take the state baseball championship trophy for Perk. On May 1, 1948, Davis pitched Perk to a south division victory over the Copiah-Lincoln Junior College Wolves. After leaving Perk, Davis played two years professional baseball for the Columbia (South Carolina) Reds and the Fitzgerald (Georgia) State League. From 1950-1955 he played on the Pensacola Alumni Semi-Professional Football Team. Davis initiated a career in law enforcement in 1951, which culminated in a 12-year stint (1960-1972) as Sheriff of Escambia County, Florida. From 1973 until his retirement in 1991, he engaged in various law enforcement-related activities and private business ventures. Throughout his career Davis served the community by coaching Little League baseball and basketball, through volunteer fire department activities, and by sponsoring various church-related activities for disadvantaged children.

Zenobia Ruth (Denson) Houston (Bay Springs) Harrison-Stone-Jackson Agricultural High School and Junior College Sept. 1927 - May 1932, Athlete 1920-1924, Coach 1927-1932

Noby Ruth (Denson) Houston, born December 24, 1901, graduated from high school in Bay Springs in spring 1920. That fall she entered Mississippi Women's College, a Baptist institution in Hattiesburg, which later evolved into William Carey College. While at MWC she excelled in women's sports, especially basketball. After her graduation from MWC in 1924, she taught one year at Magnolia Consolidated School seven miles west of Wiggins and two years at Piave in Greene County. In 1927, Lee Denson, her cousin who was then superintendent of Harrison-Stone-Jackson Agricultural High School and Junior College at Perkinston, recruited Noby Ruth to teach music and coach women's basketball. Her 1929 team won the Second Place State Trophy in the state tournament held March 16 in the Old Gym at Perkinston. The 1929 tournament was the second annual Mississippi junior college state tournament in the history of the Mississippi Junior College Athletic Association and the first one held in the facilities of a member institution. The trophy taken by Noby Ruth's team in the 1929 tournament was the initial state level women's sports trophy in the history of the Perkinston-based institution and the only one until the Perk women's basketball team won the south division title of 1953. In addition to coaching, Noby Ruth, who was the band-orchestra leader, apparently initiated the practice of playing music at sports events. Noby Ruth left Perk in May 1932. The following month she married Reuben Kidd Houston of Sylvarena. After ten years in Texas the couple returned to Bay Springs. Noby Ruth (Denson) Houston died in Bay Springs on November 7, 2000.

Matthew Lawton (Saucier) Mississippi Gulf Coast Community College Class of 1991 Athlete 1989-

Matt Lawton, born November 30, 1971, in Gulfport, grew up in Saucier. After graduating from Harrison Central High School in 1989, Lawton enrolled at MGCCC (Perkinston Campus) on a baseball scholarship. According to Coach Cooper Farris, Lawton set the MGCCC record for stolen bases with 50 in 1990. In 1991 he broke his own record by stealing 80 bases. In two seasons at MGCCC Lawton went to bat 332 times, had 141 hits, scoring 137 runs, and knocking in 78 more. While at MGCCC, Lawton was All-State and All-Region XXIII both years. He was a member of the MGCCC team that placed fifth in the nation at the 1991 National Junior College Athletic Association (NJCAA) World Series, after which he was declared a Junior College All-American. Also in 1991 Lawton was selected to play for the NJCAA All-Star Team that traveled to Cuba to play the Cuban national team in a seven game series. His performance in Cuba was such that a representative of the scouting department of the Minnesota Twins met him at the airport in Miami, Florida, with an offer that caused Lawton to refuse a baseball scholarship to the University of South Alabama. He climbed the Minnesota Twins Minor league ladder from 1991 to 1995 being the "Twins Minor League Player of the Week" several times. He was called up to the Minnesota Twins major league team in 1995. He was selected as the Twins Most Valuable Player in 1998 and made the American League All-Star Team in 2000. According to Cooper Farris, Lawton returned and practiced with the MGCCC team every January and February from 1992 to 1999.

Delores Ann (Parker) Sumrall (Biloxi) Perkinston Junior College Aug. 1951 - May 1952 Athlete 1951-1952, Coach 1968-1974

Delores (Parker) Sumrall, born April 5, 1933, in Biloxi, attended St. Martin High School, lettered four years in basketball and was co-captain of the team her senior year. She also played on amateur fast-pitch softball teams including the Gulfport Hi Neighbors softball team which won the 1950 Mississippi State Championship. Sumrall attended Perkinston Junior College for the 1951-1952 session, where she was a guard on the Perkette basketball team and was named Honorable Mention All-State for her season's performance. In addition to her intercollegiate play at Perk, Sumrall also served as captain of a campus intramural basketball team. After leaving Perk she earned a bachelor of science degree in education at Mississippi Southern College in Hattiesburg and a master of science degree in education at William Carey College located in the same city. During her 34-year career as a coach, teacher, and administrator, she coached junior high basketball and track at St. Martin for six years. In track her teams won the county and conference championships five times. Her basketball teams won the county championship four times and the conference championship three times. The 1995 Dixie Bowl was dedicated to Sumrall in honor of her decades-long commitment to the youth of the St. Martin community. In 1999, after 14 years of service to MGCCC as a Trustee (including two one-year stints as Chairperson of the Board), the Association of Community College Trustees (ACCT) elected Sumrall as a member of the ACCT National Board of Directors, which in turn elected her Southern Region Chairperson.

Appendix IV

MISSISSIPPI GULF COAST COMMUNITY COLLEGE ALUMNI ASSOCIATION

INSTRUCTOR OF THE YEAR AWARD RECIPIENTS

1971 - 2000

The MGCCC Alumni Association established the Instructor of the Year Award in 1971 to recognize selected instructors for academic excellence and contributions to the community. The first four awards were college-wide in scope. Beginning in 1975, each campus (Perkinston, Jefferson Davis, and Jackson County) named an Instructor of the Year. Beginning in 1999 the Alumni Association recognized an Instructor of the Year for the Community Campus, bringing the total awards per year to four.

According to the rules, an instructor might be named Instructor of the Year twice. In the 20th century three instructors were so honored--Bennie Van Court (JC 1979 & 1985), Charles Sullivan (Perk 1976 & 1990), and Kathryn Lewis (Perk 1979 & 2000).

In the 20th century four married couples were given the award--Woodley (Perk 1978) and Nelda (Perk 1985) Lott; Jon (Perk 1988) and Kathryn (Perk 1979 & 2000) Lewis; David (JD 1982) and Joan (JD 1987) Fitch; and Dean (JC 1980) and Edna (JC 1981) Shaw. In 2000 Dean Shaw was the longest serving Instructor of the Year having been a member of JC's first (1965) faculty. Shaw enjoyed yet another unique distinction together with his social studies division counterparts, L. A. Drago at JD and Charles Sullivan at Perk. In 2000 the social studies division was the only one in which all three sitting campus department chairmen had been named instructor of the year and also was the only division in which all three chairmen had served the institution for 30 or more years.

Each instructor's position at the time of the award was given, however, educational attainments and years of service were continued to the close of the instructor's career with MGCCC or to the close of the 20th century. The absence of a final date indicated that the instructor was still serving as of December 31, 2000.

1971
Guy D. Moffett
Science Department
Physics/Mathematics
MISSISSIPPI GULF COAST
JUNIOR COLLEGE

Employment with Mississippi Gulf Coast:
Perkinston Campus 1952-1974

Education:
Diploma, Harrison-Stone-Jackson Junior College
B.S., M.A., University of Southern Mississippi

*Date of Death: December 30, 1990

1972
Eugene Clement
Chairperson, Fine Arts Department
Choral Director/Music
MISSISSIPPI GULF COAST
JUNIOR COLLEGE

Employment with Mississippi Gulf Coast:
Perkinston Campus 1949-1986

Education:
B.M., M.M., University of Southern Mississippi
Additional study
University of Southern Mississippi

*Date of Death: December 18, 1991

1973
Betty (Peavy) Malone
Chairperson, Language Arts Department
English
MISSISSIPPI GULF COAST
JUNIOR COLLEGE

Employment with Mississippi Gulf Coast:
Jefferson Davis Campus 1965-1991
Perkinston Campus 1991-1994

Education:
B.A., William Carey College
M.S., University of Southern Mississippi
Additional study
University of Southern Mississippi

1974
William R. "Billy" Towles
Technical Department
Drafting & Design
MISSISSIPPI GULF COAST
JUNIOR COLLEGE

Employment with Mississippi Gulf Coast:
Jefferson Davis Campus 1969-1976
Adjunct 1977-1992
West Harrison County Occupational
Training Center 1993-

Education:
A.S., Perkinston Junior College
Additional study at
University of Southern Mississippi

1975
Betty June (Worrell) Lee
Business Department
Accounting
JEFFERSON DAVIS CAMPUS

Employment with Mississippi Gulf Coast:
1965-1989

Education:
B.S., Mississippi University for Women
M.Ed., Mississippi State University
Additional study
University of Mississippi

1975
Lynne (Hall) Pringle Burger
Social Studies Department
Sociology/Geography/Political Science
JACKSON COUNTY CAMPUS

Employment with Mississippi Gulf Coast:
1971-1995

Education:
Diploma, Gulf Park College
B.A., Newcomb College, Tulane University
M.S.S., University of Mississippi

1975
Robert Morris Rominger Jr.
Social Studies Department
History/Political Science/Philosophy
PERKINSTON CAMPUS

Employment with Mississippi Gulf Coast:
1970-

Education:
B.S., M.A., University of West Florida
Additional study
University of Southern Mississippi

1976
****Charlie L. Kelly***
Vocational-Technical Department
Pipefitting/Plumbing
JACKSON COUNTY CAMPUS

Employment with Mississippi Gulf Coast:
1969-1976

Education:
20 Years Experience

*Date of Death: October 12, 1976

1976
James M. Knight
Science Department
Chemistry/Biology
JEFFERSON DAVIS CAMPUS

Employment with Mississippi Gulf Coast:
1969-1991

Education:
B.S., M.A., University of Southern Mississippi
Residency for Doctorate
University of Southern Mississippi

1976
Charles Leonard Sullivan
Social Studies Department
History/Geography
PERKINSTON CAMPUS

Employment with Mississippi Gulf Coast:
1967-
(Aug. 1969-Aug. 1970 Leave of Absence
for Doctoral Residency)

Education:
B.S., M.S., University of Southern Mississippi
Residency for Doctorate
University of Mississippi

1977
Charlie Eldon Ormon
Chairperson, Technical Education Department
Electronics/ Computer Programming
JACKSON COUNTY CAMPUS

Employment with Mississippi Gulf Coast:
1967-1997

Education:
B.S., M.Ed., Mississippi State University
Additional Study
University of Southern Mississippi

1977
Randall Anastasio
Physical Education Department
Health/Physical Education
JEFFERSON DAVIS CAMPUS

Employment with Mississippi Gulf Coast:
1973-1986

Education:
B.S., M.S., University of Southern Mississippi

1977
Frank Spring
Vocational-Technical Department
Printing
PERKINSTON CAMPUS

Employment with Mississippi Gulf Coast:
Perkinston Campus 1968-1987
Central Office 1987-1998

Education:
15 Years Experience

1978
Royce B. Luke
Business and Office Administration Department
Economics/Accounting
JACKSON COUNTY CAMPUS

Employment with Mississippi Gulf Coast:
Perkinston Campus 1956-60
Jackson County Campus
1965-1966, 1969-1988, 1992-1997

Education:
A.A., East Central Junior College
B.S., M.S., University of Southern Mississippi,
Ed.D., Mississippi State University

1978
William Brewer
Chairperson, Technical Department
Criminal Justice
JEFFERSON DAVIS CAMPUS

Employment with Mississippi Gulf Coast:
1969-1987

Education:
B.S.C., University of Mississippi
M.S., University of Southern Mississippi
Additional Study
University of Southern Mississippi
Tulane University

1978
Woodley Lott
Chairperson, Language Arts Department
English/Literature
PERKINSTON CAMPUS

Employment with Mississippi Gulf Coast:
1960-1990

Education:
B.S., M.A., Ph.D.,
University of Southern Mississippi

1979
Kathryn Ann (Schledwitz) Lewis
Fine Arts Department
Speech/Theatre
PERKINSTON CAMPUS

Employment with Mississippi Gulf Coast:
1969-

Education:
B.S., M.S., University of Southern Mississippi
Additional study
University of Southern Mississippi

1979
Bennie Lynn (Taylor) Van Court
Technical Education Department
Drafting & Design
JACKSON COUNTY CAMPUS

Employment with Mississippi Gulf Coast:
1971-1998

Education:
A.S., Perkinston Junior College
B.S., M.S., University of Southern Mississippi
Additional study
University of Mississippi

1979
Paul G. McKay
Mathematics Department
Mathematics
JEFFERSON DAVIS CAMPUS

Employment with Mississippi Gulf Coast:
1967-

Education:
B.S., M.S., Mississippi State University
Residency for Doctorate
University of Mississippi

1980
Harmon Dean Shaw
Chairperson, Social Studies Department
History
JACKSON COUNTY CAMPUS

Employment with Mississippi Gulf Coast:
1965-

Education:
B.A., Millsaps College
M.A., Mississippi State University
Residency for Doctorate
Mississippi State University

1980
Norma Jane Richards
Associate Degree Nursing
Medical/Surgical Nursing
JEFFERSON DAVIS CAMPUS

Employment with Mississippi Gulf Coast:
1972-

Education:
B.S.N., Louisiana State University
School of Nursing
M.S., Texas Woman's University

1980
Mary Katherine (Morphis) Adams
Science Department
Home Economics
PERKINSTON CAMPUS

Employment with Mississippi Gulf Coast:
1970-1982

Education:
B.S., M.S., Mississippi State College for Women

1981
Edna (Hannah) Shaw
Language Arts Department
English
JACKSON COUNTY CAMPUS

Employment with Mississippi Gulf Coast:
1969-

Education:
B.S., Blue Mountain College
M.S., University of Southern Mississippi

1981
Lucas Philip Lisotta
Fine Arts Department
Speech/Drama
JEFFERSON DAVIS CAMPUS

Employment with Mississippi Gulf Coast:
Perkinston Campus 1962-1965
Jefferson Davis Campus 1965-1980
Education:
B.A. Northeast Louisiana State College
M.A., Louisiana State University
Additional study
Louisiana State University

1981
Richard J. Miller
Chairperson, Science Department
Biology
PERKINSTON CAMPUS

Employment with Mississippi Gulf Coast:
1970-1996

Education:
B.S., Southeastern Louisiana University
M.Ed, Auburn University
M.S., Oklahoma State University
Ph.D., University of Alabama

1982
Walter Elisha Mullen III
Language Arts Departmental
English
JACKSON COUNTY CAMPUS

Employment with Mississippi Gulf Coast:
1967-1994

Education:
B.A.E., University of Mississippi
M.E. Auburn University

1982
David C. Fitch
Mathematics Department
Mathematics/Engineering
JEFFERSON DAVIS CAMPUS

Employment with Mississippi Gulf Coast:
1970-1985, 1990-1999

Education:
B.S., M.S., Mississippi State University
Residency for Doctorate
Rice University

1982
Marie Antoinette (Davis) Heim
Chairperson, Developmental Studies Department
Reading/Study Skills/Leadership Development
PERKINSTON CAMPUS

Employment with Mississippi Gulf Coast:
1979-

Education:
A.A., Mississippi Gulf Coast Junior College
(Perkinston Campus)
B.S., University of Southern Mississippi
M.Ed., William Carey College
Ed.D., University of Southern Mississippi

1983
Karen A. Davis
Associate Degree Nursing
Fundamentals/Pediatric
JACKSON COUNTY CAMPUS

Employment with Mississippi Gulf Coast:
1974-1987

Education:
B.S., Northeast Louisiana University
M.S., University of Southern Mississippi

1983
Quincy Albert Long
Science Department
Biology
JEFFERSON DAVIS CAMPUS

Employment with Mississippi Gulf Coast:
1965-1996

Education:
A.S., Jones County Junior College
B.S., M.S., University of Southern Mississippi
Additional Study
University of Southern Mississippi

1983
Cheryl Lynn (Kouba) Catalano
Language Arts Department
English
PERKINSTON CAMPUS

Employment with Mississippi Gulf Coast:
1979-

Education:
B.S., M.Ed., University of Southern Mississippi
Additional study
University of Southern Mississippi

1984
Robert Comer Hudson
Vocational Education Department
Machine Shop
JACKSON COUNTY CAMPUS

Employment with Mississippi Gulf Coast:
1976-1997

Education:
B.S., M.S., University of Southern Mississippi

1984
****Evelyn Alford***
Licensed Practical Nursing
Practical Nursing
JEFFERSON DAVIS CAMPUS

Employment with Mississippi Gulf Coast:
1965-1984

Education:
Diploma, School of Nursing, New Biloxi Hospital
Additional study
University of Southern Mississippi
Texas Woman's University

*Date of Death: June 14, 1985

1984
****Wentz Batson***
Vocational-Technical Department
Ornamental Horticulture
PERKINSTON CAMPUS

Employment with Mississippi Gulf Coast:
1975-1991

Education:
B.S., Mississippi State University

*Date of Death: June 20, 1998

1985
Bennie Lynn (Taylor) Van Court
Technical Education
Drafting & Design
JACKSON COUNTY CAMPUS

Employment with Mississippi Gulf Coast:
1971-1998

Education:
A.S., Perkinston Junior College
B.S., M.S., University of Southern Mississippi
Additional study
University of Southern Mississippi
University of Mississippi

1985
Laurie Anthony Drago
Social Studies Department
History/Government
JEFFERSON DAVIS CAMPUS

Employment with Mississippi Gulf Coast:
1970-

Education:
B.A., Northwestern State College of Louisiana
M.A., Louisiana State University
Residency for Doctorate
University of Southern Mississippi

1985
Nelda (Jackson) Lott
Language Arts Department
English/Literature
PERKINSTON CAMPUS

Employment with Mississippi Gulf Coast:
1960-1990

Education:
B.S., M.A., Ph.D.,
University of Southern Mississippi

1986
Teresa (Griffis) Heidleberg
Language Arts Department
English
JACKSON COUNTY CAMPUS

Employment with Mississippi Gulf Coast:
1982-1989

Education:
B.A., Valdosta State University
M.Ed., Ph.D., University of Southern Mississippi

1986
Charles Ray Shows
Chairperson, Social Studies Department
History/Government/Psychology
JEFFERSON DAVIS CAMPUS

Employment with Mississippi Gulf Coast:
1965-1991

Education:
B.S., M.A., University of Southern Mississippi
Residency for Doctorate
University of Southern Mississippi

1986
David C. Schwab
Science Department
Biology
PERKINSTON CAMPUS

Employment with Mississippi Gulf Coast:
1973-1995

Education:
B.S., M.S., Southeastern Louisiana University
Ph.D., University of Southern Mississippi

1987
Patricia Ann "Patt" Odom
Fine Arts Department
Art
JACKSON COUNTY CAMPUS

Employment with Mississippi Gulf Coast:
1980-1999

Education:
B.S., M.A.E., University of Southern Mississippi
Additional Study
University of Tennessee
Ringling School of Art and Design
Louisiana Technical University
University of Hawaii

1987
Joan Elaine (Wilson) Fitch
Language Arts Department
English
JEFFERSON DAVIS CAMPUS

Employment with Mississippi Gulf Coast:
1972-1999

Education:
B.A., University of Southern Mississippi
M.A., University of Arkansas
Ph.D. University of Southern Mississippi
Additional study
Princeton University,
University of Virginia, Academy in Rome,
Harvard University

1987
Robert Thomas Walden
Chairperson, Science Department
Physics/Math
PERKINSTON CAMPUS

Employment with Mississippi Gulf Coast:
1973-1987

Education:
B.S., M.S., Murray State University
Ph.D., University of Southern Mississippi

1988
Thomas Ralph Smith
Mathematics Department
Math
JACKSON COUNTY CAMPUS

Employment with Mississippi Gulf Coast:
1965-1994

Education:
B.S., Louisiana College
M.S., University of Southern Mississippi
Additional study
University of Southern Mississippi

1988
****Donald E. Moore***
Chairperson, Fine Arts Department
Speech/Theatre
JEFFERSON DAVIS CAMPUS

Employment with Mississippi Gulf Coast:
1976-1987

Education:
B.S., M.S., University of Southern Mississippi
Additional study
University of Southern Mississippi
University of Mississippi

*Date of Death: July 17, 1987

1988
Jon Richard Lewis
Social Studies Department
History
PERKINSTON CAMPUS

Employment with Mississippi Gulf Coast:
1977-

Education:
B.S., M.A., University of Southern Mississippi
Additional study
University of Southern Mississippi

1989
Annette Hutcherson
Associate Degree Nursing
Medical/Surgical Nursing
JACKSON COUNTY CAMPUS

Employment with Mississippi Gulf Coast:
1978-1989

Education:
B.S., M.S., Ph.D.,
University of Southern Mississippi

1989
Susan Gayle (Stewart) Pagano
Mathematics Department
Math
JEFFERSON DAVIS CAMPUS

Employment with Mississippi Gulf Coast:
1972-1980
1984-

Education:
B.S., M.S., University of Mississippi
B.S., University of Southern Mississippi

1989
Charles Michael Acres
Fine Arts Department
Art
PERKINSTON CAMPUS

Employment with Mississippi Gulf Coast:
1976-

Education:
B.A., Jacksonville State University
M.A., M.F.A., University of Alabama

1990
Robert R. Herrington Jr.
Chairperson, Science Department
Chemistry/Biology
JACKSON COUNTY CAMPUS

Employment with Mississippi Gulf Coast:
1968-1990

Education:
B.S., M.S., University of Southern Mississippi
Residency for Doctorate
University of Southern Mississippi

1990
Evelyn Webb
Chairperson, Language Arts Department
English
JEFFERSON DAVIS CAMPUS

Employment with Mississippi Gulf Coast:
1972-1993

Education:
B.A., Jackson State University
M.S., University of Southern Mississippi
Ph.D. University of Southern Mississippi

1990
Charles Leonard Sullivan
Chairperson, Social Studies Department
History/Geography
PERKINSTON CAMPUS

Employment with Mississippi Gulf Coast:
1967-
(Aug. 1969-Aug. 1970 Leave of Absence for Doctoral Residency)

Education:
B.S., M.S., University of Southern Mississippi
Residency for Doctorate
University of Mississippi

1991
Lena Nell (Hollis) Melton
Science Department
Physical Science/Anatomy/Physiology/Biology
JACKSON COUNTY CAMPUS

Employment with Mississippi Gulf Coast:
Adjunct 1979-1985
1985-

Education:
B.S., Hampton Institute
M.S., Ph.D., University of Southern Mississippi

1991
R. Elaine (Turrentine) Schmidtling
Associate Degree Nursing
Medical/Surgical Nursing
JEFFERSON DAVIS CAMPUS

Employment with Mississippi Gulf Coast:
1976-1999

Education:
Diploma, John Peter Smith School of Nursing
B.S.N. William Carey College
M.S., University of Southern Mississippi

1991
Larry Burney
Vocational Department
Office Systems Technology
PERKINSTON CAMPUS

Employment with Mississippi Gulf Coast:
George County
Occupational Training Center
1976-

Education:
B.S., Albany State College
M.B.Ed., Jackson State University
Additional study
Alabama State University
University of Southern Mississippi

1992
Barbara Sue (Davis) Haygood
Chairperson, Developmental Studies Department
Math
JACKSON COUNTY CAMPUS

Employment with Mississippi Gulf Coast:
1985-

Education:
A.A., Mississippi Gulf Coast Junior College
(Perkinston Campus)
B.S., Mississippi State College for Women
M.Ed., William Carey College

1992
Carole Lynn (Wilson) Meadows
Business Department
Business and Office Administration
JEFFERSON DAVIS CAMPUS

Employment with Mississippi Gulf Coast:
1967-1969
Adjunct 1979-1984
1984-1994
1999-

Education:
B.S., M.B.E., University of Mississippi

1992
Alfred Leon Byrd
Chairperson, Business Department
Business Technology
PERKINSTON CAMPUS

Employment with Mississippi Gulf Coast:
Adjunct 1972-1983
1984-1993

Education:
A.A., Perkinston Junior College
B.S., M.S., University of Southern Mississippi
Additional study
University of Southern Mississippi

1993
Raymond H. Tanner
Mathematics Department
Math
JACKSON COUNTY CAMPUS

Employment with Mississippi Gulf Coast:
1983-

Education:
A.A., Mississippi Gulf Coast Junior College
(Jackson County Campus)
B.S., University of Southern Mississippi
M.Ed., William Carey College
Additional Study
University of Southern Mississippi

1993
Ouida Sue (Howell) Clark White
Chairperson, Business and Office Administration
Business Related Courses
JEFFERSON DAVIS CAMPUS

Employment with Mississippi Gulf Coast:
1966-

Education:
A.A., Jones County Junior College
B.S., M.S., University of Southern Mississippi
Additional study
University of Southern Mississippi

1993

Brenda Faye (Alexander) Batey

Language Arts Department
Foreign Languages
PERKINSTON CAMPUS

Employment with Mississippi Gulf Coast:
1988-

Education:
A.A., Mississippi Gulf Coast Junior College
(Perkinston Campus)
B.A., University of Southern Mississippi
M.A., Mississippi State University
Additional study
Instituto Centro Americano de Asuntos
Internacionales

1994

Faye (Morgan) Jones

Social Studies Department
Sociology
JACKSON COUNTY CAMPUS

Employment with Mississippi Gulf Coast:
1989-

Education:
B.S., Mississippi College
M.A., Mississippi State University
Additional study
University of South Alabama

1994

Sarah (Varnadore) Mulvaney Stopson

Vocational Department
Office Systems Technology
JEFFERSON DAVIS CAMPUS

Employment with Mississippi Gulf Coast:
Jefferson Davis Campus 1979-1984
West Harrison County
Occupational Training Center
1984-

Education:
A.A., Mississippi Gulf Coast Junior College
(Jefferson Davis Campus)
B.S., M.S., University of Southern Mississippi

1994

Noel R. Mann

Chairperson, Science Department
Chemistry
PERKINSTON CAMPUS

Employment with Mississippi Gulf Coast:
1974-1996
(Dec. 1990-Aug. 1991, Leave of Absence
to serve in Gulf War)
1999-

Education:
B.S., M.S., Delta State University
Ph.D., University of Southern Mississippi

1995

Amaryllis (Jordan) Stroud

Developmental Studies Department
Reading/Study Skills
JACKSON COUNTY CAMPUS

Employment with Mississippi Gulf Coast:
1965-1995

Education:
B.S., M.Ed., University of Southern Mississippi
Additional study
University of Southern Mississippi
Mississippi State University

1995

William Therrell

Social Studies Department
History
JEFFERSON DAVIS CAMPUS

Employment with Mississippi Gulf Coast:
1963-1998

Education:
B.S., M.A., Mississippi State University

1995
Brenda (Ragan) Shotts Nalepa
Science Department
Biology
PERKINSTON CAMPUS

Employment with Mississippi Gulf Coast:
1987-1997

Education:
A.A., Hinds Junior College
B.S., Mississippi University for Women
M.S., Mississippi State University
Ph.D., University of Southern Mississippi

1996
Kimberly Rusty (Johnson) Brown
Science Department
Biology
JACKSON COUNTY CAMPUS

Employment with Mississippi Gulf Coast:
1990-

Education:
B.A., University of Mississippi
M.Ed., University of Southern Mississippi

1996
Gloria June (Ladner) Jefferson
Vocational-Technical Department
Teacher Assistant Program
JEFFERSON DAVIS CAMPUS

Employment with Mississippi Gulf Coast:
1992-

Education:
A.A., Mississippi Gulf Coast Junior College
(Perkinston Campus)
B.S., Our Lady of Holy Cross College
M.S., University of Southern Mississippi

1996
David Paul Dueitt
Fine Arts Department
Band Director
PERKINSTON CAMPUS

Employment with Mississippi Gulf Coast:
1988-

Education:
B.S., M.M., University of Alabama

1997
Deborah Ann Hill
Associate Degree Nursing
Psychiatric and Mental Health Nursing
JACKSON COUNTY CAMPUS

Employment with Mississippi Gulf Coast:
1983-

Education:
B.S., Mississippi University for Women
M.N., University of Mississippi Medical Center

1997
Carol Ann (Dick) Holley
Chairperson, Language Arts Department
English
JEFFERSON DAVIS CAMPUS

Employment with Mississippi Gulf Coast:
Adjunct 1989-1991
1991-

Education:
A.A., Mississippi Gulf Coast Junior College
(Jefferson Davis Campus)
B.S., University of South Alabama
M.S., University of Southern Mississippi

1997
Marilyn (Porter) Smith Lott
Fine Arts Department
Vocal Music
PERKINSTON CAMPUS

Employment with Mississippi Gulf Coast:
1990-

Education:
A.A., Mississippi Gulf Coast Junior College
(Perkinston Campus)
B.M.E., M.M.E., University of Southern Mississippi

1998
Rebecca (Burkes) Moreton
Fine Arts Department
Speech and Theatre
JACKSON COUNTY CAMPUS

Employment with Mississippi Gulf Coast:
1991-

Education:
B.A., M.A., University of Mississippi
Additional Study
University of Memphis

1998
Margaret Sharon (Keith) Andresen
Language Arts Department
English/Foreign Languages
JEFFERSON DAVIS CAMPUS

Employment with Mississippi Gulf Coast:
1967-1998

Education:
B.A., M.A., University of Southern Mississippi
Additional study
University of Florida
University of Puget Sound
University of Southern Mississippi

1998
John Bowen "J.B." Brown
Vocational-Technical Department
Welding
PERKINSTON CAMPUS

Employment with Mississippi Gulf Coast:
1974-

Education:
A.S., Pearl River Junior College
B.S., M.S., University of Southern Mississippi

1999
Jeffrey Marshall Feinberg Sr.
Coordinator, Inplant Apprenticeship
Electronics/Electrical
COMMUNITY CAMPUS

Employment with Mississippi Gulf Coast:
1989-

Education:
A.A., Mississippi Gulf Coast Junior College
(Jackson County Campus)
B.S., University of Southern Mississippi

1999
Debra (Mize) Smith Matthews
Chairperson, Vocational Department
Electrical Technology
JACKSON COUNTY CAMPUS

Employment with Mississippi Gulf Coast:
1986-

Education:
A.A.S., Mississippi Gulf Coast Junior College
(Jackson County Campus)
Additional Study
University of Southern Mississippi

1999
Dorothy Lee (Robinson) Knight
Language Arts Department
English
JEFFERSON DAVIS CAMPUS

Employment with Mississippi Gulf Coast:
1978-2000

Education:
A.A., Coahoma Junior College
B.S., Jackson State University
M.Ed., William Carey College

1999
Janet Gail Moody
Science Department
Biology
PERKINSTON CAMPUS

Employment with Mississippi Gulf Coast:
1996-

Education:
A.A., Pearl River Junior College
B.S. Mississippi State University
B.S., Mississippi Baptist Medical Center
M.S., Ph.D., University of Southern Mississippi

2000
Nora Gale (Bond) Newbill
Adult Basic Education
Basic Skills/General Education Development
COMMUNITY CAMPUS

Employment with Mississippi Gulf Coast:
1994-

Education:
A.S., Mississippi Gulf Coast Junior College
(Perkinston Campus)
B.S., University of Southern Mississippi

2000
Shelia Alva Brown
Chairperson, Science Department
Biology
JEFFERSON DAVIS CAMPUS

Employment with Mississippi Gulf Coast:
1985-

Education:
B.S., Louisiana State University
M.S., Loyola University
Ph.D., University of Southern Mississippi

2000
Jane Anne (Cavaroc) Brenden
Associate Degree Nursing
Community/Mental Health Nursing
JACKSON COUNTY CAMPUS

Employment with Mississippi Gulf Coast:
1991-

Education:
A.S., Mississippi Gulf Coast Junior College
(Jackson County Campus)
B.S.N., M.S.N., University of South Alabama
Ph.D., University of Southern Mississippi

2000
Kathryn Ann (Schledwitz) Lewis
Chairperson, Fine Arts Department
Speech/Theatre
PERKINSTON CAMPUS

Employment with Mississippi Gulf Coast:
1969-

Education:
B.S., M.S., University of Southern Mississippi
Additional study
University of Southern Mississippi

MISSISSIPPI GULF COAST COMMUNITY COLLEGE

HISTORY OF THE BOARD OF TRUSTEES 1911 - 2000 INCLUDING LISTS OF PRESIDENTS/CHAIRPERSONS AND MEMBERS OF THE BOARD FROM HARRISON, STONE, JACKSON, AND GEORGE COUNTIES AND THEIR TERMS OF SERVICE

History of the Board of Trustees, 1911 - 2000

The original Board of Trustees set up in 1911 consisted of five members. The Harrison County Board of Supervisors appointed two, the Harrison County School Board appointed two and the Harrison County Superintendent of Education was the other one. Appointments to the Board were made in such a manner as to insure that a member resided in each of the county's five supervisor beats. By the terms of the compromise leading to the formation of the Bi-County Harrison-Stone Agricultural High School in 1916, Harrison County received six members to Stone County's five, thus assuring Harrison County control of the Board. In addition, whether by accident or design, all Presidents of the Board in the Agricultural High School period (September 1911-September 1925) hailed from Harrison County.

With the establishment of the Harrison-Stone-Jackson AHS and Junior College in September 1925, Jackson County appointed five Trustees to the Board. The college catalogs continued to list six Harrison County Trustees until 1929 when the number dropped to five. In summer 1933 representation on the Board rose to six members from each of the three counties. Representation in each case was composed of one member appointed by each supervisor plus the county superintendent of education. The term of service for a regular Trustee was five years with unlimited reappointment. A superintendent of education served four years with unlimited re-election opportunities. The terms of service for regular Trustees were staggered in such a manner that no county would change all of its Trustees in any one election year even if all its supervisors were defeated at the polls. All four Trustees from all four Beats 1 terminated simultaneously. All four Trustees representing all four Beats 2 terminated the following year and so on. Superintendents of education were terminated individually by defeat at the polls, retirement, or death.

On October 15, 1941, President A. L. May announced to the Board that the George County Supervisors had levied a one-half mill tax in support of the college. At the next meeting, on November 7, two George County Trustees took their seats on the Board. One of these was the current George County Superintendent of Education. From the beginning, no matter the number of Trustees allotted to a county, the county superintendent of education was one of them. On June 26, 1946, four more George County Trustees joined the original two, thus bringing the total membership of the Board to 24.

When the college began its expansion into a tri-campus college around 1960, Dr. C. C. Colvert, the architect of the expansion plan, advised reduction of the 24 member Board by half or more. Colvert recommended that the heavily populated counties of Harrison and Jackson receive proportionally greater representation than sparsely populated Stone and George Counties. The Trustees of Stone and George blocked vote after vote on the issue, forcing a compromise by which the Board added five new members thus raising the total number of Trustees to 29. Harrison County, which had the largest population and contributed the most to funding the institution at the time, received four of the new members. Jackson County received the other one. Stone and George each retained six Trustees.

Legislative action designed to restructure and decrease the number of community college Trustees throughout the state obliged MGCCC to reduce its total number of Trustees to 23 as of July 1, 1989. Accordingly, the terms of all current sitting superintendents of education in the four counties were terminated as of that date. Superintendents of education were not barred from future appointment, but they no longer held Trustee status by virtue of office.

Under the 1989 Board reapportionment plan, Stone and George Counties were reduced to three Trustees each. Harrison and Jackson Counties each received eight Trustees. In addition, in 1989, Jackson County was awarded a ninth Trustee, who served a term of five years. Five years later Jackson County's representation on the Board returned to eight while Harrison County's representation rose to nine. Thus the membership of the Board after 1989 stood at 23 with the "floater Trustee" alternating the balance of power between Jackson and Harrison Counties on the Board on a five-year cycle.

The data given in the following lists as terms of service for Trustees were derived in most cases from Trustee attendance at Board meetings. The actual term of an individual Trustee's appointment may have been longer or shorter than that inclusive of the dates in the lists. Sometimes Trustees missed the early Board meetings of their terms, thus rendering the term of service given in the lists as shorter than what had been authorized. On the other hand, occasionally a Trustee continued service after the expiration of his term because he did not know and apparently was not told that the term had expired. In those cases the Trustee served longer than his authorized term.

Presidents/Chairpersons of the Board of Trustees
Agricultural High School and Junior/Community College
1911 - 2000

Agricultural High School

Name	Hometown	County	Begin Term	End Term
Elmer Jr., Frederick William	Biloxi	Harrison	1911 (Sept. 18)	1913 (Jan. 17)
Gorenflo, William F.	Gulfport/Biloxi	Harrison	1913 (Jan. 17)	1922 ?
Temming, R. V.	Gulfport	Harrison	1924 ?	1924 (Aug.) ?

Junior/Community College

Name	Hometown	County	Begin Term	End Term
Bond Jr., Andrew Jackson	Wisdom	Stone	1925 ?	1929 (Aug. 8)
Leach, W.	Biloxi	Harrison	1929 (Sept. 5)	1936 (Jan. 8)
Smith Sr., Vinson B.	Pass Christian	Harrison	1936 (Feb. 5)	1943 (Dec.)
Heidelberg, H. P.	Pascagoula	Jackson	1944 (Jan. 12)	1952 (Jan. 23)
Wentzell, Charles S. "Vester"	Biloxi	Harrison	1952 (Jan. 23)	1957 (Dec. 28)
Malone, Maurice L.	Lucedale	George	1958 (Jan.)	1972 (Dec.)
Mauldin Jr., William S.	McHenry	Stone	1973 (Jan.)	1973 (Dec.)
Mauldin Jr., William S.	McHenry	Stone	1974 (Jan.)	1974 (Dec.)
Mauldin Jr., William S.	McHenry	Stone	1975 (Jan.)	1975 (Dec.)
Peterson, Warner	Pascagoula	Jackson	1976 (Jan.)	1976 (Dec.)
Peterson, Warner	Pascagoula	Jackson	1977 (Jan.)	1977 (Dec.)
Mauldin Jr., William S.	McHenry	Stone	1978 (Jan.)	1978 (Dec.)
Mauldin Jr., William S.	McHenry	Stone	1979 (Jan.)	1979 (Dec.)
Ward, Wilbur G.	Lucedale	George	1980 (Jan.)	1980 (Dec.)
Ward, Wilbur G.	Lucedale	George	1981 (Jan.)	1981 (Dec.)
Ward, Wilbur G.	Lucedale	George	1982 (Jan.)	1982 (Dec.)
Switzer, Eula [Mrs. C. T. Sr.]	Biloxi	Harrison	1983 (Jan.)	1983 (Dec.)
Switzer, Eula [Mrs. C. T. Sr.]	Biloxi	Harrison	1984 (Jan.)	1984 (Dec.)
Bryan Jr., James E.	Wiggins	Stone	1985 (Jan.)	1985 (Dec.)
Bryan Jr., James E.	Wiggins	Stone	1986 (Jan.)	1986 (Dec.)
Peterson, Warner	Pascagoula	Jackson	1987 (Jan.)	1987 (Dec.)
Peterson, Warner	Pascagoula	Jackson	1988 (Jan.)	1988 (Dec.)
Ward, Wilbur G.	Lucedale	George	1989 (Jan.)	1989 (Dec.)
Ward, Wilbur G.	Lucedale	George	1990 (Jan.)	1990 (Dec.)
Peden, Jean [Mrs. William A.]	Gulfport	Harrison	1991 (Jan.)	1991 (Dec.)
Dedeaux, John Randle	Perkinston	Stone	1992 (Jan.)	1992 (Dec.)
Dedeaux, John Randle	Perkinston	Stone	1993 (Jan.)	1993 (Dec.)
Sumrall, Delores [Mrs. Charles E.]	Ocean Springs	Jackson	1994 (Jan.)	1994 (Dec.)
Sumrall, Delores [Mrs. Charles E.]	Ocean Springs	Jackson	1995 (Jan.)	1995 (Dec.)
Ward, Wilbur G.	Lucedale	George	1996 (Jan.)	1996 (Dec.)
Ward, Wilbur G.	Lucedale	George	1997 (Jan.)	1997 (Dec.)
Peden, Jean [Mrs. William A.]	Gulfport	Harrison	1998 (Jan.)	1998 (Dec.)
Peden, Jean [Mrs. William A.]	Gulfport	Harrison	1999 (Jan.)	1999 (Dec.)
Massengale Jr., Donald	Pascagoula	Jackson	2000 (Jan.)	2000 (Dec.)

On February 18, 1965, the title "President" of the Board was changed to "Chairman" of the Board.

Harrison County Trustees
Agricultural High School
1911 - 1925*

Name	Supt. Of Ed.	Hometown	Begin Term	End Term
Dawsey, John Jefferson	Supt. Of Ed.	Gulfport	1911 (Sept. 5)	1915 (Dec. 31)
Jones, J. L.		Gulfport	1911 (Sept. 5)	1916 ?
Batson, William Edmond**		Recluse	1911 (Sept. 5)	1916
Bond, Rankin**		Perkinston	1911 (Sept.)	1916
Elmer Jr., Frederick William		Biloxi	1911 (Sept.)	1913 (Jan. 17)
Gorenflo, William F.		Gulfport/Biloxi	1913 (Jan. 17)	1923 ?
Wood, W. H.	Supt. Of Ed.	Gulfport	1916 (Jan. 1)	1919 (Dec. 31)
Hunt, Walter Henry "Skeet"		Biloxi	1916 (Sept. 1)	1922 ?
Wood, W. N.		Saucier	1916 (Sept. 1)	1920
Patenotte, F. L.		Beat 2	1916 (Sept.)	1919 ?
Williams, R. S.		Beat 5	1916 (Sept.)	1920 ?
Temming, R. V.***	Supt. Of Ed.	Gulfport	1920 (Jan.)	1924 ?
Scarborough, P. N.		?	1920 (Jan.)	1920 (May) ?
Adam Sr., Emile Joseph		Pass Christian	1920 (Jan.)	1923 (Dec.)
O'Neal Sr.,Eli Washington		Saucier	1920	1921 ?
Hagin, E.		Lyman	1920	1922 ?
Blackledge, Lloyd		Saucier	1922	1931
Leach, W.		Biloxi	1923 (Sept. 19)	1936 (Jan. 8)
Hopper, Dr. H. P.		Saucier	1923 (Sept. 19)	1924 ?
Darby, Cooper J.	Supt. Of Ed.	Gulfport	1924 (Jan. 1)	1929 (Sept.)
Adam Jr., Emile Joseph		Pass Christian	1924 (Jan.)	1931 (Feb.)
Howell, Posey N.		Howison	1924 (Dec.)	1936 (Jan. 8)
Curtis, L. E.		Biloxi	1925	1928

*The loss of *Perkinston Minute Book 1* and the absence of five catalogs between 1914 and 1923 rendered it impossible for the archivist to provide accurate dates for Trustees' terms of service in this era.

**Apparently William Edmond Batson of Recluse and Rankin Bond of Perkinston moved from the Harrison County Board of Trustees to the Stone County Board of Trustees at the creation of Stone County in 1916.

***R. V. Temming lost the 1923 Harrison County superintendent of education race to Cooper J. Darby. As of January 1, 1924 Temming, though no longer superintendent of education, remained on the Board as president.

Stone County Trustees
Agricultural High School
1916 - 1925

Name	Supt. Of Ed.	Hometown	Begin Term	End Term
Bass, Claude Ham*	Supt. Of Ed.	Wiggins	1916 (June 27)	1919
Swetman, Charles C.*		Perkinston	1916 (July 10)	1934 (May 23)
Hatten, R. W.*		Wisdom	1916 (July)	1920
Bond, Rankin*		Perkinston	1916 (July)	1920 (Jan.)
Batson, William Edmond*		Recluse	1916 (July)	1919 (Dec.)
Broadus, Buren	Supt. Of Ed.	Wiggins	1920 (Jan.)	1928 (Jan.)
Lott, W. W. "Wash"		McHenry	1920 (Jan.) ?	1923 (Dec.)
Brown, John B.		Perkinston	1920 (Jan.) ?	1922
Bond Jr., Andrew Jackson		Wisdom	1921 (Feb. 7)	1929 (Aug. 8)
Lott, J. R.		Bond	1923 ?	1924
Breland, George W.		McHenry	1924	1926 (July)
Batson, Clark O'Connor		Recluse	1924 (Jan.)	1932 (June 8)

*In the compromise leading to the formation of the Bi-county Harrison-Stone Agricultural High School in 1916, Harrison County was allowed six Trustees, and Stone County was allowed five. This arrangement which gave Harrison County control of the Board of Trustees continued until 1933 when all supporting counties were allowed six Trustees. Stone County's first five Trustees are the first five on this list. On June 26, 1916, Claude Ham Bass, Stone County's first elected superintendent of education, replaced P. O. Colson (who had been appointed superintendent of education on June 5). By virtue of his office, Bass became the first Stone County AHS Trustee on the day of his election. At some point in late 1919 Clark O'Connor Batson, eldest son of William Edmond Batson of Recluse, "served the county as superintendent of education for a short time while filling out the unexpired term of C. H. Bass." ("Crabology," *Daily Herald*, July 29, 1921). Since the length of this "short time" is not known, that service was not noted in the chart. Clark O'Connor Batson later served as a Trustee from 1924 to 1932. On July 10, 1916, the Stone County School Board met and elected two AHS Trustees. One of those was Charles C. Swetman as was confirmed in *Perkinston Minute Book 2*, page 152. The other one elected by the Stone County School Board was likely Judge R. W. Hatten. Rankin Bond of Perkinston and William Edmond Batson of Recluse, both of whom had served on the old Harrison County AHS Board, were probably the two confirmed by the Stone County Board of Supervisors in July 1916.

Harrison County Trustees
Junior/Community College
1925 - 2000

Name	Supt. Of Ed.	Hometown	Begin Term	End Term
Blackledge, Lloyd		Saucier	1922	1931 (Mar. 3)
Leach, W.		Biloxi	1923 (Sept. 19)	1936 (Jan. 8)
Adam Jr., Emile J.		Pass Christian	1924 (Jan.)	1931 (Feb)
Darby, Cooper J.*	Supt. Of Ed.	Gulfport	1924 (Jan. 1)	1929 (Sept. 23)
Howell, Posey N.		Howison	1924 (Dec.)	1936 (Jan. 8)
Curtis, Louis E.		Biloxi	1925	1928
Deen, George M.	Supt. Of Ed.	Gulfport	1929 (Sept. 23)	1935 (Dec. 31)
Smith, George R.		Pass Christian	1931 (Feb.)	1931 (Nov.)
Blackledge, William Luther		Saucier	1931 (July 8) 1963 (Nov. 20)	1941 (Apr.) 1972 (Jan. 15)
Smith Sr., Vinson B.		Pass Christian	1932 (Feb.)	1943 (Dec.)
Milner, John K.		Gulfport	1933 (June)	1939 (Dec.)
Ladnier, O. L.	Supt. Of Ed.	Gulfport	1936 (Jan. 1)	1947 (Dec. 31)
Pringle, Victor B.		Biloxi	1936 (Feb.)	1939 (Dec.)
Colmer Sr., M. A.		McHenry	1936 (Feb.)	1939 (Dec.)
Wentzell, Charles S. "Vester"		Biloxi	1940 (Jan. 8)	1957 (Dec. 28)
Head, W. C.		Gulfport	1940 (Jan. 8)	1943 (Dec.)
Moran, R. J.**		Lyman	1940 (Jan. 8) 1952 (Jan.)	1947 (Dec.) 1970 (Dec.)
Broadus, M. Albert		Saucier	1941 (May)	1943 (Dec.)
Richards, J. Homer***	Supt. Of Ed.	Saucier	1944 (Jan. 1)	1951 (Dec. 31)
Robinson, William V.		Pass Christian	1944 (Jan.)	1947 (July 23)
Caraway, W. H.		Gulfport	1944 (Jan.)	1963 (Dec. 31.)
Frye, J. Marshall		Pass Christian	1947 (July 26)	1953 (Aug. 1)
Carson, Robert G.		Saucier	1947 (Nov. 19)	1963 (Oct.)
Patton, Virgil D.		Saucier	1948 (Jan.)	1951 (Dec.)
Ladner, R. L. Supt. Of Ed.		Gulfport	1952 (Jan. 1)	1959 (Dec. 31)
Dantzler, A. M.		Pass Christian	1953 (Aug. 1)	1959 (Dec.)
Wentzell, J. E.		Biloxi	1958 (Jan.) 1972 (Jan.)	1962 (Dec.) 1978 (May)
Smith, Esco	Supt. Of Ed.	Gulfport	1960 (Jan. 1)	1971 (Dec. 31)
DeMetz, Donald		Pass Christian	1960 (Jan. 15)	1978 (Aug. 23)
Page, Lyle		Biloxi	1962 (June 5)	1965 (Aug.)
Starr, W. H.		Gulfport	1962 (June 5)	1976 (Apr. 8)
Furr Jr., John		Pass Christian	1962 (June 5)	1969 (June 5)
Ball, Arthur		Saucier	1962 (June 5)	1970 (Nov.)
Elder, Roy		Biloxi	1963 (Jan. 1)	1968 (Jan. 1)
Reese, James E.		Gulfport	1964 (Jan. 1)	1976 (Feb.)
Graves, J. A.		Biloxi	1966 (May 9)	1968 (June 5)
Creel, Richard		Biloxi	1968 (March)	1987 (Dec.)
Quave, Russell		Biloxi	1968 (June 5)	1986 (June 9)
Sellier, Earl		DeLisle	1969 (June 5)	1974 (June 5)
Levron, Harold J.		Saucier	1971 (Jan. 1)	1975 (June)
Milner Jr., Tom W.		Gulfport	1971 (Jan.)	1981 (June)
Ladner, Robert D.	Supt. Of Ed.	Gulfport	1972 (Jan. 1)	1979 (Dec. 31)
Hanson, Herbert C.		Pass Christian	1974 (June 28)	1979 (Dec.)
Switzer, Eula [Mrs. C. T., Sr.]		Biloxi	1975 (Sept. 17) 1988 (Jan.)	1986 (Dec. 17)
D'Angelo, Joseph H.		Gulfport	1976 (Feb.)	1992 (Jan.)
Owen Sr., Tofie M.		Gulfport	1977 (June)	1985 (Sept. 18)
Santa Cruz, Alan J.		Biloxi	1978 (May 31)	1981 (Aug. 26)

DeMetz Jr., Harold		Long Beach	1978 (Sept. 19)	1980 (Jan. 15)
Antoine, Eddie P.		Pass Christian	1979 (Nov. 30)	1989 (July 1)
Arledge, Henry****	Supt. Of Ed.	Gulfport	1980 (Jan. 1)	1989 (July 1)
Hilton, Murrell		Pass Christian	1980 (Jan.)	1993 (Mar.)
Peden, Jean [Mrs. William A.]		Gulfport	1981 (Aug. 19) 1993 (Apr.)	1991 (July)
Bankston, Alton G.		Biloxi	1981 (Oct. 12)	1988 (Jan.)
Necaise, Albert		Gulfport	1985 (Dec.)	1990 (Dec.)
Gruich, Dr. Frank		Biloxi	1986 (July)	
Allen, Gertrude [Mrs. Douglas]		Biloxi	1986 (Dec. 17) 1994 (June)	1990 (June)
Weaver, Jackie		D'Iberville	1988 (Mar.)	1999 (July 21)
Taylor, James M.		Gulfport	1990 (June)	1993 (Nov. 24)
Hewes Jr., Billy		Gulfport	1991 (Jan.) 1996 (Oct.)	1995 (Dec.) 1997 (June)
Randall, Lillian Cully [Mrs. William Aston]		Gulfport	1991 (Dec.)	1999 (June)
Cerra, James V.		Pass Christian	1993 (Apr.)	2000 (Jan.)
Williams, John C.		Gulfport	1994 (July)	1996 (July)
Watters Jr., Robert		Gulfport	1996 (Jan.)	
Estes, James N.		Gulfport	1997 (Aug.) 2000 (Feb.)	1999 (July)
Diaz, Duane M.		Biloxi	1999 (Aug.)	
Rogers, Gene		Pass Christian	2000 (Feb.)	

*Cooper J. Darby, Harrison County Superintendent of Education since January 1, 1924, was unanimously elected on September 5, 1929, to succeed J. L. Denson as superintendent of the Harrison-Stone-Jackson AHS and Junior College. Darby informed the Harrison County Board of Supervisors that he would continue to serve as superintendent of education until September 23. At that time George M. Deen replaced Darby in that position and Deen attended his first Trustee meeting on October 3.

**R. J. Moran was the longest serving Harrison County Trustee of the 20th century with a total of 26 years and 10 months.

***J. Homer Richards was a Trustee before he became Harrison County superintendent of education.

****Henry Arledge was the last Harrison County Superintendent of Education to serve as a Trustee by virtue of his office. The 1989 change in Board representation ended his service as a Trustee.

Stone County Trustees
Junior/Community College
1925 - 2000

Name	Supt. Of Ed.	Hometown	Begin Term	End Term
Swetman, Charles C.		Perkinston	1916 (July 10)	1934 (May 23)
Broadus, Buren	Supt. Of Ed.	Wiggins	1920 (Jan.)	1927 (Dec. 31)
Bond Jr., Andrew Jackson		Wisdom	1921 (Feb. 7)	1929 (Aug. 8)
Breland, George W.		McHenry	1924 1936 (Sept.)	1926 (July) 1938 (May)
Batson, Clark O'Connor		Perkinston	1924 (Jan.)	1932 (June 8)
Broadus, J. W. "Uncle Webb"		Perkinston	1926 (July)	1936 (Dec. 2)
Bond, Howard H.	Supt. Of Ed.	Wiggins	1928 (Jan. 1)	1931 (Dec. 31)
Breland, Gavin A.		Wiggins	1929 (Nov.)	1931 (Dec.)
Robertson, J. E.	Supt. Of Ed.	Wiggins	1932 (Jan. 1)	1939 (Dec.)
Lott, T. W.		Wiggins	1932 (Feb.)	1943 (Dec.)
Smith, Duncan E. "Uncle Dunk"*		Perkinston	1932 (Aug. 3)	1963 (Dec.)
Newton, Robert W.**		Wiggins	1933 (June 14)	1935 (Oct.)
Dees, Calvin Elias		Perkinston	1934 (Aug.)	1935 (July)
			1942 (Oct. 14)	1945 (Sept. 19)
Caraway, Ellis		Wiggins	1936 (Jan.)	1937 (June)
Dedeaux, J. N.		Perkinston	1936 (Feb.)	1942 (April 15)
Cherry Sr., James A.		Wiggins	1937 (July)	1943 (Dec.)
O'Neal, Ford		Perkinston	1938 (June)	1940 (Jan.)
O'Neal, Dowey D.	Supt. Of Ed.	Wiggins	1940 (Jan. 1)	1951 (Dec. 31)
Breland, J. H.		Perkinston	1940 (April 10)	1943 (Dec.)
Dees, John Clifton		Perkinston	1942 (April 15)	1942 (Oct. 14)
Lott, Bruner A.		Wiggins	1944 (Jan.)	1961 (Dec.)
Reabold, Rosa [Mrs. Fred]		McHenry	1944 (Jan.)	1944 (June)
Batson, P. A.		Wiggins	1944 (Jan.)	1947 (Dec.)
Blackwell, S. A.		Perkinston	1945 (Jan.)	1951 (Dec.)
Dees, Calvin Eugene ***		Perkinston	1945 (Sept. 19) 1952 (Jan.)	1947 (Dec.) 1964 (Dec.)
O'Neal, Attis		Perkinston	1948 (Jan.) 1956 (Jan. 21)	1951 (Oct.) 1965 (Dec.)
Taylor, W. W.		Wiggins	1948 (Jan.)	1976 (July)
Blackwell, Leonard A.	Supt. Of Ed.	Wiggins	1952 (Jan. 1)	1959 (Dec. 31)
Evans, B. A.		Perkinston	1952 (Jan.)	1955 (Dec. 31)
Breland, Boyce L.****	Supt. Of Ed.	Wiggins	1960 (Jan. 1)	1967 (July)
Bond, Gordon G.		Perkinston	1962 (Jan.)	1991 (Dec.)
Davis, Hiram J.		Perkinston	1964 (Jan. 1)	1978 (Dec. 31)
Mauldin Jr., William S.		McHenry	1965 (Jan. 1)	1984 (Dec.)
Patton, Clayton N.		McHenry	1966 (Jan. 1)	1970 (Dec. 31)
Roberts, Edwin Jack "E.J."	Supt. Of Ed.	Wiggins	1967 (July)	1967 (Aug.)
Miller, Emory Jack "E.J."	Supt. Of Ed.	Wiggins	1967 (Aug. 23)	1971 (Dec. 31)
Callahan Jr., William M.		Wiggins	1971 (Jan. 4)	1971 (Dec.)
Gordon, James V	Supt. Of Ed.	Wiggins	1972 (Jan. 1)	1975 (Dec. 31)
West, Johnnie C.*****		Wiggins	1972 (Jan. 3)	1972 (Jan. 8)
Anderson, Parnell		Wiggins	1972 (Jan.)	1990 (Dec.)
O'Neal, James A.	Supt. Of Ed.	Wiggins	1976 (Jan. 1)	1979 (Dec. 31)
Bryan Jr., James E.		Wiggins	1976 (July)	
Odom, Charles G.		Perkinston	1979 (Jan.)	1988 (Jan.)
Danzey, Eddie	Supt. Of Ed.	Wiggins	1980 (Jan. 1)	1987 (Dec. 31)
Dedeaux, John Randle		Perkinston	1985 (Jan.)	1999 (July)
Fulcher, Virgel******	Supt. Of Ed.	Wiggins	1988 (Jan. 1)	1989 (July 1)

Smith, Buford		Perkinston	1988 (Feb. 1)	1988 (Dec.)
Hall, Thomas E.		Wiggins	1992 (Jan.)	
Strickland, Clyde		Perkinston	1999 (Dec.)	

*Duncan E. "Uncle Dunk" Smith set Stone County's 20th century record for service as a Trustee with 31 years and 4 months. Smith was the institution's first Trustee to cross the 30-year service mark. No other Stone County Trustee served 30 years, but Gordon G. Bond came close with 29 years and 11 months, and W. W. Taylor served 28 years and 6 months.

**Robert W. Newton, appointed June 14, 1933, by the Stone County School Board, was Stone County's first sixth Trustee. Until that point Stone County had had only five Trustees.

***Calvin Eugene "Gene" Dees was a son of Calvin Elias Dees. Gene was not a junior, but he signed his name as "C. E. Dees, Jr."

****In July 1967, Boyce Breland resigned as Stone County Superintendent of Education to take the position of MGCJC District Assistant Director of Vocational Education. Edwin Jack "E.J." Roberts served as interim Stone County Superintendent of Education until August 1967, when Emory Jack "E. J." Miller was elected to the position. E. J. Roberts later served a four-year term (January 1, 1976 to December 31, 1979) as George County Superintendent of Education, and thus became the only person in the 20th century to serve as superintendent of education (and consequently as a Trustee) from both Stone and George Counties.

*****In December 1971, the Stone County Board of Supervisors appointed Johnnie C. West, who had that month finished his term as a Stone County Supervisor, as a Trustee beginning on January 3, 1972. In doing so the Board of Supervisors forgot that a supervisor had to wait a full year after his term as supervisor ended before he could become a Trustee. Therefore, West resigned five days after his appointment began.

******Virgel Fulcher was the last Stone County Superintendent of Education to be a MGCCC Trustee by virtue of his office. The 1989 change in Board representation ended Fulcher's service.

Jackson County Trustees
Junior/Community College
1925 - 2000

Name	Supt. Of Ed.	Hometown	Begin Term	End Term
Flurry, E. E.*		Vestry	1925 (June 5)	1946 (March)
Watson, L. B.*		Ocean Springs	1925 (June 5)	1930 (Nov.)
Booth, E. B.*		Pascagoula	1925 (July)	1932 (April)
Ezell, A. W.*		Pascagoula	1925 (fall)	1930 (Nov.)
Morgan, Marshall McClellan "Mac"*	Supt. Of Ed.	Pascagoula	1925 (Sept. 9)	1927 (Dec. 31)
Alexander, W. M.	Supt. Of Ed.	Pascagoula	1928 (Jan.)	1931 (Dec. 31)
Friar, Robert A.		Ocean Springs	1930 (Nov.)	1931 (Dec. 31)
Russum, Bennie Plunkett		Pascagoula	1930 (Nov.)	1931 (April)
Heidelberg, H. P.		Pascagoula	1931 (April 6)	1952 (Jan. 23)
O'Keefe, Mary		Ocean Springs	1931 (Dec.)	1942 (Sept. 16)
Megehee, Alfred Forrest**	Supt. Of Ed.	Pascagoula	1932 (Jan. 1)	1951 (Oct. 17)
Cumbest, M. B.		Escatawpa	1932 (June)	1952 (Mar.)
Stewart, W. G.		Moss Point	1933 (April)	1933 (Nov.)
Martin, O. H.		Moss Point	1934 (May)	1937 (Dec. 15)
Suthoff, E. V.		Moss Point	1937 (Dec. 15)	1946 (July)
Carr, Mrs. Charles M.		Ocean Springs	1943 (April)	1961 (Feb. 22)
Flurry, Norman V.		Vestry	1946 (April 17)	1977 (Jan.)
Spann, Frank George		Moss Point	1948 (Jan.)	1952 (Jan.)
Morgan, Marshall McClellan "Mac"	Supt. Of Ed.	Pascagoula	1951 (Oct. 17)	1955 (Dec. 31)
Megehee, Carl		Pascagoula	1952 (Jan. 23)	1959 (Oct.)
Mack, Lester		Escatawpa	1953 (Jan.)	1962 (Dec.)
Hamilton, Gavin Malcomb		Hurley	1953 (May)	1973 (Jan.)
Bilbo, A. C.	Supt. Of Ed.	Pascagoula	1956 (Jan. 1)	1959 (Dec. 31)
Gibson, Donald W.		Pascagoula	1960 (Jan.)	1960 ?
Gautier, Newton Perry	Supt. Of Ed.	Pascagoula	1960 (Jan. 1)	1963 (Dec. 31)
Peterson, Warner***		Pascagoula	1960 (Sept.)	1996 (Sept.)
Puhle, Gus H.		Ocean Springs	1961 (May 17)	1973 (Apr. 1)
Slaughter Jr., Robert H.		Pascagoula	1962 (June 5)	1994 (Dec.)
Roberts, Dr. Richard Angus		Moss Point	1963 (Jan. 23)	1983 (Dec.)
Mallette, Marland H.	Supt. Of Ed.	Pascagoula	1964 (Jan. 1)	1979 (Dec. 31)
Hamilton, Gavin Franklin		Hurley	1973 (Jan.)	1992 (Jan. 22)
Lemon, James Kirkpatrick		Ocean Springs	1973 (Apr.)	1985 (Dec.)
Fornea, Larry		Gautier	1977 (Feb.)	1981 (Dec.)
Smithie, Jimmy	Supt. Of Ed.	Pascagoula	1980 (Jan. 1)	1988 (Dec. 31)
George Sr., J. B.		Pascagoula	1982 (Feb.) 1989 (July 19)	1986 (Dec.) 1994 (June)
Alfred, Mary Frances Evans		Moss Point	1983 (Dec.)	1988 (Dec.)
Sumrall, Delores P. [Mrs. Charles E.]		Ocean Springs	1986 (Jan.)	
Descher, Patricia [Mrs. William H.]		Ocean Springs	1987 (Jan.)	
Barnes, Geraldine		Pascagoula	1989 (Jan.)	
Walters, Max Newton****	Supt. Of Ed.	Vancleave	1989 (Jan. 1)	1989 (July. 1)
Roberts Jr., Harry		Ocean Springs	1989 (July 19)	
Massengale Jr., Donald*****		Pascagoula	1989 (July 19)	
Ely, Frank		Lucedale	1992 (Feb.)	1993 (Mar.)
Bradley, Sylvia [Mrs. Jack R.]		Hurley	1993 (May)	
Taylor, Ariel [Mrs. Austin]		Pascagoula	1995 (Jan.)	1999 (Dec.)
Jones, T. Moreno		Pascagoula	1997 (Sept.)	
Gautier, Earl D.		Moss Point	1999 (July 21)	
Flecher, Jay		Pascagoula	2000 (Jan.)	

*The first five names on this list are Jackson County's original complement of Trustees. Marshall McClellan "Mac" Morgan,

Jackson County Superintendent of Education since 1924, became a Trustee by virtue of his office. The Jackson County Board of Supervisors appointed A. W. Ezell and E. B. Booth. The Jackson County School Board appointed L. B. Watson and E. E. Flurry. All five original appointees were listed in *Perkinston Minute Book 2*, page 151. The Jackson County Board of Supervisors considered joining in support of the AHS in September 1924, but the proposal was tabled until September 9, 1925, when the supervisors approved an appropriation of 3/10 of a mill toward the support of the school. Apparently the Jackson County Board of Supervisors and the Jackson County School Board, knowing that this action would be taken, appointed several Trustees before the appropriation was levied. When Jackson County joined the Harrison-Stone-Jackson AHS and Junior College, the Board of Trustees was composed of six members from Harrison County and five each from Stone and Jackson. That changed in 1933 when all three counties were allowed six Trustees.

**Jackson County Superintendent of Education Alfred Forrest Megehee died in office October 17, 1951. According to Nellie Schatz of Moss Point, Marshall McClellan "Mac" Morgan, who had served as superintendent of education from January 1924 to December 1927, stepped in to serve the balance of Megehee's term and then served another full term. In order to provide continuity in the listing of superintendents of education, Morgan's two terms of service are listed separately.

***Warner Peterson was not only the longest serving Jackson County Trustee, but he also set the record in the 20th century for service as a Trustee to the institution--36 years. Two other Jackson County Trustees served in excess of 30 years. Robert H. Slaughter Jr. served 32 years, 6 months. Norman V. Flurry served 32 years, 9 months.

****Jackson County Superintendent of Education Max Newton Walters was the last to serve as a Trustee by virtue of his office. The 1989 change in Board representation ended his term of service.

*****Donald Massengale Jr. was the first "floater Trustee" selected in accordance with the 1989 Board reapportionment plan.

George County Trustees
Junior/Community College
1941 - 2000

Name	Supt. Of Ed.	Hometown	Begin Term	End Term
Malone, Maurice L.*		Lucedale	1941 (Nov. 7)	1972 (Dec.)
Eubanks, M. A.*	Supt. Of Ed.	Lucedale	1941 (Nov. 7)	1947 (Dec. 31)
Pope, M. Lavelle		Barton	1946 (June 26)	1979 (Dec.)
Brown, Kenneth G.		Agricola	1946 (June 26)	1968 (Nov.)
Holland, Charles A.		Lucedale	1946 (June 26)	1949 (Feb. 23)
Maples, Florian		Perkinston	1946 (June 26)	1947 (May)
Moffett, Guy D.	Supt. Of Ed.	Lucedale	1948 (Jan. 1)	1951 (Dec. 31)
Moore, Wiley T.		Lucedale (Perk route)	1948 (Jan.)	1972 (Feb. 25)
Cochran Sr., J. L.		Lucedale	1949 (Feb. 23)	1955 (Dec. 31)
Rouse, Leo R.	Supt. Of Ed.	Lucedale	1952 (Jan. 1) 1964 (Jan. 1)	1959 (Dec.31) 1967 (Dec. 31)
Cochran, Eugene		Lucedale	1956 (Jan. 21)	1957 (July 22)
Murrah, Milton C.**		Lucedale	1958 (Jan.)	1991 (Dec.)
Cooley, John	Supt. Of Ed.	Lucedale	1960 (Jan. 1)	1963 (Dec. 31)
Dungan, Carroll	Supt. Of Ed.	Lucedale	1968 (Jan 1)	1971 (Dec. 31)
Jones, Charles Luther		Lucedale	1969 (Jan. 6)	1988 (Dec.)
Bryan, Robert E.	Supt. Of Ed.	Lucedale	1972 (Jan. 1)	1975 (Dec. 31)
Ward, Wilbur G.		Lucedale	1973 (Jan.)	
Howell, Arlie Ray		Lucedale	1973 (Jan.) 1992 (Jan.)	1990 (Dec.)
Roberts, Edwin Jack "E.J."	Supt. Of Ed.	Lucedale	1976 (Jan. 1)	1979 (Dec. 31)
Reid, William	Supt. Of Ed.	Lucedale	1980 (Jan. 1)	1983 (Dec. 31)
Ivey, William Larry		Lucedale	1980 (May 26)	1989 (Dec. 31)
Massey, Barbara P.	Supt. Of Ed.	Lucedale	1984 (Jan. 1)	1987 (Dec. 31)
Pugh, William Steven***	Supt. Of Ed.	Central	1988 (Jan. 1)	1989 (July 1)
Harwood Jr., Joe B.		Agricola	1989 (Jan.)	1993 (Aug.)
Cooley, John Ward		Lucedale	1995 (Aug.)	

*From November 1941 until June 1946 George County had only two Trustees (M. A. Eubanks and M. L. Malone). In June 1946 George County received six Trustees.

**The longest serving George County Trustee of the 20th century was Milton C. Murrah with 33 years, 11 months. Next came M. Lavelle Pope with 33 years, 6 months. Maurice L. Malone served 31 years and one month.

***George County Superintendent of Education William Steven Pugh was the last to serve as an MGCCC Trustee by virtue of his office. The 1989 change in Board representation ended his service as a Trustee.

A LIST OF THE SUPERVISORS SERVING HARRISON COUNTY 1911 - 2000, STONE COUNTY 1916 - 2000, JACKSON COUNTY 1925 - 2000, AND GEORGE COUNTY 1910 - 2000

Harrison County Supervisors

(beginning with those in office as of 1911 at the time of the establishment of the Harrison County Agricultural High School at Perkinston to 2000)
The information for this chart was supplied by
Emmanuel Bentley & Tim Barnard of the Harrison County Chancery Clerk's office

Name	Beat	Terms
Elmer Sr., Frederick William**	1	1908 (Jan.)-1915 (Dec.)
Batton, Judson Cornelius	1	1916 (Jan.)-1923 (Dec.)
Nixon, Walter L.	1	1924 (Jan.)-1939 (Dec.)
Lawrence, Dewey	1	1940 (Jan.)-1962 (Apr.)
Foster, Mary Lawrence****	1	1962 (Apr.)-1962 (July)
Quave, Laz	1	1962 (July)-1971 (Dec.)
Melvin, Ernest C.	1	1972 (Jan.)-1983 (Dec.)
Eleuterius, Robert N. "Bobby"	1	1984 (Jan.)-
Cruthirds, Thomas E.	2	1908 (Jan.)-1911 (Dec.)
Reeves, Icham	2	1912 (Jan.)-1919 (Dec.)
Pigford, C. I.	2	1920 (Jan.)-1923 (Dec.) 1932 (Jan.)-1934 (Feb.)
Evans, Paul	2	1924 (Jan.)-1931 (Dec.)
O'Neal, Oscar	2	1934 (Feb.)-1939 (Dec.)
Cassibry, O. F.	2	1940 (Jan.)-1955 (Dec.)
Dedeaux, Roy Edward	2	1956 (Jan.)-1963 (Dec.)
Simpson, Rimmer Calvin	2	1964 (Jan.)-1975 (Dec.)
Urie, Leroy	2	1976 (Jan.)-1985 (June)
Smith, Esco	2	1985 (June)-1985 (Nov.)
Moffat, Eddie	2	1985 (Nov.)-1988 (Sept.)
White, David	2	1988 (Sept.)-1989 (Nov.)
Dedeaux, Homer R.	2	1989 (Nov.)-1991 (Dec.)
Peden, William A.	2	1992 (Jan.)-1992 (Dec.)
Benefield, Larry*****	2	1993 (Jan.)-
Scarborough, John*	3	1892 (Jan.)-1911 (Dec.)
Adam Sr., Emile Joseph	3	1912 (Jan.)-1915 (July) 1924 (Jan.)-1938 (Aug.)
Andresen, Fred	3	1915 (July) - 1919 (Aug.)
Adam, C. Bidwell	3	1919 (Sept.)-1923 (Dec.)
Fitzpatrick, Hugh W.	3	1938 (Aug.)-1947 (Dec.)
Hayden Sr., Julius John	3	1948 (Jan.)-1959 (Dec.)
French, Nicholas B.	3	1960 (Jan.)-1967 (Dec.)
Hursey, Francis J.	3	1968 (Jan.)-1971 (Dec.)
Reed, Robert L.	3	1972 (Jan.)-1975 (Dec.)
McDonald, William "Billy"	3	1976 (Jan.)-1987 (Dec.)
Larosa, Frank	3	1988 (Jan.)-1989 (May)
Reeves, Thomas L. "Joe"	3	1989 (May)-1989 (Nov.)
Larosa Sr., David V.	3	1989 (Nov.)-1999 (Dec.)
Ladner, Marlin	3	2000 (Jan.)-
Brown, D. Jason	4	1904 (Apr.)-1911 (Dec.)
Hickman, John C.	4	1912 (Jan.)-1915 (Dec.)
Ramsey, W. Knox	4	1916 (Jan.)-1919 (Dec.)
Ladnier, A. W.	4	1920 (Jan.)-1927 (Dec.) 1936 (Jan.)-1936 (Apr.)
Hopper, Dr. H. P.	4	1928 (Jan.)-1935 (Dec.)
Saucier, J. Loren	4	1936 (Apr.)-1939 (Dec.)
Ladnier, Willie Mayvin	4	1940 (Jan.)-1956 (Dec.)
Ladnier, Gatha	4	1956 (Dec.)-1967 (Dec.)

Lewis, Wendell C.	4	1968 (Jan.)-1971 (Dec.)
Snowden, Hue B.	4	1972 (Jan.)-1987 (Dec.)
Allen, Phillip	4	1988 (Jan.)-1991 (Dec.)
Benefield, Larry*****	4	1992 (Jan.)-1992 (Dec.)
Midcalf, Robin Alfred*****	4	1993 (Jan.)-1999 (Jan.)
Martin, William W.******	4	1999 (Jan.)-
Bond Jr., Andrew Jackson	5	1904 (Jan.)-1915 (Dec.)
Smith, Edward Randolph***	5	1916 (Jan.)-1916 (June 5)
Broadus, M. Albert	5	1916 (July)-1923 (Dec.)
O'Neal, Loren E.	5	1924 (Jan.)-1927 (Dec.)
Fairley, Edward	5	1928 (Jan.)-1941 (May)
Blackledge, William Luther	5	1941 (May)-1955 (Dec.)
Broadus, Glen Dennis	5	1956 (Jan.)-1967 (Dec.)
Robinson, Arlan	5	1968 (Jan.)-1979 (Dec.)
Switzer Sr., C. T.	5	1980 (Jan.)-1986 (Dec.)
Switzer, Eula [Mrs. C. T.]	5	1986 (Dec.)-1987 (Dec.)
Switzer Jr., C. T.	5	1988 (Jan.)-1999 (Dec.)
Rocko, Constance "Connie"	5	2000 (Jan.) -

*John Scarborough served a two-year term (1888-1889) before his first four-year term began in 1892.

**Frederick William Elmer Sr. of Biloxi served four two-year terms--1876-1877; 1878-1879; 1880-1881; and 1890-1891. Four-year terms began in 1892, and Elmer served his first four-year term beginning in 1908.

***Edward Randolph Smith was serving as supervisor, Beat 5, Harrison County, when Stone County was created on June 5, 1916. On June 26, 1916, Smith was elected supervisor Beat 5 of the new county. The creation of Stone County took most of old Harrison County Beats 4 and 5, necessitating the redrawing of the beat lines particularly in the piney woods section of Harrison County. The residence of the Beat 4 Harrison County Supervisor remained in the parent county, but Smith wound up in Stone County. Smith thus became the only person to serve as a supervisor in both of the counties supporting the Harrison-Stone Agricultural High School.

****Mary Lawrence Foster was the first woman to serve Harrison County as a supervisor.

*****Larry Benefield served Harrison County, Beat 4, from January 1, 1992, to December 31, 1992. The redrawing of beat lines in order to provide greater African-American representation resulted in Benefield's residence being placed in Beat 2. In January 1993, Robin Alfred Midcalf replaced Benefield in "new" Beat 4 becoming the first woman and the first black to be elected to the position of supervisor in Harrison County. Benefield replaced William A. Peden in Beat 2.

******William W. Martin was the first black man elected as supervisor in Harrison County.

Stone County Supervisors

From 1916 to 2000

The information for this chart was supplied by Stone County Chancery Clerk Gerald W. Bond and Ona Mae Willingham

Name	Beat	Term(s)
Bond, Andrew Wiggins*	1	1916 (June 26)-1919 (Dec.)
Walton, Dr. T. J.	1	1920 (Jan.)-1931 (Dec.)
Smith, Edward Randolph	1	1932 (Jan.)-1935 (Dec.) 1944 (Jan.)-1949 (Dec. 12)
Miller, W. A.	1	1936 (Jan.)-1943 (Dec.)
Smith, Carl T.	1	1949 (Dec. 12)-1950 (Feb. 23)
Dees, John Clifton	1	1950 (Feb. 23)-1979 (Dec.)
Pearson, Freddie George	1	1980 (Jan.)-1991 (Dec.)
Parsons, Dana R.	1	1992 (Jan.)-1995 (Dec.)
Ainsworth, Harold B.	1	1996 (Jan.)-1999 (Dec.)
Walters, Jill	1	2000 (Jan.)-
Brown, D. Jason*	2	1916 (June 26)-1919 (Dec.)
Batson, William Edmond	2	1920 (Jan.)-1927 (Dec.)
Smith, Laden	2	1928 (Jan.)-1931 (Dec.)
Brown, Vernon E.	2	1932 (Jan.)-1935 (Dec.)
Brown, John B.	2	1936 (Jan.)-1943 (Dec.)
Brown, O. B.	2	1944 (Jan.)-1983 (Dec.)
Shaw, Buster Dean***	2	1984 (Jan.)-1991 (Dec.)
Fairley, Jerry J.****	2	1992 (Jan.)-1998 (Oct. 11)
Fairley, Pam [Mrs. Jerry J.]*****	2	1998 (Oct. 11)-
Switzer, Dr. Ross Adams*	3	1916 (June 26)-1935 (Dec.) 1940 (Jan.)-1945 (May 1)
Hickman, Peter Griffin	3	1936 (Jan.)-1939 (Dec.)
Switzer, Anne [Mrs. Ross Adams]	3	1945 (May 1)-1945 (Aug.)
Dees Sr., Calvin Elias	3	1945 (Aug.)-1947 (Dec.)
Parker, Billy	3	1948 (Jan.)-1963 (Dec.)
Overstreet Sr., Lee	3	1964 (Jan.)-1978 (Aug. 17)
Overstreet Jr., Lee	3	1978 (Aug. 17)-1983 (Dec.)
Parker, Bobby D.	3	1984 (Jan.)-1991(Dec.) 1996 (Jan.)-1999 (Dec.)
Shaw, Buster Dean***	3	1992 (Jan.)-1995 (Dec.)
Ladnier, Brian	3	2000 (Jan.)-
O'Neal Sr., Sardin M.*	4	1916 (June 26)-1919 (Dec.)
Bond, Rankin	4	1920 (Jan.)-1923 (Dec.)
Lott, W W. "Wash"**	4	1924 (Jan.)-1941 (Feb. 16)
Robinson, Roy L.	4	1941 (Feb. 20)-1941 (Sept. 1)
Robinson, Lillie (Mrs. Roy L.)	4	1941 (Sept. 10)-1942 (Mar. 2)
Bond, Emmett R.	4	1942 (Mar. 3)-1955 (Dec.)
O'Neal, Percy C.	4	1956 (Jan.)-1967 (Dec.)
West, Johnnie C.	4	1968 (Jan.)-1971 (Dec.)
Mallett, Orbin	4	1972 (Jan.)-1991 (Dec.)
Strickland, Scott	4	1992 (Jan.)-
Smith, Edward Randolph *	5	1916 (June 26)-1919 (Dec.)
Breland, Bostick Hanson "Crab"	5	1920 (Jan.)-1923 (Dec.)
Alexander, G. J.	5	1924 (Jan.)-1927 (Dec.)
Bond, Eugene H.	5	1928 (Jan.)-1931 (Dec.)
Breland, Gavin A.	5	1932 (Jan.)-1939 (Dec.)
Bond, Otis M.	5	1940 (Jan.)-1959 (Dec.)
Bond, Leland L.	5	1960 (Jan.)-1967 (Dec.)

Hancock, William Walter "Bill"	5	1968 (Jan.)-1971 (May 31)
Hancock, Vondell [Mrs. W. W.]	5	1971 (May 31)-1971 (Dec.)
Hunt, Glennis	5	1972 (Jan.)-1991 (Dec.)
Bond, Dale T.	5	1992 (Jan.)-1999 (Dec.)
Hatten, Duncan	5	2000 (Jan.)-

*Andrew Wiggins Bond of Wiggins, D. Jason Brown of Stillmore, Sardin M. O'Neal Sr. of Perkinston, Edward Randolph Smith of Powers, and J. C. Fore of McHenry were selected by a committee of Stone County citizens on May 13, 1916, for recommendation to the governor of Mississippi to be appointed as provisional supervisors until an election could be held. Second District Circuit Judge James H. Neville swore in these and all other Stone County provisional officers on June 5, 1916 (the date which came to be regarded as the birthday of Stone County). All of the provisional supervisors except J. C. Fore, who lost to Dr. Ross Adams Switzer, were elected to office in Stone County's first official election held on June 26, 1916. One of these, Edward Randolph Smith, was a current supervisor of Harrison County, Beat 5. Smith served Stone County Beat 5 from June 5, 1916 to December 1919 and Beat 1 from January 1932 to December 1935 and from January 1945 until his death in late 1949. At that time his son, Carl T. Smith, was appointed to serve his unexpired term.

**Four days after W. W. "Wash" Lott's death on February 16, 1941, Mississippi Governor Paul B. Johnson Sr. appointed Lott's 32-year-old son-in-law, Roy L. Robinson, to serve as interim supervisor until an election could be called to fill Lott's vacant Beat 4 seat. In the May 6 election Robinson ran unopposed, taking the Beat 4 seat in his own right. On September 1, less than four months after that election, Robinson died in a car-bus collision on Highway 49 one mile north of Perkinston. Nine days later Governor Johnson appointed Robinson's widow to the Beat 4 seat until yet another election could be called. Thus, Lillie Lott Robinson became the first woman to serve as a Stone County supervisor. When Emmett R. Bond succeeded her on March 3, 1942, he was the fourth supervisor to serve Beat 4 in slightly more than one year.

***Buster Dean Shaw served Beat 2 from January 1984 to December 1991. The redrawing of beat lines placed Shaw's residence in Beat 3, and Shaw defeated Bobby Parker and served that beat from January 1992 to December 1995.

****Jerry J. Fairley was Stone County's first black supervisor.

*****Pam Fairley, Jerry J. Fairley's widow, was appointed interim supervisor after the death of her husband. She won the Beat 2 seat in the next general election thus becoming the first woman elected to the position of supervisor in Stone County.

Jackson County Supervisors

(beginning with those in office in 1925 at the time of the establishment of the Harrison-Stone-Jackson Agricultural High School and Junior College at Perkinston to 2000)
The information for this chart was supplied by Betty Rodgers of the Jackson County Archives.

Name	Beat	Terms
Denson, Dr. E. A.	1	1924 (Aug. 24)-1927 (Dec.)
McLeod, R. D.	1	1928 (Jan.)-1931 (Dec.)
Cochran, H. W.	1	1932 (Jan.)-1943 (Dec.)
Cumbest, Roy O.	1	1944 (Jan.)-1957 (Aug. 5)
Cumbest, Lum	1	1957 (Aug. 5)-1981 (Nov. 6)
Hamilton, Frank	1	1981 (Nov. 25)-1982 (Feb. 1)
Pierce, A. E. "Peter"	1	1982 (Feb. 1)-1987 (Dec.)
Smith, Tommy S.	1	1988 (Jan.)-1991 (Dec.)
Moseley, Charles R.	1	1992 (Jan.)-1999 (Dec.)
Barton, Manly	1	2000 (Jan.)-
Burnham, K. W.	2	1920 (Jan.)-1947 (Dec.)
Khayat, Edward A.	2	1948 (Jan.)-1982 (May 7)
Corley, Ed	2	1982 (May 7)-1982 (Aug. 19)
Robinson, Fred**	2	1982 (Aug. 19)-1987 (July 2)
Patton, James W.	2	1987 (July)-1987 (Dec.)
Norvel, Robert R.	2	1988 (Jan.)-
Martin, William F.	3	1916 (Oct.)-1926 (Jan.)
Gautier, Hermes F.	3	1926 (Feb.)-1947 (Dec.)
Krebs, Joe V.	3	1948 (Jan.)-1951 (Dec.)
Hague, George B.	3	1952 (Jan.)-1959 (Dec.)
Bartlett, Maness	3	1960 (Jan.)-1967 (Dec.)
May, J. C.	3	1968 (Jan.)-1991 (Dec.)
Pol, Michael	3	1992 (Jan.)-1995 (Dec.)
Lee Sr., Larry O.	3	1996 (Jan.)-1999 (Dec.)
Broussard, Tim	3	2000 (Jan.)-
Lemon, J. K.	4	1919-1929 (Apr. 29)
Moran, A. P. "Fred"	4	1929 (June)-1967 (Oct. 19)
Moran, Duncan	4	1967 (Oct. 19)-1967 (Dec.)
Roberts, William T.	4	1968 (Jan.)-1982 (May 21)
Endt, Alvin	4	1982 (May 24)-1982 (Aug. 19)
Brodnax, Tommy W.	4	1982 (Aug. 19)-1991 (Dec.) 1996 (Jan.)-1999 (Dec.)
Landry, Sharon [Mrs. Robert]***	4	1992 (Jan.)-1995 (Dec.)
Leach, Frank	4	2000 (Jan.)-
Wilson, Braxton W.	5	1924 (Jan.)-1931 (Dec.)
Vaughn, R. L.	5	1932 (Jan.)-1943 (Dec.)
Cruthirds, George A.	5	1944 (Jan.)-1951 (Dec.)
Davis, Olin H.	5	1952 (Jan.)-1975 (Sept. 9)
Davis, Nell [Mrs. Olin H.]*	5	1975 (Sept. 9)-1975 (Dec.)
McElroy, Ed	5	1976 (Jan.)-1982 (May 7)
Luke, Royce	5	1982 (May 7)-1982 (Aug. 19)
Holden, Douglas	5	1982 (Aug. 19)-1987 (Dec.)
Clifford III, Carroll	5	1988 (Jan.)-1995 (Dec.)
Patterson, Burt L.	5	1996 (Jan.)-1999 (Dec.)
McKay, John	5	2000 (Jan.)-

*Nell Davis [Mrs. Olin] was the first woman to serve as a Jackson County supervisor.
**Fred Robinson was Jackson County's first black supervisor.
***Sharon Landry [Mrs. Robert] was the first woman elected as a Jackson County supervisor.

Supervisors of George County, Mississippi

1910 to 2000

Compiled by Marjorie Baxter

(With some assistance from the staff of Lucedale-George County Library)

Name	Beat	Beginning/Ending Term
Eubanks, David Clay	1	1910 (July)-1915 (Dec.)1918 (Dec.)-1919 (Dec.)
Stinson, William H.	1	1916 (Jan.)-1918 (Sept.)
Havard, Lyman Wirt	1	1920 (Jan.)-1923 (Dec.)
Cowart, Walter Scott	1	1924 (Jan.)-1927 (Dec.)
Eubanks, Charles Posey	1	1928 (Jan.)-1931 (July 2)
Eubanks, Paul Truman	1	1931 (July 2)-1931 (Dec.)
Ward, Ernest Bower*	1	1932 (Jan.)-1939 (Dec.) 1944 (Jan.)-1944 (Dec.)
Havard, Carl Thomas	1	1940 (Jan)-1943 (Dec.) 1964 (Jan.)-1967 (Dec.)
Yonge, Edward Grady	1	1945 (Jan.)-1947 (Dec.)
Read, Henry A.	1	1948 (Jan.)-1959 (Dec.)
Eubanks, Lloyd Monroe	1	1960 (Jan.)-1963 (Dec.) 1968 (Jan.)-1971 (Dec.)
Howell, Vernon E.	1	1972 (Jan.)-1975 (Dec.) 1980 (Jan.)-1983 (Dec.)
Ward, Loren Small	1	1976 (Jan.)-1979 (Dec.)
Eubanks, Clyde W.	1	1984 (Jan.)-2000 (June 4)
Eubanks, Audrey [Mrs. C. W.]**	1	2000 (June 5)-
Ward, Cornelius Ferdinand	2	1910 (July)-1911 (Dec.)
Harper, John Everett	2	1912 (Jan.)-1919 (Dec.)
Vice, John T.	2	1920 (Jan.)-1927 (Dec.)
Bonnett, Charles M.	2	1928 (Jan.)-1935 (Dec.)
Parker, Wiley J.	2	1936 (Jan.)-1947 (Dec.)
Wall, Clemon O.	2	1948 (Jan.)-1955 (Dec.)
Bufkin, Otis Rivers	2	1956 (Jan.)-1963 (Dec.)
Loftin Jr., Sam H.	2	1964 (Jan.)-1971 (Dec.)
Brannan, Keith Maborn "Snooks"	2	1972 (Jan.)-1977 (Feb. 21)
Brannan, Harriet [Mrs. K. M.]***	2	1977 (Feb. 21)-1987 (Dec.)
Christian, Robert Wayne	2	1988 (Jan.)-1999 (Dec.)
Pope, J. E.	2	2000 (Jan.)-
Goff, John Bruner	3	1910 (July)-1915 (Dec.) 1924 (Jan.)-1927 (Dec.)
Byrd, Prentice Moore	3	1916 (Jan.)-1919 (Dec.) 1928 (Jan.)-1930 (Feb. 8)
Howell, John T.	3	1920 (Jan.)-1923 (Dec.)
Fairley, Neil Godfrey	3	1930 (Mar.)-1935 (Dec.) 1944 (Jan.)-1947 (Dec.)
Parker, William Web	3	1936 (Jan.)-1939 (Dec.)
Davis, Joseph Henry	3	1940 (Jan.)-1943 (Dec.)
Howell, Willie Ernest "Pat"	3	1948 (Jan.)-1955 (Aug. 29)
Howell, Elma [Mrs. W. E.]****	3	1955 (Aug. 29)-1955 (Dec.)
Cochran Walter Woodrow "John"	3	1956 (Jan.)-1963 (Dec.) 1972 (Jan.)-1975 (Dec.)
Howell Sr., Clemon David	3	1964 (Jan.)-1971 (Dec.)
Fairley, Ralph Burge	3	1976 (Jan.)-1995 (Dec.)
Cochran, Orville Harold	3	1996 (Jan.)-
Dorsett, Jett C.	4	1910 (July)-1911 (Dec.)

Howell, James T.	4	1912 (Jan.)-1919 (Dec.) 1928 (Jan.)-1931 (Dec.)
Cochran, William Wesley	4	1920 (Jan.)-1923 (Dec.)
Woodard, John C.	4	1924 (Jan.)-1927 (Dec.)
Havard, Lyman Webster	4	1932 (Jan.)-1939 (Dec.)
Moody, Willie Thomas	4	1940 (Jan.)-1959 (Dec.)
Rouse, Robert Lee "Tut"	4	1960 (Jan.)-1967 (Dec.)
Cochran, Joseph Lynwood	4	1968 (Jan.)-1974 (May 21)
Cochran, Cornelia [Mrs. J. L.]	4	1974 (May 21)-1975 (Dec.)
Reeves, Billie	4	1976 (Jan.)-1983 (Dec.)
Havard, Larry Amon	4	1984 (Jan.)-
Broom, Wesley W.	5	1910 (July)-1911 (Dec.)
McQuagge, Frazier G.	5	1912 (Jan.)-1914 (Oct. 6)
Flurry, Rufus	5	1914 (Nov.)-1919 (Dec.)
Maples, Florian	5	1920 (Jan.)-1943 (Dec.)
Whittington, James Howard	5	1944 (Jan.)-1951 (Dec.)
Green, Reginald Jackson "Reg"	5	1952 (Jan.)-1975 (Dec.)
Williams, Ernest Clinton "Clint"	5	1976 (Jan.)-1979 (Dec.) 1984 (Jan.)-1987 (Dec.) 1996 (Jan.)-1999 (Dec.)
Howell, Norman Cedrick	5	1980 (Jan.)-1983 (Dec.) 1988 (Jan.)-1995 (Dec.)
Cochran, William Henry	5	2000 (Jan.)-

*Ernest Bower Ward was a supervisor for eight years; then he was sheriff for four years. Because he could not succeed himself as sheriff, he ran as supervisor once again. A year after he was elected supervisor, the then current sheriff resigned. Ward was then able to run for the office of sheriff and, of course, had to resign as supervisor.

**Audrey Faye (Gibson) Eubanks served as interim supervisor upon the death of her husband, Clyde W. Eubanks. In the next general election she was elected to the post in her own right.

***Harriet Brannan served as interim supervisor upon the death of her husband, Keith Maborn Brannan. In the next general election she became the first woman to be elected supervisor in George County.

****Elma Howell, widow of Willie Ernest "Pat" Howell, was the first woman to serve as a George County supervisor.

Author's note -- For the purposes of this work, only those supervisors who served George County from 1941-2000 should have been included. However, since Marjorie Baxter made available the list of George County Supervisors from the organization of the county in 1910, the list was published in its entirety due to its value to historians.

MISSISSIPPI GULF COAST COMMUNITY COLLEGE
CAMPUS CHIEF EXECUTIVE OFFICERS
(DEANS/EXECUTIVE DEANS/VICE PRESIDENTS)
1959 - 2000

The chief executive officer of a campus was known as a "dean" from June 7, 1959 until July 23, 1969 when the title was changed to "executive dean." In June 1983 the term "vice president" replaced the title "executive dean."

Perkinston Campus		
William P. Lipscomb	Dean	June 7, 1959
	Named Dean of Jefferson Davis Campus	July 1, 1964
Charles Garrus "C. G." Odom	Dean	July 1, 1964
	Executive Dean	July 23, 1969
	Retired	June 30, 1977
	Died	October 3, 1999
Dr. Clyde E. Strickland	Executive Dean	July 1, 1977
	Vice President	June 1983
	Retired	December 31, 1990
Dr. Bobby S. Garvin	Vice President	January 1, 1991
	Resigned to become President of Miss. Delta Community College	June 30, 1992
Dr. Richard Miller	Vice President	July 1, 1992
	Suffered a stroke	September 2, 1994
	Medical retirement	Fall 1995
Dr. Willis Hulon Lott	Interim Vice President	October 26, 1994
	Vice President	January 17, 1996
	Named MGCCC President	August 1, 1998
Dr. Mary (Spring) Graham	Vice President	August 19, 1998
Jefferson Davis Campus		
Dr. William P. Lipscomb	Dean	July 1, 1964
	Executive Dean	July 23, 1969
	Removed to Central Office	February 1978
	Resigned	July 31, 1978
Glen W. Cadle	Interim Executive Dean	February 1978
	Executive Dean	May 8, 1978
	Vice President	June 1983
	Retired	December 31, 1991
	Died	August 23, 1995
Dr. Clifton Donnell Taylor	Vice President	January 2, 1991
Jackson County Campus		
Curtis L. Davis	Dean	July 1, 1964
	Executive Dean	July 23, 1969
	Vice President	June 1983
	Retired	December 31, 1991
Dr. Royce Luke	Vice President	January 1, 1992
	Retired	June 30, 1997
Dr. Houshang Moradmand	Vice President	July 1, 1997
Community Campus		
Nell Murray	As Executive Assistant for Development she directed the establishment of the Community Campus, and in addition to her former duties exercised executive control of the new entity for one year. Relinquished control of Community Campus to Vice President Mary (Spring) Graham retaining her former position.	July 1, 1996 June 30, 1997
	Retired as Executive Assistant for Development	Fall 1997
Dr. Mary (Spring) Graham	Vice President	July 1, 1997
	Transferred to the Perkinston Campus as Vice President	August 19, 1998
Nell Murray	Came out of retirement to act as Interim Executive of Community Campus pending selection of new vice president.	Fall 1998
	Retired again	December 1998
J. Clifton Quinn	Vice President	January 4, 1999
	Resigned	June 2000
Anna Faye Kelley	Vice President	June 2000

PAST PRESIDENTS OF THE MISSISSIPPI GULF COAST COMMUNITY COLLEGE ALUMNI ASSOCIATION 1929 - 2000

1929-1930	Noll P. Davis
1930-1931	Searcy H. "Doc" Davis
1931-1932	Calvin Eugene Dees
1932-1933	Dowey D. O'Neal
1933-1934	Dowey D. O'Neal
1934-1935	Posey Godard
1935-1936	John Clifton Dees
1936-1937	John Clifton Dees
1937-1938	Hammond "Tom" Davis
1938-1939	Oliver Anderson
1939-1940	Billy Jack Dees
1940-1941	Randle Dedeaux
1941-1942	John Clifton Dees
1942-1943	Otis Singletary
1943-1944	Otis Singletary
1944-1945	Calvin Eugene Dees
1945-1946	Oliver Anderson
1946-1947	Clare (Sekul) Hornsby
1947-1948	Lionel Gardner
1948-1949	Lionel Gardner
1949-1950	Cooper Rouse
1950-1951	Cooper Rouse
1951-1952	Homer Dedeaux
	Guy D. Moffett
1952-1953	Boyce Holleman
1953-1954	Glendon Johnson
1954-1955	Richard Lewis
1955-1956	Joseph H. D'Angelo
1956-1957	Curtis Dedeaux
1957-1958	Dr. W. H. Starr
1958-1959	Bill Weaver
1959-1960	Louis M. Hudson
1960-1961	Louis M. Hudson
1961-1962	Richard Yarbrough
1962-1963	Jimmy McManus
1963-1964	Louis M. Hudson
1964-1965	Sam Owen
1965-1966	Sam Owen
1966-1967	Dwight Moody
1967-1968	Horace Bradley
1968-1969	Horace Bradley
1969-1970	Crawford Dees
1970-1971	Crawford Dees
1971-1972	Ed Robbins Taylor
1972-1973	Clifton Donnell Taylor
1973-1974	Dolores (McHenry) Mauldin
1974-1975	Dolores (McHenry) Mauldin
1975-1976	Dr. Stephen Pitalo
1976-1977	Dr. Frank G. Gruich
1977-1978	Dr. Frank G. Gruich
1978-1979	Cooper Roberts
1979-1980	Cooper Roberts
1980-1981	Hermes Hague
1981-1982	Hermes Hague
1982-1983	Dolores (McHenry) Mauldin
1983-1984	Dolores (McHenry) Mauldin
1984-1985	Gary L. Roberts
1985-1986	Gary L. Roberts
1986-1987	Joe Donald
1987-1988	Jimmie (McBay) Bradley
1988-1989	Jimmie (McBay) Bradley
1989-1990	Jackie Parker
1990-1991	Jackie Parker
1991-1992	Mark Maples
1992-1993	Mark Maples
1993-1994	Cheryl Lynn (Kouba) Catalano
1994-1995	Cheryl Lynn (Kouba) Catalano
1995-1996	L. D. "Buster" Stringfellow
1996-1997	L. D. "Buster" Stringfellow
1997-1998	L. D. "Buster" Stringfellow
1998-1999	James Turner
1999-2000	James Turner
2000	Chris Cumbest

Appendix IX

RECIPIENTS OF THE MISSISSIPPI GULF COAST COMMUNITY COLLEGE ALUMNI ASSOCIATION SAM OWEN TROPHY AWARD 1956 - 2000

The late Sam Owen of Gulfport, who attended Harrison-Stone-Jackson Agricultural High School in session 1927-1928, established the Sam Owen Trophy Award, which was given annually from 1956-2000 at homecoming to a person who had actively supported the college.

1956	Calvin Eugene Dees
1957	Searcy H. "Doc" Davis
1958	Joseph H. D'Angelo
1959	Clare (Sekul) Hornsby
1960	Richard "Dick" Lightsey
1961	Dr. W. H. Starr
1962	Louis M. Hudson
1963	Donald Sanders
1964	Cooper J. Darby
1965	G. L. Pemberton Mrs. Louis M. Hudson
1966	Roy B. Strickland
1967	Billy Jack Dees
1968	Ferris Batson
1969	Sam Owen, Posthumously
1970	Horace Bradley
1971	Vertis G. Ramsay
1972	Crawford Dees
1973	Hersel McDaniel
1974	Dr. Frank G. Gruich
1975	Wyvona (Bond) Scarbrough
1976	Dolores (McHenry) Mauldin
1977	Dr. Stephen Pitalo
1978	Attis L. O'Neal
1979	Cooper Roberts
1980	Guy D. Moffett
1981	John Clifton Dees
1982	George Anthony Schloegel
1983	Hermes Hague
1984	Joe Donald
1985	Jimmie (McBay) Bradley
1986	Edward A. Khayat
1987	James E. Reese, Posthumously
1988	Gary L. Roberts
1989	Gary J. Holland
1990	L. D. "Buster" Stringfellow
1991	Dr. Julius John Hayden Jr.
1992	Milton C. Murrah
1993	Henry Terry
1994	Glen W. Cadle
	Curtis Davis
	Dr. Clyde Strickland
1995	Joe Byrum
1996	Edward A. Evans
1997	Dorothy (Hague) Gilmer
1998	William A. Frantzen, Posthumously
1999	James O. Rabby
2000	Randle Dedeaux

INDEX

- T -